Culture, Self-Identity, and Work

CULTURE, SELF-IDENTITY, AND WORK

Miriam Erez
P. Christopher Earley

New York   Oxford
OXFORD UNIVERSITY PRESS
1993

Oxford University Press

Oxford   New York   Toronto
Delhi   Bombay   Calcutta   Madras   Karachi
Kuala Lumpur   Singapore   Hong Kong   Tokyo
Nairobi   Dar es Salaam   Cape Town
Melbourne   Auckland   Madrid

and associated companies in
Berlin   Ibadan

Library of Congress Cataloging-in-Publication Data
Erez, Miriam.
Culture, self-identity, and work /
Miriam Erez and P. Christopher Earley.
p. cm.   Includes bibliographical references and index.
ISBN 0-19-507580-3
1. Employee motivation—United States.
2. Self-perception—United States.
3. Work ethic—United States.   I. Earley, P. Christopher.
II.   Title.
HF5549.5.M63E74   1993
658.3'14—dc20   92-28734

9 8 7 6 5 4 3 2 1

Printed in the United States of America
on acid-free paper

PREFACE

There has been an ever-increasing demand placed on people to understand one another and to live cooperatively. Despite such a need, societal misunderstandings and strife have subverted all attempts by civilized peoples to coexist peacefully. If we trace human history to its origins, we might compare our current conflicts to those of early homo sapiens who banded together to fend off more aggressive hunters, only to turn against one another in times of scarcity. However, we know from historical evidence that primitive peoples cooperated in order to survive and developed a hierarchical structure, or ranking, in order to maintain their collective stability. Such cooperative arrangements provided the model for modern industrial organizations.

Our purpose in this book is to present a theory of behavior in work organizations utilizing a cultural perspective. Both of us share strong discipline-based perspectives on work behavior, and such an approach is reflected by the fact that we have chosen to focus on a person's psychological experience of self-identity as the fundamental building block of our theory. We have chosen this path as well since much of the existing literature on organizations that addresses intercultural issues has focused on more macro-oriented topics such as comparative organization structure, political climates, and so on. In fact, we are unaware of any existing theory of intercultural work behavior based on the individual as a conduit of culture's influence. Although we focus upon the individual's sense of self, we do not hold that individuals in all societies interpret the world in terms of themselves. Rather, the self is a universal aspect of humanity and its definition is shaped differentially according to various cultural values and perspectives.

Modern society seems largely to have ignored many of the lessons of the past. We tend to misunderstand one another as we continue to pursue specific interests often detrimental to those of others. We see manifestations of such misunderstandings in the political, religious, and cultural spheres of everyday life. Such observations might lead one to assume that people are destined to be in continual conflict and torn by competing interests. However, many scholars have not fallen prey to such negative thinking and have expressed optimism that people may improve over time.

Perhaps the most important lesson that people have learned is that they must possess a fuller understanding and appreciation for who they are, and what their place in the general social order is, if they are to achieve social stability. During the last century we have learned much about what it means to be human. Work by such scholars as Ruth Benedict, Claude Lévi-Strauss, Louis Leakey, Talcott Parsons, Frederick Strodtbeck, Harry Triandis, and Ward Goodenough has advanced our knowledge of what it means to be human and how people come together to form societies. The fundamental, embedded rules, practices, and social artifacts that underly these societies constitute what many call culture. The implicit assumption in much recent work on human interaction has been that culture is a universal but idiosyncratic aspect of society. Early in this century most work on culture was devoted to developing taxonomies and applying them to existing societies for purposes of comparison. More recently a number of scholars have adopted such an approach to better understand one particular form of human activity, namely, behavior in the workplace. Although there is great utility in this procedure, it is merely the first step in developing a more comprehensive theory of work behavior from an intercultural perspective.

Researchers in the field of management are entering an exciting new phase by exploring the psychological aspects of self and their relationship to culture and work organization. For a number of years, there has been ample evidence that various work methods were differentially effective in individual cultures, but we were only able to speculate as to why such differentiation occurred. It has proved unacceptable to rely on simplistic explanations such as "we are just different" or "the social system prevents techniques from being transferred" as a way of understanding comparative management findings. The new approach, applying a micro-organizational perspective to the study of comparative management, utilizes a rigorously controlled and systematic experimentation involving elaborate but confined theoretical perspectives in order to specifically tie psychological manifestations of culture (e.g., beliefs concerning how one should interact with others from an in-group) to emergent work behavior. It is our belief that such an approach will deepen our understanding of the role of culture in shaping individual reactions to management practices and will enable us to predict which practices will be most effective in a given cultural context.

This book consists of ten chapters. Chapter 1 discusses the underlying motives and needs for publishing a book on organizational behavior from a cross-cultural perspective.

Chapter 2 presents our theoretical model, namely, the cultural self-representation model. This model is anchored in the general framework of cognitive information processing. It proposes a link between the macrolevel of cultural factors and the microlevel of individual behavior through the self as an information processor and an interpreter of the meaning of managerial practices in light of cultural criteria.

Chapter 3 focuses on the macrolevel of culture. It summarizes various approaches to the study of culture and examines cultural values among different cultures. The purpose of this chapter is to acquaint the reader new to intercultural research with a number of conceptual frameworks from the fields of anthropology, psychology, and sociology, as well as to situate our model within this context.

Chapter 4 represents an in-depth exploration of the nature of social relatedness in society. This is often referred to as individualism-collectivism in the literature. We highlight this dimension of culture since interpersonal relations are at the heart of organizational behavior.

Chapters 5 through 10 focus on specific major areas in organizational behavior. The chapters, written in line with our model of cultural self-representation, demonstrate how cultural differences explain the effectiveness of various managerial and motivational techniques.

Chapter 5 discusses work motivation from a cross-cultural perspective. It examines the congruence between various motivational techniques and cultural characteristics in light of cultural characteristics.

Chapter 6 examines the relationship between cultural characteristics and the interpersonal communication system in organizations. The Japanese system exemplifies the corporate relationship between the cultural dimension and the interpersonal communication system. The communication system facilitates the process of shared values and hence strengthens the cultural dimension. On the other hand, a homogenous culture ensures that senders and receivers of information share the same meaning and interpretation. Hence a strong culture improves the effectiveness of interpersonal communication in organizations.

Chapter 7 focuses on group dynamics. It discusses the meaning of groups within different cultures. Differences in group processes of formation, maturity, and effectiveness across cultures is examined in relation to differences in the meaning of groups.

Chapter 8 centers on leadership. Models of leadership are examined in line with cultural differences. We propose a model derived from charismatic and transformational approaches. The major thesis propounded is that effective leadership is best understood by examining the culturally grounded symbols and myths invoked by a leader.

Chapter 9 examines conflict management as a function of cultural influences and the needs of the self. Chapter 10 presents a summary and integration of organizational behavior from a cross-cultural perspective.

ACKNOWLEDGMENTS

Many individuals contributed to the creation of this book. Needless to say, our theory represents the accumulated fund of research and experience gleaned from a number of key individuals. We have been exposed to many stimulating ideas expressed by Harry Triandis, Allan Lind, Ed Locke, Tamao Matsui, Shelly Zedeck, Al Goldberg, and Nilli Diengott—to name just a few individuals. We are grateful to our home institutions and colleagues for their continued support. In particular, P.C.E. wishes to thank the University of California, Irvine, for its patience as the book was being completed. Financial support in the form of a Fulbright Senior Research Fellowship from the United States–Israel Educational Foundation and Council for International Exchange of Scholars and a sabbatical leave from the University of Minnesota enabled P.C.E. to work with his colleague as a visiting scholar at the Technion–Israel Institute of Technology.

We would also like to thank the editorial staff at Oxford University Press for its patience and help in shaping and honing our "diamond in the rough." Particular thanks go to Herbert J. Addison and Mary Sutherland, who endured a sometimes awkward U.S.–Israel connection that slowed the completion of our book. We would also like to thank Cristina Gibson for her help in attending to the final details of our book and Henry Krawitz for his care and energy in making our prose clear and succinct.

Finally, we would like to thank our doctoral students, who over the years have stimulated our thinking about international and intercultural issues. We continue to develop, in part, because our students never tire of asking us to define what we mean by nebulous concepts such as "culture" or "self-identity."

Irvine, Calif.   P.C.E.
Haifa, Israel   M.E.
September 1992

CONTENTS

Culture, Self-Identity, and Work

1

Introduction

The search for an answer to a seemingly simple question has led to a long journey in which we have explored the available literature, theoretical models, and methodology, resulting in a new model of cross-cultural industrial/organizational (I/O) psychology. The question was: Why were successful managerial and motivational techniques not found to be uniformly effective across cultural borders? Numerous examples could be cited: quality control circles, which have been successful in Japanese companies, have had only a limited effectiveness when implemented in the United States (Lawler, 1986); methods of individual performance appraisal that are widely used in the United States have not been successfully implemented in non-American companies outside the United States; individual job enrichment programs developed in the United States have taken the form of autonomous work groups in Scandinavia; differential reward systems that motivate employees in the United States are unacceptable in the Kibbutz system in Israel, where egalitarianism is implemented. Unfortunately, present models of I/O psychology do not provide answers to this question, which takes so many forms in the work setting.

The field of organizational behavior (OB) pertains to the way individuals, groups, and organizations act to create outputs of products and services. Work behavior is a function of personal characteristics, situational factors, and the way they interact with each other. While personal characteristics have been studied extensively in psychology, scant attention has been paid to situational factors and, in particular, to culture as a determinant of organizational behavior.

Most theories of OB chiefly focus on the direct link between managerial and motivational techniques, on the one hand, and employee attitudes and behavior, on the other. Effects of goal-setting techniques, job enrichment, performance appraisal, and incentive plans have been examined with respect to employee performance, work satisfaction, work commitment, and turnover, whereas possible contextual moderators have been overlooked. Most attempts to generalize the validity of these studies have been limited to the United States, where the vast majority of such studies were conducted. For example, 1,255 out of 1,699 articles published in thirteen English-language journals between 1982 and 1989 were written by American authors (Erez, in press). Even in cases where validity generalization posed a problem, situational effects were overlooked and most likely were interpreted as artifacts. In fact there was no theoretical framework for ascribing meaning to those effects.

Cultural effects can be ignored as long as research takes place within the same cultural system. However, the process of globalization has created opportunities for transferring managerial techniques across cultures, and such attempts have not always been successful (Adler, 1986; England, 1983; Hofstede, 1980; Jaeger, 1983). Failures in transferring methods of human resource management (HRM) across cultures suggest that culture acts as a moderator in the relationship between managerial techniques and employee behavior. No theory of I/O psychology to date incorporates culture as an explanatory factor of employee behavior. This book represents an attempt at developing a conceptual framework in order to measure the effectiveness of managerial techniques from a cross-cultural perspective.

CULTURAL FACTORS INFLUENCING
ORGANIZATIONAL BEHAVIOR

The process of developing a new model of cross-cultural I/O psychology has occurred in several stages. First among these is a heightened awareness of the influence of cultural factors on OB. The last two decades have witnessed significant changes in the work environment which have highlighted these cultural variables.

Expansion of the Work Environment from Local to Global and International Markets

Globalization is defined as "the crystallization of the entire world as a single place" (Robertson, 1987:38), and this definition mainly holds true in economic terms. For example, the United States, is becoming part of an increasingly global economy. About 100,000 American companies do business overseas, including 3,500 multinational companies. It is estimated that a third of the profit of U.S. companies is derived from international business, along with a sixth of the nation's jobs (Cascio, 1989). The competitive global market sets new rules for survival.

What are the psychological repercussions of such changes on the individual employee? Employees have to become more competitive in order to help their organizations survive. Very often they have to compete outside their local environment and against unfamiliar players. The level of ambiguity and risk increases, and there is a growing need to learn about the characteristics of new markets and to adjust to them.

The growing concern over the competition between Japan and the United States has been documented from 1989 to 1991 on a weekly basis in *Fortune* and *Business Week,* as well as in more specialized management journals in the United States. American companies are eager to learn as much as possible about the cultural characteristics of the Japanese and their management practices in the hope that such knowledge will improve their competitive strategies.

Instability of the Work Environment

A substantial number of American companies have experienced mergers, acquisitions, and downsizing. Between 1987 and 1989 there were about 11,428 merger deals at a total value of $645,386 million (*Mergers and Acquisitions,* 1990). Of these, 1,412 were of foreign acquisitions of U.S. companies, with only 621 representing U.S. acquisitions overseas. Two of the more celebrated cases were the acquisition of Rockefeller Center in New York City and Columbia Pictures in Hollywood, California, by Japanese companies.

Mergers and acquisitions often result in a cultural clash between the acquiring company and the new acquisition. In such cases organizational culture becomes an important factor in the process of mutual adjustment. Furthermore, mergers and acquisitions often result in massive layoffs. A survey by the American Management Association (Offermann & Gowing, 1990) showed that 39% of the 1,084 companies surveyed reduced their work force in the past year. From 1985 to 1988 approximately 15 million workers were affected by mergers and acquisitions, and nearly three quarters of the senior executives in an acquired company left within a three-year period. These processes have a strong impact on the "survivors" as well as on those forced to leave (Offermann & Gowing). For the survivors, restructuring means a high level of uncertainty and dissatisfaction, stress, and an increasing distrust. A survey conducted by Franham in 1988 revealed that, compared to 1983, more employees complained that their companies did not treat them with respect, that they did not get enough information from top-level management, and that the management's level of ability was low. Those who were forced to leave experienced financial problems along with a high level of stress and a diminished sense of personal worth, which often resulted in physiological symptoms. This cost is paid not only by the single individual but by society at large.

Organizational Restructuring

Due to globalization, organizations no longer have distinct physical identities (Miles & Snow, 1984). Headquarters of organizations can be located in one country, manufacturing in another, sales and distribution in a third country, and service close to the customer in a nonlocal market. As a result, organizations change their structures to become flatter, with fewer layers of management and more diversification, which requires cultural adaptation. Each distinct business is responsible for the day-to-day operations, while the corporate office is responsible for the financial control of the divisions and overall strategic development (Hill, Hitt & Hoskisson, 1988). Globalization requires more joint ventures and results in a network of contracted relationships and strategic alliances (Galbraith & Kazanjian, 1988).

Another aspect of organizational restructuring is the emergence of the virtual organization, whose members do not meet face to face but are linked through computer technology. It has been estimated that about 16 million corporate employees in the United States now work in their homes (Offerman & Gowing, 1990).

Focus on Teamwork

Because organizations today rely on self-contained work groups that are in a position to learn customer preferences and can relay the information to other divisions, there is a growing emphasis on teamwork and team building (Sundstrom, De Meuse

& Futrell, 1990). This shift toward teamwork is of special interest to I/O psychologists since it is implemented in a culture characterized by individualistic values.

Growth of the Service Sector

The service sector now accounts for 71% of the work force. It creates new jobs and redefines previous ones. In addition, there is a growing emphasis on the sales and service functions. Even the largest R&D labs now take customers needs into consideration, more than they did in the past. A growing number of technicians and engineers have been required to shift their job focus from technical aspects to marketing and sales. Such companies as Proctor & Gamble, which was known as the king of mass marketers, are moving toward micromarketing, tailoring their marketing plans to the needs of individual retailers and consumers. For example, Proctor & Gamble has six different campaigns for Crest toothpaste directed toward separate consumer populations. As consumers increase their demand for time saving, product quality, and reliability, companies will need to increase their efforts in order to compete in the market. This goal becomes more difficult when customers are spread across cultural borders.

Emergence of High-Technology Telecommunications Systems

The revolution in telecommunications systems is observed everywhere. An increasing number of users rely on electronic mail, fax, cellular phones, and teleconferencing equipment to facilitate communication across borders and significantly reduce the time needed to process information. Software is now being developed that will simultaneously translate written documents from one language to another. These changes in telecommunications may help bridge the gap between different cultures.

The revolution in office and factory automation continues. In many cases automation has been implemented without considering the human operator and productivity improvement has not met original expectations (Turnage, 1990). Office and factory automation affects job design, skill requirements, and the number of employees required to perform the job. More attention should be given to the interplay between the human operator and the automated system to assure a high level of productivity and work satisfaction.

Financial Forces in the Market

The market is driven by the financial considerations of shareholders. If the value of a company drops beneath the value of its stock, shareholders may prefer to sell the company and realize its assets. The dominant forces in the market are no longer product considerations, management needs, the well-being of the employees, or even the survival of the company. The maximization of profit for shareholders is currently the main consideration (Hirsch, 1987). Shareholders worldwide can buy stocks in any international exchange and influence the market value of companies in any country. Thus, companies should learn to cope with the cultural diversity of their shareholders.

Unification and Separatism in the Political Arena

Merger in the business community takes the form of unification among countries: the unification of Europe and of East and West Germany, the end of the cold war, and the opening talks between South and North Korea are examples. Sociologists view postindustrial society as moving from small-scale communities toward a world of cultural imperialism based on economic, state, and telecommunications technology (Smith, 1990). Paradoxically, we also are witnessing the reemergence of nationalistic forces, in particular as they manifested themselves in Eastern Europe in 1992. These forces threaten the process of unification and bring culture to the fore (Acnason, 1990).

The exposure to different cultures and environments and the influx of immigration increase the need to understand the relationship between culture and behavior. The variance among situations has become as important for understanding work behavior as the variance among individuals. However, theories of OB do not provide a conceptual framework for understanding cultural effects.

THE CURRENT STATE OF THEORY
DEVELOPMENT IN OB

The field of OB pertains to the psychological study of the ways individuals, groups, and organizations behave to create output of products and services as a means for maintaining and enhancing their own survival. In line with the discipline of psychology, the vast majority of research centers on the individual, overlooking cultural and contextual effects.

Cross-cultural psychology is "the study of similarities and differences in individual psychological and social functioning in various cultures and ethnic groups" (Kagicibaci & Berry, 1989:494). Until very recently, these two fields of psychology were developed in parallel with only a limited amount of influence on each other. Cross-cultural research has focused on the relationship between psychological variables at the individual level and variables at the societal level, including cultural, social, economic, ecological, and biological variables. The field of OB has occupied only a small niche within the wide scope of cross-cultural research, and vice versa: OB research has not adopted a cross-cultural perspective on employees' behavior in organizations.

Research in cross-cultural psychology still lacks a strong conceptual framework (Kagitcibasi & Berry). On the other hand, highly developed conceptual models with strong empirical support have been developed in I/O psychology, including the goal-setting theory of motivation (Locke & Latham, 1990); expectancy models (Vroom, 1964); job design (Hackman & Oldham, 1980); the theory of behavior in organization (Naylor, Pritchard & Ilgen, 1980); decision-making models (Beach & Mitchell, 1990; Staw, 1985); and models of employee-organization interaction (Schneider, 1986). These models focus on the individual employee and attempt to explain employee behavior by examining individual goals, expectancies, self-efficacy, and need satisfaction. The models focus mainly on the individual employee and attempt to explain employee behavior by looking at individual goals, expectancies, self-efficacy, and need satisfaction. A growing body of research demonstrates that even work satisfaction, which is believed to be affected by the work environment, is likely to be modified by genetics. Research findings demonstrate that identical twins who grew up apart from each other have similar levels of work satisfaction compared to nonidentical twins or others (Arvey, Bouchard, Segall & Abraham, 1989).

This tendency to emphasize individual difference characteristics over situational factors has strengthened a universalistic approach to OB. Researchers who have sought validity generalization across situations have often treated situational effects as artifacts. However, very little research has been done on the impact of the environment and the way it interacts with different managerial practices to affect employees' behavior. A more recent theoretical development is the emergence of contingency models of OB that introduce contextual factors as moderators of the relationship between managerial practices and work behavior. These models are directed toward developing managerial actions that are appropriate for a specific situation and the people involved (Szilagyi & Wallace, 1983). However, the context is still defined in narrow terms of the immediate work environment, ignoring cultural factors.

The contingency models were developed chiefly with respect to leadership effectiveness. They propose that managerial effectiveness depends on the contingency between the managerial style and the particular characteristics of the situation. Different models of leadership examine different situational characteristics and the way they interact with participative versus nonparticipative management, or with employee versus task-oriented style. Fiedler and Chemers (1984) propose that a task-oriented leader is most effective in situations which are either very favorable or unfavorable for the leader's attempt to influence subordinates. An employee-oriented style is most effective in situations of moderate favorableness. Vroom and Yetton (1973) propose that participation in decisionmaking is contingent upon two major considerations. One is the amount of information available to the manager. Participation is effective when a manager does not have all the necessary information for decision-making and invites employees to serve as an additional pool of knowledge and information. The second criterion is managerial confidence. When a manager is not confident that a decision will be accepted, participation may increase the employees' level of commitment. Hersey and Blanchard (1982) consider the maturity level of the group as the situational characteristic which moderates the effectiveness of an authoritarian versus a democratic style.

Holland's (1973) contingency model of a person-job fit has shaped the field of vocational psychology. The model proposes that the congruence between the individual and the job is the key factor in the employee's successful adjustment to the work place, job satisfaction, and sense of well-being. Congruence is assessed by means of a typology of six personality types. Holland's model has been successfully implemented outside the work-setting as well. For example, Meir and Hasson (1982) show that the inclination to stay in a settlement is correlated to the level of congruence between the personality type of a particular member and the modal personality type of other members in the settlement.

Other contingency models focused on organizational structure and job design. Some propose that the effectiveness of different designs—for example, organic versus mechanistic organization, job enrichment, or sociotechnical design—is contingent upon situational characteristics, including technology, market, location of the plant (in rural or urban areas), and individual difference characteristics.

With the exception of a few models (Hellriegel, Slocum & Woodman, 1989; Szilagyi & Wallace, 1983), all other approaches to OB and human resource management (HRM) do not address the moderating effect of culture on work behavior. Typical models of OB and HRM consider the political, regulatory, social, economic, and technological forces in the environment but not cultural factors (Cascio, 1989). Since most of these models have been developed within a Western cultural framework dominated by individualistic values, they are chiefly concerned with individual behavior. For example, models of HRM that attempt to match individuals and jobs ignore the person–group fit or the person–organizational culture fit. Processes of communication which integrate individuals in organizations into social and cultural systems have not been considered as part of the functional activities of HRM (Cascio).

In view of the number of highly developed theories of OB, it is surprising that the cultural factor has not been addressed. A few models of OB are exceptions to this oversight. They examine the moderating effect of organizational climate and culture on the relationship between personal attributes and employees' behavior (Schneider, 1975, 1987). Some of these models suggest that organizational climate, as portrayed by the shared perceptions of organizational policies, practices, and procedures (Reichers & Schneider, 1990), can either facilitate or inhibit the display of individual difference characteristics (Schneider, 1975). Others suggest that the congruence between individual and organizational attributes has a positive effect on employees' behavior.

Cappeli and Sherer (1991) severely criticize the field of OB for ignoring the influence of the external environment on behavior. "By abandoning important [contextual] explanations for individual behavior, research in OB may actually have gotten worse overtime, at least by the standard of predictive power" (76). They warn that the field of OB is likely to miss the chance to establish any independent uniqueness if it continues to ignore contextual influences.

Traditional approaches within the field of OB may have predisposed researchers to exclude contextual factors from their theoretical models. The following represents a sampling of such approaches.

The Use of "Fixed" Research Paradigms

Psychology is the study of individual difference characteristics of individual behavior. Research paradigms of I/O psychology were developed in line with the individualistic trend in psychology. Paradigms serve as road maps for guiding research; therefore, they seriously limit the number and kind of variables under study. Research paradigms comprise the cognitive schema necessary for sampling, selecting, and interpreting empirical evidence. Information cannot be processed unless it can be recognized and interpreted.

The lack of awareness of contextual effects has led to the development of meta-analytic techniques that enable researchers to test for validity generalizations across situations while ignoring possible situational effects (Schmidt & Hunter, 1977). Situational effects often were explained as artifacts. It is therefore reasonable to argue that existing research paradigms cause biases in information search and block opportunities for collecting and interpreting data that contradict existing paradigms

The Individual as the Unit of Analysis

The focus on the individual as the unit of analysis, especially in American I/O psychology, which dominates the research literature, has distracted attention from broader units of analysis. From a historical perspective the focus on the individual is a product of liberal individualism, the dominant trend in psychology, which views individuals as self-contained, autonomous sovereigns in charge of their own lives. This approach calls for a detachment from the ties that formerly bound individuals to their community and defined who they were or could be. This detachment sets people free to determine their own self-definitions. Communal associations are established by persons who exist independently of those associations and who can withdraw their consent to belong as freely as they gave it (Sampson, 1989). According to this theory, a "well-ordered society is . . . one in which people are free to pursue their various aims" (Sandel, 1982:116), and the task of government is to assure the conditions that allow individuals to choose their own aims and purposes in life, not to set these aims for the individual.

In its extreme form an individualistic approach views individuals as self-contained and detached from their social milieu, ignoring the importance of interpersonal relationships in shaping self-identity. The self is, in fact, a product of the social system, shaped by the shared understanding of members of a particular culture of what it is to be human (Sandel, 1982; Cahoone, 1988; Cushman, 1990). This shared understanding is transmitted from one generation to another through the process of socialization. Extreme individualism limits the development of the self by mitigating the role played by interpersonal relationships in shaping self-identity.

The individualistic paradigm confines the level of analysis mainly to the individual level, disregarding sociocultural effects in I/O psychology. The neglect of contextual factors often leads to a false attribution of contextual effects to individuals (Ross, 1977).

The focus of American psychology on the individual level of analysis coincides with the dominant individualistic culture of the United States, unlike collectivistic cultures, which pay more attention to contextual and cultural factors (Boyacigiller & Adler, 1991; Triandis, in press). Citizens of large countries, such as the United States, are less likely to speak foreign languages or to know about other countries than are citizens of small countries (Hofstede, 1991) and, consequently, do not develop as great an awareness of cultural differences. In the new era of globalization the individualistic approach does not provide the conceptual framework and the methodology for understanding cross-cultural differences in the formation of cognitive schemas, self-identity, and individual behavior. A new theory is, therefore, needed for understanding individual behavior in the global era (Sampson, 1989).

The Cognitive Paradigm

The rise of the cognitive paradigm in I/O psychology is responsible for the shift in focus from external environmental factors to internal factors of cognitive information processing, including perceptions, interpretations, and evaluations (Cappeli & Sherer, 1991). The cognitive paradigm focuses on individual perceptions internal representations of the external environment, which is partially shaped by individual difference characteristics. Individual perceptions do not provide accurate information on the objective characteristics of the perceived environment; rather perceptions are the product or interaction of environmental and personal characteristics. The same situational characteristics may lead to different perceptions among individuals who differ in personality, personal experiences, and accepted social values and norms. Thus perceptions do not fully correspond to the objective environment.

It can be argued that cognitive processes mediate the relationship between contextual effects and individual behavior, and that both contextual and mediating effects have to be studied in order to understand and predict behavior. Yet the mediating role of cognitive processes has not been recognized. Some researchers contend that although endogenous theories that examine cognitive mediating processes help explain motivation, exogenous theories provide the "action lever" that can be employed to change work motivation (Katzell & Thompson, 1990). These researchers emphasize the need to improve the technology of work motivation, including such methods as incentive plans, goal-setting, and job design, rather than the need to develop cognitive mediating models.

Knowledge of the mediating processes per se does not convey specific information on the nature of situational characteristics. Hence any attempt to control or change situational effects requires the identification of situational factors, their causal relationships to the mediating processes, and consequent behavior. Unfortunately the gradual rise of the cognitive paradigm in I/O psychology has detracted attention from situational factors and eroded the role of context in ongoing OB research. According to the cognitive paradigm, "If individuals construct their own images of the environment, which vary across individuals, then why bother with the objective environment?" (Cappelli & Sherer, 1991:82). Culture is a characteristic of the social context and, as such, is not part of the existing cognitive paradigm.

Bridging the Gap Between Microlevel Behavior and Macrolevel Contextual Factors

Cappelli and Sherer argue that "there is no way to relate macro theories, with their focus on the environment, to micro behavior or vice versa (87). Their solution to the problem is to focus on the organizational level of analysis as a midpoint on the macro-micro continuum. They argue that the organizational context can more easily be related to employees' behavior than the macrolevel of societal factors. Among the organizational variables that were found to affect individual behavior are demographic, structural, and technological characteristics (Pfeffer, 1983; Pugh, 1976). Yet the mere knowledge that a relationship exists between various organizational variables and employees' behavior does not contribute to our understanding of causality. The causal link may be explained by mediating cognitive processes.

THE IDENTIFICATION OF CULTURAL CHARACTERISTICS

Despite the lack of theoretical models, forces in the real world have highlighted the importance of the cultural factor. A new research area has emerged which focuses on typologies of cultures. Among the typologies developed are those by Elizur (1984), England (1983), Hofstede (1980), Ronen and Shenkar (1985), Schwartz (1990), and Triandis et al. (1988). The typologies vary in the cultural dimensions they measure and in the methodology they use for assessing cultural differences. Hofstede developed the most popular typology to date consisting of four major dimensions of work values: collectivism versus individualism, power distance, uncertainty avoidance, and masculinity versus femininity. He used the typology to differentiate among forty I.B.M. subsidiaries across forty countries. A full discussion of each of the typologies is presented in chapter 3.

Cultural typologies contribute to our knowledge and understanding of cross-cultural differences, but they do not help us to understand how culture interacts with management practices to affect employee behavior. The attention given to cultural factors has triggered research on cultural differences in employees' work attitudes and behavior; for example, differences in perceived work burnout and coping behavior (Etzioni & Pines, 1986), in the meaning of work satisfaction (Dubin & Galin, 1991; Hulin & Mayer, 1986), in issues of morality (Zeidner & Nevo, 1987), and in motivational techniques, which will be discussed in chapter 5. The question still remains as to how the three factors—culture, managerial techniques, and individual work behavior—are interrelated.

APPLICATION OF COGNITIVE MODELS OF INFORMATION PROCESSING TO DEVELOP MODELS OF OB

One way to develop new conceptual frameworks is by questioning existing theoretical models. Cappeli & Sherer (1991) stress the inhibiting forces in the field of OB that have attenuated the development of new models. Yet their analysis does not result in a new conceptual model. They propose as a compromise to conduct research on the mesolevel of organizations because they cannot offer a conceptual model that bridges the gap between the macrolevel of the work environment and the microlevel of employee behavior.

We chose to question some of Cappeli and Sherer's own conventions in an attempt to discover the guiding principle that could lead to the development of a new model. In particular the following two conventions were selected: (1) cognitive models inhibit the integration of contextual factors into models of organizational behavior; and (2) there is no way to bridge the macrolevel of the work environment and the microlevel of individual behavior.

An in-depth examination of the nature of cognitive models leads to a counterargument to the one proposed by Cappeli and Sherer. We propose that cognitive models may facilitate rather than inhibit the development of models of OB that incorporate cultural factors. We argue that cultural and contextual factors have not been considered seriously because there was no available cognitive theory for understanding how stimuli from the work environment are selected, processed, and interpreted by the individual employee.

The lack of cognitive models of information processing in I/O psychology is admitted by Katzell and Thompson (1990), but they do not recognize the need for such models. Rather they contend that endogenous theories, which examine cognitive mediating processes, can only explain motivation, whereas exogenous theories provide the "action lever" that can change work motivation. They emphasize the need to improve the technology of work motivation by means of incentive plans, goal-setting, and job design, rather than through the development of cognitive mediating models.

Cognitive models of human information processing provide the theoretical foundation for understanding persons as processors of information and as allocators of cognitive resources. Metacognitive approaches recognize that individuals not only process information but also have knowledge about their cognitive processes. This knowledge serves as a source of influence on behavior (R. Kanfer, 1990). Individuals are capable of self-regulating their behavior toward goal attainment by taking the following steps: self-monitoring, which pertains to the attention people pay to their own behavior; self-evaluation, which takes place by personal judgement of the discrepancies between one's behavior and the goals and standards for behavior; and self-reaction, achieved by creating incentives for one's own actions and by responding evaluatively to one's behavior (Bandura, 1986).

Models of cognitive information processing within the social domain are known as models of social cognition. Such models enable us to understand how information from the social environment, as well as from internal cues, is sampled, processed, interpreted, and stored in cognitive schemas. Information that confirms the cognitive schema is more likely to be accepted than conflicting information (Wyer & Srull, 1989).

We propose that metacognitive models of self-regulation provide the necessary conceptual framework for understanding the relationship between culture and work motivation. In cognitive terms culture is viewed as a set of shared meanings, transmitted by a set of mental programs that control individual responses in a given context (Hofstede, 1980; Shweder & LeVine, 1984). Culture serves as a criterion for evaluating the meaning of various managerial techniques and the valences of their behavioral outcomes. It shapes the cognitive schemas which ascribe meaning and values to motivational variables and guide our choices, commitments, and standards of behavior. We argue that *cognitive models facilitate rather than inhibit the integration of macrolevel cultural variables into models of organizational behavior*.

It seems that Cappelli and Sherer have fallen victims of their own paradigm, believing that cognitive models downplay the role of contextual factors. By taking this approach they overlook the capacity of cognitive models to explain how contextual stimuli are sampled, processed, and interpreted and how they influence subsequent behavior.

The second convention pertains to the difficulty in linking situational factors on the macrolevel with employee behavior on the microlevel of analysis. We argue that cognitive processes of self-regulation formulate the link between macro- and micro-phenomena. They sample, process, and ascribe meaning to information received from the external milieu. Self-regulatory processes operate in the service of developing and maintaining a positive representation of the self (Gecas, 1982). These processes interpret informational cues from the environment in terms of their contribution to a person's sense of self-worth and well-being. As such they provide the link between the macrolevel of the work environment and the microlevel of employee behavior. Thus by questioning two conventions of Cappeli and Sherer, we opened the way for formulating a new model of cross-cultural I/O psychology based on metacognitive models of self-regulation.

The following case study illustrates the role of metacognitive models of self-regulation in understanding the moderating effect of culture on the relationship between managerial techniques and work behavior.

THE INTERRELATIONSHIP AMONG CULTURE, MANAGERIAL PRACTICES, SELF-REGULATORY PROCESSES, AND EMPLOYEE BEHAVIOR: A CASE STUDY

CTX is one of the most successful high-tech companies in Israel. Its main product is highly sophisticated equipment for the printing industry. Within a few years, CTX grew to become a multinational company with a total of sixteen subsidiaries in Europe, the United States, and Japan whose main purpose is to provide service and maintenance of the printing machines.

The headquarters, located in Israel, had serious problems communicating with its subsidiaries. The managers of the subsidiaries did not provide the necessary reports on daily activities or on special problems with maintenance and service. Such feedback was essential for the head office to monitor the subsidiaries and to learn about the special needs of the customers. To help overcome the communication problems, the general manager invited the managers of all the subsidiaries to participate in a workshop in Israel. The workshop was designed as a role-playing exercise to enable headquarters to express the importance of communication and to allow the subsidiaries to explain why they did not communicate properly.

Managers from the sixteen subsidiaries and the headquarters were divided into two groups—one representing the subsidiaries and the other representing the head office. Each group prepared arguments for the meeting with the other side. The representative of the Israeli headquarters started the meeting by saying: "First of all, you are all fired, and, second, you have two minutes to explain why you did not respond to our questions." The manager of the Italian subsidiary emotionally responded, "Vendetta," adding, "You, the headquarters, used to ask me to send reports and data on customers and services, but you never told me what you did with them. You have not provided any feedback or comparative data on other subsidiaries. Therefore, I refuse to provide any additional information."

The manager from Belgium politely said, "No response is also a response," meaning that he expected the home office to heed the signal and find out what bothered him. The Israeli representative, not used to the indirect style of the Belgian manager, could not understand how no response constituted a response and became very upset. He raised his voice and very angrily stated that subsidiaries should be loyal to their head office and not dare to refuse to communicate any information requested of them. Unfortunately the cultural gap was too deep, and the Israeli representative was unable to interpret the responses of the subsidiaries. Clearly their responses reflected cultural diversity, and communication could have been improved had cultural cues been understood.

The foregoing example illustrates how cultural values and norms influence the effectiveness of managerial practices: The Israeli managers of CTX had a direct and authoritative style, possibly acquired during military service. On the other hand, Israeli culture is known for its low level of power distance. Israeli employees are not threatened by the authoritarian style of their superiors, most likely interpreting it as assertiveness and decisiveness rather than as a display of power and control.

Members of the subsidiaries were unfamiliar with Israeli managerial style. The dominant values in most European countries encourage a democratic and participative approach to management. The European representatives were therefore offended by the direct and authoritarian style of the Israelis, which they interpreted as a reflection of power and control rather than assertiveness and decisiveness. They attempted to protect their egos by taking revenge, in the case of the Italian representative, or by an indirect response of denial in the case of the Belgian representative. The need to protect their egos created resentment rather than loyalty and cooperation with the Israeli headquarters.

The low level of commitment and loyalty conveyed by the European subsidiaries contradicted the expectations of the Israeli managers. Their expectations were informed by the group orientation and collectivistic values that characterize Israeli culture (Hofstede, 1980). Commitment and loyalty are also values acquired during military service. According to these values, the subsidiaries were expected to adhere to the company's goals.

The conceptual framework that helped interpret the CTX case study is based on cognitive models of self-regulation. Such models will be used as the infrastructure for our model of cross-cultural OB.

TOWARD THE DEVELOPMENT OF A NEW MODEL OF CROSS-CULTURAL OB

Recognizing the importance of situational variables, several researchers have recently criticized existing models of validity generalizations that do not take situational factors into account (James et al., 1992). In the absence of a theoretical framework that incorporates situational moderators, as well as statistical models for analyzing these effects, they were often treated as artifacts in studies of validity generalization. James et al. developed a statistical method that integrates situational variables into models of validity generalization. Yet such a statistical model can only be implemented if there is a theoretical reason for identifying situational moderators. They proposed that situational variables should be identified by taking a proactive approach "in which a theory is constructed pertaining to situational moderation of validities, in which theory is then used to design empirical investigations that include assessment of situational variables . . ." (10).

Our main purpose is to propose a new model of cross-cultural I/O psychology that examines the moderating effect of culture on the relationship between managerial practices and employee behavior. We argue that the effectiveness of motivational techniques and managerial practices depend, to a large extent, on their perceived utility and contribution to the attainment of personal and organizational goals. Their utility is evaluated according to certain norms and values, which vary across cultures. From the employee's perspective, the value of managerial techniques is determined by the extent to which they provide opportunities for maximizing the individual's potential and for satisfying self-generated needs. From the organizational perspective, the utility of implementing certain managerial techniques depends on the extent to which they harness human resources to the attainment of organizational goals.

The model we propose stems from a metacognitive approach to self-regulatory processes. Such an approach enhances our understanding of how different contextual stimuli are selected, processed, and interpreted by the individual. Our model proposes that the self, as a representative of the self-regulatory processes, constitutes the link between the macro- and microlevels of analysis: The self selects, processes, and interprets environmental stimuli with respect to their contribution to personal self-worth and well-being. Cultural criteria are used to evaluate managerial practices and motivational techniques for their potential to satisfy personal goals and self-generated needs. Thus self-regulatory processes constitute the link between the macrolevel of cultural values and norms, the mesolevel of organizational processes, and the microlevel of individual behavior.

We chose to define our OB model as a model of *Cultural Self-Representation*. It consists of four groups of variables: (1) cultural values and norms—the criteria used for evaluating managerial techniques; (2) managerial and motivational techniques—their potential contribution to individual goal attainment, self-worth, and well-being as evaluated in line with cultural criteria; (3) the self as an information processor and interpreter of organizational stimuli in line with cultural values; and (4) consequent work behavior, as exemplified by various indexes of behavior and such attitudes as performance quantity and quality, extra-role behavior, and withdrawal behavior as opposed to positive attitudes of commitment and work satisfaction.

We propose that the potential contribution of various managerial practices and motivational techniques depends on cultural values and norms. For example, managerial practices that reinforce personal competition may be highly valued in an individualistic culture but not in a collectivistic culture (Hofstede, 1980). A supervisor who encourages open criticism will be welcomed by subordinates in a culture of low power distance but will raise the suspicion of subordinates in a culture of high power distance (Hofstede).

Employees interpret the meaning and value of various managerial techniques in relation to their own well-being. They positively interpret managerial practices that provide opportunities for individual goal attainment and for the experience of self-worth. Cultural values and norms serve as criteria for making such evaluations.

New developments in three areas—intercultural research, social cognition, and the self—usher in a new stage in the study of the relationship between culture, self, and organizational behavior. It is reasonable to argue that successful managerial techniques in one culture may lose their effectiveness in another. The differences in their effectiveness can only be understood if we take into consideration the situational factors that lead individuals to interpret the same managerial techniques in different ways. As the market becomes more global, more attention should be given to cultural characteristics, because they set the norms and standards in the service of the self.

Numerous examples demonstrate how different motivational techniques and managerial practices emerge in different cultures and how their effectiveness changes when transferred across cultures. These examples will be discussed in later chapters. The paucity of conceptual models in OB which take contextual factors into consideration limits our ability to understand and predict OB across cultures. The main objective here is to develop an innovative model that integrates cultural factors with organizational behavior and proposes a link between processes on the macro and microlevels.

The theoretical framework presented in this book promotes our understanding of the relationship between cultural factors, managerial practices, self-regulatory processes, and employee behavior. It serves as a means to reexamine the major areas of OB from a cross-cultural perspective. Our intention is to demonstrate how cultural variables contribute to our understanding of OB and the prediction of work activities. The model explains why different managerial techniques are developed in different cultures. It proposes that managerial techniques congruent with cultural characteristics are more likely to endure and be effective than those which are incongruent. On the practical level the model provides criteria for predicting the successful implementation of various managerial techniques in different cultures.

2

Cultural Self-Representation Theory

Most existing models of OB and work motivation, developed in the sixties and seventies, focus on the individual employee rather than on the group or team and attempt to explain work behavior by looking at individual goals, expectancies, self-efficacy, and need satisfaction. Motivational techniques designed to reinforce the contingency between individual behavior and behavioral outcomes include the expectancy theory of motivation (Vroom, 1964), which stresses the motivational effect of maximizing personal utilities by means of high performance; the job-enrichment approach (Hackman & Oldham, 1980), which defines the motivation potential of a job in terms of its contribution to the intrinsic motivation of the individual employee; and the goal-setting theory of motivation (Locke & Latham, 1990), which emphasizes setting specific and difficult individual goals.

Human resource management (HRM) places a strong emphasis on personnel selection and employees' performance appraisals. In the eighties about 25% of all articles published in American I/O psychology journals discussed these two topics (Erez, in press). Individual incentive plans, designed to reinforce performance, and differential incentive plans, including flexible, "cafeteria style" benefits, were tailored to satisfy the needs of the individual employee (Cascio, 1989). This emphasis on the individual detracts attention from environmental factors that affect OB.

Two significant changes in the work environment—the globalization of the market and the restructuring of companies—have had a tremendous impact on employees' self-concept, work motivation, and commitment to the work place, as well as on OB and its consequent performance outcomes. From a psychological perspective these changes involve confrontation with cultural differences in customers' needs, partners' norms of behavior and work values, HRM practices, and decision-making processes. The popularity of guidebooks on how to do business with the Japanese attests to the fact that companies in Western societies are ill-prepared to do business across cultural borders.

Culture is often defined as a shared-meaning system (Shweder & LeVine, 1984) wherein members of the same culture are likely to interpret and evaluate situational events and practices in a similar way. Those outside the culture are likely to respond differently. Concerning managerial practices, those found to be effective in one culture may be ineffective in another. For example, quality control circles have been successfully implemented in Japan and the Far East (Onglatco, 1988), and sociotechnical systems are successful in North European countries (Gyllenhammar,

1987). Individual job-enrichment designs have been implemented in the United States (Hackman & Oldham, 1980); however, attempts to implement quality circles or sociotechnical systems have not been highly successful (Lawler, 1986). And whereas differential monetary reward systems are viewed negatively by members of the kibbutz movement in Israel because they contradict the ideology of equality (Leviatan & Rosner, 1980), such differential rewards are well accepted in the private sector and in individualistic cultures that are guided by the values of equity rather than equality (Erez, 1986). The successful implementation of motivational techniques and managerial practices appears to depend on their congruence within the cultural context. Culture provides the standards for evaluating certain motivational techniques and managerial practices as either positive, neutral, or negative.

Unfortunately, models of organizational behavior developed in the West do not take this aspect of cultural difference into consideration; rather, situational effects are commonly interpreted as artifacts. A recent review of the theory and practice of work motivation by Katzell and Thompson (1990) does not include any aspect of cross-cultural research on work motivation, although such research provides explanations for differential interpretations of motivational techniques. Furthermore, they downplay the importance of endogenous theories that might explain how culture is related to organizational behavior and work motivation. These theories, which deal with process or mediating variables, are based on a cognitive approach to information processing and social cognition and have not yet been the target of extensive research and application in work situations.

We argue that adaptation to changes in a complex environment requires an analysis of the cognitive mechanisms of information processing to explain how employees interpret and evaluate the situation and how their work motivation and work behavior is affected by these processes. The key factors in models of work motivation, which include job enrichment, goals, and organizational commitment, are evaluative by nature. Employees evaluate the situation, including the level of goal difficulty and the opportunities for self-enhancement and intrinsic and extrinsic satisfaction. These evaluations are constrained by culture. Based on their evaluations, employees develop intentions and make commitments to their immediate jobs and to the organizational goals.

No current theory of OB provides the conceptual framework for understanding how culture, managerial practices, and work behavior are interrelated. The lack of an adequate theoretical framework for understanding the moderating effect of culture has led to the development of the present model.

A development of a new theory is not an end in itself. Rather, a better theory is a means to an end. A theoretical model should generate a series of steps toward the diagnosis/solution of a problem (Campbell, 1990). Conceptual models can be improved by using three criteria: they can be derived analytically; they can come about as a result of evaluations by experts in the field of study; and they can be evaluated empirically (Campbell). All three criteria are considered in the process of formulating a new model of cross-cultural I/O psychology:

On the empirical level, the generalizability of present theories of I/O psychology holds true mainly in the United States. Yet the theories fail to explain the variance in research findings across cultures (Adler, 1986; Amir & Sharon, 1987). Empirical confrontation is essential for testing the meaning and validity of scientific hypotheses. What happens to a theory when it is not supported by empirical findings? The answer to this question is guided by two different approaches. One, representing the school of logical empiricism, asserts that some theories are right and other are wrong, and that the empirical confrontation is a test of whether a given theory is valid. The drive to empirically support a theoretical model may cause biases in interpretation. For example, data analysis in line with a universalistic and individually oriented model of behavior may lead to a wrong interpretation of situational effects as artifacts or they may be attributed to individual differences.

The second approach represents the position of contextualism, which maintains that all theories are right and that empirical confrontation is a continuing process of discovering the contexts under which hypotheses are true and those under which hypotheses are false (McGuire, 1983). According to the constructivist paradigm, "the role of the empirical side of science is not to test which opposite formulation is valid but rather to explore and discover the range of circumstances in which each of the opposite formulations holds" (McGuire, 1980:79). This approach enhances models of interaction which examine the boundary conditions of theoretical models. With respect to cultural effects, this approach tests the moderating effect of culture on the relationship between various managerial techniques and employee behavior.

The second criterion for evaluating the quality of theoretical models is by expert evaluation. Researchers in the field of cross-cultural psychology admit that their theoretical models are poorly developed. Although the field of I/O psychology has a longer tradition of theory development than that of cross-cultural psychology, "the state of theory in industrial and organizational psychology is not what it should be and improvement is needed (Campbell:40). In particular, theories of I/O psychology have been criticized for lacking validity generalization across cultures (Boyacigiller & Adler, 1991). On the basis of peer evaluation, present models of organizational behavior fail to account for cultural moderators.

The third criterion of theory evaluation is analytic. From an analytic perspective we chose to question three conventions in I/O psychology and to reframe them: (1) mediating processes do not serve as an action lever to boost employees' work motivation (Katzell & Thompson, 1990); (2) cognitive information processing inhibits the development of contextual models of organizational behavior (Cappeli & Sherer, 1991); and (3) there is at present no way to relate the individual-based explanations of employee behavior in microresearch to the environment or context-based explanations of organizations in macroresearch. A counterapproach proposes that cognitive, mediating, self-regulatory processes provide the conceptual framework necessary for the development of a model of cross-cultural I/O psychology. Such models help explain how employees process, evaluate, and interpret organizational cues of managerial practices in light of their cultural values and norms. Contrary to the first convention, mediating processes of self-regulation may serve to boost employees' motivation. In contrast to the second convention, cognitive processes may improve our understanding of how environmental stimuli are processed and interpreted by individuals. In contrast to the third convention, cognitive models of self-regulation may bridge the gap between the macrolevel of culture and managerial practices and the microlevel of individual behavior.

Cognitive models of information processing explain how information from the external environment is selectively recognized, evaluated, and interpreted in terms of its meaning for the individual, and how it affects behavior. Metacognitive models involve self-regulatory processes which are guided by the paradigm that individuals are aware of their own cognitive processes and can actively influence the monitoring and appraisal processes to enhance perceptions of well-being. Knowledge about one's own cognitive processes is captured by the self, which interprets managerial practices and motivational techniques according to accepted cultural values and norms and in fulfillment of self-generated needs.

We propose that the source of influence on the self-regulatory processes is the *self*. The self processes information, interprets it in line with internalized criteria, and activates the response patterns accordingly (Markus & Wurf, 1987). Self-concept is a composite view formed through direct experience and evaluations adopted from significant others (Bandura, 1986). When significant others share the same value system and norms of behavior, it can be argued that the self is modified by culture. In different cultures various aspects of self might be modified, as will be further discussed. We propose that the self is an important unit of analysis for understanding cross-cultural differences in employees' perception and evaluation of various motivational and human resource management techniques, and their consequent work behavior.

Since the self has the capacity for self-evaluation, it generates needs for self-enhancement and for the preservation of positive self-esteem. These needs are partly shaped by culture and partly by the unique, personal characteristics of the individual. It is reasonable to expect different selves to emerge in different cultures and, consequently, different managerial approaches to be effective in satisfying needs for self-enhancement.

The self seems to be the link between culture and employees' work behavior. On the one hand, it is shaped by cultural values and norms; on the other, it directs employees' behavior toward self-enhancement. Therefore it captures the cultural characteristics which are most relevant for work behavior.

Based on the metacognitive framework, we propose a *cultural self-representation model* for understanding OB across cultures. The model consists of four factors: (1) cultural values and norms which dominate the external and the internal work environment; (2) managerial practices and motivational techniques operating within a particular work environment; (3) the self, modified by culture, as an interpreter of managerial practices and motivational techniques in light of cultural values and norms and in relation to self-generated needs; and (4) employees' work motivation and work behavior. The self mediates the effect of various managerial practices and motivational techniques on work behavior. It forms the link between the contextual level and the individual behavior in organizations.

In the following sections we will elaborate on each component of this model, which is presented in Figure 2-1.

The first section examines cultural characteristics and their potential effect on the meaning ascribed by employees to managerial practices and motivational techniques. The second describes various motivational techniques that will be interpreted in light of cultural values and norms. The third portrays the self as the link

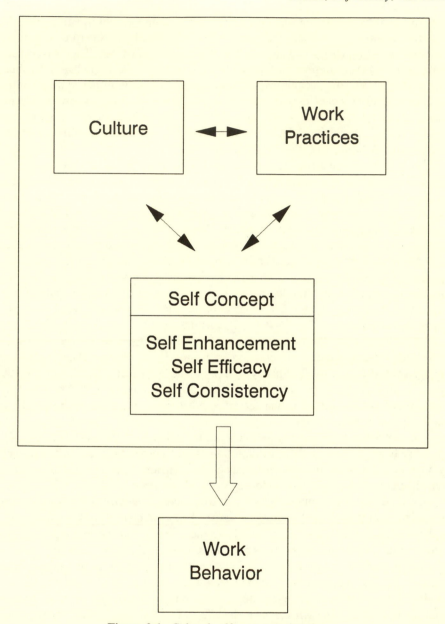

Figure 2-1. Cultural self-representation theory

between cultural values, managerial practices, and employees' behavior. The self is viewed as an information processor which selects, interprets, and evaluates the meaning of managerial practices and motivational techniques as contributing to personal self-worth and well-being in light of cultural values and norms. The fourth section centers on organizational behavior and work motivation as outcomes of the self-regulatory processes.

CULTURAL CHARACTERISTICS

The globalization of the market, the unification of Europe, massive immigration from East Europe, and the processes of mergers and acquisitions have exposed employees to different cultures. As a result cultural differences have become a focus of attention, and their effect on work behavior is becoming more evident. In the domain of OB, the concept of culture, both on the national and organizational levels, is key to understanding why American companies do not perform as well as their counterparts in Japan (Schein, 1990).

To understand why different types of managerial practices and motivational techniques emerge in different cultures, and why the modeling and transference of certain techniques across cultures is not always effective, we should learn more about the role that culture plays in our model of work behavior. Toward this end we propose a cognitive information processing approach to the understanding of culture. We view culture as a shared knowledge structure that results in decreased variability in individual response to stimuli. The cognitive approach is embedded in many definitions of culture. For example, Kluckhohn (1954) represents the anthropological approach, defining culture as patterned ways of thinking. Similarly Shweder and LeVine (1984) view culture as a set of shared meaning systems, and Hofstede (1980) defines it as a set of mental programs that control individuals' responses in a given context.

Culture itself is developed within a certain ecological environment (Berry, 1979). Since the adoption of cultural contents is selective and adaptive, different ecological environments modify different cultures. Adaptation to the environment requires different levels of sophistication and of cognitive complexity. As a result we find that cognitive schemas across cultures vary in both their level of complexity and their content parameters (Witkin & Berry, 1975). Members of different cultures develop different ways of viewing and perceiving the world. Their level of cognitive complexity was found to be positively related to indexes of economic growth (Gruenfeld & MacEacheron, 1975).

Culture shapes a society's core values and norms, which are shared and transmitted from one generation to another through social learning processes of modeling and observation, as well as through the effects of one's own actions (Bandura, 1986).

Culture can be defined on different levels of analysis, ranging from a group level to an organizational level or a national level. Independent of the level of analysis, culture can be defined as "what a group learns over a period of time as that group solves its problems of survival in an external environment and its problem of internal integration" (Schein, 1990:111). Any definable group with a shared history can have a culture, and within one nation or one organization there can be many subcultures (Schein, 1990; Schneider, 1975; Triandis, 1972). Once a group has learned to hold common assumptions about adaptation to the environment, its members respond in similar patterns of perception, thought, emotion, and behavior to external stimuli.

In homogenous societies, the norms and values of various ingroups are relatively uniform within tight cultures. However heterogenous societies have groups with dissimilar norms and values, and consequently a loose culture is formed (Triandis, 1989b). The strength and degree of internal consistency of a culture are a function of the homogeneity across groups, the length of time the groups have existed, the intensity of the groups' experiences of learning (Schein, 1985, 1990), and the degree to which norms and rules of behavior are generalized across situations. Loose cultures seem to be more tolerant of deviant behavior than tight cultures.

Cultures are differentiated in their content components. One of the most central dimensions of culture is individual's n versus collectivism (Triandis et al., 1988). Individualism versus collectivism captures the dimension by which the members of one culture relate to each other. It accounts for most of the variance in the ecological cross-cultural value data collected by Hofstede (1980). Collectivism, in contrast to individualism, conveys self-definition as part of the group, subordination of personal goals to group goals, concern for the integrity of the group, and intense emotional attachment to the ingroup. The major themes of individualism are self-definition as an entity that is distinct and separate from the group, emphasis on personal goals, and less concern for and emotional attachment to the ingroup (Triandis et al.).

Cultural values have an immediate impact on organizational structures and processes and on employees' behavior. Managerial practices and motivational techniques that are considered to be legitimate and acceptable in one culture may not be acceptable in another. Therefore culture should be taken into consideration when evaluating the effectiveness of various managerial and motivational techniques.

A developmental perspective on the cultural evolution of societies indicates a shift from traditional collectivistic cultures to modern individualistic cultures, with a focus on exchange rather than communal relations and on the independent rather than the interdependent self. The sift toward individualism is associated with high levels of gross national product (GNP) (McClelland, 1961; Hofstede, 1991; Triandis, 1989b). Hofstede suggests that the GNP/capita is positively and linearly correlated to individualism. Countries characterized by individualistic values have higher levels of GNP/capita than countries characterized by collectivistic values. Yet a careful examination of Hofstede's data suggests that several countries (e.g., Singapore, Hong Kong, and Japan) that scored above the regression line on collectivism had higher scores on GNP/capita than we might expect.

The advantage of individualistic over collectivistic countries may depend on the criteria used. For example, comparative measures of stress and health problems indicate that Western individualistic countries suffer from these problems more than do collectivistic cultures and that there is a trade-off relationship between affluence and stress in Western countries (Henry & Stephens, 1977). Keeping GNP/capita constant, the advantage of collective groups in reducing health problems and prolonging life expectancy is evident in Israeli kibbutzim. Research data collected between 1975 and 1980 by Leviatan and Cohen (1985) demonstrated that life expectancy among elderly people in the kibbutzim was significantly higher than among elderly people in Israel's urban areas. In the kibbutzim life expectancy was 74.4 years for men and 78.9 years for women compared to the total population figures in Israel of 71.9 and 75.4 years for men and women, respectively. Leviatan and Cohen attributed longevity to the social support system for the elderly people in the kibbutzim.

The emergence of Japan and other Confucian countries as economic powers in the 1980s, suggests that collectivism is compatible with rapid development. What is not clear, however, is whether rapid growth occurs *only* when countries are "catching up" with the more developed countries.

The cultural dimension of collectivism versus individualism has a direct implication for self-concept. Different selves are expected to be developed in collectivistic and individualistic cultures. Consequently different interpretations are expected to be given to HRM practices and to managerial and motivational techniques, depending on their contribution to the growth of a collective or a private self. Further elaboration of the meaning of self-concept and self-identity in relation to culture is offered in the section on the self.

MANAGEMENT PRACTICES AND MOTIVATIONAL TECHNIQUES

Employees' behavior in organizations is directed by HRM practices and by motivational techniques. A typical model of HRM in the United States contains three groups of factors: (1) strategic objectives—productivity, quality of work life, profits; (2) environmental characteristics—competitive, legal, and social issues; and (3) functions—employment, development, compensation, labor-management, support, evaluation, and international implications (Cascio, 1989). Such a model is clearly tailored for an individualistic-competitive culture. All HRM functions are oriented toward the individual employee. For example, selection of individual employees is based on individual difference characteristics; performance appraisal is centered on the individual and his/her personal achievement; individual compensation plans are commonly implemented in American companies; and jobs are designed for the individual employee.

Functions that pertain to groups and interpersonal relationships do not exist in the model. For example, team building and interpersonal communication patterns are not included among the functions of HRM. Cultural dimensions are not part of the environmental characteristics, and problems of HRM from an international perspective are discussed ad hoc with no theoretical framework.

In contrast to American models of HRM, those used in Japanese companies are based on the philosophy of familial management (Erez, 1991), which advocates mutuality between management and employees, strong ties between employees and their corporation, and the responsibility of management for the employees' well-being. The main characteristics of HRM in Japan are lifetime employment, a strong emphasis on interpersonal communication, group participation in decision-making, and team development. Compensation is based on seniority and profit sharing. Individual performance appraisal is rarely implemented, and employees are evaluated on the basis of their contribution to the group or organizational unit. It is reasonable to argue that managerial practices which are consistent with the Japanese culture may not be effective in American companies and vice versa.

The effect of various managerial techniques on an individual's sense of self-worth is interpreted by self-regulatory processes according to cultural values and norms.

Therefore, the mesolevel of managerial practices and motivational techniques should be studied in relation to the macrolevel of cultural values.

THE SELF

This section focuses on the self as modified by culture and as the interpreter of the meaning and importance of various managerial practices and motivational techniques for a person's self-worth.

"The self consists of all statements made by a person, overtly or covertly, that include the words "I," "me," "mine," and "myself" (Triandis, 1989b:506). A person's attitudes, intentions, roles, and values represent the self.

People everywhere are likely to develop an understanding of themselves as physically distinct and separate from others. Beyond a physical self, individuals have a private self which conveys the awareness of internal thoughts and feelings that are private to the extent that they cannot be directly known by others (Markus & Kitayama, 1991). Yet these thoughts and feelings are shaped to a great extent by the shared understanding within a particular culture of what it is to be human (Cahoone, 1988; Cushman, 1990). The enduring attachments and commitments to the social environment help define who we are (Sandel, 1982). The self is a composite view of oneself that is formed through direct experience and evaluations adopted from significant others (Bandura, 1986).

The self is viewed as a dynamic interpretive structure that mediates most significant intrapersonal and interpersonal processes. Intrapersonal processes include cognitive information processing, affect, and motivation, whereas interpersonal processes reflect the interaction with the social milieu—social perception, choice of situation, interaction strategy, and reaction to feedback (Markus & Wurf, 1987). The self is a person's mental representation of his/her own personality, social identity, and social roles (Kihlstrom & Cantor, 1984). The functioning of self-concept depends on both self-motives being served and on the configuration of the immediate social situation.

More psychologists have come to the realization that the self must function within a particular environment, and that there is no meaningful way to speak about persons abstracted from their particular community (Sampson, 1989). Humans are incomplete and therefore unable to function adequately unless embedded in a specific culture (Cushman, 1990). The enduring attachments and commitments to the social environment help define who a person is (Sandel, 1982).

Among sociologists there has been a similar movement to define self-concept as rooted in the social system and as a reflection of the responses and appraisals of others. The reference group's norms become the internalized standards against which individuals judge themselves. Thus, the self is modified to a great extent by social learning processes.

The mechanisms by which all self-relevant information is processed, stored, and organized into a certain structure have mainly been conceptualized by models of social cognition. According to this approach the self is viewed as a person's mental representation of his/her own personality, formed through experience and thought and encoded in memory alongside mental representations of other objects, reflected and imagined, in the physical and social world (Kihlstrom et al., 1988). It is a system of self-schemas or generalizations about the self derived from past social experiences. A schema is hypothesized to have a dual nature of structure and process. As such the self is both the knower and what is known (Markus & Wurf, 1987). The content of self-conceptions and identities form the structure and anchors the self in the social system, whereas self-evaluation deals with the dynamic dimension of the self (Gecas, 1982).

On the structural level the self is viewed as a collection of schemas, prototypes, goals, or images that are arranged in a space (Sherman, Judd & Bernadette, 1989). Each schema is a generalization about what the self is, and it contains descriptive information about traits, roles, and behavior, as well as knowledge of rules and procedures for making inferences and evaluating its own functioning and development (Kihlstrom & Cantor, 1984).

The self is viewed as multidimensional, consisting of many role identities (Gecas, 1982; Hoelter, 1985), and relevant traits and characteristics (Markus & Wurf, 1987). People differ in the components of their selves and in the relative importance of these components. The various attributes of the self seem to be organized in a hierarchical order. The general self is at the top of the hierarchy, followed by more specific self-attributes (Cantor & Khilstrom, 1987; Marsh, 1986; Shavelson & Marsh, 1986). The hierarchical structure is also conceived in terms of central and peripheral traits, with the central traits more crucial for self-concept (Cantor & Kihlstrom). Individuals are known to be more committed to their central roles because they are more consequential to their conduct of behavior (Stryker, 1968).

Not all the information about the self is accessible at any particular moment. In information-processing terms, the self represents declarative knowledge (consisting of abstract and concrete factual knowledge) of those attributes and features of which it is aware, at least in principle. The aspects of personality brought to our attention at any particular time are determined by contextual factors (Khilstrom et al., 1988). The part active at any moment is called the "working self," or "self-concept of the moment" (Markus & Kunda, 1986; Markus & Wurf, 1987). The working self directly encounters the environment. Compared to the deeper levels of self-concept, it is more accessible, active, malleable, and tied to prevailing circumstances. The configuration of the immediate social environment determines the facet of the self that is most accessible.

In addition to the structural approach, the self has been conceived of in terms of dynamic self-regulatory processes. These processes consist of the following steps: (1) the setting of goals that represent proximal and enduring self-definitions; (2) planning and strategy selection to facilitate goal attainment; (3) self-monitoring, which takes place as people attend to various aspects of their behavior, including intensity, direction, and quality; (4) judgmental processes, which evaluate behavior in line with certain standards; and (5) self-reaction, including self-reinforcement (Bandura, 1986; Kanfer, 1980; Markus & Wurf). While some theories emphasize self-reinforcement as critical for self-regulatory success (Bandura; Kanfer), others emphasize information rather than rewards as the critical determinant of attempted changes (Carver & Scheier, 1981).

Self-regulatory processes operate in the service of developing and maintaining a representation of the self. Thus, the self-concept is to a large extent an agent of its own creation (Gecas, 1982). Three motives in the service of the self can be identified (Gecas; Markus & Wurf): (1) the need for self-enhancement, as reflected in seeking and maintaining a positive cognitive and affective state about the self; (2) the self-efficacy motive, which is the desire to perceive oneself as competent and efficacious; and (3) the need for self-consistency, which is the desire to sense and experience coherence and continuity.

Self-Enhancement

The experience of self-enhancement is affected by opportunities in the environments and by cognitive self-regulatory processes of sampling, assessing, and interpreting such opportunities. Research on the information-processing consequences of self-enhancement continues to grow. This research demonstrates the existence of self-serving bias in information processing (Kunda, 1987). For example, individuals are more sensitive to self-relevant stimuli than to stimuli with a low relevance to the self; they process self-congruent stimuli more efficiently, and they resist incongruent information. Self-relevant stimuli show enhanced recall and recognition (Markus & Wurf, 1987).

Numerous studies have demonstrated that self-referent information is more highly recalled than other-referent information or semantic information (Kihlstrom et al., 1988). For example, in one study subjects were asked to recall information about a list of personal traits. In one condition they focused on the attributes of the trait (orthographic, phonemic, and semantic), and in the second condition they were asked to judge whether some traits described themselves. In the later case more items were recalled than in the former (Rogers, Kuiper & Kirker 1977). Accessibility of a memory is a function of the degree to which the stimulus information makes contact with preexisting knowledge during encoding (Kihlstrom et al.). The fact that self-referent information is more highly recalled than any other attests to the centrality of self-concept in our cognitive network.

One manifestation of the need for self-enhancement is the general tendency to distort reality, through selective perception and bias in attribution, in the service of maintaining a positive self-conception (Gecas, 1982; Kunda, in press). For example, people choose to judge others on dimensions that are personally relevant and not on other dimensions. They prefer and seek out positive information about themselves, and they selectively sample, interpret, and remember events that support positive self-concept.

Self-Efficacy

Perceived self-efficacy is "a judgement of one's capability to accomplish a certain level of performance" (Bandura, 1986:391). People tend to avoid tasks and situations they believe exceed their capabilities. Efficacy judgements promote the choice of situations and tasks that have a high likelihood of success while eliminating tasks that exceed one's capabilities. Four sources modify the perceptions of self-efficacy.

The first is enactive attainment, based on authentic mastery experiences. Success raises perceptions of self-efficacy and repeated failures lower them. Once a strong sense of self-efficacy is established, the effect of failure is attenuated. To protect positive perceptions of self-efficacy, people tend to attribute failure to situational factors. Vicarious experience is another factor which affects self-efficacy. Visualizing others performing effectively positively affects one's level of self-efficacy. People rely on other models when they have no prior experience. Convinced vicariously of their inefficacy, they are unlikely to perform well, whereas when observing the success of others similar to themselves, they are more likely to perform effectively. Verbal persuasion is a third factor that either enhances or inhibits self-efficacy. Positive persuasion leads people to believe that they are capable of obtaining their goal; consequently they become more committed to the goal and allocate more resources to their mission. Commitment and effort result in a higher level of performance (Erez & Zidon, 1984), which further increases self-efficacy. The fourth, physiological state, serves as a basis for evaluating one's capability. Symptoms of fatigue, stress, and anxiety indicate that a person is not at his or her best and attenuate perceptions of self-efficacy (Bandura, 1986). Two of the factors, vicarious experience and verbal persuasion, are expressions of social learning processes which take into consideration influences of the social environment.

Self-efficacy has been mainly developed with respect to the individual (Bandura). However a perceived collective efficacy is crucial for what people choose to do as a group, how much effort they put into it, and how persistent they are in the face of failure. The strength of groups, organizations, and nations lies partly in the sense of collective efficacy (Bandura). It is not exactly clear how collective efficacy is shaped by the social environment and whether it is more likely to develop in certain cultures than others. An analogy between self-efficacy and collective efficacy suggests that collective efficacy is shaped by the history of positive and negative experiences on the group level, as well as by the immediate situation. The relative salience of individual versus collective efficacy may be shaped by culture. In group-oriented cultures with a history of effective teamwork, collective efficacy may be higher than in group-oriented cultures with a history of failures. In individualistic cultures, collective efficacy may be lower than that of successful teams in group-oriented cultures, since their experience in team work is limited.

Self-Consistency

While such motives as self-enhancement, self-actualization, and self-efficacy have been studied extensively, self-consistency has received little empirical attention. The sense of continuity and consistency helps individuals to connect events in their current social life to past experiences and to maintain a coherent view that enables them to operate effectively in the environment (Epstein, 1973). The motivation for perceived self-consistency has two manifestations. It leads to the active construction of memories and selective perceptions in line with previous events. It also activates and directs people to behave in accordance with the values and norms implied by the identities to which they are committed.

The self-consistency motive is supported by numerous findings (Epstein; Markus & Wurf, 1987). First, individuals exhibit a continuity of motivational patterns that sustains their self-image across time, despite such life experiences as marriage and changed jobs. A self-consistency motive provides a sense of continuity and stability. Second, individuals appear to construct world views that are consistent with their self-images. These views are filtered in order to maintain a stable self-image. Finally, individuals are resistant to information that is incongruent with their self-structure. They are likely to make situational attributions for behavior that is inconsistent with their own self-image. Thus employees who are confident of their mechanical dexterity may attribute an inability to master a new machine operation to such environmental disturbances as noise rather than poor dexterity. It is important to note that stable, cognitive structures that define the self are shaped by culture. Since mechanical competency in males is prized in American culture, many American males perceive themselves as being manually dexterous and capable of operating or repairing such mechanical devices as the family furnace or lawnmower.

The need for self-consistency can also affect employees' acceptance of various managerial techniques. Techniques that are familiar and consistent with cultural traditions and norms are more likely to be accepted than others. This factor may contribute to our understanding of why certain techniques are more effective than others.

Self-enhancement, self-efficacy, and self-consistency motives are part of the self-regulatory processes. Their fulfillment depends on self-evaluation and self-worth. Cultural values provide some of the criteria and standards used for self-evaluation. These criteria vary across cultures, along with differences in cultural values, and shape different meanings of self-worth.

The process of self-evaluation requires the use of a set of criteria and guidelines. Three reference sources of criteria are recognized (Breckler & Greenwald, 1986). One is the public evaluation that a person gains from others. The second is self-evaluation, as determined by personal, internal standards. The third is based on the contribution that one makes to the collective or reference group. These criteria correspond to the three facets of the self. The public self represents cognition concerning others' view of oneself. It is sensitive to the evaluations of significant others and seeks to gain their approval (Breckler & Greenwald, 1986; Triandis, 1989b). The private self represents cognition that involve traits, states, or behaviors of the person; it seeks to satisfy internal standards of achievement. The private self represents a person's view of what makes him or her unique. The collective self seeks to achieve the goals and fulfill the role established by a reference group. The collective self corresponds to the notion of social identity, that is, "the part of the individual's self-concept which derives from his or her knowledge of his or her membership in a social group, together with the values and the emotional significance attached to this membership" (Tajfel, 1978:63).

The criteria for evaluation used by the self vary across cultures, along with differences in cultural values, and shape different meanings of self-worth. Criteria used by the private self are supported by individualistic values, whereas those representing the collective self predominate collectivistic cultures. The public self is considered to be an extension of the private or the collective self, depending on the culture (Triandis, 1989b). In individualistic cultures it is assumed that the generalized others will reinforce autonomy and independence, whereas in collectivistic cultures they will reinforce the subordination of the private goals to the collective goals.

The development of the three points of self-reference is based on the cognitive discrimination between oneself and others. The sequence of development is from the public to the collective self (Breckler & Greenwald, 1986). The first developmental stage of the public self reflects conformity to external rules, with conscious preoccupations centering on appearance and social acceptability (Piaget, 1965). The private self develops as the individual internalizes the valuative standards of others. It is seen as the conscientious stage of ego development, with an emphasis on long-term self-evaluated goals, self-set standards for achievement, differentiated self-criticism, and a sense of responsibility (Loevinger, 1976). The collective self represents a further developmental step in which the goals of the reference groups have become internalized, and the individual is capable of effective collaboration with others (Piaget, 1965). The three facets of the self have a direct correspondence to Kelman's analysis of social influence in terms of compliance, internalization, and identification (1961).

Although the structural and dynamic dimensions of the self are considered to be universal, the relative differentiation between the self and others varies across cultures. People who live in the same cultural environment share similar values and cognitive schemas, and they use similar criteria for evaluating the contribution of certain types of behavior to the development of a sense of self-worth (Triandis, 1989b). Western cultures are known for their individualistic values. In these cultures the self is less connected and more differentiated from the social context. The normative imperative is to become independent from others, self-reliant, and to discover and express one's unique attributes. Western cultures reinforce the formation of the independent self "whose behavior is organized and made meaningful primarily by reference to one's own internal repertoire of thoughts, feelings, and actions of others" (Markus & Kitayama, 1991:226).

In contrast the predominant values of Far Eastern cultures are collectivism and group orientation, with an emphasis on harmony, conformity, obedience, and reliability. These cultures tend to be homogenous, share a common fate, and emphasize interdependence and a sense of collectivity, mainly when they are exposed to external threat and competition with outgroups (Triandis, 1989b). People in collectivistic cultures stress similarities with other group members that strengthen their group identity. Collectivistic cultures emphasize the connectedness among human beings and cultivate the interdependent concept of the self (Markus & Kitayama, 1991). The interdependent self entails "seeing oneself as part of an encompassing social relationship, recognizing that one's behavior is determined, contingent on, and, to a large extent organized by, what the actor perceives to be thoughts, feelings, and actions of others in the relationship" (227). The focus of the interdependent self is its relationship to others.

Empirical findings demonstrate that people from East Asia have a greater tendency to describe themselves in terms that reflect their collective interdependent self than do Europeans or North Americans (Bond & Cheung, 1983; Trafimow, Triandis

& Goto, 1991). Students from Western cultures perceive themselves to be less similar to others compared to students from Eastern cultures. However Eastern students perceive others to be less similar to themselves than do Western students. This finding suggests that for individuals from Western cultures, self-knowledge is more distinctive and elaborate than knowledge about others, whereas for individuals from Eastern cultures, knowledge about others is more distinctive and elaborate than knowledge about the self. Among the Chinese, who are motivated by the interdependent self, social needs are stronger than needs for autonomy and personal achievement (Bond, 1988).

The typology of the three self-derived needs—enhancement, efficacy, and consistency—and the classification of private and collective selves, or independent and interdependent selves, were developed as two separate systems. The question of how these systems relate to each other has not yet been addressed. It is reasonable to argue that the fulfillment of the three self-derived needs should have different meanings for the independent self and the interdependent self. For this purpose the two systems should be integrated. The three self-derived needs are nested within the two facets of the self—the independent and interdependent self. Different criteria for evaluation are employed by the independent and the interdependent facets of the self to determine what kind of actions and situations will be perceived as satisfying self-derived needs. According to this model, self-enhancement for the independent self motivates individuals toward personal achievement. Situations and managerial practices that provide opportunities for individual success are positively evaluated by the independent self. On the other hand, enhancement for the interdependent self motivates individuals to contribute to the success of the group, to avoid social loafing (Earley, 1989), and to meet the expectations of significant others (Bond, 1988; Markus & Kitayama, 1991).

The need for self-efficacy is a salient characteristic of the independent self, whereas the perception of collective efficacy, which pertains to people's sense that they can solve their problems and improve their lives through concerted effort (Bandura, 1986), is characteristic of the interdependent self. Self-consistency is evaluated by the independent self in line with previous individual behavior. For the interdependent self, consistency pertains to the enduring relationship between a person and his or her reference group.

The self, including the self-derived needs, constitutes the link between the contextual factors of culture and managerial practices, which operate on the macro- and mesolevels, respectively, and the microlevel of employee behavior. Management practices are evaluated by the self in line with accepted cultural values and with respect to their fulfillment of the self-derived needs.

GENERALIZED WORK BEHAVIOR

The broad concept of work behavior encompasses work-related behavioral processes that take place on the individual, group, and organizational levels. These processes can be measured according to both objective and subjective criteria. Among the objective criteria are: performance quantity, performance quality, withdrawal behavior such as absenteeism and turnover, as well as extra-role behavior, that is, behavior over and above expectations. Subjective criteria involve perception and attribution, attitude formation, motivation, and commitment.

Work behavior is strongly affected by managerial practices and motivational techniques. Managerial practices are evaluated according to their contribution to employee self-worth and well-being. Cultural values and norms serve as criteria for evaluating the potential contribution of management practices to employee self-worth. A positive evaluation results in a positive effect on work behavior. Thus the self mediates the relationship between managerial practices and work behavior.

AN INTEGRATION

The dominant models of work behavior, work motivation, and HRM are cognitive by nature and tend to focus on the individual employee. A typical Western model of HRM focuses on the individual-job fit, using individual-based methods of selection and placement in the organization and techniques of individual performance appraisal as employees progress in their work (Cascio, 1989). These models overlook the sociodynamic processes in the work as part of HRM. For example, interpersonal communication, staffing work teams, and evaluating team performance are usually not considered.

In a similar vein, current theories of work motivation focus on the individual and attempt to explain motivated behavior as a function of individual goals (Locke & Latham, 1990), individual expectancies (Vroom, 1964), self-efficacy (Bandura, 1986), and need satisfaction (Maslow, 1954). Similarly the individual employee and his or her particular job serve as the units of analysis for designing enriched jobs (Hackman & Oldham, 1980).

Another example of an individually focused motivation theory is that of goal setting. Recently self-efficacy and valences were introduced as mediating variables between goals and performance (Earley & Lituchy, 1991; Eden, 1988; Garland, 1985; Locke & Latham). The core findings of the goal-setting model demonstrates that specific and difficult goals lead to high performance levels *if* accepted by the individual and *if* feedback is provided (Locke & Latham). It can be argued that goal acceptance or commitment has a stronger motivational power than goals per se since it connotes a stake in the consequences and a willingness to persevere and sacrifice to realize the goal (Novacek & Lazarus, in press). Thus an important motivational question is: How can one motivate employees to become committed to their goals?

It is reasonable to expect a high level of goal commitment when goal attainment contributes to self-enhancement. The interpretation of goal attainment and work outcomes as self-enhancing depends on accepted norms and values. Thus the value of work outcomes and of attaining certain goals may vary across situations and cultures.

Present theories of work motivation do not take cultural factors into consideration, and their prediction of outcomes is confined to Western individualistic cultures. Moreover, emphasis has been on exogenous theories of work motivation that focus on motivational factors that can be manipulated by the organization, such as incentives, goal-setting techniques, and job redesign. Yet endogenous theories that examine process or mediating variables and help explain motivation are downplayed. Katzell & Thompson (1990) argue that exogenous theories provide "action levers" that can be employed to change work motivation. They emphasize the technology of work motivation rather than causal factors that explain why a certain technique has the potential to become more effective than others.

The approach proposed by Katzell and Thompson is probably useful within a given work environment, where all employees are likely to interpret the managerial practices in the same way. However, since the self is shaped by the environment, different interpretations might be given to the same motivational stimuli in different cultures. The evaluation of goal attainment and of certain work outcomes as contributing to the enhancement of the self depends on prevailing cultural standards. For example, individual-based rewards will be more highly valued in a culture that enhances the private self over the collective self. On the other hand, group-based rewards will be more highly valued in a culture dominated by the collective self. Cultural characteristics can be identified on the national level, the organizational level, and even on the unit level of analysis.

Numerous cross-cultural studies have recently been conducted on work values, HRM practices, and work motivation. The studies clearly demonstrate that there are significant differences among cultures in collectivistic versus individualistic values, and in power distance (the psychological distance between different levels in the organizational hierarchy, Hofstede, 1980; Triandis et al., 1988; Triandis, 1989b). Such differences correspond to the differential effectiveness of various motivational HRM techniques.

One effective way to interpret the differential effectiveness of these techniques is by classifying them into two categories: those consistent with an individualistic culture that provides opportunities for experiencing self-enhancement and self-efficacy, and those consistent with a collectivistic culture that provides opportunities for the development of collective self-enhancement and collective efficacy. Such a classification promotes congruence between managerial techniques and cultural characteristics, as reflected in self-concept.

Table 2-1 summarizes the classification of various managerial techniques into two categories: group-centered versus individual-centered techniques. Managerial techniques that match such individualistic values as individual job enrichment, individual goal-setting, and individual incentives were found to be effective in individualistic cultures. In contrast, managerial techniques that correspond to such collectivistic, group-oriented values as quality circles, autonomous work groups, group goals, and participation in goal-setting and decision-making, were found to be more effective in such collectivistic cultures as Japan, China, and Israel (Earley, 1989; Erez, 1992; Erez, 1986; Erez & Earley, 1987; Matsui, Kakuyama & Onglatco, 1987).

Based on theories of social cognition, managerial techniques that are congruent with the cultural schema are more likely to be accepted than others, and motivational factors that are highly valued by prevailing cultural standards are more likely to contribute to self-enhancement than others. It is therefore reasonable to argue that successful managerial techniques in one culture may lose their effective-

Table 2-1. Group Versus Individually Centered Managerial Techniques

Technique	Individual-Centered	Group-Centered
Goal setting	Individual-based	Group-based
Incentives	Individual	Group
Performance appraisal	Individual	Group
		Company-based
Job design	Job enrichment	Sociotechnical
		Quality circles
Job analysis	Specific job requirements	General job requirements
Socialization	Low emphasis	High emphasis
Communication	Low interpersonal	High interpersonal
Problem solving	Individual-based	Group-based
Decision-making	Majority vote	Group consensus

ness in another. With the expansion of global markets, endogenous theories that focus on cultural characteristics will gain importance. The present model proposes that mediating processes of cultural self-representation link cultural factors, managerial practices, and work behavior.

The relationship between culture and effective managerial techniques has been shown in numerous studies. In Norway, French, Israel, and As (1960) attempted to replicate a study by Coch and French (1948) in the United States that found direct employee participation in decision-making to be more effective than participation by a representative or no participation. The researchers explained their failure to replicate the study by arguing that in Norway it was customary for union representatives to participate in decision-making, but not the employees themselves. Since direct participation did not fit in with the cultural schema, it was not found to be effective. Similarly Earley (1986) found that in British companies, unlike in American companies, shop stewards are more highly trusted than supervisors, and therefore their decisions are more likely to be accepted by British compared to American employees.

The effectiveness of participation on employees' commitment and performance is influenced by norms prevalent in the culture. Group participation is congruent with collectivistic, group-oriented values and with a low level of power distance rather than with individualistic values and a high level of power distance. Therefore we expect to find a differential effect of participation on goal commitment and performance in the two types of culture. Indeed, Erez and Earley (1987) tested the effectiveness of participation in Israel, a collectivistic and group-oriented culture, and in the United States, an individualistic culture. They found that the Israeli sample reacted adversely to assigned goals, as compared to participatively set goals. Individuals who were assigned goals were less committed and performed less competently than individuals who participated in goal-setting. Such differences were not observed in the American sample.

Another example can be cited in relation to group goals and group performance. Matsui and his colleagues (Matsui et al., 1987) found that group goals were effective for the Japanese. However in individualistic cultures, group goals very often result in social loafing and free riding because the group members do not share responsibility to the same extent as those in collectivistic cultures (Earley, 1989). Unless employees are personally accountable for their performance, group performance tends to be less effective in individualistic than in collectivistic cultures. Perhaps one way to make group performance effective in individualistic cultures is to require the members to be personally accountable for their performance (Weldon & Gargano, 1988).

Differences in collectivistic versus individualistic values may explain why different models of job enrichment were developed in the United States as compared to Norway, Sweden, or Japan. Hackman and Oldham's (1980) model of job enrichment, which is prevalent in the United States, focuses on designing jobs for the individual employee. The critical psychological states that mediate the relationship between job dimensions and work motivation reflect the private self. They consist of experienced meaningfulness of the work, experienced responsibility, and knowledge of results. However the model does not include psychological dimensions that enhance the collective self, such as the formation of social identity and social support.

In contrast North European countries have adopted models of autonomous work groups, and Japan has successfully implemented quality control circles. North European countries and Japan are known to have more collectivistic values than the United States (Hofstede, 1980). The use of quality control circles coincides with the collective self as it is advocated and supported by the tight group-oriented culture of Japan. In fact the whole system of interpersonal communication and decision-making, including small group activities at all organizational levels and the *ringi* system of bottom-to-top decision-making (Erez, 1992) is designed to fit in with group-oriented values. The preceding examples will be discussed further in subsequent chapters on work motivation and interpersonal communication.

Studies demonstrate that the differential implementation of managerial techniques in different countries is not a coincidence. Rather it reflects the contingency between the potential effectiveness of certain managerial techniques and cultural values as they are interpreted by our model of cultural self-representation.

SUMMARY

Our model of cultural self-representation proposes that the potential effectiveness of various managerial techniques is evaluated by the self in terms of their contribution to self-enhancement, perceptions of efficacy, and self-consistency. The criteria for evaluation are determined by cultural norms and standards. The criteria and standards of evaluation in cultures which cultivate the collective self are different than those used in cultures which emphasize the private self. These criteria are more clearly and specifically defined in tight rather than in loose cultures (Triandis, 1989b). Managerial techniques that reinforce the individual's contribution to the group are consistent with collectivistic cultures, whereas individually based reward systems are more prevalent in individualistic cultures. Therefore different managerial techniques are expected to be effective in different cultures.

The process of globalization—including the unification of Europe, the massive immigration from Eastern Europe to the West, and the mergers and acquisitions across geographical borders—exposes employees to new cultures and new situations. A company located in one country sells products and services to customers in other countries. The value system and behavioral norms of the host country have to be taken into consideration in order to satisfy customers' expectations and needs. Furthermore the same company may have a diversified labor force, mainly when different units are located in different parts of the world. As a result the motivational force of managerial and human resource management practices may change from one place to another. The model of cultural self-representation takes into account the diversification of the labor force and the customers, and it can be used for evaluating management practices across cultural borders.

From the individual perspective, the exposure to the global market activates cognitive information processing to interpret and adjust to the new environments. Members of one part of the global market encounter members of another who interpret and react to the situation differently. As a result there is a growing need to learn more about cultures. The increase in publications, research centers, and teaching programs on Japan and other countries on the Pacific Rim aims to satisfy this need.

The direct implication of the process of globalization is that cultural characteristics should be taken into consideration when implementing managerial techniques. Multinational companies and joint ventures may have to use different techniques at different branches, unless they manage to dominate the corporate values over and above cultural differences. In the same vein, companies' approach to customers should be diversified, especially in the case of multinational companies that serve local markets overseas.

The exposure to foreign cultures sharpens individuals' awareness to themselves. The ability to define the collective self through comparisons to others may be one of the great benefits of the process of globalization. American psychologists argue that their biggest challenge is to explore a new theory of the person suitable for the global era we are entering (Sampson, 1989). Perhaps cross-cultural research can be a means to enhance our understanding of the differences among cultures and to help define our own social identity.

3
Cultural Frameworks

The most important and universal aspect of being human is that people in particular localities share a number of characteristics, such as religion, political views, life-style patterns, and approaches to work. In developing a serious theory of organizational behavior within an intercultural context, we must begin with a full appreciation for the construct of culture. The essential element of such a conceptualization is the fact that people vary in the ways that they build their lives but the variation is predictable within and across groups of people. This variability is the descriptive dimension of what is termed culture.

There are many reasons to study culture in examining OB that we discussed in the previous chapter. The point we wish to make here is that the study of OB within a cultural framework is not only desirable but necessary for a number of reasons. First, the multinationalization of work organizations has become the rule rather than the exception. Second, the development of truly fundamental theories of OB requires evidence to suggest that they apply equally well in a multitude of cultures. For instance, the heavy emphasis placed on individual rewards and outcomes common to individualistic societies, such as the United States, is often viewed with curiosity and suspicion in collectivistic societies, as found in Japan. Pancultural theories demand that the parochial tests of management theory dominant in the United States be overcome. Finally, cultures and nations are not synonymous, even though many scholars treat them as such.

The field of international management often neglects specific aspects of culture in favor of a more easily defined (and less theoretically precise) parameter denoted by geopolitical boundaries. This approach is fine for nations that are highly homogeneous and the researcher is not concerned with identifying generalizations of the findings, but it is problematic for countries that experience high political upheaval, geographic dispersion, or other turbulence. In such cases, equating culture with the nation-state becomes problematic. For example, Israel and the United States have recently experienced a large influx of Soviet immigrants. If we were to conduct a study sampling the two soviet groups, we might expect to find many similarities of values, traditions, and so forth, and we might erroneously conclude that the two "nations" are the same. The illustration is not intended merely to warn the reader concerning sampling issues; rather, we must be wary of confusing *national* and *cultural* origins. Our purpose in developing a more thorough conceptualization of culture is to predict both within- and between-nation variability.

Since a broad and complete overview of "culture" is beyond the scope and aim of this book, we will limit ourselves to examining several definitions of culture and the micro- and macrolevel aspects of culture. Next, we will present cultural models representing a number of approaches—value models, attitude and subjective meaning models, and systems models—followed by a summary of the essential components of culture for studying OB. Finally, we will briefly compare and contrast various frameworks from the fields of cultural anthropology, OB, psychology, and sociology. Although we will not focus exclusively on methodology related to the study of culture, the reader is referred to the second volume of Triandis's *Handbook of Cross-Cultural Psychology* (1980) for an in-depth treatment of analytic concerns for intercultural research, as well as Malinowski's approach (1944) concerning the conduct of ethnomethodology.

As we discussed in chapter 2, our model is based on an information-processing perspective (Lord & Foti, 1985; Lord & Kernan, 1987; Miller, Galanter, & Pribram, 1960; Schank & Abelson, 1977; Wyer & Srull, 1980, 1989). Thinking, feeling, and acting in a complex social setting involve the comprehension and interpretation of events. An individual must attend to an event and comprehend its meaning. For instance, if an employee is asked to become a team player, will helping coworkers who are behind in their work satisfy the requirement, or is the employee expected to attend social gatherings after work? This comprehension or "meaning" analysis (Mandler, 1975) is guided by a schemata search. A social event or setting contains both magnitude (amount) and direction (schema for team player) components, and meaning is derived by a comparison of its direction with existing schemata (e.g., a team player schemata may include helping others at work, attending social events, or participating in company committees).

Event comprehension may occur through two types of cognitive processing: automatic, requiring little conscious awareness from the individual; or controlled, demanding great attention (Shiffrin & Schneider, 1977). If an event is familiar, automatic processing occurs, and the individual responds using existing patterns of action. When the goal is unfamiliar, or is presented within the context of a complex environment, the individual engages in controlled processing. This form of processing is typically preceded by metacognition (Brown, 1977). Metacognition consists of two general processes: conscious reflection of one's cognitive activity and conscious activities concerned with handling difficulty.

Once an event is comprehended, it stimulates an elaborate cognitive sequence by which the individual selects an action plan to react to the situation. A plan is a cognitively based routine for attaining a particular objective or reacting to a predictable social setting. It consists of multiple steps, some of which are elements needed to achieve other steps. A plan may be conceptualized as a hierarchically organized structure, incorporating goals and subgoals, along with a specification of the temporal sequencing needed to enact them (Wyer & Srull, 1985). Schema are mental structures that control attention and the subsequent reconstruction of memory. They fall into several categories, including self-schemas (self-image), person schemas (trait behavior information common to certain groups or types of people), event schemas or scripts (knowledge of the typical sequence of events for a situation), or person-in-situation schemas (information about how people should act in a particular social setting). Scripts may be weak (organizing expectations of events but not the exact sequence of events) or strong (expectations of an exact sequence of events due to the goal-subgoal relationship between script events) (Abelson, 1981; Lord & Foti, 1985).

We focus on the use of plans and scripts because they prescribe how events should proceed within a particular setting and have implications for social evaluation that enable an individual to comprehend social stimuli. This conceptualization is useful for several reasons. The hierarchical structure can be used to describe an individual's affective response to a culturally relevant situation (Lord & Kernan, 1987; Mandler, 1975; Wyer & Srull, 1985). For example, Lord and his colleagues (e.g., Lord & Foti, 1985; Lord et al., 1978) have used script theory to describe how subordinates react to their leaders. They found that scripts help subordinates predict how a leader may behave and that negative evaluations of the leader may occur if the scripts are violated. In as much as these scripts are related hierarchically, we see that changing leadership expectations through training (for example, training employees from a strong caste society to be more participative) may alter a particular script but not the hierarchically superordinate values that underly the structure. A hierarchical structure aids us in understanding why merely altering specific expectations may not be sufficient in integrating culture and work practices.

An information-processing approach is also useful for providing a consistent means of integrating cultural-level influences with individual-level actions. As we examine the definitions of culture as well as the models of culture, a common theme reoccurs, namely, that culture refers to shared knowledge and meaning systems (D'Andrade, 1984). In as much as the information-processing perspective depicts plans and scripts as ways to organize knowledge, we can view culture as a hierarchical structure of plans and subordinate scripts that are shared among individuals having a common background. As we know from schema theory, individuals' knowledge structures influence their affective reactions to events (Isen & Baron, 1991) as well as their behavioral reactions (Wyer & Srull, 1989). Thus we may view culture as a shared knowledge structure that results in decreased variability in individual interpretation of stimuli.

Perhaps the largest deviation of our approach from a traditional information-processing perspective is that we use values and the self-concept as the basis for these knowledge structures. Depending on an individual's cultural background and unique experiences, he or she will adopt a set of values that can be used to define the self and reevaluate one's self-concept as new experiences are gained. Thus values acquired through childhood and adolescence also shape an individual's way of viewing the world, interpreting events, and reacting to situations.

Another advantage of our approach is that it picks up themes from the existing frameworks on culture, yet still constitutes a middle-range theory that lends itself to empirical analysis. As will be described later in this chapter, many existing models of culture are grandiose but do not lend themselves to empirical assessment (Triandis, in press). The use of an information-processing paradigm to describe culture is not altogether new; since the seventies, cognitive anthropologists have advocated the study of culture through knowledge systems (e.g., Goodenough, 1971). The focus of attention in cognitive anthropology has been the identification of knowledge and rules that prescribe how an individual makes sense of a situation and the role of symbols and rites in transferring the knowledge systems among individuals without specific regard to an organizational context. Several organizational researchers (e.g., Barley, 1990; Bougon, Weick & Binkhorst, 1977) have used a cognitive approach to map out the communication patterns within organizations, but they have largely ignored the general cultural context in which the organization is embedded. Our approach builds on that of the cognitive anthropologists and the organization researchers by viewing the cognitive and interpretive processes of individuals in organizations in terms of their cultural context.

DEFINITIONS OF CULTURE

The various ways that researchers have defined culture are summarized in Table 3-1. A widely accepted definition proposed by Clyde Kluckhohn summarizes the anthropologist's definition of culture: "Culture consists in patterned ways of thinking, feeling and reacting, acquired and transmitted mainly by symbols, constituting the distinctive achievements of human groups, including their embodiments in artifacts; the essential core of culture consists of traditional (i.e., historically derived and selected) ideas and especially their attached values" (1951, 86:5). Other commonly applied definitions of culture include Herskovits's (1955:305) formulation that culture as the man-made part of the environment. Triandis (1972) and Osgood (1974) define it as a perception of the man-made part of the environment.

Table 3-1. Comparison of Various Definitions of Culture

Authors	Key Defining Characteristics
Herskovits (1955)	Culture is the man-made part of the environment.
Parsons and Shils (1951)	On a cultural level we view the organized set of rules or standards as such, abstracted, so to speak, from the actor who is committed to them by his own value-orientations and in whom they exist as need-dispositions to observe these rules. Thus a culture includes a set of *standards*. An individual's value-orientation is his commitment to these standards.
C. Kluckhohn (1954)	Culture consists in patterned ways of thinking, feeling and reacting, acquired and transmitted mainly by symbols, constituting the distinctive achievements of human groups, including their embodiments in artifacts; the essential core of culture consists of traditional (i.e., historically derived and selected) ideas and especially their attached values.
Hofstede (1980)	[Culture consists of] a set of mental programs that control an individual's responses in a given context.
Triandis (1972)	[Culture is] a subjective perception of the human-made part of the environment. The subjective aspects of culture include the categories of social stimuli, associations, beliefs, attitudes, norms and values, and roles that individuals share.
D'Andrade (1984) and Geertz (1973)	A culture is viewed as a pattern of symbolic discourse and shared meaning that needs interpreting and deciphering in order to be fully understood.

Some definitions are very limited and focused, such as Shweder and LeVine's (1984) view that culture is a set of shared meaning systems, whereas Herskovits (1955) represents a broad, all-encompassing view of culture as the man-made aspect of the environment. Other definitions include Skinner's (1971) view that culture is a complex series of reinforcement contingencies moderated by particular schedules of reward and Schein's (1985) view that the core of culture is the untested assumptions of how and why to behave. Hofstede (1980) defines culture as a set of mental programs that control an individual's responses in a given context, and Parsons and Shils (1951) view culture as a shared characteristic of a high-level social system.

The most general view of culture is that it is a set of characteristics common to a particular group of people. We can view culture as a function of interrelated systems (Triandis, 1980:9) including the ecology, subsistence, sociocultural, individual, and interindividual systems. The ecological system refers to the physical environment, resources, and geography of a people. The subsistence system refers to how individuals in a society use ecological resources to survive, e.g., hunting and fishing, gathering food, and creating industry. The sociocultural system refers to institutions, norms, roles, and values as they exist around the individual. The individual and interindividual systems refer to the individual (e.g., motivation, perception, and learning) and social aspects of behavior (e.g., child-rearing and social networks). These systems do not dictate culture per se; rather, we can use this type of general framework in order to understand culture and its relation to individual and collective actions (Bhagat & McQuaid, 1982).

Using the multiple-systems method as a way of approaching culture, we can see that culture refers to both objective and subjective aspects of man-made elements. Whereas traditional definitions of culture focus on the tools and artifacts that people produce (Herskovits, 1955), we agree with recent work in cultural anthropology (e.g., Shweder & LeVine, 1984) and psychology (e.g., Triandis, 1972, 1980, in press) that the subjective aspects are important as well. The subjective aspects of culture include the categories of social stimuli, associations, beliefs, attitudes, norms and values, and roles that individuals share.

A series of studies examining the role of individualism and collectivism as a moderator of the display of social loafing (Earley, 1989, 1990) found that collectivists do not socially loaf (reduce performance as the result of a group performance context) when working with their ingroup or clan, whereas individualists socially loaf in any group context. When the research findings were described to individualists, they concluded that the collectivists in the research study were probably motivated by individual interests acquired through group success. Collectivists, however, react quite differently: "Well of course this is the expected reaction in a group context. A group member is responsible for his or her group". In other words, the values and beliefs held by members of the two cultural groups leads to fundamentally different behavior and reactions to the same work setting and information.

The shaping influence of cultural beliefs on individuals' actions is aptly demonstrated in Bunzel's description of how the Zuni Indians approach deer hunting:

Man is not lord of the universe. The forests and fields have not been given him to despoil. He is equal in the world with the rabbit and the deer and the young corn plant. They must be approached circumspectly if they are to be persuaded to lay down their lives for man's pleasure or necessity. Therefore the deer is stalked ritualistically; he is enticed with sacred esoteric songs, he is killed in a prescribed manner, and when brought to the house is received as an honored guest and sent away with rich gifts to tell others of his tribe that he was well treated in his father's house. (1932:488–89 as cited by Kluckhohn and Strodtbeck, 1961)

The Zuni's focus on "harmony with nature" is consistent with the dominant, man-nature value described by Kluckhohn and Strodtbeck (1961). To a typical Anglo-Westerner, the Zuni approach to hunting might be viewed as quaint or eccentric; however, this attitude ignores the basic relationship of man to nature according to the Zuni view. The typical reaction to the hunting of a deer by an Anglo would neither include the ritual aspect of the hunt nor the view that a symbiotic relationship exists between the hunter and the hunted.

Needless to say, there are a variety of cultural influences on the institutional and organizational levels of human endeavor. Culture shapes the type of organizations that evolve and the nature of social structures as they grow and adapt (Hofstede, 1980). Societies shape their collectives and social aggregates according to the rules implied by culture. Just as a highly individualistic society places a low emphasis on broad, social networks of extended families and friends, their organizations reflect an emphasis on individual reward and action (Triandis, in press).

Other aspects of culture will emerge in further detail when we discuss specific views of culture addressed in the literature. These characteristics include time, language, and locality variables as well as historical and ecological commonalities. However all of these variables need not be identical for two societies to share a number of common cultural characteristics. For example, Israel is experiencing a very active immigration of individuals with different ecological and language backgrounds, who share a common religion and philosophy. The shared history of Israelis and the new immigrants is a cultural glue that binds all together. What is crucial to understanding this cultural heritage is that the common religious and philosophical backgrounds of the Jewish Diaspora have led to shared knowledge systems, scripts, and so forth. This is one example of a cultural influence on individual action that ecology alone cannot account for, given the geographic dispersion of the Diaspora.

A final point that warrants attention is the pervasiveness of culture. Culture refers to the core values and beliefs of individuals within a society that are formed in complex knowledge systems during childhood and reinforced throughout life (Lachman, 1983; Triandis, in press). Whereas a great deal of management research has been directed toward understanding corporate culture (also referred to as organizational culture, a topic that we will turn to later in our discussion), this refers to the peripheral or more easily influenced values and beliefs that an individual holds. Thus an organization's culture has a relatively weak influence on an individual's core beliefs and values; if these beliefs and values are threatened by organizational practices, we can expect dysfunctional work behavior or maladjustment (Adler, 1986).

Cultural values and beliefs are encompassing but not immediately apparent to society members. They can be understood at an individual level of analysis, if we consider that individuals possess both cultural knowledge structures as well as individual or specific structures. Thus an individual's behavior within an organizational setting is a product of both culturally acquired as well as individually acquired (via unique life experiences) knowledge systems.

PERSPECTIVES ON CULTURE

In this section we provide a review of culture models from a number of approaches, including value models, subjective culture, cognitive structures and interpretive systems from cognitive anthropology, general systems, and organizational culture. Within each section we highlight a number of approaches from a historical perspective in order to illustrate the trends in the study of culture. After describing existing frameworks, we summarize them using our information-processing approach as an organizing theme.

Value Models: Parsons and Shils

One of the earliest views of culture was Parsons and Shils' (1951) extension of Parsons's *The Structure of Social Action.* Although a complete review of Parsons and Shils' General Theory of Action is beyond our means, we will review the key components of their model in relation to their value-orientations of culture.

Their model posits that social or individual action occurs within the constellations of three interdependent systems—social, personality, and cultural. The social system has three basic characteristics: interaction between two or more actors; the situation includes others who are the object of cathexis, or *alters;* and the actors behave in concert as a function of a collective goal-orientation. The personality system refers to several characteristics: it consists of interconnections of actions for a given actor; the actor's actions are organized according to a structure of need-dispositions; and, the goals and actions of the individual are not random but operate according to a specified structure. The cultural system comprises an organization of values, norms, and symbols that guide the choices made by actors and direct their interactions; it is more abstract than either the individual or social systems but elements can be transmitted to the other systems; the pattern of regulatory norms is made up of coordinated, rather than random elements, which in combination form value systems, belief systems, and systems of expressive symbols.

The basic framework, represented in Figure 3-1, consists of the actor-subject (either a person or a social group); the object (either social, personalities, and social groups or nonsocial, physical, and cultural objects); the interplay of personalities and social groups with objects; and the framing of this interplay within the context of the cultural systems. The most relevant aspect of the action model for culture is the value-orientation component of the actor's orientation and commitment to particular norms, standards, and criteria of behavior. Parsons and Shils argue as follows:

Whenever an actor is forced to choose among various means objects, whenever he is forced to choose which need-disposition he will gratify, or how much he will gratify a need-disposi-

	THE SUBJECT		THE OBJECT

THE SUBJECT

1. An actor-subject: the actor whose orientation of action is being analyzed. (In an interaction situation, this actor is called "ego.")

   The actor-subject is sometimes called simply the "actor" and is always an "action system." Thus the actor-subject is either:

   a. a personality
   b. a social system

THE OBJECT

2. Objects: those objects to which the actor-subject is oriented. These are (i) social objects and (ii) nonsocial objects.

   i. Social objects are actors (i.e., action systems) but here they are objects rather than subjects in a given analysis. (In an interaction situation, these actors are called "alters.") Social objects are:

      a. personalities
      b. social systems

Personalities and social systems fit together in the following fashion whether they are subjects or objects.

	Personality A	Personality B	Personality C
Social system 1	Role 1-A* Motivational aspects Value aspects	Role 1-B Motivational aspects Value aspects	Role 1-C Motivational aspects Value aspects
Social system 2	Role 2-A Motivational aspects Value aspects	Role 2-B Motivational aspects Value aspects	Role 2-C Motivational aspects Value aspects
Social system 3	Role 3-A Motivational aspects Value aspects	Role 3-B Motivational aspects Value aspects	Role 3-C Motivational aspects Value aspects

   ii. Nonsocial objects may be:
      a. Physical objects
      b. Cultural objects (i.e., symbols or symbol systems).

Cultural Systems

Cultural systems are the common values, beliefs, and tastes of the actors (as either subjects or objects) interacting with symbol systems (as objects). Thus the underlined components above show the abstraction of cultural systems from the action frame of reference.

*Each of these roles is a subsystem of orientations. This subsystem can be analyzed with respect to either (i) the personality's motives, of which the orientations are a function, or (ii) the values which the personality respects in this specific social system. Thus roles are divided into motivational aspects and value aspects.

Figure 3-1. Simplified version of Parsons and Shils' general theory of action (SOURCE: Parsons and Shils: *Toward a General Theory of Action,* Harvard University Press, 1951).

tion—whenever he is forced to make any choice whatever—his *value-orientations* may commit him to certain norms that will guide him in his choices. . . . On a cultural level we view the organized set of rules or standards as such, abstracted, so to speak, from the actor who is committed to them by his own value-orientations and in whom they exist as need-dispositions to observe these rules. Thus a culture includes a set of *standards*. An individual's value-orientation is his commitment to these standards. (1951:59–60)

There are three general modes of value-orientation. The cognitive mode involves the commitments to standards or norms through which cognitive judgements are validated. The appreciative mode refers to the commitments to standards or norms through which the appropriateness or consistency of judgements concerning the gratification of a given object is established. The moral mode refers to commitments to standards or norms which affect particular actions or systems of action. Specifically, the moral mode guides the actor's choices for action based on how the action will affect the integration of the actor's own personality system and the integration of the social groups in which he or she is a member.

According to Parsons and Shils, there are five fundamental value-orientations that define and categorize cultures. These value-orientations, or pattern variables, include: affective versus affective neutrality; self-orientation versus collectivity-orientation; universalism versus particularism; ascription versus achievement; and specificity versus diffuseness. (Parsons and Shils refer to these five dichotomies as pattern variables and the specific resultant combinations of all five variables as the value-orientation.) Affective versus affective neutrality refers to the extent it is acceptable for individuals to experience immediate gratification. In an affective culture individuals are permitted to indulge in immediate gratification, whereas in an affectively neutral culture individuals restrain from such excesses. Self-orientation versus collectivity-orientation is discussed at great length in our next chapter. Briefly, it refers to the relation of an individual's pursuit of self versus collective interests. In a self-oriented society individuals pursue their own interests and "do their own thing," whereas in a collectively oriented society individuals view their own actions in terms of their impact on others in their collective or group. Universalism versus particularism refers to the role of general rules in guiding action. In a universalistic culture a broad set of rules and policies will guide all individuals' actions, and conformity to these standards is expected, whereas in a particularistic culture individuals are guided by the unique aspects of the situation and its relevance to specific aspects of the actor. Ascription versus achievement refers to how an individual is judged in a society. In an ascriptive culture individuals are judged by attributes that they possess (e.g., social group membership and possessions), whereas in an achievement culture individuals are judged by their actions and performance (e.g., skills and work habits). Finally, specificity versus diffuseness refers to the degree to which relations among actors and objects are limited. In a diffuse culture the relation of the actor to the social object can be quite indirect, whereas in a specific culture this relation is quite narrow and limited.

These pattern variables are often presented as the five "dimensions" (e.g., Hofstede, 1984:36) of culture according to Parsons and Shils, but this is somewhat misleading since they emphasize that the pattern variables together constitute a system. Their argument is that these variables represent five general choices that an individual must make to give a situation specific defined meaning. To be a pattern variable, a given set of alternatives must derive directly from the problem of which mode of orientation will be dominant. Thus it is the unique combination of pattern variables that aids us in distinguishing among cultures. The isolation of a specific pattern variable without regard to the other ones (and the general system) may be misleading.

Value Models: Kluckhohn and Strodtbeck

Kluckhohn and Strodtbeck (1961) argued that there are five basic value-orientations underlying cultures. These orientations include: human nature (good versus mixed versus evil crossed with the mutability of the goodness); man-nature (subjugation to nature, harmony with nature, and mastery over nature); time (past, present, and future); activity (being, being-in-becoming, and doing); and relational (lineality, collaterality, and individualism).

Human nature refers to the innate goodness of people. The view that people are evil is exemplified by traditional Puritan thought. Emphasis was placed on controlling and regulating behavior to prevent the evil from spreading. The man-nature aspect refers to the individual role in coping with nature. For instance, many Asian cultures stress the view that man must be in harmony with nature, whereas the orientation of most Anglo-Westerners is that of man over nature, that is, dominance of nature through technological means. The time orientation refers to the time frame salient to a group. For example, Chinese culture places a great emphasis on ancestral obligations and rites. Such a past orientation is contrasted with the future orientation of Westerners who are often discontent with their current setting and seek change for the better. An activity orientation refers to self-expression in activity. In a being society emphasis is placed on immediate gratification and spontaneous action much like Morris' (1942) Dionysian dimension. A being-in-becoming society focuses on action and accomplishment—measurable achievements. Finally, relational-orientation refers to an individual's relation to his or her collective, similar to Parsons and Shils's self-orientation versus collectivity-orientation. The addition of the lineality component is interesting because it adds a temporal dimension to the value-orientation concept. (We discuss this dimension in greater detail in the next chapter.)

There are several interesting differences between F. Kluckhohn and Strodtbeck's approach and that of Parsons and Shils. F. Kluckhohn and Strodtbeck argue that any combination of the five orientations (three levels each) may occur and can be viewed separately without losing meaning. They make no assumptions concerning the relative importance of certain value-orientations over others. An important element of their model concerns the rank ordering of various value-orientations. A value-orientation is presumed to have a particular rank order in a given society. For instance, U.S. Anglo culture generally places individualism over collaterality and collaterality over lineality, whereas other cultures may rank order the levels of each value-orientation differently. F. Kluckhohn and Strodtbeck emphasize that *all* levels of any value-orientation will be present in a given culture. What is crucial in understanding differences between cultures is the rank ordering of each value-orientation. Cultural assimilation is aided by congruence of these rank orderings as well.

Values Model: Rokeach

Although not originally intended as a model of culture, Rokeach (1973) developed a general model of values and the self that has been used by a number of researchers in describing intercultural variations in values (Feather & Hutton, 1973; Hofstede, 1980; Rokeach). He compared samples of people representing various ethnic and social origins within the United States as well as samples of students from a number of different countries.

The relation of values to an individual's belief system and definition of the self is central to Rokeach's model. He defines value as "an enduring belief that a specific mode of conduct or end-state of existence is personally or socially preferable to an opposite or converse mode of conduct or end-state of existence. A *value system* is an enduring organization of beliefs concerning preferable modes of conduct or end-states of existence along a continuum of relative importance." (5).

A number of important characteristics can be derived from this definition. First, a value is an enduring but malleable construct. If it were unchangeable, an individual would be static and consequent experiences would not have an effect on his or her values, which we know is incorrect. Likewise, if an individual's values were not somewhat stable, this would be problematic as well since continuity of interaction would be impossible. The relative stability of values can be traced to the manner in which we typically adopt these values, namely, during early socialization experiences as a function of childhood. As a child matures and is exposed to settings of increasing complexity, he or she is likely to reaffirm particular values congruent with the settings and weaken or change other values that are inconsistent with the settings.

Second, a value is a belief that is prescriptive or proscriptive, that is, it forms the basis for judging the desirability of some means or end of action. It is the belief that is the basis of preferences that guide action (Rokeach, 1973:7). Third, a value refers to a mode of conduct or an end-state of existence. Values can be instrumental or terminal in their function, although there is not necessarily a one-to-one correspondence between an instrumental and a terminal value. Rokeach argued that there are two types of instrumental values (moral and competence) and two types of terminal values (personal and social). Moral instrumental values mainly refer to modes of behavior (e.g., behaving honestly), and they do not necessarily correspond to particular end-states. Competence instrumental values refer to personal accomplishment and self-actualization. The personal and social terminal values refer to the self-centered versus the society-centered focus of valued end-states. In a collectivistic culture we assume that individuals will focus primarily on their social terminal values, although this does not imply that they disregard personal ones—it merely argues a prioritization of desired end-states.

A fourth characteristic of values is that they imply a preference pattern and a conception of preferability. The object or end-state is desirable rather than simply something that is desired. Fifth, a value is a conception of something that is personally or socially preferable for an individual. The relevance of this dimension is that an individual does not necessarily apply a personal value to others. For example, a person may value honesty and, as a consequence, not cheat on paying taxes. However this individual may not expect colleagues to adhere to the same practice in order to be viewed as "honest."

Values are organized into systems that have a number of implications for an individual. After an individual learns a particular value, it becomes integrated into an organized system of interrelated values in some hierarchical structure. Just as with values, value systems are relatively stable but not permanent. The personal, social, and cultural experiences of an individual shape the value system and create both intracultural variability and uniqenesses as well as intercultural similarities. The value systems described by Rokeach bear a strong resemblance to the value-orientations described by F. Kluckhohn and Strodtbeck (1961) in as much as there exists a complex structure and interdependence among an individual's values. The major difference between the two frameworks is that Rokeach does not specify a priori prototypic value structures and, in fact, has an empirically based "shopping list" of values. He does argue, however, that the number of terminal and instrumental values that individuals have is finite, perhaps limited to several dozen.

Values and value systems serve a number of functions for an individual. Values are standards that lead individuals to take positions on issues, predispose them to favor particular ideologies, guide self-presentations, influence how individuals evaluate and judge themselves and others, act as a basis for morality and competence comparisons with others, and direct individuals to challenge certain ideas and to rationalize beliefs and actions that would otherwise be unacceptable so as to preserve self-image (Rokeach: 13). Value systems act as general plans for conflict resolution and decision-making as well, and they motivate our actions in daily situations. According to Rokeach, values are motivational in several ways:

> Instrumental values are motivating because the idealized modes of behavior they are concerned with are perceived to be instrumental to the attainment of desired end-goals. If we behave in all the ways prescribed by our instrumental values, we will be rewarded with all the end-states specified by our terminal values. Terminal values are motivating because they represent the super goals beyond immediate, biologically urgent goals. Unlike the more immediate goals, these super goals do not seem to be periodic in nature; neither do they seem to satiate—we seem to be forever doomed to strive for these ultimate goals without quite ever reaching them.
>
> But there is another reason why values can be said to be motivating. They are in the final analysis the conceptual tools and weapons that we all employ in order to maintain and enhance self-esteem. They are in the service of what McDougall (1926) has called the master sentiment—the sentiment of self-regard. (1973:14).

Thus values serve as a powerful motivational influence in three ways: they are instrumental in attaining desired end-states, they are desired end-states, and they help us define and reinforce our sense of self.

Rokeach developed a general model of belief systems in which an individual's values play a preeminent role. An individual's belief system is composed of ten subsystems that can be conceptualized as a series of concentric circles. At the innermost circle is the individual's cognitions about the self, or self-image. The next layers that follow are (in sequence moving away from the self): terminal value system, instrumental value system, attitude system, attitude, cognitions about one's own behavior, cognitions about significant others' attitudes, cognitions about significant others' values or needs, cognitions about significant others' behavior, and cognitions about behavior of nonsocial objects.

From this scheme there are a number of interesting issues that can be highlighted. First, value systems play a key, central role in an individual's belief system. Second, a belief system is a functionally interconnected system; a change in one subsystem will have an impact on other subsystems. Third, the ultimate purpose of the total belief system, including value systems, is to maintain and enhance an individual's self-image or self-regard. Fourth, changes in one subsystem will impact other related subsystems in both directions of the subsystem hierarchy and the individual's self-image as well. Fifth, contradictions among subsystems will usually result in a change in the subordinate system. If an individual's attitude is changed through some organizational intervention (e.g., conveyed through socialization during meetings) but is in conflict with an existing value, the attitude change will be temporary and the attitude will return to a more consistent position. Finally, the model suggests that values are not necessarily harder to change than attitudes since a value that conflicts with an individual's self-image will likely change, whereas an attitude that conflicts with behavior will be less likely to change.

The impetus for change, according to Rokeach's value model, is self-dissatisfaction arising from contradictions among subsystems. The greater the extent that these contradictions imply an influence on individual's self-image, the more likely is change to occur. Rokeach further argues that it is the affective experience of self-dissatisfaction, and not the cognitive contradiction itself, that gives rise to changes. The underlying change occurs as an experience of negative affect arising from self-dissatisfaction due to moral or competence issues. As suggested earlier, self-dissatisfaction arising from conflicting subsystems implies that the hierarchically subordinate system will be most likely to change. Again, however, the exception lies in the relation of the conflicting subsystems to other more superordinate systems, particularly the self-image. Thus an attitude and a value that are contradictory will likely be resolved by the attitude changing unless the attitude is more consistent with the individual's self-image. In this case, an individual will be most likely to change the conflicting value in order to maintain the attitude that is consistent with the image of self.

We have discussed the Rokeach model at length because it offers two facets that will play a central role in our conceptualization of behavior in organizations. First, the relevance of values and value systems for distinguishing similarities and differences among cultures is apparent from the vast literature on culture. Second, Rokeach provides an explicit role for an individual's sense of self in the value model, a theme that plays a major role in our framework.

Despite many positive features of Rokeach's model, it is not without its critics. One major drawback is that the complexity of the model has not been adequately tested by Rokeach's empirical methodology (Zavalloni, 1980). The primary instrument he developed and used is the Rokeach Value Survey (1973, appendix). This instrument consists of two separate checklists in which a respondent is asked to rank order thirty-six value statements. The first list measures terminal values represented by eighteen constructs, such as world peace and social recognition. The second list of eighteen items assesses instrumental values using such adjectives as courageous, honest, and polite. The respondent's rankings establish a preference pattern.

The relative ranking procedure gives rise to a number of interpretation problems. For example, if two cultures differ on a particular terminal value, such as social recognition, but both are relatively low in preference ranking (e.g., country A ranks social recognition as a 12.5 and country B ranks it as a 13.0), we do not know if this is due to an artifact arising from preferences higher in the rankings or if it is just not important to either group. Another problem concerns the choice of adjectives from the instrumental values list since adjectives will frequently connote different meanings across cultures (Osgood, 1977). Finally, the scale itself does not capture the implied theoretical interdependencies of the value model. Each of the values in the survey are taken separately rather than in some more complex configuration that we would expect for an individual's value system.

Zavalloni (1980) makes the additional observation that Rokeach used student samples in his comparison of the United States, Australia, Canada, and Israel and that such a practice may underestimate within-culture variability. We find this criticism somewhat less compelling since it is inherent in any sample but can be overcome, in part, by increasing sample size and breadth within a country. Just as Hofstede's (1980) reliance on a particular organization for his sample limits generalizability, Rokeach's work is limited but not invalidated by his sampling procedure.

Value Models: McClelland's Need for Achievement

Although McClelland's (1961) model of achievement focuses on an assumed need rather than value, we include it in this section because it is consistent with a general paradigm of culture in which personality dispositions are influenced by cultural and economic forces. This influence, in turn, impacts behavior in culturally predicted patterns.

The basic premise of McClelland's model is that three facets of personality—striving for success in competition with some standard of excellence or need for achievement, striving to acquire power or need for power, and a desire to establish relationships with others or need for affiliation—influence many aspects of individual and societal actions. Of the three, the need for achievement construct has played a central role in McClelland's theorizing about cultures. He accepts the Freudian assumption that child-rearing practices shape adult personality structure and that an ideal method for identifying this powerful personality determinant is through the use of projective methods and fantasy. McClelland argues that the achievement motive directly affects the economic structure of a society and it can transform it through reorientations in achievement motives.

The model proposed by McClelland posits three major classes of variables related to economic achievement: background factors (middle-class status, mesomorphic physique, such child-rearing variables as warmth, cultural variations, religious values, temperate climate, and absence of slavery); psychological variables (high need for achievement in individual protocols, high need for achievement in cultural products such as folk literature); and factors related to economic achievement (such entrepreneurial role functions as risk-taking, entrepreneurial status and success, spirit, restlessness and mobility). These classes of variables are sequentially linked, and they have an impact on a country's economic growth factors, such as the number of full-time entreprenurs in preliterate cultures, trade, national consumption of resources, and growth of GNP.

A key element in McClelland's model is an elaboration of Weber's thesis that the Protestant Reformation gave rise to modern capitalism (Jahoda, 1980). McClelland reasoned that the new values engendered by the reformation were translated into new child-rearing practices that, in turn, provided the impetus for modern capitalism. In his empirical work, he used achievement imagery from children's stories across different countries and scored them for the presence of achievement themes. He correlated these achievement scores with measures of economic growth and found a very high and positive correlation between the two indices.

McClelland's work is subject to a number of criticisms concerning conceptual and empirical shortcomings. For example, the choice of children's stories as a measure of achievement motivation and his use of the Thematic Apperception Test (TAT) are subject to criticism. TAT is difficult to score and interpret and its images are culturally biased (Holtzman, 1980; Kornadt, Eckensberger & Emminghaus, 1980). The use of children's stories is problematic as well since it precludes comparisons with preliterate cultures. It is not clear that achievement themes in these stories necessarily imply a comparable level of achievement motivation in the children (or the society).

To test his theory empirically, McClelland and his colleagues (e.g., McClelland & Winter, 1971) conducted an ambitious effort in the United States and India in order to train achievement motivation. However, results of these studies failed to provide consistent support for his model. In an unpublished study Barrett and Franke (1971, as cited in Hofstede, 1984:127) argue that the relation underlying McClelland's model was fortuitous, an artifact of his methods of measurement. Additionally, Hofstede points out the instability of McClelland's rank ordering of country scores from his 1925 to 1950 time points and suggests that the high variations across a single generation are unlikely to be attributable to societal shifts alone; rather, the shifts reflect an unreliability in the measurement system.

Despite a number of methodological criticisms of McClelland's approach, it warrants comment that his work has been both ambitious and fruitful as a theoretical framework for integrating personality, cultural practices, and societal outcomes. We view this work as a crucial step toward the development of a model that links individuals' actions with their culture and environment.

Value Models: Hofstede

Perhaps the most widely cited work on culture developed for the study of organizations is that of Geert Hofstede (1980, 1980b, 1983, 1984). Hofstede developed a four-dimension overview of cultural variation in values based on data from over forty countries in which a single multinational organization had subsidiaries and over 100,000 questionnaires from individuals representing a wide variety of occupations, ages, and other demographic backgrounds measured at two different time periods.

Hofstede's model is based on the idea that culture can be viewed as a series of mental programs. He defines culture as "the collective programming of the mind which distinguishes the members of one human group from another" (1984:21). These mental programs refer to prescribed ways of doing things or acting, and they range according to levels of uniqueness. At the least unique level are universal mental programs that are shared by all people. This refers to the biological system of the human body and includes such actions as flight-or-fight responses, emotional displays, and so on. A somewhat higher level of uniqueness is the collective level, which refers to mental programming shared among individuals belonging to a certain group or category and is similar to Triandis's (1972) concept of subjective culture (which will be discussed in the next section). Collective programming is shared among individuals who have a common time, place, and language (Triandis, in press). The individual level of programming refers to those aspects of individuals that determine their unique personalities. These mental programs are transferred through genetic linkages as well as learned by individuals through their cultural system, particularly during childhood and early development. The middle or collective level refers to the programming that is most often transferred via socialization mechanisms. In *America and the Americans* John Steinbeck (1966) observed that despite the genetic and cultural potpourri that constitutes American society there is something uniquely "American" to the non-American that allows for immediate identification. Steinbeck argued that the concept of American culture is both embedded and elusive while still immediately recognizable by someone outside of the culture. The distinctiveness of being an American can be read as if it were a neon sign.

At the core of mental programs are values and culture. Hofstede defines values as "a broad tendency to prefer certain states of affairs over others" (1984:18). They are an attribute of individuals as well as collectivities. Hofstede's research on cultural values is framed within a general model of forces on cultural patterns, beginning with exogenous influences (e.g., forces of nature, trade, conquest) that affect cultural origins (e.g., historical, technological, and urbanization effects). Origins, in turn, influence societal norms (e.g., value systems of major groups in the population), followed by consequences (e.g., education, religion, family patterns) that reinforce the origins and societal norms. Hofstede argues that outside influences rarely have a direct impact on norms; rather, they influence norms through such cultural origins as technology. The key role played by values is that they regulate the impact of these origins on such consequences as institutional practices. Thus one needs to study the impact of technological infusions into a developing nation to understand its impact on societal norms and, in turn, the impact on lifestyle or emergent organizational structures.

According to Hofstede's empirical work, the four value dimensions on which cultures vary are power distance, uncertainty avoidance, individualism, and masculinity versus femininity. Power distance refers to the extent members of a culture accept inequality and large differentials between those having power (e.g., superiors) and those having little power (e.g., subordinates). Hofstede offers a number of antecedents of power distance, including child-rearing patterns, environment, and historical events. For example, in low power distance cultures (e.g., Israel) less emphasis is placed on obedience of children, whereas in a high power distance cultures (e.g., Mexico) parents strongly emphasize obedience of children. Hofstede suggests several interesting implications of power distance for management practices. In a high power distance culture subordinates are more satisfied and expect a directive style of management from their superiors, whereas in a low power distance culture more participatory practices are expected.

Uncertainty avoidance reflects the emphasis on ritual behavior, rules, and labor mobility within a culture. High uncertainty avoidance is found in countries that report high levels of stress, such as Japan and Belgium. Possible antecedents of uncertainty avoidance may include such factors as invasion from neighbors or soil infertility (Triandis, in press). From an organization's perspective the consequences of uncertainty avoidance suggest that managers should be selected because of their seniority and a strong emphasis on loyalty to the firm.

Individualism reflects the extent to which individuals emphasize their goals over those of their clan or group. Individualistic cultures are characterized by members who strive to achieve their own goals, who have narrow family structures, and whose movement among groups is a function of self-interest, whereas collectivistic cultures are characterized by members who emphasize the needs of the group over self-interests and live in extended family structures. (Interestingly, the most individualistic cultures identified by Hofstede are English speaking (e.g., United States, Canada, and Great Britain), and one wonders about the linguistic implications of such a finding.) The antecedents and consequents of individualism are discussed in greater detail in chapter 4.

Masculinity/femininity refers to societies that differentiate on the basis of activity and gender. For instance, a masculine culture emphasizes differences between genders whereas in a feminine culture gender differentiation is minimal. The centrality of work in a person's life is greater in a masculine than in a feminine culture, and the general quality of life over work is emphasized more in a feminine culture. In high masculine cultures people prefer salary over working hours, and they emphasize achievement in the work context. The feminine culture is characterized by individuals who "work to live" rather than "live to work" (Hofstede, 1980; Triandis, in press).

From a purely management perspective, Hofstede's work has been of great benefit to researchers because it is "approachable"; it is sufficiently clear and parsimonious to lend itself to empirical test. For example, Hofstede has used his four dimension approach as a way of relating management practices to culture. Among other hypotheses, Hofstede argues that economic theories of self-interest can be related to: power distance and individualism; the priority of task- or work-group relations related to individualism; efficacy of participatory management methods such as Theory Z and Managerial Grid related to power distance; the expression of affect in organizational contexts related to uncertainty avoidance; emphasis on competitiveness, equity, and equality norms related to power distance and individualism; achievement versus affiliation motives related to masculinity versus femininity; sex roles and occupation structures related to masculinity versus femininity; economic development related to individualism and masculinity; and the nature of worker-manager relations related to power distance and individualism.

Although there are many empirical studies using Hofstede's dimensions of culture cited throughout this book, we draw attention to a few examples here. Bond et al. (1985) examined the relation of power distance and individualism to ingroup behavior. They found that a high status ingroup member could insult a low status ingroup member with relative impunity in a collectivistic and high power distance culture such as Hong Kong but not in an individualistic and low power distance culture such as the United States. Earley (1984) related the individualistic versus collectivistic orientation of Americans, British, and Ghanaians to the frequency of social interaction (and perceived value of it) in a factory setting. These studies suggest that distinguishing among management practices based on Hofstede's classification scheme has potential for clarifying the impact of culture on work.

There are a number of potential problems with Hofstede's work that we will touch on briefly. Perhaps the most frequent criticism levied against his typology is that it is based on responses from a single organization and reflects the peculiarities of the company. This criticism is not overly compelling since the assumption that the results are "homogenized" assumes that (1) the organization used in the study has an identical structure and operating pattern in all of its locales (extremely high formalization and rigidity), and (2) the "culture" conveyed by the multinational organization overwhelms the unique national cultures sampled in the study. It is not clear that either of these conditions are met since we doubt that *any* organization can so effectively direct its foreign affairs as to overwhelm national culture, and we doubt even more seriously that the organization's culture has an overwhelming impact on an individual's own cultural background.

Another criticism levied against Hofstede is that the items used to represent the four dimensions are not face valid, and they capitalize on chance. In some cases the restricted items used by Hofstede may lead the researcher to wonder what they mean (one of the uncertainty avoidance items actually assesses an individual's propensity to leave his/her job within a several-year period, and it is not clear that turnover intentions actually measure uncertainty avoidance) and whether or not the dimensions are applicable in all cultures. For example, Hofstede and Bond (1988) published an addendum to the original four dimensions suggesting that uncertainty avoidance might best be replaced with a Confucian dynamism in Asian cultures. However we might argue that additional scales constructed on the general constructs forwarded by Hofstede (e.g., Erez & Earley, 1987) may overcome these limitations.

Other Value Models

There are a number of additional models that have been proposed and tested using a values approach. In this section, we will mention a number of them briefly so as to provide the interested reader with an overview.

Morris (1956) conducted a series of studies on philosophical orientations across cultures. His empirical work was a logical extension of his philosophical work, and he developed a values scale using this background. He used a tripartite framework to correlate the various ways that people live and their values. The basic values reflected in the various lifestyles were Dionysian (indulgence of desires and overt expression of enjoyment), Promethean (tendency to actively shape the world and adapt it to man's interests), and Buddhistic (self-regulation and control as well as temperance of one's desires). These three values were combined into the following thirteen statements (Zavalloni, 1980:85) and respondents were asked to state whether or not they approved.

Way 1: preserve the best that man has attained.
Way 2: cultivate independence of people and things.
Way 3: show sympathetic concern for others.
Way 4: experience festivity and solitude in alternation.
Way 5: act and enjoy life through group participation.
Way 6: constantly master changing conditions.
Way 7: integrate action, enjoyment, and contemplation.
Way 8: cultivate capacity for simply enjoyment.
Way 9: attain joy and peace through receptivity.
Way 10: control unruly impulses.
Way 11: cultivate the self through the contemplative life.
Way 12: use body energy for daring deeds.
Way 13: cultivate humility and closeness to persons and nature.

Applying his lifestyle scenarios to student samples from the United States, India, Japan, China, and Norway, Morris found that American students were activist, self-indulgent, and less subject to social restraint and self-control, whereas the Japanese students had a general orientation toward people and society. The Chinese students showed a strong tendency toward enjoyment and activity as well as self-sufficiency. In a follow-up study by Prothro (1958), it was found that Arab students showed a preference for activity, group participation, and self-control but rejected receptivity, contemplation, and carefree enjoyment.

Another approach, taken by Allport, Vernon, and Lindzey (1960), argues that the values of theoretical man (discovery of truth through critical and rational thought), economic man (emphasis on practical and tangibly useful things), aesthetic man (values placed on beauty and harmony), social man (values placed on altruism and philanthropic love), political man (emphasis on power and influence), and religious man (emphasis on communion with the cosmos) captures the essence of differences among individuals. Ronen (1978) used Sarnoff's scheme (a human value index in which Western Society's values are placed into two general categories: values of aggrandizement (wealth, prestige, power) and values of realization (humanitarian, egalitarian, aesthetic, intellectual)) as a basis for studying the values of Israeli kibbutzim and privately owned organizations. Murdock (1945) developed a list of seventy cultural universals that he argued were exhaustive and could be used to describe differences and similarities among cultures. These universals included such variables as food taboos, hospitality, trade, etiquette, and folklore.

More recently Glenn (1981) proposed a cognitive value approach to examining associative versus abstractive cultures. In associative cultures people use their own associations among categories when they interact and assume that others share their associations. For example, if a supervisor tells an employee to "get the work done soon," it is assumed that the subordinate implicitly understands what work should be performed, what "soon" means, what the consequences of failing to perform will be, and so forth. There is a strong assumption of shared meaning and that the context of the interaction conveys much of its meaning. In an abstractive culture, people tend to be very explicit in their interactions, and they define their terms carefully.

Associative cultures are characterized by face to face communication, whereas abstractive cultures are characterized by communication in the mass media. Additionally, in associative cultures an appropriate response to someone's action may not appear to be directly linked to the original behavior (e.g., helping someone to understand a new word processor may be reciprocated with an invitation to lunch several weeks later). In abstractive cultures, actions are often linked to immediate and corresponding reactions (for example, one worker helping another to complete a job results in a direct reciprocation). Thus the exchanges in an abstractive culture tend to be characterized as tit for tat or direct exchange, whereas in an associative culture they may be more diffused.

Glenn also discusses ideologists versus pragmatists as a dimension of culture. Pragmatists focus on information that is useful or practical, whereas ideologists begin with a broad framework and sample facts to see if they fit into an existing framework.

Other studies of values include work by Ronen and his colleagues (Ronen, 1978, 1982, 1986; Kraut & Ronen, 1975; Ronen & Shenkar, 1985) which focuses on cluster and small space analysis of various countries using a number of basic values. Whitely and England (1980) used England's Values Questionnaire to survey managers from the United States, Japan, Korea, India, and Australia. Although they found numerous differences in values among the cultures, it is not altogether clear what these differences mean without a strong, underlying theory (Triandis, in press).

A highly regarded study of managerial values that still serves as a basis for many current studies was the massive work of Haire, Ghiselli, and Porter (1966). In this study managers from fourteen countries were surveyed concerning their values and attitudes toward work relationships, organizations, leadership, and work goals, among others. Maehr and Braskamp (1986) developed a Personal Incentives Model to describe the responses of 575 American and 467 Japanese managers. They found that Americans emphasized affiliation, recognition, and social concern more than the Japanese, who emphasized financial incentives, task, and excellence. Unfortunately the results seem at odds with other literature (e.g., Hofstede, 1980) concerning these cultures, although Triandis (in press) argues that ingroup versus outgroup differences in the two countries may explain the discrepancy. Without a stronger cultural knowledge of the countries involved, it appears that the Maehr and Braskamp findings are of limited utility.

Several studies of values address component aspects of culture. Bond and his colleagues (e.g., Bond, 1988; Leung & Bond, 1984) focus on equity and equality norms or values held in Asian versus Western cultures. Bond (1988) developed a Chinese Values Survey consisting of forty items, and his study of twenty cultures demonstrates several clusters of values: Confucianism (emphasis placed on filial piety, moderation, humbleness, and sense of shame); Oriental tradition (emphasis placed on industry, kindness, loyalty to superiors, and courtesy); and, relationship orientation (tolerance of others, harmony with others, solidarity, patience, and courtesy). By correlating his factor scores with those of Hofstede, Bond found only a significant relationship.

Another ambitious program, undertaken by the Meaning of Work (MOW) research team (1986), examined the valued aspect of work and life by individuals from eight countries. They split work centrality into identification with work, involvement and work commitment, and choice of work as a means of self-expression. Unfortunately the differences obtained by the MOW team are not easily understood without a thorough understanding of the various cultures, and the research endeavor is atheoretical.

Finally we wish to note the work of Schwartz and Bilsky (1987), who developed a model of a universal structure of values. Their theory views values as cognitive representations of three universal requirements: biological needs, interactional requirements for interpersonal coordination, and societal demands for group welfare and survival. The core of their model is the interaction among three facets of values: goal, interests, and motivational domain. Goals refer to the instrumental versus the terminal aspects of values, and interests refer to an individualist versus a collectivist versus a "both" orientation. (It is not really clear what the "both" category refers to since the interest construct is discussed in light of Triandis et al. (1985) and Hofstede's (1980) work on individualism versus collectivism, suggesting that it is a bipolar construct. Perhaps this indicates that a "both" category would be a midpoint between the extremes of individualism and collectivism.) The third facet, motivational domains, consists of eight aspects: enjoyment, achievement, self-direction, maturity, security, prosocial, restrictive conformity, and social power.

Schwartz and Bilsky combine these facets of values through the use of a mapping sentence. They define value as, "an individual's concept of a transituational goal that expresses interests concerned with a motivational domain and evaluated on a range of importance from range [*sic*] as a guiding principle in his/her life" (1987:553). The unique combinations of levels of the three facets can be used to characterize individuals from particular cultures. For example, an ambitious individual can be represented by an instrumental goal, individualistic orientation, and achievement motivational domain. Schwartz and Bilsky used small space analysis to analyze value data from 455 Israeli schoolteachers and 331 German students. The results provide support for their model in a number of respects. Their work represents a renewed interest in studying cultures from a value perspective but, unlike many of its predecessors, it is founded on a theoretical framework that aids in interpreting the results. The question remains, however, how this model will hold up to replication in other cultures in which the assumed motivational domains may not be equivalent. The interests domain does not seem sufficiently well developed to constitute a pancultural construct.

To summarize, we have examined a number of approaches to studying culture that utilize a values perspective. The basic rationale underlying these models is that culture manifests itself in the values held by the society's members. These values are thought to influence an individual's attitudes, cognitions, and behavior.

Recently there has been a more cognitive orientation in the study of culture. In the next section we describe a number of theoretical models from anthropology and psychology that represent the cognitive approach to the assessment and understanding of culture.

Subjective Culture Models

The approach used by a number of intercultural researchers has been based on the argument that culture is an enacted phenomenon tied to the collective perceptions and interpretations of people within a society or subjective culture. Osgood (1964) discusses subjective culture in terms of language:

The denotative or referential uses of terms—the way the lexicon carves up the work—appear largely arbitrary and unique to particular languages until the ethnolinguist discovers a framework of semantic components that can be imposed comparably on these phenomena. In closely analogous fashion, our own researchers over the past few years provide evidence for a universal framework underlying certain affective or connotative aspects of language. These findings enliven the possibility of constructing instruments for measuring these aspects of 'subjective culture' comparably in diverse societies—in effect, circumventing the language barrier. (171)

This definition was later elaborated by Triandis (1972) and formed the basis for his model of subjective culture, which we will discuss shortly. Building on Herskovits's (1955:305) definition of culture. Triandis defines subjective culture as "a cultural group's characteristic way of perceiving the man-made part of its environment. The perception of rules and the group's norms, roles, and values are aspects of subjective culture" (4). He argues that individuals who share a common language, work in related activities, and so on, are likely to share the same subjective culture. Individuals who interact frequently because of shared physical locale or who share common demographic characteristics are likely to share a similar subjective culture since it is likely that they will have positive social interactions with one another.

Osgood's primary work in the realm of subjective culture has been the development of his Atlas of Semantic Meaning (1964, 1977; Osgood, May & Miron, 1975). The purpose of his research program was to develop a general index of semantic meaning that might be used to interpret such constructs as justice or freedom across a variety of cultures. He sought to develop comparable instruments—semantic differentials—to measure semantic meanings across cultures.

Among other findings, Osgood identifies three underlying dimensions of affective meaning: evaluation, potency, and activity (EPA). Evaluation refers to the "good/bad" aspect of a concept; potency refers to the strength of a concept; and activity refers to the energy underlying a concept. Although all three dimensions are present in all cultures' concepts, the distinguishing feature among cultures is the relative value of the three dimensions. Thus far Osgood and his colleagues have compiled the semantic ratings for numerous concepts in several dozen cultures. The findings seem to suggest a similarity of concept meaning across cultures, i.e., a concept such as freedom will get positive ratings across most of the cultures.

A second approach to subjective culture is presented by Triandis (1972). This model concerns itself with the way people in different cultures perceive their social environment as well as the impact of environmental factors on these processes. Perhaps the most notable aspect of his model is its breadth in trying to assess the relations among environment, social environment, values, and psychological process. Given its comprehensive nature, we feel it warrants special attention. The model is reproduced in Figures 3-2 and 3-3.

The distal antecedent of subjective culture is physical environment—resources as well as historical events. The physical environment has a direct impact on a society's economic activities which, in turn, influence more proximal antecedents such as occupations and labor structure. As we will discuss in a subsequent section of this chapter, occupational communities have a number of important effects on individuals. An oft cited example of the impact of physical environment on a collective or group is the tragic case of the lk tribe in Africa. Due to a variety of political complications combined with severe drought conditions, the tribe has degraded from a close-knit community to an aggregation of people unwilling to share or interact. Family and tribal structures have collapsed, and children as young as two and three years old are abandoned to fend for themselves.

Perhaps a more appropriate example (albeit, mundane) for our management context is the relationship of population to the use of labor-intensive production methods. In the People's Republic of China it is more common to see several score laborers digging a ditch for a drainage system than a crew of five or six people using earth-moving equipment. In this case, the combination of an abundance of people and scarce technological resources leads to production methods that emphasize labor-intensive methods. Barry, Child, and Bacon's (1959) work, in which they studied over one hundred fishing, hunting, and agricultural communities, provides another example. They found that in hunting and fishing economies which have low food accumulation, the adults are individualistic and assertive. In agricultural societies which have abundant food resources, adults are conscientious, compliant, and conservative. These results suggest that food availability is associated with competitive versus cooperative behavior. We will explore other aspects of Barry's systems approach in a subsequent section of this chapter.

Historical events have an impact on the social and political organizations that evolve in a society as well as on more proximal aspects of culture, including language, religion, location, and feedback from own behavior. For example, as a result of World War II, Japan's militaristic orientation changed to an industrial one. Likewise the emphasis on rugged survivalism characteristic of settling the Wild West in the United States is thought to have contributed to the strong individualistic orientation of Americans. Historical events play a role in the type of organizations that evolve in a society as well. For instance, Mao's cultural revolution rejected the economic control system of feudal China and replaced it with the communist/collective system. The Chinese cultural revolution led to an egalitarian ideology and a focus on the welfare of Chinese society. The profound impact of the revolution on Chinese society serves to illustrate that historical events can have marked effects on a society even during a relatively short time frame.

With regard to other effects, Triandis posits that proximal antecedents have an impact on pancultural psychological processes which, in turn, create subjective culture. For example, religion and language influence the types of categorizations that individuals make, the number of categories they use, as well as the consistency with which a particular label is assigned to a particular object (1964). Little (1968) showed that Mediterranean people prefer shorter distances for social interaction than do northern Europeans. This difference in social behavior reflects different religious norms concerning interaction and the impact of these norms on cognitive scripts for behavior in a social context. The famous Whorf-Sapir linguistic hypothesis argues that language has a profound impact on sociocultural behavior. Its theme is reflected in such popular works as George Orwell's *Animal Farm* ("All animals are created equal but some animals are more equal than others") and *Nineteen Eighty-four*.

Occupation and social setting also influence aspects of subjective culture since the roles that individuals enact as well as the tasks they perform are dependent on their occupations. For example, such trades as carpentry that involve mentoring and apprenticeship encourage hierarchically differentiated roles within the context of a communal group (Van Maanen & Barley, 1984). The impact that such basic psychological processes as learning (cognitive and instrumental), categorization, and conditioning have on subjective culture is illustrated through a variety of more specific sociological and psychological constructs, including roles, tasks, norms, cognitive structures, values, affect, behavioral intentions, habits, and utilities.

The determinants of action in Triandis's model are an individual's behavioral intentions and habits. Patterns of action are a function of behavioral intentions which are influenced by subjective culture. It is the link between subjective culture and behavioral intentions that provides an explicit relation lacking in value-based models. In a subjective culture approach, values influence behavioral intentions through an individual's affective states as well as cognitive structures (although values are reciprocally determined by cognitive structures). Patterns of action and behavioral intentions resemble other information-processing models (e.g., Ajzen & Fishbein, 1980), although many of the details concerning roles, norms, and tasks remain as unspecified antecedents in these other models. Triandis adds nonvolitional antecedents of action not typically incorporated in others' models. Habits, he argues, represent the impact of repeated feedback concerning particular actions. In associative cultures linguistic cues often convey rank among people, and these nuances of language are enacted habitually. Social behavior and protocol, such as social distance, similarly reflect habit rather than cognition. Anyone familiar with a culture that uses a large social distance knows how uncomfortable it can be to interact face to face with someone who is from a small social distance culture.

Earley recalls an incident in meeting his sponsor for the first time in Kumasi, Ghana. It is Ashanti custom for friends to hold hands and remain physically close to one another while they speak. He was extended this compliment of friendship by his

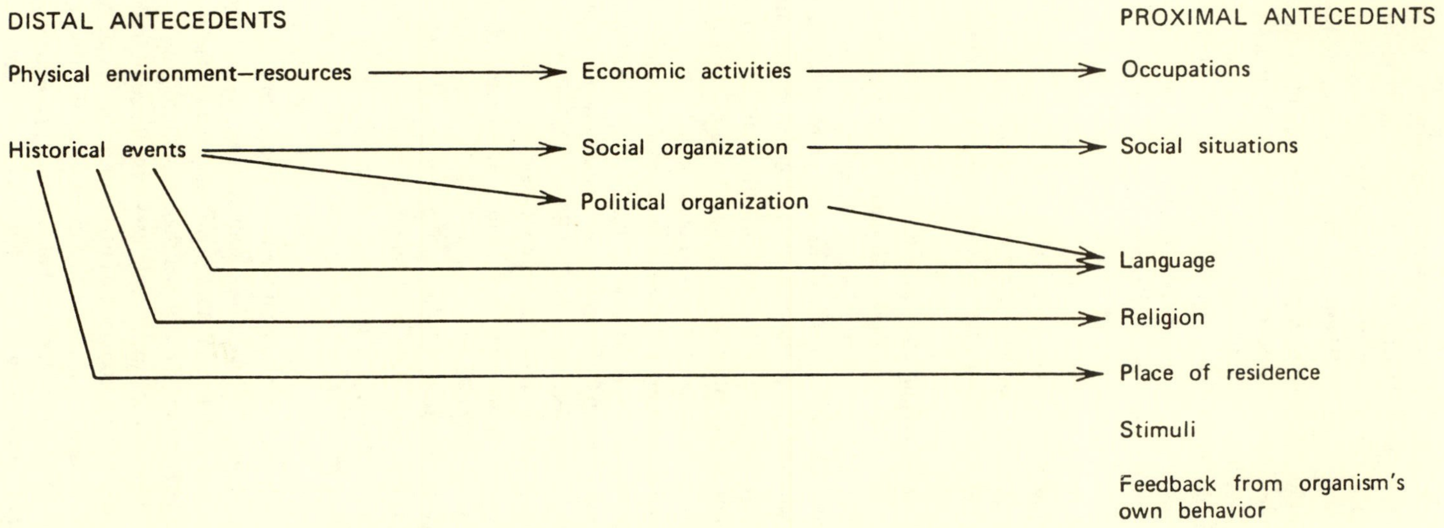

Figure 3-2. Distal antecedents of subjective culture (SOURCE: Triandis, 1972)

62

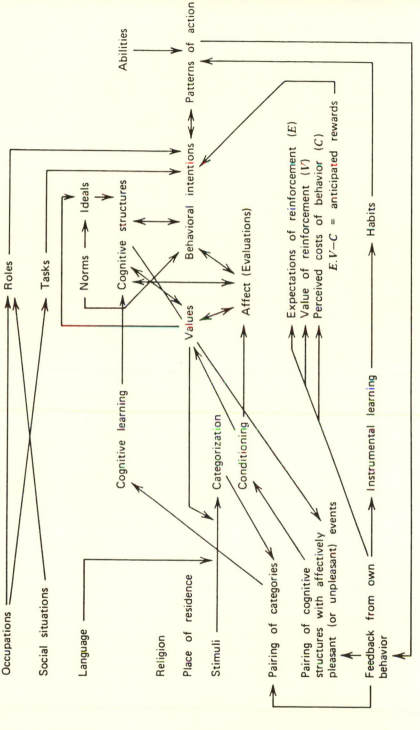

Figure 3-3. Proximal antecedents and consequences of subjective culture (SOURCE: Triandis, 1972)

colleague; however the close physical contact violated a social distance to which he was accustomed and made him feel discomfort. Social habits clearly are reaffirmed by cultural values and norms.

The core of Triandis's model is the specific action of behavioral patterns as a function of distal and proximal antecedents that impact subjective culture. His model captures the relation of macro, societal-level influences on specific individuals' responses through psychological process. However this model remains a general sketch concerning many global relationships. As Triandis himself points out,

The utility of this framework is limited. It only states the concepts we wish to study and hypothesizes the probable relationships between them. A more useful framework will go further and specify how particular variables subsumed under each of these concepts are related to variables subsumed under adjacent concepts. Such middle-range theories are only now beginning to develop and will have to be tested quite thoroughly before they can be incorporated into the present framework as established relationships rather than mere hypotheses. (1972:24)

Despite this concern, his model of subjective culture is an important extension and elaboration of Parsonian theory and the value frameworks that have dominated much of the work on cross-cultural organizational behavior.

Cognitive Anthropology

An approach related to subjective culture is reflected in a movement within anthropology often referred to as cognitive anthropology. Although a comprehensive review is beyond our means, we will provide a general overview of this movement. We suggest that the interested reader see D'Andrade (1984), Goodenough (1971), and Spradley (1979) among others concerning a strong cognitive perspective, and Geertz (1973) and Shweder and Levine (1984) for a collection of essays on culture theory describing shared meaning systems and symbols. Two recent trends in anthropology focus on the perceived nature of culture from a cognitive structuralist view and an interpretive meaning view. These trends are in striking contrast to more historical approaches that focus on linguistic styles in the study of culture (Durbin).

The cognitive structuralist approach views culture as a complex set of shared knowledge systems and structures. It is well represented by Cole and Scribner (1974), Goodenough, and Spradley as well as D'Andrade, who presents a synthesis of the strictly cognitive approach with the interpretive style of Geertz. Cole views the heavy emphasis on hypothesized differences in cognitive process as a primary shortcoming of cross-cultural theory. He sharply criticizes Piaget's work on cognitive development, arguing that cognitive development is the same across cultures but Piaget's methods are inconsistent with the cultures he studied. Cole argues that many of Piaget's observations were biased by his constructs and that only through a detailed assessment of the relevant cognitive processes would clear understanding occur. Goodenough and Spradley have shaped cognitive anthropology using the conceptualization of culture as a knowledge system. According to this perspective, the key to understanding culture and subjective meaning is knowing the rules or scripts that guide action—how people make sense of their situation and how this influences patterned action?

In the organizational realm, the cognitive anthropology approach is well illustrated by Bougon and his colleagues (Bougon, Weick & Binkhorst, 1977; Donnellon, Gray & Bougon, 1986; Weick & Bougon, 1986). According to this approach, the behavior of communities, such as Bougon's, can be interpreted using a cognitive map or cognitive knowledge system of interpersonal relationships. The key to understanding the culture of a community is to understand how rules of conduct and relationships are represented as a knowledge system shared among its members. A similar approach is taken by the social network theorists to determine the communication and interaction networks that bind together individuals from a social system (Barley, 1990). Thus we can view culture as a complex network of rules and schema concerning all aspects of how communal members interact with one another.

Another movement within cognitive anthropology concerns the use of shared meanings and symbols as the core of culture. Championed by Geertz (1973), this view has been espoused by a number of organizational researchers studying corporate culture (later in this chapter organization culture will be discussed more fully). According to this view, the cross-cultural researcher functions as an interpreter of explicit and implicit aspects of a culture. The significance of symbols in meaningful relationships is determined by interpreting the interactions among societal members. Thus a culture is viewed as a pattern of symbolic discourse that needs interpretation and deciphering in order to be fully understood. The methodology for such research is primarily descriptive, involving extensive interviews and observations of members from within the culture. The researcher is also concerned with determining the dominant themes that specify the linkages among values, attitudes, and action as well as how the specific symbols within a subgroup or community reflect those of the society at large.

Within an organizational context, Harris and Sutton (1986) examine the rituals and ceremonies that mark the departure of individuals from their organizations, such as farewell parties or testimonials. A striking example that conveys a culture of distrust and conflict is exemplified by the way a Southwest-based electronics company fires its employees. After returning from lunch the dismissed employee is surprised by a security guard standing by his or her desk. The guard's function is to ensure that no company property is removed as the person clears out the desk. The guard escorts the employee out of the facility, and the various security badges and passes are taken away—much like the symbolic breaking of the calvary officer's sword when he was dishonorably discharged. This symbolic ceremony instills a norm of distrust and reinforces in employees who remain in service fear of the high price they will pay should they become disloyal to the organization.

The differing roles of researchers in the cognitive versus interpretive approaches to understanding cultural systems is striking. Whereas the cognitive researcher actively devises systematic examinations of cognitive process using a strong positivist approach, the interpretivist argues that the positivist approach is doomed to failure since it neglects the sociodynamic inherent in the complex nature of relationships. By definition the interpretivist is an active observer and interpreter of cultural phenomena rather than a scientist who presumes to impose causal structure on dynamic and embedded social systems. Perhaps it is best to view these approaches as complementary rather than competing, as some writers seem to assert (e.g., Smircich & Calas, 1986), much in the same way that the field of strategy business has attempted to integrate case analysis with more quantitative approaches.

Systems Models

The primary characteristic of the systems approach to the study of culture is that culture is viewed as a series of interlocking systems of variables. Earlier in this chapter we identified a general systems approach advanced by Triandis (1980:9) that included several general systems: ecology, subsistence, sociocultural, individual, interindividual, and projective. A systems approach represents these subsystems as interlocking facets of larger systems to describe culture and its effect on societal members.

One of the earliest systems models that attempted to link levels of systems was proposed by Whiting and his colleagues (Whiting & Child, 1953; Whiting, 1964, 1974). A specific model proposed by Whiting in 1964 and later revised in 1974 suggests that culture can be represented by six sets of systems: environment, history, maintenance, a child's learning environment, individual and projective expressive. According to this model, environment (e.g., terrain and climate) is reciprocally related to history (e.g., migrations and inventions) and both are antecedent to maintenance systems (e.g., economy, social structure, division of labor, and settlement patterns). Maintenance systems have a direct effect on a child's learning environment (e.g., tasks assigned, status of caretakers and teachers) which feeds into the individual component (e.g., adult and infant learners). Finally, the individual component influences the projective expressive system (e.g., magic beliefs, rituals and ceremonies, religious dogmas, art, and recreation).

Although there are a number of potential problems with the Whiting model (e.g., static nature and heavy reliance on psychoanalytic theory in the connection of child-rearing practices to projective expressive systems), it represents an important step toward linking the macro to the microlevel and back to the marco. Unlike other models of culture that link societal and environmental systems to more microlevel ones, such as values, personality, and subjective culture, Whiting's model takes this unidirectional linkage and turns it back toward more macrolevel aspects of society, such as religious institutions as influenced by the expressive system. In one test of the model, Whiting, Kluckhohn, and Anthony (1958) used the concept of Oedipal rivalry in describing the emergence of male initiation rites. He assumed that certain social conditions (e.g., mother-son sleeping arrangements) would lead to a strong dependence on the mother in early life. This dependence would manifest itself in powerful hostility between father and son when the father comes between the mother and son. The function of the initiation rite was to reduce tension during the son's adolescence following his separation from the mother.

A second systems model, proposed by LeVine (1984) is an elaboration of a Darwinian variation-selection model. One of the nicest innovations of his model is

the extensive use of feedback loops among the systems. According to this model, ecology exerts an influence on child-rearing customs by imposing certain constraints. A genertic component of the model enters into the shaping of an individual's personality through a coinfluence with the shaping from parental influences. Thus personality is shaped by variations in genetic predispositions (genotypes) as well as variations in the normative environment attributable to parental influence through child-rearing customs. LeVine argues that individuals must adapt to such normative subenvironments (secondary adaptations) as occupational roles and that they will adjust with greater or lesser success depending on their genotype. He further posits that the adaptation to subenvironments is an active adjustment through a system of self-regulation. The self-regulatory system leads to changes in personality as a result of the social sanctions and norms prevalent in the culture.

Another model specifically designed to analyze culture and organizations developed by Harris and Moran (1979, 1987). According to their perspective, there are eight interdependent systems that constitute culture: kinship, education, economy, politics, religion, association, health, and recreation. Unfortunately Harris and Moran do not provide an extensive analysis of how these subsystems interrelate but they do describe how each subsystem will impact an organization in isolation from other systems. For instance, the kinship system refers to such family patterns as the tight nuclear family found in individualistic cultures versus the broad extended family found in more collectivistic cultures. In an extended kinship culture, emphasis is placed on nepotism in hiring practices, which is not seen as negative or problematic. The education system refers to both formal and informal methods of providing knowledge and skills. Harris and Moran argue that the education system may have a strong impact on the training and leadership programs available to organization members. Another example is the association system, which refers to the network of social groupings in society. Some cultures emphasize organizations and create formal or informal associations for a wide variety of activities. Joining such associations may be important if managers consider them to be a useful source of support and loyalty (Ronen, 1986:29).

Our major concern with the Harris and Moran model is that the systems are not adequately integrated, and many aspects of some subsystems appear to be values rather than systems. For example, the kinship and association subsystems seem to reflect the value of individualism and collectivism rather than dynamic, freestanding subsystems.

Organizational Culture

We will begin with a general review of the notion of corporate or organizational culture, followed by a brief critique. As our presentation is abbreviated, we refer the interested reader to reviews by Frost, et al. (1985), Kilmann, Saxton, and Serpa (1985), Pondy et al. (1983), Sathe (1985), Schein (1985), Smircich and Calas (1986), and Tichy (1982) as well as a number of special issues of journals, including *Administrative Science Quarterly* and *Organizational Dynamics*. Research on this topic peaked during the 1980s stemming from the popularity of management books,

threats of international competition (most notably from Japan), the proliferation of multinational and joint ventures, and a counterreaction to the positivist tradition of analyzing systems into their component parts (Smircich, 1983; Smircich and Calas).

The basic definition of organizational culture is captured nicely by Smircich and Calas's description of corporate culture as the sociocultural dynamics that develop within organizations; culture is viewed as an internal attribute of an organization rather than an external force that intrudes upon the organization.

The idea of corporate culture has led to a number of different research streams. Some individuals view culture from an engineering perspective, insisting that it refers to a coordination of systems within an organization, such as culture and reward systems (Cummings, 1984), or an element essential for effective organizational change (Sathe, Tichy). Others view an organization as a living or dying system having an organization-level personality. For instance, Kets de Vries and Miller (1986) developed a typology of organizations based on manifestations of pathological personality types.

Smircich and Calas categorized the following frameworks for studying organizational culture: themes, paradigmatic perspective, and theory of knowledge perspective. The themes perspective refers to culture as a root metaphor. The five themes identified by Smircich and Calas are comparative and corporate cultures, cognition, symbolism, and unconscious processes. The first two themes refer to culture as a variable denoting relationships between or within organizations. The other three themes refer to the use of an organization as a culture, that is to say, culture is what constitutes an organization from an expressive and symbolic process perspective.

The paradigm framework attempts to link culture and communication to organizational context, and it consists of two major approaches. The functionalist paradigm is characterized by the objectivist or positivist approach used in most of the social sciences. Its purpose is to develop useful law-like statements that enable the researcher to understand behavior within the context of specific corporate cultures. The second approach is the interpretive paradigm from an antipositivist view. In essence, interpretive research centers on understanding the dynamics of a corporate setting through the subjective perceptions of the viewer. The third framework is the knowledge perspective, or the interests embedded in the organizational symbolism literature.

Stablein and Nord (1985) use this approach to describe three cognitive interests derived from Habermas (1979). Technical interest focuses on the manipulation and control of the environment consistent with a functionalist approach. Practical interest refers to a desire to understand meaning in a specific situation so that a decision can be made and action undertaken. The focus is on a consensually agreed upon decision rather than a more generalizable rule. Emancipatory interest refers to an interest in enhancing human liberties and responsibility in the world. The purpose of this approach is to determine the shared meanings of culture that have the potential to free individuals and give them liberty in individual action.

The following brief descriptions of current empirical assessments of organization culture are intended to give the reader a general flavor for this research. At a conceptual level, Morgan and Smircich (1980) discuss concepts of people as responding mechanisms or as adaptive mechanisms. Powell (1985) provides a general

overview of the publishing industry in his institutional analysis of organization culture and social structure. Peters and Waterman's popular work *In Search of Excellence* (1982) details case organizations that depict effective organizational cultures. Although the book is plagued by conceptual inconsistencies and poor methodology (see Carroll, 1983 and Triandis, in press, for critiques), it illustrates how critical organizational culture is to performance and worker well-being. More scientifically defensible studies of culture have been conducted by Harris and Sutton (1986), Jaeger (1983, 1986), Martin (1982), Martin and Siehl (1983), and Trice and Beyer (1984), although, with the exception of Jaeger, these studies appear somewhat ignorant of the general culture in which the organizations are embedded.

Empirical work suggests that national or societal-level culture must be considered along with organizational culture in order to fully understand the relation of an organization's culture to organizational functioning (England, 1983). For example, Lincoln, Hanada, and Olson (1981) found that matching organizational culture with societal culture results in high job satisfaction. Ferris and Wagner (1985) found that a congruence of Japanese organization structure with Japanese values was positively related to the effectiveness of quality circles. A similar idea is put forward by Ouchi and his Theory Z analysis (Ouchi, 1981; Ouchi & Jaeger, 1983). Another good example of the relationship between societal and organizational cultures is presented by Misumi (1984) who examines participatory decision-making and Japanese values. He argues that such decision-making styles as the *ringi* system are consistent with the early Meiji era of Japan.

We have a number of rather significant concerns with the notion of organizational culture in general. Our first concern is best expressed by Ruth Benedict (1934, 1946) who cautioned researchers in the field of anthropology that "topical studies" of particular institutions (e.g., marriage, initiation, or economic) are misguided since the significant unit is not the institution but the general cultural configuration. This theme is also put forward by Tyler, who states that cultures . . . are not material phenomena; they are cognitive organizations of material phenomena. Consequently, cultures are neither described by mere arbitrary lists of anatomical traits and institutions such as house type, family type, kinship type, economic type, and personality type, nor are they necessarily equated with some over-all integrative pattern of these phenomena" (1969:3).

The study of organizational culture is misguided in the sense that organizations do not possess cultures of their own; rather, they are formed as a function of societal culture. Perhaps the distinction between culture and norms will illuminate our point. D'Andrade (1984) argues that culture and norms differ in that norms tell people how they should behave in a particular context, whereas culture tells them the inherent meaning of the context. As Schneider points out, "Where norms tell the actor how to behave in the presence of ghosts, gods, and human beings, culture tells the actor what ghosts, gods, and human beings are and what they are all about" (1975:203). Since organizational culture refers to the norms that regulate action within a particular organization, the heavy emphasis on the study of myths and rituals simply reflects the sense-making that individuals engage in given these institutional norms. Perhaps the most important lesson to be learned is that organizational norms, rules, and functioning need to be consistent with a society's culture to prevent the individual from experiencing role ambiguity and alienation. Similar observations have been made by Van Maanen and Barley (1984) in their work on occupational communities.

Triandis (in press) argues that organizations may have a weak effect on an individual's peripheral values but no lasting impact on his or her deep-seated values. Such a conclusion is evident if we consider a values model such as Rokeach's. Organizational norms that conflict with an individual's values will have an impact on the self-image only if they are consistent and reinforced. Rather than perpetuating the view that organizations need to develop creative cultures or achievement-oriented cultures or motivation-by-positive-results cultures, we recommend that attention be directed toward reconciling organizational practices with those of the society's culture (see Hofstede, 1980 for a similar argument expressed in a more eloquent fashion). This need may become increasingly apparent as democracy and capitalism are spread to countries in Eastern Europe and Asia that are fundamentally collectivistic. What impact will a capitalist system relying on principles of self-interest have for a collectivistic culture? Just as the apparent economic successes of the capitalist experiments taking place in the People's Republic of China are beginning to waiver (Bao, 1991 personal communication), we may find long-term failures due to the overly rapid exportation of capitalism to collectivistic societies.

SUMMARY OF APPROACHES AND PRESENT FRAMEWORK

We have discussed a large number of perspectives and briefly traced the way scholars have approached the concept of culture in anthropology, organizational behavior, psychology, and sociology. In order to understand this plethora of frameworks and theories, we offer an abbreviated trend analysis of each discipline in Figure 3-4.

As can be seen from our figure, the emphasis on cultural frameworks differs somewhat across disciplines, but many similarities exist as well. For instance, many of the disciplines have chosen to move away from an emphasis on values as a way of describing cultures, although this approach is still prevalent in organizational behavior. Perhaps this strong bias is attributable to the vast nature of Hofstede's work or the ease with which individuals can address his dimensions of culture. Unfortunately most work with his model, along with other value models, typically consists of comparisons of management methods (e.g., leadership model X) between cultures A and B looking for differences that can be attributed to values. Another form of analysis is the simple mapping out of a new typology of values rather than a more theoretically satisfying integration of antecedents and consequences of the values. Even though Hofstede (1980, 1984) used a cognitive framework in conceptualizing culture as a set of shared, mental programs and provided a number of hypothesized connections with antecedents/consequences, few researchers have attempted to develop empirical tests of this aspect of his work.

Interestingly the field of sociology appears to have lost serious interest in the concept of culture, viewing it as an implicit result of structure best understood through the careful study of institutions, norms, and social structure (Goldberg, 1990, personal communication). However, some sociologists argue that it is again

	approx. 1900 - 1920	1920 - 40	1940 - 60	1960 - 80	1980 - present
Cultural anthropology	culture via ethnography (Tylor, 1889)	use of rules and norms for culture; participant observation (Malinowski, 1933)	cognitive beliefs and experimentation (Goodenough, 1956); pattern variables (Kluckhohn & Strodtbeck, 1961)	shared cognitive structures (Goodenough, 1971; Spradley, 1979); interpretivist view (Geertz, 1973)	script/schema theory; interpretive meaning systems (D'Andrade; Shweder & LeVine, 1984)
Organization behavior				values approach (Haire et al., 1966; Hofstede, 1980)	"corporate culture" & comparative mgt. (Schein, 1985; Smircich, 1983)
Psychology	cultural rites explained by psychological process (Levy-Bruhl, 1910)	studies of need structure and values (Murray, 1932)	needs and values approaches (Allport et al., 1960; Murdock, 1951)	subjective culture (Osgood, 1964; Triandis, 1972); achievement motive (McClelland, 1961)	values model (Ronen, 1986; Schwartz & Bilsky, 1987); self concept (Triandis, 1989)
Sociology	social structure determining culture (Radcliffe-Brown, 1922)		values approach and use of pattern variables (Parsons & Shils, 1951; Kluckhohn, 1951)	Reduced emphasis on concept of culture as an explicit variable and emphasis on culture as an implicit result of social structure -- development of institution's impact on norms. Very recent rediscovery of culture as explicit variable (Wuthnow & Witten, 1989)	
(time period)	approx. 1900 - 1920	1920 - 40	1940 - 60	1960 - 80	1980 - present

Figure 3-4. Trends of cultural frameworks across time

71

gaining significance as an explicit influence on organizations and social process (Wuthnow & Witten, 1988). The reemergence of sociological interest in culture is evident in the organizational work of DiMaggio (1982) Hirsch and Andrews (1983), and Powell (1985), among others. We would disagree with the structuralists' view that culture is merely an implicit product of social structure. As we argued earlier, norms are an important aspect of how culture manifests itself but are not synonymous with culture. However the impact of social structure and the resulting norms on individuals' shared knowledge structures appears to be gaining interest in the literature.

The interest in culture from a psychological perspective has followed two primary paths, namely, subjective culture and values models, with the latter gaining much attention in recent work. The revival of interest in a values perspective seems to have limited potential since these broad approaches do little for the development of the middle-range theories needed for advancing specific findings (Triandis, in press). The value model of Schwartz and Bilsky (1987) offers some hope for a value approach since it provides a theoretical linking of motives, goals, and interests as a means of describing values in societies. Perhaps their approach can be used to describe how values impact shared knowledge structures, thus providing needed linkages between the macro- and the microrealms. What we do not need are more studies that classify countries based on a researcher's favorite value scheme.

Recent work conducted in the field of organizational behavior seems to mimic and lag behind other fields (a perpetual dilemma for organizational behavior research in many regards). The organizational behavior approach used in the 1960s followed the value approaches of sociology and anthropology, whereas more recent research on corporate culture borrows heavily from cognitive and interpretive anthropology from the 1970s. Ironically, recent approaches to cultural anthropology have relied on many psychological process theories that seem distasteful to organizational culture researchers (Smircich and Calas, 1986). Perhaps the biggest difference between organizational culture researchers and intercultural psychologists is the methodology employed (experimentation versus ethnomethodology) rather than true paradigm clashes. Triandis (in press) argues that "the use of qualitative methods is essential in the *early* phases of a research project. These are situations where such methods provide useful data, but the problem is that many researchers stop there. The more quantitative methods should be used also to test, confirm, and refine hypotheses. The importance of multimethod approaches needs to be emphasized" (39).

These models of culture consistently utilize shared values and knowledge as a way of describing culture and its impact on behavior. Our model uses these principles by positing that culture, an individual's conception of self (knowledge structures unique to the individual), and work behavior interact. Without consideration of these three facets, we cannot fully understand why individuals behave in particular ways within an organizational context.

Present Framework

At the most general level, our model can best be described as a psychological approach focusing on the interplay of an individual's self-concept, culture, and work environment. It is not our intent to portray our model as a "grand" theory depicting all aspects of society; rather, we wish to provide a theoretical framework to capture how culture and self interact within the context of an organizational setting. In doing so, we will employ many of the concepts put forward by information-processing approaches (e.g., Lord, 1985; Schank & Abelson, 1977), Triandis's (1972) model of subjective culture, and work on the self (e.g., Marcus & Wurf, 1987; Rokeach, 1973; Triandis, 1989). Using an information processing approach, we focus on the "micro" aspects of organizational behavior, including such applied topics as work motivation, group dynamics, leadership, and conflict management.

Perhaps what distinguishes our approach most from others is its intended application domain—work behavior in organizations. Although a number of models have addressed the impact of culture on institutions, scant attention has been directed toward the development of an intercultural theory of organizational behavior. Our view is that behavior within the context of an organization has its own eccentricities that define organizational behavior but that cannot be fully understood removed from a general cultural context. This separation becomes salient when organizations are "internationalized" through joint ventures and multinational corporations.

While our approach is intended to clarify how management techniques may be adopted/adapted across cultures, its focus is on understanding the dynamics of work behavior in varying cultural contexts. Our model utilizes a fundamental value that has been depicted in every model we have encountered, namely, the social-relatedness of individuals—the so-called individualism versus collectivism theme. In the next chapter we will develop and refine this concept at length since it plays such a central role in our model. We believe that the dynamic between individualism and collectivism is crucial because it gets at the heart of an organization—the interaction among parties for the purpose of producing outputs or providing services. A final element of our model is a temporal component not often employed in models of culture. The absence of feedback loops and a dynamic perspective is often viewed as a shortcoming of culture models, and we think that such an omission should not be made.

In summary, our model uses a psychological approach, relying on the concept of the self along with a central value of how people relate to one another. Its intended application domains are the intrapersonal, interpersonal, and intergroup dynamics that define organizational behavior.

4

Individualism and Collectivism

Although societies differ along many cultural dimensions, a key distinguishing characteristic of work behavior is the way in which members relate to one another as a group. The pattern of responses with which individuals relate to their groups reflects their degree of individualism or collectivism. Put simply, humans are a collectivistic species, collecting together for mutual support around the lone fire. In contrast, mountain lions or black widow spiders are species that require solitude and avoid collective action. From an evolutionary perspective, a collective orientation has given humans the capacity to aggregate knowledge, develop a shared history, and protect evolutionary adaptations. At the extreme, a number of sociologists and anthropologists argue that people do not exist except within a social context (e.g., Etzioni, 1968).

The interconnection between what we are and our social context is clearly evident. We govern ourselves by social laws that guide our actions despite the obvious freedom we exercise to fulfill our unique and individual desires. Our social reality is based on a number of consistent rules and principles that serve to bridle an individual's initiative toward collective goals and outcomes. Despite the individualism expressed by some and a desire to pursue individual goals, our actions take place within a carefully orchestrated social reality of interconnected individuals. As Etzioni points out, "Man is not unless he is social; what he is depends on his social being, and what he makes of his social being is irrevocably bound to what he makes of himself. He has the ability to master his internal being, *and the main way to self-mastery leads to his joining with others like himself in social acts*" [italics added] (1968:2).

The aspect of culture that captures this emphasis on social relations is commonly referred to as individualism and collectivism (Hofstede, 1980). As we described briefly in Chapter 3, the individualism versus collectivism orientation refers to the extent of social connectedness between an individual and his or her social memberships, clans, or collectives. The extent of social integration is not invariant across societies. In some cultures people live in limited kinship units consisting of such immediate family as husband, wife, and children. In other cultures the immediate family include one's grandparents, uncles, aunts, cousins, or even close friends. These relationships can be determined by bloodlines or kinship ties based on loose and distant relations (Hofstede, 1984:149). Thus one universal aspect of how humans live concerns the manner in which they aggregate into collectivities or clans.

An example may aid to clarify the level of social relations among individuals from different individualistic and collectivistic cultures. In an individualistic culture such as is found in the United States, the family typically includes the parents and the children. Grandparents often live by themselves until some point when they can no longer care for themselves, after which they are relegated to a "retirement community" or what in the past was less euphemistically called the "old folks home." These institutions are evolving to extend adult care from the active senior years through ambulatory or bed-ridden stages. Even the traditional nuclear family in the United States has given way to single-parent households and reliance on outside daycare for the children of working parents. In a collectivistic culture such as is found in the People's Republic of China, emphasis is placed on extended family relationships; parents, children, grandparents, and other relations often will live together even if no economic necessity is present (Li, 1978).

Our emphasis on the individualism versus collectivism dimension lies in its universality and integral nature to work. More so than other cultural dimensions, the individualistic versus collectivistic orientation of a society has profound implications for how individuals work (Hofstede, 1980; Triandis, 1989b, in press). However our discussion of intercultural aspects of organizational behavior is not strictly limited to the individualism/collectivism dimension; rather, we utilize it as an organizing element for our theoretical model.

COLLECTIVITIES AND CLANS

Prior to discussing individualism and collectivism, it is necessary to define what is meant by a collective or a clan. We utilize Etzioni's (1968) and Parsons and Shils' (1951) description of collectives and their functioning in determining social structured as the basis for our presentation.

According to Etzioni (96–105), social collectives consist of individuals who are bound together by a number of different relationships. A normative relationship is based on shared values and norms. Individuals are bound together by common goals and interests, and their mutual commitments are not strictly rational; rather, they are bound by affection and loyalty to one another. A utilitarian relationship is one in which individuals have complementary interests but treat one another as means to mutually compatible ends. In this relation the commitments of individuals to one another are based on rational interests and are stable so long as the individuals provide mutually beneficial actions. The utilitarian relationship is instrumental for achieving compatible ends. A coercive relationship entails the use of threat or force to bind parties to one another. The actors treat one another as objects to be exploited, and commitments can be either rational or nonrational but the relations are typically unstable. Collectives are usually based on a combination of these three relationships, although one will tend to dominate the others. For instance, a mentor has a normative relationship with his disciples that includes an element of a utilitarian relationship as well (e.g., the mentor can help the disciples receive the training and guidance needed to attain a good job).

A collective refers to a group of individuals bound together through a common set of values and norms. Etzioni defines a collective as "a macroscopic unit that has a potential capacity to act by drawing on a set of macroscopic normative bonds which tie members of a stratification category" (98). Individuals within a collective are bound to one another through emotional predispositions, common interests and fate, as well as mutually agreed upon social practices. In such a relationship the temptation to defect and pursue self-interests over those of the collective are minimal. This point is particularly important since the degree of shared values is positively related to a collective's stability.

Durkheim (1933) argues that collectives based on a purely utilitarian basis are inherently unstable and require extensive precontractual agreements in order to facilitate stability. Since such agreements inevitably fail to consider all contingencies, when a new situation arises that benefits some parties more than others, defection or pursuit of self-interest is likely in the utilitarian-based collective. For instance, Williamson (1975) developed an extensive model of transactions costs to describe the dynamics that individuals engage in to ensure that they will experience sufficient costs in their exchanges to bind them to these agreements. He argued that for exchanges among individuals to be stable, intragroup transactions must be associated with costs that bind the parties to the transactions.

Some transactions cannot be adequately regulated by imposed costs because passions and emotion dictate individuals' actions. According to Frank's commitment model (1988), individuals do not always act efficiently in the pursuit of self-interest; rather, they operate according to emotional dispositions that help them solve commitment problems. A commitment problem is exemplified by someone who threatens retaliation against his or her transgressor. Unless the transgressor really believes that the injured party will carry out the threat, the threat (imposed costs of transaction) will have no meaning. This becomes particularly salient if the cost of retaliation is great to both parties. In such a case, an individual motivated purely by self-interest would choose not to retaliate. However if the injured party is known to be predisposed to retaliate regardless of the personal costs, then the injury may be forestalled since it is known that retaliation will be inevitable. The "irrational" emotional predisposition to retaliate regardless of self-interests inoculates the individual from external threat. Thus Frank argues that emotional predispositions may be highly useful even if they run counter to self-interests.

Given the large size of some collectivities (e.g., national college fraternities), members cannot always interact with all other members. This is why stability occurs only if members of the collective share values and norms. Collectivities are large entities that consist of hierarchically organized subcollectivities that interact with one another through a number of means (Etzioni, 1968) in order to achieve common goals. Subcollectivities can interact with one another directly across unit boundaries by individuals or groups. For example, a local union will interact with representatives of other locals at annual meetings or contract negotiation talks. Members of subcollectivities may also share a belief in certain symbols. An example of this is the religious practice of communion in Christianity which takes place in many diverse settings while retaining a common, symbolic meaning to all members. Leaders from subcollectives may interact with one another in front of group meetings of the subcollectives. An example of this is the often misguided bipartisan effort of the U.S. Senate to pass tax reforms. Republican and Democratic leaders stand together as a gesture of commonality and community in front of the broad senate constituency.

What is crucial about these distinctions concerning collectives is that all individuals participate in them but the relative number of subcollectivities to which an individual belongs and his or her commitment to the goals of the subcollectives will vary as a function of individualism and collectivism. We now turn to the specific definition of individualism and collectivism and its ramification for individuals' actions within a social context.

OVERVIEW OF INDIVIDUALISM AND COLLECTIVISM

The distinction between individualism and collectivism was introduced to modern organization theory by Parsons and Shils (1951:248) who distinguished between a self-orientation, or focus on ego-integrative morals, and a collectivity-orientation, or focus on the social system. Others use the cultural labels of cooperation versus individualism (Mead, 1967), collaterality versus individualism versus lineality (F. Kluckhohn & Strodtbeck, 1961), and individualism versus collectivism (Hofstede, 1980; Triandis, 1989b; in press; Wagner & Moch, 1986). Although individualism-collectivism is a multifaceted construct (Triandis, 1989a; Triandis et al., 1988), an important attribute of a collectivistic society is that individuals view and identify themselves through a very limited number of group memberships or ingroups. An essential aspect of individualism and collectivism is that it describes the relation of an individual to these ingroups.

Individualism and collectivism can have a number of implications for social behavior based on facets of the construct. For instance, Triandis (1989a) reported having generated sixty-six separate hypotheses for the relation of individualism and collectivism to social behavior, values, attitudes, among others. The primary characteristics of individualism and collectivism include: relation of personal to collective interests and goals; family structure; individual discretion for action; locus of decision-making; emotional dependence on the collective; identity based in the social group; *Gemeinschaft* (community-based) versus *Gesellschaft* (society-based) social order; and emphasis on belonging (Hofstede, 1984:171). In addition, Triandis (1989b) suggests that other important dimensions of individualism and collectivism include: membership in a limited number of ingroups, sharing of resources, interdependency of relations among group members, and feelings of involvement in one another's lives (Hui & Triandis, 1985; Triandis, 1989b, in press).

Perhaps the most important aspect of individualists and collectivists concerns their goals and interests relative to the goals and interests of their collective. Individualists give priority to self-interests over those of their collective, whereas collectivists do not distinguish between the two. To the collectivist a collective goal *is* the individual's goal, and if self and collective interests do differ, he or she will subordinate personal interests to those of the collective. For instance, Bontempo, Lobel, and Triandis (1989) examined the reactions of individualists (American sample) and collectivists (Brazilian sample) to performing acts costly to the individual (e.g., visit a sick friend in the hospital). In order to determine potential differences between conformity and internalization of group norms, the subjects were asked, at a public forum and in private, how they would act and whether or not it would be enjoyable to perform the action. The researchers found that the individualists reported the socially desirable response (e.g., to visit and enjoy the visit) in the public format but not in the confidential format. In the latter condition, individualistics indicated that it was unlikely that they would engage in the behavior and even less likely that they would enjoy doing so. However the collectivists (Brazilian sample), both in public and in confidence, reported a high likelihood of performing the act and enjoying. Bontempo et al. concluded that this difference was due to the internalization of group norms by the collectivists and that their actions reflected deep commitment to the group.

Another major component of individualism and collectivism concerns the nature of group memberships. In a collectivistic culture, the self is defined by ingroup memberships. A key characteristic of an ingroup is represented by Durkheim's (1933:365) distinction between contractual relations and organic solidarity in describing a clan. He argues that contractual relations can only regulate predictable exchanges among individuals and are inadequate to control the conflicts that inevitably arise as individuals interact over time. A clan is characterized by an "organic solidarity" such that, under most circumstances, members of a clan will function together to attain objectives desired by the group and avoid or minimize any new conflicts that might arise over time. Thus organic solidarity refers to the normative bonds that hold clan members together and prescribe the ways they should interact with one another to achieve group goals (Etzioni, 1968:102). Ouchi and Jaeger (1978) refer to a clan form of organization in their paper concerning Type Z organizations. Such an organization can be thought of as a clan since the individuals share many common goals and there are embedded social structures and procedures to minimize interpersonal conflicts (see also Etzioni:103–8).

As discussed earlier, collectivists will subordinate their personal interests to the goals of their collective or ingroup, and ingroup membership is stable even when the ingroup places high demands on the individual (Triandis, 1989a). An individual belongs to only a few ingroups, and behavior within the group emphasizes goal attainment, cooperation, group welfare, and ingroup harmony. Collectivists are concerned about the implications of their actions on their ingroups, and they feel interdependent on ingroup members. They also emphasize the integrity and harmony of the ingroups (Hui & Triandis, 1985) over self-interests. The ingroup influences a wide range of the collectivist's social behaviors, and he or she responds more fully to such guidance than do individualists (Davidson et al., 1976). In addition collectivists are thought to view outgroup members with suspicion and distrust (Triandis et al., 1988). One explanation for this reaction is offered by Tajfel's Social Identity Theory (1982) according to which, ingroup members derive a positive self-identity from their group membership. The need to achieve positive group distinctiveness causes people to compare their ingroup with the outgroup and to perceive the ingroup as preferable, even if the ingroup and the outgroup are not in direct conflict. The result of this comparison process is a general denigration of outgroup so as to enhance self-identity and ingroup status (see also Brewer & Kramer, 1985, for a comprehensive review).

In an individualistic culture emphasis is placed on self-sufficiency and control, the pursuit of individual goals which may or may not be consistent with ingroup goals, and membership within multiple ingroups. Individuals from an individualistic society will often drop out of an ingroup if membership becomes a burden or inhibits the attainment of individual goals. In addition, individuals who are not members of an ingroup are not necessarily treated as an outgroup; the competitive actions directed toward outgroup members exhibited by a collectivistic culture are not as likely in an individualistic one (Triandis et al., 1988).

Another important characteristic of a collectivistic society is that families are extended, and the actions of group members are coordinated. For instance, Hofstede (1984:150) suggests that in modern China, a highly collectivistic society, ideological conversions often take place collectively. He argues that such a collective change does not take place merely due to a powerful change agent, such as a family household master, but due to a sense of collective identity. The relation of the extended family to a collectivist's behavior within an organizational setting often leads to perceptions of corruption by individualists who observe the interactions. For instance, it is both accepted practice and expected that family members are given positions and promotions in Saudi Arabian companies. Such practices are a logical extension of the strong collectivism observed in the Middle East. Yet in the West nepotism is viewed as corrupt and unjust.

The extension of family and clan into the organizational realm is also evident in a collectivistic culture such as Japan. For example, Nakane (1978) suggests that in Japanese organizations a group of co-workers shows allegiance to its leader provided that the leader demonstrates paternalism toward the group. By showing care and concern for their subordinates, leaders elicit hard work, cooperation among workers, and sacrifice for the good of the group. There is even some evidence to suggest that modern industrial Japan reflects the basic society structure of feudal times; its companies represent the lines of ancient feudal lords and shogun (Pascale & Athos, 1981).

Individualism and collectivism reflect fundamental themes of autonomy and group action as well. In an individualistic society emphasis is placed on individual freedom of action and preferences, whereas in a collectivistic society it is assumed that the pursuit of individual interests is morally wrong if they conflict with collective interests. There are numerous reasons why individuals may sway in one direction or another concerning moral stances of individual autonomy but these are beyond the scope of this discussion. The morality of individual versus collective action may be the most intangible aspect of culture because it strikes at the very heart of a society's moral stance.

The distinction between individualism and collectivism also holds for differences between communal and exchange relations (Triandis, 1989b). A communal relation is similar to Durkheim's (1933) use of organic solidarity, namely, the relation is based on shared norms and values. A communal versus an exchange relation is characterized by concern for other's needs versus concern for equity, the importance of maintaining equality of affect as opposed to emotional detachment, and the evaluation of benefits according to an equality or an equity standard. An individualistic society adheres more closely to the equity principle, whereas a collectivistic society follows an equality norm (Leung, 1987).

In collectivistic cultures role relationships are often more nurturant and intimate than they are in individualistic cultures, although this tendency is limited to ingroup members (Triandis, 1989b). In fact evidence suggests that collectivists may express hostility or communicate ineffectively with outgroup members. Triandis (1967) found that collectivists do not communicate effectively with members of their own organization if they are not ingroup, and others argue that bureaucracies in collectivistic cultures function poorly because people hoard information within ingroups. Espinoza and Garza (1985) reported that collectivists compete with outgroup members, even if it is not in their self-interest to do so. Likewise, Pandey (1986) reported that outgroup members are often exploited by collectivists.

Clearly the relation of an individual to his or her ingroup is a key feature of individualism and collectivism. The individualist belongs to many ingroups and flows easily between them when it is in his or her interest to do so. Individualists are more accepting of strangers and deviance than are collectivists. Collectivists, however, place great devotion to their ingroup, and they will subordinate their own interests to those of their ingroup.

PERSPECTIVES ON INDIVIDUALISM AND COLLECTIVISM

A large number of scholars have used the concept of individualism and collectivism to describe the relations of people to one another in society. We now turn to a brief overview of several prominent perspectives on individualism and collectivism, including: Parsons and Shils (1951), Kluckhohn (1951) and F. Kluckhohn and Strodtbeck (1961), Hofstede (1980, 1984), and Triandis (1989b, in press), along with several other commentaries.

Parsons and Shils

The distinction used by Parsons and Shils (1951:80–81) concerning how individuals relate to one another with regard to shared interests is called self-orientation versus collectivity orientation. This dimension refers to the dilemma of private versus collective gains, that is, the disharmony created by the choice of actions that will benefit individual interests (to attain own goals) over actions that will benefit the collective. According to Parsons and Shils, this dilemma is resolved by an actor who gives priority to either self-interest or collective goals and actions.

As we described earlier, Parsons and Shils's theory describes action within three basic systems—personality, social, and cultural. At the personality level, self-orientation refers to a need disposition on the part of individuals that permits them to pursue personal goals or interests. A self-interest is pursued regardless of its implications for the collective. A collectivity orientation argues that an individual's need disposition guides actions according to the goals or interests of his or her collectivity. Individual actions take into account the shared values of the collectivity, and the actor accepts responsibility for the well-being of the collectivity even if it requires the subordination of self-interests.

The relation of self-orientation versus collectivity orientation to action at a social-system level refers to the role expectations of the actors, that is, what actions are permissible or should receive priority under various settings. A self-orientation suggests that role incumbents are free to pursue private interests regardless of their impact on the interests or values of their collectivity. A collectivity orientation suggests that role incumbents are obliged to take into account the values and interests of the collectivity. The role incumbent is expected to subordinate self-interests to those of the collective should the setting require it.

At a cultural level self-orientation refers to a normative pattern that prescribes a range of permissible actions in the pursuit of self-interests. Such an allowance permits the individual to pursue self-interests even if they have a direct bearing on other collectivity members. A collectivity orientation refers to a normative pattern prescribing a domain of actions which an individual is obliged to pursue in order to attain the interests and goals of the collective. It defines the responsibilities that an individual feels toward the collective across a wide range of settings.

The essential element of Parsons and Shils's discussion of individualism and collectivism is the tendency of an actor to pursue self-interests versus those of his or her collective. Their emphasis on goals and interests constitutes a limited view of individualism and collectivism that was later broadened by other authors.

Kluckhohn and F. Kluckhohn and Strodtbeck

The distinction used by Kluckhohn (1954) and described in more detail by F. Kluckhohn and Strodtbeck (1961) defines the relational aspect of value orientation as individualism versus collaterality versus lineal. F. Kluckhohn and Strodtbeck's distinction is an extension and clarification of the basic dichotomy between *Gemeinschaft* (folk societies) versus *Gesellschaft* (complex, urban societies) that was first introduced by Tonnies in 1887. The dichotomy was used to describe a distinction between societies that are based on relatively simple social order, structure, and tradition typical of more primitive cultures (*Gemeinschaft*) versus the more complex social structure and order typical of modern, industrialized cultures (*Gesellschaft*). F. Kluckhohn and Strodtbeck note, that their trichotomy— individualism versus collaterality versus lineal—has the advantage of providing fine distinctions both within and across systems. They argue that societies must adhere, to varying degrees, to all three relational principles as opposed to just one end of a bipolar continuum.

Individualism refers to the autonomy over action afforded to the individual. If a culture is individualistic, individual goals have primacy over the goals of specific collateral or lineal groups. This does not imply, however, that an individual is free to selfishly pursue personal interests and disregard those interests of society. F. Kluckhohn and Strodtbeck point out that

each individual's responsibility to the total society and his place in it are defined in terms of goals (and roles) which are structured as *autonomous*, in the sense of being independent of particular lineal or collateral groups. For example, the man who joins a business firm in the United States is expected, in pursuing his own goals of moneymaking and prestige, to be cooperative with other similarly oriented fellow workers and, in addition, is expected to have a positive attitude toward the overall goals (purposes) of the organization. Yet it is not expected that this man remain in cooperation with these particular workers or dedicated to the goals of the particular firm if he receives an offer from another firm which will increase his salary or prestige." (18–19)

A strong collateral orientation refers to the primacy of the goals and welfare of the extended group over those of the individual. Since the reference group is typically independent of other similar groups, the pursuit of goals for the extended group does not usually interfere with other groups. F. Kluckhohn and Strodtbeck illustrate the collateral orientation with a description of the Navaho, who have numerous autonomous roles and goals but give priority to those of the extended household or clan.

Finally, a lineal orientation refers to a prioritization of group goals over time. Continuity of the group and an ordered positional succession are central to lineality. An example of lineality is the British aristocracy, which is maintained through time by kinship lines and a select system of ascension from the middle class to the aristocracy. Individuals can be members of the aristocracy through their bloodlines or by a very limited and strictly administered succession through the middle class (e.g., knighthood for special service to the crown). The difference between mere collaterality and lineality is that the latter captures a strict hierarchy of ordered positions along with movement within the hierarchy, whereas the former merely refers to the adherence to commonly held goals or interests of the group.

F. Kluckhohn and Strodtbeck's value orientation model of individualism and collectivism suggests that we need not think of the dimension as strictly dichotomous or bipolar; rather, we may consider relative emphasis as a determining influence on individuals' actions. Their concept of lineality imposes an hierarchical succession of roles capturing a temporal component to collaterality, or a group emphasis.

Hofstede

Perhaps the most highly cited intercultural researcher in the field of organizational behavior today is Geert Hofstede. His concept of individualism and collectivism does not really diverge substantially from prior work by sociologists and anthropologists, although it is based on a comprehensive empirical study incorporating responses from over forty countries. We will discuss his general definition of individualism and collectivism and his empirical operationalization of the construct. Our description of the antecedents and consequences of individualism and collectivism will rely heavily on Hofstede's work (1980, 1984).

According to Hofstede, individualism and collectivism is a conglomeration of values concerning the relation of an individual to his or her collectivity in society. An individualistic society is one in which self-concept is defined in individual or trait terms, whereas a collectivistic society is one in which an individual is defined with reference to a societal and cultural context. For instance, an individualistic self-concept would argue that religious conversion takes place as an individual act. In a more collectivistic culture such a conversion may be instigated by a few individuals, but it will often result in the conversion of the entire collective.

Individualism and collectivism has moral implications as well. Mao Tse-tung argued that individualism is evil and that the selfishness associated with it would harm the collective. Such a view argues that self-interests are not inconsequential; rather, that the success of the collective ensures the well-being of the individual. However many individualistic countries (e.g., the United States) consider their success based in their self-orientation and its presumed beneficial impact on creativity and initiative.

Individualism and collectivism is related to a number of organizational characteristics as well. Individuals from a collectivistic society call for greater emotional dependence on one another than individuals from individualistic societies, and their organizations are expected to play a stronger role in their lives. For example, in many Asian cultures an individual's company is not only expected to provide a salary, medical coverage, and other benefits common to the West but also housing, childcare, education, and even moral and personal counseling and political indoctrination. Using Etzioni's (1961, 1968) distinction of moral versus calculative involvement (essentially, moral involvement refers to an interaction based on internalized standards, whereas calculative involvement is based on the expectation of exchange and equity), Hofstede suggests that calculative involvement is characteristic of individualistic societies, whereas the social aspect of moral involvement is characteristic of more collectivistic ones. The social form of moral involvement refers to the horizontal relationships within collectives.

Other influences of individualism and collectivism on an organization include: admittance of individuals to influential positions in the organization, the kind of reward system employed, and the structure of the organization, among others. A more detailed description of these consequences is provided in the next section.

From an empirical viewpoint, Hofstede defines individualism and collectivism by individuals' perceived importance of six work goals: work that is challenging and that gives a personal sense of accomplishment is positively related to the degree of individualism; having training opportunities to improve or learn new skills is negatively related to individualism; having good physical working conditions (e.g., good ventilation and lighting in a factory) is negatively related to individualism; having freedom to adapt your own approach to your job is positively related to individualism; having a job that fully uses your skills and abilities on the job is negatively related to individualism; and having a job that leaves you sufficient time for personal or family life is positively related to individualism.

Although it may seem confusing that job challenge is positively related to individualism, whereas use of skills is negatively related, Hofstede reasons that the distinction is based on the role of the individual versus the organization. For example, challenge emphasizes individual achievement, whereas use of skills emphasizes contribution toward the organization's goals. Likewise personal time and freedom stress the independence of the worker from the organization, whereas physical conditions emphasizes what an organization can provide for an individual. Thus, Hofstede's individualism and collectivism dimension seems to capture, to a large extent, an individual's dependence (in the case of collectivists) or interdependence (in the case of individualists) on the organization.

Triandis and His Colleagues

Triandis' definition of individualism and collectivism is particularly useful since it describes the theoretical relation of the individualism and collectivism construct to a number of antecedents and consequences relevant for the study of behavior in organizations.

According to Triandis, individualistic and collectivistic societies vary on a number of relevant dimensions germane to organizational behavior. Before describing these specific aspects, we will discuss Triandis' distinction between the cultural and individual levels of individualism and collectivism. At the individual level people can be described as *allocentric* or *idiocentric*. Allocentrics are concerned with social support and experience low alienation, whereas idiocentrics focus on achievement but are lonely (Triandis et al., 1988). At the cultural level we can describe societies as having an individualistic versus a collectivistic orientation comparable to the distinction provided by the other scholars discussed earlier. The advantage of this distinction across levels is the explicit realization that people form a collectivistic culture may, on a person to person basis, be quite idiocentric and vice versa. The distinction emphasizes that cultural values describe shared attributes of societies rather than the values of individual X from culture Y.

According to Triandis, collectivistic societies emphasize a number of characteristics: priority is given to group goals, which are viewed as a means for attaining individual goals; concern for how one's actions will impact ingroup members; tendency to share resources with ingroup members; interdependence among ingroup members is desirable; involvement in other ingroup members' lives; perception that ingroup values/norms are universally valid and a willingness to fight for these values; social behavior is strongly influenced by ingroup rules; relationships are viewed as nurturing, respectful, and intimate; relationships are based on a principle of equality and altruism rather than exchange and equity; and, ingroups tend to be small, tightly knit, and quite stable across time.

The first characteristic, subordination of personal goals to those of the group, is posited as the most important. In individualistic cultures, people will put their own needs over those of the group. Triandis argues that individualists belong to many groups and flow between them so as to attain personal interests; they will avoid a particular ingroup should it place too many demands on the individual. The collectivist has a stable ingroup membership, whereas the individualist belongs to multiple ingroups and has to refresh membership and status in the group constantly.

According to Triandis, the number of ingroups to which an individual belongs is a key aspect of individualism and collectivism:

The individualist forms his own ingroups, conforms in order to be accepted by ingroups, stays with an ingroup as long as it serves his purposes, and drops it for another ingroup when a better "deal" can be made somewhere else. A similar point can be made when interpreting findings that the frequency of compliments is higher in the U.S. than in Japan. In collectivistic cultures one may not have to "work as hard" to get into ingroups (one is already a member) or to stay in them, as in individualistic cultures. Compliments presumably "lubricate" social relationships and are more needed by the individualist, who has to enter many, diverse ingroups, than by the collectivist, who is secure in his ingroups. (in press).

Other Work

There are a number of research efforts concerning individualism and collectivism that merit comment, particularly given their relation to organizational functioning. Breer and Locke (1965) developed an eighty-three-item measure that assesses many aspects of individualism and collectivism, including a mix of attitudinal, belief, value, and normative items. Their measure, developed for administration to college students, was related to the construct of task interdependence. They found that subjects who performed disjunctive tasks reported greater individualism and that subjects who performed conjunctive tasks reported greater collectivism.

Using the Breer and Locke measure, Wagner and Moch (1986) further refined a conceptualization and an empirical measure of individualism and collectivism, separating the measure into three categories: beliefs, values, and norms. Their reasoning suggests that conceptual differences among beliefs (statements held to be true), values (statements that denote evaluations of goodness or evil), and norms (standards for behavior shared by a given group) lead to different assessments of individualism and collectivism focusing on the concept of self-interest versus group interests. For example, a worker who holds individualistic values and beliefs may behave collectively (e.g., by adhering to production shutdowns imposed by co-workers) depending on his or her work group norms. Based on their conceptualization, Wagner and Moch called for additional theorizing concerning the relevance of individualism and collectivism to organizational behavior theories.

A recent values study by Meindl, Hunt, and Lee (1989) examines the effect of individualism and collectivism on work values. They found marked differences in a number of work values related to individualism and collectivism not limited to national "culture" (i.e., country). Although we disagree with their conclusion that cross-cultural comparisons can be viewed as an alternative way of examining individual differences (culture becomes a proxy for group membership in which groups are homogeneous with respect to particular individual differences variables), their study demonstrates several interesting patterns of work values related to individualism and collectivism.

ANTECEDENTS AND CONSEQUENCES OF INDIVIDUALISM AND COLLECTIVISM

In order to develop a more thorough understanding of the individualism and collectivism construct, we now turn to a general model depicting a number of antecedents and consequences of individualism and collectivism in society. We are particularly indebted to the work of Hofstede (1980), Triandis (1989b, in press), and Wagner and Moch (1986).

The antecedents and consequences of individualism and collectivism are presented in Figure 4-1. The figure describes these antecedents and consequences as correlates, although it is not clear that these are direct causes and effects. The precise relation of these factors to individualism and collectivism remains vague and awaits further empirical research. The figure is organized using two basic dimen-

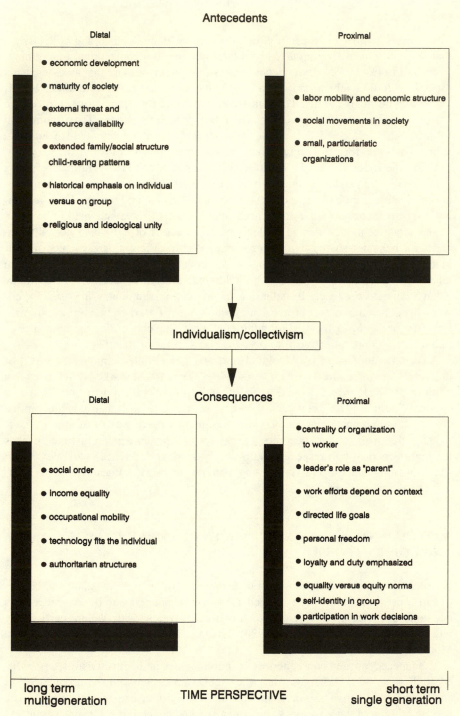

Figure 4-1. Antecedents and consequences of individualism and collectivism

sions, proximity to the individual and time perspective, as a way of discussing these influences and consequences. Proximity to the individual refers to how much direct effect a factor plays on an individual within his or her organization as well as the congruence with the level of the individual. For example, a distal factor such as economic growth and development in a society is rather far removed from an individual, whereas a proximal factor such as self-identity in group is within an individual's immediate organizational experiences. Our second dimension is a temporal component based on a simple distinction. If an antecedent (or consequent) requires multiple generations to show its influence (or view its resulting nature) then it is long-term. A more immediate effect refers to a change that takes less than a single generation to show its impact on the individual and his or her environment. This dimension captures the linearity aspect of F. Kluckhohn and Strodtbeck's constraint of individualism and collectivism. We now turn our discussion to describing the major antecedents of individualism and collectivism.

Antecedents

There are a number of antecedents of individualism and collectivism, ranging from economic development and child-rearing patterns to social movements. Our discussion begins with such distal influences as historical antecedents of individualism and collectivism followed by more proximal (to the individual) and transient antecedents.

At the most general level, individualism and collectivism are related to the wealth and economic development of societies. Hofstede found a generally high correlation of individualism with gross national product (GNP) ($r = .82$) such that the wealthier nations were more individualistic. Interestingly, Hofstede found that economic growth for the nineteen wealthiest countries in his sample was *negatively* related to individualism. He speculated that this relation might be explained by the following logic: if a country becomes excessively wealthy (high growth) then it become overly individualistic and hence growth becomes stunted. This suggests that there should be a balancing of wealth among nations, a conclusion that Hofstede points out is not currently warranted.

Individualism and collectivism are related to the agriculture/hunter origins of a society as well (Triandis, in press). A traditional argument is that societies that depend on agriculture and farming for their survival are likely to form in aggregates or collectives based on farm plots. The hunter/gatherers, however, have a need to wander; therefore a well-developed and complex social context is dysfunctional. In such a setting individuals survive best by hunting alone or in small groups. This distinction has also been applied to agricultural-collectivist versus industrial-individualist societies as well (F. Kluckhohn & Strodtbeck, 1961; Triandis). Although it has been thought that societies initially have a collectivistic orientation to deal with the threats of nature and the environment, followed by movement toward an individualistic orientation as wealth increases, it is interesting to note that a number of countries that are reported to be collectivistic (e.g., Sweden) are economically affluent as well. We would hypothesize that the relation of wealth to individualism is positive *to a point,* after which society members can afford to act for the welfare of all individuals in the society. In other words, the self-interest associated with prosperity is temporary, and societies eventually shift to caring for all citizens.

Another antecedent of individualism and collectivism concerns immigration patterns. We would anticipate that highly homogeneous cultures will be collectivistic since they share a common heritage and background and therefore operate as an "extended family." For example, Japan has remained a relatively "pure" society for quite some time, and it is collectivistic as well. At the other extreme, the United States was founded as the great "melting pot" and is among the most individualistic of all cultures (Hofstede, 1980). Societies do not need to be long-established for homogeneity to influence collectivism. Modern Israel is a relatively young nation yet the underlying religious belief system of Judaism has resulted in a highly collectivistic society. A related factor concerns the relation of the society to its surrounding neighbors. If a country has a number of friendly neighbors and an open border, we would expect a more individualistic society since the people will tend to give and take from one another and form a large number of associations with others. However a country that is threatened or unfriendly with its neighbors will likely be quite collectivistic, drawing on its own people as resources.

Family structure and child-rearing practices are related to the collectivistic orientation found in a society. Collectivism is associated with an emphasis on conformity, obedience, and dependability. Extended family structure is associated with collectivistic cultures, and individuals views themselves in terms of the larger family context. Emphasis is placed on how each family member's contributions will influence the family and benefit it. In addition, an emphasis on the importance of a harmonious clan creates the distinction between ingroup and outgroup.

There are a number of more proximal antecedents of individualism and collectivism. A society that has a large number of small organizations is likely to be more collectivistic. Small organizations are logical extensions of the family or clan into an individual's work life. In such organizations the worker is cared for and helped just as he or she was guided as a child. It should be noted, however, that these organizations are often extensions of clan or tribal structures (e.g., Japan) and that the critical feature is not their size, but their role as a central element in the worker's life (Misumi, 1984). Organizations that care for all of the needs of their employees are characteristic of collectivistic cultures.

Other antecedents of individualism and collectivism include the labor mobility patterns of individuals as well as social movements in a culture. For example, some sociologists have argued that the ease of labor movement found in American industry fosters the "lone wolf" or individualistic orientation of its workers. People who are unable to move easily between organizations will logically adapt to their organization by becoming highly committed to the success of the organization. Social movements and trends can have a strong influence on individualism and collectivism as well. Futurists have often speculated that the increasing computerization of the workplace and the advent of "work at home" may foster a self-interested, isolated workforce. An emphasis on egalitarian themes may foster collectivistic attitudes as well. For example, the social movement and attempted secession of French Canada may further foster a highly collectivistic French segment within the general Canadian population.

Consequences

Although there are a number of distal consequences of individualism and collectivism, such as democratic versus socialistic political systems, market versus planned economies, and religious philosophies that emphasize equality norms (Hofstede, 1980), our emphasis is on the proximal consequences of individualism and collectivism for organizational behavior. We begin this section by discussing the implications of individualism and collectivism for social norms and worker values followed by the more distal consequences on occupational mobility and general social order.

There are a number of proximal consequences of individualism and collectivism. Organizations in highly collectivistic cultures often have systems of participative decision-making and workplace democracy (Wilpert, 1984). Such systems of democracy include worker participation through coordinated work teams found in Sweden, quality circles in Japan, and worker collectives in the People's Republic of China. A comprehensive review of worker participation is available in Erez (in press) and Wilpert (1984).

Individualism and collectivism are related to attitudes concerning leadership and conflict management. There has been a resurgence in the importance personal charisma and presence in American models of leadership (e.g., House's Charismatic Leadership Theory, 1991). In a collectivistic culture a leader is expected to play a more paternalistic role (Hofstede, 1980) and guide subordinate actions. This may seem inconsistent with the egalitarian norms of collectivists, but it is consistent if we assume that the leader is perceived as someone who will help a group attain its goals. For example, Israeli kibbutzim rotate the "leader" position throughout its membership so that a hierarchy exists (Tannenbaum et al., 1974) but the formally appointed leader does not exist as a permanent feature. In an individualistic culture a leader is often viewed as an autonomous and charismatic person who draws upon his or her employees through a romantic or idealized connection. Interestingly, Fiedler's Contingency Model of Leadership (1964) is one of the few Western theories of leadership that merges aspects of the individual with those of the group, and it has received empirical support in both individualistic and collectivistic cultures; yet it reflects a strongly individualistic theme, with the key agent being the leader and his or her actions in the work setting. A more thorough discussion of this model is presented in the chapter on leadership.

As we discuss in greater detail in chapter 9, conflict management and negotiation styles vary across individualistic and collectivistic clusters. For instance, collectivists typically utilize an equality norm in dealing with ingroups but an equity approach in negotiating with outgroups. Individualists, however, use an equity approach in their negotiations regardless of group memberships. These differences have received empirical support from Leung and his colleagues (Leung, 1986; Leung & Bond, 1984).

Individualism and collectivism have a number of implications for the relation of an individual to his or her work group. A collectivist derives self-identity through the ingroup and its successes. Interestingly, many theories of group interaction (Turner, 1987) use an individualist perspective, focusing on how individuals are attracted to a group according to the benefits they derive. If we assume that collectivists remain in relatively stable ingroups, then it is evident that a group is not "chosen" by a collectivist in the same fashion as by an individualist. However we do not mean to imply that collectivists are not "free" to choose their group memberships. Just as individualists are born into particular groups (i.e., family) so are collectivists; and, just as with individualists, collectivists can join ingroups of their choosing.

As we discuss in the chapter on group dynamics, the key difference in the perception of what membership entails is in terms of timeframe. Collectivists view group membership as more long-term and permanent than do individualists. Thus many of the actions of collectivists in the workplace center around the long-term aspect of their work group memberships. This is reflected by an emphasis on insider contacts, ingroup promotion, and actions directed at benefiting the ingroup. For example, in Chinese culture great emphasis is placed on the connections and contacts one has with others, or what is called *guanxi*. Although *guanxi* is somewhat less heavily emphasized in modern China (Boisot & Child, 1988), an individual's contacts still play an important role in promotions, awarding of contracts, and so forth.

The most obvious distal consequence of individualism and collectivism for an organization concerns the nature of social order and structure. In a highly collectivistic society organizations tend to be hierarchically flat and arranged along family or tribal lines. Organizations are highly integrated into an individual's life. For instance, workers in a collectivistic culture such as Japan will often vacation together and eat evening meals together as an extension of their life within the organization.

Individualism and collectivism also have an impact on work values. In individualistic societies work goals emphasizing pleasure and affection, autonomy, and equity in exchange are salient, whereas collectivists emphasize skill development, prestige, and the well-being and goals of their ingroup. Individualist stress the opportunity to "do their own thing," which is reflected in autonomous work, decentralized decision-making, and incentive systems that reward individual action and accomplishment.

Another general consequence of individualism and collectivism is the flipside of an antecedent, namely, labor mobility. To the degree that individualists feel free to flow between ingroups based on the benefits they offer, we would expect to see higher labor mobility in individualistic than in collectivistic cultures. This is related to a number of more specific consequences that we will discuss shortly, such as loyalty to the organization. Of course, such endogenous influences on labor mobility as labor supply and demand, industry absorption rates, and so on are independent of cultural influences or removed from their direct effects.

Collectivistic cultures have paternalistic organizations that expect worker loyalty to duty. This paternalistic role in an employee's life is not viewed as intrusive; quite the contrary, workers expect their organization to play a significant role in their lives and expect their superiors to participate as a parental or guiding figure.

In collectivistic cultures work is structured around the needs of the collective or workgroup, whereas work in an individualistic culture stresses individual action and autonomy. Perhaps the most explicit contrasts is the approach to job design theory in the United States (individualistic) and Sweden (collectivistic). The dominant model of job design in the United States is the Hackman and Oldham (1980) Job Characteristics Model, which stresses such aspects of an individual's work as autonomy and individual performance feedback. This is in contrast to the sociotechnical systems approach (Rousseau, 1977) prevalent in Sweden. This approach emphasizes a merging of technology with the needs of the work group rather than the individual. Emphasis is placed on the social processes needed to maintain a work group's well-being and harmony.

Some Exemplar Studies Using Individualism and Collectivism

We conclude our discussion of individualism and collectivism with a description of a few studies that illustrate the impact of individualism and collectivism on a number of organizational behaviors and processes.

As we discussed earlier, Hofstede (1980) found a positive relation between individualism with per capita GNP. He found that individualistic countries such as the United States and England attach importance to freedom and challenge in jobs, and managers rate autonomy very highly. In contrast collectivists emphasize job training, conformity, and duty and loyalty to their organizations. He related individualism and collectivism to organizational factors ranging from self-actualization theory (less valid in collectivistic cultures) to the use of performance-appraisal systems (more prominent in individualistic cultures) and the role of nepotism and family contacts for internal promotions in organizations (acceptable in collectivistic cultures).

Using an ipsative personal incentives inventory, Maehr and Braskamp (1986) examined the various factors that individuals from the United States and Japan find important as personal incentives. They found that the Japanese (collectivists) emphasized financial incentive, task accomplishment, and excellence of performance, whereas the Americans (individualists) stressed affiliation, recognition, and social concern most highly. Although this result seems counter to the stereotypes we often hold about Japanese work values, Triandis (in press) explains it by pointing out the role of ingroup membership. He suggests that collectivists are not as concerned about affiliation and social concerns as individualists since they belong in a stable ingroup that satisfies those needs. Individualist need to satisfy affiliation needs as they move among various ingroups; therefore it is a salient factor.

Another example is reflected in the Japanese *ringi* system of decision-making (Erez, 1986; Misumi, 1984). In this scheme individuals from lower levels in an organization must develop and clear ideas up through the hierarchy. If the issue is stopped at a particular node, it goes back to the bottom of the hierarchy and is reshaped to address the concerns that were raised, then once again sent up to the hierarchy. By the time it travels to the top successfully, it has been endorsed by a number of individuals who are committed to it. This system also reinforces a sense of continuity and harmony in decision-making that is consistent with the collectivistic orientation of Japanese society (Pascale, 1978).

SUMMARY AND PRESENT DEFINITION

The definitions of individualism and collectivism we have discussed share a number of similar dimensions. For the sake of discussion we have categorized these definitions into six categories: breadth of construct, time frame, level of analysis, underlying motives or interests, affective and loyalty aspects, and specification of collective or ingroup.

Breadth of Construct

The construct of individualism and collectivism has evolved from a general relational component (e.g., F. Kluckhohn & Strodtbeck, Parsons & Shils) to a more specific component analysis. For example, Triandis emphasizes in his definition that the key component of individualism and collectivism is the subordination of individual goals to those of the collective. Likewise Hofstede empirically bases his individualism factor on a limited number of work-related values such as skill development and physical conditions (although his conceptual development of individualism is much broader). Hui's (1984) development of an individualism and collectivism scale again suggests an approach that specifies particular aspects of individualism and collectivism (e.g., family, life-style).

Table 4-1. Comparison of Individualism and Collectivism Constructs

Authors	Key Defining Characteristics
Parsons and Shils (1951)	Terminology: *self-orientation versus collectivity orientation* refers to the dilemma of private versus collective gains and the disharmony created by the choice of actions that benefit the individual over the collective.
F. Kluckhohn and Strodtbeck (1961)	Terminology: *individualism versus collaterality versus lineal* refers to the prominence of individual versus collective goals. The addition of lineality captures a temporal component of embedded hierarchies and the prioritization of group goals over time.
Hofstede (1980)	Terminology: *individualism* refers to broad conceptualization of self-concept rooted in individual action and definition versus self-concept rooted in collective terms. It attempts to capture definition of self incorporating multiple aspects of society and lifestyle.
Triandis (1990, in press)	Terminology: *individualism versus collectivism* refers to broad set of characteristics with strong emphasis on ingroup membership and self versus collective goals. Collectivists are thought to subordinate own goals for those of ingroup. Additional emphasis is placed on distinguishing between cultural and individual-level referring to allocentric versus idiocentric for individual-level and collectivistic versus individualism for cultural level.
Erez and Earley (1993)	Terminology: *individualism versus collectivism* refers to relational aspects used by F. Kluckhohn and Strodtbeck in relating own actions to those of the group. Relation of individual to ingroup is crucial aspect of dimension as are self versus group interests. Additional emphasis is placed on temporal dimension of individual's relation to ingroup across time.

It is interesting to note that as researchers attempt to conduct specific research, they are evolving specific, component definitions of individualism and collectivism to match the middle-range theories underlying their constructs. Also, much of the empirical work on individualism and collectivism has focused on identifying work values with component aspects of individualism and collectivism in order to explain why particular values cluster together for particular countries (e.g., Meindl et al., 1989). This empirical work fails, however, to advance our understanding of individualism and collectivism and its relevance to organizations because it is not placed within a broader nomological network nor is it being used to make concrete predictions of work behavior.

Time Frame

The time-dependent nature of interpersonal relations in individualistic and collectivistic cultures has important implications for organizational behavior. An oft cited example concerns the time perspective of Americans and Japanese (Lincoln, Hanada & Olson, 1981). Americans are often accused of being short-sighted and unwilling to commit to long-term relationships and contracts. Certainly we can use individualism and collectivism as one correlated factor in such a finding since the individualist feels free to move among ingroups and will not commit for a prolonged period to any particular relationship unless it remains rewarding (Triandis, in press). Collectivists view group membership as stable and long-term; each interaction is viewed as an element in an extended (sometimes across generations) relationship. The definition put forward by F. Kluckhohn and Strodtbeck captures a temporal component via the lineality aspect of individualism and collectivism. To Kluckhohn and Strodtbeck, lineality refers to the relational aspect of individualism and collectivism that is embedded within multiple generations of a people. We believe that individualism and collectivism should be viewed as temporally anchored since heritage and ancestry may be important but overlooked aspects of different types of collectivism.

Level of Analysis

The definitions show a high degree of convergence with regard to level of analysis (e.g., society versus individual). They all propose that individualism and collectivism refer to a society-level (or, in the case of Wagner and Moch [1986] a workgroup level) construct with Triandis distinguishing between society-level and individual-level constructs and terminology. Interestingly much of the empirical work conducted on individualism and collectivism in organizations has relied on individual-level measures of the construct, including those studies using Hofstede's "ecological level" analyses (e.g., Earley, 1989; Meindl et al., 1989). In as much as most value-based models of culture discuss shared perceptions of work values, it seems reasonable that individualism and collectivism can be examined at both the individual and societal levels provided that researchers are careful to maintain consistency of individualism and collectivism with respect to other constructs in their models.

Underlying Motives

Individualism and collectivism is often depicted as a dichotomy between self-interest versus group interest (Hofstede, 1980; Triandis et al., 1988; Wagner & Moch, 1986). Such a simple categorization can overlook numerous subtleties of behavior. For instance, Hofstede argues that collectivists can pursue self-interests as well as group interests as long as priority is given to the group, and Triandis argues that self interests may coincide with group interests or be instrumental in attaining them. Traditional economic arguments posit that the pursuit of self-interest leads to collective benefits, whereas the literature on collective action and social dilemmas (e.g., Dawes, 1972; McKie, 1974; Olson, 1971) warns against pursuit of self-interests in certain circumstances because it imposes collective costs.

A rationalist might argue that pursuit of group interests reflects the collectivist's desire to ensure his or her own personal well being through a culturally acceptable mechanism. Perhaps the most reasonable conclusion is that *all* individuals have self- and group interests; culture influences which of these interests will manifest themselves in a particular setting. Throughout childhood and adolescence the collectivist is reinforced and rewarded for cooperative actions with group-focused outcomes, whereas the individualist is rewarded for engaging in actions that have positive personal outcomes (Earley, 1991). Rather than viewing self- and group interests as opposing motives, we can view them as separately linked to knowledge structures that are evoked in a culturally prescribed fashion (Goodenough, 1971).

Affective Attachment and Loyalty

Most authors consider the affective attachment of an individual to his or her collective to be implicit. If we are discussing individualism and collectivism from a family perspective, then it seems reasonable to assume that affect and loyalty are implicit; however affect and friendship may mean very different things for the individualist and the collectivist within a work group. For example, Japanese managers are reported to spend their dinners and evenings with their work colleagues as a natural extension of work. Americans interpret this action as work fanaticism and selflessness, but an alternative explanation is that there exists a positive, affective bond between the managers and their subordinates that makes such after-hours activities very desirable. A related idea that has not received much attention in the intercultural literature is the lifecycle of an ingroup. Although some work has been conducted on group life stages (for specific examples, see Brewer & Kramer, 1985; Gersick, 1988), it is not at all clear how attachments to ingroups are formed in individualistic and collectivistic cultures and how individuals adapt and form loyalties to their groups. By ignoring the affective component of an individual's affective attachment to his or her ingroup, and how the permanence of these attachments influences behavior, we miss an important aspect of organizational behavior.

Specification of the Reference Group

There has been a useful trend in defining individualism and collectivism in terms of a specific reference group rather than "society" in general. A common misconception is that collectivism is synonymous with socialism and that all collectivists are harmonious and homogeneous. The recent work on individualism and collectivism by Earley (1989, 1991), Espinoza and Garza (1985), and Triandis (1989b) suggests that individualists and collectivists may not differ in kind with regard to behavior toward ingroup but that they may differ with regard to behavior toward ingroup membership (e.g., size, who is included, number of in-groups). Thus an individualist's ingroups may be small and numerous, whereas a collectivist's ingroups are large but few in number. At present the conceptual work by Triandis (1989b, in press) appears to be the only extensive discussion focusing on the nature of the ingroup and individualism and collectivism. We think this work is important because the size of an individual's ingroup and how ingroups are formed have significant implications for optimal structuring of work groups to keep them aligned with cultural values.

Present Definition

Building on the conceptualizations discussed by Parsons and Shils, F. Kluckhohn and Strodtbeck, Hofstede, and Triandis, we define individualism and collectivism as a set of shared beliefs and values of a people concerning the relationship of an individual to aggregates or groups or individuals. It represents the way individuals relate to others in their society, and it reflects their emotional and cognitive attachments to particular networks of individuals. Our cultural self-representation model posits that culture manifests itself in an individual's self-identity through his or her basic motives for action. In the case of individualism and collectivism, we can trace its impact on these motives as well. Since collectivists have a high concern for ingroup welfare, their enhancement motives will be directed toward activities that provide for ingroup successes. A collectivist will achieve a positive self-concept through contributions to the group. It seems reasonable to argue that self-efficacy will be greatest for the collectivist who works within a group context since earlier successes in life most likely were reinforced in a group setting (Bandura, 1986; Earley, 1991).

The self-consistency motive presents a number of interesting possibilities for individualism and collectivism. In as much as collectivists experience stable ingroup membership, their sense of lineality should be quite strong. Consistent with this, many collectivistic cultures emphasize ancestral connections as a basis for current relationships (Hofstede, 1980). However an individualist's sense of self-consistency is likely to be more responsive to generational changes because he or she maintains multiple group memberships and defines his or her identity based on self-actions rather than the actions of ingroup members. Thus the individualist views practices as nepotism and "paybacks" with disdain and impatience.

Our definition is based on the relational aspect of F. Kluckhohn and Strodtbeck's work, although we do not view the lineal component as independent of the individualism and collectivism spectrum. We do agree, however, that all cultures possess varying amounts of *both* individualistic and collectivistic tendencies. It is important to keep in mind that the temporal component of individualism and collectivism is not uniformly applicable to both ends of the continuum. For collectivistic cultures the temporal component is an important contribution of an individual's relation to the group. Since their sense of membership is long term and extended (through multiple generations), the behavior of collectivists will reflect pursuit of group goals for both the short and the long term. However, individualistic cultures view relationships as short term and unpredictable. The multiple and changing group memberships of individualists leads to a seemingly low commitment to group interests, even though this may merely reflect a short-term perspective. An individualist may be just as committed to a group goal as a collectivist *during the time for which the goal is relevant to a particular ingroup and it satisfies self-interests*. Thus if we ignore the temporal dimension underlying the individualist and collectivist orientations, we may erroneously conclude that individualists are incapable of committing themselves to the goals of their ingroups.

Our purpose in this chapter has been to review the construct of individualism and collectivism. In general terms individualism and collectivism refer to the relation of an individual to his or her collective, reflected by an emphasis on self-interests (individualistic) or group-interests (collectivistic). The antecedents of individualism and collectivism include child-rearing patterns, industrial versus agriculturally-based economies, and social movement within the culture. The consequences of individualism and collectivism include work designed around the individual versus the work group, autonomy in work, participative decision-making, and a paternalistic leadership pattern. Individualism and collectivism can be used as a construct to explain a variety of organizational behaviors such as work efforts, leadership, and motivation across cultures. We now turn to a more complete theoretical development of individualism and collectivism and discuss how our model of self-representation can be applied to various aspects of OB.

5

Work Motivation

The role of motivation in the work context has been studied to understand what causes employees to try hard to do well, or more specifically, what causes the arousal, direction, and persistence of voluntary actions that are goal directed (Mitchell, 1982).

Several theories of motivation were developed to answer the above questions, including theories of needs (Maslow, 1954), goal-setting (Locke & Latham, 1990), and expectancy (Mitchell, 1973; 1982). These theories, which focus on individual performance analysis, fail to examine culture as a potential influence on motivation and behavior. It is reasonable to ask why culture should play any role in understanding work motivation. The key to this question is in understanding the relationship between needs, values, and culture.

THE RELATIONSHIP AMONG NEEDS, VALUES, AND CULTURE

Needs and Values

A need is defined as "an internal state of disequilibrium or deficiency which has the capacity to energize or trigger a behavioral response" (Steers & Porter, 1991). The cause of the deficiency could be physiological, such as hunger; psychological, such as need for achievement; or sociological, such as need for affiliation. The motivational sequence is activated by the emergence of needs which motivate individuals to take actions toward need satisfaction (Locke, 1991; Steers & Porter). Need satisfaction in its broadest sense is the organism's survival and well-being (Locke). The state of disequilibrium influences the level of arousal, whereas the actions toward anticipated outcomes set the direction.

Two major typologies of needs are often implemented in the field of work motivation. Maslow's need hierarchy (1954) classifies needs into five groups in a hierarchical order, from the basic level of physiological and safety needs, through the relational needs, and up to the high order needs of self-esteem and self-actualization. McClelland's typology (1961), distinguishes between three basic needs: achievement, which is defined as "behavior directed toward competition with a standard of excellence; affiliation, which is the desire to establish and maintain friendly and warm relations with others; and power, which represents the desire to control others and influence their behavior. A modification of McClelland's typology is proposed by Kuhl (1992) who distinguishes between three F's of motivation: *flirt*—sex and affiliation; *flow*—hunger and achievement; and *fight*—aggression and power. *Flow* describes a motivational state of self-forgetful immersion in a task (Csikszentmihalyi, 1975).

Kuhl's typology suggests that the motivational phenomenon is experienced on both the level of bodily instantiation and that of cognitive representation. The bodily instantiation is the immediate translation of needs into physiological correlates during early (subcortical) levels of brain function. For example, subjects whose Thematic Aperception Test stories contain many fantasies related to needs for autonomy and power show higher concentrations of norepinephrine (an adrenal gland hormone) after being exposed to power-related incentives, whereas subjects with a strong need for affiliation show increased dopamine concentrations after having viewed a romantic movie (McClelland et al., 1980, 1987). On the other hand, the cognitive representation of needs takes the form of values and implies that people have a conscious awareness of their motives.

The link between needs and values occurs at the level of cognitive representation. Values are considered to be "the cognitive representations and transformations of needs, and man is the only animal capable of such representations and transformations" (Rokeach, 1973:20). While needs and motives exist on both biological and cognitive levels, values are exclusively a product of consciousness (Locke, 1991).

Values are defined as "enduring beliefs that a specific mode of conduct or end-state of existence is personally or socially preferable to an opposite or converse mode of conduct, or end-state of existence" (Rokeach, 1973:5). The immediate functions of values are to give expression to human needs and to guide action. Concern for end-states of existence, such as "peace," "freedom," and "equality," is expressed by terminal values, whereas concern for modes of conduct, such as "ambitious," "capable," and "helpful," is expressed by instrumental values. Values and needs correspond to each other. For example, the instrumental values "independent" and "intellectual" are highly rated by individuals who score high on need for achievement, and it is negatively related to "honest" and "obedient." On the other hand, the need for affiliation is highly related to the terminal values "true friendship" and "a world of peace" (Rokeach).

As the cognitive representation of needs, values mediate the relationship between needs, goals, and intentions in the motivation sequence. The complete motivational sequence consists of six steps: Needs → values → goals and intentions → performance → rewards → satisfaction (Locke, 1991). Since goals and intentions are conscious formulations, needs cannot be translated into goals unless they have a cognitive representation in the form of values. Thus values play a necessary role in ascribing cognitive meanings to needs and in transforming needs into goals and intentions for action. Goals can be viewed as applications of values to specific situations. Goals and intentions serve as the immediate regulators of behavior, and they regulate the intensity, direction, and persistence of action.

Values have both a direct and an indirect effect on rewards and satisfaction. The indirect effect is through the sequence of goals, performance, rewards, and satisfaction. The direct effect occurs because values determine what actions will be personally rewarding and satisfying (Locke, 1991).

The Role of Values in Motivational Theories

The goal-setting model. Although values are recognized to be part of the motivation sequence (Locke, 1991), their effect on goals has not been studied explicitly. Yet the opposite causal relation pertaining to the effect of goals on the valence of goal attainment has been examined. Goal difficulty and specificity were found to affect the valence of goal attainment (Locke & Latham, 1990). Valences are measured in terms of expected satisfaction from goal accomplishment when no extrinsic incentives are offered for performance. Among the reasons given by subjects for agreeing to try for assigned goals were: to improve their skills; to gain a sense of achievement; and to prove themselves to be competent. Thus specific and difficult goals make actions oriented toward the accomplishment of these goals more meaningful and valuable to the performer.

Goals acquire values by affecting the individual's self-efficacy expectations. They provide a sense of purpose, direction, and clarity concerning performance expectations (Bandura, 1986; Wood & Bandura, 1989). The setting of specific and difficult goals raises expectations and triggers a self-fulfilling prophecy of high performance in organizations (Eden, 1988).

Positive evaluation of goals leads to the development of goal commitment; therefore it is argued that goal commitment implies that the goal itself, as well as the process of goal-setting, is of high value to the performer. Research on participation in goal-setting demonstrates that participation enhances the level of goal-commitment (Erez, Earley, & Hulin, 1985; Latham, Erez & Locke, 1988). One possible explanation for the positive effect of participation on commitment is that it allows employees to experience control and influence over the decision-making process (Latham, Erez & Locke).

The expectancy model. One of the few theories of work motivation that explicitly focuses on values, the expectancy theory (Mitchell, 1982) proposes that people are motivated to choose a course of action that maximizes their utilities. Utility is determined by the sum of all the values of outcomes that individuals expect to obtain by taking a particular action. The expectancy model takes into consideration the intensity of expected values in a particular situation but not the content of values as predictors of choice and action. Thus the expectancy model is not domain-specific but rather situation-specific.

Content domain theories. Theories of work motivation that are domain-specific are postulated in terms of needs and motives rather than values, and they often use projective measures to assess underlying motives. For example, the need for achievement, power, and affiliation can be assessed using TAT. Such assessments often serve as a means to distinguish managers from nonmanagers (McClelland & Boyatzis, 1982). Successful managers are characterized by a high need for power, a moderate need for achievement, and a low need for affiliation. Miner (1978) investigated the motives of successful line managers by using an incomplete sentence test.

The results indicated that respect for authority figures, competitiveness, the desire to impose one's wishes on others, preference for traditional "masculine" roles, and routine administrative work, and enjoyment of standing out in a crowd are distinguishing characteristics. The use of projective tests implies that needs and motives operate on a subconscious level; unlike values, they are not fully represented in consciousness.

Needs, Values, and Self-Regulatory Processes

Values operate on the cognitive level. Both sensory-perceptual and cognitive processes operate on this level. The process that underlies perception is neurophysiological and unconscious. But at the conceptual level of awareness, the process of cognition is conscious, and based on reason. This process does not operate automatically but volitionally (Binswanger, 1991). Volition reflects the free will to choose to utilize or not utilize one's conceptual faculty. It is defined as "the ability to maintain and enact an action tendency the organism is committed to despite the impulsive nature of competing action tendencies" (Kuhl & Kraska, 1989:344).

Values are conceptual representations of needs and, as such, are part of the conceptual, volitional system. The causal path from values to goals and intentions is purposeful and self-regulated. Self-regulatory processes are based on the premise that persons act both as processors of information and as sources of influence on behavior (R. Kanfer, 1990:152). The self-regulatory process comprises three major components: self-observation, self-evaluation, and self-reaction (Bandura, 1986; Kanfer, 1980). The process of self-monitoring allows people to pay adequate attention to their own activities and performances. Self-evaluation is determined by reactions of significant others, by referential comparisons with others, and by personal standards. Activities that are relevant to one's value preference and sense of personal adequacy are more likely to elicit self-evaluative reactions than others (Bandura). The ultimate purpose of the total belief system is to maintain and enhance an individual's self-image. Self-evaluation activates self-reactions mainly in areas affecting one's welfare and self-esteem. Thus the more relevant performances are to one's value preferences and sense of personal adequacy, the more likely self-evaluative reactions are to be elicited (Bandura).

The meaning of events and actions for the individual self is understood by means of models of attribution. The basic premise is that individuals attribute causes for important instances of their behavior and that of others (Duda & Allison, 1989). Attributions are often guided by self-derived needs for enhancement and efficacy, and for avoiding threat and failures. The motivation to protect the self against negative evaluation often leads to biases in reasoning and to the "illusion of objectivity" (Kruglanski, 1980; Kunda, in press). To this end people search memory for those beliefs and rules that could support their desired conclusions. For example, achievement-oriented people are likely to attribute negative-response outcomes to such external factors as task difficulty or luck, whereas positive-response outcomes are attributed to such internal factors as effort and ability (Weiner, 1986).

Cross-cultural research has demonstrated that concepts of ability and effort vary across cultures (Holloway, 1988). For example, the Japanese emphasize effort as the main cause of high or low performance, whereas Americans emphasize ability. Furthermore, the concept of intelligence varies across the two cultures: the Japanese place greater emphasis on social competence as a component of intelligence than do Americans. These differences in the attribution schema of Japanese and Americans are meaningful once the differences in cultural values and in the formation of the self are taken into consideration. Ability is a salient individual difference characteristic, and perhaps for this reason it is highly emphasized by the individualistic culture of the United States. On the other hand, the salience of the collective self in Japan emphasizes social competence as a component of intelligence. In keeping with their individualistic values, Americans tend to use self-serving attributions. They attribute success to themselves more often, and failure less often, than do the Japanese (Kashima & Triandis, 1986; Markus & Kitayama, 1991). Hence the cultural factor is essential for understanding the nature of attributions once we cross the borders of a particular culture.

Needs, Values and Culture

Values are the cognitive representations not only of individual needs but also of societal and cultural demands (Rokeach, 1973). On the individual level, values differ from needs in the sense that needs are considered to be fundamentally the same for all people, whereas values make each person a unique individual and guide his or her personal choices and actions (Locke, 1991). An extrapolation from the individual level to a higher level of aggregation suggests that members of the same culture are likely to share similar values acquired in the process of socialization. These values represent the acceptable modes of conduct and end-states of existence of a particular culture. Thus values differentiate not only on the individual level but on the cultural level as well.

The correspondence between personal values and cultural values is illustrated by the following example. Equality and freedom, two of the central values in Rokeach's typology (1973), correspond to two of the major cultural values of high versus low power distance and collectivism versus individualism in Hofstede's typology (1980a). The former pertains to equality versus inequality, and the latter pertains to personal freedom versus social control. Empirical research demonstrated that Americans, as compared to Israelis, rate higher on individualism and power distance; correspondingly, they rate higher on freedom and lower on equality (Hofstede; Rokeach).

A study of the underlying motivational structure of Rokeach's value system across cultures was recently conducted by Schwartz and Bilsky (1987). They argue that a comprehensive typology of content domains of values should cognitively represent three universal human requirements: biological needs, requisites of coordinated social interaction, and survival and welfare needs of groups. Using the Small Space Analysis they found that Rokeach's thirty-six values are organized in a circular structure of seven motivational types. Enjoyment, achievement, and self-direction are located in adjacent regions, all three domains forming one contiguous interest region of individualism. Located opposite to the individualistic region are three adjacent domains representing the motivational types—prosocial, conformity, and security—and they form the collectivistic region. The maturity type is located on the boundary between the individualistic and the collectivistic regions.

The universality of the motivational structure was tested by comparing the structure of the motivational types in seven different cultures: Australia, Hong Kong, the United States, Spain, Finland, Germany, and Israel. These societies differ substantially in the cultural values of collectivism and individualism (Hofstede, 1980). Nevertheless, the major structure of motivational types was supported in all seven societies. Of special interest is the finding that the location of achievement is always in the individualistic zone, even in the more collectivistic cultures of Hong Kong and Spain. It seems that the primary goal of achievers everywhere is to attain recognition for themselves (Schwartz & Bilsky, 1990). Yet eleven of the single values were not consistently located in the same motivational domain across cultures. For example, in Finland the two values, "responsibility" and "a world of beauty," are located in the prosocial zone, suggesting that responsibility is perceived as behaving reliably to promote others' interest, and "a world of beauty" means active concern for preserving nature.

An expansion of the research samples to twenty cultures has resulted in a further elaboration of the model. Content dimensions which did not appear in the original typology of values (Rokeach, 1973) were added to the questionnaire and resulted in a structure of ten motivational types: self-direction ("freedom," "creativity," "independent"); stimulation ("an exciting life," "a varied life"); hedonism ("pleasure," "enjoyable life"); achievement ("ambitious," "capable," "successful"); power ("social power," "wealth," "authority"); security ("national security," "family security"; conformity ("obedient," "self-discipline"); tradition ("respect for tradition," "humble"); spirituality ("a spiritual life," "inner harmony"); benevolence ("helpful," "forgiving"); and universalism ("equality," "social justice").

Power, achievement, and tradition types appear in all twenty countries and are considered to be universal. Hedonism, universalism, and security types are found in 95% of the countries, and stimulation, benevolence, and conformity types appear in 90% of the countries. The findings lead to the following conclusions: that a) with respect to the content dimension, ten distinct motivational value types are likely to emerge within and across cultures; with respect to the structural dimension, the ten types are organized in a circular value structure with consistent value compatibilities and conflicts—the major conflict is between individualistic and collectivistic zones; with respect to the priorities of the motivational types across cultures, more empirical research is needed to detect cross-cultural variation in value priorities. The findings suggest that the greatest differences in value priorities emerge in comparisons between collectivistic and individualistic societies: We can expect such values as tradition, conformity, and benevolence to be more important in collectivistic societies, whereas self-direction, stimulation, and universal values will be more important in individualistic societies.

The close relationship between values and motives is expressed in numerous typologies that use motivational terms to study work values (Elizur, 1984; Mannheim & Dubin, 1986; Rim, 1970; Ronen, 1986; Ronen & Shenkar, 1985).

Since values serve as cognitive representations of needs, determining also which actions and behavior will satisfy those needs, it is reasonable to argue that differences in cultural values reflect differences in motivation. Members of different cultures will respond to different motivational techniques and different types of rewards. For example, Americans can be expected to value motivational techniques designed to emphasize differentiation and to reward employees on an individual basis. In contrast, participative management can be expected to be more highly valued by Israelis than by Americans.

Individual merit pay the compensation method commonly in use in American companies, is inconsistent with a new managerial philosophy, Total Quality Management (TQM), which emphasizes collective responsibility for an entire production line or service process. Thus, companies that elect to implement TQM should replace their individually based pay system with one based on compensation for collective performance, such as gainsharing, profit-sharing, or stock ownership (Bowen & Lawler, 1992).

The following section examines the emergence of various motivational techniques and their effectiveness across cultures within the conceptual framework of the model of cultural self-representation.

WORK MOTIVATION WITHIN A
CROSS-CULTURAL FRAMEWORK

Cultural values serve as criteria for evaluating the meaning of various motivational techniques and the valences of their behavioral outcomes. Culture is viewed as a set of shared meanings, transmitted by a set of mental programs that control individual responses in a given context (Hofstede, 1980a, 1991; Shweder & LeVine, 1984). Culture shapes the cognitive schemas that ascribe meaning and values to motivational variables and guide our choices, commitments, and standards of behavior.

Cultural values convey enduring beliefs, shared by the members of a particular culture, concerning preferable modes of conduct or end-states of existence along a continuum of relative importance (Rokeach, 1973:5). As the internal representation of culture, values serve to evaluate the potential contribution of managerial practices and motivational techniques to employees' sense of well-being and self-worth. Motivational techniques that are congruent with the value system are positively evaluated and are most likely to facilitate behavior that leads to self-satisfaction. However, motivational techniques are likely to be rejected when they are incongruent with the cultural values, and fail to facilitate behavior that enhances self-satisfaction. For example, the implementation of an individually based incentive plan is incongruent with cultural values of equality and team cooperation and is likely to result in negative motivation and negative emotional responses. Within a value system that advocates loyalty and support of colleagues, a new manager's attempt to pressure employees to report any negative behavior among their peers will not be successful. According to the model of cultural self-representation, managerial techniques are evaluated by the self using criteria provided by the cultural values and norms. Therefore, managerial techniques that are not consistent with the cultural values are negatively evaluated by the self and are likely to result in negative motivation. As the examples given suggest, culture moderates the relationship between management practices and employees' behavior.

In the next section we will review some of the common methods of work motivation within a cultural perspective. The cultural dimensions of collectivism and power distance serve as criteria for evaluating the motivation potential of various managerial practices. As defined by Hofstede, "collectivism pertains to societies in which people from birth onward are integrated into strong, cohesive ingroups, which throughout people's lifetime continue to protect them in exchange for unquestioning loyalty. Individualism, as its opposite, pertains to societies in which the ties between individuals are loose: everyone is expected to look after himself or herself and his or her immediate family (1991:51). Collectivism has been found to explain most of the variances across cultures (Triandis, in press). Power distance is defined as "the extent to which the less powerful members of institutions and organizations within a country expect and accept that power is distributed unequally" (Hofstede: 28). The moderating effect of these two cultural characteristics on the relationship between motivational approaches and employees' behavior will be examined with respect to four motivational techniques: participation in goal-setting, quality control circles, job enrichment, and reward allocation.

Participation in Goal-Setting

Participation, as a motivational technique, was originally developed to overcome resistance to change. The technique involves three psychological processes: sociodynamic group processes, motivational processes, and cognitive processes of knowledge and information sharing. Lewin (1951) emphasized the socio-dynamic aspect of participation and defined it as a "group discussion leading to a decision" (1943:63). Making a joint decision and publicly voting for it puts pressure on group members to adhere to the group decision.

The motivational component of participation has five main derivations. (1) It satisfies intrinsic motivational properties of work by allowing employees greater influences, autonomy, and responsibility (Dachler & Wilpert, 1978; Lawler, 1986; Wilpert, 1984). (2) It clarifies performance expectations (Mitchell, 1973), and the link between actions and performance outcomes (Lawler, 1986; Schuler & Lee, 1982), as well as performance expectations (Mitchell, 1973). (3) It allows for personal control over one's course of behavior (Erez & Kanfer, 1983; Staw, 1986). (4) It enhances one's sense of self-efficacy through verbal persuasion, vicarious experiences (e.g., the opportunity to see how similar others successfully develop strategies for goal attainment), and peer modeling (Earley & Kanfer, 1985). (5) In situations of technological and organizational change, participation helps to reduce the level of anxiety, and consequently employees are more willing to enact changes and become committed to their new goals (Coch & French, 1948; Lewin, 1951).

The cognitive mechanism of participation allows for a larger pool of information and a larger variety of perspectives compared to nonparticipation. Participation enhances upward communication, utilization of information, understanding of the job, and the rationale of underlying decisions (Strauss, 1982). The cognitive mechanism has the potential for improving the quality of decisions and performances.

A careful examination of the early psychological research on participation suggests that the effect of participation on individual behavior is a two step-process. Participation affects commitment, which further affects behavior and performance. It is reasonable to assume that when goal commitment is high, regardless of the way a goal is set, no significant differences will to be found between participation and nonparticipation in assigning goals. The two-step model was tested and supported in a series of studies conducted by Erez and her colleagues (Erez & Arad, 1986; Erez, Earley, & Hulin, 1985; Erez & Earley, 1987). Results clearly demonstrated that participation led to a higher level of goal commitment than nonparticipation and resulted in a higher level of performance.

However a series of studies conducted in the United States by Latham and his colleagues (for a review, see Locke & Latham, 1990) failed to find a significant effect for participation. The common denominator of each of Latham's studies was a high level of goal commitment, irrespective of the level of participation. Latham, Erez, and Locke (1988) conducted a series of studies in an attempt to resolve the inconsistencies in their results. They reasoned that the differences in their results should be explained by differences in their experimental manipulations, which resulted in contextual differences. In fact, they were able to identify a number of variables that differed between the two lines of research. (1) Goal difficulty was higher in Erez's than Latham's studies, leading to a lower level of goal commitment in Erez's research. (2) Task importance was higher in Latham's than Erez's research, leading to higher levels of intrinsic motivation and goal commitment in the former case. (3) In Erez's research only, participants were advised that they did not have to accept unreasonable goals. (4) Conflict between personal and externally set goals was experienced in the work of Erez, Earley, and Hulin (1985) but not in Latham's studies. (5) Instructions for assigned goals were given by Erez in a direct, brief "tell" style (goal merely assigned), whereas Latham used a "tell and sell" style (goal assigned and rationale given), presented in a polite and friendly manner; he also emphasized that task was important and reachable. The common denominator among each of the above variables was that they either enhanced or inhibited goal commitment. In studies conducted by Erez and her colleagues, these variables reduced the level of goal commitment, whereas in studies by Latham et al. goal commitment was enhanced. As a result of the a priori high level of goal commitment, there was no differences between participation and nonparticipation in Latham's research. In Erez's studies the a priori low level of goal commitment was maintained only in the nonparticipation condition. Commitment was enhanced through participation, and consequently the two groups significantly differed in their performance level.

Latham, Erez, and Locke (1988) jointly studied the effect of the five variables on goal commitment and performance. Of all the variables, the difference between the "tell," "tell and sell," and participation styles was the major causal variable that explained the differences in their results. The "tell" style and brevity of instructions created perceptions of low influence and support, which resulted in low levels of goal commitment, self-efficacy and subsequent performance. The empirical findings concluded that (1) the effect of participation is explained by the two-step model, with commitment and self-efficacy as mediators of the relationship between participation and performance, and (2) that the contrast between participation and the "tell" style is chiefly responsible for significant differences in commitment and self-efficacy, and consequently in performance.

The research efforts of Latham et al. (1988), conducted in the United States and Canada, did not look into cross-cultural differences, while most of Erez' research (Erez, 1986; Erez & Arad, 1986; Erez & Zidon, 1984; Erez, Earley & Hulin, 1985) was conducted in Israel. It is reasonable to expect that cultural characteristics may affect the commitment to certain motivational techniques. Participation, in particular, is not value-free. From a political perspective, it increases workers' control over production and conveys the belief that participatory democracy is a social value in itself. In fact, "no issue in the field of organizational behavior and industrial relations is more loaded with ideological and moral connotations than that of worker participation in decision-making" (Locke & Schweiger, 1979:266). Ideological differences between the United States and Europe led the proparticipation voice in the United States to advocate voluntary adoption of participative practices, whereas in Europe compulsory participation is advocated through a government legislation. In comparison to the United States European countries are generally known to be more collectivistic and to have a lower level of power distance between different organizational levels (Hofstede, 1980). It is therefore reasonable to propose that cultural background can influence support for participatory management. In fact, European researchers have suggested that the strongest predictors of attitudes toward participation and of actual involvement are values, institutionalized norms, and experience with a participative approach (Heller & Wilpert, 1981; Heller et al., 1988; England, 1983). In the next section we review a number of studies on participation in goal-setting and decision-making from this perspective.

An early study of participation in the work setting was conducted in the United States by Coch and French (1948). They found that group participation resulted in a higher level of goal commitment and performance than did nonparticipation or participation by a representative. A replication of the study in Norway was not successful: group participation was found to be no more effective than participation by a representative. A cross-cultural perspective helped resolve the inconsistencies between the two studies. The authors identified institutionalized differences between the United States and Norway with respect to participation. Since Norwegian workers were unionized, union representatives were perceived to be the legitimate management liaisons. On the other hand, voluntary participation was more acceptable in the United States than was institutionalized participation. Direct group participation coincided with the American philosophy of participation but not with the Norwegian philosophy, which viewed direct group participation as a threat to the legitimate power of union representatives.

In a more recent study Earley (1986) discovered that cultural differences explain the differential effectiveness of a goal-setting method implemented in the United States and England. A goal-setting technique initiated by shop stewards was more effective than one initiated by supervisors in England. No such differences were found in a U.S. sample. Earley concluded that English workers, as contrasted with American workers, place greater trust in their shop stewards than in their supervisors and therefore responded more favorably to a goal program sponsored by a steward than by a manager. Using our theoretical mode, it can be argued that the managerial practice that is more congruent with cultural norms satisfied the self-derived needs. It satisfied the need for self-enhancement by making the workers feel good about the collaboration with the stewards whom they trusted. It satisfied the need for self-efficacy because employees in England trusted their stewards and were more confident of accomplishing the goals they had set. It also satisfied the need for self-consistency by being consistent with previous norms of behavior.

Erez and Earley (1987) conducted a cross-cultural study in the United States and in Israel to test for the moderating effect of culture on the relationship between participation in goal-setting and performance. The United States is known for its individualistic values and moderate levels of power distance in organizations. In contrast Israel is known for its collectivistic values and low level of power distance (Hofstede, 1980). In Israel employee participation programs are institutionalized. They take the form of work councils in the private and public sectors and the form of employees' management representatives in the Histadrut sector, which is the general federation of unions and the employer of about 23% of the industry (Rosenstein, Ofek & Harel, 1988). The highest level of participation is implemented in the kibbutz sector, which symbolizes the value of collectivism, group orientation, and egalitarianism. Ultimate decision-making power in the governance of the kibbutz resides with the general assembly of all the kibbutz members (Leviatan & Rosner, 1980).

Participants in Erez and Earley's study included 180 university students, of whom 120 were Israeli (60 of these were kibbutz members), and 60 were Americans. They were all asked to perform a task under one of three goal-setting conditions: group participation, participation through a representative, and no participation. The results, illustrated in Figure 5-1 demonstrate that the performance of the Israeli students were significantly lower when goals were assigned to them than when goals were participatively set. In addition Israeli students who were assigned goals performed significantly lower than their American counterparts. There were no differences between the Israeli and the American students when goals were participatively set. This finding clearly demonstrates the moderating effect of culture. The more collectivistic and lower power distance Israeli students reacted adversely to nonparticipative assigned goals as compared to the more individualistic and higher power distance American students. A nonparticipation approach was inconsistent with Israeli cultural norms, and hence was negatively interpreted by the self. The results lead to the conclusion that the difference between Israelis and Americans is not their attitude toward participation but their reaction to assigned goals.

Cultural differences can exist between subcultures within one country and may lead to a differential effect of participation. Erez (1986) examined the effectiveness of three levels of participation in three industrial sectors within Israel, representing three different points on a continuum of participative values: (1) the private sector, guided by utilitarian goals with no explicit policy of employee participation; (2) the Histadrut, which is the federation of most unions in Israel; and (3) the kibbutz sector, known for its strong collective values, emphasis on group welfare and egalitarian approach to profit sharing (Leviatan & Rosner, 1980). The three sectors represent different work environments and provide different opportunities for par-

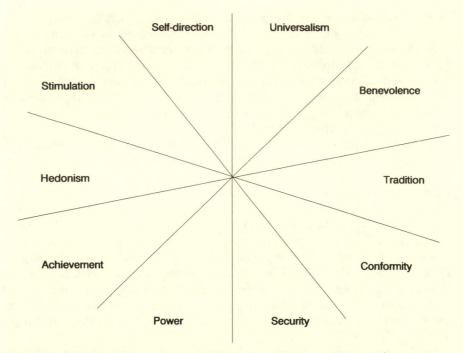

Figure 5-1. Theoretical structure of relations among motivational types of values (SOURCE: Schwartz, 1990)

ticipation. Results of this study, illustrated in Figure 5-2, demonstrate that group participation was most effective in the Kibbutz sector, participation by a representative was most effective in the Histadrut sector, and nonparticipation was most effective in the private sector. Once again the contingency approach was validated and direct group participation was found to be most effective in a group-centered collectivistic culture.

The effectiveness of group goals versus individual goals varies across cultures. In Japan the combination of group and individual goals was found to be more effective than individual goals alone (Matsui, Kakuyama & Onglatco, 1987). However in individualistic cultures group goals very often result in social loafing and free riding because group members do not share responsibility to the same extent as group members in collectivistic cultures (Earley, 1989). Perhaps one way to make group performance effective in individualistic cultures is to encourage group members to become personally accountable for their performance (Weldon & Gargano, 1988).

Participative management can constitute a subculture within an organization (Schneider, 1975). For example, French, Key and Meyer (1966) examined the effect of participation in the setting of goals as part of a performance appraisal system in the General Electric Company. They found that participation in goal-setting was more effective in a department with a participative climate. Assigned goals were more effective in a department with a nonparticipatory climate, particularly when employees felt threatened by the appraisal process.

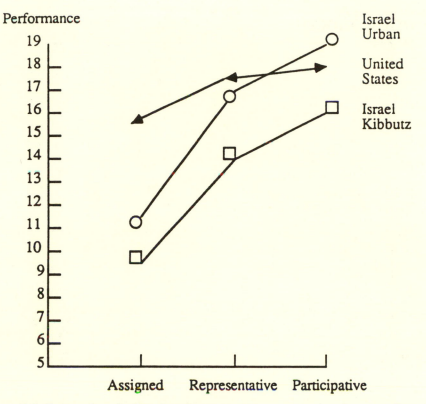

Figure 5-2. Presentation of adjusted performance means across goal-setting strategies and countries (SOURCE: Erez & Earley, 1987)

A study conducted in Israel on the implementation of quality circles demonstrated that it was successful in industrial plants where other mechanisms of employee participation such as labor-management councils already existed (Erez, Rosenstein, Barr, 1989).

Participatory management is effective when it is supported by the cultural values of group collectivism and by a low level of power distance. Prior experience with employee participation and appropriate training facilitates the implementation of participative methods.

Quality Control Circles

The contingency between participation and culture is clearly exemplified by the success of participatory management techniques in Japan. The Japanese set of values is characterized by collectivism, group orientation, and respect for seniority (Hofstede, 1980; Odaka, 1986; Triandis, 1988). Group orientation conveys the priority given to the continuity and prosperity of the social system. Collectivism is reflected in self-definition as part of a group, subordination of personal goals to group goals, concern for the integrity of the ingroup, and intense emotional attach-

Performance

Figure 5-3. Analysis of covariance showing the interaction of goal-setting strategies and sectors (SOURCE: Erez, 1986)

110

ment to the group (Triandis, 1988). This culture nourishes the collective-self, which has a central role in processing and interpreting information (Triandis, 1989b). Its core values inform Japanese management practices.

Concern for the continuity of the organization and the integrity of the group has led to the development of a system of lifetime employment. The terms "management familism" (Kume, 1985), or "corporate collectivism" (Triandis, 1989b) are used to describe the lifelong commitment that Japanese management and employees share. Managers attribute their success to the lifetime employment system that sustains mutual commitment between employees and employers and encourages team work and group cohesiveness (Erez, 1992). Employees' participation demonstrates the value of corporate collectivism. It takes the form of small group activities, including quality circles on the shop-floor level, and management improvement activities at higher organizational levels. Quality control (QC) circles are based on the implicit recognition that workers understand their work better than almost anyone else and can significantly contribute to its improvement (Canon, 1987; *Q.C. Circle Koryo: General Principles of the QC Circle,* 1980; *How to Operate Q.C. Circle Activities,* 1985).

QC circles are small groups in the same workshop that voluntarily and continuously undertake QC activities, which include the control and improvement of the workplace (Onglatco, 1988:15). In Japan QC circles are designed to enhance quality company-wide and to contribute to the employees' self-growth. Over the years they have increased from about six thousand circles in 1975 to almost two hundred and thirty thousand circles in 1985 (Onglatco). QC circles in Japan have significantly improved product quality and efficiency, reduced costs, and facilitated innovation. For example, a software company reported a 70% reduction of error rate since the implementation of the QC system, and a bank reported a significant relationship between circle activation and efficiency indices (Onglatco). QC circles have enhanced social understanding and employees' sense of participation and fulfillment of higher order needs.

In an attempt to compete with the Japanese, many American companies have implemented QC circles. Their limited success in the United States is attributed to the lack of top-level managerial support (Cole, 1980). In the long run, quality circles raise employees' expectation of higher-level participation, which cannot be fulfilled. American management is driven by a different philosophy than the Japanese. Participation does not necessarily fit in with American individualism, the lack of lifetime commitment, and the high level of specialization, according to which employees are evaluated as specialists rather than as whole persons. Successful implementation of QC circles requires the staff support or the involvement of middle-level management; without such support the circles fail to fulfill their purpose. The successful implementation of QC circles requires an infrastructure of participatory management.

The Japanese example demonstrates that when motivational techniques are congruent with cultural values, they satisfy self-derived needs and result in a high-performance level. In Japan, the collective self was found to be more complex and more dominant than the private self. Therefore self-enhancement, self-efficacy, and self-consistency are experienced when an individual makes a contribution to the group and gets recognition for his or her contribution. Motivational techniques that facilitate the contribution of the individual to group success are found to be effective. Reciprocally, effective group performance reinforces perceptions of collective efficacy, which furthers group and organizational performance.

Job Enrichment

The underlying theme of the job enrichment approach is that work can be structured so that it is performed effectively, and at the same time job holders find the work personally rewarding and satisfying. The critical psychological states that mediate the relationship between job dimensions and work motivation reflect the private self. They consist of experienced meaningfulness of the work, experienced responsibility, and knowledge of results. Certain job characteristics determine the motivation potential of a job and the extent to which it enhances intrinsic motivation and its consequent performance. Skill variety, task identity, and task significance contribute to the experienced meaningfulness of work. Autonomy at work strengthens the sense of responsibility, and feedback on performance outcomes provides knowledge of results (Hackman & Oldham, 1980).

The job enrichment approach is mainly designed for individual employees, but the model does not include psychological dimensions that enhance the collective-self, such as the formation of group identity and social support (Lawler, 1986). Although Hackman and Oldham examine the manifestation of the principles of job enrichment on the group level, they recommend that "unless the case of self-managing work groups is compelling, it may be more prudent in traditional organizations to opt for the less radical alternative of enriching the jobs of individual employees" (225).

The difficulties associated with the group level stem from the lack of knowledge and experience on the part of American managers in managing teams and in dealing with the interpersonal aspects of team work. This problem may be less prevalent in such collectivistic and group-oriented societies as Japan, Sweden, and Israel.

Parallel to the development of the individual job-enrichment approach in the United States, a similar approach, known as the sociotechnical system or autonomous work groups, was developed on the team level in such northern European countries as England, Sweden, and Norway (Thorsrud, 1984). The sociotechnical approach attempts to optimize the integration of the social and technical aspects of the work system. It takes into consideration the interplay between the organization and its environment and, in particular, the cultural values that specify the norms, rules, and regulations of behavior in organizations. Sociotechnical interventions usually involve job design on the group level that incorporates five principles of individual job enrichment: team autonomy, team responsibility, feedback on performance, and task meaningfulness enhanced by skill variety and by task identity and significance. One of the disadvantages of the sociotechnical system, as viewed by American experts, is that it "does not adequately deal with differences among organization members in how they respond to work that is designed for the sociotechnical perspective" (Hackman & Oldham, 65). This critique is an outgrowth of cultural values that emphasize individual difference characteristics over group concerns.

We propose that the same principle of enhancing internal motivation by improving the motivation potential of the job has taken two different forms on the basis of cultural differences. In the United States, which is an individualistic culture, it has taken the form of individual job enrichment design, while in Europe, which is more collectivistic, it has taken the form of autonomous work groups. We would like to note that in Israel there is a special Unit of Sociotechnical Design which develops and implements sociotechnical projects in the kibbutz industry. This approach was adopted by the kibbutz sector because it conforms to its cultural values.

The most famous sociotechnical project has been implemented in the Volvo auto industry. A sociotechnical system has been substituted for the traditional assembly line in the Kalmar plant. The work is organized in teams, each responsible for a particular, identified portion of the car—electrical systems, interior doors, and so on. Team members have the opportunity to develop task identity by assuming responsibility for an identifying portion of the work. In addition all group members develop multiple skills which allow them to rotate tasks among themselves and substitute for each other. The multiple-skills approach has enhanced task meaningfulness. A sense of responsibility is developed by self-inspection of product quality. The immediate feedback on quality performance available through inspection provides knowledge of results and enhances work motivation and performance.

In another Volvo plant located in Torslanda, a similar approach has been implemented on the departmental level by delegating to the four main departments (pressing, body work, painting, and assembly) as much autonomy as possible. Each department has formed working groups to solve unique problems. On the managerial level, industrial democracy has taken the form of work councils, consultation groups, and project groups. These groups have their own budgets to spend for the improvement of working conditions. The implementation of the sociotechnical system has helped to reduce turnover and improve the level of product quality compared to the traditional assembly line. The function of management at Volvo has been redirected to create of climate "where the people who matter will be able to have ideas and try them out" (Gyllenhammar, 1977:501).

The development of individual job enrichment in the United States, autonomous work groups in northern Europe, and QC circles in Japan is not a coincidence. Rater, it supports our main theme, that different cultures promote the development of different forms of motivational techniques. Cultural criteria are used for evaluating the motivational techniques. Motivational techniques which contribute to the fulfillment of self-derived needs are presumably congruent with the culture. In the United States individual job enrichment satisfies the private self, which is cultivated by the value of individualism. In north Europe the sociotechnical system provides opportunities for the enhancement of the collective self, which is supported by the collectivistic values, while in Japan, QC circles are congruent with the values of a group orientation and provide opportunities for the fulfillment of the collective self.

Reward Allocation

Rewards can be allocated on the basis of equity—to each according to contribution, equality, or need. Theories of motivation and managerial practices developed in the United States are mainly guided by the equity rule, namely, that the rewards are differentially distributed and are contingent upon performance. This applies to the expectancy model of motivation, the equity model, and models of merit-based compensation plans. Methods of individual performance appraisal have been developed and implemented extensively in the United States because performance appraisal serves as a major criterion for compensation. The scientific management school advocates performance-based compensation and the use of individual wage incentive plans (Taylor, 1967). The superiority of the equity rule over the rule of equality or the rule of need has continually been advocated by American managers and has never been questioned. When a rule is so widely applied within a particular culture that it becomes obvious, we never question it; however the same allocation rule may not be taken for granted when implemented in a different culture. Thus decisions regarding allocation rules are a meaningful research topic for a cross-cultural study.

Allocation preferences are influenced by three factors: beliefs about the personal utilities of specific distributions; situational demands; and cultural influences (Leventhal, Karuga & Fry, 1980). Motivational research has mainly been concerned with personal beliefs and, to a lesser extent, with specific situational factors. Interest in the third factor has stemmed from research in cross-cultural psychology. This research has mainly been published in cross-cultural journals and has not been incorporated into the mainstream of research on work motivation. In the following section we will discuss the relevance of culture for understanding the process of reward allocation and its effectiveness.

The value of collectivism and group orientation has a strong influence on reward allocation. The rule of equality is best suited to cultures with group-oriented, collectivistic values, whereas the rule of equity is suited to individualistic values. It was found that individuals with high interpersonal orientation used equality norms to a greater extent than individuals who scored low on interpersonal orientation (Adler, Brahm & Graham, 1992; Leung & Bond, 1984). The opposite was found for the rule of equity (Swap & Rubin, 1983). Since interpersonal orientation is a facet of the collective-self, the equality rule should be more highly accepted in collectivistic than in individualistic cultures. Indeed research has demonstrated that the Chinese, who have collectivistic values, use the equality rule in allocating rewards to ingroup members more than do Americans who are guided by individualistic values (Leung & Bond, 1984; Bond, Leung & Wan, 1982).

Additional research has demonstrated that there are boundary conditions for the implementation of the rule of equality in collectivistic cultures and the rule of equity in individualistic cultures. Collectivists make clear distinctions between ingroup and outgroup members. Therefore in collectivistic cultures the rule of equality may not hold for outgroup members. In individualistic cultures a distinction can be made between public and private reward allocation. Public allocation emphasizes the interpersonal dimension, which may attenuate the use of the equity rule and enhance the use of the rule of equality. The study conducted by Leung and Bond demonstrated that in both the Chinese and the American samples participants allocated to themselves more resources in the private condition when the social pressure was removed. Furthermore high performers in both cultures allocated to themselves more rewards than did low performers. Chinese males used the rule of equality more than their American counterparts, both for ingroup and outgroup members. However for outgroup allocation they used the rule of equality when the allocation was public and the rule of equity when allocation was made privately. Thus in addition to the main effects of culture and situation (level of publicness and in-group/outgroup), cultural characteristics interacted with the level of publicness to affect allocation decisions.

The specific characteristics of the situation may determine the primacy of collective or the private self. The collective self prefers the rule of equality, whereas the private-self supports the rule of equity. Leung and Park (1986) compared two environments within the United States and Korea: a work setting guided by performance goals and a neighborhood guided by the goal of enhancing friendship. They hypothesized that the rule of equity would be implemented in the work-setting and the rule of equality would dominate the neighborhood. Their findings supported the situational effect. In both countries the rule of equity was more highly regarded in the work setting, and allocators who used the equity rule in the work setting were more highly evaluated on social competence than others. In contrast, in the neighborhood situation the equality rule was more highly preferred than the equity rule. Yet compared to Americans, Koreans ranked allocators who used the equality rule higher on social evaluation than those who used the equity rule. Again, both cultural and contextual attributes influenced the rule of reward allocation.

Of special interest is a case involving the implementation of a management by objective (MBO) program in the Israel National Water Company (Gluskinos, 1988). The MBO program consisted of set performance goals, individual performance appraisals, and individual monetary incentives. At the end of one year the results demonstrated that the setting of goals had led to a significant cost reduction, mainly in energy costs. However attitudes toward the individual appraisal system and monetary rewards were mixed. The appraisal procedure was perceived to be threatening. In fact, the local union used allegations of improper appraisal to demand a halt to the written appraisal procedure. The opposition to the written appraisal procedure existed despite the fact that the mean evaluations were above average and only a few employees received negative evaluations. The bonus system was opposed by 40% of the employees even though it increased their net income. The objections reflected envy among those who were not rewarded and could not demonstrate excellence in certain jobs. Most comments on how to improve the bonus system suggested rewarding teams rather than individuals.

The negative responses to the differential system of performance appraisal and rewards become meaningful only when they are interpreted in light of the dominant cultural values in the company. The company is in the public sector, its employees are all unionized, and they have lifetime employment. Salary and compensation are distributed according to the rule of equality, and promotion is usually determined by seniority. The organizational culture in the company reflects the dominant cultural values in Israel: collectivism and low power distance. The differential reward and performance appraisal systems, designed for an individualistic culture, were not congruent with the cultural values of the company. This incongruence resulted in negative responses to parts of the MBO system. Such an outcome could have been avoided by taking into consideration the organizational culture and adjusting the MBO system accordingly.

Tornblom, Jonssons, and Foa (1985) compared the use of the three allocation rules in the United States and Sweden. The Swedish value system (Tomasson, 1970) is more oriented toward equality than the American system. The Swedish education system discourages competition in favor of cooperation. Teamwork and solidarity are encouraged rather than individual achievement. The equality rule is most appropriate to the Swedish cultural values, whereas the equity rule is congruent with American culture. Tornblom et al. hypothesized that the order of preference of allocation rules among Swedes would be equality, followed by needs and equity last and that the three rules would be more highly differentiated among Swedes than among Americans. The result clearly supported the predicted preference order. The equality rule was significantly stronger among Swedes compared with Americans; the equity rule was stronger in the United States than in Sweden; and the need rule was viewed negatively by Americans, whereas Swedes were indifferent to the rule. The degree of differentiation among rules was higher for Swedes than Americans. One possible explanation is that the Swedish value system is more integrated and consistent, whereas in the American system internal conflicts may exist between the values of individual freedom and achievement on the one hand, and equality by law on the other.

The high value given to interpersonal orientation in Sweden is evidenced in the criteria for advancement. A positive correlation was found between cooperativeness and rate of advancement in the Scandinavian countries and Japan but not in ten other countries, including the United States, the Netherlands, Belgium, and Germany (Rosenstein, 1985).

The three allocation rules were examined with respect to positive and negative allocation—bonus and cut in pay, respectively—both in the United States and India (Murphy-Berman et al., 1985). Results demonstrated that for Indians the order of preference of the three rules was need, equality, and equity across situations. On the other hand, Americans preferred allocation on the basis of equity in the positive resource condition but on the basis of need in the negative resource condition. Several explanations could be offered for the results. First, allocation on the basis of need predominates in collectivistic cultures because of the high level of personal interdependence and a greater sensitivity to other people's needs (Murphy-Berman et al., 1984). Second, the rule of need is more likely to be implemented when needs become visible, as in the case of India. A third explanation is that Indians are less responsive to merit because status in their society is determined by affiliation and not so much by achievement (Berman & Singh, 1985; Murphy-Berman et al., 1984).

The preceding studies clearly demonstrate that cultural factors influence preferences concerning rules of reward allocation. The application of an inappropriate distribution rule may cause feelings of injustice and demotivate employees. Therefore knowledge about cross-cultural differences with regard to preferences of allocation rules is vital for implementing motivational techniques.

SUMMARY AND IMPLICATIONS

The study of work motivation is no longer limited to one particular culture. Motivational techniques that were once taken for granted are not obvious when examined from a cross-cultural perspective. The existing models of work motivation are culturally bound and, therefore, limited in their capacity to explain cross-cultural differences in work motivation. Fortunately new developments in metacognitive models of self-regulation offer a conceptual framework for examining the moderating effect of culture on the relationship between motivational techniques and employees' behavior. Cultural values direct individuals' selective attention to stimuli in the work environment, and they serve as criteria for evaluating and interpreting motivational techniques.

Our model of cultural self-representation proposes that the motivation potential of various managerial techniques is evaluated by the self according to cultural criteria and with respect to their contribution to the fulfillment of the self-derived needs. The collective self is more visible in collectivistic cultures. Therefore, motivational practices are evaluated on the basis of their fulfillment of collective self-derived needs. In individualistic cultures the private self is salient and the motivation potential of various managerial techniques is evaluated with respect to their fulfillment of the private self-derived needs. In collectivistic cultures self-fulfillment is experienced by contributing to group success, whereas in individualistic countries it is experienced by personal achievements. In different cultural environments different motivational techniques are expected to be effective.

The West should learn from Japan, not by borrowing specific techniques but by developing motivational techniques that provide opportunities for satisfying self-derived needs in Western cultures. In Japan cultural values cultivate the collective-self and its derived needs: collective self-enhancement is satisfied by the contribution of the individual to the group; collective efficacy is experienced when the group is perceived as capable of attaining group goals; and collective self-consistency is satisfied by maintaining the equilibrium between a person's view of him or herself, the way he or she is viewed by members of the reference group, and the way the reference group is viewed by others.

Japanese management philosophy and practices create the culture and the opportunities for satisfying collective self-derived needs. Employees are evaluated according to their contribution to the success of their group. Perceptions of collective efficacy are enhanced by managing teamwork rather than individual work, by developing a system of small group activities, and by providing feedback on the team and on the company level. Collective self-consistency is maintained by the enduring relationship between the individual employee and the employing organization. Status and recognition in organizations are heavily determined by seniority. This criterion reduces ambiguity and maintains the stability of one's place in the hierarchy. Thus the effectiveness of the Japanese management system can be attributed to the provision of opportunities for the fulfillment of collective self-derived needs in line with Japanese cultural values.

Our model of cultural self-representation offers a conceptual framework for evaluating the motivation potential of various managerial practices across cultures. The model draws the link between culture, self, motivational practices, and motivated behavior.

Certain universal principles of motivation seem to cut across cultural borders. The content domain of human needs and motives is universal. Needs for enhancement, efficacy, and consistency are universal human characteristics. Yet the salience of the various needs, as well as the means for satisfying them, vary across cultures. The content domain and structure of the motivational types of values seem to be universal (Schwartz, in press). Yet the relative strength of the various motivational types differ across cultures. The motivation sequence is universal (Locke, 1991). Goals and intentions are the immediate regulators of behavior and mediate between values and performance. However the relative importance of values and the meaning of specific goals may change according to cultural values.

The main principles of the goal-setting model, which emphasize specific and challenging goals accompanied by feedback and goal commitment, seem to be applicable across cultures. Clear and specific goals are important, particularly in a changing and competitive environment. Specific and challenging goals create opportunities for satisfying self-derived needs (driven by either the independent or the interdependent self). However the nature of goals, whether individual or group goals, and the way goals are set, whether assigned, participatively set, or self-set, seem to have a differential effect across cultures.

The attainment of complex-task goals depends to a great extent on the use of effective strategies (Locke & Latham, 1990). Therefore training employees to develop and use strategies for the attainment of challenging goals is gaining importance across cultures. The acquisition of knowledge and skills strengthens perceptions of self- or collective efficacy and leads to higher performance levels. Training should have a universal positive effect on work motivation and performance.

The principle of linking performance to outcomes, advocated by the expectancy model, seems to have a universal effect on motivation and performance. Yet the valence of various reward outcomes is partially determined by cultural values and, therefore, varies across cultures.

In a changing and unstable work environment, the provision of opportunities to exercise control over one's behavior is important for self-enhancement. Perceptions of control may be enhanced by motivational techniques that encourage personal or group accountability and responsibility. Such motivational techniques may lead to higher levels of organizational commitment and to extra-role behavior (Organ, 1987).

6

Culture, Self, and Communication

Culture and communication are closely related. This relationship can be viewed three different ways: culture as a communication phenomenon, communication as a manifestation of culture, and culture and communication as a reciprocal relationship.

Communication is commonly defined in terms of information processing. The process begins with a source of information who decides which message to send and what signals and symbols to use for encoding the message. The message is then transmitted through certain channels to a receiver, who decodes the information, interprets it, and reacts accordingly. A smooth flow of communication occurs when the signal transmitted is interpreted as intended by the source. Anything added to the signal, between its transmission and reception, that is not intended by the source is considered to be noise (Fiske, 1990).

The process of communication is affected both by bottom-up and top-down processing. The former contains information that comes up to the brain from the sensory receptors, whereas the latter contains information that is guided by high-level cognitive processes that involve expectations, motivation, and values, as they are represented in the self. These processes are molded into a cognitive schema that is internal to the perceiver (Neisser, 1976). In interpersonal communication at least two persons are involved, the sender and the receiver of information. Top-down processes occur in both modes of the communication channel. In this case, the fit between the encoding and decoding of information depends on a coding system shared by both the sender and the receiver. Top-down processes that are shared by members of the same social group can be viewed as elements of the subjective culture (Triandis, 1972). Culture conveys shared knowledge, information, and meaning; therefore the flow of interpersonal communication depends to a great extent on the mediating processes of cultural self-representation, as portrayed in our model in chapter 2.

The purpose of this chapter is to introduce a cognitive framework for integrating the three perspectives on culture and communication: culture as a communication phenomenon, communication as a manifestation of culture, and the reciprocal relationship between culture and communication as mediated by cultural self-representations.

CULTURE AS A COMMUNICATION PHENOMENON

Most definitions concur that communication is the transmission of information, ideas, emotions, skills, and so on, by the use of symbols (Littlejohn, 1988). Communication is the study of the actual social process wherein significant symbolic forms are created, apprehended, used, and preserved (Carey, 1988). It is "the thread by which the fabric of society is held together. A culture's reality is defined in terms of its meanings, which arise from interaction within social groups" (Littlejohn: 110). Therefore society can be viewed as a form of communication and communication as a basis for human organizing (Weick, 1979).

Weick's theory of organization illustrates how organizations and environments, including the cultural environment, are shaped by communication. Organizing activities involve interlocked behaviors or double-interacts which consist of an act followed by a response and then a follow-up act by the first person. A smooth flow of organizing activities depends on the common meaning given by the actor and the respondent to their activities. The interaction or communication among organizational members serves to achieve common meanings. Organizing activities are based on three premises: enactment, which reflects the notion that environments are enacted by the process of attending to selective environmental stimuli that formulate a cognitive representation of the environment—thus environments have no preexistence; selection, which means that certain actions are selected and others are rejected; and retention, which decides which aspects of the event will be retained for the future. Retained information is integrated into the existing body of information that forms the basis by which individuals and organizations operate.

Attention, selection, and retention are the underlying processes of sensemaking. When these processes are shared by members of a certain group they form the subjective culture of that particular group (Triandis, 1972). Thus it is proposed that the formation of culture is enacted by the process of communication.

The definition of culture in terms of shared meaning is consistent with the symbolic interactionist approach, which stresses the role of shared meaning and symbols as the binding factor of societies. The term symbolic means interpretive, having interactive meaning and value (Schall, 1983). Symbolic interactionism is based on four core assumptions. First, the basic social unit of analysis is the social act. This involves an initial gesture from one individual, a response to that gesture by another individual, and a resulting action, which is perceived or imagined by both actors (Littlejohn). Societal action is the extended process of many individuals accommodating their action to one another. Second, individuals use symbols for communication. The symbols are interpreted by the receiver and gain their meaning through interactions with others. For a society to exist symbols must possess shared meaning. Third, meaning is derived by conscious interpretation. "An object has meaning for a person when he or she consciously thinks about or interprets the object" (98). Fourth, the meaning is determined in light of one's situation and the direction of one's actions. Cooperation among people enables them to correctly interpret each other's intentions and actions and to respond in an appropriate way.

Symbolic interactionism views culture as "a process defined by the communication practices members use to create subjective interpretations of organizational life

(Sypher, Applegate & Sypher, 1985). Accordingly, communication behavior is viewed as the primary vehicle for the active creation and maintenance of cultures. A smooth flow of communication creates a strong culture (Deal & Kennedy, 1982).

Shared meaning is feasible when individuals share certain rules for interpreting experience and for acting. Goodenough (1970) defined culture in terms of sets of standards for perceiving, believing, evaluating, communicating, and acting. Communication rules are considered to be "tacit understanding about appropriate ways to interact with others in given roles and situations" (Schall, 1983:560). Communication rules focus on prescribed message exchange, whereas norms deal with expected behavior. Communication rules are selectively activated according to what seems to be most appropriate in a given situation. If interacting individuals define the situation differently, they will apply different communication rules, which will result in miscommunication. For example, when the boss of a loan department in a bank was absent, his immediate subordinate thought he should resume responsibility and make a decision concerning a big loan for one of the clients. Yet his boss thought that such a major decision was his personal responsibility and should have been postponed until he returned to work. The application of two different rules of communication resulted in miscommunication between the boss and his subordinate.

Communication rules are identified either on a tactical or a thematic level. The former prescribes specific behavior, whereas the latter reflects values and beliefs. A thematic rule might require, for example, that employees be active participants in their organization. A specific rule derived from it would allow subordinates to assume responsibility when their boss is away.

Schall conducted a field study identifying communication rules as a cultural phenomenon. Members of an information system division (group A) and an investment department (group B) in one corporation participated in the study. A multimethod design was implemented using five different sources of data: an influence-style questionnaire; official documents that reflected formal rules of influence; observations and interactions of the chief researcher with the group members during a one-month period; in-depth, relatively unstructured interviews with group members; and card sorting by importance of influence tactics and of potential power sources.

The overall findings of this study revealed a number of intergroup similarities and differences. Both groups had a strong task focus and a sense of urgency. They valued technical competence, information, explanations, and recognition for performance. Both groups valued pleasant, nonconfrontational, on-the-job relationships with co-workers, and managers from both groups valued control of resources. However the groups differed significantly in the meaning they assigned to the above attributes. A sense of urgency in group A was associated with long-term projects, whereas in group B it was associated with short-term daily deadlines. To increase resource control, managers in group A built alliances, whereas managers in group B increased resource control by personal involvement in day-to-day operations. Members of group A valued the seeking and sharing of information, whereas in group B information flow was restricted to certain subgroups.

In addition to the differences between groups there were notable differences between managers and nonmanagers in both groups. In group A managers' first priority was given to meeting deadlines, whereas nonmanagers' first priority was given to producing the highest quality possible. In group B managers' first priority centered on coordinating efforts toward accomplishing group-wide results, whereas nonmanagers' priorities centered on independent efforts toward accomplishing particular tasks and assignments. The respect managers and nonmanagers showed toward each others' priorities was higher in group A than B. As a result members of group B experienced frustration, tension, and a sense of anomie. Members of group A saw their group life conforming more closely to the formal rules than did group B members. When the two groups interacted, they faced problems of coordination and frustration since they enacted different rules of communication.

The study by Schall demonstrates that communication rules capture the essence of subcultures in organizations. However it raises questions concerning the nature of the relationship between shared meaning and communication flow. It is reasonable to expect that the absence of shared meaning would result in miscommunication. Yet findings demonstrate that the notable differences in perceived priorities between managers and nonmanagers did not result in communication problems in group A, and managers and nonmanagers were sensitive and sympathetic to each others' priorities. In group B the split between managers and nonmanagers resulted in frustration, tension, and a sense of anomie. Thus the differences between managers and nonmanagers in both groups do not provide an explanation for the different patterns of communication that were developed in the two groups.

One possible explanation may be derived from a theory proposed by Weick (1979), which was empirically supported by Donnellon, Gray & Bougon (1986). Weick proposed that the sharing of beliefs is not essential to the perpetuation of interlocked behavior; organized action continues to occur based on the knowledge that the exchange among group members will continue. What must be shared are expectations about what will be exchanged and a code of the production, along with comprehension of the behavior through which the exchange is enacted. The code is a repertoire of behavioral options that members of a given society recognize, respond to, and use to interact with one another (Donnellon et al.). The relationship between meaning and action is described in terms of "equifinality" (Donnellon et al.), meaning that different interpretations have similar behavioral implications. Thus organization members may take similar actions for different reasons.

The case presented by Donnellon et al. provides an empirical support of their argument. In this case members of the personnel department decided to lay off four group leaders in the production department. Members of the production department discussed the possibility of going on strike. Two metaphors for strike were offered: "Striking is getting revenge" and "Striking is principled behavior" (52). Strike action was actively opposed by several group members who disagreed with the first metaphor. However when the second metaphor was introduced into the discussion, they unanimously agreed to go on strike. Organized action did not result from a shared meaning among the department members but rather from a shared knowledge that the exchange process would continue. The use of metaphors, along with such other means as logical arguments and affect, were found to be effective for creating equifinal meaning leading to joint action. The researchers conclude that organizational members have two alternative sets of organizing tools—shared meaning and shared communication mechanism. In the latter case it is plausible for two persons to "agree to disagree" as part of a continuous process of organized action. When two persons say, "we disagree," the continuous flow of communication and of organized action is effectively stopped.

In summary, theoretical arguments and research evidence support the notion that communication is the essence of culture. A strong culture develops when societal members share the same meaning and interpretation of stimuli and situations. Communication is a necessary condition for shared meaning to occur. However culture and its elements of organizing actions can be formed, even in the absence of shared meaning, as long as there is an agreement to continue the exchange process among group members, and as long as they share similar codes of encoding and decoding information.

COMMUNICATION AS A CULTURAL PHENOMENON

While numerous studies have examined the impact of culture on communication, conceptual models that integrate the myriad research hardly exist. Our purpose is to develop a conceptual framework that would allow the research to be integrated into one model.

Gudykunst, Ting-Toomey, and Chua (1988) developed a multivariate model that portrays the paths between culture and communication. According to this model, culture affects communication through two levels of mediating variables. The first level of mediators includes four factors: social cognitive processes consisting of information processing, persuasive strategy selection, conflict management styles, personality, social relationships, and self-perceptions; situational factors, including the structure of language, roles, and environmental settings; affect, which conveys emotional expressions and responses; and habits, which are reflected in the set of automatic responses acquired through the process of socialization. These factors further affect a second level of mediators: intentions, which are instructions about how to communicate; understanding, which is the interpretation of incoming stimuli and the ability to describe, predict, and explain these stimuli; and facilitating conditions, which enable an individual to carry out an act. All these factors further affect communication.

Sociocultural variability is reflected in differences in all the above factors, which further affect communication. The complete model of Gudykunst et al. has not been tested empirically. One possible explanation is that the number of variables included in the model limits one's ability to empirically test all the possible paths and interactions between variables. However portions of the model were tested in numerous studies and will be further reported.

Triandis and Albert (1987) propose a more focused model that centers on cognitive frames. They postulate that communication is shaped by culture since it requires a certain degree of shared meanings, shared understanding of linguistic and nonlinguistic symbols, and similar frames of reference. Cultures provide their members with cognitive frames to help focus their attention on certain environmental stimuli and evaluate and interpret the processed information. Triandis and Albert used the following frames to capture cultural variations: emphasis on people, ideas, or action; different values; process versus goal orientation; and patterns of information processing. Yet they did not clarify the rationale for choosing the above categories and whether these categories are mutually exclusive or not.

In line with the model of Gudykunst et al. and of Triandis and Albert, we suggest focusing on two cognitive factors: cultural values and cognitive styles. Cultural values ascribe meaning to information and capture a major part of cultural variation. Cognitive styles reflect the level of differentiation, cognitive complexity, and abstraction, and as such, clearly influence cognitive information processing. These two cognitive factors have been widely studied in relation to cultural variation and communication. In addition cognitive styles modify the private and collective self, which in turn affect communication patterns. The communication dimensions that have been examined most often are communication styles, decision-making processes, and conflict resolution. An integration of existing research leads to the following conceptual framework for studying the relationship between cultural cognitive frames and communication (see Table 6-1).

The conceptual framework consists of two dimensions: a dimension of cultural variation in cognitive frames, including cultural values, cognitive styles, and the self; and a communication dimension consisting of communication styles, patterns

Table 6-1. A Model for Studying the Relationship Between Cultural Variability in Cognitive Frames and Communication

Cognitive Frames	Communication Patterns		
	Communication Style	Decision-Making	Conflict Resolution
Cultural values			
Individualism	Explicit style	Individual rational confrontation	Direct confrontation
Collectivism	Implicit style	Group intuitive consensus	Avoiding confrontation
Low power distance	Informal/direct	Bottom-Up	Networking
High power distance	Formal/direct	Top-Down	Compliance
Low uncertainty avoidance	Implicit	Delegation	Implicit
High uncertainty avoidance	Explicit	Centralization	Explicit
Masculinity	Rational	Factual	Rational
Feminnity	Emotional	Affective	Emotional
Cognitive styles			
Field dependence	Social cues Information seeking	Participative	Affective
Field independence	Internal reference	Individual	Self-controlled
High context culture	Concrete/affective	Face-saving	No separation between conflict issue & person
Low context culture	Abstractness	Confrontational	Separation between conflict issue & person
The self			
Private self	Self-face maintenance	Personal goals	Self-face concern
Collective self	Other-face maintanence	Collective goals	Other-face concern

of decision-making, and conflict resolution. The cultural values most frequently studied in relation to communication are collectivism versus individualism, power distance, uncertainty avoidance, and masculinity versus femininity. The cognitive styles most often studied with respect to cultural variation are field dependence versus independence and low versus high context cultures. The private and collective selves are shaped by the cognitive frames and influence the formation of certain communication patterns. The model serves to explain how the cognitive dimension conveys cultural variation and how it affects communication styles, decision-making processes, and conflict resolution.

Cultural Values

According to Hofstede's typology (1980a), cultures differ from one another in at least four dimensions of values: collectivism versus individualism, power distance, masculinity versus femininity, and uncertainty avoidance. *Collectivism* is characterized by a tight social framework and by subordination of individual goals to the group goals. In contrast individualism implies a loose social framework in which people are supposed to take care of themselves and subordinate group goals to individual goals. *Power distance* reflects the extent to which a society accepts an unequal distribution of power in organizations. *Uncertainty avoidance* is the extent to which a society feels threatened by uncertain and ambiguous situations. Societies try to avoid such uncertainty by establishing more formal rules and believing in absolute truths. *Masculinity* expresses the extent to which the dominant values in the society are "masculine," that is, assertive, rational more than emotional, valuing materialistic outcomes, and so on.

Chapter 5 on work motivation described how cultural values moderate the effectiveness of various managerial techniques. In particular the values of collectivism versus individualism and power distance were found to be important determinants of the effectiveness of reward allocation, job design, participation in goal setting, and small group activity. In this chapter we are going to discuss how cultural variation in values and cognitive styles affects patterns of decision-making and conflict resolution.

Collectivism and Individualism

The need to preserve group harmony in a collectivistic culture can be seen in the communication style. For example, Japan and Korea are known for their collectivistic values and for their emphasis on interdependence and group harmony. To preserve group harmony they adopt an implicit style of communication, including the use of ambiguous words to avoid confrontation and disharmony. Such qualifiers as "maybe," "perhaps," "probably," and "somewhat" are frequently used by the Japanese (Okabe, 1983:36). Similarly, Koreans do not make negative responses while communicating with others in order to preserve group harmony (Park, 1979). Canadians and Americans, who are known for their individualistic values, have less concern for group harmony. They are more likely to use explicit words for interpersonal communication, including such terms as "absolutely," "certainty," and "positively" (Okabe).

Decision-making in collectivistic cultures resides in the group rather than in the individual. Corporate communication in Japan is based on personal, oral communication and on a two-way flow of communication (Ruch, 1985). The Japanese management system is known for its bottom-up communication methods, such as the *ringi* system and small group activity. The *ringi* system requires the approval of all employees who are involved in implementing decisions. Before a decision is implemented, it is discussed in small groups for the purpose of smoothing implementation and facilitating coordination.

Meetings in Japan are longer and more frequent than in Western cultures. They are designed to clarify decisions and strategies and to coordinate activities both horizontally and vertically. The style of conducting meetings differs from those in the United States. Americans invite open and honest confrontation; the Japanese avoid it and will discuss disagreements prior to the meeting which merely gives formal approval to decisions reached during informal consultations. Decisions in Japan are reached by consensus, whereas in the United States they are reached by majority rule (Ruch).

Kume (1985) compared American versus Japanese decision-making styles on six dimensions: (1) locus of decision: groups in Japan versus individuals in the United States; (2) initiation and coordination: bottom-up in Japan versus top-down in the United States; (3) temporal orientation: adjusted to changes, slow decision but immediate implementation in Japan versus planning ahead, quick decision but slow implementation in the United States; (4) mode of reaching decisions: consensus in Japan versus individual decisions, majority decision, or split decision in the United States; (5) decision criterion: intuitive, group harmony in Japan versus rational practical empiricism in the United States; (6) communication style: indirect in Japan versus direct confrontation in the United States. All six dimensions of decision-making seem to be affected by the values of collectivism and group harmony.

Power Distance

Power distance may explain differences in the perception of legitimate authority. Power distance in England was found to be smaller than in France (Hofstede, 1980a). English managers perceive authority as vested in the person and therefore highly value personal autonomy. On the other hand, French managers perceive authority as vested in the role and value compliance with the rules of the organization (Graves, 1972). Conflict resolution in both countries is affected by perceptions of authority. In the French factory conflict is resolved by compliance with a strong central authority. In the British factory managers use personal networks and coalitions in an attempt to solve problems (Graves).

A comparison between American subsidiaries in South America and local companies demonstrated significant differences in delegation of authority. Power distance in South America is higher than in North America (Hofstede, 1980a). The differences in cultural values may explain why managers in American subsidiaries were more likely to delegate responsibilities than managers in local South American companies. It is interesting to note that 80% of the managers in the subsidiaries were South Americans, yet they assimilated the American culture that predominated in the subsidiaries (Negandhi & Prasad, 1971).

In Japan the hierarchical structure of the society affects the patterns of communication. In particular communication is affected by status, age, and sex differences. Young people pay respect to their elders, juniors to seniors, and low-level employees to managers in higher organizational levels. Age, seniority, and organizational level are highly correlated in Japan as age is a major criterion for promotion.

Uncertainty Avoidance

High uncertainty avoidance is reflected in a direct style of communication that does not leave much room for ambiguity. For example, Gudykunst and his colleagues (Gudykunst et al., 1988) found that cultural variability along this dimension explains differences in the use of elaborate versus succinct verbal styles. A high level of uncertainty avoidance is more likely to enhance an elaborate style, whereas a succinct style is more prevalent in cultures with low uncertainty avoidance.

The use of a direct style is another characteristic of high uncertainty avoidance. For example, Israelis are highly driven by uncertainty avoidance (Hofstede, 1980a). This characteristic may explain why they use a direct style of communication. Israeli Sabra culture uses the direct style of *Dugri* speech ("straight talk"), which implies a concern for sincerity in the sense of being true to oneself (Katriel, 1986). Israelis are likely to tell each other directly and very explicitly what they have in mind, even if it leads to confrontation.

Whereas high collectivism enhances a preference for implicit style and high uncertainty avoidance lends itself to an explicit style, this is not always borne out in practice. In Israel, as well as in Japan, the dominant values are ones of collectivism and high uncertainty avoidance (Hofstede, 1980a); yet the dominant communication styles in the two countries differ. In Japan the implicit style fits the concern for harmony, but it does not fit the high need for uncertainty avoidance. In Israel the explicit style fits the high need for uncertainty avoidance, but it does not fit the need to preserve group harmony. One possible explanation is the moderating effect of a third value of power distance which differs between the two cultures. Power distance is high in Japan and low in Israel. This may explain why the Japanese are more careful of avoiding open communication that may conflict with the social hierarchy. On the other hand, the low power distance in Israel encourages the use of an open and explicit style. Thus different combinations of values lead to different preferences of communication styles.

Masculinity Versus Femininity

This is related to the level of affect that is manifested in communication. The expression of emotions is more highly tolerated in feminine cultures than in masculine cultures (Glenn, Witmeyer & Stevenson, 1977).

Cognitive Styles

Field independence is the ability to highly differentiate between stimuli and to think analytically, whereas field dependence refers to lower levels of differentiation and global thinking. The ability to differentiate and to think in analytic and abstract terms reflects a high level of cognitive complexity. Field dependence is sometimes described as an apperceptual style, that is, the manner in which an individual sorts,

processes, and reacts to environmental cues (Larson, 1978). The unique characteristic of field-independence is the ability to perceive parts of a field as discrete
from the surrounding field, rather than as embedded in the field (Witkin, 1949).

Field dependence or independence is associated with cultural variation. Witkin &
Berry (1975) identified four antecedent factors of field dependence or independence: ecology, social pressure, socialization, and biological effects. Ecological
adaptation refers to the characteristic relationship between man and nature. Traditional societies are classified into hunters and gatherers, and agriculturalists and
pastoralists (Berry, 1971). Ecological demands force members of a society to develop certain perceptual abilities. For example, hunters need to locate food and to
return safely to their homes. Since they need to distinguish the stimuli from the
environment, they develop field-independence.

Social pressure pertains to social conformity and sociocultural stratification. In
tight societies intense pressure is put on the individual to conform. In loose societies
such pressures are few, allowing self-control to operate. Field independent societies can be differentiated from field dependent ones on the basis of family structure (nuclear versus extended, respectively); social structure (egalitarian versus
hierarchical–stratified); and social relation patterns (reserved–fragmented versus
mutual dependence–integrated). It is suggested that agriculturalists, who cultivate
the land and become permanent residents, develop tighter social relationships than
to hunters. They live in extended families and experience a high level of interdependence.

The parent–child relationship influences the development of a certain cognitive
style: a demand for adherence to parental authority, encouragement of reliance on
others, restriction of exploration, and lack of emphasis on achievement constrain the
development of psychological differentiation. This style of child rearing is known as
status oriented, or person-oriented. On the other hand, the growth nurturing style
enhances self-reliance, supports interaction, positively reinforces curiosity, achievement, and verbal articulation, all of which promotes the development of field
independence.

Biological factors also seem to affect cognitive style. Research indicates that
androgen, which promotes the development of secondary male sex characteristics,
is associated with field independent behavior, whereas estrogen, which promotes
the development of secondary sex characteristics in the female, is associated with
field dependent functioning (Boverman et al., 1968; Dawson 1972). To summarize,
field dependence is prevalent in cultures characterized by adherence to authority and
the use of strict socialization rules, whereas a field independence style is developed
in cultures that encourage autonomy, have more lenient child rearing practices, and
have loose social organization (Gudykunst et al., 1988).

Field-dependent and field-independent persons have different personality characteristics. They vary in the level of psychological differentiation. Field-dependent
persons are likely to use the field as a referent for behavior, whereas field-
independent persons perceive their identity as separate. According to Witkin (1949)
a sense of separate identity entails the existence of stable internal frames of reference for self-definition and for viewing, interpreting, and reacting to the world. It is
reflected by the capacity to establish and maintain attitudes and judgements without

continuous reference to external standards, and in the face of contradictory expressions by others. Conversely the continuous use of external frames of references for the definition of one's feelings, attitudes, and needs suggests a poorly developed sense of separate identity.

A second distinguishing characteristic of field dependence versus field independence is the extent of reliance upon external social referent. Field-dependent persons rely more on external social referent, particularly in ambiguous situations when they use information from others to resolve ambiguity. Field-independent people are less likely to be engaged in information-seeking behavior than field dependent people. (Mausner & Graham, 1970). Again, this is particularly true in ambiguous situations.

A third characteristic of field dependency is socially facilitative behavior. Individuals who have to be attentive to social cues to insure direct access to others are more likely to have an interpersonal orientation than are field-independent people. They are sociable and altruistic, seek affiliations with others, and show interest in social occupations. In contrast, field-independent people are individualistic, cold and distant in their relations with others, concerned with ideas and principles rather than with people, task oriented, and most interested in technical occupations (Witkin & Goodenough, 1976).

Field independence is hypothesized to be a developmental variable comprising patterns of thought and behavior that vary along a scale, with the most global or diffused pattern at one end and the most articulated or differentiated pattern at the other. Individuals at the global end of the continuum are likely to be intellectually intuitive, perceptually holistic, emotionally expressive, socially dependent, and other-directed. Those at the articulated end are likely to be intellectually analytical and systematic, perceptually discriminating, emotionally self-controlled, socially independent, and self-reliant (Gruenfeld & MacEachron, 1975). According to Gruenfeld and MacEachron, positive relationships exist between certain growth-nurturing styles of child-rearing, socioeconomic class, and field articulation. Generalizing from the particular to the general, they hypothesized that the level of performance on measures of field articulation among managers from a particular country will correlates with indices of that country's economic development. The results clearly supported their hypothesis.

High- Versus Low-Context Cultures

Field dependence versus independence seems to be associated with a cultural dimension of high- versus low-context dependence. This dimension distinguishes between context-dependent communication and abstract communication. Content-dependent cultures use context to ascribe meaning to messages, whereas noncontext cultures use abstract concepts to convey their messages. A high-context message is one in which "most of the information is either in the physical context or internalized in the person, while very little is in the coded explicit transmitted part of the message; a low-context message is one in which "the mass of information is vested in the explicit code" (Hall, 1976:79).

Members of high-context cultures tend to use an affective-intuitive style, resembling the style used in poetry. They use associative communication which focuses on the experience of the communicator with the subject that is being communicated (Glenn, 1981; Gudykunst & Kim, 1984; Ting-Toomey, 1985). This distinction is similar to the one between field-dependent and field-independent persons. Field-dependent persons, compared to field-independent persons, are more likely to pay attention to the source of messages than to the message itself, and they are more affected by the social appeal of the source of information (Larson, 1978).

The Japanese, Chinese, and Arabs are identified as members of high-context cultures, whereas Swiss, Germans, Scandinavians, and Americans are members of low-context cultures (Gudykunst et al., 1988). Low-context communication pre-dominates individualistic cultures, whereas high-context communication resides in collectivistic cultures. High- and low-context cultures influence the style of commu-nication in conflict resolution. Individuals in low-context cultures are better able to separate the conflict issue from the person involved in the conflict than are indi-viduals in high-conflict cultures (Ting-Tommey, 1985). In high-context cultures to disagree openly or confront someone in public is a severe blow and an extreme insult, causing both sides to "lose face," particularly in the case of communication between superiors and subordinates. Individuals in high-context cultures perceive the conflict situation as expressive. For them the conflict issue and the conflict person are hardly separable from each other. In high-context cultures individuals are sup-posed to engage in a normative process of reciprocal sensitivity toward one another. Persons in low-context cultures characterize conflict as primarily instrumental.

The rules for handling conflict differ across the dimension of high versus low context. In high-context cultures there are prescribed ways of handling conflict, and once the cultural scripts are mastered, a relatively low degree of uncertainty and risk prevails. A potential for conflict is relatively higher between strangers in low-context cultures than in high-context cultures because, in the latter case, it is more likely that individual normative expectations of acceptable behavior are violated. On the other hand, interaction which deviates from cultural normative expectations is more easily identified in a normative homogenous system than in a normative heterogenous system.

High- and low-context cultures promote different attitudes toward conflict resolu-tion. In low-context cultures, characterized by action orientation, the players in a conflict are likely to assume a direct confrontation. In high-context cultures they try to avoid direct confrontation by employing a calculated degree of vagueness, typ-ically when tension and anxiety mount. Low- and high-context cultures differ in their style of argument. People in the United States typically engage in the factual-inductive style of argument; in Russia they use the axiomatic-deductive style of logic; and in Arab cultures people primarily engage in the affective-intuitive style of emotional appeal (Glenn, Witmeyer & Stevenson, 1977). The factual-inductive style is based on facts and moves inductively toward conclusions, while the axiomatic-deductive style proceeds from the general to the particular.

In conflict situations members of low-context cultures handle conflicts by using the factual-inductive style or axiomatic-deductive style more than members of high-context cultures. Low-context cultures tend to avoid direct confrontation. For exam-ple, an executive in China is advised to solve a conflict between two subordinates by meeting separately with each of them, whereas in the United States the supervisor is advised to meet jointly with the two sides of the conflict (Bond, Leung & Giacalone, 1985). Similar results were found in comparisons of conflict resolution among Mexicans and among Anglo-Americans (Kagan, Knight & Martinez-Romero, 1982). Differences between high- and low-context cultures affect communication between superiors and subordinates. In low-context cultures superiors directly criticize subordinates for poor quality work. In a high-context culture superiors are careful not to hurt the feelings of their subordinates when they have to criticize their work. For example, a North American supervisor is likely to say, "I cannot accept this proposal as submitted. You should come up with some better ideas" whereas a Japanese supervisor might say, "While I have the highest regard for your abilities, I would not be completely honest if I did not express my disappointment at this proposal. I must ask that you reflect further on the proposal you have submitted to me" (Miyahara, 1984:9).

In collectivistic, high-context cultures, "face" is an important psychological construct that is closely tied to "honor," "shame," and "obligation." Therefore members of high-context culture are more concerned with saving face than are members of low-context cultures, and they try to avoid direct confrontation (Lebra, 1976; Ishida, 1974; Nomura & Barnlund, 1983).

COGNITIVE FRAMES AND THE SELF

Non-Western cultures have been described as concrete owing to their focus on situation-bound behavior and social role rather than on abstract personality traits or dispositions (Cousins, 1989). Concreteness is usually ascribed to a cognitive inability to engage in analytic thinking, that is, to abstract features of behavior from the context. It refers to a reliance on perceptual stimuli—a tendency to perceive things as part of the real life settings from which they normally take their meanings rather than to mentally isolate objects from their attributes and generalize across contexts on the basis of conceptual similarities. It is assumed that the stimuli-bound perception is more primitive than the mature thought capable of abstracting veridical categories.

Cognitive shortcomings are believed to prevent individuals from certain non-Western cultures from perceiving a person as independent from the concrete contexts of daily life (Bond & Tak-sing, 1983).

Several recent studies, while confirming the presence of concrete thinking in non-Western cultures, point to the influence of cultural values on social perception (Cousins, 1989; Miller, 1984; Shweder & Bourne, 1984). A comparative study of India and the United States found that Indian Hindus use more concrete and contextually qualified descriptions of people they know than do Americans. Miller found that Americans tend to attribute behavior to personal disposition, whereas Indian Hindus attribute behavior to the situation. Yet, there are no significant differences between the two groups in tests of abstract thinking. This finding rules out cognitive shortcomings and confirms the influence of indigenous cultural meanings. Cultural attitudes associated with individualism and collectivism may explain such differences. Americans stress autonomy and self-reliance, whereas Indian Hindus view the person in relation to others. Sociocentric cultural premises rather than a lack of abstract skills are believed to cause Indians to focus on interpersonal context and actual behavior.

Another intriguing case is that of Japan. Comparable to Western societies in industrial and economic achievement, its students far surpass their American counterparts in the abstract fields of science and math; yet their mode of thought is often described as concrete. In view of the inconsistency Cousins (1989) examined the role of culture as an alternative explanation for context-bound versus context-free perceptions of the self. Individualistic premises describe a person as situation-free, a discrete agent, whereas sociocentric premises locate a person in relation to others. Cousins hypothesized the Japanese can generate abstract concepts of the self, given a frame of reference conducive to a sociocentric idiom.

To test the above hypothesis, two questionnaires were administered to American and Japanese students. A Twenty-Statement Test (TST) self-description questionnaire asked the students to write twenty statements on "Who am I?." The other questionnaire used a contextual format, asking subjects to describe themselves in a specific setting, such as home or school. Responses were classified into two categories: qualified psychological attributes made in reference to others, and pure attributes free from contextual qualifications. The results of the TST questionnaire demonstrated that American subjects referred more frequently to purely psychological attributes than did Japanese students (i.e., "I am easy-going"). Japanese students referred more often than their counterparts to the physical self, social categories, preferences, wishes, and regular activities; however the Japanese subjects described themselves in highly abstract, global terms significantly more often than did Americans (i.e., "I am a living form"). Results of the contextual questionnaire demonstrated that the Japanese used a greater number of pure attributes ("I am diligent") than Americans, who used more qualified attributes ("I am often lazy at home").

These findings illustrate the priming effect of culture. The format of the TST questionnaire lends itself to expressions of ego-autonomy. From the Japanese perspective, "Who am I?" is an unnatural question if divorced from context. Therefore, Japanese subjects on the TST described themselves in terms of social affiliations or reference to concrete attributes. Yet this relational context was expressed in such abstract terms as, "I am a member of the twentieth century." The Japanese students' responses on the TST were both significantly more abstract and more concrete than the American responses.

The contextual format of the other questionnaire is conducive to sociocentric conceptions of self. Situational cues made it unnecessary for Japanese subjects to fill in the context integral to their sense of self, providing leeway for more abstract self-reflection. It is here that the Japanese were more likely to experience themselves as distinct agents with personal styles and dispositions ("cheerful," "quiet"). In contrast, American subjects responded to contextual cues with a more concrete interpretation of self. For them, trait terms lose some of their meaning in the contextual format, (for example, "at home I am usually open with my brother"). Abstract processes occur in both cultures but serve different ends—different experiences of being a person.

A study conducted by Trafimow, Triandis, and Goto (1991) provides additional confirmation of the priming effect on the sampling of private versus collective self. In this study American and Chinese students were primed to sample either a private or a collective self. The priming effect was introduced by asking participants to think of what makes them different from others—a private self—or what they have in common with others—a collective self. Subjects then responded to a self-description questionnaire, and their responses were coded either as idiocentric or group related. Results demonstrated both cultural and priming effects. American students gave more idiocentric responses than did Chinese students. In addition, subjects who received the private-self prompt made a greater proportion of idiocentric responses than those who received the collective-self prompt.

The Self as Related to Patterns of Communication

Cultural variations, and in particular variations in values and cognitive frames, shape different self-concepts. The private self dominates cultures that have individualistic values, cognitive styles of field independence, and low-context orientation. The collective self is modified through social transactions and is more prevalent in collectivistic cultures with cognitive styles of field dependence and high-context orientation.

In individualistic cultures the private self has an existence apart from the society, whereas in collectivistic cultures the collective self acquires its meaning through relations with others (Gudykunst et al., 1988). For example, the Chinese concept of human is *jen,* or *jin* for the Japanese. This term reflects the individual's interaction with his or her fellow human beings (Hsu, 1985). Terms like "good man" (*hao jen*) or "bad man" (*huai jen*) mean that one's behavior is good or bad in relation to others. Self-esteem of members of collectivistic cultures is shaped through interaction with other human beings.

Collective and private selves are two dimensions of the self, but their salience varies across cultures. In Japan a distinction is made between *tatemae,* which corresponds to the public self and entails behavior that is open to observation by anyone, and *honne,* which corresponds to the private self and refers to mental processes that are unobserved by others (Tedeschi, 1986). Behavior corresponding to the public, collective self is more prevalent in Japan and China than behavior corresponding to the private self.

The collective and the private self are expected to enhance different patterns of communication. The collective self is shaped through interactions with others. This process of shaping one's public self is known as "facework" (Gudykunst et al.). "Face, in essence, is a projected image of one's self in a relational situation. It is an identity that is conjointly defined by the participants in a setting" (Gudykunst et al., 85). In collectivistic cultures the self is maintained through the active negotiation of facework, whereas in individualistic cultures the self is often defined as an intrapsychic phenomenon.

Ting-Toomey (1988) developed a two-dimensional model of facework maintenance: self-face concern versus other-face concern, and seeking association-positive self versus seeking dissociation-negative self. Self-positive face (SPF) employs communication strategies for inclusion and association. Other positive face (OPF) elicits communication strategies to support the other person's need for inclusion and association. On the other hand, self-negative face (SNF), and other negative face (ONF) enhance communication strategies for maintaining freedom and autonomy.

Face negotiation reflects cultural variation in values and cognitive styles. Individualistic cultures are concerned with self-face maintenance, the protection of personal autonomy and control over oneself and others, reflecting negative-face needs. On the other hand, collectivistic cultures are concerned with other-face maintenance, and they value positive-self needs of inclusion. In high-context cultures face negotiation is more ambiguous, and every face-support or face-violation has a strong social impact.

Cultures modify the cognitive frames that influence communication. Communication style and patterns of decision-making and of conflict resolution differ across cultures. Certain combinations of cultural characteristics are more likely to occur than others. For example, collectivistic values are associated with cognitive frames of field dependence, high-context orientation, and the dominance of the collective self. Individualistic values are associated with cognitive frames of field independence, low-context orientation, and the private-self. The former combination promotes an implicit communication style, more emotional than rational, with an emphasis on group decision-making, conflict avoidance, and concern for other-face maintenance. The second combination of cultural dimensions promotes an explicit style, more rational than emotional, with an emphasis on individual decision-making, confrontation, and concern for self-face maintenance.

The Reciprocal Relationship Between Culture and Communication: The Case of Japanese Corporations

Advocates of the third approach view communication and culture as reciprocally influencing each other (Erez, 1992; Gudykunst, Ting-Toomey & Chua, 1988). Gudykunst et al. advocate the reciprocal approach but, in fact, focus on a one-way path from culture to communication. Erez adopts the reciprocal approach for examining communication patterns in Japanese corporations. The reciprocal approach proposes that the communication network forms the connecting links among group members, transmits social values, and facilitates value sharing. Conversely, shared meaning and values facilitate the flow of communication. Shared communication mechanisms and shared meaning are the essence of collective action (Donnellon, Gray, & Bougon, 1986). A strong culture is developed through a high level of agreement and shared meaning among all members (Wiener, 1988). Conversely, a strong culture facilitates the smooth flow of communication by improving the mutual understanding of the coding system of communication.

These reciprocal relationships have been studied extensively in Japanese corporations. Japan is known for its long tradition of group-oriented values, the strong need for affiliation, and emphasis on interpersonal communication (Hofstede, 1980a). Odaka (1986) proposes the concept of "groupism" to describe the Japanese set of values. Groupism refers to the priority given to continuity and prosperity in the organization as a whole. Conversely, the organization is duty-bound to all of its members' needs.

The codes of behavior operating in Japanese society, whether rural or urban, are guided by the following values of groupism: (1) lifelong membership; (2) selfless devotion to the community to ensure its continuity, prosperity, peace, and happiness; (3) discipline and seniority-based rank to maintain social order in the community; (4) harmony and concerted effort through cooperation; (5) concern for the person's total welfare: peace and happiness in the life of the group cannot be achieved unless its members' needs are satisfied; and (6) authoritarian management and participative management. The elderly hold the highest status and positions in the community; however, all important decisions are taken in council with all members participating. The elders' duty is to pass final judgment on the results reached by the council. Responsibility for implementation of the decisions is borne not by individual members but by the group as a whole.

The strong emphasis on groupism is supported by the high value given to consensus, harmony, and cooperation. All these are essential for maintaining the group. Even the individual self in Japan is defined in relation to others rather than as distinct from others, as in Western societies (Kume, 1985; Triandis, 1989b).

Groups serve as the unit of analysis in Japanese society. The basic unit is the father-son dyad called *ie,* the household. A more complex level is the *dozoku,* consisting of a principal household with branches (Nakane, 1967). It is a goal-oriented corporation concerned with the results of its activities and with its own definite perpetuation (Hsu, 1975).

The urban counterpart of the *dozoku* is the *lemoto.* It is basically a system of school organizations of arts and crafts. The curriculum includes flower arranging, tea ceremonies, judo, painting, calligraphy, dancing, Kabuki, and so on. *Lemoto* is a family system, with the master regarded as its head. The master exercises supreme control, and his dyadic relationships with his students are analogous to the father-son relationship. The interlinked hierarchy of the *lemoto* is similar to the relationship between the principal household and its branches. Disciples are interlinked with other disciples through their masters, who are in turn interlinked through senior masters. In this way a vast structure is built up. This hierarchic pattern characterizes Japanese society at large. It dominates the father-son dyad, the relationship between the inheriting son and his brothers and sisters, between the principal household and the branches, and between the master and his disciples.

The symbiotic interrelationships between social structure, value system, and communication network have existed throughout the history of Japanese society, up to the present. During the Edo era (seventeenth century), Japan comprised a large number of fiefs—villages inhabited by patriarchal families forming close-knit communities with a common destiny. The members of the community were completely bound to it for the duration of their lives. The combination of close-knit relationships, geographical proximity, and ownership of the land helped preserve the group-oriented values which have dominated Japanese society.

Japan's group-oriented values and communication system is modeled on that of the large mercantile houses—originally family businesses—that emerged in the eighteenth century and preceded the period of industrialization which began in the nineteenth century. Here the tradition of close-knit relationships was reflected in lifelong employment, seniority-based hierarchy, apprenticeships, training and discipline, harmony, consensus, and group decision-making.

Modern Japanese corporations adopted the cultural values of the society at large and developed their communication patterns accordingly. Erez (1992) examined the communication patterns in ten large Japanese corporations by conducting thirty-seven in-depth interviews and by analyzing official documents and publications. A content analysis of the interviews lead to the following findings. The Japanese system of corporate management is guided by the following principles: lifelong tenure; compassionate concern for employees, including their personal problems; participative management and group responsibility; a decision-making system that operates from the bottom to the top known as *ringi;* emphasis on harmony; a seniority-based reward system; a combination of both authoritative and participative management; standardized training to ensure uniform competence; job rotation to produce generalists; and employment not confined to the employee's specialized work functions. These values are clearly reflected in the intensive corporate communication system which encompasses top-down, bottom-up, horizontal, formal, and informal channels of communication, as presented in Figure 6-1.

Top-Down Communication

The hierarchical order that exists in Japanese society at large is extended to the work place. Japanese employees show respect to their top managers even outside the job premises (Odaka, 1986). There is strong emphasis on face-to-face communication, including the relationships between top-level managers and rank-and-file employees (Triandis et al., 1988). It is common practice for nonmanagerial employees to talk directly to top-level executives on work-related matters (Kume, 1985). In addition, there are occasions when the president of the company himself meets with the employees and talks directly to them. These inspirational talks are aimed at strengthening the organizational culture and work ethic. For example, a series of talks by President Sono Fukujiro of TDK in 1981 covered topics related directly to the work environment, such as "Being Creative" and "The Smart TDK Man," and themes concerning family life and society in general, such as "The Ideal Couple" and "Japan's Aesthetic Culture" (Erez, 1992).

The personal approach of top-level managers is also demonstrated by their active role in selection interviews, in orientation courses for new employees, and in training programs. This direct top-down communication serves a dual purpose: first, it emphasizes the importance of the subject matter under discussion; secondly, it demonstrates the high consideration top management has for its employees.

A strong emphasis is placed on information sharing and on shared meaning and understanding, which enhance the formation of a strong culture. This emphasis is reflected in the procedures of admission and training. All newly hired employees participate in an introductory program for a period of up to six months during which they rotate assignments in the various departments and become acquainted with different organizational functions (Takagi, 1985). The experience provides them with a general overview of the organization and helps to familiarize them with the

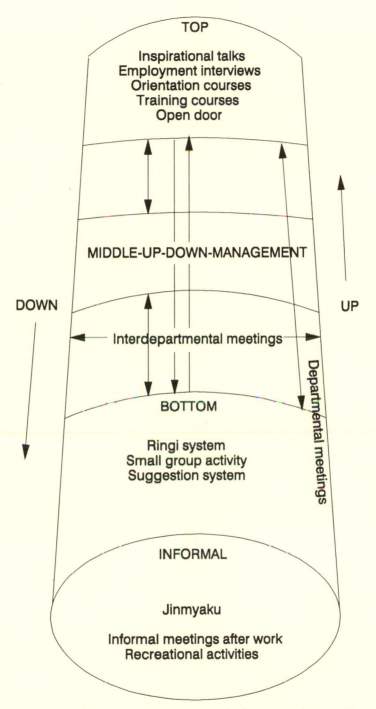

TOP

Inspirational talks
Employment interviews
Orientation courses
Training courses
Open door

MIDDLE-UP-DOWN-MANAGEMENT

DOWN

Interdepartmental meetings

UP

BOTTOM

Ringi system
Small group activity
Suggestion system

Departmental meetings

INFORMAL

Jinmyaku

Informal meetings after work
Recreational activities

Figure 6-1. Model of Japanese corporate communication system (SOURCE: Erez, 1992)

137

specific "language" of each department to enable them to communicate fluently throughout the organization once they have settled down. New recruits attend special courses and lectures on the various aspects of the organization, some given by top-level executives, including the president. At Hitachi, for example, the introductory program involves an orientation course, visits to some of the company's major factories, three-months instruction in manufacturing sections, and a twenty-month advanced program that includes on-the-job training, classroom study, and voluntary self-development courses (Hitachi, 1986).

The importance of the training system is emphasized by its position in the organizational structure. At Hitachi the president assumes chief responsibility for education throughout the company and is supported by committees that identify the training needs of the employees. The training system serves as a formal channel of communication that helps the employees adjust to their jobs and to technological changes. The socialization process facilitates cultural adaptation by the new employees, and the training process supports and strengthens the organizational culture.

Bottom-Up Communication

These channels of communication convey the belief in group harmony and in the joint responsibility of all group members for the successful operation of the organization. It is manifested in several forms.

The *ringi* system is a decision-making process initiated at a low-level managerial position. The idea itself may originate with a high-level manager, but a subordinate undertakes to develop it further and prepares the draft as a basis for the decision. The written proposal is circulated among the different levels for approval, each member affixing a stamp of approval called *hanko,* indicating basic acceptance. The number of *hankos* varies according to the number of people who would be affected by the decision and are involved in the process. Simultaneously, there is a process of preparatory communication through informal discussion and consultation (*nemawashi*). This process reflects the spirit of consensus and takes place before the formal proposal is presented at the official meeting (Ballon, 1988; Kume, 1985; Odaka, 1986; Takanaka, 1986).

Small-group activity involves teams of about eight to ten employees engaged in problem-solving and implementation of solutions. The most popular form of small group activity is the quality control (QC) circle. Its purpose is to increase productivity and improve the level of quality through direct participation. Each group begins by selecting a specific goal and each group member has a role in its attainment. The problem is analyzed and its causes are identified. Solutions are sometimes sought with outside help. Once all members understand what has to be done, the solution is carried out and the results are checked. Results have official recognition, including awards. QC circles solve problems of quality improvement, work efficiency, overhead reduction, safety, and so on (Canon, 1987).

The intangible results of small-group activity include a strong sense of security, acquisition of interpersonal skills, and the development of a knowledgeable workforce. The experience QC leaders gain improves their capacity for leadership and, in the longer run, enhances their chances of promotion. Small-group activity in Japan continues to survive due to strong support by top management and a supportive culture, fostered by such special events as competitions, kick-off conventions, prizes, intra- and extramural publications, and nationwide participation in quality circles.

Suggestion System

This communication system enables individuals to put forward ideas for improvement. Their suggestions are examined and ranked according to their level of contribution
by the evaluators who also provide feedback. Awards are granted annually, and the best proposals rate a special presidential award. For example, in Canon an all-expenses-paid two-week tour of overseas plants is granted for the best suggestions.

Middle-Up-Down Management

This form of communication serves to bridge the gap between the visionary but abstract concepts of top management and the experience-based concepts originating on the shop floor (Nonaka, 1988). The role of the middle level consists of generating information by integrating the strategic macro-level with its hands-on micro counterpart—the deductive top-down process with the inductive bottom-up process. In addition, it provides a horizontal link across specialties, such as research and development, manufacturing, and marketing.

Formal and Informal Horizontal Communication

On the formal level horizontal communication involves departmental and inter-departmental meetings. These meetings serve several purposes: to announce work goals in public and increase the level of commitment to publicly set goals; to monitor group members' activities; to provide mutual feedback; to stimulate new ideas; and to coordinate activities.

Interdepartmental meetings, for example, serve the purpose of developing new products. In Pfitzer, a pharmaceutical company, the development of new products is jointly discussed by representatives of the R&D center and the manufacturing and marketing departments. The joint discussion ensures that the proposed product has a potential market and that the cost of development and production can be offset by the market price. This procedure enables the company to avoid possible pitfalls due to lack of interdepartmental communication. Departmental and interdepartmental meetings facilitate the development of a strong organizational culture and of a smooth flow of communication across departments.

Informal meetings among peers is another form of horizontal communication. Several times a week employees who work together meet for drinks after working hours. These meetings are basically social but also serve as an exchange of information and ideas—sometimes as part of the small-group activity or *nemawashi* process referred to earlier.

The companies encourage the social communication network since it contributes to the smooth flow of information, shared meaning, and mutual support in decision-making. Again, informal communication channels strengthen the culture which reciprocally facilitates the flow of communication.

A unique form of informal communication system in organizations is the *jin-myaku*. It is defined as the connection among people belonging to the same group or the same series of groups in the political, business, and academic worlds (*Dictionary, 1974*). *Jinmyaku* represents a hierarchical array of informal networks across groups within and outside the organization that facilitate the exchange of information and provide mutual support (Takezawa, personal communication, 1988). In this sense, *jinmyaku* follows the traditional social structure of the *dozoku* and *Iemoto*. *Jinmyaku* is sometimes formed among graduates of the same school and becomes exclusive and out of bounds to outsiders. In this case it is known as *gakubatsu* (Matsui, personal communication, 1990). Members of a *jinmyaku* help one another in obtaining promotion and support each other's decisions. In conclusion, belonging to a *jinmyaku* is a symbol of security and status. There is actually a saying, "Know-who is more important than know-how."

The closest analog to *jinmyaku* in Western organizations is mentoring, in which a senior helps a young employee make his or her way in the organization (Olian et al., 1988). However, these mentor-employee relationships are purely dyadic, whereas in Japan *jinmyaku* is a social network. Surprisingly there is no specific mention of this term in the Western research literature on Japanese management, although the phenomenon was described by Drucker, who felt unable to characterize it properly: "It has no name—the term 'godfather' is mine, not theirs" (1971:120).

Interorganizational Communication Networks
Communication in Japanese industry encompasses both intraorganizational and interorganizational networks. The latter form is characterized as a network economy (Lincoln, 1990). The economic networks in Japan are institutionalized. Identifiable industrial groupings, called *keiretsu* (Gerlach & Lincoln, 1990), are formed around vertical and horizontal networks. The vertical network consists of a hierarchy of suppliers and distribution outlets beneath a large, industry-specific manufacturer. The horizontal network is clustered into economic groups involving manufacturers, trading companies, large banks, and insurance companies. These large groups provide their members reliable sources of loan capital, a stable core of long-term shareholders, and a partially internalized market. The *keiretsu* systems operate by means of strong social bonds and obligations to manage and coordinate transactions. A similar system of economic networks exists in such collectivistic cultures as Korea and Taiwan but not in individualistic Western countries.

The interorganization communication networks strengthen the shared meaning and cultural values on a macrosocietal level. The Japanese market can be viewed as concentric circles form the inner level of the work group through the level of organizational units, corporations at large, *keiretsu,* and Japanese society at large. The communication network serves as the glue that binds Japanese society together and interlinks the Japanese corporations with the society at large. The Hitachi company book is titled *Introduction to Hitachi and Modern Japan*. This title symbolically represents the ties between the corporations and the society at large. The collective identity of the individual employee is developed through interactions with others while Japanese corporate identity acquires its meaning in relation to the society at large.

The Japanese case demonstrates the reciprocal relationship between cultural values and communication. Cultural characteristics shape the patterns of both intra- and intercorporate communication. The communication system facilitates the sharing of cultural values by the participants, which in turn further strengthens the corporate culture and employees' commitment to corporate goals. The implication for Western organizations is that effective communication relies on the congruence between the cultural values and the communication system. In the West companies often attempt to apply managerial practices and communication systems that have been proven successful in other cultures. Such appropriated methods may be ineffective if they are incongruent with the organizational culture. Changes in the communication system should be carefully adjusted to fit the cultural environment (Hofstede, 1980b; Jaeger, 1983; Lincoln, Hanada & Olson, 1981; Odaka, 1986; Takanaka, 1986).

An interesting case in which a group decision-making process was adjusted to fit an individualistic culture was implemented in such American companies as Boeing, IBM, and Marriott (Kirpatrick, 1992). This method, known as Groupware, allows a group of people to participate in a decision-making process through the keyboard and the computer screen, as illustrated in Figure 6-2. All participants communicate at once by typing in their ideas and comments, sending them simultaneously to the computer screens of all other participants, and at the same time, receiving on their own personal screen ideas and comments from all other participants. This form of communication saves a significant amount of time, up to 90%, and allows all participants to share ideas and influence the decision-making process. Companies that implemented the Groupware method reported a significant improvement in the quality and productivity of meetings. They found that groups were able to reach a

Figure 6-2. Illustration of computer-based communication system (SOURCE: Kirkpatrick, 1992)

genuine consensus, and their members became more committed to decisions than they would have been with conventional methods. It is concluded that cultural characteristics should be identified in order to adjust communication methods to a particular work environment.

COMMUNICATION ACROSS CULTURES

Patterns of communication style, decision-making style, and conflict resolution vary across cultures. The cultural characteristics which shape the communication pattern are values, cognitive styles, and self-concept. Communication stimuli activate attitudinal and behavioral responses. Since communication stimuli are processed and interpreted according to cultural characteristics, their effect on behavior is moderated by culture. The same communication stimulus may elicit different responses in different cultures.

It is reasonable to ask whether cultural differences in cognitive frames interfere with a smooth flow of communication. In reference to Weick's (1979) concept of equifinal meanings, we suggest that communication across culture may continue because dissimilar interpretations may lead to similar behaviors. Furthermore, action (typical of individualistic cultures), social affiliation (typical of collectivistic cultures), and ideas are interrelated; the intersection among them serves as a common denominator for a continuous exchange of communication.

In action-oriented, individualistic cultures, what a person does influences who the person is and which groups he or she is able to join. Similarly, in people-oriented cultures, who the person is and which groups he or she can join depend to a great extent on what the person does. In Japan, for example, the leading industrial companies admit only job applicants who are affiliated with ivy league universities. However, affiliation with a leading university depends on one's academic achievement. For Americans, the fact that someone graduated from a prestigious university is an indication of his or her academic achievement. However, it also means that the person is affiliated with an ivy league university. Thus, people in two different cultures can ascribe different meanings to the same phenomenon and yet end up making the same decisions.

In a similar vein one could argue that ideology and reality are mutually dependent. The ten commandments, which serve as the infrastructure of many juridical systems, were originally developed to enable the continuous existence of human society. Yet many religious laws were modified and given different interpretations over the years, in keeping with the changing reality. Since the essence of both ideology-driven cultures and pragmatic cultures is to maintain the continuous existence of the society, they may end up making similar decisions for different reasons. Furthermore, different ideologies may lead to similar actions. For example, in 1977 President Anwar Sadat initiated a peace agreement with Israel to restore the honour of the Arab nation and reclaim the Egyptian territories occupied by Israel, even though most of the land was desert. Israel accepted the agreement because peace was of utmost importance to the Israelis, more so than the occupied Egyptian lands or the pride of the winners. Both countries signed the peace agreement but perhaps for different reasons.

Cross-cultural differences in communication have a direct effect on any activity that requires joint efforts across cultures. A necessary condition is the shared ability to encode and decode rules. One way to develop an understanding of the cultural coding system is through training (Triandis & Albert, 1987). An effective training program enables the participants to acquire general principles which guide their behavior in specific situations. The present conceptual framework can be used for identifying the key variables that need to be included in a training program on communication. We identified the relationships between values and cognitive styles, as well as the relationships between these two cognitive frames and the self, and between all three and communication patterns. A training course developed in accordance with this framework will help the participants to learn deductively how to communicate across cultures in specific situations they have not faced before.

7

Group Dynamics

As we have argued in earlier chapters, people do not work within a social void; rather they interact and are interdependent upon others as they work and behave in an organization. People work together so as to perform various tasks (e.g., assembly of an automobile), but they work together for social needs as well. In chapter 4 we provided extensive discussion concerning the crucial role of the collective to human interaction. In this chapter we apply our cultural self-representation model to the dynamics of the social group with special attention to applications in work settings such as participative decision-making, sociotechnical systems, and work cooperatives.

Given the prevalence of groups, it is clear that they are an essential element in understanding intercultural aspects of behavior. Our lives are organized around such groups as families, work crews, religious societies, and sports teams. Much of what we do for business and pleasure revolves around the group. This is not to say that all of our behavior occurs within a group context; many of our actions occur within aggregates rather than natural groups. As we will define shortly, groups are psychologically and sociologically distinct from casual aggregates of individuals. Whereas a group has specific qualities involving roles, structure, and so on, aggregates simply refer to a collection of individuals who gather for individual purposes and needs (e.g., an audience at a movie). We can think of individual behavior as distinct from group behavior as well. We perform actions for our individual needs in an individual context such as purchasing a favorite dessert, playing solitaire, watching a movie on television alone, and so on. These behaviors do not constitute group behavior nor does their explanation fully apply to the dynamics of a group. Thus our focus is on the social context of work behavior in which individuals gather to perform some task or maintain intragroup stability and relations.

We know that the study of groups in intercultural settings has yielded interesting similarities and differences among group types. For example, the famous studies of Asch (1956) concerning conformity and social influence have been replicated in a number of cultures and societies. In his classic paradigm, Asch examined conformity effects by having individuals judge the length of one line relative to another. A subject initially made a judgment concerning the relative length of the line after which he or she was placed in a room with other "subjects" (confederates). The next phase involved the "subjects" reporting that one line (the shorter one in reality) was longer than another one contrary to the real subject's earlier judgment. The conformity effect is reflected by the subject's second judgment and the extent to which it falls in line with the other "subjects'" judgments. This basic study has been replicated in a number of countries (as we will discuss in more detail later) demonstrating conformity effects. Findings suggest that conformity effects are observed to a similar degree in many different cultures (e.g., United States, Germany, Japan, Brazil), and it is typically found that 30–35% of the subjects conform to the group standard.

Group research also has been applied to the study of work teams as they develop and evolve (Hackman et al., 1975, 1989; McGrath, 1984; Gersick, 1988, 1989; and Guzzo & Waters, 1982). In recent years there has been a call to understand the dynamics of group development. It has been claimed that such understanding cannot be gained within a laboratory context (Goodman et al., 1986). Ironically such critics often neglect the cultural context from a societal viewpoint, focusing instead on the "culture" of the organization itself or emergent norms within the group as if they arise independently of cultural context. As we will argue, this assumption is as damning to the study of "real" groups as the use of a laboratory context. Neither intervention (laboratory versus culture-ignorant field) demeans the study of work groups; rather they impose limits on theory generated from such approaches.

Out of many recent theories of group interaction the first to provide full consideration of dynamic groups and the concept of the self is the approach by Tajfel and Turner (1986) and their colleagues (Turner, 1987) called Social Categorization Theory (SCT). We will discuss this approach at length and use it as a basis for integrating our cultural self-representation theory within current work on group dynamics. Where it falls short is where we intend to extend and refine it, namely, the integration of cultural context and various alternative needs that shape the self.

We begin our chapter with an overview of the concept of a work group and a brief history of the field. We will emphasize work from the fields of psychology and sociology, although our emphasis will remain primarily psychological. Next we will review recent trends in the study of groups, including the work emerging in organizational behavior. As we will discuss shortly, current research efforts are intended to capture "real" group dynamics, but these efforts are still deficient from a cultural viewpoint. Another shortcoming that we will discuss is the heavy individualistic orientation reflected in current work, even in such approaches as Misumi's research (1985) on the study of leadership behavior in Japan. After presenting our conceptual model and explaining its significance for the study of groups in social and work contexts, we will apply our group model to a number of application domains, including conformity and deviance, group decisions, social motivation, and work teams.

DEFINITION AND BRIEF HISTORY

Definition

Needless to say, a full review and history of research in group dynamics is not our intention. We wish to present a general background for the reader in order to provide a context for our model. The research literature on groups is voluminous. The interested reader is referred to such recent reviews of group research as Brewer and Kramer (1985), Moreland and Levine (1987), Messick and Mackie (1989), and Tajfel (1982), as well as books by McGrath (1984), Turner (1987), and Zander (1983), among others.

There are many definitions of a group and how it differs from an aggregate. McGrath defines a group as a social aggregate that involves mutual awareness and potential mutual interaction. He uses families, work crews and task performance teams, and friendship (or social) groups as examples of groups. He emphasizes that groups differ from other social aggregates in their potential for mutual interaction. McGrath (1984) argues as follows:

For an aggregation to be a group, it must include two or more people, but it must remain relatively small so that all members can be mutually aware of and potentially in interaction with one another. Such mutual awareness and potential interaction provide at least a minimum degree of interdependence; that is, members' choices and behaviors take one another into account. Interdependence, in turn, implies some degree of continuity over time: these relationships have, or quickly acquire, some history, and some anticipated future. A *time-based, mutual interdependence can reasonably be termed "dynamic."* In other words a group is an aggregation of two or more people who are to some degree in dynamic interrelation with one another. . . . [T]his definition of group would normally include families (at least the residential unit core), work crews, and many social or friendship groups, but would normally not include units that fit all of the other kinds of aggregations in that list (cultures, communities, organizations, etc.).

Thus McGrath distinguishes a group from other types of social aggregates based on three dimensions: size, interdependence, and temporal pattern.

Turner et al. (1987:1) take a somewhat different view of a group. They define a psychological group as one that is a source of reference for its members, who subjectively compare themselves to others in the group and adopt their norms and values. When individuals accept membership in a group, it influences their attitudes and behavior. Turner et al. distinguish the group from other social aggregates by viewing an individual's attachment to the group as a reference point rather than mere membership. However, their definition is not restrictive in size or temporal considerations, as is McGrath's, and they even discuss crowd behavior as a manifestation of "group behavior." Thus, Turner et al.'s definition can be applied to social aggregates of various sizes as well as at various stages of group formation. This aspect of their definition is appealing for our model since we wish to look at an individual's group memberships at various levels in society and across time frames.

Recently a number of definitions of groups have emerged that focus on the cognitive aspects of group membership (Messick & Mackie, 1989). Cognitive representations of groups consist of complex, hierarchical structures that contain such elements as category labels, attributes, and exemplars. A category representation refers to a category label (e.g., college professor), an abstracted prototype (list of features such as old and grey, beard, glasses, befuddled), and the projection of these characteristics to the group as a whole (stereotype). For example, Linville's (1982) multiple-exemplar model argues that category and abstracted stereotypes are used as a basis for forming judgements about the nature of groups. Researchers have used these models for the study of groups, and in particular, the study of individual's judgements concerning existing groups.

From a cultural viewpoint, Mann (1980) points out a number of interesting features of "natural groupings." A natural group is one that exists of its own accord rather than as the result of a laboratory manipulation. What is important about such a group is that it helps us understand the relevance of culture and society in a more direct fashion than through the use of laboratory or ad hoc groups. Although we may take a position of slight disagreement with this stance, Mann raises a valuable point, namely, that natural groups offer more direct generalizations to mature groupings found in society such as family units, long-term work groups, and so on. However Mann does not specify what constitutes a natural group nor when an ad hoc group becomes a natural group.

Based on these definitions, we adopt the major facets of McGrath's and Turner et al.'s definitions. A group refers to two or more individuals who interact directly or indirectly for the accomplishment of a common goal. Additionally, a group shares a common set of beliefs and values, and these characteristics form the basis for membership, although selection into (or out of) a group is not necessarily a voluntary action on the part of a member. For example, an individualist may choose to leave a family group (e.g., sever all ties with a critical parent or disown the family), whereas such an option does not exist for a collectivist (Triandis, 1988; Triandis et al., 1988). Our definition does not require an aggregate to be a particular size or age for it to constitute a group, although groups will vary qualitatively according to these dimensions. Our definition requires that we consider the nature and structure of a group separate from the individual members. This final point seems necessary since much research on groups takes an individualistic perspective focusing on individual needs and motives (Turner et al.).

Group Research: Historical Perspective

The earliest work on groups can be traced to LeBon's (1895) work on crowd behavior. LeBon viewed the dynamics of a crowd as a psychological attachment based on mental unity among group members. According to this view, crowd behavior is distinct and inferior to individual behavior in that crowds are driven by emotion and a collective mind that relies on base motives and reactions. Three processes guide the emergence of a crowd mentality: deindividuation of personality, contagion, and suggestibility. As a crowd forms, an individual becomes an anonymous player with a reduced feeling of responsibility. Emotions and irrational impulses that spread through a crowd rapidly and are accepted by others provide the opportunity for contagion. Interestingly LeBon argued that a mob might be constructive as well as destructive since its primary characteristic is one of impulsiveness rather than maliciousness. Thus a properly guided crowd might demonstrate heroic and altruistic actions on behalf of the collective instead of the violence often thought to be the outcome of crowd behavior.

Triplett's (1898) studies of social presence is often cited as the earliest experimental work in the study of group influence. Triplett examined human performance characteristics of bicycle racing and found that the presence of competitors was sufficient to stimulate a particular individual's performance. This finding was one of the first documented studies of social motivation, namely, a social facilitation response.

McDougall (1908) considered the group as reflective of a paradox of social life. Although the group lowers the mental processing of individuals to those of the brutal and impulsive crowd, it is only through participation in society that people can rise above it and fulfill their true potential. He argued that a society is comprised of the relations among the minds of individual members and that "the individual minds which enter into the structure of the group mind . . . do not construct it; rather, as they come to reflective self-consciousness, they find themselves already members of the system, molded by it, sharing in its activities, influenced by it at every moment in every thought and feeling and action. . . . [T]his system . . . does not consist of relations that exist external and independently of the things related, namely the minds of individuals . . ." (McDougall, 1921 as quoted in Turner, 1987:7). Thus a group was thought to possess either good or bad characteristics, but it clearly transcended the mental functioning of the individual.

According to McDougall, the nature and complexity of groups increases as its development increases. This view suggests that a group is more complex and stable to the extent that individuals share common foci of attention, emotional reactions to those foci, interdependence of mental processes, and an awareness of one another's mental processes. He argued that these collective minds are more stable and sophisticated than the more primitive crowd.

A rather different approach to the study of groups was proposed by Allport (1924) in his work on a stimulus-response approach to groups. In essence Allport viewed a group as nothing more than an aggregate of individuals who could be fully understood through the individual. He argued that a group context might be viewed as a particular kind of environmental context that influences an individual's behavior. A group context might be thought of as an antecedent condition for an individual's behavior much in the same way that a physical context (e.g., finding oneself in a large, open stadium and being tempted to shout to hear an echo) might elicit particular behaviors. Perhaps the most crucial aspect of Allport's approach was the devaluation of the concept of a group; a denial of the group as an entity that transcends the individual. For example, Allport's theory of social facilitation posits that the presence of others performing an action similar to oneself acts as an antecedent social stimuli that aids in the release of a previously learned behavior. Thus the group's influence on an individual is not an emergence of new behavior but simply the enhancement of an individual's behavior.

Research on groups that was later adopted and applied within a cross-cultural framework was pioneered by Asch, Lewin, and Sherif in their work on social behavior. The earliest work was conducted by Sherif (1936) in his studies of group influence and perception. He studied the nature of group influence on conformity using on optical illusion referred to as the "autokinetic effect," or apparent movement of a light source in the absence of visual reference points. He found that when several individuals were placed together, their judgments of light movement tended to converge on a collective judgement and that these supraindividual judgments have a subsequent effect on an individual's personal mental structures. Using a Gestalt perspective he argued that the entire experience field had properties that transcended individual parts. Rejecting Allport's reductionistic view of the group, Sherif stated that "the properties of any part are determined by its membership in the total functional system" (84).

Perhaps the most important abstraction from his view for our thesis is that judgments and evaluations are relative to a frame of reference from the perceptual field. This suggests that judgments such as temperature are relative to a reference frame (e.g., the authors of this book differ greatly concerning what constitutes cold weather since they live in very different climates—temperate Israel versus frigid Minnesota). He also argued that individuals have their own internal frame of reference conveyed through societal norms and values, customs, fashions, and so on. Thus an individual's sense of self is derived through a shared value system. In Sherif's view, "Values are the chief constituents of the ego. . . . These values are the social in man." (185).

Asch (1951) provided further elaboration that the group transcends the individual. He argued that the social relations observed in a group do not exist within the mind of an individual; rather they are processes that take place simultaneously and are interdependent. The group becomes real and interactive as individuals are capable of mutual reference, seeing their relations to one another as part of a common social field. In his studies of conformity (to be discussed later) Asch found that the social field has an effect on an individual's judgements. This finding has been replicated in a number of different cultural contexts.

Lewin (1951) proposed a field theory of social action in which an individual is exposed to a number of forces such as group influence, task context, and so on. The total field encompassing the forces on an individual is the "life-space," and the individual and the group constitute an interdependent system. His definition of a group as an interdependent system of individuals forms the basis of his work on social norms, leadership styles, and cohesiveness. In his classic study on participation in decision-making, Lewin found that the emergent group norms resulting from participative interactions changed the behavior of individuals more easily than the use of individual-based persuasion. He established that an individual's behavior is a function of the person and the social environment—the result of social and psychological forces tied to group membership.

What is clear from the Gestalt influence found in Sherif, Asch, and Lewin's work is that they understood a group to be a dynamic system that is more than the sum of its individual members. As opposed to Allport's individual-based approach to the study of groups, these theorists viewed the study of groups as an interdependent system. This approach provides an important integrating mechanism for understanding the interplay of individual behavior within a group and societal values and norms. Thus the individual approach taken by early researchers does not provide an adequate way to integrate cultural influences into group dynamics without an excessive reliance on stimulus generalization.

Recent Emphases on Groups

The historical view of groups emphasized motivational approaches that stress the role of attitudes toward one's own group and those of others in maintaining individual self-esteem and image (Brewer & Kramer, 1985). The focus has been on the role of the individual and his or her attachment to the group as well as on the structure and stability of the group. The primary features of group formation and maturity are identity, interdependence, and social structure (Cartwright & Zander, 1968; Turner, 1987). The identity component refers to a collective awareness among group members that they constitute a distinct social entity. The group must be able to identify itself as unique and feel that its members share a common identity. Interdependence within a group allows members to maintain their interactions with one another. Finally, a group must have a social structure such that interactions become stabilized and regulated by role and status differentiations and members come to share social norms and values that prescribe beliefs and attitudes relevant to the group.

A number of emphases in recent literature are relevant to our work. The motivation-based approaches described by such early theorists as Sherif and Asch have been displaced by more cognitive approaches. The work of Thibaut and Kelley (1959) can be viewed as an initial step in this direction in as much as they described a theory of social exchange based on the cognitive processing of utility considerations. As the wave of excitement continued concerning cognitive orientations in the field of psychology and its applications for the study of groups, increasingly cognitive approaches emerged. In as much as our intent is not to present an overview of group research, we will illustrate current trends that relate to our model of culture and work.

New theoretical models of group formation and development and of intergroup relations have emerged. As we described earlier, a number of models draw upon social cognition, more specifically schema theory, as a basis for describing group formation and membership. For instance, Linville (1982) proposed the multiple-exemplar model in which prototypes or exemplars are used to classify individuals into particular groups. Judgments about a group are made by retrieving and integrating information about such exemplars as individual members. However research seems to suggest that Linville's model is not fully accurate. Park and Hastie (1987) found that judgments about the variability of individual outgroup members were unrelated to judgments about the group as a whole. From this it appears that individuals will sometimes think of groups based on specific exemplars, but this is not a completely determined process. Another shortcoming of the model is that most processing is thought to occur as a function of memory-feature comparisons rather than online processing, so it appears overly static (Messick & Mackie, 1989).

Tajfel and Turner's (1986) Social Identity Theory (SIT) provides a different framework wherein individuals' self-evaluations are shaped in part by their group memberships. Individuals will develop and foster a positive self-image by accentuating the positive attributes of their ingroup and the negative attributes of their outgroups. Tajfel and Turner's extensive research on intergroup bias often employs a methodology referred to as minimal group technique in which individuals are assigned to groups on a random basis. Their work demonstrates that an individual assigned to a group, even on a random basis, will discriminate in its favor.

The difficulty with SIT is to provide an empirical test of its basic tenets. One implication of SIT is that an individual's self-image will be enhanced as a result of intergroup comparisons. Oakes and Turner (1980) examined this proposition and found support for the self-image enhancement effects of outgroup discrimination. Yet subsequent research by Lemyre and Smith (1985) suggested that the Oakes and Turner findings did not reflect an enhancement of self-image (self-esteem in these studies was used as a surrogate for self-image); rather the classification into groups decreased self-esteem, and the outgroup bias restored an individual's self-image to a level comparable to the precategorization condition. Another problem with the model is illustrated in a study by Vanbeselaere (1987) in which subjects were cross-categorized into two subcategories. SIT offers little explanation concerning this situation, and it was found that cross-categorization reduced intergroup bias and discrimination. It remains unclear what role social identification and self-enhancement actually play in group processes.

An extension and generalization of SIT, called Social Categorization Theory (SCT), was proposed by Turner (1987). According to this model, people perceive themselves as belonging to a hierarchy of groups. At the most general level, people distinguish themselves from nonhumans; social groups are based on intraclass similarities and interclass differences. SCT proposes that (1) self-concept is the fundamental component of a cognitive system; (2) an individual's self-concept has many interrelated facets; (3) particular facets of the self are activated by specific settings; (4) cognitive representations of the self take the form of self-categorizations; (5) these self-categorizations exist as part of a hierarchical system; (6) self-categorization occurs at a minimum of three abstraction levels, namely, human versus nonhuman, ingroup versus outgroup, and personal self-categorizations that define and differentiate individual group members from one another; (7) self-categorizations at any level tend to form and become salient through comparisons of stimuli defined as members of the next higher level of self-category; (8) the salience of self-categorization leads to an accentuation of intraclass similarities and interclass differences; and (9) there is a functional antagonism between the salience of one level of self-categorization and other levels such that the salience produces perceived intraclass similarities and interclass differences at other levels as well. Further, Turner et al. assume that individuals are motivated to maintain a positive self-evaluation of self-categories through a comparison of their own and other members' characteristics with prototypes of the next higher level of categorization.

From our perspective SCT has several interesting features that can be used to describe cultural influences. Turner et al. argue that group formation can occur as a result of spontaneous or emergent social categorizations from the immediate situation. They can also occur as a result of some preformed, internalized categorization scheme available from such cultural sources as class, gender, and race. SCT does not provide much information concerning the latter antecedent of group formation, which is the focus of our model. The basic premise, that individuals use preformed categories in forming ingroups and making judgements about outgroups, is crucial for understanding group processes in various cultures. For example, Bontempo, Lobel, and Triandis (1989b) examined the relation between ingroup identification and internalization of goals using Brazilian and American samples. As we discussed in chapter four, collectivists will remain active within their ingroup even if it places great demands on them, whereas individualists will exit from a particular ingroup in favor of a less demanding ingroup under these circumstances. This suggests that the nature of group membership, what norms emerge for member behavior, varies across cultures and so must the critical features that define self-categorization and group formation. Thus the features defining self-categorization are likely to vary culturally.

Another criticism that can be raised about the validity of SCT for intercultural use is the lack, from an empirical vantage, of an adequate motivational basis for SCT operation. Turner et al. argue that self-categorization leads to perceptual distortions (increased ingroup evaluation and degradation of outgroup) and that this distortion leads to a positive self-image much in the same fashion as SIT argues. However SCT posits a tendency to maintain a positive self-image (and comparable image of other ingroup members) to the extent that the individual's categorization of self and ingroup match the prototype or ideal from the next higher level of categorization. Messick and Mackie's (1989) review of SIT suggests that enhancement of self-esteem is not a sufficient explanation of empirical tests of SIT (or SCT).

In the next section we will argue that self-enhancement is only one aspect of group membership; therefore SCT is incomplete in describing the motives underlying group processes. If we include self-efficacy and self-consistency motives, we gain a more thorough understanding of groups. The cultural significance of group membership is not addressed by traditional theories. For example, the nature of ingroup membership is largely dictated by cultural norms in collectivistic societies. Since these memberships are both preformed and stable, the group formation process described by SCT may be, in part, moot. The nature and precision (salience) of categorization may vary as well. To the individualist, ingroup membership is variable and categorizations may be quite "fuzzy," or ill-defined. An individualist who is asked if a friend constitutes "family" may be uncertain and judge the friend in terms of many characteristics before deciding. A collectivist may respond to the question with an immediate affirmation because his or her categorization of ingroup is more restrictive and well defined. We now turn to a discussion of our model of group processes.

GROUP ACTION MODEL

Overview

In keeping with our cultural self-representation theory, we have outlined a more specific model of group process within a cultural context, shown in Figure 7-1. The group model is an elaboration of our more general model, which is based on a general information-processing approach to behavior.

The model describes the antecedents of group formation as well as the interaction of group and task setting within an organizational and cultural context. The use of boxes that encompass process aspects of the model (e.g., cultural context encompasses all of the group processes) is intended to show that these effects are pervasive yet embedded. For example, group interactions are embedded in an organizational context, suggesting that an organization's managerial practices will influence group interactions as well. Decision-making in an organization renowned for participatory practices such as I.B.M. will differ substantially from a more autocratic organization such as AT&T (Pascale & Athos, 1981).

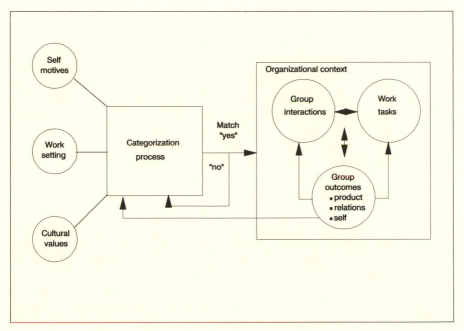

Figure 7-1. Group process model

Our model begins with a categorization process similar to that described by Turner et al. (1987) in their SCT model. We argue that categorization will vary on two dimensions: content of characteristics used in classification and the breadth of category items. These dimensions refer to a quality and quantity aspect of classification much like SCT, but we add another aspect: match certainty versus degree of "fuzziness" (McGrath, 1984). It is assumed that an individual will continue to search for group matches if a particular match is unsuccessful. Again, self-motives provide the basic impetus for individuals to seek out group membership.

If a group match is made, we enter the next phase of the model. We pose this second stage as the enacted group since this is where organization members perform their work. Group interactions consist of self-motives, roles and norms, social structure and power, communication patterns, and so on. The unique patterns of interaction, given a particular work or task context, constitute a blueprint of group performance. We argue that these performances show commonalities and consistent variation for given societies and organizations within societies.

The authors conducted a study (1987) of goal-setting methods (assigned versus participative versus representative) using one American and two Israeli samples (kibbutzim and urban subjects). The study consisted of a laboratory experiment in which subjects were asked to construct a class schedule for a student using a provided list of classes. In the assigned-goal condition subjects were provided with a specific and challenging goal for performance. In the representative-goal condition, a group of five subjects elected one of their members to represent them in a dyadic exchange with the experimenter to set a performance goal. The participative condition consisted of a five-person group discussion and decision concerning what the performance goal would be in the experiment. Among the findings it was noticed that the kibbutz sample consistently set low goals for themselves in the participative-goal condition. The subjects explained that they wanted to set a low goal to make certain that each member of their group would successfully achieve their goal. In the American sample the subjects in the participative-goal condition tended to compete with one another (*intra*group) and challenge one another to set difficult goals. In essence the American sample sought to push one another via the participative intervention, whereas the kibbutz sample sought to protect one another. The same managerial intervention produced markedly different group interactions as a result of intercultural variation.

The final aspect of our model is the feedback loop of group interaction outcomes. These outcomes include products of task performance as well as intragroup and intergroup relations. It also includes the self-evaluation of member drives and needs even though these are individual evaluations. We note that these outcomes may not be mutually compatible; they sometimes have unpredictable effects on performance and subsequent group interactions. For example, a highly task-oriented work group may insulate itself from others with the intention of being productive. This isolation, however, might be viewed as competitive or malevolent by interrelated work groups who might, in turn, isolate the group from needed resources. Eventually the once productive work group may become unproductive because it lacks resources from others. Thus, the feedback loops suggest that group outcomes will have a significant impact on a group's continuing existence.

These feedback loops also demonstrate that a group's outcomes will have an influence on a member's propensity to search for new group affiliations. If the outcomes suggest a frustration of self-motives (e.g., enhancement, efficacy, or consistency), then an individual will search for new affiliations in some cases. We add the qualifier "in some cases" because the evaluation occurs within the context of a given culture, and the choice to change group affiliation is not identical in varying cultural settings. An individualist whose self-motives are frustrated may change affiliations (or expand by adopting others), but a collectivist is not likely to do so; rather, he or she will try to change subsequent group outcomes to satisfy those motives. (Additionally, the self-motives of individualists and collectivists manifest themselves in very different ways. Whereas an individualist may satisfy a need for self-enhancement through individual glory, we would predict that a collectivist would do so through his or her ingroup's successes. Perhaps a collectivist will redouble efforts to aid the ingroup because he or she does not view changing groups as a viable alternative. The individualist does not view changing affiliations as a problem and, therefore, chooses to change groups to satisfy self-evaluation motives.)

Categorization and Group Formation

As we described earlier, we have adopted a general information-processing framework similar to one popular in the social cognition literature (Brewer & Kramer, 1985; Moreland & Levine, 1987; Messick & Mackie, 1989; Turner et al., 1987). Category representations can be thought of as a category label associated with an abstracted list of features representing a prototype for the category. This group-level information is derived from learning opportunities about a category that is not fully formed (Messick & Mackie).

Categorization does not occur in some deterministic or certain fashion. An individual's category contains central tendency, variability, and exemplar information. Upon encountering a new individual (or group), classification may be based on multiple criteria. When confronted with a categorization judgment (e.g., a person introduced to a novel work group) an individual will recall characteristics of an acceptable group and match the features of the new group with the prototypic group. The central tendency and variability information implies that an individual will consider possible deviations before a final categorization is formed. If an employee is introduced to a work group member who is judged to deviate from the work group as a whole, then he or she may not reject the group as an appropriate fit. As described earlier, Park and Hastie (1987) argue that the mixed model (including variability information as well as exemplars) is the most useful in predicting an individual's judgment of fit.

According to our model, categorization occurs as a result of several influences that affect category salience and content. First and foremost are the three fundamental motives of the self: self-enhancement, self-efficacy, and self-consistency. The relation of self-enhancement to categorization has been described in the literature through Tajfel's SIT model. Individuals will categorize an appropriate fit if they perceive that a given group will enhance their sense of self. This is reflected by a self-selection system whereby individuals seek out others who will reaffirm their own images. Further, an individual will accentuate positive attributes and derogate those held by the outgroup (but not ingroup) so as to maintain and strengthen this enhancement. In this sense, individuals are attracted to groups that will provide reaffirmation of their own traits. The second motive is that of self-efficacy, or personal development. Bandura (1986) argues that individuals seek mastery over tasks in order to build their sense of efficacy. Similarly we would argue that individuals will base their categorizations of others on the expectation that the group will provide them opportunities to develop their potential and efficacy. The self-consistency motive suggests that individuals will seek out groups (make categorization judgments) based on their desire to maintain a certain stability and continuity in life.

An important facet of these motives is that they may work in concert, independently, or even against one another at times. For example, an individual from a high power-distance culture (Hofstede, 1980; Hofstede et al., 1990) may categorize a highly hierarchical and authoritarian group as a good fit consistent with cultural norms of power differentials. However this group structure may not be appropriate for personal growth opportunities in which individual autonomy is needed. An individual's judgement of fit will be equivocal and will in the end be based on the self-motive(s) characteristic of a given culture. These motives may be complementary as well in an individual's categorization. For example, an individual from an associative culture (Glenn, 1981; Triandis, 1989b) will infer contextual and symbolic meanings in communication. If such a person encounters a highly egalitarian group that stresses free exchange and harmony, then it may be a good fit since the free exchange of ideas may provide a rich forum for expressing oneself. At the same time, this group may provide the individual with growth opportunities needed for self-enhancement. Thus, the motives of an individual may work together or independently, and the particular combination will reflect an individual's cultural background and personal experiences.

Another influence on categorization is the work setting as an element that makes group features salient. As Turner et al. (1987) discuss, attribute salience is a key determinant of feature matching. If we use our formation-processing approach, we see that a work setting can make various features of a group salient while suppressing other features. According to this view, when confronted by external stimuli, an individual will process this information by recalling related concepts (Wyer & Srull, 1980). External stimuli, combined with information stored in memory (often abstracted or in a prototypic form), inform an individual's categorization judgments; once activated these memories will be readily available for subsequent processing. The earlier information becomes easily accessed (or "primed") and is likely to be used in subsequent judgments.

The relevance of priming in a work context is that particular features of an individual's work may influence his or her categorization judgements. For instance, an employee whose work is very restrictive and routinized may seek out groups that are similarly structured and whose actions are predictable. However an employee whose routine work is oppressive may be very quick to shun a group whose members seem banal or predictable. We find indirect evidence for this from Salancik and Pfeffer's (1977) model of social information processing as well as subsequent work by others who argue that job characteristics are socially interpreted. Our model shows how the work setting, managerial practices, and the nature of the work itself tend to highlight particular characteristics that influence an individual's categorization judgments.

The final component that influences an individual's categorization judgements is cultural background. This feature is alluded to in various models of group formation (e.g., SCT), but it does not seem to receive formal integration. Turner et al. (1987) argue that one aspect of group formation is the internalization of some preformed, culturally available classification such as class, occupation, or race. Unfortunately, their theory does not address how these preformed characteristics come to be or how they might be changed by group membership, although they do argue that internalization can be likened to attitude change. They suggest that internalization of a group's preformed categories is similar to attitude change processes, with the categorizations being analogous to the cognitive or belief aspect of an attitude. Thus they argue that individuals will internalize a group's preformed categories as a result of attitude change brought about by persuasion, public commitment to positions, and so on.

This argument ignores the individual's own preformed characteristics based on his or her own culture. It does not consider the relation of person A (raised in culture A) to a group whose members are from culture B. A concrete example will demonstrate our point. A black Philadelphia business leader recently addressed a problem in community relations between blacks and their new neighbors from South Korea. It appeared to some blacks that the Korean shopowners were not showing them respect because, among other problems, the Koreans would not make eye contact with the customers. In black culture (as well as in American culture in general), avoiding eye contact is seen as a slight, implying that the person is not worth looking at. For Koreans eye contact between strangers is considered impolite and is reserved for closer relations. Similarly the Korean employees giving change avoided handing it directly to the customers since physical contact is considered an intimacy—particularly between female and male. These differences in preformed characteristics led the members of the respective groups to view the other as an outgroup; as a result, hostility and resentment erupted. Cultural background can influence the preformed categories of both an individual and an existing group.

We argued earlier that the nature of categorization judgements may differ as a function of cultural background as well as content. The fuzziness of categorizations is likely to differ according to cultural backgrounds. According to Triandis (1989b) individualists are members of many ingroups and flow between these ingroups, whereas collectivists have few but stable memberships (culturally determined in some instances). It is likely that the categorizations of individualists are uncertain and fuzzy, whereas those of collectivists are more clear and determined. Although Triandis argues that individualists move between ingroups if they place excessive demands on members, it may be that they move because they do not have a well-developed identity with their ingroups and move around as they search for an ideal fit. Collectivists may not change ingroup membership often because of social structure (unavailability of alternative ingroups) or because the memberships are so clearly defined that movement between groups is rejected.

As a result of categorization comparisons, an individual will choose whether or not to affiliate with a group. If he or she does not join a group then the search process continues to the extent that self-motives remain unsatisfied without group membership. Interestingly, it may be that a lack of available matches will stimulate an individual to seek individual actions that may satisfy such self-motives as learning a new language on one's own—for self-efficacy or self-enhancement—or maintaining present group memberships for sake of self-consistency. Assuming that the categorization indicates a good fit, we continue by examining the nature of group interactions within the group as well as with the work itself.

Group Interactions

Once a group has been formed and its members interact, a number of patterns can be observed. Although specific forms of interactions will be discussed in the final part of this chapter, we will address general forms and aspects of group interaction in our model.

Group interaction is guided by the individual actions of members in accordance with their self-motives. These motives not only influence formation but direct behavior within the group context. An individual who has a strong motive for self-consistency is likely to function as a group facilitator and help to maintain group harmony. Such a person is likely to engage in actions that facilitate interpersonal interactions and smooth out conflicts as they arise. An individual who has a high degree of self-efficacy motivation is likely to direct his or her efforts toward group performance since such actions enhance the sense of personal efficacy. The behavior of someone who has a strong self-enhancement motive will be directed toward attaining positive self-evaluative information. Such individuals will seek out information that reflects positively on themselves. This motive has been posited by Tajfel, Turner, and others as the driving force (and consequence) behind group formation and interaction. We argue that the intergroup bias observed in Tajfel's work with minimal groups may reflect the self-enhancement motives for group members.

SCT and SIT theories overlook the point that self-enhancement is not the only motive underlying group interactions (Messick & Mackie, 1989). We might expect dominant themes to emerge for each member, but their secondary motives will have an influence as well. For instance, an individual who is highly motivated toward self-enhancement and self-consistency may try to gain self-glory by developing the cohesiveness of a group. By securing a reputation as a great facilitator, the person receives recognition as an emergent leader and also maintains the continuity and stability of intragroup relations. Interestingly, an individual with this profile may choose to focus on intergroup competition so as to gain glory from the "battle" and secure a safe environment for his or her ingroup.

An individual's self-motives have implications for the stability of group membership as well. It seems reasonable that an individual with a strong self-consistency motive will tend to remain with an ingroup longer than one with a weak motive. Similarly an individual who has a strong self-efficacy motive may move among ingroups in order to maximize growth opportunities. The combination of individuals who have various motives merits serious investigation. We might speculate that individuals with various dominant motives will complement one another to ensure the survival of the group. Such a position is reflected in such theories of group process as Bales' (1953) two-process schema, the Bion-Thelen Interaction Theory (Bion, 1961; Thelen, 1956) among others. However if we assume that the motives of individuals vary as a function of cultural background, and that homogeneous groups are unhealthy for group survival, then we would expect systematic problems in group formation and development as a function of culture. For example, collectivists such as the Chinese who stress group harmony and have strong self-consistency motives should have difficulty maintaining stable and productive groups; yet this is quite counter to reality. We conclude that the composition of a "successful" group does not make a big difference, either because the secondary motives of members enable the group to survive or else the homogeneity/heterogeneity issue is just not relevant. Individualists might assume that heterogeneity is necessary for group success. A collectivistic view might argue that homogeneity is preferred in order that the group operate (in whatever fashion) as a unified entity rather than the pseudo-coordinated efforts of individuals who have their own agendas.

The next major aspect of group interaction concerns the roles that group members occupy as they interact. Our argument is that these roles have an emergent as well as predetermined aspect. The emergent component largely reflects an individual's self-motives, as we have just discussed. For example, an individual who has a strong self-enhancement motive may emerge as a group's leader so as to receive group attention. The position itself, however, will have its own constraints dictated by the social structure of the group. As a result a leadership position may provide ample opportunity for self-enhancement in an American work group but less opportunity in a culture in which individuals rotate the position as an expected duty (e.g., Israeli kibbutz). Emergent roles will reflect the demands of the task environment as well. If a particular task setting requires role differentiation (e.g., a team that works on assembling an automobile), these roles will emerge as the group copes with performance demands. Similarly roles will emerge as a group faces uncertainty in the general environment, such as conflict with other groups or technological change. If a group is confronted with strong intergroup competition, we would expect roles to emerge that aid the group in coping with the external competition.

Another important aspect of role formation in groups is the impact of culture on social structure. This is illustrated by an examination of leadership roles in various cultures. As we discuss in chapter 8, the behavior of an effective leader varies by culture. In a high power-distance culture (one that emphasizes an unequal distribution of power among superiors and subordinates), an effective leader is autocratic and dominant, whereas in a lower power-distance society an effective leader uses persuasion rather than domination to direct followers (Hofstede, 1980). Not only does the content of a leader's role vary according to culture but its existence may vary as well. In a society that stresses equality and participation a single leader may not exist; rather a group of individuals may share leadership. Not only the content but also the existence and patterns of roles will change.

Related to the question of roles is the social structure that encompasses those roles. If we view roles as interconnected in some social network (Barley, 1990; McGrath, 1984) then group interaction can be seen as regulated by this network. According to social network theory, the pattern of interactions among individuals in terms of the roles they occupy will largely determine their interpersonal relations and the outcome of interactions. The network of role connections tends to regulate intragroup dynamics, and these connections may be choreographed by cultural influences. In the famous *ringi*-sei system of decision-making in Japan (Misumi, 1984; Triandis, 1989b), consensual support for a decision is gained by informally testing the decision at increasingly higher levels of the organization in order that all affected members "buy into" the decision. The progression of the decision process is culturally dictated, and the lowest member in the chain has the role or obligation to move the decision through the system. Cultural influences on role structure are also evident in the contrast between the American and the Chinese (People's Republic of China) military. In the United States, uniforms, badges, and insignias, distinguish among ranks but in the People's Republic of China all uniforms are the same and differential insignias are not worn. (Through personal conversations with former Chinese soldiers, Earley learned that the lack of insignias does not mean that differences in uniforms go completely unnoticed. High-ranking officers often have a uniform made out of very fine cloth compared with those of infantry soldiers.)

Communication patterns similarly influence the nature of group interactions. Most of the early work on communication networks emphasized the impact of structure on group member satisfaction and group output (Shaw, 1978). In summarizing the findings Shaw suggested that the key to understanding communication networks is through the concepts of independence and saturation. The notion of independence suggests that individuals who are free of intragroup obligations are more likely to be satisfied with their group interaction, whereas individuals who are saturated by a large number of tasks and role demands, including message processing, will be less satisfied. In decentralized networks saturation is higher for simple tasks, and satisfaction and efficiency will suffer. This distinction between network types and load requirements is interesting but of limited usefulness since it fails to capture the impact of culture on communication networks. Networks that are highly centralized may be efficient but inconsistent with an individual's cultural background. A centralized communication system in an egalitarian society may alienate network participants (Hofstede, 1980). Productive efficiency may be low even in efficient networks if they disrupt expected interaction patterns.

Group interactions are influenced by the nature of exchange within the group as well. The most well-developed aspect of group process research has resulted from the exchange theories of Adams (1963), Homans (1958), Thibaut and Kelley (1959), Kelley and Thibaut (1978) and, more recently, from the procedural justice research of Lind and Tyler (1988) and Thibaut and Walker (1978). The basic proposition of social exchange theory (Thibaut & Kelley) suggests that individuals interact in such a way as to obtain "fair" exchanges in their relationships, and that these exchanges incorporate the perceived rewards and costs of interaction. Their interactions are governed by multiple principles, including maximization, risk minimization, satisficing, and so on.

A number of allocation rules may be used to predict exchanges among group members, such as equity, individual effort, equality, and need. Relevant to our model, the exchanges that occur within a group may be guided by several different rules or norms that vary according to cultural characteristics. Leung and Bond (1984) found that in collectivistic cultures equity or equality norms are preferred depending on whether one is dealing with ingroup or outgroup members. When dealing with an ingroup, their subjects (Chinese) preferred to use the equality norm for allocation and exchange, whereas in dealing with an outgroup they followed a strong equity norm. Tornblom, Jonsson, and Foa (1985) found that an equality norm was preferred over a need and equity norm for exchange in Sweden. Clearly the preferred exchange relationship varies as a function of cultural background.

A more recent development in the area of exchange relationships is procedural justice. The basic finding from this field is that the opportunity to present information relevant to a decision enhances judgments of the fairness of the decision-making procedure (Lind & Tyler; Thibaut & Walker). Research suggests that such "process control" enhances reactions to allocation decisions and performance even if the outcome is not determined by the person having process control (Lind, Kanfer & Earley, 1990). Although we will discuss this topic at greater length we note that several studies by Lind and his colleagues have produced interesting intercultural findings concerning procedures and exchange relationships. For example, Leung and Li (1990) examined the relation of cultural background to reactions to procedural fairness interventions and found convergence with Western findings.

The Group-Value Model, a theory forwarded by Lind and Tyler to account for a process control effect, argues that the opportunity to provide input into a procedure (even if the input has no influence on the outcomes derived from the procedure) has a positive impact on an individual's reactions to the procedures and outcomes. It is argued that this benefit occurs because the opportunity to provide input affirms that an individual is a full-fledged and valued member of his or her group. People value input opportunities which suggest that their views are worthy of being heard (230–40). We would expect cultural variations to influence what individuals expect, in terms of providing input ("voice"), as well as their satisfaction with it. In a highly collectivistic culture we might find that provision of input does not produce a strong return since such input is expected, whereas it may have a stronger impact in cultures lacking such opportunities (unless cultural norms are so severe that input would be aversive to the individual). Thus the nature of exchange in groups reflects cultural differences and similarities in allocation rules as well as procedural influences.

Group Tasks

There has been a great deal of work on the development of task typologies (e.g., Hackman & Morris, 1978; Laughlin, 1980; McGrath, 1984; McGrath & Altman, 1966; Shaw, 1973; and Steiner, 1972). A thorough overview of this work is available in McGrath (chaps. 5–11). We will briefly describe his categorization scheme in relation to our model.

McGrath uses a task circumplex having eight task types and four quadrants. The group task circumplex, presented in Figure 7-2, uses two fundamental dimensions—conflict versus cooperation and conceptual versus behavioral—and four processes—generate, choose, negotiate, and execute. The tasks in the circumplex range from planning (high generate and high cooperate with moderate behavioral) to contests or battles, competitive tasks (high behavioral, high execute, and moderate to high conflict). The dimension of conflict versus cooperation refers to the nature of intragroup and intergroup dynamics. For instance, an intellective task refers to intragroup cooperation, whereas mixed-motive tasks are most often marked by intergroup conflict. The dimension of conceptual versus behavioral refers to thought versus action. For example, problem solving is a conceptual task, whereas collective shouting used in social loafing research (Latane et al., 1979) is a behavioral task. The quadrants refer to generating ideas or plans, choosing among alternatives, negotiating outcomes, and executing actions. McGrath's circumplex is a useful way to describe task types and predict their relation to self-motives and culture.

Although management and production methods have been exported to other cultures from the West (and, more recently, from the East back to the West), there is clear evidence to suggest that group-work context varies across cultures. Perhaps the most dramatic example is the sociotechnical system of group work found in Sweden (Katz & Kahn, 1978; Rousseau, 1977). In the famous Saab experiment, methods of production were reorganized to support the work-group ethic emphasized by their collectivistic culture. It is important to realize that group interaction will vary

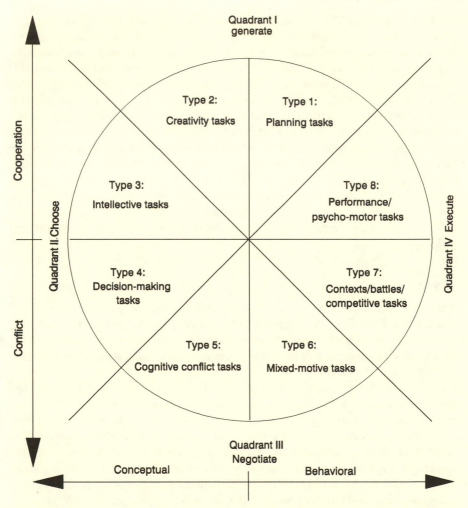

Figure 7-2. Group task circumplex (SOURCE: Figure adapted from McGrath, 1984:61)

according to the nature of the task undertaken and the cultural context. Indeed some researchers posit that task characteristics may be the dominant theme in group interaction.

Harnett and Cummings (1980) examined the impact of negotiation structure (number of participants), individual differences (trust in opponent), strategy variables (differences in opening bids), and national origin on negotiation behavior and outcomes using student and manager samples from several countries. Their key finding was that the bargaining behavior seemed to operate comparably, regardless of national origins, and they concluded that these structural variables may overwhelm potential cultural differences. This work, which we will discuss in greater detail in the chapter 9, illustrates that national differences may not emerge given the constraints of task considerations. (A problem with this particular study is that it overlooks the possibility that the demand for the task chosen may be a self-selection effect attributable to culture). Regardless, the task will strongly influence group interaction, but task selection may reflect cultural differences.

Group Interaction Outcomes

In our groups model, there are three basic types of group interaction outcomes: product, relations, and self-evaluation relative to motives. Research on group interactions often uses a product-interpersonal relations dichotomy, but we have added the self-evaluative component as well to reflect the self-concept aspect of our general model.

By "product" we refer to any tangible or intangible outcome produced by a group as a function of its interactions. Products can include physical output (e.g., automobile or computer-assembled products), behavior (e.g., a group march protesting government policies), and decisions or problem solving (e.g., group forecasting of market investments). These products reflect group interaction (interdependence), and they are intentional and directed toward group goals.

The nature of group interaction and output has been the focus of research for quite some time. Early work on social process argued that the presence of others facilitated the display of behavior (Triplett, 1898; Geen & Gange, 1977). This work was concerned with individual performance within a social context. More recent theorizing on group outcomes has pointed to a problem of group interaction resulting in a loss of output, or process loss (Steiner, 1972). It is argued that the coordination often lacking in group performance contexts reduces the group's efficiency. Instead work by Hackman and Morris (1978) suggests that groups will often begin working on a task without even planning a strategy for the effective coordination of their members. They argue that this process loss is not inevitable and can be overcome with proper coordination and group training. In fact groups might be more productive than a comparable additive function of individual members' efforts since members can learn from one and motivate one another.

A related group-performance phenomenon is called social loafing (Latane et al., 1979). This refers to the reduced efforts of individuals who perform as part of a group rather than alone (Harkins & Petty, 1983:153; Latane et al.). Individuals who believe that they are taking part in a task with others reduce their efforts, independent of any potential loss attributable to distraction or lack of coordination during actual group performance (Harkins & Petty). An individual may loaf because he or she assumes that the actions of others will ensure the attainment of the collective good (i.e., from greed) or, in anticipation that others will loaf, to avoid appearing the "sucker" (i.e., fear of embarrassment) (Kerr, 1983). Social loafing is related to such organizational concepts as the attainment of the public or collective good (Olson, 1971:14–15). For instance, Olson argued that, although group members may share an interest in attaining a collective benefit, they do not share a common interest in paying the cost of attaining the benefit (21). Individuals whose individual contributions are shared equally and unnoticed among the group have little incentive to contribute. Thus a self-interest motive leads to the dilemma of collective action; individuals withhold contributions to collective action in order to pursue personal interests. As a result the collective good may not be attained and the individual's self-interest suffers.

Olson argues that as group size increases and individuals' efforts go unnoticed, their feelings of dispensability increase. Since increased individual effort produces an inconsequential gain that is shared equally among the group, an individual loafs (redirects effort away from attaining the collective good) so as to pursue personal goals, thereby benefitting from both the collective and the personal good. Individual efforts are increasingly difficult to monitor as group size increases, therefore the social consequences for low effort are reduced and loafing increases.

The nature of group products will vary with the type of task undertaken. From a cultural perspective group products can be influenced by members' efforts, the strategy chosen, and their choice of task. As we will discuss in the next section, the effort of individuals in a group setting will vary as a function of culture. Gabrenya et al. (1985) and Earley (1989) found that social loafing was less prevalent (or nonexistent) in collectivistic cultures than in individualistic ones. Hackman and Morris (1978) point out that task strategies for a group may be preformed based on individuals' cultural backgrounds. It may be that groups from various cultures structure their tasks (or choose certain structures over others) according to their cultural preferences. Thus we might expect more reciprocally interdependent tasks in a collectivistic culture that stresses equality and participation and more sequential or pooled interdependence in an individualistic culture.

Another outcome of group interaction is the relationships developed within the group and toward the outgroup. A general outcome of group formation is intergroup bias and discrimination, as we have already discussed (Tajfel, 1982; Turner, 1987). Certain cultures accentuate intergroup differences. The positive side to intergroup relations is the relationships formed within a group. The bonds of friendship and loyalty to the group produce qualitative differences in intragroup relations. For example, Israelis display a form of blatant honesty. Good friends are quite willing to criticize one another in a truthful but abrupt fashion. Americans, however, will avoid such a direct approach, relying more on indirect cues. This does not mean that Israelis form "true" friendships and Americans do not (or vice versa). It does suggest that intragroup relations will manifest themselves in a variety of ways and that we can expect intercultural variations. Interestingly, a single dimension of culture is not always adequate for predicting these intragroup relations. For example, the Chinese and the Israelis are both collectivistic but the abrupt honesty of the Israelis would not be considered appropriate by the Chinese. Their emphasis on group harmony (Chinese Culture Connection, 1987; Hofstede & Bond, 1988), results in different manifestations of social behavior.

Another aspect of group interaction outcomes is the self-evaluation that occurs as a result of group activity. Individual members self-evaluate the group's interaction, product, and relations in order to assess their own motives and needs. Individuals who have a strong motive for self-efficacy will examine their own contribution to group products and assess their current efficacy expectations. In the case of self-consistency, individuals will focus on the functioning of the group within a given context across time (e.g., how the group is acting now compared with last week). In general individuals will assess their own self-motives as a function of group interaction.

Feedback Loops

Our model has two primary feedback loops. The first is the result of group interaction that leads to group outcomes, which, in turn, have an effect on subsequent interactions. This point seems rather obvious, but it is less clear how these interaction loops may differ culturally. If a group of American workers receives feedback on how well they have performed a task will this information impact them the same way it would a group of Chinese workers? On the surface we might answer "yes," but there is reason to believe that this will not necessarily be the case. From an information-processing perspective, it may be that individuals form different attributions as a function of their cultural backgrounds. In a superstitious culture, where luck or faith in supernatural forces is a strong attributional factor, group failures may be attributed to external forces. For example, the religious determinism associated with Islamic beliefs may lead to an attribution that outcomes are predestined as the "will of Allah" and impel a group to disregard preventive measures that could forestall unpleasant outcomes. Instead of adjusting their own performances, the group may rely on offerings to the gods and prayer. Thus, feedback may have quite different effects as a function of culture.

The second feedback loop focuses on group outcomes and subsequent group membership. Outcomes impact on an individual's desire and intention to remain in a group as well as the intention to seek out alternative group memberships. From our discussion of individualism versus collectivism we can see that this feedback effect will vary across cultures. In collectivistic societies group memberships are long-term and few in number, whereas in individualists cultures persons belong to multiple groups and freely move among them (Triandis et al., 1988). Feedback that suggests group goals have not been met or self-evaluations that are troubling may encourage an individualist to seek out new group memberships. A collectivist does not have the immediate recourse of changing groups if outcomes are unsatisfactory; rather he or she must continue this affiliation and work toward subsequent successes. For this reason we would expect that group membership stability in a collectivistic culture requires an emphasis on group structure and survival.

APPLICATION TO SELECTED TOPICS

In this section we will describe a number of different group processes and suggest how intracultural and intercultural research relate to our general model. Our listing of applications is not exhaustive; rather our intention is to present a number of illustrations, including conformity and deviance, group decisions, social motivation, and work teams.

Conformity and Deviance

The purpose of socialization is to induce individuals to conform to society's practices and to those of the group to which they belong. Organizations socialize their employees for much the same reason (Van Maanen & Schein, 1977). Conformity is an important element in social behavior and group membership.

Intercultural research on conformity often employs the Asch paradigm or a variant on it. Whittaker and Meade (1967) studied conformity in Brazil, Hong Kong, Lebanon, and Rhodesia. In three of the four countries the frequency of conformity was similar to Asch's results using American samples (31% to 34% of the subjects exhibited conformity). In the case of the Rhodesian sample (Bantu tribespeople), the subjects were very conformist (51%). Other studies conducted in Germany (Timaeus, 1968) and Japan (Frager, 1970) obtained conformity but to a lesser extent. The finding for Japan is particularly interesting since it is often assumed that the Japanese are highly conformist; Frager found only 25% conformity. One explanation for this finding is that the ad hoc groups used in the experimental procedure may not have captured the important ingroup–outgroup distinction (Nakane, 1970). In other words, nonconformity may have occurred because the subjects were placed among a group of strangers (Mann, 1980). In the case of Whittaker and Meade's work with the Bantu, the participants' familiarity with one another's background and heritage may have functioned as an ingroup identification.

Berry's (1980) work on subsistence societies offers an explanation for the impact of culture on conformity. He argues that high food accumulators exhibit high conformity because they have a high degree of interdependence. He further argues that conformity is tied to a society's economy and ecology. Berry found positive but somewhat mixed evidence for his approach (1980; Berry & Annis, 1974). Our model describes conformity effects from a more proximal framework, namely, an individual's self-consistency motive and attachment to a group. Simply stated, conformity is the result of an individual's desire to maintain consistency in his or her interactions with others and a propensity to maintain group membership.

The level of conformity observed in societies will depend on both factors. For example, a collectivist who has a low need for consistency may still conform because his or her propensity to maintain group membership is high. An individualist may have a lower need for consistency and less propensity to stay in a group; therefore we would observe less conformity and a higher likelihood that the individualist will leave the group should it apply normative pressure for conformity. Conformity is also a function of task. Tasks that promote high interdependence are likely to stimulate conformity as a way to coordinate members' actions. Perhaps the biggest shortcoming of conformity research has been the heavy reliance on the Asch paradigm. Subsequent research might well be redirected to observe the interactive nature of task, self-motives, and culture.

Group Decisions

The greatest influence on intercultural research on group decision-making has been Lewin's Field Theory (1951). The essence of his approach to that participation in the decision-making process will enhance individuals' acceptance of and commitment to a decision. In follow-up work using Lewin's framework, Misumi (1984) and his colleagues (Misumi & Haroaka, 1960; Misumi & Shinohara, 1967) have shown that the group-decision method is highly effective in inducing attitude and habit changes among Japanese workers. Consistent with the research on conformity, Misumi found that the participation influence was more effective using natural groups than ad hoc ones.

A more naturalistic form of decision-making for the Japanese work environment is referred to as the *ringi-sei* system (Erez, 1992; Kerlinger, 1951; Nakane, 1970; Triandis, 1989b). In this consensus system decisions are made "anonymously," and subordinates and leaders are bound together in obligations and loyalty. Decisions are made according to a bottom-up procedure whereby subordinates devise tentative solutions or decisions concerning a problem and proceed to "clear it" through the next level of superiors who adjust the decision and pass it on up. By the time the decision makes it to the top, it has been altered and endorsed by all individuals who will be involved in its implementation. This system reflects a strong self-motive of consistency and self-enhancement through group loyalty and commitment. It also reflects a ritualistic style of decision-making that reinforces a strong hierarchy within a particular social structure.

A second form of decision-making is the so-called "risky-shift" (Wallach & Kogan, 1965). It has been observed that individuals who band together in a group will make more extreme judgements than individuals who remain by themselves (Lamm & Myers, 1978) and that this effect is attributable to the presentation of new information (Burnstein & Vinokur, 1975) or social comparisons (Jellison & Riskind, 1970; Sanders & Baron, 1977). The shift in judgement has been found to occur in a risky as well as a cautious direction. If it results in a permanent opinion shift, it is referred to as attitude polarization (see Lamm & Myers, 1978, for a review). Turner et al. (1987) argue that the polarization phenomenon can be explained, in terms of their SCT model, as a shift in the direction of the most prototypic group member and who he or she represents; that is, members adjust their opinion in line with their image of the group position (conformity) and more extreme, preformed, and prototypical responses of this image. Polarization occurs as a result of the self-categorizations that create a common identity in a group.

We can use our model to expand on these findings. Self-categorizations reflect more than just a need for self-enhancement. The shifts observed in attitudes due to the choice-shift influence reflect self-categorizations according to our self-motives. For example, it has been argued that individuals shift toward risk (or caution, depending on cultural values) so as to appear highly capable (Jellison & Riskind, 1970; Lamm & Myers, 1978). Gologor (1977) examined this prediction in an intercultural context and found that a Liberian sample tended to make more cautious decisions consistent with their cultural values. This is consistent with both self-consistency and self-enhancement motives in a conservative (avoiding risks) culture. However we would predict that the self-efficacy and enhancement motives would be strongest for a high risk culture, resulting in more shifts toward risk, since these decisions will fulfill the growth opportunities sought by societal members. Choice shifts differ across culture not simply because of different cultural values but due to the interaction of culture and self-motives.

Social Motivation

Two aspects of social motivation are facilitation and inhibition. Social facilitation is illustrated by research on group presence (for an extensive review, see Geen & Gange, 1977) as well as more recent theorizing by Paulus (1984). Our model can be used to describe facilitation as a motivational manifestation of the self-enhancement and self-efficacy motives. The presence of others activates such concepts as self-image and individual competence since these "others" are observing the individual. The result of such social pressure is increased arousal that translates into enhanced performance for well-learned behavior or decrement in the use of novel behaviors. The desire to look good and bolstered efficacy creates an impetus to perform well. From a cultural viewpoint, we might argue that a facilitation effect will depend on the relative importance of self-enhancement, group membership, and performance norms. An individual who is culturally inured to group presence (e.g., an Israeli kibbutz member) may not experience the same degree of increased motivation as one for whom it is a cultural novelty.

Another aspect of social motivation refers to social loafing—losses in performance as a function of group interaction independent of process losses (Latané et al., 1979). A few studies of social loafing have been conducted in cultural contexts other than the United States. Gabrenya, Latané, and Wang (1983) reported loafing among Taiwanese school children in a study that replicated one by Latané et al. involving a clapping and shouting task. This result was in contrast to an earlier study by the same authors (1981) who found a facilitation effect for group-based performance among Taiwanese and Hong Kong graduate students attending United States universities. In their more recent study, the Gabrenya et al. speculate that the loafing effect may have occurred as an artifact of the sound-generation task. They argue that such a task may not have been sensitive to group-oriented cultural differences since the group members were not permitted to communicate with one another nor did they share a joint sense of purpose. Support for this alternative hypothesis was found in a subsequent study (1985) although the findings were not related to specific aspects of culture; instead they relied on national differences among the samples.

Matsui, Kakuyama, and Onglatco (1987) examined the differential impact of individual and group responsibility for work performance (though the study did not examine social loafing). They argue that the superiority of group-based versus individual-based performance in their study may be a function of the collectivistic background of their subjects (Japanese students). The collective orientation of the Japanese may have enhanced the sense of comraderie among group members. The hypothesis that social loafing is mediated by individualistic–collectivistic beliefs was tested by Earley (1989) using Chinese and American managerial trainees as samples. His results demonstrated that loafing effects occurred among the individualists (i.e., primarily the American sample) but not the collectivists (i.e., primarily the Chinese sample). He conducted a follow-up study (in press) using samples from the United States, Israel, and the People's Republic of China. Utilizing a process model of social loafing, he found that loafing did not occur among collectivists if they worked in the context of an ingroup, but it did occur if they worked alone or in an outgroup. Individualists socially loafed regardless of group membership, but they did not loaf in an individual performance condition. Further, Earley found that the effect of interaction within a group context (ingroup, outgroup, or individual) and individualism–collectivism on performance (loafing) was mediated by individuals' rewards for performing as well as their individual and group efficacy.

Our model suggests several explanations for these findings. Most obviously ingroup membership activates concepts of group survival and self-efficacy as described by Earley (1989, in press). Additionally ingroup membership is more effective in activating these concepts of survival and efficacy in a collectivistic as opposed to an individualistic culture, probably due to differences in self-categorizations associated with cultural norms (Turner, 1987). Thus an individual's response to the social context will not necessarily reduce his or her contribution to group efforts.

Work Teams

Intercultural research on work teams is sufficiently voluminous that any single overview would be inadequate. We will simply focus on a few major topics in order to illustrate our group model.

The use of individual-based versus group-based job design has received considerable attention (Davis, 1973; Hackman & Oldham, 1980; Trist & Bamforth, 1951; Tannenbaum, 1980). The focus of much of this work has been on the sociotechnical approach to job design (Rousseau, 1977; Thorsrud & Emery, 1970). According to this approach, an emphasis is placed on maintaining intact work groups by integrating the methods of production with the needs of a group. This allows group members more discretion in their work, more control over their nonwork activities, and so forth. The advantage of this approach for group-oriented cultures is that workers do not experience alienation. The basic features used in the famous Saab engine factory experiment (Tannenbaum) include: (1) assembly groups rather than assembly lines; (2) assembly of a whole engine by a group; (3) determination by group members how work is to be allocated within the group; (4) a cycle time of thirty minutes rather than 1.8 minutes that is typical of the assembly line; and (5) selection of workmates by team members. Rubenowitz (1974) provides a summary of several Scandinavian experiments in the sociotechnical system and reports favorable reactions to the system by managers and employees. This approach is clearly consistent with the self-motives of efficacy and consistency, reflecting collectivistic values of group unity and functioning.

For an individualist, however, self-efficacy and individual growth are achieved through individual accomplishment rather than group effort. This accounts for the popularity of Hackman and Oldham's Job Design Model (1980), which examines the redesign of work from an individual's perspective. As with its collectivistic counterpart, the merging of technology and work emphasizes human needs but focuses on such individual needs as personal autonomy and knowledge of results, rather than on group needs. Such an approach will be effective to the extent that it satisfies an individual's desire for personal growth.

Participation in goal setting has also received considerable attention. The impact of participation in decision-making and goal setting is an effective way to enhance group members' attachment to a goal. Work by a number of researchers (e.g., Earley, 1986; Erez, 1986; Erez & Earley, 1987; Matsui et al., 1987) has demonstrated that participation in goal setting has a positive impact on goal commitment and performance and that these effects differ somewhat across cultural settings. Our group model suggests that such intervention may satisfy self-consistency needs and reaffirm an individual's membership in the group. Participation also provides information concerning task strategies (Campbell & Gingrich, 1986; Earley, 1986; Erez & Arad, 1986) which acts to further satisfy self-efficacy motives.

Substantial research has been conducted on Japanese management systems that employ quality circles (Cole, 1980; Lincoln, Hanada & Olson, 1978; Tannenbaum, 1980; Triandis, 1989b). This approach to production emphasizes quality control (QC) techniques and opportunities for participation. Although some critics suggest that quality circle participation is coercive (Cole), the system does lend participants prestige and provides them occupation opportunities and limited financial incentives through bonuses. The basic principle of the quality circle is the provision of group-based suggestions for the improvement of the work environment and production (Cole). What is unique about the quality circle system is that it appears to enhance worker commitment and loyalty to an organization through a participative system of work involvement. Since QC is taught to all employees, manufacturing rejection rates are low and fewer product inspectors are required.

Using our model, we can identify a number of facets that apply to the quality circle principle, suggesting that it may be useful in various cultures (but for different reasons). The success of the quality circle technique is consistent with Japanese ideology. It reaffirms an individual's sense of group membership and provides an important self-efficacy opportunity for personal growth. It is effective because it provides Japanese workers with a growth opportunity within a group context (growth is tied to benefits for the ingroup). An important question for American managers is to what extent these methods can be adopted. Although American workers may not have as strong an ingroup identity as the Japanese, the quality circle technique may be useful if it enhances an individual's sense of growth (self-efficacy motive) and personal image (self-enhancement motive). Key to the successful use of quality circles is the understanding that both collectivists and individualists have similar self-enhancement motives; however, collectivists seek it through the group's welfare, whereas individualists seek individual growth potential.

SUMMARY

This chapter has focused on the development of a model of group formation and maintenance. We have provided a brief background on group research as well as a conceptual model for examining group processes in a cultural context. The model has applications for such topics in group research as conformity and deviance, group decisions, social motivation, and work teams.

The essence of group formation and membership is not a simple exchange of resources, as implied by early theories of group behavior. Individuals attach themselves to groups through a self-categorization process that involves a number of motives in addition to the self-enhancement benefit described by Tajfel and Turner's models of SCT and SIT. For example, collectivists form stable ingroups because they have a strong self-consistency motive, whereas the fluid movement of individualists among ingroups reflects a strong motive for self-enhancement and self-efficacy but a lower self-consistency motive.

In discussing the impact of group dynamics on outcomes we have distinguished among types of outcomes and tasks undertaken by a group. We would expect a certain degree of homogeneity among tasks, given the exportation of production methods across cultures; yet unique methods are evident as well. For example, critics argue that the success of the Japanese system is tied to the heavy American support of post-World War II Japanese manufacturing. If this were the case we would expect a strong similarity between Japanese and American methods of management. It is clear from extensive research on the Japanese system that the management techniques are quite different than in the United States and much of the Japanese success is tied to an effective blending of cultural background with production methods.

Our model demonstrates that group formation and processes are influenced by various self-motives that are culturally determined. The tasks chosen by groups, their approach to task performance, and the outcomes associated with group functioning will vary according to cultural values. Not only do different motives operate in group dynamics according to cultural background, but the same motives may manifest themselves in very different ways.

8

Leadership

Perhaps no topic within the field of organizational behavior excites and incites more than that of leadership. It is a topic that has long captured the imagination of theologians, historians, and philosophers, and much of history concerns vivid descriptions of such great military figures as Alexander the Great, Julius Caesar, Joseph Stalin, and George Patton as well as such political visionaries as Gandhi, Mohammed, Mao Tse-tung, and Karl Marx. We ask ourselves how these individuals led their armies, built their empires, and led their people. These questions have long been the subject of scientific work and our focus in this chapter is to provide some sense of how culture influences the leadership process in an organization. We begin our discussion with an overview of the construct of leadership.

Leadership is one of the most confusing terms that exists in the organizational behavior literature. It is a general term that means such things as power, authority, administration, control, and supervision, depending on who is asked. There are many definitions of leadership in the literature. In the most general sense, leadership involves a number of characteristics, including interactions among two or more people, a leader's intentional influence on a follower's behavior, and the movement of individuals according to some specified objective (Yukl, 1989). Some researchers refer to leadership as a perception that one member of a group has the right to tell other group members what to do within the group. Jacobs (1970:232) takes a more exchange-oriented perspective, defining leadership as, "An interaction between persons in which one presents information of a sort and in such a manner that the other becomes convinced that his outcomes . . . will be improved if he behaves in the manner suggested or desired." According to Roach and Behling (1984), leadership refers to the process of influencing a group's activities toward goal achievement. Burns (1978) contrasts transformational and transactional forms of leadership. Under transformational leadership, the role of the leader is to provide followers a growth environment in which both leader and followers will "raise one another to higher levels of motivation and morality" (20). In contrast, transactional leadership is concerned with the tangible goods and outcomes that followers might attain by following a leader. Burns argues that only in the case of transformational leadership is a bond between leader and follower established that may remain permanent.

Related to Burns's definition concept of transformational leadership is the charismatic theory of leadership. We will develop this distinction to a larger extent later in this chapter since it provides an important link between leader-follower relations and cultural context. Charismatic leadership refers to a leader's influence on the emotions, self-esteem, and self-concept of the followers. House and Singh (1988) make the following distinction between transactional and charismatic definitions:

> The difference between transactional theories and transformational or charismatic theories of leadership behavior lies in the components of the subordinate's motivation that are affected by the leader's behavior and in the specific behaviors of the leader that affect components of the subordinate's motivation. Transactional leaders have their primary effects on follower cognitions and abilities. Charismatic leaders have their major effects on the emotions and self-esteem of followers—the affective motivational variables rather than the cognitive variables. . . . despite some danger of oversimplification, transactional theories describe actions of leaders that result in work behavior becoming more instrumental in followers reaching their *existing* goals while at the same time contributing to the goals of the organization. In contrast, charismatic or transformational theories address the actions of leaders that result in subordinates *changing* their values, goals, needs, and aspirations. (101)

Thus we see that leadership is defined by the mediating processes through which it is assumed to influence a subordinate's behavior.

A current debate concerning the construct of leadership can be illustrated by the transactional versus transformational approaches, namely, the type of influence exerted. For example, Zaleznik (1977) argues that leadership and management differ; a leader determines the "right thing" to do (important to the followers as well as the organization), whereas a manager knows how to do the "right thing." Leaders are forward-looking visionaries, whereas managers carry out duties and responsibilities much in the same way as a technician performs a routine job (Bennis, 1989; Sashkin, 1988; Selznick, 1957; Yukl, 1989). This is a restatement of the distinction between supervision versus leadership described by Katz and Kahn (1978) who defined leadership as influence above what can be attained through organizationally derived power.

It is not clear that transactional and transformational approaches are as distinct as their advocates argue. Yukl (230–31) points out that charismatic leaders often provide their followers with tangible outcomes and that transactional leaders can instill an ideological commitment in their followers. The clear boundary assumed by the charismatic and transformational theorists, including Bennis (1989), Bass (1988), Burns (1978), Conger and Kanungo (1987), and House, Spangler, and Woycke (1991), among others, does not appear to be quite so firm.

Another limitation of this distinction concerns an implicit cultural bias that the "leader" should manipulate, guide, or direct followers' reactions much like a shepherd and flock. Such an elitist assumption is characteristic of Western thought, but it may be an erroneous assumption for other cultures. The popularity of charismatic and transformational theories in the Western literature (primarily the United States and Canada) seems to reflect a cultural theme—a "savior" or "great leader" who will bring Western societies to greatness.

The study of leadership has taken a number of approaches, including power-based, trait, behavior, situation, and contingency methods. The power-based approach focuses on how a leader gains and utilizes power to influence others. The trait approach focuses on those personal characteristics of a leader that are assumed to provide the leader with his or her ability to lead. Although this approach was used extensively from the 1930s to the 1950s, it failed to provide any traits that were consistently useful in identifying leaders from nonleaders. More recently the charismatic leadership theorists have relied on this approach in their work. The behavior approach attempts to identify leaders by focusing on the behaviors they engage in, resulting in the dimensions of initiating structure versus consideration (Fleishman & Harris, 1962), task- versus relationship-oriented (Katz, Maccoby & Morse, 1950; Katz & Kahn, 1978), performance- versus maintenance-oriented (Misumi, 1985; Misumi & Peterson, 1985), and concern for people versus concern for task (Blake & Mouton, 1964; 1982). This approach examines two dimensions of leadership behavior: a focus on the task and its effective performance versus a focus on the relational aspect of the work group. These distinctions bear a striking resemblance to Bales's (1950) categorization of small group functioning into group locomotion (movement toward group-goal attainment) versus group-maintenance functions (maintaining intragroup harmony and relational functioning).

The interactive approach that has received the most empirical testing and support is undoubtedly Fiedler's Contingency Theory of Leadership (1967, 1970, 1971, 1978). This model and others in this category focus on the interactive influence of person and situation in determining leadership effectiveness. Research using a contingency approach has taken a number of directions but two major groupings are apparent (Yukl, 1989:9). One examines how the leader's behavior interacts with the work setting to determine group effectiveness. The other considers how the setting influences the nature of the leader's behavior through role expectations, information-processing demands, and so forth.

In this chapter we will describe a general model of leadership using the principles derived from our Cultural Self-Representation Theory and the dominant themes in the literature. As might be expected, our approach will emphasize how cultural influences and self-concept magnify and clarify the leader–follower(s) relationship. It is our intent to highlight a number of different aspects of leadership in terms of cultural background as well as to describe some potential shortcomings of existing models that lack a pancultural approach. In addition we will provide a brief review of several leadership studies that address cultural issues. However our purpose is to develop new theory rather than to survey existing work.

BASIC FRAMEWORK OF LEADERSHIP

Overview

Our general framework, presented in Figure 8-1, is loosely based on Yukl's (1989:269) integration model. The model is based on three major focal points: leader, follower, and intervening processes. We represent these foci in an interrelated network embedded within a "cultural frame" or general societal context. The cultural frame does not refer to an organization's "culture"; rather we view organizational culture as inherent in the intervening processes. The cultural frame refers to

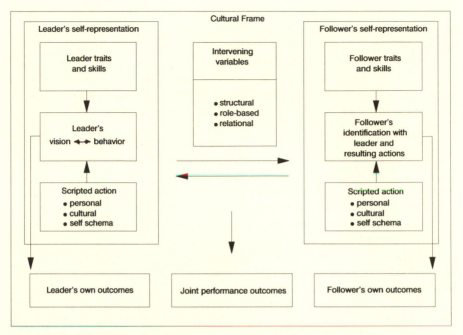

Figure 8-1. Leadership and cultural self-representation theory

the society in which the organization operates. Its influence pervades all aspects of leadership in the various relationships individuals form with one another.

The framework depicted in Figure 8-1 is an extension and elaboration of our general theory of cultural influence. The relation of leader to follower is determined by each person's self-concept and its relation to culture. For example, in a highly collectivistic culture a leader is perceived (and evaluated) to the extent that he or she moves a group toward valued goals. The attachment of followers to the leader hinges on the leader's importance for group success. In an individualistic culture an emotional bond is formed between the leader and follower. This relationship takes the form of an intimate relationship between the two, and the follower views the leader as a source of personal outcomes and recognition. The leader and follower's self-concepts help outline the nature of their interaction with one another.

We use the approach advocated by Lord and his colleagues (1985; Lord et al., 1978) in describing the information-processing aspects of the model. This approach utilizes script theory to describe how individuals interact with one another and how they behave in various settings. Many aspects of a leader's or a follower's behavior can be described using script and schema theory since many of the interactions between leaders and followers are routine or scripted. Even if we consider a dramatic example, such as John F. Kennedy's speech on American patriotism (emphasizing the individual's contribution to the country rather than the country's contribution to the individual), the setting, nature of presentation, and the behavior of the leader and his followers can be viewed as scripted. No one observing the president's speech needed to be told to remain quiet during its presentation (with the exception, perhaps, of some disapproving Republicans); nor did the president need to be told to use dramatic pauses to heighten emotional responses in the listeners. (We are not arguing that all leaders are able to enact their scripts as effectively as Kennedy but this does not negate the existence of the scrips.) The actions of leaders and followers are not as "free form" as many leadership theories would lead us to believe because the scripts and schemata have cultural as well as personal roots. Thus the impact of culture on leadership processes can be traced, in part, through a more thorough understanding of information processing (Lord & Foti, 1985).

With regard to self-concepts, our approach to leadership emphasizes both the leader and follower as important actors. A number of leadership theories have neglected such issues as empowerment, attribution, upward influence, and post-action rationalization. Current views appear to be myopic concerning the over-whelming importance of a leader's personality in producing joint outcomes (e.g., Bennis & Nanus, 1985; Conger & Kanungo, 1987). The dynamics of the follower's actions seem to be ignored in these models; a leader can only "lead" if followers provide such an opportunity. In our view, the actions of the leader and follower are unique and equally powerful and they produce collective as well as individual outcomes.

Another general aspect of our framework concerns the endemic nature of culture. We do not view culture as some antecedent or cause of leader/follower actions since this form of direct influence operates through the self-concept. The embedded nature of leadership within a general cultural context is reflected in the nature of the intervening processes, including structural, relational, and role-based aspects of the work setting. For example, the Japanese decision-making system refers to a struc-turally based style that has its roots in Japanese tradition (Misumi, 1985; Triandis, in press). It would be a mistake to view leadership in this system separate from the structure of decision making or to interpret the leadership style used in Japan as inherently participative since it is quite directive and paternalistic in many other respects (Misumi).

An important component of leadership concerns the nature of individuals' rela-tionships with one another. Such interactions are influenced by culture as well. Hofstede (1980, 1981) argues that power distance influences the efficacy of particu-lar leadership styles. He suggests that more participative styles are appropriate for cultures in which egalitarian values are dominant (i.e., low power distance). Bass's (1981) review of Margaret Mead's anthropological work suggests that leadership styles vary according to culturally based relations. For example, traditional Eskimo culture emphasizes equality among individuals, whereas Samoans view individuals as part of a hierarchy, which they enforce. Clearly cultural influences on how individuals relate to one another is a key aspect of understanding leadership.

Leader's Self-Representation

Traditional models of leadership emphasize motives, traits, and skills. We view a leader's self-representation as a function of individual traits and skills as well as scripted action and self-schema. This section will discuss the major influences that determine a leader's behavior.

The earliest models of leadership sought to identify the key characteristics of a leader. Based on an extensive review by Stogdill (1974), a number of traits and skills were identified. An effective leader is often thought to be adaptable, ambitious, aware of the environment, persistent, confident, and tolerant of ambiguity. The skills possessed by effective leaders include intelligence, creativity, organization, social skills, and persuasiveness. Stogdill offers the following generalized description of an effective leader:

The leader is characterized by a strong drive for responsibility and task completion, vigor and persistence in pursuit of goals, venturesome and originality in problem solving, drive to exercise initiative in social situations, self-confidence and sense of personal identity, willingness to accept consequences of decision and action, readiness to absorb interpersonal stress, willingness to tolerate frustration and delay, ability to influence other persons' behavior, and capacity to structure social interaction sytsems to the purpose at hand. (81)

A number of researchers have sought to identify the key traits associated with effective leaders. For example, the work conducted by Bray, Campbell, and Grant (1974) concerning American Telephone and Telegraph assessment centers identifies a number of skills associated with effective management, including oral skills, human relation skills, planning and organizing skills, and creativity. Additionally, they identify a number of traits, such as a desire for advancement, resistance to stress, tolerance for ambiguity, motivation, broad interests, self-set (challenging) goals, and a readiness to make decisions. In their findings these traits and skills alone did not guarantee success unless they were coupled with a situation that provided an individual an opportunity to develop the skills further, and he or she had a superior acting as a role model to demonstrate how an achievement-oriented manager should act.

In a review of assessment center work, Dunnette (1971) identifies six traits associated with managerial effectiveness: energy level, organizing and planning skills, interpersonal skills, cognitive skills, work-oriented motivation, and personal control of feelings and resistance to stress. Based on his review of several studies, Dunnette concludes that there is a great deal of convergence concerning these traits. Researchers at the Center for Creative Leadership (McCall & Lombardo, 1978) identify a number of traits for effective leaders by looking at "derailed" managers who advanced to middle management but failed to continue their rise in the organization. The traits associated with successful managers include emotional stability and composure (calm, confident, and able to handle crises), defensiveness (willingness to admit mistakes and accept responsibility to correct the situation), interpersonal skills (sensitive, tactful, and considerate), and technical and cognitive skills (broad work experiences and perspectives in handling a number of different problems).

Perhaps the most extensive analysis and development of a leadership trait characteristic is Fiedler's (1964) concept of least preferred co-worker (LPC). The construct of LPC has proven to be difficult for Fiedler's contingency model since it is still not altogether clear what it really is. The LPC measure is based on an individual's choice of bipolar adjectives to describe the co-worker with whom he or she would least prefer to work. Fiedler (1978) argues that LPC represents an individual's motive hierarchy, although Rice (1978) suggests that it is most likely an attitudinal measure. The low LPC leader is motivated by task objectives and emphasizes task-oriented behavior, whereas a high LPC leader focuses on affiliation motives and emphasizes interpersonal relationships. A secondary motive of interpersonal or affiliation concerns for a manager will only come into play for a low LPC leader if a task setting is favorable and structured. Similarly a secondary achievement motive will only influence a high LPC leader if personal relationships are strong among subordinates and peers.

As attention shifted from the person to behavior, research moved from personality to situational attributes. However, the understanding of cultural influences on work behavior can only occur through a knowledge of personality since it is through the personalities of the leader and followers that culture is manifested. Theoretical work by researchers such as Weiss and Adler (1984) has been very helpful in understanding the nature of personality in a work setting. It is through the personality patterns and preferences of followers that leaders may espouse valued symbols of culture. Thus if we understand personality patterns common to a group of individuals, we may better understand the cultural patterns underlying their society and how a given leader might influence their actions in an organizational context.

Recently a trait and skill approach to the study of leadership has rekindled interest in the personalities of leaders and followers. This approach is referred to as charismatic leadership. The concept of charismatic leadership is derived from Weber's (1947) use of the term "charismatic authority." Weber argues that this form of authority is not an inviolate trait of the individual; rather it refers to a transitory characteristic that emerges as a revolutionary force to reorient a system toward a new social order. He describes charismatic authority as derived from a faith in the leader's exemplary character rather than through formal rules and traditions. The role of the charismatic leader is to create and institutionalize new orders of rules, traditions, and procedures that eventually supplant him.

Weber distinguishes between charismatic and other forms of authority, e.g., traditional—an established belief in the sanctity of immemorial tradition—and rational–legal—a belief in the legality of rules. He posits that charismatic authority refers to control derived from a particular position within a social structure tied to qualities of the position holder. Eisenstadt suggests additional characteristics of charismatic authority: "In contrast to any kind of bureaucratic organization of offices, the charismatic structure knows nothing of a form or an ordered procedure of appointment or dismissal. It knows no regulated 'career,' 'advancement,' 'salary,' or regulated and expert training of the holder of charisma and his aides. It knows no agency of control or appeal, or local bailiwicks or exclusive functional jurisdictions; nor does it embrace permanent institutions like our bureaucratic 'departments' which are independent of persons and purely personal charisma . . ." (1968:20). Thus charismatic authority refers to an aspect of social structure in which a particular leader (elected or emergent position holder) influences the actions of followers.

More recent attention (e.g., Bass, 1985; House, Spangler & Woycke, 1991; Westley & Mintzberg, 1988) has focused on charisma as personality trait of particular individuals. For example, House et al. examined the biographies of U.S. presidents, contrasting the effectiveness of charismatic and noncharismatic leaders. They view charismatic leaders as ones who "articulate a mission or vision in ideological terms, demonstrate a high degree of self-confidence and a high degree of involvement in the mission, set a personal example for followers to emulate, create and maintain a positive image in the minds of followers, peers, and superiors, communicate high performance expectations to followers and confidence in followers' ability to meet such expectations, behave in a manner that reinforces the vision and the mission of the leader, show individualized consideration toward followers, and provide intellectual stimulation to followers" (1991:104–05). Although there are questions concerning their empirical procedures (e.g., the use of a small panel of expert raters whose judgements serve as the source of behaviors weakly linked to a rather broad and highly evaluative definition of charisma), the study illustrates that the charismatic leader is viewed as one who has a vision of some desired future state, empowers his or her followers, and provides challenging growth opportunities for his or her followers.

Perhaps the most relevant view of charismatic leadership from a cultural perspective is Sashkin's (1988) adaptation of Parsonian theory. Using Parsons' action framework, Sashkin argues that charismatic leadership can be thought of as a fundamental, internal aspect of value orientation. The charismatic leader is one whose work is "defining, constructing, and gaining commitment to a set of shared values, beliefs, and norms about change, goals, and people working together—that is, defining, building, and involving people in the organization's culture" (136). According to this view, the behavior of a charismatic leader depends on the existence of a shared culture between the leader and the followers. Although it may be possible for a leader to nurture and enhance general cultural values (as Sashkin and others suggest), we disagree with the idea that the charismatic leader shapes an organization's "culture" independent of general societal values. Thus the effective leader is one who can identify (or merely advocate) values that are shared with followers rather than assume a more proactive role. A corporate leader such as Iacocca was able to lead because he addressed themes and issues that were culturally relevant to his work force, not because he changed their cultural values. His emphasis on product quality did not instill new values in his employees (it seems ludicrous to assert that American automobile workers did not value quality work); rather he achieved these aims by tapping such cultural themes as improving oneself (self-efficacy concept) and pride in work (self-enhancement concept).

The view that a charismatic leader instills a vision in his or her followers is particularly important from a cultural perspective. The premise of all charisma theories is that a shared vision guides followers in their actions. What is not made clear is the relevance of underlying cultural themes in the creation of a leader's vision. An exception is the European approach to charisma theory. Kets de Vries (1988) uses a psychoanalytic approach in which he identifies underlying cultural themes that emerge as collective symbols. He argues that for leaders to be effective there must be a congruence between their own and societal concerns. The essence of the charismatic leader is a projection of personal struggles into a shared or universal concern which societal members (followers) try to solve collectively. For example, in an individualistic society such as the United States, a leader must struggle against the situation as an autonomous agent. An effective leader projects the image of an "underdog" among followers who then adopt the leader's struggle as their own. In a collectivistic society such as the People's Republic of China, the social relation of leader to follower (and social protocols) dominates the leader's attention. The collectivistic leader must struggle to maintain the social structure of his or her ingroup in order for it to confront external challenges. Individualistic and collectivistic charismatic leaders transfer struggles to their followers through very different mechanisms although both types of leaders rely on a personalized relationship with their followers.

One of the most effective ways charismatic leaders transfer these struggles to their followers is through myths and symbols. Kets de Vries argues that leaders are ideal recipients for the "crystallization of primitive and unstable identifications" as a result of transference (243). A charismatic leader becomes a group's ego and conscience to ease followers' anxieties, as well as the embodiment of their favored past relationships. A paternalistic leader assumes the role of father figure in a society that endorses a strong and controlling relationship among parents and children. The charismatic trait reflects different characteristics or themes across cultures. Thus the struggles of Gandhi represent relevant facets of Indian culture but not necessarily of American culture. Similarly the charismatic leader of one organization does not necessarily capture the hearts and minds of followers in a different organization. It might be argued that if culture were to entirely dominate leader characteristics, we would see no intracultural variation (e.g., across organizations from the same country). This is misguided; a single culture has many themes, and different leaders are likely to espouse different themes as a function of their unique experiences (self-schema and personal views).

The relationship of a charismatic's vision to cultural myths and beliefs is important since these visions are informed by culture and constitute a leader's self-representation. In our model we argue that the leader's vision and the behavior chosen to enact the vision are derived from self-representation. Given that cultural background helps shape the self, culture plays an important role as an antecedent to a leader's vision and acts as an integrator of leaders and followers. For example, a highly prominent managerial consultant from the United States is famous for his ability to stimulate business audiences to develop excellence in their organizations. His presentation taps into such cultural symbols and themes as the heroic entrepreneur, independence, and risk-taking, and his behavioral style includes dramatic gesturing, getting followers to become physically involved (clapping and shouting support). As a charismatic presence he uses cultural themes to legitimate his vision of the successful United States corporation and his behaviors are consistent with those of American society. Much to his surprise, a lecture tour in the People's Republic of China proved unsuccessful because he failed to realize that the cultural themes and physical gesturing that he relied on in the United States was no longer appropriate. The physical involvement of followers that the consultant relies on is considered to be quite rude by the Chinese. Managers are expected to be unemotional and restrained under such circumstances (Onglatco, 1990).

Much of the power derived from charismatic authority relies on qualities that followers attribute to their leader. These attributions of charisma are enhanced by a manager who can effectively invoke cultural myths and heroic deeds in accordance with followers' belief system (Willner, 1984:15). Some researchers (e.g., Conger, 1988) mistakenly argue that this is evidence that context is not as crucial as relational/personality dynamics. In as much as context is embedded in culture, we would assert that it is overwhelmingly crucial for understanding the effectiveness of a charismatic leader. Simply stated, charisma (in this usage) is not a personality trait but a label denoting the overlap of an individual's self-representation with cultural beliefs and the extent to which this overlap is consistent with followers' sense of self (Bass, 1988:57).

We have focused a great deal on the charismatic's vision and its relation to culture, but it is important to understand the implications of scripted behaviors if we want to predict leader behavior for enacting vision. Sashkin (1988:138–45) posits three major avenues through which vision is enacted: strategic, tactical, and personal.

A strategic approach refers to the development of a clear organizational philosophy that provides a leader the strategic goals to shape an organization's culture. (Our only dispute here is that a leader does not have free reign concerning the development of an organization's culture.) The emergence of charismatics and their approach must be rooted in the cultural tradition (Kets de Vries, 1988; Sashkin, 1988). The concept of participation based on individual input used in the United States may be inconsistent with the approach to participation used in a more collectivistic culture such as the People's Republic of China.

A tactical approach refers to the actual policies and programs used to enact vision. To be effective it is essential for these programs to involve middle- and lower-level management. As we will discuss shortly, such commitment hinges on a follower's self-representation.

The personal approach to enacting vision includes focusing the attention of followers on key issues, effective communication skills, demonstrating trustworthiness, displaying respect for followers, and taking risks rather than dwelling on failure avoidance.

Ultimately leader behavior will take many forms but it is consistent with cultural norms. Sashkin argues that risk taking is an important personal characteristic of a charismatic leader; yet such an assumption is erroneous for certain Asian cultures in which risk taking and avoidance are not dominant cultural themes (Hofstede & Bond, 1988). Similarly in a collectivistic culture the need to demonstrate trustworthiness is not salient since it is a definitional aspect of an individual's attachment to his or her ingroup. If we examine the facets of the self (viz. enhancement, efficacy, and consistency), it becomes clear that leader behavior will be directed by a desire to maintain the self. For instance, a leader in an individualistic culture such as the United States, whose vision includes helping employees develop their own potential, may provide employees with individual growth opportunities, even pitting one employee against another to "let the cream rise." This approach would not be successful in a collectivistic culture that stresses group harmony. More importantly, it is unlikely that a leader would enact an approach that violates the motive for self-consistency with cultural themes. Rather, a leader will develop visions and enact behaviors that are consistent with his or her past experiences.

So far our discussion suggests that a leader will search for, critically examine, and rationally enact particular behaviors that are consistent with his or her sense of self.

However this overly rational approach is unrealistic and ignores the schematic structure of the self (Markus & Wurf, 1987). The self can be represented as a hierarchical structure in which the most central traits of the self are superordinate and organized in schema along with procedural knowledge concerning how the world operates. Much of the behavior enacted by a leader can be understood if we consider how the self-structure operates in accordance with self-motives. An example of the self-organization of a leader is presented in Figure 8-2.

The example is intended to illustrate a simplified structure of a leader's sense of self organized around the cultural theme of collectivism. At the highest level, we have the cultural value itself, with a number of specific contexts in which the self operates. We might argue that the collective and public selves are most likely to operate within a family or ingroup setting. However these distinctions become blurred as ingroup structure extends to the work and societal contexts, as is the case of the collective self.

Within a work context a leader's endorsement of a cultural value, such as collectivism, manifests itself in specific cognitive structures, including beliefs about participation in decision-making, work-group structure, sociotechnical interventions, and so on. Our diagram highlights participative decision making as one exemplar of substructure. A leader's self-concept might include numerous beliefs associated with participation: (1) it helps employee grow, (2) it is just and necessary, (3) it reaffirms the leader's membership in society, and (4) it promotes a positive self-image for the leader by advocating values respected by society. The first two examples are related to a self-efficacy motive, the third example to a self-enhancement motive, and the fourth to a self-consistency motive.

A leader's beliefs and feelings inform the specific actions he or she will take to enact vision. For example, a leader may provide subordinates an opportunity to speak out on their own behalf or allow them decision control through the delegation of authority or restructure their work to provide them autonomy and control. The example we provided in chapter 2 concerning job-redesign efforts in the United States (individualistic) versus Sweden (collectivistic) illustrates how scripted actions relate to cultural frames. A leader from an individualistic culture will provide job restructuring that maximizes individual discretion and autonomy, whereas a leader from a collectivistic culture will provide restructuring that gives discretion to the group or collective. Leaders may share ideological concerns based on common cultural themes (egalitarianism) yet manifest those themes in very different ways since other cultural themes (collective versus individual focus) will influence the scripted actions as well. The unique experiences of a leader should also be considered. Our intent is not to argue that culture is the sole determinant of a leader's behavior and vision. There is no reason to expect two leaders who share a common cultural background to enact identical leadership behaviors, but we would expect to see consistencies in the underlying themes that drive these actions.

A leader's sense of self informs his or her behavior and particular vision of the organization. Taken together these factors contribute to outcomes unique to the leader as well as joint outcomes based on follower and setting characteristics. Before turning to the outcomes for the leader and followers, we describe the nature of the follower within our model.

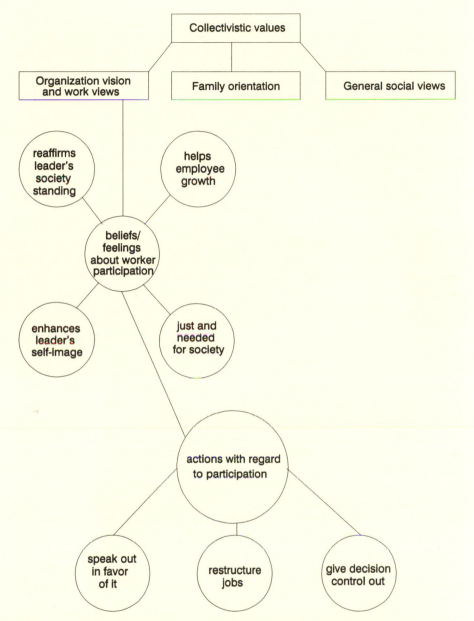

Figure 8-2. Schematic representation of leader's cultural values

Follower's Self-Representation

Followers have certain traits and skills that promote their commitment to a leader's vision and subsequent outcomes. In this section, we will describe these factors and how they influence a follower's commitments from the perspective of self-concept. We will argue that the commitment phenomenon does not merely reflect an individual's judgement of efficacy to contribute; rather it reflects a cognitive readjust-ment based on the challenges inherent in the leader's vision. Thus the more chal-lenging the vision, the more efficacious the follower will feel. Next we will describe the nature of scripted action and how this relates to cultural background as well as to personal aspects of the self. Finally, we will discuss the nature of follower identifi-cation with a leader and the leader's vision and how this may predict various outcomes.

The approach of many researchers to the study of leadership seems to take the followers as a given, that is, the role of the leader is to shape the followers as though they were clay. The strong theme of leader autocracy (so-called "take charge" style) espoused in North American societies is reflected in these approaches to leadership. For instance, path-goal theory (House, 1971) argues that the role of a leader is to clarify the uncertainties concerning how to produce and what the outcomes of production will be for the followers/subordinates. Graen's Vertical Dyad Linkage Model (Scandura & Graen, 1984) discusses the relationship of a leader to groups of subordinates who are "ingroup" or "outgroup." The model describes how the relationship of a leader to an ingroup member leads to the member receiving more discretion, better work assignments, higher attributions of competence, and so on. What seems to be less emphasized in these models is the active role of a follower in the development and maintenance of the leader–follower relationship.

Charismatic and transformational theories of leadership are guilty of the "passive follower" assumption as well. These models argue that the leader captures the mind and heart of a follower who comes to the leader's summons. Even the idea of empowerment suggests that the leader instigates some exchange that provides a subordinate with greater influence, as if it were a gift (Burke & Day, 1986). To their credit the transformational theorists such as Burns (1978) and Bass (1985) argue that the transformational process is an exchange between leader and follower. According to Burns, transformational leadership takes place "when one or more persons raise one another to higher levels of motivation and morality" (20). There is, however, an implicit assumption that this transformation takes place *because* of the leader and that the follower acts as a facilitator. (This point is axiomatic since the follower who instigates the transformation is, by definition, the transformational leader.) Etzioni (1961) makes this point even more salient by arguing that charismatic-like qualities are needed in organizations to induce subordinates to accept guidance and in making value judgements and decisions. He even argues that charismatic-like qualities are dysfunctional anywhere in an organization except at the top of a hierarchy (Etzioni 317).

In our model we argue that leadership is best viewed as an exchange between leader and follower. If followers do not accept and commit themselves to a leader's vision then the leader is ineffective. A critic might argue that if followers do not commit themselves to the leader's vision and/or goals then the leader is not truly a "leader." This argument, however, reminds us of the tautological definitions of "reinforcers" offered by the behaviorists (i.e., anything that increases the frequency of the behavior it follows is a reinforcer—not particularly helpful in a predictive fashion). We argue that a leader may be charismatic and still not stimulate a follower in a particular setting for a number of reasons. The role of the follower is proactive and not merely reactive. The follower also shapes the leader's vision based on his or her self-representation.

The primary influences on followers' identification with a leader are their self-enhancement and self-efficacy motives. These motives function together in shaping their actions and commitment to a leader. A sense of efficacy is determined, in large part, by past experiences (Bandura, 1986), that gave definition to an individual's skills and traits. These experiences also determine how individuals view themselves (self-enhancement). An engineer who has had a number of past experiences supporting her belief that she is a competent mathematician and logician will be more likely to commit to a leader's vision of developing a new system of computer chip fabrication using sophisticated mathematics than will an engineer who does not possess this same sense of efficacy. The underlying motive is that an individual will engage the environment so as to enhance the sense of self. Thus the mathematically inclined engineer is attracted to such a setting (likely to gain from other successes that will further enhance the self), whereas the less mathematically inclined engineer is repelled by such a setting. The leader's capacity to attract a follower is dependent on the follower's self-representation and desire to maintain a positive sense of self.

We can apply this logic to the other motives of the self. With regard to self-consistency, an individual's tendency to engage in similar patterns of behavior is invoked. Many leadership theories describe the difficulty a leader has in overcoming the inertia or apparent complacency of followers. Such inertia is not unexpected since it is a natural part of an individual's self-representation. A leader must remember that followers may be reluctant to change their activities because the sense of continuity that comes with inertia supports his or her self-consistency. This continuity is not isolated from other aspects of a follower's life; changes in one part of a lifestyle (e.g., altering work responsibilities through a job transfer) may impact on the consistency experienced in other parts of the follower's personal and family life. The development or nurturing of traits is likely to have this type of ripple effect. A leader may be able to overcome this inertia during a time of turbulence for the follower when consistent behaviors are no longer functional. At such a time an effective leader can introduce protocols for "dysfunctional" behaviors (dysfunctional according to the old system but functional under the new environmental conditions) that help ease the transition for the followers under stress. President Mikhail Gorbachev's development of a "new social order" for the Soviet Union is an example of such an introduction; capitalistic market systems are substituted for the centrally planned economy.

Requiring a follower to make additional investments in education (e.g., continue on for a graduate degree) to help a group or organization develop will have serious implications for the follower's relationship to his or her ingroup(s). The extra time commitment and implicit change in perspective may disrupt a follower's relationships with others. For example, French, Israel, and As (1960) attempted a partial replication of the classic Coch and French (1948) study of participation. They found that the effectiveness of participatory practices was moderated by the perceived legitimacy of such an intervention according to existing social structures. The apparent ineffectiveness of participation in their study was attributed to the threat it appeared to pose to the labor unions and system of worker representatives existing in their sample's country. Although the participatory techniques provided every worker with additional skills and opportunities for growth, they were rejected. An important implication of this argument is that self-consistency may be threatened by skill enhancement and, more important, the impact on self-representation may have consequences for the effectiveness of a leader's attempt to "empower" or "transform" the subordinate. Much like the character Charly in the short story "Flowers for Algernon" (Rogers, 1969) a newly developed sense of self provides insights that threaten what has provided comfort in the past.

The follower's self-representation also is influenced by such factors as scripted actions, cultural symbols, and attributions about self and leaders. For the sake of comparison, we present a hypothetical schematic representation of a follower's cultural values and associated cognitive structure in Figure 8-3. In our example the follower shares the collectivistic values espoused in his or her culture and by the leader. Under work role and values, we see that one result is a general endorsement of, and belief in, participative management practices, including participation in decision-making, goal-setting, and so on. This set of beliefs is supported by certain assumptions concerning participation, e.g., it demonstrates the employee's worth (self-enhancement), it provides growth opportunities (self-efficacy), and so on. A more behavior-oriented aspect of this general focus is illustrated by the follower's reactions to participation. A follower may speak out in its favor, develop positive affect toward someone who provides the opportunity for participation, and search for ways to make effective use of it. A follower who endorses participation is likely to engage in actions that will provide future opportunities for participation, by using upward influence methods as one example.

There are two important considerations with regard to our model of leadership. One concerns the role of culture in shaping an individual's self-concept. We have discussed how collectivism can permeate an individual's beliefs about work and appropriate behavior in a variety of work settings. The relationship of culture to leadership can be direct or indirect; an action such as searching for information to make good work decisions may be related to values and beliefs other than collectivism (e.g., established work habits or definitions of quality work). An endorsement of collectivistic values may result in radically different behavioral responses to participation among individuals.

A second aspect of the model is that culture impacts the leadership process *because* it shapes the individual's self-representation. For example, a leader from an authoritarian culture who is asked to manage a foreign subsidiary operating in a culture that endorses egalitarian and participative styles may attempt to implement techniques that are likely to fail because they are inconsistent with the followers' belief systems, sense of self, and so on. However these beliefs are shaped by personal experiences as well as by culture. Thus a follower who endorses egalitarian values may adapt to normative pressures and go along with the leader's authoritarian style because his or her specific cognitive structure contains a node endorsing conformity to superiors and co-workers. We must *fully understand* an individual's self-representation if we wish to make accurate predictions of leadership effectiveness.

Related to this second point is the role of an individual's schema and scripts in

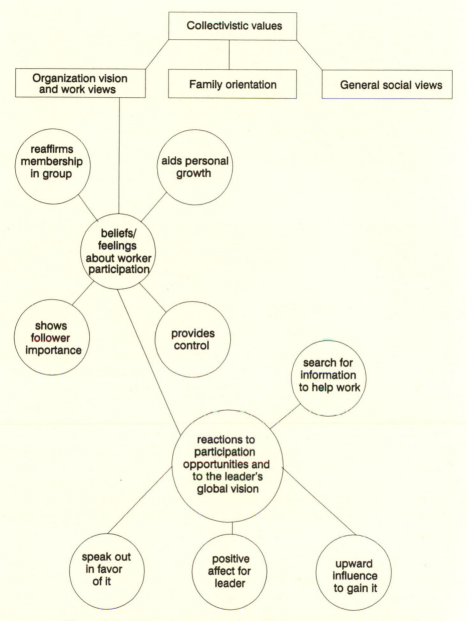

Figure 8-3. Schematic representation of follower's cultural values

determining a leader's effectiveness. Just as eating at a restaurant can be described as scripted (Schank & Abelson, 1977), so can a follower's reaction to particular leadership visions. The major difference is that a leader's vision and guidance will often be expressed in vague ways, allowing opportunities for the use of multiple scripts. A follower's reaction to particular aspects of a leader's vision and action will be scripted and automatic but seemingly erratic. For example, an employee may automatically work longer hours as job demands require if his or her leader projects an image of trust, respect, and competence. The worker's reaction to such an image (working long hours) is the scripted response for that employee. Cultural values and norms shape these scripts by directing an individual's actions in a general way so that, over time, some scripts are adopted over others.

Another major influence on a follower's response to a leader is his or her identification with the symbols underlying the leader's presence. As we discussed earlier, European leadership theorists relate the significance of symbols to psychoanalytic processes (Kets de Vries, 1988). During the process of transference, it is argued, followers may attempt to relive bygone relationships so as to complete them in a satisfying manner. Kets de Vries (1988) asserts that leaders are prime candidates for such transference: "Followers may endow their leaders with the same magic powers and omniscience they attributed in childhood to parents or other significant figures. Moreover, transference reactions can be acted out in different ways and may affect both leaders and followers" (244). He suggests that transference can take one of three forms: idealizing, or ascribing unrealistic qualities to a leader; mirroring, or a desire to be the central focus of attention; and, persecutory, or a vengeful devaluation of a leader as the result of tacit promises left unfulfilled. These transferences are interrelated in a number of ways. Followers actively shape the leader according to their own myths; culture shapes the "ideal" image manifested in the myths. As this relationship continues, a leader tends to feed on the follower's approval and develop a sense of grandiosity captured in the myths, perhaps taking on burdens that are unrealistic and unattainable. As it becomes clear to the leader that a work goal is unattainable, he or she may subject followers to cruel circumstances; they, in turn, shift to a persecutory transference as promises are not met. The result can be a total breakdown in the leader–follower relationship.

The nature of transference is related to the symbols and relations inherent to a particular culture. Willner (1984:15) describes four factors that enhance the attribution of leadership, including the invocation of cultural myths and actions that are heroic or extraordinary. The key to understanding the role of culture in the attribution of leadership is identifying the cultural myths and symbols relevant for a particular group of followers. For example, Westley and Mintzberg (1988) point out that Lee Iacocca drew many comparisons between Chrysler's problems and those of the United States during such crises as wars and economic depressions. He also described Chrysler as an amalgam of many "little" people (e.g., suppliers, dealers) who needed a "helping hand" from the government and not a "hand out." These images tap into many aspects of American culture, including the shared image of war and fighting for just principles, self-sufficiency as opposed to a welfare society, and the importance of individual liberty. Iacocca was able to enlist a strong following by using the images and values prominent in American culture. The effective leader utilizes the shared symbols of followers to ensure their identification with the leader's vision.

Westly and Mintzberg also argue that Iacocca's use of myths and symbols created connections for followers that helped legitimate his ideas and vision. Relying on Lévi-Strauss's (1963) work on structural equivalents, they describe the sequence as "Iacocca's family = America; Chrysler = America; therefore Chrysler = Iacocca's family" (1988:193). Although this particular connection is more easily described by transitivity rules of attitudes (Fishbein & Ajzen, 1975), the point is that the structure of an individual's self-representation enables us to understand the connections between cultural and personal experiences.

The nature of leader–follower relationships is influenced by a number of other cultural factors. In our model the cultural value of individualism and collectivism plays a crucial role in work relationships. We have illustrated one facet of individualism and collectivism in Figures 8-2 and 8-3, and we wish to reemphasize the importance of this cultural value for an individual's self-representation. In a collective society an effective leader must provide followers with the opportunity for contributing to ingroup welfare, whereas a leader in an individualistic society must provide followers with opportunities for personal growth and public approval. It is not the case that individualists do not wish to contribute to their ingroups; rather self-representation is most strongly shaped by their evaluations derived from external and internal sources of personal growth. Thus an effective leader not only recognizes the relevance of common ideology, beliefs, and values but provides followers self-evaluative opportunities that are applicable to their self-concept.

A follower's identification with a leader and commitment to his or her vision is also influenced by the attributions made about the leader and the setting. Much work has been done in this area by Calder (1977) as well as by Mitchell and his colleagues (e.g., Mitchell & Liden, 1982; Mitchell & Wood, 1980; Wood & Mitchell, 1981). Briefly, an attributional perspective argues that the qualities of leadership are projected onto a leader as a result of a follower's perceptions of the leader. The attributions of a follower may influence how he or she will react to the leader's vision and goals. For instance, a socially unskilled leader may make a verbal faux pas and not evoke a negative reaction from followers if it is attributed to poor social skills rather than general incompetence. Although it is not clear how attributional processes differ across culture, we suggest that similar attributional processes operate across cultures but utilize different informational cues. Thus we might expect followers from different cultures to focus on different aspects of their leaders' actions and to make different types of attributions. To the allied forces Saddam Hussein appeared to be a megalomaniac who placed his people on the brink of disaster, but to the Palestinians he was a hero who was willing to take on seemingly insurmountable odds for the sake of a united Arab people.

Leader and Follower Outcomes

Until now we have focused on the nature of the leader–follower relationship and the antecedents to this relationship by examining the congruence of self-representation and cultural values. We now turn to the implications of leader–follower dynamics for the personal outcomes of leaders and followers, individually and jointly.

From a cultural perspective, the most important outcome for a leader is the affirmation of status in the ingroup. As a leader gains favor within a group, followers will reaffirm the leader's position through attention, praise, admiration, and so on. These outcomes reinforce a leader's self-representation through all three self-motives. For example, praise satisfies the leader's self-enhancement motive by producing a positive self-image. The self-consistency motive is satisfied by a leader's continuing status within a group. Perhaps the most interesting aspect of the leader's personal outcomes is the impact of follower and institutional outcomes on the leader's sense of self-efficacy. For instance, the transformational leader who produces a general environment conducive to the mutual growth of both leader and followers experiences self-efficacy and a desire to take on increasingly more challenging tasks (Bennis & Nanus, 1985). The self-efficacy motive may be a key to success (assuming that the leader is capable) since the leader will set increasingly challenging goals for self and group, more actively engage the work environment, and develop a grander vision of the future. Researchers such as Locke & Latham (1990) emphasize the importance of setting challenging goals and developing a long-range vision for successful organizational performance. The leader who receives follower support is encouraged to develop further challenges which, in turn, will lead to even greater successes and follower admiration. These successes help satisfy the leader's self-efficacy, self-enhancement, and growth motives.

Kets de Vries (1988:240–41) argues that an effective leader is one whose personal struggles reflect the problems of society at large. By equating personal struggles with societal crises, a leader creates a bond with his or her followers (Lasswell, 1960:186). This displacement of private for collective problems depends on the leader's ability to use cultural myths and symbols to commit the follower to the leader's preferred mode of action (Willner, 1984). The use of cultural myths and symbols reinforce a follower's sense of continuity or self-consistency.

The use of projection not only provides a leader with an effective commitment mechanism but also provides an outlet for the leader's own problems. We should not overlook the relevance of self-purging as an outcome as well as a motive for particular leadership actions. A leader who desires to reassert himself as a paternal figure will use an authoritarian leadership style as a way of satisfying his self-concept. The potential for cultural conflicts exists since the society that stresses equality will not provide a paternalistic leader a work context that is beneficial to the leader's self-concept.

The personal outcomes of followers are the subject of many leadership models. We will discuss these outcomes with regard to a follower's self-representation. Certain outcomes build a follower's sense of self-efficacy and growth. The essence of effective transformational leadership is the provision of growth opportunities for followers. An effective leader will identify a follower's weaknesses and strengths in order to structure work opportunities that favor success and allow a follower to develop personal skills. Challenging assignments, on-the-job training, and meaningful work can help a follower grow (Hackman et al., 1975). There is, however, an important cultural distinction that must not be overlooked. For collectivistic followers, growth opportunities must not be gained at the expense of collective welfare. In a collectivistic culture an effective leader provides work opportunities that will allow an individual to grow within the ingroup. For example, quality circles not only promote productive efficiency but provide collectivists an opportunity to improve their ingroup's work context. By aiding the work group, a collectivist experiences personal growth and the group benefits. In such a case, self-efficacy does not imply "isolated" efficacy.

Among the many outcomes that affect a follower's self-enhancement motive, the development of a sense of contribution to the work group is perhaps the most culturally relevant. By following a leader, an individual gains a chance to improve ingroup conditions through personal accomplishment. These opportunities promote a stronger sense of capability and help maintain a positive self-image. An effective leader can recognize the important facets of a worker's life and give the worker ample opportunity to succeed in these areas. Such an approach sounds like a formidable task. It implies that all work opportunities must be tailored to each individual; however a leader may rely on cultural facets as a universal (and unifying) theme for followers. In the United States a leader should provide personal challenges for employees. Such an approach is supported by the vast literature on goal-setting. Without question, employees in the United States respond to individual challenges which help build a strong sense of efficacy (Bandura, 1986; Earley & Lituchy, 1991; Locke & Latham, 1990).

Concerning personal outcomes that affect a follower's motive of self-consistency, Kets de Vries (1988) suggests that the transference process provides followers with a powerful way to confront their own problems and resolve them. Many individuals, particularly in stressful circumstances, use transference onto leaders as a way of resolving personal problems dating back to childhood or adolescence. Managers in Western cultures may feel uncomfortable being cast in the role of a parent figure by a subordinate who needs to resolve childhood jealousies, but the follower's need for consistency suggests that the leader may be key to working through conflicts and discontinuities from earlier times. As authority figures, leaders provide an ideal outlet for unresolved conflicts. A follower may endow the leader with special attributes that can provide the follower consistency and resolve these conflicts.

The joint outcomes of leader and followers are the universal topic of leadership models. The outcomes discussed in the literature include group and individual performance, worker satisfaction, pay, work conditions and absenteeism, cognitions and abilities, motivation and self-esteem, and goals and aspirations of followers (House, Spangler & Woycke, 1991; Yukl, 1989). Most organizational behavior theories of leadership (including the recent focus on transformational approaches) emphasize the individual's outcomes somewhat devoid of a general social context. This seems ironic given the argument posed by these theorists that leadership is a construct best understood within the complexity of a dynamic work setting.

We will highlight the joint outcomes of leader–follower interactions from a cultural perspective. The most pertinent joint outcome is the reaffirmation of social structure and interpersonal relations. Sashkin's (1988:134–35) application of Parsonian theory comes close to providing an explicit role of social structure in the leader–follower interaction. However he fails to complete the link between existing values and the leader–follower relationship as a means of reaffirming these values. An important joint outcome of a leader–follower interaction is that it maintains a consistency of hierarchy and intercourse that society recognizes. It legitimatizes differentiation among people and provides continuity for the varying roles that individuals occupy. Such interactions also reinforce the nature of social relationships within an organizational context by signalling the legitimacy of an organization to govern these relationships. This argument is not new; Tannenbaum et al. demonstrated in their study of hierarchy (1974) that such structural relations exist in all societies.

Joint outcomes not only reaffirm the significance and legitimacy of social structure but also assert the legitimacy of group relationships. The interactions between leader and follower send a signal to these individuals that they are functioning within an existing social group. Such legitimation gives rise to the social bonds that Durkheim (1933) described as organic solidarity. The social fabric that binds people together is the basis for all exchanges, and even in highly individualistic and trade-oriented societies (e.g., United States), the thread of this fabric is strengthened by leader–follower interactions.

Another joint outcome of a leader–follower exchange is mutual growth, or what might be called a collective efficacy. Just as individuals learn and grow, so do societies. The exchange of ideas and the development of mutual goals provide the foundation for a collective to develop a group structure. This is especially true for heterogeneous groups whose members have complementary but differing perspectives. For example, a development team of engineers, whose leader has a vision of a new computer system interface, may build on various team members' strengths in order to collectively develop the new system. It is not merely a transaction, after which a computer system emerges; rather the group develops a joint purpose and interpersonal relationships to fulfill the collective goal. Along with emerging relationships comes a social structure, shared history (albeit short-term), rules and norms, and evolved interpersonal commitment. The various followers will need to decide what role they will play within the group (as well as adapting to existing roles), how to relate to the leader, what attachments they will form to one another, and how new members to the team can "join in." Although many of these processes are heavily influenced by existing social rules and practices within a culture (and organization), each group will develop its own unique form as it evolves. Thus collective-efficacy refers to the group social structure, rules, and norms that emerge as leader and follower interact.

Another joint outcome, the release of societal anxieties can be described using a psychoanalytic model. Although this may sound quite removed and esoteric, an example drawn from recent history illustrates this type of outcome. During the early and mid 1980s, a resurgence of patriotism was evident in the United States under President Reagan. Many of the symbols and myths the president used to build his popularity were based on the concerns many Americans faced about their nation's weakening world status. Given the competitiveness of the Pacific Basin countries and the declining technological edge of American businesses, many Americans felt anxiety (and perhaps still do) about their nation's status in the world order. During his administration, President Reagan used patriotic themes and "America the great" metaphors as a way of helping people deal with their uncertainties. Dramatic shifts occurred in the American mentality, such as the purging of guilt concerning the Vietnam war and the treatment of Vietnam veterans. Images and themes of America reemerging as the great world leader dominated people's thoughts and they were able to move beyond concerns that they were second class world citizens.

The president's leadership allowed the American people to vent many societal concerns over the loss of world status, guilt over Vietnam, a failing economy, and so on. Similar observations can be made concerning the recent trauma facing the Soviet Union. Although Mikhail Gorbachev's initial economic reforms were met with enthusiasm and adopted as the "new" consistent system, a number of citizens are now calling for the emergence of a Stalinist leader to restore order and structure. Stalin is becoming the societal symbol of order and security while Gorbachev's (and Boris Yeltsin's) "new" system has become the symbol of turbulence and difficult times.

On a less grand scale, a leader and his or her followers can help one another purge more localized (e.g., organization specific) concerns and anxieties, including company identification, role ambiguity, and a lack of work commitment. Participative management styles often induce strong commitment because they provide workers with a legitimate channel for venting frustrations with their work, even if this does not result in actual changes in the work environment. The work of Lind and Tyler (1988) on the group-value model of procedural justice posits that "voice" (the expression of opinions in a procedurally identified fashion) results in enhanced commitment and perceptions of outcome fairness independent of instrumental influences (see also Earley & Lind, 1987; Lind, Kanfer & Earley, 1990).

Intervening Variables

A final aspect of our model concerns intervening variables that moderate the relationship of a leader to his or her followers. We highlight a few of the variables that we view as culturally important.

Leaders and followers operate within the context of organizational structures that are influenced by culture. Although intracultural variations exist, there are systematic differences in the structures of organizations. For example, manufacturing organizations in the People's Republic of China are typically bureaucratic and hierarchically differentiated ("tall"). In the United States, organizations are often decentralized and less hierarchically differentiated. The reasons for these differences are beyond our scope and the topic of debate (e.g., Adler, 1986; Triandis, in press), but structural differences will influence how a leader and follower interact. In a highly bureaucratic organization the leader will be far removed from his or her followers. When this structure emerges in an egalitarian society (e.g., due to a multinational corporation exporting its structure to other societies), communication problems emerge in the leader–follower interaction and an incongruous image is projected. If, however, the leader compensates for structural incongruities by interpersonal style (e.g., by "walking around," as suggested by Peters & Waterman, 1982) then structure does not limit the effectiveness of a leader's interaction with followers.

A second intervening variable is the role of structure within a given society. We know from sociology and social psychology that roles represent a powerful influence on an individual's behavior in work settings. For example, it is considered inappropriate for a Japanese subordinate to criticize his or her superior during work; yet it is not only acceptable but expected that criticisms will be voiced after working hours when the superior and the subordinates go to dinner or have drinks. The roles enacted by the superior and subordinates are fundamentally different during the evening when the subordinate is permitted to criticize the superior. Further, it is expected that the superior will listen to the criticism but not acknowledge it the next day during work (Erez, 1992).

Roles dictate the types of interactions that are available to the leader as well. One of the cultural biases built into much of the work on charismatic leadership is the view that such a leader is a "risk taker." Such a romantic view is consistent with a Western perspective but it does not necessarily apply to other cultures that do not view risk taking as desirable. In this sense the charismatic leader is restricted to particular kinds of role-based behaviors recognized by his or her culture. Thus a risk-taking leader in the United States may be viewed as overly hasty, unwise, and neglectful of the welfare of the group in a more collectivistic culture.

Inherent in all societies are relational aspects that capture how people interact. Using Kluckhohn and Strodtbeck's (1961) concept of lineality, we can see that the relationship of a leader to followers is influenced by the continuity of relations over time. One might argue that lineage influences management/leadership capabilities analogous to Kluckhohn and Strodtbeck's (1961) discussion of the lineal aspect of individualism versus collectivism. The notion that great leaders are truly born and not made and the "great man" approach to leadership (see Yukl, 1989, for a detailed discussion) are quite inconsistent with the American and Canadian view that leadership, even charismatic leadership (see Sashkin, 1988), is an acquirable skill. A culture's view of relations among individuals can moderate the relationship of a leader to his or her followers.

The relational component of ingroup to outgroup is an important aspect of leadership in a collectivistic culture. As we described in chapter 4, collectivists view outgroup with suspicion and distrust, whereas they are committed to the welfare of ingroup members. A leader who needs to unite ingroup with outgroup must realize that the various parties will be hesitant to interact since they are relationally antagonistic. In the extreme, a leader may opt to keep competing groups apart and play the role of coordinating agent or facilitator rather than attempt to integrate the groups. This approach seems to fly in the face of the American philosophy that everyone can be reconciled ultimately. This individualistic view holds that since group memberships are transitory, there is no reason why new groups cannot be constructed if all parties "try." Recent developments in the Middle East suggest that the United States' desire for a unified region may be unrealistic, and the differing views of individualists and collectivists with regard to group structure and leadership may account for some of the incongruent perceptions among various groups.

SUMMARY

Our purpose in this chapter has been to apply the Cultural Self-Representation Theory to understanding the nature of leadership from a cultural viewpoint. We have focused on the significance of structure, roles, and self-definitions of leader and followers in describing leadership. Portions of our model are supported by previous research. For example, Shamir, House, and Arthur (1991), propose that charismatic leadership achieves its effects by implicating the self-concept of followers and recruiting their self-expressive motivation. Although they do not explicitly examine cultural dimensions, it is implied that charismatic leaders have the ability to empower their followers by identifying the factors that promote their followers' sense of self-enhancement and self-efficacy. They increase their followers' intrinsic motivation by emphasizing the symbolic and expressive aspects of the effort required for goal attainment. Thus charismatic leaders should be sensitive to cultural values in order to ascribe meaning to the behavioral outcomes they expect from their followers.

From a structural viewpoint, the nature of leader–follower interactions is delimited by the type of organization. Decentralized organizations may inhibit a leader's effectiveness if he or she depends on interpersonal interaction. Similarly an authoritarian leader who wishes to operate in a flat-structured organization is likely to become frustrated. In describing a cultural model of leadership, the importance of roles cannot be overlooked. Roles of leader and follower are strongly influenced by the social structure in a given society, and individuals operate within the context of these roles. Although some leadership theories portray the dynamic leader as one who is role-making rather than role-taking, it seems naive to assume that a leader operates outside of the cultural context. In our view not only does intracultural variation occur but systematic intercultural variation in leadership occurs as well. Thus the ways that individuals interact in different cultures varies as a function of the expected roles of leaders and followers.

We described the importance of individuals' self-definitions and how culture impacts them. Individuals possess cognitive structures of self-concept that incorporate personal and societal experiences. We argue that the congruence between leaders' and followers' self-concepts enable us to predict leader effectiveness. Such congruence can be achieved by reliance on shared symbols, transference, and the purging of individual and societal anxieties. This does not imply that effective leadership is merely an angst-driven process; leader and follower reconcile themselves to adverse issues and move toward mutually desired goals.

9

Negotiation and Bargaining

With the continuing expansion of organizations across geopolitical boundaries, the necessity of understanding negotiation and bargaining is obvious. Recent events in the Middle East, Eastern Europe, and the Soviet Union illustrate the centrality of negotiation to societal action. Negotiation occurs in work and social environments, ranging from the establishment of new joint ventures to decisions concerning family vacations. Clearly negotiation is a pervasive form of social interaction (Adler et al., 1992; Lewicki & Litterer, 1985; Thompson, 1990).

The topic of negotiation has been addressed in a number of fields, including psychology, economics, sociology, political science, and industrial relations. Much of this research has focused on prescriptive approaches to effective bargaining (Raiffa, 1982; Thompson, 1990). Frequently raised questions concern outcome maximization (single party as well as joint), avoidance of impasse, and procedural aspects. The major theoretical approaches include economic, game theoretic, and behavioral-cognitive schemes.

In its most basic form negotiation refers to the process by which individuals attempt to allocate scarce resources according to some transactional scheme (Rubin & Brown, 1975). A negotiation setting has five characteristics: (1) people believe they are in conflict with one another; (2) communication is possible; (3) compromises are possible; (4) offers and counteroffers can be made; and (5) these offers and counteroffers do not determine the outcomes unless all parties accept them (Chertkoff & Esser, 1976; Rubin & Brown, 1975; Thompson, 1990). We would add a cultural aspect of negotiations in as much as the criteria for judging outcomes and making offers is culturally based. As a result the pattern of transactions that underlies offers and counteroffers is prescribed by the parties' social and normative backgrounds.

The basic negotiation scenario consists of the negotiation parties, their constituencies and interests, the transaction process, available resources, and the negotiation outcome. The party refers to an individual (or group of individuals) who has defined preferences and acts according to them. A constituency refers to individuals whom a party has a responsibility to represent in the pursuit of particular interests. A party may represent constituents with a single nonoverlapping interest or overlapping interests (Jensen & Meckling, 1976; Neale & Northcraft, 1991). The transactions process refers to the procedures and practices used by the parties during a negotiation. For example, collectivists are very concerned with ingroup survival and, therefore, will often begin negotiations by stating which issues are nonnegotiable (ingroup threatening). Individualists, however, are more concerned with appearances and the *means* through which outcomes are achieved (Triandis, 1989a). Thus individualists are more likely than collectivists to seek compromise positions in order to appear reasonable and earnest in their negotiations. Resource availability refers to those tangible and intangible materials available for distribution among the various parties.

Perhaps the most crucial concern in negotiations is the identification and definition of resources that are available for distribution. Outcomes refers to the distribution of available resources after the negotiation is completed. These outcomes are the product of bargaining, but they will not result if a negotiation reaches an impasse. Outcomes are referred to as pareto optimal or efficient if a single party's outcomes cannot be improved without hurting the outcomes of the other party (or parties) (Nash, 1950). Distribution outcomes are related to the structure of the bargaining context. If the parties' interests are perfectly correlated, the negotiation refers to "pure conflict" or a fixed-sum (zero-sum) context (Galbraith, 1973; Walton & McKensie, 1965). If the parties' interests are perfectly positively correlated, the negotiation refers to "pure cooperation," although this situation suggests that a negotiation context may not really apply (e.g., the parties are not competing for scarce resources). If the parties' interests are somewhat competing but not entirely so, the negotiation refers to an "integrative" setting.

Integrative contexts are posited to be the most common in negotiations (Raiffa, 1982; Thompson, 1990; Walton & McKensie, 1965) since it is likely that the parties' interests are not completely overlapping and that their preferences and values are not fully redundant. The *potential* for integrative bargaining outcomes is highest if the parties come from different cultural backgrounds, even though the use of different transaction processes may prevent the attainment of an integrative solution. Individuals from different cultures are likely to have differing preference structures; therefore a pure conflict context is less likely to be observed. However differing preferences for transaction processes (e.g., how offers and counteroffers are made) may create an impasse despite the potential for an integrative bargaining outcome.

Theoretical approaches to the study of negotiation can be grouped into three categories: economic, game theoretic, and behavioral-cognitive (Bazerman & Carroll, 1987; Bazerman & Neale, 1992; Neale & Northcraft, 1991). The economic approach relies on the assumption that individuals are rational and that rational outcomes are a function of a zone of agreement and efficiency. A party's zone of agreement refers to the minimum and maximum levels of outcomes he or she is willing to accept. If both parties have overlapping zones, a positive zone of agreement is said to exist and a negotiated settlement should occur. If the settlement point is pareto optimal, the agreement is said to be efficient.

A game theoretic approach to negotiations focuses on the structure of payoffs and its role in determining negotiation outcomes. According to Rapoport (1959), an "elementary game situation" is one in which "two individuals whose interests are not coincident are in control of different sets of choices and endeavor to make their respective choices in such a manner as to emerge with an advantage" (51). In the classic Prisoner's Dilemma (Rapoport & Chammah, 1965), two players compete for resources and typically end up with pareto inefficient outcomes. If they cooperate with one another they can obtain a pareto efficient outcome, but the risk of personal loss to one player typically drives individuals to compete with one another. The research literature discusses hypothetical situations in which the players' appropriate choices are deduced based on mathematical calculations of how "rational" players would operate under complete information. The focus of game theory is the development of theorems about appropriate competitive choices given various game contexts (Neale & Northcraft, 1991; Roth, in press).

Both economic and game theoretic approaches operate with an emphasis on rationality and logic that is not consistently supported in actual negotiations (Bazerman & Carroll, 1987). Although the experimental results of traditional game-theroretic models are weak predictors of actual negotiator behavior (Roth, in press), economic and game theoretic approaches provide a means of identifying appropriate prescriptive outcomes for negotiations.

In the behavioral–cognitive framework the negotiator is seen as a dynamic but imperfect processor of information in the negotiation context. We will examine ways of expanding this approach. Our basic supposition is that a negotiation is influenced by culture through its impact on the negotiators, transactions process, and context. Thus our focus will not be primarily prescriptive, as it is for the economic and game theoretic approaches, but descriptive, tracing the cultural influences on methods of negotiation. We will discuss some prescriptive aspects of negotiations as well since the value embedded aspects of culture seems to warrant a "what should be" approach.

BEHAVIORAL-COGNITIVE FRAMEWORK

We will begin our discussion of the behavioral–cognitive framework of negotiations by reviewing the recent work of Bazerman, Neale and Northcraft. In particular we will discuss the Behavioral Negotiation Theory (BNT) proposed by Neale and Northcraft (1991) as a basis for our cultural model of negotiations.

The BNT model, presented in Figure 9-1, consists of two major categories of variables—context and negotiators. Context refers to the background of the negotiation and consists of such structural influences as power, deadlines, and integrative potential as well as other people involved in the negotiation but not directly involved in the transaction process, such as constituencies and third parties. The negotiators component refers to the psychological dispositions and experiences of the parties involved in the negotiation, including planning, information-processing demands, affective states, and individual differences. It also includes such interaction processes as communication and influence tactics employed by the parties in the exchange of offers. In addition the BNT model incorporates negotiated outcomes.

Neale and Northcraft's BNT model posits that the context of negotiation is static whereas the negotiators are dynamic. They use a football game as a metaphor for this distinction. The rules of the game, setting, crowd, and coaches' instruction

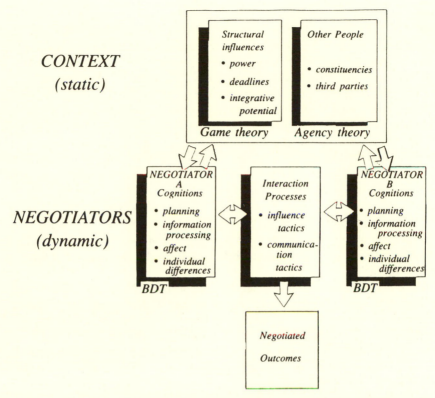

Figure 9-1. Neale and Northcraft's Behavioral Negotiation Theory (SOURCE: Adapted with permission from Neale and Northcraft, 1991)

represent the context and the players' thoughts and interactions represent the dynamic level—the vehicle through which the context influences negotiated outcomes.

Context

The context of a negotiation consists of structural influences and other parties. These aspects are considered to be static since they are the backdrop to negotiations.

BNT argues that there are at least three sources of structural influence. Power differentials among the parties will impact negotiation outcomes. McAlister, Bazerman, and Fader (1986) found that dyadic negotiations in a competitive market are more likely to reach an integrative outcome when the parties are equal in power. Faley and Tedesehi (1971) found that parties of equal power make more cooperative choices than parties of unequal power. However, Komorita, Sheposh, and Braver (1968) found that unequal power leads to more cooperative choices than equal power.

Deadlines have been found to impact negotiated outcomes. Pruitt and Drews (1969) found that time pressures reduce initial demand levels, aspirations, and bluffing. Carnevale and Lawler (1986) found that the effect of time pressure is related to the cooperative orientation of the parties. In their study time pressures impeded the ability of individualistically oriented negotiators (i.e., focused on self-gain) to attain an agreement. Cooperative negotiators (i.e., focused on both self-gain and gain for others) were not adversely influenced by time pressures. Carnevale and Lawler conclude that time pressure may cower aspirations (conducive to reaching a settlement) but lower information exchange and the use of trial-and-error strategies (a hindrance to reaching a settlement).

The integrative potential of a negotiation is an important structural variable. The simplest example of integrative potential is presented in the following scenario. Two negotiators must agree on the disposition of a shipment of oranges. Both parties want the full shipment, and the simple distributive solution is to give each party half. However party A wants the shipment for the juice of the orange and party B wants the orange peel. The integrative solution (i.e., pareto efficient) is for party A to receive all of the juice and party B to receive all of the peel. Such a solution is possible because each party's subjective utilities for available resources are complementary.

The other parties involved in a negotiation constitute the second major aspect of context. BNT uses a simplified version of Agency Theory to capture the potential influence of constituency and third party influences on negotiation behavior. Agency theory is concerned with the differences in perspective of principals (e.g., owners of capital) and agents (e.g., such representatives of the owners as firm managers) and how these differences may impact the actions of agents on behalf of principals.

In negotiation research there are two categories of "other people" that influence negotiator behavior. The constituency of a party refers to individuals who hold the negotiator accountable. These individuals may or may not have a direct influence on the party yet still have an impact (Rubin & Brown, 1975). Interestingly, the presence of a constituency has been found to reduce the likelihood that a negotiator will demonstrate a problem-solving orientation (Neale & Northcraft, 1991). We might speculate that a collective orientation would moderate this effect. Whereas individualists might be distracted by the constituency, collectivists would be familiar with a constituency presence (e.g., ingroup). However a collectivist whose constituency is made salient (assuming that it consists of ingroup) may be inhibited in negotiations by the responsibility he or she feels for the constituency and tend to overprotect its interests. We will return to the importance of constituencies in our model later in this chapter.

The second category of "other people" in the BNT model is the third party. Such an individual may or may not have binding influence over the negotiators but is assumed to be neutral. The hallmark of a third party is impartiality and neutrality. Research generally supports the finding that arbitration facilitates negotiated settlements by imposing additional costs that parties are unwilling to incur. From a cultural viewpoint, the nature of third party participation may vary dramatically. For example, French, Israel, and As (1966) were unable to replicate the original Coch and French (1948) findings (on the benefits of participation) because the later study used direct participation. Earley (1986) found that a goal-setting program introduced to British tire tread layers was more effective if implemented through recognized agents (e.g., shop steward) than others (e.g., supervisor). We might argue that third party intervention would be more appropriate in high power distance societies than in those that have low power distance because subordinates would be unfamiliar with direct negotiations with their superiors. The third party would provide a useful and legitimate buffer in a high power distance culture.

Negotiators

The second level of the BNT framework is the psychological disposition of the parties involved in a negotiation. There is a strong trend in negotiation research toward a behavioral and cognitive view of action. Individuals are not simply inanimate objects that play out "games" according to prescribed rules of superrationality; rather they think, react, and act nonrationally (Bazerman & Carroll, 1987; Thompson, 1990). BNT posits that negotiator cognition can be classified into three groups of variables: planning, information processing, and affect.

Planning refers to the tactics and methods a party uses during negotiation. Roloff and Jordon (1989) examined the nature of negotiator plans and outcomes and found that plan structure and aspirations influence outcomes and integrative orientations. They also found that negotiators generally are unwilling to switch strategies during a session and become increasingly entrenched in their strategies after they revise their approach.

The information-processing aspect of negotiation has received considerable attention. Utilizing a behavior decision-theory perspective, researchers have found that negotiators are subject to various cognitive processing limitations, including framing (Neale and Bazerman, 1985; Neale & Northcraft, 1991), anchoring and adjustment (Huber & Neale, 1986), availability (Taylor & Thompson, 1982), overconfidence (Bazerman & Neale, 1982), reactive devaluation (Bazerman & Carroll, 1987), and "fixed pie" assumptions (Thompson & Hastie, 1990). This vast literature demonstrates that negotiators are subject to many cognitive processing limitations. As Bazerman and Carroll argue, the rationality assumption of an economic perspective is unwarranted. There are numerous studies that illustrate the nonrationality of negotiators' behavior.

A negotiator's affective state influences cognition, yet little research has focused on its impact on outcomes. Carnevale and Isen (1986) found that a positive mood (induced through the receipt of a small gift prior to the negotiation) facilitated creative problem solving and integrative agreements. Pruitt and Rubin's (1986) Dual Concern Model posits that integrative outcomes are obtained if negotiators have a high concern for self *and* others. Thus the degree of empathy that a negotiator exhibits for the opposition will facilitate joint outcomes. From a cultural perspective, Triandis (1989a) points out that collectivists do not consider it a virtue to put themselves in someone else's shoes. This suggests that the integrative orientation required by the Dual Concern Model may be problematic at times.

Although they do not explicitly incorporate individual differences as a form of negotiator cognition, Neale and Northcraft argue that these individual differences may indirectly influence cognition. They suggest that Machiavellianism (an interpersonal style characterized by domination and manipulation) is negatively related to integrative outcomes, whereas perspective-taking ability (similar to empathy in the Dual Concern Model) is positively related. In their ten-country study of negotiation and bargaining, Harnett and Cummings (1980) examined a number of personality variables in a cross-cultural context and found that those individuals who were the most averse to taking risks and who strongly believed in internal control were the strongest bargainers and attained the highest individual outcomes. Although Harnett and Cummings conclude that cultural differences do not account for a great deal of variability in bargaining strategies and outcomes, it is interesting to note the conceptual overlap between their "individual differences" construct of risk-taking propensity and Hofstede's (1980) cultural dimension of uncertainty avoidance.

Interaction Process and Outcomes

The interaction process of negotiation involves the way individuals communicate and attempt to influence one another. The research on communication in negotiation has focused on two aspects of the negotiation process, namely, the way communication is related to the negotiation outcome and its role in the negotiation process.

Research has demonstrated the importance of communication so that parties reduce mutual threat (Krauss & Deutsch, 1966; Theye & Seller, 1979). In their classic "trucking game" experiment Deutsch and Krauss (1962) demonstrated that the nature of communication opportunities influenced participants' negotiated outcomes. More specifically, they found that individuals who were provided an opportunity to communicate with one another, but not tutored how to use this opportunity, did not benefit from the communication. Without proper training, the subjects in the trucking game often used the communication channel as an opportunity to threaten one another for personal gain.

Communication is crucial for the exchange of offers during a negotiation. Harnett and Cummings (1980) found that individuals are more likely to reach integrative settlements when they exchange frequent offers and solicit reactions to their proposals than if they do not exchange proposals. Another aspect of communication is the flow of information. Schelling (1960) has argued that "information is weakness" since the fully informed bargainer is more likely to anticipate stalemates and will give more concessions to insure that negotiations continue. On the other hand Hamner and Harnett (1975), building on Seigel and Fouraker's (1960) level of aspiration research, have argued that information can make negotiation outcome aspirations more realistic (in line with their negotiating partner) and, therefore, facilitate the attainment of a settlement. Thus the mere presence of communication channels is not sufficient to guarantee negotiated settlements. As Rubin and Brown (1975) argue,

A well-known adage concerning the value of communication in a broad range of conflict situations states that "If you can get the parties to communicate with one another, their conflicts will resolve themselves." This maxim has a familiar ring in bargaining, too, being typical of the sort of curative that both naive observers and armchair diagnosticians readily prescribe for the amelioration of conflict. Yet if one puts such advice to empirical test, one is likely to find that its applicability is somewhat limited—for experimental research as well as day-to-day bargaining incidents make it quite clear that [the mere availability of communication channels provide no guarantee that they will be used or used effectively]. (92)

The interaction process also includes the use of influence tactic by negotiators. Work in this area has focused on the bases of power (e.g., French and Raven's (1959) taxonomy) and their relation to settlements. The results indicate that three primary tactics are used—assertion, rational argument, and manipulation (Kipnis & Schmidt, 1983)—and that effective negotiators use these tactics differentially. In general more assertive tactics are preferred when dealing with someone of lower status, whereas rational argument is best used in dealing with superiors. As we will discuss shortly, the choice of influence tactics used varies by culture as well. Maxwell and Schmitt (1975) found that among Norwegian negotiators, a cooperative strategy in a prisoner's dilemma game led to a cooperative strategy by an opponent; yet among American negotiators, a cooperative strategy led to exploitation by an opponent. Druckman et al. (1976) examined the bargaining styles of Indian, Argentinean and American negotiators. They found that Indians negotiated longer and were more competitive in their bargaining than Americans or Argentineans. Hofstede (1980) argues that individuals from a high power distance culture are more likely to use assertive and manipulative influence styles in dealing with their subordinates than individuals from a low power distance culture.

The final aspect of Neale and Northcraft's BNT model are the negotiated outcomes. Traditional research in economics and game theory has focused on tangible assets that are exchanged among participants, such as money, poverty, and so on. More recent work suggests that individuals may have preference structures for intangible assets that are revealed through their actions and behavior. The typical criticism by psychologists is that economics only deals with tangible outcomes (e.g., Thompson, 1990) or "super-rational" behavior. A countercriticism from the economist's viewpoint is that psychologists ignore the recent work by economists on revealed preference structures. It would be more appropriate at this point for scholars to refocus their attention on research that expands our understanding of cultural influences on outcomes rather than focusing on the shortcomings of other disciplines. For example, Neale and Bazerman (1991) have pointed out that personal relationships play an important role in negotiations, and in fact, the outcome of a negotiation may include the development of relationships between the negotiating partners. American managers have been criticized because they fail to establish the interpersonal bond that is customary in a collectivist culture such as Japan's (Harris & Moran, 1987). A cultural model of negotiations needs to incorporate such relationships as important outcomes, particularly in a dynamic model of interaction.

We now turn to our model of negotiation and bargaining, which is based on Neale and Northcraft's BNT approach. First we will discuss a dyadic model which focuses on the general context, reframing it as a dynamic influence on negotiation. Our model differs from the BNT approach primarily in its greater emphasis on variables that are likely to be culturally linked, such as a shared history among the parties, norms and practices, social systems, and so on. We will extend this dyadic model to a multiparty approach that addresses the complexity of such interactions. However, our multiparty model is a simplistic representation of multicultural interactions and negotiations.

CULTURAL MODEL OF NEGOTIATION

Overview

Our model is intended to highlight the role of culture in a conceptualization of negotiation. As shown in Figure 9-2, this model can be conceptualized as two general systems—a general frame and a localized one. The general frame consists of such distant influences as social and regulatory procedures, stakes, cultural values, shared histories of the parties, and constituencies or interested parties. The local frame consists of the negotiators' cognition, self-concept, and local work practices and norms for negotiation. We present the localized frame as an embedded one since the effect of culture on various components of the model are often subtle and indirect. For example, the cultural background of the negotiators may influence negotiated outcomes through the parties' application of resource allocation rules. Leung and Bond (1984) found that Chinese collectivists differed in their reward allocation rules (equality versus equity) depending on their relationship to the negotiator (ingroup versus outgroup), whereas these differences did not occur for individualistic American negotiators who generally preferred an equity-based allocation scheme. This study illustrates that cultural norms may have an indirect effect on negotiations depending on more localized variables (e.g., relationship between negotiators).

There is also a dynamic component to our model. The nature of negotiated outcomes at time t may bear a direct impact on subsequent relationships at time $tt1$. As we mentioned earlier, American managers have been criticized for their superficial and abbreviated approach to interactions with their Japanese and Middle Eastern counterparts. In these more collective societies, attainment of ingroup status is time-consuming but essential for effective negotiation. Thus the embeddedness of the local frame reflects the need to adhere to cultural practices. There is also a reciprocal influence, namely, the local frame reinforces the general norms and values of a culture (Adler, 1986; Harnett & Cummings, 1980; Hofstede, 1980; Triandis, 1989b). Negotiations will be more successful if they adhere to cultural practices, and these successes, in turn, will reinforce existing cultural practices.

General Context

The general frame of our model consists of four general factors as well as the constituencies of the parties. The general factors are the social and regulatory procedures of a society, general values of culture, shared history of parties, and stakes of interested parties.

The social and regulatory procedures of a society refer to those legal and institutionalized practices used in negotiations (Rubin & Brown, 1975). For example, the United States has a system of negotiation and arbitration legally endowed to handle disputes arising between labor and management. Practices in labor-management negotiations within the United States has focused heavily on the role of third party interventions in settling disputes. Fact finding, conventional arbitration, and final-offer arbitration represent formal legal procedures in the American system. Other

Social and regulatory procedures   General values of culture

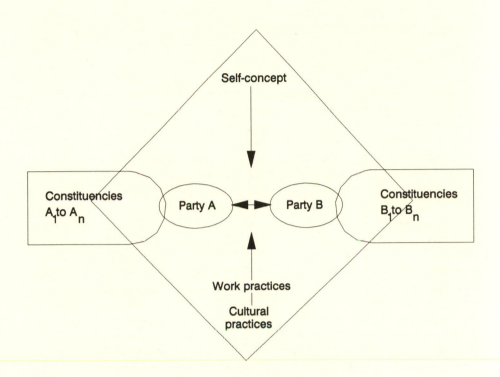

Shared history of parties   Stakes of interested parties

Figure 9-2. Dyadic model of negotiation

cultural systems employ various forms of representation, such as stewardship in the United Kingdom, worker collectives in Sweden, and the kibbutz movement in Israel (Stevens, 1963; Summers, 1965). Thus the legal systems underlying negotiation will have a direct influence on the negotiation process itself.

The general values of a culture influence the context of negotiations as well. This facet of our model refers to the societal norms governing power differentials, group identity, conflict orientation, and so on. In an associative culture (Glenn, 1981;

Triandis, 1989b), emphasis is placed on context-specific meaning. Individuals communicate using various associations that they assume are shared by their partners. For example, if one is told, "The boss wants you to do X," the consequences of not doing X, such as getting fired are implicit. In an abstractive culture communication is more explicit. Thus an American manager (abstractive culture) who negotiates with a Japanese manager (associative culture) will want to "clarify all of the details" at the expense of the assumed underlying commitment of the Japanese manager. The legitimacy of negotiation and conflict varies as a function of cultural values and practices as well. Triandis (1989b) argues that individuals want to avoid excessive conflict because they perceive themselves as moving from group to group. They do not want to anger any particular group that, in the future, might be an ingroup.

The third aspect of the general frame is the stakes of the interested parties. The size of the stakes will affect the desire of participants to achieve their negotiation aspirations (Rubin & Brown, 1975). As the size of the stakes increases, so does the likelihood of impasse and the difficulty of attaining a satisfactory settlement for the parties involved in the negotiation (Greenhalgh, 1987). The stakes are often tied to cultural values and norms. Clearly the Israeli-Palestinian conflict is tied to large stakes, defined, in part, by the historical and social claims to the territory in dispute. The claim to this land is measured in terms of very large stakes dating back many centuries.

A final aspect of the general context is the shared history of the parties. In many negotiations the parties involved in a conflict share a common history that is relevant to the nature of a negotiation. For instance, the negotiations concerning the return of Hong Kong to the People's Republic of China involve the common history of the Chinese people during the turn of the century. In negotiations it is not only important to recognize that the parties share a common history but to identify how negotiation practices may overlap due to this common background. A common background may be a source of conflict if the original separation of the parties was a difficult one. Recent attempts to reconcile the People's Republic of China and the National Republic of China have been difficult and slow because the ideological and political basis of their separation imposes a serious obstacle to overcome. In this case, a shared sense of collectivism and familialism that underlies each group does not help to integrate the two societies; rather it perpetuates the ingroup-outgroup distinction that separates them. It is interesting to note that in Germany, a more individualistically oriented culture, unification of East and West was achieved more easily. Thus the shared history of the parties may be a facilitator or an inhibitor of a negotiation, depending on the cultural nature of the parties.

Constituencies

The significant role of constituencies in our model is related to the concept of individualism-collectivism. An overlooked aspect in negotiation research is the negotiator's attachment to a culturally determined constituency. Research on constituencies suggests that the psychological salience or physical presence of a constituency can have various influences on a negotiator, such as seeking positive evaluation, reduced problem-solving capacity, and an unwillingness to provide concessions to an opponent (Rubin & Brown, 1975). The effect of a constituency on a negotiator's behavior is evidenced in a number of studies. For example, it can be argued that as a negotiator's commitment to constituency-advocated positions increases, the negotiator's ability to evaluate alternative proposals, either self-generated or offered by the opponent, decreases (Neale & Northcraft, 1991). A negotiator's need to be positively evaluated is likely to impede transactions as well. McKersie, Perry, and Walton (1965) found that labor and management negotiators had to answer to their respective constituencies or fear sanctions and/or possible removal from their position.

One theoretical explanation underlying the potential adverse impact of constituency effects on negotiator behavior and problem-solving ability is impression management (Davis & Triandis, 1970; Neale and Northcraft, 1991). Since negotiation implies that concessions must be made as offers and counteroffers are generated, it stands to reason that a negotiator who is making progress may be viewed with some suspicion by a constituency that assumes something is being given away or compromised. The problem is particularly acute if the negotiators share a common work history. If the constituency begins to question the loyalty of a negotiator and monitor his or her behavior, it will constrain the negotiator. Imposed controls can reduce the effectiveness of the negotiator and, as a result, reduce outcomes for the constituency. Diminished outcomes fuel the constituency's suspicions and lead to a downward spiral of distrust and control. This phenomenon is referred to as the dilemma of the boundary role person described in Adams' (1963) work.

The intervention of a third party in a negotiation is thought to relieve some of the pressure constituencies place on their negotiators. Rubin (1980) found that negotiators were more likely to make concessions if they were at the request of a third party. The ability to make a concession and attribute it to the third party may relieve some of the social pressure from constituencies and provide the negotiator with a face-saving mechanism (Neale & Northcraft, 1991).

There is evidence to suggest that cultural background will influence negotiators' relationships to their constituency and their negotiating behavior. Glenn (1981) argued that Russians (collectivists) and Americans (individualists) will negotiate differently in a number of ways. Collectivists see more differences between ingroups and outgroups than do individualists (Earley, 1989, 1991; Triandis, 1989b, 1989a). As a result, collectivists see conflict as a natural course of events and compromise with outgroups as a threat to the ingroup. A distributive solution to a negotiation is seen as an unacceptable position (Triandis, 1989a).

A distributive or simple compromise solution is unacceptable to a collectivist because it is viewed as a threat to ingroup welfare, whereas the individualist is concerned with the procedures and means by which solutions are derived. If a negotiator is representing his or her ingroup, then the "ends" of a negotiation take on a particularly strong significance and communication with the opponent (outgroup) is kept at a minimum. As Triandis (1989a) argues, the individualist is concerned primarily with procedural justice (cf. Lind & Earley, 1992; Lind & Tyler, 1988), whereas the collectivist is concerned primarily with distributive justice. It is interesting to speculate how ingroup members might negotiate with one another in a collective culture (assuming that the negotiation does not center on issues of ingroup welfare) since ingroup conflict is acceptable in some but not all collective cultures. The characteristic emphasis on ingroup harmony in such collective Asian cultures as Japan and the People's Republic of China (cf. Adler, 1986; Hofstede, 1980; Hofstede & Bond, 1988; Triandis, 1989b) does not appear in Israeli collective groups such as kibbutzim. In the case of the kibbutzim, ingroup members stress a frank honesty with one another that might seem harsh to an American (individualist) or Japanese (collectivist) manager. Israeli collectivists believe that frankness is conducive to ingroup longevity. Thus collectivists may also differ in their style of conflict negotiation with outgroup versus ingroup members, probably due to cultural differences that vary across collectivist societies.

The devotion and attachment a negotiator has for his or her constituency is likely to influence behavior, and this attachment is influenced in large measure by a negotiator's cultural background (see chap. 7; Tajfel, 1982). The effect of a constituency is likely to have a stronger impact on the collectivist than the individualist for other reasons as well. The impact of these differences in group membership stability suggests that the collectivist will not risk ingroup welfare and assume an antagonistic approach to outgroup. An individualist's willingness to move among ingroups suggests that ingroup welfare (outcome) is not as central as outcomes or procedures that reaffirm an individualist's legitimacy as a unique person. This "affirmation as a unique member in society" perspective underlies Lind and Tyler's (1988) Group Value Model of procedures. They argue that procedures provide an individual with a means of reaffirming his or her position and status within a group (or social structure). The individual gains a sense of group/social identity through his or her participation in group activities and procedures. Applying this argument to the collectivist is somewhat problematic since group identity is a given (stable). It is unclear that collectivists have a need to reaffirm their membership status. Although the results of procedural justice appear to generalize across cultures (e.g., Leung, 1985; Leung & Li, 1990; Lind et al., 1978), it is not known whether the group value explanation holds comparably for individualists and collectivists.

Based on our discussion we could expect the effect of a constituency on a negotiator to be stronger for collectivists than for individualists. However the relation of cultural background to propensities for conflict and negotiating style is unclear.

Self-Concept

Our self-representation model includes three self-motives that influence negotiation behavior—enhancement, efficacy, and consistency. We use an extended version of Bazerman and Carroll's (1987) schema-based model of negotiation to incorporate these self-motives.

Social cognition research focuses on the information-processing capabilities of individuals (Carroll & Payne, 1976; Wyer & Srull, 1989). As we described in chapter 2, the self can be conceptualized as a cognitive structure having a number of persons, events, and times as relevant nodes. This cognitive structure has information based on individuals' past experiences, values, and norms obtained through socialization, and reasoned linkages based on problem-solving skills. If asked to define an effective negotiator, an individualist might respond, "someone who is fair with others," whereas a collectivist might respond, "someone who is concerned with the welfare of the work group."

The extension of a mental-structure approach to the self implies that these structures, their shape and content, are influenced by an individual's self-motives. For example, a negotiator with a strong need for consistency may seek quick resolutions to problems in order to avoid conflict that threatens to change the group's social structure. In terms of the shape of a mental structure, a single dominant self-motive may lead to a narrow set of associations and a rather fixed perspective. The negotiator's strong need for consistency may be reflected by a tendency to interpret social outcomes in terms of variations on past negotiation practices or traditions.

A negotiator who has a strong motive for self-enhancement and who represents a collective culture (emphasis on sampling behavior from the collective self) may seek to gain a positive evaluation by acting in an ingroup's favor. The notion of "face" in Asian cultures reflects such a motive. A Japanese manager who negotiates on behalf of his company must be careful to appear to be negotiating on the ingroup's behalf to avoid suspicion and loss of face (Triandis, 1989b). The Japanese manager will monitor his fellow organization members as a means of assessing his successes in a negotiation. Their support and approval serve to enhance self-image.

The self-efficacy motive influences cognitive structures as well. A negotiator who has a strong self-efficacy motive and who samples from the private self will seek out self-generated cues that reflect individual growth and capability during negotiations. Thus a large concession made by an opponent may be seen as a personal triumph and bolster self-confidence. A large concession may not have the same effect on a collectivist negotiator whose sense of efficacy is tied to the constituency's reaction and not the negotiation itself.

Our extension of social-cognitive theory includes the nature of script processing (Schank & Abelson, 1977; Wyer and Srull, 1989). According to this view, we can describe an individual's cognitive structures as temporally linked or scripted (Abelson, 1976). For example, in the United States the script for purchasing an automobile can be described as

entering the showroom, meeting a salesperson, viewing cars, focusing on one car, test driving, assessing any trade-in allowance, haggling over price, settling on a price, and signing contracts. . . . There are subscripts or "tracts" such as whether a trade-in is possible. If the buyer provides a low offer, the salesperson may enter a track where the offer is taken to the sales manager, whereupon the salesperson comes back and says that he could not convince the sales manager to accept such a low amount, followed by more haggling. (Bazerman & Carroll, 1987:269)

The script concept is very useful for providing negotiators with preset ways of interacting during negotiations. An individual's self-concept strongly influences the type of script that evolves during a negotiation. An individual who has a strong motive for self-consistency will likely evoke negotiation scripts in a very consistent way, even if it is not the ideal script. These scripts indirectly reflect self-motives since they are patterned after an individual's experiences and knowledge of the world, and these experiences are shaped by self-motives.

If we consider the combined effects of script processing and self-motives, we can see how culture shapes negotiating behavior. In Bazerman and Carroll's car purchase script, a collectivistic negotiator who has a strong self-enhancement motive will interpret self-evaluations from ingroup social cues. These social cues will be heeded by the negotiator provided that they reinforce his or her perceived contribution to the collective or ingroup. This may explain Triandis' (1989b) finding that collectivistic negotiators focus on negotiation outcomes (relative to ingroup needs and desires), whereas individualistic negotiators focus on negotiation means. To the individualist, the concessions and offers made during the course of negotiation, and its progress, reflect the private self and individual accomplishment. As an individual enters into a negotiation he or she will evoke a script (and self-concept) that not only reflects the content of the situation but the individual's self-motives as well.

An individual's sampling (private versus collective) may have an additional effect. Not only will the type of script evoked differ according to an individual's self-motives, but the source of information used in deciding an appropriate script will vary as well. The individualist will rely on self-generated cues and processing, whereas the collectivist will look to the ingroup in deciding the appropriate negotiation script. Thus an individualist may view consultation with a constituency as a weakness or a lack of confidence, whereas the collectivist views it as an expected aspect of information gathering during a negotiation. The actions of the opponent may similarly be interpreted according to the sampling that an individual engages in. The collectivist may view an individualist's consultation with a constituency as a strength and evoke a script or schema that signifies "negotiator is respectful of collective."

Work Practices and Culture-Specific Work Norms

An additional influence in negotiation behavior is the role of adopted work practices as influenced by culture-specific norms. In this section, we will discuss a number of practices that shape bargaining and negotiation.

An early study on negotiation and bargaining by Porat (1969) examined conflict issues in Denmark, Spain, Sweden, Switzerland, and the United Kingdom. Using a union-management exercise, the results demonstrated that Spanish negotiators were the least willing to deviate from a preplanned strategy; they ended up with the least gain for the company and the greatest gain for the union. The Swedish negotiators were the most flexible (willing to deviate from a preplanned strategy). The United Kingdom, Switzerland, and Denmark exhibited behavior between the extremes of Spain and Sweden. Concerning international negotiations, Sawyer and Geutzkow (1965) argue that the national character or culture of a negotiator results in different negotiation practices.

Perhaps the most comprehensive study of negotiation behavior in a multicultural context was reported by Harnett and Cummings (1980). Using a bargaining game they examined the behavior of individuals from the United States, England, France, Belgium, Finland, Spain, Greece, South Africa, Thailand, and Japan. The game consisted of dyadic negotiations in which the participants assumed the role of a buyer or seller of a fictitious commodity. The research design included the following variables: geographical origin (grouping the European participants into a single group due to small sample sizes); personality differences (using the dimensions of conciliation versus belligerence, risk taking, locus of control, and suspicion versus trust); bargaining strategy used; and information available. Their results suggest that the structural and personality aspects of the game accounted for most of the variability in the results. Culture played a significant but minor role in the findings. It is interesting to note that several significant personality variables can be interpreted as psychological manifestations of cultural variables. For instance, risk taking is highly related to Hofstede's dimension of uncertainty avoidance and trust versus suspicion is related to individualism versus collectivism. Thus Harnett and Cummings's use of overlapping constructs, as well as the use of geopolitical boundaries as surrogates for culture, may explain the rather limited effect of culture in their findings.

It remains unclear how culture influences negotiations. Studies that have examined the effects of national differences on negotiation behavior do not explain cultural versus national effects. For example, a particular organization might have strong norms of work participation, collectivity, and egalitarianism and yet engage in labor-management negotiations that are very antagonistic and competitive because of existing labor laws. From our perspective of culture-specific work norms, it is important to understand the *propensities* that negotiators might exhibit toward other negotiators. For example, the collectivist negotiator is likely to consult with his or her ingroup members as often as possible and assess their reactions to determine whether or not a negotiation is going well. Similarly an individual from a high power distance culture will respond well to the imposed authority of a third party or arbitrator, and someone from an associative culture will loosely tie propositions together since the underlying relations will be assumed or implicit. Thus it is important to distinguish bargaining behavior that is tied to personality versus culture versus context (Harnett & Cummings, 1980).

Interaction Processes and Outcome Allocation

Our premise is that interaction processes and outcome allocation differ as a function of cultural background. We begin our discussion with a description of interaction and procedures recently proposed by Lind and Earley (1992).

The dominant theory of groups and organizations is exchange theory. According to this view, individuals seek to understand their actions and those of others based on their outcomes and how their actions may influence these outcomes. Individuals maintain group memberships in the belief that they are instrumental in attaining valued outcomes otherwise not easily attained. In the last fifteen years, however, a growing body of literature has examined the implications of procedures on individuals' social decision-making. Research on procedural justice has demonstrated that some procedures are perceived as more fair than others regardless of the outcomes they produce (e.g., Lind & Tyler, 1988; Tyler and Lind, in press).

The basic findings from procedural justice are attributable to three general effects. The *process control* (Thibaut and Walker, 1978) or *voice* effect (Folger, 1977) describes how perceptions of procedural fairness are enhanced when individuals are provided an opportunity to express themselves. Recent research demonstrates that the voice effect operates independently of its instrumental effect on outcomes (Earley & Lind, 1987; Lind, Kanfer, and Earley, 1990). The *dignitary process* effect (Lind & Tyler, 1988) refers to individuals' enhanced perceptions of fairness when they are treated in a dignified and respectful fashion. The *fair process* effect (Folger, 1977) refers to enhanced perceptions of fairness and greater compliance with decisions following positive evaluations of procedural outcomes (Lind & Earley, 1992).

The relevance of procedural effects in the study of negotiation and culture hinges on the role of procedures as a means of symbolizing group or collective membership. Before discussing the specifics of this argument, we will briefly review the cross-cultural literature on procedural justice. For example, Leung and his colleagues (Leung, 1987; Leung & Li, 1990; Leung, Earley & Lind, 1990) have examined the role of voice effects in Hong Kong Chinese culture. Leung has demonstrated the pancultural effect of voice. Takenishi and Takenishi (1990) found that evaluations of new laws by Japanese citizens were linked to relational attributions about authorities. They demonstrated a fair process effect on attitudes toward taxes similar in magnitude to that of Americans. Leung et al. (1990) examined the relations among procedural justice judgments, organizational altruism, commitment, and job security. They found that the relation of justice judgments to organizational attitudes of their U.S. and Hong Kong samples was roughly comparable.

For our purposes a more important question is why these procedural effects occur. Lind and Earley (1992) suggest that procedural effects and the cultural value of individualism versus collectivism jointly influence the extent to which individuals operate according to self- versus group-oriented motives. For instance, if an individual perceives a group's procedures as unfair or unjust, then self-oriented processes (exchange based) will dominate. However if procedures are seen as just, an individual will tend to focus on group-oriented processes in a quasicollectivistic fashion. Thus we observe what appears to be a collectivistic orientation for an individualist who is operating under just or fair procedures. This person will focus on adhering to group rules, maintaining existing authority structures, and so on.

Fair procedures may evoke similar perceptions of justice among individualists and collectivists but for somewhat different reasons given the differences in group-membership stability. Individualists may respond favorably to procedures because they reflect on their personal achievements, whereas collectivists may respond favorably because they perceive just procedures as an important way to maintain group harmony and existence. Thus individualists and collectivists may respond comparably to procedural interventions but for very different reasons.

The second major aspect of interaction processes is the allocation of outcomes relative to cultural values. A number of scholars (e.g., Berman et al., 1984; Samuelson & Messick, 1986) have conducted studies examining the allocation rules for outcomes as they relate to an individual's cultural background. Leung and Bond (1984) conducted two studies examining the allocation rules (equality versus equity) used by Chinese (collectivist) and American (individualist) samples. Berman et al. (1984) found that Indian subjects were more likely to allocate rewards on the basis of need and less on the basis of merit or equality than were the American subjects. Finally, Mann (1980) examined the allocation rules of children from Osaka, Japan, and Adelaide, Australia. They found that children from the collectivistic culture (Japan) were more likely to use an equality rule for allocating chances to obtain a group reward (chocolate) than were children from the individualistic culture (Australia).

Taken together these studies demonstrate that the outcome allocation rules used by negotiators will vary as a function of culture. An allocation rule of equality was employed typically by collectivists, whereas a rule of equity was employed by individualists. This principle, however, appears to vary, given the ingroup versus outgroup composition of the negotiating parties.

Extension to Multiparty Context

In this section we will extend our discussion from a dyadic negotiation to a multiparty context. For the sake of simplicity, we will discuss a single variation of the negotiation, namely, a negotiation with multiple parties, each of whom represents an independent constituency (i.e., each member represents a different group, such as a Security Council debate at the United Nations). Our model is presented in Figure 9-3.

Multiparty negotiations is a topic that is beginning to receive research attention (Bazerman, Mannix, & Thompson, 1988; Mannix, Thompson & Bazerman, 1989; Neale and Bazerman, 1991). A group negotiation can be thought of as a decision-making process in which three or more persons, representing their own interests, make decisions about how to resolve conflicting preferences (Bazerman et al.). The multiparty negotiation differs from the dyadic case in two major ways: information processing demands increase, and interpersonal processes become increasingly complex (Neale & Bazerman). As the number of parties involved in the negotiations increases, the information-processing requirements increase as well. The negotiators must be aware of additional preference structures and how to combine them (according to unspecified decision rules that may vary by cultural preferences) into joint outcomes. Interpersonal interactions and interaction styles become problematic as communication channels are overburdened, coalitions form, and group equilibria become unstable.

In the context of our model there are several key extensions of the dyadic form. Coalition formation plays an important role in negotiating outcomes (Murninghan, 1978; Murninghan & Brass, in press). However coalition interests do not always reflect the interests of the total group; they may form based on the shared histories of the negotiating parties. Since coalitions are often unstable, the outcomes they decide (and force on the other parties) may be rejected if the coalition falls apart. We would

Social and regulatory procedures   General values of culture

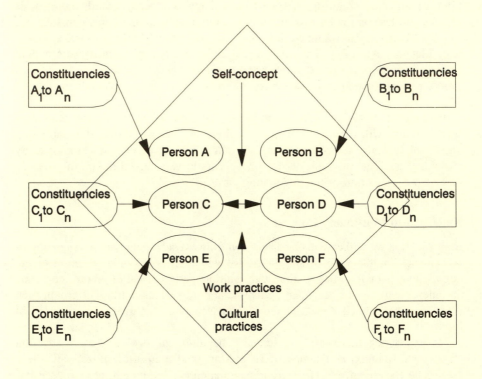

Figure 9-3. Multiparty model of negotiation

expect culture to influence the formation of coalitions as well. Individualists will be more likely to join other groups in forming coalitions than will collectivists, unless the collectivists can join with relatively similar parties and/or share a common opponent.

Another extension of our dyadic model concerns the adoption of interactional processes and allocation rules. Some compromise in rules that apply in the dyadic context would be impossible in a multiparty context. Communication mode and pattern may be a problem as well since particular modes (e.g., face to face) may be threatening to some, but not all, parties and may lead to particular coalitions being formed. Multiparty negotiations also are subject to group-decision biases that do not necessarily appear in the dyadic context, e.g., choice-shift phenomenon (Lamm & Myers, 1978) or groupthink (Janis, 1982). Although we might argue that dyadic negotiators are subject to group-decision biases to the extent that they emphasize consultation with their constituency, the coalitions that form during multiparty negotiations will inevitably be subject to decision bias.

SUMMARY

We have presented an overview of the negotiation literature with an emphasis on how culture might enhance this research stream. Three primary points have been raised in discussing dyadic and multiparty negotiations.

The self can be thought of as a conduit of cultural influences in a negotiation. An individual's self-motives and sampling impact how he or she views the negotiation context and reacts to offers and counteroffers. For instance, an individualist who has a strong self-enhancement motive will use his or her success in the negotiating process (i.e., making successful offers) as a means of maintaining a positive self-image. Such a negotiator will emphasize (and respond to) negotiation practices that highlight individual initiative and accomplishment.

We have emphasized the role of constituencies in influencing a negotiator's behavior. Our discussion differs from earlier work on constituencies (e.g., Rubin & Brown, 1975) in as much as we argue that the cultural background of a negotiator will influence how he or she relates to a constituency. The individualist listens to the constituency as an agent or as a representative, whereas the collectivist *is* the constituency in the case of ingroup. The collectivist does not distinguish his or her interests from those of the ingroup constituency. We have also expanded the role of interaction and allocation practices to a cultural context, based on the literature on procedural justice and allocation of rewards (e.g., Leung & Bond, 1984; Lind & Earley, 1992; Lind & Tyler, 1988). We have argued that the allocation rules employed in a negotiation will vary based on an individual's cultural background. For instance, collectivistic cultures place an emphasis on equality allocation rules in an ingroup context, whereas individualistic cultures emphasize equity rules.

According to our view, the positive effect of fair procedures on various cultures may operate for different reasons. The same procedures seem to be judged "fair" across very different cultures. Finally, we extended our discussion of dyadic negotiations to a multiparty context, examining coalition formation based on cultural preferences, group decision biases, and communication demands. The information-processing demands attributable to group negotiations, discussed by Bazerman, Mannix, and Thompson (1988) and Neale and Bazerman (1991), are complicated exponentially if we consider that parties must not only know others' preferences but understand why these preferences arise. Fundamental assumptions concerning why parties act and respond become problematic in a cultural context. Coalitions that form may be based on cultural factors and shared histories that are not the usual basis for coalition.

Research on negotiation will benefit from a more active consideration of cultural effects. As our understanding of others' perspectives increases, we will gain more insight on intracultural negotiations.

10

Summary and Conclusions

The model of cultural self-representation is the last stage in a developmental process which was initiated by the authors in an attempt to understand, explain, and predict OB across cultures.

The first stage in the process was stimulated by the recognition that attempts to transfer managerial techniques across cultures have often been unsuccessful and that, in some cases, managerial techniques had to be modified in order to be effective. From a psychological perspective this recognition has directed attention to the cultural factor. Companies that used to operate in a local market and now compete in the global market have realized that customers in one part of the world have different preferences and norms of behavior than customers elsewhere. Common managerial practices and motivational techniques in their home countries proved to be ineffective in other countries in which the companies operated. Thus the variance among cultures has become as important for understanding work behavior as the variance among individuals.

The second step in the process involved a search for cultural dimensions that could be used to analyze cultural effect on OB. We identified a number of typologies of culture that were developed during the 1970s and 1980s (Elizur, 1984; England, 1983; England & Lee, 1973; Hofstede, 1980; Ronen & Shenkar, 1985; Schwartz & Bilsky, 1987; Triandis et al., 1988). It is interesting to note that the vast majority of researchers who developed typologies for identifying cultural variation were non-Americans. Perhaps these researchers had more exposure to cultural variation, were more sensitive to the effect of culture on behavior, or were not strongly influenced by the dominant theoretical framework in the United States, which stems from an individualistic approach and disregards situational effects. Cultural typologies contributed to our understanding of cross-cultural differences in work values and preferences, but they did not help us understand the causal relationship between culture and employees' behavior, or the moderating effect of culture on the relationship between managerial and motivational techniques and work behavior.

The third stage involved a search for an existing theoretical model that could serve as a conceptual framework for understanding cultural effects. Unfortunately all existing models of OB did not take the cultural dimension into consideration. These theories reflect the traditional trend in psychology, which focuses on individual difference characteristics and their effects on behavior. Situational effects are often ignored. In studies of validity generalization, situational effects often have been treated as artifacts or attributed to individual differences. Theories serve as cognitive frames that guide the process of selection, evaluation, and interpretation of information. Therefore cultural effects go unrecognized in the absence of an appropriate theoretical model.

A number of researchers have criticized the lack of situational factors in existing models. Cappeli and Sherer (1991) analyzed the main weakness in existing models, but they have not offered an alternative model. In fact they believe there was no way to bridge the gap between the macrolevel of situational factors and the microlevel of employees' behavior. They compromise by focusing on situational factors at the mesolevel of the organization. However this does not account for the differential validity of various managerial practices across situations, since macrolevel situational factors are not part of the model.

James et al. (1992) criticized existing models of validity generalization for not taking situational effects into consideration and proposed an alternative statistical model that analyzes situational effects on validities. They admitted that a theoretical framework is necessary for proactively identifying potential situational moderators, but such a theoretical model was not available.

The development of new metacognitive models of self-regulation helped to inform our model of cultural self-representation (Kuhl, 1992; Locke, 1991). However, potential contribution of a cognitive framework for situational models was not self-evident. In fact Cappeli & Sherer (1991) attribute the erosion of the role of context in models of OB to the gradual rise of cognitive models. They argue that this is because cognitive models stress the importance of the subjective reality as it is cognitively framed in the individual mind while underemphasizing the importance of the external context.

Unlike Cappeli & Sherer, we discovered the potential contribution of cognitive models toward understanding how situational variables are sampled, processed, and interpreted by the individual and how they affect employees' behavior. Cognitive models of self-regulation propose that individuals not only process information but are aware of their cognitive process and can actively influence the monitoring and appraisal processes to enhance perceptions of self-worth and well-being.

Self-regulatory models propose a link between such macrolevel factors as culture and mesolevel organizational factors, such as management practices, and employees' behavior, including attitudinal and performance outcomes. Cognitive processes of self-regulation reside in the self, which serves as the interpreter of external stimuli. External stimuli consist of cultural values on the macrolevel and management practices on the mesolevel. Using the framework of cognitive self-regulation, we searched for a way to link these two levels and employees' behavior.

The fourth developmental stage concerned the need to understand the moderating effect of culture on the relationship between managerial practices and employees' behavior. At this stage, our model of cultural self-representation was postulated. We doubt that this model could have been postulated without going through the preceding three stages of theory development.

Our model of cultural self-representation builds upon the self-regulatory models. It consists of four core variables: (1) culture, which is viewed as a set of shared meanings, transmitted by mental programs that control individual responses in a given context (Hofstede, 1980); (2) management practices and motivational techniques which affect individual behavior in organization; (3) the self, which is shaped by a shared understanding within a particular culture of what it is to be human, is a composite view of a person's mental representation of his or her own personality and, as such, it is both the knower and what is known; and (4) generalized work behavior as an outcome of the self-regulatory processes.

Self-regulatory processes aim at enhancing a sense of self-worth and well-being. The self links the parts of the model. It evaluates and interprets managerial practices and motivational techniques, which are directed to affect work behavior with respect to their contribution to the individual's sense of self-worth. Positive evaluations of managerial practices result in the desired behavior, whereas negative evaluations hinder the desired behavior. Cultural values, as they are represented in the self, serve as criteria for evaluating managerial practices. Effective managerial practices adhere to cultural values and lead to behavior that enhances perceptions of self-worth. Management practices that are not perceived by the self as enhancing perceptions of self-worth will be ineffective. Culture determines the value of various managerial practices and, as such, it moderates the relationship between managerial practices and employees' behavior.

The value and potential contribution of the present model may be evaluated in line with the different roles that theories should play (Campbell, 1990).

Theories Tell Us That Certain Facts Among the Accumulated Knowledge Are Important and Others Are Not

The present model tells us that culture is an important determinant of the effectiveness of managerial techniques. Cultural values provide the criteria for determining whether certain motivational techniques will be perceived as enhancing or inhibiting self-worth and well-being. Positive evaluations result in desired behavior, whereas negative evaluations result in undesirable behaviors. Thus the model identifies culture as an important moderator of the relationship between management practices and employees' behavior.

Theories Can Give Old Data New Interpretations and New Meaning

The present model helps to understand the boundary conditions of culture and why certain managerial techniques are effective in certain cultures but not in others. Prior to the development of our model, situational effects were ignored because there was no conceptual framework to capture their effects. The model gives old data new interpretations and meanings by discovering the moderating effect of culture on the relationship between management practices and employees' behavior. We have re-examined such core topics of organizational behavior as motivation, leadership, groups, and communication from the perspective of the new conceptual model.

Theories Identify Important New Issues and Prescribe the Most Critical Research Questions That Need to Be Answered to Maximize Understanding of the Issue

Our model was developed in response to theoretical and practical questions. On the practical level it addresses two major concerns: the lack of validity generalization of various motivational techniques across cultures, and the failure to successfully transfer managerial techniques from one culture to another. On the theoretical level it aims at identifying the cultural parameters and their effect on employees' evaluation of various managerial techniques' contribution to their self-worth and well-being.

Theories Provide a Means by Which New Research Data Can Be Interpreted and Coded for Future Use

We hope that the present model will be used to design new research and to interpret new data. Two ongoing studies conducted in Israel will benefit from its use. One focuses on the ability of Russian scientists and engineers to adapt to the Israeli culture. The second examines the implementation of new motivational techniques in the kibbutz sector. We hope the model will stimulate a new wave of research in cross-cultural organizational behavior.

Theories Provide a Means for Identifying and Defining Applied Problems and for Prescribing and Evaluating Solutions to Applied Problems

The present model provides criteria and guidelines for evaluating the potential effectiveness of motivational techniques and managerial practices in different cultural environments.

Theories Provide a Means for Responding to New Problems That Have No Previously Identified Solution Strategy

The present model provides such a means. It incorporates culture as a factor that influences the evaluation of various motivational techniques by employees. It defines the role of cognitive information processing in mediating the effects of cultural values and motivational techniques with respect to the individual's self-concept. The model introduces the self as the link between the macrolevel of context and the microlevel of employee behavior. It also defines the relationship between cultural values, motivational techniques, the self, and work behavior. These relationships determine the potential effectiveness of motivational techniques that are transferred across cultures.

The successful implementation of managerial techniques depends on their congruence with cultural values. Cultural values serve as criteria for evaluating the contribution of various managerial practices to employees' well-being. Employees are motivated to allocate all their resources to the attainment of work goals when management practices are perceived to contribute to the enhancement of perceptions of self-worth and well-being.

PREVIOUS RESEARCH IN OB REEXAMINED IN LIGHT OF CULTURAL SELF-REPRESENTATION

Work Motivation

The model of cultural self-representation sheds light on the process by which motivational techniques acquire their value. The model accounts for the differential effect of motivational techniques across cultures and allows validity generalization to be tested by taking into consideration the moderating effect of culture. Research demonstrates that attempts to transfer motivational techniques across cultures have not been very successful. Previous models did not provide the conceptual framework for analyzing cases of success and failure. The present model allows us to analyze the reasons for past failure or success and to predict potential failure and success in the future.

Values are key to understanding cross-cultural variations in work motivation because they are the cognitive representations of needs (Rokeach, 1973), mediating between needs and goals (Locke, 1991). Values are the cognitive representations not only of individual needs but also of cultural demands. Since differences in cultural values determine what will be rewarding to employees, it is to be expected that members of different cultures will be motivated by different techniques.

The research literature demonstrates that the basic processes of self-regulation are universal, as is the motivation sequence (Locke, 1991), the content domain of human needs, and the content domain and structure of the motivational types of values (Schwartz, in press). Yet the relative strength of needs and motivational types differs across cultures and influences the effectiveness of various motivational techniques.

Chapter 5 reexamined the effectiveness of four motivational methods from the perspective of the new model: participation in goal-setting, QC circles, job enrichment, and reward allocation.

Participation

Whereas current models of motivation fail to explain why participation in goal-setting and decision-making produces inconsistent results, a cultural perspective allows us to understand the differential effectiveness of participatory management. Our model proposes that cultural background can either facilitate or hinder the effect of participation. Since participation often takes place in a group setting, it is endorsed by group-oriented, collectivistic cultures. It provides opportunities for each participant to influence the decision. Participation is more likely to be regarded positively in cultures of low power distance and high collectivism than in cultures of high power distance and high individualism.

Participation contributes to a sense of self-worth by providing the opportunity to influence decisions and to be a part of the group. These benefits are highly valued in cultures characterized by collectivism and low power distance. A reexamination of previous research in chapter 5 provided support for the model; participation was found to be most effective in cultures that value collectivism and low power distance (Erez, 1986; Erez & Earley, 1987; Matsui, Kakuyama & Onglatco, 1987).

Quality Control Circles

Quality control (QC) circles are a form of participatory management that has been found to be highly effective in Japan. Many American companies, particularly in the auto industry, have attempted to transfer the method to their own companies in the hope of improving the quality of their products, yet these attempts have been unsuccessful for no apparent reason. An analysis of these failures from a cross-cultural perspective provides the explanation. QC circles were developed in Japan, which is characterized by group orientation and collective values. The unit of analysis in Japanese corporations is the group rather than the individual, and the Japanese management philosophy is described as corporate collectivism (Triandis, 1989). Employees are guaranteed lifetime employment, and they develop a strong sense of identification with the organization.

In collectivistic and group-oriented cultures, the individual's sense of self-worth is enhanced by making a contribution to the group and receiving group recognition. The QC system is effective in Japan because it provides opportunities for enhancing a sense of collective self-worth. However in individualistic cultures the collective self is less salient than the private self. Hence a managerial technique which enhances the collective self is less valued than one which enhances the private self.

The present model could serve to predict the effectiveness of QC circles in new settings and to identify the conditions under which this method will be effective. Organizations could create suitable subcultures or adapt the method so that it could be effective in their own culture. For example, many companies in Israel are now implementing a technique known as Total Quality Management (TQM). Israeli society is more collectivistic than the United States, though less than Japan, and it has a lower level of power distance compared to both the United States and Japan. Thus QC circles within TQM could be successful in Israel. The particular characteristics of the organizational culture should be examined and adapted to fit the underlying philosophy of TQM. Our reanalysis of previous research demonstrates that the effectiveness of a particular managerial technique depends on its congruence with the cultural values of the work context.

Job Enrichment

Job design has taken different forms in different cultures. A reexamination of previous research reveals that cultural characteristics determine the particular type of job design. Job enrichment was developed in the United States, which is known for its individualistic values, whereas autonomous work groups were developed in Scandinavia, which is characterized by collectivistic values and a lower power distance than the United States. The same five principles of job enrichment are implemented in both designs. Individual skill variety, task significance, task identity, personal autonomy and responsibility, and individual feedback comprise the individual job enrichment design. Job rotation among group members, task significance, task identity on the group level, group autonomy and responsibility, and feedback to the group are part of the autonomous work group or the sociotechnical system. Both methods enhance intrinsic motivation. Yet in the case of individual job enrichment, the method contributes to the enhancement of a sense of private self-worth, whereas in the case of autonomous work groups the method enhances a sense of collective self-worth. Thus culture shapes the dominant and effective motivational techniques. Since effective techniques are culture bound, they may lose their effectiveness when transferred across cultures.

Reward Allocation

A person raised in the United States might think that there is only one rule of reward allocation, namely, the equity rule: to each according to contribution. This rule increases the level of differentiation and individualism. However a review of the cross-cultural literature reveals that there are three basic rules: the equity rule, the principle of equality, and the principle of need. A reexamination of these three rules and where they apply points to the direct effect of culture on the development of reward allocation principles.

Such individualistic cultures as the United States recognize the rule of equity and encourage differentiation. Employees are motivated by a differential reward system. The rule of equity can hinder the development of group harmony, which is a major characteristic of collectivistic cultures. Thus in a collectivistic culture the rule of equality is more likely to be implemented. Although the formation of ingroups and outgroups in collectivistic cultures may invite opportunities for differentiation, the basis for differentiation is not what a person does but who the person is.

Allocation on the basis of needs takes place in collectivistic countries, where there is greater sensitivity to other people's needs, and in societies where per capita income is low. Needs dominate the allocation rule when they become visible, as is the case in India. Subcultures may also influence allocation rules. The application of an inappropriate allocation rule may cause feelings of injustice and demotivate employees. Therefore a knowledge of relevant cultural dimensions is vital for the effective implementation of various compensation techniques. For practical reasons, cultural values, both on the societal and the organizational level, should be examined before implementing any particular compensation method.

To summarize, the effect of various motivational techniques on employees' behavior is moderated by culture. Motivational techniques are evaluated by the self according to cultural criteria and with respect to their contribution to the fulfillment of self-derived needs. The collective self is salient in collectivistic cultures; therefore motivational techniques which strengthen the ties between group members and enhance perceptions of collective self-worth are positively evaluated and have a positive effect on behavior. In individualistic cultures motivational techniques that strengthen the contingency between personal behavior and work outcomes enhance perceptions of self-worth; hence they are more effective than other methods. The reanalysis of previous findings in light of the present model sheds a new light on the moderating effects of culture. It offers new criteria for judging the potential effectiveness of various motivational techniques.

Communication Patterns in Work Organizations

Extensive research has been conducted on the relationship between culture and communication. However, most of the studies were conducted in the field of cross-cultural psychology rather than OB. The research questions raised in the studies do not have a direct implication to OB. The vast majority of studies are concerned with the causal relationship between culture and communication. Three different approaches have been identified. The first approach, represented by the school of symbolic interaction, views culture as a communication phenomenon, because the formation of culture is enacted by the process of communication. The creation of shared meaning and symbols that reflect the existing culture can only take place through the process of communication. Several studies empirically investigated organizational culture as a communication phenomenon. One approach, developed by Schall (1983), identified communication rules that captured the essence of organizational subcultures. In this study communication between managers and subordinates continued to flow even in cases when they did not share the same information. For example, the first priority of managers was to meet deadlines, whereas the first priority of nonmanagers was to maintain quality. This finding suggests that the sharing of beliefs is not crucial for a continuous communication flow.

Another important factor that accounts for the smooth flow of communication is the knowledge that the exchange will continue. Communication can continue as long as the parties share the same expectations of what will be exchanged and have a common code for interpreting the behavior through which the exchange is enacted. This finding has important implications for communication across cultures, particularly for conflict resolution. It implies that cross-cultural differences in values and preferences should not necessarily impede communication. This dimension of communication allows people to agree not to agree while they continue to communicate with each other.

The second approach views communication as a cultural phenomenon. Cultures provide the cognitive frames that guide members' attention to particular stimuli and information which they select to be processed. The literature review revealed three groups of cultural attributes that shape the patterns of communication: cultural, which refers to collectivism versus individualism, power distance, uncertainty avoidance, and masculinity versus femininity; cognitive styles, as expressed by the level of field dependence or independence and by the degree of context dependence; and the self, which takes either a private or a collective form. These cultural attributes directly influence communication style, patterns of decision-making, and conflict resolution. Table 6-1 summarizes communication styles and patterns of decision-making and conflict resolution as they are shaped by cultural attributes. It reveals four dimensions of communication patterns that are shaped by culture: (1) level of ambiguity: explicit versus implicit; (2) orientation: self versus other; (3) expression: rational versus emotional; and (4) cognitive style: abstract versus concrete.

These four dimensions could form sixteen different combinations; however the empirical findings point at two major clusters. The first is characterized by an implicit style, orientation toward others, conflict avoidance, affective expression, and concrete thinking. The second cluster consists of an explicit style, self-orientation, confrontation, rational expression, and abstract thinking. The first cluster is shaped by values of high collectivism, low power distance, low uncertainty avoidance, and femininity. In addition, it is shaped by a high context, field-dependent cognitive style and by the dominance of the collective self. The second cluster is shaped by values of individualism, high power distance, high uncertainty avoidance, and masculinity. The cognitive styles are characterized by field independence and low context dependence, and the private self is dominant. Thus a cultural perspective on communication reveals a parsimonious typology of communication patterns.

The third approach proposes reciprocal relationships between culture and communication. According to this approach the communication network forms the connecting links among group members, transmits social values, and facilitates their sharing. Conversely shared meaning and values facilitate the flow of communication. Communication patterns in Japanese organizations serve as a case study in support of the reciprocal approach (Erez, 1992). It demonstrates how cultural dimensions shape the patterns of both intra- and interorganizational communication. The communication system facilitates the sharing of cultural values by the participants; this in turn strengthens the corporate culture and increases employees' commitment to corporate goals and shared values.

The implication for Western organizations is that effective communication relies on the congruence between the cultural values and the communication system. An incongruent communication system imposed by consultants or adopted because of its popularity may not be effective. New communication patterns should be shaped in accordance with the organization's cultural values. For example, the groupware method, which was described in chapter 6, exemplifies the adjustment of a group-decision approach to an individualistic culture. Team members communicate through keyboards and computer screens and benefit from the group process without getting involved in a face-to-face communication. This method may be appropriate for organizations in individualistic cultures, and in fact, is successfully operated in high-tech companies in the United States. The method may not be effective in collectivistic and high power distance cultures because it does not provide opportunities for interpersonal interaction and does not maintain hierarchical order in organizations.

We conclude that culture shapes the communication system in organizations, and reciprocally, the system enhances the organizational culture by facilitating the communication of shared values. In addition culture moderates the relationship between communication and behavior.

Group Dynamics

In chapter 8 we applied our cultural self-representation model to the dynamics of the social group with special attention to its applications in such work settings as participative decision-making, sociotechnical systems, and work cooperatives.

Given the prevalence of groups, it is clear that they are an essential element in understanding intercultural aspects of behavior. Our lives are organized around such groups as families, work crews, religious groups, sports teams, and so on. Much of what we do for business and pleasure revolves around the group. We have focused on the social context of work behavior in which individuals gather to perform tasks or to maintain intragroup stability and relations. The study of groups in intercultural settings has yielded interesting similarities and differences. For example, the famous studies by Asch (1956) concerning conformity and social influence have been replicated in a number of cultures and societies. Group research on the development and evolution of work teams has been conducted by Hackman and his colleagues (1975; 1989), Gersick (1988; 1989), Guzzo and Waters (1982); and McGrath (1984). In recent years there has been a call to study the dynamics of group development, yet some researchers claim that it cannot be done in a laboratory context (Goodman et al., 1986). Ironically such critics often neglect the cultural context of a societal viewpoint, focusing instead on the "culture" of the organization itself or emergent norms within the group, as if they arise independent of cultural context. As we argued, this assumption is as damning to the study of "real" groups as it is to work conducted in a laboratory context. Neither intervention (laboratory versus acultural field work) demeans the study of work groups; rather such approaches impose limits on the validity generalization of the theories they generate.

We used Tajfel and Turner's (1986) Social Categorization Theory as a basis for integrating our cultural self-representation theory with current work on group dynamics since it provided the first full consideration of dynamic groups and the concept of the self. We further refined and extended their approach through the formal integration of cultural context and various alternative needs that shape the self.

Current research efforts directed toward capturing "real" group dynamics have been deficient from a cultural viewpoint. Earley's work on the social loafing phenomenon (1989, in press) illustrates that culture plays a crucial role in understanding group dynamics. Our cultural self-representation model provides new insights on how a loafing context might induce workers to reduce their efforts in one cultural context but not in another. Another shortcoming of the literature is its individualistic orientation, reflected even in such approaches as Misumi's research (1985) on leadership behavior in Japan.

In keeping with our cultural self-representation theory, we have proposed a more specific model of group process within a cultural context. The model is intended to serve as a process model, describing antecedents of group formation as well as the interaction of group and task setting within an organizational and cultural context. Group interactions take place in an organizational context. This suggests that an organization's managerial practices will influence group interactions as well. In this chapter we have presented our conceptual model and explained its significance for the study of groups in social and work contexts. We also applied it to such domains as conformity and deviance, group decisions, social motivation, and work teams.

Conformity and Deviance

The purpose of socialization is to induce individuals to conform to society's practices and to the group to which they belong. Using our model, we described conformity effects as a function of an individual's self-consistency motive and attachment to a group. Simply stated, conformity is the result of an individual's desire to maintain consistency in his or her interpersonal interactions and a propensity to maintain group membership. The actual level of conformity observed in societies will depend on both of these factors. For example, a collectivist may have a low need for consistency but still conform since the propensity to maintain group membership is high. An individualist may have a lower need for consistency and less propensity to stay in a group; we would therefore expect to observe less conformity and a greater likelihood that the individualist will leave a group that applies normative pressure for conformity. Conformity is also a function of task; tasks that promote high interdependence are likely to stimulate conformity as a means to coordinate members' actions.

Group Decision-Making Research

The major influence on intercultural research on group decision-making has been Lewin's Field Theory (1951). The essence of his approach is that participation in the decision-making process will enhance individuals' acceptance of, and commitment to, a decision. Utilizing Lewin's framework, Misumi and his colleagues (e.g., Misumi, 1984; Misumi & Haroaka, 1960; Misumi & Shinohara, 1967) have shown the group-decision method to be highly effective in inducing attitude and habit changes for Japanese workers. We also discussed the Japanese form of decision-making referred to as the *ringi-sei* system (Erez, 1992; Kerlinger, 1951; Nakane, 1970; Triandis, 1989b). This system reflects a strong self-motive of consistency and self-enhancement through group loyalty and commitment. It also reflects a ritualistic style of decision-making that reinforces a strong social hierarchy. A second form of decision-making is the so-called "risky-shift" (Wallach & Kogan, 1965). The shifts observed in the choice-shift paradigm reflect self-categorizations according to our self-motives. For example, it has been argued that individuals shift toward risk and caution in certain cultural environments in order to appear highly capable (Jellison & Riskind, 1970; Lamm & Myers, 1978). This is consistent with self-consistency and self-enhancement motives in conservative (risk avoidant) cultures.

Social Motivation

Our model describes facilitation as a motivational manifestation of self-enhancement and self-efficacy motives. It suggests several explanations for social inhibition or loafing. Ingroup membership activates concepts of group survival and self-efficacy (Earley, 1989; in press). It is more effective in activating these concepts in a collectivistic culture than in an individualistic culture, probably due to the differential effect of self-categorization in various cultures (Turner 1987). Thus an individual's response to the social context will not necessarily reduce his or her contribution to group efforts.

Work Teams

A great deal of attention has been focused on the use of individual-based versus group-based job design (Davis, 1973; Hackman & Oldham, 1980; Tannenbaum, 1980; Trist & Bamforth, 1951). The focus of much of this work has been on the sociotechnical approach to job design (Rousseau, 1977; Thorsrud & Emery, 1970). This approach is consistent with self-motives of efficacy and consistency, which reflect collectivistic values of group solidarity and cooperation. For an individualist, however, self-efficacy and individual growth are achieved through individual accomplishment rather than group effort. This explains the popularity of Hackman and Oldham's Job Design Model (1980), which approaches the redesign of work from the individual's perspective.

In discussing the impact of group dynamics on outcomes we have distinguished among types of outcomes as well as types of tasks undertaken by a group. Our model shows that group formation and processes are tied to different self-motives, depending on the cultural background. The tasks chosen by groups, their approach to task performance, and the outcomes associated with group functioning will vary according to cultural values. We have used our model as a way of identifying new areas for group research, given the interest in group choice and categorization that we see in the literature. Our group model also provides a new way of addressing some of the problems concerning team intervention that are discussed in the literature. It offers a more complete understanding of team members' culture as a predictor of group dynamics.

Leadership

Leadership is one of the most central yet confusing terms in OB literature. It is a general term that may connote power, authority, administration, control, or supervision. Among the many definitions found in the literature, leadership generally involves the following characteristics: interactions among two or more people; a leader's intentional influence on a follower's behavior; and the movement of individuals according to some specified objective (Yukl, 1989).

In chapter 8 we critically examined the concept of leadership using a cultural perspective. In this chapter we built a general model of leadership using the principles derived from our Cultural Self-Representation Theory and the dominant themes in the literature. Our approach emphasized how cultural influences and self-concept magnify and clarify the leader-follower(s) relationship. We discussed how various leadership styles are informed by cultural values and norms, and we described some potential shortcomings of existing models that lack a pancultural approach. In addition we provided a brief review of leadership studies that address cultural issues.

Our general framework, loosely based on Yukl's (1989, 269) integrating model, is based on three major focal points: leader, follower, and intervening processes. We have represented these foci in an interrelated network embedded within a cultural frame or general societal context. The cultural frame does not refer to an organization's "culture"; rather, we have presented organizational culture as inherent in the intervening processes. The cultural frame refers to the society in which the organization operates.

The relation of leader to follower is determined by each person's self-concept, as moderated by culture. For example, in a highly collectivistic culture leaders are recognized and evaluated by their ability to move a group toward valued goals. Followers' attachment to leaders hinges on their relevance to a group's success. In an individualistic culture the emotional attachment occurs as an intimate bond between the leader and follower. The leader is viewed as a source of personal outcomes and recognition. For both leader and follower, self-concept helps outline the nature of how each should interact with the other.

Our analysis of leadership emphasized both the leader and follower as important actors. Leadership theories often neglect such issues as empowerment, attribution, upward influence, and post-action rationalization. Instead they focus on the role of personality and charismatic leadership style in producing joint outcomes (e.g., Bennis & Nanus, 1985; Conger & Kanungo, 1987). The dynamics of the follower's actions seem to be ignored in these models, even though a leader can only "lead" if followers provide the opportunity. Our view presents the actions of both leader and follower as unique, equally powerful, and capable of producing collective as well as individual outcomes.

We used our tripartite approach to leadership to examine a number of interesting themes that have emerged in the literature. One important theme in the notion that charismatic leaders instill a vision within their followers. This concept is particularly important from a cultural perspective. All charismatic theories agree that a shared vision provides followers guidance for their actions. However they fail to explain how underlying cultural themes influence a leader's vision. For example, in an individualistic society such as the United States, a leader must confront difficult situations as an autonomous agent. An effective leader uses the image of "underdog" to persuade followers to adopt the leader's struggle as their own. In a collectivistic society such as the People's Republic of China, the social relationship between leader and follower (and social protocols) dominates the leader's attention. The collectivistic leader must struggle to maintain the social structure of his or her ingroup in order that it will confront external challenges. Thus individualistic and collectivistic charismatic leaders transfer struggles to their followers through very different mechanisms, although both types of leaders rely on a personalized relationship with their followers.

One of the most effective ways for charismatic leaders to transfer these struggles to their followers is through myths and symbols. Kets de Vries (1988) argues that leaders are ideal recipients for the "crystallization of primitive and unstable identifications" (243) as a result of transference. A charismatic leader serves as the group's ego and conscience and resolves followers' anxieties. The leader also represents the embodiment of the followers' favored past relationships. A paternalistic leader assumes the role of father figure in a society that endorses a strong and controlling relationship among parents and children. From a cultural viewpoint, it is clear that the charismatic trait reflects different characteristics or themes across cultures.

In our model, we argued that leaders' vision, and the behavior they chose to enact that vision, are derived from their self-representation. Given that cultural background helps shape the self, we believe that culture plays an important role as an antecedent to leadership vision and action and as an integrator of leaders and followers. Much of the power invested in charismatic authority is derived from attributions made by followers. These attributions of charisma are enhanced by a manager who can effectively invoke cultural myths and heroic deeds according to the follower's belief system (Willner, 1984:15). Some researchers (e.g., Conger, 1988) mistakenly argue that this is evidence that context is not as crucial as relational/personality dynamics. In as much as context is embedded in culture, we would assert that context is overwhelmingly crucial for understanding the effectiveness of a charismatic leader. Charisma in this sense is not a personality trait but rather a label denoting the overlap of an individual's self-representation with cultural beliefs and the extent to which this overlap is consistent with followers' sense of self (Bass, 1988:57).

We described the traits and skills of a follower and how, from the perspective of the individual's self-concept, they influence commitment to a leader. We argued that the commitment phenomenon does not merely reflect an individual's judgment of efficacy to contribute; rather, it reflected a cognitive readjustment based on the challenges inherent in the leader's vision. Next, we described the nature of scripted action and how it relates to cultural background as well as to personal aspects of the self. Finally, we discussed the nature of a follower's identification with a leader and the leader's vision and how this may predict various outcomes.

The approach many researchers have taken to the study of leadership suggests that followers are passive lumps of clay waiting to be shaped by the leader. The acceptance of leader autocracy—the so-called "take charge" style—espoused in North American societies is reflected in these approaches to leadership. Charismatic and transformational theories of leadership assume that the leader captures the mind and heart of a follower who comes to the leader's summons. Even the concept of empowerment suggests that the leader instigates some exchange that provides a subordinate with greater influence, as if it were a gift (Burke & Day, 1986). We argue that leadership is best viewed as an exchange between leader and follower within a social context.

Our purpose in this chapter was to apply the Cultural Self-Representation Theory to understanding the nature of leadership from a cultural viewpoint. We have focused on the significance of structure, roles, and self-definitions of leader and followers in describing leadership. From a structural standpoint, the nature of leader-follower interactions is delimited by the type of organization. We described the importance of individuals' self-definitions and how culture helps define them. Individuals possess cognitive structures of self-concept that incorporate personal and societal experiences. The congruence between a leader's self-concept and that of his or her followers enables us to predict the leader's effectiveness.

Negotiation and Bargaining

Our purpose in chapter 9 was to critically examine negotiation and bargaining from a cultural perspective. The topic of negotiation has been addressed in a number of fields, including psychology, economics, sociology, political science, and industrial relations. Much of this research has focused on prescriptive approaches, examining how individuals might bargain more effectively (Raiffa, 1982; Thompson, 1990). The questions frequently raised focus on outcome maximization (single party as well as joint), avoidance of impasse, and procedural aspects. We focused on a cultural aspect of negotiations, in as much as the criteria for judging outcomes and making offers is culturally based, and concluded that the pattern of transactions that underlies offers and counteroffers is prescribed by the parties' social and normative backgrounds.

The basic negotiation scenario consists of the negotiation parties, their constituencies and interests, the transaction process, available resources, and the negotiation outcome. The party refers to an individual (or group of individuals) who has defined preferences and acts accordingly. A constituency refers to individuals whom a party represents in the pursuit of particular interests. A party may represent constituents with a single nonoverlapping interest as well as overlapping interests (Jensen & Meckling, 1976; Neale & Northcraft, 1991). The transactions process refers to the procedures and practices used by the parties as they interact during a negotiation. For example, collectivists are very concerned with ingroup survival and, therefore, will often begin negotiations by stating what issues are nonnegotiable (ingroup threatening). Individualists, however, are more concerned with appearances and the *means* through which outcomes are achieved (Triandis, 1989a). They are more likely than collectivists to seek compromise positions in order to appear reasonable and earnest in their negotiations. Resource availability refers to those tangible and intangible materials available for distribution among the various parties. Outcomes refer to the distribution of the available resources after the negotiation is complete.

We proposed a model intended to highlight the role of culture in a negotiation. This model can be conceptualized as two general systems—a general frame and a localized one. The general frame consists of such distant influences as social and regulatory procedures, stakes, cultural values, shared histories of the parties, and constituencies or interested parties. The local frame consists of the negotiators' cognition, self-concept, and local work practices and norms for negotiation. We present the localized frame as embedded, since the effect of culture on various components of the model are often subtle and indirect. For example, the cultural background of the negotiators may influence negotiated outcomes through the parties' application of resource allocation rules (Leung & Bond, 1984). For instance, Leung and Bond found that Chinese collectivists differed in their reward allocation rules (equality versus equity) depending on their relationship to the negotiator (ingroup versus outgroup), whereas these differences did not occur for individualistic American negotiators, who generally preferred an equity-based allocation scheme. This study illustrates that cultural norms may have an indirect effect on negotiations, depending on more localized variables (such as the relationship between negotiators).

There is a dynamic component to our model as well since the nature of negotiated outcomes at time *t* may bear a direct impact on subsequent relationships at time *tt1*. American managers have been criticized for their superficial and abbreviated approach to interactions with their Japanese and Middle Eastern counterparts. In these more collective societies, attainment of ingroup status is time-consuming but essential for effective negotiation. The local frame both reflects the need to adhere to cultural practices and reinforces the general norms and values of a culture (Adler, 1986; Harnett & Cummings, 1980; Hofstede, 1980; Triandis, 1989b). Negotiations will be more successful if they adhere to cultural practices, and these successes will, in turn, reinforce existing cultural practices.

A gap in the literature on negotiation is the absence of discussion of cultural influences on negotiator's reactions to constituencies. There is evidence to suggest that the cultural background of a negotiator will influence the nature of his or her relation to the constituency and, consequently, affect negotiating behavior. Glenn (1981) argued that Russians (collectivists) and Americans (individualists) will negotiate differently in a number of ways. Collectivists see more differences between ingroups and outgroups than do individualists (Earley, 1989, 1991; Triandis, 1989b, 1989a). As a result collectivists consider conflict to be a natural course of events and view compromise with an outgroup as a threat to the ingroup. A distributive solution to a negotiation is seen as an unacceptable position (Triandis, 1989a).

In keeping with our self-representation model, we examined the local frame of negotiation from a self-perspective. There are three aspects of the self (enhancement, efficacy, and consistency) that influence negotiation behavior. The extension of a mental structure approach to the self implies that these structures, their shape and content, are influenced by an individual's self-motives. For example, a nego-tiator who has a strong need for consistency may seek quick problem resolutions to avoid conflict, if conflict implies a change in the group's social structure. Concern-ing the shape of a mental structure, a single, dominant self-motive may lead to a narrow set of associations and a rather fixed perspective. The negotiator's strong need for consistency may be reflected by a tendency to interpret social outcomes as a variation of past negotiation practices or traditions. A negotiator who has a strong motive for self-enhancement and who is from a collective culture, which empha-sizes sampling behavior from the collective self, may seek a positive evaluation by acting to gain an ingroup's favor. The notion of "face" in Asian cultures reflects such a motive. A Japanese manager who negotiates on behalf of his company must be careful to appear to be negotiating on the ingroup's behalf so as to avoid suspi-cion and loss of face (Triandis, 1989b). The Japanese manager will monitor his fellow organization members as a means of assessing his successes in a negotiation and use their support and approval as a way to enhance self-image.

The self-efficacy motive will influence the nature of cognitive structures as well. A negotiator who has a strong self-efficacy motive and who samples from the private self will seek out self-generated cues that reflect individual growth and capability during negotiations. Thus a large concession made by an opponent may be seen as a personal triumph and will bolster self-confidence. A large concession may not build the efficacy of a collective-self negotiator since this person's efficacy is tied to the constituency's reaction and not to the negotiation itself.

We also presented an overview of multiparty negotiations. Here, too, the self is viewed as a conduit of cultural influences in a negotiation. An individual's self-motives and sampling impact how he or she views the negotiation context and reacts to offers and counteroffers. We used our model to identify new areas of research such as an expanded view of the interaction of constituencies with their dependent parties and a better understanding of how negotiation positioning might relate to cultural background. Research on negotiation will benefit from a more active con-sideration of cultural effects and the role of an individual's self-concept in shaping negotiations.

PRACTICAL IMPLICATIONS

The reexamination of the research literature in light of our model of cultural self-representation has several practical implications. Cross-cultural relationships are facilitated by the communication system. Therefore a necessary condition for a cross-cultural communication flow is that members of different cultures share an understanding of encoding and decoding rules. These rules are derivations of cultur-al characteristics. Shared understanding can be acquired through a learning process in which the participants develop a common understanding of each others' encoding and decoding rules.

Managers and nonmanager employees who are transferred from their home coun-tries to foreign countries should develop an awareness of cultural differences in managerial practices and rules of behavior. They should be able to identify the moderating effect of culture on the relationship between managerial practices and behavior. Such knowledge will enable managers to predict employees' acceptance or rejection of managerial techniques they might try to implement.

Cultural characteristics should be taken into consideration when decisions are made to transfer managerial practices and motivational techniques across cultures. Management practices should be congruent with cultural values in order to be smoothly adopted and to have a positive effect on behavior. If the adopted methods are not congruent with prevailing cultural values, they should be modified to fit the unique characteristics of the environment. The successful implementation of new managerial techniques requires a knowledge and understanding of the cultural characteristics of the organization and of the specific characteristics of the adopted method.

The practical implications proposed above are direct derivations of the model of cultural self-representation. Kurt Lewin once said that there is nothing more practical than a good theory. We believe that our model proves to be practical because of its strong conceptual framework. A good theory starts with an explicit diagnosis of a problem. The problem which stimulated this work concerns the differential effect of management practices across cultures. On a theoretical level this problem pertains to issues of validity generalization across situations. On a practical level it pertains to the attempt to effectively transfer managerial techniques across cultures.

The next step in the process of model development was to review the literature to learn how others dealt with the problem and whether they have already found a solution. The literature search was disappointing. Existing models of OB not only did not have a solution to the problem but failed to identify the problem; culture was not part of their cognitive schema. Our aim was to develop a conceptual framework that explains the differential effect of managerial techniques across cultures. At this stage it was clear that culture should be incorporated into future models of OB.

In our search for a conceptual framework, we examined the latest theoretical developments in the field of I/O psychology, namely, the cognitive model of self-regulation, trying to fit the cultural factor into that framework. This step has led to the development of our new model of cultural self-representation. The model consists of four major factors: culture and management practices as macro- and meso-level factors; the self as the link between the macro-meso levels and employees' behavior, whereby the self serves as an interpreter of managerial practices in line with cultural values and with respect to their contributions to the satisfaction of self-derived needs; and employees' behavior.

The final step was to test the model by reexamining the existing body of research and reinterpreting the empirical findings in line with the new model. The reanalysis of the existing body of knowledge improves our understanding of organizational behavior across cultures.

The steps we have taken in the process of model development are those recommended by Campbell (1990) for developing a problem-analysis model. We learned about the recommended series of steps only at the end of our journey and therefore believe that these steps are inherent to the process of developing a problem-analysis model. We hope that, on the theoretical level, the model of cultural self-representation will stimulate future research on cross-cultural OB and that on the practical level, it will serve to predict the effectiveness of managerial and motivational techniques prior to their implementation across cultures.

REFERENCES

Abelson, R. P. 1976. Script processing, attitude formation and decision making. In J. S. Carroll and J. W. Payne, eds., *Cognition and social behavior*, 33–46. Hillsdale, NJ: Erlbaum.

———. 1981. Psychological status of the script concept. *American Psychologist* 36:715–29.

Adams, J. S. 1963. Toward an understanding of inequity. *Journal of Personality and Social Psychology* 67:422–36.

Adler, N. J. 1986. *International dimensions of organizational behavior*. Boston: Kent.

Adler, N. J.; Brahm, R.; and Graham, J. L. 1992. Strategy implementation: A comparison of face-to-face negotiations in the People's Republic of China and the United States. *Strategic Management Journal* 13:449–66.

Ajzen, I., and Fishbein, M. 1980. *Understanding attitudes and predicting social behavior*. Englewood Cliffs, NJ: Prentice-Hall.

Allport, F. H. 1924. *Social psychology*. Boston: Houghton-Mifflin.

Allport, G. W.; Vernon, P. E.; and Lindzey, G. 1960. *A study of values*. Boston: Houghton Mifflin.

Amir, Y., and Sharon, I. 1988. Are social psychological laws cross-culturally valid? *Journal of Cross-Cultural Psychology* 18:383–470.

Arnason, J. P. 1990. Nationalism, globalization and modernity. In M. Featherstone, ed., *Global culture-nationalism, globalization, and modernity: A theory of culture and society*. Special issue, 207–36. London: Sage.

Arvey, R. D.; Bouchard, T. J.; Segal, N. L.; and Abraham, L. M. 1989. Job satisfaction: Environmental and genetic components. *Journal of Applied Psychology* 74:187–92.

Asch, S. 1951. Effects of group pressure upon the modification and distortion of judgment. In H. Guetzkow, ed., *Groups, leadership and men*. Pittsburgh, PA: Carnegie Press.

———. 1956. Studies of independence and conformity. A minority of one against a unanimous majority. *Psychological Monographs*, 70(9) (Whole No. 416).

Bales, R. F. 1953. The equilibrium problem in small groups. In T. Parsons, R. F. Bales, and E. A. Shils, eds., *Working papers in the theory of action*, 111–62. Glencoe, IL: Free Press.

Ballon, R. J. 1988. *Japanese decision-making: A circular process*. Business series 117. Tokyo: Sophia Institute of Comparative Study.

Bandura, A. 1986. *Social foundations of thoughts and action: A social cognitive theory*. Englewood Cliffs, NJ: Prentice-Hall.

———. 1989. Perceived self-efficacy in the exercise of personal agency. *The Psychologist: Bulletin of the British Psychological Society* 10:411–24.

Bao, J. M. 1991. Personal conversation. August 28.

Barley, S. R. 1990. The alignment of technology and structure through roles and networks. *Administrative Science Quarterly* 33:24–60.

Barry, H.; Bacon, M. K.; and Child, I. L. 1957. A cross-cultural survey of some sex differences in socialization. *Journal of Abnormal and Social Psychology* 55:327–32.

Bass, B. M. 1981. *Handbook of leadership: A survey of theory and research*. New York: Free Press.

———. 1985. *Leadership and performance beyond expectations*. New York: Free Press.

———. 1988. Evolving perspectives on charismatic leadership. In J. A. Conger and R. N. Kanungo, eds., *Charismatic leadership*, San Francisco: Jossey-Bass.

Bazerman, M. H., and Carroll, J. S. 1987. Negotiator cognition. In B. Staw and L. L. Cummings, eds., *Research in organizational behavior*, Vol. 9, 247–88. Greenwich, CT: JAI Press.

Bazerman, M. H., and Neale, M. A. 1982. Improving negotiator effectiveness: The role of selection and training. *Journal of Applied Psychology* 67:543–48.

———. 1992. *Negotiating rationally*. New York: Free Press.

Bazerman, M. H.; Mannix, E. A.; and Thompson, L. L. 1988. Groups as mixed-motive negotiations. In E. J. Lawler and B. Markovsky, eds., *Advances in group processes: Theory and research*. Vol. 5: 195–216. Greenwich, CT: JAI Press.

Beach, L. R., and Mitchell, T. R. 1990. Image theory: A behavioral theory of decision making in organizations. In M. B. Staw and L. L. Cummings, *Research in organizational behavior*. Vol. 12, 1–41. Greenwich, Conn: JAI Press.

Beer, M., and Walton, E. 1990. Developing the competitive organization: Interventions and strategies. *American Psychologist* 5:154–61.

Benedict, R. 1934. *Patterns of culture*. Boston: Houghton Mifflin.

———. 1946. *The chrysanthemum and the sword*. Boston: Houghton Mifflin.

Bennis, W. (1989). *Why leaders can't lead*. San Francisco: Jossey-Bass.

Bennis, W. G., and Nanus, B. 1985. *Leaders: The strategies for taking charge*. New York: Harper & Row.

Berman, J. J.; Murphy-Berman, V.; Singh, P.; and Kumar, P. 1984. *Cross-cultural similarities and differences in perceptions of fairness*. Journal of Cross-Cultural Psychology 16:55–67.

Berman, J. J., and Singh, P. 1985. Cross-cultural similarities and differences in perceptions of fairness. *Journal of Cross-Cultural Psychology* 16:55–67.

Berry, J. W. 1971. Ecological and cultural factors in spatial perceptual development. *Canadian Journal of Behavioral Science* 3:324–36.

———. 1979. A cultural ecology of social behavior. In L. Berkowitz, ed., *Advances in experimental social psychology*. Vol. 12, NY: Academic Press.

———. 1980. Social and cultural change. In H. C. Triandis and R. W. Brislin, eds., *Handbook of cross-cultural psychology*. Vol. 5:211–80. Boston: Allyn & Bacon.

Berry, J. W., and Annis, R. C. 1974. Ecology, culture and psychological differentiation. *International Journal of Psychology* 9:173–93.

Bhagat, R. S., and McQuaid, S. J. 1982. Role of subjective culture in organizations: A review and directions for future research. *Journal of Applied Psychology Monograph* 67:653–85.

Binswanger, H. 1991. Volition as cognitive self-regulation. *Organizational Behavior and Human Decision Processes* 50:154–78.

Bion, W. R. 1961. *Experiences in groups: And other papers*. New York: Basic Books.

Blake, R. R., and Mouton, J. S. 1964. *The managerial grid*. Houston, TX: Gulf.

———. 1982. Management by grid principles or situationalism: Which? *Organization Studies* 7:207–10.

Blasi, R. J. 1988. *Employee ownership: A revolution or rip off?* Cambridge, MA: Harper & Row.

Boisot, M., and Child, J. 1988. The iron law of fiefs: Bureaucratic failure and the problem of governance in the Chinese economic reforms. *Administrative Science Quarterly* 33:507–27.

Bond, M. H. 1988. Invitation to a wedding: Chinese values and global economic growth. In P. Sinha and H. Kao, eds. *Social values and development*. New Delhi: Sage, 197–209.

Bond, M. H., and Cheung, T. S. 1983. College students' spontaneous self-concept: The effect of culture among respondents in Hong Kong, Japan, and the United States. *Journal of Cross-Cultural Psychology* 14:153–71.

Bond, M. H.; Leung, K.; and Wan, K. C. 1982. How does cultural collectivism operate? The impact of task and maintenance contributions on reward distribution. *Journal of Cross-Cultural Psychology* 13:186–200.

Bond, M. H.; Wan, K.; Leung, K.; and Giacalone, R. A. 1985. How are responses to verbal insults related to cultural collectivism and power distance? *Journal of Cross-Cultural Psychology* 16:111–27.

Bontempo, R.; Lobel, S. A.; and Triandis, H. C. 1989. *Compliance and value internalization among Brazilian and U.S. students*. Typescript. Univ. of Illinois, Champaign, IL.

Bougon, M.; Weich, K.; and Binkhorst, D. 1977. Cognition in organizations: An analysis of the Utrecht jazz orchestra. *Administrative Science Quarterly* 22:606–39.

Boverman, D. M.; Klaiber, E. L.; Kobayashi, Y.; and Vogel, W. 1968. Roles of activation and inhibition in sex differences in cognitive abilities. *Psychological Review* 75:23–50.

Bowen, D. E., and Lawler, E. E., III. 1992. Total quality-oriented human resources management. *Organizational Dynamics* Spring: 29–41.

Boyacigiller, N., and Adler, N. J. 1991. The parochial dinosaur: Organizational science in a global context. *Academy of Management Review* 16:262–90.

Bray, D. W.; Campbell, R. J.; and Grant, D. L. 1974. *Formative years in business: A long-term AT&T study of managerial lives*. New York: Wiley.

Breckler, S. J., and Greenwald, A. G. 1986. Motivational facets of the self. In R. M. Sorrentino and E. T. Higgins, eds., *Handbook of motivation and cognition: Foundations of social behavior*, 145–64. New York: Guilford.

Breer, P. E., and Locke, E. A. 1965. *Task experience as a source of attitudes*. Homewood, IL: Dorsey.

Brewer, M. B., and Kramer, R. M. 1985. The psychology of intergroup attitudes and behavior. *Annual Review of Psychology* 36:219–43.

Brown, R. H. 1977. *A poetic for sociology*. New York: Cambridge University Press.

Burke, M. J., and Day, R. R. 1986. A cumulative study of the effectiveness of managerial training. *Journal of Applied Psychology* 71:232–46.

Burns, J. M. 1978. *Leadership*. New York: Harper & Row.

Burnstein, E., and Vinokur, A. 1975. What a person thinks upon learning he has chosen differently from others: New evidence for the persuasive-arguments explanation of choice shifts. *Journal of Experimental Social Psychology* 11:412–26.

Cahoone, L. E. 1988. *The dilemma of modernity: Philosophy, culture and anti-culture*. Albany: State University of New York Press.

Calder, B. J. 1977. An attribution theory of leadership. In B. M. Staw and G. R. Salancik, eds. *New direction in organizational behavior,* 179–204. Chicago: St. Clair.

Campbell, D. J., and Gingrich, K. F. 1986. The interactive effects of task complexity and participation on task performance: A field experiment. *Organizational Behavior and Human Decision Processes* 38:162–80.

Campbell, J. P. 1990. The role of theory in industrial and organizational psychology. In M. D. Dunnette and L. M. Hough, eds., *Handbook of industrial and organizational psychology,* 2nd ed. Vol. 1, 39–73. Palo Alto, CA: Consulting Psychologists Press.

Canon. 1987. *Canon handbook.* Corporate Communication Centre, Tokyo: Canon.

Cantor, N. and Kihlstrom, J. F. 1987. *Personality and social intelligence.* Englewood Cliffs, NJ: Prentice-Hall.

Cappeli, P., and Sherer, P. D. 1991. The missing role of context in OB: The need for a meso-level approach. In B. Staw and L. L. Cummings, eds. *Research in organizational behavior.* Vol. 13, 55–110. Greenwich, CT: JAI Press.

Carey, J. W. 1988. *Communication and culture.* Boston: Unwin Hyman.

Carnevale, P. J., and Lawler, E. J. 1986. Time pressure and the development of integrative agreements in bilateral negotiations. *Journal of Conflict Resolutions* 30:636–59.

Caroll, D. T. 1983. A disappointing search for excellence. *Harvard Business Review* (Nov.–Dec.), 78–88.

Carroll, J. S., and Payne, J. W. 1976. The psychology of the parole decision makeup process: A joint application of attribution theory and information processing psychology. In J. S. Carroll and J. W. Payne, eds., *Cognition and social behavior,* 13–32. Hillsdale, NJ: Erlbaum.

Cartwright, D., and Zander, A., eds. 1968. *Group dynamics: Research and theory.* 3rd ed. New York: Harper & Row.

Carver, C. S., and Scheier, M. F. 1981. *Attention and self-regulation: A control theory approach to human behavior.* NY: Springer-Verlag.

Cascio, W. F. 1989. *Managing human resources: Productivity, quality of work life, profits.* New York: McGraw Hill.

Chertkoff, J. M., and Esser, J. K. 1976. A review of experiments in explicit bargaining. *Journal of Experimental Social Psychology* 12:464–86.

Chinese Culture Connection. 1987. Chinese values and the search for culture-free dimensions of culture. *Journal of Cross-Cultural Psychology* 18:143–64.

Coch, L., and French, J. R. P. 1948. Overcoming resistance to change. *Human Relations* 1:512–32.

Cole, M., and Scribner, S. 1974. *Culture and thought.* New York: Wiley.

———. In press. Theorizing about socialization of cognition. *Ethos.*

Cole, R. E. 1980. *Work, mobility, and participation: A comparative study of American and Japanese industry.* Berkeley: University of California Press.

Conger, J. A. 1988. Theoretical foundations of charismatic leadership. In J. A. Conger and R. N. Kanungo, eds., *Charismatic leadership* (pp. 12–39) San Francisco: Jossey-Bass.

Conger, J. A., and Kanungo, R. 1987. Toward a behavioral theory of charismatic leadership in organizational settings. *Academy of Management Review* 12:637–47.

Constitution of the United States of America: Amendments to the Constitution of the United States, Article I and Article XIV. In *The 1989 information please almanac,* 598–99. Boston: Houghton Mifflin.

Coon, C. S. 1946. The universality of natural groupings in human societies. *Journal of Educational Sociology* 20:163–68.

Cousins, S. D. 1989. Culture and self-perception in Japan and the United States. *Journal of Personality and Social Psychology* 56:124–31.

Csikszentmihalyi, M. 1975. *Beyond boredom and anxiety.* San Francisco: Jossey-Bass.

Cummings, L. L. 1984. Compensation, culture, and motivation: A systems perspective. *Organizational Dynamics* 12 (3):33–44.

Cushman, P. 1990. Why the self is empty: Toward a historically situated psychology. *American Psychologist* 45:599–611.

D'Andrade, R. 1984. Cultural meaning systems. In R. A. Shweder and R. A. LeVine, eds., *Culture theory: Essays on mind, self, and emotion,* 65–129. New York: Cambridge University Press.

Dachler, H. P., and Wilpert, B. 1978. Conceptual dimensions and boundaries of participation in organizations: A critical evaluation. *Administrative Science Quarterly* 2:1–35.

Davidson, A. R.; Jaccard, J. J.; Triandis, H. C.; Morales, M. L.; and Diaz-Guerrero, R. 1976. Cross-cultural model testing: Toward a solution of the ethic-emic dilemma. *International Journal of Psychology* 11:1–13.

Davis, E. E., and Triandis, H. C. 1970. An experimental study of white-black negotiations. *Journal of Applied Social Psychology* 1:240–62.

Davis, J. H. 1973. Group decision and social interaction: A theory of social decision schemes. *Psychological Review* 80:97–125.

Dawes, R. M. 1972. In defense of "bootstrapping." *American Psychologist* 27:773–74.

Dawson, J. L. M. 1972. Effects of sex hormones on cognitive style in rats and man. *Behavioral Genetics* 2:21–42.

Deal, T., and Kennedy, A. 1982. *Corporate culture: The rites and rituals of corporate life.* Reading, MA: Addison-Wesley.

Deutsch, M., and Krauss, R. M. 1962. Studies of interpersonal bargaining. *Journal of Conflict Resolution* 6:52–76.

Dictionary of the Japanese language. 1974. Tokyo: Shogakkan.

DiMaggio, P. 1982. Cultural entrepreneurship in nineteenth-century Boston. Parts 1–2. *Media, Culture, Society* 4:35–50, 303–22.

Donnellon, A.; Gray, B.; and Bougon, M. G. 1986. Communication, meaning, and organized action. *Administrative Science Quarterly* 31:43–45.

Drucker, P. F. 1971. What we can learn from Japanese management. *Harvard Business Review* 49:110–22.

Druckman, D., Benton, A. A., Ali, F., and Bagur, S. J. 1976. Cultural differences in bargaining behavior: India, Argentina and the United States. *The Journal of Conflict Resolution*, 20, 413–52.

Dubin, R., and Galin, A. 1991. Attachment to work: Russians in Israel. *Work and Occupations* 18:172–93.

Duda, J. L., and Allison, M. T. 1989. The attributional theory of achievement motivation: Cross-cultural considerations. *International Journal of Intercultural Relations* 13:37–55.

———. 1989. The attributional theory of achievement motivation: Cross-cultural considerations. *International Journal of Intercultural Relations* 13:37–55.

Dunnette, M. D. 1971. Multiple assessment procedures in identifying and developing managerial talent. In P. McReynolds, ed., *Advances psychological assessment.* Vol. 2, Palo Alto, CA: Science and Behavior Books.

Durkheim, E. 1933. *The division of labor in society.* Trans. G. Simpson. New York: Free Press.

Earley, P. C. 1984. Social interaction: The frequency of use and evaluation in the U.S., England, and Ghana. *Journal of Cross-Cultural Psychology* 15:477–85.

———. 1986. Supervisors and shop stewards as sources of contextual information in goal-setting: A comparison of the U.S. with England. *Journal of Applied Psychology* 71:111–18.

———. 1989. Social loafing and collectivism: A comparison of the United States and the People's Republic of China. *Administrative Science Quarterly* 34, 565–81.

———. In press. East meets West meets Mideast: Further explorations of collectivistic and individualistic work groups. *Academy of Management Proceedings*, 205–9.

Earley, P. C., and Kanfer, R. 1985. The influence of components of participation and role models on goal acceptance, goal satisfaction, and performance. *Organizational Behavior and Human Decision Processes* 36:378–90.

Earley, P. C., and Lind, E. A. 1987. Procedural justice and participation in task selection: Control-mediated effects of voice in procedural and task decisions. *Journal of Personality and Social Psychology* 52:1148–60.

Earley, P. C., and Lituchy, T. R. 1991. Delineating goal and efficacy effects: A test of three models. *Journal of Applied Psychology* 76:81–98.

Earley, P. C., and Shalley, C. E. 1991. New perspectives on work performance: Merging motivation and cognition. In: Rowland and Ferris, eds., *Research in Personnel and Human Resource Management.* Vol. 9, 121–58. Greenwich, CT: JAI Press.

Eden, D. 1988. Pygmalion, goal-setting, and expectancy: Compatible ways to boost productivity. *Academy of Management Review* 13:639–52.

Elizur, D. 1984. Facets of work values: A structural analysis of work outcomes. *Journal of Applied Psychology* 69:379–89.

England, G. W. 1983. Japanese and American management: Theory Z and beyond. *Journal of International Business Studies* 14:131–41.

England, G. W., and Lee, R. 1973. Organizational size as an influence on perceived organizational goals: A comparative study among American, Japanese, and Korean managers. *Organizational Behavior and Human Performance* 9:48–58.

Epstein, S. 1973. The self-concept revisited, or a theory of a theory. *American Psychologist* 28:408–16.

Erez, M. 1986. the congruence of goal-setting strategies with socio-cultural values and its effect on performance. *Journal of Management* 12:83–90.

————. 1992. Interpersonal communication systems in organizations and their relationships to cultural values, productivity and innovation: The case of Japanese corporations. *Applied Psychology: An International Review* 41:43–64.

————. In press. Towards a model of cross-cultural I/O psychology. In M.D. Dunnette and L. Hough, eds. *Handbook of Industrial and Organizational Psychology.* 2nd ed. Vol. 4. Palo Alto, CA: Consulting Psychologists Press.

Erez, M., and Arad, R. 1986. Participative goal-setting: Social, motivational and cognitive factors. *Journal of Applied Psychology* 71:591–97.

Erez, M., and Earley, P. C. 1987. Comparative analysis of goal-setting strategies across cultures. *Journal of Applied Psychology* 72:658–65.

Erez, M.; Earley, P. C.; and Hulin, C. L. 1985. The impact of participation on goal acceptance and performance: A two-step model. *Academy of Management Journal* 28:50–66.

Erez, M., and Kanfer, F. H. 1983. The role of goal acceptance in goal-setting and task performance. *Academy of Management Review* 8:454–63.

Erez, M.; Rosenstein, E.; and Barr, S. 1989. *Antecedents and supporting conditions for the success of quality circles.* Research report no. 193–720. Haifa: Israel: Technion Institute of Research and Development.

Erez, M., and Zidon, A. 1984. Effect of goal acceptance on the relationship of goal difficulty to performance. *Journal of Applied Psychology* 69:69–78.

Espinoza, J. A., and Garza, R. T. 1985. Social group salience and inter-ethnic cooperation. *Journal of Experimental Social Psychology* 231:380–92.

Etzion, A. 1961. *A comparative analysis of complex organizations.* New York: Free Press.

————. 1968. *The active society.* New York: Free Press.

Etzion, A., and Pines, A. 1986. Sex and culture in burnout and coping among human service professionals: A social psychological perspective. *Journal of Cross-Cultural Psychology* 17:191–209.

Faley, T., and Tedeschi, J. T. 1971. Status and reactions to threats. *Journal of Personality and Social Psychology* 17:192–99.

Farnham, A. 1988. The trust gap. *Fortune* December 4, 56–7.

Feather, N. T., and Hutton, M. A. 1973. Value systems of students in Papua, New Guinea, and Australia. *International Journal of Psychology* 9(2), 91–104.

Ferris, G. R., and Wagner, J. A. 1985. Quality circles in the United States: A conceptual reevaluation. *Journal of Applied Behavioral Science* 21:155–67.

Fiedler, F. E. 1964. A contingency model of leadership effectiveness. In L. Berkowitz, ed., *Advances in experimental social psychology,* 150–90. New York: Academic Press.

————. 1967. *A theory of leadership effectiveness.* New York: McGraw-Hill.

————. 1970. Leadership experience and leader performance: Another hypothesis shot to hell. *Organizational Behavior and Human Performance* 5:1–14.

————. 1971. Validation and extension of the contingency model of leadership effectiveness: A review of empirical findings. *Psychological Bulletin,* 76, 128–148.

————. 1978. The contingency model and the dynamics of the leadership process. In L. Berkowitz (ed.), *Advances in experimental social psychology.* New York: Academic Press.

Fiedler, F. E., and Chemers, M. M. 1984. *Improving leadership effectiveness: The leader match concept.* NY: Wiley.

Fishbein, M., and Ajzen, I. 1975. *Belief, attitude, intention and behavior: An introduction to theory and research.* Reading, MA: Addison-Wesley.

Fiske, J. 1990. *Introduction to communication studies.* 2nd ed. London: Routledge.

Fleishman, E. A., and Harris, E. F. 1962. Patterns of leadership behavior related to employee grievances and turnover. *Personnel Psychology* 15:43–56.

Folger, R. 1977. Distributive and procedural justice: Combined impact of "voice" and improvement on experienced inequity. *Journal of Personality and Social Psychology* 35:108–19.

Foreign Press Center. 1985. *Facts and Figures of Japan* 1985. Tokyo: Foreign Press Center.

Frager, R. 1970. Conformity and anti-conformity in Japan. *Journal of Personality and Social Psychology* 15:203–10.

Frank, R. H. 1988. *Passions within reason.* New York: Norton.

French, J. R. P.; Kay, E.; and Meyer, H. H. 1966. Participation and the appraisal system. *Human Relations* 19:3–20.

French, J. R. P.; Israel, J.; and As, D. 1960. An experiment in a Norwegian factory: Interpersonal dimension in decision-making. *Human Relations* 13:3–19.

French, J. R. P., and Raven, B. 1959. The bases of social power. In D. Cartwright, ed., *Studies in social power,* 150–67. Ann Arbor: Institute for Social Research, University of Michigan.

Frost, P. J.; Moore, L. F.; Louis, M. R.; Lundberg, C. C.; and Martin, J. 1985. *Organizational culture.* Beverly Hills, CA: Sage.

Gabrenya, W. K., Jr.; Bibb, L.; and Wang, Y. 1981. Social loafing among Chinese overseas and U.S. students. Paper presented in August at the Second Asian Conference of the International Association for Cross-Cultural Psychology, Taipei, Taiwan, R.O.C.

————. 1983. Social loafing in cross-cultural perspective. *Journal of Cross-Cultural Psychology* 14:368–84.

————. 1985. Social loafing on an optimizing task: Cross-cultural differences among Chinese and Americans. *Journal of Cross-Cultural Psychology* 16:223–42.

Galbraith, J. 1973. *Designing complex organizations*. Menlo Park, CA: Addison-Wesley.

Galbraith, J. R., and Kazanjian, R. K. 1988. Strategy, technology, and emerging organizations. In J. Hage, ed., *Futures of Organizations,* 29–41. Lexington, MA: Lexington Books.

Garland, H. 1985. A cognitive mediation theory of task goals and human performance. *Motivation and Emotion* 9:345–67.

Gecas, V. 1982. The self concept. *Annual Review of Psychology* 8:1–33.

Geen, R. G., and Gange, J. J. 1977. Drive theory of social facilitation: Twelve years of theory and research. *Psychological Bulletin* 84:1267–88.

Geertz, C. 1973. *The interpretation of cultures*. New York: Basic Books.

Gerlach, M. L., and Lincoln, J. R. 1990. The organization of business networks in the U.S. and Japan. Paper presented at the Networks and Organizations Conference at Harvard University, Cambridge, MA.

Gersick, C. J. G. 1988. Time and transition in work teams: Toward a new model of group development. *Academy of Management Journal* 31:9–41.

————. 1989. Marking time: Predictable transitions in task groups. *Academy of Management Journal* 32:274–309.

Glenn, E. 1981. *Man and mankind: Conflicts and communications between cultures*. Norwood, NJ: Ablex.

Glenn, E.; Witmeyer, D.; and Stevenson, K. 1977. Cultural styles of persuasion. *International Journal of Intercultural Relations* 1:52–56.

Gluskinos, U. M. 1988. Cultural and political considerations in the introduction of Western technologies: The Mekorot project. *Journal of Management Development* 6(3):34–46.

Goldberg, A. 1991. Personal conversation. October 17.

Gologor, E. 1977. Group polarization in a non–risk taking culture. *Journal of Personality and Social Psychology* 15:203–10.

Goodenough, W. H. 1956. Componential analysis and the study of meaning. *Language* 32:195–216.

————. 1970. *Description and comparison in cultural anthropology*. Chicago: Aldine.

————. 1971. *Culture, language and society*. Reading, MA: Addison-Wesley.

Goodman, P. S., et al. 1986. *Designing effective work groups*. San Francisco: Jossey-Bass.

Graves, D. 1972. Cultural determinism and management behavior. *Organizational Dynamics* 1:46–59.

Greenhalgh, L. 1987. Relationships in negotiation. *Negotiation Journal* 3:235–43.

Greenwald, A. G. 1980. The totalitarian ego: Fabrication and revision of personal history. *American Psychologist* 85:53–57.

Gruenfeld, L. W., and MacEachron, A. E. 1975. A cross-national study of cognitive style among managers and technicians. *International Journal of Psychology* 10:27–55.

Gudykunst, W. B., and Kim, Y. 1984. *Communicating with strangers*. New York: Random House.

Gudykunst, W. B.; Ting-Toomey, S.; and Chua, E. 1988. *Culture and interpersonal communication*. Beverly Hills, CA: Sage.

Guzzo, R., and Waters, J. A. 1982. The expression of the affect and the performance of decision-making groups. *Journal of Applied Psychology* 67:67–74.

Gyllenhammar, P. G. 1977. How Volvo adapts work to people. *Harvard Business Review* July–August: 102–13.

Habermas, J. 1979. *Knowledge and human interest*. Boston: Beacon Press.

Hackman, J. R. 1990. Introduction. In J. R. Hackman, ed., *Groups that work (and those that don't),* 1–14. San Francisco: Jossey-Bass.

Hackman, J. R., and Morris, C. G. 1978. Group process and group effectiveness: A reappraisal. In L. Berkowitz, ed., *Group processes,* 57–66. New York: Academic Press.

Hackman, J. R., and Oldham, G. R. 1980. *Work redesign*. Reading, MA: Addison-Wesley.

Hackman, J. R.; Oldham, G. R.; Janson, K.; and Purdy, K. 1975. A new strategy for job enrichment. *California Management Review* 17:57–71.

Haire, M.; Ghiselli, E. E.; and Porter, L. W. 1966. *Managerial thinking: An international study*. New York: Wiley.

Hall, E. T. 1976. *Beyond culture*. Garden City, NY: Doubleday.

Hamner, W. C., and Harnett, D. L. 1975. The effects of information and aspiration level on bargaining behavior. *Journal of Experimental Social Psychology* 11:329–42.

Harkins, S. G., and Petty, R. E. 1983. Social context effects in persuasion. In P. B. Paulus, ed., *Basic group processes,* 149–78. New York: Springer-Verlag.

Harnett, D. L., and Cummings, L. L. 1980. *Bargaining behavior: An international study.* Houston, TX: Dame.

Harris, P. R., and Moran, R. T. 1987. *Managing cultural differences.* Houston, TX: Gulf.

Harris, S. G., and Sutton, R. I. 1986. Functions of parting ceremonies in dying organizations. *Academy of Management Journal* 29:5–30.

Heller, F. A.; Drenth, P.; Koopman, P.; and Ruz, V. 1988. *Decisions in organizations: A three-country comparative survey.* Newbury Park, CA: Sage.

Heller, F. A., and Wilpert, B. 1981. *Competence and power in managerial decision making: A study of senior levels of organization in eight countries.* Chichester, NY: John Wiley.

Hellriegel, D.; Slocum, J. W.; and Woodman, R. W. 1989. *Organizational Behavior,* 5th ed. St. Paul, MN: West Publishing Company.

Henry, J. P., and Stephens, P. M. 1977. *Stress, health, and social environment.* NY: Springer.

Hersey, P., and Blanchard, K. 1982. *Management of organizational behavior: Utilizing human resources,* 4th ed. Englewood Cliffs, NJ: Prentice-Hall.

Herskovits, M. J. 1955. *Cultural anthropology.* New York: Knopf.

Hill, C. W. L.; Hitt, M. A.; and Hoskisson, R. E. 1988. Declining U.S. competitiveness: Reflection on a crisis. *Academy of Management Executive* 2:51–60.

Hirsch, P. M. 1987. *Pack your own parachute: How to survive mergers, takeovers, and other corporate disasters.* Reading, MA: Addison-Wesley.

Hirsch, P. M., and Andrews, J. A. Y. 1983. Ambushes, shootouts, and knights of the roundtable: The language of corporate takeovers. In L. R. Pondy, P. J. Frost, G. Morgan, and T. Dandridge, eds., *Organizational symbolism,* 145–55. Greenwich, CT: JAI Press.

Hitachi. 1986. *Introduction to Hitachi and modern Japan.* Tokyo: Hitachi Ltd.

Hoelter, J. W. 1985. The structure of self-conception: Conceptualization and measurement. *Journal of Personality and Social Psychology* 49:1392–1407.

Hofstede, G. 1980a. *Culture's consequences: International differences in work-related values.* Newbury Park, CA: Sage.

———. 1980b. Motivation, leadership and organization: Do American theories apply abroad? *Organizational Dynamics* (Summer): 42–63.

———. 1983. The cultural relativity of organizational practices and theories. *Journal of International Business Studies* 14:75–89.

———. 1984. The cultural relativity of the Quality of Life concept. *Academy of Management Review* 9:389–98.

———. 1991. *Culture and organizations: Software of the mind.* London: McGraw-Hill.

Hofstede, G., and Bond, M. H. 1988. The confucius connection: From cultural roots to economic growth. *Organizational Dynamics* (Spring), 4–21.

Hofstede, G.; Neuijen, B.; Ohayv, D. D.; and Sanders, G. 1990. Measuring organizational cultures: A qualitative and quantitative study across twenty cases. *Administrative Science Quarterly* 35:286–316.

Holland, J. 1973. *Making vocational choices: A theory of careers.* Englewood Cliffs, NJ: Prentice-Hall.

Holloway, S. D. 1988. Concepts of ability and effort in Japan and the United States. *Review of Educational Research* 58:327–45.

Holtzman, W. H. 1980. Projective techniques. In H. C. Triandis and J. W. Berry, eds., *Handbook of cross-cultural psychology.* Vol. 2, 245–78. Boston: Allyn & Bacon.

Homans, G. C. 1958. Social behavior as exchange. *American Journal of Sociology* 63:597–606.

Honigmann, J. S. 1959. *The world of man.* New York: Harper & Row.

House, R. J. 1971. A path goal theory of leader effectiveness. *Administrative Science Quarterly* 16:321–38.

House, R. J., and Singh, J. 1988. Power and personality in organizations. *Research in organizational behavior.* Vol. 10, 305–57. Greenwich, CT: JAI Press.

House, R. J.; Spangler, W. D.; and Woycke, J. 1991. Personality and charisma in the U.S. presidency: A psychological theory of leader effectiveness. *Administrative Science Quarterly* 36:364–96.

Hsu, F. 1985. The self in cross-cultural perspective. In A. Marsella, G. DeVos, and F. Hsu, eds., *Culture and self: Asian and Western perspectives,* 24–55. New York: Tavistock.

Huber, V., and Neale, M. 1986. Effects of cognitive heuristics and goals on negotiator performance and subsequent goal setting. *Organizational Behavior and Human Decision Processes* 38:342–65.

Hui, C. H. 1984. Individualism-collectivism: Theory, measurement and its relation to reward allocation. Ph.D. diss., University of Illinois, Urbana-Champaign.

Hui, C. H., and Triandis, H. C. 1985. Measurement in cross-cultural psychology. *Journal of Cross-Cultural Psychology* 16:131–52.

Introduction to Hitachi and modern Japan. 1986. Tokyo: Hitachi Ltd.

Hulin, C. L., and Mayer, L. J. 1986. Psychometric equivalence of a translation of the JDI into Hebrew. *Journal of Applied Psychology* 71:83–94.

Isen, A. M., and Baron, R. 1991. Positive affect in organizations. In L. L. Cummings and B. M. Staw, eds., *Research in organizational behavior*. Vol. 14, 91–137. Greenwich, CT: JAI Press.

Ishida, E. 1974. *Japanese culture: A study of origins and characteristics*. Trans. T. Kachi. Honolulu: University of Hawaii Press.

Jacobs, T. O. 1970. *Leadership and exchange in formal organizations*. Alexandria, VA: Human Resources Research Organization.

Jaeger, A. M. 1983. The transfer of organizational culture overseas: An approach to control in the multinational corporation. *Journal of International Business Studies* 14:91–114.

————. 1986. Organizational development and national culture: Where's the fit? *Academy of Management Review* 11:178–90.

Jahoda, G. 1980. Theoretical and systematic approaches in cross-cultural psychology. In H. C. Triandis and W. W. Lanbert, eds., *Handbook of cross-cultural psychology*. Vol. 1, 69–142. Boston: Allyn & Bacon.

James, L. R.; Demaree, R. G.; Mulaik, S. A.; and Ladd, R. T. 1992. Validity generalization in the context of situational models. *Journal of Applied Psychology* 77:3–14.

Janis, I. L. 1982. *Groupthink: Psychological studies of policy decisions and fiascoes*. Boston: Houghton Mifflin.

Jellison, J. M., and Riskind, J. 1970. A social comparison of abilities interpretation of risk-taking behavior. *Journal of Personality and Social Psychology* 15:375–90.

Jensen, M. C., and Meckling, W. H. 1976. Agency theory. *Journal of Financial Economics* 3:305–60.

Kagan, S.; Knight, G.; and Martinez-Romero, S. 1982. Culture and the development of conflict resolution style. *Journal of Cross-Cultural Psychology* 13:43–59.

Kagicibasi, C., and Berry, J. W. 1989. Cross-cultural psychology: Current research and trends. *Annual Review of Psychology* 40:493–531.

Kanfer, F. H. 1980. Self-management methods. In F. H. Kanfer and A. P. Goldstein, eds., *Helping people change*. 2nd ed., 334–89. New York: Pergamon.

Kanfer, R. 1990. Motivation theory and industrial and organizational psychology. In M. D. Dunnette and L. Hough, eds., *Handbook of industrial and organizational psychology* (2nd ed.). Vol. 1, 75–170. Palo Alto, Ca: Consulting Psychologists Press.

Kanfer, R., and Ackerman, P. L. 1989. Motivation and cognitive abilities: An integrative/aptitude-treatment interaction approach to skill acquisition. *Journal of Applied Psychology* 74:657–90.

Kashima, Y., and Triandis, H. C. 1986. The self-serving bias in attributions as a coping strategy: A cross-cultural study. *Journal of Cross-Cultural Psychology* 17:83–97.

Katriel, T. 1986. *Talking straight: Dugri speech in Israeli Sabra culture*. Cambridge: Cambridge University Press.

Katz, D., and Kahn, R. L. 1978. *The social psychology of organizations*, 2nd ed. New York: Wiley.

Katz, D.; Maccoby, N.; and Morse, N. 1950. *Productivity, supervision, and morale in an office situation*. Ann Arbor, MI: Institute for Social Research, University of Michigan.

Katzell, R. A., and Thompson, D. E. 1990. Work motivation: Theory and practice. *American Psychologist* 45:144–53.

Kelley, H. H., and Thibaut, J. W. 1978. *Interpersonal relations: A theory of interdependence*. New York: Wiley.

Kelman, H. C. 1961. Processes of opinion change. *Public Opinion Quarterly* 25:57–78.

Kerlinger, G. 1951. Decision making in Japan. *Social Forces* 30:36–41.

Kerr, N. 1983. Motivation losses in small groups: A social dilemma analysis. *Journal of Personality and Social Psychology* 45:819–28.

Kets de Vries, M. F. R. 1988. Origins of charisma: Ties that bind the leader to the led. In J. A. Conger and R. N. Kanungo, eds., *Charismatic leadership*, (pp. 237–252) San Francisco: Jossey-Bass.

Kets de Vries, M. F. R., and Miller, D. 1986. Personality, culture, and organization. *Academy of Management Review* 11:266–79.

Kihlstrom, J. F., and Cantor, N. 1984. Mental representations of the self. In L. Berkowitz, ed., *Advances in experimental social psychology*. Vol. 17, 2–48. N.Y.: Academic Press.

Kihlstrom, J. F.; Cantor, N.; Albright, J. S.; Chew, B. R.; Klein, S. B.; and Niedenthal, P. M. 1988. Information processing and the study of the self. *Advances in Experimental Social Psychology*. Vol. 21, 145–78. San Diego, CA: Academic Press.

Kilmann, R.; Saxton, M.; and Serpa, R. 1985. *Gaining control of the corporate culture*. San Francisco: Jossey-Bass.

Kipnis, D., and Schmidt, S. M. 1983. An influence perspective on bargaining within organizations. In M. Bazerman and R. Lewicki, eds., *Research on negotiation in organizations* 1:303–19.

Kirkpatrick, D. 1992. Here comes the payoff from computers. *Fortune* (March), 51–57.

Kluckhohn, C. 1951. The study of culture. In D. Lerner and H. D. Lasswell, eds., *The policy sciences*. Stanford, CA.: Stanford University Press.

———. 1954. *Culture and behavior*. New York: Free Press.

Kluckhohn, F., and Strodtbeck, F. 1961. *Variations in value orientations*. Westport, CT: Greenwood Press.

Komorita, S. S.; Sheposh, J. P.; and Braver, S. L. 1968. Power, the use of power and cooperative choice in a two-person game. *Journal of Personality and Social Psychology* 8:134–42.

Kornadt, H. J.; Eckensberger, L. H.; and Emmingaus, W. B. 1980. Cross-cultural research on motivation and its contribution to a general theory of motivation. In H. C. Triandis and W. W. Lonner, eds., *Handbook of cross-cultural Psychology*. Vol. 3, 223–322. Boston: Allyn & Bacon.

Krauss, R. M., and Deutsch, M. 1966. Communication in interpersonal bargaining. *Journal of Personality and Social Psychology* 4:572–77.

Kraut, A. I., and Ronen, S. 1975. Validity of job facet importance: A multinational, multicriteria study. *Journal of Applied Psychology* 60:671–77.

Kruglanski, A. W. 1980. Lay epistemology process and content. *Psychological Review* 87:1–44.

Kuhl, J. 1992. Motivation and volition. A paper presented at the XXV International Congress of Psychology, Brussels, Belgium.

Kuhl, J., and Kraska, K. 1989. Self-regulation and metamotivation: Computational mechanisms, development, and assessment. In R. Kanfer, P. L. Ackerman, and R. Cudeck, eds., *Abilities, motivation, and methodology*. Hillsdale, NJ: Lawrence Erlbaum.

Kume, T. 1985. Managerial attitudes toward decision-making: North America and Japan. In W. P. Gudykunst, L. P. Stewart, & S. Ting-Toomey, eds., *Communication, culture and organizational processes,RR, 231–57*. Beverly Hills, CA: Sage.

Kunda, Z. 1987. Motivated inference: Self-serving generation and evaluation of causal theories. *Journal of Personality and Social Psychology* 53:636–47.

———. (in press). The case for motivated reasoning. *Psychological Bulletin*.

Lachman, R. 1983. Modernity change of core and peripheral values of factory workers. *Human Relations* 36:563–80.

Lamm, H., and Myers, D. G. 1978. Group-induced polarization of attitudes and behavior. In L. Berkowitz, ed., *Advances in experimental social psychology*. Vol. 11, 145–97. New York: Academic Press.

Larson, A. W. 1978. Aperceptual style and intercultural communication. In F. L. Casmir, ed. *Intercultural and international communication*. Washington, D.C.: University Press of America.

Lasswell, H. D. 1960. *Psychopathology and Politics*. Rev. ed. New York: Viking Penguin.

Latané, B.; Williams, K. D.; and Harkins, S. 1979. Many hands make light the work: The causes and consequences of social loafing. *Journal of Personality and Social Psychology* 37:822–32.

Latham, G. P.; Erez, M.; and Locke, E. A. 1988. Resolving scientific disputes by the joint design of crucial experiments by the antagonists: Application to the Erez-Latham dispute regarding participation in goal setting. *Journal of Applied Psychology* 73:753–72.

Laughlin, P. R. 1980. Social combination processes of cooperative, problem-solving groups as verbal intellective tasks. In M. Fishbein, ed., *Progress in social psychology*. Vol. 1, 46–82. Hillsdale, NJ: Erlbaum.

Lawler, E. E., III. 1986. *High involvement management*. New York: Jossey-Bass.

Lebon, G. 1895. *Psychologie des foules*. Paris: F. Oléan. (English trans. *The crowd*. London: T. Fisher Unwin, 1896.)

Lebra, T. S. 1976. *Japanese patterns of behavior*. Honolulu: University of Hawaii Press.

Lemyre, L., and Smith, P. M. 1985. Intergroup discrimination and self-esteem in the minimal group paradigm. *Journal of Personality and Social Psychology* 49:660–70.

Leung, K. 1985. Cross-cultural study of procedural fairness and disputing behavior. Ph.D. diss., University of Illinois, Urbana-Champaign.

Leung, K. 1987. Some determinants of reactions to procedural models for conflict resolution: A cross-national study. *Journal of Personality and Social Psychology* 53:898–908.

Leung, K., and Bond, M. 1984. The impact of cultural collectivism on reward allocation. *Journal of Personality and Social Psychology* 47:793–804.

Leung, K.; Earley, P. C.; and Lind, E. A. 1990. *Organizational justice in the United States and Hong Kong*. Working paper. Chinese University of Hong Kong.

Leung, K., and Li, W. 1990. Psychological mechanism of process-control effects. *Journal of Applied Psychology* 75:613–20.

Leung, K., and Park, H. J. 1986. Effects of interactional goal on choice of allocation rule: A cross-national study. *Organizational Behavior and Human Decision Processes* 37:11–120.

Leventhal, G. S.; Karuza, J.; and Fry, W. R. 1980. Beyond fairness: A theory of allocation preferences. In G. Mikula, ed., *Justice and social interaction: Experimental and theoretical contributions from psychological research:* 167–218. NY: Springer-Verlag.

Lévi-Bruhl, L. 1910. Les fonctions mentales dans les sociétés in inféreures. Paris: Alcan.

Levi-Strauss, C. 1963. *Structural anthropology.* Trans. New York: Basic Books.

Leviatan, U. 1983. Work and aging in the kibbutz: Some relevancies for the larger society. *Aging and Work* 6:215–26.

Leviatan, U., and Cohen, J. 1985. Gender differences in life expectancy among kibbutz members. *Social Science Medicine* 21:545–51.

Leviatan, U., and Rosner, M. 1980. *Work and organization in kibbutz industry.* Norwood, PA: Norwood Editions.

LeVine, R. 1984. Properties of culture: An ethnographic view. In R. A. Shweder and R. A. LeVine, eds., *Culture theory: Essays on mind, self, and emotion.* New York: Cambridge University Press.

Lewicki, R., and Litterer, J. 1985. *Negotiation.* Homewood, IL: Irwin.

Lewin, K. 1943. Forces behind food habits and methods of change. *Bulletin of the National Resource Council* 108:36–65.

———. 1951. *Field theory and social science.* New York: Harper.

Li, D. J. 1978. *The ageless Chinese.* New York: Charles Scribner's Sons.

Likert, R. 1961. *New patterns of management.* NY: McGraw-Hill.

Lincoln, J. R. 1990. Japanese organizations and organization theory. In B. M. Staw and L. L. Cummings, eds., *Research in organizational behavior.* Vol. 12, 255–94. Greenwich, CT: JAI Press.

Lincoln, J. R.; Hanada, R.; and Olson, J. 1981. Cultural orientation and individual reactions to organizations: A study of employees of Japanese-owned firms. *Administrative Science Quarterly* 26:93–115.

Lincoln, J. R.; Olson, J.; and Hanada, M. 1978. Cultural effects on organizational structure: The case of Japanese firms in the United States. *American Sociological Review* 43:829–47.

Lind, E. A., and Earley, P. C. 1992. Procedural justice and culture. *International Journal of Psychology* 27:227–42.

Lind, E. A.; Erickson, B. E.; Friedland, N.; and Dickenberger, M. 1978. Reactions to procedural models for adjudicative conflict resolution: A cross-national study. *Journal of Conflict Resolution* 22:318–41.

Lind, E. A.; Kanfer, R.; and Earley, P. C. 1990. Voice, control, and procedural justice: Instrumental and noninstrumental concerns in fairness judgments. *Journal of Personality and Social Psychology* 59:952–59.

Lind, E. A., and Tyler, T. R. 1988. *The social psychology of procedural justice.* New York: Plenum.

Linville, P. W. 1982. Self-complexity as a cognitive buffer against stress-related illness and depression. *Journal of Personality and Social Psychology* 52:663–76.

Little, K. B. 1968. Cultural variations in social schemata. *Journal of Personality and Social Psychology* 10:1–7.

Littlejohn, S. W. 1988. *Theories of human communication.* 3rd ed. Belmont, CA: Wadsworth.

Lobel, S. A. 1986. Effects of intercultural contact on variance of stereotypes. Typescript. University of Illinois, Urbana-Champaign.

Locke, E. A. 1968. Toward a theory of task motivation and incentives. *Organizational Behavior and Human Performance* 3:157–89.

———. 1991. The motivation sequence, the motivation hub, and the motivation core. *Organizational Behavior and Human Decision Processes* 50:288–99.

Locke, E.A.; Frederick, E.; Lee, C.; and Bobko, P. 1984. Effects of self-efficacy, goals, and task strategies on task performance. *Journal of Applied Psychology* 69:241–51.

Locke, E. A., and Latham, P. G. 1990. *A theory of goal setting and task performance.* Englewood Cliffs, NJ: Prentice-Hall.

Locke, E. A.; Latham, G. P.; and Erez, M. 1988. The determinants of goal commitment. *Academy of Mangement Review* 1:23–39.

Locke, E. A., and Schweiger, D. M. 1979. Participation in decision-making: One more look. In B. M. Staw, ed., *Research in organizational behavior.* Vol. 1, 265–339. Greenwich, CT: JAI Press.

Loevinger, J. 1976. *Ego development.* San Francisco: Jossey-Bass.

Lord, R. G. 1977. Functional leadership behavior: Measurement and relation to social power and leadership perceptions. *Administrative Science Quarterly* 22:114–33.

Lord, R. G.; Binning, J. F.; Rush, M. C.; and Thomas, J. C. 1978. The effect of performance cues and leader behavior on questionnaire ratings of leadership behavior. *Organizational Behavior and Human Performance* 21:27–39.

Lord, R. G., and Foti, R. J. 1985. Schema theories, information processing, and organizational behavior. In H. P. Sims and D. A. Gioia, eds., *The thinking organization,* 21–48. San Francisco: Jossey-Bass.

Lord, R. G., and Kernan, M. C. 1987. Scripts as determinants of purposeful behavior in organizations. *Academy of Management Review* 12:265–77.

Maehr, M. L., and Braskamp, L. A. 1986. *The motivation factor: A theory of personal investment.* Lexington, MA: Lexington Books.

Malinowski, B. 1944. *A scientific theory of culture.* Chapel Hill: University of North Carolina Press.

Mandler, G. 1975. *Mind and emotion.* New York: Wiley.

Mann, L. 1980. Cross-cultural studies of small groups. In H. C. Triandis and R. W. Brislin, eds., *Handbook of cross-cultural psychology.* Vol. 15, 155–210. Boston: Allyn & Bacon.

Mann, L.; Radford, M.; and Kanagawa, C. 1985. Cross-cultural differences in children's use of decision rules: A comparison between Japan and Australia. *Journal of Personality and Social Psychology* 49:1557–64.

Mannheim, B., and Dubin, R. 1986. Work role centrality of industrial workers as related to organizational conditions, task autonomy, managerial orientations and personal characteristics. *Journal of Occupational Behavior* 39:359–77.

Mannix, E. A.; Thompson, L. L.; and Bazerman, M. H. 1989. Small group negotiation. *Journal of Applied Psychology* 74:508–17.

Marcie, D. 1990. *Organizational behavior: Experiences and cases.* 2nd ed. St. Paul, MN: West.

Markus, H. R., and Kitayama, S. 1991. Culture and the self: Implications for cognition, emotion, and motivation. *Psychological Review* 98:224–53.

Markus, H., and Kunda, Z. 1986. Stability and malleability of the self-concept. *Journal of Personality and Social Psychology* 51:858–66.

Markus, H., and Wurf, E. 1987. The dynamic self-concept: A social psychological perspective. *Annual Review of Psychology* 38:299–337.

Marsh, H. 1986. Global self-esteem: Its relation to specific facets of self-concept and their importance. *Journal of Personality and Social Psychology* 51:1224–36.

Martin , J. 1982. Stories and scripts in organizational settings. In A. H. Hastorf and A. M. Isen, eds., *Cognitive social psychology,* 255–306. New York: Elsevier.

Martin, J., and Siehl, C. 1983. Organizational culture and counterculture: An uneasy symbiosis. *Organizational Dynamics* 12:52–64.

Maslow, A. H. 1954. *Motivation and personality.* New York: Harper and Row.

Matsui, T. 1990. Personal communication. Saitama, Japan: Surugadai University.

Matsui, T.; Kakuyama, T.; and Onglatco, M. L. 1987. Effects of goals and feedback on performance in groups. *Journal of Applied Psychology* 72:407–15.

Mausner, B., and Graham, J. 1970. Field dependence and prior reinforcement as determinants of social interaction in judgement. *Journal of Personality and Social Psychology* 16:486–93.

Maxwell, G., and Schmitt, D. R. 1975. *Cooperation: An experimental analysis.* New York: Academic Press.

McAlister, L.; Bazerman, M. H.; and Fader, P. 1986. Power and goal setting in channel negotiations. *Journal of Marketing Research* 23:228–36.

McCall, M. W., Jr., and Lombardo, M. M., eds. 1978. *Leadership: Where else can we go?* Durham, NC: Duke University.

McClelland, D. C. 1961. *The achieving society.* Princeton, NJ: Van Nostrand.

McClelland, D. C., and Boyatzis, R. E. 1982. Leadership motive pattern and long-term success in management. *Journal of Applied Psychology* 67:737–43.

McClelland, D. C.; Davidson, R. J.; Saron, C.; and Floor, E. 1980. The need for power, brain norepinephrine turnover, and learning. *Biological Psychology* 10:93–102.

McClelland, D. C.; Patel, V.; Stier, D.; and Brown, D. 1987. The relationship of affiliative arousal to dopamine release. *Motivation and Emotion* 9:1–10.

McClelland, D. C., and Winter, D. G. 1971. *Motivating economic achievement.* New York: Free Press.

McDougall, W. 1908. *An introduction to social psychology.* London: Methuen.

McGrath, J. E. 1984. *Groups: interaction and performance.* Englewood Cliffs, NJ: Prentice-Hall.

McGrath, J. E., and Altman, I. 1966. *Small group research: A synthesis and critique of the field.* New York: Holt, Rinehart & Winston.

McGregor, D. 1960. *The human side of enterprise.* NY: McGraw-Hill.

McGuire, J. 1980. The development of theory of social psychology. In R. Gilmour and S. Duck, eds., *The development of social psychology,* 54–80. London: Academic Press.

———. 1983. A contextual theory of knowledge: Its implementations for innovation and reform in psychological research. In L. Berkowitz, ed., *Advances in experimental social psychology,* 1–47. Orlando, FL: Academic Press.

McKersie, R. B.; Perry, C. R.; and Walton, R. E. 1965. Intraorganizational bargaining in labor negotiations. *Journal of Conflict Management* 9:463–81.

McKie, J. W. 1974. *Social responsibility in the business predicament*. Washington, DC: Brookings Institution.

Mead, M. 1967. *Cooperation and competition among primitive people*. Boston: Beacon Press.

Meindl, J. R.; Hunt, R. G.; and Lee, W. 1989. Individualism-collectivism and work values: Data from the United States, China, Taiwan, Korea and Hong Kong. *Research in Personnel and Human Resources Management*. suppl. 1, 59–77.

Meir, E. I., and Hasson, R. 1982. Congruence between personality type and environment type as a predictor of stay in an environment. *Journal of Vocational Behavior* 21:309–17.

Mergers and Acquisitions. 1990. M&A demographics of the decade: The top 100 deals of the decade. *Mergers and Acquisitions* 25:107–12.

Messick, D. M., and Mackie, D. M. 1989. Intergroup relations. *Annual Review of Psychology* 40:45–81.

Miles, R. E., and Snow, C. C. 1984. Fit, failure, and the Hall of Fame. *California Management Review* 26:10–28.

Miller, G. A.; Galanter, E.; and Pribram, K. H. 1960. *Plans and the structure of behavior*. New York: Holt, Rinehart.

Miller, J. G. 1984. Culture and the development of every-day social explanation. *Journal of Personality and Social Psychology* 46:961–78.

Miner, J. B. 1978. Twenty years of research on role-motivation theory of managerial effectiveness. *Personnel Psychology* 31:739–60.

Misumi, J. 1984. Decision-making in Japanese groups and organizations. In B. Wilpert and A. Sorge, eds., *International perspectives on organizational democracy,* 92–123. New York: Wiley.

Misumi, J. 1985. *The behavioral science of leadership. An interdisciplinary Japanese research program*. Ann Arbor: University of Michigan Press.

Misumi, J., and Haraoka, K. 1960. An experimental study of group decision-making (III). *Japanese Journal of Educational Social Psychology* 1:136–53.

Misumi, J., and Peterson, M. F. 1985. The performance-maintenance (PM) theory of leadership: Review of a Japanese research program. *Administrative Science Quarterly* 30:198–223.

Misumi, J., and Shinohara, H. 1967. A study of effects of group decision on accident prevention. *Japanese Journal of Educational Social Psychology* 6:123–34.

Mitchell, T. R. 1973. Motivation and participation: An integration. *Academy of Management Journal* 16:670–79.

———. 1982. Motivation: New directions for theory, research, and practice. *Academy of Management Review* 7:80–8.

Mitchell, T. R., and Liden, R. C. 1982. The effects of the social context on performance evaluations. *Organizational Behavior and Human Performance* 29:241–56.

Mitchell, T. R., and Wood, R. E. 1980. Supervisor's responses to subordinate poor performance: A test of an attributional model. *Organizational Behavior and Human Performance* 25:123–38.

Miyahara, A. 1984. A need for a study to examine the accuracy of American observers' perceptions of Japanese managers' communication styles. Paper presented at the Eastern Communication Association Convention, Philadelphia.

Moreland, R. L., and Levine, J. M. 1987. The composition of small groups. In E. J. Lawler, B. Markovsky, C. Ridgeway, and H. A. Walker, eds., *Advances in group processes*. Vol. 9, 237–80. Greenwich, CT: JAI Press.

Morgan, G., and Smircich, L. 1980. The case for qualitative research. *Academy of Management Review* 5:491–500.

Morris, C. W. 1956. *Varieties of human value*. Chicago: University of Chicago Press.

MOW International Research Team. 1986. *The meaning of working: An international perspective*. New York: Academic Press.

Murdock, G. P. 1945. The common denominator of cultures. In R. Linton, ed., *The science of man in the world of crisis,* 123–42. New York: Columbia University Press.

———. 1957. World ethnographic sample. *American Anthropologist* 59:664–87.

Murninghan, J. K. 1978. Models of coalition behavior: Game theoretic, social, psychological and political perspectives. *Psychological Bulletin* 85:1130–53.

Murninghan, J. K., and Brass, D. In press. Intraorganizational coalitions. In M. Bazerman; R. Lewicki; and B. Sheppard, eds., *The handbook of negotiation research*. Vol. 3. Greenwich, CT: JAI Press.

Murphy-Berman, V.; Bernan, J.; Singh, P.; Pachuri, A.; and Kumar, P. 1984. Factors affecting allocation to needy and meritorious recipients: A cross-cultural comparison. *Journal of Personality and Social Psychology* 46:1267–72.

Murray, H. A. 1938. *Explorations in personality*. New York: Oxford University Press.

Nakane, C. 1967. *Human relations in vertical society*. Tokyo: Sophia Institute of Comparative Study.

————. 1970. *Japanese society*. Berkeley: University of California Press.

————. 1978. Trans. Yoshi Kashima. Tokyo: Kodansha.

Nash, J. 1950. The bargaining problem. *Economerica* 28:155–62.

Naylor, J. C.; Pritchard, R. D.; and Ilgen, D. R. 1980. *A theory of behavior in organizations*. NY: Academic Press.

Neale, M. A., and Bazerman, M. H. 1985. The effect of framing on conflict and negotiation overconfidence. *Academy of Management Journal* 28:34–49.

————. 1991. *Cognition and rationality in negotiation*. New York: Free Press.

Neale, M. A., and Northcraft, G. B. 1991. Behavioral negotiation theory: A framework for conceptualizing dyadic bargaining. In L. L. Cummings and B. M. Staw, eds., *Research in organizational behavior*. Vol. 13, 147–90. Greenwich, CT: JAI Press.

Negandhi, A. R., and Prasad, S. B. 1971. *Comparative management*. New York: Appleton-Century-Crofts.

Neisser, U. 1976. *Cognition and reality: Principles and implications of cognitive psychology*. San Francisco: W. H. Freeman.

Nomura, N., and Barnlund, D. 1983. Patterns of interpersonal criticism in Japan and the United States. *International Journal of Intercultural Relations* 7:1–18.

Nonaka, I. 1988. Toward middle-up-down management: Accelerating information creation. *Sloan Management Review* (Spring), 9–18.

Novacek, J., and Lazarus, R. S. 1990. The structure of personality commitments. *Journal of Personality* 58:693–715.

Oakes, P. J., and Turner, J. C. 1980. Social categorization and intergroup behavior: Does minimal intergroup discrimination make social identity more positive? *European Journal of Social Psychology* 10:295–301.

Odaka, K. 1986. *Japanese management: A forward-looking analysis*. Tokyo: Japan Productivity Organization.

Offermann, L. R., and Gowing, M. K. 1990. Organizations of the future: Changes and challenges. *American Psychologist* 45:95–108.

Okabe, R. 1983. Cultural assumptions of East and West: Japan and the United States. In Gudykunst, W., ed., *Intercultural communication theory*, 123–45. Beverly Hills, CA: Sage.

Olian, J. D.; Carroll, S. J.; Giannantonio, C. M.; and Feren, D. B. 1988. What do protégés look for in a mentor? Results of three experimental studies. *Journal of Vocational Behavior* 33:15–37.

Olson, M. 1971. *The logic of collective action*. Cambridge, MA: Harvard University Press.

Onglatco, M. L. U. 1988. *Japanese quality control circles: Features, effects and problems*. Tokyo: Asian Productivity Center.

Organ, D. W. 1987. *Organizational citizenship behavior: The good soldier syndrome*. Lexington, MA: Lexington.

Osgood, C. E. 1964. Semantic differential technique in the comparative study of cultures. *American Anthropologist* 66:171–200.

————. 1974. Probing subjective cultures. Parts 1, 2. *Journal of Communication* 24:21–34, 82–100.

————. 1977. Objective indicators in subjective culture. In L. Loeb Adler, ed., *Issues in cross-cultural research*. Annals of the New York Academy of Sciences 285:435–50.

Osgood, C. E.; May, W.; and Miron, M. 1975. *Cross-cultural universals of affective meaning*. Urbana: University of Illinois Press.

Ouchi, W. G., and Jaeger, A. M. 1978. Type Z organization: Stability in the midst of mobility. *Academy of Management Review* 5:305–14.

Pandey, J. 1986. Sociocultural perspectives on ingratiation. *Progress in Experimental Personality Research* 14:205–29.

Park, M. 1979. *Communication styles in two different cultures: Korean and American*. Seoul, Korea: Han Shin.

Park, B., and Hastie, R. 1987. Perception of variability in category development: Instance- versus abstraction-based stereotypes. *Journal of Personality and Social Psychology* 53:621–35.

Parsons, T., and Shils, E. A. 1951. *Toward a general theory of action*. Cambridge, MA: Harvard University Press.

Pascale, R. T., and Athos, A. G. 1981. *The art of Japanese management*. New York: Simon & Schuster.

Pascale, R. T. 1978. Personnel practices and employee attitudes: A study of Japanese- and American-managed firms in the U.S. *Human Relations* 31:597–615.

Paulus, P. B. 1984. *Basic Group Processes*. New York: Springer-Verlag.

Peters, T. J., and Waterman, R. H. 1982. *In search of excellence*. New York: Harper & Row.

Pfeffer, J. 1983. Organizational demography. In L. L. Cummings and B. M. Staw, eds., *Research in organizational behavior*. Vol. 5, 357–99. Greenwich, CT: JAI Press.

Piaget, J. 1965. *The moral judgement of the child*. NY: Free Press.

Pondy, L. R.; Frost, P. J.; Morgan, G.; and Dandridge, T. C., eds. 1983. *Organizational symbolism*. Greenwich, CT: JAI Press.

Porat, A. M. 1969. Cross-cultural differences in resolving union-management conflict through negotiations. Experimental Publications System no. 2, ms. 069A.

Porter, L. W. 1990. Overview of OB. Paper presented at the annual meeting of the Society for Industrial Organizational Psychology, April 1990 at Miami, Fla.

Powell, W. W. 1985. *Getting into print: The decision-making process in scholarly publishing*. Chicago: University of Chicago Press.

Prothro, E. T. 1958. Arab students' choices of ways to live. *Journal of Social Psychology* 47:3–7.

Pruitt, D. G., and Drews, J. L. 1969. The effect of time pressure, time elapsed, and the opponent's concession rate on behavior in negotiation. *Journal of Experimental Social Psychology* 5:43–60.

Pruitt, D. G., and Rubin, J. Z. 1986. *Social conflict: Excalation, impasse, and resolution*. Reading, MA: Addison-Wesley.

Pugh, D. 1976. The Aston approach to the study of organizations. In G. Hofstede and S. Kassem, eds., *European contributions to organization theory*, 62–77. Assen, Germany: Van Garcum.

Q. C. Circle Headquarters. 1980. *General principles of the Q. C. circle*. Tokyo: Q. C. Circle Headquarters, JUSE.

————. 1985. *How to operate Q. C. circles activities*. Tokyo: Q. C. Circle Headquarters, JUSE.

Radcliffe-Brown, A. R. 1922. *The Andaman Islanders*. Cambridge: Cambridge University Press.

Raiffa, H. 1982. *The art and science of negotiation*. Cambridge, MA: Belknap Press.

Rapoport, A. 1959. Critiques of game theory. *Behavior Science* 4:49–66.

Rapoport, A., and Chammah, A. 1965. *Prisoner's dilemma: A study in conflict and cooperation*. Ann Arbor: University of Michigan Press.

Reichers, A. E., and Schneider, B. 1990. Climate and culture: An evolution of constructs. In B. Schneider, ed., *Organizational climate and culture*, 5–39. San Francisco, CA: Jossey-Bass.

Rice, R. W. 1978. Psychometric properties of the esteem for least preferred co-worker (LPC scale). *Academy of Management Review* 3:106–18.

Rim, Y. 1970. Values and attitudes. *Personality* 1:243–50.

Roach, C. F., and Behling, O. 1984. Functionalism: Basis for an alternate approach to the study of leadership. In J. G. Hunt, D. M. Hosking, C. A. Schriesheim, and R. Stewart, eds., *Leaders and managers: International perspectives on managerial behavior and leadership*. Elmsford, NY: Pergamon Press.

Robbins, R. H. 1973. Identity, culture, and behavior. In J. Honigmann, ed., *Handbook of social and cultural anthropology:* 1199–222. Chicago, Il: Rand-McNally.

Roberts, K. H. 1970. On looking at an elephant: An evaluation of cross-cultural research related to organizations. *Psychological Bulletin* 74:327–50.

Robertson, R. 1987. Globalization and societal modernization: A note on Japan and Japanese religion. *Sociological Analysis* 47(S):35–43.

Rogers, D. 1969. *Flowers for Algernon*. Chicago: Dramatic Publishing Co.

Rogers, T. B.; Kuiper, N. A.; and Kirker, W. S. 1977. Self-reference and encoding of personal information. *Journal of Personality and Social Psychology* 35:677–88.

Rokeach, M. 1973. *The nature of human values*. New York: Free Press.

Roloff, M. E., and Jordon, J. 1989. Strategic communication within bargaining plans: Forms, antecedents, and effects. Paper presented at the Second Biannual Conference of the International Association for Conflict Management, Athens, GA.

Ronen, S. 1978. Personal values: A basis for work motivational set and work attitude. *Organizational Behavior and Human Performance* 21:80–107.

————. 1982. *Clustering countries on attitudinal dimensions: A review and synthesis*. Paper presented at the 20th International Congress of Applied Psychology, Edinburgh, Scotland.

————. 1986. *Comparative and multinational management*. New York: Wiley.

Ronen, S., and Shenkar, O. 1985. Clustering countries on attitudinal dimensions: A review and synthesis. *Academy of Management Review* 10:435–54.

Rosenstein, E. 1985. Cooperativeness and advancement of managers: An international perspective. *Human Relations* 38:1–21.

Rosenstein, E.; Ofek, A.; and Harel, G. 1988. Organizational democracy and management in Israel. *International Studies of Management and Organizations* 17:52–68.

Ross, L. 1977. The intuitive psychologist and his shortcomings: Distortions in the attribution process. In L. Berkowitz, ed., *Advances in experimental and social psychology*. Vol. 10, 174–221. NY: Academic Press.

Roth, A. E. In press. An economic approach to the study of bargaining. In M. Bazerman, R. Lewicki, and B. Shephard, eds., *Research on negotiation in organizations*. Greenwich, CT: JAI Press.

Rousseau, D. M. 1977. Technological differences in job characteristics, employee satisfaction, and motivation: A synthesis of job design research and sociotechnical systems theory. *Organizational Behavior and Human Performance* 19:18–42.

Rubenowitz, S. 1974. *Experiences in industrial democracy and changes in work organizations in Sweden.* Psckologiska Institutionen, 2. Göteborg: Göteborgs Universitet.

Rubin, J. Z. 1980. Experimental research on third-party intervention: Toward some generalizations. *Psychological Bulletin* 87:379–91.

Rubin, J. Z., and Brown, B. R. 1975. *The social psychology of bargaining and negotiation.* New York: Academic Press.

Ruch, W. V. 1985. *Corporate communications: A comparison of Japanese and American practices.* Westport, CT: Quorum Books.

Salancik, G. R., and Pfeffer, J. 1977. Who gets power—and how they hold on to it: A strategic contingency model of power. *Organizational Dynamics* 5:3–21.

Sampson, E. E. 1989. The challenge of social change for psychology: Globalization and psychology's theory of the person. *American Psychologist* 44:914–21.

Samuelson, C. D., and Messick, D. M. 1986. Alternative structural solutions to resource dilemmas. *Organizational Behavior and Human Decision Processes* 37:139–55.

Sandel, M. J. 1982. *Liberalism and the limits of justice.* Cambridge: Cambridge University Press.

Sanders, G. S., and Baron, R. S. 1977. Is social comparison irrelevant for producing choice shifts? *Journal of Experimental Social Psychology* 13:303–14.

Sashkin, M. 1988. The visionary leader. In J. A. Conger and R. N. Kanungo, eds., *Charismatic leadership,* 122–65. San Francisco: Jossey-Bass.

Sathe, V. 1985. *Culture and related corporate realities.* Homewood, IL: Irwin.

Sawyer, J., and Guetzkow, H. 1965. Bargaining and negotiation in international relations. In H. C. Kelman, ed., *International Behavior,* 464–520.New York: Holt.

Scandura, T. A., and Graen, G. B. 1984. Moderating effects of initial leader-member exchange status on the effects of a leadership intervention. *Journal of Applied Psychology* 69:428–36.

Schall, M. S. 1983. A communication-rules approach to organizational culture. *Administrative Science Quarterly* 28:557–81.

Schank, R. C., and Abelson, R. P. 1977. *Scripts, plans, goals, and understanding: An inquiry into human knowledge structures.* Hillsdale, NJ: Erlbaum.

Schein, E. H. 1985. *Organizational culture and leadership:* A dynamic view. San Francisco: Jossey-Bass.

Schein, E. H. 1990. Organizational culture. *American Psychologist* 45:109–19.

Schelling, T. 1960. *The strategy of conflict.* Cambridge, MA: Harvard University Press.

Schlenker, B. R. 1985. *The self and social life.* New York: McGraw-Hill.

Schmidt, F. L., and Hunter, J. E. 1977. Development of a general solution to the problem of validity generalization. *Journal of Applied Psychology* 62:590–601.

Schmitt, N. 1990. *What else should we do?* Presidential address at the annual meeting of the Society for Industrial Organizational Psychology, Miami, FL, April 1990.

Schneider, B. 1975. Organizational climate: An essay. *Personnel Psychology* 28:447–79.

Schneider, B. 1987. The people make the place. *Personnel Psychology* 40:437–53.

Schuler, R. S., and Lee, C. 1982. A constructive replication and extension of a role and expectancy perception model of participation in decision making. *Journal of Occupational Psychology* 55:109–18.

Schwartz, S. H. (in press). Universals in the content and structure of values: Theoretical advances and empirical tests in two countries. In L. Berkowitz, ed., *Advances in experimental and social psychology.* San Diego, CA: Academic Press.

Schwartz, S., and Bilsky, W. 1987. Toward a universal psychological structure of human values. *Journal of Personality and Social Psychology* 53:550–62.

Schweiger, D. M.; Ivancevich, J. M.; and Power, F. R. 1987. Executive actions for managing resources before and after acquisition. *Academy of Management Executive* 1:127–38.

Seigel, S., and Fouraker, L. 1960. *Bargaining and group decision making: Experiments in bilateral monopoly.* New York: McGraw-Hill.

Selznick, P. 1957. *Leadership in administration: A sociological interpretation.* New York: Harper & Row.

Shamir, B.; House, R. J.; and Arthur, M. B. 1991. The transformational effects of charismatic leadership: A motivational theory. Typescript.

Shavelson, R. J., and Marsh, H. W. 1986. On the structure of self-concept. In R. Schwarzer, ed., *Anxiety and cognitions:* 305–30. Hillsdale, NJ: Erlbaum.

Shaw, M. E. 1973. Scaling group tasks: A method for dimensional analysis. *JSAS catalog of selected documents in psychology* 3:8.

————. 1978. Communication networks fourteen years later. In L. Berkowitz, ed., *Group processes*, 351–62. New York: Academic Press.

Sherif, M. 1936. *The psychology of social norms*. New York: Harper.

Sherman, S. J.; Judd, C. M.; and Bernadette, P. 1989. Social cognition. *Annual Review of Psychology* 40:281–326.

Shiffrin, R. M., and Schneider, W. 1977. Controlled and automatic human information processing: II. Perceptual learning, automatic attending, and a general theory. *Psychological Review* 84:127–90.

Shweder, R. A., and Bourne, E. J. 1984. Does the concept of the person vary cross-culturally? In R. A. Shweder and R. A. LeVine, eds., *Culture theory: Essays on mind, self, and emotion*, 158–99. New York: Cambridge University Press.

Shweder, R. A., and LeVine, R. A. 1984. *Culture theory: Essays on mind, self, and emotion*. New York: Cambridge University Press.

Skinner, B. F. 1971. *Beyond freedom and dignity*. New York: Knopf.

Smircich, L. 1983. Concepts of culture in organizational analysis. *Administrative Science Quarterly* 28:339–58.

Smircich, L., and Calas, M. B. 1986. Organizational culture: A critical assessment. *Annual Review of Sociology* 2:228–63.

Smith, A. D. 1990. Towards a global culture? In M. Featherstone, ed., *Global culture—nationalism, globalization and modernity: A theory, culture, and society special issue*, 171–92. London: Sage Publications.

Sono, F. 1981. *Stages of growth: Reflections on life and management*. Tokyo: TDK Electronics.

Spradley, J. P. 1979. *The ethnographic interview*. New York: Holt, Rhinehart and Winston.

Stablein, R., and Nord, W. 1985. Practical and emancipatory interests in organizational symbolism: A review and evaluation. *Journal of Management* 11:13–28.

Staw, B. M. 1986. Beyond the control graph: Steps toward a model of perceived control in organization. In R. N. Stern and S. McCarthy, eds., *The organizational practice of democracy:* 305–21. New York: John Wiley.

Staw, B. M., and Boettger, R. D. 1990. Task revision as a form of work performance. *Academy of Management Journal* 33:534–59.

Staw, B. M., and Ross, J. 1987. Behavior in escalation situations: Antecedents, prototypes, and solutions. In L. L. Cummings and B. M. Staw, eds., *Research in organizational behavior*. Vol. 7, 39–78. Greenwich, CT: JAI Press.

Steers, R. M., and Porter, L. W. 1991. *Motivation and work behavior*, 5th ed. New York: McGraw-Hill.

Steinbeck, John. 1966. *America and Americans*. New York: Viking.

Steiner, I. D. 1972. *Group process and productivity*. New York: Academic Press.

Stevens, C. M. 1963. *Strategy and collective-bargaining negotiation*. New York: McGraw-Hill.

Stogdill, R. M. 1974. *Handbook of leadership: A survey of the literature*. New York: Free Press.

Strauss, G. 1982. Workers participation in management: An international perspective. In B. M. Staw and L. L. Cummings, eds., *Research in organizational behavior*. Vol. 4, 173–263. Greenwich, CT: JAI Press.

Stryker, S. 1968. Identity, salience, and role performance. *Journal of Marriage and Family* 30:558–64.

Summers, C. W. 1965. Labor relations in the common market. *Harvard Business Review* 43:148–60.

Sundstrom, E.; DeMeure, K. P.; and Futrell, D. 1990. Workteams: Applications and effectiveness. *American Psychologist* 45:120–33.

Swap, W. C., and Rubin, J. Z. 1983. Measurement of interpersonal orientation. *Journal of Personality and Social Psychology* 44:208–19.

Sypher, B. D.; Applegate, J. L.; and Sypher, H. E. 1985. Culture and communication in organizational contexts. In W. B. Gudykunst, L. P. Steart, and S. Ting-Toomey, eds. *Communication, culture and organizational processes*, 13–29. Beverly Hills, CA: Sage.

Szilagyi, A. D., and Wallace, M. J. 1983. *Organizational behavior and performance*. 3rd ed. Glenview, IL: Scott Foresman.

Tajfel, H. 1978. *Differentiation between social groups: Studies in the social psychology of intergroup relations*. London: Academic Press.

————. 1982. Social psychology of intergroup relations. *Annual Review of Psychology* 33:1–39.

Tajfel, H., and Turner, J. C. 1986. The social identity theory of intergroup behavior. In S. Worchel and W. G. Austin, eds., *Psychology of intergroup relations*, 7–24. Chicago: Nelson-Hall.

Takagi, H. 1958. *The flow in Japanese management*. Ann Arbor, MI: UMI Research Press.

Takanaka, A. 1986. Some thoughts on Japanese management centering on personnel and labor management: The reality and the future. *International Studies of Management and Organizations* 15:17–68.

Takenishi, M., and Takenishi, A. 1990. *Why Japanese citizens evaluate the tax as unfair?* Fairness criteria and their relative importance. Typescript, Kochi University, Japan.

Takezawa, S. J. 1988. Personal interview. School of Social Relations, Rikkyo University, Tokyo.

Tannenbaum, A. S. 1980. Organizational psychology. In H. C. Triandis and R. W. Brislin, eds., *Handbook of cross-cultural psychology*. Vol. 5, 281–334. Boston: Allyn and Bacon.

Tannenbaum, A. S.; Kavcic, B.; Rosner, M.; Vianello, M.; and Weiser, G. 1974. *Hierarchy in organizations*. San Francisco: Jossey-Bass.

Taylor, F. W. 1967. *Principles of scientific management*. [Originally published, 1967.] NY: Norton.

Taylor, S. E., and Thompson, S. 1982. Stalking the elusive "vividness" effect. *Psychological Review* 89:155–81.

Tedeschi, J. 1986. Private and public experiences and the self. In R. Baumeister, ed., *Public and private self*, 76–97. New York: Springer-Verlag.

Thelen, H. A. 1956. Emotionality of work in groups. In L. D. White, ed., *The state of the social sciences*, 184–200. Chicago: University of Chicago Press.

Theye, L. D., and Seller, W. J. 1979. Interaction analysis in collective bargaining: An alternative approach to the prediction of negotiated outcomes. In D. Nimmo, ed., *Communication Yearbook 3*, New Brunswick, NJ: Transaction Press.

Thibaut, J. W., and Kelley, H. H. 1959. *The social psychology of groups*. New York: Wiley.

Thibaut, J. W., and Walker, L. 1978. A theory of procedure. *California Law Review* 66:541–66.

Thompson, L. 1990. Negotiation behavior and outcomes: Empirical evidence and theoretical issues. *Psychological Bulletin* 108:515–32.

Thompson, L., and Hastie, R. M. 1990. Social perception in negotiation. *Organizational Behavior and Human Decision Processes* 47:98–123.

Thorsrud, E. 1984. The Scandinavian model: strategies of organizational democratization in Norway. In B. Wilpert and A. Sorge, eds., *International perspectives on organizational democracy*: 337–70. Chichester: Wiley.

Thorsrud, E., and Emery, F. E. 1970. Industrial democracy in Norway. *Industrial Relations* 9:187–96.

Tichy, N. M. 1982. Managing change strategically: The technical, political, and cultural keys. *Organizational Dynamics* 11(2):59–80.

Timaeus, E. 1968. Untersuchungen zum sogenannten konformen Verhalten. *Zeitschrift für experimentelle und angewandte Psychologie* 15:176–94.

Ting-Toomey, S. 1985. Toward a theory of conflict and culture. In W. Gudykunst, L. Stewart, and Ting-Toomey, S., eds., *Communication, culture and organizational processes*, 71–86. Beverly-Hills, CA: Sage.

———. 1988. A face negotiation theory. In Y. Kim and W. Gudykunst, eds., *Theory and intercultural communication*. Newbury Park, CA: Sage.

Tomasson, R. F. 1970. *Sweden: Prototype of modern society*. New York: Random House.

Tonnies, F. 1887. *Community and society*. New York: Harper and Row.

Tornblom, K. Y.; Jonsson, D.; and Foa, U. G. 1985. Nationality, resource, class, and preferences among three allocation rules: Sweden vs. USA. *International Journal of Intercultural Relations* 9:51–77.

Trafimow, D.; Triandis, H. C.; and Goto, S. G. 1991. Some tests of the distinction between the private self and the collective self. *Journal of Personality and Social Psychology* 60:649–55.

Triandis, H. C. 1964. Cultural influences upon cognitive processes. In L. Berkowitz, ed., *Advances in experimental social psychology*, 2–48. New York: Academic Press.

———. 1967. Toward an analysis of the components of interpersonal attitudes. In C. Sherif and M. Sherif, eds., *Attitudes, ego-involvement and change*, 227–70. New York: Wiley.

———. 1972. *The analysis of subjective culture*. New York: Wiley.

———. 1977. *Interpersonal Behavior*. Monterey, CA: Brooks/Cole.

———. 1980–81. *Handbook of cross-cultural psychology*. Boston: Allyn and Bacon.

———. 1980. Values, attitudes and interpersonal behavior. In H. Howe and M. Page, eds., *Nebraska symposium on motivation*, 195–260. Lincoln: University of Nebraska Press.

———. 1984. Toward a psychological theory of economic growth. *International Journal of Psychology* 19:79–96.

———. 1988. Collectivism vs. individualism: A reconceptualization of a basic concept in cross-cultural social psychology. In G. K. Verma and C. Bagley, eds., *Cross-cultural studies of personality, attitudes and cognition*, 60–95. London: Macmillan.

———. 1989a. Cross-cultural studies of individualism and collectivism. In J. Berman, ed., *Nebraska symposium on motivation*, 41–133. Lincoln: University of Nebraska Press.

———. 1989b. The self and social behavior in differing cultural contexts. *Psychological Review* 96:506–20.

———. In press. Culture: Theoretical and methodological issues. In M. D. Dunnette and L. Hough, eds., *Handbook of industrial and organizational psychology*, 2nd ed. Vol. 4. Palo Alto, CA: Consulting Psychologists Press.

Triandis, H. C., and Albert, R. D. 1987. Cross-cultural perspectives. In F. M. Jablin, L. L. Putman,

K. H. Roberts, and L. W. Porter, eds., *Handbook of organizational communication: An Interdisciplinary perspective*, 264–95. Beverly Hills, CA: Sage.

Triandis, H. C.; Bontempo, R.; Vilareal, M. J.; Masaaki, A.; and Lucca, N. 1988. Individualism and collectivism: Cross-cultural perspectives on self–in-group relationships. *Journal of Personality and Social Psychology* 54:328–38.

Triandis, H. C., McCusker, C., and Hui, C. H. 1990. Multimethod probes of individualism and collectivism. *Journal of Personality and Social Psychology* 59:1006–20.

Trice, H. M., and Beyer, J. M. 1984. Studying organizational cultures through rites and ceremonials. *Academy of Management Review* 9:653–69.

Triplett, N. 1898. The dynamogenic factors in pace-making and competition. *American Journal of Psychology* 9:507–33.

Trist, E. L. 1981. *The evolution of a socio-technical system*. Toronto, Ontario: Quality of Working Life Center.

Trist, E. L., and Bamforth, K. W. 1951. Some social psychological consequences of the longwall method of goal-getting. *Human Relations* 4:3–38.

Turnage, J. J. 1990. The challenge of new workplace technology for psychology. *American Psychologist* 45:171–78.

Turner, J. C. 1987. *Rediscovering the social group*. Oxford: Basil Blackwell.

Tyler, S. A. 1969. *Cognitive anthropology*. New York: Holt, Rinehart and Winston.

Tyler, T. R., and Lind, E. A. (in press). A relational model of authority in group. In M. Zanna, ed., *Advances in experimental social psychology*. Vol. 25. New York: Academic Press.

Tylor, E. B. 1889. On a method of investigating the development of institutions, applied to laws of marriage and descent. *Journal of Anthropological Institute of Great Britain and Ireland* 18:245–69.

Van Maanen, J., and Barley, S. R. 1984. Occupational communities: Culture and control in organizations. In B. M. Staw and L. L. Cummings, eds., *Research in organizational behavior*. Vol. 6, 287–365. Greenwich, CT.: JAI Press.

Van Maanen, J., and Schein, E. H. 1977. Toward a theory of organizational socialization. In B. M. Staw, ed., *Research in Organizational Behavior* 1:209–64.

Vanbeselaere, N. 1987. The effects of dichotomous and crossed social categorization upon intergroup discrimination. *European Journal of Social Psychology* 17:143–56.

Vroom, V. H. 1964. *Work and motivation*. NY: Wiley.

Vroom, V. H., and Yetton, P. W. 1973. *Leadership and decision-making*. Pittsburgh: University of Pittsburgh Press.

Wagner, J. A., III, and Moch, M. K. 1986. Individualism-collectivism: Concept and measure. *Group and Organization Studies* 11:280–304.

Wallach, M. A., and Kogan, N. 1965. The role of information and consequences in group risk-taking. *Journal of Experimental Social Psychology* 1:1–19.

Walton, R. E., and McKersie, R. B. 1965. *A behavioral theory of labor negotiations*. New York: McGraw Hill.

Weber, M. 1947. *The theory of social and economic organizations*, T. Parsons, trans. New York: Free Press.

Weick, K. E. 1979. *The social psychology of organizing*, 2nd ed. Reading, MA: Addison-Wesley.

Weick, K. E., and Bougon, M. 1986. Organizations as cognitive maps. In H. P. Sims, Jr., and D. A. Gioia, eds., *The thinking organization*. San Francisco: Jossey-Bass, 102–35.

Weiner, B. 1986. *An attributional theory of motivation and emotion*. New York: Springer Verlag.

Weiss, H. M. and Adler, S. 1984. Personality and organizational behavior. In B. M. Staw and L. L. Cummings, eds., *Research in Organizational Behavior* 6:1–50.

Weldon, E. and Gargano, G. M. 1988. Cognitive loafing: The effects of accountability and shared responsibility on cognitive effort. *Personality and Social Psychology Bulletin* 14:159–71.

Westley, F. R., and Mintzberg, H. 1988. Profiles of strategic vision: Levesque and Iacocca. In J. A. Conger and R. N. Kanungo, eds., *Charismatic leadership*. San Francisco: Jossey-Bass.

Whitely, W., and England, G. W. 1980. Variability in common dimensions of managerial values due to value orientation and country differences. *Personal Psychology* 33:77–89.

Whiting, J. W. M. 1964. Effects of climate on certain cultural practices. In W. H. Goodenough, ed., *Explorations in cultural anthropology*, 496–544. New York: McGraw-Hill.

———. 1974. A model for psycho-cultural research. *Annual Report 1973*. American Anthropological Association.

Whiting, J. W. M., and Child, I. L. 1953. *Child training and personality*. New Haven: Yale University Press.

Whiting, J. W. M.; Kluckhohn, R.; and Anthony, A. S. 1958. The function of male initiation ceremonies at puberty. In E. E. MacCoby, T. Newcomb, and E. Hartley, eds., *Readings in social psychology*. New York: Holt.

Whittaker, J. O., and Meade, R. D. 1967. Social pressure in the modification and distortion of judgment: A cross-cultural study. *International Journal of Psychology* 2:109–13.

Whyte, W. F. 1959. An interaction approach to the theory of organization. In M. Haire, ed., *Modern organization theory*, 39–86. New York: Wiley.

Wiener, Y. 1988. Forms of value systems: A focus on organizational effectiveness and cultural change and maintenance. *The Academy of Mangaement Review* 13:534–45.

Williamson, O. E. 1975. *Markets and hierarchies*. New York: Free Press.

Willner, A. R. 1984. *The spellbinders: Charismatic political leadership*. New Haven: Yale University Press.

Wilpert, B. 1984. Participation in organizations: Evidence from international comparative research. *International Social Sciences Journal* 36:355–66.

Witkin, H. A. 1949. The nature and importance of individual differences in perception. *Journal of Personality* 18:145–70.

Witkin, H. A., and Berry, J. W. 1975. Psychological differentiation in cross-cultural perspective. *Journal of Cross-Cultural Psychology* 6:4–87.

Witkin, H. A. and Goodenough, D. R., 1976. Field dependence and interpersonal behavior. *ETS Research Bulletin*, RB–76-12. Educational Testing Service.

Wood, R. E., and Bandura, A. 1989. Social cognitive theory of organizational management. *Academy of Management Review* 14:361–84.

Wood, R. E., and Locke, E. A. 1990. Goal setting and strategy effects on complex tasks. In B. M. Staw and L. L. Cummings, eds., *Research in organizational behavior*. Vol. 12, 73–110. Greenwich, Conn: JAI Press.

Wood, R. E., and Mitchell, T. R. 1981. Manager behavior in a social context: The impact of impression management on attributions and disciplinary actions. *Organizational Behavior and Human Performance* 28:356–78.

Wuthnow, R., and Witten, M. 1988. New directions in the study of culture. *Annual Review of Sociology* 14:49–67.

Wyer, R. S., Jr., and Srull, T. K. 1980. The processing of social stimulus information: A conceptual integration. In R. Hastie; T. M. Ostrom; E. B. Ebbesen; R. S. Wyer, Jr.; D. L. Hamilton; and D. E. Carlston, eds., *Person memory: The cognitive basis of social perception*, 227–300. Hillsdale, NJ: Lawrence Erlbaum Associates.

———. 1989. *Memory and cognition in its social context*. Hillsdale, NJ: Lawrence Erlbaum.

Yukl, G. A. 1989. *Leadership in organizations,* 2nd ed. Englewood Cliffs, NJ: Prentice Hall.

Zaleznik, A. 1977. Managers and leaders: Are they different? *Harvard Business Review* 55 (5):67–78.

Zander, A. 1983. The value of belonging to a group in Japan. *Small Group Behavior* 14:3–14.

Zavalloni, M. 1980. Values. In H. C. Triandis and R. W. Brislin, eds., *Handbook of cross-cultural psychology*. Vol. 5, 73–120. Boston: Allyn and Bacon.

Zeidner, M., and Nevo, B. 1987. The cross-cultural generalizability of moral reasoning research: Some Israeli data. *International Journal of Psychology* 22:315–30.

INDEX

OUR PARTNERSHIP

Our Partnership

by Beatrice Webb

———

edited by
Barbara Drake and Margaret I. Cole
with an introduction by
George Feaver

*Professor of Political Science
in the University of British Columbia*

London School of Economics and Political Science
Cambridge University Press

Published by the Syndics of the Cambridge University Press
The Pitt Building, Trumpington Street, Cambridge CB2 1RP
Bentley House, 200 Euston Road, London NW1 2DB
32 East 57th Street, New York, NY 10022, USA
296 Beaconsfield Parade, Middle Park, Melbourne 3206, Australia

Text of the 1948 edition, copyright
London School of Economics and Political Science
Introduction © London School of Economics and Political Science
This edition © London School of Economics and Political Science

ISBN: 0 521 20852 1

First published 1948
This edition 1975

Printed in Great Britain
at the University Printing House, Cambridge
(Euan Phillips, University Printer)

CONTENTS

CONTENTS

PLATES

INTRODUCTION TO THIS EDITION

GEORGE FEAVER

BEATRICE POTTER was born on 2 January 1858 at Standish House in the Cotswolds. Before the year was out Lord Palmerston's first ministry had fallen and the Government of India passed from the East India Company to the Crown. Sidney Webb was born in central London on 13 July 1859, a year which witnessed the publication of two of the great classics of nineteenth-century thought, Darwin's *Origin of Species* and Mill's *On Liberty*. The Webbs' origins were thus unmistakably mid-Victorian, and indeed, in the first volume of her autobiography, Beatrice was to recall how as a young woman she had watched fascinated from the visitor's gallery in the Commons while Gladstone and Disraeli vied for domination of the House.

Yet because so many of their projects as intellectuals in politics were destined to bear fruit in our own time, we somehow do not think of the Webbs as Victorians. As Fabian pioneers in the Labour Party, as founders of the London School of Economics and the *New Statesman*, as authors of multifarious schemes of far-reaching social, political and educational reform, they seem to belong essentially to the twentieth century. The impression is strengthened by their longevity. Both were in their fifth decade when Queen Victoria died in 1901 but fully half of their long lives still lay ahead of them. They lived to see the desolation wrought by the two world wars. The Beveridge Report was published a year before Beatrice's death in 1943, and Sidney, who lingered on, was still alive when the postwar Attlee government set about in earnest to implement a British welfare state.

Today, a quarter of a century later, the Webb presence is still felt, perhaps nowhere more so than in the fabric of their great institutional legacy, the London School of Economics and Political Science. If they left no 'auto-icon' of themselves as Bentham did at University College London, the LSE with its deliberate plainness remains every bit as much a permanent memorial to their personalities and their style of living. In the Founders' Room at the LSE there is Sir William Nicholson's portrait of them, depicting them in their later years in a casual scene before the brick fireplace at their country retreat, Passfield Corner. They are busy over galley proofs. The floor is littered with blue books and papers. Their white terrier 'Sandy' is stationed in the foreground, staring apparently intrigued at Sidney, who, wearing his inevitable three-piece suit, stands next to the grate. His eyes are directed towards Beatrice in an uncomplicated expression of affection.

The artist's treatment of Beatrice is more complex. 'He has taken an incredible time over me', she wrote in her diary after a sitting, 'I have been painted in and painted out half a dozen times . . . now at last the figure satisfies him and is quite good enough for me.'[1] She is shown seated, perched rather stiffly forward in her chair. Her white hair is untidy, her clothing (she borrowed her pink blouse for the occasion from the gardener's wife) casual to the point of abandon. Her right hand is outstretched towards the flames yet it remains somehow distant from the fire's warmth. She is gazing straight ahead in an attitude of melancholy reverie, lost in private thought.

Beatrice *was* more complex than her husband. The privileged offspring of newly-moneyed but cultivated stock, she had been a moody and unhappy child. By nature imperious and strong-willed, she grew to womanhood restless, erratically industrious and morbidly attracted to the great insoluble questions of life and death. She was physically striking . . . a 'tall commanding figure', as H. G. Wells described her, in the character of 'Altiora Bailey' in *The New Machiavelli*, 'splendid but a bit untidy . . . with dark eyes that had no depths, with a dark hard voice that had an almost visible prominence, aquiline features and straight black hair that was apt to go astray . . . like the head feathers of an eagle in a gale.'[2] There is a certain untamed defiance in her features that is wonderfully captured in a well-known photograph of her taken by G. B. Shaw as she sat brooding in a porch chair.[3]

Sidney's beginnings and his personality were less glamorous. There was something bizarre about his appearance that made it a ready target for political cartoonists. The bright star of a family only marginally middle-class, he learned early that his prospects in life hinged directly on hard work and the disciplined cultivation of his talent. He entered upon his maturity a committed socialist of the moderate 'Stuart Millite' variety, and matched his political faith to an apparently unquestioned sense of direction. Some saw in his air of self-assurance a certain pedantic arrogance: W. T. Stead of the *Pall Mall Gazette* once said of him that he was 'a very remarkable man, much more remarkable than anybody thinks, excepting himself'.[4] But his friends thought his qualities were those of a skilled committee man. He was even-tempered, doggedly persistent, and in many respects unimaginative . . . so much so that Friedrich Engels, impatient with his cautious Fabianism, once described him in a letter to Karl Kautsky, in terms not meant to be flattering, as 'a genuine British politician'.[5]

Beatrice, of course, recognised the differences between Sidney and herself, but thought they contributed positively to their capacity for what she termed 'joint-thinking'. She once wrote in an oft-quoted passage that 'We are both of us second-rate minds, but we are curiously combined.'[6] She was the architect and philosophical investigator, she said, and he the practical-minded executor. He had his blue books, his statistical abstracts, and his fascination with the *minutiae* of political and administrative history; she had her dreams. And as we all know, they combined these diverse temperaments into such an extraordinarily productive union that even in a nation whose modern history has been rich in successful teamwork, it is still 'the firm of Webb' that comes to mind as the perfect model or paradigm of an intellectual partnership.

.   .   .

The celebrated unity of purpose within the Webb partnership was accorded its crowning accolade in Beatrice's own moving portrait of 'The Other One' in the early pages of *Our Partnership*. Yet in point of biographical fact, each of them had already passed through the formative stage of their lives before they first met. Certainly, long before Sidney Webb became a full-fledged partner in the firm, other major influences had exerted themselves on Beatrice Potter and contributed substantially towards the future direction of her career. There were, for example, other men in Beatrice's life. The first of these was her father. She once claimed to be 'a sort of weak edition' of him, and said that he was the only man she ever knew who genuinely believed women to be superior to men. Richard Potter was a happy, active man and a model father. A hard-headed businessman, a Conservative in politics with a wide circle of friends in public affairs, he entertained many of the leading thinkers of the day. He believed in progress, and turned his household into a laboratory for the pursuit of experiments in cultural improvement. He tirelessly encouraged Beatrice in the belief that her sex mattered little to what she might accomplish in life. The message was not lost on her, the eighth of nine daughters, a girl who felt her mother resented her because she had not been born a boy. Beatrice's mother was indeed a rather superior person who preferred the company of clever men to women and wrote a novel about herself. She was a remote figure in the eyes of her daughter, who tells us in *My Apprenticeship* that her mother described her in childhood as 'the only one of my children who is below the average in intelligence'.[7]

It was Herbert Spencer, a regular visitor in the Potter household and the 'philosopher of the hearth' of Beatrice's otherwise lonely and withdrawn childhood, who first convinced her of her intellectual promise; he told her that she reminded him of George Eliot. The eccentric sociologist's rigidity of mind and his unswerving dedication to evolutionary social science set before Beatrice an example of 'intellectual heroism' that she was to emulate in her own lifework. Reading his books when she was very young inspired in her the ambition to become a social investigator. She resolved to take up the torch of science from the old 'metaphysician of the homemade intellectual',[8] and make its light burn brighter through her efforts; to develop Spencer's highly theoretical sociology into a more practical human science by grounding it in a firmer foundation of social fact. She rejected his extreme anti-statism, but her own social and political thought still had its starting-point in Spencer's organic analogy.

The Liberal politician Joseph Chamberlain was the third man in Beatrice's early life. If Spencer was allowed to open intellectual vistas for her that would have been unthinkable in the education of a female in a more orthodox Victorian household, her father nonetheless sensed the dangers of an exclusively intellectual upbringing. He scolded his 'busy Bee' for her absorption in Spencer's theories, exclaiming on one occasion: 'Words, my dear, mere words . . . he lacks instinct, my dear, he lacks instinct.' When she met the rich and dashing Chamberlain at Spencer's annual garden party in the summer of 1883, Beatrice came to understand what her father meant. Spencer and Chamberlain were fundamentally antipathetic characters and Beatrice was at first disconcerted. Spencer, to her impressionable young mind, epitomized reason and intellect, and was in politics an iconoclastic individualist and anti-democrat. Chamberlain struck her as a man of passion and was politically a radical critic of the established order. 'Curious and interesting character', she mused, 'dominated by intellectual passions, and with little self-control but with any amount of purpose.'[9] Beatrice was 25, Chamberlain 47, at the time of their first encounter. Twice widowed, he was again actively seeking a wife. He aroused in Beatrice hitherto unexperienced emotions and soon she was writing of her feelings of 'floating towards a precipice'. She had fallen in love.[10]

But it was to be an unrequited love. Alike strong-willed, ambitious, and domineering, they soon clashed. In the course of a stormy courtship Chamberlain told her that what he sought from women was 'intelligent sympathy', and he made it clear he would not tolerate the contradiction of his views. Beatrice was understandably attracted by the prospect of life at the side of this rising political star, if only she could impress strongly enough upon him her disapproval of his masculine self-possession. As the struggle for dominance moved back and forth, she threw aside her reservations, and in a moment of desperation openly declared her love. Chamberlain retreated, and soon afterwards married the daughter of an American politician. Beatrice was humiliated. Moreover, this major disaster in love coincided with her arrival at what she later characterised as 'the dead point'[11] of her search for a creed.

Beatrice had been raised as a Unitarian. Her mother was a pious and puritanical woman much attracted to religious disputation. In later life, largely withdrawn from society in self-imposed atonement for the death of her only son and her apparent inability to produce further male offspring, she had poured out to her diary her longings for a union of the mystic and rational elements in religious belief. The religious tastes of Beatrice's father were less severe. They were also less certain, and the Potter household in Beatrice's childhood was a haven for a varied succession of agnostics, positivists and orthodox Christians. He eventually gave up Unitarianism and became an Anglican. Beatrice, whose hold on the orthodox Christian faith had at best been shaky, found in regular exposure to such variety of religious opinion only further grounds for abandoning it altogether. By 1876, the year of her 'coming out' in London society, she had been converted to a new religion. Its God was The Unknowable: its prophet Herbert Spencer: its Bible his *Synthetic Philosophy*.[12]

Yet the Spencerian religion of science could never of itself comfort Beatrice's restless urge to get at the ultimate mysteries of human life. She was to muse over this theme on the very day of her mentor's death. Acknowledging Spencer's influence in her conversion from orthodox Christianity, she nonetheless confessed her continued inclination to doubt scientific materialism more than spiritualism. She was convinced that science was bankrupt in face of the larger questions of individual and social existence. A private solution lay in prayer and the search for voices in the Great Unknown. But how, she wondered, could one arrive at a social faith that would overcome the barren formalism of science and the terrible spiritual isolation of individualism, while avoiding the pitfall of ideological obscurantism?

What intervened to resolve her dilemma was the discovery during the 1880s of the idea of salvation through disinterested social service. Convinced that leading middle-class intellectuals were developing a 'class-consciousness of sin' towards the economically deprived lower orders,[13] she resolved to dedicate herself to the service of others. She would toil as a sociological brainworker in the neglected vineyards of suffering mankind. The die was cast in the autumn of 1883 when, dissatisfied with her purely academic studies of social class, she persuaded her childhood nurse and housekeeper, Martha Mills, to take her to visit some of her less well-to-do relations in Bacup, Lancashire.[14] Disguised as a Miss Jones, farmer's daughter, Beatrice intended to observe first-hand the routine of the cotton-operatives and mill-hands of the grim northern town. The experience came as a revelation. She saw in their frugal lives a dignity and purpose that she was certain was altogether lacking in her own strata of society. The social egalitarianism and 'one-idea'd-ness' of their religious socialism made her feel as if she were living through a page of puritan history. At Bacup, she felt, one could bear witness to a social order in which thought and action were really guided by religious faith.

Yet it struck Beatrice as sadly inevitable that the old-world virtues of Bacup would be steadily undermined by the new social values of an advancing scientific culture. She pondered aloud in letters to her father as to how, with the religious channel closing up, political convictions might come to take the place of Christian faith.[15] In raising the question in Beatrice's mind, Bacup provided a decisive turn in her self-development and brought into sharper focus a set of questions which had for long been forming themselves in her private thoughts. She referred to these questions in the well-known Introduction to *My Apprenticeship*: 'Can there', she asked,

> be a science of social organisation in the sense in which we have a science of mechanics or a science of chemistry . . . ? And secondly, assuming that there be, or will be, such a science of society, is man's capacity for scientific discovery the only faculty required for the reorganisation of society according to an ideal? Or do we need religion as well as science, emotional faith as well as intellectual curiosity?[16]

Fully half a dozen years before she met Sidney Webb, Beatrice Potter had settled on a craft and was groping towards a creed by which to live. Socialism lay still in the future. But already she had resolved to dedicate her talents to the service of a new political order which, should it eventuate, would owe its birth to the powerful vision of a committed social science linked to a broader religion of humanity.

Beatrice's commitment to political radicalism grew steadily in the years after Bacup. First as a volunteer charity worker, later as an apprentice researcher with her cousin Charles Booth's great survey of *The Life and Labour of the People of London*, and later still as a scholar in her own right preparing her study of the co-operative movement in Britain, she became increasingly aware of working-class people and their problems. Afterwards she recalled these as 'the critical years of my life'. She had become 'a divided personality', a *déclassée* middle-class female who roamed the slums of the East End of London by day, and talked about her experiences in fashionable drawing-rooms by night. By February 1890, as she later claimed, she had passed through 'the successive stages of socialist evolution' and wrote in her diary: 'At last I am a socialist!'[17] Shortly before, on 26 November 1889, her dying father had urged upon her: 'I want one more son-in-law . . . I should like to see my little Bee married to a good strong fellow.'[18] Within a matter of weeks Beatrice met Sidney. Afterwards she confided to her diary: 'a loop-hole into the socialist party: one of the small body of men with whom I may sooner or later throw in my lot for good and all'.[19]

Sidney and Beatrice first met in person during January 1890, in the flat of one of her friends near the British Museum. On that occasion, Sidney provided her with a list of research sources which she needed for her study of the co-operative movement. In 1928, Beatrice recollected of this period that, if she had to answer in half a dozen words why she became a socialist, 'I should say "because I discovered the Co-operative Movement"; and were I allowed another six words to complete this tabloid confession, I should add "and discussed it with Sidney Webb" '.[20] Beatrice's interest in co-operation dated from Bacup, where she had grown convinced that the co-operative societies contained the seed of an alternative to capitalism. She felt, however, the need for a scheme to preserve the spirit of voluntary co-operation while protecting the producers from outside exploitation. She rejected the notion of the self-governing workshop as impracticable and argued for a system of ' "government from above" . . . supplemented by "government from below" '.[21] This meant in practical terms, as Sidney was at pains to impress upon her, the protective arm of a beneficent political state kept honest in its dealings with the co-operators by the incessant pressure of organized Trade Unions.

For his part, Sidney had by the time of their first meeting already made something of a name for himself as a leading theoretician among the small band of earnest intellectuals who comprised the newly-founded Fabian Society. He was generally accounted a key influence in the victory of the Progressives in the London County Council elections of 1889, the ground having been prepared in advance by his influential Fabian pamphlets *Facts For Socialists* (1887) and *Facts for Londoners* (1889). And in 1889, both his *Socialism in England* and his contribution to *Fabian Essays in Socialism* had appeared. In the last of these, Sidney had set out to demonstrate the inevitability of the modern movement towards socialism. His method was historical and positivistic, his political ideology reformist rather than revolutionary. Drawing on Comte, Darwin and Spencer, he first described the disintegration of the 'Old Thesis' of the eighteenth-century European feudal state, with its social nexus of ascriptive status relations. He then passed to a discussion of the 'Period of Anarchy', when free contractual relations and individualism triumphed, and utilitarianism became 'the Protestantism of Sociology'. Gradually, Sidney argued, there was emerging a 'New Synthesis', accompanied by a social nexus in which the individual would be increasingly superceded by the community of which he formed a part. Classical political economy was therefore fast becoming an outmoded perspective for inquiry. With the focus shifting to the social organism, the appropriate science for investigating the conditions of social health must be sociology. And, as Sidney concluded, this entailed a revision of the relative importance assigned to liberty and equality as principles informing social administration, a point which, he contended, was foreseen by J. S. Mill when he converted to socialism in successive editions of his *Political Economy*.[22]

Sidney Webb was born in Cranbourn Street near Leicester Square, and he remained throughout his life a devoted metropolitan. He once remarked in a memoir that no place on earth could content him more for habitation than that very middle part of London he had come to love in boyhood.[23] As Sidney was by nature reticent in discussing his private affairs, we know relatively little of his origins. But what we do know is that his mother was the proprietress of a hairdressing establishment and that his father, as Beatrice comments in *Our Partnership*, was 'a public accountant in a humble way'.[24]

From his earliest years Sidney was a voracious ingestor of facts. He once recalled how as a lad it would take him a full hour to traverse the length of Fleet Street, so absorbed would he become in the periodicals displayed on newsstands and in newspaper office windows. Characteristically, he found joy and enlightenment in poring over the entries in *Kelly's London Directory*. His unusual aptitude for swift reading and his photographic memory became legendary. Edward Pease recollected how Sidney had read through the *Encyclopedia Britannica* from beginning to end in his idle moments.[25] In *Our Partnership* Beatrice notes at one point that while on holiday in the country 'Sidney must have devoured some fifty or sixty books: I only accomplished two or three'.[26] Shaw remembered an episode in a French post office while travelling with Sidney. The postal clerk had disagreed with Sidney's assertion that his papers could go through the post for the equivalent of a halfpenny. Sidney insisted, and cited para. x on p. x of Vol. x of the relevant regulations that entitled him to despatch official papers at this rate. When the clerk's superior was called in and the regulations examined, Sidney was shown to have been correct.[27]

It thus came as no surprise when Sidney distinguished himself as a young scholar at the City of London College and later as a student at the Birkbeck Institute. Earlier, his mother had scraped together the money to send him and his brother Charles to Switzerland to study French and then to the home of a German pastor at Wismar to learn German. But while still at Birkbeck, a family crisis, the details of which we know little, forced Sidney to abandon his studies and become a wage-earner at the age of sixteen. Undeterred, he carried on with evening classes at London University while working for a City broker during the daytime. In 1878 he sat successfully for the first of a series of Civil Service competitive examinations which enabled him to advance rapidly from a junior clerkship to a senior administrative appointment at the Colonial Office. In his spare time he completed studies for an extra-mural London University law degree. At around this time Shaw met Sidney at the meetings of the Zetetical Society, and as Shaw recalled:

He knew all about the subject of the debate; knew more than the lecturer; knew more than anybody present; had read everything that had ever been written on the subject; and remembered all the facts that bore upon it. He used notes, read them, ticked them off one by one and threw them away, and finished with a coolness and clearness that to me, in my then trembling state, seemed miraculous. This young man was the ablest man in England ... Sidney Webb.[28]

Recognising his freakish scholarly capacities, Shaw formed a fast friendship with 'the unassuming young cockney prodigy', and it was through Shaw that Sidney became a member of the Fabian Society. By the date of his introduction to Beatrice, the trio of Webb, Sydney Olivier and Graham Wallas were known as 'The Three Musketeers' of the Society, while the impish Shaw, on his own account, enacted the role of D'Artagnan.[29]

Shortly after meeting Beatrice, Sidney ventured to send her a copy of a recent pamphlet he had written and a regular correspondence between them began. Already, months before, a 'mysterious penumbra' seemed to hint at their destiny. In October 1889 Beatrice had read Sidney's contribution to *Fabian Essays*, and commented afterwards: 'by far the most significant and interesting essay is the one by Sidney Webb'. Earlier, in a review notice of Booth's survey of the London poor in *The Star*, Sidney had concluded that 'the only contributor with any literary talent is Miss Beatrice Potter'.[30]

Beatrice cannot be said to have been immediately smitten with love for Sidney. As some candid entries in her diary suggest, she thought his appearance peculiar, with his huge head and tiny body, oversized nose, eyes and mouth, unkempt hair, and 'a most bourgeois black coat shiny with wear'. He struck her as a cross between a London card and a German professor. And yet there was a quality in Sidney Webb that kindled her interest from the start. 'I like the man', she conceded. 'There is a directness of speech, an open-mindedness, an imaginative warm-heartedness which should carry him far.'[31] In a further entry she mused: 'If the opportunity comes I think the man will appear. In the meantime, he is an interesting study. A London retail tradesman with the aims of a Napoleon! A queer monstrosity to be justified only by success.'[32]

Sidney had none of Beatrice's initial reservations. By the late spring of 1890 the two had come to a 'working compact' while attending a conference in Glasgow. But Miss Potter was to prove herself no easy prize. She made the moonstruck Sidney promise that if his work suffered he must give her up. He was to think of her as 'a married woman, as the wife of a friend'. Nonplussed, he agreed to try to look upon their relationship strictly from 'the point of view of Health', and to do his best to suppress his 'purely personal feelings' towards her. Beatrice duly reported the terms of the compact to her diary and concluded the entry on a triumphant note: 'One grasp of the hand . . . and we were soon in a warm discussion on some question of Economics.'[33]

Despite her best intentions, Beatrice soon found herself weakening before Sidney's persistent efforts. On an outing to Epping Forest he apparently read aloud to her from Keats and Rossetti, and she in turn gave him leave 'to think of me, when you would be thinking of yourself . . . but not when you have sufficient power to work'.[34] He was now her new-found counsellor, grown so impetuous with love that he occasionally forgot his own theory of the inevitability of gradualness. When she sent him proofs of her book on the co-operative movement, he responded by pointing out that, if only they worked together, they could accomplish much more. She retorted: 'I am a piece of steel.' Undaunted, his passion stronger than his logic, Sidney answered that 'one and one placed together, in a sufficiently integrated relationship, make not two but eleven'.[35]

Beatrice had been so badly stung by Chamberlain that she was not easily persuaded that marriage could ever mean anything other than suicide. In the end, however, Sidney's powers of persuasion won out and the two became secretly engaged on 20 May 1891. That summer they went to Norway for a holiday and Beatrice's diary reflects how thoroughly she had by then abandoned her reservations and replaced them with an almost disconcertingly analytical attitude towards their relationship. 'Our marriage', she suggested,

will be based on fellowship . . . a common faith and a common work. His feeling is the passionate love of an emotional man, mine the growing tenderness of the mother touched with the dependence of the woman on the help of a strong lover . . . and in the background there is the affectionate comraderie, the fun, the strenuous helpfulness, of two young workers in the same cause.[36]

Strolling hand in hand over the Norwegian moorland at sunset, the two social investigators eagerly discussed the outlines of their partnership-to-be. Sidney recounted how his great ambition in life was to take part in the governing of Britain on socialist principles. Beatrice suggested that he begin by seeking a place on the London County Council, where he would gain valuable practical experience of politics and administration. A second step lay in helping her own work, where through researches into the history of public administration, he would acquire useful technical knowledge. As they walked on, Sidney wondered aloud whether his fiancée was not perhaps too ambitious for him. Beatrice answered that much depended on whether the right opportunities presented themselves. In the meantime, she reminded him (and she reiterates the point at the beginning of *Our Partnership*), their joint talents and their varied experiences of life, combined with the high degree of financial independence that her unearned income of £1000 per annum made possible, conferred upon them certain initial advantages in the struggles that lay ahead.[37]

The secretly betrothed couple were now constant companions. Sidney posed as a sort of amanuensis to Miss Potter . . . 'amply rewarded', she confessed quaintly to her diary, by 'brief intervals of human nature'.[38] Many of Beatrice's old friends were scandalized. The Booths grew cool, and Herbert Spencer was so aghast at her attachment to a socialist that he withdrew her name as his literary executor. Beatrice had expected as much. During the Norwegian sojourn she had acknowledged to herself that:

The world will wonder. On the face of it it seems an extraordinary end to the once brilliant Beatrice Potter . . . to marry an ugly little man with no social position and less means . . . whose only recommendation, so some may say . . . is a certain pushing ability.[39]

She admitted too that she was 'not "in love", not as I was'. But she went on to reaffirm her conviction that in his intellect and his warm-heartedness, in his 'power of self-subordination and self-devotion for the "Common Good"', Sidney offered something every bit as worthy of her affectionate devotion. He held out the prospect of a more certain, more objective, and more enduring relationship, and one of infinitely greater potential worth to mankind, than one based upon the fickle sentiments of mere romantic love.

On New Year's Day 1892, Beatrice's ailing father died and she was at last free to embark upon her new life with Sidney. They were married at the St Pancras Vestry, London, on 23 July 1892. From that date she seems never again to have entertained serious doubts about the rightness of her decision. By the following summer she could record that 'my husband and I grow nearer to each other each hour of the day. A beautiful pact, marriage. Personal love and tenderness, community of faith, fellowship in work . . . a divine relationship.'[40] Some years later, in a 1911 diary entry marked '4 a.m.', she reflected that Sidney was 'the most perfect of lovers, by night and by day, in work and in play, in health and in sickness'.[41] And when in 1926 she embarked on the preparation of *Our Partnership* by composing a prefatory tribute to her partner, she concluded it with the touching observation that 'The days of his absence are weary to get through; and the sleepless hours of the night are haunted, not by the fear of death, but by the dread of life without him.'[42]

Our Partnership recounts the story of the first two decades of the Webb collaboration. It begins when Beatrice, aged 34, and Sidney, aged 33, had just embarked on their joint career. It ends with the Webbs aged 53 and 52. They were by then celebrities, and they could look back on a record of prodigious achievement. A checklist of their printed books, pamphlets, articles and miscellaneous publications for 1892–1911 includes over 170 separate entries and lends substance to A. G. Gardiner's reference to the Webbs as 'two typewriters clicking as one'.[43] Among their publications in the period are some of their most famous books, including *The History of Trade Unionism* (1894), *Industrial Democracy* (1897), the first volumes of their ambitious *English Local Government* series (1906–10), and the *Minority Report of the Poor Law Commission* (1909). At the same time Sidney was heavily involved in the affairs of the Fabian Society. He also sat as a councillor on the London County Council, steered the business of its Technical Education Board, played an important role in the reorganisation of London University, and engineered the creation of the London School of Economics. Beatrice's service on the Poor Law Commission involved heavy demands on her time. Yet she managed during these years to establish herself as the hostess of one of London's leading political *salons*. Even so, the gruelling pace of their lives was seldom allowed to interfere with Beatrice's diary-keeping. The typescript for the period, exclusive of the large 1911 travel diary, runs to some 1446 pages.

They managed to do so much by cultivating an attitude that Leonard Woolf described as one of 'open-minded dogmatism'.[44] Anything that fell within their interests was pursued with tireless intensity; anything that fell outside their purposes was ruthlessly excluded. They combined this attitude with a regimen of puritanical plain-living. 'One thing is clear', Beatrice says in a passage that summarizes a recurrent theme in the diaries, 'we must live the plainest, most healthful life in order to get through the maximum of work; and one must economize on all personal luxuries in order to have cash to spend on anything that turns up to be done.'[45] Working with research assistants, they gathered their materials together on endless slips of paper, then set to work writing for three or four hours every morning. 'It is a curious process, this joint-thinking', she wrote of their work at the time, 'we throw the ball of thought one to the other, each of us resting, judging, inventing in turn. And we are not satisfied until the conclusion satisfies completely and finally both minds.'

The Webbs' experiences in social investigation during the *Partnership* years lent themselves to an adumbration of their general political philosophy. 'We realize every day, more strongly', Beatrice wrote in 1900, 'that we can never hope to get hold of the "man in the street": we are "too damned intellectual".'[46] While themselves socialists, their researches left them with little patience with the egalitarian shibboleths of dogmatic socialism. They came to the conclusion that the rank and file of socialists were 'feather-headed failures' and that the leaders of organized labour were as often as not ignorant obstructionists.[47]

The Webbs' ideal state took shape as a beneficent 'housekeeping state'[48] in which extensive public services would minister to men's needs and guarantee a national minimum of civilized life. And just as the Webbian theory of administrative elitism may be said to constitute a secularized variation of the Calvinist doctrine of the elect, so too is the preferred social morality of the Webbian state, at least in Beatrice's formulation, distinctly reminiscent of the Puritan values of disciplined hard work and simple living that they pursued in their private lives. Happiness, at least in the sense of physical enjoyment, Beatrice comments in a passage comparing her views with those of the Benthamites, 'is an end which does not recommend itself to me'.[49] There are infinitely more important aims in social healing, and elsewhere she explains the Webb firm's vision of a state in which the individual is stimulated and constrained 'by the unfelt pressure of a better social environment, to become a healthier, nobler and more efficient being'.[50]

The achievement of their goals, the Webbs believed, required a two-fold strategy. In the first place they must find recruits for their new administrative elite, as well as social scientists to advise them. This, they thought, meant permeating the young middle-class men, 'catching them for collectivism before they have enlisted on the other side'.[51] And secondly, as convinced gradualists, they must persuade leading spokesmen for the major political parties of the desirability of their reformist schemes. The first goal would be achieved by the foundation of a new school of Webbian social science, the second by the steady cultivation of the politicians in the drawing-room of their home.

In the course of her narrative of these years, Beatrice described the foundation of the London School of Economics as 'perhaps the biggest single enterprise of *Our Partnership*'.[52] Certainly it was a remarkable achievement. Begun on a shoestring in two rented rooms at 9 John Street, Adelphi, the School had grown by the dates of their deaths into one of the world's leading centres of teaching and research in the social and political sciences.

During the summer of 1894 Sidney learned that he had been named executor of the estate of an eccentric Fabian personally unknown to him, a Mr Henry Hunt Hutchinson, who had blown his brains out. In his Will, Mr Hutchinson directed that £10000 be applied by Webb and four Fabian associates 'to the propaganda and other purposes of the [Fabian] Society and its Socialism'.[53] Graham Wallas, who was staying with the Webbs and Shaw at Borough Farm, Godalming, at the time, later recollected that the morning after receiving the news, Sidney and Beatrice awakened early, had a long discussion, 'and at breakfast told us that part of the money would be used to found a school in London on the lines of the *Ecole Libre de Sciences Politiques* in Paris'.[54] Beatrice's own version does not occur in her diary until 21 September 1894. Recounting the background to the 'odd adventure', she proceeded to list some of the suggestions which had been made for disposing of the windfall. The money might be used to pay for the ordinary work of the Fabian propagandists, or to underwrite the costs of the entire Fabian executive standing for Parliament, or to subsidize ILP candidates in their constituencies. But she then sets out Sidney's view: 'His version is to found, slowly and quietly, a *London School of Economics and Political Science*'. The evening before they had sat by the fire jotting down plans, and had decided that 'Above all, we want the ordinary citizen to feel that reforming society is no light matter, and must be undertaken by experts specially trained for the purpose.'[55]

Both of these accounts seem in retrospect slightly romanticized. Sir Sydney Caine's judgement, after an examination of the School records, was that 'they do not quite support the idea of a fully fledged scheme emerging at once'.[56] At any rate, years after the foundation of the LSE, Sidney Webb commented to Lord Beveridge that he had had no idea of a school of economics prior to the Hutchinson bequest. In

October 1888, it is true, he had written to Graham Wallas from America, telling him how impressed he had been with the teaching of economics at the Massachusetts Institute of Technology. And in 1893–4 a Commission appointed to look into the prospects for a teaching university in London had referred pointedly in their report to the manner in which the *Ecole Libre de Sciences Politiques* in Paris had 'raised with great success the standard of political education in France', a point which would not have escaped Sidney's attention from the vantage point of his position on the Technical Education Board.[57]

At a meeting of the Hutchinson trustees over which he presided on 8 February 1895 Sidney presented a memorandum which makes it clear that by that date he had formulated a definite scheme. He urged that the trustees 'should make it our main object to promote *education* . . . not mere propaganda in the parties of the hour, but solid work in economic and political principles'.[58] He was convinced that 'Ten years of this work might change the whole political thinking of England.' He attached an outline of *'The London School of Economics and Political Science'*, which he proposed to start on an experimental basis in October, with the help of a £500 grant from the Hutchinson bequest. To allay the suspicions of any trustees who thought his scheme inconsistent with the intent of the will, he added a request for £150 for a series of Fabian lectures around the country. Thereafter he took his scheme before the Technical Education Board of the LCC (which had been created on a motion by Webb in 1893, and of which he was conveniently chairman) and got £500 more, on the understanding that the lectures of the new institution would include instruction in commercial subjects. Meantime, he arranged for the free use of the lecture halls of the Royal Society of Arts and the London Chamber of Commerce. Sidney's adroitness in manoeuvring these sources of funding and good will suggests one reason for his reputation on the LCC as 'wily Webb'.[59] For while he gave the Hutchinson trustees to understand that his School would be a centre conducive to the spread of Fabianism, through its emphasis on research and the fundamental study of social and political institutions, he told the Technical Education Board that its value would lie in teaching of a practical commercial value; and with equal gusto he assured the Education Committee of the London Chamber of Commerce that 'the School would not deal with political matters and nothing of a socialist tendency will be introduced'.

At the end of May the trustees approved a short-term lease of premises in John Street; student fees were set at three pounds and 203 students were enrolled. With a director, a secretary, a porter, and eleven lecturers, the LSE opened its doors in October 1895. Within a year the School's British Library of Political and Economic Science was launched and the School moved to expanded premises at 10 Adelphi Terrace, at the corner of Robert Street overlooking the Thames. The rent was £350: the Webbs induced Miss Charlotte Payne Townshend, a millionaire Irish socialist who shortly afterwards became Shaw's wife, to take over the second and third floors for a rent of £300 ('We, knowing she was wealthy, and hearing she was socialistic', Beatrice wrote with characteristic candour, 'interested her in the London School of Economics . . . It was on account of her generosity to our projects and "for the good of the cause" that I first made friends with her.').[60] The School remained in these premises for six years. The Webbs gave School receptions that brought students into contact with the staff and with supporters from the outside world, and the Shaws were much in evidence. One of the early chairmen of the Students' Union recollected that if Union debates sometimes flagged he would 'send a chit to Bernard Shaw upstairs, who frequently responded with an appearance'.[61] As well as the regular staff there were occasional lecturers who supplemented the basic calendar offerings. Bertrand Russell appears on an early list of occasional lecturers, with 'Political and Economic Theory' as his subject. At that time a young Fellow of Trinity College, Cambridge, he donated most of the proceeds of his fellowship to the School.

In 1900–1901 the School was formally established as a

teaching institution of the reorganised London University, and with the help of a grant of land from the LCC, and generous gifts from philanthropists such as Mr Passmore Edwards and Lord Rothschild, the School constructed its first permanent building on its present site in Aldwych, only a fifteen-minute walk from Sidney's birthplace. There were then still three years to run on the original Hutchinson bequest. Looking back on the frantic pace of the LSE's earliests days its first director, W. A. S. Hewins, felt he had been privileged to have taken part 'in a great romance'.[62] Sidney himself said of its dramatic progress that 'it is said that on the buildings of the School of Economics the concrete never sets'.[63] Private as well as public monies continued to be contributed to the School's early funds. Sir Ernest Cassel gave a quarter of a million pounds, and by the 1930s the Rockefeller Foundation had contributed close to half a million more, and there were further substantial gifts from the Carnegie U.K. Foundation and other benefactors. In the curious logic of events, the financial treasures of leading capitalist enterprises were solicited to help build up an institution that to many has seemed a byword for socialism, just as it was a sizeable capital endowment proffered by her business-minded father that assured Beatrice and Sidney of the independence to pursue their joint career as socialist reformers.

In an assessment which has been corroborated in the testimony of many others, Beatrice wrote in *Our Partnership* that it was primarily Sidney who 'engineers the School'.[64] Dame Margaret Cole has similarly concluded that, from the nature of the case, Beatrice's role in the foundation of the LSE was as 'an adjutant rather than a prime mover'.[65] Sidney dominated its early financial administration and much of the day to day policy. When preparations were underway for the removal of the School to Adelphi Terrace, Beatrice noted in her diary: 'poor Sidney trudges over there directly after breakfast and spends his mornings with painters, plumbers and locksmiths, interviewing would-be students to whom he gives fatherly advice'.[66] His legendary obliviousness to aesthetic considerations found its way into the School's very physical constitution. The architect A. J. Penty was shocked to learn that the winning design in a competition for the LSE's first permanent building was decided by simply adding up the floor space in the various plans and awarding the contract to the one with the greatest square footage: Sidney called it 'decision by the statistical method'.[67]

The Webbs turned their energies to the creation of the LSE at a time when they were becoming discouraged over the slow inroads that the Progressive Party had made in the LCC. In December 1894 they had suffered a 'crushing defeat' in the Westminster vestry elections, in which Beatrice herself had stood as a candidate. And in the main LCC elections of March 1895 there was a standoff in which an even number of Moderates and Progressives were returned. Beatrice, at least, seemed to view the scheme for founding the LSE as a way to regain their lost momentum. At Christmas 1895, she wrote defiantly in her diary: '. . . we are creating the London School of Economics as a wider foundation than street-corner preaching'.[68]

By March 1898 she could assure herself that the LSE was 'growing silently though surely into a centre of collectivist-tempered research and establishing itself as *the* English school of economics and political science'. Along with their efforts in the Fabian Society, on the LCC, and through their writings, Beatrice saw the foundation of the School as the capstone of a plan under which 'no young man or woman who is anxious to study or to work in public affairs can fail to come under our influence'.[69]

Without overdrawing the picture, it is at least interesting to observe that Beatrice's plans for the School were originally more ambitious than Sidney's. Certainly some of their friends felt that the LSE scheme opened up a golden opportunity for socialistic propaganda. Shaw, for example, wrote (significantly, perhaps, to Beatrice rather than to Sidney) urging that the School's new director be urged to 'speak as a Collectivist, and make it clear that the School of Economics will have a Collectivist bias. Any pretence about having no bias at all, about "pure" or "abstract" research, or the like evasions and unrealities must be kept for the enemy.' He wanted a Collectivist teaching staff and 'the Collectivist flag . . . waved, and the Marseillaise played if necessary in order to attract fresh bequests'.[70]

But Sidney held adamantly to the view that the LSE should be an impartial research and teaching institution. Believing, as he had argued in his contribution to *Fabian Essays*, that the 'irresistible progress of Democracy' in the nineteenth-century entailed an 'irresistible glide into collectivist Socialism',[71] he was ready to let the facts adduced by social research speak for themselves. As Professor von Hayek has remarked, politics entered into Sidney's thinking only insofar as he believed, perhaps naively, that a careful study of the facts 'ought to lead most sensible people to socialism'.[72] The facts, for Sidney, were always the facts of economic and administrative analysis developed in an historical framework. From the outset Beatrice viewed the School as a vehicle for achieving the elusive science of society of which she had dreamt since joining Charles Booth's research team in the 1880s. It would be a centre of *'research really done . . .* with a high degree of accuracy and exhaustiveness in work', divorced from 'metaphysics and shoddy history', and eventually, a place of 'pure learning and culture'.[73] Notwithstanding his ringing tribute to sociology in the *Fabian Essays*, Sidney's approach was less abstractly theoretical. In a memorandum launching an appeal for the British Library of Political and Economic Science, he envisaged political studies as a field in which economics, jurisprudence and general history formed departments around 'the actual facts and experiences of public administration'. It is not insignificant that Sidney himself was for many years an unpaid Professor of Public Administration in the LSE, and that sociology was not introduced as a subject at the School until the session of 1904–5. He was an institutional scholar more interested in the practical machinery of government than in abstract ideas. Hence Graham Wallas' well-known remark that the Webbs were interested in town councils while he was interested in town councillors, and Sidney's own comment that the kind of statistics he wanted taught at the School was 'not statistical theory, but statistics for junior civil servants'.[74]

Sidney lived up to his commitment to keep the School a centre for impartial study. He recruited lecturers who were critical of prevailing scholarly orthodoxy rather than spokesmen for particular political ideologies. Few of them were socialists. The LSE's first two directors went on to careers as Conservative MPs, and when, in 1910, the Railway Companies which had been early benefactors demanded Sidney's resignation as Chairman of the Governors of the School after he had delivered a speech critical of the low wages of railway servants, he gave in rather than risk the loss of their support. He was succeeded by a young Conservative politician. Beatrice mused: 'It is always sad when a favourite child grows up and *seems* to escape influence and control. But one has had one's day and we must not repine. In some ways the School has been too successful, it has outgrown our tutelage.'[75] But she added that they had succeeded in putting an imprint on the LSE that it would not easily lose, a point amply confirmed by the destiny of such School figures as Hobson, Tawney, Laski and the Coles in socialist lore. But there is also a case to be made, as Sir Sydney Caine has argued, that the LSE has perhaps on balance been an influence against as well as for Socialist policies.[76] The Webbs' achievement in founding the School goes far beyond partisan considerations. As another director, Sir Walter Adams, observed, in paying tribute to Sidney's prescience and his fairness in overseeing the amazingly rapid establishment of 'his child' as a major centre of learning in the social sciences, the LSE has been paradoxically a centre both of academic innovation and of the best in traditional scholarship. In this respect, he concludes, Sidney's engineering of its early maturity gave the School 'the self-confidence and courage to be conservative'.[77]

If the foundation of the LSE was the highlight of Sidney's career during these years, Beatrice's service on the Poor Law Commission and the subsequent campaign to propagandize the findings of their *Minority Report* placed her for a time in centre stage. Fully a third of the text of *Our Partnership* is devoted to the topic. As Dame Margaret Cole has observed, appointment to the Commission came 'at exactly the right moment . . . having for over thirteen years played second fiddle, albeit a loud and imposing second fiddle, she was more than ready to make an advance in her own proper person'.[78]

Beatrice was appointed to the Poor Law Commission in 1905. The Balfour Government, which made the appointment, had previously been the subject of intense 'permeation' at the Webb *salon*. The Commission was established to inquire into the workings of the existing system of poor relief, based on statutes dating from 1834, and to assess its suitability to the conditions of twentieth-century society. It was under the aegis of the Poor Law that the notorious nineteenth-century workhouses had flourished, and while local efforts had been made to alleviate the worst abuses, there was a growing feeling that the old procedures for ministering to the plight of the destitute were unsuited to contemporary conditions. Beatrice quickly surmised that the composition of the twenty-man Commission was such as to dispose it to recommend, at most, moderate changes. She seemed to view this as a challenge to goad them into producing a more innovative report . . . one, indeed, which would break entirely with the prevailing philosophy of relief. With financial aid from Charlotte Shaw, the Webbs set to work researching various specialized aspects of the Commission's work, and they circulated reports based upon their findings among the Commissioners. Whereas most of the members saw their task as that of finding answers for the best means of relieving destitution, the Webbs wanted to expand the Commission's inquiry to include an examination of its causes. The modern state, they urged, had an obligation to work towards the eradication of poverty. And since they believed that the causes of poverty were varied, they called for the ending of the Poor Law and its replacement by local agencies providing specialized services. Moreover, the Webbs wanted the able-bodied recovered for active social roles, and to this end, proposed the creation of labour exchanges organized by a Ministry of Labour, which would co-ordinate regional fluctuations in the labour force and run training establishments. Under the Local Authorities, there would be Registrars of Public Assistance who, in keeping with the moral tone of Webbian reform, would have wide discretion in deciding whether or not services were to be free. The Webbs wanted people to pay according to their means, and evidently believed they would do so willingly out of a sense of obligation to their fellows. They also believed that the benefits rendered by the state under their schemes would not be mere material benefits, but would contribute to the moral as well as the physical well-being of the citizen . . . would 'ensure to the workers by hand and by brain steady progress in health and happiness, honesty and kindliness, culture and scientific knowledge, and the spirit of adventure'.[79]

It is a commonplace that the *Minority Report* which sets out these arguments anticipated in many respects the later development of the welfare state. But when it was submitted in 1909 (it was written by Sidney at the Herefordshire estate of a friendly millionaire, Sir Julius Wernher, a fact which struck Beatrice as 'really rather comic')[80] it was signed by only four members of the Commission. Beatrice's efforts had undoubtedly made inroads on the main body of the Commissioners, as they brought in a majority report which threw out the infamous principle of 'less eligibility', according to which the poor were made to work by ensuring that relief was kept below the lot of the worst-paid workman. But while a reformist document, the majority report fell far short of Beatrice's vision of a new social system, in recommending as it did the relief of the poor by a combination of voluntary bodies and statutory authorities. Beatrice expected that their report would be accorded a bad reception 'from all sides'. But within a month the press had hailed the *Majority Report* for its tone of enlightened reform, and generally ignored the Webbs'. Beatrice was indignant and resolved to carry their case to a wider audience. She wrote in her diary on 13 May:

'Enter the National Committee for the Break-Up of the Poor Law.'[81]

Soon the organization's name was changed to the National Committee for the Prevention of Destitution. It was a remarkable propaganda effort. Within a short time the Committee had some 16000 members. Housed in offices in The Strand, 'wedged between the Fabian Office close on its right and the London School of Economics a few yards to its left', it was, Beatrice reflected, 'a sort of middle term between avowed Socialism and non-partisan research and administrative technique'.[82] The Committee produced letters, tracts, leaflets and other literature expounding its views, and the Fabian Society brought out a cheap annotated edition of the *Minority Report*. A monthly newspaper, *The Crusade*, was founded to further the cause, and out of it later grew the *New Statesman*. But with the great Liberal electoral victory of 1911, the campaign petered out. The public seemed satisfied with Lloyd George's unemployment and sickness insurance schemes, which were enacted in the Insurance Act of 1911. Many felt, with the iconoclastic labour leader John Burns, that the Webbs had been dished.

Beatrice looked back on the Poor Law campaign with mixed feelings. For the first time the partners had set aside private 'permeation' to engage in public propaganda . . . had become in a more positive sense intellectuals in politics. She wrote that she sometimes regretted the turning point. But she wondered if she had had any real choice between the rival calls of social research and practical politics. At any rate, in the aftermath of the campaign she wrote in her diary on 7 May 1911, that the time had arrived 'for a genuine Socialist Party with a completely worked out philosophy and a very detailed programme'.[83] But the intellectually symmetrical party she had in mind when she sought a place on the Executive of the Fabian Society during the following year . . . a party led by bright university men who would serve as brain-workers on behalf of the labouring classes . . . was to fare little better than had her plans for the eradication at a stroke of poverty and its replacement by the housekeeping state.

There was to be precious little symmetry in the fratricidal relations of the Webbs with the guild socialists, the ILP and the trade unions; and out of such disparate materials it was to be Sidney, the ideal committee man, rather than Beatrice, the philosophical schemer, who would play a central role in engineering the creation of the modern Labour Party in 1918.

Beatrice was never to publish *Our Partnership* in her lifetime, and from the date of its ostensible ending in 1911 until her death in 1943 a period of 32 years was to elapse. And while the time span of *Our Partnership* encompassed the most intense years of the Webbs' collaboration, Beatrice brought the book to end not with the close of the Poor Law campaign in 1911, but with a brief *résumé* added in 1938 of the events leading up to their conversion to Russian communism. Their massive and controversial *Soviet Communism, A New Civilisation* appeared in 1935, and on the very last page of *Our Partnership* Beatrice refers to it as 'the final and certainly the most ambitious task of "Our Partnership" '.[84]

By the end of the Poor Law campaign the Webbs' popularity was at a low ebb. They were thought too radical by their old Liberal and Conservative friends and too intellectual by working-class leaders. They came to be regarded as ambitious and ruthless manipulators, a view of them given its classic expression in H. G. Wells' portrait of them as the Baileys in his *The New Machiavelli*. Beatrice was frustrated at the apparent lack of direction in their joint career, and her mood only deepened with the onset of war. After August 1914 Sidney was as busy as ever in behind-the-scenes advisory work, helping to draft emergency regulations and plotting with Arthur Henderson and others the creation of a postwar Labour Party. Beatrice brooded; and so depressed did she become over the war that she suffered a serious breakdown from which she recovered only gradually. When she did so it was in response to the challenges of postwar reconstruction, which held out the prospect of a revival of her full working-relationship with Sidney.

In 1915 the partners had projected a major work on the

nature of socialism on which they set to work in earnest after the war. It was to be, as Beatrice noted in her diary, 'a summary of our knowledge and our faith . . . our Last Testament'.[85] As the work progressed it became divided into two parts, which appeared respectively as the *Constitution for a Socialist Commonwealth* (1920) and the *Decay of Capitalist Civilisation* (1923). The books were markedly different in tone from the characteristic Webb production of the *Partnership* years. The *Constitution*, while still professing adherence to Sidney's gradualist line, was more programmatic, more abstractly theoretical, in its holistic blueprint for a government of the future. The *Decay* was more virulently polemical in its critique of the capitalist *ethos* than anything the two partners had hitherto written.

These were for Beatrice halcyon days, in which her partnership with Sidney was revived. She wrote eagerly in her diary about being 'back in our old style of partnership' after a protracted period of despondency.[86] She was especially happy over the *Constitution*, the idea for which had come to Beatrice while listening to H. G. Wells deliver a lecture on utopianism; she called the *Constitution* 'the jointest of our joint efforts'. Its ambitious social engineering made the book's composition seem to her a form of enjoyment: it was 'real sport', she felt, 'thinking out each separate part and making each part fit the others'.[87] Beatrice was disappointed when the *Constitution* was accorded no more friendly a reception than had been the case with the *Minority Report* a decade earlier. But her appetite had been whetted by the exhilarating experience of writing in a format that allowed more scope for her imagination than that of their usual work. Certainly there is evidence that she sometimes found her formal sociological studies with Sidney stultifying; she once declared roundly that she was 'sick to death trying to put hideous facts, multitudinous details, exasperating qualifications, into a readable form'.[88]

For if Sidney's self-professed goal in life was to be one of the socialist governors of Britain, Beatrice confessed to her own 'secret ambition', settled on long before she met Sidney, 'to write a book that would be read'.[89] As early as September 1889, she recorded in her diary that 'This last month or so I have been haunted by a longing to create characters and move them to and fro among fictitious circumstances.'[90] And indeed, she had tried writing a joint novel with Auberon Herbert, which was to be entitled *Looking Forward* and take the form of a response to Edward Bellamy's *Looking Backward*. But she had concluded she must set it aside 'until I have discovered my laws', a decision that prompted Herbert to taunt her playfully as 'A woman without a soul, looking upon struggling society as a young surgeon looks on a case as another subject for diagnosis.'[91]

Beatrice returned to the idea of creative literature during her idleness in the war years. On 3 January 1917, she noted that she had 'bought a small cheap typewriter and I am using up some of my spare hours in the afternoon in copying out and editing my MSS diaries so as to make a "Book of My Life" '.[92] She worked away at her 'secret and pleasurable occupation' until, with the reactivation of the partnership in the reconstruction period, when they embarked on the *Constitution*, she set it aside. Then, in 1922, Sidney realized his ambition to enter Parliament, when he was returned as Labour member for Seaham. Two years later he was called into the first Labour Cabinet as MacDonald's President of the Board of Trade. He remarked to Beatrice on the eve of Parliament in 1924 that so far as their working partnership was concerned, it seemed like 'the blank page between the Old and the New Testament'. And Beatrice, who had for long been reluctant to encourage Sidney in his ambition for fear of its inroads on their joint work, concluded a description of the new Cabinet in her diary with the observation: 'Here ends the Old Testament.'[93] Earlier, on New Year's Eve 1922, a month after Sidney entered the House, she had declared her renewed intention to 'get on with "*My Craft and My Creed*" '. 'I have done so much drudgery', she mused, 'that I think I have a right to let myself go on a work of art! But have I the capacity . . . at sixty-five years of age . . . of anything approaching a work of art?'[94]

Beatrice originally budgeted two years for the preparation of the text of *My Apprenticeship*. But the book did not appear until 1926, and it is perhaps significant that, of all her voluminous writings, she felt the most anxious for the success of this, her first book of sole authorship since her marriage. She worried that Sidney would disapprove of its subjectivity, observing, in a diary passage of March 1925, that 'all that part which deals with "my creed" as distinguished from "my craft" seems to him the sentimental scribblings of a woman, only interesting just because they are feminine'.[95] As she worked away, she alternated between moods of 'panic that the book would fall dead' and a 'delusion that I was going to make a little fortune out of it'.[96] When she finished the draft finally on 29 October 1925, she could not forbear warning herself of the possibility of ridicule at the hands of reviewers who knew her as a writer of works of information rather than art. But when the book appeared in the early summer of 1926, she was relieved to find that her anxiety over 'this child of my old age' had been exaggerated. She was generally pleased with the notices and recorded with satisfaction that it now seemed clear that 'the book will influence thought and be read by students and thinkers and be quoted by future historians'.[97]

Even before completing *My Apprenticeship*, Beatrice had pretty well settled on the idea of following it up with several further volumes of autobiography. She wanted to work out more completely 'my conception of the place of religion in the life of man'.[98] She started in immediately after the publication of the *Apprenticeship*, for in the Passfield Papers there is a 16 page typescript entitled 'Prologue: Sidney Webb', which is headed with a note: 'An attempt at a portrait written mostly in the night and early morning during July, 1926.' At the end is added: 'Re-copied and finished September 29th, 1926.'[99]

But after that time work on *Our Partnership* proceeded sporadically. A period of research intervened, when the Webb partnership was revived in order to complete their *Poor Law History*. Then, in 1929, Sidney was elevated to the peerage as Baron Passfield and re-entered the Cabinet in MacDonald's second Government as Secretary of State for the Colonies . . . an achievement which, following on his earlier Cabinet position at the Board of Trade, prompted Beatrice to note in her diary the curious parallel between the political careers of 'her boy' and Joseph Chamberlain, who had earlier held the same two portfolios.[100] Sidney's return to active politics inevitably trapped Beatrice in a time-consuming routine of social obligations. There were also bouts of ill health, and the general distraction of their removal from their London home to Passfield Corner.

But by May Day 1931 Beatrice had finished the first chapter of *Our Partnership*. Heartened by Sidney's apparent enthusiasm for her latest efforts in autobiography, she pressed on, and noted on 19 June that 'I dictated the last words of the second chapter of the book, which ends the period 1892–98.'[101] She confessed she was enjoying herself, in contrast to the agonies of composition she had experienced over *My Apprenticeship*. 'The writing of this book . . . is comparatively easy', she wrote, adding that 'I don't care a little damn what other people say of it: probably I shan't be alive when it is published; anyhow, I am too aged to care.'[102] At her current rate of progress, she estimated, she could finish the volume in another two years: 'by that time I shall be $75\frac{1}{2}$ . . . leaving me $4\frac{1}{2}$ years before 80 to write the last volume, 1912–1932'.[103]

But Beatrice was never to realize her projected completion dates. She was struggling with old age, haunted by periodic doubts about her continued capacity for first-rate intellectual work, and increasingly disillusioned with spiralling unemployment and the general direction of British affairs . . . a disillusionment which culminated in the abrupt fall of the Labour Government in August 1931, and the formation of a National Coalition Government under MacDonald, 'The Great Betrayer', as she called him. Beatrice was personally relieved that Sidney was able to shed the burden of office, but the general view that he had been an unsuccessful Colonial Secretary cannot have comforted either of them. She felt more than ever that outside of one's own immediate concerns there was 'a tragic bewilderment', and that 'no one now talks of progress'.[104] She wondered whether it was a sign of un- mistakable decadence, or if there was any hope for a new social order arising out of the old. Her usual daydreams were now replaced by the recurring nightmare she had had during the Great War . . . that European civilization was in the process of dissolution. Sidney, according to Beatrice, scoffed at her fears. 'Even if Europe fails', he submitted, 'there is always the U.S.A.', which he thought not likely to develop the British social disease of class conflict and social disorder. 'Anyway', he added, 'there is nothing *we* can do . . . all that remains for us is to finish up all our books.'[105] But Beatrice felt the inevitability of his gradualism no longer an appro- priate response to the realities of the world, and by April 1926, was asking herself: 'When will such a leader arise who will unite the intellect of an Aristotle, a Goethe or an Einstein, with the moral genius of a Buddha, a Christ, or a St Francis of Assisi?'

At this juncture a new distraction intervened to assuage Beatrice's doubts. It began with a dinner party at their London flat during February 1930, when the Webbs had the Russian Ambassador, Gregori Sokolnikov and his wife to dine with the Shaws, Arthur Ponsonby and P. J. Noel-Baker. The Sokolnikov dinner brought back in a rush the sentiments she had felt at Bacup as a young woman search- ing for a creed. The Russians neither smoked nor drank their wine, and their naive faith and their asceticism rendered them in Beatrice's eyes 'veritable puritans'. In their simpli- city and their unpretentiousness, she mused afterwards, the Sokolnikovs belonged to 'the very best type of young work- man of good character in quest of knowledge'.[106] Assuredly, Beatrice was aware – at least rationally – of the dangers of an uncritical approach to Soviet Russia. The rigid orthodoxy of its 'creed autocracy' would have to be somehow reconciled with the freedom of men's souls: what was needed was 'a church without a dogma'. But Beatrice's mind had been stimulated by her old dream of uniting science and mysticism

into a solid social faith. What attracted her to Soviet Russia
was her feeling that it might supply the kind of soul for
government that was so patently lacking in the West. 'It is',
she wrote, 'the invention of the religious order, as the determining factor in the life of a great nation, that is the magnet
that attracts me to Russia. Practically that religion is
Comteism . . . the Religion of Humanity. Auguste Comte
comes to his own.'[107] Five days after the Sokolnikov party
Beatrice began her next diary entry with a complaint that
'The life I lead is displeasing in its restlessness.' Soon she
was reading everything she could get her hands on to do with
Russia, and put Sidney to work helping her. The publication
of *Our Partnership* was set aside for the pursuit of a more
pressing task, one which was to provide the Webb partnership with a dramatically climactic ending. By the time the
Webbs sailed for Stalinist Russia in May 1932 to gather
materials for their *Soviet Communism*, as Desmond McCarthy
later recorded,[108] Beatrice's new faith was fanatical. She got
Sidney to help her draft out a memorandum containing their
hypothetical conclusions before they had even left London.[109]

'We have no incompatible desires, either together or apart',
Beatrice once wrote of the firm of Webb, 'our daily existence
and our ideal are one and the same . . . we sail straight to our
port over a sunlit sea. But the point we make for seems sometimes an unconscionable way off!'[110] The point seemed
closer when she found her haven in Soviet Russia. But she
never lost her inquisitiveness about the larger point of her
journey through life. She yearned for certainty and with the
passage of years turned increasingly from public affairs to
muse on the meaning of the end at hand. She pronounced
herself prepared, but was saddened at the thought that death
would mean terrible loneliness for the surviving partner. With
characteristic hubris, she suggested that a solution which had
occurred to her was that they might both be shot to death
simultaneously by an anarchist on the day of their golden
wedding anniversary.[111]

It was an extraordinarily intimate partnership. And yet, as

Kingsley Martin[112] and others have pointed out, there flourished such profound differences beneath its surface appearance: Sidney the incurable optimist, the Benthamite fact-grubber and incrementalist, the intrepid rationalist: Beatrice a brooding pessimist, a mystic, her intellectual roots, through Spencer, in St Simon and Comte and grand theoretical positivism.[113] There was assuredly something for both of them in their intense collaboration. For if the partnership involved risks, it also served to preserve the integrity of the partners in a manner more profitable to each than would have been possible had they gone their separate ways. And thus the jibe of Sir William James:

> How wise it was of Mrs. Webb
> To mate with little Sidney
> A man of slightly lower class
> But one of her own kidney.[114]

But in the end, the best achievements of the celebrated pair were less the products of their joint efforts than of the talents of each of them as individuals.

Leonard Woolf has said of Beatrice that she had 'the temperament strongly suppressed, the passion and the imagination, of an artist, though she would herself have denied this'.[115] And indeed, Herbert Spencer was perhaps closer to the truth than he appreciated when he told Beatrice that she reminded him of George Eliot. For in her moralistic search for a craft in *My Apprenticeship*, there is more than a little that is evocative of Maggie Tulliver in *The Mill On The Floss*. Like Beatrice Potter, Maggie was

a creature full of eager, passionate longings for all that was beautiful and glad; thirsty for all knowledge, with an ear straining after dreamy music that died away and would not come near to her; with a blind unconscious yearning for something that would link together the wonderful impressions of this mysterious life, and give her soul a sense of home in it.[116]

Beatrice's description of her personal development in *My Apprenticeship*, in which she travelled from uncertain beginnings through adversity to love and companionship at Sidney's side, was a Tulliverian literary triumph of no mean proportions. And when she turned to continue her story in

Our Partnership, now as a defiant intellectual in politics united with her partner in a pilgrim's progress[117] towards a creed to live by, it was the same Maggie Tulliver of Beatrice's deep imaginative instincts that led her to the dramatic, indeed theatrical, ending of their journey in *Soviet Communism, A New Civilisation*.[118]

Notes

Abbreviations

M.A. *My Apprenticeship*, London, Longmans Green, 1926.
O.P. *Our Partnership*, London, Longmans Green, 1948.
D.(3) *Diaries, 1912–1924*, London, Longmans Green, 1952.
D.(4) *Diaries, 1924–1932*, London, Longmans Green, 1956.
P.P. Passfield Papers (LSE).
Work *The Webbs and Their Work*, London, Muller, 1949.

1 D.(4), p. 170. Kingsley Martin, in 'The Webbs in Retirement', in *Work*, pp. 295–6, recounts a wonderful allegory centring on 'Sandy'. Weekend guests at Passfield Corner would be taken on walks, but, he recollected, there was always an 'incomprehensible incident' with 'Sandy' at the outset: 'Just before the walk started, he began to bark at Mrs. Webb, while she hit the ground with a walking stick. While she shouted loudly and repeatedly, "Sandy! Sandy!", Sidney stood silently by, watching. I could never make out who won this odd battle of wills or why it had to be fought. Dogs do bark with excitement when they are going out. I never dared to question Mrs. Webb on the subject. It was a ritual behind which lay some mysterious emotional satisfaction. In the end Sandy made a final and tragic rebellion. I suppose he reached the end of his patience. Anyway he bit Mrs. Webb and had to be destroyed.'

2 H. G. Wells, *The New Machiavelli*, London, The Bodley Head, 1911, p. 203. He added (206) that 'her soul was bony'.

3 The photograph is reproduced in Kitty Muggeridge and Ruth Adam, *Beatrice Webb, A Life*, London, Secker & Warburg, 1967, as the frontispiece.

4 Cited in Anne Fremantle, *This Little Band of Prophets*, N.Y., Mentor Books, 1960, p. 41.

5 See Lewis S. Feuer (ed.), *Karl Marx and Friedrich Engels: Basic Writings on Politics and Philosophy*, N.Y., Anchor Books, 1959, p. 448.

6 M.A. p. 412.

7 M.A. p. 11. 'My mother was nearing forty years of age when I became aware of her existence', Beatrice wrote, 'and it was not until the last years of her life, when I was the only grown up daughter remaining in the home, that I became intimate with her. The birth of an only brother when I was four, and his death when I was seven years of age, the crowning joy and devastating sorrow of my mother's life, had separated me from her care and attention; and the coming of

my younger sister, a few months after my brother's death, a partial outlet for my mother's wounded feelings, completed our separation.' For background discussion, see Kitty Muggeridge and Ruth Adam (n. 3 above), pp. 24–31.

8 Richard Hofstadter, *Social Darwinism in America*, Boston, Beacon Press, 1964, p. 32.

9 M.A. p. 123.

10 There are very few references to Chamberlain in *My Apprenticeship*, but the MSS diaries are full of passages dealing with the abortive affair. For two rather different assessments of the impact of the infatuation on Beatrice's life, see Dame Margaret Cole, 'Appendix: Beatrice Webb and Joseph Chamberlain', in D.(4), pp. 311–16, and Kitty Muggeridge and Ruth Adam (see n. 3 above), chapter 6. At any rate, Beatrice was still thinking about Chamberlain for some time after meeting Sidney. Thus, she wrote in her diary on 1 December 1890: 'personal passion has burned itself out, and what little personal feeling still exists haunts the memory of that other man. Why did I watch for hours at the entrance to the South Kensington museum for two days last summer unless in the hope of seeing him . . . a deplorable weakness for which I despised myself too much to repeat the third time.' P.P., 1 December 1890, vol. 14, ff. 63–5.

11 M.A. p. 279.   12 M.A. p. 90.

13 M.A. p. 180.   14 M.A. p. 152 *passim*.

15 M.A. pp. 160–2.   16 M.A. p. xiv.

17 M.A. p. 408.   18 M.A. p. 401.

19 P.P., 26 April 1890, vol. 14, ff. 35–6.

20 Cited in Mary Hamilton, *Sidney and Beatrice Webb*, London, Sampson Low, 1933, p. 64.

21 M.A. p. 387.

22 Sidney Webb, 'Historic', in G. B. Shaw (ed.), *Fabian Essays in Socialism* (1st pub. 1889), N.Y., Dolphin Books, n.d., pp. 46–83.

23 See Mary Hamilton (n. 20 above), pp. 18, 26.

24 O.P. p. 2. But Sidney's birth certificate lists the profession of his father, Charles Webb, as "Hair Dresser". P.P.III,1.5.

25 Edward Pease, 'Webb and the Fabian Society', in *Work*, p. 25. In the same collection Kingsley Martin writes of Sidney: 'a story is told of his reading the whole of Chambers' *Encyclopedia of English Literature* in the train between London and Edinburgh'.

26 O.P. pp. 174, 176.

27 The story is recounted in Mary Hamilton (n. 20 above), p. 22.

28 Ibid. p. 14.   29 G. B. Shaw, 'Early Days', in *Work*, pp. 4, 8.

30 M.A. pp. 404–5.   31 M.A. p. 408.

32 P.P. 26 April 1890, vol. 14, f. 35.

33 P.P. *circa* May 1890, vol. 14, ff. 42–3.

34 P.P. 27 September 1890, vol. 14, ff. 63–5.   35 M.A. p. 411.

36 P.P. 20 June 1891, vol. 14 (2), ff. 2–3. 'Marriage, we always say', Beatrice commented to Virginia Woolf, 'is the waste paper basket of the emotions.' Too often, she felt, it interfered with one's work: 'I am not prepared to make the minutest sacrifice of efficiency', Beatrice wrote in her diary in a passage describing marriage as 'another word for suicide'. In another place she observed that 'It pains me to see a fine intelligent girl, directly she marries, putting aside intellectual things as no longer pertinent to her daily life.' P.P. 25 July 1894,

vol. 15, ff. 11–12. She added as an afterthought: 'And yet the other alternative . . . so often nowadays chosen by intellectual women . . . of deliberately foregoing motherhood seems to me to thwart all the purposes of their nature. I myself . . . or rather we . . . chose this course in our marriage . . . but then I had passed the age when it is easy and natural for a woman to become a child bearer . . . my physical nature was to some extent dried up at 35 after ten years stress and strain of a purely brainworking and sexless life. If I were again a young woman and had the choice between a brainworking profession or motherhood, I would not hesitate which life to choose (as it is I sometimes wonder whether I had better not have risked it and taken my chance).' Ibid. vol. 15, f. 12 (page 20). While their marriage was childless, Beatrice was in the habit of referring to their pet project of the moment as their 'child'.

37 P.P. 7 July 1891, vol. 14 (2), ff. 3–6.   38 M.A. pp. 413–14.

39 P.P. 20 June 1891, vol. 14 (2), f. 2.   40 P.P. Summer 1893, vol. 14 (2), f. 47.

41 O.P. p. 472.   42 O.P. p. 11.

43 Cited in Margaret Cole, 'The Webbs and Social Theory', *British Journal of Sociology*, vol. 12 (June 1961), p. 102.

44 Leonard Woolf, 'Political Thought and The Webbs', in *Work*, p. 259.

45 O.P. p. 65.   46 O.P. p. 202.

47 O.P. pp. 125, 134.   48 O.P. p. 149.

49 O.P. pp. 210–11.   50 O.P. p. 229.

51 O.P. p. 125.   52 O.P. p. 84.

53 The Will is reproduced in Sir Sydney Caine, *The History of the Foundation of the London School of Economics and Political Science*, London, Bell, 1963, p. 18.

54 Cited in O.P. p. 86, from Wallas' essay on the foundation of the School in *The Handbook of the Students' Union*, 1925.

55 O.P. p. 86.

56 Sir Sydney Caine (n. 53 above), p. 20.

57 See F. A. Hayek, 'The London School of Economics, 1895–1945', *Economica*, vol. 13 (February 1946), pp. 1–31.

58 Sir Sydney Caine (n. 53 above), p. 37.

59 O.P. p. 67.   60 O.P. pp. 90–1.

61 Cited in F. A. Hayek (n. 57 above), pp. 9–10.

62 O.P. p. 89.

63 Quoted in M. Cole, *Beatrice Webb*, N.Y., Harcourt Brace, 1946, p. 86.

64 O.P. p. 185.

65 Margaret Cole, *Beatrice Webb* (n. 63 above), p. 85.

66 O.P. p. 94.   67 See Anne Fremantle (n. 4 above), p. 128.

68 O.P. p. 92.   69 O.P. p. 145.

70 The letter is reproduced in Sir Sydney Caine (n. 53 above), pp. 45–7.

71 Sidney Webb, 'Historic' (n. 22 above), pp. 50, 82.

72 F. A. Hayek (n. 57 above), p. 5.

73 O.P. pp. 92, 95, 195. Leonard Woolf, apropos the seriousness with which Beatrice approached the subject of education as civics training, tells the story in his autobiography of a luncheon at Grosvenor Road: 'The conversation drifted, if conversation with the Webbs can ever accurately be said to have drifted, into the subject of education. Beatrice said that she thought it would be a good idea if Education Authorities provided for the small children in government schools sets of "municipal bricks" inscribed with the names of various organiza-

tions; in playing continually with these the children would more or less unconsciously "learn their civic duties".' Beatrice was quite serious, but Leonard's wife, Virginia Woolf, said afterwards in her diary that 'even Sidney had his mild joke at her'. Leonard Woolf, *Beginning Again, An Autobiography of the Years 1911–1918*, London, Hogarth Press, 1964, pp. 115–16.

74 F. A. Hayek (n. 57 above), p. 7.   75 O.P. p. 464.

76 Sir Sydney Caine (n. 53 above), p. 95.

77 Walter Adams, 'Letter From the Director', *LSE Magazine*, November 1972, pp. 1–2.

78 Margaret Cole, *Beatrice Webb* (n. 63 above), p. 105.

79 O.P. p. 477, cited in J. S. Clarke, 'The Break-Up of the Poor Law', in *Work*, p. 101. In O.P. p. 430, Beatrice notes that 'The *unconditionality* of all payments under insurance schemes constitutes a grave defect. The state gets nothing for its money in the way of conduct, and may even encourage malingerers.'

80 O.P. pp. 412–14.   81 O.P. p. 428.

82 O.P. p. 434.   83 O.P. p. 471.

84 O.P. p. 491.   85 D.(3), pp. 50, 154.

86 D.(3), p. 163.   87 D.(3), pp. 178–9.

88 P.P. 1 February 1895, vol. 15, ff. 58–9.

89 M.A. p. 109.   90 M.A. pp. 398–9.

91 M.A. pp. 190, 399.   92 D.(3), p. 80.

93 D.(3), p. 264; O.P. p. 117.   94 D.(3), p. 232.

95 D.(4), p. 58.   96 D.(4), p. 108.

97 D.(4), p. 107.   98 D.(4), p. 76.

99 P.P. Sec. VII, 2 (14), Box I.   100 D.(4), p. 205.

101 D.(4), p. 273.   102 D.(4), p. 272.

103 D.(4), p. 273; See also O.P. p. 482 *et seq.*

104 D.(3), p. 203.   105 D.(4), p. 99.

106 D.(4), p. 236.   107 D.(4), p. 299.

108 Desmond MacCarthy, 'The Webbs as I Saw Them', in *Work*, p. 128.

109 See D.(4), pp. 308–9.   110 O.P. p. 177.

111 D.(3), p. 234.

112 Kingsley Martin, 'The Webbs in Retirement', in *Work*, p. 297.

113 See, for example, Gertrude Himmelfarb, 'The Intellectual in Politics: The Case of the Webbs', *Journal of Contemporary History*, vol. 6 (3), 1971, pp. 3–11.

114 *The Spectator*, 18 March 1953, quoted in Anne Fremantle, (n. 4 above), p. 112.

115 Leonard Woolf, *Sowing, An Autobiography of the Years 1880–1904*, London, Hogarth Press, 1960, p. 49. But see also Shirley Letwin, *The Pursuit of Certainty*, Cambridge University Press, 1965, pp. 352–7, for a somewhat different view of Beatrice as a literary figure.

116 Book 3. v.

117 In the P.P. Sect. VII, 2 (xv) there are two boxes of materials for a projected work, never published, to be entitled *Our Pilgrimage*. It was to have been divided into *The Three Stages of Our Pilgrimage*. In Beatrices hand there is written atop the title page of Chapter I: 'The First Stage of the Pilgrim's Progress.'

118 See, for example, F. R. Leavis, 'Mill, Beatrice Webb, and the "English School" ', *Scrutiny*, XVI, June 1949, pp. 104–26.

PREFACE

WE have been asked by Sidney Webb to prepare for publication this first volume of *Our Partnership* by the late Beatrice Webb, and to write a short preface.

The book, which is a sequel to *My Apprenticeship*, first published in 1926, relates to the earlier years of her marriage, 1892–1911, and was originally intended by her, had she lived, as a first instalment of other volumes to follow, but this was not to be. The plan of the book, like that of *My Apprenticeship*, was to interweave extracts from her contemporary diaries with the narrative of events. The work was actually begun in 1926, immediately after the publication of the earlier volume, but was soon interrupted owing to the pressure of research and to the political activities connected with the second Labour Government. It was resumed in 1931, only to be interrupted again by the Webbs' visit to Russia, the work on *Soviet Communism*, and by periods of ill-health. The main lines and arrangement of the book were settled at the beginning and maintained; additions and alterations were made at intervals almost up to her death in April 1943, but the text was never finally revised.

We have ventured to omit from the book a chapter on " Round the English-speaking World " (1898). While the chapter contains much interesting matter, it has little or no bearing on the main concerns of the present volume. We have also omitted some passages from the diaries on technical subjects, which were either of great length or had appeared in substance in earlier publications; again, a few phrases are left out which we felt that Beatrice herself would have withdrawn as they might have given offence to persons now still living. Otherwise, and apart from minor verbal corrections and the addition of some explanatory footnotes, the text remains exactly as she left it.

My Apprenticeship, in its first edition, included a number of footnotes on the principal characters which appeared in it, and a few such notes had already been added by Beatrice to *Our Partnership*. We have appended instead, for the convenience of the student, a biographical index of the persons mentioned in so far as they are concerned with the matter of the book.

For the rest, we leave Beatrice herself to write her own introduction. The full book as planned by her, and of which *My Apprenticeship* and this volume are only the two first instalments, was originally to be called *My Creed and My Craft*, but in her desire to describe truthfully her lifelong pursuit of a living philosophy, her changes of outlook and ideas, her growing distrust of benevolent philanthropy as a means of redeeming " poor suffering humanity ", and her leaving of the field of abstract economic theory for the then practically unexplored paths of scientific social research, she felt it necessary to reveal something of her own experiences and personality, of the restless and lonely phase of *My Apprenticeship*, of the loving companionship and deep peace of *Our Partnership*. The book became, in fact, an autobiography.

" I mean ", she writes in her diary (May 1922), " to finish this book before taking up my other work, and I mean to write it according to my conscience, not shamefacedly in fear of scoffing remarks. The difficulty is to tell the truth without being self-conscious about it. I have been reading through my diaries and dictating extracts so as to base my autobiographical element on it, not on memories but on contemporary evidence exactly as if it were about somebody else. It is amazing how one forgets what one thought and felt in the past, and even what one did and with whom one was intimate. Reading of all our intrigues over the Education Bill (1902) was a shock to me, not so much the intrigues themselves as our evident pleasure in them! How far is intrigue permissible? "

She writes again (February 1923): " There is a certain morbidity in writing this book—it is practically an autobiography with the love affairs left out—the constantly recurring decision of what degree of self-revelation is permissible and desirable. The ideal conduct would be to treat the diaries exactly as I should treat them if they were someone else's—of course a contemporary person with the same objective requirements about other people's feelings. But it is almost impossible to get into that frame of mind—one's self-esteem is too deeply concerned—also Sidney's feelings have to be considered. On the other hand, many personal traits and experiences may seem significant to the author which are really uninteresting—mere flashes of personal vanity."

Later, in 1926, when she had begun to prepare the present volume, she records her difficulty in expressing her philosophy of life, her belief in the scientific method, but its purpose guided always by religious emotion. " I am perpetually brooding ", she writes (April 1926), " over my inability to make clear even to myself, let alone to others, why I believe in religious mysticism, why I hanker after a Church—with its communion of the faithful, with its religious rites, and its religious discipline, and above all with its definite code of conduct." She rejects " scientific materialism " as a rival metaphysic or as a guide to human conduct. " The trend of scientific thought is to discourage the mind of man from searching for absolute truth with regard to the meaning of life, and to regard metaphysics as an aid to living rather than as an extension of objective knowledge. . . . Then there is the complaint that what seems right to-day seems wrong to-morrow and that the great religions of the world have differed in their moral codes. This uncertainty in the verdict is equally true of science; what seems proved to-day is disproved and rejected to-morrow. Indeed, the ideal of infallibility is and can never be realised by faculties that are evolving; each stage and conclusion will be a jumping-off place for a new departure. Why should not our discernment of *what ought to be* become clearer and broader exactly as our own discernment of *what is true* becomes more extensive and complete and more completely verified? What we have to consider is not the occasional lapses in the development of morality through religion, but whether history shows any constant relation between the presence of religious mysticism and the progressive development of what we consider right living."

The appeal made to her later by Soviet Communism may be traced, at least partly, to the passionate, almost religious, faith of its founders in the " brotherhood of man "—" from each according to his faculty, to each according to his need " —and their deliberate use of science as a means of achieving this end. Its political intolerance and fanaticism during its bitter struggle against enemies, both at home and abroad, she was wont to compare with the religious intolerance and savage persecutions of earlier centuries. " When it is objected ", she writes again (April 1926), " that, as a matter of fact, religious mysticism has itself led to meanness and cruelty, I answer, this is only another way of saying that all human faculties are imperfect and that the religious faculty, like the faculty of observation and reason, is subject to degeneration and even to death by disease." A question that then perpetually vexed her was: " Can we have the moral results of a religious faith without religious rites and religious discipline, without a communion of the faithful pledged to practise these rites and to carry out a definite moral code, *i.e.* without a Church? I doubt it. And the longer I live the more doubt tends to become a settled conviction. Somehow or other we must have the habit of prayer, the opportunity for the confession of sin and for the worship of goodness if we are to attain personal holiness. Otherwise we suffer from a chronic devitalisation of the religious faculty. But how can we get a Church without a dogma—a dogma which will offend intellectual integrity and moral sincerity? No such Church seems within sight. Like so many other poor souls I have the consciousness of being a spiritual outcast. . . . I have failed to solve the problem of life—of man's relation to the universe and, therefore, to his fellow-men. But I have a growing faith that it will be solved by a combination of truth-seeking and personal holiness—of the scientific mind with the religious life. When will such a leader arise who will unite the intellect of an Aristotle, a Goethe or an Einstein, with the moral genius of a Buddha, a Christ or a St. Francis of Assisi? "

Beatrice continued to write her diaries—awake in the early morning hours—to within a few days of her death in her eighty-sixth year. She knew that her strength was rapidly failing and the end was near; but, even after the tragedy of the second World War, she never lost her faith in the power of man to follow the light within him and, by the use of science, to create a social, economic and international order which would bring out what was best in him—the spirit of co-operation and service—and so overcome the great stumbling-blocks of fear and greed. She herself was ready to go—sad only at the parting from her beloved—and to pass on her task to others. The *Partnership* has already left its mark on the social legislation of to-day, and the revolutionary ideas of the early campaigns are now the commonplaces of all political parties.

We are indebted to the Cambridge University Press for permission to use extracts from a Report of the Pilgrim Trust on *Men Without Work*; to Messrs. Cassell & Company, Ltd., and the Yale University Press for an extract from *Politics from Inside* by Sir Austen Chamberlain; to Messrs. Constable & Company, Ltd., for "Lord Rosebery's Escape from Houndsditch" from *The Nineteenth Century and After*, September 1901, and for an extract from *The Apologia of an Imperialist* by W. A. S. Hewins; to Messrs. J. M. Dent & Sons, Ltd., and E. P. Dutton & Company, Inc., New York, for extracts from *Pillars of Society* by A. G. Gardiner; to Sir William S. Haldane and Messrs. Hodder & Stoughton, Ltd., for lengthy extracts from *An Autobiography* by R. B. Haldane; to Mr. Alexander MacLehose for extracts from *From One Century to Another* by Elizabeth Haldane; to Messrs. Macmillan & Company, Ltd., for an extract from *History of the London County Council* by Gibbon and Bell, and for an extract from *Life of Joseph Chamberlain* (Vol. III) by J. L. Garvin; to the *Manchester Guardian* for two reports from the *Manchester Guardian*; to the *News Chronicle* for an extract by H. W. Massingham from the *Daily Chronicle*; to the Students' Union of the London School of Economics and Political Science for an extract from the *Handbook of the Students' Union* by Professor Graham Wallas; and to the *Times* for an extract from the report of the Conference of the National Union of Women Workers, October 29, 1897.

For assistance in compiling the Biographical Index our thanks are due also to the following: Lord Beveridge, George M. Booth, Ivor Brown, Miss Mildred Bulkeley, Sir Arthur Cochrane, Professor G. D. H. Cole, Dr. Alfred Cox, Dr. Hugh Dalton, F. W. Galton, Philip B. Dingle, Town Clerk of Manchester, G. E. Haynes of the N.C.S.S., Stephen Hobhouse, P. F. Jupe of the Establishment Board of H.M. Treasury, Commissioner David Lamb and Colonel Carvosso Gauntlett of the Salvation Army, Mrs. C. M. Lloyd, L. M'Evoy, Town Clerk of Leicester, Dr. J. J. Mallon, John Moss of the Kent County Council, Dr. Stark Murray, Edward R. Pease, Dr. Karin Stephen, Herbert Tracey of the Trades Union Congress, and Miss May Wallas.

B. D.

M. I. C.

London
September 1947

AN INTRODUCTION

THE OTHER ONE

In the summer of 1926, a few weeks after the publication of *My Apprenticeship*, thinking that I might continue the story of my life, I set down my impression of the Other One; the circumstance of his upbringing, his personality as it appeared to me, and the character of his influence on his contemporaries. Other tasks intervened and it was not until 1931 that I started to write the first chapter of this book. To-day, after another lapse of time, bringing with it advanced old age, I insert without correction the informal sketch of 1926 as an introduction to *Our Partnership*.

Sidney Webb was born of parents neither rich nor poor, neither professional brain-workers nor manual workers, neither captains of industry nor hired hands. His people belonged to the part of England (Kent and Essex), and to the social class that had escaped out of the feudalism of the countryside, without being transformed by the industrial revolution. The social environment of his parents and grandparents was, in fact, typical of the industrial development of the first half of the nineteenth century; a somewhat stagnant population of traders and fisher-folk, of master craftsmen and little cultivators—all alike living outside the ancient chartered towns. His paternal grandfather, who brought up a large family and accumulated a fortune of something like ten thousand pounds, for fifty years kept the village inn that served a Kentish hamlet; a vigorous old Radical. His mother's family were little property-owners in Essex and Suffolk, cultivating land or sailing wooden ships between the ports of the East Coast, and occasionally venturing across the North Sea and the Channel, sometimes blossoming out into yeomen stockbreeders or owners of fishing smacks and trading vessels. So far as I have been able to ascertain, there was only one person within the family connection who was, in any way, distinguished—a first cousin—Fred Webb, the famous jockey who won the Derby, afterwards becoming a well-known trainer. Among uncles, aunts and cousins, there were apparently no members of the older and more dignified professions; no beneficed clergyman, no physician or surgeon, no solicitor or barrister, no naval or army officer. The families concerned belonged almost exclusively to the lower middle-class; some rose temporarily to be small land-owners and " rentiers ", others fell into dependence and poverty; but none became directors of great undertakings, whether of profit-making enterprise or in public administration.

The father and mother of Charles, Sidney and Ada Webb were thus what the worldly call " little folk ", without social influence, but with a certain amount of backing from better-off relations. The mother had been left an orphan at a tender age, to be brought up by one or other of her aunts. In 1848, a brother-in-law advanced her a few hundred pounds to open a retail shop in a street of shops in central London which became, after her marriage in 1854, the home of the little family and the principal source of the family income. Meanwhile, the father, who had gained sufficient education to become a public accountant in a humble way, looked after the neighbouring shopkeepers' ledgers and settled the affairs of little companies and societies which had got into trouble, thereby earning a small and irregular income. He gave the greater half of his time gratuitously to serve on the local vestry and the board of guardians, or to acting as trustee or executor for humble folk. I doubt whether the family income ever reached £500 a year, and I doubt whether the family expenditure ever went below £300, in an era of cheapness.

But the most important part of a child's environment is the character of its parents. The Webb parents were both of them beyond reproach; they were, in fact, the last word in respectability. The father, who died a few months before I became engaged to Sidney, was, from all accounts, singu-larly refined in character—modest and unassuming, remarkably public-spirited, always ready to do unpaid work either for public bodies or friends who were in trouble. He was a diligent reader of newspapers and political pamphlets. But throughout life he suffered frail health and was managed by his far abler and more energetic wife. For Sidney's mother was a woman of character and capacity; a clever shopkeeper and excellent housekeeper, giving her children good fare, open windows and cold baths, and training them in good habits. Graham Wallas, who knew her before her breakdown in health, described her as " wise and witty, with a remarkable memory ". It was she who, after consulting with a friendly customer, sent the two boys, at a considerable sacrifice of income, first to a Swiss school to learn French and then into the family of a German pastor at Wismar to learn German—an accomplishment which indirectly led to Sidney getting into the first division of the Civil Service, and to his brother becoming the foreign correspondence clerk in Marshall & Snelgrove and other firms, and eventually graduating into a successful profit-making venture of his own. The intellectual atmosphere of the home was made up of the Radical politics of the father—he was, for instance, an ardent supporter of John Stuart Mill's candidature at Westminster in 1865—and the broad evangelical religious feeling of the mother, who took the children to one church or chapel after another in search of an eloquent preacher free from sacerdotalism. It remains to be added that the family " kept itself to itself " and had few relatives in London, and practically no friends. The Webb family was not socially attractive: there was no margin of income for entertaining; the home, though comfortable, was cramped and ugly; its inhabitants, if not ugly, were homely and plain in appearance and manners; the sister attractively plain, the brother just commonplace. Though I never saw the father, and only saw the mother when she was aged and crippled, it was clear that neither one nor the other had a fine appearance or peculiar charm—except the charm of essential goodness, of honesty, personal kindliness and public spirit. But the outstanding characteristic of this family circle was the absence

of the " will-to-power ", or the desire to be conspicuous.
Even Charles, who had not inherited the public spirit and
intellectual interests of his father, who was just a clever and
honest tradesman and a good family man, never wanted to
make more money than was necessary to give him a small
but comfortable home, a little rough shooting and a few
weeks' annual tour on the Continent. When he had secured
£1500 or £2000 a year, he retired from active business. As
for exercising authority over other people, he quite obviously
disliked it; neither had he been tempted by social ambition.
This absence of any desire to climb up the social ladder, or
to enjoy luxury, as distinguished from comfort, was to me
the most attractive feature of the family life of the Webbs.
They neither admired nor objected to social superiors—they
ignored them. A life of distraction and luxurious leisure, of
conspicuous expenditure, would have merely worried and
bored them past endurance. Thus Sidney's environment did
not encourage class bitterness, nor lead to the conception of
class war; there was certainly no consciousness of family
failure; and, as it happened, there was, so far as he and his
brother were concerned, from their early youth upwards, a
growing consciousness of personal success. The material and
mental environment of the Webb family was neutral in its
politics and economics, a neutrality shown by the subsequent
opinions of the two brothers and sister. Charles became and
remained a City Tory, Sidney became a Socialist and Ada a
mugwump—predominantly progressive but not " Labour ".

So much for family circumstances. Edward Pease, who
knew Sidney's parents and his brother and sister, more than
once observed that Sidney was one of the few men whom he
had known, whose remarkable brain power could not be
explained by the brains of his parents or forebears: his far-
reaching and always working intellect must have been a
physiological freak. Superficially, he resembled his family.
" Undistinguished and unimpressive in appearance " would
be the verdict of a qualified reporter. In an English crowd
he would pass unnoticed unless someone asked whether he
was a foreigner. " At an International Congress ", wrote an

American journalist, " Sidney Webb might be found among the intellectuals of any nation's delegation." On the Continent, he is usually assumed to be French. At the Hamburg International Socialist Congress in 1923, for instance, he was followed and abused as such; and a hotel porter rudely refused to believe he was English until he showed his passport as a British M.P., when effusive apologies were tendered.

Regarded as a public personage, Sidney Webb has always been the delight of caricaturists. With his big head, bulgy eyes, bushy moustaches and square-cut short beard (it is this latter feature which gained him the name of " Nannie " in the House of Commons), small but rotund body, tapering arms and legs and diminutive hands and feet, he lends himself to the cubist treatment of the ridiculous. These ill-looks, however, are not represented in photographs; for the photographer always selects the profile or half-face. Taken in profile, with the disproportion between head and legs corrected by the falsified photographic perspective, he is not only remarkable but attractive in appearance. The massive head, covered with thick wavy hair (originally black, now streaked with white), the broad finely-moulded forehead, large kindly grey eyes, imposing Roman nose together with the afore-mentioned bushy imperial, would look well on a coin! Assuredly this head-piece indicates brain power—a fine intellect tempered by visionary idealism and lit up with benevolence.

As a speaker he is not prepossessing. He has a husky voice, made less articulate by a rapid delivery; at times, in his haste, he omits a syllable or clips his words. When he hesitates, either in talk or in public speaking, there are ugly intervening " ers " and " ums ". His diction, though fluent and coherent, lacks style; he has none of the graces or tricks of the orator; when addressing a popular audience he is apt to be prosy and monotonous. But he has his own kind of effectiveness. In argument he is ingenious and often convincing; he is always informative and logical. In short, he is a first-rate class lecturer; he raises rapidly, and in their right order, all the relevant issues, and either settles them there and then, or gives his students some notion how to do so; he insinuates wise thoughts and suggests subtle qualifications; with advanced students he is often witty. At question time he is overwhelming; no heckler has ever got the better of him! Whilst honest enquirers get what they want. And, if he says he does not know, he tells them where to go for the best information.

But it is as a committee man that Sidney Webb excels. He is always on the spot; he thinks twice as fast as his colleagues; he so foresees the drift of the discussion that he can lie in wait, and open or block the way according to his aims. He is the ideal draftsman; able to express the desired conclusion in a dozen different phrases so as to disarm suspicion or prejudice and to suit diverse temperaments. He can accept, or even suggest, amendments which satisfy troublesome opponents without achieving their hostile ends.

Have I made it clear that, admirable as a social engineer, Sidney Webb has not the make-up of a popular leader? He lacks personal magnetism; he has no liking for personal prominence; he is, in fact, not a public personage at all, he is a private citizen with public aims and expert knowledge. Hence, the continuous depreciation of him by journalists like H. W. Massingham, who specialised in the melodrama of public affairs, and amused themselves and their readers by setting up idol after idol for the people to worship. For Sidney Webb did not lend himself to this game; he has always been a " behind the scenes " man, and even on committees he has succeeded best with fellow-researchers and fellow-administrators, in fact, with his intellectual equals. For it must be admitted he has not always been able to suffer fools gladly; he has had neither the patience nor the itch for power, needful for manipulating coarse characters and common minds by deception and flattery. I will not say he has courted unpopularity—he has been too unselfconscious for that—moreover, he would have thought it silly. If he has courted any state of being, it has been anonymity and inconspicuousness. But he has always had the courage of his opinions; and time after time he has " used himself up " for a cause in which he believed.

Of course, he has changed in manner and method after middle-life. When he was young and enthusiastically convinced that mass poverty could be abolished and the economic circumstances of the world transfigured by collective control and collective administration, his keenness took the form of persistent permeation; of endless intrigues to persuade those in authority to go his way. By friends and enemies alike, he was acclaimed an accomplished wire-puller. Perhaps the cleverest caricature—about 1900—was a picture of Balfour and Asquith bobbing up and down at the end of wires handled by the " wily Fabian ". But, in later years, he has become too philosophical, too much the researcher and, therefore, the doubter, to persist in getting his own way—even behind the scenes. After sixty he gladly took a back seat in all affairs, and on all the occasions when his colleagues were in the limelight, he was busying himself about matters which, though important, the other leaders felt irksome and were inclined to leave undone. Hence, his apparent failure in the House of Commons relatively to his reputation on entering it as *the* Intellect of the Labour Party —a reputation which served him ill, seeing that it roused the vulgar insolence of the baser type of Tory. Hence, also, the odd ups and downs in the esteem of well-known contemporaries. " Son Éminence Grise " was Camille Huysmans' nickname when that clever Belgian statesman was resident in London during the last two years of the Great War, observing the reconstruction of the Labour Party by Henderson and Sidney. " I never can see what people see in him," remarked John Morley to a friend—who forthwith reported it! " The worst of Webb ", wrote G. D. H. Cole in a character sketch, " is that he is *permanent*; when you think you have disposed of him he confronts you in another part of the field." There were times when " the Webb myth " took the form of a sinister and hidden presence, manipulating the activities of Church and State, of the Tory and Liberal press, of the Trade Union and Co-operative Move-

7

ments in the direction of fanatically held ideals. At other times he has been dismissed as a " back number ", as " an exploded myth ", as " a bourgeois pedant ", hopelessly out of touch with the virile democracy. As a matter of fact, the " all-powerful " and the " insignificant " verdicts were equally beside the mark; his influence has been limited but steady; it has varied little from time to time; and it has never taken the form of personal power; he has insinuated thoughts which fructified, he has never actively dominated other people's activities; he has never been (except to his wife!) *a man of destiny*. What he has achieved, either in organisation or in thought, has been slow but continuous constructive work, carrying out elastic but definite and consistent plans of social reconstruction. Public spirit, personal disinterestedness, tenacity of purpose, accurate knowledge and sound reasoning, have been the faculties whereby he has attained such success as he has had in bringing about, by propaganda, in legislation, or through administration, the social reorganisation in which he has believed. Fullness of knowledge, sense of proportionate value of facts and issues, lucidity in expression and a tireless industry, have been his peculiar contribution to our joint work.

So far I have described the Other One as a public servant —for a public servant he has been in the fullest meaning of the term. In his intimate relations, he is singularly free from faults and he has certain delightful gifts. He has always been healthy in body and mind, he has had no day-dreams, his very sleep is dreamless. He has had no vindictiveness and he has never been obsessed by particular persons or events. To use topical jargon, he never suffered from " suppressions " or "complexes "; he never felt himself to be either inferior or superior to other people; in his own eyes he is just one among equals. He has never claimed to be in the front rank; he does not push his way into the corner seat of a railway carriage—as I invariably do!—he watches the others seat themselves, and takes the place that is left. Likewise he is no respecter of persons, except in so far as one man may need more help or be better able to serve a common cause than another. Such personal sensitiveness as he has —and I think he is largely unconscious of the effect of his own personality—takes the form of withdrawing from the contest, retiring into the background to go on with his own researches complacently. In his outlook on men and affairs he is impersonal—an amused and amusing observer, giving the benefit of the doubt to erring mortals, generous in appreciation of moral and intellectual gifts, but not a hero-worshipper. Indeed, he dislikes reputed heroes and heroines, and he laughs at Bernard Shaw's " Superman ". He is on friendly terms with many people; they trust him and he trusts them; but he is too absorbed in disentangling questions and promoting causes to have intimate friendships. This absence of friendships in his life has, I think, been a loss to him. Perhaps Bernard Shaw and, some way down the scale of frank intimacy—Haldane—but I can think of no other but these two who have been lifelong friends as well as colleagues. He is apt to be bored by women; especially by sentimental or " temperamental " women and by professional beauties; they don't interest him and he resents their claims to admiration and attention. When I placed the handsome but metallic Lady Desborough beside him at a luncheon at our house, he remarked afterwards that he thought her " unpleasing with her artificial and insincere talk and silly trick of shutting her eyes at you ". His absence of mind with another charming lady was signalised by her ejaculation, as she noticed him listening to the conversation at the other end of the table, " And what is *she* saying now, Mr. Webb ? " How he detested Mrs. Pat Campbell when she was brought to see us by Lady Elcho! G. B. S.'s subsequent infatuation he regarded as a clear case of sexual senility! Sophie Bryant, the hard-headed and accomplished principal of the North London Collegiate School, who sat with him on the Technical Education Board and on the Senate of London University, is the only woman I remember to have interested him, and the generous and noble-minded Alys Russell the only one for whom he has expressed affectionate concern. Casual conversation in truth does not amuse him; he prefers reading and he dislikes " unnecessary communications " from those he lives with. If he married a chatterbox as a " second ", Heaven help her!

The plain truth is that his emotional life—all his capacity for personal intimacy, and for over-appreciation of another's gifts—has been centred in his wife and partner, and his wife just because she is also his partner. One of his most attractive gifts as a life companion is his gaiety of nature, he is nearly always happy. One refrain recurs continuously in his consciousness and he does not hesitate to express it—an almost childlike gratitude for his good luck in life. " We ought to do good work," he often says as we wander arm-in-arm together or I sit on his lap by the firelight, " we have been so amazingly fortunate." Content with his lot in life, enjoyment of the daily round of research and the writing of books, the interest of an observer in the tasks of an M.P. and party leader; a varied outlook on life, a pleasant sense of humour, above all a continuous helpfulness to other people, are delightful characteristics in a constant companion—they make life seem worth while. And, if there be a touch of absurdity in his adoration of a helpmate, it is a flaw in his reasonableness which she discounts to his credit! Also, he has her " on the lead " and, when she strays into morbid ways, or darts off in a panic, she is firmly but gently pulled back with deprecating chaff combined with soothing reflections on the relative unimportance of any particular happening and even doubts as to the significance of her own frame of mind. Thus the monstrous self fades off the screen of her consciousness to be replaced by refreshing vistas of the past history and future prospects of the human race, as if the life-force were as beneficent as he is himself. For the Other One is an unrepentant optimist in big things and small! Sometimes he mocks at his own confidence in the well-meaning of the universe. " When I was a child," says he, " haunted by a future Hell, I remember casting out the fear once for all by thinking to myself—perhaps derived from Martin Elginbrod, if I had then read him—' If I were God, and He were I, I should forgive Him His trespasses '. He is not worse but better than I." And he adds, " In our criticism of Nature's doings why should we not give the Almighty God ' the benefit of the doubt '? But the doubt must be an honest doubt and not contrary to evidence."

The days of his absence are weary to get through; and the sleepless hours of the night are haunted, not by the fear of death, but by the dread of life without him.

CHAPTER I

STUDIES IN BRITISH TRADE UNIONISM
1892–1898

WE opened Our Partnership with certain assets. An unearned income of £1000 a year, and a liking for the simple
life, ensured unfettered freedom in the choice of a career.
We were in the prime of life and in good health; we felt
assured of loving companionship without end, a confidence
which proved singularly well-founded; we shared the same
faith and practised the same craft; we enjoyed laughing at
ourselves and at other people. " Two second-rate minds but
curiously complementary ", I had recorded in my diary on
our engagement to be married. Sidney had unique aptitude
for documentary research; he could rush through MS. and
printed pages at an incredible rate, turning out sheafs of
separate sheets whereon were methodically inscribed, in
immaculate handwriting, tables of statistics, minutes of proceedings, series of events, rival hypotheses as to causal connection, apt quotations, each paper complete in itself with
reference and date—all essential material for the discovery
of the attributes of various types of organisations. He was a
good linguist; he spoke and wrote fluently. He had an
amazing capacity for memorising facts, and developing, in
logical sequence and lucid phrase, arguments and conclusions. Skill in social intercourse was my special gift. An
experienced hostess, I had never felt the sensation of shyness
in any company of men and women, whatever their character or intelligence, their status or occupation; I could insinuate myself into smoking-rooms, business offices, private
and public conferences, without rousing suspicion. I may
observe in passing that, in those days of unemancipated
females, to be a woman and, therefore, at the start-off, not
taken seriously, yielded better innings, whether through
cross-examination, disguised as light conversation, or by a

happy-go-lucky acquisition (by guile, not theft) of confidential documents. I revelled in observing and recording the sayings and doings of men and describing their reactions to particular kinds of industrial or political institutions; and I jumped quickly out of old categories into fresh lines of enquiry. The two together had a wide acquaintance with men and women of all grades of poverty and affluence—of varied occupation and professions. Sidney had graduated as a civil servant through three government departments—the War Office, the Inland Revenue and the Colonial Office. As successful journalist, lecturer and pamphleteer, he was acquainted with the newspaper world, with the Radical caucus of the metropolis and provincial towns, and he was intimate with many of the rising intellectuals of his own generation. A few months before our marriage, he had become one of the leaders of the Progressive Party then dominating the London County Council. Born and bred in the world of the big business of two continents, I had, as a young girl, dashed about the outer ring of London " society ", spent week-ends at the country houses of bankers and brewers and, more rarely, in the homes of county magnates. In these delectable places, I had associated with men of science and distinguished ecclesiastics; with Cabinet Ministers and leading lawyers; with " society " dames and university dons. For the six years prior to our marriage, I had devoted my free time to getting an inside knowledge of the homes and work-places of representative groups of manual workers; as rent collector and " would be " sweated worker in the slums of East London, as collaborator in Charles Booth's [1] great enquiry into the *Life and Labour of the People*, as a welcome visitor in the homes of my cousins among the Lancashire cotton operatives; [2] and, most important of all, through friendly intercourse with the leaders of the co-operative and trade union movements.

There were, I must admit, disabling gaps in our knowledge of Victorian England. We ignored and were ignored by fashionable " society "—not to mention " the smart set ".

[1] See *My Apprenticeship*, chapters v and vi. [2] See *ibid*. pp. 152-71.

Our minds were blank about the professionals and the multi-tudinous amateurs of high and low degree, of sport, games and racing. Few and far between were the diplomatists who sought us out; and foreign affairs, generally speaking, were a closed book to us. And alas! owing to our concentration on research, municipal administration and Fabian propaganda, we had neither the time nor the energy, nor yet the means, to listen to music and the drama, to brood over classic literature, ancient and modern, to visit picture galleries, or to view with an informed intelligence the wonders of architecture. Such dim inklings as we had of these great human achievements reached us second-hand through our friendship with Bernard Shaw. Our only vision of the beautiful arose during our holiday wanderings, at home and overseas, sometimes walking, sometimes cycling, by river and forest path, over plain and mountain, in mist, cloud and sunshine.

Thus, we started Our Partnership with an agreeable independence of the world's opinion and delicious dependence on each other. From an old woman likely to know, an ingenuous youth enquired: " After love-making and sufficient income, what's necessary for a happy marriage? " " Identity of taste in seemingly unimportant matters," I rapped out somewhat heedlessly, " such as, open or closed windows, regular or irregular hours, simple or elaborate meals, spells of silent fellowship or continuous talk about nothing in particular." Then, after reflection: " Unity of temperament on the one vital issue, self-expression or self-control. Is the way of life to be governed by the impulse of the moment for or against particular persons or places, occupation or amusements; or is it to be determined according to an agreed plan adhered to by both parties, irrespective of momentary likes or dislikes? " " Oh! " retorted the youth, " the old quarrel of reason *versus* emotion? " " Not at all," I answered; " patterns of behaviour, codes of conduct, general plans, whether for ten years or a lifetime, arise, so far as I know, from unreasoning, though not necessary *unreasonable*, emotion. Is not a general plan of conduct inspired and dominated by emotion the epicentre of all religions? However that may be, living according to plan is a surer basis for happy marriage than the perpetual shifting desire for self-expression. The impulse of the moment, noble or ignoble, aesthetic or philistine, is apt to differ every time, and all the time, from individual to individual. Living according to a deliberately thought-out plan, however tiresome and thwarting it may occasionally be, is an automatic aid to continuous comradeship."

Now a plan of life involved in our view not merely a deliberately designed method or style of living, but also an object to be sought, and as far as possible attained, as the result of our living. This is what is sometimes called a philosophy of life. Fundamentally, we agreed about this, though minute introspection might discover from time to time some variation of emphasis, and even differences of outlook. From many of the common ends of life we were saved by circumstances. Our income sufficed for our needs; and we felt none of the usual temptations to increase our joint little fortune, and (as we realised) thus become entangled in the trammels and trappings of wealth. The fact that our marriage proved to be childless made easy what other people sometimes called our " financial disinterestedness ". We had no objection to receiving payment for articles or lectures when it was offered to us; and we welcomed, as enabling us to engage additional assistance, the few hundreds a year which, as time went on, accrued from the sale of our solid but unreadable books. Indeed, we sometimes sought payment when it did not hinder our work or prevent us from saying what we liked, especially at times when the expenses of our investigations threatened to exceed our current account. We even scrupled sometimes at " spoiling the market " for others whose livelihood depended on writing or lecturing. We enjoyed our work quite as much when it brought no cheque as when we peddled fragments for payment; for it was not only our vocation willingly rendered in return for our unearned income, but served also as our daily sport—the particular game of life we preferred to play. It remains to be added that Our Partnership was an indissoluble combination of two strong and persistent aims. We were, both of us, scientists and at the same time Socialists. We had a perpetual curiosity to know all that could be known about the nature and working of the universe, animate as well as inanimate, psychical as well as material, in the belief that only by means of such knowledge could mankind achieve an ever-increasing control of the forces amid which it lived. We were, both of us, secularists, in the sense that we failed to find in the universe anything that was supernatural, or incapable of demonstration by the scientific method of observation, hypothetical generalisation and experimental or other form of verification. Like other scientists, we were obsessed by scientific curiosity about the universe and its working. But, unlike the astronomers and the physicists, the chemists and the biologists, we turned our curiosity to the phenomena that were being less frequently investigated, namely, those connected with the social institutions characteristic of *homo sapiens*, or what is called sociology. We accordingly devoted ourselves as scientists to the study of social institutions, from trade unions to Cabinets, from family relationships to churches, from economics to literature—a field in itself so extensive that we have never been able to compass more than a few selected fragments of it.

At the same time, we were active citizens; and, as such, we had to have a practical policy of public life. Our growing knowledge of social institutions led us to a policy of transforming the organisation of wealth production and distribution, from its basis of anarchic individual profit-making to one of regulated social service. That is to say, our action as electors, administrators and propagandists was that of Socialists, instead of that of Liberals or Conservatives. Looking back on half-a-century of scientific investigation and public activity, it seems to us in retrospect that every discovery in sociology and, indeed, every increase in our own knowledge of social institutions has strengthened our faith that the further advance of human society is dependent on a considerably further substitution of institutions based on public service for those based on profit-making. We have, accordingly, had the enjoyment of harmony between the two halves of our lives, between our scientific studies and our practical citizenship. At the same time, it must be admitted that our reputation or notoriety as Socialists has more than once aroused obstruction or hostility to our efforts, whether as individual investigators, or as promoters of adequately equipped sociological research, as an essential condition for the progress of mankind to ever higher levels of individual distinction and communal welfare.

At this point some readers may question whether it is desirable to combine scientific research into social institutions with active participation in their operation. Is the professional administrator or legislator made more efficient or less efficient as such by being also a practised observer, reasoner and verifier in the domain in which he is temporarily an actor? Conversely, is the scientific investigator, concerned essentially to discover the truth about the working or development of a particular type of economic or political organisation, rendered more likely or less likely to arrive at verifiable conclusions because he finds himself temporarily " behind the scenes ", or at the very centre of the current activities of the social institution in question, by his membership of the elected authority, or his appointment to its executive staff? I am disposed to think that there is something to be said on each side of the question. But I suggest that, if the human unit in the case is not a single individual but an intimate and durable partnership, the balance is wholly in favour of the combination of purposes. If one partner is predominantly and continuously the scientific investigator, with only slight and occasional participation in active life, whilst the other partner is more continuously entangled in administration or legislation, with only secondary and intermittent personal work in investigation or research, their incessant intimate discussions may well increase the efficiency and augment the yield of both sides of each other's intellectual activities. I believe that, from time to time, we had evidence of this happy result in Our Partnership. In the earlier years, when I was almost wholly engaged in studying the records and the working of trade unionism, the Other One, whilst intermittently sharing in different parts of England in this absorbing quest, was chairman of the Technical Education Board, and (as described in a following chapter) was mainly engaged, during three-quarters of each of six successive years, in laying the foundations of a unified educational system for the whole of London, and watching very closely the reactions upon schemes of vocational training of all the trade unions of the metropolis. Our duality was, in this instance, of reciprocal advantage. In another instance, about quite a different social institution, the Royal Commission or Select Committee, our experience yields a similar result. Both partners devoted much time and thought to the voluminous records and published criticisms of a whole century of these bodies, of various types and diverse compositions. But we never got a satisfactory hold on the conditions and the expedients that determined success, or failure, in each of the hundred or more specimens that we studied, until we both had enjoyed brief and intermittent experiences of actual membership of these bodies—membership in which the knowledge gained from investigation of the past was joined with incessant watchfulness of the happenings in which we were taking part. This was markedly seen when, from 1905 to 1910, I was a member of the Royal Commission on the Poor Law and the Relief of Distress from Unemployment; and the Other One was free for incessant consultation and enquiry outside.

TRADE UNION ENQUIRY

For the first six years of our married life—the part covered by this and the following chapter—our energies ran in three channels. There was the enquiry into the British trade union movement and the publication of *The History of Trade Unionism* in 1894, and *Industrial Democracy* in 1898; there was Sidney's administrative work on the London County Council and the establishment and chairmanship of the Technical Education Board; and, towards the end of the time, there was the initiation of the London School of Economics and Political Science. Finally, always and everywhere, there was propaganda of Fabian collectivism. In the following pages I describe the first of these activities, our researches into the constitution and working of British trade unionism and our consequent association with trade union officials and representatives, as these experiences were reflected in the pages of my MS. diary supplemented by our joint memories.

And here I must revert to my unmarried days a few months before I met the Other One. In *My Apprenticeship*, I have described how my investigations into the sweated industries of East London had convinced me that if the capitalist system was not to lead to " earnings barely sufficient to sustain existence; hours of labour such as to make the lives of the workers periods of almost ceaseless toil, hard and unlovely to the last degree; sanitary conditions injurious to the health of the persons employed and dangerous to the public "—to quote the words of the House of Lords Committee on Sweating in 1889–90—capitalist enterprise had to be controlled, not exceptionally or spasmodically, but universally, so as to secure to every worker prescribed minimum conditions of employment. Even in the co-operative movement, which had been started by working-men in the interests of the producers, but had developed into a consumers' organisation bent on getting the best quality for the lowest price, some such control was clearly necessary. This control was, in organised industries, such as cotton and mining and, to a lesser extent, engineering and shipbuilding, already operative, either through the specific device of trade unionism—collective bargaining—or by the legislative enactment secured by the pressure of the trade unions and their advisers and sympathisers. But, brought up as I had been, in a stronghold of capitalism, under the tutelage of the great apostle of *laisser-faire*, Herbert Spencer,[1] I was

[1] Herbert Spencer (1820–1903), " the household saint and philosopher of the hearth " of Beatrice's youth. An uncompromising individualist, he cancelled her appointment as his literary executor on the announcement of her marriage to a Socialist. See Biographical Index. (Ed.)

fully aware of the various objections to trade unionism: how it prevented, or at least hindered, the introduction of new inventions and the better organisation of the workshop; how it had fomented strikes and compelled employers to resort to lock-outs; how it had restricted output, either by rule or indirectly by limiting the number of apprentices; and how it had thus checked the mobility of labour from place to place and industry to industry, and damaged Great Britain's capacity to compete in the markets of the world. And it so happened that, at the very time I was meditating on the virtues and vices of trade unionism, there broke out the great London Dock Strike of 1889, which, for the first time, united in one solid phalanx the thousands of casual labourers I had watched, day after day, at the gates of the dock companies, and in the tenement houses of East London. Moreover, this movement had secured an unusual amount of public sympathy among all classes of the community and financial support from the manual workers as far off as Australia. Hence it was not surprising that I used up a fortnight in August 1889 in attending the Trades Union Congress at Dundee, a Congress at which there was a battle royal between the " Old Unionists " and the " New ".[1]

Dundee, August 1889.—This morning, while I was breakfasting, Shipton—the chairman of the parliamentary committee of the Trades Union Congress, and secretary of the London Trades Council—joined me. His view of the Dock Strike is strongly adverse to the men; he is visibly biassed by his antipathy to, I might almost say hatred of, Burns. Ben Tillett is, he says, an enthusiast who, however, has " made a good thing " out of his enthusiasm. The way the strike was started, he told me, was illegitimate. No responsible official of a trade union which had funds of its own to lose, would treat employers in that fashion. Ben Tillett drew up a letter demanding certain concessions and sent it with a letter announcing that, if these demands were not con-

---

[1] " The leaders of the New Unionists (1884–89) . . . sought to bring into the ranks of existing organisations—the trade unions, the Municipality, or the State—such masses of unorganised workers who had hitherto been entirely outside the pale, or inert elements within it. They aimed, not at superseding existing structures, but at capturing them all in the interests of the wage-earners. Above all, they sought to teach such masses of undisciplined workers how to apply their newly acquired political power so as to obtain in a perfectly constitutional manner, whatever changes in legislation or administration they desired."—*History of Trade Unionism*, by S. and B. Webb, p. 404. (Ed.)

ceded by 12 o'clock that morning, the men would come out. " Just
fancy," he added, " expecting a manager to decide a question of enormous financial importance without consulting his directors! " Then
Burns came on the scene with his intense desire for notoriety and his
foreign ideas of the solidarity of labour which he is trying to foist on
British trade unionists. But it won't work. Each trade has its own
interests and technicalities; and all organisation, to be permanently
successful, must be based on the appreciation of these interests and on
a knowledge of the facts of the special trade concerned. " Look how the
' Knights of Labour ' [1] have failed (in the United States)—that sort
of thing is bound to break up in the end. The capitalist has only to
sit still with folded hands. If the dock companies stand out—if they
are able to resist the other capitalist interests which are using the
strike to get their own way—if they are able to resist this pressure
the whole organisation will break down and the workers will dribble
back."

So spoke Shipton. Clearly, whatever may be his sympathy for dock
labour, his dislike of a Socialist victory was the stronger feeling. . . .

Shipton is not an attractive man. Small, with a weasel-like body and
uncertain manner, and an uneasy contorted expression; grey eyes without candour or freshness, and with that curious film over them which
usually denotes an " irregular " life; deep furrows under the eyes and
round the mouth; bald-headed with a black beard neatly trimmed; a
general attempt at middle-class smartness completes the outward man.
An ambitious disappointed man, a certain feeling of uncertainty as to
his own position. Ability, divided aims, are the characteristics which
seem most marked to the observer. I should imagine that in his heart
of hearts he has little sympathy with the working-man, that he prizes
his position as an official because of the power it brings. . . .

Tuesday. Dundee, Sept. 1889.—A battle royal at Congress between the supporters of Broadhurst and old-fashioned methods, on the
one hand, and the Socialists led by Burns and Mrs. Besant, on the other.
These two leaders, however, were absent: the Socialist Party was led
by two somewhat foolish young men, delegates of the London compositors, and suffered in consequence. The battle raged round the personal abuse of Broadhurst. The Socialists have apparently spent the last
year in spreading calumny of all sorts, besides trying to persuade the
rank and file that Broadhurst is a reactionary. But I think they have

, [1] Though trade unionism was legalised in the U.S.A. in 1845, the " Knights
of Labour " were founded in 1869 as a secret organisation " to secure and maintain
the rights of working-men against their employers ". They organised a general
strike of colliers and railwaymen in 1887, involving some 50,000 strikers, but the
strike collapsed before the end of the year. (Ed.)

carried it too far. Among English working-men of the better type there is a rooted dislike to desert old leaders; an intense suspicion of the mere talker who has not proved his faculty for steady work. Then the Socialist at present labours under the disadvantage of relying on outside money and outside brains. "Why should I be dictated to by an ex-artillery officer? (Champion)" was one of Broadhurst's most effective points. Trade unionists are jealous of interference and are intensely exclusive. ("Why are you here," I am frequently asked, "come with mischief in your pocket, to plot and plan?")

So the whole Congress set its back up; the Socialists dwindled down to eleven while Broadhurst's supporters numbered 177. A brilliant victory for the conservative section—conservative, not in politics but in the methods and aims of their own organisation.

With Broadhurst I lunched afterwards, and smoked a cigarette. His suspicions of my intentions were completely dissipated when he heard I was an anti-suffrage woman: he immediately thought me sensible and sound. "When I hear a woman's name talked of I am immediately prejudiced against her; but I can see that you are as different as pitch from diamonds!" So he chatted on about societies, trade unionism, and his own complaints and showed every sign of becoming confidential. A commonplace person: hard-working no doubt, but a middle-class philistine to the back-bone: appealing to the practical shrewdness and high-flown, but mediocre, sentiments of the comfortably-off working-man. His view of women is typical of his other views: he lives in platitudes and commonplaces.

In spite of the prejudices and exclusiveness of the leading trade unionists, the frank fellowship, the absence of personal animus and personal rivalry, the general loyalty to leaders and appreciation of real work, as distinguished from talk, are refreshing. Then, among the veterans, the officials of the largest, oldest and most influential unions, there is a knowledge of facts, and realisation of industrial problems, an appreciation of commercial and financial matters, which makes one feel hopeful of the capacity for self-government in the working-class. Very different from the Socialist leaders, with the dirty personalities with which they pelt each other; with their envy and malice against any leader, and with their ignorance, one might almost say their contempt and hatred of facts. A crew of wrecked reputations, politicians on the make, and paid intriguers from the Tory caucus, interspersed, it is true, with beardless enthusiasts of all sorts and conditions, and redeemed by a John Burns, who seems to be a man with a conscience and a will. But is he not departing from the Socialist camp?

Another scene. Breakfast table. On my right Broadhurst, beaming over his ham and eggs and the delightful memories of yesterday's triumph over his enemies. " Yes, we are now going to take our stand against the intrusion of strangers into our body on false pretences. They blame us for being exclusive; they have made us ten times more exclusive. We have cleared the platform of outsiders, we will now clear the press table from intriguers."

All this muttered loud enough for my neighbour on the left to hear. Cunninghame Graham is pouring over the *Labour Elector*. (Cunninghame Graham is a cross between an aristocrat and a barber's block. He is a *poseur*, but also an enthusiast, an unmitigated fool in politics, I think.) " I have a letter from Kropotkin," Cunninghame Graham whispers to me; " he says, and I agree with him, if Burns with 80,000 men behind him does not make a revolution, it is because he is afraid of having his head cut off. Burns is a grand fellow tho', different from these miserable slaves of bourgeois trade unionists," he adds, with a wave of his hand towards Broadhurst, a wave of the hand which gradually settles down upon a loaf of brown bread which C. G. believes to be common property, but which, unfortunately, happens to be specially prepared for her great man's over-taxed digestion by Mrs. Broadhurst. The bourgeois slave watches with indignation the delicately tapering fingers of the anarchist clutch hold of his personal property, and with a large perspiring palm of the outstretched hand grasps the whole thing in his fingers. " No, no, Sir, not that," he roars; " this is my *own* bread, made by my *own* wife, in my *own* house, and carried here in my *own* portmanteau, that you cannot have." Cunninghame Graham withdraws with the apologies of a gentleman. " Not my bread; I'd rather he destroyed my reputation than took my bread," roared the dyspeptic but somewhat gluttonous Broadhurst. Cunninghame Graham looks unutterably disgusted, and wipes his aristocratic hand with soft cambric. . . .

Other scenes in the private smoking-room of the leading trade unionists, to which I was introduced by Broadhurst's favour. Not altogether a nice atmosphere; with a good deal of lobbying apparent in the background, resulting in the return of the old parliamentary committee with only one change. " Dirty work," said Burnett,[1] with a look of unutterable contempt in his clear grey eyes, " the sailor [2] brought twenty votes, practically exchanging them for a seat on the committee. Too much of that sort of thing."

Altogether the later scenes of the Congress did not impress me so favourably as the opening days, when only loyalty to the old leaders was apparent. The trade unionists are a fine body of men; but they

[1] John Burnett, former secretary of the Amalgamated Society of Engineers and afterwards Labour correspondent of the Board of Trade.
[2] Havelock Wilson, organiser of the National Sailors' and Firemen's Union.

are lacking in the naïve enthusiasm and open-hearted cordiality of the co-operators. They are officials, and officials who live by manipulating their constituents; they have the vices of officials combined with those of popular representatives. The majority of them are aiming at the dignity of the J.P., or the more solid preferment of the factory inspectorship. . . . The upshot of the Congress was the rehabilitation of Broadhurst and the old gang and the discomfiture of the Socialist outsiders. There are signs that the victorious leaders, warned by the Socialist attack, will try to tighten their hold by placing the Congress on a more representative basis with regard to members and payment. At present, every delegate has one vote; and a union may send any number of delegates irrespective of their membership and contribution. This gives undue influence to mushroom unions which may be created in order to swamp solid trade union organisations. On the other hand, if membership were duly represented, the great conservative unions of Lancashire would exclude from all power the new blood. The officials of these old standing unions have become intimately connected with the employers. Many of them are J.P.'s and most of them Conservative in politics. They believe in arbitration and conciliation and in dealing with each trade separately. All action is to be based on technical knowledge of the special trade. They are fully alive to foreign competition, and even versed in all the intricacies of the currency question. With them trade unionism is rapidly assuming the form of a union of all the producers in one trade against the outside world. The differences between the two great classes of producers, capitalist brain-workers, on the one hand, and on the other, manual wage-earners, are to be settled by experts from both sides. Mere ideas, such as the solidarity of labour, are to them absurd. " We lived through all that," said Birtwistle (the veteran leader of the cotton weavers); " they imagine themselves the advance guard, they are really the babies of trade unionism."

Thus, one of the cleavage lines in the Congress between the old and the new school was the question of sending representatives to foreign and international congresses. The younger school maintains that the very difficulty of foreign competition would be solved by the solidarity of labour; and that the fossil trade unions are diverted from vigorous action by the mere pedantry of technical knowledge of the " ins and outs " of one tiny specimen of industry.

The eight-hours question was fought on these lines and the specialists won by a fair majority.

The following two years were spent in nursing my father; using any free time in attending Co-operative Conferences and touring Co-operative Societies. Meanwhile, we had entered into an early phase of Our Partnership. As described in *My Apprenticeship*, we met for the first time in January 1890, and at Whitsun of that year we found ourselves together at the Glasgow Co-operative Congress. A telegram from a leading weekly, asking me to contribute a signed article on Lord Rosebery's presidential address, ended in Sidney helping me to write it. The joint article proved too long; the " editor " cut my stuff out and put his stuff in: consequence—mingled annoyance and pleasure! " I had no idea that Beatrice was such an accomplished journalist," observed one brother-in-law to another; " is she going to take to it as a profession? " At the Lincoln Co-operative Congress of 1891, we were privately pledged to marriage; and the following August holiday finds me care-taking Herbert Spencer's house in St. John's Wood (the philosopher being away in the country), a convenient meeting-place with a civil servant care-taking the British Empire from Whitehall!

St. John's Wood, August 14th, 1891.—A succession of trade unionists to dine here [I record in my diary]. Poor Herbert Spencer—to think that his august dining-room is nightly the scene of Socialist talk, clouds of tobacco smoke aided with whiskey. Maxwell, Broadhurst's secretary, the shrewdest of mortals, who is friendly to me in the extreme, and anxious to help; but a cynic: the trade union world, according to him, is by no means lovely—more intriguing, it seems, than the co-operative world.

" I do not believe that there was a single secretary of a trade union that did not write to the governor (Broadhurst) to ask for an appointment as factory inspector " (Broadhurst had been Under-Secretary for the Home Office in 1885). By the way, the whole influence of the Home Office has been thrown against appointing working-men as factory inspectors. " You have no idea—working-men will do anything or give anything in order to be free of manual labour. There is no effort they won't make, no meanness they won't stoop to, to turn themselves into 'office men '. It is feeling conscious of this that makes them so suspicious of each other's effort."

He is fat and good-natured, with a detached intellect; never gives you his views, except about persons, and then he has humour and a sharp stinging tongue. He works for Broadhurst night and day; for very little pay, but with an apparent devotion; his motive is a riddle; he is unmarried, with no apparent convictions except a general scepticism of things divine and human.

I shall have some trouble to get my information. Most of the trade union officials are hard-headed, suspicious men, with an anti-feminist bias. Moreover, where they themselves are friendly, there is often on their part a dread of their assistant secretary. The latter is usually himself elected by the members as a sort of check on the general secretary. If you have one for you, you usually have the other against you. But we shall see. . . .

September 15th, 1891.— . . . And for Sidney [I note a few weeks later on, when I am again in attendance on my father, studying the material I had gathered], this enquiry will be of untold use. The politician of the future must understand all the details of industrial life; he must be, before all things, a practical economist. For economics in the widest sense are rapidly becoming the technical side of the politician's work. Also, he is learning through this wider intercourse with facts and men, a more proportionate sense and a wider judgement than was possible to a London civil servant. Thus, from a strictly personal point of view, an acquaintance with the leaders of working-class organisation throughout the country will be a highly-desirable connection, not to be despised. So that, in helping me, he does not feel, nor am I conscious, that this work is my particular concern. . . .

On New Year's Day, 1892, my father died and in a week's time our engagement was communicated to my family and friends.[1] But we were in no hurry to get married. Sidney had

---

[1] Here are three entries from the MS. diary of my sister, Kate Courtney, January 1892. The first from a description of her eight sisters, written whilst staying with me for my father's funeral; the other two a few days after hearing of my engagement to S. W.

". . . Beatrice—handsome and slightly Jewish-looking with a very intellectual face—gives herself up to investigating social questions—has written a book on Co-operation, is writing a larger one on trade unions—is in close alliance and friendship with the Fabian Socialists—particularly one of them—a great friend of Mrs. J. R. Green—she is much admired by many people though some of the family shake their heads a little over her emancipated ways and advanced views,—but with half admiration also. Father's death frees her to follow her own career without a tie of any sort. . . ."

". . . A letter comes from Beatrice, which is a great surprise to me and not at first quite a welcome one! She announces her engagement to Sidney Webb—the Fabian Socialist leader. The day before, in answer to a note from the *Pall Mall*, I had absolutely contradicted the rumour, supposing I should certainly have heard something if it were true. But Bee judged, rightly I think, that father's funeral should pass off without this new excitement. . . . On the Sunday night, Bee brought S. Webb to dinner and the A. Cripps came also. I had never seen him, but

TRADE UNION INVESTIGATION

resigned from the Civil Service and was busy writing the literature for, and helping to organise the victory of, the Progressives at the London County Council election of March 1892, at which he won by a large majority the Deptford seat from the Tories. Anxious to complete the enquiry into Lancashire and Yorkshire trade unions, I settled down in a lodging in Manchester and was immediately elected an honorary member of the club of trade union officials which met every Thursday in a Deansgate public-house. Aided by our newly engaged secretary, F. W. Galton, who was not only a bright and attractive youth but also the secretary of the trade union of highly-skilled silver crest engravers, I started out to attend trade union meetings whilst superintending Galton's work on trade union documents.

Manchester, February 11*th,* 1892.—Exactly three weeks since I set my foot in Manchester. Have been working hard; looking through minute books, interviewing and attending business meetings of trade unions. It was stupid of me not to think of this idea before. One learns so much more by observing men at their work, than by simply reading reports, etc. But it never struck me that I could get into the private executive meetings of societies and see for myself the sort of questions that arise. But, at present, it is difficult to see the wood for the trees; I am groping about, catching on first to one trunk and then to another; trying to follow the lines of growth of the branches, and the lie of the roots; and getting sadly mixed up in my ideas. But I am working hard and well. My engagement to S. W. has not injured me in the least; except, perhaps, with Birtwistle. . . .

There were, however, days of relaxation in the midst of all this drudgery, and I give two entries:

Manchester, February 28*th,* 1892.— . . . Two days utter exhaustion. Last Sunday was delightful; I need him once a week to rest me in the sublime restfulness of love, and he needs me to soothe him and

only heard various accounts not at all flattering. He was quiet, perhaps shy—but he looks strong and able though not much of a figure of a man, and I hope we may like him. Beatrice seems quietly happy and confident of the future, and she has a softness of expression and manner which looks as if her feelings were engaged."

"*Tuesday* 19*th.*—We met him again at Theresa's [Cripps] with Daniel [Meinertzhagen], W. Cripps, and Lallie [Holt], who was in great form in her most genial mood. Yes I *think* we may like this new brother-in-law whom we certainly should not have chosen. . . ."

reduce his world of cross-purposes to its proper calm. But alas! Our work keeps us apart. . . .

May 4th, 1892.— . . . Severe attack of influenza broke into my work; a fortnight in bed, just at the time of his triumphant return to the County Council, but the last week he was with me and we both went on to Liverpool. There I rested in the luxurious Holt mansion [my sister's, Mrs. Robert D. Holt] for a week and then back again to work. I found Galton working on the piles of material I had left. A good deal of his work had to be re-done, and the ensuing two weeks I spent in training him, he working all day under my eye. A sharp, attractive boy and assiduous worker, and as keen as a razor; a former pupil of Sidney's in economics. But all my appointments to attend [trade union] executive meetings had to be given up: a grievous disappointment to me.

Then a fortnight's holiday. . . . We spent four days at Arundel with Graham Wallas and the light-hearted Bernard Shaw, and then back again to our cosy lodging. Here for ten days: it seemed two. We have been working hard—shaping together the material into a rough history—and then he working at the reference library, whilst I casually interviewed trade unionists and superintended Galton. To-day, he left me and I feel a bit lonesome. . . . We are certainly supremely fortunate. We love each other devotedly; we are intensely interested in the same work; we have freedom and means to devote our whole lives to the work we believe in. Never did I imagine such happiness open to me. . . .

The last six weeks of solitary unmarried life were spent in Leeds attending the delegates' meeting of the Amalgamated Society of Engineers to revise their rules; to which I had been admitted by special resolution.

July 2nd, 1892.—The delegates sat (68 of them) for six hours a day. This delegate meeting will be a crisis in the history of the A.S.E. For some time past, under the guidance of a weak secretary, there has been trouble within and without. The spirit and aspirations of the New Unionism have infected even this conservative and aristocratic body which, until a few years ago, has been little better than a great benefit society. Not that the A.S.E. has not fought its battles. The nine hours' movement of 1872 was the beginning of a great revival of trade unionism and was initiated by the A.S.E. But, except for one or two pitched battles at long intervals, the even tenor of benevolent claims has been uninterrupted. The A.S.E. has appeared to its members, scattered about—some in remote country districts—simply as one more great friendly institution for mutual help in common needs. . . .

The scene has changed in the last two years. The two foremost figures in the Labour world, Tom Mann and John Burns, both happen to be members of the A.S.E. Though they won their reputation in organising unskilled workers, and in the political propaganda of the Socialist movement, their fellow-members have become proud of them and have been greatly influenced by their powerful cry of " Forward! " . . .

In the more populous districts, and especially on the North East Coast, the A.S.E. have been stimulated to strike for new privileges. This has led to serious friction between the local district authorities, with a definite trade policy, and the central and unrepresentative executive in London, fitted by its constitution only to administer a friendly society. No guidance and no control, yet irritating repudiations or dilatory acceptance of the already acted on decisions of the local district committees. The London council has, in fact, fallen into universal disrepute; and to make confusion worse confounded, the elaborate complicated local organisations, branches, local district committees, central district committees, grand committees, and joint committees, have thrown up a mass of divergent views for different and overlapping areas. Hence, the public discredit of the A.S.E. and the dissatisfaction and discord among its members.

The recent disasters on the North East Coast have ripened discontent into a determination to change the constitution of the Society fundamentally. Last year, the members voted, by a large majority, for a delegate meeting (the last one was in 1885), and for the past six months committees of revision have been sitting in all the centres of the engineering industry. The result is a " book of suggestions ", 258 pages of closely printed amendments to the present rules: emanating from all parts of the U.K., and even from America and Australia. The delegates are confined to these suggestions: they cannot propose an amendment which does not appear in the book. I listened to a six hours' debate on the subject (a proposal to create a permanent salaried executive committee, which was carried). One of the most level-headed discussions I have ever heard.

I omit the greater part of my report of the discussion on most of these suggestions, which lasted for some weeks.

There are half-a-dozen delegates who are quite admirable debaters: clear, forcible, concise. The language and arrangement of some of the subjects are quite excellent and I longed to see some of the speakers in Parliament. There is no limitation of time; but this freedom to prose and rant has not been abused and I listened for six hours with no sense of boredom or impatience.

The Conference is more or less divided up into sections or caucuses, pledged to a particular programme or reform—though, on the whole, there is a *bona fide* discussion of all the proposals. London and the North East Coast are found to stand for efficiency and inclusion; Manchester and Lancashire delegates represent a solid conservative reactionary vote and have opposed, tooth and nail, any radical change. Scotland would follow suit if it were not for a certain " home rule " tendency. Belfast is ultra Tory and has but one principle to promote—restriction of output in methods of work and exclusiveness in membership. The Midland delegates and the Yorkshire scatter their votes indiscriminately for and against progressive proposals. But, undoubtedly, the most level-headed as well as the ablest speakers are Socialists: for instance, Evans (Brighton); Sellicks (Woolwich); Barnes (Chelsea); Fletcher (Newcastle); Halston (Gateshead). This is altogether an agreeable surprise to me. Hitherto, my experience has been that the more feather-headed workmen are Socialists. But then Socialism is rapidly changing in character; it is losing its revolutionary and class-bitter character, and becoming constitutional effort based on hope and not on hatred. The Manchester men, and the Scotch and Irish, are for the most part individualists; but, with the exception of Fergusson of Glasgow who is a canny Scotsman, they have no remarkable men among them; though they exhibit a certain shrewd caution, they are narrow-minded and illiberal. In fact, they are not good examples of their creed. Whether this is chance, or whether it signifies a general conversion of the more generous-hearted and intellectual workmen to Socialist economics, is a moot question. Such Socialism as there is, is of a decided Fabian type; and one realises that the facts and figures and general arguments are taken from Fabian literature.

Some pleasant evenings I have had chatting with selected delegates. Yesterday evening I had a North East Coast man, an enthusiastic supporter of Sidney's possible candidature for the Gateshead vacancy when it occurs.

Altogether it has been a most fortunate coincidence—this A.S.E. delegate meeting and my visit to Leeds. Galton drudges away in the board room of the Co-operators (we always secure an office out of the Co-operators) at the minutes, etc., of local societies. He works very hard but he needs more training. Sidney is indulgent and flattering in manner, I have to be critical. . . .

The next entry is emphatic, and written in large letters:

Exit Beatrice Potter, July 23rd, 1892.
Enter Beatrice Webb, or rather Mrs. Sidney Webb, for I lose alas! both names.

It certainly never occurred to me that, near forty years after-wards, I should be again asked to change my name and its prefix—and by the same man![1] The answer has been in the negative, with the approval of the Other One.

The honeymoon was spent investigating on the spot the ramshackle trade societies of Dublin: nineteenth-century combinations of Catholic artisans, claiming direct descent from the exclusively Protestant guilds established in the seventeenth century by Royal Charter for the express purpose of preventing Papists gaining an honest livelihood. One of the societies, the Dublin Bricklayers' Society, paraded the old parchment charter, bereft of its seal, and apparently handed over by the lawyer's clerk to the society when the ancient companies were dissolved in 1843. Thence to Belfast, interviewing hard-fisted employers and groups of closely organised skilled craftsmen; many of them Scotch, veracious and cautious in their statements about their own conditions of employment, and contemptuous and indifferent to the Catholic labourers and women who were earning miserable wages in the shipyards and linen factories of Belfast.

The honeymoon holiday ended at Glasgow, attending the Trades Union Congress, collecting trade union documents and interviewing trade union secretaries.

August 1892.—Ugly certainly are the banks of the Clyde [I enter in my diary], and very hideous are the results of enormous earnings by certain sections of men, brutalised by want in bad times, and long hours of working during the spells of prosperity. The Clyde is the home of piece-work and contract work, of poverty, drunkenness, stupidity and competition. It is the paradise of the able, pushing man, who rises out of the slums to own a deer forest. . . .

This time the Congress meant eight hours and no mistake [I enter later on]; a large majority of delegates were pledged to it owing to change of front of the cotton operatives. . . .

The sting of the New Unionist movement has been effectively drawn out by the adhesion of the cotton officials to the eight-hour day; on all other points, stalwart Old Unionists. The fact that the

[1] When in 1929 Sidney was created Baron Passfield, Beatrice flatly refused to change her name and remained Mrs. Sidney Webb. (Ed.)

cotton unionists have always been legalists was overlooked. The labourers' unions too, are rapidly shrinking up with bad trade; while the Socialists, instead of being scurrilous and aggressive, are (under the influence of Fabianism) pursuing the policy of permeation—most successfully, I think. At the first Congress I attended, Dundee, only three years ago, Broadhurst reigned supreme, and the Socialists were at daggers drawn with all the Old Unionists, resorting to what Champion, with apparent approval, used to call " political assassination ", that is the destruction of personal reputation by slandering. Now Sidney hobnobs with all the older men, and we are as friendly with Mawdsley as with Tillett. The last bit of permeation—rather a joke—Mawdsley the Tory individualist, having been invited to address the Church Congress, begs us for hints. A Socialist discourse is promptly supplied him: it remains to be seen whether he accepts it.

The hopeful side of the Labour movement seems to me a growing collectivism of the Miners' Federation and the Cotton Unions. Here, at last, we are on solid ground and among men who, if they take a thing up, do it with the intention and capacity to carry it through.

Exactly four weeks at Glasgow—the last ten days a rush of work— Sidney working the whole day on documents except the hours he spends trudging out to the far-off suburbs to interview trade union secretaries. Out of the four weeks we have had two holidays—a Sunday on Loch Awe with Auberon Herbert,[1] and a week-end visit to R. B. Haldane.

Memory recalls the tall figure [of Auberon Herbert], wrapped in an old shawl, with vague blue eyes, soft high voice, flowing white beard—the Don Quixote of the nineteenth century, waving one hand at us, while pushing his sailing boat away from the shore; giving us his final blessing: " You will do a lot of mischief and be very happy in doing it."

But to resume the diary :

August 1892.—Sunday with Haldane was more remunerative. He is now an influential man: willing to stand in the background, to counsel the Ministers and act as go-between [I remind the reader that, in July 1892, the Liberal Party had taken office with a narrow majority]. Talked incessantly about the possibilities of reorganising the Home Office as the Ministry of Labour; perfecting the factory department. Ended in pressing us to write a memorandum for Asquith

---

[1] The Hon. Auberon Herbert: see *My Apprenticeship*, pp. 187, 188, 189, 190, 219, 322, 396.

(a request since repeated by Asquith). Wrote it the other day, but stress of work made us keep it over till Edinburgh. Haldane not hopeful of the future—" constituencies not converted to collectivism—at least not in Scotland ". Sunday afternoon a fair bevy of " Souls "[1] came over to tea. Haldane prides himself on hovering between the fashionable paradise represented by the " Souls " and the collectivist state represented by the Fabians. " Souls " good to look at; gushing and anxious to strike up acquaintanceship with an unconventional couple. A charming pair—the Alfred Lytteltons—graceful, modest, intelligent, and with the exquisite deference and ease which constitutes good breeding. But to me the " Souls " would not bring " the peace that passeth understanding ", but a vain restlessness of tickled vanity. One would become quickly satiated.

I leave Glasgow with no regrets. The working-men leaders here are an uninteresting lot; without enthusiasm or much intelligence. The Scotch nature does not lend itself to combination; the strong men seek to rise and push for themselves and not to serve others. And apparently the Co-operators have absorbed the finer intelligence and warmer hearts among the Scotch working-men of the official cast.

41 Grosvenor Road

A " hard little house ", so H. G. Wells described, in *The New Machiavelli*, the home of the Oscar Baileys (*alias* Webbs) in Grosvenor Road, Westminster. To which I may add that it was ten-roomed, rent £110, served by two maids, and that we occupied it on lease for near forty years. I think I must have broken records in having had, during that period, only five separate servants, one of whom was with

[1] The following description of the " Souls " is taken from *An Autobiography*, by Lord Haldane (1928), pp. 120-21: " I began in 1893 to move a good deal in what is called London Society. There was a group of well-known people nicknamed the ' souls '. They sometimes took themselves much too seriously, and on the whole it is doubtful whether their influence was on balance good. But they cared for literature and art, and their social gifts were so high that people sought much to be admitted into their circle. Among the men were Arthur Balfour, the late Lord Pembroke, George Curzon, Harry Cust, George Wyndham and Alfred Lyttelton. Among the women were Lady Ribblesdale, her sister Margot Tennant (afterwards Mrs. Asquith), Lady Elcho, Lady Desborough and Lady Horner. Week-end parties at which the ' souls ' assembled were given at Panshanger, Ashridge, Wilton and Taplow. Among the hostesses on these occasions were Lady Cowper, Lady Brownlow and Lady Pembroke, older but attractive women, who were gratefully but irreverently called the ' Aunts ' of the ' souls '. One or two outside men were welcomed and were frequently guests on these occasions. Among them were John Morley, Sir Alfred Lyall, Asquith, and myself. We were not ' souls ', but they liked our company, and we liked theirs because of its brilliance." (Ed.)

me for over thirty years: another consequence of living according to plan; housemates like to know exactly what to expect, when and where? Our workroom on the ground floor, which served also for meals, a long narrow room running east to west, in early morning and late afternoon welcoming sunshine, was lined with books and blue-books; the space left over covered with engravings and enlarged photographs of three generations of my family; from my grandparents and their children, to a selection from among a hundred or so nephews and nieces, with here and there a portrait of a near friend: Herbert Spencer, R. B. Haldane, Mandell Creighton, Bernard Shaw and Marie Souvestre; and two brothers-in-law, Leonard Courtney and Alfred Cripps (afterwards Lord Parmoor), I recall. On the half-landing the secretary's office: oil-clothed floor, large deal writing-table, from floor to ceiling shelved with pamphlet boxes. As years went by, these hundreds of boxes, filled with tens of thousands of quarto-sized research notes, overflowed into an overhead box-room of identical shape. Not less utilitarian in its furnishings was the conventionally shaped sitting-room on the first floor; long seats fitted into alcoves and, under the western window, an escritoire, table heaped with books, three easy-chairs but no sofa: all designed to accommodate the largest number of guests standing or sitting. This harsh interior was redeemed by the unique interest and beauty of the outlook. To spring out of bed on a summer morning and see, spread out before you, the sun rising behind Lambeth Palace, on clear days the Dome of St. Paul's and the spires of the City churches, its rays lighting up the tiny waves breaking the surface of the swift-flowing tidal river, whilst oar-steered barges, some with red or yellow sails, drifting rafts of timber and steaming colliers passed under the Vauxhall and Lambeth bridges, was a joyful greeting to another day. Other scenes from the balcony of the sitting-room I remember: on still autumn days the river, in ebbing tide, sulking among the mud banks and lapping the anchored river-craft; or, in full tide, losing itself in fog, white, yellow or black, thus seeming as boundless in its expanse as the Mississippi; or, again, at night, city and river lights far and near, hardly distinguishable from the stars, sometimes the glow of brilliant moonlight, illuminating the moving waters, whilst blackening the bridges and their shadows. Other recreations were the walks along the Thames embankment, to the right past the Tate Gallery, the two Battersea bridges, the Royal Hospital and the Physic Garden, to the upper reaches of old Chelsea, where my sister Kate Courtney lived ; or to the left through the resort of Lords and Commons, the dwelling-place of the British Civil Service, the stately Inns of Court and their winsome gardens, citywards to the Cathedral of St. Paul's to seek peace in the music of old-world Christian rites. Or, again, an evening stroll, under St. Thomas's Hospital, watching the sun set across the river behind the terraced Houses of Parliament and the five towers of Westminster, secular and ecclesiastic. Even to-day, living in a delightful countryside, I sometimes feel homesick for the river Thames sweeping through the splendour and squalor of the birthplace of the nineteenth-century capitalist dictatorship.

Our plan of life was to spend eight or nine months of the year in our London home; working together in the mornings at the book; Sidney devoting a long afternoon to L.C.C. administration; the evenings either alone together, browsing over periodicals and light literature, or discussing research, municipal administration or Fabian propaganda with friends and associates. The other months, especially the long summer recess of the County Council, were spent either in some countryside working up our material or in provincial towns carrying on our investigations; whilst every two or three years, usually on the publication of another volume, we treated ourselves to a few weeks' complete holiday on the Continent.

Here are a few entries from the diary, mainly concerned with *The History of Trade Unionism* and *Industrial Democracy*, and our consequent association with trade union officials:

December 30th, 1892.—How gloomy other Christmas Eves have been: always the low-water mark of a year's despair; at best an arid time of family gossip, over-eating, preparation for heartless winter games. Now I have won a vantage ground of wonderful happiness: and, even when physical energy ebbs low, I still feel fundamentally happy. And Sidney also has found a resting place. No need now to struggle for happiness or success: all energy can be given to work. . . .

We have actually begun the book.[1] But, after writing the greater part of the first chapter, we are reading at the British Museum to get fresh ideas of eighteenth-century industry. It is still to be proved—the experiment of writing a book together—sometimes our ideas clash and we fall between the rival ideas; but on the whole we get on. My only trouble is that I can work such short hours compared to him and I feel a mere dilettante, but when spring comes I shall feel better. . . . Sidney for his part is enthusiastically happy. He seems to have settled down to the County Council administration work; at present largely engaged in planning the Technical Education Board. Parliament seems further off than ever; but we are getting used to the prospect of intellectual study, and the humble rôle of county councillor. But, I think, more is to be done by administrative experiment, on the one hand, and educating the constituencies, on the other, than by entering into the political game carried on in Parliament. . . .

The Argoed, Sept. 17*th*, 1893.—The first fortnight [I write nine months later when we are at The Argoed, our old Monmouthshire home: still in the hands of my father's executors], we spent finishing the sixth chapter of our book. Then Graham Wallas came, read our first chapter and severely criticised the form of it. He made me feel rather desperate about its shortcomings. So I took it and wrestled with it: writing out a complete new syllabus with a quite different arrangement of the subject. This Sidney "wrote to " with my help. Bernard Shaw came ten days after and has stayed with us the remainder of our time working almost every morning at our book. The form of the first chapter satisfied him, and he altered only words and sentences. The second chapter he took more in hand and the third he has to a large extent remodelled. Sidney certainly has devoted friends. But then it is a common understanding with all these men that they use each other up when necessary. That is the basis of the influence of the Fabian Society on contemporary political thought: the little group of leaders are practical communists in all the fruits of their labours. While Bernard Shaw was working on the book, Sidney and I set about separate tasks. I attempted to write a lecture on the sphere of trade unionism; he worked at Tom Mann's minority report.[2] My attempt

[1] *The History of Trade Unionism.*
[2] The Minority Report of the Royal Commission on Labour.

proved to be a hopeless fiasco. I struggled vainly under my great mass of information: historical lore, statistics, analysis—the stuff overwhelmed me. After five days' work I read to S. what I had written. He looked puzzled, and suggested that he should write it out. Then we had a bit of a tiff. For, when my miserable meanderings appeared in his clear hand, it was so obviously out of place for a lecture and that mortified me and I was in a devil of a temper. Next morning he sat down patiently to recast it, and we worked four days together and made a rough draft. Now I am working it up into lecture form. But my failure made me feel a bit of a parasite. So much for a holiday task. . . .

The Fabian Junta

As a relief from these entries about ourselves, I give my first impressions of S. W.'s friends and fellow-Fabians: Graham Wallas and Bernard Shaw, together with casual observations on John Burns and his relation to the Fabian Junta.

The Argoed, September 17th, 1893.—Graham Wallas—six feet with a slouching figure—good features and genial, open smile—utterly unselfconscious and lacking in vanity or personal ambition. Without convictions he would have lounged through life—with convictions he grinds; his natural sluggishness of nature, transformed by his social fervour into a slow grinding at anything that turns up to do. In spite of his moral fervour, he seems incapable of directing his own life, and tends to drift into anything that other people decide. This tendency is accentuated by his benevolence and kindliness and selflessness— almost amounting to a weakness. Thus, while his intimate friends love him and impose on him, superficial strangers of poor character often actually despise him. To some men and women he appears simply as a kindly, dull fellow—an impression which is fostered by a slovenliness of dress and general worn-out look. He preaches too, a habit carried over from his life as usher and teacher of boys. To his disciples he appears a brilliant man, first-rate lecturer, a very genius for teaching, a great thinker and a conscientious writer. It remains to be seen what else he will become beyond a successful propagandist and an admirable and most popular University Extension lecturer. He has two books on hand—but, owing to his constant running off on other people's business, they stand a poor chance of being finished within a year or so. If enthusiasm, purity of motive, hard if somewhat mechanical work, will make a man a success, then Graham Wallas has a great career before him. He has plenty of intellectual ability too; what he lacks is deliberate concentration and rapid decision what to do and how to do it. A loveable man.

Bernard Shaw I know less well than Graham Wallas, though he is quite an old friend of Sidney's. A fellow with a crank for not making money, except he can make it exactly as he chooses. Persons with no sense of humour look upon him as a combination of Don Juan and a professional blasphemer of the existing order. An artist to the tips of his fingers and an admirable craftsman; I have never known a man use his pen in such a workmanlike fashion, or acquire such a thoroughly technical knowledge of any subject upon which he gives an opinion. But his technique or specialism never overpowers him: he always translates it into epigrams, sparkling generalisations or witty personalities. As to his character, I do not understand it. He has been for twelve years a devoted propagandist—hammering away at the ordinary routine of Fabian executive work with as much persistence as Wallas or Sidney. He is an excellent friend, at least to men (" a perfect house friend ", I add two years later, " self-sufficient, witty and tolerant, going his own way and yet adapting himself to your ways "). But beyond this I know nothing. I am inclined to think that he has a slight personality; agile, graceful, and even virile; but lacking in weight. Adored by many women, he is a born philanderer; a " soul " so to speak; disliking to be hampered either by passion or convention and, therefore, always tying himself up into knots which he has to cut before he is free for another adventure. Vain is he? A month ago I should have said that vanity was the bane of his nature. Now I am not so sure that the vanity itself is not part of the *mise en scène*, whether, in fact, it is not part of the character he imagines himself to be playing in the world's comedy.

A vegetarian, fastidious but unconventional in his clothes; six feet in height with a lithe, broad-chested figure and laughing blue eyes. Above all a brilliant talker and, therefore, a delightful companion. To me he has not yet a personality: he is a pleasant but somewhat incongruous group of qualities. Some people would call him a cynic: he is really an idealist of the purest water.

These two men with Sidney make up the Fabian Junta. Sidney is the organiser and gives most of the practical initiative, Graham Wallas represents morality and scrupulousness, Bernard Shaw gives the sparkle and flavour. Graham Wallas appeals to those of the upper and educated class who have good intentions: no one can doubt his candour, disinterestedness, enthusiasm and extreme moral refinement. Sidney insinuates ideas, arguments, programmes and organises the organisers. Bernard Shaw leads off the men of straw, men with light heads—the would-be revolutionaries, who are attracted by his wit, his daring onslaughts and amusing paradoxes. He has also a *clientèle* among cynical journalists and men of the world. What the Junta needs to make it a great power are one or two personalities of *weight*; men of wide experience and sagacity, able to play a long hand, and to master the movement. If John Burns would get over his incurable suspicion and if he could conquer his instinctive fear of comradeship, I know no man who could so complete the Fabian trio and make it thoroughly effective. If Burns would come in and give himself away to the other three as they do to each other—the Fabians could dominate the reform movement. Burns is, in some respects, the strongest man of the four, though utterly ill-equipped in his isolation for leadership. But that contingency, I fear, is past praying for. Collectivism will spread, but it will spread from no one centre. Those who sit down and think will, however, mould the form, though they will not set the pace or appear openly as the directors. . . .

Grosvenor Road, October 17*th,* 1893.—Spent a whole morning with John Burns [I write when we are again in London] looking over the trade union documents he has. Our relationship with John Burns has never been a cordial one; it promises to be more so in future. I began with a prejudice against him. At the Newcastle Congress he seemed an intriguer who suspected everyone of intrigue. His unfriendly attitude towards Tom Mann also displeased me. Possibly, he heard of my dislike, for he treated me with marked suspicion. Of Sidney he has, until lately, been jealous and was anxious that he should not come on the L.C.C. But, for one reason or another, this unfriendliness has much lessened. On my part, I have long since seen reason to alter my opinion of him as a public man. His capacity, straightforwardness, power of reason, has given him a permanent position, which poor Mann forfeited by his light-headed change of front on all questions human and divine. Sidney has always had a high opinion of him. Burns, on his side, sees now that Sidney does not seek to play the rival Labour leader, and that his influence (Burns') will not be diminished by Sidney being on the L.C.C. If Sidney went into Parliament, it might be that the old jealousy would revive.

For jealousy and suspicion of rather a mean kind are John Burns' burning sin. A man of splendid physique, fine and strong intelligence, human sympathy, practical capacity, he is unfitted for a really great position by his utter inability to be a constant and loyal comrade. He stands absolutely alone. He is intensely jealous of other Labour men, acutely suspicious of all middle-class sympathisers; whilst his hatred of Keir Hardie reaches the dimensions of mania. He is a born ruler of barbarians, impressing his followers with his will and determination, not guiding them by reason. And yet he is essentially an intellectual man; one of his finest qualities is the constant testing of questions by intellectual methods rather than by sentimental considerations. It is pitiful to see this splendid man a prey to egotism of the most sordid kind; an egotism that seeks not so much to fill the world with its own doings as to diminish all other reputations in order that his own work may stand out in relief. . . .

ROYAL COMMISSION ON LABOUR

Meanwhile, Sidney had been helping trade union officials by drafting minority reports for royal commissions, notably for the much-advertised Royal Commission on Labour, about which I find the following caustic entry:

Grosvenor Road, December 24th, 1893.—Royal Commission on Labour a gigantic fraud.[1] Made up of a little knot of dialecticians *plus* a carefully picked parcel of variegated Labour men, and the rest landlords or capitalists, pure and simple. The dialecticians—Gerald Balfour, Frederick Pollock, Alfred Marshall and Leonard Courtney —have had it their own way: they have puzzled the workmen with economic conundrums, balked inconvenient evidence by cross-questions, and delivered themselves of elaborate treatises on economics, history and philosophy to bewildered reporters—equally in the form of questions. Spent a somewhat painful day there, the first day of Sidney's examination. He was irritated by the bad faith of the Commission, and treated them to a little of their own game. His answers read well, and were richly deserved; but his manner was objectionable and pained me. Also the Charles Booths, Kate Courtney, Mrs. Dugdale and others of that set were listening to him and, as they agreed with the dialecticians, they showed their disapproval markedly. However, the next day the dear boy made a pretty apology and bore the cross-examination with perfect good humour. It ended in an amicable discussion between him and Gerald Balfour for an hour-and-a-half, on abstract economics, pleasant to listen to, but fit only for after-dinner talk, and not the sort of questions and answers to be delivered at the public expense. Utter waste of time to all concerned except that it woke us up to the harm the Commission might do if their report is taken in good faith. Hence, the inspired article in the London [*Daily*] *Chronicle* written by Massingham after a long talk with us. . . .

[1] For an analysis of the defects of the Royal Commission on Labour, as a method of investigation, see *The Failure of the Labour Commission,* XIX Century, July 1894, by Beatrice Webb.

Grosvenor Road, Christmas Day, 1893.—Another chicken hatched here last summer—Tom Mann's minority report. . . . Sidney has spent quite three weeks on it; but, though we think it of importance, we cannot help regarding it as a practical joke over which we chuckle with considerable satisfaction. Poor Labour Commission, having carefully excluded any competent Socialists from its membership, having scouted the idea of appointing me as a humble assistant commissioner, will now find a detailed collectivist programme, blazoned about as the minority report of its Labour members! Dear old Leonard [Courtney], who told us with pompous superiority that they were all agreed: and that there was no prospect of any minority report—and we had it lying all the time on our table and had been putting the last touches to it that very morning. Certainly, persons with brains and independent means may have a rare good time. . . .

Grosvenor Road, March 13*th,* 1894.—Amusing afternoon. Mann came in in the morning to say that he was bringing Mawdsley, Austin and Abraham [1] to discuss the minority report at 5 o'clock—the excuse

---

[1] The scene at the Royal Commission when the Labour men produced their report was extensively noticed in the press.

"This report was produced at yesterday's sitting of the Commission [the *Westminster Gazette* of March 16, 1894, reports], and it created (says the *Manchester Guardian*) almost as much consternation as if a bomb had been exploded in Westminster Hall. The Duke of Devonshire was clearly unprepared for it. It altered the whole situation so far as his draft recommendations were concerned, and he suggested that the Commission should have time to consider the new report, for which purpose he then adjourned the Commission until after Easter. The minority report, it is reported, will propose among other matters a legal eight-hour day, with certain limitations, the amendment of the Factory Acts in the direction of the abolition of home work, the relief of the unemployed by empowering Boards of Guardians to acquire land and to till it by the labour of persons temporarily unemployed, the improving of the conditions under which female workers in certain trades are employed, the improvement of the lot of the dock labourers and other casual workers, and the amelioration of the condition of the agricultural labourer. The same report will also express regret that the nationalisation of the land cannot be dealt with. These questions bristle with opportunities for controversy, and it will not be possible to conclude the work of the Commission by the end of the month. It is expected that five members of the Commission at least will subscribe to this report."

Apparently Mawdsley was under no delusion about the authorship of the report. When a member of the majority of the Royal Commission observed with a sneer that the signatories had obviously not written the report, Mawdsley answered sharply: "Certainly not: nor has the Duke or any of you written the majority report. The only distinction between us and you is that you have paid your man, and we have been sharp enough to get it done without payment, and better done too." On the close of the Commission, Mawdsley insisted on the three Labour members, Tom Mann, Michael Austin and himself, signing a formal letter of thanks to S. W. for enabling them "to submit a report which we believe will prove to be of great value to the cause of Labour in the future, also in some sense a guide to the industrial and political policy to be endorsed by the workers".

Among the other documents drafted for the trade union officials by Sidney Webb was the minority report presented by Broadhurst as a member of the Royal Commission on the Aged Poor, 1895.

being that he had left it with Sidney to look over it from a legal point of view. We were both rather taken aback: thinking that Mawdsley, whose adhesion was most important, would not only refuse to support it but would, perhaps, join the rest of the Commission in trying to keep it out altogether. We could not imagine Mawdsley, a staunch Conservative, adopting it " all of a heap ". When Mawdsley turned up early to write his copy for the *Factory Times*, I was relieved to find that he was supremely disgruntled with the majority report and felt in a fix as to what he should do. Sidney took the matter in hand, and asked leave, as a lawyer, to give the others the gist of Mann's report. Standing in front of the fire, he began reading out all the parts which would affect Mawdsley most, he making comments on it, Mann playing into his hand by suggesting more advanced statements, Sidney supporting Mawdsley in many of his criticisms. As he read on Mawdsley expressed his approval and was apparently delighted with the practical and detailed character of the suggestions. It ended by Mawdsley considering the report his own and taking it on himself to announce to the Commission that they were drawing up a minority report and would present it in a couple of days. The only alteration he insisted on was the omission of the word " Socialism ", though he agreed to the substitution of the words " public administration, national and local ". So much is in a word. . . .

Industrial Democracy

Our first book—*The History of Trade Unionism*—was published in the spring of 1894, and we rewarded ourselves for the two years' work by a three weeks' holiday in Italy.

Grosvenor Road, April 30th, 1894.—It is the first complete break in our work that we have had since those happy days in Norway three years ago. Of course, I have had days and weeks of " lazing " from sheer incapacity to work—but I think I have used up all my energy during the last three years in work—I have never had sufficient over to enjoy anything but a somewhat depressed *rest*. The last weeks I have slacked off so that I may have plenty of spirits for our holy-day. We need to rid ourselves of the turmoil of the life here during the last three months, so as to set to our next bit of work with a clear head and clean conscience!

Grosvenor Road, May 21st, 1894.—Back from a delightful three weeks' holiday. Nine days in Venice. Charming rooms overlooking an Alma Tadema court, with canal and bridge between us and it and old marble gateway and well, whither Venetian women with their soft-coloured clothes went to draw water. Our days were spent on the water with an old gondolier whom we engaged by the day, and in St. Mark's Piazza and in St. Mark's itself—that vision of sumptuous beauty which it is a glory to recall. Very sweet hours of companionship—not thinking, but simply feeling the beauty around us—a true honeymoon of love and common enjoyment. Then to Como (Menaggio) where we met the Richard Stracheys—the General, an old experienced Indian administrator, and Mrs. Strachey, a strong, warm-hearted, enthusiastically literary woman. But, though our evenings were spent with them, smoking cigarettes and sipping coffee on the terrace, our days were spent together wandering over the hills and in the lovely gardens of the Villas. Then a long journey back, and we are again in our little house, beautifully cleaned up by our two maids, and with Galton keenly anxious to be at the next volume. The holiday has been just what we needed; it has swept away all the cobwebs of secret minority reports, and all the tatters of the last bit of work, so that we can begin fresh and clear, a new subject. One day spent over our correspondence, and this morning I started off to plan the new volume. We propose to rough-hew the whole before either perfecting any part of it or completing our investigation; since we do not know exactly which points want clearing up. It will be a difficult and delicate piece of work, and need a great deal of hard hammering to weld it into anything like form. But we are encouraged—if, indeed, such a labour of love needed encouragement—by the appreciation of our labour and patience in the first volume. Perhaps I feel a bit of a humbug when the reviews talk of the " endless labour " entailed in the work—we have taken the work lightly, Sidney giving only half-time to it, and I the miserable few hours which I am capable of giving to any sort of work. But I must pull myself together and work harder at this volume—work hard and live simply.

To us *The History of Trade Unionism* seemed little more than an historical introduction to the task we had set before us: the scientific analysis of the structure and function of British Trade Unions, in order to discover the tacit assumptions and social implications underlying their activities; and, what appeared to us of crucial importance, the relation of manual-working trade unionism to other forms of social organisation: notably, to profit-making enterprise, to political democracy, and to the consumers' co-operative movement. The following entries from my diary, scattered over four years, reveal the intolerable toil of thought involved in working out a theory of trade unionism consistent with the facts we had observed and the hypotheses we believed we had verified.

Grosvenor Road, July 10*th,* 1894.—Not getting on with our book. It is a horrid grind, this analysis—one sentence is exactly like another, the same words, the same construction—no relief in narrative. And then the facts often do not admit of clear and definite classification— they are not grouped in distinct and separate classes, they are mixed up together in a fine tangle, and any attempt to place them in nice little maps seems purely artificial. No doubt the sequence involved in history writing is as artificial as are the groups involved in classification (how silly it is to suppose that facts *ever tell their own story*—it is all a matter of arranging them so that they may tell something—and the arrangement is purely a subjective process). I sometimes despair of getting on. with the book—I feel horribly vexed with myself for loitering and idling as I do morning after morning; looking on while poor Sidney drudges along. London, too, is beginning to get on my nerves, with the heat and the continual noise and movement and the distraction of seeing one person and another. When we get to the country, it may be better: we must make an effort.

Borough Farm, Surrey, July 25*th,* 1894.—Overlooking a little country lane with heather-covered moorland on one side and a thicket of young trees behind, stands the farm-house we have taken for three months. The farmer and his wife, hard-headed, somewhat grasping folk, who make us pay more than London prices for all their produce, and whom I rather suspect of taking toll on our groceries! and a grim old labourer who serves them and does menial offices for us, and whom we meet in the late evening with a coat puffed out with concealed rabbits, are our co-occupants of the substantial red-brick old-fashioned house. Tho' only one hour and a few minutes by rail from London, it is too remote for postal delivery and we have to fetch our letters some $1\frac{1}{2}$ miles from a village! But this and other drawbacks are out-weighed by the exceeding charm of the country. Heather-grown moor-land studded with firs and intermixed with broad expanses of wooded pasture, occasionally a grove of glorious forest trees with thorn and holly bush nestling under—all open and free to wander, mile after mile, without a single fence, ditch or " trespass board ". Here we shall be for three months resting, reading and writing as hard as we can at our book. These first ten days, Sidney has been working at his paper for the British Association, on *The Heresies of the L.C.C.,* and I have been somewhat despairingly spending my mornings over the chapter on " Apprenticeship ". But he has been up and down to London, and even I had to rush up to two committees.

Borough Farm, Surrey, August 10*th,* 1894.—Either the Surrey climate is enervating, or I am no good at this analytical deductive work which goes to make up our second volume. Rightly or wrongly, we are writing our analysis of facts before we have completed our investigation, with a view of concentrating our attention, when we begin to investigate, exactly on those points which need clearing up and which we are certain to use. Consequently, we are perpetually working without sufficient or adequate material: our descriptive analysis lacks definiteness; the lines of our argument become shaky; each division, as we turn it out, seems unsatisfactory. Then our work suffers from being an almost unconscious attempt to unite three things: (1) a descriptive analysis of modern trade unionism with as much analytical history of separate trade unions as will light up the statistical account and show the direction of growth as well as the present structure; (2) a criticism of trade unions (for the good of the unionists!); (3) an apology for, or defence of trade unions (for the enlightenment of the middle-class and economists). These three objects do not amalgamate well. It spoils the descriptive analysis, which ought to be absolutely cold, for authors or readers to feel that these facts will presently be used to support a thesis. But this is not all. When we come to the thesis we find the facts, tho' they can be used as illustrations, are not much good as the basis of our structure—they are only the ornament. The whole structure of our argument turns out to be deductive in form, with psychological hypotheses or inductions used as its material. So the facts we have laboriously detailed seem somewhat *de trop*. Whether, that being so, we ought not to begin with the theory of trade unionism, instead of demonstrating the need for it, or whether we ought not to begin with the descriptive side—the facts— and then deal with the theory as a second division?

October 8th, 1894. *Borough Farm.*—It is some years since I have watched summer turn into autumn and felt the first breath of winter creeping over the country. This year the summer left us early, the sky closing over with cold grey clouds, only now and again they break, and the sun slants out and lights up the sombre blues and browns of the landscape. Perhaps, it is the rich tones of the heath and bracken which recall some of those lovely Rusland [my father's house in Westmorland] autumns; for, as I stand and watch the clouds drifting across the moor and try to fathom the glorious depths of colour of land and sky, memories of old days jostle each other and seem to take me back to the thoughts and feelings and daily life of struggling girlhood—the inevitable melancholy of the autumn months, the brooding over books, the long walks with Father, afternoon tea in the little hall at Rusland after a trudge in the mist, Mother's bright welcome to Father, her keen relish of her cup of tea before she went to her boudoir to study her grammars, or settled herself down to a talk with Father over his business affairs and the family prospects—all the strange medley of good and evil one lived through as a girl. But, in chewing the cud of those old memories, I am impressed, not with the *past-ness* of the old life but with the perfect continuity of the present and the past: these autumn months of years ago were always devoted to study, ·were always stimulated by a restless desire to conquer new strands of thought. After nearly twenty years of adult life, I am still living the same daily life, still using my whole energy in unravelling ideas and attempting to clear issues—the practical affairs which occupy most people's middle life are no more now than they were then—at least, not during our three months' holiday. There is an inexpressible delight in this consciousness of continuity, in feeling that those hours of lonely and painful study are linked on to the settled occupation—perhaps one might almost say the settled profession—of a productive brain-worker. If one could only have foreseen that this daily intellectual effort would one day be set in a frame of loving companionship and constant sympathy, one would have been less restless and morbidly self-conscious.

Of course, one gets discouraged at one's incapacity as of old. Each chapter of this book needs a certain amount of hard and vigorous thinking, and I feel dispirited when I have to knock off work an hour after I have begun, or when I have to lay by for a whole day. But it is vastly different working after one has some assurance of the worth of one's work and toiling, day after day, not knowing whether one has special capacity or not. And then what light love brings to the daily task: it turns that black despair of the over-strained brain-worker into calm quiescence. When first I was married, I feared that my happiness would dull my energies and make me intellectually dependent. I no longer feel that; the old fervour for work has returned without the old restlessness. Of course, my life in London, with its other claims, leaves me with less physical energy—but this, I think, is almost counterbalanced by the absence of any waste through mental misery. On the whole, then, I would advise the brain-working woman to marry—if only she can find her Sidney!

Borough Farm, October 11*th*, 1894.— . . . For all that, I leave this quaint little home with regret. The last months I have pulled myself together and done some hard thinking. We have roughed out four or five chapters of our book. I am beginning to see that, if we can only put enough work into it, this volume will be far more instructive than the *History*—a far bigger achievement. I dread the dullness that comes over me in London, the sheer incapacity to grapple with a hard bit of complicated analysis. However, I must save myself as much as I can for the book—I can only do my best. And I must, in order to be able to work, resolutely refuse to *worry*; otherwise I shall not do my share of the labour and shall be a source of fatigue and not of rest to Sidney. The next six months—with the vestry and L.C.C. elections added on to all the administrative business—seems likely to be somewhat trying for my Boy.

The last months of 1894 were largely taken up by the Westminster vestry elections, whilst our joint energies in the two first months of 1895 were completely absorbed in the London County Council election; all activities which will be described in the following chapter. Indeed, I gather from my diary that it was not until the August recess of 1895 that we disentangled ourselves from our political environment and returned to our special task of investigating the trade union movement.

The Argoed, August 8th, 1895.—I wonder whether other brainworkers make as many futile starts as we do. Here I have been painfully labouring to fashion a first chapter on the " Objects of Trade Unionism " and have wasted hours of Sidney's time in executing it and now the *idea* turns out not good enough—too thin and insignificant. It is hard to foretell the worth of an idea until you have expressed it fully with all its attendant facts in all their ramifications. After spending hours, if not days, on it, you find either that it is not true or absurdly insignificant and banal. It is this process, experimenting in working out ideas, that entails the length of time spent on analysis as compared with history. With history, the threads are supplied by the chronological order—you can weave these threads into any pattern; bring one of them to the surface and then another. But with analysis of facts, the threads are hypotheses: to be tested in strength and consistency before you dare weave them into conclusions and illustrate them with facts. . . .

Grosvenor Road, Sept. 9th, 1895.—At Cardiff [Trades Union Congress] we were in the usual whirl of talk. The hotel we were in was actually attached to the hall so that it was the centre where all the delegates congregated—especially as there were three entertainers quartered there—Lady Dilke [1] with her attendant ladies—Gertrude

---

[1] Representing the Women's Trade Union League, of which Lady Dilke was then president, and her niece, Miss Tuckwell, honorary secretary. (Ed.)

Tuckwell, Mary Abraham (factory inspector), Sir Hickman Bacon and ourselves. Lady Dilke entertained on a large, I might almost say gross scale—her young women asking every trade union official they came across to champagne lunches and elaborate dinners. The dear good baronet, with his doglike devotion to Sidney, provided us with a private sitting-room, where we had our trade unionists and he had the I.L.P.—we going in for little confidential lunches and suppers for the purpose of extracting information and insinuating useful suggestions. But all this is the background. The drama was fought out in the hall on the second day. The minority of the parliamentary committee inspired by Broadhurst, and led by J. Havelock Wilson, led the attack on the new " standing orders ". There was no defence—delegate after delegate got up and denounced the action of the parliamentary committee. No defence except bad language and abusive epithets from John Burns. But, when it came to the vote, the cotton and coal men showed their cards silently and with that vote collared the Congress and its organisation for their own purposes.

Mawdsley comes out now as the hero of the *coup d'état*.[1] Poor Burns has allowed himself to be used as the tool, his egregious vanity, virulent hatred of Keir Hardie and Tom Mann, suspicion of everyone else, prompting him to destroy the representative character of the Congress, to oust himself in order to oust certain other men, leaving Mawdsley and Cowey (Miners' Federation) in possession of the whole political influence of trade unions. Whether these men make anything of their power depends on whether the alliance stands good and whether Mawdsley shows more statesmanship than his predecessors. We had Mawdsley to dinner after the vote had been taken. Without disguising our opinion of the *coup d'état* we suggested to him that he might make the parliamentary committee a much more efficient instrument and that we should be glad to help. He rose to the suggestion, and I am not at all certain whether this parliamentary committee will not prove much more amenable to our influence than its predecessors. Mawdsley is a cool-headed man, quite aware of his own deficiencies and far too cynical to be suspicious. Whether or not we use Mawdsley, we may rest assured that he will use us: which after all is all we desire. Poor Burns, to have ousted Keir Hardie from the Congress and let in Sidney Webb to the parliamentary committee! Brought home a good deal of material. Must now turn to our book again. . . .

Now it so happens that this arbitrary alteration, by the parliamentary committee, without the consent of Congress, of the " standing orders " determining its constitution, re-

[1] See p. 49.

sulted in the domination of the " block vote " not only over the general policy of the trade union movement, but also, eventually, over that of the British Labour Party destined to become, from 1918 onwards, alternately His Majesty's Opposition and His Majesty's Government. Hence, I turn back the pages of my MS. diary to an entry, dated January 15, 1895, describing how this *coup d'état* came about.

Grosvenor Road, January 15th, 1895.—Meanwhile, there is an intrigue going on inside the P.C. which may affect the future of trade unionism, and which has already roused a storm in that little world. This much can be gathered from the newspapers. " Standing orders " have been issued to the trade unions which the parliamentary committee have declared shall govern the next Congress. Shortly stated, these orders amount to this: trades councils are to be excluded: the voting is to be on the plan of the Miners' Federation—the delegates of each trade, however few or numerous, are to have voting power according to the numerical strength of their society; one vote for every 1000 members; and, lastly, no man is to be a delegate who is not working at his trade, or serving as the *salaried* official of his union. Of course, this is a revolution in the constitution of Congress. These " orders " of the P.C. have been backed up by the *Daily Chronicle* and the *Factory Times,* denounced by the *Clarion* and the *Labour Leader.* So far as one can judge, they would mean that Congress would consist of a few salaried officials, each of whom would carry in his pocket the proxy of his whole trade.

It was on this question that Broadhurst came to consult us. He spent the first hour in giving us, with graphic but somewhat lengthy detail, the inner history of this *coup d'état.* How there had been a vague instruction by Congress to the parliamentary committee to consider all the resolutions with which Congress could not deal, how among these there appeared some minute alteration of " standing orders ", how Burns had got a sub-committee of five (himself, Woods, Mawdsley, Holmes and Jack) appointed to see what could be done, how at the November meeting of the P.C. these new " standing orders " were placed before the committee suddenly, without any notice, for their approval. So far Burns had had it all his own way. Broadhurst immediately rallied the other side and fought the question for three days. Six voted for, six against: Holmes gave his casting vote in favour of " revolution ". So far Burns had gained a hazardous victory; but relied on keeping back these " orders " until a month before Congress. Broadhurst waited till Burns and Holmes were gone to America, and having a majority at the P.C. insisted on circulating the " standing orders " to all trade unions. " I wanted to issue a circular explaining their full nature, but that little vain imp Tillett would not stick to me. But I have taken care to let it be widely known that these 'orders' would exclude from Congress not only myself, but Keir Hardie, Tom Mann and Hammill; and would practically exclude from any say, not only the trades councils, but all the small trades of the country. Now Mr. Webb, I have told you the tale, let me know your frank opinion as to the orders in themselves? "

Then we set to, and discussed the whole constitution of Congress. Broadhurst had evidently come, not only to get Sidney's advice, but to get him to draft alternative " standing orders " to be submitted to Congress. It is going to be a duel between Burns and Broadhurst. Burns has acted in a very unwise if not a mean way. Seeing he cannot control the present Congress, and cannot work the parliamentary committee, he has decided to reduce both to the smallest dimensions, or (as he would say) to save them from becoming the instruments of " Labour politicians " and " agitators ". Of course, there is a good deal to be said against the present constitution of Congress; and, on the face of it, one of the " orders " is a self-denying ordinance on Burns's part, since he would be technically excluded. But, as Sidney says, it was a curious fact that the " self-denying ordinance " known to history did not exclude Cromwell who proposed it. And so with Burns. He is not technically a T.U. official; but, since he already receives £100 from the A.S.E., a stroke of the pen would make him one; whilst there is not the slightest chance of Broadhurst, Mann, Keir Hardie or Hammill getting a salary from the unions. That being the case, Sidney virtually agreed to Broadhurst's request to draw up suggestions for his private use. . . .

One cannot help admiring also the shrewdness of his [Broadhurst's] attitude towards us. He has read our book with minute care—he has swallowed our very severe criticism of his conduct of the P.C. between 1880–9 with perfect good temper. The fact that our account discredits him, and elevates Burns, has not apparently affected his determination to make full use of us. He is lazy, not quick in drafting, with no intellectual skilfulness; he realises that without some middle-class help he can do nothing—so finding no one he can trust more than us he unreservedly places himself in our hands and so doing places us in a very delicate position.

For Burns, though unscrupulous, incurably suspicious, and rather mean in his methods, has some splendid moral and intellectual qualities. So long as he does not fear any diminution of his personal prestige, his judgement is very fine—far more warmth, insight and intelligence than Broadhurst. We do not wish to detract from his influence. On nearly all questions he is instinctively on the right side. He honestly tries to think out problems. But, for the last year, it has been apparent that on all questions bearing on the trade union movement his intelligence and conscience have been completely *paralyzed* by a dominant terror that some other Labour leader will eclipse him by means of it. It looks as if he were deliberately trying to diminish the political force of the trade unions as great corporations. Of course, it would be possible to hold that that was a good thing to do from the point of view of the common weal—that associations of producers ought not to concern themselves with general politics. But that is not our view, more especially not Sidney's, whose whole political policy has been to stimulate this activity. It looks as if we should have to choose between backing Burns and backing the trade union world. He will not in any way consult us, or explain his meaning; he is never open with us; in spite of our genuine desire to work with him both on London and Labour questions, he always shows an undercurrent of jealousy and suspicion. For all these reasons, it will be almost impossible for us to refuse Broadhurst's appeal to help him to carry out our views. The hurry-scurry of politics and Broadhurst's discretion may save us from coming directly across Burns, but it will be rather of the nature of egg-dancing if we succeed in preventing him mischief-making without incurring his anger. . . .

Suffolk, September 16th, 1896.—Last day of our stay in the Suffolk rectory. For the first three weeks I was seedy—mooned and dreamed my life away, chatting with our visitors, or sitting in the little study watching Sidney work on with our chapter on " Apprenticeship ", or straining after the party on my bicycle—feeling all the time somewhat miserable and woe-begone. The last four weeks we have worked well together, and have really got within sight of the end of our book and the completion of our theory. Now that we have finished the elaborate technical analysis of each set of regulations—our own theory of trade unionism is emerging. It is exciting, this clearing-up of one's thought after two years of patient plodding. And, as far as we can tell, the ideas we are evolving seem to be fruitful and likely to breed others. Out of our study of trade unionism we are developing a new view of democracy and, I think, quite an original set of economic and political hypotheses. For the first time since we began this book I am feeling intellectually keen and absorbed in my work. . . .

The Argoed, January 18th, 1897.— . . . The hill enveloped in cold mist. But it has been a splendid time for work: have written the best part of two chapters. Have worked both together and apart, Sidney reading through the thirty volumes we brought with us on abstract economics and writing, with occasional suggestions from me, the chapter on the " wage fund ", whilst I spent hours scheming the chapter giving our synthesis of the " higgling of the market ". Then he and I would write it out clearly, he criticising my ideas; sometimes we would get at cross purposes, but our cross purposes would always end in a shower of kisses. I doubt whether two persons could stand the stress and strain of this long drawn-out work, this joint struggle with ideas, a perpetual hammering at each other's minds, if it were not for the equally perpetual " honeymoon " of our life together. These three weeks, with the peaceful grey days and long evenings, the wanderings over the moorland and up and down dale, the cosy evenings by the log fire, he reading *Brand* and *Peer Gynt* to me, have been a delicious holy-day—a relief from the noise, bustle and news of London. And, as if to reward us for being so happy enshrouded in cold mist, the sun, the last three days, has come out gloriously shining in red splendour over the whitened landscape; followed at sunset by an equally glorious moon lighting up in an absolutely still air the long lines of highland, their night's shroud of white mist creeping stealthily up from the village. I am so well and blessedly happy. Again those morbid troublings of last autumn seem to me amazing!

Looking back on the year, I am satisfied with our work. We are nearly through with our book, three months more grind of our little minds, and we shall have turned out all that they can yield on this subject. Of course, the worth of our work will be only temporary; all our hypotheses will be either truisms or fallacies in a generation's time. Still, I think, we shall have left a solid substratum of fact for others to reason on. Our descriptive analysis of special facts is, I believe, the best part of our work and likely to be most permanent. . . .

Dorking, May 1st, 1897.—I have been especially vigorous, completely absorbed in thinking out the last chapter of our book. To me the unravelling of a consistent theory of industrial regulation (in the chapter on " Economic Characteristics of Trade Unionism ") has been extremely exciting. Now that we have found our theory, every previous part of our analysis seems to fit in perfectly, and facts, which before puzzled us, range themselves in their places as if " by nature ". We alternate between thinking that the work will be as great, in its effect on political and economic thought, as Adam Smith's *Wealth of Nations,* to wondering whether the whole of it is not an elaborate figment of our imagination. Anyway, the elaborate analysis of the facts contained in the second part of the work, an analysis which we made by pondering over the facts and trying to get an exhaustive description of what actually exists, must be useful; for it was not until the whole diagnosis was complete that we began to see clearly the principles which seemed to spring from it. The companionship over the book in these latter parts has been delightful; the constant testing of the thought by the two minds, the act of *combined thinking* in which the experience and the hypotheses of the two intellects becomes inextricably mingled, so that we are both unconscious of what we have each of us contributed, has been extraordinarily stimulating. But I doubt whether the English reading public will understand or be impressed; if there is to be a *succès d'estime*, that appreciation will come from Germany.[1] The background of our lives—the pleasant friendships, the beautiful spring, with all its sweet sounds, sights and scents, and the pretty house and garden, the long hours of leisure—is luxurious almost to a fault. One broods at times over the question whether our work is worth all the happiness and well-being we are extracting from the life of the community, and at times one feels uneasy lest we are taking more than our share. Happily, the supreme luxury of love and close comradeship does not abstract from other people's chances of enjoyment. Our life at present is like the early summer, growth and delight in growing, love and the delight in loving. We are getting middle-aged, and yet we feel young in our intellectual life, always on the threshold of new discovery, and almost childish in our revelling in each other's adoration and tenderness. How full and brimming over with happiness human life can be. How could this happiness become universal or nearly universal—that is the problem. . . .

The Argoed, August 27th, 1897.—The first fortnight or three weeks Sidney and I struggled painfully with re-writing the " Economic Characteristics "—the stiffest chapter in the whole work—both of us feeling that we had " bitten off more than we could chew " in our *Theory of Trade Unionism.* At last we got into such a hopeless state of continuous argument that it was clear that we were wasting energy. So he agreed to go on by himself, whilst I should begin to plan out the last chapter. So he is grappling with it alone, I think, successfully. He is stronger-brained than I am, and can carry more things in his mind at once; I was getting hopelessly befogged with utter weariness. We are working really too hard to enjoy it: we are bent on getting the book done with and out with autumn; and this last chapter has proved far more complicated than we thought. The weather is one continual south-west rain storm which adds a touch of gloom to our overstrain. Bernard Shaw, too, is working continuously revising his plays. . . . We are a very middle-aged party this autumn—inclined to drudge at our work. For all that, Sidney and I are peacefully happy.

[1] Through the accident of a compositors' strike in the autumn of 1897, *Industrial Democracy* appeared in German a month before it was published in English.

Now that I feel the crucial chapter is really getting on, I can sit and calmly think out the last chapter and the preface. . . .

The Argoed, Sept. 10*th,* 1897.—The last day at the Argoed! Turned out to make room for a tenant and transplanting ourselves " over the way " to " Moorcroft " for the remainder of the vacation. Spent another ten days hammering away together at the " Economic Characteristics ". Sidney got over the kink, but his stuff was rough hewn and had to be polished up. Now, at last, we are sending the last instalment of the chapter to the printer. It has been by far the hardest bit of reasoning that I have ever attempted and it remains to be seen how much of it stands against hostile criticism. What will be said is that we have seized on certain characteristics of the " common rule " and magnified them out of all proportion to others that we have not even so much as mentioned. That is to some extent true. Our chapter is really " *an analysis of certain characteristics of the common rule* ". But then these are exactly the characteristics which have been hitherto completely overlooked and, therefore, want to be given all the prominence of isolated treatment. Other investigators will come along and set our little discoveries (if discoveries they prove to be) in their proper place. . . .

Grosvenor Road, December 10*th,* 1897.— . . . Also, the engineers' lock-out—Sidney constantly drafting letters and conditions, I sometimes egging him on. A wretched business! It is only those who know the rotten constitution of the A.S.E., and their guerilla policy, who realise the badness of the whole business, the hold that employers have over the public opinion of all classes in the general dislike of the A.S.E. This morning we drafted letters to the *Daily Chronicle* and the *Manchester Guardian*, and wrote private letters to the leading officials of the great unions begging them to take the matter up on the ground that collective bargaining is attacked. We may be on the eve of a big convulsion—a Conservative Government is always favourable to the growth of revolutionary feelings—and for the last five years working-class opinion has been lying dormant. Meanwhile, our portentous book is still in the press, will appear on January 4th. We must prepare ourselves for disappointment, or rather we must try not to think of success or failure, simply feel that we have done our level best and there it is—to be taken or left. Anyway, we have learnt enormously from our six years' investigation, and the life has been a happy one— full of love and interest. What more can we ask for? . . .

Grosvenor Road, December 14*th,* 1897.—Asquith called here this morning and spent half-an-hour discussing the engineering dispute. He has for the last few years been cold to the Labour movement, and unfriendly to us, so his anxiety to be informed was an interesting sign of the times. He is a shrewd able lawyer: coarse-grained and unimaginative, but sensitive like all politicians to the changes in the political atmosphere. Sidney explained the engineers' contention and also their weakness, and coached him up on the technical side of the question; gave him our chapter on the "Standard Rate". We did our best: we shall see whether it bears fruit in his speech at Stockport. . . .

A month later I give the outcome of the engineers' lock-out:

Grosvenor Road, January 1898.—Sidney and I have spent much thought and time on the engineers' dispute, but all to no purpose. No sooner had we worked up public opinion against the original terms of the employers than the officials of the A.S.E. gave us all completely away by offering to accept practically the same terms if the employers gave 51 hours. The employers, of course, refuse the 51 hours, but point triumphantly to the men's proposal whenever it is suggested that these terms are inconsistent with the continuance of trade unionism. It is of no avail that the members reject these terms by overwhelming majority: public opinion, only too glad to escape from censuring capitalists, backs up the employers' logic. After the event Barnes comes and consults us—but it is useless advising when advice is not understood. This set of officials are hopelessly incompetent—feather-headed I.L.P. or obscurant old-fashioned unionists of the Allan type [1]—a type all right in its day but now bygone in usefulness. So the weary business drags on, and all friends stand aloof feeling that it is useless to move in any direction since the officials of the A.S.E. may drift in the other. The employers have, as regards immediate victory, played their cards with remarkable astuteness. But they are over-reaching themselves. Their victory, even if they attain their end of making the union agree as a corporation to their terms, will be a mere paper victory. It is childish to expect good results from a consent wrung from thousands of men by threats of absolute starvation. The best they can look for is that, under the stress and strain, the A.S.E. will go to pieces—discontented classes and districts breaking away and repudiating the society, its agreements and its debts. But that will be no advantage. Instead of one union to deal with, they will have a dozen irresponsible, semi-secret bodies fighting in guerilla wherever and whenever they get a chance. And they forget the polling booth! . . .

---

[1] William Allan, General Secretary of the A.S.E., 1851–74; typical of the "Old Unionist" official. An administrator of friendly benefits rather than a militant trade unionist. Consequently uninfluential in trade union politics. See Biographical Index and *History of Trade Unionism*, by S. and B. Webb, p. 458. (Ed.)

Here is the final entry, recording our partnership in the study of British Trade Unionism: the reader will forgive its naïve self-complacency.

Grosvenor Road, January 11*th,* 1898.—Our big book has had a brilliant reception. The *Times* gave us two columns on the day of publication; the *Standard* an abusive leader; the *Daily Chronicle,* the *Daily News,* and half-a-dozen big provincials were all properly enthusiastic. Other papers followed suit and produced their reviews the next day: the weeklies treated us quite handsomely. Altogether a small triumph in its way. The scientific character of the work is recognised, though of course the critics chaff us for our " pompous phraseology ". It is a big plant on the public: a new method and a new theory!

CHAPTER II

MUNICIPAL AND UNIVERSITY
ADMINISTRATION
1892–1898

At this point in the narrative I turn aside from the narrow track of social investigation, which we pursued together, the direction determined by ourselves, to the broad and crowded highway of municipal administration. If the foregoing chapter recalls the habitual morning's work from 1892 to 1898, the following pages account for the Other One's afternoons. And here I fall from the status of equal partnership to that of a humble servitor of my lord, with the added zest of being an observer and recorder of his doings. But alas! this essay in biography will not be accepted as impartial so I give the portrait by the well-known editor of the *Pall Mall Gazette* of Sidney Webb as he first appeared at the L.C.C. election of 1892 before the footlights of municipal democracy.

Mr. Sidney Webb is a very remarkable man, much more remarkable than anybody thinks, excepting himself. Since Mr. Chamberlain arose in Birmingham there has been no man so like him as Mr. Sidney Webb, who aspires to be Mr. Chamberlain of London—only more so.[1] For to all the energy and perseverance and municipal spirit of Mr. Chamberlain, Mr. Sidney Webb adds a great literary gift and a philosophic conception of social progress to which Mr. Chamberlain can lay no claim. He is a socialist; but he is no utopian dreamer, he is a man crammed with facts. He is no fanatic, but a wily, shrewd,

---

[1] *The Elector's Guide*, p. 50. Edited by W. T. Stead. Beyond the fact that S. W. endorsed and developed Chamberlain's doctrine of " high rates and a healthy city ", I see no likeness in character, opinion or circumstances, of the social investigator and Fabian permeator to the outstanding politician, orator and imperialist statesman of the last quarter of the nineteenth century. There is, however, a superficial coincidence in political career. Alike, they entered the Cabinet for the first time without previous subordinate office, as President of the Board of Trade, and alike they retired from the Cabinet, when Secretary of State for the Colonies; the significant distinction being that S. W. entered the Cabinet at about the same age at which Joseph Chamberlain retired from it, when the great man became the propagandist of a new fiscal policy.

adroit wirepuller, whose hand is felt in a great many quarters where it is not seen. The next three years will be a test as to whether he is as capable in taking part in a public body as he has shown himself to be in writing pamphlets, inspiring editors, and in general wire-pulling. . . . At present there is some doubt as to whether he is not the most dangerous candidate in the field for the cause which he has at heart. His contributions to the Fabian Society and the *Star* newspaper, and his interesting book on *The London Programme*, are so many red rags to the Conservative bull; and there is no doubt that if Mr. Sidney Webb's programme could be fathered upon every progressive candidate in the constituencies, the moderates would sweep London. Mr. Webb is not a candidate for to-day, he is one for the day after to-morrow. But, for that very reason, it is urgently to be desired that he should be elected to the County Council without more ado. There is nothing like putting such a man in harness to take the nonsense out of him, and to make him understand the wisdom of the old adage, *festina lente*. . . .

THE LONDON COUNTY COUNCIL

The establishment of an elected governing body for the metropolis in the guise of a county council was incidental to the scheme of reform of county government throughout England and Wales, which the President of the Local Government Board (Ritchie) passed into law as the Local Government Act of 1888. For the administration of the justices of the peace in quarter sessions, there was substituted administration by a directly elected county council. In the metropolis, comprising, besides the ancient corporation of the City of London, parts of the counties of Middlesex, Surrey, Essex and Kent, the indirectly elected Metropolitan Board of Works, representing the congeries of vestries and district boards throughout London, had been established thirty years earlier (1855).[1] In 1888, Mr.

---

[1] The establishment in 1855 of the Metropolitan Board of Works by Sir Benjamin Hall (Chief Commissioner of Works in the then Whig Ministry) may be ascribed to the pressing necessity for a new Main Drainage authority to prevent the Thames becoming a common sewer, a task in which the Metropolitan Commissioners of Sewers, appointed by the Government in 1848, had lamentably failed. The new Board was, on the whole, an efficient body, largely directed by a salaried chairman (Sir J. McGarel Hogg) who was imposed on it by the Government. Besides a successful main drainage scheme which took nearly twenty years to complete the Board has to its credit, during its thirty years' life, the construction of the Thames Embankment; the systematic administration of the London Building Act which had

Ritchie saw no practicable alternative to the definite excision of these parts of four counties from the remainder of their areas, and the transformation of the indirectly elected Metropolitan Board of Works into a directly elected county council, corresponding to those which elsewhere superseded the justices in quarter sessions. This transformation, revolutionary as it seemed to the Conservative Party, was the more readily accepted because the Metropolitan Board of Works had recently been besmirched and discredited by the exposure of certain exceptional cases of graft in which one or two of its members, in collusion with one or two of its principal officials, had been implicated. This exposure led to a revulsion of feeling, which co-operated with the desire to give London a municipal government worthy of its pre-eminence, induced a number of distinguished men of philanthropy and goodwill to come forward as candidates for the new body. So outstanding a personality as Lord Rosebery agreed to stand for the City, with a view to assuming the chairmanship.

The first election, in January 1889, was, from the standpoint of the experienced politician, an unorganised scramble. Neither the Liberal nor the Conservative Party used the party electoral machinery. Candidates spontaneously offered themselves to the electors, mainly as advocates of " good government ".[1] There were no deliberately formulated party

been passed in 1855; the organisation of the Metropolitan Fire Brigade after 1866; the clearance of large areas of the worst slums, various great street improvements, and many minor services. In its last years, the Board's record was stained by the cases of graft mentioned above, which were investigated by a Royal Commission. It is only fair to say that these were shown to have been quite exceptional, and that most of the Board's administration was not only honest but also fairly well organised.

[1] Elizabeth Haldane in *From One Century to Another*, 1937, describes the rise of the Progressive Party in London administration: " The development of the social services was seen in the new London County Council, with its rather advanced programme. There were at least a majority of 'Progressives ' and John Burns advocated what he called ' Practicable Socialism ' which made a good cry, so that socialism thus became something less to be feared than it had been so far. Sidney Webb was its principal supporter and he gave it a certain intellectual flavour; though his programme was advanced enough. Sidney and Beatrice Webb became our friends, and visited us at Cloan. There was always great discussion as to which was the abler, but no conclusions were arrived at, for both were extraordinarily able and yet more extraordinarily diligent. They made one feel heartily ashamed of one's idle hours when one saw how they worked from morning to night, producing volumes of carefully verified matter. They had great influence on politics on both

programmes among which the voters could choose. Almost the only lead as to policy was given by what was then an obscure body of young men and women, the Fabian Society,[1] which, by what was then an original device, caused all the candidates to be importuned by showers of printed lists of questions, sent by electors demanding answers to every issue of what ought to be " municipal politics ". These were accompanied by pamphlets explaining in detail the policy afterwards known as municipal Socialism. In the absence of any contrary policy, a large proportion of the candidates, who had thought only of " good government ", found themselves subscribing to this programme.

The first three years' term of the London County Council was chiefly occupied in framing the elaborate constitution required for so great an administration, and with tentative efforts towards increased efficiency and avoidance of waste. When the second election approached (that of 1892 at which the Other One became a candidate for a seat held by a Conservative), party organisation on both sides became definite and powerful. The Conservative Party saw the importance of controlling so influential a local authority as the London County Council had become. Opposing the Conservatives were those councillors who called themselves the Progressives, with a view to uniting for municipal purposes, along with the Liberals (largely Nonconformists), also the Conservative and Liberal Unionist sympathisers with an active policy in London administration; the churchmen and Roman Catholic philanthropists who wanted the slums and the mean streets reformed; and the trade unionist workmen who sought to insist on fairer conditions of employ-

sides because they saw nearly as much of Balfour, the Bishop of London and the Conservatives as they did of Liberals like my brother, though there were indeed those like Asquith who turned a deaf ear to their theories " (pp. 135-6).

[1] The Fabian Society, the oldest living Socialist society in this or any country, was founded in 1884. Bernard Shaw and Sidney Webb both joined it in the first year of its existence, and Webb was a member of its Executive Committee for fifty years, from 1885 to 1935. Beatrice became a member of the Fabian Society shortly after her marriage. In the 1945 election, over 200 of the 394 Labour members returned to Parliament were Fabians. (Ed.)

ment. This heterogeneous host was marshalled by a professedly non-political body (the London Reform Union), and was supplied with a programme—the Other One says by the Fabian Society—a programme which, somehow or other, found its way into six months' issues of *The Speaker*, then the weekly organ of intellectual Liberalism.[1]

It is difficult to bring home to the perplexed, pessimistic and jaded mind of post-war England the mental climate of the London Progressive movement of the 'nineties. Honest indignation at the mass misery of the working-class quarters of London, ardent hopefulness of what might be, and assured confidence in the way of betterment—this union of pity, hope and faith underlies *The London Programme* of 1892.

First the rousing of the sense of shame in the better-off citizens of London:

Twenty thousand of its citizens fight in the fearful daily struggle for bread at the dock gates, and even after the Pyrrhic victory of the great dock strike of 1889, one-third of them, on an average, struggle in vain. Thirty thousand of its children are at school entirely breakfastless. One in every five of the five millions who began again to-day the weary round of life will eventually quit that life in the workhouse or the hospital, for want of a better refuge. One in ten of them had to accept the bitter bread of official pauper charity last year. And all this in the richest and most productive city in the world, paying an annual tribute, or ground rent, of fifteen millions sterling for mere permission to occupy the low hills and swampy marsh by the Thames, which labour alone has rendered productive! . . . The million households, immersed in constant toil, and for the most part pinched by sordid cares, have long had no common standard, no conscious common action. Without effective municipal or political organisation, without unity of taxation or representation, a mere loose aggregate of shifting sand, this great community has lain almost helpless in its anarchy before the forces of spoliation. . . . We dare not neglect the sullen discontent now spreading among its toiling millions. If only for the sake of the rest of the Empire, the London masses must be organised

[1] These articles were afterwards published in book form (*The London Programme*, by Sidney Webb, 1892). They had been preceded by the Fabian Society's *Facts for Londoners* (56 pp., 1889), described as " an exhaustive collection of statistical and other facts relative to the metropolis, with suggestions for reform on socialist principles ".

for a campaign against the speculators, vestry jobbers, house farmers, water sharks, market monopolists, ground landlords, and other social parasites now feeding upon their helplessness. Metropolitan reform has become a national, if not an imperial question.[1]

By himself [pleads the author of *The London Programme*] the typical Londoner is a frail and sickly unit, cradled in the gutter, housed in a slum, slaving in a sweater's den, and dying in the work-house infirmary. Collectively he is a member of the greatest and most magnificent city which the world has known, commanding all the latest resources of civilisation, and disposing of almost boundless wealth. Accepting the principle of municipal co-operation, which has proved so advantageous in the larger provincial towns, what can Londoners as citizens do for themselves collectively to make the metropolis a pleasanter home for its million families?[2]

The London County Council was, to quote from *The London Programme*, " born in chains ". The powers with which it had been endowed did not approximate to those of a provincial county borough:

It had nothing to do with paving, cleansing or lighting the streets; waterworks, gasworks, markets, and tramways were completely out-side its province; its police formed an army as alien as the Irish con-stabulary; it was functionless and almost powerless in valuation and assessment; it did not collect its own rates; it had no more control over the Thames than over the tides; it was neither the sanitary nor the burial authority; and it could not even prepare or supervise the registration of the voters who elected it. It was, in fact, simply a cross between the county justices and the Metropolitan Board of Works, and its chief occupations were a strange hotch-potch of lunatic asylums and the fire brigade, main drainage and industrial schools, bridges and baby-farms.[3]

The embittered conflict at each election between Pro-gressives and Moderates, usually backed up by the Liberals and Conservatives respectively, raged round the question of increasing the authority of the L.C.C., on the one hand, and, on the other, checking, if not superseding, its powers by establishing minor municipal bodies similar to the non-county boroughs scattered about the English counties. For it must be noted that *The London Programme* of 1892 did

[1] *The London Programme*, by Sidney Webb, p. 7 (1891).
[2] *Ibid.* p. 207.   [3] *Ibid.* p. 10.

not stop at improvements in the machinery of government. The London County Council of the future was to make energetic use of its existing and future powers. According to the programme that was suggested, it was to become like the Manchester or Birmingham County Borough Council, the water authority, the gas authority, the tramway authority, the market authority, the housing authority, the dock authority and the hospital authority, and, most preposterous of all—the police authority, for the metropolitan area. As I shall describe in another chapter, one at least of the Progressives desired and intended, already in 1892, to unify London education and, for this purpose, to make the L.C.C. also the education authority for London, in supersession of the directly elected London School Board, which was confined to elementary education.

New sources of revenue were to be secured by the equalisation of rates between rich and poor districts, by the taxation of ground rents and by a municipal death duty. Above all, the unearned increment, due to the mere growth of the population or to public improvements, was to be partially absorbed by the community, either through betterment rates, or by the County Council having the power of compulsory purchase of land on the basis of a special valuation as a source of revenue. To quote Joseph Chamberlain, the London County Council of those days was a volatile body " whose ambition soars far above those details of local government upon which the health and happiness of the people mainly depend ".[1]

Glimpses of the L.C.C. at work and of the reaction set up by the doings and doctrines of the Progressives, at the polls and in the press—extending even to the august circles of the Cabinet and ex-Cabinet—appear in the MS. diaries 1892–98, and may interest the student of municipal institutions.

The Argoed, July 30th, 1893.—The London County Council looms large in our lives because it takes up so much of Sidney's energies. Every day he comes home he tells me about his various

[1] *The Speaker,* February 9, 1895.

committees and gives me glimpses of the internal working of the machine. Let me see whether I can sum up some of the impressions he leaves on my mind. First, the L.C.C. consists of the Progressive portion of it. The Moderates, as a party, are simply out of it. Individual Moderates become chairmen of committees, but only because in those particular departments they are more progressive than the Progressives. Indeed, the conversion of the abler Moderates to definite portions of the Progressive programme is one of the notable features of the County Council, and a token of the triumph of the idea of public administration as against private enterprise. That is, of course, the whole significance of the L.C.C.—the growing faith in and enthusiasm for public service. It is not that the L.C.C. does so much more than its predecessor the Metropolitan Board of Works, but that it does all its work efficiently and with zeal, and with a view to increasing and not diminishing its functions. There is no one man at the L.C.C. who dominates the organisation. I imagine in the last Council Lord Rosebery took a pre-eminent part. But, though Lord Rosebery continues a member, he seldom attends; and his swooping down on the Council, with regard to a proposed site the other day, was much resented. The Council is really run by various groups of county councillors, circling round the three office-holders—who are all county councillors—the chairman, vice-chairman and deputy-chairman of the Council. The most prominent of these groups is the one directing the parliamentary and political policy of the County Council—among whom are B. F. C. Costelloe, Sidney and J. W. [afterwards Sir John Williams] Benn. Then come the chairmen of the non-political committees—such as housing, parks, asylums, etc., all of whom are in touch with the chairman of the Council. John Burns occupies a quite unique position, owing, not to his committee work, but to his powerful personality and Labour following outside the Council. His influence, moreover, is diminishing since he has become an M.P.

It is, perhaps, a sign that the County Council is still young that the whole direction of its administration is in the hands of the councillors and not relegated to the paid servants. There are twenty or thirty men who make a profession of the Council, in the sense of spending their whole energies on its work. This, of course, means that the L.C.C. is a middle-class body; composed of men of sufficient means to work for nothing. And, even those working-men who are on it, contribute little to its government; they speak in the weekly meetings of the Council, but they take little or no part in committees.

The weekly Council meetings are, perhaps, the least important part of the Council's proceedings. The aim of the able chairman of a committee is to pass his reports through Tuesday's meeting without raising contentious questions. It is only the badly-managed committees that get their activities talked about and their policies discussed. The Council is a machine for evolving a committee; the committee is a machine for evolving one man—the chairman. Both alike a machine for dodging the democracy (in a crude sense) by introducing government by a select minority instead of the rule of the majority. . . .

Grosvenor Road, June 20th, 1894.—Haldane just been here: says the Unionist Party will make a determined attack on the L.C.C. and attempt to break London up into separate municipalities. That this has been in the mind of Chamberlain, Balfour and Salisbury is clear from their recent utterances. But Sidney says that it is an impossibility; you could not divest the L.C.C. of the great bulk of its powers though, of course, it would be possible to change its constitution and reinstate the Metropolitan Board of Works. But that would be too much to propose. Meanwhile, it is of the utmost importance to carry the vestries. I must see whether I can get the London Reform Union to take the matter up. Cannot help thinking that Chamberlain is leading his party very wrong and that he will knock his head against a blank wall both on the London question and on that of the trade unions. It looks like sheer political idiocy to throw the trade unions and the London Progressives into the arms of the Liberals—but, I suppose, he thinks he sees his game! Personally, one would regret being forced into the fight—as we shall both be if the attack is serious. It is so much pleasanter to investigate and write rather than organise and speak. Just now our life is so perfect; it might easily become strained, and dissipated in mere manipulation. But one thing is clear: we must live the plainest, most healthful life in order to get through the maximum of work; and one must economise on all personal luxuries in order to have cash to spend on anything that turns up to be done. With so much love and personal happiness, one ought to be able to do much for others.

The malignant desire of the Conservative Party of 1894 to destroy the County Council that its own Ministry of 1888 had set up, in order to break up the great metropolitan area into an unspecified number of independent municipalities, seems to have provoked us to widen our sphere of electioneering activity. For the triennial election of the London School Board in 1894, the Fabian Society threw itself into the " Fight against Diggleism ",[1] which our close friend,

[1] See p. 67. (Ed.)

Graham Wallas, was successfully organising, and which the Other One helped by various journalist activities. Our own main attention was given to the most neglected part of the electoral field, that of the five or six thousand members of the hundred or so vestries,[1] whose triennial term of office expired shortly after that of the members of the School Board. The vestry election campaign throughout London was taken in hand, not very efficiently, by the London Reform Union, the body formed primarily to look after the Progressive Party's electioneering for the County Council. We ourselves could do little more than lead the forlorn hope in our own Tory Westminster (at that time the united parishes of St. Margaret and St. John), where we both offered ourselves as candidates.

Borough Farm, Surrey, July 25th, 1894.— . . . We have the organisation of the vestry elections on our hands—I having instigated the London Reform Union to take it up, having got Sidney appointed as chairman of the sub-committee, feel that we must pull the fight through successfully. Also, started a " Citizen Sunday " for next October in the hope of drawing in the clergy of all denominations into London reform.[2] But all this casual work means taking time from our book, and I am glad to be down here to concentrate on this very tough bit of analysis. If we get on to the Westminster Vestry, that will take up even more time, and Heaven only knows when we shall

---

[1] It is hard to convey to the present generation the confusion and obscurity of the local administration of the several parishes of London outside the one square mile of the City Corporation during the whole of the nineteenth century. The ratepayers of the twenty-five large parishes elected vestries of 24 to 120 members, who administered (without any other supervision or control than, after 1871, that of the very perfunctory Local Government Board) the paving, lighting, cleansing and draining of the streets; all that existed of the sanitation of the dwellings and the removal of refuse, and many miscellaneous services. They had authority to levy an unlimited rate on the householders. Nearly a hundred smaller parishes were grouped in 1855 under fourteen district boards, of from 27 to 84 members, which were nominated triennially by the elected vestries of the constituent tiny parishes. When the London County Council was established in 1888, these vestries and district boards were spending nearly £2,000,000 annually.

[2] " Citizen Sunday ", a chosen day on which all churches and chapels are invited to unite in prayer for social reform, and to devote a sermon to some aspect of the citizen's duty, has since [1936] continued annually. It was at first sponsored by the Christian Social Union, which became the Industrial Christian Fellowship. A circular appeal, signed by about a hundred leading citizens, including, besides ministers of all denominations, prominent trade unionists, employers of labour and politicians, is addressed annually to all places of worship.

get the book to the printer: at present the thought of it undone and not visibly growing oppresses me much.

Grosvenor Road, December 1st, 1894.—Galton's little study turned into the central office of the Progressive candidates for the Westminster vestry elections. Certainly, we have created our organisation and selected our 90 candidates with singularly little trouble. The first stage was to create a branch of the London Reform Union—Sidney, chairman, Galton secretary; the second to call, in the name of the L.R.U. branch, a conference of all the temperance, trade union and political organisations and to form a Progressive council—Sidney chairman, Galton secretary; the final step to select our candidates and to form these into one organisation: Sidney chairman, Galton secretary. These three organisations, under their respective chairmen and secretaries, have worked with wonderful harmony; and have between them, at a cost of £30, initiated a really vigorous campaign. The Westminster Radicals, a poor down-trodden lot, perpetually licked at all elections, hardly know themselves with their 90 candidates. Sidney has drafted the address, Galton is acting as election agent, and the working-men candidates are doing the canvassing and even the clerk's work. If by some marvellous chance we get returned to-day fortnight, we shall have our work cut out to drill them into working shape.

Altogether we have been living in the atmosphere of elections. Graham's candidature for the School Board gave us a personal interest in the fight. Of course, the result of the School Board elections is most satisfactory, from the point of view of the Progressives generally, and most exasperating for the Progressive Party on the School Board. Graham Wallas is making friends with the " left wing " of the enemy in the hope of detaching the majority of them from the educational policy of Diggle, and turning the scale.[1] It is very curious, that both Sidney and Graham, though very advanced in their views, are better liked by the Moderates of the L.C.C. and L.S.B. than other members of the Progressive Party. " Wily Webb ", as Sidney is called on the L.C.C., is always colloguing with the more sensible of the Moderates with a view of getting them to agree to things *in detail* which they could hardly accept in bulk. That seems also to be Graham's policy which he is carefully beginning on the London School Board. The truth is that *we want the things done* and we don't much care what

[1] The School Board election in November 1894 resulted in the virtual defeat of the policy so long pursued by the Rev. J. R. Diggle, the leader of the Church party. But his opponent, the Hon. Lyulph Stanley (later Lord Stanley of Alderley), failed to secure a " Progressive " majority, though Graham Wallas came in with a notable reinforcement. This produced an almost evenly divided Board, in which a few enlightened and well-disposed churchmen often voted with the Progressives; a situation giving scope for skilful compromises!

persons or which party gets the credit; we are pretty confident that, if it comes to a fight, we know the arts of war as well as our enemies; but, between the battles, our cause may be advanced by diplomacy—even by a frank alliance with our former enemies if they be willing to take one little step forward in our direction. The Fabians are still convinced believers in the policy of permeation.

Meanwhile, the book hangs fire. With both Sidney and Galton completely absorbed, I feel helpless. Moreover, as a candidate myself for the vestry, I have caught a little of the election fever and am growing rapidly excited and perturbed. The L.C.C. elections, upon which so much depends, are looming in the distance. It might be better to give myself up frankly to electioneering and use these weeks as an opportunity for observing how elections are fought and won. It is all part of our subject-matter—democracy. Surely we shall end by constructing the great " Webb " chart of the modern democratic state?

December 1894.—Crushing defeat at Westminster vestry elections; only 5 Progressives out of 96! We had persuaded ourselves that we should at least carry St. John's II. solid, and make some show in St. John's I. and III.—the St. Margaret's Ward we recognised as hopeless. But, apparently, the slums of Westminster are as completely Tory as the palaces. I do not think there has been any lack of energy or even of skill in engineering such forces as we had. But it is obvious that our attempt to collar the constituency with three weeks' work—mostly amateur—was a fiasco, which we ought to have expected. Against us we had a perfect organisation with a permanent staff, a local paper and unlimited money, we had all the wealthy residents, nearly all the employers of labour, and the whole liquor interest—no fewer than ten publicans and five other persons connected with the Trade, running as Conservative candidates. We had a register from which every known Liberal had been knocked off, year by year, without a protest from the feeble flickering little Liberal Association. Behind all this, we had Burdett-Coutts's charities and churches. And to fight these potent powers Galton stood single-handed with a mob of working-men and small tradesmen candidates—some of them good talkers, but like most Labour men full of gassy optimism, caring only to fore-gather in the rooms of the Liberal Association and talk big of the victory they are going to win. Our one strong card was the corruption of the last vestry—" squalid jobbery amounting to corruption ". But the Conservatives very rightly preferred a little " jobbery "—infinitesimal burden on the rates—to a possible defeat of their party in one of its fastnesses. Deeply-rooted distrust of entrusting business to a lot of " small folk " of no standing operated, too, against our candidates; working-men—other things being equal—prefer an employer to a fellow-worker as a candidate; other things were in this case unequal—to our disadvantage.

Add to these causes the perfectly legitimate grudge the Westminster ratepayers have against the Progressives for the 6d. extra imposed by the Rate Equalisation Bill.

All that I have heard of vestrydom in this election and its doings, discourages me from hoping much from the new state of things. In London, there is no public opinion and no public knowledge about the government of these small areas. The L.C.C. has to submit itself to full publicity, its every action is scanned by a hostile press, its proceedings are witnessed by the whole metropolitan community. But in a vestry area there is no public supervision; you may live in a district 50 years and hardly know of the existence of your vestry—the ordinary working-man or professional man would not know any one of the vestrymen by name, will hardly know when and at what time they hold their meetings, still less what is the weekly or yearly record of work. It is only within three weeks of the election that we discovered that there had been an appalling amount of corruption and jobbery. The whole government is left practically in the hands of small tradesmen and one or two political wire-pullers largely interspersed with publicans and builders. Here the worst form of local feeling manifests itself—a local feeling which is in itself incipient jobbery. If there is a sanitary inspector to be appointed, a local man is most likely to be chosen quite irrespective of his qualifications. Of course, it does not stop at this comparatively innocent precept of " Westminster work for Westminster men " (to my mind a most rotten maxim), it soon degenerates into preference for a friend or relation of a popular vestryman. And, against this, the citizen has no chance of redress for the simple reason that he never knows what is going on. Probably the best governed London parishes are the purely aristocratic vestries—where the retired Indian civil servant, the officer, the rector, the medical man, rule undisputed. You cannot trust a democracy without any provision for *full and effective publicity*. That was why one felt half-hearted as to the results of this election. The little tradesmen or working-men whom we were supporting were no better than their Tory fellows. If they had got elected without a strong leader they would have sunk to the same level of mean local feeling and petty jobbery. Is it possible to create civic patriotism in a small *metropolitan* area, with no common life and no local press read, as a matter of course, by all classes of the community? I fear not—at least not in our day.

Grosvenor Road, February 10*th*, 1895.—Three weeks off the L.C.C. elections. Sidney spending all his mornings writing articles for all sorts of papers—especially the religious organs, such as the *Guardian*, the *Church Times*, the *Christian World*, the *Methodist Times*, etc. We are, in fact, making a vigorous attempt to get the Church, the Catholic and the Nonconformist ministers on our side. As all the " sinners " are against us, we might as well get the saints to support us. Moreover, we resolutely refuse to believe that any good person *properly informed* could be otherwise than a Progressive! If we are beaten—*i.e.* if a Moderate majority is returned—it will not be for lack of organisation. We are better *organised* than our opponents— if they win it will show that the common opinion is against us. . . .

Grosvenor Road, March 5th, 1895.—An anti-climax! After all the heat on both sides, after the blowing of both the big party trumpets, the calling to arms of saints and sinners by their respective champions, the rousing, on the one hand, of all the threatened interests, the appeal, on the other hand, to the forces of piety and democracy, London citizens send back an exactly even number of Moderates and Progressives—a bare half of registered electors taking the trouble to vote. In so many words, our constituents laugh in their sleeves, and say " tweedledee, tweedledum ". As far as Sidney personally is concerned, it is " as in 1892 ", his poll becoming fractionally higher, his majority fractionally lower. In a Conservative constituency, he retains a Progressive majority of eighteen hundred votes.

The loss of the second seat, too, means practically no change since it is fully accounted for by Keylock's stupidity and Elliott's [Social Democratic Federation candidate] superior poll.[1] In Deptford at least the mind of the electors is apparently unchanged. But, though this is most satisfactory, yet we do not disguise from ourselves that there is nothing like the enthusiasm of 1892. The same proportion of the electors went to the polling booth and voted for Sidney—largely because we insisted on it. . . .

Grosvenor Road, March 1895.—Sidney low about the L.C.C.— brooding over the defeat. It is not unnatural now that we should hear rumours of the magnificent organisation of our opponents—of £30,000 collected for the election, of an electoral council composed of delegates from the central Conservative Association and the Municipal Society, and the Moderate Party sitting daily receiving reports from constituencies; of swarms of convassers, of, in fact, a perfect electioneering kit for each candidate. There may be some basis for these reports—

---

[1] H. Keylock and J. Elliott split between them the Progressive vote and let in the Moderate candidate. H. Keylock represented Deptford on the L.C.C., 1892–95; he was said to be strong in support of municipal services, but timid in facing any consequent rise in the rates. (Ed.)

but, if all this happened, then why did not the Moderates poll a higher vote? No, there is no accounting for the defeat except the falling away of our supporters—in some cases, their transference to the other side, but usually their abstention. From reports, the explanation seems to be largely the lack of employment during a time of fearful cold—with the indifference and even savage hostility to all existing institutions which this state breeds. " Everybody is either out of work or only half employed and, consequently, out of sorts with everybody else, and some think if they could have a change of any sort, it must be an improvement." These words I read yesterday by chance in a report from a London branch of a great trade union; acting on this soreness—this feeling of quite unmerited misery—we have the I.L.P. abuse of the Progressives, and the cunning appeals of the Moderates for support to begin great public improvements without waiting for such fanciful reform as betterment rates. But the general conclusion that comes out of it is that an empty belly is, from our point of view, a bad politician. These times of physical want and mental despair are either the seed times of angry revolutionary feeling or of colourless despairing quietude. We forget that it was not until the dark years of 1881–85 were well over that *constitutional socialism*, as distinguished from *revolutionary socialism*, began to grow. It was no coincidence that the great Progressive victory came in the year of the greatest prosperity. We must educate and wait for fat years.

It has added to Sidney's discomfiture that the mercurial H. W. Massingham has turned against him. Massingham has had fits of admiration for Sidney, of more or less duration! Only the other day we heard of him dilating on his greatness, and asserting that any day he cared he could be in the Cabinet! All through the L.C.C. campaign he has been more than friendly—both publicly and privately. But the results of the fight have brought about a reaction against Sidney; and strangely enough it has been Sidney's personal success which seems to have tipped the balance. The fall of Burns' majority has angered Massingham, and the fact that Sidney—a middle-class collectivist— has not received the same snub from the multitude has made him still angrier. For Massingham has a hero-worship for John Burns. His excitable unstable nature has always been attracted by the boisterous vigour and immense self-conceit and assurance of our great Labour leader. As a dramatic critic, he has infinitely preferred the stalwart demagogue, with his picturesque language and bracing personality, to Sidney's quiet, unpretentious little figure, with its even flow of statistics, arguments and diplomatic persuasiveness (or as some would say evasiveness!), and, like a good critic, he is sore and angry that the audience do not take his view and favour his favourite. For the rest,

Burns has always disliked and suspected the pair of us and has instilled some of his prejudices into Massingham's mind. But Sidney will write a soft answer—and in a few months, perhaps weeks, the tantrum will be over.

There is no use blinding ourselves to the setback to our ideas. Tom Mann said that the victory of the Progressives would redound to the glory of official Liberalism. Quite the contrary, it is our defeat which will give them secret joy. "No more of your collectivism for us ", the Liberal capitalist will say—" it cannot even buy votes for our party." It will doubtless harden the heart of the old gang: militate against the reconstruction of the Liberal Party on the collectivist basis. And, while it will delay permeation, it will also weaken the chances of an Independent Labour Party becoming any force in the land. F. Hammill and Peter Curran have discredited themselves—by their success and failure. They have injured the Progressives, without showing any strength of their own. No class of Englishman can long tolerate the simple wrecker. . . .

Grosvenor Road, March 13*th,* 1895.—Yesterday at the L.C.C. was an exciting scene. When we arrived at half past two the entrance was crowded and all the galleries filled—the inside of the building leading to the Council chamber thronged with councillors and their immediate friends and relations. By Charles Harrison's kindness, I was passed on to the dais where I sat between Lady Farrer and Mrs. Beachcroft on the Moderate side of the chair. All the councillors were in their places before the clock struck three. To everyone's surprise Sir J. Hutton, though in the building, refused to take the chair, sulking at his non-re-election by his own party—Charles Harrison, vice-chairman, opening the proceedings in his hoarse guttural. The election of the chairman [Sir Arthur Arnold] was a foregone conclusion—the aldermen an agreed compromise. Both parties had their men in attendance, and they were ushered in by the two whips and welcomed by the new chairman. A distinguished company, three retired heads of great government departments, a bevy of peers— Ritchie, the stepfather of the Council, E. Hubbard, an aristocratic director of the Bank of England, Whitmore, the leader of the Tory M.P.'s for London and the organiser of the Moderate forces; in fact, only one nonentity among the new aldermen, the Progressive Hubbard, a rough and ready temperance member of the old Council. Certainly, if the Progressives have accomplished no other good, they have made the L.C.C. the most accomplished, distinguished, and even the most aristocratic, local body in the world! A strange effect of the Labour and Socialist onslaught on London! And we must admit that the Moderate victories have raised the standard of good looks of the L.C.C.

Slim aristocrats, well-fed and slightly dissipated-looking frequenters of London drawing-rooms and clubs, are, from a scenic point of view, welcome contrasts to the stunted figures of the Labour representatives and the ungraceful corpulence of the Progressive men of business. But the manners are as distinctly deteriorated. The " gentlemen's " party are loud and insolent in their ways—an insolence which is possibly a reaction from their long term of servitude to an overwhelming Progressive majority. Our side was subdued, sitting tight and forcing their way through, by their bare majority to the deputy-chairmanship—thus retaining the three executive offices. Over Dickinson's appointment raged a fierce debate—his rejection by Wandsworth, his partisanship, and finally his former acceptance of a salary, being alternatively advanced as arguments against his re-election. When Sidney rose to defend him (I noticed Ritchie turn round to scrutinize the speaker with quick curiosity), the interruptions of the Moderates reached their climax—Sidney being, for the nonce, the *bête noire* of the opposition. All we could do was to save Dickinson by promising a committee of enquiry into the whole subject of the deputy-chairmanship.[1] Whether we shall save him and his salary in the end, I much doubt.

It is quite obvious that the brunt of the battle will be over in a few months. The Moderates will make a determined attempt to reverse the policy of the late Council in all its controversial points. If they do not succeed in capturing, or, at any rate, obstructing the machine, they will tire in their efforts. Their party, though well equipped with able men, has no staying power—their attendance will fall off rapidly as the novelty wears off and the game of imperial politics becomes more absorbing, or the delights of sport and pleasure more enticing. Of course, there will still be powerful critics who are able to push us forward whither we do not desire to go, and pull us backward from our own course. All this will mean more strain, more temper, and more judgement. Whether, when the three years have elapsed, and the fourth Council takes its place in Spring Gardens, we shall have survived the ordeal, remains to be seen! But, whatever else

---

[1] The office of deputy chairman of the L.C.C. has an interesting history. Unlike the chairmanship, or vice-chairmanship, it was at one time a paid post. The appointment in its early form originated in the Progressive distrust of permanent officials, whom they suspected of being under Tory influence. A deputy chairman was, therefore, appointed from among the Council's members. He was expected to exercise personal control over the staff, and paid a substantial salary to enable him to give his whole time to the job. The post was first held by F. B. Firth, M.P., leader of the Progressive Party, and on his death by A. H. Haggis, 1889–91. The salary was abolished in 1895, when W. H. Dickinson completed his term, and a tradition has since then developed of appointing a member of the opposition to the post. See *History of the London County Council*, by Gibbon and Bell, p. 35. (Ed.)

may happen, we are not the kind of folk to say to the electorate, " Lord, let thy servants now depart in peace ". If we die, we will die fighting—and leave marks behind us!

Grosvenor Road, July 8th, 1895.—Meanwhile, the L.C.C. proceeds satisfactorily in spite of the fact that the Moderates have now a majority of one of the elected members. The Moderates have failed to wreck the Progressive Party policy—whenever they have been led out to do battle, they have ended in running away from the issue. Of course, new enterprise in the direction of municipalisation has been damped down; but, wherever the lines have been already laid, the machine runs smoothly on—with, perhaps, less friction than when the Moderates felt themselves a trampled down minority and cried out piteously to outside authorities, like the House of Lords, to help them. It is much more difficult for the peers to refuse to pass a proposal which is brought before them by Lord Cadogan than when it was promoted by Charles Harrison. And, if the truth must be told, the peers are the least reactionary of the new Moderate recruits and are apt to act as a centre between the Tory rump and the Progressive vanguard. So works our English society—progressivism may yet be saved by the priests and the lords. . . .

Grosvenor Road, March 2nd, 1898. [Three years later.]—A great meeting at St. James's Hall—Lord Rosebery to the rescue. I sat behind him and watched him narrowly. He had lost that drugged look—heavy eyes and morbid flesh—that he had as premier. He is at once older, healthier and *better* looking. His speech had vigour, astuteness and flashes of dramatic genius. But he was woefully full of himself; his whole expression and attitude was concentrated self-consciousness and sensitiveness—not sufficient of an actor to lose himself in his part, not sufficient of a patriot to lose himself in his cause. Throughout there was an undercurrent of complaint—of personal grudge against the political world. He is not a leader. Outside foreign politics he has no creed and only a scrappy knowledge; his very egotism is ineffective egotism—an egotism that shrinks from the world's touch, not the egotism that forces itself on the world. For my part, if a man is to be full of himself, I like him to have the will and the capacity to make the world full of him also!

No one knows how the L.C.C. election will turn out: both sides suffer in turn from hope and depression. The Conservative organisation is straining every nerve to get the Moderates in: whilst we, on our side, are beating up every available Progressive force wheresoever it is located. There is a good deal of beating of big drums over this election: the Conservatives say Lord Salisbury's Government is at stake, the Progressives that the L.C.C. is to be damned or saved. As a matter of fact, neither will happen: and sensible persons on both sides feel somewhat ashamed of the exaggeration. Apart from the result as a symptom of public opinion, it is doubtful whether it would not suit the Progressives that the Moderates should get a small majority, and the Conservatives that the Progressives should hold office on insecure tenure. An overwhelming defeat would naturally be disastrous to either side, but we imagine that public opinion is too divided for that. We incline to believe in a small Progressive majority; the Moderate whip, on the other hand, expects to win six seats. But there is no index to the public opinion of that anonymous creature— the London elector. . . .

Grosvenor Road, March 1898.—*The L.C.C. Election.* We sallied forth about 8.30 A.M. (Sidney having voted first in Westminster) laden with sandwiches, teapots and oranges, to fit up the committee rooms. It was a glorious morning, the Westminster buildings rising out of the blue atmosphere and the river dancing in the brilliant morning sun. At 9.30, I had settled down at one of the six committee rooms, spent an hour arranging the bringing-up cards, and learning my way about on the map of the district. Throughout the morning working-men helpers dribbled in, and voters turned up anxious to find out their polling district. About 3.30, the bringers-up trouped in; at 5, it was a crowd in the little room, each waiting to report progress. Then came on a heavy fall of snow; but the feeling of the Progressives was so hot that they trudged on through the sleet and the slush—not one of my fifteen workers gave up working. But I felt that the Lord had meant to test the strength of the conviction of the working-man and I trembled with doubt—would he go to the poll in spite of the rain? That was the question which agitated the heads of the organisa-tion for the next two hours. Directly we learnt that the working-class districts had polled 60% we knew we were safe—and hoped that Deptford was a sample this time of London. Then the hurried dinner— nineteen of our West End helpers; then the exciting hours of the count; then the midnight visit to the National Liberal Club all aglow with Progressive victories—and then to bed, oh! so tired, far too tired to sleep.

The Moderates are hardly snowed under as in 1892, but they are soundly beaten, leaving us in a great majority for the next three years. They owe their defeat to the foolhardy attack on the L.C.C. led by Salisbury and Devonshire, to the apathy of the Conservative voter during a Conservative Government, and the negative character of the Moderate programme. Last time, the Moderates declared themselves in favour of Chamberlain's social programme: this time, as a Conservative Ministry was in power and doing little or nothing to carry out the programme, they could not pretend to be in favour of it. The workman, too, who is sentimentally attached to the Works Department (which represents his old shibboleths of standard rates and hours and direct employment), rallied to the defence of the Progressives with great enthusiasm. And the reaction against the Conservative Government was greater than the reaction against the Progressives. Probably, therefore, we are in for another six years' power—for so long as the Conservatives remain at Downing Street we shall not be turned out of Spring Gardens. It is a question whether the country does not advance more quickly with the Conservatives in power at the centre and the Progressives capturing local authorities, than with a weak Liberal Government, and a provincial reaction. . . .

THE TECHNICAL EDUCATION BOARD

It is a trite saying that it is the unexpected that happens in the development of institutions. The Progressive leaders of 1892 would have been mightily surprised if they had been told that the L.C.C. of the twentieth century would be far less concerned with material things such as gas and water, docks and markets, tramways and tunnels, than with the education and recreation, medical treatment and adequate maintenance of the five millions of inhabitants within the metropolitan area. And yet the main task accomplished by the Other One during his eighteen years' service on the L.C.C. was its development as the greatest educational authority in the world; its first beginnings being the establishment of the Technical Education Board covering alike elementary, secondary and university education by means of grants-in-aid and the establishment of a gigantic scholarship ladder; and then, through the 1903 Education Act, absorbing into itself as the practically unrestricted single education authority, for the whole metropolitan area, the School Board with its colossal network of elementary schools.

A series of accidents started the L.C.C. on its career as the education authority. The first of these was a mishap to the Conservative budget of 1890, which had included an addition to the spirit duties, to be credited to the county and county borough councils, partly for a scheme of police superannuation, and partly for the purchase of publicans' licences in order to get rid of redundant public-houses. To the latter proposal a storm of opposition arose, mainly from the temperance movement, which objected to such a recognition of property in licences. Towards the end of the session, after the increased taxes had been voted, and were in course of collection, the Government found itself constrained to abandon the proposed appropriation to the purchase of licences. The constitutional point was then pressed that the new tax revenue could not be left unappropriated in the same session in which it was authorised. At this stage, A. H. D. Acland,[1] a much underrated British statesman, an enthusiast for public education and one of the few adepts in the new subject of technical education, jumped in. For three days he fought to get the " whiskey money " definitely allocated, in England, to technical education, and in Wales to the execution of the Welsh Intermediate Education Act. In the end, the Government agreed to the proposal for Wales, and for England handed the money over to the county councils to expend as they thought fit; but with a distinct intimation that definite charges would hereafter be laid on them for educational purposes.

The newly established London County Council had not found time in its first term to take action under the Technical

---

[1] " A. H. D. Acland," writes R. B. Haldane in his autobiography (pp. 93 and 103), ". . . a real reformer in elementary and secondary education and to whom I was attracted on this account, was another of our members. Mr. Gladstone never cared for him much because, having once been a clergyman, he had renounced his clerical orders so as the better to be able to enter public life effectively. But, partly I think in response to the strong appeals some of us made to him, Mr. Gladstone, when he next came in in 1892, made Acland Minister of Education, a position in which he did splendid work. . . . Arthur Acland was also a stimulating personality, full of knowledge, particularly about primary and secondary education." To this appreciation I may add that from the first days of Labour representation and throughout the career of the parliamentary Labour Party right up to his death in 1926, Arthur Acland was a generous supporter of the new movement. In the general elections of 1918, '22, '23 and '24 he gave considerable sums to enable young university men to run as Labour candidates; and by a donation of £1600 he made possible the establishment of the National Labour Club in 1919. Finally, he left £10,000 on trust to enable young Labour men and women to pursue research in political and economic subjects. His lifelong connection with the consumers' co-operative movement is well known. Though he was not among the brilliant or dominant, he was assuredly the most enlightened and far-seeing of all the Liberal politicians of the last decade of the nineteenth and the first decade of the twentieth century.

Instruction Act; not even when in 1890 it found itself endowed with the funds thus vaguely allocated for the purpose. It so happened that S. W.'s first motion on the Council was one proposing that a committee should be appointed to consider whether the Council should not proceed under the Act. So cautiously worded a resolution, not taken seriously, was adopted unanimously; and the mover was left to choose the committee, subject to the usual exact representation of the party balance on the Council. S. W. has often explained how, in his anxiety to put on the ablest members from the various sections, he found he had not provided for a chairman, as practically all his nominees proved to be already chairmen of other committees. He was, therefore, virtually driven to preside himself. This committee was persuaded not to rely on its inner consciousness but to engage a young man—Hubert Llewellyn Smith— then acting temporarily as lieutenant to Arthur Acland in the promotion of technical education, to prepare a report, setting forth the existing position, and sketching out a possible policy for the Council. Within a year this comprehensive report—a volume in itself—was approved by the committee as a general outline. Meanwhile, the committee had been led to accept a new constitution. For the Council simply to add one more to its score of committees, wholly composed of members of the Council, would have antagonised the School Board and the City companies, and jeopardised the support of the teachers and the trade unionists. Far better, suggested Sidney, create a new instrument, which might conciliate opponents, and even enlist their assistance. This took shape in the Technical Education Board—a title not known to the law—composed of twenty members of the Council, with fifteen nominated outsiders. Moreover, explained the Fabian, if the Council was going to nominate outsiders at all, it was better to let the rival or sectional interests choose their own representatives than for the Council to impose its choice. Hence, the Council was recommended to allow the School Board, the City and Guilds Institute, the Head Masters' Association, the Head Mistresses' Association, the London Teachers' Association, and even the London Trades Council, to nominate their own representatives on what thus became a hybrid body. Incidentally, it seemed to follow almost automatically that this Technical Education Board, unlike the score of ordinary committees of the Council, had to be freed, once its annual estimates were approved, from the necessity of seeking specific approval of every expenditure exceeding £50, and even of reporting its proceedings more than once a quarter, and then only for the information of the Council.

One of the most effective instruments in the Board's policy of co-ordination was its elaborate scholarship system. In its popular aspect, this was an educational ladder of unprecedented dimensions. It was, indeed, among educational ladders, the most gigantic in extent, the most elaborate in its organisation of "intakes" and promotions, and the most diversified in kinds of excellence selected and in types of training provided, that existed anywhere in the world. But, in the policy of the T.E.B., the system of scholarships and bursaries was more than a "capacity-catching" device. The scholarships brought a steady stream of clever boys and girls to the languishing endowed secondary schools, to the expanding technical institutes and to the unfilled classes of the university colleges. Payment for these county scholars was made the basis of a system of annual grants to institutions under all sorts of independent administrations, justifying expert inspection of their work, and a carefully devised code of regulations to ensure their continued efficiency. What had previously been a chaos of isolated institutions, largely unaware of one another's existence, became gradually welded—without suppression of local administration by separate bodies of governors—into a graded educational system covering every part of London. Into such a system it became possible for the Council gradually to introduce new and additional secondary schools and technical institutes, to fill geographical gaps and relieve local congestion, without destroying or even weakening the older institutions, or arousing their opposition. Finally, in calling into being the Central School of Arts and Crafts and the London Day Training College, the T.E.B. set a standard in technology and pedagogy by which the whole kingdom has profited.

Under the initial inspiration of Arthur Acland and Hubert Llewellyn Smith, Sidney induced the Board to begin by appointing a bevy of highly expert officers—the scientist William Garnett as secretary and chief officer; Dr. Kimmins as chief inspector; G. J. Frampton and W. R. Lethaby as art advisers. Technical education was not to be cramped or fettered by limitations of grade or age or even of subject. The Board, indeed, could not go beyond the Council's statutory limitation. This, however, was found to be, when looked at in the right light, not unduly narrow! Every subject aided by the Science and Art Department was within the definition; and also any other subject that the Department might sanction at any time. Sidney chuckled when he described how he went to see Acland—then the Minister in charge of education—and represented that London was a kingdom in itself in which practically every occupation was represented. Would the Minister, accordingly, in order to save official time and trouble, at once sanction as " technical instruction in London " every subject that the department had already sanctioned anywhere? " I think we can do that, cannot we? " asked Acland of (Sir John) Donnelly, his permanent head. The outcome was an order adding, for London, a long list of subjects to the already lengthy array of the Science and Art Department, including all the sciences and all the arts, all foreign languages together with modern history, economics, geography, commercial education, domestic economy and what not. " We can now lawfully teach anything under the sun except ancient Greek and theology ", observed Sidney complacently.

The scope of the work thus defined, the most important issue, in the mind of the chairman of the Board, if not in that of the less observant members, was the method of organisation. It was important not merely to add odds and ends of classes and schools and institutes to the multifarious and diverse confusion of educational equipment already in existence. What was essential was to have in view, from the first, and to work steadily towards it, though not necessarily to talk about it, a scheme of education for London, as a whole, in which all grades and kinds of formal education, from the kindergarten to the university, in all subjects and at all ages, would find appropriate place, and be duly co-ordinated and connected. Such a vision involved an immediate decision at the outset; between a policy of utilising and assisting existing agencies as far as they could be made to go, on the one hand, and, on the other, a policy of confining the Council's work to setting up its own institutions in unabashed rivalry with established institutions, over which the Council would then gain no control. Needless to say, the Board was guided to the larger view of comprehension and control ; and the existing technical institutions, evening classes, secondary schools and university colleges, with any additions that philanthropic enterprise made to their numbers, were gradually brought into a systematic organisation. Some critics objected that the T.E.B. had, by its lavish subventions, saved the decayed endowed secondary schools from supersession by upgrowths from the elementary schools under direct public administration. Others declared that the T.E.B. had bought, by its grants, the recruiting, inspection, supervision, control and virtual direction of these ancient foundations, for which an unexpected *renaissance* in desirable variety was thereby assured.

I have set down rather fully what I have been told of the work of the T.E.B.[1] because, though the work of the Board was quite sufficiently praised by educational experts and uncritically applauded by the public, I do not believe that justice has been done to the amount of deliberate policy that underlay its multifarious decisions. The T.E.B. had the wisdom to equip itself from the outset with a considerable staff of the ablest experts it could enlist for love or money. The County Council had the sense to give the Board

[1] For an authoritative account of the T.E.B. and the development of the County Council into the Local Education Authority for London, see *A Retrospect*, by Dr. William Garnett, from the *Educational Record*, April 1929.

a free hand, and to receive its quarterly reports with due appreciation without party dissensions or hampering instructions. I recall with some pride that the Board, unlike the other committees of the Council which annually changed their chairmen, re-elected Sidney without opposition for six successive years (1892–98). I know that he attended every one of its meetings and nearly all the innumerable sub-committees. I have heard him say that, in the early years, he habitually wrote out before each meeting the exact words of the resolutions that he thought should be passed on all the subjects on the agenda—a practice which usually enabled him to steer the discussion to the desired conclusion, and at any rate gave him control over the drafting. It remains to be added that he insisted on signing every one of the thousands of cheques by which the Board's payments were made, in order, as he explained, to " look at each with the eye of the district auditor ", so that he might ensure (as throughout the whole six years he did ensure) that no payment was so described as to attract a surcharge—the bug-bear of inexperienced authorities working under indefinite powers.

Here is one of the few entries in the MS. diary referring to Sidney's afternoons at Spring Gardens:

Grosvenor Road, July 30th, 1893.—Five afternoons of the week he is engrossed in committee work.[1] Besides the general business of the

---

[1] The following list of committees on which S. W. served between 1892 and 1898 show that his afternoons were not entirely absorbed by the T.E.B. Throughout this period he was also a member of the party committee which acted as a sort of informal Cabinet deciding the policy of the progressives on all controversial subjects:

    Member of the Appeal Committee, 1892–93;
    Corporate Property Committee, 1895–98;
    County Rate Committee, 1896–98;
    Establishment Committee, 1892–93;
    Finance Committee, 1893–95;
    General Purposes Committee, 1892–98;
    Local Government and Taxation Committee, 1892–98;
        (Vice-chairman, 1892–94);
    Parliamentary Committee, 1892–98;
    Public Health and Housing Committee, 1892–93;
    Rivers Committee, 1894–95;
    Water Committee, 1892–95;

and of the Special Committees on—

    London Government, 1894–95;
    Thames Conservancy, 1893–94;
    Chairman of the Technical Education Board, 1892–98.

Council, he has been giving persistent work to starting the Technical Education Board and guiding its various sub-committees. Kind friends tell me he is an extraordinarily clever chairman of a troublesome Board of experts and obstructives. Besides this—his special work— he has had to draw up the plan to be submitted to the London Unifica- tion Commission and give constant attention to the special L.C.C. committee which has been somewhat at cross-purposes with the Com- mission presided over by our esteemed relative Leonard Courtney. . . . With his life I am more than satisfied. The work he is doing, creating machinery for collective action, is the work I desired to see him do: and the fact that his work is unostentatious, that it cannot be seen or estimated except by his fellow-workers, makes it all the finer. . . . And as, in spite of this purely administrative effort, he still finds energy to think, reconstruct past history, to disentangle ideas—I do not feel that his life has been narrowed by becoming mainly practical. To adapt the present machinery to the facts of to-day, to think out the new machinery for to-morrow by the light of yesterday's experience —this combination of practice and theory is, I think, the ideal life for him. . . .

The Other One's work on the T.E.B., and Graham Wallas's service on the London School Board, seem to have led me to ponder over the question whether we were not putting the cart before the horse in concentrating on the education of the child and the training of the youth, without trying to solve the problem of the right breeding of the human race.

All this points [I enter in my diary in July 1894] to the endow- ment of motherhood and raising the " generation and rearing " of children into an art through the elaboration of a science. Sometimes, I imagine how the men and women of a hundred years hence will wonder at our spending all our energy and thought on the social organisation of adult men and women, and omitting altogether the vastly more important question of the breeding of the generation that is to succeed them. " How could you hope to improve (they will say) the organisation of society without attending to the quality of the men and women to be organised? The success or failure of your collectivist organisation depended on the characteristics of the democracy, and these characteristics you left to the chances of the unregulated and haphazard breeding of the slums." And their criticism will be true. What can we hope from these myriads of deficient minds and deformed bodies that swarm in our great cities—what can we hope from them but brutality, meanness and crime; whether they are struggling for subsistence at the dock gates, or eking out their days in the poor law or penal colony? To enlist the loafer at trade union rates, in the service of the community, will probably enable him to work less and eat more than under the lash of the slave-driver. On the other hand, the vigorous-minded artisans, with their well-educated wives, are abstaining from child rearing because it is an unpaid service rendered to the community, seriously impairing their strength for the struggle to gain their own bread. These facts will seem so obvious to the social reformer of 1994 that he will wonder at our endless discussions of present-day problems much as we wonder at the metaphysical politics which absorbed the whole energy of the French thinkers on the eve of the Revolution. But for all that, we cannot take up the woman's question. We cannot hope to attack individualism, or, as we prefer to call it, anarchy, in its stronghold of the home and the family, entrenched behind current religious morality and custom, before we have replaced it by deliberate collective rule in the factory, the mine— in the whole machinery of wealth production, where anarchy stands condemned by the great bulk of the people as meaning oppression and gross injustice between man and man. Possibly, too, woman will have to go through the same social stages as the labourer, on her way to freedom; she will have to exchange the servitude of *status* for the servitude of *contract*, to rise out of personal dependence before she gains social protection and recognition. We can but leave this problem reverently to our children: preparing their way by cutting at the roots of prejudice, superstition and rotten custom. Often, I wonder whether we do our full duty in this respect; whether we do not acquiesce timidly in the prevailing thought and feeling on these remote issues in order to diminish the friction for those reforms we have in hand? If so, we are short-sightedly practical—we attain our means but lose our end.

The London School of Economics

At this point I recall the first steps in what was perhaps the biggest single enterprise in Our Partnership—the initiation of the London School of Economics and Political Science.

An odd adventure! [I write in my diary on September 21, 1894]. A few weeks ago, Sidney received a letter from a Derby solicitor informing him that he was left executor to a certain Mr. Hutchinson. All he knew of this man (whom he had never seen) was the fact that he was an eccentric old gentleman, member of the Fabian Society, who alternately sent considerable cheques and wrote querulous letters about Shaw's rudeness, or some other fancied grievance he had suffered at the hands of some member of the Fabian Society. " Old Hutch " had, however, been a financial stay of the Society and the executive was always deploring his advancing age and infirmity. When Sidney heard he was made executor he, therefore, expected that the old man had left something to the Fabian Society. Now it turns out that he has left nearly £10,000 to five trustees and appointed Sidney chairman and administrator—all the money to be spent in ten years. The old man blew his brains out, finding his infirmities grow upon him. He had always lived a penurious life and stinted his wife and by no means spoilt his children—and left his wife only £100 a year which Sidney proposes should be doubled by the trustees. The children are all provided for and do not seem to resent the will.

The public-spirited attitude of the Hutchinson family deserves record. Owing to its extreme informality and the suicide of its author shortly after its signature, the will, we were informed, would probably not be upheld in a court of law, if the family chose to dispute it. But, with one accord, the widow and her children demanded that it should be carried out; one of the sons joining the Fabian Society to show his acquiescence. Moreover, the unmarried daughter, who had been given £1500 by her father, and who was one of the trustees, demurred to the proposed purchase of an additional annuity for her mother as inconsistent with her father's will, and, when overborne by the other trustees, made a will leaving her tiny fortune to Sidney and Edward Pease on a wide trust, practically in order to reimburse the original trust for the cost of the extra annuity. She died within a few months.

Now the question is how to spend the money [I continue]. It might be placed to the credit of the Fabian Society and spent in the ordinary work of propaganda. Or a big political splash might be made with it—all the Fabian executive might stand for Parliament! and I.L.P. candidates might be subsidised in their constituencies. But neither of these ways seem to us equal to the occasion. If it is mainly used for the ordinary work of the F.S., then it will merely save the pockets of ordinary subscribers or inflate the common work of the organisation for a few years beyond its normal growth. Moreover, mere propaganda of the shibboleths of collectivism is going on at a rapid rate through the I.L.P.—the ball has been set running and it is rolling down the hill at a fair pace. It looks as if the great bulk of the working-men will be collectivists before the end of the century. But reform will not be brought about by shouting. What is needed is *hard thinking*. And the same objection applies to sending nondescript Socialists into Parliament. The Radical members are quite sufficiently compliant in their views: what is lacking in them is the leaven of knowledge. So Sidney has been planning to persuade the other trustees to devote the greater part of the money to encouraging *research* and economic study. His vision is to found, slowly and quietly, a *London School of Economics and Political Science*—a centre not only of lectures on special subjects, but an association of students who would be directed and supported in doing original work. Last evening we sat by the fire and jotted down a list of subjects which want elucidating: issues of facts which need clearing up. Above all, we want the ordinary citizen to feel that reforming society is no light matter, and must be undertaken by experts specially trained for the purpose. . . .

To which contemporary account I add a reminiscence which Professor Graham Wallas contributed to the *Handbook of the Students' Union* in 1925:

So many causes go to every effect that it is generally impossible to assign the invention of any important institution to a precise date. There is no such impossibility in the case of the School. It was invented at Borough Farm, a couple of miles south-west of Godalming, early in the morning of a certain day in August 1894. . . . Mr. and Mrs. Webb, Mr. G. B. Shaw, and I were staying at the little farm. The day before, Mr. Webb learnt that, by the will of Mr. Henry Hutchinson, he had been given the duty of directing the expenditure of a sum of money. He and Mrs. Webb woke up early, had a long discussion, and at breakfast told us that part of the money would be used to found a school in London on the lines of the École Libre des Sciences Politiques in Paris.

For two relatively unknown persons, without academic distinction, holding outrageously heterodox opinions in the very branch of knowledge that they were intent on promoting, and provided with no other resources than the few thousand pounds that Sidney could allocate from the Hutchinson Trust—such an enterprise seemed an impertinence. The first step was to find a young economist, indifferent to the frowns of the orthodox, sanguine, enterprising, and, above all, sufficiently disinterested, to devote himself whole-heartedly to the creation of the proposed institution in return for a minute and uncertain salary. A queer accident had already marked out our man. A year or so previously, whilst writing *The History of Trade Unionism*, we had visited the Bodleian Library in order to discover whether among its miscellaneous collections it had happened to preserve any pamphlets, petitions or broadsheets making mention of combinations, other than those we had found in the British Museum, or in the well-equipped libraries at Dublin, Glasgow and Manchester. Although we had written in advance to Bodley's librarian, explaining our object, and also had provided ourselves with a personal letter of introduction from the Fellow of an Oxford College with whom we were staying, he received us with a discourtesy, not to say a downright rudeness, that we afterwards learned to be a personal characteristic. He, finally, repelled our enquiries with the remark that we should find all we required in Howell's *Conflicts of Capital and Labour*! At this point we were politely accosted by a young man, an obvious intellectual, with an attractive countenance and pleasant manner, who was reading in the library, and had noticed our discomfiture. He quietly took us into a corner, saying he would himself get out everything we wanted. We learned who he was and read with appreciation the volume that he had published on *English Trade and Finance chiefly in the 17th Century*. The mutual attraction between W. A. S. Hewins and the Webbs was not similarity in political outlook. His views sprang from an instinctive sympathy with mediaevalism which led him spiritually, in the course of a few years, to join the Roman Catholic Church, and politically into a lifelong advocacy of a scientific tariff. We were democratic collectivists, believing in the eventual triumph, in so far as social environment is concerned, of the principle of equality between man and man; if only by the roundabout way of the " inevitability of gradualness ". But there was a wide field of agreement for active co-operation. First, our common dislike of the so-called Manchester School, of its unverified deductive reasoning and abstract generalisations, of its apotheosis of " the economic man ", exclusively inspired by the motive of pecuniary self-interest, and of its passionate defence of the rights of property as against the needs of humanity. And, secondly, our common faith in the practicability and urgent necessity of a concrete science of society implemented through historical research, personal observation and statistical verification. I quote from the account that Hewins has himself given of his eight years' connection with the London School of Economics, at first a sickly infant, of doubtful parentage, born into an indifferent if not hostile world, for whose survival, through the first years of infancy and steady progress in size and stature, he was so largely responsible.

It was at the close of 1894 [W. A. S. Hewins writes], when I was giving a course of lectures at Hove on Social History, that Sidney Webb asked me if I would go and see him and his wife, as they wanted to consult me about the organisation of certain lectures. Sidney Webb was then chairman of the Technical Education Board of the London County Council. I found he had become executor of the will of a Mr. Henry Hutchinson, who had recently died leaving £10,000. . . . After consulting counsel, Webb had decided to devote part of this money to the foundation of an institution on the lines of the École des Sciences Politiques, Paris. Further, the Technical Education Board of the London County Council decided to organise lectures on higher commercial subjects, and Webb wanted my advice as to the way in which these two schemes might be combined to form a new institution in London for the higher study of economics and political science and training suitable for those engaged in administration or business. I drew up this scheme and we discussed it at 41 Grosvenor Road. There was then no idea that I should organise the proposed new institution; Webb consulted me as an outside expert, as I have no doubt he consulted other people. . . . On March 29th, 1895, I received another letter formally asking me to undertake the organisation of the proposed school, and accepted.

The work proceeded rapidly. This depended mainly upon Sidney and Beatrice Webb and myself, and I shall always look back on the period during which I worked with them as one of the happiest and most productive in my life. We met almost daily and never had a dispute during the eight years I was so closely associated with them. We desired that the lectures and investigations held at the School should be representative of all branches of economics and political science, and no differentiation against persons was to be allowed on the grounds of sex, religion, or economic or political views. Full provision was to be made for training for business administration, and for the central or local governments; for library work; the higher forms of research; the publication of monographs upon special subjects.

The first business was the acquisition of suitable premises. We began on a small scale and took the ground floor of No. 9 John Street, Adelphi, for class work, and official business, and obtained the co-operation of the Society of Arts and the London Chamber of Commerce for numerous courses of lectures. . . . Within two months of my acceptance of the Directorship of the School, we were in a position to announce provisional arrangements for the autumn session. . . . We quickly moved from No. 9 John Street, Adelphi, to 10 Adelphi Terrace. As we did not require the two top floors, we let them to a great friend and benefactor, Miss Charlotte Payne Townshend, who soon afterwards became the wife of George Bernard Shaw. The generosity of Mr. Passmore Edwards and Lord Rothschild then enabled us to build a new School in Clare Market. Since those days the building has been vastly extended and the entrance changed from Clare Market to Houghton Street, and there the work is still carried on. Mrs. Bernard Shaw and Bertrand Russell generously helped by enabling us to give research studentships. . . . When I think of the first days of the School of Economics at No. 9 John Street, Adelphi, and contemplate the great organisation which has grown from those beginnings, I can only feel that I was privileged, along with my colleagues, to take part in a great romance. Difficulties appeared from day to day, only to be overcome. Although we represented different schools of thought and were on different sides of politics, I cannot remember any incident which disturbed the harmony of our relations during those early years or which interfered in any way with the rapid progress of our great undertaking. . . .[1]

The truth implicit in W. A. S. Hewins' demure and discreet statement lies in the fact that he and we were far too absorbed in pushing the School into a sound position to have either the time or the inclination to quarrel over political and economic dogmas. For there were overt and hidden enemies, not a few of them, intent on blocking the way for this new departure in university teaching, this new laboratory of sociological research. They were beaten, bless

[1] *The Apologia of an Imperialist,* by W. A. S. Hewins, pp. 24-8.

them! so I won't mention names. If I did, the survivors might find themselves summoned to appear as defendants in a specially staged series of " mock trials ", for which high-brow performances, in aid of the funds of the London hospitals, the present London School of Economics [1931], with its 120 professors and lecturers and its 3000 students, has accidentally achieved a newspaper notoriety.

Stray sidelights on Sidney's day-by-day participation in building up the School appear in the MS. diary between 1895 and 1898. In the first of these, I introduce another of the founders of the School, described by a contemporary journalist as " the elusive personality of Mrs. Bernard Shaw ". An apt term, for this lady has hitherto escaped publicity by dexterously dodging, on all occasions, behind the figure of her famous husband. But she could not escape my mental camera, the imaginary snapshots being duly translated into words in the MS. diary.

Grosvenor Road, September 16*th*, 1896.—In person she is attractive, a large graceful woman with masses of chocolate-brown hair, pleasant grey eyes [" They are green," she observed, on reading this entry], *matte* complexion which sometimes looks muddy, at other times forms a picturesquely pale background to her brilliant hair and bright eyes. She dresses well; in flowing white evening robes she approaches beauty. At moments she is plain. By temperament she is an anarchist, feeling any regulation or rule intolerable, a tendency which has been exaggerated by her irresponsible wealth. She is romantic but thinks herself cynical. She is a Socialist and a Radical, not because she understands the collectivist standpoint, but because she is by nature a rebel. She has no snobbishness and no convention; she has " swallowed all formulas " but has not worked out principles of her own. She is fond of men and impatient of most women; bitterly resents her enforced celibacy but thinks she could not tolerate the matter-of-fact side of marriage. Sweet-tempered, sympathetic and genuinely anxious to increase the world's enjoyment and diminish the world's pain. . . . Last autumn she was introduced to us. We, knowing she was wealthy, and hearing she was socialistic, interested her in the London School of Economics. She subscribed £1000 to the library, endowed a woman's scholarship, and has now taken the rooms over the School at Adelphi Terrace, paying us £300 a year for rent and service. It was on account of her generosity to our projects and " for the good of the cause " that I first made friends with her. To bring her more directly into our little set of comrades, I suggested that we should take a house together in the country and entertain our friends. To me she seemed at that time, a pleasant, well-dressed well-intentioned woman; I thought she would do very well for Graham Wallas! Now she turns out to be an " original ", with considerable personal charm and certain volcanic tendencies. Graham Wallas bored her with his morality and learning. In a few days she and Bernard Shaw were constant companions. For the last fortnight, when the party has been reduced to ourselves and Shaw, and we have been occupied with our work and each other, they have been scouring the country together and sitting up late at night! . . .

To cut a long story short, the two married each other in the summer of 1898, while we were journeying round the world studying Anglo-Saxon democracy. This meant that for some years the Bernard Shaws were " at home " just one flight above the class-rooms and library of the new institution.

Here are other entries in the MS. diary between 1895 and 1897:

Grosvenor Road, April 9th, 1895.—Have settled down quite comfortably to work again, spending all mornings over our book and Sidney at the L.C.C. in the afternoon. Re-elected chairman of Technical Education Board, and giving a good deal of time to that and the starting of the London School of Economics and Political Science. Selected Hewins (a young Oxford don) as director, engaged Wallas and Schloss as Hutchinson lecturers, and Acworth and probably Foxwell as L.C.C. lecturers. Also, in treaty with Chamber of Commerce and Society of Arts for rooms free of charge. Great good luck that Sidney happens to be chairman of Technical Education Board, able to combine the two sources. Promises well just at present, but impossible to tell whether the old gang won't wake up and cry out before the institution is fairly started—which would delay, possibly baulk, our plans. . . .

Grosvenor Road, May 8th, 1895.—The London School looks promising. Hewins has talked over the principal economists including Marshall and Edgeworth; we have secured Foxwell; the Society of Arts and Chamber of Commerce are giving us their rooms free; the Technical Education Board has voted the £500 a year; the trustees are amenable—and apparently there is no hitch of any kind. I myself am anxious that the " show lecture " side should not be too much developed, and that we should concentrate on getting *research really done*. For that object, I should like to gather round us all the able young men and women who are taking to economics, free their minds of prejudices and start them with a high ideal of accuracy and exhaustiveness in work. If there is one thing I have believed " from the beginning to the end ", it is that no progress can be made except on the basis of ascertained fact and carefully thought out suggestion. Despite our theory, bias, creed and prejudice, we are all equally wandering in the labyrinth, searching for the clue of true facts to bring us out on the right side of each particular problem. It is pitiful to see the narrow sectarian view most Socialists take—binding themselves hand and foot by a series of shibboleths. The working-men are especially afflicted with the theological temperament—the implicit faith in a certain creed which has been " revealed " to them by a sort of inner light. " Why is it that I, a poor ignorant man," said [H. W.] Hobart, one of the I.L.P., to me yesterday, " have perceived ' the truth ' whilst educated men with leisure and brains are still adhering to the old errors; unless I am right in saying they are mostly knaves! " . . .

Welcombe, Christmas, 1895.—We have recovered from our feelings of depression at the widespread reaction—we have turned our hopes from propaganda to education, from the working-class to the middle-class. It is only fools who refuse to make to themselves a " Paradise "! Having been beaten back in our endeavour to make a London Progressive Party with a permanent majority, we are creating the London School of Economics and Political Science as a wider foundation than street-corner preaching. Hewins is making a success of the School— 200 to 300 students attending the different classes and lectures. It is honestly scientific—served, indeed, by more individualist lecturers than collectivists—because the individualists are still the better men. But collectivists are encouraged—and the younger men and women are brought under collectivist influence. We are to some extent trying our best to attract the clever men from the universities; Sidney and Wallas lecturing at Oxford and Cambridge; and letting it be known that any one coming up who is interested in economics will have a warm welcome at Grosvenor Road. Leonard Hobhouse recruits for us at Oxford, the young Trevelyans at Cambridge. All this means a good deal of expenditure of time, sympathy, and alas! money. One cannot keep open house and live economically.

Grosvenor Road, March 26*th,* 1896.—Our time, for the last five weeks, a good deal taken up with writing " begging letters " for the Political Science Library. This winter the rapid growth of the School of Economics made new premises inevitable. But how to raise the money? The Technical Education Board which, under Sidney's chairmanship, subsidises most of the lectures, could not be asked to find premises, the funds of the Hutchinson Trustees are not inexhaustible. A brilliant idea flashed across Sidney's mind. We needed, for the use of the students, books and reports—why not appeal to the public to subscribe to a Library of Political Science? At first we thought we could get a millionaire to subscribe the whole amount on condition that he called it by his own name. In vain I flattered Passmore Edwards; in vain Sidney pressed Sir Hickman Bacon; in vain we wrote " on spec " to various magnates. The idea did not impress them. So we decided to scrape money together by small subscriptions. Sidney drafted a circular; Hewins secured the adhesion of the economists and then began a long process of begging letter writing. Sidney wrote to all the politicians; I raked up all my old ball partners, and between us we have gathered together a most respectable set of contributions— a list which is eloquent testimony to our respectability! Next week the appeal goes out for publication to the press. Even if we collect a comparatively small sum, the issue of the appeal has been a splendid advertisement for the School; and whatever we do get is so much spoil of the Egyptians. Not that we want to deceive the contributors. We are perfectly *bona fide* in our desire to advance economic knowledge, caring more for that than for our own pet ideas. And anyone who knows us knows our opinions, and all the money has been practically sent to *us* personally—so that the contributors are fully aware in whom they are placing their confidence. [Eventually Passmore Edwards put down £10,000 for a new building and the L.C.C. allowed us to put it up on a vacant site.]

Here I may interpolate that there was another reason for starting the British Library of Political Science as a separate entity. Among the stray facts caught up in Sidney's memory was the little-known Literary and Scientific Institutions Act of 1843, by which the Prince Consort had endeavoured to lead the British public in the direction of " Wissenschaft ". This measure provided that such institutions should be exempt from local rates. The Treasury and the lawyers in due course saw to it that neither universities, nor municipal free libraries, came within the scope of the Act; but Sidney had observed that the London Library still enjoyed the exemption. Why not also a specialist library in economic and political science? On this precedent, exemption was actually granted for a number of years for the premises over which the library spread itself. Eventually, however, the local rating authority objected that the School, then become a constituent part of a university, was the dominant element in the occupation; and consequently withdrew the exemption.

Grosvenor Road, July 14th, 1896.—Making arrangements to start the London School in its new abode at Adelphi Terrace in October. Engaged a bright girl as housekeeper and accountant. Advertised for political science lecturer—and yesterday interviewed candidates—a nondescript set of university men. All hopeless from our point of view—all imagined that political science consisted of a knowledge of Aristotle and modern! writers such as De Tocqueville—wanted to put the students through a course of Utopias from More downwards. When Sidney suggested a course of lectures to be prepared on the different systems of municipal taxation, when Graham suggested a study of the rival methods of election from *ad hoc* to proportional representation, the wretched candidates looked aghast and thought evidently that we were amusing ourselves at their expense. One of them wanted to construct a " Political Man ", from whose imaginary qualities all things might be deduced; another wanted to lecture on " Land under the Tudors ", but had apparently read only the ordinary textbooks. Finally, we determined to do without our lecturer—to my mind a blessed consummation. It struck me always as a trifle difficult to teach a science which does not yet exist.

Grosvenor Road, October 5th, 1896.—The last fortnight we have been a good deal absorbed in preparing Adelphi Terrace for the opening of the School. Found Hewins in a state of nervous collapse threatening severe illness. Sent him away with his wife and child, and took over the work of preparing for the coming term. Poor Sidney trudges over there directly after breakfast and spends his mornings with painters, plumbers and locksmiths, interviewing would-be students to whom he gives fatherly advice—comes home to lunch and then off to the L.C.C. In the interval of arranging the details of the housekeeping of the School, I am getting on slowly with the book, preparing the ground for work with Sidney next week when Hewins is back. Obvious that this institution will take up much of our time for the next few years. We are convinced it is worth while, in spite of the harassing character of the work. We want to create a centre of intellectual work and comradeship from which our views will radiate through personal intercourse. It remains to be seen how we succeed.

Cliftonville, Margate, November 8th, 1896.—School promising, but not assured. Successful classes and lectures are those giving purely technical instruction to professionals—methods of statistics and railway economics—such subjects as commercial law and currency proving rather too abstract for the clerk to see in what way they make for his bread and butter. Pure learning and culture, such as growth of political theory, is at present a " frost " except for the attendance of the full student who has paid his guinea and attends all the lectures. It is this class we want to encourage—until we have a regular *clientèle* of 300 full students, our success will be problematic in the extreme. Hewins, who expected great things, has been depressed and irritable and it has taken all Sidney's good temper and tact to keep things smooth. Hewins is a sanguine enthusiast—pulls hard and strong when he feels the stream with him. . . . However, with the rise of the students to 220, Hewins' spirits have gone up and he is now again prophesying great things. But I see that this School, if it is to be made a permanent success, will mean a good deal of work and thought for Sidney and myself.

The Argoed, January 18th, 1897.—The London School is progressing. Sidney has contrived to edge it in to any possible London University. It is still a speculation in money, students and output, but it promises well.

The London University

Out of the chairmanship of the T.E.B. and the founding of the L.S.E. sprang Sidney's collaboration, in so far as the metropolis was concerned, with that foremost pioneer in modern university education—R. B. Haldane. And here I recall a potent personality. As lawyer, politician and administrator, R. B. Haldane came to be recognised as one in the first rank. An ardent amateur in philosophy, his writings reveal a passion for deducing from given premises first principles, justifying an emotional faith in the vital as against the mechanistic interpretation of the behaviour of man. Thus, in the secret places of his heart, Haldane believed in the spiritual interpretation of the universe.[1] But it was pre-eminently as a big public personage, in some ways the

---

[1] The following passage from R. B. Haldane's autobiography bears out this view of his state of mind: ". . . My religious outlook was a genuine one. Its origin was a deep conviction that the more experience is spiritual the more it is real. My old master, Lotze, had influenced me towards this conviction, and so had Hegel, whom I had been studying as closely as the state of my then knowledge permitted. With all this had come the further conviction that not only in philosophy but in science it

biggest and most genial of his time, that he will be remembered by those who knew him. Plenitude, mental and physical, seemed to me his dominant feature, leading to a large intake and a like output. A big head on a bigger body —generous expenditure on the good things of life, not least among them choice edibles and the accompanying portions and potions of nicotine and alcohol, also of select quality; long hours of work; endless documents and books mastered and remembered; a multitude of interests, and an ever-widening circle of friends and acquaintances, extending from Emperors and Kings, distinguished diplomatists, and famous men of science and learning, to representative manual workers and scientific and administrative experts of all sorts and kinds: any adequate picture of his life would entail a large and crowded canvas. He had a thin small voice, he was no platform orator; he did not cultivate the press; he was not a fluent journalist; thus he never became a popular figure; he was, in fact, the exact antithesis of a demagogue. Though, successively, Secretary of State for War and Lord Chancellor in two Governments, he remained throughout his life a behind-the-scenes man. Unattractive as a young man, he became as he grew in years, owing to his wit and wisdom and courteous manners, a social charmer, equally at home in the smartest society set or in drab groups of professional men and women. He had a notable gift for manipulating his fellow-men and for the organisation of business; for getting the best out of his subordinates; mainly because, whilst being somewhat cynical, he was always good-humoured and considerate, tempering rebuke and approval with kindly humour. Thus, it was in personal intercourse that he excelled; in successful intrigue, always for public and not for private ends. About Haldane's personal disinterestedness there can be no doubt. He loved power,

was true that no systematic knowledge is sufficient in itself unless it leads up and points to first principles. This doctrine later became valuable to me even as a guide in work at the Bar. It did not help in the business of cross-examination. I was never good at that, nor in the conduct of *nisi prius* cases. But it was invaluable in preparation for the presentation of great questions to the Supreme Tribunals, where the judges were keen about first principles and were looking out for help from the advocate " (*Richard Burdon Haldane—An Autobiography*, pp. 29-30).

especially the power of the hidden hand; or shall I say of the *recognised* hidden hand? But he frequently sacrificed his own prospects if he could thereby serve a friend or promote a cause he believed in. To sum up my memories: a powerful and beneficent personality, a great citizen, above all a loyal and generous colleague.

Amongst all our common friends, R. B. Haldane takes precedence alike in the length of his friendship and in its bearing on the Other One's administrative and political career. He had known each of us before we knew each other; and, as he described, with a humorous gloss, in his autobiography, he had " covered " by the accommodating rôle of a desirable suitor, Sidney Webb's appearance in my father's house when we were, unbeknown to my family, engaged to be married. Our first intrigue with Haldane! After thirty years of uninterrupted friendship the two found themselves in 1924 colleagues in the first Labour Cabinet. It was Haldane who created and fostered the flattering " Webb myth " that flowered so agreeably and advantageously for us and our schemes in the first decade of the twentieth century. Even when the myth, being a myth, faded away, to be replaced by the myth of an " exploded myth ", he remained a steadfast fellow-conspirator for the public good. What bound us together as associates was our common faith in a deliberately organised society: our common belief in the application of science to human relations with a view to betterment. Where we differed was in the orientation of political power. Haldane believed more than we did in the existing governing class: in the great personages of Court, Cabinet and City. We staked our hopes on the organised working-class, served and guided, it is true, by an *élite* of unassuming experts who would make no claim to superior social status, but would content themselves with exercising the power inherent in superior knowledge and longer administrative experience.

Here is an entry in the MS. diary giving my contemporary impression of Haldane's personality before he had become a political personage:

Grosvenor Road, May 3rd, 1897.—Haldane here for a Sunday. Difficult to estimate what amount of influence that man exercises in public affairs. He has never held office; but during the last Liberal Government he was the chief instigator of their collectivist policy— serving to carry information and suggestions from specialists like our- selves to the heads of departments. He was also responsible for many of their appointments. In this Parliament he is in constant confidential intercourse with Balfour and other Conservatives over the many non- party questions dealt with by a Government—and even in some purely political questions his advice is asked. He attracts confidence where he is at all liked—once on friendly terms, you feel absolutely secure that he will never use personal knowledge to advance his own public career to the detriment of any friend. The rank and file of his own party dislike him intensely; partly because he detaches himself from party discipline and acts according to his own inner light, and partly because he seems dominated by some vague principle which they do not understand and which he does not make intelligible. His bulky form, and pompous ways, his absolute lack of masculine vices or " manly " tastes (beyond a good dinner), his superiority and constant attitude of a teacher, his curiously woolly mind would make him an unattractive figure if it were not for the beaming kindliness of his nature, his warm appreciation of friends and a certain pawky humour with which he surveys the world. And there is pathos in his personality. In spite of the successful professional life, the interest and entertain- ment of constantly mixing with the most powerful minds and in the most stirring affairs, the enjoyment of luxurious living to a man with a first-rate digestion, he is a restless, lonely man—in his heart still worshipping the woman who jilted him seven years ago. All the sadder that genuine affectionateness—pleasure in intimate and entirely confidential relations, a yearning towards some sort of *permanence*— is really the strongest side of Haldane's character. He was made to be a husband, father and close comrade. He has to put up with pleasant intercourse with political friends and political foes.

When we are together we are constantly discussing hotly. He has been converted, in a sort of vague metaphysical way, to the principles of collectivism. But, whether it is that his best brains are given to his professional work, or whether it is that he is incapable of working out or even fully comprehending *concrete* principles, he never sees the right side of a question until you have spent hours dinning it into him. Even then he does not admit it, and will go on bringing entirely irrelevant matters wilfully into the discussion in order to " keep you off ", so to speak. But it is quite worth while hotly debating the question with him, because he always comes right in the end, and when you meet him a month hence he repeats your own arguments. As a retort *he* would say that *we* were narrow and limited to our own questions, quite forgetting their proportionate value to other wider issues—and that it is impossible for the cultivated " representative " to do more than grasp certain large principles. Further, that mere logic and mere information are all very well, but they are of little service to move the world without a great personality and long-continued knowledge of affairs. With a pretty significant hint that we have neither, he always ends an encounter. " What *we* think to-day, *you* will think to-morrow " is usually my last hit. All the same, we two and he remain genuinely fond of each other.

Now it so happened that R. B. Haldane and Sidney, united by friendship, made a good combination for the task they undertook: to get carried into law the necessary Bill for the reorganisation of the London University. To begin with, they were, in their several ways, both entirely free from the subtly pervading influence of the Oxford and Cambridge of those days, with their standards of expensive living and enjoyable leisure, and their assumption of belonging to an aristocracy or governing class. Haldane had graduated at Edinburgh and Göttingen, among students living sparely in uncomfortable lodgings, undistracted by games, who looked forward to no other existence than one of strenuous brain-work. He believed intensely in the university, not only as a place for " great teaching " but also as a source of inspiration by " great minds ", producing, in the choicer spirits, a systematic devotion to learning and research. The Other One, on the other hand, with little formal schooling, had known what it was to gain education in adolescence whilst earning a livelihood; he realised the advantages of guidance and attraction that were, by a series of university examinations, brought to bear on myriads of lonely students, to most of whom a full-time undergraduate career, not to mention a residential university, was not within sight. Haldane, to gain his higher aim, would willingly have scrapped the system of external examinations by which alone London University awarded its coveted degrees. In his eyes, even the best-equipped public library, and the most highly organised evening classes, counted for nothing in comparison with the inspiration he had found in personal intimacy with Stuart Blackie and Lotze. But he realised, under Sidney's influence, if not the undesirability, at any rate the political unpracticability, of overthrowing what had already taken deep roots. He, accordingly, designed a scheme of combining in a single university, of a new type, all three elements, namely: the external students influenced by a system of examinations which could be improved; an organised hierarchy of evening classes which, so far as London was concerned, the Technical Education Board was raising to the highest grade; and the group of autonomous colleges, in which a professoriate in no way inferior to those of Germany and Scotland could be trusted to inspire self-selected groups of earnest students in every subject of study and research. For such a university in the greatest of all metropolitan cities, the two conspirators believed that the necessary millions of money would be forthcoming; and the experience of the past thirty years has justified their faith. Possibly, not without its effect on the negotiations (and these I leave Haldane to describe) was the promise which Sidney induced the London County Council to make that, out of the technical education " whiskey money ", the reconstructed university should be straight away endowed with £10,000 a year towards the support of four of its faculties, namely, science, the education side of arts, and two new faculties of engineering and economics, on condition that neither evening students nor the growing polytechnics were excluded.

For me [relates Haldane in his account of these years] the absorbing political subject was higher education. . . . I approached Balfour about the University of London. It was then a mere Board for examining outside students who got from it external degrees by means of examinations without teaching. Valuable as the work of extending degrees to external students had been in the past, it was no longer sufficient. The system lent itself to the purposes of the crammers, and the school teachers in particular used it for obtaining what were virtually little more than trade-marks. The real purpose of university training, the development of the mind in the atmosphere of the teaching university, where teachers and taught could come into close relation, was lacking.

So strongly was this felt that many of the professors in the London colleges had set their hearts on the establishment of a second, the professorially-run university, with no external examinees at all. I knew that the opposition to so far-reaching a measure would be too strong to overcome in the then indifferent state of public opinion. I saw that, as a first step at all events, the only way was to pass an Act enlarging the existing University of London by giving it a powerful teaching side. This might be relied on in the end to absorb the other side by reason of its quality. Of this opinion, also, was my friend Sidney Webb, who as the successful chief of the Technical Education Board of the London County Council had great opportunities of studying the practical problem. Sidney Webb and I took counsel together. He was a very practical as well as a very energetic man. We laid siege to the citadel. We went round to person after person who was prominent in the administration of the existing University. Some listened, but others would not do so and even refused to see us. In the end, we worked out what was in substance the scheme of the London University Act of 1898. The scheme was far from being an ideal one. It provided by way of compromise for a Senate which was too large to be a really efficient supreme governing body for the new composite University, and it had other shortcomings of which we were well aware. But it did set up a teaching university, although Convocation, with its control of the external side, would remain unduly powerful. We saw that the scheme thus fashioned was the utmost we could hope for the time to carry, in the existing state of public opinion about higher education in London. I went to Balfour as soon as we were ready, and explained what we had done and why we had done it in this form. He was both interested and sympathetic, and, after consideration, said that his Government would take the matter up and introduce a Bill fashioned on our lines, although the Government could not pledge itself to stand or fall by it. The Bill was ultimately, after much consultation with me, introduced to the House of Commons by Sir John Gorst on behalf of the Government. He explained it to the House, and concluded by saying that it was on the whole a Bill which the Government recommended.

There was a storm. Sir John Lubbock, the member for the University, opposed it in the interest of the convocation by whose members he had been elected. Sir Charles Dilke and others attacked it fiercely on various grounds. For some time in the course of the discussion not a speech was made in its favour, and the prospects of the Bill seemed hopeless. I sprang to my feet when an opportunity at last offered, and I spoke for once like one inspired. I told the House of Commons of the scandal that the metropolis of the Empire should not have a teaching university to which students from distant regions might come as to the centre for them of that Empire. I showed how far we were behind continental nations, and what a menace this was to our scientific and industrial prospects in days to come. I knew every inch of the ground, and displayed its unsound condition. We were far away from the days in which a step forward had been made by calling into being the examining body named London University, a creation which had given degrees by examination to those whom the Church had in the old days shut out from university status. That reform was in its time a most valuable service to the state, but it was a service which had become superseded in the light of new standards in university education which demanded much more.[1]

In the course of the next few months, in circumstances which taxed to the uttermost Haldane's ingenuity and persuasiveness, the Bill became law. In the summer of 1897, the Government appointed a small executive Commission to draft the constitution and statutes—a vitally important body which happened to have as one of its leading members my old friend Dr. Mandell Creighton (the first President of the School of Economics), who had just been appointed Bishop of London; and, for its chairman, an old acquaintance, Lord Davey. In my diary, I find an entry summarising the doings of the spring of 1897.

Grosvenor Road, July 26th, 1897.—Sidney and Haldane rushing about London trying to get all parties to agree to a Bill for London University. If it goes through, it will be due to Haldane's insistence and his friendship with Balfour—but the form of the Bill—the alterations grafted on the Cowper Commission Report are largely Sidney's. He thinks he has got all he wants as regards the Technical Education Board and London School of Economics. The Commission appointed to carry the Act out is largely favourable, or at any rate " susceptible " to right influence. . . .

[1] *Richard Burdon Haldane—An Autobiography,* pp. 124-7.

CHAPTER III

SOCIAL AND POLITICAL ENVIRONMENT
1892–1898

HITHERTO I have described our specialised activities: first the joint enquiry into British Trade Unionism and the consequent publication of *The History of Trade Unionism* in 1894, and *Industrial Democracy* in 1898, and secondly the administrative work of the Other One on the L.C.C., his chairmanship of the Technical Education Board for six years, and the foundation of the London School of Economics and Political Science. I turn now to the outermost strand of our activities: the propaganda of Fabian collectivism, within the social and political life of our day.

Let me first remind the reader of the outstanding political events of Great Britain during the first spell of Our Partnership, 1892–98. For six years prior to this period the Salisbury administration held office, but it depended for its majority on the seventy Liberal Unionist members led by Joseph Chamberlain; and he, it is needless to add, gave the Government loyal support in return for an effective influence on home and foreign affairs. In July 1892, the month of our marriage, a general election left the Conservatives and Liberal Unionists in a minority in the House of Commons. " There never was so depressed an election ", one historian relates. " The country was tired of the Unionist Government, but without enthusiasm for its successors. The Irish quarrel had taken all the glamour out of Mr. Gladstone's crusade; British Radicals saw no prospect for the causes they had at heart. By heroic efforts Liberals and Irish scraped together a majority of 40 which, as their opponents pointed out, left them absolutely at the mercy of the Irish party in the teeth of a British majority against Home Rule."[1] " The

[1] *Great Britain, Empire and Commonwealth, 1886–1935*, by J. A. Spender, pp. 58-9.

interlude of Liberal administration from 11th August 1892 to 24th June 1895 ", we are told by another Liberal historian, " was only half the length of a normal Government's life in those days; and the two Cabinets which filled it were paralysed for want of any real majority either at Westminster, or in the constituencies." [1]

But this was not all. Mr. Gladstone, whom the Queen was compelled to accept as Prime Minister, was wholly out of sympathy with the projects of social reform vaguely adumbrated in the Newcastle Programme, upon which the election had been fought; proposals more clearly set forth by the little group of Liberal collectivists led by Haldane, Acland, Asquith and Grey.[2] Had not the great man asserted, during his last administration, that unemployment was actually an improper subject even for discussion by the representatives of the people, seeing that it was a necessary incident in profit-making enterprise, and, therefore, should not and could not be dealt with by the political state? Moreover, Gladstone was an anti-militarist and anti-imperialist, and objected to increasing expenditure on the armed forces almost as much as he did on social reform. Hence, when the Home Rule Bill was cast out by the House of Lords in the autumn of 1893, and his colleagues objected to a dissolution on that question, still more when in the spring of 1894 the First Lord of the Admiralty proposed an addition to the Navy, Gladstone threatened to resign: " He had supposed that there were several members of the Cabinet who shared his views and would follow his example, and it was a shock to him to discover in the end that he stood alone. ' Resigned! ' he said in after years, ' I did not resign, I was put out.' " [3]

There ensued a sharp and short struggle, reflected in the entries in my diary, between those Liberal M.P.'s who were at once collectivists and imperialists, who favoured Lord

---

[1] *England 1870–1914*, by R. C. K. Ensor, 1936, p. 209.

[2] Haldane was the only one who approached to a Socialist or remained a true collectivist. The others could more properly be termed "radical reformists". The same group, together with Lord Rosebery, formed the "Limps" or Liberal Imperialists. (Ed.)

[3] *Great Britain, Empire and Commonwealth, 1886–1935*, by J. A. Spender, p. 69.

Rosebery as Premier, on the one hand; and, on the other, the *laisser-faire* and anti-imperialist group, who insisted that Sir William Harcourt should not only lead the House of Commons, but also be Prime Minister. Apparently, the Queen took the matter into her own hands and sent for Rosebery. The Rosebery administration, with its chief standing aloof and resentful, lasted thirteen months and was terminated, in June 1895, by a catch vote on whether or not we had a sufficient stock of cordite! Whereupon Salisbury took office and dissolved Parliament, gaining a majority of 152 over the opposition (340 Conservatives and 71 Liberal Unionists, against 177 Liberals and 82 Irish Nationalists). The Liberal Unionist leaders accepted office in the Conservative Government, and for the next seven years the national policy at home and abroad was directed by Salisbury, Chamberlain and Balfour.

Such was the political framework within which we carried on our propaganda of Fabian collectivism. But what exactly was this peculiar brand of Socialism? In answer to this question, I give a few extracts from a lecture by Sidney Webb on " Socialism: True and False ", given to the Fabian Society in January 1894, on the tenth anniversary of its foundation.

Though we took the title of the Fabian Society [1] in January 1884, it was two or three years before we had quite found out what our instinctive choice of a title really portended. In 1884, the Fabian Society, like the other socialist organisations, had its enthusiastic young members—aye, and old ones too—who placed all their hopes on a sudden tumultuous uprising of a united proletariat, before whose mighty onrush, kings, landlords and capitalists would go down like ninepins, leaving society quietly to re-sort itself into utopia. The date for this social revolution was sometimes actually fixed for 1889, the centenary of the opening of the French Revolution. . . . It was against all thinking and teaching of this catastrophic kind that the Society gradually came to set its face—not, as I believe, because we were any less in earnest in our warfare against existing evils, or less extreme in

---

[1] The explanatory quotation of the name " Fabian " is given on the title-page of the early Fabian Tracts (see No. 7): " For the right moment you must wait, as Fabius did most patiently when warring against Hannibal, though many censured his delays; but when the time comes you must strike hard, as Fabius did, or your waiting will be in vain, and fruitless ".

our remedies, but because we were sadly and sorrowfully driven to the conclusion that no sudden or simultaneous transformation of society from an individualist to a collectivist basis was possible or even thinkable.

On the other hand, we had but little sympathy with schemes for the regeneration of mankind by the establishment of local utopias, whether in Cumberland or in Chili. To turn our back on the unearned increment and the machine industry seemed a poor way of conquering them. We had no faith in the recuperative qualities of spade husbandry, or in any devices for dodging the law of rent. In short, we repudiated the common assumption that socialism was necessarily bound up with insurrectionism, on the one hand, or utopianism, on the other, and we set to work to discover for ourselves and to teach to others how practically to transform England into a social democratic common-wealth. . . . What we Fabians aim at is not the sub-division of property, whether capital or land, but the control and administration of it by the representatives of the community. It has no desire to see the Duke of Bedford replaced by five hundred little Dukes of Bedford under the guise of enfranchised leaseholders, but prefers to assert the claim of the whole community to the land, and especially to that unearned increment of value which the whole community creates. It has no vain dream of converting the agricultural labourer into a freeholder, farming his own land, but looks to the creation of parish councils empowered to acquire land for communal ownership, and to build cottages for the labourers to rent. The path to its town utopia is that of Mr. Chamberlain's early career, though not of his political programme —unlimited municipalisation of local public services and a wide extension of corporate activity. London, in particular, has caught up the old Birmingham cry of " high rates and a healthy city ", but with a significant difference. Our modern economists tell us that the first source of public revenue for a rising city is the growing rental value of its site, which at present falls into private hands. Hence, the new demand for the gradual municipalisation by taxation of urban land values—a demand still so little understood by most of our statesmen that they fondly imagine it to have something to do with a division of rates between house-owner and occupier. It is coming to be remembered, in short, that Bentham himself, the great father of political radicalism, urged that taxation need not be limited to the supply of funds for the bare administrative expenses of the state, but that, wisely handled, it also supplied a means of gradually securing the great end of equality of opportunity to every citizen.

For the rest, the Fabian Society studiously avoided any quotations from Karl Marx, preferring indeed Robert

Owen; they translated economics and collectivism into the language of prosaic vestrymen and town councillors. They dealt largely in statistics; they talked about amending factory acts, and municipalising gas and water supplies. Above all, they were prolific of facts, ideas and practical projects of reform. They were, indeed, far more extreme in their opinions and projects than their phrases conveyed to the ordinary citizen. Their summary of Socialism, which was found in the ensuing decade to have a strong appeal, was put in the following terms. It comprised, they said, essentially collective ownership wherever practicable; collective regulation everywhere else; collective provision according to need for all the impotent and sufferers; and collective taxation in proportion to wealth, especially surplus wealth.[1]

At this point I had better confess that in the propaganda of Fabian collectivism, 1892–98, I was more an observer than a colleague. For it was with some misgiving that I joined the Fabian Society on my engagement to Sidney Webb. To discover the processes of social organisation, to observe and record the behaviour of man in society, had been my primary object in life; and it seemed to my cautious temperament that any pronounced views about social changes to be aimed at, might hamper these researches; partly

---

[1] Rather than give my own view of the place of the Fabian Society in British politics, I quote the estimate of G. M. Trevelyan in his well-known *British History in the Nineteenth Century*, p. 403:

" The third current of *fin de siècle* Socialism, and the most important, was the Fabian doctrine, specially connected with Mr. and Mrs. Sidney Webb. The Fabian Society was founded in 1883. Its name recalls a Roman general whose motto was ' slow but sure '. Eschewing revolution, and intent on the actualities of England at the end of the nineteenth century, Fabians exonerated socialists from the heavy obligation of reading Karl Marx. Without dogmatising as to the ultimate future of industrial organisation, they preached practical possibilities, here and now—municipal socialism and state control of conditions of labour. Equally far from Marx and Morris, they left the New Jerusalem alone, and sought to impregnate the existing forces of society with collectivist ideals.

" The Fabians became experts in bringing electoral, journalistic and personal pressure to bear on local bodies, and on the Liberal or Conservative government of the hour—somewhat after the methods of action of Francis Place, but with the added power of the democratic franchise. By the end of the century it is in Fabianism that we find the nearest approach to a body of doctrine directly affecting the laws and administration of the time, like the doctrines of Bentham and Mill in the past. The Fabians were intelligence officers without an army—there was no Fabian party in parliament—but they influenced the strategy and even the direction of the great hosts moving under other banners."

because it might bias my own selection of facts and hypotheses, but also because the way of discovery might be
blocked by those who held contrary opinions. As years went
by neither of these objections held good. I soon realised
that complete detachment from current politics was impracticable unless you were indifferent to the public welfare,
or had come to the conclusion that human society was
beyond human control. For the longer I studied the social
organisation in which I had been born and bred, the stronger
became my conviction that the distribution of power and
wealth among my fellow-citizens was being controlled, and
very deliberately controlled, in the interests of the propertied
classes, to the detriment of the vast majority of the people,
thus preventing any adequate rise in the health and happiness, the manners and the culture, of the community as a
whole. Nor did I find that Fabian collectivism stood in the
way of getting information. Students, as we happened to
be in those years, of working-class organisation and local
government, an avowed preference for legal enactment and
municipal development helped more than it hindered our
quest for knowledge. For the rest, the British governing
class of the 'eighties and 'nineties, enveloped in self-complacency and enjoying the consciousness of power and a
leisurely life in luxurious surroundings, was innately indifferent to the workings of the intellect. To the typical
politician and lawyer, landlord and financier, to the wealthy
manufacturer and trader, elaborate and accurate descriptions of the poverty of the poor, such as Charles Booth's
Life and Labour of the People in London, or carefully reasoned
arguments in favour of specific reforms, seemed equally
negligible. Men were, and always would be, governed by
their appetites or by conventional views of right or wrong;
if they were exceptionally self-controlled and intelligent,
they might be guided by their pecuniary self-interest and
their desire to found a family; in which case they would be
promptly enrolled in the governing class. Hence the group
of young intellectuals who were, between 1885 and 1892,
getting resolutions passed by Liberal associations and

Radical working-men's clubs, in favour of the eight-hour day, old-age pensions, a minimum wage for those in public employment, and increased health and educational services; or who were reading papers at the British Association and at other reputable gatherings on *The Difficulties of Individualism*, *The Necessary Basis of Society* and *The Transition to Social Democracy*, were welcomed with benevolent smiles and kindly words by distinguished members of the governing *clique*. Some Fabian phrases were actually incorporated in the platform speeches and election addresses of the leaders of the Liberal Party at the general election of July 1892. Had not Sir William Harcourt proclaimed from a public platform that " we are all Socialists now "? had not the rising Liberal lawyer, H. H. Asquith, solemnly stated in his election address: " I am one of those who believe that the collective action of the community may and ought to be employed positively as well as negatively; to raise as well as to level; to equalise opportunities no less than to curtail privileges; to make the freedom of the individual a reality and not a pretence "? [1]

The following entries from the MS. diary show rapid disillusionment with the policy of permeation leading to the publication, in the *Fortnightly Review* of November 1893, of the Fabian Manifesto entitled: " To Your Tents, O Israel ", drafted by Bernard Shaw.[2]

December 24th, 1892.—Have seen something of politicians [I write a few months after our marriage]. Haldane and Asquith to dinner; Sydney Buxton and Acland coming later on. . . . All the younger men in the Government hard at work introducing administrative reforms, yet uncertain whether the old gang will not dictate a policy of evading all legislative proposals. No leader to the new reform movement; a mere upheaval in favour of doing something, met by tight sitting on the part of the provincial capitalists. And when they do give way, they give way on the wrong points; they are as likely as not to skedaddle in face of some preposterous demand, whilst refusing even to consider some quite sound scheme. And the result is that the political world

[1] *Memories and Reflections*, by the Earl of Oxford and Asquith, K.B., vol. i. p. 113.
[2] But very considerably peppered by us with sallies which passed as characteristically Shavian.—G. B. S.

is simply chaotic at present, at least on the reform side. Men like Balfour know well enough what they are playing for and succeed in leading a compact party. If chaos continues they will have a still larger mass of voters. . . .

Grosvenor Rd., Christmas Day, 1893.—The excitement of the autumn [I write exactly twelve months afterwards] has been the issue of the Fabian Manifesto which for a week or so loomed large to us. With Shaw's reproduction of Sidney's facts, it boomed in the press: the Tory democratic papers quoted it freely; the Radical papers denounced it; only the *Spectator* and the *Standard* refusing to notice it out of sheer perplexity how to deal with it. I am not sure whether after the event I altogether approve of it. There is some truth in Graham Wallas's original observation that we were rushed into it by fear of being thought complacent and apathetic by the Independent Labour Party. Whether it is wise to do anything simply from fear of being left behind? But that was not the whole of the motive. All through the spring Sidney and Shaw have been feeling the need of some strong outspoken words on the lack of faith and will to go forward manifested by the majority of the Cabinet. They could hardly go on supporting the Liberals if these were deliberately fooling the Progressives with addled promises. Perhaps the Fabian junta chose the right time to speak: anyway they said only what they thought; they spoke to the world exactly what they had been saying in private. So far the manifesto was justified. . . .

It would be an impertinence to summarise the words of Bernard Shaw. Here are a series of extracts which give the gist of the Fabian Manifesto:

It is not for the Fabian Society to betray the secret history of the desperate efforts made from 1886 to 1892 to bring the Liberal Party up to the poll in some semblance of democratic condition. That red spectre, the Newcastle Programme, vanished on the morrow of the general election, having served its turn; and nobody now wants to hear the story of the infinite pains with which it was raised and brought to the uneasy bedside of Mr. Gladstone himself. The heroic speeches made by the Liberal leaders when, rallying to the revolutionary flag, blazoned with payment of members, death (by taxation) to the ground landlord and royalty owner, home rule for London and relief to the ratepayer, and municipalisation of every monopoly under the sun, they hauled it to the high top-gallant of the great Liberal Party amid the inspiring strains of " we are all Socialists now ", are not usually alluded to at present, having also served their turn; and it is not for the Fabian Society to spoil a stirring page of political history by bringing the public behind the scenes to see those eagle-eyed statesmen carried to the platform, kicking, screaming and protesting, in the arms of the collectivist radicals of London, who offered them the alternative of saying as they were told or spending another seven years in opposition. As the world knows, they said as they were told; and they just scraped through at the election by abandoning Home Rule to the Irish constituencies, and ruffing " Integrity of the Empire " and Tory democracy with collectivist trumps conveyed from the sleeves of the London Liberal and Radical Union and the Fabian Society.

There follows a detailed exposure of the reactionary doings of the Whig Ministers, notably in the administration of the Post Office under Arnold Morley, and of Public Works under Shaw-Lefevre: too long to quote.

Lord Spencer, at the Admiralty [proceeds the indictment], also had his opportunities. The scandal of the starvation wages at the Deptford and other victualling yards had become too great to be any longer ignored. . . . The Government's brand-new Labour Department made him a special report as to what he ought to pay, and brought forcibly to his notice the damning facts as to what he did pay. Like Mr. Acland in the Science and Art Department, he might frankly have accepted for all the dockyard workmen the recognised standard rates of the various trade unions concerned. Like the London County Council, he might have resolved to pay no wage on which a family could not decently exist. He might have put a stop to the practice, recently exposed in a tragic case, of not paying the labourers until their wages are a week overdue, thus driving them to the pawnbroker to borrow at heavy interest the money due to them by the British Government, which pays them no interest at all on the compulsory loan. He might have " abolished " the middleman who at Deptford drove poor Pluck to suicide at the very moment of the departmental enquiry, and taken all the Admiralty workmen into direct public employment. He might have established the eight hours' day in all the government dockyards. . . . Had Mr. Fowler been but a little less than a quarter-of-a-century behind his time, what a field he would have found in other directions! Had he been really in sympathy with the House of Commons' repeatedly expressed desire to put down sweating, what a circular he could have issued to all the local authorities in the kingdom, commending to their notice the model clauses of the London County Council; stimulating them to the establishment of an eight hours' day for all their employees; and urging them to follow the House of Commons in abandoning the competitive rate for a living wage! And with local authorities everywhere eager for guidance on the menacing problem of the unemployed, what really democratic president of the local government board would have let himself be put to open shame by ignoring the very existence of acts of parliament enabling the guardians to set the poor to work, or have refused to come to any decision as to whether local authorities should or should not be allowed to try their own experiments in this direction!

But all the Ministers are not found wanting: there are words of encouragement, or are they words of apology, for those members of the Cabinet who were deemed to be permeated with Fabianism:

Now Mr. Asquith and Mr. Acland, like Mr. Sydney Buxton, hold their portfolios as representatives of that Liberal dilution of collectivist radicalism which made itself felt in the last parliament on the memorable occasion when the three gentlemen in question, with Sir Edward Grey and Mr. Haldane, suddenly checkmated a reactionary Whig job put forward under the specious title of leaseholds enfranchisement, to the unspeakable astonishment and confusion of the Liberal leaders, whose sole objection to the measure was that it was too advanced. Without the collectivist movement outside parliament it is certain that Messrs. Asquith, Acland, Sydney Buxton and Sir Edward Grey would never have displaced members of the " old gang " in the ministry, and one can only surmise the intensity of the friction that must have been created in the Cabinet between administrators of their way of thinking and a reactionist like Sir William Harcourt holding the purse-strings. The situation is so obvious that the Fabian Society may, without indiscretion, say that when the secret history of Mr. Gladstone's administration comes to be written, it will be found that since the very formation of the Cabinet, the progressive party, led by Mr. Asquith and Mr. Acland, and joined by Lord Rosebery, Lord Ripon, Mr. Mundella and Mr. Bryce, has been hampered, blocked, and eventually overborne, firstly, by Mr. Gladstone's complete absorption in Home Rule; secondly, by the active hostility of such seasoned Whigs as Sir William Harcourt and Mr. Fowler; thirdly, by the doctrinaire " Manchesterism " and pettish temper of Mr. John Morley; and fourthly, by the ignorance, indifference and inertia of the Whig peers, Lords Spencer and Kimberley, backed by such obsolescent politicians as Mr. Shaw-Lefevre and Mr. Arnold Morley.

The Manifesto ends with a plan of campaign: the creation of a Labour Party securely anchored in the trade union movement.

To those working-men who look solely to the interests of labour we need not address any lengthy argument for putting the Reform Bill of 1885 to its proper use by largely increasing the representation of labour in parliament. The fact that, in the House of Commons, governing a country where four men out of every five are wage workers, only fifteen out of six hundred and seventy are labour members, is altogether disgraceful to our great labour organisations. . . . The case for the fifty candidates, the £30,000 and the prompt and energetic organisation of the labour vote, is unanswerable. The question is, who is to do it? There is, unfortunately, no such thing as completely effective and general organisation of the working-classes in this or in any other country. But there is one organising agency, which is so much more effective and advanced than any other, that its superior fitness for the political work in hand is beyond all question; and that is the trade union organisation. There is nothing in the labour world that can compare even distantly with it. . . . There is no other combination able to cope with a general election. Attempts have been made, and are still being made from time to time, especially by Socialists, to establish general societies of the whole working-class to relieve the trade unions of their political duty; but, at the present moment, if the unions polled their entire voting strength at a general election, they could put not less than two thousand voters into the field for every single voter in the ranks of the most successful of their rivals.

The money difficulty, which is the great bar to parliamentary representation of the working-class, does not exist for bodies which can raise a thousand pounds by a levy of from a penny to sixpence per member. A subscription of a penny a week for a year from every member of a trade union in the country would produce at least upwards of £300,000; and, though such a subscription is not completely practicable, the calculation shows how easily the larger unions alone, with their membership of a million, could provide £30,000 to finance fifty labour candidates at £600 apiece, and to force forward the long-deferred legislation for payment of members and election expenses.

On the whole then, we may take it that the representation of the working-classes at the general election will depend on the great national trade unions, and not on the Socialist bodies. Neither the Fabian Society nor the Social Democratic Federation, neither the Labour Electoral Association nor the society known as the Independent Labour Party, has the slightest prospect of mustering enough money to carry through three serious candidatures, much less fifty. Their part will be to provide the agitation which will enable the trade union leaders to obtain the support of the rank and file in rising to the occasion. [*Fortnightly Review*, November 1893.] [1]

The Fabian Manifesto, so I judge from a batch of letters from our personal friends among Liberal politicians and Liberal journalists, hurt feelings and roused anger.

The manifesto is a heavy blow to us [writes R. B. Haldane on November 2, 1893]. We younger men were striving to bring those with whom we were immediately in contact into relation with you. We were making an impression. The liberal machine was in course of modification. The work was very difficult. . . . It was easier to persuade the older men, like Harcourt and Fowler, than to coerce them. . . . It hurts *us* far more than the old gang, for weak as we were we could point, in the old days, the days of a week ago, to the support of your party. And now the Whig element will smile and go its way, and rely on what is really the substantial back-ground of the purely political working-man, who cares much where Liberalism is still comparatively strong, for things like Welsh Disestablishment and Home Rule.

Even more exasperated by the Manifesto was H. W. Massingham, the political editor of the *Daily Chronicle*.

Its appeal to trade unions is absurd and ill-timed; it is already being universally interpreted in the press (see the *Pall Mall* and the *Dundee Advertiser*) as a mere Unionist dodge, and it is in particular a retrogression (in the matter of the advice to trade unions—*who won't respond*) from every political principle that the Fabians have upheld. I think it a terrible mistake, which may have serious consequences. " Not that it is easy to discuss seriously a manifesto chock full of levity, of unreal and insincere argument, of unverified statements, and of purposeful exaggeration ", he writes to G. B. S. ". . . You have perpetrated a schoolboy jest—a mere freak of mischievous tom-foolery." [I may observe in passing that within two years, as will be seen in the following pages, our correspondents had become as critical as we had been of the spinelessness of the Liberal Cabinet.]

I gather from the MS. diary that, during the next four years, we became increasingly intimate with politicians and

[1] For details as to the organisation of the Labour Party and its relation to trade unionism see *The History of Trade Unionism*, S. and B. Webb, 1920 edition, chapter xi., " Political Organisation, 1900–1920 " (p. 677). See also *History of Socialism*, by Thomas Kirkup, revised by Edward Pease, 1913, section on " The Labour Party " (pp. 384–92). (See, too, *British Working-Cass Politics*, G. D. H. Cole. Ed.)

civil servants. But, immersed as we were in our researches into British Trade Unionism and in S. W.'s municipal and educational administration, this contact with the greater world of politics has left few traces in our joint memory. So I restrict myself to giving, for the most part without comment, a long string of entries; which may well seem to the reader scrappy and inconsequent, unduly personal and therefore lacking in perspective and sense of proportion. As a set-off these contemporary notes will, at any rate, be free from the distortion of being " wise after the event ": the one irredeemable flaw, regarded as evidence of past states of mind, of all political reminiscences.

March 12*th*, 1894.—Last Thursday I was sitting down to work after breakfast when Haldane was announced. " I have come to see you and Webb about the political situation ", he began, looking grave and disturbed. I called Sidney in, and we both sat down feeling that we were expected to condole with some grievance but not quite certain which. " These are dreadful appointments ", he continued. " Shaw-Lefevre is fatal to the Local Government Board; couldn't be worse: George Russell at the Home Office, too." And then Haldane unburdened his soul to us. He described how the last ten days had been in reality a pitched battle between the old and the new Radicals. The common run of Liberal members were strongly in favour of Harcourt; the little gang of collectivist Radicals (which included Asquith, Acland, Sydney Buxton and Grey) had forced Rosebery on the parliamentary Radicals with the aid of such outside forces as the London Progressives and the *Chronicle*. John Morley had joined them from personal dislike of Harcourt, so that the hand of the Labouchere lot had been forced by the threat of the retirement of the most vital part of the Ministry. But the old gang had had their revenge. They had promoted Fowler, forced into the L.G.B. Shaw-Lefevre (Fowler and Harcourt's nominee), and effectually barred the way to Haldane's entry into the Cabinet. It was natural enough that poor Haldane, having sacrificed himself by incurring the hatred of the rank and file by his successful Rosebery intrigue, should not be satisfied with this result. He had come to us to suggest that the *Chronicle* should be more critical in its attitude towards the new Government, and that the Progressives generally should not give themselves away. It was a quaint episode, when one remembered his grave remonstrance about our hostile attitude last autumn, that he should be instigating us to be independent. I saw, however, that it was more the *Chronicle* that he was after than ourselves. So I arranged that he should meet Massingham here on Sunday night and talk it over.

Massingham came in before Haldane arrived, and confirmed his account of what had taken place. Asquith and Haldane, he says, are hated by the House of Commons Radical, who feels the ground slipping from under him without knowing why. Haldane incited Massingham to keep the *Chronicle* an independent force. They and Sidney more or less determined on a plan of campaign. . . . " It is war to the knife, now," said Haldane impressively, " either they or we have to go down." But what amused me was the way in which the present crisis had completely healed the strained feeling caused between Sidney and Massingham, and to some extent Haldane, by the Fabian Manifesto. Massingham, who had told us firmly that he would never work with us again, was now taking counsel about his conduct of the *Chronicle*, and his ultimatum to the nominal editor that he would stand no interference in the political editorship. It shows how right we were to treat his angry outburst of private and public abuse with imperturbable good temper, and turn our left cheek when he struck our right. I like Massingham immensely: I like him more than I respect him. His excitability, impressionableness, his quick appreciation of anything you say, and clever reproduction of it—all this is attractive —but one feels that to be safe with him one ought to keep him very much in tow. In that respect he resembles Tom Mann: he needs ballast.

Our little plan of writing the minority reports of the two Commissions [1] seems to be coming off all right. Tom Mann hands in his elaborate Socialist manifesto and programme to-morrow. Broadhurst swallowed his part quite complacently, and Sidney has prepared him an excellent document on old-age pensions and the reform of the poor law. But we tremble lest some inadvertence should spoil our little game and Sidney's work be wasted. But these sort of risks one has to run with these Labour men. They are not efficient. Broadhurst a good deal more so than Tom Mann; but then one likes him less in other ways, which makes working through him less pleasant. Whether we shall succeed in making our little home the intellectual headquarters of the Labour movement depends a good deal on the success, from the point of view of the two men concerned, of these minority reports. If it becomes generally known among the working-men leaders that Sidney is always ready to give them their stock in trade, and that no discredit comes to them from accepting his help, then we shall be able to direct the aims and methods of the popular party on the questions which we understand. This behind the scenes intellectual leadership is, I believe, Sidney's especial talent.

[1] Royal Commissions on Labour and on the Aged Poor.

Sidney is discouraged about the political situation [I write in July 1894]. Absorbed in the L.C.C. administrative work and in the book, he has little time for wire-pulling. He feels that there is a backwarda-tion. The Conservative Unionist Party is now fully alive to the issue of individualism and property as against collectivism and labour legislation, and is making preparations to fight hard; whilst the Liberal Party, though vaguely collectivist, is not led by collectivists, and has even among its leaders the most bigoted individualists. We have to some extent roused our natural enemies without having secured our natural allies. The Independent Labour Party, with its lack of money, brains and, to some extent, moral characteristics, is as yet more a thorn in the side of the Liberals than an effective force on our side. Tom Mann is putting a good deal of steam into its propaganda and is lending to the cause some of his high character and personal purity; but at present there is no chance of its being more than a wrecking party, to some extent contradicting the permeating policy of the Fabians. Still, it has its uses: it may be a question of the surgeon's knife rather than of a sustained regimen.

I sometimes wonder whether I am right in inclining Sidney *not* to go into Parliament. Hardly a month passes but some constituency or other throws out a fly for him; but so far he resolutely refuses to consider it, and that largely because I discourage him. Personally, I feel that he is doing real work on the L.C.C., work which is not only useful to London, but useful to him, in that it gives him problems of administration to think out instead of pure wire-pullers' work. Is there any distinction? Is not all administrative work wire-pulling, with a clear conception of your ends? Perhaps the distinction is that in administration your ends must be practicable and desirable; in political wire-pulling, you may be highly successful in your machinery but have altogether misunderstood the object of it. I do not feel confident that he would be a big success in the House; I do not think the finest part of his mind and character would be called out by the manipulation and intrigues of the lobby. And then a parliamentary career would destroy our united life; would cut at the root of a good deal of our joint effort. Perhaps that is why I distrust my dislike of his going into Parliament; it would take so much away from me, personally, would add so many ties and inconveniences. Sooner or later I suppose he will have to make the sacrifice—but better later than sooner.

Borough Farm, Surrey, July 1894.—How far, I wonder [I write a few days later], will the collectivist principle carry us? The thinkers of fifty years ago believed as firmly in individualism as we believe in collectivism—probably more uncompromisingly; for the men and

women of to-day distrust general principles even though they be prepared to use them. And yet it is easy to see now that the settled conviction of the individualists that government should be limited to
keeping the ring clear for private individuals to fight in, was based on
the experience of a one-sided and corrupt participation of the government in industrial organisation, and not on any necessary characteristic
of state action. Face to face with the government action of their own
day, they were to a large extent right. Is it not possible that it is the
same with collectivism? Public administration is the alternative to
private enterprise, and since private enterprise is corrupt and selfish
we propose to supersede it by democratic control. But it is, on the face
of it, as unlikely that the collectivist principle will apply all round as
that the individualist principle would solve all the social problems of
fifty years ago. I do not think that we Fabians believe in more than a
limited application of the collectivist principle; though, as practical
politicians, we think that we are as yet nowhere near the margin of
cultivation, that we can cultivate this principle vigorously for all that
it is worth, in all directions without exhausting its vitality. But of
one thing I feel certain. The controversy which seems to us now so
full of significance and import will seem barren and useless to our
great-grandchildren; they will be amazed that we fought so hard to
establish one metaphysical position and to destroy another. And that
is why I value diagnosis so much more highly than controversy and
propaganda. How eagerly one searches in old pamphlets, articles and
speeches for the chance fact which has been used to illustrate some
utterly bygone argument or principle; how much more highly one
values accurate and vivid description to subtle argument and slashing
logic. But even here one is discouraged. The selection of facts is
governed by the hypotheses of the investigator. Just those facts, which
would have been most illuminating to the student of the next century,
may be overlooked, or even, if noticed, may be carelessly thrown on
one side. One must be content to work for one's own day. . . .

December 29th, 1894.—Spent our Christmas at Parmoor, with
Alfred Cripps, the children, the [Leonard] Courtneys and various
Cripps nieces. Alfred's home is strangely attractive—with a dash of
sadness in it—especially to Theresa's sisters.[1] A charming house,
designed largely by Theresa, the soft luxurious colouring, the quaint-
ness of the furniture, the walls covered with her portraits, all bring
back to me the memory of her gracious personality, so full of sympathy,
wit and vivid imagination. And yet the home seems complete without
her—the children revel in high spirits and health, the servants are

---

[1] Beatrice's sister Theresa Cripps died in 1893, leaving five young children.
(Ed.)

contented. Alfred himself has regained all the lightheartedness of his charming disposition. Possibly it is the rebound from the sadness of his most intimate thoughts, but to the mere spectator he seems more lighthearted than of old. He is again the young man—unattached—absolute master of his own life. And he is in the full tide of great prosperity. An enormous professional income (he told Arthur [1] that he made £1000 a week during the session) has enabled him to buy the family estate and sit down in front of a promising constituency. Doubtless he sees before him a brilliant career. Dear old Father used to call him " the little jewel of an advocate "—a term which just fits him. There is something jewelled in his nature; intellectual *skilfulness* raised to the highest degree, a perfect deftness in execution, a loving disposition, unruffled temper, a cheery optimism; all these bright qualities set in a solid determination that all things shall fit in with his view of what is desirable—for himself and others. He is a delightful father—the children obeying him implicitly with no consciousness of being ruled or regulated; a charming host—seeming to place his whole establishment at the service of his guests; a most indulgent master and landlord; and, yet for all that, he gets his own way in life, and takes a very large share of the good things of the world both material and spiritual. With this disposition he could hardly be a reformer. He has become of late years more and more a Conservative opportunist—bent on keeping the soft places of the world for his own class—but ready to compromise and deal whenever his class would lose more by fighting. He has almost a constitutional dislike of economic or social principle. In the management of his own estate he creates the maximum of personal dependence on himself, not only scattering his money freely, but almost preferring to give it when it is least deserved so as to get the greatest amount of personal gratitude. And yet he is a determined opponent of any kind of public help—opposes it on the ground that it would undermine personal effort; in his heart of hearts he feels that it would render impossible the exercise of that power which he loves—the love of binding people to you by ties of obligation and personal gratitude. I doubt whether Alfred ever thinks out an economic or political problem. Why should he? He knows on which side he is retained, and there will be time enough to get up the advocate's facts when the question turns up. This superficialism, of course, takes from his conversation all the deeper interest—he never weighs what you say, he simply listens to it to get the cue for a bright repartee or a quick turn of the subject. Discussion with him becomes a pretty play of words, he refuses to consider your position and will not permit you to look round his. Perhaps it is this part of Alfred's development

---

[1] Arthur Playne, married to Beatrice's sister Mary. (Ed.)

with which I am most disappointed. When I first knew him—for those three or four years I was intimate with him—he was *thinking* hard, trying to ascertain facts and draw conclusions. He has now ceased to think. All the intellectual energy he can spare from his money-making advocacy is spent in the enjoyment of his own prosperity, and in that baser form of advocacy—the manufacture of electioneering speeches. With his skill and charm he will succeed in politics as he has succeeded at the Bar—he will " make money or its equivalent "—and that is all. For all that, he remains an essentially lovable man. And without doubt he will one day find another mate, and then we shall lose sight of him.

It is curious to see the three brothers-in-law together. Each one has, for the opinions of the other two, tolerant contempt. Leonard Courtney likes Alfred far better than he does Sidney, thinks him a pleasant, attractive fellow with all the antecedents of a gentleman and a scholar. But for his opportunist Toryism—his demagogic anti-democratic attitude—he has, I think, an even greater intellectual contempt than for Sidney's collectivism. Alfred frankly defends class privileges and as frankly appeals to the prejudices of the masses— favours protection and publicans as well as priests and peers, and is as bitterly opposed to popular education, or even any stimulus to citizenship, as he would bè to unlimited outdoor relief. Beyond all he is a purely party man and looks on every proposal as a move in the party fight.[1] All this is as intensely repugnant to Leonard as Alfred's lax management of his estate, or his scarcely veiled bribery of the Stroud constituency. To Leonard the means whereby you carry through a proposal, the arguments with which you support it, are as important as the end itself. And to do Leonard justice he is a democrat at heart, in that he honestly desires that the government of the country should be the reflection of the free desires and views of the whole body of the people. Possibly he is more of a democrat than we are ourselves; for we have little faith in the " average sensual man ", we do not believe that he can do much more than describe his grievances, we do not think that he can prescribe the remedies. It is possibly exactly on this point that Leonard feels most antagonism to our opinions. We wish to introduce into politics the professional expert—to extend the sphere of government by adding to its enormous advantages of wholesale and compulsory management, the advantage of the most skilled entrepreneur. Leonard agrees with us, I think, in believing that the happiness of the mass is the end to be aimed at, but he has no faith

[1] During the War 1914–18, Alfred Cripps, on the ground of pacifist principle, left the Conservative Party and later joined the Labour Party. See Biographical Index. (Ed.)

in our methods because he holds a radically different economic creed. Alfred, on the other hand, refuses seriously to discuss with us, because he recognises at once that we desire different ends—Leonard he holds to be a cranky faddist who cannot make up his mind which side of things he is really going to support. The attitude of the three brothers-in-law may therefore be described thus: Alfred looks on Sidney as a traitor to the brain-working and propertied class; Sidney looks on Alfred as a " kept " advocate of the *status quo*; Leonard looks on Alfred as a somewhat selfish, thoughtless and superficial conservative; on Sidney as a shallow-minded, self-complacent, half-educated democrat; whilst both Sidney and Alfred have much the same opinion of Leonard —an upright but wrong-headed man, dominated by a worn-out economic creed and shackled by lack of sympathy and quick intelligence. To some extent all opinions are equally true—as a summing-up of each individual they are all equally false.

January 20*th*, 1895.—Haldane, utterly discouraged with condition of the Liberal Party; says there is now no hope that the Cabinet will pull themselves through. With the exception of Acland, none of the Ministers are doing any work: Rosebery sees no one but Eddy Hamilton, a flashy fast Treasury clerk, his stud-groom, and various non-political fashionables; Sir W. Harcourt amuses himself at his country place and abroad, determined to do nothing to help Rosebery; even Asquith, under the dominance of his brilliant and silly wife, has given up attending to his department and occupies his time by visiting rich country houses and learning to ride! " Rot has set in," says Haldane; " there is no hope now but to be beaten and then to reconstruct a new party. If only you Progressives can hold your own at the L.C.C. elections, you would be a plank saved from the wreck upon which we could build a new combination."

The same strains from Massingham, now much under Haldane's influence. He spent three or four hours here the other day being coached for the *Daily Chronicle* on the L.C.C. election. Urged Sidney to go into Parliament and become one of the leaders of the reconstruction party. But Sidney will bide his time. At present, the L.C.C. is a better platform from which to bring about collectivism than the House of Commons.

January 23*rd*, 1895.—Last night we had an informal conference with the I.L.P. leaders; MacDonald and Frank Smith (who are members both of the Fabian Society and the I.L.P.), having been for some time harping on the desirability of an understanding between the two societies. To satisfy them Sidney asked a little dinner of Keir Hardie, Tom Mann, Pease and Shaw, and the two intermediaries. I think the principals on either side felt it would come to nothing. Nevertheless, it was interesting. Keir Hardie was reserved, and merely reiterated the burden of his speech to the Fabians. But Tom Mann gushed out his soul. The practical issue before us was the action of the I.L.P. at the L.C.C. elections. Tom Mann, with the concurrence of Keir Hardie, advised the I.L.P. to abstain from voting. The Progressives on the L.C.C., he said, were not convinced Socialists and, even those who were, chose to run as Progressives and not as purely Socialist candidates. Therefore, the I.L.P. should be hostile to their return. He would not support John Burns (or presumably Sidney), " because Jack played to get the vote of the mere Liberal ". " No one could get the votes of the I.L.P. who did not pledge himself to the nationalisation of the means of production, and *who did not run overtly in opposition to all who were not socialists.*" He would accept no alliance. When we cross-examined his reasons they amounted to this. First, even if the Progressives were trying their best to use the L.C.C. for socialist purposes, the I.L.P. of the provinces regarded them as mere Liberals; and, as a fact, if the Progressives were elected, it would redound to the credit of the official Liberals. Secondly, the amelioration brought about by the collectivism of the L.C.C. retarded the growth of the I.L.P. movement; set back the social revolution.

It was melancholy to see Tom Mann reverting to the old views of the S.D.F. and, what is worse, to their narrow sectarian policy. Keir Hardie, who impressed me very unfavourably, deliberately chooses this policy as the only one he can boss. His only chance of leadership lies in the creation of an organisation " agin' the Government "; he knows little and cares less for any constructive thought or action. But with Tom Mann it is different. He is possessed with the idea of a " church "—of a body of men all professing the same creed and all working in exact uniformity to exactly the same end. No idea which is not absolute, which admits of any compromise or qualification, no adhesion which is tempered with doubt, has the slightest attraction to him. And as Shaw remarked, he is deteriorating. This stumping the country, talking abstractions and raving emotions, is not good for a man's judgement; and the perpetual excitement leads, among other things to too much whiskey.

I do not think the conference ended in any understanding. We made clear our position. The Fabians in no way competed with the I.L.P. We were purely an educational body—we did not seek to become a political party. We should continue our policy of inoculation—of giving to each class, to each person, coming under our influence, the exact dose of collectivism that they were prepared to assimilate. And we should continue to improve and enlarge such machinery of government that came into our hands. Of course, this slow imperceptible change in men's opinions and in the national institutions, is not favourable to the growth of a revolutionary party. There is some truth in Keir Hardie's remark that we were the worst enemies of the social revolution. No great transformation is possible in a free democratic state like England unless *you alter the opinions of all classes of the community*—and, even if it were possible, it would not be desirable. That is the crux between us!

In the last chapter I described the stalemate of the London County Council election in the first days of March 1895; the Progressives deprived of their majority of elected members, and dependent, for their administrative control, on the Progressive aldermen overhanging from the outgoing Council. A fortnight later, there occurred an event which, because it affected one of the family group, lent acidity to the following entries in the MS. diary. My brother-in-law, Leonard Courtney, who had served for six years as Deputy Speaker, was pressed by Sir William Harcourt and his colleagues to accept the Government nomination for the Speakership: he felt compelled, out of loyalty to his own party, to enquire whether or not they wished him to accept it. The answer was decisively in the negative.[1]

March 19th, 1895.—Poor dear Leonard diddled out of the Speakership by his own party. A mean and discreditable intrigue of Chamberlain's, who has had an animus against him ever since I can remember—first because Leonard was too much of a Whig, then because he retained too much of the Radical. Most likely, however, it has been all through a personal animus dating from Leonard's refusal fifteen years ago to enrol himself as Chamberlain's follower. It is only fair to say that Leonard has had a contempt for Chamberlain's intelligence and character—and Leonard is not a man to hide his opinions. Leonard's bad manners, his supercilious depreciation of other people's claims, and his lack of graciousness, have been Chamberlain's opportunity. We are grieved not only for his and Kate's sake but because we really believe we have lost the most democratic Speaker available. For, with all his faults, Leonard has an honest desire for the maximum *efficiency* in democratic machinery; and he judges each change on its own merits and not on what it may lead to. He has *faith in democracy*—a quality which covers many sins.

[1] See *Life of Lord Courtney*, by G. P. Gooch, chapter xv., "The Speaker's Chair" (pp. 316-28).

March 26th, 1895.—Beatrice Chamberlain [1] paid me one of her annual visits, and we had a long talk on politics, carefully avoiding the L.C.C. and the Speakership. She was anxious to know our opinion of the Factory Bill—was it a good Bill—did it go far enough? I gather from her attitude that J. C. is friendly to regulation of private enterprise and has no prejudices in favour of free trade in labour. I told her that the Bill was excellent so far as it went, but might easily be made better by certain amendments. I felt inclined to offer to send her the amendments; but I am not sufficiently certain of J. C.'s *bona fides* to be completely confidential. One great advantage of the Bill is that at last we get recognised the principle I have been fighting for for five years, the responsibility of the *giver out of work* for conditions of employment: my own pet invention in labour legislation, I am glad to see it at last embodied in the black and white of a Government Bill.

May 27th, 1895.—A grey outlook in political situation, a heavy reaction setting in against the Liberal Government—the " haves " thoroughly frightened, the " have-nots " unsatisfied. Within the Liberal Party each man complaining of the other—no comradeship or cohesion—all at sixes and sevens with regard to opinions.

July 8th, 1895.—On the eve of the election, the Fabians are sitting with their hands in their laps [I write just before the general election]. From our point of view, no result can be satisfactory. The Liberals, on the eve of dissolution, show no signs of grace, they go unabsolved to their grave: if anything, rather inclined to repent their good deeds, not to regret their lost opportunities. Lords, Home Rule and Local Veto are their battle cries—Rosebery, Morley and Harcourt voicing each separately. The I.L.P. is splashing about in a futile ineffectual fashion, the S.D.F. turning all its energies into a fanatical crusade against John Burns! We wish the Liberals to be beaten, but we do not wish the Tories to win. A tie, or something near a tie, would suit us best. But it looks like a triumphant majority for the Tories. Nor does there seem much hope in the future. The Liberal Party is pledged to three measures which offend all the conservative instincts of the people—Home Rule, Local Veto and Church Disestablishment—without exciting the slightest enthusiasm among the advanced section of their party. Sometimes we think we are in for a long spell of strong Conservative rule beginning with 1895, and lasting possibly for another twenty years with only short interregnums of weak Liberal Government. For the Liberals have no leaders inspired with a new faith. Asquith has been ruined by marrying a silly ignorant wife; and

---

[1] Daughter of Joseph Chamberlain by his first wife and intimate friend of Beatrice before her marriage. (Ed.)

there is no other man who has at once capacity, character and conviction. The Labour men are mere babies in politics; judging from our knowledge of the Labour movement we can expect *no* leader from the working-class. Our only hope is in permeating the young middle-class man—catching them for collectivism before they have enlisted on the other side.

Though the situation looks bad for our side of things, it is impossible not to be amused and interested in the political drama. Chamberlain is the man of the moment. He has kept the little band of Liberal Unionists separate and compact for ten years; and now, just before they must of necessity melt away, he has deftly used them to ride into power, dragging into the Government the faithful Jesse Collings, the servile Powell Williams and the amiable youth, Austen. The humour of the situation is the fact that the majority of the Liberal Unionists in the House of Commons have been anti-Chamberlainites—more hostile in their hearts to " Joe " than the bigoted Tories! It is a testimony to the marvellous force of Chamberlain's personality that he pervades this election—no one trusts him, no one likes him, no one really believes in him, and yet everyone accepts him as the leader of the united Unionists. His position in the Tory Party is, in fact, very similar to his position in 1885 in the Liberal Party. Is it equally unstable? Will he play again the rôle of the usurper to keep his seat on the throne, or does he believe sufficiently in his new party to serve it faithfully? I am inclined to think that, barring accidents from evil temper, the cause of private property is sufficiently attractive to Chamberlain's mind to keep him from wilful wrecking; and that, on the whole, Salisbury has got a fair consideration in the bargain of the last few days. But alas! for the poor dear Liberal Unionists—that little company of upright, narrowly enlightened, well-bred men—who drifted away from the Liberal Party ostensibly on Home Rule, but mainly because of the shoddy social schemes Joe had imposed on Gladstone. To be used as the ladder up which Joe climbs into a Conservative Government, waving aloft his banner of shoddy reform, then to be thrown ignominiously aside. A fit ending for a company of prigs!

July 10*th*, 1895.—Attended London Trades Council meeting last Thursday. Printed agenda of platonic resolutions on all manner of questions. But the business done was exclusively on minutes of the executive. For two-and-a-half hours some 100 delegates wrangled over an accusation of *sweating* brought against the Salvation Army by the Printing Trades Federation and reported by the printing trades group of the L.T.C. Quite obvious that the delegates of the Printing Federation had made numberless exaggerated statements: equally clear that the printing trades group had given a clean bill of health to the Salvation Army in spite of manifold signs of sweating in the past, if not in the present. No conclusion—referred to another committee.

But the most astounding fact about this meeting was the total absence of any reference, or even a by-the-way allusion, to the approaching general election. It is almost inconceivable that a meeting of the representative working-men of London should be held within four days of the general election without taking apparently the slightest notice of it. It is another proof of the disastrous political incapacity of the present T.U. leaders. The T.U. world seems half-paralysed. The faked-up conference at Manchester on the 11th, held because it was ordered by the last Congress, has had not the remotest effect on any single election. The *Cotton Factory Times*, the organ of the cotton operatives, has dilated on cotton duties and bi-metallism, but not a word on the more general interests of the wage-earners; the I.L.P. journals—*Clarion* and *Labour Leader*—have published no programme, have given no lead [I record, as the returns for the long drawn-out election drop in], except Keir Hardie's futile suggestion that I.L.P. voters should spoil their ballot papers by writing the name of some woman as candidate. Even the miners seem to be in a state of political suspended animation.

Of course, this has meant a rout for the anti-Conservatives (really that is the only generic term wide enough to cover the numberless groups) all along the line—Sir W. Harcourt being smashed at Derby, and Keir Hardie at West Ham! The rout is quite indiscriminate: if the official Liberals have been extinguished, the Labour Party has certainly not won. Some dozen seats have probably been lost by Labour candidatures; but, where the Liberal has stood aside, the Labour man has failed to win the place.

To us the result is not altogether unsatisfactory. From our point of view the field had to be cleared. The official Liberals had rucked up. For the last year, there were numberless signs that our opinions were discounted—that there was a backwardation. This has been especially obvious since the L.C.C. elections—the Harcourts, Morleys, Hibberts and Fowlers have sneered, have as good as said that they were not any longer going to be bamboozled, that Home Rule, Local Veto, Church Disestablishment and anti-Lords were to be the only battle cries of the Liberal Party. The utter rout, the annihilation, one might almost say, of the Harcourt faction—the hopeless discredit into which such reforms as Local Veto, Home Rule, Church Disestablishment have fallen clears the field of a good deal of cumbrous débris. On the other hand, the I.L.P. has completed its suicide. Its policy of abstention and deliberate wrecking is proved to be futile and absurd; Keir Hardie has probably lost for good any chance of posturing as M.P., and will sink into the old place of a discredited Labour leader. So long as the I.L.P. existed as an unknown force of irreconcilables, the more reasonable policy of permeation and levelling-up was utterly checkmated.

I do not mean to say that events have gone as we wished. Two years ago we hoped not only to go on levelling-up the great body of Liberals, but also to weed out of the party, by a reasonable and discriminating Labour policy, the reactionaries; and thus possibly bring about a small Tory majority. But directly we discovered the ruck-up of official Liberalism, on the one hand, and the utterly unreasonable attitude of the I.L.P., on the other, we saw plainly that *our* game was up. *We were beaten* in the local elections of last autumn and this spring. From the general election we held aloof, refusing either to back the I.L.P. or support the Liberals. The rout of both, therefore, is no defeat for us. It leaves us free, indeed, to begin afresh on the old lines—of building up a new party on the basis of collectivism. Whether the English nation desires the change or can be brought to desire it; whether, if it does desire it, it will have the patience to work it out, is to my mind still an open question. In any case it will be a long business—and mainly dependent on the levelling-up of character and intelligence in the mass of the people. Meanwhile, the affairs of the nation are in the hands of an exceptionally able set of men who have been elected as trustees of the *status quo*. There is little danger of reaction, either in administration or legislation. The Conservatives are pledged up to the hilt to a policy of social reform, and the worst they can do is to stand still.

Grosvenor Hotel, Manchester, October 8th, 1895.—Sidney and I journeyed down here to cultivate Rochdale—Sidney speaking to the I.L.P. and I holding forth from the pulpit of a large Congregational church on the ethics of factory legislation. Rochdale, if ever Sidney thought of going into Parliament, is a possible constituency, at present held by a Tory owing to a split between Labour and Liberal. But Parliament seems further off than ever. We are loth to give up our quiet life of thought and enquiry, and we are discouraged by the hopeless state of progressive politics. Those who form the backbone of the Liberal Party, who dominate the party machinery, who own the wealth, who to a large extent monopolise the intelligence, have no convictions on the questions that interest working-men. At the best they are timid empiricists, who if they are assured that collectivism is the coming creed give it a faint-hearted support. For the most part, they are secretly hostile; they dare not proclaim their hostility so they remain dumb trying to evade the questions as outside practical politics.

These men would rather see a Conservative Government in power than allow the leaders of their own side to push forward social democracy. I am not sure that this hostile force is not still the strongest element inside the Liberal Party; none the less strong because they remain silent as regards the public, expressing themselves forcibly to the official leaders whom they surround like a body-guard keeping out all outside influence. The trick of forcing on the party an advanced programme, and then calling them traitors because they did not carry it out, is played out so far as we are concerned. It served its purpose; it was a wedge driven into the party and has discovered the true line of cleavage between the old and the new. But that is done and finished with. Now we collectivists have to assert ourselves as a distinct school of thought, taking up each question separately and reviewing it in the light of our principles. But the first need of a school of thought is *to think*. Our special mission seems to be to undertake the difficult problems ourselves, and to gather round us young men and women who will more or less study under inspiration. At present we have a certain set of young people all more or less devoted to the Fabian junta. Herbert Samuel, Charles Trevelyan, Bobby Phillimore, Bertrand Russell; all rich men of the upper or middle-class, and MacDonald, Martin, Macrosty of the lower middle-class. The London School of Economics should furnish others. But, in order to occupy this position, we must to some extent hold ourselves aloof; and, above all, we must be, and what is more or at least equally important, we must *appear* absolutely disinterested. At present that position seems inconsistent with any attempt to push forward a political career. If Sidney goes into Parliament he must go as an independent elected on account of his peculiar opinions and more or less the leader of a new party either within the Liberal organisation or outside it. No other position would compensate to the cause for his loss as an active thinker and administrator; no other position could make up for the personal sacrifice of giving up our joint work and the life of learned leisure for the inconvenience, separation and turmoil of a political career.

January 5th, 1896. *Parmoor.*—Two other visits, and we are back to-morrow at our work. Five days at Hadspen—Sidney's first introduction to the Hobhouse household. For Henry [1] he has always had an honest liking, admiring his public spirit and his refined view of life, and his painstaking industry. Henry's great lack is intellectual initiative and moral experience—he is narrow and limited—so to speak, blind to whole sides of life and quite incapable of discovering new lights and meanings. But he tries his level best to *be* enlightened, never

---

[1] Henry Hobhouse, married to Beatrice's sister Margaret. See Biographica Index. (Ed.)

consciously allows personal or class interest to bias him, and is quite incapable of unworthy motive. In this imperfect world these high and chivalrous qualities are admirable. Perhaps it has weighed with us that alone among my brothers-in-law he has welcomed Sidney with grave courtesy into the family, has always treated him with respect and friendliness, has apparently never felt that repulsion which most of my brothers-in-law have shown to him—either on account of his lack of social status or because of his opinions. Maggie,[1] of course, is the same high-spirited, rather vulgar and sharp-tongued woman—has cut her nature down to suit her husband's intellectual limitations without raising it to conform to her husband's moral standard. There is always therefore a jar in the house—Maggie protesting against Henry's quixotic principles—Henry silently resenting her plots and plans for social advancement and pecuniary saving. The family life suffers a little from this jar and loses in grace and charm. But this is only superficial. The two are honestly fond of each other, and Margaret is a capable and wholly devoted mother. Stephen, the eldest boy, now scholar at Eton, is a tall, lanky, ugly boy—unspoilt and simple-minded, with none of the public school boy's " side "—industrious, discreet and interested in men and things. No charm of body or mind—except an unsullied honesty and purity of nature. The little girls are correct and well-mannered, bright and happy, very pleasant to look at and quite sufficiently intelligent. The other children are too young to be judged. The most marked general feature of all of them is the lack of that introspective morbid character that distinguished most of us. Neither Stephen, nor the two girls, show any curiosity about religion, they all conform and never ask questions. They seem at present to have some of the limitations in intellectual and moral experience that is so marked a characteristic of their father. I should imagine that Stephen Hobhouse is destined by his character to be a civil servant— in which case we may hope to see something of this boy—to whom I feel drawn.

After five days at Hadspen we came on here. A charmingly attractive house—an atmosphere of "promise and expectation". Alfred [Cripps], after a brilliant professional career, is entering political life with all the self-assurance and ambition of the man who has never failed. And what a contrast to Henry! With a wide tho' superficial knowledge of human affairs, with the typical advocate's temperament, Alfred has chosen his political party and means to abide by it. No nonsense

[1] Margaret was Beatrice's most intimate companion among the sisters and, while they differed widely in outlook, Beatrice often expressed her admiration for her sister's intellectual integrity, her outspokenness and courage in defence of what she believed to be right. See Biographical Index. (Ed.)

about enlightenment, or any impartial study of the common weal. He deliberately shuts his eyes to the other party's case except in so far as knowledge of it will help him to controvert it. With infinitely more intelligence, knowledge and sympathy than Henry, he is far less capable of a sound political judgement. Whereas Henry in nine cases out of ten will be more enlightened than the rank and file in his own party, Alfred will probably range himself among the prudent and able reactionaries. He is, of course, far too clever not to compromise— but his compromise will always be the best compromise for his class and not the best for the community. He will never hesitate to start false issues and use false arguments in order to throw dust in the face of the people. Love of *truth*, at one time so prominent in his nature, now hardly exists; he is utterly uninterested in economic or political research. Sharp wits are all that are required to perceive an attack on the fundamental principles of " private property and the growth of the Empire "—sharp wits, and physical force are all that is needed to defend them. That being so, whether this evil, or that evil, prevails is an immaterial issue. Still more fantastic, to his mind, is that elaborate dissection and diagnosis of social and economic facts which enables a politician to deal with them. All this discovery and analysis are in his mind purely mischievous, not because *these evils cannot be cured* (Leonard Courtney's position), but for the far simpler reason that it is not worth while curing them. Having decided to stand by his class, being honestly (and no doubt justly) convinced that that class has everything to lose and nothing to gain by an alteration in the *status quo*, the one thing needful is to appeal to the popular suspicion, fear, prejudices and fallacies to keep back any further reforms. I do not mean this as a moral indictment. Alfred's original conviction that it is desirable that an upper class, owning most of the property and keeping the control of the nation, should exist is a proposition which can be perfectly well defended. But it is a proposition which, in face of a political democracy, it is impossible to state overtly and equally useless to attempt to prove. Foolish persons, like Auberon Herbert or Herbert Spencer, only injure the cause they are attempting to defend; since their conclusions render all their logic and all their facts suspect. That is, after all, not their fault, but the fault of the political public which is, let us admit at once, grossly biased. We, on the other hand, having arrived at the popular conclusion, are willing enough to uncover the facts and the reasonings which have led us there, and are supremely intent on finding out more facts so that we may proceed yet further. Alfred Cripps is far too clever not to perceive that the real interest of the people is hostile to that of the classes—to meander about like Henry Hobhouse attempting to discover the common weal argues simply, to his mind, a lack of capacity. There is no common weal—there is a solution which will suit the " haves ", and a solution which will suit the " have-nots ", and there is, of course, a compromise. It is this superior clear-sightedness which has transformed Alfred into a mere political advocate habitually ignoring facts and distorting issues. In a political democracy, no really intellectual politician who disagrees with the assumptions of democracy—still less one who agrees with the principles of a plutocratic or aristocratic state—can possibly remain an honest thinker and honest speaker. It is not the fault of Alfred's nature—it is the inevitable result of the conflict between his first principles, and the political circumstances in which he is forced to live.

Alfred's temperament and intellectual position is interesting because I think it is typical of the intellectual tone of the genuine conservative. And this means that the whole onus of economic discovery and political education will be thrown on those who desire complete democracy, still more on those who desire complete *social* democracy. This means a terrific intellectual strain on the progressive party. It is intensely difficult to be at once investigators and agitators—men of science and administrators. We are trying, in our humble way, to lead both lives— to keep our head clear to see the facts—without losing that touch of the political market which leads to effective propaganda. We shall probably fail at both pursuits—that is to say, we shall do each far less well than we might have done if we had specialised. Sooner or later there must needs be division of labour—if it comes in our time, we, I think, shall become investigators and not politicians.

The whole mind of the country is at present absorbed in foreign politics. There has been a dramatic interest in the Transvaal events. Secrecy in international matters has, I think, been finally discredited so far as England is concerned. And the occasion has found the man. Joe Chamberlain is to-day the national hero. Only a small section— the extreme Tories of the Alfred Cripps type—withhold their admiration for the swiftness and courage with which he has grappled with the crisis. Whether his Cabinet altogether appreciates the autocratic way in which he deals single-handed with every event is an interesting question of Cabinet politics. But his ways—his strong will, assiduity and reasonableness—have certainly given the nation confidence not only in his administration of the colonies but in the Conservative Government. In these troubled times, with every nation secretly disliking us, it is a comfortable thought that we have a Government of strong, resolute men—not given either to bluster or vacillation—but prompt in taking every measure to keep us out of a war and to make us successful should we be forced in it.

131

April 18*th*, 1896.—Whilst we were at the Lakes, we had furious letters from J. R. MacDonald on the " abuse of the Hutchinson Trust " in the proposal to contribute to the Library of Political Science. J. R. M. is a brilliant young Scot—lately I.L.P. candidate for Southampton—whom we [through the Fabian executive] have been employing as Hutchinson Trust lecturer in the provinces. These lectures are avowedly socialistic, but from the first Sidney has insisted that both MacDonald and Enid Stacy should make them educational: should issue an elaborate syllabus of a connected course, with bibliographies, etc. And, apparently, they have been extremely successful. But MacDonald is personally discontented because we refused to have him as a lecturer for the London School. He is not good enough for that work; he has never had the time to do any sound original work, or even learn the old stuff well. Moreover, he objects altogether to diverting Socialist funds to education. Even his own lectures, he declares, are too educational " to make Socialists "; he wants an organiser sent about the country. " Organise what? " asks Sidney. MacDonald dare not reply " I.L.P. branches ", which he meant. Neither could he suggest organising Fabian societies as it has always been against the policy of the Fabians to organise people; its function being to permeate existing organisations. The truth is that we and MacDonald are opposed on a radical issue of policy. To bring about the maximum amount of public control in public administration do we want to organise the unthinking persons into Socialist societies, or to make the thinking persons socialistic? We believe in the latter process.

The Liberals being hopelessly out of court whilst the Conservatives seemed firmly established for many years ahead, the practical question arose, shall we or shall we not mend our fences on the Conservative side of the field of politics? From the following entries I gather that the answer was in the affirmative:

Whitsun, 1896.—Sidney much enjoyed colloquy with Sir John Gorst [acting Minister for Education], Michael Sadler, Llewellyn Smith and others about Education Bill. On the whole, he is favourable to the central idea of the Bill: that is, replacing *ad hoc* bodies by one set of representatives chosen to manage all the business of the locality (but doubtful whether the Bill, as it stands, will effect this): also, not against helping voluntary or denominational schools in return for a measure of control, which is bound to grow. Other clauses, enabling public authorities to subsidise private venture schools, he looks upon as radically bad. He, however, recognises that it is no good *for him* to oppose the Bill—far better to appreciate the good in it and, by appreciating it, get some influence in amending it in our direction. And he is fortunately placed for this purpose. As originator and chairman of the most successful educational authority in London, as a friendly acquaintance of Gorst's—as a friend of Llewellyn Smith and Sadler, and acquainted with all the educationalists in London, he is able to be constantly suggesting amendments which are favourably considered by those in authority.

This work, and pushing the London School and the Political Science Library, combine to force us more into political society on both sides. On Monday, for instance, we dined at the House with Haldane and Asquith and other Liberals; on Tuesday, with Sir John Gorst and Lord George Hamilton, two Conservative Ministers. Becoming too, every day more connected with the superior rank of civil servants, such as, Sir Alfred Milner, Sir George Kekewich, Henry Cunynghame and others (Sidney's old connection with the Civil Service stands him in good stead—he knows the ropes of almost every office). All this is in a way pleasant (I do not hide from myself that I am pleased and flattered that my boy is recognised as a distinguished man!), but it means less intellectual absorption in our work. Still we go plodding on with our analysis—making up our minds on each separate subject as we go along, more than ever convinced that we must write a *Textbook of Democracy*—crisp and authoritative— as our next work. We are always abusing the Liberal Party for not knowing its own mind—it would be more to the purpose if we made it up ourselves!

Whitsun, 1896.—Came back and found the Education Bill practically dead. . . . The discreditable failure of this complicated measure only another instance of how impossible it is nowadays to succeed in politics without technical knowledge of the great democratic machine. The last Liberal Government went out discredited because their members were mere prigs thrust into office—the present Government are going the same way. " In these matters I am a child ", says Balfour! We do not want clever school boys at the head of our great departments. We want grown men, " grown up " *in the particular business they have taken in hand*, doing their eight or nine hours' work for ten months in every year, whether in office or out of office; behaving towards their profession as the great civil engineer, lawyer or medical man behaves. In political life the standard of natural ability is remarkably high, the standard of acquirements ludicrously low. Who would trust the building of a bridge to a man who started with such an infinitesimal knowledge of engineering as Balfour or

Gorst have of national education and its machinery? There seems to be a settled conviction that any clever man, trained to any profession whatsoever, will succeed in politics whether or no he knows anything about the details of public administration, or the facts of the common life he has to attempt to reform. That impression we must try to destroy.

August 14th, 1896. *Saxmundham.*—A whole fortnight wasted in illness—rheumatic cold combined with general collapse. This must excuse the absence of the brilliant account which I looked forward to writing of the International Congress! To us it was, as we expected it to be, a public humiliation. The rank and file of Socialists—especially English Socialists—are unusually silly folk (for the most part feather-headed failures) and heaped together in one hall with the consciousness that their every word would be reported by the world's press, they approached raving imbecility. The confusion of tongues, of procedure, the grotesque absurdity of masquerading as " nations ", and you have all the factors for a hideous fiasco from the point of view of public opinion. The Fabians sat silent taking notes as reporters for the capitalist press; Sidney writing descriptive accounts for the *Manchester Guardian*, Shaw for the *Star*, Bland for a weekly paper, Clem Edwards for the *Daily News*, and another Fabian for the *Chronicle*. The Fabians at any rate write history if they do not make it!

But, though we were ashamed of the " British nation " as represented by the callow youths and maidens of the I.L.P. and S.D.F., the Socialists of other lands were exceptionally enlightening. The German political Socialists are substantial persons—their intellects somewhat twisted by their authoritarian dogmatism—but with strong sterling character and capable of persistent and deliberate effort. Among them, too, are thoughtful cultivated men such as Kautsky and Adler. The party is closely knit together, and apparently free of the frothy irresponsibility of our English movement. The Belgians in their responsible attitude resemble the Germans—both parties, one feels instinctively, are preparing themselves (perhaps prematurely) to become H.M. Opposition. Vandervelde, moreover, the leader of the Belgians, is a man of quite exceptional charm and distinction—a scholar and a gentleman. Among the French, Swiss, Dutch and Italians, there are individuals who are really " thinking ": we felt, perhaps, for the first time, how much the collectivist movement would gain by a quiet exchange of thought and experience between the cultivated and intellectual Socialists of all countries. Such a conference will be one of our likely plans for the future.

October 5th, 1897.—Had to attend Manchester Conference of Women. Usual large gathering of sensible and God-fearing folk—

dominated by the executive of Bishops' wives, who give to the proceedings an atmosphere of extreme decorum and dignity. I have
resigned from the executive owing to their persistence in having
prayers before all their business meetings which, I suggest, is wanting
in courtesy to the Jewesses and infidels whom they wish to serve
with them. Some of them agree but say that the Union would lose
membership if it were not understood to be deliberately Christian.
Very well: then I have no place on its executive. I remain on sub-
committees and will keep the Union straight on industrial questions.[1]

The Bishops' wives are a nice lot—and I regret parting company
with them. In spite of their piety they are large-minded—take broad
views and have the pleasant manners of the great world. They are,
in fact, " gentlemen " to deal with: very different from the narrow,
intriguing, fanatical little Nonconformists who sit on the Council.
Possibly it is the predominance of the Lyttelton family that gives
the governing body of the conference such a sweet and wholesome
flavour—there being at least three Lytteltons on the executive, whilst
the sub-committees swarm with younger members of the family. The
Lytteltons and Louise Creighton are the presiding spirits of the
conference.

Louise Creighton now becomes—as wife of the Bishop of London
—one of the great hostesses of London " society ". In spite of the
fact that she is a fervent Christian and I an avowed agnostic, we have
a warm respect for each other. She is an absolutely straight woman,
who never swerves from what she believes to be right—is sometimes
ugly in her brusque directness. She hides with difficulty her dislike or
disapproval, and so has many enemies, or rather, persons who dis-
parage her and call her " bourgeois " and thick-minded. To Alice
Green, with her tortuous mind and uncertain ways, Louise is anathema,

---

[1] Report of Conference of National Union of Women Workers, *The Times*,
October 29, 1897.
" . . . Mrs. Sidney Webb moved a resolution to the effect that the business of
the meeting should not commence with prayers as stated on the agenda. Speaking
as a ' religious-minded agnostic ', she felt, when she saw the word ' prayers ' at the
head of the agenda, that if she had not been elected on the committee on false
grounds, she had been treated with discourtesy by the other members. While
members of the Jewish persuasion did not object to be present at Christian prayers,
the sect to which she belonged were not free to take part in them. Roman Catholics
were differently placed. Agnostics were in an extremely difficult position; if present
at Christian prayers they did not like to protest or leave the room or make themselves objectionable. She hoped those who participated in the business of the association would not be compelled to take part in the prayers.
" Mrs. Greenlees, in seconding, asked Mrs. Webb to substitute ' ladies of all
shades of religious opinion ' for ' Christians '.
" Mrs. Webb : ' That will suit me better as it includes Roman Catholics '."

though possibly now that she is the wife of the Bishop of London Alice Green may see " quality " in her. A calm fine face, a cool manner, a somewhat dictatorial mind towards those whose intellects or characters she does not respect, Louise is not likely to become a popular woman—but she will raise " society " to a higher level of intellectual sincerity and warmheartedness, and make the world value sterling qualities rather than fashion and mere sparkle.

October 30*th*, 1897.—So ended my official connection with the Bishops' wives [I write afterwards, when my resolution to dispense with religious rites was rejected]. I felt, rightly or wrongly, that it was necessary to clear up the situation: either the association was distinctively Christian or not; if the latter, the executive had no right to impose the religious rites of a particular sect on a non-religious body; if the former, I was gaining influence on false pretences. It is difficult to know when and where it is wise to make a stand, and insist on equality of treatment as a matter of principle. But I have a distrust of slipping into a sort of quagmire of latitudinarianism, in which only the narrow-minded and uneducated persons are allowed to have strong convictions. And I feel one must fight against the temptation of pushing one's particular hobbies by sacrificing straightforwardness and intellectual honesty in all other issues. It is strange how a meeting is influenced by the *way of putting it*. My resolution had given great offence; and when I rose to move it I felt hostile feeling all around. But, with a few frank and gentle words, all the hostility vanished; and, though the meeting supported the executive, I had won their sympathy and respect, which again reacted on me and I felt rather a brute to object to their prayers! The association otherwise strikes me as doing good work: Louise Creighton has distinctly a statesmanlike mind—and the group of women who now control the policy are a good sort: large-minded and pleasant-mannered. The " screeching sisterhood " are trying to invade them, but Louise's battalions of hard-working religious and somewhat stupid women will, I think, resist the attack.

To return to the entry of October 5, 1896:

One reason I am so fagged is the growth of the social side of our work. We are perpetually entertaining—and the opening of the School has added a long list of students whom we feel it our duty to see and talk to. The usual visit to Oxford—48 hours talking—propaganda of collectivist views and the expediency of research—enjoyable enough this bright discussion with young dons and undergraduates, but oh! how exhausting. Sidney lectured twice and we both talked incessantly from the breakfast party to the last smoke late at night.

The Argoed, January 18th, 1897.—The Conservative Government finds itself paralysed. Except for its sordid grant to landlords it has not been able to move backward or to move forward. The Liberal leaders are as feeble and half-hearted as ever. But neither party are putting forward any alternative policy to collectivism—neither party *dare* take any step, or even make a proposal that contradicts this policy. The Conservative Government is being dragged by its own Arbitration Act into regulating the conditions of labour: it is being coerced by its promises into spending additional money on public education. It will presently have to confess itself bankrupt in proposals, or accept the collectivist solution of employers' liability and old-age pensions. In all probability it will do nothing in these matters, and the Chamberlain programme of social reform is becoming far too complicated for the actor-politician or the accomplished *littérateur*. That fact works our way: the collectivists alone have the faith to grind out a science of politics—and I think they will prove to have the capacity.

February 3rd, 1897.—Last night, being the second night of the education debate, Gorst entertained a lively party of young people at dinner, retiring afterwards to his private room where we laughed and smoked, whilst division bells were ringing and count-outs were threatening. As we sat on the sofa, Gorst became confidential in a curious spasmodic way. " The newspapers say this is a humiliation for me, the Education Bill. But it's the Duke [of Devonshire] who is humiliated. Salisbury told me from the first that I was to be under-secretary, and that the Duke would be responsible for the educational policy in the Cabinet. The Duke is quite as much against this Bill as I am. He told the Cabinet so: and when they insisted he shrugged his shoulders! " From the Education Bill, we passed to the general situation. I ventured to say that Balfour was discredited—at which Gorst looked pleased. " He doesn't know anything," he remarked contemptuously, " we are on the eve of a crisis: there will be a revolt presently of the urban Tories. They can't go on watching their seats being taken from under them. As for social reform: all chance of that is gone. When first this Government came into office, they honestly intended to do something. I know, as a matter of fact, that Salisbury said to Chaplin soon after the Government was formed, ' Chaplin, can't you do something for the unemployed? ' " At this my gravity gave way, and Gorst's eyes twinkled merrily; but, when the others looked up at my laughter, he checked himself and became demure and began to talk Indian administration and colonial policy.

February 6th, 1897.—A great gathering last night in Queen's Hall —900 L.C.C. scholars receiving their certificates from the Prince of Wales. Sat close to H.R.H. and watched him with curiosity. In his performance of the ceremony, from his incoming to his outgoing, he acted like a well-oiled automaton, saying exactly the words he was expected to say, noticing the right persons on the platform, maintaining his own dignity whilst setting others at ease, and otherwise acting with perfectly polished discretion. But, observing him closely, you could see that underneath the royal automaton there lay the child and the animal—a simple kindly unmoral temperament which makes him a good fellow. Not an English gentleman: essentially a foreigner— and yet an almost perfect constitutional sovereign. From a political point of view, his foibles and vices, his lack of intellectual refinement or moral distinction, are as nothing compared to his complete detach- ment from all party prejudice and class interests, and his genius for political *discretion*. But one sighs to think that this unutterably common- place person should set the tone of London " society ". There is something comic in the great British nation, with its infinite variety of talents, having this undistinguished and limited-minded German bourgeois to be its social sovereign. A sovereign of real distinction, who would take over as his peculiar province the direction of the *voluntary side of social life*, who could cultivate in rich and leisured society a desire to increase the sum of real intellectual effort and eminence, what might he not do to further our civilisation by creating a real aristocracy of character and intellect? As it is, we have our social leader proposing in this morning's papers, as a fit commemora- tion of his august mother's longest reign, the freeing of the hospitals from debt—the sort of proposal one would expect from the rank and file of " scripture readers " or a committee of village grocers intent on goodwill on earth and saving the rates!

My boy spoke a few words to the 900 children at the end, worth all the rest of the speeches put together—urging them to remember that, as London had helped them, they must seek, in their future lives, to serve London.

May 7th, 1897.—Accident Compensation Bill satisfactory—a sort of revolutionary proposal which only a Conservative Government could bring in. We should have preferred the state to find the money, but that is a detail. Moreover, there are plenty of objects to which our extra income-tax can be devoted directly it becomes feasible to exact it. The main point—*universal compensation without contribution from workmen*—is secured to a certain number of trades only, but extension only a matter of time. The limited application of a complete principle is far better than the universal application of a dwarfed or incongruous principle.

The Argoed, January 18th, 1897.—Christmas with Alfred Cripps. Last year he was starting his political life; this year he is well on the road to office. He is in splendid spirits: talks with easy critical familiarity of Balfour and other leading Conservatives, and gives one to understand incidentally that he is constantly consulted by them. He is, in fact, rapidly becoming a sort of legal adviser, " a little jewel of an advocate " (as Father used so affectionately to call him) to the Conservative Party. His tone is the same: save the *status quo* as regards property, and keep the Government in the hands of the upper classes, but compromise right and left on all immaterial points and don't let bigots and zealots get the upper hand. Vested interests must be curbed and regulated—but preserved. No nonsense from Church dignitaries about bossing education, or high-handedness from railway managers about their employees—preserve the world from sensations and then all will be well. Just at present he is irate about the Financial Relations Commission. " Another piece of Gladstone's mischief: setting commissions to work to make grievances." He is still as uninterested as ever in investigation. " Life is a process of cram from the university to the Bar, from the Bar to the Front Bench; of course you and Sidney who have the good fortune to be able to do original research," he pleasantly remarked, " are exceptions; but we practical men, who look to professional success, know that it is only a question of cram— of getting up your case—that is all there is time for." He is still making a large income at the Bar, and spending it lavishly on his constituency, home and children. The eldest boy, Seddon, is exhausting pleasures at a tremendous rate: this year his bicycle was discarded and he was driving about in the smallest dogcart covered with his initials, with rug, lamps, etc. to match. Ruth has become more thoughtful and looks on rather wistfully—the mother in her is creeping into view. A year's school has made Leonard commonplace: a year's home has made " Daddy "[1] more exuberant than ever. The Playnes were staying there; Arthur cross and uncivil; Mary extremely affable and uncomfortably anxious to be pleasant. Refused a half-hearted invitation to take Longfords on the way here.

Here follows the first entry about the series of dramatic events which led to the South African War; and, incidentally,

[1] The Rt. Hon. Sir Stafford Cripps at the age of eight. (Ed.)

to splitting of the Liberal leaders into two embittered factions: the Liberal Imperialists on the one hand, and, on the other, the pro-Boers, with Sir Henry Campbell-Bannerman balancing himself uncomfortably between the two. Meanwhile the Tories and the Liberal Unionists were finally merged in the powerful Conservative Party which swept the country at the general election of 1900.

June 25th, 1897.—Back in London. Imperialism in the air—all classes drunk with sightseeing and hysterical loyalty. Our morning, hard at work proof-correcting: in the afternoon and evening friends drop in to welcome us back—Sidney absorbed in catching up arrears of L.C.C. work.

July 8th, 1897.—Dined last night with Alfred Cripps and Margaret Hobhouse. Alfred full of Workmen's Accident Bill. He is organising opposition, and scheming with the employers to get in amendments. His feelings are a queer combination of anger at the Bill and at Chamberlain, helplessness in face of a Government majority, backed by the united forces of the opposition, and self-complacency that he, at least, perceived the danger and outrageousness of the proposal and was doing his lawyer's best to spike the wheels of this abominable legislation. " It is only the party's loyalty to Balfour that would carry it through," he said piteously, " not only is the principle of the Bill preposterous but the whole drafting of it is crude in the extreme." He asserted that it killed " contracting out "; " not one scheme of the many that I have seen will stand this Bill ". He admitted that it meant state compensation at no very distant date (I do not feel quite so cocksure about this, it *might* work out into trade groups). " It is a Trade Union Bill—it makes all in the direction of large establishments—I know you like that, I don't." Of course, I chaffed him—complimented him on the revolutionary character of Conservative reforms. " If the S.D.F. had proposed it, it would have been laughed out of court; and the Fabian Society would never have thought of such barefaced spoliation of one particular class." " You are a cynic, Beatrice," Alfred responded pleasantly, but looking extremely sore. " It is one of the triumphs of the underground force of the democracy," said I; " what we are now discovering is that a Conservative majority is a more effective instrument of this force than a Liberal Government." " It is those wretched urban towns—they are the force behind Chamberlain." How he dislikes and distrusts Chamberlain.

July 26th, 1897.—Spent Sunday with Alfred Cripps at Parmoor. Obviously disgusted with the ways of Parliament this session. " Balfour

has no principle," he plaintively repeated. "He is perpetually asking
'why not?' to the proposals of the Radical wing of the Unionist Party."
"Chamberlain has beaten us; he twirls Balfour round his little finger
and Salisbury is cynically indifferent to home affairs—except, perhaps,
to the interests of the Church and of land." At other times, Alfred
asserted that they had succeeded in getting 80% of their amendments
into the Workmen's Accidents Bill—but it was quite clear that he
felt the champions of liberty and property had been done in the play
of the parliamentary hand. "It is hateful fighting your own party:
you are not free to use the most telling weapons: if only I could have
fought Chamberlain from the opposite side of the House! But the
feeling is growing against him: he will break up the Unionist Party
and you will have him back leading your side before this Parliament
is out."

"He is much more useful to us fighting from within the Conservative ranks, my dear Alfred, we shall do our very best to keep
him there. It is only Conservatives who can make revolutions nowadays, and they are, if anything, more susceptible to democratic pressure
than the Liberals."

Alfred Cripps is, I think, beginning to discover that a Government
will be flattering and considerate towards an able young lawyer who
is ready to advise them and defend them whenever asked; but that
these amenities cease when he begins to oppose them either overtly
or privately.

He talked a good deal about the South African Committee, of
which he is a member. He was against the production of the telegrams [1]
on the ground that telegrams passing between co-conspirators were
not evidence! Throughout the proceedings he had evidently taken a
somewhat tight-drawn legal view which had been combated by
Chamberlain. He signified that Harcourt had first been led by
Labouchere but, having been landed by the latter into some impossible
position, he had turned round. "We were surprised at his attitude;
but, of course, we did our utmost to meet him, it was all-important
to get the two front benches to agree on one report." The two witnesses
who left the worst impression on Alfred's mind were Hawksley and
Flora Shaw. But he is evidently disgusted with the whole Rhodes
party: in spite of his plea that now they are being unfairly treated as
the result of the reaction.

July 29th, 1897.—This was a typical Haldane dinner on the night
of the South African debate, typical of Haldane's weakness—his

---

[1] Probably a reference to the seven "missing telegrams" withheld by Cecil
Rhodes from the Select Committee of Enquiry into the Jameson Raid. (Ed.)

dilettante desire to be in every set; and of his strength—his diffusive friendship which enables him to bring about non-party measures.

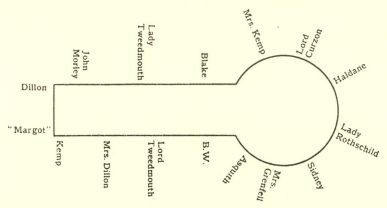

July 15*th*, 1897.—A great gathering of distinguished dames entertained at dinner a corresponding number of distinguished men.[1] It was a brilliant and polished set of people—representing a good deal of hard work. The dinner, the rooms, the flowers and the dresses were soberly luxurious and charmingly tasteful—the three speeches, Mrs. Steel, Lady Henry Somerset and the Bishop of London, were eloquent and witty—the Bishop excelled himself in the polished " man of the world " style. Strange person—my friend the Bishop—a scholar, a cynic, an admirable man of business, and a staunch believer in the Church—possibly also a believer in religion as a necessary element in society. But his faith is the other side of complete scepticism. His attitude towards all things is one of steady depreciation—no good in intellect, no good in sentiment, no good in science, no good in politics. Since " good " exists, there is only one place left for it—the Church! The faith that originates in cynical scepticism is not an altogether wholesome constituent towards the making of a church.

[1] The dinner referred to in the above entry was the Women's Jubilee Dinner and Soirée, July 14, Grafton Galleries, given by 100 distinguished women to 100 distinguished men, arranged by Mrs. Humphry Ward and the following ladies: Dr. Garrett Anderson, Miss Agnes Clerke, Mrs. Mary Davies, Mrs. Fawcett, Mrs. J. R. Green, Miss Jane Harrison, Lady Jeune, Miss Mary Kingsley, Lady Dorothy Nevill, Miss Flora Shaw, Miss Ellen Terry, Miss Maude Valerie White and Mrs. Flora Annie Steel.

Seeing that it was difficult to discover 100 distinguished women, some other ladies, among them myself, were called in to advise. I remember that my contribution was the principal factory inspectors and the heads of different educational institutions. My guest was the Bishop of London. What was remarkable in this dinner was that the 100 men were extremely distinguished, including practically all the leading politicians with the exception of Lord Salisbury, and many other persons of distinction; the difficulty being that so many distinguished men were left out, who in consequence were offended.

To which account I add another from the diaries of Sir Algernon West.[1]

On July 14th I was asked by Lady Henry Somerset to be one of her guests at the dinner of a hundred distinguished ladies of the Queen's reign. The interest was lost from the fact of my not knowing who was who, and I wished they had all been labelled! However, Lady Henry made a lovely speech and Dr. Creighton a very frivolous one, not at all suited to the occasion. Mrs. Annie Steel, the author of *On the Face of the Waters*, made a poor speech, and that was all, but the occasion was a remarkable one, and I fear there was some heart-burning among those who were not included in the chosen hundred.

July 30th, 1897.—Massingham dined here last night. Greatly excited about South African debate. " Superb rope dancing—Chamberlain's speech. Hawksley in the House ready to produce telegrams and letters unless Chamberlain repudiated condemnation of Rhodes. Harcourt completely taken in, consented to back up Government if they condemned Rhodes, and now Chamberlain declares that he accepted condemnation as a compromise and, as far as he was concerned, he always thought Rhodes a fine fellow. It is superb: it is a delight to watch such a man." And Massingham bubbled over with the joy of the political dramatic critic. " Chamberlain's career is extraordinarily interesting—every day brings its own trick. The career is more interesting than the man," added Massingham more gravely; " he has neither the knowledge nor the convictions to make him more than a great political artist." " Surely," I rejoined, " we shall look back on the last fifty years of the nineteenth century as the peculiar period of political artists: we have no statesmen: all our successful politicians, the men who lead the parties, are artists and nothing else. Gladstone, Disraeli, Randolph Churchill, Chamberlain, and the unsuccessful Rosebery—all these men have the characteristics of actors: personal charm, extraordinary pliability and quick-wittedness."

October 18th, 1897.—Met John Morley at a *tête-à-tête* dinner at the Courtneys. He and Sidney anxious to be pleasant to each other. A charming person for a talk on literature: but a most depressing spectacle as a Liberal leader. In sympathy with no single one of the progressive ideas, he clings to his old shibboleths of non-intervention and non-expansion abroad, and Church disestablishment and a sort of theoretical " home rule " at home. When I suggested that, if I had supreme power, I would hesitate before I disestablished the

[1] *Private Diaries of the Rt. Hon. Sir Algernon West, G.C.B.*, edited by Horace G. Hutchinson, 1922, p. 339.

Church he seemed aghast. And yet he dare not pronounce in favour of his own convictions: he feels instinctively the country is against him. To do nothing, and to say nothing, to sit and wait for the tide to ebb from this Government is the long and short of his policy. Naturally enough he is pessimistic: thinks that all things are going to the bad and that the country has lost its intellect and its character. On politics he is like a theologian who has begun to doubt his theology: in argument he always shrinks away from you, as if he suspected you of laying traps for him out of which he could not struggle. A closed mind and a lack of pluck in asserting the dogmas that dominate him, give a most unpleasant impression of narrow-mindedness and nervelessness. I shall send him our book: if he reads it, it may *antagonise* him into some living thought. Leonard Courtney, one felt instinctively, was infinitely more open-minded as well as more robust in intellect: was fully prepared to consider new propositions and not in the least inclined to run away because he might have to change his mind if he stayed to look at them. John Morley is a pitiable person as a politician; all the more so because he is conscientious and upright. It makes one groan to think of that moral force absolutely useless.

December 10*th*, 1897.—Perhaps part of my chaotic frame of mind is due to dabbling in " society ": thought it good opportunity to invite some people to dinner since it did not much matter whether I felt seedy or not the next day. [We had just passed *Industrial Democracy* through the press.] My little parties are said to be successful, but they don't please me. Directly you entertain for entertaining's sake, then they become hollow and unpleasant. An element of vanity enters in and you begin to wonder what impression you make; what your friends think of each other, and so on. My conclusion from this last month is that the dross in my nature is not yet eliminated! There is a good strong strain of the vain worldling left. Thank the gods, there is no trace of such feeling in Sidney. Work and love are the only gods he lives for. Oh! my boy, how I love you—past understanding!

March 1898.—Perhaps the most striking fact of the L.C.C. elections [I record a few days after the Progressive victory of March 1898] has been the complete eclipse of the Liberal leaders. The Progressive election committee has spurned their help, has fought the whole battle on the non-political line. And this contempt for the Liberal leaders has not sprung from the extreme left (Sidney thought they were carrying it too far and himself had down Lord Ripon at New Cross), but from the little knot of Progressive Radicals—Collins, McKinnon Wood, Dickinson, etc. Rosebery, it is true, came forward, but expressly as a past Progressive chairman of the L.C.C., and himself disowned any official connection with the Liberals. The official London Progressives, men who six years ago would have been only too proud of the patronage of an ex-Liberal Cabinet Minister, now stand completely divorced from their allegiance to the Liberal leaders, and talk of them with habitual contempt as men of no conviction and no knowledge. Even Rosebery, whom they are glad enough to use, has no influence with them. This victory will strengthen this feeling of independence, if not superiority, to the official Liberal leaders on the part of the L.C.C. Progressives. They will more and more regard themselves as able and experienced administrators, actually working out political problems, whilst they will look on men like Bryce, Asquith, Harcourt, Fowler, either as mere members of a debating society, or as London " society " men with whom they have little or nothing in common. Asquith especially has lost all his prestige in the eyes of the London Radical.

We gather, on the other hand, that there is no repentance on the part of the front bench Liberals, at least there was not before the L.C.C. election. Not a member of the front bench seems to be working at politics: they are either following their own professions or dancing attendance on London " society ". Their whole attitude is certainly astounding: beyond cavilling at the Government, chiefly on foreign questions, no one is ever the wiser for their appearances in public. . . . I think most Progressives have ceased to read their speeches: even the I.L.P. find it precious difficult to criticise " a negation in opposition ".

We, therefore, close this portion of our life with considerable complacency and start on our long journey with a light heart.[1] Our book has been extraordinarily well received; our party has recovered a good working majority on the L.C.C.; the London School of Economics is growing silently though surely into a centre of collectivist-tempered research, and establishing itself as *the* English school of economics and political science. We can now feel assured that with the School as a teaching body, the Fabian Society as a propagandist organisation, the L.C.C. Progressives as an object lesson in electoral success, our books as the only elaborate and original work in economic fact and theory, no young man or woman who is anxious to study or to work in public affairs can fail to come under our influence. Massingham of the *Daily Chronicle* is again our friend: the *Manchester Guardian* and the *Echo* are practically our organs through Leonard Hobhouse and W. M. Crook, the provincial Liberal papers are extremely friendly. It is only the *Westminster*, the *Daily News*, the *Star* which remain somewhat cold and suspicious towards the rising of a new party. But all this does

---

[1] Between April and December 1898, Beatrice and Sidney were touring America and Australasia. (Ed.)

not mean that " our set " is anywhere near office or nominal political power. The crust of London Society Liberalism is, as yet, far too hard for us to break, and I doubt whether we are not always likely to work underground at foundations, upon which a younger generation will build, perhaps not quite in the form we intended!

To which hubristic passage I will add another entry from the diary, revealing the presence of personal vanity coupled with a sophisticated conscience:

February 1898.—The old " Eve " in me is delighted [I write a few weeks before our departure] with buying a trousseau for our nine months' journey. It is a long time since I have had a really good " go " at clothes: I am revelling in buying silks and satins, gloves, underclothing, furs and everything that a sober-minded woman of forty can want to inspire Americans and colonials with a true respect for the refinements of collectivism. It is a pleasure to clothe myself charmingly. For the last ten years, I have had neither the time nor the will to think of it. For this tour, I harmonise extravagance with my conscience by making myself believe that I must have everything new, and that I must look nice! I believe that it is a *deliberate* expenditure. For six months ago I determined that I would do myself hand-somely. . . . But I daresay one or two of the specially becoming blouses are the expression of crude vanity; my delight in watching these bright clothes being made is a sort of rebound from the hard drudgery of the last two years. But it is rather comic in a woman of forty—40 all but two weeks. Forty, Forty, Forty! What an age! Almost elderly. I do not feel a bit old!

CHAPTER IV

ENQUIRY INTO ENGLISH LOCAL GOVERNMENT
1899–1905

ONCE again, in January 1899, we were back in our little home on the Thames Embankment, resuming our work in the triple capacity of investigators into social institutions, promoters of the newly established London School of Economics, and, in the case of the Other One, as chairman of the Technical Education Board, a determined organiser and agitator, intent on unifying all public education, whether elementary, secondary or university—more especially in the metropolis—under one local government authority—that of the London County Council.

In this and the following chapter, I shall attempt to describe successively these three separate activities from 1899 to 1906: a difficult task as they seem inextricably entangled together in the main sources of my information: the entries in my diary.

Why did we decide on English local government as our next subject for detailed investigation and analysis? Our main reason was that in the course of our previous investigations we had found ourselves coming to a new view of the scope and purpose of the compulsory association of men as citizens, whether national or local. Hitherto, we had investigated and described social organisation based on voluntary association: the co-operative and trade union movements. Already before my marriage I had studied a form of voluntary association lauded at the time by idealists of all classes, by leading trade unionists, by the more benevolent of employers, by Liberal and Conservative philanthropists and even by revolutionary Socialists—the ideal of Robert Owen, the self-governing workshop—as an alternative to the capitalist organisation of industry. This ideal was assumed to be the aim of the contemporary co-operative movement.[1] During my two years' enquiry into this remarkable manifestation of working-class organising capacity, I had made two separate discoveries. The Co-operators, who, with the assent of their intellectual supporters and admirers, kept on asserting that the object of their movement was the abolition of the wage system and the organisation of industry in the interest of the manual working *producers*, had, in fact, by 1889, built up a great industrial organisation of hierarchical character exclusively in the interest of the working-class *consumers*. In doing this, they had offered to the community a clear-cut alternative to capitalist retail and wholesale trading, and less completely, in the productive enterprises of the Co-operative Wholesale Society, to capitalist manufacturing. Unwittingly, the Co-operators had performed what is now known as the " Marxian operation ": they had cut out of the body politic the individual profit-maker, exploiting the producer and the consumer alike in order to build up his own fortune. Far from abolishing the wage system, what they had done was to extend it to the brain-worker. What they had abolished was the profit-making entrepreneur! Yet, at congress after congress, the Co-operators refused to recognise the transfiguration of

---

[1] For an analysis of the ideal of the self-governing workshop, and the reason for its failure, as an alternative to capitalist enterprise, not in Great Britain only, but also in France and Germany, in spite of a whole century of experiments, see *The Co-operative Movement in Great Britain*, chapter v., on " Associations of Producers " (pp. 127-69), by Beatrice Potter, 1891. It is instructive to note that this species of organisation flourishes in the industry of the USSR, whilst it is actually the dominant type in Soviet agriculture. The success of the industrial co-operatives (*artels*) as well as of the collective farm (*kolkhosi*) under Soviet Communism seems to be due (1) to the elimination from the environment of the private profit-maker, whether as financier, capitalist employer or wholesale or retail trader; (2) to the constant supervision and assistance of the collective farms by the USSR Commissar of Agriculture, the Communist Party and the local authorities, in the supply of water through irrigation, of unlimited tractors and combines and of plentiful fertilisers, supplemented by the continuous advice of scientific experts, almost irrespective of cost. The guiding principle is that wherever the self-governing association of producers is successful in fulfilling its obligations and in creating a peaceful and educational life for its members, it is left free to manage as it chooses; it is only interfered with when failure threatens, either through the break-up of the community through internal discord, or through the failure of its productive activities through lack of managerial ability, technical skill or the requisite machinery.

their own movement. What I did was to point out this trans-figuration, whilst at the same time I explained and justified it. My second discovery was that democracies of consumers, if they are to be a desirable as well as a practicable alternative to private profit-making, must be complemented by demo-cracies of workers by hand and by brain—that is, by trade unions and professional societies. Hence, when Our Part-nership was set up, our first job was to turn the searchlight of investigation upon the associations of producers, in their most obvious form of trade unionism.

Meanwhile, the Other One, who had already served thirteen years in three different departments of the Civil Service, including a whole decade of supervision of half-a-hundred separate governments overseas, became a leading member of the London County Council, one of the greatest of the world's social institutions divorced from the profit-making motive. It was borne in upon us, not merely that compulsory association in government had necessarily to be added to voluntary association both as producers and as consumers, but also that this inevitable compulsory associa-tion of man as a citizen was demanded for much more than national defence and the maintenance of internal order. We saw that to the Government alone could be entrusted the pro-vision for future generations, to which neither producers nor consumers would attend as such. Moreover, such obvious social utilities as public health and universal education, the provision for the destitute, the sick and the defectives, like that for the orphans and the aged—all of them based on pro-vision according to need—involved enterprises to which no profit-making could usually be attached, and which were, for the most part, outside the characteristic activities or desires either of the associated consumers or of the associated producers. In short, we were led to the recognition of a new form of state, and one which may be called the " house-keeping state ", as distinguished from the " police state ". This gave us a new vision of social development. The pro-vision of services according to need were, as we thought, destined to grow and develop. It was hard to imagine how this extension could possibly be undertaken and administered on the basis of the motive of profit-making, even if that motive was held to be essential to every undertaking of economic character. Moreover, the start had already been made on the contrary principle of a public service. The social institutions which had gradually undertaken most of what had been done in the way of provision according to need, notably for the destitute and the persons of unsound mind, were, in England and Wales, the parish vestries, the county justices and the municipal corporations, to which had been added in 1834 the boards of guardians—that is to say, they belonged to local rather than to national government. If social institutions based on the motive of profit-making were to be increasingly supplemented, or superseded, by social institutions conducted by a salaried public service—rewarded not by the making of private fortunes, but by public honour and special promotion; if local administration was destined to rival and even to surpass in importance the national Civil Service, it was important to discover by what means the various parishes and counties and municipalities were, in fact, governed; how their several administrations had arisen in the past and how they were now developing; and by what extensions and improvements these social institutions could be best fitted for the additional tasks that they would find themselves undertaking. Thus it was that we decided in 1898 to investigate the structure and functions of English local government, intending at the outset to concentrate our attention upon the period from the Municipal Corporations Act of 1835, and the Poor Law Act of 1834, to the present day.

So far, so good: but alas! at this point I had better confess that we failed to fulfil our plan of analysing and describing the local government of England from 1834 to the present time.

What we had contemplated was an analysis of the local government of this generation, with merely a preliminary chapter about the antiquities, anterior to 1835, which it had superseded. But, in the course of our journeyings up and down the country, we found even the present local government so firmly rooted in the past, and the past so complicated and obscure, that it became indispensable to us to make a special study of the period immediately preceding the reforms of 1832–35. At first, we intended to restrict ourselves to the first three decades of the nineteenth century. Further study convinced us that we could neither understand nor make intelligible by itself what was but the tag-end of a period opening with the Revolution of 1688.

The century-and-a-half lying between the dismissal of the Stuarts in 1688 and the Reform Parliament of 1832, constitutes, for the historian of the internal administration of England and Wales, a distinct period of extraordinary significance. For the first time, and perhaps for the last time in English history, the national Government abstained from intervention in local affairs, practically leaving all the various kinds of local governing bodies to carry out their several administrations as they chose, without central supervision or central control. Even when Parliament was appealed to for legislation, it allowed the different localities to have practically whatever constitutions and whatever powers they asked for; contenting itself with ratifying, in the innumerable local acts of the eighteenth-century statute book, the particular projects and compromises of the local interests concerned. The experiments in poor law and municipal enterprise thus initiated were, we thought, instructive to the reformers of to-day. But, besides these experiments in function, the diverse origins and varied constitutions of the eighteenth-century local authorities seemed to us vital to our understanding of the more uniform pattern of modern local government, based on an electorate, at first restricted by property qualifications, but becoming, as time went on, practically inclusive of all adult inhabitants.

What sort of output grew out of this miscalculation, what exactly did we fail to do, and what did we actually achieve, during these six years of strenuous investigation?

Our initial purpose—an analysis of English local government as it existed in our own time for the use of would-be reformers as well as students—was, as I have already indicated, not carried out. At the beginning of 1906, we published a ponderous volume on the development of the parish and the county between 1689 and 1834, to be followed in 1908 by two volumes on the manor and the borough for the same period. It was not until 1920 that we issued the most original and, certainly, the most significant of our series on the constitution of English local government prior to 1834. In this last volume—*Statutory Authorities for Special Purposes* —we describe the gradual supersession of feudal institutions based on mutual obligations of lord and tenant, and of the newer mutualities of chartered corporations and guilds, of craftsmen and merchants, all alike owing allegiance to the King, by a new species of authority, arising directly out of the needs of this or that section of the community: such as the need for land drainage, and town sewers, for highways, for street-lighting and policing, for the regulation of markets, and last but not least, for the better relief of destitution and the suppression of vagrancy. Many of these authorities started as voluntary associations of the consumers of the required services, to be subsequently transformed by local Acts into compulsory associations of citizens. It was this slow but fundamental change, alike in the organism, the function and the environment of local authorities, that was brought to a climax by the Reform Parliament in the Poor Law Amendment Act of 1834, and the Municipal Corporation Act of 1835.

Apart from these four volumes, mainly concerned with the constitutional development of local government authorities, and only incidentally with their activities, we published from time to time during the next twenty years, special studies of the doings of local authorities such as *The Story of the King's Highway*, *English Prisons under Local Authorities* and *The History of Liquor Licensing*. In only one department did we complete our task of discovering and analysing the structure, function and social environment of a particular species of local government from its first inception in the dark ages to its latest development in our own times. In this case, our own researches during the six years described in this chapter were continued as part of my work as a member of the Royal Commission on the Poor Law, 1905–9. In another chapter, I shall tell how I dovetailed our own enquiry into that of the Commission; thus enabling me to circulate to my colleagues reports on English poor law policy from 1834 to 1906, the municipal health service, and other matters, culminating in the Mino:ity Report issued as part of the final Report of the Royal Commission on the Poor Law in 1909. But, owing to this and other distractions, it was not until 1925 that we published the first volume of *The History of the English Poor Law* (the old poor law), and not until 1929 that we were able to issue the second and third volumes (the new poor law), describing the doings of elected boards of guardians from their inauguration by the Poor Law Amendment Act of 1834 to their final abolition by the Local Government Act of 1929.

Such was the output from this long drawn-out enquiry into English local government. What were our instruments and methods of research?

Our first step was to find a colleague, free to leave London and carry out independently, but according to our plan, the investigation into the structure, activities and environment of local authorities in this or that part of England. We were singularly fortunate in securing straight away, and for six years, the services of F. H. Spencer,[1] to which were added

---

[1] Frederick Herbert Spencer, the son of a chargeman engineer at Swindon railway works, had graduated into the profession of elementary school teacher at the Borough Road Training College. During his time with us he took his LL.B., and afterwards, by a thesis based on his researches with us, on the Origins of Municipal Government, his D.Sc.(Econ.). He left us to become examiner for the L.C.C. scholarship system, and head of the commercial school of the City of London College. From that position he became one of the Board of Education inspectors on commercial subjects, and was stationed in Liverpool. After the war he was promoted to be H.M. Divisional Inspector of Schools for the N.W. Division. Subsequently he was appointed, at a salary rising from £1250 to £2000 a year, chief inspector for the whole educational service of the London County Council, from which he retired at the end of 1933. Even then he continued his work as educational adviser in more than one direction, being, for instance, invited in 1935–36 to lecture successively to all the universities of the Dominion of Canada, and to visit South Africa and Australasia to investigate certain educational problems.

He remained with us for some six years, and married our other research secretary, Miss Amy Harrison, a B.A. of the University of London, Aberystwyth College,

in the course of the following year those of Miss Amy Harrison. These two investigators settled down, together or separately, in town after town, taking elaborate notes of the minutes and reports of the local authorities, and making an equally detailed study of contemporary local newspapers and pamphlets, whilst attending the meetings of the local authorities concerned, and interviewing the representatives and officials. It is, perhaps, not surprising that, after one or two years of this close companionship, they married each other. " We have had constantly to put our heads together to read your illegible instructions; is it surprising that in due course our hearts grew together? " one of them wrote to us, in announcing their engagement. I may add that they became our lifelong friends.

At this point, it seems worth while to give to those readers who are interested in sociological research, a brief account of our method of note-taking. It is hard to persuade the accomplished university graduate, or even the successful practitioner in another science, that an indispensable instrument in the technique of sociological enquiry—seeing that without it any of the methods of acquiring facts can seldom be used effectively—is an exceptionally elaborate system of making notes, or what the French call *fiches*. This process serves a similar purpose, in the study of social institutions, to that of the blow-pipe and the test-tube in chemistry, or the prism and the electroscope in physics. That is to say, it enables the scientific worker to break up his subject-matter, so as to isolate and examine at his leisure its various component parts, and to recombine the facts when they have been thus released from all accustomed categories, in new

and joint author with Miss B. L. Hutchins of the *History of the Factory Acts*. On obtaining her B.A., Miss Harrison was for three years a teacher in a Welsh Intermediate School, after which she settled in London, at first attending evening lectures at the London School of Economics, and there being awarded the Lucy Rose Research Studentship enabling her to become a full-time student at the School. There her research into the effects of Factory Act regulation upon the labour of women resulted in a thesis with which she obtained the D.Sc.(Econ.) of the University of London.

From time to time we engaged extra assistants, and in 1905 Miss Bulkley, B.Sc.(Econ.) took the place of Mr. F. H. Spencer as our permanent research secretary, and continued with us in this capacity until 1912.

and experimental groupings, in order to discover which coexistences and sequences of events have an invariable and, therefore, possibly a causal significance. The first item in the recipe for scientific note-taking in sociology is that the student must be provided, not with a note-book of any sort or kind, but with an indefinite number of separate sheets of paper of identical shape and size (we found large quarto the most convenient form), and of sufficiently good quality for either pen or typewriter. The reason why detached sheets must be employed, instead of any book, is, as will presently be demonstrated, the absolute necessity of being able to rearrange the notes successively in different orders; in fact, to be able to shuffle and reshuffle them indefinitely, and to change the classification of the facts recorded on them, according to the various tentative hypotheses with which the investigator will need successively to compare these facts. Another reason against the note-book is that notes recorded in a book must necessarily be entered in the order in which they are obtained; and it is vitally important, in the subsequent consideration of the notes, to be set free from the particular category in which the note-taker has found any particular fact, whether of time or place, sequence or coexistence. In sociology, as in mineralogy, " conglomerates " have always to be broken up, and the ingredients separately dealt with. To put it paradoxically, by exercising your reason on the facts separately recorded and displayed in an appropriate way, on hundreds, or perhaps thousands, of separate pieces of paper, you may discover which of a series of tentative hypotheses best explains the processes underlying the rise, growth, change or decay of a given social institution, or the character of the actions and re-actions of different elements of a given social environment. The truth of one of the hypotheses may, by significant correspondences and differences, be definitely proved; that is to say, it may be found to be the order of thought that most closely corresponds with the order of things.[1]

[1] The interested student will find deposited in the library at the London School of Economics a number of pamphlet boxes containing the sheet of notes, mostly

Guided by the subject-catalogue of our ten volumes on English local government and this summary account of our methods of research, my readers may find some interest in the following entries in my diary from 1899 to 1906, giving some more intimate and personal reactions of Our Partnership in this voyage of discovery.

March 7th, 1899. *Grosvenor Road.*—Now that I spend my time in taking notes vigorously all the morning from the minutes of town councils as well as writing such letters as are absolutely necessary, I have little inclination to make entries in my diary. . . . Meanwhile, we are well into our new enquiry and have elaborated a syllabus for the use of investigators. We have engaged as secretary a clever ambitious elementary school teacher—F. H. Spencer—about twenty-eight years old. We tried a nice young man straight from Oxford, but he was a dead failure, not realising what constituted a day's work, and presenting us with little essays instead of research notes. At present, we seem to be nibbling at the outermost corner of our subject. In a year's time, I suppose we shall feel that we have got some sort of grasp of it. I am aiming at living a student's life: withdrawing from any social excitement inconsistent with regular work, regular exercise, plain food and abundance of sleep.

April 28th, 1899. *Bradford.*—Sidney and I left London on our first investigating tour into local government on Thursday before Easter Sunday, and chose Leeds as our destination, as S. had promised to preside over a conference of elected persons to be held there on

in the handwriting of Mr. and Mrs. Spencer, and of other assistants, but also of the Webbs themselves, on the constitutions, activities and social environment of the town councils of Leeds and Leicester, of Newcastle and Liverpool, and many other boroughs, together with many Quarter Sessions and other county authorities. These slips of paper, which must number in the aggregate many tens of thousands, amount, in the case of Leeds, to about 800, and in that of Newcastle to 650; whilst in some cases there is a short summary of the development of the councils from 1835 to 1900. Even more voluminous are the notes relating to boards of guardians. These include an analysis, according to the type of pauper dealt with, the able-bodied, the sick, the children, the mentally defective, not only of the treatment afforded by the boards of guardians, but also of the policy laid down in the first instance by the Poor Law Commissioners and Poor Law Board, and by its successor the Local Government Board, whether in general or special orders, or in the private letters of the government inspector to the board of guardians concerned. This research enabled me to present to my colleagues a long memorandum on English Poor Law policy, 1834–1906, demolishing once and for all the fiction that the local government board had adhered, throughout this period, to the dogma of "less eligibility" laid down by the Royal Commission of 1834. (See the subsequently published volume entitled *English Poor Law Policy*, by S. and B. Webb, 1910.) For samples of these notes see Appendix.

Good Friday.[1] His speech and the conference were an unexpected success: all the papers giving full reports. Otherwise, the first week of our stay at Leeds was wasted seeing that all the officials were holidaying and the public offices—even the public library—closed. Sidney had an exceptionally bad cold, and the boarding-house we were in was dreary after our bright little home. On Thursday of Easter week we got to work, having persuaded the Lord Mayor to place a room in the Town Hall at our disposal and to give us free use of the minutes and reports. For another week Sidney, Spencer and I were hard at work on these documents. Then we tackled the West Riding County Council at Wakefield, and the Board of Guardians and School Board of Leeds. In the middle of my stay Sidney had to return to London, leaving me and our new secretary to finish up as best we might.

The personalities of Leeds public life are neither interesting nor attractive. Leeds and its inhabitants strike me as equally unlovely. " Getting on ", measured in money, is the dominant idea: the rich are conventional and purse-proud; the working-man dull, and without fight or faith. In fact the Tory squire and the Tory brewer are more public-spirited and more progressive than the lower middle-class Liberal. Leeds' Liberalism is the crudest individualism: negative and destructive—anti-state church, anti-public expenditure, the sweeping away of what they call " privilege " and the bringing in of political machinery for securing the equal value of all men's votes. No faith in any motive but that of pecuniary self-interest; no conception of any more complicated structure than the universalised ballot box. " There's not a man at this table, except yourself, that is not worth his £60,000 ", is the reported tactful remark of a Leeds alderman to a young London barrister who was dining with him. The saving grace, which has kept Leeds municipal government free from the grosser forms of corruption, has been the childish vanity which makes the ordinary Leeds shopkeeper desire to hear himself called " Alderman ", still more " my Lord Mayor ". Social ambition has prevented the motive of pecuniary self-interest from Americanising Leeds municipal life. After all, social ambition is a form of reverence for something better than yourself— the lowest form because the end aimed at is self-advancement—still a leaven because it means a recognition that some men are superior to yourself: which is true.

There will clearly be no difficulty in getting our material: our hardest task will be to determine what material to select, and where to stop. Between this diary and myself, I get on better at the actual

[1] Note, February 1920. This conference was held in connection with the I.L.P. Conference. I do not seem to have been interested in the latter.

investigation when Sidney is not there: he is shy in cross-examining officials, who generally begin by being unwilling witnesses and need gentle but firm handling: he hates life in provincial lodgings and seeing each day new people, and this repugnance reacts on me and I get disheartened and wonder whether I have not led him into a useless adventure. In dealing with documents he is far more efficient than I; but, in the manipulation of witnesses with a view of extracting confidential information, his shyness and scepticism of the use of it give me the advantage. And I am more ruthless in the exercise of my craft when he is not there to observe and perchance disapprove of my little tricks of the trade.

At the beginning of May 1899, I am back again in London recalling the six weeks' investigation into Yorkshire local government.

May 16th, 1899. Grosvenor Road.—Mrs. Gray of Gray's Court was my hostess at York. Almost a beautiful woman: fine features, queenlike figure, generous sympathy and warm-hearted public spirit—a perfection made less perfect by dramatic attitudes and an untrained mind. The old-world house, built into the city walls, and overlooking the Dean's garden, was a welcome change from the Leeds boarding-house with its ugly furniture and still uglier inhabitants. But, though unspeakably pleasanter, the few days I spent at York were less fruitful because I had to talk in return for my entertainment and came tired each day to work on the minutes. Mrs. Gray is a guardian, and her tales of the way in which outdoor relief is administered confirmed my observations of the relief work of the Leeds Board of Guardians, when I sat and watched them. The lay representatives of the ratepayers make a bad court to administer money payments which ought to be given according to definite principles—according to a code of law.

From York I went on to Beverley to look into the administration of the East Riding County Council. John Bickersteth, with whom I stayed, is the son of a Bishop, married to Lady Margaret, a pious old-maidish little woman. He is an athletic, attractive man of the country gentleman type, who bicycles into Beverley about 11 o'clock and comes out by the 3.30 train: takes life in a leisurely fashion and accepts with kindly tolerance the " little people " who have joined the country gentlemen in county administration since the election of the new county councils. He is a Yorkshire Whig, far too gentlemanly to share the old radical shibboleths, but quite unaware that there is a new school of radical collectivism growing up. Fortunately, he endowed me with all his reports, otherwise my visit would have been wasted, as he insisted on entertaining me the whole time; and, eventually despairing of getting to work, I went off for a ride with him and extracted what information I could about county government between pleasant gossip about men and affairs. He took me to see the town clerk of Beverley, a cynical, vulgar, but able man who was obviously delighted to call the aristocratic county clerk " Bickersteth ".

How much have I learnt in my six weeks' investigation? A vision of the tangle of local government: of the independence of the county boroughs, the recalcitrant defiance of the non-county boroughs, the shadowy authority exercised over them by the county councils; the grumblings of the district councils at the C.C.'s proddings, the appeals of the parish councils to the C.C. against the neglect of work by the district councils—the universal rivalry and sometimes actual litigation between various grades of sanitary authorities over incorporations and extensions of boundaries, over water catchment areas, tramways and hospitals. Then again, the mechanical grindings of the school board and the short-sighted stinginess of the boards of guardians, and in the dim and distant Whitehall the old-womanish L.G.B. threatening, obstructing, auditing and reporting—mostly without effect. It is not a vision of lucid beauty: but it is intensely human.

The town chosen for our next centre of investigation was Manchester, where I spent most of the summer, the Other One joining me now and again, and permanently for the August recess.

June 15th, 1899. *Manchester.*—The third week here. Sidney stayed for a fortnight, and has now returned to his L.C.C. work. We got straight away into our enquiry and we have been working every day, Spencer at the minutes of the Town Council, and Sidney and I at interviewing officials and abstracting reports lent or given to us. Two delightful Sundays we spent in the lanes of Cheshire: one night at Tarporley where, seven years ago, he and I stayed as an engaged couple with Mrs. [Alice Stopford] Green as chaperone. Those Sundays were very happy days, honeymoon rambles, dodging the high-roads and finding ourselves in farmyards.

At times we get discouraged at the bigness of our task: then we console each other by repeating " Well, if we cannot do it no one else can ", a conceited reflection. To-day I am feeling somewhat lonely in the little lodging—a whole fortnight away from him. . . .

Here I will insert an entry which does not directly concern the subject-matter of this chapter, but which gives a glimpse of the background of social distraction in which I lived.

July 24th, 1899. *Grosvenor Road.*—This last month of hot dry weather has been spent mostly in entertaining American and colonial friends. Some four mornings of each week have been spent at the British Museum scanning files of the *Manchester Guardian* and taking copious notes. Miss Fairchild, a charming Boston girl, has been staying with me and I have had a succession of little dinners for her entertainment. Our small circle of acquaintances is pleasant enough: easy-going, unconventional and somewhat distinguished. We are sought but do not seek—the most agreeable way of seeing people. Not that " society " pays us continuous attention: we are only casually found out by persons belonging to the great world—we live in a pleasant back-water of our own. But our social status, such as it is, is distinctly advantageous to the local government enquiry: it enables us to see any official from whom we want information. We are not going to have any trouble about getting access to facts: the task will be to select out of the mass of material submitted to us.

To return to our Manchester investigation, here is the impression I got from five weeks' work on workings of municipal government in that city:

September 9th, 1899. *Grosvenor Road.*—Five weeks in Manchester in a little rented house, with our own maids to look after us, and our secretary to help us—a peaceful happy time, collecting material and, by a well-regulated life, keeping fit for persistent work. We are more interested in this enquiry than in trade unionism: the problems are multitudinous and the machinery intricate. The least invigorating part of the subject-matter are the persons engaged in the work of local government: in the present administration of English provincial local government there is a singular lack of idealism and charm, of efficiency and force.

The Manchester Town Council turns out to be no better than that of Leeds. The most marked feature is the way in which the magnitude and importance of its work has outgrown its organisation. The different parts of the machine are out of joint; it rumbles on in some sort of fashion because it is pushed along by outside pressure, but it is always breaking down in the efficiency of its administration. The Council, judged by this test, would seem to be inefficient or corrupt or both. The men running the organisation are not a bad lot: one or two of the officials are distinctly able. But there is no head to the concern, no one who corresponds to a general manager of a railway company, still less to its paid chairman. The Mayor, elected for one year, has all his time absorbed by public meetings, social functions or routine administration: he is far more the ceremonial head of the city than the chief of the executive of the city government. The town clerk and his deputy are exclusively engaged in legal and parliamentary business; they spend most of their time in the lobbies of the House of Commons, in presenting the corporation's case at L.G.B. enquiries, in preparing leases and drafting agreements or in submitting bye-laws to government departments.

The suggestion that the town clerk of a great city like Manchester can be anything more than its solicitor and parliamentary agent—can fill the place of its chief executive officer—is, as things are at present, an absurdity. All the other city officers are technicians, accountants, engineers and medical men. The city surveyor and the M.O.H. are neither of them markedly competent and they have the status, not of administrators, but only of consultants called in whenever the chairman or secretary of one of the standing committees deems their advice necessary. The city treasurer is a promoted clerk; the chief constable a promoted policeman. With one exception, the administrative head of a department is the secretary of the committee supervising its work. Hence, the services of gas and of water, of tramways and markets, and even the rivers department, are all managed by promoted clerks with no professional training for their work. In fact, there is only one real executive officer who understands the technique that he has to supervise—a man named Rook, the superintendent of the sanitary department who, though he entered the Council's service at 30s. a week, has become a technician at his own job, and may be trusted to see that any given piece of work is carried through from its inception to its completion. To make confusion worse confounded, each committee considers itself like an independent company, and reports as little as it dare to the Town Council, which meets once a month, and is regarded by the chairman and members of each committee as a superfluous body which ought not to intervene.

These committees nominate their own members for election each year, and the tradition is that the committee must always be united in face of the Council. Hence, the atmosphere of secretiveness towards the Council, and of suspicious hostility on the part of those members of the Council who do not happen to be elected on the leading committees. Some of the committees are dominated by persons who are grotesquely unfit: for instance, the markets committee has had for years an illiterate tailor as chairman. In other cases the committee is run by a really able and upright man, but even he will pride himself on managing it " as I should my own business "; he resents mightily any criticism of his policy or methods. In short, there is nobody whose special business it is to see that all parts of the organisation are co-ordinated and working to a common end. Friction and petty scandals, accusations and recriminations, dog the Council's work. All this secretiveness and jealousy of control does not attain its object—if that be a quiet administrative life. Tales of peculation and jobbery, most of which are, I believe, untrue, get abroad through a malicious member or a resentful [elective] auditor who finds the accounts too much for his understanding. The rejoinder of the committees to all these stories, true or false, is always still more secrecy, with the result that the Council becomes enveloped in a permanent cloud of presumed stupidity and corruption.

So far as we have made the acquaintance of the councillors there are none very good, and none very bad. I have not picked out any who seem to be " rotters ". The abler among them are all old men— a little gang of Liberals who are still the salt of the Council. The social status is predominantly lower middle-class, a Tory solicitor and an I.L.P. journalist being the only men with any pretension to culture. The abler administrators have no pretension to ideas, hardly any to grammar: they are merely hard-headed shopkeepers, divided in their mind between their desire to keep the rates down and their ambition to magnify the importance of Manchester as against other cities. There is no cleavage on the Council according to policy—the Council drifts into subsidising the [Ship] canal or working its own tramways, or into " direct labour " in its public works, almost without deliberate thought, and certainly without any discussion either of principles, or of the special circumstances, which make for or against the proposal before the Council. The Council, in fact, fumbles along by the method of trial and error; but it has its head in the right direction pushed by outside force. But who is initiating this force? There seems no person, or group of persons, at work. It is more like the result of an impersonal current of ideas affecting all the persons concerned without their being conscious of them.

October 10*th*, 1899.—We saw little of the city government of to-day [I note after staying with Sister Holt in Liverpool], spending all our energies on the most interesting minutes of the old select vestry and on the documents of the town hall. Liverpool strikes us as more efficient than Manchester, a close ring of officials having replaced the petty incompetence of the committee system characteristic of Manchester town government. But there is a long tradition of corrupt dealing with publicans and other propertied sinners—at least so say the Liberal families of Holts and Rathbones. Munificent public work has been done at Liverpool by some of the wealthy Unitarian families, but these families are petering out, and the sons are not worthy of the fathers. Whether this is inevitable to all families, or the bad effect of two or three generations of luxury, I do not know. The present generation of rich folk want to enjoy themselves, find nothing to resist, no class or creed interest to fight for, so that they have ceased to consider anything but their pleasures.

October 1899. *Grosvenor Road.*—So far we see straight in front of us the way we shall go for the next few years. Our enquiry is stretching out before us, arduous, requiring patience and persistency, but by no means impracticable. For the rest there is the Economic Faculty to build up, and our share in administration and propaganda. Our finances are sound, our health good, and there is no reason for anxiety. We must spend, if need be, our capital on our work, and we must not be disheartened by its magnitude. We are fast becoming elderly, we have not so many years left, we must make the best of our talents and leave the future to take care of itself. And it is useless to be down-hearted because of the indifference and stupidity of the world, even as regards its own true interests. And it is childish to yearn after some sanction to the worth-whileness of human effort. For us who " know not ", this sanction is unattainable: we can but follow the still small voice of moral instinct which insists that we shall seek truth and love one another. Is the sanction the calm happiness in work: the peaceful delight in living?

November 30th. *Grosvenor Road.*—Immersed every morning in the reading of documents in some municipal office: can't manage more than four good hours. Two afternoons I am due at the School: to lecture or to see students. Another afternoon I am at home, and the other afternoons get filled up with calls, casual committee meetings and exercise. But we are sufficiently advanced in our work to contemplate beginning to write when we return from Plymouth in January.

December 14th. *Grosvenor Road.*—Spencer, Mildred Sturge and I spent a week over the St. Pancras vestry minutes. We have taken on Mildred Sturge, a Newnham graduate, as a sort of paid apprentice. She is not able, but accurate and painstaking. An expedition to Norwich in bitterly cold weather to start a Miss Watson on the Norwich records ends our autumn campaign. Next week we go to Plymouth for the Christmas recess to undertake the records there. I begin to grasp the character of local government at the beginning of this century. When we return we shall hew out of our accumulated material the first draft of our first chapter.

January 31st, 1900. *Torquay.*—Here for three nights attending an enquiry into borough extension.

A month at Plymouth at work together, with Spencer to help us, at the Plymouth records [I recall, before reporting on the extension enquiry]. For recreation we had two days' wanderings on bicycles over Dartmoor in mist and rain, one or two walks with Sidney on Mount Batten, and pacing alone over the Hoe watching the setting sun after the day's work was done. Otherwise, we stuck closely to our note-taking and interviewing. I remember when we were steaming through the tropics and I was visualising our work for the next few years, I dreaded the thought that we should have to spend all our time out of London in towns: I feared that my health and my spirits would break down with sedentary office work in places like Leeds, Manchester and Liverpool, without the long holidays in the country we were accustomed to. But our life during the last year turned out not half bad: the enquiry has been unexpectedly interesting: my health excellent, and the occasional 48 hour cycling in country lanes round about the towns, a joy and a delight—making up in intensity of pleasure for the longer holidays in the country. Sidney has been well, interested, and happy: every day brings greater confidence in the worth-whileness of this continuous study of facts and careful reasoning from them.

And here is a somewhat denigrating report of what seemed to me futile proceedings:

Three days sitting in bad atmosphere listening to the argument whether or not St. Mary Church and Cockington shall be included in the borough of Torquay. I had an introduction from T. W. Russell of the L.G.B. to the inspector who was holding the enquiry, one General Crozier; and I happened to light on the hotel where he and two of the leading counsel engaged in the case were staying. Unfortunately, the hotel was small and crowded, so that there was not much opportunity for confidential talks with judge and counsel; and the local men were too flustered to give me much information. But I quickly made friends with three out of the five counsel—Littler, Richards and Duke; Littler being a useful acquaintance seeing that he is chairman of Middlesex Quarter Sessions, the records of which we have to go through. General Crozier is a gouty and slow-minded old West End clubman, past his work, even if he were ever capable of it—a relic, I imagine, of the era of barefaced jobbery of appointments. I am not impressed with the quality of the legal ability present at the enquiry. Perhaps these extension cases do not lend themselves to a careful mustering of proven facts or to subtlety of argument. Hearsay evidence as to the wishes of this or that section of the population and jumbles of irrelevant considerations, the reiteration of stock arguments for or against extensions of boundaries in general, such as,

" the larger areas mean more efficient administration ", or, " a smaller area is more conducive to keen interest ", that a particular district is or is not the outgrowth of an older inhabited area, that borough government is more desirable than that of an urban district council, that the amenities of the borough are or are not shared with the surrounding districts—I felt that I could have reeled it all off mechanically if I had just been told on which side I was to plead. As to the evidence it was all of the nature of personal opinions, obviously *ex parte* opinions: no attempt was made to prove the truth or the falsehood of all this assertion, and counter-assertion. Then there is the silly badgering of inexperienced witnesses. " Will you answer yes or no, Mr. Jones? " when in the opinion of the nervous witness " Yes " would be misleading, and " No " inaccurate. It was easy to see that any facts obtained, and many not obtained, by this expensive process could have been got by a couple of experienced investigators examining witnesses quietly in their homes as well as documents which had not been faked for the occasion. Littler and Richards lent me their briefs to read and it was quite clear to me, as I sat and listened to the proceedings, that the K.C.'s drawing huge fees had added nothing whatever to the facts or the arguments prepared for them by the local solicitors. The culminating absurdity of the proceeding is that, if the decision of the L.G.B. inspector (who by the way took little or no interest in the talk of the counsel) is not accepted by the parties concerned, the whole case will have to be argued out again before a parliamentary committee. Personally, I came out of the court not having heard one of the issues raised adequately cleared up—certainly not the general issue of larger or smaller areas of administration. At present I am divided in my mind between the desirability of large municipal boroughs and the expediency of keeping alive the old historic county and, therefore, the minor local authorities under county jurisdiction.

June 12*th*, 1900. *Leicester*.—Staying in a rough boarding-house, the best in Leicester, for a fortnight's investigation. It is kept by a woman of character and intelligence but a bad housekeeper. House dirty, meals rough and monotonous, and service inefficient but willing. We pay £2 : 2 : 0 a week each and have a good bedroom and small sitting-room; our meals with some half-a-dozen other lodgers, four harmless business men and two women of the usual boarding-house type. Everyone is good-tempered and well-mannered; and the other lodgers either do not feel the roughness, or are too good-tempered to object to it. Sidney feels the discomfort more than I do. No doubt my greater intentness on the enquiry makes up for a good deal in my case. In his case the need for investigation is not a part of his personal life and aims, which are administrative.

In our MS. notes in Sidney's handwriting, I find the following summing-up of our general impressions of Leicester municipal government:

Summing up at the end of a fortnight, our general impression confirms our particular notes.

The new corporation started in 1835 with a remarkably able town clerk (Stone), and a set of able, honest and socially influential men—wholly Liberal and Nonconformist, mostly Unitarian—belonging industrially to the upper middle-class of the time—bankers, hosiery manufacturers and professional men. Partly in reaction against the prodigal and corrupt Tory administration, their dominant idea was to administer the public property honestly and economically—to pay low salaries, to contract wherever possible, to pay off debt by prudent sales of land. Notwithstanding this bias, and the hard times of the " forties ", when sanitation came up they were (under Whetstone) ahead of public opinion—appointed a medical officer and a staff of temporary inspectors to discover nuisances, which they peremptorily ordered to be abated. They had (under Whetstone) a horror of overgrown establishments, and thus shrank from enlarging functions—subsidised a Water Company (eventually taken over). They were, in fact, more like Leeds and Manchester.

Intensely political—always voting petitions in Liberal and Nonconformist interest—appointed all Liberal mayors and aldermen and, apparently, Liberal chief officials. The procedure was good, and reports of committees full; but it was adapted to a group of personal friends—Stone, town clerk, was friend and solicitor to all the leading councillors. The relationships would have been invidious, if they had not been men of high honour; they were simultaneously chairmen and directors of railway, water and gas companies, which they, as a corporation, had to control and deal with, they bought land of themselves, they were related with Stone and everyone else by marriage. But they left a tradition of highest integrity and always doing their best for the town.

This state of things continued certainly until Stone's death about 1870. After interregnum of unsatisfactory successors for a couple of years or so, the Council fell back on Stone's clerk (Storey), a shrewd but uncultivated man of no social position or professional status. He was assiduous in the office, attended all committees, and carried on traditions of Stone. During this 20 years (1874–1894) there was an involuntary expansion of corporate activity, taking over water and gas, flood prevention and sewerage works, etc., and finally in 1891 extending boundaries.

This was a period of great industrial expansion of Leicester; and, with the boot trade, the uprise of a new and somewhat rough class of employer. Gradually, the old families of Paget, Whetstone, Ellis, Johnson, etc., dropped out of municipal life—becoming M.P.'s and semi-county people—if remaining in Leicester, tending to become an aristocracy.

In 1891, with the election of the whole Council on the extension [of boundaries], the remnants of the above either retired, or were pushed on one side. Two new elements came to the front—the new capitalist traders and boot manufacturers (*e.g.* Hart, Wood, Lennard, Marshall), and the workmen. All evidence shows there was a great change. It is said that the new capitalists were more influenced by desire to improve their social position through municipal office than the old. At the same time, the workmen, as electors and as councillors, brought in motives of social improvement, propaganda, and conscious class interest.

The net result, since 1891, is that the Council has become much more progressive and democratic in sympathy; and, as the defect of this quality, more discordant and worse-mannered. This has been a further bar to any of the old " aristocracy " entering it.

The procedure, well enough adapted for a little party of friends, has not changed. The committees are now too secret, and have too much delegated to them—no provision for adequate publicity, or adequate control by Council. This leads to government by a *clique* (Wood, Lennard and Vincent), not on party lines, but on basis of satisfying personal power and ambition, and mutual protection. This has led to suspicions of the clique, and their friends getting indirect financial advantages, but no actual corruption is alleged.

Our impression is that the chief officers have, during the past decade, not been chosen on political lines, but rather for their probable sub-serviency to the clique. The ablest is evidently Colson, the gas manager. The new town clerk (Bell) did not improve on acquaintance; and we now judge him to belie his appearance of ability and solid qualities, by lack of experience, industry and zeal. He is, however, immensely thought of by many people in the town, and through his gentlemanly manners and good appearance carries great weight with rank and file of the Council.

The School Board is said to have begun in 1871, by having able educational enthusiasts and to have had two good chairmen in suc-cession; then a steady-going business man, and now a weaker ditto—the clerk is a mere clerk. One great aim seems to be to avoid publicity. It strikes us as an inferior edition of Leeds.

The Board of Guardians has always been considered far inferior to the Council and School Board—is said now to be rather like the rank and file of the Council, several small men are on both. Rather a rise since 1894—advent of six women, vote by ballot, and real election. [S. W.'s entry.]

At this point I will again insert an entry which, while reflecting my permanent interest in our joint investigations, relates to our other activities and describes the social environment of our daily existence.

May 22nd, 1900. Grosvenor Road.—The next eight years seem likely to settle how useful we shall be to our generation. Our effort is now directed to one end—to establish on a firm basis a science of society. We are trying to bring this about partly by the School of Economics. Sidney's persistent energy has attained at least a formal success for the School. We have gained university status, we have secured a building and a site, and we have the prospect of a regular income; we have attracted students, and we are training teachers. But how far the new activity will prove to be genuine science and not mere culture or shallow technical instruction, remains to be seen. The same doubt with regard to our own work. We are lavishing time and money on the investigation, doing it in an extravagantly complete manner. Shall we have the intellectual grasp to rise superior to our material—or shall we be simply compilers and chroniclers? It is only in rare moments that I have any vision of the book as a whole; at most times I am dazed by the intricacy and technical detail of the subject. Have we " bitten off more than we can chew "? It may be the time is not yet come for a sound science of social organisation. Anyway, we have faith that the beginning will be brought nearer by our effort, even if it fails to attain for us any kind of personal success. But, if we are to think out the development of local government in all its different phases, from our chaotic notes, it is clear that I must be free from the distractions of London life. Relations, old friends, continental and American admirers, students and persons who can help us in our investigation—all have to receive their due amount of attention. I am on excellent terms with the family—the sisters have taken to us and are beginning to wish that we should see much of them and their children: this means the giving and taking of dinners, chaperoning girls on bicycling parties, putting up public schoolboys on their trips to London. The old friends seem to look reproachful when one evades their offers to call or refuses blankly to lunch or dine with them. Then again students. Here I acknowledge a duty—one is bound to do one's little to helping forward younger persons, less fortunately placed than oneself, to the pathway of research and investigation. Lastly, there are a multitude of persons one ought to see in connection with local government. And, as a penalty for possessing a social conscience, in the background of all other distractions, the ghostly forms of all sorts and conditions of men, who have helped me in the past to get information on the subjects I was investigating—employers, philanthropists, trade unionists, co-operators. The only way out of the whole tangle is to get out of London. This we will do next spring.

The eight weeks' recess from London County Council administration was spent in Northumberland.[1]

September 25th. Newcastle-on-Tyne.—Staying here to start Miss Kitson on the local minutes. Our vacation at an end. Five weeks in St. Philips Vicarage, the home of a high church Anglican priest, who is also a socialist, up on the high ground in a working-class quarter. The house was badly built and designed, but pleasantly appointed,

---

[1] After turning over the 650 or so separate pages of notes I recall our general impression of Newcastle municipal government between 1835 and 1900.

(1) The exceptional potential wealth in land ownership, in port facilities and in the right to levy town dues, which the corporation possessed when it started on its career as a representative body.

(2) Not unconnected with this exceptional corporate wealth was the continuous presence on the town council of distinguished local capitalists, including, for instance, chairmen and vice-chairmen, directors and shareholders of the railway company and of the local joint-stock companies that supplied the inhabitants with gas and water, with toll bridges and tramways; together with the principal local ship-owners, ship-builders and important traders.

(3) The outstandingly favourable terms which these business men habitually obtained from the corporation as buyers and lessees of its land and its port facilities, and in their arrangements for the composite payment of town dues, and in the control of the gasworks, waterworks and tramways.

(4) The absence of party politics and the infrequency of electoral contests, owing to the current agreement between the local Tories and the local Whigs not to contest seats on the town council unless the holders voluntarily retired.

(5) The complete absence of any consciousness, on the part of these eminent business men, that they were in any way acting otherwise than strictly honourably in their continuous stream of dealings with the corporation that they controlled in getting something for nothing at the expense of their fellow-citizens. In this way they contrasted with the "professional politicians" in New York and other cities, who were fully aware that they were selling " franchises " and other favours to big business, and failing to enforce the laws regulating the sale of alcoholic liquor and suppressing immorality.

(6) In contrast with the Birmingham Town Council, and in the last decade of the century also with the London County Council, the capitalists who dominated the Newcastle Town Council were honestly devoted to the doctrine of *laissez-faire,* which yielded conclusive arguments against undertaking improvements in the housing, education and sanitation of the poorer inhabitants of their city, as matters of public concern and common well-being. It was this naïve synthesis between their economic creed and their pecuniary self-interest which enabled them to carry out the policy of exploitation of the corporate wealth for private profit without self-condemnation, and even without public blame from their fellow-citizens. This self-complacency became impossible with the rise of a new political party inspired by the growth of municipal socialism practised in Birmingham and London.

with a good library of theological and devotional books. Our impressions of Newcastle local government, not flattering—even worse than Leeds or Liverpool—are given fully in our notes. The weather was detestable so that we had little temptation to desert our work; and, by the end of the time we were both of us ready for our delightful holiday at Bamborough.

Three weeks we spent lying in a tent on the sand, watching the sea, or cycling over moorland and mountain, or wading out to rocks or islands—a quite enchanting holiday. We took with us masses of books, chiefly works on the Oxford movement—a continuance of the theological taste we acquired at the Vicarage: also Perthes' memoirs, lent us by a remarkable Newcastle man, Dr. Merz (whose acquaintance we had made), and his own *History of Thought*.

I have found true refreshment in this theological reading—a change of thought and an exercise of feeling. Specially interested in the Catholic religion as mental hygiene and discipline of the emotions, an authoritative guidance to the *motive* of conduct. There is so much energy and happiness wasted in everyone's life through lack of single-heartedness, through the presence of evil or unworthy feelings. The Catholic discipline has a traditional—and no doubt empirical—wisdom in training of character and the direction of the emotions. I have no special sympathy with the ascetic saint, yet the world could do with a good deal more physical self-control, humility and disinterested love, without human beings losing their effectiveness. All this experience was, it seems to me, thrown clean away with the Protestant Reformation. Perhaps other qualities were gained: but it is easier for me to see the loss than the gain.

Sometimes Sidney and I feel that we can hardly repay by our work the happiness and joy of our life. It seems so luxurious to be able to choose what work one will do, according to one's faith in its usefulness, and do that work in loving comradeship. The next ten years will prove whether we are right in devoting our energies to the establishment of a science of society, and whether the amount of scientific work we have mapped out for ourselves is not beyond our powers. But all that we are responsible for is the single-hearted devotion of our talents, whether of capacity, means or position, to the work one believes in. With Sidney this is comparatively easy; with me it is always a struggle to keep my mind from wandering off into foolish romancings. It is in this self-discipline that I find the need and the truth of prayer.

From January 1901 to December 1905, the date of my appointment as a member of the Royal Commission on the

Poor Law and Unemployment, the MS. diary is mainly concerned with the two other activities of Our Partnership: the furtherance of the London School of Economics, and the propaganda, open and concealed, for the unification of all education from the infant school to the university, under the London County Council. But, in order to complete the tale of our local government enquiry before it was merged in that of the Royal Commission on the Poor Law, I give the following entries, which can be skipped by all those who are not interested in the tiresome struggle with masses of material involved in sociological research.

April 24th, 1901. Churchfield, West Lulworth, Dorset.—A large thatched cottage with low straggling rooms, plain, clean but not too comfortably furnished, has been our living place for the last three weeks. The village is in a hollow of the chalk downs, without trees, and cut off from the sight of the sea. From our sitting-room window we look on to the road, then a hedge and then an orchard, beyond— other thatched cottages. But, once on the downs, there are glorious stretches of well-shaped hill and abrupt chalk cliff, expanses of sea and sky, and, on the other side, the most beautiful plain of heath and moor and wooded promontory, with bright little rivers running in all directions except sea-ward. The colouring these last days has been exquisite, the sea—sapphire, amethyst, emerald, moonstone—the white chalk cliff rising out of it in mysterious lines of white, pink, grey, the brilliant yellow gorse in the foreground and, on the other side, the dark russet of the yet unfolded beech buds, the dull green-black of the fir, and the rich tones of heather and scrub covering the plain and creeping up the little valleys of the bare neutral-tinted chalk downs.

The first fortnight was wet and cold, and, beyond our regulation two hours' walk in the afternoon, we stayed in and worked at " the book ". We had brought with us ten pamphlet boxes of material, MS. minutes of vestries, etc. The first three days I spent struggling with the draft of our first chapter, rearranging each section and when I had rearranged it submitting it to Sidney. Then he would begin (I sitting by his side) to rewrite it: both of us breaking off to discuss or to consult our material. Indeed, this constant consultation of our " specimens " is the leading feature of our work. We are always handling our material: one of us will object, " that is not so ", or " that is not always the case ", and then forthwith it becomes a question of evidence, and how far the facts we have under our hands are representative of the whole. The last three or four days we have gone systematically through all the ten boxes over every specimen, so as to be sure that we have included all the facts and accounted for all the similarities and divergencies between our " specimen " vestries. At last our chapter on the parish is complete, and I sent it off to be typewritten this afternoon.

January 30th, 1902. *Grosvenor Road.*—I have been so hard at work on the book that I have had no energy left over for diary writing. . . . Then we went to Margate into lodgings taking the devoted Emily [1] with us—which made the lodgings quite homely. We worked well together and almost ended the difficult chapter on " Municipal Corporations ". The number of times Sidney and I have laboured through these four volumes of the Royal Commission Report of 1834 is tiresome even to think about, arranging and rearranging the evidence, and arranging our facts in endless ways so as to find coincidences and perhaps causes. Our conclusions from the evidence are almost too favourable to please us: they are hardly *vraisemblable*. Since we came back we have either been tidying up the chapters, or I have been at the Guildhall working with Spencer through the minutes of the Court of Common Council of the City of London.

April 25th, 1902. *Crowborough Beacon, Sussex.*—A pleasant four weeks here, camping out in the large rooms of a girls' school at Crowborough Beacon. We have had a happy and successful time here: writing the chapter on the " Commissioners of Sewers ", sorting the material from structure into function (a tiresome job which will have occupied one or other of us for ten days). I have been thinking out the " assumptions " underlying the working out of local government prior to 1834. At present, I have the following principles: obligation of all to contribute service; desirability of common agreement; supervision by superior authority, calling in the counsel of inferiors; and *co-option and nomination of successors* by the existing governing body. It is clear that the principle of " obligation " referred to old services or general statutory services; and the principle of " common agreement " to new services or pseudo-voluntary services. I shall doubtless see other principles when we come to work out the functions. The book is getting into the interesting and philosophical stage, and I am looking forward with hopefulness and happiness to the ten weeks with the Russells.

May 4th, 1902. *Friday's Hill, Fernhurst.*—Settled again for our nine weeks' sojourn with the Bertrand Russells. Hard at work on the

---

[1] Emily Wordley, for many years parlourmaid at 41 Grosvenor Road. (Ed.)

Poor Law Report of 1834. I had to break into the work to help Sidney through with his University of London article. . . .

June 1902. *Friday's Hill.*—I have worked well, but with small result in actual stuff written. Of the eight weeks we have been here, nearly two were spent on the university article—counting exhaustion and proof-correcting, another two in reading through and analysing the whole of the Poor Law Commission evidence of 1833–4. Another week has been more or less spent in entertaining and resting, so that not more than a fortnight has been actually consumed in writing. But what I have done is to get the whole poor law section planned out and about half written, as well as the general scheme of Part II. of the book conceived, so that now the work will go straight forward. Sidney has only been able to write out (he always elucidates and completes my rough draft) what I have done, spending only one or two days a week down here.

July 1902. *Grosvenor Road.*—Four fruitful weeks at Campden, Gloucestershire, whither we return for another three to-morrow. We have done good work completing our chapter on the Poor Law. We see now that our first work will be the history of English local government from the Revolution down to 1835, practically the eighteenth and nineteenth centuries. It has been impossible to separate the early nineteenth from the eighteenth century, of which it was a mere continuation, without any deliberate change in constitution. Administrative inefficiency was one of the features of the eighteenth century, and it was only in the reform movement of 1832–5 that we have the first sign of a desire for efficient administration; and that only in the minds of " cranks " like Chadwick. The reactionary and the radical parties were alike against efficiency, the first for corrupt and the second for doctrinaire reasons. Our work on local government will be a big indictment, not only of the eighteenth century, but also of the present-day local government.

November 10*th*, 1902. *Grosvenor Road.*—Meanwhile, we are hammering out our conclusions and throwing them at the head of the public in the form of massive historical analysis. It is a time, we think, for big artillery in the way of books. But hard thinking takes time. For a whole month I played about with propositions and arguments, submitting them, one after another, to Sidney, before we jointly dis-covered our own principles of poor law administration. And each of the services will have to be taken up in the same exhaustive manner! How could we do it, if working together were not, in itself, delightful? It is a curious process this joint thinking: we throw the ball of thought one to the other, each one of us resting, judging, inventing in turn. And we are not satisfied until the conclusion satisfies completely and finally both minds. It is interesting too, to note that we never discover our principles until after we have gone through the whole labour, not only of collecting, classifying and marshalling our facts, but of sitting down in front of them, until we discover some series of hypotheses which accounts for all the facts. This final process seems to me to be not at all unlike testing in a laboratory; or manipulating figures in the working out of a mathematical problem. It is experimentation, constantly testing the correspondence between the idea and the fact. I do most of this experimentation and Sidney watches and judges of the results, accepting some, rejecting others. It is he who finds the formula that best expresses our conclusions.

January 16th, 1903. *Overstrand, Cromer.*—The last afternoon here. . . . A happy time: spent the first ten days sorting and pondering over the material on vagrancy and classifying the subject under " devices "; Sidney, meanwhile, clearing up odds and ends of work—Technical Education Board, University and [School of Economics] business. Then we started work together, and roughed out the greater part of the vagrancy chapter—I lazing over the fire while Sidney did the real work. This would take up our mornings—four hours; in the afternoon, there would be a walk on the beach or more rarely a ride, and then a quiet read at 18th-century literature. Sidney must have devoured some fifty or sixty books: I only accomplished two or three together with a few novels borrowed from Lady Battersea. Half-a-dozen times we went in for a chat with our neighbours in their resplendent villa, or Lady Battersea came to see us. She is a good and true-natured woman, and quite intelligent, though like all these " society dames " quite incapable of anything but chit-chat—flying from point to point. . . .

January 1903. *Grosvenor Road.*—This year has been both happy and fruitful. We have got on well with the book—though the task grows bigger and more complicated as we toil to complete it. We find ourselves really writing the internal history of the eighteenth century —and for this purpose I am reading eighteenth-century literature— trying to discover what were the good features of the time. A certain kind of veracity seems its leading moral quality; a perfected form in prose, its intellectual achievement; and I suppose certain discoveries as to the contents of men's minds; appreciativeness of human motive, cynical, but at least open-eyed. In fact, short-sighted and limited truth-seeking. As to conduct, human nature seems to have sunk pretty low—at any rate in England. Selfish, self-indulgent, corrupt, and slack in all kinds of effort except dissipation—even cruel, at least compared to the present day. But what a lot of the eighteenth century survives in the twentieth! Progress seems to have been made chiefly by the lower middle-class and upper artisans.

March 2nd, 1903. Grosvenor Road.—I took the chair for H. G. Wells's lecture on " Areas of Administration " at the Students' Union. Like ourselves, he is impressed with the need for some scientific adjustment of units of administration to functions or services—the obvious absurdity of Newcastle and Jarrow, for instance, being separate units of tramway administration, instead of the whole of Tyneside. He suggested some ideal areas for all purposes based on the function of locomotion. In summing up the debate, I threw out, on the spur of the moment, the suggestion of sweeping away all fixed areas; of instituting one unit of representation: *e.g.* one representative for every 10,000 persons for all purposes whatsoever, and of combining these units with each other according to function in many different groups or governing bodies. Thus, the five representatives of Deptford would sit together for street cleansing and lighting purposes, would sit with the other London representatives for education, main drainage, and with these and those of the home counties for water, etc., etc. The grouping would be done by Order in Council according to the service and according to fixed or changing conditions with regard to population, industry, climate, etc. The local government through the country would thus be fluid, indefinitely elastic, the same units grouped in any number of ways. Each constituency would fix its eyes on the one man, and take precious care to get a good representative. This would involve a great development of statutory committees with co-opted members, as some of the groups would be too large in member-ship to admit of direct administration by the whole body. Also, it might be necessary in rural districts to provide for the election or nomination of purely subordinate administrative bodies, who would manage the local affairs under the supervision of a large body. G. B. S. was delighted with the suggestion. There may be some grain of use-fulness in it.

June 15th, 1903. Aston Magna, Gloucestershire.—Meanwhile, our big work on local government grows slowly and surely; but still there is a good deal of ground to cover. Since we have been down here—sixteen days—I have mastered the whole of our notes on licensing of public houses by the justices, and the evidence and reports of four parliamentary enquiries, and we have actually written the greater part of the section—some twenty pages of printed matter, I suppose. It reads a straightforward narrative now—but oh! the mental struggle of getting the facts disentangled and marshalled one after another! Four hours every morning have we worked either together or separately. I getting the scheme right and Sidney getting the details correct and revising my scheme. We have worked all the harder because we have been absolutely undisturbed and the weather has been bad, so that Sidney has worked on in the afternoon, and I have brooded over the chapters trudging in the rain along the dripping lanes. Some delightful rides we have had together in the few fine days—happy hours of light-hearted companionship, arguing about our book or plotting our little plans.

August 1903.—While I spend four whole mornings in mastering the contents of one little book, and rest the whole afternoon and evening in order to work again the next day, Sidney will get through some eight or ten volumes bearing on local government, or likely to contain out of the way references to it. . . . The continuous activity of his brain is marvellous: unless he is downright ill, he is never without a book or a pen in his hand. He says that he cannot think without reading or writing, and that he cannot brood; if he has nothing before him more absorbing, he finds himself counting the lines or spots on some object. That is why when he is in a street or a bus he sees and reads and often remembers the advertisements. If I would let him, he would read through meal times. A woman who wanted a husband to spend hours talking to her, or listening to her chit-chat, would find him a trying husband. As it is, we exactly suit each other's habits. Long hours of solitary brooding is what I am accustomed to, and without which I doubt whether I could be productive. It is restful for me to wander off in moor, in lanes and field, or even to sit silently by his side in our tent, or by the fire. I have my thoughts, and he has his book, and both alike go to complete and fulfil our joint task. Of course, it is exactly the eager effort, taken together, the discussion, the planning and the execution, the continuous mutual criticism of each other's ideas and each other's expression of these ideas—all this vigorous co-operation for three or four hours at a stretch—that makes the silent companionship possible, even when this last is continued, perhaps, for three or four days at a time. Sometimes I am a bit irritated because at some time he will not listen to what seems to me a brilliant suggestion—dismisses it with " that is not new ", or with a slight disparaging " hmm ". But I generally smile at my own irritation, and take back any idea to clear up or elaborate or correct with other thoughts, or to reject as worthless; sometimes I flare up and scold—then he is all penitence and we kiss away the misunderstanding. Our love gives an atmosphere of quiescent happiness (to use Rogers' classification), and our work gives us periods of restless or energetic happiness. And when we are alone in the country together there is no other thought or feeling to intrude on this peaceful activity. We have no incompatible desires, either together or apart; our daily existence and our ideal are one and the same—we sail straight to our port over a sunlit sea. But the point we make for seems sometimes an unconscionable way off!

November 1903. *Grosvenor Road.*—Exactly a month to-day we returned to London. I have worked regularly at the book, but until the last week my brain seemed like wool, and my daily effort was more painful than productive. The net result is half the chapter on prison administration written, and most of the material mastered—but Sidney has really done the better part of the work though occupied with other matters.

November 1903.—Becoming obsessed with my scheme of transforming English local government, by sweeping away all areas, paying skilled men as representatives and adding, by co-option, residents and expert amateurs for different purposes. Such a body—say 600 representatives for England—would make a Grand Council for all England's internal affairs—a similar Grand Council for Wales, Scotland and Ireland—breaking up into smaller units of local government according to function. Salaries of £1000 a year out of national funds.

Perceive now that it would be desirable to have a Part III. to our book on theory of local government, giving an analysis of the assumptions upon which the 18th century and early 19th century local government was based—with the rise of new assumptions. With our mass of facts needful to have a brilliant and dogmatic theoretical part, quite apart from the concrete narrative, and based on a personal creed. Working well.

December 6th, 1903.—Finished the prison chapter to-day: for the last six weeks have worked well and hard at it—re-written it many times, improving it both in form and substance—Sidney the substance (which he is always adding to), I the form, which I model and remodel until I am satisfied with it. To-morrow I begin on another function—the suppression of nuisances. Meanwhile, Sidney will get out his little book on *London Education.*

January 17th, 1904. *Grosvenor Road.*—For the last fortnight—ever since I returned from our short Christmas holiday—I have been struggling with our material on municipal regulation. We have now decided to issue three volumes—I. on *Structure,* and II. and III. on *Function*—the two latter consisting respectively of poor law, police and prisons, and municipal regulation, municipal enterprise, and municipal finance. The two first volumes are done—in the first draft—and we have finished most of the separate chapters on municipal regulation, and the last chapter on the suppression of nuisances. The former I sketched and Sidney wrote out on Saturday—but I am still at work scheming the chapter on nuisances, without as yet seeing much light. It took a whole week pondering, analysing and indexing the material—then some days sorting out in my own mind the notions that belonged to a general introduction to regulation, and those belonging specifically to nuisances. This preliminary work is the hardest of all—one wanders far and wide in thought before one hits on exactly the right limits and right order of one's subject-matter. And it is work that one practically has to do alone, though directly one has got some limits and order satisfactory to oneself, Sidney's criticism or elaboration are an immense use. Indeed, I often feel that his " finish " is far more important than my preliminary framework.

October 1904. *Grosvenor Road.*—Since we returned a fortnight ago, I have been working for six hours a day, re-sorting the material back into structure—so that we may begin to re-write our first volume—and, by the way, clearing up my mind as to the arrangement of the subject-matter of each volume. It is hard driving work—a good deal is mere mechanical drudgery, but it has the advantage of a broad view of the whole subject-matter, structure and function, law and administration, origins and changes in the lines of development. . . . But, in the main, we lead the student's life—at least I do—the rest being taken as recreation in the odd times left over from the working day.

November 8th.—The sorting is finished—the two secretaries (Mrs. Spencer and Miss Crick) have completed it, working two days a week for the last six weeks. I, meanwhile, have superintended and helped—going over every page in the pamphlet boxes—and have looked up odds and ends of parish law in the British Museum. Now I have settled down to reconsider the chapter on the parish. I shall index the whole of the material under the four new heads of the parish and its office, the open vestry, the close vestry, the representative vestry, with innumerable subheads for each of the four chapters—varying the work with re-drafting the text of the chapter.

November 1904.—I am analysing all our material on vestries during the four morning hours and reading eighteenth-century literature for two odd hours in the afternoon—altogether I find I can manage six or seven hours' study now, as against the three or four hours of old days.

December 22nd, 1904.—Off to Felixstowe for a three weeks' recess —during which time we hope to finish off the parish chapter to be re-typewritten. We might do indefinitely more research, but it is time to be getting on if we ever are to complete our whole work on English local government up to the present time. Moreover, it is necessary for Sidney's administrative work to increase his reputation by publishing a big work of research.

January 1905. *Grosvenor Road.*—Since we returned ten days ago from our recess at Felixstowe, I have been hard at work analysing all our select vestry material, and reading at the British Museum everything that bears on it—Sidney going on to poor law pamphlets with occasional digressions to the matter I have in hand.

March 9th, 1905. *Grosvenor Road.*—Begun on the material for the county. Sidney another two weeks' work on the close vestry, annotating and completing it. . . .

March 15th.—Made an uncomfortable discovery this morning. In considering our material for our chapter on the county, I became aware that we have omitted to ask for and examine the presentments of grand juries, high constables, petty courts, etc. Also petitions from inhabitants and individuals. All we have looked at and abstracted are the orders of the quarter sessions. The mistake is due to our limited view at the beginning of our investigation: we started out with no systematic survey of our sources—merely allowed these to turn up anyhow. It is not too late, though troublesome, to remedy it. But I shudder at the thought of how bad our work was three years ago. We ought to have known better, with Cox's *Derbyshire* on our bookshelves. But I tend never to read a book until I actually want it, and Sidney does not regard discovering of sources as part of his duty. Damned stupid of me!

April 1905. *Grosvenor Road.*—Three or four weeks more after that spent either amassing new material at the British Museum for our chapter on the county, or in analysing our twelve boxes of material at home.

June 1905.—While we were at Aston, Sidney took the initiative and wrote hard at the chapter on county administration—I followed in his wake, supplying him, from my index, with all the instances in our material. But my work was mechanical. Now I have to pull the whole together—the county must be finished before we leave for Scotland a month hence. A strong sharp pull will do it.

July 1905.—Almost finished the county—but a few more pages to write—just the tag end of our last chapter.

October 1905. *Grosvenor Road.*—Five days' hard grind at MS. records of the Bristol Corporation of the Poor, and Municipal Corporation: encouraging Mrs. Spencer with my presence and leaving her to finish. Now at work sorting, indexing and scheming Book IV. of our work: seignorial franchises and municipal corporations. Sidney, meanwhile, gives all his spare time preparing *The Parish and the County* for the press, but much occupied with the L.C.C. work.

December 1905. *Grosvenor Road.*—Meanwhile, the thought of the work on the Royal Commission on the Poor Law added to the pressure of finishing our book, is not altogether a happy outlook. Our enquiry for Book III. is not yet completed—there are many gaps in our knowledge which I, aided by three private secretaries, am trying to fill up. But one hardly dare relax one's grip of the complicated subject, and how I shall manage to run a public enquiry side by side of our own, on a different subject, for a different period, I hardly care to think.

CHAPTER V

THE UNIFICATION OF LONDON EDUCATION
1899–1902

" How can I produce the next act in Our Partnership? " I ask the Other One. " So far I have disentangled and grouped together all the entries in the diaries displaying our joint investigation into English local government. But this uses up a mere fraction of the diaries of 1899–1906. Here is a mass of entries about your participation in the daily doings of the London County Council; your continued work, as vice-chairman, on the Technical Education Board, and the further development of the scholarship scheme and the co-ordination of the various grades and kinds of educational institutions; the part you played in reconstructing London University, and, as a senator, linking it up with the polytechnics, on the one hand, and the secondary schools, on the other. More interesting to me is the record of our devoted nursing of that delicate infant, the London School of Economics; its rapid growth and admission into the University of London, as part of the Faculty of Economics and Political Science, a new faculty on which you had insisted. And, last but not least, there are, from 1902 onward, all your manœuvres, which were certainly extensive and peculiar, on the London County Council, in the lobbies of the House of Commons, and even in the Tory press, to make the London County Council the supreme authority for the education of London citizens, whether elementary or secondary, secular or denominational, technical or university. And, all the while, as a background to our personal aims and efforts, there are entries about the South African War, the discords within the Liberal Party, the triumphant endorsement of aggressive imperialism at the polls in 1900, the Nonconformist outcry against putting the Catholic and

Anglican voluntary schools on the rates, the break-away of Chamberlain from the Conservative Government in 1903, and the starting of the tariff reform campaign (which incidentally deprived us of Hewins as Director of the School of Economics)—all this political, economic and religious ferment, ending in the outstanding triumph of the Liberal Party at the polls early in 1906, giving us a firmly established Liberal Government right up to the outbreak of the Great War. How can I mould this medley of events into a single act in the absorbing drama of Our Partnership? "

" Why not have one chapter on the unification of London education, and another on the social and political environment in which this unification took place? " suggests the Other One. " That sounds sensible; also it follows the pattern of the three chapters dated 1892–8." Then, after a pause: "It might be possible, though difficult, up to 1901–2. But, when once you took to wire-pulling about the proposed London Education Act, our social environment changed. For good or for evil, we were compelled, if we wished to succeed, to seek out those personages who could help to carry out our policy. How else can we explain our association with Anglican bishops, other than Dr. Creighton who was an old friend, and even with Catholic priests? Why did we become intimate with Conservative Cabinet Ministers? And how else could we have secured Rosebery as second president of the School of Economics, and Lord Rothschild (of all persons in the world) as third president, with a handsome donation of £5000? Why did our dear friend Haldane insist on introducing us to other members of the Liberal League, even to the uncongenial Perks? The explanation is simple. It chanced that with all these personages we happened to find, during that particular period of Our Partnership—a common purpose—the unification of education, and its wide extension under a directly elected authority. No: I am afraid I must keep all the entries together for each successive year in chronological order. What I think I will do is to split the period of 1899–1906 into two chapters. The first, 1899–1902, will be concerned in the main with the unification of secondary, technological and university education, including scientific research, all departments which you happened to be administering in one way or another. The second chapter, 1903–5, will centre round your successful wire-pulling for the re-drafting of the London Education Bill, which proposed to make the metropolitan boroughs the education authority, into the London Education Act of 1903, which established the London County Council as supreme authority over all rate-supported or subsidised education and research throughout the metropolis. To which I shall add entries from the diary recounting your patiently pursued persuasion of the Progressive Party during the last three years of its dominance, 1903–6, in favour of working the Act whole-heartedly in the interests of maximum efficiency. Meanwhile, will you kindly sit down and write out exactly what you meant by the unification of London education? " Here is the slip he presently handed to me:

What we had dimly in view from the outset, although this was only gradually formulated, was the desirability of bringing about, so far as London's vast population was concerned, a three-fold unity of educational activity. It seemed necessary, if any substantial progress was to be made, to unify the government of London education, placing all of it under the direction of a single elected municipal organisation. It was equally important to bring all grades and kinds of educational institutions, literary and technical, academic and professional, elementary and secondary, university and postgraduate, into harmonious co-operation with one another, for what was, after all, a dominant purpose which they had in common. These two unities, horizontal and vertical, involved essentially problems and methods of administration. A third, and some would say, a more important unification to effect, concerned the substance and method of education, that of combining teaching with research, "pure" science with applied, intellectual development with artistic expression, instruction with training for life.

1899

For the first six months after our return to England,[1] we had to separate. Whilst I settled down in one provincial town

[1] The return home from their nine months' tour abroad. See p. 145 n. (Ed.)

after another, to start our colleague, F. H. Spencer, in our particular methods of research, the Other One resumed his various administrative activities in the metropolis. This enforced parting we found somewhat hard to bear.

" I have been horribly impressed all this week ", writes the Other One during one of our longer separations, " with the *loneliness* of life except when you are there. I can't bear to think of what it would be if there were an accident to your train, or when you were bicycling, which left me really alone. I get thoroughly nervous and depressed, and am miserable; unable to work, or read in the evenings, and wanting my colleague and companion, my helpmate and playmate. Fortunately, there is now little more than a week of it. . . ." Then again three days later: " The apparent advantage of dividing our forces is delusive, as I am afraid my work falls off by nearly as much as the gain. I have been able to do nothing towards the book this evil fortnight. Partly this must have been the case owing to the arrears of other business. But partly (and I am afraid in no small degree), it has been due to my own failure. I have been strangely incapable. It has been almost a failure of will-power. Of course, it is not easy to be sure this is not idleness. But, after all, if idleness is so strong as to incapacitate, it does not matter what you call it. What is annoying is that it is a miserable state. If one is idle, one ought at any rate to enjoy the idleness! I am afraid, therefore, we must not count on being able to increase our output by working apart. I am sure the very opposite is the case: a much more agreeable prospect! . . ."

Fortunately, there were the London County Council recesses: ten days at Easter and at Whitsuntide, a month at Christmas, and more than two months in the summer. Settled together in lodgings or in a rented house in a suburb of some provincial city, we spent the week-days in investigation and the week-ends in cycling in the neighbouring countryside; all of which is described in the preceding chapter. With these few words of introduction, I present the following entries of the diary of 1899, selected in order to give a vision of our life as a whole, apart from our specialised tasks of research. I begin with the very first entry in the MS. diary for 1899.

February 5th.—Since we returned to England I have been disinclined to write in my diary, having nothing to relate and having lost the habit of intimate confidences, impossible in a joint diary such as we have kept together during our journey round the world. One cannot run on into self-analysis, family gossip, or indiscreet and hasty descriptions of current happenings, if someone else, however dear, is solemnly to read one's chatter then and there. I foresee the sort of kindly indulgence, or tolerant boredom, with which Sidney would decipher this last entry! And this feeling would, in itself, make it impossible to write whatever came into my head at the time of writing without thought of his criticism. . . .

March 7th.—Sidney has been principally engaged in engineering the School of Economics into its proper place in the new University, bargaining alternatively with the Royal Commission to recognise it as a School of the University and to create a separate Faculty of Economics and Political Science, with the T.E.B. to endow the proposed Faculty with an income, and with Passmore Edwards to present a new building. Everything seems to be going excellently. . . .

May 15th.—Whilst I am mainly occupied in this enquiry, Sidney engineers the School and to a lesser extent the University. He is in the background of the County Council, partly because he has been so long away; partly because he is considered a specialist in education. On educational matters he leads without dispute; the T.E.B. and the Council doing anything that he asks them to do. He no longer evokes hostility: the Moderates respect him, the leading Progressives ask his advice, but do not regard him as a rival for the position of leadership. No doubt this is due to his growing disinclination to push himself forward for any position desired by anyone else; his refusal to take any steps to start a career of political advancement. His dislike of the personal struggle for leadership becomes, in fact, greater and greater. He is as energetic and persistent as ever, but his energy is perpetually seeking the line of least resistance for the cause he believes in—and the line of least resistance for his cause is the line of least advancement for himself. . . .

Haldane dined with us last night to talk over University affairs—especially the possibility of getting Carnegie to endow London University with some of his millions. We loathe what we saw of Pittsburg and explained that we could not possibly approach " the reptile ": but thought that others could do so who knew less or thought differently. John Morley for instance? So Sidney agreed to draft some kind of description of what might be done. Haldane was down-hearted, more down-hearted than I have ever seen him about the prospects of the Liberal Party. He tried to explain away Rosebery's last speech—crying quits to Home Rule, Socialism, Temperance and other social reforms, but could not do so even to his own satisfaction. The present situation —all the leaders of the party on strike—is becoming ludicrous—no one understanding what they are striking against unless they are striking against each other. Haldane brought a cordial invitation from Herbert Gladstone to Sidney to stand for Deptford, or any other London constituency, all expenses to be paid by the party: " a sign not of grace, but of dire necessity ".[1] " They think your standing would do them good," said Haldane, " but I told them ", he added in a half-bitter, half-playful tone, " that, like Rosebery, you would neither come in nor go out." " Until we know who is to be the company," I retorted, " we shall stand in the doorway and help to block the door by standing there."

Ten days in London have been dissipated by social duties. Three days I had to spend at Brighton with Herbert Spencer, he becoming insistent that I must visit him. Poor old friend: I verily believe that he thinks it is a treat for me to spend so many hours in his stuffy house, subsisting on his stingy housekeeping, so stingy that sometimes I spend no little time in considering whether I can manufacture an excuse to get a good

[1] In a letter 21/6/99, the Other One refers to this flattering desire to rope him into the Liberal Party:

" Last night's dinner was curious and interesting. Lord Tweedmouth had 40 to dinner, in his gorgeous house, on gorgeous plate. There were present Campbell-Bannerman, all the London Liberal M.P.'s except Stuart and Burns, Herbert Gladstone, and all the chosen Liberal candidates and probable candidates for London—including 24 County Councillors. I was given a very high place—put next to Sir H. Campbell-Bannerman at the main table! There was a most gorgeous dinner, and after it, to my surprise, and I think unexpected by others, Lord Tweedmouth invited us all to make suggestions how to win London. In response to cries Dr. Collins and Dickinson spoke, and then there were cries for me. So I rose, and being quite unprepared rather missed my opportunity I am afraid. It was difficult to say what one should have said. But I managed very politely to express my feeling that the leaders would have to make it clear that they meant business on London questions, especially taxation of Ground Rents and water: and that I was not myself a candidate. This led to rather a funny result—Causton, Herbert Gladstone and Bannerman in speaking later, all insisted with ludicrous iteration, that I *must* become a candidate. It became the ' note ' of the evening, to everybody's amusement. Steadman, Dr. Napier, Lawson also spoke, saying not much. The fact is we were all unprepared to speak, and of course rather hampered by our position as guests. I am sorry now that I did not say more ' for their good ', but I felt bound to try to be extra-courteous. Of course I told Causton and H. Gladstone afterwards very decidedly that I quite certainly would *not* stand—and I don't feel in the least inclined to do so. But it was evident that last night they meant to make a dead set at me."

meal out. However, on this visit there was no actual lack of nourishment. Two innocuous young women are in perpetual attendance—one a pianist, the other a housekeeper; the same secretary, half-secretary half-valet—three maid-servants, and a coachman—all at the call of the poor old man's money. He told me that during the last years he has been drawing from the sales of his books, eight hundred a year from England, and five hundred a year from America. All his savings are in the Linotype Company, in which he invested in order to break the trade union—an investment which yields high interest. So that he is more than well off considering his narrow needs. Notwithstanding all this mean living, there is the stamp of heroism on his daily life. At eighty years of age he still struggles on, in pain and depression, revising his biology in the firm faith that his words are the truth.

June 18th.—Spent Sunday with the Holts. Dear old Lallie most affectionate. Hers is a nature which improves with years—her character has softened, deepened, and she has gained in intellectual interests. At present, in the intervals of keeping a luxuriously comfortable house for a large family with many friends, she reads theology, trying to find a creed which combines rational thought with religious emotion. She has a strong mind, but she has neither intellectual training nor experience of thought, and it is pathetic to watch her struggling with wrinkled brow to reach conclusions which have been reached long ago by persons of her temperament. For the metaphysic we adopt is mainly a matter of temperament. She is a thorough-going puritan—pious but hating authority or intellectual or emotional self-subordination. Between her and us, there is a genuine regard: she admiring our persistency and strength of conviction, and we—Sidney especially—liking the orderliness and public spirit of the Holts. We go there again in September to study the Liverpool Town Council.

July 3rd.—Back in London in time for the International Women's Congress. The American and continental women took it quite seriously: but the more experienced English women, whilst organising it admirably, mocked at it in private: the press sneered at it, and the public generally ignored it—always excepting the entertainments of the duchesses and countesses who had been drawn in to patronise the Congress. It was not a failure, but hardly a success. The council meetings were stormy and unbusinesslike (I represented New Zealand owing to our recent visit to that land), resolving themselves into a duel between Mrs. Creighton, backed up by the N.U.W.W.[1] set of English women, on the one hand, and, on the other, Mrs. Wright Sewell (an

---

[1] National Union of Women Workers. (Not a trade union body, but a group of women interested in women's organisations. Ed.)

autocratic and self-assertive American), supported by Lady Aberdeen and the American and continental delegates. Great Britain and her faithful colonies were routed, which is what Mrs. Creighton desired, as she wished the National Council of Great Britain to withdraw from the International. It would have been better if the N.U.W.W. had refused to let itself be drawn into this adventure: it believed neither in Woman with a big " W ", nor in Internationalism with a big " I "; it is distinctly parochial and religious—most emphatically insular. To the well-bred and conventional ladies who dominate it, the " screeching sisterhood " demanding their rights represents all that is detestable. The public conferences were some of them informing and all of them decorous, and, owing to the predominance of the N.U.W.W. *clique*, the discussions were practical, even technical in character. I took the chair at one of the conferences and spoke at another, and turned up at the council meetings to support Great Britain. But with Mary Playne [my sister] in the house, and friends drifting in to see me, my week was wasted and my strength dissipated. Americans and colonials turn up and claim our attention, and the completion of our enquiry seems far off and unattainable.

October 10*th.*—This past summer [I note after staying with Sister Holt], so far as personal life is concerned, has been full of enjoyment of work, health and love. But it has been marred by the nightmare of the Dreyfus case and the Transvaal crisis. I took a feverish interest in the Dreyfus trial—Sidney grew impatient and would not read it, but to me it had a horrible fascination—became a morbid background to my conscious activities. Equally unsavoury have been the doings of our own people in the Transvaal—an underbred business, from the Jameson Raid to the South African Committee of Enquiry, from the hushing up of the Enquiry and the whitewashing of Rhodes, to the flashy despatches of Milner, and the vulgarly provocative talk of Chamberlain resulting in war with the Transvaal Republic, that remnant of seventeenth-century puritanism.

October 30*th.*—Haldane spent an hour or so with us this evening. Significant is the transformation in his attitude from a discreet upholder of Liberal solidarity to that of a rebel against the views of the majority, determined to assert himself. " The Liberal Party is completely smashed, Mrs. Webb ", and he beamed defiance. He had spent a month reading Transvaal blue-books and was convinced that Milner was right, and that war was from the first inevitable. The cleavage goes right through the Liberal Party into the Fabian Society, Shaw, Wallas and Whelen being almost in favour of the war, J. R. MacDonald and Sydney Olivier desperately against it, while Sidney occupies a middle position—thinks that better management might have prevented it, but that now that it has begun recrimination is useless, and that we must face the fact that henceforth the Transvaal and the Orange Free State must be within the British Empire.

Sidney lecturing at Oxford: I stayed here for my usual Wednesday afternoon at home. This is rapidly becoming a series of interviews with members of my class at the School of Economics. I enjoy lecturing every Thursday: the preparation of my lecture takes the best part of two mornings either in actual preparation or in resting so that my brain may be clear. The weekly class brings me into close connection with the work of the School: I see some half-dozen students every week and talk over their work with them. I am glad that our life becomes every day more that of students and teachers, our intercourse with general society shrinking up to occasional meetings with casual acquaintances. I sometimes long for more physical enjoyment, bright exercise and the still beauty of the countryside: for leisure as distinguished from the inertia of exhaustion. Indeed, when we are both a little weary we talk of the time when we shall be free to retire to the country and plan an ideal cottage with a large library, with lounges and room for endless book shelves, with a couple of spare bedrooms, and an open sunny verandah. Silence, beauty and physical exercise seem to me the supreme luxury; the mental superlatives we have already—mutual love and keen intellectual interest.

The Shaws have taken up their residence in Charlotte's attractive flat over the School of Economics, and Sidney and I meet there on Thursdays to dine sumptuously between our respective lectures. Charlotte and Shaw have settled down into the most devoted married couple, she gentle and refined, with happiness added thereto, and he showing no sign of breaking loose from her dominion. What the intellectual product of the marriage will be, I do not feel so sure: at any rate he will not become a dilettante, the habit of work is too deeply engrained. It is interesting to watch his fitful struggles out of the social complaisancy natural to an environment of charm and plenty. How can atmosphere be resisted?

December.—John Burns dined here last night. He is mellowed in temperament, he has lost his restless egotism and personal hatreds, and something of his force: lost his emphatic faith and his fierce sympathies with suffering. Of course, he will go on being " progressive ", and will back up anything that can be put into an Act of Parliament. But, like most untrained enthusiasts, experience of affairs has unhinged his faith and dulled his enthusiasm. All the common or garden objections to specific reforms, which were the trite commonplaces of one's childhood, which one learnt to discount, realising the prejudices from which they sprang, seem brand-new truths to him. His special bugbear to-day is the pressure exercised on representatives by municipal and state employees to improve the conditions of their employment at the cost of the community (he having in his constituency some 3000 persons drawing maintenance from rates and taxes). These men and women might retort that John Burns, L.C.C., M.P., had become accustomed to postmen earning 18s. a week and denied the right of collective bargaining. His past utterances as a Labour leader—as a strike leader—hamper him in his reaction: it is assumed that he must necessarily be always on the side of the wage-earners, whatever their claims may be, and however fierce their resentment. When he insists on his freedom to judge the rightness and expediency of any demand he is denounced as a renegade. Certainly, there is no such pressure on Sidney. I do not think there is any danger of undue pressure. If public servants were to press for better conditions than were enjoyed by the majority of the voters, it would bring about its own reaction. These doubts and difficulties are fast paralysing Burns as a progressive leader.

December 1899.—Massingham, Vaughan Nash and Harold Spender have been dismissed from the *Daily Chronicle*; W. P. Reeves is out of spirits; and, generally, Liberals of all types are depressed and uncertain of themselves. The dismissal of Massingham from the editorship, and of the others from the staff, of the *Daily Chronicle* reflects the strong patriotic sentiment of its readers; any criticism of the war at present is hopelessly unpopular. The cleavage of opinion about the war separates persons hitherto united and unites those who by temperament and training have hitherto been divorced. No one knows who is friend and who is enemy. Sidney does not take either side and is, therefore, suspected by both. He is against the policy that led to the war, but that issue being past he believes in a policy of thorough in dealing with the Boers. And who can fail to be depressed at the hatred of England on the Continent: it is comforting and easy to put it down to envy and malice, but not convincing. To those who, like Massingham, Leonard Hobhouse and Frederic Harrison believe the indictment of British policy to be justified, the times look black, and the fact that those with whom they are accustomed to agree regard them as suffering from hysteria does not improve their temper. To my mind, given the fact that the Boers were fully armed, confident in their strength, and convinced of our weakness, war was inevitable. Whether this condition of affairs was in itself inevitable, or whether it was brought about by the impossible combination in British policy of Gladstonian sentimental Christianity with the blackguardism of Rhodes and Jameson, is another matter. But I doubt whether the partisanship of Milner, and the bad manners of Chamberlain, have had much to do with it. Chamberlain has injured himself with the thinking men of all parties by his lack of kindliness, courtesy and discretion, but he is still the " strong man " of politics: and the political " pit " of men from the street likes the strong man and has no desire that he should mend his manners. Besides, he has convictions and he expresses them honestly and forcibly—qualities at present rare in the political world. I should gather from the growing irritability of his speeches that his splendid physique is giving way.

1900

Kruger's ultimatum of the 11th October 1899, which demanded the withdrawal of British troops from any proximity to the frontiers of the two Boer Republics, produced immediately a state of war, beginning with an unexpected invasion of the Cape Colony by the Boer forces. British feeling was further embittered by the manifest pleasure of France and Holland, and by the even more humiliating episode of patronising advice from the German Emperor as to how we should conduct the campaign. Hence the year 1900 found British public opinion tense and angry, making even social intercourse difficult. The Conservative Party was solidly behind the determination of Chamberlain and Milner to " beat the Boers " and extend the British Empire. The Liberal Party, already enfeebled by a series of quarrels among rival leaders, was shattered by a definite split into three fiercely warring groups. The "Liberal Imperialists ", organised in the Liberal League under Lord Rosebery, and including Haldane, Asquith and Sir Edward Grey, gave full support to the Conservative Government in waging the war. A mixed group of distinguished individuals —the so-called pro-Boers—drawn equally from the Liberal Unionists and the Liberals—under the leadership of my brother-in-law Leonard Courtney, and enlisting many non-political intellectuals, upheld the right of the Boer Republics to complete independence, and denounced the policy and action of the Conservative Government as wicked aggression. An intermediate position was held by the newly chosen leader of the Liberal Party, Sir H. Campbell-Bannerman; supported by Sir William Harcourt and the central body of the Liberal Party, he found himself unable to deny the necessity of the war, but dissented alike from the policy which had led up to it, and from the objects and methods by which it was being pursued.

Looking back on this long and bitter controversy, and consulting the speeches and memoirs of the leading personages in all three camps, I am struck with an extraordinary omission, which seems to have passed unnoticed at the time. Amid all the angry argument as to whether the territories of the Transvaal and the Orange Free State should be governed by the resident Boer farmers or by the legislative assemblies at Capetown and Westminster; and as to whether or not the Boer farmers had an indefeasible moral right to independent sovereignty, or the Johannesburg [Uitlander] citizens a fundamental right to a vote, no one in Great Britain or South Africa seems to have remembered that these various claimants to power, whether Boer or British, agriculturist or gold-miner, were only a minority, a million or so strong, amid a vast majority of Kaffirs, five or six millions in number, amid whom this variegated white minority had intruded itself. With one exception, presently to be recorded, not one of the contending factions in Britain or South Africa—not one of the outstanding persons in the controversy—ever mentioned the claim of the native population whose conditions of life were at stake, even to be considered in the matter, let alone to be admitted to the government, or even to be given a vote, in the vast territories in which they had been living for generations.

How did the little group of Fabians react to this heated controversy? " The majority of the Society ", we are told by its historian and former general secretary, Edward Pease, " recognised that the British Empire had to win the war, and that no other conclusion to it was possible." But a considerable minority, including two members of the executive, J. R. MacDonald and J. F. Green, and George Barnes and Peter Curran, future Labour M.P.'s, together with Walter Crane, H. S. Salt, Mrs. MacDonald and Mrs. Pankhurst, were fervent pro-Boers. Hence, in December 1899, a special meeting of the members was called at which S. G. Hobson submitted a resolution—" That the Society should dissociate itself from the imperialism of capitalism and vainglorious nationalism and condemn the war ": the result being that the previous question was carried by a bare majority of 59 to 50. This inconclusive result reflected, we are told, " a great diversity of opinion in the Society, and the executive committee, for the first, and so far the only time, availed itself of the rule which authorised it to submit any question to a postal referendum of all the members ". As there was never any question of the Society issuing a pronouncement in favour of the war, the resolution submitted in February 1900, with arguments for and against, was: " Are you in favour of an official pronouncement being made now by the Fabian Society on imperialism in relation to war? " The membership at that time was about 800, of whom 50 lived abroad, and in all only 476 votes were cast, 217 in favour of a pronouncement and 259 against. Whereupon, as stated above, the MacDonalds and thirteen other members resigned from the Society.[1]

This, however, did not settle the matter. Within a few months of the secession which was jestingly referred to as " the Boer trek ", it became apparent that a general election in Great Britain would be forced by the Government. The Society would necessarily have to take a hand in a contest in which not the Boer War alone, but the whole policy of Joseph Chamberlain's imperialism, would be the dominant issue. The executive committee accordingly deputed a small committee to prepare the necessary election manifesto, and persuaded Bernard Shaw to act as draftsman. What, after prolonged discussion, he supplied, with incomparable skill, was a pamphlet of 100 pages, which brought out the Fabian position, but also did justice to the various valid criticisms and necessary qualifications expressed by all the most fanatical partisans of the Boers, on the one hand, and the patriots, on the other. The draft was again submitted to a full meeting of members, at which all sorts of criticisms

[1] *The History of the Fabian Society*, by Edward Pease, pp. 128-30.

were made and diligently noted by the draftsman, the meeting ending by adopting the statement by acclamation. The resulting pamphlet, published at one shilling as *Fabianism and the Empire*, was naturally ignored by the party newspapers and the rival parliamentary candidates. But it had its educational effect on those whom it reached, and it reads to-day, as, perhaps, the most prescient and permanently instructive public document of its date, notably as regards the relative rights and duties of the white and the coloured citizens of the Empire.

To this introduction I may add a domestic detail. My eight brothers-in-law, all of them more or less political-minded, represented every grade of opinion in favour of and against the war, from die-hard Tory imperialists to stubborn pro-Boers; we two sitting comfortably in the middle, speaking soothing words to each and all—an agreeable circumstance which tended to make our little house in Grosvenor Road, for the first time, a common centre for my sisters and their children.

Torquay, January 31st.—The last six months, and especially the last month at Plymouth, have been darkened by the nightmare of war. The horrible consciousness that we have, as a nation, shown ourselves to be unscrupulous in methods, vulgar in manners as well as inefficient, is an unpleasant background to one's personal life—a background always present, when one wakes in the night and in the intervals of leisure during the day. The Boers are, man for man, our superiors in dignity, devotion and capacity—yes, *in capacity*. That, to a ruling race, is the hardest hit of all. It may be that war was inevitable: I am inclined to think it was: but that it should come about through muddy intrigues and capitalist pressure and that we should have proved so incapable alike in statesmanship and in generalship is humiliating. I sometimes wonder whether we could take a beating and be the better for it? This would be the real test of the heart and intellect of the British race: much more so than if we succeed after a long and costly conflict. If we win, we shall soon forget the lessons of the war. Once again we shall have " muddled through ". Pecuniary self-interest will be again rehabilitated as an Empire-building principle. Once again the English gentleman, with his so-called habit of command, will have proved to be the equal of the foreign expert with his scientific knowledge. Once again our politicians and staff officers will bask in the smiles of London " society ", and will chatter bad metaphysics and worse economics in country house parties, imagining themselves to be men of the world because they have neither the knowledge nor the industry to be professional administrators and skilled soldiers.

To us public affairs seem gloomy; the middle-classes are materialistic, and the working-class stupid, and in large sections sottish, with no interest except in racing odds, whilst the Government of the country is firmly in the hands of little cliques of landlords and great capitalists, and their hangers-on. The social enthusiasm that inspired the intellectual proletariat of ten years ago has died down and given place to a wave of scepticism about the desirability, or possibility, of any substantial change in society as we know it. There may be the beginnings of intellectual curiosity, but it is still a flicker and not a flame. And, meanwhile, the rich are rolling in wealth and every class, except the sweated worker, has more than its accustomed livelihood. Pleasure and ease are desired by all men and women: science, literature and art, even social ambition and party politics, have given way to the love of mental excitement and physical enjoyment. If we found ourselves faced with real disaster, should we as a nation have the nerve and persistency to stand up against it? That is the question that haunts me.

February 20*th*.—Meanwhile, our little schemes with regard to the new University of London prosper. We have got the School recognised as a Faculty of Economics, we have secured a site and a building, free of cost, and an income of £2500 devoted to economics and commercial science. Sidney will be a member of the Faculty and will probably represent the County Council on the Senate. Best of all he has persuaded the Royal Commission to recognise economics as a science and not merely as a subject in the Arts Faculty. The preliminary studies for the economics degree will, therefore, be mathematics and biology. This divorce of economics from metaphysics and shoddy history is a great gain. We have always claimed that the study of the structure and function of society was as much a science as the study of any other form of life, and ought to be pursued by the scientific methods used in other organic sciences. Hypothesis ought to be used, not as the unquestioned premiss from which to deduce an unquestioned conclusion, but as an order of thought to be verified by observation and experiment. Such history as will be taught at the School will be the history of social institutions discovered from documents, statistics and the observation of the actual structure and working of living organisations. This attainment of our aim—the starting of the School as a department of science—is the result of a chapter of fortunate accidents. There was the windfall of the Hutchinson Trust, then the selection of Hewins as director, the grant from the T.E.B. towards commercial education, the coming of Creighton to London as Bishop, and the successful packing of the University of London Commission. Then again we are humble folk whom nobody suspects of power; and Sidney's opinions on educational matters are considered moderate and sound as neither anti- nor pro-ecclesiastic. And we have had two very good friends helping us—Haldane and the Bishop of London, both of them trusting us completely in our own range of subjects. Of course, the School is at present extremely imperfect: its reputation is better than its performance. But we have no illusions, and we see clearly what we intend the School to become and we are convinced that the science will emerge.

February 23rd.—Beatrice Chamberlain came to lunch on Wednesday, ostensibly to tell me about poor Clara Ryland,[1] but really to find out what we felt about the Transvaal. She was as vigorous and attractive as is her wont, a fine generous nature, reflecting the best side of her father. Her tone about the Transvaal was far more moderate and magnanimous than I expected—not nearly so partisan as some of my sisters. Against Steyn of the Free State she was distinctly venomous and she was deprecatory of Schreiner and the Cape Government. " They have been deplorably weak, they have run from one side to the other, imploring each alternately to climb down. And, though Schreiner eventually slipped down on our side, he did so not out of loyalty but merely to save himself." All this I disputed with some warmth. When her carriage was announced, I noticed a look of nervous dissatisfaction on her face and she went to put on her veil, I following. With an effort she broke out: " You will congratulate Papa on having smashed his detractors last night? "[2] " We have never attached much importance to the telegram," I answered affectionately. " What other people say Mr. Chamberlain said is not evidence," I added. Her face brightened and she said something about misunderstandings of conversations when two persons were referring to different things—from which I gather that we are right in assuming that the telegrams are similar in character to those already published. If only Chamberlain

---

[1] Clara Ryland, youngest sister of Joseph Chamberlain. She had recently lost her husband. (Ed.)

[2] On February 20, D. H. Thomas (afterwards Lord Rhondda) moved in the House for a " full enquiry to be made into the origin and circumstances . . . of the incursion into the South African Republic of an armed force in 1895 ". To old arguments about the whitewashing of Rhodes and " missing telegrams ", the anti-war party added references to these documents stolen by a clerk from Bourchier Hawksley's office. Chamberlain's reply was volcanic. " It was a splendid exhibition of parliamentary genius ", reported the old *St. James' Gazette*, " and cannot fail to enhance even Mr. Chamberlain's reputation "; while the *Daily Chronicle*, which loved him not, described the speech as " a brilliant rhetorical feat, however much or little it answered the point of the indictment ". See *Life of Joseph Chamberlain*, J. L. Garvin, vol. iii. pp. 550-55. (Ed.)

had not whitewashed Rhodes! Though I am inclined to believe that his defence of Rhodes sprang from a defiant loyalty to a man in whose devotion to the Empire he has complete confidence, this explanation is not quite convincing.

March 8th.—A week with Herbert Spencer at Brighton. Combined a visit to him with some days' work at vestry and municipal records. The old man is better and more benign than I have seen him for years. But, about the world in general and England in particular, he is terribly pessimistic. " Heading straight towards military despotism: the people will get what they deserve. I remember ", he continued, " being angry many years ago with an Irishman for saying that the English were a stupid race. I should not be angry now, I should only add that they are brutal as well as stupid." He still retains his personal affection for me—more out of habit, I think, for every year he becomes more suspicious of our aims and of our power of reaching these aims. His housekeeping has become quite comfortable: two bright young persons as housekeeper and pianist respectively, three maids, a house-boy, coachman and a secretary, all dancing attendance on the old man. His secretary has not had a holiday for ten years and his two young ladies are kept close at it all day and every day, " making a pleasant circle for me ", he calls it. He is despotic—humanely despotic, anxious for their health and for his view of what ought to be their pleasures. But he is intensely suspicious that he is being done by his housekeeper or his servants, and certain that he is chronically cheated by his trades-men. " Interests, interests, interests, that is what dominates the world: if you are to get your rights, you must be perpetually distrusting every one. And it is your duty to exact your rights ", he added with a snarl. Poor old man, it is pathetic to see a nature so transparently sincere, so eager to attain truth, warped by long-continued flattery and subordina-tion of others to his whims and fancies into the character of a complete egotist, pedantic and narrow-minded—a true Casaubon.

March 16th.—Utterly done up with a week of dissipation. The day I came back I dined with Alfred [Cripps] at the House of Commons in a private room without ventilation—a veritable hole of Calcutta. Margaret Hobhouse had to leave, finding it unbearable. I struggled on, chatting with Carson, a clever, cynical and superficial Irishman—an ultra Tory on all questions. " Gerald Balfour, the worst Irish Secretary we have had: he and his brother have done more to make Home Rule possible than all the preceding governments put together. When he leaves, he will leave all parties united clamouring for Home Rule by making it clear that it is not worth while being loyal ", was his emphatic summing-up of the situation. It was not surprising to me that Carson thought that John Morley had been an admirable Secretary: " In all his administration he followed the advice of the Unionists ". On Friday, we had a little dinner of friends here: on Sunday, we supped with Willie Cripps: on Monday, I debated in the Chelsea Town Hall with an anti-regulationist; on Tuesday, we had to dine with us the Creightons and Professor Ramsay to talk London University, and on Wednesday, we dined with Haldane to meet a select party of Rose-berites including the great man himself. Haldane sat me down next Lord Rosebery against the will of the latter who tried his best to avoid me as a neighbour, but all to no purpose, Haldane insisting on his changing places. He is a strange being, self-conscious and sensitive to a more extreme degree than any mortal that I have ever come across. Notwithstanding this absurd self-consciousness, he has a peculiar personal charm, the secret, I imagine, of his hold on a section of the Liberal Party and of the public. At first he avoided speaking to me. But, feeling that our host would be mortified if his little scheme failed utterly, I laid myself out to be pleasant to my neighbour, though he aggravated and annoyed me by his ridiculous airs: he might be a great statesman, a Royal Prince, a beautiful woman and an artistic star, all rolled into one. " Edward," called out Lord Rosebery to Sir Edward Grey as the latter, arrayed in Court dress, hurried away to the Speaker's party, " don't tell the world of this new intrigue of Haldane's." And I believe Lord Rosebery winked as he glanced at me sitting by him. Which showed that he has at least a sense of humour. For the party *was* an intrigue of Haldane's—an attempt to piece together an anti-little-England combination out of the most miscellaneous morsels of political influence. " I feel deeply honoured at the place you gave me, Mr. Haldane," said I, as he saw me out of his luxurious flat, " but, if I were four-and-twenty hours in the same house with that man, I should be rude to him." Haldane is now amusing himself by weaving, from his gossiping imagination, a Rosebery-Webb myth.

Consequent on all this dissipation no work at the book and a feeling of disconsolate blankness when I look at our accumulating material. My brain is all wool, and my thoughts are woolgathering.

July 19*th*.—A month in London entertaining, especially seeing sisters, and snatching from the waste of energy two or three mornings at the British Museum over local newspapers. Longing to get back to quiet days of absorption in our subject. Sidney struggling on, engineering the School, its site, its buildings, its income and its status as a university institution. Breakfast 8, sharp: reading together at British Museum from 9.15 to 1 o'clock: then back to lunch and he off to his committees, I to waste my time—always someone to lunch or to dinner, or dining out or calling—some distraction taking one's thoughts from profitable brooding over local government. For our present work —pushing the School, and our enquiry into local government—some social connections are needful. The same old problem, how much sacrifice of personal efficiency to personal influence? In England, all power to establish new undertakings rests on your influence over the various ruling cliques. The more cliques you are in touch with the easier it is to lay broad foundations. On the other hand, your power for good depends, in the long run, on the quality of your special product; and this last depends on whole-hearted devotion to your subject. The sort of compromise I make is to take the summer weeks in London as my holiday, and to turn the times that would be holidays into periods of sustained research. But we both look forward to the time when long months in the country will give us at once time for work and delightful recreation.

We have seen much of the Leonard Courtneys this spring. Leonard's determined support of the Boers' plea for independence, even more his denunciation of the war, has alienated him from both political parties. The Tories regard him as a wholly unendurable person; the vast majority of Liberals consider him to be a quixotic crank; even the tiny group of pro-Boer Radicals think that his speeches and manifestoes are often out of season. It is only among the I.L.P. and S.D.F. working-men that he finds enthusiastic followers in his anti-Government crusade. A strange turn in the wheel of political popularity! He is too absorbed in the consciousness of a great wrong done, too fervently convinced that there is only one way out of the tragedy, to care much for his own political career. What hurt him most, oddly enough, is the social boycott: Leonard has always enjoyed the leisurely society of persons of culture and position, and to-day he and Kate find themselves without the accustomed invitations.[1] The disinterestedness and robustness of his convictions has impressed some of the elect; but a cynical public has been annoyed and irritated by his tone of moral indignation and his assumption of moral superiority. He has flung in

[1] Leonard Courtney was returned for Liskeard at a by-election of 1877 and held the seat until the 1900 election, when he retired from the candidature owing to the refusal of both parties, Conservative and Liberal, to support him. " When Courtney was elected ", wrote Justin M'Carthy, " I remember having a talk with an experienced Member of the House, who set himself up as an authority on all political questions. ' Mark my words,' he said to me with an air of portentous wisdom, ' he will be a dead failure in the House of Commons.' I did mark his words, and Courtney was not a dead failure, but a very live success." (*Reminiscences*, ii. p. 369.)

" We are completely and entirely out of it ", wrote Kate Courtney in her diary, September 24, 1900: " my great man is in splendid isolation. To Ripon to stay at Studley Royal. We were met by telegrams, and telegrams continued for the two days we were there, mostly from various hopeless constituencies, suggesting he should stand. Two requests for a speech from Exeter and Battersea, which we acceded to after some hesitation."

the face of a nominally Christian, but really unbelieving world, Kruger's faith in God; and the majority of good citizens have resented it because they have not dared to answer back what they think, that such a faith in God unfits a man to be the ruler of an independent state. This very morning Kate produced from a blue-book a nobly felt and finely expressed letter from Kruger to an Englishman in January 1900, tense with religious fervour. " Kruger really believes in God, and God's government of this world ", I cheerfully admitted, a sentiment accepted by Kate as granting the whole case for the Boers. " Which proves to me ", I added sadly, " that he is an impossible person for the rest of this wicked world to treat with." Kate looked shocked, and almost asked me to leave the house on the spot. Dear Kate is an incurable sentimentalist and has no sense of humour: she gives happiness and increased self-assurance to Leonard; but she aggravates his one big fault—his inveterate mental habit of thinking everyone who disagrees with him immoral and unenlightened. All the same, there are few mortals for whom I have so continuous an affection and respect as I have for Leonard Courtney and his loving satellite.

Political parties become daily more chaotic. The Tories are, as a party, complete cynics bound together by a rampant imperialism, alternately protecting vested interests and appealing to demagogic passions they do not themselves share. But, at any rate, they understand the game of " follow the leader ". The great Liberal Party—" the engine of progress "—has lost its old faith and has no notion in which direction progress lies. The rank and file mete out contempt impartially to all their titular leaders. Captain Lambton, for instance, who believes neither in Home Rule nor Local Veto, still less in Disestablishment, and is an enthusiastic supporter of the Government's South African policy, is standing as Liberal candidate for Newcastle—John Morley's old constituency. Meanwhile, Leonard Courtney and John Morley are acclaimed as the only honest politicians by the recognised Labour leaders, who have one and all gone pro-Boer. The Fabian Society, it must be admitted, is completely out of it, the majority believing in the inevitability of the war, whilst the minority regard the majority as being the worst kind of traitors.

September.—On our way down to-day [from local government investigation up North] we found Haldane at Newcastle and travelled with him to York. He was full of political talk. " Not a single issue is being discussed at this election that will be remembered two years hence ", was his summing-up of the situation. For the last four months he has spent all his time, left over from his income-earning at the Bar, on building up the Liberal Imperialist Party. He obstinately maintains that no frontal attack on social and industrial evils is possible for the Liberal Party: they must gain the confidence of the electors on foreign policy and any social reform must come by " turning movements ". The Tory majority, he thinks, will be diminished; and the present Government will not last more than two or three years more. Balfour is tired of it, Chamberlain is the only strong man and he is universally distrusted as supreme ruler. " This Government is rotten: no young shoots and much dead wood. Moreover, it is tainted with jobbery and corrupt contracting: the Birmingham ring has made money out of the war: though little is said, the electors don't like it. It is only the emergency of the Transvaal settlement, and the uncertainty as to who and what the Liberal leaders are, that will make the elector continue the Tories in office." He intimated that the Liberals would reform after the election, with Rosebery as leader, Asquith as first lieutenant, and Perks as organiser. " Then money will flow in and everyone who dreams of a peerage or a baronetcy will send in his cheque ", added Haldane with a cynical shrug.

October 7th.—Haldane's anticipation of a diminished Government majority seems hardly likely to be fulfilled. The Liberal Party divided against itself, uncertain as to its policy, is being badly routed at the polls. The " strong man " of the Government has played it down low to the " man in the street ": the " street " has answered back with emphatic approval. And, in doing so, the electors have shown common sense. Who could trust a party with a lay figure as ostensible leader, and as the real leaders of its sections men who hate each other, and each other's ideas, more than they do the persons or the views of the enemy. And there seems little hope for the Liberals in the near future. To win back the large towns they have to give up Home Rule, Local Veto, and Disestablishment; they have to become imperialists and develop some kind of social programme. In giving up the old politics, they alienate the Celtic fringes, and all the provincial Liberal politicians: in imperialism, they cannot outbid the Tories: in all social questions, they lack knowledge or conviction and fear to lose their remaining rich men. So they will fall back on the Rosebery plan of " no policy ", hoping that they may be accepted as the only alternative to the Government gone stale. That may cause the adhesion, one by one, of men (mostly of the upper and middle classes) who are personally offended with the Government: or who belong to interests that are threatened by the expenditure and innovation of Tory democracy. But it will not bring back to their ranks the great mass of town workers who want some strong lead: something blatant and positive in return for their votes.

Meanwhile, we go on, little concerned with the stress and storms of politics. Now and again we have a qualm lest the huge Conservative majorities in London constituencies may mean a Moderate victory in L.C.C. elections in March. Otherwise a Conservative Government is as good for us as a Liberal Government, presided over by such men as Sir Henry Fowler. We realise every day more strongly, that we can never hope to get hold of the " man in the street ": we are " too damned intellectual ", as a shrewd journalist remarked. All we can hope to do is to find out for ourselves the actual facts and embody them in a more or less scientific form, and to trust to other people to get this knowledge translated into popular proposals. What is more probable is the silent use of this knowledge in the unperceived transformations of law and government by men and women of goodwill. Our business is to be friendly to men of all parties—to *try* to be charitable and unassuming, and to go on with our own work persistently and loyally. Sidney, in his administrative work, has considerable power to build up London secondary and university education on the lines he believes in; with the London School of Economics we have, in our own hands, the forming of the economic and political science teaching of the new university, and through the new faculty the gradual establishment of a new science and a new art. That, with our own research work, ought to be sufficient for our faculties, indeed, it may prove to be beyond them!

November.—One sad result of this election is the exclusion of Leonard Courtney from Parliament. He and Kate have fought splendidly for the cause they believe in, and though they accept the fact that the country is dead against them—they have accepted it with quite magnificent cheerfulness. And yet to Leonard it means probably an end to his career, the loss of an occupation which gave him public influence, agreeable society, and which minimised the results of his loss of sight. Fortunately for him, he has a devoted and sympathetic wife who lives for him and for his ideas, shares every feeling and every thought, and whose faith in his essential greatness is only increased by the world's neglect! And he has the staying power of strongly religious feeling, and a firm faith (though its particular form I have never been able to discover) enabling him to dismiss questions of personal gain as irrelevant alike in thought and action. If Leonard had been endowed with more intellectual humility and sympathy, with more desire for work, he might have become a great power for good. As it is, he has been " a voice crying in the wilderness ", ennobling and stimulating those who have chanced to hear and understand him.

December 9th.—A delightful Sunday with the Bertrand Russells and Haldane—talking philosophy, university organisation and politics.

Early Days of the Partnership

Sidney Webb (*ætat circa* 32)

Haldane still devotedly attached to Rosebery: trying hard to make friends for him even among such humble folk as ourselves and the Russells. And we used our opportunity to press for the adoption of this policy of a national minimum of health, education and efficiency, leaving free play to the competition between private enterprise and public administration *above* that minimum. " Rosebery has his back to the wall and will not be forced into a premature declaration of policy: all he is pledged to, is that there shall be no tampering with the Empire." But we are to meet Rosebery again: apparently, the great man is an admirer of *Fabianism and the Empire* and has sent various gracious messages to Shaw.

December.—Our autumn has been dissipated with odds and ends. Sidney has been absorbed in his administrative work. London University proves to be the most formidable addition to the L.C.C. and Technical Education Board. The Senate of 50 more or less distinguished folk, many unknown to each other, and drawn from all sections of society, without procedure and with extraordinarily incompetent officers inherited from the old " examining board ", is the most difficult body to get into working order. The Chancellor, Vice-Chancellor and Registrar are simple obstructionists, and represent respectively apathy, stupidity and ill-will, each carried to its nth. All that is done has to be done in spite of them; and, of course, as far as Lord Kimberley and Sir H. Roscoe are concerned, it is impossible to be otherwise than outwardly acquiescent and respectful. Sooner or later the running of the University will, I think, fall largely to Sidney and Hewins and one or two others: at present it is chaos. Meanwhile, we have been spending our substance on giving little dinners to diverse senators: trying to make them understand each other and accept Sidney's view of university organisation.

1901

January 2nd, 1901.—Back in London after a few days with the Playnes and Hobhouses. The sisters do not grow apart as years roll on: indeed, the last few years have seemed to bring us all nearer together. Blood relationship is a very tenacious tie: it outlasts many relationships of choice—wears better than any other relationship (except marriage), though it is seldom so close or satisfying as the special intimacy of the moment. For, as one gets middle-aged, intimate friendships seem to fade away, and one is too much occupied and, in a sense, too utilitarian, to make new friends. One sees persons who are for the time one's fellow-workers and these individuals are not necessarily sympathetic. Old friends die, or marry, or become estranged or indifferent: of my early friendships few remain: the Booths and Margaret Harkness estranged, Carrie Browne dead, the Barnetts, Ben Jones, Ella Pycroft, Alice Green, Bella Fisher and Marie Souvestre all extremely friendly when we meet, but we meet, perhaps, once a year: in the case of these latter, perhaps, two or three times a year. There is, it is true, Herbert Spencer whom I occasionally visit, out of piety towards an old sentiment. Then the " two dear comrades and friends " who for some half-dozen years regularly spent their holidays with us—Wallas and Shaw—are both of them married; and, though here again when we meet we meet as old friends, we seldom see each other. . . . And, possibly, they would all of them say that we were too much absorbed in each other to care for others and that our friendliness was more an overflow of our happiness than any special love for them. In fact, a sort of universal benevolence to all comers seems to take the place of special affection for chosen friends. It is only the persistent yet slack tie of sisterhood that seems to survive these inroads of indifference.

The man we see most of nowadays is Hewins: every Tuesday he lunches with us to discuss the affairs of the School. He is original-minded and full of energy and faith. Shaw always declares he is a fanatic. So he is. But he is also a born manipulator. We never know whether he is telling us his real opinion, or his real intention. We feel that we are being " handled " just as we watch him handling others. He ought to have been an ecclesiastic: and would have entered the Church if it had not been for the 39 Articles to be swallowed, just at a time when physical science and historical criticism made these tenets seem intellectually contemptible. In thought, he would be a reactionary if the present trend of Liberal opinion did not happen to be a reaction from the doctrine of " individual freedom ". He hates disorder; he detests protestantism; or following the " inner light ", or any other rebellion against the reasonable will of the community. He is a great admirer of Chamberlain; dislikes all the Liberal leaders equally; votes Progressive, and is a member of the National Liberal Club. He is a Churchman and an ardent believer in the scientific method in economics and politics. He is disinterested with regard to money: he is ambitious of power—altogether he is one big paradox. But the most characteristic paradox of his nature is the union of the fanatic and the manipulator. With such a character it is difficult to be intimate, however much it may excite one's admiration, liking and interest.

Naturally enough we have a large circle of friendly acquaintances, some of whom might be considered friends. Haldane, the Reeveses, the Bishop of London and Louise Creighton, the women factory inspectors, Lion Phillimore, the Bertrand Russells, the staff of the London School of Economics, the senators of the new University, the

Bishop of Rochester [Talbot] and his wife, Sir Alfred Lyall, the Richard Stracheys, and other more or less interesting folk—come and go: a still larger circle leave cards and force me, by so doing, to trudge to all the quarters of residential London. But, for the most part, we have been left to ourselves and allowed to spend our energies on our own special work.

At present, I am writing the opening chapters to a small book on *Factory Legislation: its Theory and Practice*, or rather adapting portions of our Part III. of *Industrial Democracy* to a more popular audience. I have also undertaken to edit the remaining chapters, and to see the whole through the press. It is to be a counterblast to the persistent opposition to factory legislation on the part of the " women's rights " movement reinforced by the employers' wives. This opposition has for the last ten years blocked all progress in the effective application of the Factory Acts to other industries. It is led by a few blatant agitators, who would not count for much if they were not backed up by many " society " women who belong to the governing clique, and by a solid opposition to further reform from vested interests. What we have to do is to detach the *great employer*, whose profits are too large to feel the immediate pressure of regulation and who stands to gain by the increased efficiency of the factors of production, from the ruck of small employers or stupid ones. What seems clear is that we shall get no further instalments of reform unless we gain the consent of an influential minority of the threatened interest. I feel sometimes in despair about the book. Beyond a little mechanical research, my mind has been entirely off the subject of local government, either preparing lectures on industrial competition, or on methods of research, or brooding over the religious question and the provision of a metaphysic and a mental hygiene. I have been reading at large on these questions: theology, saints' lives, James' *Will to Believe*, and his *Psychology*, various works on scientific method, and so on. The one subject my mind revolts at is local government. But we shall have to set to and *do it* directly the L.C.C. election is over. I am making elaborate arrangements for a good five months in the country, and hope to accomplish at least the first part (prior to 1835). We have masses of material, but all the thinking has to be done.

January 15th, 1901.—Mandell Creighton—Bishop of London—dead. One of our best friends. When we returned to London this autumn we found him invalided. He had broken down on his holiday, and was by the doctor's orders confined to the house. Three or four times I went down to Fulham to see him either with Sidney or alone. He was singularly gentle and sympathetic: eager to talk: the same delightful combination of banter and deep philosophy: the same strange enigmatical view of all things, whether of God or man. The very last time, in fact, just before Christmas, I had a long talk with him whilst the other guests were at tea. I told him our plan for reforming the Church; our idea of religion as mental hygiene, and the way in which we thought the High Church doctrine more consistent with it, than the Evangelical. To all of which he listened, and half seriously and half playfully agreed. Then I sent him James' *Will to Believe* and this note was the last word from him.

I first knew the Creightons in August 1887. I remember so well that visit to Worcester: my interest in the versatile and pleasant ecclesiastic and don, my attraction to the handsome and direct-minded Louise, so different from each other, and yet so completely complementary. From that time forward I remained a friend, and until they came to London used constantly to visit them. These visits to Cambridge and Worcester were among the happiest days of my life—during the long and trying time of Father's illness: the friendship, coming just at a time when I was suffering intensely, seemed a new opening into the world of distinguished men and women. And from the first they liked and trusted me—liked me for my best side. When I engaged myself to Sidney, they accepted him as their friend without hesitation; saw him through my eyes, and trusted him as they had trusted me.

Meanwhile, Dr. Creighton had changed the life of a professor and author for that of a bishop. There are many of his friends who regretted the step. The freedom of view, the brilliant dialectic, the subtle paradox, which often covered a daring hypothesis—all these were in place in a Cambridge don; they became impossible, or at any rate most baffling, in a bishop. Agnostic friends, sensitive to the proprieties of life, no longer dared to join in this intellectual adventure, with one who ought to feel himself to be a successor of the apostles. And, owing to a strange contrariness and rebellious audacity, a reaction possibly from the daily routine of a bishop's life, the change of position seemed for a time to accentuate the frivolous side of his intercourse with the outer world. Smart stories, somewhat cynical repartee, took the place of free and easy discussion of metaphysical questions. It was not possible to treat as " open questions " matters upon which a bishop had to lay down the law according to his pledges. On the other hand, he was not willing to give up his position as a member of the republic of letters, tolerant of all views and ready to be convinced by evidence. Hence, between him and the more serious-minded of his heterodox friends there arose a certain atmosphere of constraint. In our case, this was neutralised by his unfailing interest in our educational and research work. For, outside the spiritual side of life, Creighton believed implicitly in the scientific method of observation and verification. And he believed in organisation and machinery, in the regulation of conduct by law or public opinion, according to some deliberately conceived idea of social expediency. He had no faith in democracy; though he accepted it as necessary: his contempt for the politician amounted almost to intolerance. Lack of brains was to him the greatest social danger: with brains and goodwill no change was impracticable. Without intellectual leadership, the average man, however good his conduct, would remain in a state of squalor and mediocrity.

Is Dr. Creighton a convinced Christian? was the question perpetually canvassed by his friends. I always felt it an impertinence for an agnostic to raise the question. His tolerance, his desire to find a common basis with all his friends, made him deliberately stow away his Christian assumptions when he talked with heretics. " Let us find something on which we can agree, and argue on that basis ", was always his attitude of mind. He realised that the ultimate convictions of serious-minded persons could not be altered by a conversation: that they were rooted in their experience of life, or in the constitution of their minds. He never, therefore, tried to convert: all he did was to endeavour to sympathise and to justify. Probably this uncommon willingness to accept any person's fundamental assumptions, as a basis for argument, was the root of the feeling of many persons that he was intellectually insincere. Personally, I believe he had a firm belief in the validity of the Christian faith, and in its ultimate victory over other forms of thought.

Rightly or wrongly, Creighton believed that, for a state Church you must put forward a lay as well as a spiritual justification. " Baptism is the finest system of birth registration; Christianity is popular metaphysic; missions are a method of teaching the subordinate races the assumptions of their governors "—these and other sayings crept up in his conversation, addresses and charges. All this was sadly secular. The clergyman was not only a priest of the mystical body of Christ, he was also an extra official of the state charged with a certain supervision over education, poor law, and even sanitary work. Hence, during his reign in London, the Church was encouraged to throw itself bodily on the side of good, and even progressive, government in all local concerns. His own daughter he encouraged to become a manager, not of the voluntary schools, but of the board schools in Fulham. His conception was that the Church was to take its part in the secular affairs of the nation; its part being to keep up the standard of integrity, energy, scrupulousness and exact knowledge. In his short term of office he had assumed, to a large extent, the leadership of London life in secular as well as in spiritual matters; Nonconformists and secularists read his addresses with as much interest and, perhaps, even more edification than fervent churchmen. The last time I saw him he playfully remarked that he would resign his bishopric and retire to a cottage and " write messages to the English people ". These messages would, I am convinced, have mainly consisted in advice on secular matters.

Our intimacy with Dr. Creighton, and to a lesser extent with Dr. Talbot, has brought constantly before us the Church, its present difficulties and its future. Any outside demand for disestablishment and disendowment is dead at the present moment. A few political dissenters and Radical political workers in the smaller provincial towns still hold to the old doctrine of the iniquity of a union between Church and State. But, as far as the bulk of the people are concerned, this doctrine is obsolete. The town workman is now neither a Nonconformist nor a secularist, he is simply indifferent to the whole question of religion or metaphysic. On the other hand, he is inclined to think the hardworking curate, who runs his club, looks after his children on Sundays and holidays, stirs up the sanitary inspector and is sympathetic because acquainted with the struggle for better conditions of employment, a good fellow. He sees the dissenting parson moving out to the suburbs, the rich congregation preferring a new and fine building there to the old meeting-place down town. But the priest of the established Church remains in the old city parish, and is constantly abroad in the slums. The workman sees no distinction between the appropriation of the Church income by the clergy and the appropriation of mining royalties or ground values by the landlords, except in the expenditure of the income—a comparison immensely in favour of the clergyman. " The majority of them do a day's work for us and live among us, and it is precious poor pay they get for doing it ", is a frequently heard remark. " If we take to disendowing and disestablishing, we will deal with the landlords first ", is the half-conscious thought of the revolutionary workman. The educated classes who are not Church members are also losing their objections. " Nature abhors a vacuum: all metaphysic is equally untenable if you require scientific proof: the Christian metaphysic no more than the Hegelian. Why not leave the people with the old traditional faith? " are the dictates of the enlightened. " If the people wanted three state churches, I see no reason why they should not have them ", remarked Lord Rosebery. Moreover, state endowment, state control, state ownership, are all the order of the day.

Hence, there is no fear of destruction from without. But within there are disruptive tendencies. No man of culture can nowadays be a Protestant churchman of the old type—the dogma and doctrine, the written word of revelation are too ugly and impossible taken in their crudity. To be acceptable to the cultivated person the whole thing must be transformed by mysticism, by vague emotion, by the charm of tradition, on the one hand, and the hope of doctrinal development, on the other. Christianity must have its past and its future; and each alike must be different from its present. Hence, unrest in the Church and the initiation and elaboration of ritual and discipline, to cover up diversity of thought and feeling. " More room," cries the young churchman, " freedom from the limitations of the Elizabethan compromise." " Let us push forward where thought and feeling lead us." " Impossible," says the lawyer, " here are the 39 Articles, and I am charged as the representative of the state to interpret them, and eventually to enforce them."

Our suggestion is briefly this: we want no more vexatious prosecutions. Hence, abolish the right of the individual to prosecute, make prosecution the function of the vestry of ratepayers. If the inhabitants of the parish are satisfied with the clergyman, let him have absolute freedom to develop. If, on the other hand, he has failed to satisfy them, give them the power to prosecute him for breaches either of doctrine or ritual, or for non-performance of his duties. Let the court be, in the first place, his bishop, and ultimately the bench of bishops; if either party appeals, sweep away the bishop's veto on prosecutions—it is sheer nonsense to give a judge a veto on prosecutions and, unnecessary, if you otherwise provide against mere capricious prosecutions from individuals. Sweep away the civil jurisdiction over the Church. We do not want a lawyer's interpretation of the 39 Articles in the prayer book—we want a sympathetic interpretation by persons whose whole duty and life is to consider the national needs in the matter of religion. The secular state gets its control over the Church by the Prime Minister's nomination of the bishops and by parliamentary power to legislate. That is sufficient. Give such a Church, deriving its authority directly or indirectly from the people, freedom to develop along its own lines.

Of course, our object is to enable the Church to grow out of its present superstitious doctrine and obsolete form. We have faith that the development would be along the right lines. No doubt, at first, the direction would be sacerdotal and ritualistic. Personally, I do not altogether object to this. The more ritual, the more mystery, the more indefiniteness of thought, the greater the play for emotional purposes. Exactly, as in practical life, in the choice of ways and means, the scientific method, full and undefiled, must be exclusively relied on, so it seems to me in the higher ranges, in the choice of motives and ideals, it is a mistake to intellectualise, the expression must be obscure and elastic so as not to debase the purpose in the act of expression. And, though there are aspects of the priest which are distasteful, yet I desire to see the minister of religion practising the art of mental hygiene. I do not believe that the ordinary man is capable of prescribing for the diseases of the soul any more than they are for the diseases of the body. We need the expert here as elsewhere. Religion, to my mind, should consist in the highest metaphysic, music and ritual, and mental hygiene.

And I desire that the national life should have its *consciously* religious side. If, as a state, we are purely rationalistic and selfish in our motives and aims, we shall degrade the life of the individuals who compose the state. I should desire the Church to become the home of national communal aspirations as well as of the endeavour of the individual towards a better personal life. Meanwhile, I prefer the present Church, with all its faults, to blank materialism or competitive sectarianism.

To this short essay on Dr. Creighton, I add a more definite statement of my own outlook on life in the early years of the twentieth century.

January 25th, 1901.—Reading Leslie Stephen's *Utilitarians.* Always interesting to compare one's own point of view with that of one's parents! For Bentham was certainly Sidney's intellectual god-father; and though I have never read a word of him, his teaching was transmitted through Herbert Spencer's very utilitarian system of ethics, and his method through Spencer's deductive reasoning from certain primary assumptions. How has the position of the disciples shifted from that of their past teachers?

First, we agree that human action must be judged by its results in bringing about certain defined ends. There is no other sanction that we care to accept but results, though we should be inclined to give, perhaps, a wider meaning to results. For instance, the formation of a noble character, the increase of intellectual faculty, stimulus to sense of beauty, sense of conduct, even sense of humour, are all ends that we should regard as " sanctioning " action; quite apart from whether they produce happiness of one or all, or none. We altogether reject the " happiness of the greatest number " as a definition of our own end, though other persons are perfectly at liberty to adopt it as theirs. I reject it, because I have no clear vision of what I mean by happiness, or what other people mean by it. If happiness means physical enjoyment, it is an end which does not recommend itself to me—certainly not as the sole end. I prefer to define my end as the increase in the community of certain faculties and desires which I happen to like— love, truth, beauty and humour. Again, I have a certain vision of the sort of human relationships that I like and those that I dislike. But we differ from the Benthamites in thinking that it is necessary that we should all agree as to ends, or that these can be determined by any science. We believe that ends, ideals, are all what may be called in a large way " questions of taste " and we like a society in which there is a considerable variety in these tastes.

Science and the scientific method can be applied, not to the discovery of a right end, *but to a discovery of a right way of getting to any particular ends*. And here it seems to me the Benthamites fell lamentably short in their understanding of the scientific method. They ignored the whole process of verification. They deduced their ways of arriving at their own particular end—human happiness—from certain elementary observations of human nature: but they never sought to test this "order of thought " by the " order of things ". They never asked, Is it so? Now they were right in taking as their premiss an observation of human motive; they were right in forming a hypothesis deduced from this premiss. Where they went wrong, and most perniciously wrong, was in never attempting to verify and correct their hypothesis, and by this verification to discover other premises. Hence, they omitted from their calculation some of the most powerful impulses of human nature: reverence for mystery, admiration for moral beauty, longing for the satisfaction of an established expectation, custom and habit, tradition, sense of humour, sense of honour, passionate longing for truth, loyalty—besides a host of mean vanities and impulses none of which produce happiness or aim at producing it, but are just blind impulses.

February 9th.—Met Lord Rosebery at Haldane's again: Asquith, W. P. Reeves, Prof. Hewins, Prof. Massie and ourselves made up the party. I sat next to the great man who was gracious and less self-conscious than last time. But the entertainment was a futile business: we talked and laughed—" showed off "; we never got anywhere near a useful discussion on questions in which we were interested. Prof. Hewins, Sidney and I had hoped to talk about the School with Lord Rosebery who is probably to be President, but we got nowhere near it. He is a strange capricious creature, always posing to himself and others, anxious only to attain right *expression*. I was angry with myself afterwards, and was strangely enough a bit vexed at being the only lady! That would not have mattered had we talked seriously—but in mere light banter—" the eternal feminine " will intrude, and in that case one likes companionship!

But, undoubtedly, our excursions into " society " advance the interests of the School. We are to have a meeting at the Mansion House with the Lord Mayor in the chair; Lord Rosebery to make a great pronouncement in favour of commercial education in the abstract and the School in the concrete, Lord Rothschild to act as treasurer and other great persons to play up—the whole intended to raise a building and endowment fund for the School. All this is Haldane's doing, partly out of friendship for us, partly because he wants to interest his chief in *uncompromising* advance movements. Also, he delights in intrigue, and is amusing himself with putting into one company the most unlikely co-workers. An institution which has united as its supporters ourselves, Rosebery, Rothschild, the Bishop of London and the Fabian Society, is just the sort of mixed party which Haldane revels in. " My dear Hewins," said Haldane, " you ignore the personal factor in politics." For Hewins, though he willingly accepts the result, does not wholly like this " society " development.

And, in truth, it has its unpleasant side. It is much wholesomer to win by hard work than by these capricious gusts of fancy in great folk. I feel that I am skating on rotten ice which might suddenly give way under me. I am not afraid of losing the support of the " personages ", because one does not count on its continuance and takes gratefully all one can get, knowing that it will come to an end. What I do fear is weakness in my own nature: incapacity to keep my intellect and heart set on our own work, undistracted by personal vanity or love of admiration. Fortunately, Sidney is absolutely single-minded. But, like Hewins, he does not quite like it.

March 8th.—Brilliant victory at the L.C.C. election. For the last three or four months (indeed since October) Sidney has been organising the election: writing the election literature, insinuating articles in the press, gathering up the Progressive forces all through London, as well as engineering the Deptford fight. We fully expected to lose seats in London, and a portion of our own Deptford majority. But the Water Companies, at the last moment, won our battle for us by their proposed water regulations.[1] Directly these appeared we knew the tide was in our favour; the only problem was to make it flow as swiftly as possible. Hence the articles contributed to all the halfpenny press, so that by the election day, every " halfpenny " was on our side and even the *Daily Telegraph* came out in our support! Still, the sweeping majority for the Progressives means that the London elector has confidence in the old gang which has now ruled London for twelve years; and that, in spite of the fact that the old gang are exclusively Radicals, whilst the vast majority of electors are Tories. It is a striking testimony to the industry and capacity of a small body of administrators. The Moderates, on the other hand, are mediocrities, the larger number of them will not work; as a party they suffer from the same fatal defect as the Liberal Party in national politics; the majority of them have un-

---

[1] These regulations imposed new and highly unpopular restrictions on what was already an inadequate water supply in many working-class districts. " *Vote for Monopoly and Bung—Unionist Candidates for the L.C.C.* ", ran a Progressive election pastor. (Ed.)

popular convictions and run away from them. To have unpopular convictions is bad enough: to run away from them is fatal.

And now that the election is over, we can at last turn to the book. I have already begun to sort both the material and my ideas for our country sojourn. I am not satisfied with myself, but hope to be more so after a course of country air and exercise and concentration on our subject. London life, with its constant clash of personalities—its attractions and repulsions, its manipulations and wire-pulling, is distracting and somewhat unwholesome. And this last year I seem to have passed into an emotional and imaginative phase, which, whilst it gives me a certain magnetic effect on others, knocks me to pieces myself. Indeed, I am becoming mediumistic. Country life and intellectual concentration will, I trust, bring back a saner frame of mind. Brainwork is a wonderful specific against the manifold forms of hysteria.

March 22nd.—Our long-planned meeting at the Mansion House came off yesterday. As far as we were concerned, there was no hitch in the arrangement. But, from Lord Rosebery's black looks when he came on the platform, something had evidently gone wrong, and afterwards we gathered that he had intended making the meeting an occasion to answer the somewhat futile remarks of Lord Salisbury on commercial education, but the Lord Mayor had intimated that such a course would be undesirable and that Lord Rosebery had, therefore, found himself cut off from the most effective part of his speech. It was not an able pronouncement but it sufficed, and has been a great advertisement for the School. Haldane spoke with real enthusiasm, and Harvey (of Glyn Mills) with knowledge of the subject. Lord Rothschild was unable to come but heads the contributions with £5000. The whole affair is an audacious advertisement and appeal. It will be a marvel if it does not provoke an attack on the management and teaching of the School. We are sufficiently firmly seated in the saddle to risk it. I feel that now we have done our utmost to give the School an independent life, it is time that it toddled out of our nursery and to some extent took its own line. Sidney is now turning his mind to the University and has drafted a scheme for its complete reorganisation as a great centre of applied science.

And now we can, or at any rate I can, turn my thoughts wholly to the book. Fortunately, my mind has become clear of the romancing which perturbed it a few weeks ago. One of those strange and mysterious alternations which go on seemingly uncaused in our mental life— a sudden regaining of complete control over thought and feeling and a positive *desire* to concentrate all mental energy on intellectual work. It is as if a hidden influence had been withdrawn and the mind again moved freely. But the mere physical exhaustion of London life prevents me doing good and sustained work. I am longing for our three months in the country.

Meanwhile, my boy is exceptionally well and happy. He is full of active thought and work: his health is excellent, he is conscious of success, and each day he seems more supremely happy in his love for me. All asperity and harshness has left him—he is always eager, but has lost the note of exasperation which used to characterise him. There is no slackening in his effort: he is perpetually working. He has as much if not more faith; though possibly faith in science has increased, and faith in any particular economic doctrine has decreased. He is less of a doctrinaire than of old, more of an investigator. He is not a leader of men, but he is an initiator of policies: his influence is not concentrated in his own personality, it ramifies through many organisations and persons, the outcome of multitudinous anonymous activities. And I think the setting I have given him, of simple fare and distinguished friends, suits him—both in reputation and taste. It satisfies his sense of consistency to adhere to a democratic standard of expenditure; and yet he reaps many of the advantages, in the scope and variety of social intercourse, of belonging to the inner circle of the political and scientific world.

April 2nd.—Hewins came as usual to lunch to-day: he was in thoroughly bad humour. No money to speak of has come in as the result of the Mansion House meeting, and he declares that the Mansion House meeting was a big failure. The plain truth is that, in the first place, he expected far too much from the meeting; in the second place, he managed with less skill than usual. He seems to have got on Rosebery's nerves, he failed to impress the Lord Mayor, and he delayed in sending out the appeal until five or six days after the meeting (we having understood that it went out on the very night of the meeting). Now he puts down the ill-success to the connection of the School with Lord Rosebery and the Fabian Society! We tried to calm and cheer him: suggested that Lord Rothschild's £5000 was more than we had originally thought of raising, and that at least the meeting had advertised the School. But he was not to be comforted. Hewins has three weak points: he suffers from attacks of quite unreasonable impatience and depression; he is a slack organiser of his staff; and he seldom takes his chiefs into his confidence as to what he really intends to do. This destroys any complete reliance on him. But he has a magnificent energy and persistence, loyalty to his own ideas (which are in the main the same as our own), and personal disinterestedness.

The three months between the first days of April and the beginning of July were spent, so far as I was concerned, with the Bertrand Russells at their house near Friday's Hill, working on our local government book: the Other One spending the mid-week in London on L.C.C. and other business. Here is a vision of the Bertrand Russells as they seemed to us in the spring of 1901.

July 1st. Friday's Hill.—The Russells are the most attractive married couple I know. Young and virtuous, they combine in the pair, personal charm, unique intelligence, the woman having the one, the man the other, in the superlative degree. Romantically attached to each other, they have diverse interests; Alys concerns herself with social reform, Bertrand with the higher mathematics. The scheme of their joint life is deliberately conceived to attain ends they both believe in, and it is persistently yet modestly carried out. The routine of their daily existence is as carefully planned and executed as our own. They breakfast together in their study at nine o'clock (we breakfast at 8!), then Bertrand works at mathematics until 12.30, then three-quarters-of-an-hour reading together, a quarter-of-an-hour stroll in the garden together. Lunch with us, 1.30; chat in our sitting-room or out of doors, over cigarettes and coffee. Then Bertrand plays croquet with Logan [Pearsall] Smith (Alys's brother who lives here) until tea at 4.30. After that mathematics until 6 o'clock, reading with Alys until 7.30, dine at 8 o'clock, chat and smoke with us until 9.30, another hour's reading aloud with Alys until 10.30. They sleep and dress in the same room, and they have no children. . . .

As individuals they are remarkable. Alys comes of an American Quaker family: she is charming to look at—tall, graceful, with regular features, clear skin, bright blue eyes, and soft curly nut-brown hair—always smiling, often laughing, warm-hearted and sympathetically intelligent. She has not the gift of intimacy except with her husband; her manner is the same to everyone—at least so far as I have seen. She has no arts of flirtation, if anything she prefers women to men—and I think really likes the womanly woman better than the professional. She has no moods, or they are controlled, she seems always happy and grateful for happiness and yet perpetually thinking how to make others happier. Since we have been here she has spent days away nursing a friend at Cambridge, with no consciousness of virtue, responding to a call of friendship as readily as most women respond to a call of pleasure. If she has a defect, it is a certain colourlessness of intellect and a certain lack of " temperament ". But in a woman are these defects?

So much for our hosts. Besides these two, Logan Smith, a refined and gentle-natured bachelor, with a pretty talent for turning out sentences and a taste for collecting bric-a-brac, is a daily visitor and chats with us over afternoon tea. He, like his sister, is tall, delicate-featured and always smiling. But, behind this smile there is a deep-seated melancholy, due to a long record of self-conscious failure to become an artist of words. The world has proved too complex for him to grasp—he is perpetually breaking off before he has mastered even the smallest portion of it. He was meant, like Alys, to be a complementary being: as a man he cannot find a career, or even a wife, to suit him.

Bertrand is a slight, dark-haired man, with prominent forehead, bright eyes, strong features except for a retreating chin; nervous hands and alert quick movements. In manner and dress and outward bearing, he is most carefully trimmed, conventionally correct and punctiliously polite: in speech, he has an almost affectedly clear enunciation of words and preciseness of expression. In morals, he is a puritan; in personal habits almost an ascetic, except that he lives for efficiency and, therefore, expects to be kept in the best physical condition. But, intellectually, he is audacious—an iconoclast, detesting religious or social convention, suspecting sentiment, believing only in the " order of thought " and the " order of things ", in logic and in science. He indulges in the wildest paradox and in the broadest jokes, the latter always too abstrusely intellectual in their form to be vulgarly coarse. He is a delightful talker, especially in general conversation, when the intervention of other minds prevents him from tearing his subject to pieces with fine chopping logic. He is always fruitful, especially in clearing up definitions and distinctions, or in following out logical conclusions. He is fastidious with regard to friends and acquaintances: he dislikes bores and hates any kind of self-seeking selfishness or coarse-grainedness. He looks at the world from a pinnacle of detachment—dissects persons and demolishes causes. And yet he recognises that, as a citizen, you must be a member of a party; therefore, he has joined the Fabian Society! He more or less accepts Sidney as his " representative " man. But the kernel of his life is research into the processes of reasoning. Of this new and highly abstract form of logic, more abstract than mathematics, I have no vision. All that one can say is that the effect on his own mind of these processes of pure reasoning is to make him singularly helpful in clearing up more concrete issues, even when he starts with no specialised knowledge of facts. To sum up, he is an expert in the art of reasoning, quite independently of the subject-matter.

A vigorous intelligence, at once subtle and honest, with the best kind of pride—the determination not to swerve from his own standards of right and wrong, truth or falsehood, are perhaps his finest characteristics. What he lacks is sympathy and tolerance for other people's emotions;

and, if you regard it as a virtue, Christian humility. The outlines of both his intellect and his feelings are sharp, hard and permanent. He is a good hater.

I observe in Bertrand a curious parallel between his intellectual and moral nature. He is intolerant of blemishes and faults in himself and others, he dreams of perfection in man: he almost loathes lapses from men's own standards. So in his thought he is almost violently impatient of bad reasoning: a right conclusion come to by bad arguments is offensive to him: it is the *perfection of the reasoning* that he seeks after, not truth of the conclusions. Now it seems to me that there is the same sort of connection between an intellectual concentration on applied science, and a tolerant, if not lax, judgement of men. Just as I am always striving to adjust my " order of thought " to the " order of things "—exactly as I am always looking to results as the test of right reasoning (power of prevision, for instance, as the result of shockingly bad reasoning?), so I am perpetually excusing myself and others for any lapses in morality. I analyse and describe my own and others' faults. But these faults seldom offend me in themselves, but only because they result in what is unpleasant and ugly. I have no "sense of sin", and no desire to see it punished. Bertrand, on the other hand, is almost cruel in his desire to see cruelty revenged.

July 9th.—Haldane spent yesterday at Friday's Hill, and brought us news of the Liberal split and enlisted Sidney on the Asquith side. We had been watching with half indifference, half annoyance, the " retreat " of the Liberal Party within the old lines of Gladstonianism, under the leadership of Campbell-Bannerman nominally, but of the pro-Boers actually. The whole of the spring, the vacuum left by lack of any clear thinking among those who can think has been filled with pro-Boer sentiment of an extravagant kind, and the old sort of secularist individualist Radicalism. Morley and Harcourt, supported by the *Daily News*, were showing signs of returning to political life; Campbell-Bannerman, a weak vain man who all along has been in his heart pro-Boer, had been entertaining Sauer and Merriman. The Liberal Federation meeting at Bradford had been strongly pro-Boer in sentiment, though passing lukewarm resolutions of the official type. Meanwhile, the Imperialist section—Haldane, Asquith, Grey—had been working at the Bar, enjoying themselves in London " society " and letting things slide. Suddenly, they woke up to find the Liberal Party in the House of Commons under the leadership of Lloyd George, declaring itself definitely against the war, accusing Milner and the army of gross inhumanity and asserting the right of the Boers to some kind of independence. Campbell-Bannerman had been captured.

Under the influence of his old friend Lord Milner (now in London),

Asquith came down heavily, declared that the war was inevitable, that there had been no wilful cruelty, and that independence, in any sense the Boers would understand it, was impossible. He followed up his speech by voting against Campbell-Bannerman and the Irish and Welsh contingent, and led out of the House some thirty Liberal M.P.'s (the bulk of the English Liberals seem to have abstained either by accident or with intent). Then to emphasise this protest the more enthusiastic Liberal M.P.'s insisted on giving a dinner to Asquith—to fête him for his defiance of C. B. Hence the uproar: the uncomfortable spectacle of Asquith, Grey, Haldane, supported by the Tory press, in flat rebellion against C. B., the chosen leader of the Liberal Party, supported by Morley, Harcourt and the whole force of pro-Boers. " We are fighting for our lives ", said Haldane to me: " both Asquith and I would attach much importance to Sidney being present at the dinner: we do not like to press it, because the whole movement may be a failure." A dilemma: Sidney is pro-Boer in sentiment: he agrees with Asquith and Haldane, by reason; but he has not thought out the question, has paid little or no attention to it. It suits him infinitely better to keep out of the whole affair: he has already made his position among the Radicals " suspect " owing to his attitude with regard to school boards. Moreover, in many details, such as the retention of Lord Milner as administrator, he is not convinced that he would be prepared to risk complete colonial self-government in the Orange Free State and the Transvaal. On the other hand, Haldane has always trusted him in matters he cared about, has been the most loyal friend in all educational projects. " I attach little importance to the dinner," Sidney said to me when I told him of Haldane's desires, " and no importance to my being there. If Haldane wants me to go, I certainly will. I would rather, of course, have kept out of the whole affair, but one must be ready occasionally to step forward for one's friends if one has no conviction to the contrary. As between the two sections of Liberals, my sympathies are with them. I think very little will come of either party, but Haldane and Asquith are at least not hostile to our views: the others are. I will go. But you need not imagine it of any importance, one way or the other."

And now that he has agreed to go I am worrying about it. First and foremost, I know he loathes the war; he thinks the whole episode of the Rand and the Chamberlain negotiations a disgrace to this country (though he attributes the inevitability of the war to the granting of the Charter to the S.A. Co., and the discovery of gold on the Rand); he distrusts Milner; above all he feels uncertain as to his own opinions, having carefully avoided reading anything on the subject. " It is not my show ", he has often said when I have suggested he should read blue-books. From a more selfish point of view, it suits him better not to be on either side so as to get what he can from both for his projects. Then I don't believe in the genuineness of the Liberal M.P.s' own questions: they live in the wrong atmosphere and are incurably lazy. They are desperately in awe of the City, consider the opinion of the *Times*, and have their eye on the goodwill of manufacturers—even on that of the brewers. Intellectually, they are more with us than the more Radical section: but they have no pluck and no faith. All these considerations rushed through my mind as I half deprecated Sidney accepting; but my instinctive wish was that he should accept in order to please Haldane, who has been so good to us. But no doubt, as Sidney says, his going or not going is of no importance.

July 28*th.*—On the night Rosebery issued his famous letter to the City Liberal Club and to the press, Sidney was pacing the terrace of the House of Commons with Haldane and Grey, explaining to them the attitude they ought to adopt on home affairs, having been called in to consult with them. At the time when the journalists in the lobby were humming with excitement about the letter, Rosebery's devoted lieutenants were absolutely unaware of its existence! "We are not in communication with Rosebery", Haldane had said to Sidney. Again on the Friday afternoon just before the Asquith dinner, I met Haldane in the House (whither I had gone to escort a young American lady) looking terrifically grave—almost agitated. "He has made a great speech to the City Liberal Club: has repudiated the Liberal Party, has announced his intention of ' ploughing his own furrow '—all within a few hours of Asquith's speech to-night—without a word of consultation. He is a Puck in politics ", added Haldane with almost a note of exasperation.

The dinner, however, went off all right. It was a scratch assembly and Sidney was among the most distinguished of the guests. Margaret Hobhouse and I viewed it from the gallery. Asquith's speech was manly and sensible, finely phrased and spoken with considerable fervour. But, read in cold blood the next morning, it suffered in comparison with Rosebery's artistically sensational utterance. We did not take the tragic view of Rosebery's intervention taken by the little set of his immediate followers. If Lord Rosebery really means business, really intends to come forward with a strong policy, then he has done his lieutenants a good service by stepping boldly out of the ranks of an obsolete Liberalism. Asquith, Grey and Haldane can only proclaim their own freedom within the Liberal Party, they cannot denounce the other sections of it, for the simple reason that it is not business for them to step away from the front bench. To the front bench they must stick so long as they can stick also to their own principles. But Rosebery is bound by no ties, and can do the necessary work of the iconoclast of the Gladstonian ideals. Rosebery's business is to destroy Gladstonianism. Whether or not he is to become a real leader depends on whether he has anything to put in the place of a defunct Liberalism. Mere imperialism will not do: that the other side have. Now supposing he fails, as I think he will fail, to be constructive, then he leaves the field open to Asquith, Grey and Haldane with a good deal of the rubbish cleared away.

Whether this sort of reasoning glimmered into Haldane's brain, I know not. But when he came in on Monday evening he was in high spirits. Asquith and he had made it up with Rosebery (they are forgiving mortals!). It was agreed, he said, that Rosebery and Asquith were to plough parallel furrows. Meanwhile, G. B. S. writes urging us to plunge in with Rosebery as the best chance of moulding home policy. We have succumbed to his flattery; and now Sidney, with occasional suggestions from me, is engaged on an article entitled " Lord Rosebery's Escape from Houndsditch ".

What was the thesis displayed in " Lord Rosebery's Escape from Houndsditch ", published in the September number of the *Nineteenth Century*, 1901? The answer is: debunking Gladstonian Liberalism in order to clear the way for Fabian collectivism. Instead of ploughing his furrow in lonely grandeur, Lord Rosebery is respectfully incited to offer himself as titular leader to the progressive group of Liberals led by Asquith, Haldane, Grey and Acland, " a group of men of diverse temperaments and varied talents, imbued with a common faith and a common purpose, and eager to work out, and severally to expound, how each department of national life can be raised to its highest possible efficiency. If he does nothing but plough his own furrow," the author adds, " Lord Rosebery will, I fear, have to plough it alone " (p. 386).

Here are a few extracts, out of the twenty-paged article explaining its title and indicating the course to be taken by a reinvigorated and up-to-date Opposition to the Conservative Government:

Mr. Gladstone, as we now learn upon the unexpected testimony of Lord Tweedmouth, regarded the last twenty years of his life as having been spent in " patching up old clothes ". His achievements as a sartorial artist in politics approached, it must be admitted, the miraculous. But the patched-up suits of 1880, 1885 and 1892, though they served their immediate purpose, have, under the expanding conditions of contemporary politics, proved wretched wearing material. Not even Mr. Gladstone could have patched them up again. With amused dismay the new generation of progressives have lately witnessed Sir Henry Campbell-Bannerman piecing together the Gladstonian rags and remnants, with Sir William Harcourt holding the scissors, and Mr. John Morley unctuously waxing the thread. Mr. Asquith and Sir Edward Grey are sufficiently up-to-date resolutely to refuse even to try on the re-patched garment, but they are not in a position to decline to associate with those who still believe the Gladstonian cut to be fashionable. Lord Rosebery is the only person who has turned his back on Houndsditch and called for a complete new outfit. This is the first step towards the regeneration of the Opposition. I say the Opposition advisedly, for the political opportunity of the moment is not for a regeneration of Gladstonianism, or of " the Liberal Party ", or of anything else that had its day in the last century, but solely for a live Opposition. That Opposition, when it comes, may call itself the Liberal Party or any other name that may be convenient. But it is certain that it will not be the old Gladstonian party—quite the contrary, in fact—and that it will not become a political force until, meeting the new needs and expressing the new aspirations of the twentieth century —dealing, as Lord Rosebery rightly says, " in a new spirit with the new problems of the age "—it thereby makes itself into a practicable alternative to the Conservative Government.

What then is the matter with the Liberals? For fifty years, in the middle of the last century, we may recognise their party as " a great instrument of progress ", wrenching away the shackles—political, fiscal, legal, theological and social—that hindered individual advancement. The shackles are by no means wholly got rid of, but the political force of this old Liberalism is spent. During the last twenty years its aspirations and its watchwords, its ideas of daily life and its conceptions of the universe, have become increasingly distasteful to the ordinary citizen as he renews his youth from generation to generation. Its worship of individual liberty evokes no enthusiasm. Its reliance on " freedom of contract " and " supply and demand ", with its corresponding " voluntaryism " in religion and philanthropy, now seems to work out disastrously for the masses, who are too poor to have what the economists call an " effective demand " for even the minimum conditions of physical and mental health necessary to national wellbeing [pp. 366-7]. . . . The England of this generation is changing because Englishmen have had revealed to them another new world of relationships, of which they were before unconscious. This time it is not a new continent that the ordinary man has discovered, but a new category. We have become aware, almost in a flash, that we are not merely individuals, but members of a community, nay, citizens of the world. This new self-consciousness is no mere intellectual fancy, but a hard fact that comes home to us in our daily life. The labourer in the slum tenement, competing for employment at the factory gate, has become conscious that his comfort and his progress depend, not wholly or mainly on himself, or on any other individual, but upon the proper organisation of his trade union and the activity of the factory inspector. . . . The freedom for his trade union to bargain collectively, freedom for his co-operative society to buy and sell and manufacture, freedom for his municipality to supply all the common needs of the town, freedom, above all, from the narrow insularity which keeps his nation backing, " on principle ", out of its proper place in the comity of the world. In short, the opening of the twentieth century finds us all, to the dismay of the old-fashioned individualist, " thinking in communities ". . . .

Now the trouble with Gladstonian Liberalism is that, by instinct, by tradition, and by the positive precepts of its past exponents, it " thinks in individuals ". It visualises the world as a world of independent Roundheads, with separate ends, and abstract rights to pursue those ends [p. 369]. . . . Their conception of freedom means only breaking somebody's bonds asunder. When the " higher freedom " of corporate life is in question, they become angrily reactionary, and denounce and obstruct every new development of common action. If we seek for the greatest enemy of municipal enterprise, we find him in Sir Henry Fowler. If we ask who is the most successful opponent of any extension of *the common rule* of factory legislation to wider fields of usefulness, the answer is Mr. John Morley. And, when a leader is needed by those whose unalterable instinct it is to resist to the uttermost every painful effort towards the higher organisation of that greatest of co-operative societies, the state itself, who than Sir William Harcourt, at his most eloquent, can be more surely depended upon? Not that I have any right to reproach these eminent ones for standing by their principles. The principles were fresh once—in the last quarter of the eighteenth century. Their exponents' minds were fresh, too, about the middle of the nineteenth. But Adam Smith is dead, and Queen Anne, and even Sir Robert Peel; while as to Gladstone, he is by far the deadest of them all [pp. 370-71]. . . . And I confess that I feel the hopelessness, even the comic absurdity, of seeming to invite his more elderly lieutenants, at their ages, to change their spots—to turn over a new leaf and devote themselves to obtaining the greatest possible development of municipal activity, the most comprehensive extension of the Factory Acts, or the fullest utilisation of the government departments in the service of the public. I know too well that they quite honestly consider such aims to be mischievous. They are aiming at something else, namely, at the abstract right of the individual to lead exactly the kind of life that he likes (and can pay for), unpenalised by any taxation for purposes of which he individually disapproves. They are, in fact, still " thinking in individuals " [p. 370].

No leader will attract the support of the mass of unpolitical citizens —who in this juncture, at any rate, alone can give a decisive vote— without expanding his thesis of national efficiency into a comprehensive and definite programme. Nay, he must do more. He must understand his programme, believe in his programme, be inspired by his programme. He will, in fact, lead the English people—eager just now for national efficiency, they care not how—only by becoming a personified programme of national efficiency in every department of life.

Here Mr. Asquith is on the right tack: " What is the use of an Empire " (he asks) " if it does not breed and maintain in the truest and fullest sense of the word an imperial race? What is the use of talking about Empire if here, in its very centre, there is always to be found a mass of people, stunted in education, a prey to intemperance, huddled and congested beyond the possibility of realising in any true sense either social or domestic life? " [p. 375].

So far Lord Rosebery and Mr. Asquith, Mr. Haldane and Sir Edward Grey are right in their diagnosis. The nation sees that these men, in their different opportunities, have had the courage to cast off the old clothes. But, at present, we are all in the dark as to what is to be the new outfit. . . . What steps would their alternative government take to ensure the rearing of an imperial race? What action have they in mind for healing the open sore of the sweated trades: what do they intend to do with the poor law: what plan have they thought out for stimulating and directing the utmost possible municipal enterprise in sanitation and housing: what is their scheme for a comprehensive national system of education from the infant school to the university: what are their practical conclusions as to increasing the grants-in-aid, and assessing site values: how do they intend to transform the present silly procedure of the House of Commons: do they propose to simply neglect the military situation? It is on questions of this sort that they must, during the next few years, mark themselves out from their opponents, and convince us that they have a faith and a programme rooted no less in knowledge than in conviction. To think out such a programme is, of course, irksome, and, as every political Polonius will advise, to commit yourself to it is inconvenient—if you do not believe in it. But, to create a live opposition—still more, to construct an alternative government—this new thought and this new propaganda must be undertaken. If even one-half of the study and conviction, money and capacity, were put into such a campaign for the next five years that Cobden and Bright put into the Anti-Corn Law League, the country could be won for a policy of national efficiency. Without the pledge of virility which a campaign of this sort would afford, the nation will not be persuaded [pp. 385-6].

October 1st.—Sidney's article in the *Nineteenth Century* has been a brilliant success. No doubt there are some who found the self-assertiveness and contempt of others somewhat intolerable; but everyone has read it and found it new and full of substance (G. B. S. corrected the proof and inserted some of the brilliance). The Asquith, Haldane, Grey lot are delighted with it: Rosebery evidently pleased. The newspapers have taken it seriously, and it has improved his standing, I think, and made people feel that he is to be reckoned with. Now I am urging him to publish the positive side in a Fabian tract, and I intend to give the substance of it in a lecture at Oxford.

Meanwhile, we have no illusions about the Liberal Imperialists. We think that neither Rosebery nor Asquith mean to declare themselves in favour of our measure of collectivism. But they hold no views that are inconsistent with it—have nothing to offer but a refusal to take up the distinctive side of the old Liberalism. The time will come when, if they are to be a political force, they will have to " fill up " the political worker with some positive convictions. Then, we think, for the needful minimum of nourishment they will fall back on us and not on the other section.

But national affairs are not invigorating at present: the wretched war drags on, the newspapers nag and scold, and the Government seems helpless and the Opposition are more and more divided. The pro-Boers are very naturally rubbing their hands and saying " I told you so ". Personally, if there is no danger of intervention, I do not think the S.A. situation so intolerable as other persons do, and the longer and more determined the resistance, the more complete and thorough-going will be the collapse of the Boer nationality. And, with a race with so much patriotism, stubbornness and superstition, one wonders whether any more easy settling down would be permanent.

October 13th.—Sidney and Hewins in first-rate spirits about the School; building nearly complete and paid for, equipment provided from the hung-up grant of the T.E.B., a small but certain income from the same source and plenty of students. Hewins, who now sees before him a fine position and £600 p.a. secured, is somewhat elated and would, I think, tend to have a swelled head if it were not for the amount of skill and self-subordination required to engineer the business over the shoals of the university organisation. Again, one realises how, in a large and complicated society like the London educational world, the whole power of moulding events falls into the hands of the little *clique* who happen to be in the centre of things. Ten years ago Sidney could no more have influenced the teaching of economics and political science in London than he could have directed the policy of the Cabinet. But now no one can resist him: he wields the L.C.C. power of making grants, he is head of the one live institution; he is, on his own subjects, supreme on the University Senate (because he is thought to have the L.C.C. behind him), and he knows every rope and has quick and immediate access to every person of influence. Somehow I doubt whether such a state of things is quite wholesome: of course, one believes that in this case the hidden hand is beneficent and efficient! But the converse—the feeling of absolute helplessness against the doings of less efficient cliques!—is not so pleasant. One wonders whether it would be possible to conduct a country's government with efficiency and yet with free access and no favour to all concerned.

November 1st.—Asquith and Haldane dined here alone on Monday —the latter proposing to bring the former for a quiet chat. The talk did not come to much. They are, I think, somewhat depressed. Rosebery had " carted them ", so Haldane said, and was going to take his own line quite aloof from anything they might think or write. Asquith was preparing set speeches on social questions. But Haldane was still keen on winning the centre, a term which he always uses as synonymous with the non-political voter, in whose ultimate power we believe. In reality, these two sections—the centre and the non-political voter— are entirely different and to my mind very unequal in importance. What Haldane sees is the moderate politician: the capitalist or professional man who desires little social change and the Empire maintained. But the class we wish them to appeal to is the great lower middle-class and working-class, who want change, but don't know in what direction. Any party that knew its own mind as well as the facts, and had will to apply the one to the other, would succeed, in the long run, in getting hold of these classes for its policy of reform.

Rosebery is really on the same line as Haldane, though playing a different tune. Altogether the position seems somewhat hopeless.

Asquith impressed me with his manliness and unselfconsciousness, also with his shrewd open-mindedness; but he is a coarse-grained instrument and will never strike the imagination of any large section of men.

The last entry of the diary is a preface to a new friendship which opened out in the following year:

December 1901.—Wells' *Anticipations.* The most remarkable book of the year: a powerful imagination furnished with the data and methods of physical science, working on social problems. The weak part of Wells' outfit is his lack of any detailed knowledge of social organisations—and this, I think, vitiates his capacity for foreseeing the future machinery of government and the relation of classes. But his work is full of luminous hypotheses and worth careful study by those who are trying to look forward. Clever phrases abound, and by the way proposals on all sorts of questions—from the future direction of religious thought, to the exact curve of the skirting round the wall of middle-class abodes.

1902

January 30*th.*—We spent Christmas with Alfred [Cripps] and the Courtneys. Our host was in splendid form: well in health and full of public affairs. He had been in close communication with Balfour and Chamberlain trying to arrange some sort of compromise between them with regard to the Education Bill. Joseph Chamberlain was against state aid, fearing the recrudescence of the " church-rate " crusade. Balfour felt the force of the Church's cry " now or never ". He and Sidney discussed the question: as usual the " little jewel of an advocate " had not thought out the position and, though he and Sidney agreed on main points, Cripps was inclined to leave all knotty points to be settled by the House: a counsel of despair when the knots are so complicated. Dear old Leonard kept out of all this confidential talk: he and Kate spending their time with the young people, while Alfred, Sidney and I sat over the library fire. I fancy that Alfred feels his feet again in politics, and sees office near at hand should the opportunity for a new man arise. We laughingly decided that, if the three brothers-in-law were in leading positions in the House, it would end in Sidney and Alfred arranging compromises between the two front benches, with Leonard always in opposition![1] The Courtneys were as self-righteously pro-Boer as ever, but more subdued. " We are passing through some smoke (effect of Lord R.'s speech)," said Leonard, " but it will clear off."

February 28*th.*—We are at present very thick with the " Limps ". Asquith, Haldane, Grey, Munro Ferguson and the [Jack] Tennants, form a little family group into which they have temporarily attracted Sidney by asking him to their little dinners and informal meetings.

[1] It is amusing to recall that Alfred and Sidney became fellow-members of the two Labour Cabinets of 1924 and 1929–31 (Oct. 1937).

Close acquaintance with them does not make one more hopeful. Asquith is wooden, he lacks every kind of enthusiasm, and his hard-headed cold capacity seems to be given, not to politics, but to his legal cases. His brother-in-law, Jack Tennant, and Haldane both assure us that he could retire to-morrow from the Bar if he chose and that he only stays at it " for an occupation ". Strange lack of imagination not to see that there is an over-abundance of hard persistent work ready to his hand in politics, alike in thinking out reforms and in preaching them, and organising a party to push them. That lack of imagination and sensitiveness to needs lies at the root of Asquith's failure as a leader of men. For the rest, he has neither charm nor personal magnetism: he has to gain his position by sheer hard work, and that work he is not inclined to do in politics. Grey is a slight person; he has charm of appearance, of manner and even of character; but he is I fear essentially a " stick " to be used by someone else! " Politics have completely changed," he said plaintively to me when he was last dining here, " formerly you had your cause made for you, all the politician had to do was to preach it; now you have to *make your cause.*" Beyond foreign and colonial policy (whatever that may mean), Grey has no original ideas and finds it hard even to appreciate the ideas of others. And he has no notion of work as the main occupation of life; politics is merely with him an episode in his daily life, like his enjoyment of nature, books, society, sport (mostly nature and sport be it said). Neither Asquith nor Grey are, as politicians, well served by their respective wives. Margot is, I believe, a kindly soul; but, though she has in-telligence and wit, she has neither intellect nor wisdom. She is incurably reactionary in her prejudices: her two delights are hunting and other out-door exercises, and fashionable society. She is said to be ambitious for her husband; but, if so, her method of carrying out her ambition lacks intelligence as well as intellect. Lady Grey is a fastidious aristocrat, intensely critical of anyone to whom work is the principal part of life. She is clever enough to see that work alone counts, and yet knows, in her heart of hearts, that neither she nor her husband are capable of it. As for Haldane, to whom we are both really attached, he is a large and generous-hearted man, affectionate to his friends and genuinely enthusiastic about the advancement of knowledge. But his ideal has no connection with the ugly rough and tumble work-a-day world of the average sensual man, who is compelled to earn his livelihood by routine work and bring up a family of children on narrow means. Unmarried, living a luxurious physical but a strenuous mental life, Haldane's vital energies are divided between highly-skilled legal work and the processes of digestion—for he is a Herculean eater. He finds his relaxation in bad metaphysics and in political intrigue—that is, in trying to manipulate influential persons into becoming followers of Rosebery and members of the *clique*. Be it said to his credit, that he has to some extent manipulated us into this position. Munro-Ferguson is merely a pleasant young aristocrat. Perhaps, the most keen of the lot are the Jack Tennants. Mrs. Jack (formerly an inspectress of factories) is a fine-natured woman, with real knowledge and enthusiasm. She has inspired her husband with the same helpful attitude towards social questions. But Jack is a *little* man physically and mentally, and the notion of his being a force approaches the ridiculous. There remains the mysterious Rosebery. At present he is an enigma. Whether on account of his social position or of his brilliancy, or because of his streaks of wit and original thought, he can make all the world listen. He has imagination and sensitiveness, and he is a born actor. He is first-rate at appearances. Moreover, he seems to be developing persistency and courage. But as yet he shows no signs of capacity for co-operation, or even for leadership of a group of subordinates. All he has yet done is to *strike attitudes* that have brought down the House at the time, and left a feeling of blankness a few days later. To be a great leader, a man must either understand problems himself or be able to handle men who do understand them. Rosebery sees many persons, but only in order to extract from them the essence of public opinion so as to appear before the world in a popular attitude. He never asks how actually to work the machinery of government so as to get the best results. Has he any clear and definite view of the character of the results he wants to get? I fear not.

And why are we in this galley? Partly because we have drifted into it. These men have helped us with our undertakings, they have been appreciative of our ideas, and socially pleasant to us. They have no prejudice against our views of social reform: whilst their general attitude towards the Empire as a powerful and self-conscious force is one with which we are in agreement. Moreover, the leaders of the other school of Liberalism are extremely distasteful to us: we disagree with them on almost every point of home and foreign policy. Before we can get the new ideas and new frame of mind accepted, we must beat out the old. That is why we are not against the policy of the " clean slate ". We want to be rid of all the old ideals and enthusiasms —we want to stamp out the notion that the world can be bettered by abolition of some of the existing institutions; we want, on the contrary, to set people to work to build up new tissue which may in time take the place of the old. In Ireland, for instance, we don't want to abolish the union with England, but so to reconstruct the internal government that it will make the bond of union of secondary importance. We do not want to abolish or remodel the House of Lords, but to build up precedents for their non-intervention with national expenditure—all collectivism coming under this head. We do not want to disestablish the Church, but to endow science and secular ethics and any other form of intellectual activity that may seem desirable. We don't want to abolish or restrain the development of private enterprise, but, by creating dykes and bulwarks, to control its mischievous effect on the character of the race. We do not want to unfetter the individual from the obligation of citizenship, we want on the contrary to stimulate and constrain him, by the unfelt pressure of a better social environment, to become a healthier, nobler and more efficient being.

To these ideals the old Liberalisms of Leonard Courtney, Morley, Campbell-Bannerman, and the bulk of Celtic members of Parliament, are not only unsympathetic, but really hostile. Asquith, Haldane, Grey and, I think, Rosebery, are sympathetic though timorous. They will not themselves push these ideals (Rosebery is as likely as any to do it), but they will follow any one who does, *if there seems to be the least response from public opinion.* And, if Sidney is inside the *clique*, he will have a better chance of permeating its activities than by standing aloof as a superior person and scolding at them. So I am inclined to advise him to throw in his lot with them in the days of their adversity and trial, when an addition to their ranks from the democratic side is of great value to them. Half the art of effective living consists of giving yourself to those who need you most *and at the time of their most pressing want.* And, seeing that politics is a mere bye-product of our life, our own special work to-day being administration or investigation, there seem few reasons against this course of action. If we came to throw our main stream of energy into political life, we should have to choose our comrades more carefully.

The Technical Education Board is a source of worry and anxiety to Sidney. The hostility of the Conservative Government to the School Board, and the threat to abolish it, have reacted on the Radical L.C.C. and made it inclined to refuse to compete with the Radical School Board for the administration of education. J. R. MacDonald, Sidney's old enemy in the Fabian Society, slipped into the Council at an uncontested bye-election and apparently spends his time in working up the feeling against the Technical Education Board and Sidney's administration of it. He is anxious to get on to it, and Sidney is doing his best to get him in, believing that an enemy is always safer inside than outside a democratic body. But it means friction and a good deal of bickering. MacDonald does not hesitate to accuse Sidney of taking advantage of his position to favour the School of Economics [1]—an accusation which

[1] *July* 1921.—More than a year after this entry Sidney was told by a fellow-member of the Technical Education Board that J. Ramsay MacDonald had been

is perfectly true, though we think absolutely harmless. In administration, you must advance the cause which you think right and are, therefore, interested in. The unpleasant sound of the accusation is conveyed by the double meaning of the word " interested " which in most men's mouths means *pecuniarily* interested. We believe in a school of administrative, political and economic science as a way of increasing national efficiency; but we have kept the London School honestly non-partisan in its theories. Otherwise " interested " we are not, unless the expenditure of our own energy and money on an institution be termed " interested ". And Sidney's energies have by no means been exclusively devoted to the subjects he is intellectually interested in. He has, I think, been quite exceptionally catholic in his organisation of secondary, technical and university education in London, alike in the class of students to be provided for and the range of subjects taught. Heaven knows there were arrears to be made up in politics, economics and the science of administration.

The Progressives are not very happy among themselves. The more eminent of them have served as chairman, or refused to do so; and there comes the question whether the hard-working little " cads " of the party shall succeed to the chair, or whether some well-bred nonentity shall be promoted. Sidney, though willing to back up the majority of the party in any course they think fit (he does not attach much importance to the whole business), is inclined to advise a frank recognition of the plebeian character of the L.C.C., and to take an excellent and devoted member who drops his *h*'s rather than an insignificant lord. The matter has been compromised by the choice of a plebeian as chairman and a lord as vice-chairman. But it has left heart-burnings and ill-feeling within the party committee: Sidney acting as peace-maker. By his colleagues he is considered a non-competitor: he has made education his province and rules over it undisturbed; he has no desire to be chairman or vice-chairman, or leader of the party in the Council itself.

We have seen something lately of H. G. Wells and his wife. Wells is an interesting though somewhat unattractive personality except for his agreeable disposition and intellectual vivacity. His mother was the housekeeper to a great establishment of 40 servants, his father the professional cricketer attached to the place. The early associations with the menial side of a great man's establishment has left Wells with a hatred of that class and of its attitude towards the lower

spreading a report that Sidney and I were making an income by lecturing for the School. As he was perfectly well aware that, far from taking money from the School, we had been spending our surplus on the School and the library, and that Sidney and I only lectured there in order to relieve the School from paying lecturers, this libel was inexcusable.

orders. His apprenticeship to a draper, his subsequent career as an assistant master at a private venture school, as a state student at South Kensington living on £1 a week, as an army crammer, as a journalist and, in these last years, as a most successful writer of fiction, has given him a great knowledge of the lower middle-class and their habits and thoughts, and an immense respect for science and its methods. But he is totally ignorant of the manual worker, on the one hand, and of the big administrator and aristocrat on the other. This ignorance is betrayed in certain crudities of criticism in his *Anticipations*: he ignores the necessity for maintaining the standard of life of the manual working population; he does not appreciate the need for a wide experience of men and affairs in administration. A world run by the physical science man straight from his laboratory is his ideal: he does not see that specialised faculty and knowledge are needed for administration exactly as they are needed for the manipulation of machinery or [natural] forces. But he is extraordinarily quick in his apprehensions, and took in all the points we gave him in our 48 hours' talk with him, first at his own house and then here. He is a good instrument for popularising ideas, and he gives as many ideas as he receives. His notion of modern society as " the grey ", not because it is made of uniform atoms of that shade, but because of the very variety of its colours, all mixed together and in formless mass; his forecast of the segregation of like to like, until the community will become extraordinarily variegated and diverse in its component parts, seems to us a brilliant and true conception. Again, democracy as a method of dealing with men in a wholesale way—every man treated in the bulk and not in detail, the probability that we shall become more *detailed* and less *wholesale* in our provision for men's needs—that again is a clever illumination. Altogether, it is refreshing to talk to a man who has shaken himself loose from so many of the current assumptions, and is looking at life as an explorer of a new world. He has no great faith in government by the " man in the street " and, I think, has hardly realised the function of the representative as a " foolometer " for the expert.

March 19*th*.—Met " Imperial Perks " at Mr. Haldane's—a repulsive being—hard, pushing, commonplace, with no enthusiasms except a desire to have his "knife into the Church "—a blank materialist although a pious Protestant, who recognises no principle beyond self-interest. I confess the thought that Perks was a pillar of the new Liberal League staggered me: how could we work with such a loathsome person! A combination of Gradgrind, Pecksniff and Jabez Balfour. And the choice of this man as their first-lieutenant throws an ugly light on Lord Rosebery. Anyway, we and Perks are incompatible in views, in tastes, and in all our fundamental assumptions as to ends and methods. This is no doubt an exaggerated statement; but regarded from a strictly matter-of-fact point of view, I doubt whether a leader who found Perks a delectable companion would really tolerate us and our ways when he came to know us and realise what state of things we were working to bring about. The situation is made worse by the fact that Perks is the only man in the group who is in deadly earnest and, therefore, *if the group succeeds*, is likely to come out top. To think of Perks as an English Cabinet Minister: Ugh! The very notion of it degrades political life.

Two months' sampling of the Liberal Imperialists has not heightened our estimate of them. Asquith is deplorably slack, Grey is a mere dilettante, Haldane plays at political intrigue and has no democratic principle, Perks is an unclean beast, and as for Rosebery, he remains an enigma. He, at any rate, has personal distinction, originality and charm; but he seeks only appearances, has no care for or knowledge of economic and social evils, lives and moves, and has his being, in the plutocratic atmosphere, shares to the full the fears and prejudices of his class. Moreover, he is a bad colleague, and suffers from lack of nerve and persistent purpose. As for the rank and file, they are a most hetero-geneous lot, bound together by their *dislikes*, and not by their positive convictions: they have no kind of faith in any of their leaders, and are in constant fear as to their political future and personal careers. And rising up against them is a force which will become apparent at the next election—Labour candidates officially run by the great trade unions, backed up by pro-Boer capitalists. That combination will have no constructive power. Here, again, the two elements are bound together, not by a common faith, but by a common hatred. But it will be able, in many places, to smash the Liberal Imperialists. Thus the Liberal Party seems cleaved into two equally unpromising sections— Rosebery appealing to the grey mass of convictionless voters on the broad and shallow ground of Empire and efficiency; C. B. relying on every description of separatist interest, on all the " antis "—anti-war, anti-United Kingdom, anti-Church, anti-capitalist, anti-Empire. Both combinations seem to me equally temporary and equally lacking in healthy and vigorous root principles.

Having done our little best to stimulate the " Limps " into some kind of conviction, and having most assuredly failed, we now return to our own work. Three months' peaceful and strenuous effort in the country seems a delightful prospect. And between me and this diary, I think the " Limps " will be glad to be rid of us! Our contempt for their " limpness " and our distrust for their reactionary views are too apparent.

April 25th. Sussex.—Poor Sidney is somewhat distracted with anxiety with regard to the future of the School, the development of opposition to the Technical Education Board and the L.C.C. His principal concern is the exact constitution of the educational authority for London to be proposed next year. It so happens that he can use the fear of the borough councils as the authority to frighten the opponents of the T.E.B. on the Council. It is an open secret that a strong section of the Cabinet is in favour of a joint-committee of the borough councils which would be a disaster of the first magnitude to the whole of higher education in London. To avert this disaster we are moving all the forces we have any control over—our friends in the Church, university educationalists, permanent officials and any one having influence over Ministers, against the proposal of an education authority elected by and from the borough councils.

It is, perhaps, fortunate that Sidney is known to approve the lines of the present Bill applying to the country outside London. Indeed, our Radical School Board friends scoff about " Webb's Bill "—which, of course, is an absurdity. They will scoff the more if next year we are hoist by our own petard! Meanwhile, he is writing an article for the *Nineteenth Century* for June on the London University in the hope of catching a millionaire! Beit is biting!

Friday's Hill, May 4th.—Settled again for our nine weeks' sojourn with the Russells. Hard at work on poor law reports of 1834. I had to break into this work to help Sidney through with his University of London article. . . . Sidney is somewhat distracted with his undertakings and feels himself at times unequal to them. " I am not a big man," he says plaintively to me, " I could not manage any larger undertakings." But, as I tell him, it is exactly this consciousness of imperfection, whilst others find him competent, that shows that he is more than equal to his task. We only feel completely complacent with our effort when we have ceased to grasp the *possibilities* of the situation.

Enjoyed my week's work on the University article, a relief from the grind of facts—a chance for scheming, an intellectual occupation I dearly love.

At this point I think it well to interpolate some explanation of our scheme for a reconstructed London University. The University of London, founded in 1837, was merely a corporation to confer university degrees. It had no professors; it gave no teaching; it conducted no research; it awarded its degrees to persons coming from all parts, on their passing examinations on papers set by examiners whom they had never seen. It is true that there were various colleges scattered over London's vast area; the oldest entitled University College, being (as the Anglicans declared) " godless ", at which my father, a Unitarian debarred from Oxford and Cambridge, got his academic education; and King's College, established avowedly in opposition to University College, in order that young men of Church families should not be tempted to resort to the " godless " college. To these had gradually been added a dozen hospital schools of medicine and surgery; and also colleges for teaching science, mostly in its practical applications, or for training science teachers. Many of the students of these London colleges sat for the London University examinations, and were awarded its degrees. But they had no better chance than students from other cities or other countries. All the graduates of the University of London were alike " external students ". Most of those responsible for the management of the University gloried in this " externality " of their graduates, and were proud of the fact that there was absolutely no contact between those who examined and the aspirants for degrees. And all London's millions lacked the encouragement, the fertilising influence of contact with educated minds, the intellectual direction and the development of research into the unknown, with all its inventions and discoveries.

Now this lack of university inspiration and direction to London's intellectual life had been complained of for many years by all sorts of people, and a whole generation of efforts had failed of achievement. There had been many plans for university reform, and more than one Royal Commission had reported on one scheme after another. At last the Government got through Parliament an Act re-establishing the University of London on the basis of a complicated compromise between the conflicting parties, combining the examining board awarding the external degrees with the various autonomous colleges giving the necessary instruction

Beatrice Webb (*ætat circa* 33)

Days of the Poor Law Campaign

to internal students.[1] This, however, came to little better than
formal binding together of college professors and university

[1] The passing of the Act was due to R. B. Haldane. " My great question ", he
writes in his autobiography, " was how to extend University organisation in
England. There were some excellent colleges, but outside Oxford and Cambridge
very little of University life.

" I approached Balfour about the University of London [1898]. It was then a
mere board for examining outside students who got from it external degrees by
means of examinations without teaching. Valuable as the work of extending degrees
to external students had been in the past, it was no longer sufficient. The system
lent itself to the purposes of the crammers, and the school teachers in particular used
it for obtaining what were virtually little more than trade-marks. The real purpose
of University training, the development of the mind in the atmosphere of the teaching
university, where teachers and taught could come into close relation, was lacking.

" So strongly was this felt that many of the professors in the London colleges
had set their hearts on the establishment of a second and professorially run university, with no external examinees at all. I knew that the opposition to so far-
reaching a measure would be too strong to overcome in the then indifferent state of
public opinion. I saw that, as a first step at all events, the only way was to pass an
act enlarging the existing University of London by giving it a powerful teaching
side. This might be relied on in the end to absorb the other side by reason of its
quality. Of this opinion also was my friend Sidney Webb, who as the successful
Chief of the Technical Education Board of the London County Council had great
opportunities of studying the practical problem. . . . Sidney Webb and I took
counsel together. He was a very practical as well as a very energetic man. We
laid siege to the citadel. We went round to person after person who was prominent
in the administration of the existing University. Some listened, but others would
not do so and even refused to see us. In the end we worked out what was in substance
the scheme of the London University Act of 1898. The scheme was far from being
an ideal one. It provided by way of compromise for a senate which was too large to
be a really efficient supreme governing body for the new composite University,
and it had other shortcomings of which we were well aware. But it did set up a
teaching university, although Convocation, with its control of the external side,
would remain unduly powerful. We saw that the scheme thus fashioned was the
utmost we could hope for the time to carry, in the existing state of public opinion
about higher education in London."

Some years later R. B. Haldane was again at work improving London University
education: " During this period the affairs of London University were approaching
a crisis, and in the end I undertook the Chairmanship of the Royal Commission,
which sat for four years and finally reported. I managed to carry this on through the
later period of my tenure of the War Office and during the earlier part of my Lord
Chancellorship until the Report was signed. That Commission was a very interesting
one. Among my colleagues were Lord Milner, Sir Robert Morant, Sir William
M'Cormick, my old friend the ex-judge Sir Robert Romer, and Mrs. Creighton.
. . . I ought to say that my investigations in Germany had at an early stage impressed me unfavourably with the separation which had been made there between
the universities and the great technical colleges, and when subsequently, after studying the organisation of Charlottenburg on the spot with the aid of my friend
Geheimrat Witt, the Professor of Chemistry there and head of the school, I set to
work in London, along with Mr. Sidney Webb and Sir Francis Mowatt, to found
the new Imperial College of Science and Technology, I decided to press for the
application of a different principle. The new college was to be fashioned so as to
be brought as quickly as possible into a reconstructed University of London. I
presided over the departmental committee which prepared the Charter, or rather
presided over it during the second and final year of the inquiry " (*Richard Burdon
Haldane—An Autobiography* (1929) (pp. 124-6 and 90-92).

examiners, under a composite Senate having the smallest possible financial endowment, or administrative control. The reorganised University started on what was little more than a formal existence, in which all the several parts wrangled over and largely counteracted each other's projects and proposals. Some fresh convulsion, amounting perhaps to a new birth, was required to give the organism a genuine life.

What exactly was our scheme for the reconstructed London University: what kind of university was possible in London? Here are a few extracts from the article by the Other One in the *Nineteenth Century*, June 1902:

> Any practical policy for a London University has, it is clear, to have regard to the limitations, the needs and the opportunities of London life. It may at the outset be admitted that, for any university of the Oxford or Cambridge type, the metropolis is perhaps more unfit than any other spot that could be chosen. By no possible expenditure could we create at South Kensington, in the Strand, or at Gower Street, the tradition, the atmosphere, the charm or the grace of collegiate life on the Isis or the Cam. Nor is it possible to secure, amid the heterogeneous crowds of London and all its distractions, either the class selection or the careful supervision required by the parents of boys fresh from Eton or Harrow, with two or three hundred a year to spend in pocket-money. . . . With the exception of country students coming to study medicine or engineering, the undergraduate class of London University will, we may infer, be confined to London residents, and, among these, to students from the 99 per cent of London homes which are maintained on incomes under £1500 a year. . . .
>
> What, now, should be the policy of the new London University? First and foremost we must accept, as the basic principle of its structure, an organisation by faculties, not by colleges or other institutions. Only on this principle can we develop a university structure adapted to the needs and opportunities of the metropolitan area. London, it is clear, can have but one university. For the small German town or provincial English centre, the university may suitably be of simple and, so to speak, unicellular type. Oxford and Cambridge, with their close aggregation of separate colleges of identical pattern, present us with what may be called a multicellular development of the same elementary type. By no such simple repetition of parts could we create a university for the huge area and dissimilar conditions of the metropolitan districts. Its unique combination of a widely dispersed undergraduate population

and centrally segregated materials for research, its union of the most democratic student life with the most perfectly selected intellectual aristocracy of science, necessarily call for a more highly organised structure. This is found in the establishment, as the principal organs of the university, of separate faculties, each of them highly differentiated in structure, so as to fit it for dealing, in its particular department of learning, with all the teaching and all the research from one end of London to another, and capable of indefinite expansion, without interfering with any other faculty, to meet the requirements of every part of the area and every development of the subject-matter. So long as the several colleges or other teaching institutions regard themselves, and are regarded, as the units of university organisation, their instinctive megalomania is a disruptive force, creating internecine jealousy and competition for students, and impelling each particular institution, irrespective of its local conditions or special opportunities, to strive to swell itself into a complete university on a microscopic scale. Make the faculty the unit, and the same megalomania impelling the professors to work for the utmost possible extension and improvement of the faculty as such, serves only to extend the influence and enhance the reputation of the university as a whole. This is not to say that there is no place in the London University for separately organised institutions and autonomous governing bodies. It is impracticable and undesirable for the University Senate or the University faculties to undertake the vast business of managing all the colleges and other teaching institutions within the metropolitan area. Whether these institutions devote themselves to particular departments of research, to special grades of teaching, to distinct subjects of study, or to the local requirements of their districts, the University will with advantage leave to their governing bodies a large autonomy in business management and finance, and concern itself only with seeing that such portions of their teaching staff and students, their courses of instruction and equipment, as are recognised by the University, are properly organised and co-ordinated with the larger life of the whole. The lines along which this co-ordination must necessarily proceed are marked out by the subjects of teaching or research; that is to say, by faculties. At present there are eight such faculties—namely, arts, science, medicine, law, music, theology, engineering and economics. But the number of separate faculties will gradually increase, either by simple additions, such as pedagogy and philosophy, or, with the advance of the subjects, by the further differentiation into separate organisations of such large and comprehensive divisions as " science " or " arts ". . . .

Thus, instruction will have to be provided in the evening as well as in the day-time, and it should be carried on, with proper relays of teachers, practically continuously throughout the whole year. There is no harm, and indeed great advantage, in these University courses being attached to polytechnics or technical institutes whose other departments are of less than university rank. The University will, of course, take care to appoint or recognise none but thoroughly competent teachers; it will see that the courses of instruction are given the genuine university spirit: it will maintain a high standard in laboratory accommodation: and it will naturally admit, as university students, only those who satisfy its matriculation and other requirements. Subject to these conditions, there can be nothing but advantage in an indefinite multiplication of opportunities for undergraduate study in the whole of the vast area extending from Maidenhead to Gravesend, from Guildford to Bishop's Stortford. In the popular faculties of science and engineering, there will, not improbably, soon be an effective demand—measured by the presence of fifty to a hundred undergraduate students at each place—for complete degree courses at forty or fifty such centres. Even such a multiplication would give, for each centre, a population as great as that of Aberdeen or Plymouth. The teachers at these exclusively undergraduate centres, who will be chosen, it may be hoped, from the ablest post-graduates of London or other universities, must, of course, be members of the faculties and boards of studies in their respective subjects, and every possible opportunity should be given for them to meet, for the discussion of how best to advance their particular branch of learning, not only their contemporaries, but also their more distinguished colleagues, the chief university professors, whose pupils they will probably have been. Only by the frank acceptance of some such policy of extreme local dispersion of the mere undergraduate teaching, coupled with a highly organised intellectual intercourse between all the university teachers in each subject, can the London University rise to the height of its opportunity as the university for seven millions. . . .

But a university is, or ought to be, much more than a mere place for teaching. Its most important function in the state is the advancement of every branch of learning. . . . For the advancement of learning in this, the Baconian sense, the conditions of London life, far from being adverse, are, in reality, in the highest degree favourable. Even without the staff or equipment of a great university, London has always contributed much more than its quota to scientific discovery. It was by no mere accident that Davy and Faraday, Huxley and Tyndall, Sir Joseph Hooker and Herbert Spencer, had all worked in London. London's unparalleled wealth in " material " for observation and study necessarily makes it the principal centre for every branch of English science. The intellectual environment is no less favourable than the wealth of material. The fact that all the learned societies meet in London is significant. No place provides, in each subject of study, so highly specialised a society, in which the ablest thinkers and investigators in any department of learning can meet in friendly converse, not only their foreign colleagues visiting the great city, but also those who are, in the practical business of life, both needing and using the newest discoveries. Add to these natural resources of metropolitan life a university of the type required by London's needs—a large closely knit and highly specialised professoriat in each faculty directing the researches of assistants and post-graduate students in the different branches of each science—and we shall have created, in the very heart of the British Empire, an almost ideal centre from which future generations of investigators and inventors may explore new realms of fact, discover new laws, and conquer new applications of knowledge of life. In the whole range of the physical and biological sciences, in the newer fields of anthropology, archaeology, philology, pedagogy and experimental psychology, in the wide vistas opening out for applied science and the highest technology, in the constantly changing spheres of industrial and commercial relations, administration and political organisation, we may predict with confidence that a rightly organised and adequately endowed London University will take a foremost part in the advancement of learning. . . .

It may be that we must forego in London University the culture born of classic scholarship and learned leisure. But, if we can show that there is no incompatibility between the widespread instruction of an undergraduate democracy and the most effective provision for the discovery of new truth; between the most practical professional training and genuine cultivation of the mind; between the plain living of hardworking students of limited means and high intellectual achievements, we shall not, I venture to believe, appeal in vain. London University must take its own line. They are futile dreamers who seek to fit new circumstances to the old ideals; rather must we strive, by developing to the utmost the opportunities that the present affords us, to create out of twentieth-century conditions new kinds of perfection.[1]

April 1902. *Friday's Hill.*—Sidney had Morant to stay here. Morant is the principal person at the Education Department. He has occupied the most anomalous position the last six months. Taken into the office as a nondescript in a humble capacity some years ago, Gorst picked him out for his private secretary. In that way he became acquainted with the politicians—Cabinet Ministers and Conservative private members, who were concerned with Education Bills and educa-

[1] " London University : A Policy and a Forecast ", by Sidney Webb, *Nineteenth Century*, 1902.

tion policy. Presently these folk—specially the Cabinet Ministers, found him a useful substitute for Kekewich (permanent head), who was deadly opposed to their policy, and even for Gorst with whom they were hardly on speaking terms, the situation being complicated by the fact that Gorst and Kekewich were complete incompatibles, having no communication with each other! So Morant has been exclusively engaged by the Cabinet Committee to draft this present Bill, attending its meetings and consulting with individual members over clauses, trying to get some sort of Bill through the Cabinet. Both Kekewich and Gorst have been absolutely ignored. Neither the one nor the other saw the Bill before it was printed. Just before its introduction in the House, Morant wrote to Gorst saying he assumed he " might put his name at the back ". Gorst answered: " I have sold my name to the Government; put it where they instruct you to put it! " Morant gives strange glimpses into the working of one department of English government. The Duke of Devonshire, the nominal Education Minister, failing through inertia and stupidity to grasp any complicated detail half-an-hour after he has listened to the clearest exposition of it, preoccupied with Newmarket, and in bed till 12 o'clock; Kekewich trying to outstay this Government and quite superannuated in authority; Gorst cynical and careless, having given up even the semblance of any interest in the office; the Cabinet absorbed in other affairs, and impatient and bored with the whole question of education. " Impossible to find out after a Cabinet meeting," Morant tells us, " what has actually been the decision. Salisbury does not seem to know or care, and the various Ministers, who do care, give me contradictory versions. So I gather that Cabinet meetings have become more than informal—they are chaotic—breaking up into little groups, talking to each other without any one to formulate or register the collective opinion. Chamberlain would run the whole thing if he were not so overworked by his own department."

Sidney and Morant discussed for many hours the best way of so influencing the Cabinet and its advisers that we get a good authority for London. Decided to send out the T.E.B. report widely with personal letters, and to set on foot quiet " agitations " among the Church folk and other Conservative circles. Among others, Sidney has written a short note to Chamberlain drawing his attention to the policy of " delegation " in the T.E.B. [report], leaving it to be understood that he would be prepared to delegate management of the elementary schools (properly safeguarded) to borough council committees. Also to Balfour—in fact, I think he has written to every prominent personage, to each according to his views and degree of influence.

May 30th.—Yesterday the formal opening of the new building of the School of Economics, a day of satisfaction to Sidney, Hewins and myself. Our child, born only seven years ago in two back rooms in John Street, with a few hundreds a year, from the Hutchinson Trust, despised by the learned folk as a young man's fad, is now fully-grown and ready to start in the world on its own account. There is the building and equipment, all admirably planned to suit the sort of work and life we have built up; there are the staff of teachers modestly but permanently endowed, there are the formidable list of governors, over which Sidney presides, and last but not least the School has attained university status with its own curriculum, its own degrees, and with even a prospect of its own gown. Meanwhile, Sidney's personal work has broadened out into the administration of university affairs as a whole, his position on the Senate is strong and seems destined to become stronger, since he is always mentally on the spot long before the others have arrived there. He and Hewins too are a strong combination among the warring atoms, and are reinforced by Dr. Robertson of King's and such outside members as W. P. Reeves, and Lord Davey, whilst Sidney is one of Dr. Rucker's (the new principal) more confidential advisers. Should he become one of the trustees of the fund that Haldane is trying to raise, still more should he persuade the L.C.C. to " go " a ¼d. or ½d. rate, his influence with the Senate will become alarmingly strong and no doubt create anger and envy in various quarters. He will then have to walk warily, and not abuse his predominance. Fortunately for his work, he never suffers from inflation, he is too completely absorbed in getting things done and too sincerely modest to lose his head. All his aggressiveness has disappeared with his good fortune, that is his personal aggressiveness, he remains a good fighter when he has his back to the wall. In his opinion, fighting should always be the last resource before being beaten on some main issue of real importance.

Peace with the Transvaal: political burial of the pro-Boers. Immediate increase in popularity of Government: rise of Rosebery " futures ". He is playing the game of leading the Liberal Party on his own terms with consummate deftness.

June 5th. Friday's Hill.—Graham Wallas spent the afternoon and evening here without Audrey. He is more in his old form than I have seen him for years. The approaching abolition of the School Board, in which he acquiesces (on general grounds of objection to *ad hoc* bodies and I think on the particular experience of the L.S.B.), has detached his mind from the minute details of school management and left it freer to turn back to the student's life. He and I had a long discussion— walking on Marley Common—as to our respective position with regard to denominational religion. He recognises but deplores the growing tolerance of it, if not sympathy with religious teaching, on the part of confessed agnostics. He distinguished with some subtlety between the old broad Church party, who wished to broaden the creed of the Church to one which they could emphatically accept, and those religious-minded agnostics who accept Church teaching, not because they believe its assertions to be true, but lest worse befall the child's mind in the form of a crude materialistic philosophy. " I cannot see the spirit of genuine reform, if there is no portion of the Church's teaching which you object to more than any other; if you cease to discriminate between what you accept and what you reject, denying all and accepting all, with the same breath, denying the dogmas as statements of fact, accepting them as interpreting a spirit which pleases you. Dean Stanley and the broad churchmen were in quite different position: they denied the Athanasian Creed and wished it ousted, they believed the Apostles' Creed and fervently and sincerely desired it to be taught." I admitted there was much in his contention. I could only shelter myself by the argument that the reform of the Church was not the work I had undertaken to do, or which I was trained to consider. The practical alternatives before us constituted a very simple issue; whether we were to throw our weight against the continuance of the present form of religious teaching and help to establish pure materialism as the national metaphysic; or whether we would accept, provisionally, as part of the teaching in the schools, the dogmas and ritual of the Christian Church of to-day. For my own children, and for those of other people, I deliberately believed the lie of materialism to be far more pernicious and more utterly false than the untruths which seem to me to constitute the Christian formula of religion. Moreover, we are face to face with the fact that the vast majority of the English people are, as far as they think at all, convinced Christians. By insisting on secular education, I should be not only helping to spread what seems to me a bad kind of falsehood, but I should be denying to others the right to have their children taught the creed they hold to be positively true. I see no way out of the dilemma, but the largest variety possible of denominational schools, so that there may be the utmost possible choice for parents and children, and, let me add, the widest range of experiment as to the results of particular kinds of teaching on the character of the child and its conduct of life.

June 5th.—For about three weeks out of the eight, Bertrand Russell has been away staying with his friends the Whiteheads, and poor Alys has been too unwell to be here. A consciousness that something is wrong between them has to some extent spoilt our sojourn here, both Sidney and I being completely mystified. We became so concerned about the situation that I suggested that I should take Alys off to Switzerland to complete her cure, and Sidney acquiesced out of affection for her and genuine admiration for Bertrand. It would be a sin and a shame if those two should become separated, and altogether wanton misery for both. Our impression is that they have both erred in sacrificing themselves and each other to an altogether mistaken sense of obligation to other people. It is quite clear to me that Bertrand is going through some kind of tragedy of feeling; what is happening to her I suppose I shall discover in the next three or four weeks. It is the wantonness of this unhappiness which appals me: saddens and irritates both of us.

Bertrand Russell's nature is pathetic in its subtle absoluteness: faith in an absolute logic, absolute ethic, absolute beauty, and all of the most refined and rarefied type—his abstract and revolutionary methods of thought and the uncompromising way in which he applies these frightens me for his future, and the future of those who love him or whom he loves. Compromise, mitigation, mixed motive, phases of health of body and mind, qualified statements, uncertain feelings, all seem unknown to him. A proposition must be true or false; a character good or bad; a person loving or unloving, truth-speaking or lying. And this last year he has grown up quite suddenly from an intellectual boy into a masterful man, struggling painfully with his own nature and rival notions of duty and obligation. His hatred of giving pain and his self-control will, I think, save him from the disaster of doing what he would feel afterwards to have been wrong. But it is always painful to stand by and watch a struggle one cannot help. The background of life here has, therefore, not been happy—especially for me, as I have had time and opportunity to observe and brood over it. Sidney, though most anxious and willing to give a helping hand (even to the extent of letting me leave him for three weeks!), is somewhat impatient with this quite unnecessary pain. However, the problems of human relationship have a way of unravelling themselves when those concerned are intelligent, warm-hearted and healthy in body and mind. The first thing to be done is to get Alys well. I am myself looking forward to the complete change and rest. My cure is not complete: I still suffer from eczema in one of my ears, due I believe to my greedy persistence in drinking coffee which I believe is rank poison to me. Also my recent attempts to companionise Bertrand so as to keep him here (which I believe to be Alys's desire) have meant more mental exertion than is consistent with regular work. And I have not always been quite faithful to the regimen: now and again a naughty greedy feeling overtakes me at a meal and I exceed! But I am improving in that respect; keep always before me the scale and the weights. I wanted, having spent yesterday in packing, to get back to the book, but I cannot stand the knocking and cleaning going on in the house—so off I go into the woods with *Mrs. Warren's Profession*—just sent me by G. B. S.

July 1902. *Friday's Hill.*—The last days of our stay—Sidney in London and I packing up our MSS. and blue-books preparatory to the advent of a large party of Berensens, etc.

I have worked well, but with small result in actual stuff written. Of the eight weeks we have been here nearly two were spent on the University article, counting proof-correcting, and another two in reading through and analysing the whole of the Poor Law Commission evidence of 1833–34. Another week has been more or less spent in entertaining and resting, so that not more than a fortnight has been actually consumed in writing. But what I have done is to get the whole poor law section planned out and about half-written, as well as the general scheme of Part II. of the book conceived, so that now the work will go straight forward. Sidney has only been able to write out (he always elucidates and completes my rough draft) what I have done, spending only one or two days a week down here. It has been a broken time for him, absorbed in University and T.E.B. committees, consultations, redrafting of Garnett's and Hewins's reports, writing memoranda for Haldane on university matters, for Conservative M.P.'s and Bishops on " The New Education Authority for London ", and keeping our eye on the Fabian Society and the Liberal League, altogether a somewhat distracted life. But he is very happy in his activity, feels ways opening out before him of getting at least some things done in the direction he believes right. Sometimes he is weary and longs to retire to " a cottage " with me and " write books ", but more often he is happily active—unconscious of anything but his desire to transact the business in hand, successfully. He has a delightful unselfconscious nature: he has (thank the Lord!) no " subconscious self ": when not at work, or asleep, or talking, he reads—reads—reads— always ready for a kiss or a loving word, given or taken. " I am frightened at my own happiness ", he often says.

July 21*st.*—Mr. Haldane came to lunch with us yesterday. He has been immersed in writing his Gifford lectures and was absorbed by his peculiar and personal vision of the " Absolute ". He is still keen on the University and full of energy and hopefulness. But much depressed about politics; does not evidently trust Rosebery. Thinks the Conservatives are going to pieces; that the leaders would even like to be defeated and retire for a year or two; that C. B. would grasp at office on any terms, and that it would end in the fresh discredit of Liberalism with the " Limps " forced into the position of Liberal

Unionists. If asked, Rosebery might accept a coalition with the younger Tories and leave his lieutenants in the lurch and the Liberals in a discredited opposition. For the present he is chiefly concerned to prevent the defeat of the Education Bill and came to consult Sidney about it. Sidney advised a demonstration in the *Nineteenth Century* of educationalists in favour of the Bill, to strengthen Balfour's hand, and again to urge the inclusion of London. Sidney has to write a memorandum on London situation to go through Hugh Cecil to Balfour.

Attended one or two meetings of the Trades Union Congress and had delegates to tea for three days. Dominant note of the Congress is determination to run Labour candidates on a large scale, and faith in the efficacy of this device for gaining all they require. The notion is to have Labour men in the field in a number of constituencies before the Liberal candidate is selected. There is no leadership in the Congress; little respect of one man more than another; but a certain unanimity of opinion among the delegates; less cleavage between trade and trade, or between Old and New Unionists than in any Congress I have before attended. Practically the Congress has been captured (as far as its formal expression of opinion is concerned) by the I.L.P. We find ourselves quite out of harmony with it collectively, though on cordial and confidential terms with many of the delegates.

Odd letter from Rosebery. I sent him a card for my trade union teas, more to let him know what we were doing than expecting him to come. Foolish of him not to have responded to the request from the trade unionists for an entertainment at his house. He needs strengthening on the democratic side, and it would have cost him so little! The half-heartedness of these leaders to their work of leadership annoys us. If it is worth our while at great inconvenience and expense to us—we who have nothing to gain politically—how much more is it their game. Asquith, too, with a house at St. Albans within one hour of London, cannot bestir himself to come up for one day for the Congress, let alone entertain the delegates in his empty house in Cavendish Square. He, too, with the memory of Featherstone to wipe out! Why play the game at all if you mean to play so carelessly, and with so little enjoyment of the process or concern for the result?

October 14th.—All our Radical friends bitter or sullen with us over Sidney's support of the Education Bill. Certainly, if he had political ambitions, it would have been a suicidal policy on his part. Fortunately, we enjoy the incomparable luxury of freedom from all care for ourselves. We are secure in our love for one another and we are absolutely content with our present daily life, as far as our own interest and happiness is concerned. Well we may be! I have a constant wonder whether we are earning our excellent maintenance. Sidney certainly does, assuming that his work is in the right direction, for he is at it from nine o'clock in the morning continuously until 7.30, and once or twice a week lectures in the evening as well. For myself, I peg along every morning at the book for three or four hours, sometimes putting in half-an-hour in the afternoon. But, generally, I find it pays better to do nothing in the afternoons except take exercise, especially as almost every day we have someone to lunch or to dine to talk shop. We have had the whole professoriate of the School (25) to dinner in detachments, and a selection of the students in afterwards. As president of the [Students'] Union, I am trying to develop the social side of the School and have arranged to be " At Home " to students on alternate Wednesdays next term.

November 10th.—The School has opened with éclat. There are now actually at work five hundred students and the staff is hard put to it to meet the new strains. The railway companies have at last come into it with a determination to make use of the lecturing both as an educational training and as a test of capacity of their staff of clerks. For the last three years the Great Western Railway has sent some thirty or forty and paid their fees, but the attendances have been perfunctory and usually tailed off towards the end of the term. This year Wilkinson (Great Northern) [?] took the matter up with vigour: selected groups of courses for each clerk, sent an inspector to see that they attended and to listen to the lectures, required shorthand notes of the lectures to be submitted to him, and gave it out that he would read the three best essays contributed by his staff submitted to him by the Director of the School. The writer of the best essay, an unnoticed clerk in a minor department, has been promoted to the general manager's office. The Great Northern general manager, at the instigation of Lord Rosebery (who is said to talk of " our School " at the meetings of the directors), has had a long talk with Hewins, and arranged to send a contingent to the classes and to require them to pass examinations before being promoted. If this precedent be followed by other business undertakings and by public bodies, we shall have done a good deal to promote efficiency in administration. Hewins, of course, is a little bit over-confident and elated, but that is his temperament. He inspires confidence in men of affairs and has, in fact, more the business than the academic mind; though sufficiently intellectual to state concrete facts in terms of general principles. His weak point is lack of accuracy and rapidity in the despatch of business; he is slovenly in such matters as proof-correcting and dilatory in getting certain things done. But there is usually method in his carelessness, and things left undone or mistaken are usually matters about which his judgement has been over-ruled or to which his aims are slightly different from those of the governors. His carelessness is, in fact, instinctively selective if not intentionally so. It is aggravating because he always agrees to do the job.

But he and Sidney, and to a lesser extent I myself, make a good working trio. The whole internal organisation of the School is left to him with suggestions from Sidney; the whole financial side is in Sidney's hands, whilst my domain has been roping in influential supporters from among old friends and connections. Every Tuesday Hewins lunches here and we discuss the affairs of the School in all its aspects; he consults Sidney about the curriculum; Sidney tells him the requirements for securing L.C.C., Technical Education Board and University support, I submit to both my little schemes for entertaining various persons likely to be useful. Almost every week since early in October we have had dinners of eight to ten—lecturers and governors, likely friends and supporters, and students to lunch. . . . The rest of our social life, which is both lively and interesting, is deliberately designed to help forward the University, the Progressive Party on the L.C.C., and to a slight extent to give Haldane and his friends a friendly lift whenever an opportunity comes that way. The Liberal League, notably Haldane and Rosebery, have been good friends to us, and we feel bound to return in kind.

Haldane and Sidney are constantly co-operating in educational matters. Haldane has taken a bold line in supporting the Government Bill (Education) and breaking from his political friends. His position as a party politician was so damaged before that I doubt whether it has been much worsened. Undoubtedly, if Rosebery goes under and the Campbell-Bannerman lot romp in, Haldane is pretty well done for, unless they should be desperately short of men. On the other hand, he has improved his status as a leader of opinion, has shown that he knows and is keen about the higher branches of education. And the higher branches of education are one of the coming questions. It seems likely that the beginning of the twentieth century will be noted as the starting point of the new form of university training and university research—the application of the scientific method to the facts of daily life, politics and business. In this movement, Haldane will have played one of the principal though unseen parts. His career is interesting as combining that of a considerable lawyer, an education reformer and an intriguing politician (though the intrigues are always to promote a cause, never to push himself). It is a paradox that a mind that is essentially metaphysical, laying stress on the non-material side of human thought and feeling, should have been, as a matter of fact, chiefly engaged in promoting applied physical science.

Rosebery is not making way in the country and is, I imagine, having a bad time with himself. He has no grip of anything except appearances. He is so intent on trying to find out which course will *appear right* to the ordinary man of affairs, that he forgets altogether to think out which course will work out best in social results. He seems positively frightened at the thought of any such enquiry. Publicly and privately Sidney has pressed on the Liberal League the necessity of its leaders making up their minds as to what they would do if they had the power. Rosebery and Haldane hang back—they do not want to be committed. " Quite so," says Sidney; " don't publish anything or decide on any course, but let us at least have the facts at our command and know all the alternative courses." He is, however, a voice in the wilderness.

November 15th.—I took the Prime Minister [Arthur Balfour] in to dinner! I say " took " because he was so obviously delivered over into my hands by my kindly hostess who wished me to make as much use as possible of the 1¼ hours he had free from the House. It was a little party of eight at the house of the charming Mrs. Horner—High Priestess of the "Souls ", in their palmy days, now somewhat elderly and faded but gracious to those she accepts as distinguished. The other diners were Lady Elcho and Haldane, Mr. Horner and a handsome daughter.

Balfour has the charm of genuine modesty and unselfconsciousness, and that evening he seemed in earnest about education. He is delightfully responsive intellectually—a man with an ever open mind—too open, perhaps, seeing that on no question has it been sufficiently closed by study and thought to have developed principles. There comes a time in life when surely the mind should be made up conclusively as to the particular questions with which it is mainly concerned; man's work in life is action and not enquiry? Balfour's intellect has not the organic quality; there is no determinate result from the combination of his reason with his knowledge of facts. His opinions shift uneasily from side to side; the one permanent bias being in favour of personal refinement of thought and feeling. But I doubt whether he has any clear notion of how he would attempt to bring about this refinement in other people, except by personal example and influence. On the other hand, he has no bias in favour of *laisser-faire*. Action or inaction are open questions, and it is a chapter of accidents on which side he throws himself. But he *intends* to work on the side which at the moment he *thinks right*—not merely on the side that will appear right to other people—which I fear is Lord Rosebery's predicament. All this elaborate analysis based on one hour!

I set myself to amuse and interest him, but seized every opportunity to insinuate sound doctrine and information as to the position of

London education. Sidney says I managed skilfully, but then he is a partial judge! We found ourselves in accord on most questions. Perhaps that is only another way of saying that Arthur Balfour is a sympathetic and attractive person who easily tunes his conversation to the other minds. I can understand how colleagues in the House of Commons forgive his incapacity for transacting business: the flavour of his personality is delightful.

Three dinners and two evening parties at one's house in eight days is severe! But it seemed desirable to give a Conservative–L.C.C. dinner and a London University reception; and also a " Limp " dinner, and a " Limp " reception. Then there was a dinner to Lady Elcho to acknowledge her kindness to us in Gloucestershire and our introduction to Balfour; an introduction which may have good results. So I asked her to meet John Burns, the Shaws, H. G. Wells and Asquith. John Burns took the palm; his unselfconscious exuberance, dramatic faculty and warmth of feeling amounted to brilliancy; he gave us vivid pictures of prison and other episodes; views on the army; Eton and the aristocracy; on working-class and middle-class life; all fresh and interesting with a certain romantic sentiment for what was ancient and distinguished. Shaw and Wells were not at their ease—G. B. S. was jerkily egotistical and paradoxical, though he behaved well in encouraging Burns to take the stage; Wells was rather silent; when he spoke he tried hard to be clever—he never let himself go. Asquith was simply dull. He is disheartened with politics, has no feeling of independent initiative, and is baffled by Rosebery, snubs and is snubbed by C. B. He has worked himself into an unreal opposition to the Education Bill. He is not really convinced of the iniquity or unwisdom of the Bill he is denouncing. He eats and drinks too much and lives in a too enervating social atmosphere to have either strenuousness or spontaneity. Clearly he is looking to the money-making Bar for his occupation in life. As a lawyer he is essentially common quality; no interest in, or understanding of, legal principles; no ingenuity or originality in making new influences or adapting old rules to new conditions. However, he is under no delusion about himself; he has resigned himself to missing leadership.

The dinner was successful and thrilling to Lady Elcho, enjoying the new sensation of meeting such strange forms of distinction as Burns, Wells, Shaw at the house of the Sidney Webbs.

The " education " and " Moderate " dinner consisted of Sir Alfred Lyall and wife, Sir Owen Roberts (clerk to the Clothworkers and an excellent friend of ours) and wife, Sir John Dickson Poynder (L.C.C. Moderate and Conservative M.P., a simple-hearted, public-spirited country gentleman of attractive mien), Sir Lacy Robinson (L.C.C.

Moderate, former civil servant and a new governor of School of Economics), Mrs. J. R. Green, Beatrice Chamberlain and Charles Booth (whom I happened to meet in the street the day before). After dinner, we had some 30 or 40 of the educationists and University men-folk—Sir John Gorst and some eight L.C.C. Moderates. They all knew each other, or wanted to know each other, so that talk was incessant.

Finally, we had one " Limp " dinner yesterday—Sir E. Grey, Haldane, B. Russell, Wilberforce and Wiles (two L.C.C. Progress-ives), Harben (a promising young Liberal Leaguer), Isaac Mitchell (one of the ablest of the younger trade union officials) and Perry (the most influential of the university medicals and a Liberal Progressive). Lion Phillimore—the one lady to keep me company. In the evening some sixty men came in—trade union officials, L.C.C. Progressives, journalists and " Limp " M.P.'s. I introduced vigorously and they all chatted and chattered sometimes in confidential *tête-à-têtes*, sometimes in groups. Haldane, who had dined with us, chaffed me about the resurrection of the " Souls " in Grosvenor Road.

The interest of the evening to me was a long talk during dinner with Sir Edward Grey. Like Balfour he is a man of exquisite flavour; he is high-minded, simple, kindly and wise, without being able or clever—an ideal element in a Cabinet containing some strong master-mind. *But he is not the master-mind*: I doubt whether it would be physically or mentally possible for him to work eight hours a day, for, say, ten months of the year; he has neither the knowledge, the depth of feeling, nor the personal grip on life, to have a strong will or deeply-rooted convictions. His temperament is an exquisite poise—far above human passions and human prejudices—in an atmosphere rarefied by public spirit, fastidious honour and widely diffused human fellowship, essentially a passive and receptive nature, revelling in the beauties of nature, the interest of books, and the charm of one or two intimate friendships with men and women of like character in simple and refined surroundings.

The last entry in the diary of 1902 forecasts the leading preoccupation of the Other One during the following three years, 1903–5, signalised in the following chapter.

December 1902.—Morant dined here last night alone to talk over chances of London Education Bill. Wearied out with the autumn campaign and the prospect of having to superintend the working out of the new Education Act with a rotten staff and a hostile minority in each district determined to wreck the Act. He says that Balfour is furious with the Church, and the Church disconsolate with its bargain;

Londonderry a bull in a china shop, and Anson too academically clever to be a comfortable fifth wheel in the coach. He had drafted a Bill for London of two clauses applying the Act. " Quite satisfactory to you ", he observed. But alas! Walter Long, elated with his triumph over the constitution of the Water Board, says " he will be d——d before he sees the L.C.C. the education authority ". Morant doubts whether anyone wants any particular change sufficiently to get discordant views into line—the Church hesitates as to the worth-while of it, the Unionist members are terrified at the N.U.T., on the one hand, and the Tory political worker, on the other; no member of the Cabinet is keen to enhance the dignity of the L.C.C., though all except Long realise that the borough councils would be impossible. But Long is a loud-voiced persistent creature, who talks his colleagues down at Cabinet and committee meetings and is in touch with the commoner kind of obscurant Tory. So matters look dark and the present unsatisfactory situation is likely to persist, at least for the forthcoming year.

CHAPTER VI

THE LONDON EDUCATION ACT
AND AFTER
1903–1905

THE passage of the London Education Act of 1903 proved to be a landmark in Our Partnership: a successful achievement which entailed some consequences that were unpleasant. Without the broad base of universal compulsory elementary education, including within its ambit the denominational schools, the whole under the control of the London County Council, the unification of London education would have been both incomplete and unsubstantial. But this drastic reform involved not only the supersession of the *ad hoc* school board, but also " putting Rome on the rates ", not to mention also the Anglican established Church schools abhorred by the more fanatical Nonconformists. Hence, Sidney Webb's support of the Education Act of 1902, which abolished all school boards and handed over not only the board schools with their undenominational Christianity (subject to a conscience clause) but also the denominational schools, Catholic, Anglican and Wesleyan, to the provincial county councils and county borough councils, nearly all of them Conservative outside the metropolis, had already offended both the orthodox Liberals and the powerful Nonconformist element in the nascent Labour Party. And this contradiction of orthodox Liberalism seemed even more offensive when applied to the metropolis. Here, at any rate, the Conservative Party was divided in its policy, and there might be some hope of keeping the School Board as the education authority. Gradually the Progressive Party realised that the Conservative Cabinet was being encouraged by a leading member of the party to go forward with the abolition of the London School Board, with the important qualification that the London County Council was to be substituted for the indirectly elected federation of metropolitan borough councils which had been the original Conservative proposal. This willingness to accept the placing of denominational schools on the rates, and thus give them a position of permanence in the British educational system, seemed to be all the more objectionable seeing that the Webbs were known not to belong to any Christian denomination, Protestant or Roman Catholic, but to be nothing better than agnostics.

How did we come to take up this position? We realised the strength of the common British objection to making the taxpayer maintain the teaching of a religion in which he did not believe, and which he often regarded as damnably injurious both to his children and to the community. But, rightly or wrongly, we were convinced that, at that time and probably for many years afterwards, there was no alternative way of securing for every child throughout the kingdom, irrespective of class or creed, the maximum duration and efficiency of educational facilities that the House of Commons could be induced to afford.

What were the alternative ways of solving this difficult problem of creating a universal compulsory system of elementary education, paid for out of rates and taxes, and administered by a public authority, without offending the conscience of parents or teachers? I may note in passing that, in the early years of the twentieth century, it was only rival religious creeds, concerned with man's relation to the universe and with life after death, which raised questions of conscience. It was at that time never suggested, as is the case in many countries to-day, that the child should be taught deliberately to prefer one political constitution or economic system rather than another. This absence of conscientious objection was in the main due to a general agreement among contemporary educationalists that political and economic problems were not fit subjects for children of school age. But it was also a sign that there was no practical objection among the inhabitants of Great Britain to the *status quo*, as represented in the school text-books, historical or geographical, which were used in the course of education.

So far as we knew there were three or four solutions actually practised in the Anglo-Saxon world. In England, part of the curriculum in all rate-supported schools included the teaching of undenominational Christianity—whatever that may mean—with a conscience clause for teachers and the children of conscientious objectors, the persons concerned being absolved from taking part in these particular classes. Outside the publicly supported and administered schools, there were the denominational schools which were aided by Government grants, though not by the rates. There was no provision from public funds for those parents or teachers who objected to the faith in the miraculous embodied in all Christian sects. In Scotland, on the other hand, where only two Christian sects were recognised, the Presbyterian and the Roman Catholic, the custom was that the head master should belong to the same denomination as the majority of the children, and the assistant master should represent the other recognised sect of Christians. In that way Presbyterian and Roman Catholic children alike had the specific religious dogmas in which their parents believed as part of their training.

In most of the states of the U.S.A. the schools were secular, and there was no provision of any kind for Catholics or Evangelicals, who desired that their children should be brought up in a religious faith. Hence, one or two million children were being brought up outside the state school system, mostly in Roman Catholic schools, without any public provision and with no public inspection, the result being, as we had discovered in our recent tour in the U.S.A., that both teachers and schools were disastrously below any decent standard of efficiency. The same principle was pursued in New Zealand and in some of the states of Australia: in its most rigid form in Victoria. In the Victoria of the 'nineties the Roman Catholics had succeeded, whilst maintaining their own schools, in preventing the publicly supported schools from teaching any history (which they asserted must be partial either to the Protestant or to the Roman Catholic religion), or reciting any poetry in which God was mentioned. When, for instance, Wordsworth's " Ode to Immortality " was objected to on the ground that it mentioned the Deity, the Minister of Education telegraphed: " Insert ' the Gods ' ". On the other hand, one of the American states insisted on " fundamentalist " Christian doctrine, and would not permit the teaching of biological science, because research into the evolution of life contradicted the Old Testament story of the creation of the world with all the living creatures it contains in six days, with God resting on the seventh, surveying with complacency the result of his creativeness.

What was proposed in the Acts of 1902 and 1903, applying to England and Wales only, was that all schools which provided elementary education up to a certain standard should come on the rates, and be controlled by the public authority; but that such of them as had been provided by a religious denomination should be permitted to choose teachers of their own creed provided that they were efficient in secular subjects, and that, subject to a conscience clause, there should be religious teaching according to the creed of the denominational school. This solution seemed to us, *in the then state of public opinion*, the most likely to be accepted and loyally carried out while maximising the efficiency and duration of the educational opportunities for the mass of the children of the United Kingdom.[1]

---

[1] It is a curious reflection that this unwillingness or inability to give religious instruction is far more common in council schools than in the avowedly denominational schools, where the teachers are chosen because they belong to the Roman Catholic or Anglican churches. This reluctance, on the part of teachers, leaves the child's mind in a state of bewilderment, leading in many cases to cynical indifference or hypocritical make-believe. The question arises: what is the alternative? It seems impracticable to teach a child how to behave—an important part of education—without some sincerely held scale of ethical values arising out of some definite conception of man's relation to man, and man's relation to the universe. Have we, in Great Britain, yet developed any genuine science of ethics arising out of observation, generalisation and verification, and based on a sincerely held vision of man's destiny? In the middle of the nineteenth century Auguste Comte and his followers believed that they had invented a religion of humanity, for which they actually started churches with rites and sermons. But this Comtist sect, though including some distinguished minds, petered out, perhaps because it was mixed up with economic and political speculations which failed to gain acceptance. In the past decade the USSR

1903

The narrative of our daily life, excluding our researches into English local government which have already been described in Chapter IV, will be found in the following entries in my diary, whether these relate to the administrative activities and the manipulation of public opinion by the Other One, or to our intercourse with relatives, friends and fellow-workers. To these I have added a few criticisms of books and my own reflections on the destiny of man and his instinctive reaction to the unknown or the unknowable. I do this, not because these casual notes have any value in themselves, but merely because they indicate a conflict in my mind between a conscientious desire to be strictly rationalistic, and an instinctive longing for some sanction other than scientific reasoning, for believing in the eternal worthwhileness of human life. For it was to this latent " religiosity " in one of the partners that some critics attributed our dubious association with Anglican bishops and Catholic priests, not to mention Conservative politicians and civil servants, in our pursuit of the educational policy embodied in the London Education Act of 1903.

January 16th. Overstrand.—For the first time for many years the three old friends—Sidney, Bernard Shaw and Graham Wallas—spent a week together with their wives as chorus—the Shaws at the big hotel nearby and the Wallases with us. Three delightful evenings we spent listening to G. B. S. reading his new work—*Man and Super-Man*. To me it seems a great work; quite the biggest thing he has done. He has found his *form*: a play which is not a play; but only a combination of essay, treatise, interlude, lyric—all the different forms illustrating the same central idea, as a sonata manifests a scheme of melody and harmony. I was all the more delighted with it, as I had not been impressed with the bits I had heard before, and Sidney had reported unfavourably of the play itself. Possibly, the unexpectedness of the success has made me over-value it—a reaction from a current in my mind of depreciation of G. B. S. Then I am so genuinely delighted at

thinks it has evolved in its political and economic structure, and its steadfast pursuit of science, in all its applications to social life, not only a fresh code of conduct, but also a new vision of man's future.

his choice of subject. *We* cannot touch the subject of human breeding —it is not ripe for the mere industry of induction, and yet I realise that it is the most important of all questions, this breeding of the right sort of man. G. B. S.'s audacious genius can reach out to it.

Graham was somewhat depressed, physically and mentally; and, though affectionate and pleasant to us, he has a deeply-rooted suspicion that Sidney is playing false with regard to religious education. He wants all religious teaching abolished. As Sidney is not himself a " religionist ", Graham thinks that he too should wish it swept away. Politically, this seems to Sidney impossible, whilst I do not desire it even if it were possible. So between us we are prepared for a working agreement with the mammon of ecclesiasticism. Poor dear Wallas consequently sees this working agreement writ large in every act of the T.E.B., however irrelevant it may be to the religious issue (an issue which appears to Sidney to intervene as only a minute part of public education). Whether the T.E.B. takes action or omits to take action on any question there is always in Graham's eyes the priest behind the policy. This suspicion makes frank co-operation between Sidney and our old friend impossible—and though personal relations remain affectionate and appreciative, I fear there must be some official friction if not actual hostility. As Sidney's side is bound to win, though possibly Sidney himself will be sacrificed, it is to be hoped that Graham will retire from educational administration. He tried to talk G. B. S. round to his view, but failed. G. B. S. is too rootedly sceptical about all alternative philosophies to be inclined to oust Christianity by *force majeure*.

Meanwhile, we fear we shall lose on the question of the authority for London education. Inspired by Haldane the *Times* came down on our side and Sidney is seeing the *Daily Mail*. But the political Conservative is dead against the L.C.C. for London. . . . Moreover, the official opposition has declared in favour of an *ad hoc* body. The Progressives on the L.C.C. have not liked to claim education as their province; they have only been frightened by Sidney with the bogey of the borough council into holding their official tongue!

February 1st.—Sidney hard at work making public opinion as to the education authority. He interviewed Harmsworth and his " boy " editors, and the former handed over the direction of the campaign in the *Daily Mail* to Sidney.[1] He has seen Buckle of the *Times* and

---

[1] S. W. says (in 1937) that what he remembers is that, almost despairing of inducing the Cabinet to give London education to the L.C.C., he wrote at a venture to Harmsworth, whom he had never met, stating that he happened to know that the draft Bill proposed to entrust London education to a body formed by indirect election, like the old Metropolitan Board of Works. He said that he was convinced

Lawson of the *Telegraph* and Spencer Wilkinson of the *Morning Post*. He is stimulating the Church and educationalists generally to put pressure on Balfour. Haldane reports that it is still undecided, Walter Long holding out for a borough educational authority—or at any rate a majority of borough councillors on the L.C.C. committee. Progressives of L.C.C. sulky: some jealous of Sidney, others conscientiously opposed to any compromise with regard to Church schools. If L.C.C. finds itself the authority, it will be, I believe, entirely due to Sidney—to the excellent reputation of the T.E.B. under his guidance, and to his persistent efforts to stir up public opinion in favour of the L.C.C. But all this means Sidney's distraction from the book. And as it also entails a good deal of entertaining, it is a serious drain on my energy. However, the aim is worth the labour. From the standpoint of the book the worst is that, if we succeed, it will result in a big, difficult and continuous task for Sidney. All the more reason for me to keep in the highest degree of efficiency. Abstemiousness of body and calmness of mind the one way. . . .

Read through Haldane's *Pathway to Reality* on the journey to and fro—out of friendship for the author. To me his metaphysic seems an attempt to " intellectualise " the emotional assertion of a " beyond " which is bound to fail. What is called " verification " is impossible; there is no conceivable external test of the truth of your thought, and therefore no way of convincing those who do not think the same thought as you. If you are conscious of a great reality, this consciousness *may* be as valid as any other part of your consciousness? But its validity remains your own secret, not communicable to those who are not already in possession of it. Possibly, by attempting to put it into words, you rouse in other minds the knowledge that they *do* possess the secret somewhere—in the recesses of their souls—but for this purpose the emotional assertion of poetry and piety seem to me more effective than ratiocination. However, there are minds who can only accept the

that this would be disastrous for education, and what was more, he was sure that the London Conservative M.P.'s would not stand it. Hence the Government would have to give way; and why should not the *Daily Mail* have the credit of making the Government give way? To his intense surprise and delight, Harmsworth answered at once, asking him to call on Monday at 4.30 P.M. He was ushered in and found Harmsworth looking amazingly youthful, seated in conference with four still more boyish-looking assistant editors. Harmsworth asked several sharp questions, and then said, " Very well, Mr. Webb, we'll do it. But we don't know anything about the subject. You must come in every night at 11 P.M. for a week, and see that we say everything just right." Needless to say, S. W. jumped at the chance, and for a week sat with Thomas Marlowe, who was then the chief acting editor, and corrected the reports and paragraphs on London education. " I never revealed to anyone ", he laughingly said, years afterwards, " that one of my experiences had been to edit the *Daily Mail* for a week." How much this episode contributed to the formation of opinion on the Conservative side of the House of Commons no one can compute.

assertion when clothed in the form of a syllogism; and it is to these minds that metaphysics, I imagine, appeal. You must feel the need for this assertion, and you must have an intense predilection for reasoning and then you will find salvation in metaphysics. Emily Brontë's " Last Lines " are to me more convincing than the *Pathway to Reality*:

> " There is not room for death,
>> Nor atom that his might could render void,
> Thou, thou art Being and Breath,
>> And what thou art may never be destroyed."

February 25th.—A succession of dinners over the Education Bill, mostly Conservative and Church. Among our guests the Bishop of Stepney,[1] a remarkable man, who will go far. He is Creighton, without either his defects or his finest qualities; but, for that very reason, far more effective as an ecclesiastical statesman. The new kind of ecclesiastic with his eye on the *new social classes*, intent on winning for the Church democratic support. An Erastian in doctrine, anxious to see the 39 Articles and all other inconveniently obsolete documents regarded simply as formulae of historical interest, but not binding on the conscience. The Dean of Westminster, a scholar and mystic, is more attractive to me but not nearly so efficient.[2]

Met Sir William Anson at C. A. Cripps' (our brother-in-law has come out as an L.C.C. man), a pleasant subtle-minded don, a perfect head to a college, but singularly out of place in an administrative position.[3] Far more interested in discussing the relation of the Privy Council to the local authorities of the seventeenth and eighteenth centuries than the proper authority for dealing to-day with London's education. Indeed, one felt he knew so little of the elements of the latter subject, that it was barely worth while talking to him. Still it is desirable to have him not " agin us " and he must be asked to dinner. The interests of the School and the University and the smooth working of the L.C.C. have all to be considered in our little entertainments. Meanwhile, we try to get a morning's work, however perfunctory, at the book. We often long for that cottage in the country and the peaceful existence of a student life. We sometimes wonder whether such an existence would not be, in the long run, more useful. But then someone must do the rough and tumble work of government. It is a tiresome fact that to get things done in what one considers the best way, entails so much—to speak plainly—of intrigue. There is no such thing as spontaneous public opinion; it all has to be manufactured from

[1] Cosmo Gordon Lang.　　　　[2] Dr. Joseph Armitage Robinson.
[3] Vice-President of the Committee of Council on Education; M.P. for Oxford University.

a centre of conviction and energy radiating through persons, sometimes losing itself in an unsympathetic medium, at other times gaining additional force in such an agent as the Bishop of Stepney, or the *Daily Mail*. Of course, there is always the element of " sport " in this life of agitation: watching the ideas one starts (like, for instance, " the dominance of the National Union of Teachers over the borough councils ") wending their ways through all sorts of places and turning up quite unexpectedly as allies in overthrowing counter interests and arguments. It is fortunate when one happens to believe in one's own arguments: one always does so in a fashion, the most one does is to suppress the qualification. Is that " debasing the currency " or is it permissible to accept the position of an advocate to tell the truth but not the whole truth? As a matter of fact, with regard to administrative work, we plunge without hesitation on to the position of an advocate pledged only to display the arguments which tell in favour of the cause we believe in. In our scientific work, however, we honestly seek to tell the truth, the whole truth, and nothing but the truth; a distinction in standards which puzzles and perplexes me. . . .

March 14th.—The L.C.C. Progressives, or some of them, are playing the fool about the London education authority. So determined are they to " spite the Government " and so anxious for a good battle cry, that they are steering straight into a " Water Board " authority for education. A little *clique* headed by J. R. MacDonald and fighting all they know how Sidney's influence on the T.E.B.; some of the weaker of the rank and file, somewhat jealous of Sidney, are playing into their hands. Sidney thought it better to offer himself to the Progressive cause for election as chairman of the T.E.B. this year, in order to facilitate negotiations with the Government, but has given it to be understood that he does not wish to be chairman except with the full consent of the Progressive members of the Board. J. R. MacDonald has set to work to detach them from him and has succeeded with the Labour men (who are secularist, *ad hoc*, and anti-higher education) and one or two other middle-class members who are ambitious to be chairmen themselves. It remains to be seen whether he carries the caucus to-morrow. Sidney has refrained from canvassing and stood on his dignity—we both thought that, if the L.C.C. Progressives deserted him, it would be better to play for a " reaction " in his favour by having an inferior man elected chairman, under whom the Board would chafe. Of course, these dissensions will injure the chances of the Bill being on the right lines, as it will be open to the Moderates to say to the Government, that the one good man ready to carry out the Act has been rejected by his own party. It is strange that these personal enemies don't see that Sidney's position will be immensely stronger on a mixed board of borough councillors, L.C.C. and outsiders, than on a genuine L.C.C. committee, and that if he were playing for his own dominance he would go straight for that. Meanwhile, it will be a big misfortune for democratic government, even of the kind they believe most in, if the L.C.C. is put on one side as unfit to be the education authority.

I have been pondering over the question whether I could have done anything to stop the " slump in Webbs " on the Progressive side. Of course, our attention has been absorbed in getting hold of forces in the enemy's camp, and our frequent coming and going has excited suspicion in our own. They have not the wit to see that, if a Government is in power with an overwhelming majority, it is no use fighting it—at least not unless the other way has proved unavailing. Whether or not he is elected chairman to-morrow, I shall turn my attention seriously to the Progressive members of the T.E.B. when we come back from Longfords, and see what can be done to counteract J. R. MacDonald's machinations. I have suggested that whatever happens Sidney adopts an attitude of beneficent helpfulness. In only one eventuality would he fight the Progressive caucus—that is if J. R. MacDonald got himself nominated for chairman. In that case Sidney would propose Dr. Leaf, or failing him stand himself. But J. R. MacDonald is too shrewd to try that little game.

The complaint against Sidney resolves itself into this: (1) he is " in " with the Government; (2) he might sacrifice the interests of primary to secondary and university education; (3) he ignores the " religious " difficulty and is willing to be impartial between Anglican and " undenominational " Christianity. Numbers (1) and (3) are true in essence; (2) is not true, at least in our most impartial moments we believe not. We don't believe you can raise the standard of elementary education and save it from mere mechanical efficiency unless you have the university in organic connection with it—unless you have mobility between all classes of teachers from the assistant master of the present elementary school to the research professor. The same with the students: the university must be open to them in fact as well as in theory. It lacks imagination to think that elementary education can be stimulating and progressive except as the broad base to the higher learning. Those who feel themselves specifically the representatives of Labour, fail through lack of ambition for their own clients and, be it added, through self-complacency with themselves as ideal reformers of society.

March 15*th.*—The " slump " in Webbs proves to be serious: Sidney was defeated by only four to three in a little caucus of Progressives on the T.E.B. But then, the others had not troubled to turn up, or had stayed away purposely, which means indifference if not hostility. The Board, after a little spluttering, acquiesced in the election of Shepheard and Leon, both *ad hoc* anti-voluntary school men, but not personally hostile to Sidney. There are indications, too, that this feeling of antagonism is not confined to this little group—the rank and file of the Progressives do not want the L.C.C. to be the authority and they think Sidney with his press and back-stair influence is bringing it about. The Crooks[1] election has swelled the Progressive head, and they feel inclined to fight for an *ad hoc* body and unsectarian education. The position has been worsened by an indiscretion of Dr. Garnett, the able secretary of the T.E.B. (which would not have occurred if Sidney had been chairman!), in circulating a memorandum in favour of a definite scheme of L.C.C. administration. Everyone believed Sidney to have had a hand in it.

But there is a very real cleavage between our views and those of the rank-and-file Radicals, and I do not see my way honestly to bridge it. We are not in favour of ousting religion from the collective life of the state; we are not in favour of the cruder form of democracy. And we *do* believe in expenditure on services which will benefit other classes besides the working-class, and which will open the way to working-men to become fit to *govern*, not simply to *represent* their own class; and we are in favour of economy as well as expenditure. But then what is the good of having means of one's own and some intelligence, unless one is prepared to advocate what is unpopular?

March 27th.—Matters not much mended. Hubbard, an honest Nonconformist rank-and-file member of the L.C.C., had put down a resolution in favour of *ad hoc* authority some weeks ago. McKinnon Wood and Collins, both in their hearts anxious for the L.C.C. authority as unifying London government, called a party meeting to try and get a decision against bringing the question up before the Government produced their Bill. With great skill Collins succeeded in getting the party to vote thirty to twenty on non-committal resolutions in favour of a directly elected body, understood to mean the L.C.C., but blaming the Government for attacking school boards and subsidising voluntary schools; and, by an overwhelming majority, for adjourning Hubbard's resolution. Meanwhile, the Government, scared by electoral results at bye-elections at Woolwich and Rye, took fright. Morant wrote begging Sidney to let him know the result of the meeting. Londonderry's private secretary came down to ask for permission to attend, with shorthand writer, the L.C.C. debate, so that the Cabinet might have a correct and complete version of the L.C.C. views. Last

---

[1] William Crooks, L.C.C., won a notable bye-election for Woolwich in 1903.

Tuesday the Council, as a whole, prevented the taking of Hubbard's resolution by talking at length on other matters. Sidney went at Haldane's request to see Sandars (the confidential private secretary to the Prime Minister) and the Conservative Whip, and to encourage them to introduce the L.C.C. Bill. But to-day we learn in confidence that the Cabinet yesterday decided that it would not introduce their Bill giving the L.C.C. the whole of education and complete control of its committee unless they could, by this means, secure the support of the L.C.C. Progressives. Failing this, it is to be the *status quo* and the settlement of London education left over to some future Government. Now it remains to be seen whether the official leaders of the Progressives are willing and able to get Hubbard's resolution negatived. Sidney does not believe that they can carry the rank and file with them, even if they plank themselves down on the policy of L.C.C. authority.

Haldane tells us that the rot has set in severely within the Cabinet. They are panic-stricken—all except Joe (Chamberlain) who holds himself somewhat detached from the rest and lets them stew in their juice of muddle and mistake. They have been so shaken by Woolwich and Rye, and the rising tide of Nonconformism (N.U.T. agitation in London), that they were actually considering the making of an *ad hoc* authority for London—a complete capitulation. However, they were shaken out of that by Sidney's assertion that not only would Dr. Clifford and Macnamara dominate such an authority, but it would light up the flame throughout the country against the 1902 Act, and encourage a persistent refusal to accept the Act by all sorts and conditions of malcontents. So they were prepared to throw themselves into the arms of the L.C.C., if they had been able, by so doing, to get a rest from virulent opposition. The L.C.C. has not been able to rise to the emergency. Possibly it has proved that it would not be equal to running the concern. The success of the T.E.B. is largely owing to the fact that Sidney removed it from the first out of the practical control of the L.C.C. But he lost consent in gaining efficiency.

Gave my presidential address to the Students' Union, which cost a good four days to prepare, on the relative function of the investigator, the man of affairs and the idealist. The upshot of the analysis was that the investigator or scientific man has to discover the process by which a given end can be obtained within a given subject-matter. This means specialisation and all the patient methods of observation, generalisation and verification. The man of affairs has to select the processes, to adapt and adjust them in order to bring about a " state of affairs ". This entails a knowledge of and capacity to control men, and perception of general ends, which would be actually obtained by the dovetailing of the processes of the various sciences. But neither the investigator

nor the man of affairs could act, unless there was a conception of an end or purpose to be attained. This was given by the idealist. Where did he discover his ideals? Not in science, seeing that science can give processes and processes only. Not in affairs: that meant opportunism. In metaphysics or in religion? In choice of ideals within our own inner consciousness, or perhaps in communion with a higher and nobler life than that of common humanity?

April 3rd.—Listened from the Speaker's Gallery to (Sir William) Anson introducing the London Education Bill. Met with cold reception. Opposition jeering and supporters gloomily silent. An inept speech. As it stands the Bill is a bad one, though rather than the *status quo* or an *ad hoc* authority *we* would accept it as it stands. But it is clear to us that the borough council representatives on the central committee have been stuck in to be knocked out, and that the control of the L.C.C. over the local administration of elementary education will be indefinitely strengthened in committee of the House. If our prophecy be proved correct, the Bill is much what Sidney would have himself drafted, except that he would have defined in the Bill the outside element to be co-opted by the L.C.C. committee and not left it to the free will of the L.C.C. But this may be unduly distrustful of his Progressive colleagues! But, of course, the Bill as it stands has been received by every section of Progressives with contemptuous disapproval—almost delight, because it is considered so bad that it will not pass. Hewins and Pease have, however, been so indoctrinated by Sidney that they are almost enthusiastic about the present draft. Sidney goes up to-day to a meeting of the parliamentary committee of the L.C.C. to reconnoitre the position and see how far he can modify the outburst of L.C.C. disapproval.

April 29th.—L.C.C. Progressives rapidly coming round to notion of L.C.C. being the authority—the natural desire of a public body to increase its dignity and power overcoming the party feeling in favour of an *ad hoc* authority. Clear also that Government intend to give way if pressed. All the Conservative Party organs on our side agree as to strengthening of the L.C.C. position, though they differ about borough representative on the central committee, and the powers of the borough local committee. Looks as if Sidney would get his way all along the line even with regard to the constitution of the education committee.

June 15th. Aston Magna, Gloucestershire.—We left London seventeen days ago, tired out but with the restful consciousness that our plans had come off. The School gets its grant of £1100 from the T.E.B. renewed without opposition, J. R. MacDonald not being there. The Education Bill passed through committee the day before we left, in

almost exactly the shape Sidney would have given to it: the L.C.C. absolutely supreme, the borough councils relegated to the quite subordinate part of selecting the majority of the local managers; but these latter having no more power than the L.C.C. choose to give them. In fact, the Bill endows the L.C.C. with rather more freedom of action than Sidney would have suggested as the ideal arrangement: he would have preferred a statutory constitution for the education committee, instead of leaving it open to the L.C.C. [as to co-option of] other outside interests. It was very easy to get the L.C.C. ten years ago to appoint a reasonably broad committee for technical education—when none of the Council were interested in the matter. It is another thing to persuade the Progressives, with their enormous majority and strong Nonconformist element, to be fair and sane about the outside interests. Hence, our anxiety is now passed from Parliament to the L.C.C. itself. So long as we can get the present Council to consent to frame a scheme under the Act, and so long as the scheme is not outrageously one-sided, that is as much as we can do. The working of the Act will be a matter for the 1904 Council. We are concerned now to see to it that this Council has the right complexion. The whole controversy between the Progressives and Moderates is stale and has lost its significance. The Progressives, beyond sticking to some old shibboleths, have lost all impetus to further action. The Works Department, the old symbol of collectivism, is a mere device for keeping the contractors in order; the taking over of the tramways has been accomplished in principle, if not in fact; but water is lost to the L.C.C., at any rate for the next decade or two, and with regard to asylums, to housing, to sanitary and building bye-laws committee, the work of the Council has become mere routine. In fact, it is asserted by some, that the old gang who ran the administrative departments have become cautious and economical to the last degree. On the other hand, while the Council has lost the impetus to do constructive work, it has accreted a good deal of destructive radicalism of the old type. Some thirty members of the Progressive Party are standing for Parliament, and owing to the latter-day developments they are, many of them, likely to get in. This will increase the disinclination of the Progressive leaders to a vigorous municipal policy, and identify them more completely than ever with parliamentary Liberalism. And all these general considerations have been enormously heightened by the raging controversy over the Education Bill. In this, the old nihilistic spirit of the 1843–1870 Nonconformist who deliberately preferred *no education* to the teaching of a rival dogma, is rampant. A powerful rump of L.C.C. Progressives imagine themselves to be in favour of education, with a big E, but at best it is only primary education of the most mechanical and uniform type that they

want to promote. Behind them, and working with them, are two other more sinister forces—the Labour men who want no money spent on secondary or university education, and the N.U.T. who want all appointments—secondary as well as elementary—to fall into the hands of the superior elementary school teachers.

Meanwhile, the Moderate Party has become even more stale than the Progressives. Beaten down and divided by their last crushing defeat, they no longer have any heart for their work of opposition. Moreover, there is nothing for the most moderate of the Moderates to oppose in the thoroughly businesslike cautious and economical ways of the Progressive administrators. Just as the Progressives have permeated the Moderates with all that was immediately practicable in their schemes, so the Moderates have permeated the Progressives and forced them to adopt economical and businesslike methods. This mutual permeation is exactly what is accomplished by the English system of committees, in which party cleavages are lost sight of, the actual outcome being always a compromise—in a good body the " better reason " of both parties. All this, from the point of view of efficiency, is very encouraging but, when both sides feel that they have got a good deal of what they wanted and have persuaded themselves to give up the remainder, the spirit both of reform and of criticism is apt to go dead.

Now it is a question which Sidney and I have been mooting between ourselves, whether out of these elements we can produce a new party— formally or informally held together by a broad catholic and progressive educational policy. The planks would be (1) fairness to the voluntary schools, complete freedom for them to teach their religious doctrine in their own way; (2) unsectarianism in the board schools— these latter constituting, broadly speaking, the supply for the Nonconformist and secularist children—and, as regards all kinds of elementary teaching, thorough efficiency in staff and structure; (3) development of secondary and technical education on the present lines of independent governing bodies aided and inspected by the L.C.C. and kept up to the mark on their educational side; but completely free to be as denominational or anti-denominational as the governing body chose. And, last but not least, a great London University— independent of L.C.C. but subsidised and influenced by it—not only a leading university organised on a democratic basis, but a great centre of the highest and most useful science, scholarship and metaphysics.

Meanwhile, our own little schemes have been submerged, even in our own minds, by the new ferment introduced by Chamberlain into imperial politics. Protection *versus* free trade is going to supersede all other political issues for many years to come. From the public point of view, we do not regret the advent of the new ferment. Here again controversies between parties had got stale. This issue at least will force people to think, will force them to consider new facts, and to apply new assumptions. The absurd notion that the " natural " channels of trade are necessarily the best will be quickly given up; the notion that " cheapness " is the only aim in a nation's commerce will also be demolished; the need for investigation and the desirability of deliberate collective regulation will be enormously advertised. All this is to the good and makes towards economic science, and, we think, collectivism of the best sort. To Joe's specific proposals—a tax on food and eventually " protection all round ", we are, as at present advised, opposed, as politically impracticable, unnecessarily costly to the consumer and likely to lead to international friction and internal uncertainty. We do not agree, however, with the extreme hostility to these proposals; our trade depends on quite other considerations than tariffs or no tariffs. But we think Chamberlain's aim, the Empire as a unit, could be better and more cheaply and conveniently attained by other devices. Sidney, at present, inclines towards bounties on colonial imports as a likely compromise between the British consumer, the British manufacturer and the colonial producer. Viewed from the standpoint of our own little projects, the diversion of public interest from the educational controversy to the tariffs is wholly to the good. It will require, however, careful steering to prevent the School of Economics from being indiscreetly identified with either side. Hewins, somewhat impetuously, has decided to throw in his weight with Chamberlain; this will mean that Sidney must be, as he fortunately is, against the new proposals. All he will do is to get the Fabian Society at work to prepare the ground for some intermediate plan combining imperialism with sound national economy.

Just before leaving London Sidney was appointed on the small expert Royal Commission to enquire into trade union law.[1] This was our friend Haldane's doing—made easy by Mr. Balfour's kindly view

[1] This small Royal Commission, presided over by Graham Murray, afterwards Lord Dunedin, proved a fiasco. The Parliamentary Committee of the Trades Union Congress, hurt at not having been invited to nominate one of themselves as a member of the Commission, and rightly regarding it as a political device for staving off a difficult problem, resolved to boycott it, and to prevent any trade unionist from giving evidence. This did not matter much, as the problem was dealt with entirely as one of law. As the Conservative Cabinet did not want any immediate decision, or indeed any report at all until after the general election, the Commission went to sleep for a couple of years, and eventually (in 1906) made a unanimous report, with a lengthy reservation signed by me only. The Liberal Government brought in a Bill on the lines of the report; but the trade unions had utilised the general election to get most of the M.P.'s to commit themselves simply to a reversal of the Taff Vale judgement, which the Government was compelled to adopt,—a too sweeping legalisation which led, in after years, to an inconvenient reaction. [S. W.]

of us. The job is eminently one for him to do, and will have the incidental advantage of bringing us again into communication with the trade union world. Sidney's relation with the Labour men of the L.C.C. having been strained by J. R. MacDonald's ill service, it is all the more necessary to be on good terms with other sections. The parliamentary committee of the Trades Union Congress has never forgiven us our scathing description of them and their doings in *Industrial Democracy*. With John Burns we are very friendly; but this is only because he is jealous of Macnamara and Crooks, and has an old grudge against MacDonald. Next spring we shall resume our intercourse with the Co-operators in preparation for an official history of the movement.

July 8th.—Fagged with combination of work and entertaining. Before the " Charlottenburg " scheme [1] was launched, we spent ourselves, money and energy, in tuning the press and trying to keep the Progressives straight. But, of course, they unconsciously resent having situations " prepared " out of which there is only one way—*i.e.* ours! But there is so little statesmanship in the party that it is only by an elaborate preparation of the ground that they can be induced to take up the right position. Latterly I have been sampling the Progressive members—they are not much to be proud of—a good deal of rotten stuff; the rest upright and reasonable but coarse-grained in intellect and character. Even the best of them are a good deal below the standard of our intimate associates—such as Hewins, Mackinder, Haldane, Russell, etc., and the ordinary Progressive member is either a bounder, a narrow-minded fanatic, or a mere piece of putty upon which any strong mind can make an impression, to be effaced by the next influence—or rather the texture is more like gutta-percha, because it bounds back to the old shapeless mass of prejudice directly you take

---

[1] S. W. writes (1937): What was called, for short, " Charlottenburg ", needs explanation. Haldane, in his enthusiasm for German scientific education, had been immensely impressed by the success of the great technical Hochschule at Charlottenburg, near Berlin, to which Great Britain had nothing similar. Meanwhile Sir Julius Wernher (of Wernher, Beit & Co.), a South African millionaire who had bought a large estate and settled in England, was prepared to give a large sum to promote technical education of the highest degree. Haldane induced the Government to hand over the Royal College of Science and the School of Mines; and the City Companies to transfer the City and Guilds Institute which they had founded at South Kensington, to form, with the half-a-million which Wernher was to contribute, what we called, in intimate discussion, " Charlottenburg " but which eventually became the Imperial Technical Institute, now a constituent college of the reformed London University. It was part of the scheme that the London County Council, through its Technical Education Board, should contribute £20,000 a year to create additional professorships and equip laboratories, etc. All this took years to arrange, including a lengthy enquiry by a Departmental Committee, on which I sat, before the various complications were smoothed out.

your will away. It is very tiring for poor Sidney and he comes back from the L.C.C. or T.E.B. meeting exhausted though usually victorious, always so when he has had time to prepare the ground—when he does this the enemy usually don't turn up or collapse immediately and his trouble seems thrown away.

Hewins has complicated matters of the L.C.C. and School by his vehement adhesion to Chamberlainism; not only " letting out " his authorship of the *Times* articles, but resigning sensationally from the National Liberal Club. Fortunately the articles have been ineffective —but the fact of his partisanship makes our position more difficult and has necessitated Sidney flying the free trade flag. He would have preferred to keep quiet and not to take part, but that is impossible in view of Hewins' and G. B. S.'s indiscretions. Meanwhile, we struggle on in a lame way every morning; for three days I have been off with strained eyes—strained not with work but with dissipation of strength at four dinners last week. My diet saves me from worse ills than mere fatigue. Unfortunately, I don't always stick to my regimen—specially when I am bored.

Went into dinner with Winston Churchill. First impression: restless—almost intolerably so, without capacity for sustained and unexciting labour—egotistical, bumptious, shallow-minded and reactionary, but with a certain personal magnetism, great pluck and some originality—not of intellect but of character. More of the American speculator than the English aristocrat. Talked exclusively about himself and his electioneering plans—wanted me to tell him of someone who would get up statistics for him. " I never do any brainwork that anyone else can do for me "—an axiom which shows organising but not thinking capacity. Replete with dodges for winning Oldham against the Labour and Liberal candidates. But I daresay he has a better side—which the ordinary cheap cynicism of his position and career covers up to a casual dinner acquaintance. Bound to be unpopular—too unpleasant a flavour with his restless, self-regarding personality, and lack of moral or intellectual refinement. His political tack is economy: the sort of essence of a moderate; he is at heart a little Englander. Looks to *haute finance* to keep the peace—for that reason objects to a self-contained Empire as he thinks it would destroy this cosmopolitan capitalism—the cosmopolitan financier being the professional peacemaker of the modern world, and to his mind the acme of civilisation. His bugbears are Labour, N.U.T. and expenditure on elementary education or on the social services. Defines the higher education as the opportunity for the " brainy man " to come to the top. No notion of scientific research, philosophy, literature or art: still less of religion. But his pluck, courage, resourcefulness and great tradition may carry him far unless he knocks himself to pieces like his father.[1]

July 24th.—One sometimes wonders whether all this manipulating activity is worth while: whether one would not do almost as much by cutting the whole business of human intercourse and devoting oneself to thinking and writing out one's thoughts. It would certainly be far pleasanter, because a far less complicated life, with fewer liabilities for contraventions against personal dignity, veracity and kindliness. It is so easy to maintain these qualities in a vacuum! In rubbing up against others, one's vanity, one's self-will and any strain of spite gets uncovered and revealed in all their ugliness to oneself, one's friends and one's opponents. But someone has to do this practical work: and possibly it is just as well that it should be done by those who have the other life to withdraw into, so as to keep up their standard of thought and feeling. That disgust with oneself which always follows a time of turmoil—the consciousness that one has lamentably fallen short in dignity, gentleness, consideration for other people's lives and feelings, and in transparent truthfulness, is a wholesome reminder of one's own radical shortcomings. If one frankly realises one's own moral incapacity during spells of activity, it makes one more careful not to admit unworthy desires and thoughts in the times of withdrawal from the world—and the whole level of one's mental life is raised and supported by the wholesome fear of the eternal fall of the man of action. From an intellectual standpoint it is good, too, because one is constantly testing one's hypotheses by the course of events; proving whether a given social process does, as a matter of fact, bring about a given social result. Nevertheless, it is with a sigh of relief that we look forward to some months of restful intellectual work before the hubbub of next spring, and if Sidney *is* turned out of London administration, the lot will bring its compensations. It would be a mental luxury to give the whole of our joint strength to the completion of our big task, especially if we felt that we had fought hard and were in no way responsible, by carelessness, for affairs taking the wrong turn—that we had not resigned the heavier and more disagreeable work but had been dismissed as " not wanted " by the people of London.

Our season ended with a brilliant little dinner here to meet Mr. Balfour. Naturally enough I talked almost exclusively at dinner to the guest of the evening. A man of extraordinary grace of mind and body —delighting in all that is beautiful and distinguished—music, literature, philosophy, religious feeling and moral disinterestedness—aloof from

---

[1] This hasty estimate was reconsidered when W. C. became a Cabinet Minister in the Liberal Government, 1906–15 in that administration he was one of the ablest and most progressive.

all the greed and grime of common human nature. But a strange paradox as Prime Minister of a great Empire! I doubt whether even foreign affairs interest him: for all economic and social questions, I gather, he has an utter loathing—whilst the machinery of administration would seem to him a disagreeable irrelevance. Not a strong intellect and deficient in knowledge; but I imagine ambitious in the sense that he feels that being Prime Minister completes the picture of the really charming man—gives tone to the last touch of colour—piquancy to his indifference as to whether he is in or out of office. I placed Charles Booth next him—I doubt from his manner whether he knew who Charles Booth was—wondered perhaps that a Salvationist should be so agreeably unsettled in his opinions! Bright talk with paradoxes and subtleties, sentiments and allusions, with the personal note emphasised, is what Mr. Balfour likes—and what I tried to give him! From 19th-century schools of philosophy to 18th-century street life, from university to tariff, from Meredith to G. B. S., we flashed assertions and rejoinders; and " Bernard Shaw, the finest man of letters of to-day ", was one of his dicta. But he did not read *Mrs. Warren's Profession*: " It is one of the unpleasant plays. I never read unpleasant things ", he added apologetically, and looked confirmed in his intention when I asserted that it was G. B. S.'s most " serious work ". " I am reading Haldane's *Pathway to Reality* and should like to answer it; but somehow or other I don't get any time for philosophy ", he added with a note of graceful surprise. " I had hoped that the tariffs issue would turn us out, but I am beginning to doubt it." Then I explained to him with much benignity the powerful forces of the cotton trade and the Co-operative Union which would, I thought, bring about his release from office. Haldane and he returned to the House soon after 10.0, and I had a pleasant chat with Sir J. Wolfe Barry—the engineer.

July 25th.—Sidney got through the £20,000 grant to the " Charlottenburg " scheme, having drafted a careful report. Of the leading Progressives, some really approved, others dare not refuse Rosebery—only eight of the rump actually went into the lobby against it. J. R. M. made long and virulent attack on Sidney. " Mr. Haldane and Mr. Sidney Webb had presented a pistol at the head of the Council." He was supported by the Labour men. The farce of Sidney not being the chairman of T.E.B., when every agenda or report is obviously drafted by him, is becoming glaring and will make J. R. M. more angry than ever. Massingham and Macnamara too are trying to work up opposition to him in London. But Macnamara, in laying down authoritatively the issues upon which the L.C.C. election next March is to be fought, has overshot himself and disinclined the Progressive leaders to follow him.

The I.L.P. is making the Liberals very angry: and in that direction J. R. M. will not increase his influence. Meanwhile, the Moderates show some signs of working to capture Sidney for their side; and the moderate Progressives are beginning to fear they may lose him and are inclined to be more on-coming. It looks as if the rump would try to turn him out of the party, the Moderates would try to claim him, and the centre Progressives make some sacrifices to keep him. So long as he keeps his temper and head, and goes on quietly asserting his own education policy, his position is a strong one. But it is clear that the next election will be a scrimmage and we may go under. What would suit us least well (assuming that Sidney keeps his seat) would be a large Nonconformist majority; what would suit us best would be either a small Moderate or small Progressive majority—perhaps the former best of all. At this juncture the Progressive forces are really against a constructive policy or a large expenditure on education—more particularly in that direction in which it is most needed—higher education. Class, sectarian and professional jealousy leads them to a desire to stint education. Labour, Nonconformity and the N.U.T. dislike the advent of the university professor as part of publicly maintained instruction.

Our general social policy is to construct a base to society in the form of a legally enforced " minimum standard of life ", and to develop all forms of shooting upwards—whether of individuals or of discoveries and refinements. Doubtful which party in the state will help us most; protection is all to the bad, so is Nonconformist fanaticism —that is to say the positive policy of both Chamberlain and Campbell-Bannerman is bad and retrograde: and they are equally indifferent if not hostile to our programme. We have, in fact, no party ties. It is open to us to use either or both parties.

August 26th.— . . . Meanwhile, we have been entertaining and being entertained. We cycled over to the Elchos and spent a couple of hours chatting with them and Mr. Balfour and a clever Cambridge doctor—the P.M. charming as usual, but absorbed in the state of the weather and the chance of getting his golf, also awaiting sadly the death of his great-uncle (the Marquess of Salisbury). Then the Playnes came for two days, and we took them to see the Ashbees at Campden and to a formal lunch at our neighbour's, Lord Redesdale, afterwards spending a tiring afternoon standing about in his pretty gardens of bamboos. A melancholy household—this handsome, vain and autocratic elderly gentleman absorbed in his hobbies and somewhat hazardous enterprises—his wife mad at intervals, and usually away, and a family of nine young people. The two elder girls simple, attractive, but living an isolated and useless life shut up in their great house and park, kept too short of money to see life as aristocrats, and too dignified to see it as ordinary folk. When we asked them to tea at the home of their own tenant, within half-a-mile of their gate, they thought it necessary to drive here—a carriage and pair with footman—keeping it for two hours awaiting them. And yet clearly not able to go up to London for more than a week in the year!

On Monday, Sidney and I went to dine and sleep at Bishops House, Worcester. Dr. Gore, a delightful-natured pious ecclesiastic—without guile, with extraordinary fervour and earnestness—a mystic, a reformer, a preacher—but with no natural turn for administration or Church politics. He is not a wholly satisfactory bishop in the ordinary English sense. Refuses utterly to take up his position as a social magnate: he has given up his palace (Hartlebury) and settled in a large plain villa on the outskirts of Worcester, where he lives, with three other priests, a life of austere work and fervent worship. We found him deeply depressed, hating the administrative drudgery of the Bishop's position, not caring for its dignity and feeling how hard it was to be a simple missionary when clothed in bishop's purple. Into this monk's abode Sidney and I broke for one long evening's talk about the Education Bill, and the position of the Church generally. It was a strange proceeding—we non-Christians talking with these " true men of God " as to possible co-operation between them and us in any reform of society. When we woke in the morning we heard mass being said in the room beneath us, and when we came down to breakfast three out of the four were robed sacerdotally. But they were eating a hearty breakfast, whereas I was fasting, and I amused myself by upsetting their consciences on the simple food question, and the desirability of living on six ounces a day. So, in spite of my heterodoxy, I left in an odour of personal abstemiousness akin to an odour of sanctity!

On our way home, we picked up Beatrice Chamberlain, who had come to discuss the question of London school management. In the afternoon, a party assembled itself in our little parlour for tea—Lady Elcho bringing Mrs. Pat Campbell (the actress), the Freeman-Mitford girls, the Ashbees—a gay and talkative affair developing an antagonism between the actress and the economists. This morning Beatrice and I wandered over Lord Redesdale's garden and during the walk she formally proposed that I should make the acquaintance of her stepmother—she would " bring her to call ", etc. Of course, I insisted that I should come some Thursday when she returned to London—which appeared to relieve the mind of my old friend of a difficult negotiation. The next day Lord Redesdale drove us over to see the Ashbees' works, and in the afternoon she left.

October 5th.—A refreshing holiday in Normandy and Brittany—lasting the best part of three weeks—first a week with the Bertrand Russells, and then two weeks alone together. The Russells we found settled in uncomfortable lodgings in a little Normandy village—riding and reading together but not serenely happy—a tragic austerity and effort in their relations. They are both so good in the best and most complete sense, Alys has so much charm and Bertrand so much intellect, that it is strange they cannot enjoy light-hearted happiness in each other's love and comradeship—but there is something that interferes, and friends can only look on with respect and admiration and silent concern. Perhaps, they will grow into a more joyful union; certainly, they have the big essential condition—a common faith so far as personal conduct is concerned.

We two thoroughly enjoyed our time—cycling abroad is a new discovery to us—sight-seeing completes each day, and alternating with lively exercise rests instead of tiring one. And here we are back in London and thoroughly fit for an autumn's work.

November 1st.—Haldane dined with us alone: gather that events are pointing (in that circle) to Asquith as Prime Minister with Rosebery serving under him as Foreign Secretary. Our friend was very vague as to politics. Not very definite as to the " Charlottenburg " scheme, which Professor Ramsay is crabbing in all directions, and the low state of South African finance making more difficult of attainment. Had secured young Lord Lytton to run about for him, and wanted us to come and meet him—but that proved impossible.

November 3rd.—Dined at the Asquiths'. Lord Hugh Cecil, the Lyttons, Sir A. Lyall and the Birrells—our host and hostess most gracious; Lord Hugh disappointing—a bigot even on fiscal questions, dominated entirely by a sort of deductive philosophy from *laisser-faire* principles held as theological dogma; the Lyttons a charming young couple with the delightful gracious deference of the well-bred aristocrat; Sir Alfred glowing, the Birrells somewhat hack diners out; but on the whole a pleasant party gratifying to one's social vanity. Margot (Mrs. Asquith) certainly has vitality and was full of fervour for the free-trade cause and scepticism of all other aspects of the progressive programme —told us plentiful gossip about " Arthur " and called all the élite of high political society by their Christian or pet names. It is a strange little *clique*—in which the bond of union is certainly not common conviction or desire for any kind of reform. (I fancy we are admitted to it—strange to say—not as reformers and experts, but as persons with a special kind of *chic*.) I suggested that why Chamberlain would make headway, in spite of his bad arguments, was because he had a vision;

desired to bring about a new state of affairs; and was working day and night for a cause—that no one else wished anything but a quiet life and the *status quo*. Whereupon Lord Hugh and Margot exclaimed, " Why change the present state of things—all was well ". Whereupon I burst out " That's all right for you, Lord Hugh—a convinced ultra-Tory—but is that a possible attitude for the leader of the Liberal Party who, one would think, was, or ought to be, ' professionally ' aware of the mass of misery, vice and distorted human nature of our present state of society? " But, conscious of the absurdity of indignation whilst eating and drinking at the Asquiths' table, I calmed down and tried to make up for my useless and somewhat self-righteous indignation. I suppose it is well to be on good terms with these people, but I come back from their society to our shabby little home and regular hard work with a deep sigh of gratitude that I am an outsider, and have not the time nor the energy to become one of them, even if they opened wide their doors. Probably the door is kept open because we do not try to enter in.

Alfred Cripps called in splendid form. Very discontented with the Archbishop's attitude towards Education Act. Gave him the names of the bitterest opponents of the Act on L.C.C.—the rotten part of the Progressive Party which would be best lopped off. Took care not to compromise Sidney.

Reading Gladstone's Life. Interesting to note that when, after ten years' political experience, he became convinced that the state had to be an infidel state, and could not be used to promote religious truth—he turned straight away into a *laisser-faire* democrat holding persistently to the policy of diminishing the function of government and doing nothing but what every individual consented to in advance. Hence, his doctrine of nationalities and, in the end, Irish Home Rule. Add to this genuine alteration of intellectual creed, the heady emotion of feeling himself in accord with crude democracy and, owing to his superlative talent as a revivalist preacher, leading it; and you have the Gladstone of 1869–80. After 1880, he was out of sympathy with the collectivist trend of the newer democracy of town workmen, and became a reactionary, appealing pathetically to the Nonconformist middle-class in terror of the new creed and hating the new apostles. His soul was wrapped up in his own principles—religious and economic—each set in a water-tight compartment; he never realised the new order of ideas. Moreover, he was socially an aristocrat and disliked the *parvenu* in riches and political power—such as Chamberlain.

Progressives gained considerably, as I predicted, at [November] borough council elections—which will perhaps wake up the Catholics and Church to action, and possibly lull the Progressives into confidence for L.C.C. election in March. We shall lie low and say nothing, and look after our own constituency. It is vital to London education that the Nonconformists should be chastened; if they come back triumphant, the outlook will be serious. At present, the L.C.C. Progressives feel confident that there will be no turnover, and the Nonconformists are playing their game with discretion.

November 18*th.*—A strange piece of luck! J. R. MacDonald knocked off the register [during his absence abroad] and thus disabled from standing for the L.C.C. at the next election—an iniquitous flaw in the law, but not for us an ill wind.

November 26*th.*—Bryan, the late Democratic candidate for the U.S.A. presidency, dined with us last night. A most attractive personality, a large bodied and large brained man, with great simplicity and directness of nature, a delightful temper and kindly attitude towards life. Knew nothing of administration and was, in all the range of political and social questions, dominated by abstractions—by words and not by things as they actually are. A Jeffersonian democrat like Altgeld. But shrewd in his estimate of men and women, and with a strong unselfconscious and vivid faculty of speech.

November 28*th.*—Kept my pledge against coffee and alcohol for the month—treated myself to a cup after lunch to-day, and retake the pledge for two months from this evening. I am better without either and, though coffee is a temptation, I have practically got over the worst part of giving it up and might as well stick to it. Have taken cream inadvertently two or three times in the month, but shall avoid it in future, without insisting on total abstinence. Should like to get into the habit of never taking a mouthful more after I feel that my hunger is satisfied. I have reduced myself as a rule to three cigarettes a day. Health better than ever before.

December 1*st.*—Mr. Arthur Acland has been in once or twice lately to talk over education with Sidney and to arrange for interviewing Austen Chamberlain and Morant. We got on to Rosebery—Acland not cordial to his leadership; intimated that he had been intolerable as head of the Cabinet 1894–5, shy, huffy and giving himself the airs of a little German king towards his Ministers. Had neither the equality of public-school Englishmen nor the courteous and punctilious formality of the well-trained *grand seigneur*, which is the best substitute for it. " He complained that his colleagues never came to see him, but when we did go he had hurried off to the Durdans or to Dalmeny. Then after a Cabinet he might ask one of us to come to lunch—but of course we had, as busy Ministers, already mapped out our day with deputations and parliamentary work. If we pleaded a previous engagement, he would seem offended." Then he gave us a vision of the strange weird ways which Rosebery indulged in at home —delighting in surrounding himself with some low fellows and being *camarades* with them—then suddenly requesting one of his free-thinking colleagues to go to church with him, or insisting that some elderly conventional guest should drive out at 10 o'clock at night for a couple of hours in an open victoria, with a postillion galloping at high speed through the night air. " Always posing," was Acland's summary, " imagining himself to be an extraordinary being with special privileges towards the world." It is odd how that impression exactly corresponds to my memory of him on board the *Russia*[1] thirty years ago, and with my estimate of his attitude towards us during the last four years. For instance—a very considerable amount of pose—fictitious senti-ment obviously a source of enjoyment to himself. He is certainly unique—whether for good or for evil—an asset or an incubus to the Progressive Party is a question.

December 6th.—Haldane looked in this afternoon to consult on University business. Reproached him half-seriously and half in chaff about Rosebery's attitude. " If Joe were to take up the notion of a national minimum of wages, health and education, and run it alongside of preferential duties or a protective tariff, you would be done, Mr. Haldane." " But *Joe* won't do that," he retorted with a self-complacent emphasis, " he would break up his party if he did." Obviously the Liberal leaders do not seriously want social reform, and would only take it up in a practical manner if they were forced to do so by com-petition. They are, in fact, relying on the stupid Conservatism which they profess to despise and to fight. And I fear our friends the " Limps " are in this respect the worst sinners. The others have some sort of hazy notion that, after pulling down existing structure, they would build up something in its stead on the basis of more equal distribution of wealth. We cannot join with them because we don't want to pull down the existing structure—all we want is slowly and quietly to transform and add to it. So that we remain isolated from all political parties, so far as party cries are concerned, though willing and eager to work with any party who are consciously or unconsciously engaged in constructive work. But it is unpleasant, this perpetual transit from camp to camp, however bitterly hostile these camps feel to one another. It is perilously near becoming both a spy and a traitor—or rather, being considered such by the camp to which we officially belong. No

[1] 1937: Father, Kate and I crossed the Atlantic with him on the *Russia*, Christmas, 1873, and he and I sat opposite each other on either side of the Captain.

wonder the Progressives are beginning to feel uncomfortably disposed towards Sidney!

December 18*th*.—Bertrand Russell published a short article, " The Free Man's Worship ", in the *Independent Review* which throws an illuminating light on his character and conduct. In it he adopts, as a starting point, the pessimistic hypothesis of the universe—that it is " blind, mechanical, cruel ", lower than man, that man alone has, by accident, attained to morality and intelligence (much the same hypothesis as that in Metchnikoff's *Nature of Man*). Upon this hypothesis he bases, by a process of reasoning which it is not easy to follow, a fine morality, tender towards others, stoical towards self— a morality devised to sustain us in this tragedy of life. The interest of the article does not lie in the fine passages on conduct but in his betrayal of the purely agnostic attitude, and his deliberate acceptance of an hypothesis which cannot be proved to be true by the scientific method. This course he has always declared to be immoral in cases in which the choice has fallen on the religious hypothesis—hence his indignation at William James's *Varieties of Religious Experience*, or at such Hegelians as McTaggart, Haldane, Schiller. I thought he held that, as pure reason and scientific verification could not be applied to anything but phenomena, it was a betrayal of the integrity of the intellect to accept *any explanation* of the universe as a whole. But it is clear that his personal bias towards the tragic in life has made him select and dogmatically affirm the most tragic of all the hypotheses of the nature of the great " unknown "—the one in which man poses as the supreme martyr of life—condemned to suffer until extinguished as an individual or a race. Realising this bias towards the tragic explanation of the universe, one feels less perturbed at what he conceives to be the concrete tragedy of his present life. Tragedy is a pose with him, and both the facts of the universe and the facts of matrimony must live up to it. As a matter of fact, his marriage is an amazingly fortunate one —but if the facts are not such as make up a tragedy so much the worse for the facts! Fortunately his splendid morality outweighs his tragic propensities and I doubt whether Alys realises that he thinks his married life an heroically lived tragedy.

The Nature of Man, by Metchnikoff—a book just now causing some sensation—is based on the same pessimistic hypothesis. But it is more practical in its deductions: which are to find out " the secret of physical health ", " longevity ", and " the desire for death, when death becomes inevitable ". And towards the solution he throws out a brilliant scientific hypothesis—that, owing to bad regimen, we never attain physiological old age but always die a violent death, eaten up prematurely by our own phagocytes; and, therefore, we object to and resist the process—exactly as a healthy-minded man usually does object to violent death. His moral is a simple life—above all things simple food and little of it. . . . I believe both in his account of what does happen, and his suggestion of what would happen if we lived the wisest kind of life. But he seems to me to transcend the sphere of the scientific method when he asserts that science alone will discover " the goal of human existence ". The book, of course, is rank materialism of the crudest sort, and Metchnikoff would have as little patience with Russell's " The Free Man's Worship " as he would have of Catholic Christianity. Indeed, he hints that the teaching of any *unverified knowledge* should be prohibited like the consumption of poisons. How far his own book with its daring excursions into the land of conjecture would survive the application of this principle is doubtful?

December 20th.—The effect created by the accession of Charles Booth to the protectionist ranks proves what power, nowadays, is wielded by a non-party expert who is free to throw himself on one side or the other, and who is widely known to be personally disinterested, if not, indeed, philanthropic in his ends. Intrinsically, I do not attach much importance to C. B.'s opinion on the fiscal question— he has no special knowledge, a great deal of prejudice, and by no means any marked capacity for intricate reasoning. But for the world at large his credentials are 17 volumes, a public life of 30 years' service, and a great expenditure of private means for public objects. A platform which even a more powerful politician might well envy. Such a position is the sort of thing I aim at for Sidney.

1904

In December 1903, the Other One published a handbook on *London Education* which was freely circulated to all whom it might concern. In its 200 pages, he foreshadowed the establishment of a systematically co-ordinated educational system from the infant school to the university, including polytechnics, research institutes and public libraries ; and he pleaded for a whole-hearted endeavour to bring this new national culture within the reach of every inhabitant of the metropolis. Here are a few extracts:

The new authority [the author declared] is called upon to endow London with a complete educational system. To give to each of London's 800,000 children during the years of compulsory school attendance the most effective physical, moral, and intellectual training; to develop in them the utmost mental acquisitiveness; to arouse in as many as possible of them the indefinable quality that we call resourcefulness, initiative, inventiveness, or the capacity for meeting new conditions by new devices; to provide for the whole of them the widest possible opportunities for continuing their studies after leaving the day school; to carry on, by a " capacity-catching " scholarship system, all whose brains make it profitable for the community to equip them with more advanced instruction; to organise, as well for these scholarship-holders as for all others able to benefit by it, an efficient and duly varied system of secondary and university education, whether predominantly literary, scientific, artistic, commercial, technological, or professional in type; to provide the best possible training for teachers of every kind and grade; and so to organise the whole machine, as, while increasing knowledge and efficiency, to promote everywhere the development of character and culture, and ultimately to encourage the highest scholarship and the most advanced research—all this, and nothing less than this, is the duty which Parliament has committed to the London County Council [pp. 10-11].

In a final chapter on " The Lion in the Path " he visualises the one big obstacle to the vigorous administration of the new service.

But it would be idle to ignore the fact that, at this juncture, there are forces at work which may make the carrying-out of any efficient policy absolutely impracticable. It is a peculiarity of educational politics that, in some countries, at some stages of their development, the clash of religious controversy rouses feelings of such intensity that the rival partisans would occasionally rather wreck the whole machine, waste all the millions of public money, and even let the little children suffer, than permit their respective adversaries to gain a seeming triumph. Keeping strictly to my standpoint as an administrator, I end this little book by a few words with regard to the fundamental conditions without which London can have no efficient administration in education or in any other public service.

The first condition of administrative efficiency is the loyal co-operation of the whole administrative machine, from the humblest official up to the directing committee, in carrying out the purpose for which it is framed, *and no other*. If we consider the extreme case of absolute refusal, on the part of a member of the civil service, to execute the policy laid down by his official superior, or his setting himself deliberately to thwart it, we see at once that such conduct makes impossible any sort of efficiency. What is not so clearly perceived is the disastrous effect which is produced on the whole administrative machine, when any part of it seeks, not to fulfil the purpose of its being, but to twist or contort the law in order to bring about some other result. This is true no less of the controlling and directing committee-men than of the officials who serve them. When the law seeks to effect one result and the administrator another, the whole service suffers. The knowledge of any such duality permeates to the minutest ramifications of the organisation. Every officer, however humble his sphere, feels himself entitled to interpret the law and the administrative policy according to his own predilections, it may be his own conscientious conviction as to what Parliament ought to have decided; it may be, on the other hand, the interpretation which he thinks likely to serve his personal interest. This anarchic influence will be intensified by the fact that the attempts made by this or that section of the administration to twist or evade the law cannot be openly avowed, and must remain (unless they pass into the phase of sheer rebellion, which is the negation of administration) in the plane of suggestion, favouritism, or intrigue. Nor is it only the majority in power, or their executive officers, who are demoralised. The members in a minority feel that, in addition to being outvoted at the polls, they are being outwitted in the committee room, and their resentment of this fraud adds acrimony to their enforced submission. They are tempted to adopt similarly illegitimate devices of covert obstruction, intrigue with officers of their own way of thinking, and illicit connivance with outside authorities. Thus, in such an atmosphere, whilst the salaried staff becomes honeycombed with suspicion, uncertainty, and disloyalty, the directing committee itself becomes the scene, not of honest working together and mutual enlightenment, but of " sharp practice " of one sort or another, mutual antagonism and a partisan favouritism in promotion which, in its destructive results on administrative efficiency, is nearly as bad as pecuniary corruption itself. The Lion in the Path of London education is this peril of administrative perversion [pp. 196-8].

I resume the diary extracts:

January 17th, 1904.—Seven letters he [S. W.] wrote yesterday to editors enclosing his book and turning their minds to an anti-Nonconformist movement—to end in a considerable reduction of the Progressive majority, if not in a Moderate victory. If he brings off his plan and becomes responsible for the administration of the Act, I shall get still less of his time and thought for the book. Fortunately, I keep splendidly fit and can work steadily every day—but I am deplorably slow in getting over the ground and have to be constantly stopping to call for clearer and more copious evidence.

Except for four dinners of the staff of the School of Economics with gatherings of the students afterwards, which I have arranged for February and March, I am keeping myself free from social engagements. It is not the time but the energy I lack—unless I deliberately abstract it from my work. In the afternoons I take exercise, ponder and read—about twice a week I walk along the Embankment to St. Paul's and listen to the anthem and join in the beautiful liturgy of the evening prayer. Sidney's news, letters and newspapers, an occasional friend or student to lunch, now and again a few friends to dinner, or a dinner out, are sufficient from the standpoint of the greatest output. How any sane mortal with resources of their own and a few intelligent friends can exert themselves to get into " society " passes my comprehension. And yet I have just expended 21 guineas on an evening dress! I hasten to add that it is four years since I paid the same amount for my present evening garment. Still I might have done without it—if I had been quite single-minded in my indifference to social glamour. The cold-drawn truth is that though I am honestly indifferent as to whether or not I see the great world, when I do enter it I like to do credit to my reputation—an unworthy desire I own—unworthy of an ascetic student and a collectivist reformer!

February 27*th.*—Sidney and [Robert] Phillimore returned unopposed for Deptford—a somewhat striking comment on the threats of last summer that " he shall lose his seat ". He is now turning his attention to getting G. B. S. in for St. Pancras. What effect G. B. S.'s brilliant slashing to the right and the left among his own nominal supporters will have, remains to be seen—the party organisers have long ago given up the seat as lost. Sidney has written to every clergyman in the St. Pancras constituency (about 21), sending them a copy of his book and imploring them to go hard for Shaw; he has even got the Bishop of Stepney's blessing sent to the Rural Dean. He has now taken charge of two-thirds of the constituency, installed the Spencers [our own secretaries] in a committee room, and called up the whole of the Fabian Society on Shaw's behalf. Whether this effort will win what would be a forlorn hope to any other Progressive candidate, and will counteract the enemies G. B. S. makes in our own ranks, we cannot tell. The Shaws have been good friends to us, and we would not like them to have a humiliating defeat. What that erratic genius will do, if he gets on the L.C.C., heaven will know some day—but I am inclined to think that in the main he will back up Sidney. And he will become the *enfant terrible* of the Progressive Party, and make Sidney look wisely conventional. In the Fabian Society, they have certainly managed to supplement each other in a curiously effective way—let us hope it will be the same on the L.C.C. But he is not likely to get in!

March 1st.—Dined with the Munro Fergusons one day, Haldane the next; little parties of " Limps ". There is a depression in those ranks; within the Liberal Party, the Campbell-Bannerman, [Lord] Spencer, Morley crew followed by Reid, Lloyd George, Macnamara, are in the ascendant and are asserting their right to make the future Cabinet, and include as much or as little of the Roseberyites as they choose. Specially against Haldane is there a set; Rosebery, also, is at a discount—a heavier discount than he has been since he came back to speech-making politics. Partly due to growing discredit of the results of the war (Chinese labour!), dislike for expenditure on the forces; partly to Rosebery's disclaimer of social reform and to the quite opposite reason—the rehabilitation of *laisser-faire* by the free trade propaganda. Little Englandism, crude democracy, economy, secularism, are all again to the front in the official Liberal Party—are, in fact, the only actively militant forces with a policy to push. The vacuum over which the " Limps " have zealously watched cannot be kept intact; and the old creed and the old cries are rushing in, in default of better stuff.

The success of Sidney in wheeling the Progressives round to promise the energetic and prompt administration of the Act has been enormously helped by the publication of his little book with its extensive and detailed constructive programme. It has made it quite impossible for anyone to fight him as an obstructive or reactionary as the C. B. Liberals are fighting Rosebery and Haldane. Whatever space there is in the mind of the enquirer for thoughts about London education, Sidney has filled it up—packed one proposal on the top of the other, till the question whether or not Anglican or Nonconformist Christianity is to be taught for a few hours every week in certain elementary schools seems of quite minor importance.

March 3rd.—As I sat at home this morning, working at the book (Sidney having gone up to G. B. S.'s committee room), three typical interruptions occurred. Gomme, the clerk of the L.C.C., came down in haste to consult Sidney on new information before the committee met this afternoon, as to exact wording of the reference to the education committee by the new L.C.C.; a messenger came with a note from the editor of the *Daily Mail* urgently begging Sidney to write the leader telling the citizens of London how to vote on Saturday; and Robert Harcourt broke in to beg Sidney's advice and help to stave off a Labour candidate against his brother in Rossendale—the latter an altogether mistaken estimate of our influence with Labour leaders! But the discreet guidance of important officials, and hidden influence in the press, are both characteristic of Sidney's peculiar gift for " getting his own way " without anyone quite realising how.

March 5th.—Sidney wrote a signed Progressive article for the *Daily Mail*—mildly and impartially Progressive, ending with a puff of G. B. S. Now off to work for a more than doubtful result.

March 7th.—G. B. S. beaten badly; elsewhere the Progressives romping back with practically undiminished numbers. As to the first event, we are not wholly grieved. G. B. S., with a small majority, might have been useful; with an overwhelming one, would simply have been compromising. He certainly showed himself hopelessly intractable during the election: refused to adopt any orthodox devices as to address and polling cards, inventing brilliant ones of his own; all quite unsuited to any constituency but Fabians or " Souls ". Insisted that he was an atheist; that, though a teetotaller, he would force every citizen to imbibe a quartern of rum to cure any tendency to intoxication; laughed at the Nonconformist conscience; chaffed the Catholics about transubstantiation; abused the Liberals, and contemptuously patronised the Conservatives—until nearly every section was equally disgruntled. His bad side is very prominent at an election—vanity and lack of reverence for knowledge or respect for other people's prejudices; even his good qualities—quixotic chivalry to his opponents and cold drawn truth, ruthlessly administered, to possible supporters, are magnificent but not war. Anyway, we did our best for him, Sidney even puffing him outrageously in the *Daily Mail*—and he and Charlotte are duly grateful. He will never be selected again by any constituency that any wire-puller thinks can be won.

As for the general result—it is perturbing. The Church and the Catholics have apparently exercised no kind of influence—those sent to Coventry by the ecclesiastics being apparently no whit the worse. The Moderates in many constituencies, deserted by the official Conservatives, have had to bear the full brunt of the Government's unpopularity—they come back as they went out, virtually powerless. Of course, the Progressives have vowed to administer the Act impartially —but if they do so they will show real statesmanship and patriotism. I confess to a lively admiration for the " junta " who have beaten us in our underground attack on the size of the Progressive majority. For, to be absolutely honest, it was only when he [S. W.] saw that the " game was up " that he slipped down in the columns of the *Daily Mail* (Sidney would say I exaggerate his disaffection) on the Progressive side. Now it is his turn to be a " good boy " and be content with what's given him!

Yesterday Morant came to dine, and he and Sidney are working to get the pedantic Anson to approve the scheme (for the L.C.C. Education Committee) so that the Council may get to work without any sense of obstruction from the Education Department. To rebellion in Wales and hostile administration in the West Riding, there is no reason to add a newly elected and overwhelmingly popular but recalcitrant London County Council. Moreover, co-opted members would be futile if forced on the present County Council.

March 11th.—To our delighted surprise the Progressives—so far as the leaders are concerned—have returned to Spring Gardens in admirable temper, they seem literally *chastened* by their prosperity. At the lengthy party committees that have been held prior to the party meeting to-day, they have welcomed Sidney back into their counsels with great cordiality—quite disposed now that they see that the party is safe and sound, to listen to his advice on educational matters. They have even gone the length of suggesting that he should be chairman of the education committee, though they realise the difficulties; but he has decidedly negatived that notion, if anyone else can be found who will take the job on and let him work under them. It would be adding insult to injury to appoint the executioner as executor or trustee of the dead man's property—an insult which might jeopardise the smooth working of the concern. But what is really surprising is the almost unanimity with which the party committee has decided *not* to make Lord Stanley an alderman, but only to offer him co-option on the committee as a late School Board member—an offer which we know he won't accept. As for Macnamara, there has not been a whisper of having him on in any capacity—not even as a co-opted member. Meanwhile, within the party committee there has been much more trouble on what seems to us to be the unimportant question—whether Cornwall or Benn should be chairman of the Council this year—a question which seems immaterial since the other will be chairman next year! But they are both candidates for London constituencies, and both want to run as " Chairman of the Council ". The Progressive Party would like to pass both over—but there is a strong feeling, which Sidney has always upheld—that they have both earned the right, by hard administration and party work, to sit in the chair.

Meanwhile, we have been pulling the strings to get the Government to sanction the scheme, and I think we have succeeded in overcoming Anson's pedantry—Haldane, Cripps, the Bishop of Stepney and the Archbishop of Canterbury have been moved to intervene. Altogether matters look far more promising than we could have hoped with a thumping Progressive majority—it really seems as if Sidney had converted his own party by his book, at the infinitesimal cost of not being chairman for the first year, or perhaps not at all—in many ways a positive advantage. Going to open an educationist address book of persons likely to be useful in that sphere. I must *organise* our contact with them—we must learn the facts ourselves and spread our own ideas.

March 19*th.*—The last week there have been continuous sittings of the selection committee of the L.C.C., comprised of the party committee of each side *plus* a few others—a committee nominally elected by the L.C.C. at its first sitting but practically selected previously by the party whips. This committee is like an American Congress committee in that it never meets except formally—the two halves of it, Progressive and Moderate, meeting separately to select their respective members to serve on all the Council's committees. Sidney describes the Progressive meetings as extraordinarily frank and friendly; the dozen select members canvassing, with perfect candour, the qualities of all the others and planting them out where they will do most good or least harm. Jephson, an old member of the School Board, and new member of the L.C.C., who had been put on the selection committee, told me that he had never heard such a barefaced " assessment " of colleagues, and was taken aback at the autocratic manner in which the party " cabinet " disposed of or dispensed with the services of their fellows. Sidney reports great friendliness towards him and anxiety to accept his suggestions as to the education committee—Wood and Dickinson especially being somewhat remorseful over making Collins chairman—a remorse which is strengthened by their jealousy, in the political sphere, of Sir William. But, assuming that the latter bears out his reputation of letting others do the work and taking all the credit, Sidney will think it an excellent bargain—for all he wants is to have an outlet for his thought and experience and policy in London education—and, if he can get this without creating jealousy and hostility, so much the pleasanter and more effectual. Moreover Collins, being an able man, with great weight on the Council—liking, moreover, ceremonial occasions, will really free Sidney from a good deal of work and leave him free to think out the detail of educational administration, or to get on with the book. The disadvantage is that in the next weeks of transition the chairman will almost necessarily have to decide things off-hand, without consultation, and it is not yet apparent whether Collins will be able and willing to make Sidney into a deputy or at least a confidential adviser in these crucial new departures. But looked at from the point of view of efficiency and consent . . . I doubt whether the party leaders could have handled the matter more wisely than they have done. They have secured Sidney's service without raising the hostility which his chairmanship would have caused among the rank and file. They have " placed him out " in the way in which he will do most good and least harm! Certainly McKinnon Wood has shown, within the sphere of municipal administration on party lines, real statesmanship, and the party have had the sense to follow his leadership both as to policy and as to persons. " After all, Webb," he said in soothing and confidential tones, " with the exception of the somewhat unimportant matter of the co-opted members, we have done exactly what you said we ought to do; which, considering the composition of the party and their temper last spring, is more than you were justified in expecting."

The truth is the Progressives have come back very pleased with themselves, having converted themselves in the course of their electioneering to the pose they took up, for the purposes of the election, of the plain man refusing to be moved by the clamour of Church or Chapel—the Turk guarding the Holy Sepulchre of the child's intellect. Moreover, the more they look at the Education Act the more they like it, and the less fault they are inclined to find in it even with regard to denominational teaching. So Sidney is back in their favour and they all turn to him to instruct them in their new duties; not caring to take their instructions from the members of the School Board. Nine of the leading men among them dined last night at Evan Spicer's to discuss a way out of the religious difficulty, and it is significant that none of the school board L.C.C. members were invited. " The truth is," said Cornwall, " I see no better solution than the *status quo*—we must keep some denominational schools as a safety valve, else there will be a perpetual struggle to get hold of the provided schools. So far as London is concerned it is a very good Act! " " Look at Webb smiling ", chaffed Williams Benn, the new chairman of the L.C.C. and a stalwart Nonconformist.

March 25th.—" The committee has gone adversely ", reported Sidney of the first meeting. Collins had insisted on Shepheard being elected vice-chairman, and had showed signs of letting everything slide, whilst keeping Sidney at arm's length. His old antagonism to Sidney, partly jealousy and partly real disagreement on university policy—a matter on which he has been beaten—is rising pretty obviously to the surface and may develop into a nasty business. Hitherto, however, Collins has never come into the open, we have heard rumours of his unfriendliness to the London School of Economics and to the lines of Sidney's educational policy, without this hostility bearing much fruit in positive opposition. What is, perhaps, more serious is his disinclination to grasp the matter himself, so that it is inevitable that the School Board members will, by their superior assiduity and knowledge, capture large parts of the organisation and keep on the old tradition. However, so long as the new committee keeps its reputation intact as a sane and efficient administrative body, and no retrogression about higher education takes place, we must be content to mark time until a more balanced Council gives the experts a chance. In watching a public body it is amusing to note that each success or failure brings about an almost immediate reaction—we are now suffering the reaction from excluding Lyulph Stanley and Stewart Headlam. Moreover, the rank and file of the Progressives, feeling themselves in the majority, but at the same time face to face with an extremely complicated business which they don't understand, are suffering from a fear of being " bossed ". At first it was Stanley, yesterday it was Webb, to-morrow it is as likely as not they will react against the School Board members. Middle-class demos is very sensitive as to its equality in capacity for administrative work, even compared with the most experienced expert. At the finance committee a few days ago, when Lord Welby (the chairman) turned to consult Sidney on an important item in the education estimates, the worthy but stupid Leon burst out into a hot protest. " The matter has not yet been discussed by the education committee, I don't see that Mr. Webb can have any opinion as to what should be done." But, as the question had to be settled, Lord Welby quietly accepted Sidney's proposals, and passed on to other business.

I tell Sidney he had better sit back in his chair and take it easy—he has changed the form of the authority and enormously extended its powers—the substance of its action had better remain as it is until a more seasonable time. Let Collins and Shepheard and the School Board men manage elementary education as they will—if they do it with efficiency so much the better, if they muddle it up there will come an inevitable reaction. Meanwhile, we can get on with the book, and he can keep an eye on university and secondary education. It will be as much as he can do to prevent a bad reaction in that quarter—and a possible withdrawal of the University grant or of the subsidy to the School.

April 15th.—Ten days at Felixstowe—and only one lazy one—Good Friday. For the first three, we worked hard finishing the chapters on *Nuisances*—the last five or six we spent on county, town and vestry records with the Spencers at Ipswich and Woodbridge—a happy and really restful time because it turned the current of Sidney's thoughts away from the little intrigues and jealousies of the L.C.C. and its education committee, on to the bigger currents of past developments in local government. We have quite settled to devote the next year and possibly three years to the book. Sidney to slack off the L.C.C.; I intend to take him off the scene early in July as it is clear that, so long as he is there, there is always a tendency on the part of officials and even on the part of the malcontents of the education committee, to make him do the work of drafting and negotiating. That won't suit our present book—in the metaphorical sense—and will not help to get the future book—in the real sense—finished. So I am considering Scotland and the possibility of a really long sojourn there with our material, and the Spencers looking up things for us in London. The next five weeks we shall devote to getting our material on municipal enterprise into order so as to see what we require for completion.

April 19th.—We have had a couple of days with H. G. Wells and his wife at Sandgate, and they are returning the visit here. We like him much—he is absolutely genuine and full of inventiveness—a " speculator " in ideas—somewhat of a gambler but perfectly aware that his hypotheses are not verified. In one sense, he is a romancer spoilt by romancing—but, in the present stage of sociology, he is useful to gradgrinds like ourselves in supplying us with loose generalisations which we can use as instruments of research. And we are useful to him in supplying an endless array of carefully sifted facts and broad administrative experience.

I asked him to tell me frankly why Wallas and some others were so intensely suspicious of us, and seemed bent on obstructing every proposal of Sidney's. He threw out two suggestions: first, that Sidney (and no doubt I) was too fond of " displaying " his capacity for " tactics ", that he gave a " foxy " impression—that he had better fall back on being an enthusiast; secondly, that we were always regarded as a " combination " working into each other's hands, but not impelled by *quite* the same motives, or inspired by quite the same purpose—that I was regarded as a " reactionary " with an anti-Radical creed, and it was suspected that Sidney would eventually veer round to my side.[1] Of course, we have got to be ourselves, whatever

---

[1] Here is a kindly characterisation of the Webbs and their methods by one of the most distinguished journalists of his time, A. G. Gardiner:

" Among the acolytes of the Fabian order there is a constant controversy as to which of the two is before or after the other. It is an idle theme, for you can never tell where one ends and the other begins—how much you are yielding to the eloquence of Mrs. Webb, and how much to the suggestion of Mr. Webb. It is she who weaves the spells, but he who forges the bolts. Between them they have an uncanny power of persuasion. Their knowledge overwhelms you, their sweet reasonableness disarms you. You are led captive in the chains of their silken logic, and they have the victories that fall to those whose knowledge is the instrument of relentless purpose, whose patience is inexhaustible and whose urbanity is never ruffled. . . . It is this sleuth-like pursuit of their purposes that makes them so powerful and so often distrusted. There is nothing that men dislike so much as being ' managed '. And Mr. and Mrs. Webb are always ' managing ' you. They sit behind the scenes, touching buttons, pulling wires, making the figures on the stage dance to their rhythms. To their modest table come the great and the powerful to learn their lessons, and to be coached up in their facts. Some fear to enter that

may be the drawbacks, but his criticism increased my inclination for a somewhat severe abstinence from trying to " run the show "—for a quiet and unselfconscious withdrawal into other work for the next three years. Directly the grant for the School is safe we will go into retreat with our papers and books until the October session.

April 20th.—For the Wellses we had a little dinner—carefully selected—Mr. Balfour, the Bishop of Stepney, the Bernard Shaws, Mrs. Reeves, and a Mr. Thesiger, a new L.C.C. Moderate. The P.M., finding himself in a little party of intimates (Thesiger was the only stranger), belonging to a strange world completely detached from party politics, let himself go, and, I think, thoroughly enjoyed the mixture of chaff and dialectic which flew from G. B. S. to Wells and round the table to Sidney, the Bishop of Stepney and myself. There is always method in our social adventures, and at my instigation Sidney, after we had left, backed up by the Bishop and Wells and Shaw, gave an elaborate argument in favour of our half-time scheme for boys.[1] As I had told Mr. Balfour that the grand distinction between him and the Liberal leaders was that his attitude towards proposals of social reform could be expressed by " Why not? " and theirs by a grudging " Why? " he felt bound to be sympathetic and was, I think, somewhat taken with the notion. He is honestly concerned about the alleged degeneracy of the race, and inclines to, at any rate, " flirt " with new proposals. And in these days, when the mind of every Liberal leader is as closed as a live oyster, one must be grateful for small mercies.

May, Bramdean.—In the life of a little village one notes how far happier and more dignified is the existence of the hard-working daughter of the middle-class farmer or shopkeeper than that of the rich young woman who drifts through life in the big upper middle-class houses dotted about the country. There are seven Miss Legges—in the big house next door—there are five Meinertzhagens at Brockwood—

parlour of incantations, and watch the Webbs with unsleeping hostility. A mere suspicion that they are prompting behind the curtain is enough to make them damn the most perfect play " (*Pillars of Society*, by A. G. Gardiner, pp. 204-6).

[1] In our *Industrial Democracy*, 1897 (vol. ii. p. 769), we had suggested that (instead of pleading for an extension for one or two years of the compulsory attendance at the elementary school, at that time ending, as regards some occupations, at 10 years of age) there should be demanded universal compulsory, all-round training, including physical and technological, for both boys and girls up to 18 years of age, but only half time, either by alternate days or half-days, or by alternate seasons. It could be assumed, we urged, that such a halving of the supply of labour between 10 and 18 would lead to an increase in the hourly rate of wages which would render unnecessary any but a tiny scholarship in partial maintenance. We had discovered such an idea in the apprenticeship laws of certain Swiss Cantons; and it had somehow (!) found its way into the Report of the Trade Union Minority of the Royal Commission on Labour, C. 7421, 1894.

there are countless young ladies all " awaiting " with more or less self-possession the lot of the marriage market, or a useless old-maidenhood. Compare these listless young persons to pretty energetic Dolly Hawkins who " runs " our little lodgings, helps her father the post-master, and thoroughly enjoys her casual flirtations, restricted to her few spare hours or afternoons. The cottager lives at too low a level of health and intelligence—the men are brutalised, the women prematurely old; but the respectable and successful lower middle-class country-bred person now combines physical comfort, personal freedom and a considerable education, and stimulus to activity—a rising standard of ease and comfort, but not too high for efficiency. . . .

In the middle of our stay we ran up to London to take the Joseph Fels' to the University reception to the foreign academies—for once breaking our rigid rule of refusing to appear at evening parties. One reason for so doing was the desire to be polite to the Fels'. Dowdy little Americans to look at—he a decidedly vulgar little Jew with much push, little else on the surface, she a really refined and intellectual and public-spirited little body who, by mere force of character, has dragged her husband and his partner into the Fabian Society and other advanced movements. The partner, Coates, who lives with them, is a mild-mannered and dowdy Yorkshireman—a refined and gentle-spirited young clerk who has been made by Fels a partner in his concern—the concern being *Fels Naptha Soap*. Perhaps, after all, it was to the soap that we gave the dinner? Certainly, if it could have been demonstrated to us that the soap was a lie that would be found out—that dinner would not have been given. But a subscription of £100 to the Fabian Society and the report of golden soap-suds, set us thinking of the Fels' as possible founders, yet uncaptured; while the lunch made us take a genuine fancy to her, and not finding him repulsive, so we speculated an evening on them—more than that, a journey up to London!

I note a certain change in our surroundings. Some of our old comrades of ten or even eight years ago have become indifferent or even hostile to our ideas. . . . On the other hand, there is a new group of friendly young men disposed to take our views seriously—Masterman, Morgan, Ensor, Bray, Isaac Mitchell, T. E. Harvey, Basil Williams, Bron Herbert, and with a certain reservation, George Trevelyan, are all anxious to see more of us. What is, perhaps, a less wholesome sign is the accession of " society " folk—the Hubert Parrys, Batterseas, Elchos, Lyttons, [Munro] Fergusons, Monteagles, Alfred Lytteltons, Asquiths, Thesigers, Stamfords, Sydney Buxtons, Bryces and Gorst, have been added to those who ask and are asked to dinner—but all of these have a certain usefulness. Some new *friends* we have made within the same period—H. G. Wells the foremost, and the George Protheros; H. J. Mackinder is a new colleague and then there are the outer circle of senators, L.C.C., and school lecturers, and educational administrators, and bishops and distinguished foreigners. On the whole, it is an extraordinarily varied and stimulating society. The dominant note in our intercourse with these people is *social reconstruction*—in all the little dinners at Grosvenor Road and the *tête-à-tête* talk at other people's dinners—it is always round some project that the conversation ranges. What is utterly lacking is art, literature for its own sake, and music—whilst physical science only creeps up as analogous and illustrative matter; history appears in much the same aspect. The relation of man's mind to the universe is constantly present as a background in my own thought and with some of our more intimate acquaintances—with T. E. Harvey, Masterman, Haldane, Russell— I have long talks; but the subject bores Sidney as leading nowhere and as not capable of what he considers valid discussion—exactly as he dislikes discussing what train you will go by, before he has got hold of the Bradshaw. He prefers reading a statistical abstract, or an L.C.C. agenda. His relation to the universe—in the spiritual sense, he mockingly suggests, consists in his relation to me!

June 8th.—Turned from roads to help Sidney to write an article on *The Policy of a National Minimum*. Before we left London we had a little series of young progressives to discuss the possibility of pushing the policy of creating an artificial bottom to society by collective regulation and collective expenditure—" canalising " the forces of competition so that all the individuals in the community should be pressed upwards not cast downwards. The upshot of this was that we had an urgent request for an article to embody our doctrine—five thousand words, necessarily topical, are a poor medium; we were tired and disinclined to turn from our own proper business, but we felt obliged to accept. I thought it better for Sidney to sign the article singly—the double signature overloads so slight a thing, and it is too political in its tone to warrant the intervention of the female partner. I believe in mere " wife's politics "—only in research do I claim equality of recognition!

June 17th.—We lunched yesterday with the Chamberlains—to introduce the Irvines—others there were the Bonar Laws and a certain Sweet-Escott, Governor of British Honduras. I sat on one side of my old friend and we talked without constraint. He is obsessed with the fiscal question—has lost his judgement over it—refuses to think or talk of anything else. He looks desperately unhealthy, rather thin too; a restless look in his eyes, bad colour, and general aspect of " falling in ". But I should imagine that there is plenty of force in the man yet; an almost mechanically savage persistence in steaming ahead. I tried to suggest the " national minimum " as a complementary policy to import duties. " I have no prejudice against it," he answered, " but it would not do for me to suggest it—it would be said that I was trying to bribe the working-class. But there is no reason why it should not be added on by someone else." Then we drifted on to the Education Acts 1902 and 1903, which he clearly does *not* favour—he is afraid of the advent of the bureaucrat. The trail of the profit-maker in industry is in everything that Chamberlain proposes or opposes—he detests the salaried expert. Like many others who share this dislike he tries to ignore the inevitability of the officials' (salaried administrators) government of society, instead of devising safeguards against the evils of it. " If I had been Prime Minister, you would not have had the Education Act." " The one and only reason for my not regretting that you are *not* Prime Minister ", I answered pleasantly; and we passed on to other things. Sidney says that after the ladies left, Chamberlain urged on Irvine almost passionately the need for preferential tariffs (S. W. devoting himself to Sweet-Escott, as it was clear that Chamberlain wanted to talk confidentially to Irvine. Bonar Law had left). Upstairs, we four ladies had conversation—gossip about Rosebery and the Liberal Cabinet—and discussing the relative merits of Protestantism and Catholicism. I like Mrs. Chamberlain; there is a lot of sincerity and simple feeling in her face—a somewhat pathetic expression, as if life were too much for her, though she obviously enjoys, to its full, the social side of the position. I imagine she worships her great man. But there must be times when the great personage with his irritability, one-sidedness, pitiful unhealthiness and egotism and vulgarity, is rather a heavy handful for that refined and charming little lady.

All goes well with the L.C.C. and the education committee. First-rate officials are being selected, the routine administration is being digested and the plain man is learning his lesson. Sidney finds himself on agreeable terms with all parties: the School Board women being apparently the only persons who bear him a grudge. I have been somewhat assiduous in my cultivation of the Progressives—successfully, so I think; and, by leaving London at the end of June, we have at least convinced them that Sidney does not want to run the show. Antagonisms are being developed between some of the members, but Sidney has kept well outside them. He has been re-elected on the party committee, the grant to the University and the School went through without a word, and some of the leading Progressives have signified that they think he has acted " nobly " in subordinating his claims to the chairmanship of the education committee. He has given the impression that he really does not care for the distinctions of office, and as we have other work which we actually prefer doing, we are glad enough that he should be absolved from close attendance. So we go off to Scotland with our books and our papers for our three months' recess, with a good conscience and good hope.

June 20th.—Sidney's influence on the joint-life is wholesome in curbing my lower desires. There have been three separate entertainments that I should like to have gone to—Lady Wimborne's, Mr. Balfour's and the Duchess of Sutherland's evening parties. Feeling secure in the possession of an attractive garment I should have liked to have paraded myself. But S. was obdurate. " You won't be able to work the next morning, and I don't think it is desirable that we should be seen in the houses of great people. Know them privately if you like, but don't go to their miscellaneous gatherings. If you do, it will be said of us as it is of Sir Gilbert Parker—in the dead silence of the night you hear a distant but monotonous sound—Sir Gilbert Parker climbing, climbing, climbing." And I recognised the better voice and tore up the cards.

The last weeks Sidney's days have been over-filled with committees and the work arising from them. Yesterday, for instance, 8.45–11.0, drafting a report for the chairman of one of the sub-committees of the education committee of the L.C.C.; 11 o'clock Royal Commission on Trade Disputes; 12.30 sub-committee at School Board offices; 1.30 took train to South Kensington, lunching in the train, for 2 o'clock Departmental Committee on Royal College of Science; 4.30 took the chair at the London School of Economics at meeting of railway magnates to decide on railway department (secured £1000 a year to start department); 6 o'clock arrived late at higher education committee at School Board office and transacted, as chairman, remainder of business; 8 o'clock dinner here—Bernard Shaws, Jack Tennants, John Burns, Munro Fergusons and Stephen Hobhouse; after dinner group of young Progressives to be introduced to John Burns and G. B. S.; to bed 12 o'clock; began work again at book at 8.45. Very naturally there is not much brain left for the book, and until we get right away from London we shall only muddle on. But muddling on is better than leaving off; the stuff one gets on to the paper contains the necessary quotations and gives one something to bite.

October 16th.—The three months in Scotland were so completely a joint existence that there was neither the desire nor the opportunity to record it in this book. When Sidney is with me I cannot talk to the other self with whom I commune when I am alone—" it " ceases to be present and only reappears when he becomes absent. Then the old self, who knew me and whom I have known for that long period before Sidney entered into my life—who seems to be that which is *permanent* in me—sits again in the judgement seat and listens to the tale of the hours and days, acts, thoughts and feelings, which the earthly one has experienced.

Beautiful and peaceful have been the scenes of our long working holiday—especially enchanting the hill-side of Fyrish, with heather and fir-clad mountains rising up behind us, and Cromarty Firth and the North Sea rolled out beneath us; the " Golden Gate ", as we called the North and South Suters, will remain in my memory as one of the most beautiful expanses of water, land and sky. Especially beautiful the week before we left when the sun rose midway between the two promontories, right out of the ocean, its rays lighting up, one by one, each feature of the Firth until the whole landscape of cornfields, heather and rich foliage was one soft glow of gold, brown and green.

Except for four days' cycling on the West Coast and the two days broken by our change of quarters at the end of July (from Nethy Bridge near Grantown, to Fyrish near Evanton), we worked steadily six days out of seven at the book, for the four morning hours—spending the afternoons in reading and exercise. Once a week we would take a Sabbath and go some thirty miles to see friends or explore the mountains of the Black Isle. Excellent health, and greater bodily and mental vigour than I have ever known before, made me feel as if I were still in the very prime of life, and Sidney too seemed unreservedly happy. We saw a good deal of neighbours; made friends with the elementary teachers and ministers in both places, and at Fyrish had, as agreeable acquaintances, the mother and daughter of the Laird of Novar— Munro Ferguson.

We made some superficial and scattered observations on Scottish education and social life, but I doubt whether they are worth recording. I brooded, in lonely walks, over the book, or over the new philosophy which is gradually taking shape in my mind; or praised the unknown for our exceeding happiness; or prayed for strength to be abstemious, persistent in work, and clear-sighted and constantly kind to others. But I was working so hard at technical detail (roads, pavement and cleansing) that I had little strength left over for other reading or writing, and was glad to let myself be absorbed in the mere enjoyment of light, air and colour.

November 8th.—Sidney has been busy drafting his *scholarship scheme* and getting it accepted by his higher education committee. He has found his Progressive colleagues in a most kindly humour. Cornwall thanked him the other day for his self-abnegation—intimating that the junta recognised his delicacy in so retiring from view that it could not be said that he was " running them " and practically asking him to continue the same policy for a little longer, and then all would be well. And the policy has at least the advantage of enabling him to spend half his time in reading at the British Museum—all to the good of the book.

We spent last Sunday at the Sydney Buxtons with Haldane and the Birrells—endless discussions as to the future of the Liberal Party. It is clear that they are unrepentant in their determination to run into place on the old lines of economy and freedom of trade, and anti-priest bias— they refuse even to contemplate any other policy—dismiss all social reform from their minds except, perhaps, a revision of the incidence of taxation in favour of the small consumer.

They are not optimistic—look forward to a bare majority over the Irish and a tenure of one or two years—" let us get a front bench " is their cry. Haldane told us as we drove to the station early on Monday morning, that there had been a move to exclude the " Limps " last spring, but that it had collapsed and the dominant note now was a Cabinet of all sections.

December 6th.—We stayed Saturday and Sunday with the Thesigers, an attractive young couple, he a son of the General, Lord Chelmsford, and she a daughter of Lord Wimborne, both tall and pleasant to look at, intelligent, public-spirited, and versed in all the little amenities of hospitality and conversation. He is a leading Moderate on the L.C.C., also a member of the Dorset County Council; together they run the church, the school, the library, the glee-club, of their hamlet—all activities which militate against his getting on over much at the Bar. Indeed, it is this willingness to spend themselves on social service, this apparent absence of political, professional or social ambition, which lends a peculiar attractiveness to the *ménage*, in spite of a lack of any special distinction in the way of forceful administrative capacity or intellectual curiosity or subtlety. Our fellow-guests were Professor Ker—professor of English and English literature at University College, and a young Cecil [1]—a son of Lord Eustace Cecil. The former was distinctly of the *owl* type—his qualifications to teach the higher forms of his own language judged by his own conversational powers were not considerable. He was mostly silent, when he did speak one barely understood him; sometimes there seemed to glimmer through his badly chosen words and awkward sentences a sort of pawky Scotch humour, but one had to puzzle it out. Sidney says that on the Senate he never gets his proposals carried from lack of power of lucid or even correct expression. Imagine a university professor of French in Paris being

[1] Note, 1936.—Algernon Cecil; he joined the Roman Catholic Church some years afterwards.

remarkable for an utter absence of the power to talk good French![1]
Young Cecil was interesting because he was able to describe or imply
the Cecil philosophy of life. For him society was cloven in two—the
Church and the world. The Church was governed by spiritual illumination; the world outside of this radius was exclusively dominated by
the motive of pecuniary self-interest. To attempt to run the secular
world on any other motive was not only contrary to the commandment
" Give unto Caesar the things which are Caesar's " but was almost
blasphemy. All real progress was confined to *progress of the individual
soul under the influence of the Church.* Any increase of honesty or
kindliness, of honour, public spirit or truth-seeking brought about
otherwise, was merely a higher stage of self-interest (equally damnable
as the lower stages)—merely the discovery by each individual that those
qualities paid better. Accompanying, and to some extent coinciding
with this cleavage, was that between the hereditary and landed aristocracy represented by the Cecils, and " the others ". The Cecils
governed by spiritual illumination (inherited through a long line of
noble ancestors) were to direct the policy of the state, making use of
the lower motives of vulgar folk to keep the state going on its material
side. The odd part of the whole scheme was the almost fanatical objection to any attempt to alter the motives of human nature, otherwise
than by the action of the Church on the individual soul—and a
complete complacency with the one secular motive of enlightened self-
interest as the basis of everyday life. It was almost as wicked to tamper
with this motive by introducing other considerations into the industrial
or political organisation of the state, as it was to introduce the pecuniary
motive into the Church—as for instance in the sale of indulgences or
simony. Altogether I began to see the current Radical objection to the
Toryism of the Cecil type. The boy himself was both pure in heart
and intellectual in tastes, and with that delightful modesty of manner
and easy deference which robbed the creed of any *appearance* of class
insolence or religious intolerance. He was suffering from an extremity
of bad health—appendicitis and its results—and was quite obviously
being villainously treated on the physic and " much food " plan of the
ordinary doctor. I did my best to upset both his philosophy and his
régime by a combination of serious discussion and rap-dazzle repartee

---

[1] Later I realised that this hasty and superficial impression did injustice to a fine
intellect, the master of massive erudition in fields of which I knew nothing. Walter
Paton Ker (1855–1923) held the Chair at University College, London, in
English Language and Literature, and published many learned books and articles
on the mediaeval literature of England, which had a great reputation. He was a shy
and unassuming, but very kindly teacher; and I have been told that, with intimate
friends, he was witty as well as wise. He was elected a Fellow of the British Academy
in 1903.

—but I doubt success in either direction—the philosophy and the regimen were both too congenial to the fastidious and subtle self-indulgence of his temperament to be undermined in 48 hours by an elderly free-thinking woman. If the creed and the regimen remain unqualified he will be a waste product in society—interesting only as an obsolete type.

December 22nd.—An outburst of jealousy among the leading Progressives at the scholarship scheme, which has attracted much attention and is almost universally praised. Collins, Cornwall and Dickinson have not been making much of a success of their special functions—getting a good deal of odium for sins of commission and omission from Nonconformists and Church alike—Sidney on their instructions lying low. Then out he comes as chairman of the higher education committee with his great scholarship scheme carefully thought out in detail, with arguments showing that it is inevitable. They don't like to oppose it because the need for more teachers is urgent and the trend of opinion all in favour of increased facilities for the lower middle-class—they can't object to the detailed proposals because they don't know sufficient to suggest others to take their place—but it is offending the N.U.T., backing up the secondary schools, and spending the rates. Moreover, as Collins naïvely remarked to the Council, " If it is a success, the credit will be Mr. Webb's "—he said it in a complimentary tone but it was clearly an uncomfortable thought. However, though it is adjourned, Sidney thinks it is certain to go through because of the general outside approval, and because they cannot suggest an alternative. But he was a wee bit hurt at the lack of frankness and generosity on the part of the governing *clique.* I have given up trying to propitiate them as I don't find my cordiality makes any difference to their jealousy of Sidney's influence with the press and the powers that be. I tell him that he must put up with the defects of his qualities: if he goes in for hidden influence he must expect hidden obstruction. It is worth while " preparing positions " so as to carry measures one believes in—if one's talent lies in that direction one *ought* to do it. But very naturally the persons who find themselves in these prepared positions—unable to get out except through his way—naturally do not like it, and try to make the way as unpleasant as they can for him personally. Our amazing good fortune and perpetual happiness an ample reward for these vexations.

Kate Courtney remarked the other day that she always wondered, in reading the published diaries or confidential writing of private persons, why they seemed so little concerned with the great question of peace and war—so infinitely more important than their own little doings or narrow range of interests, solemnly recorded in their diaries.

And I bethought me that there is hardly a reference to the Russia-Japanese war in these pages. The answer I gave on the spur of the moment, is, I think, the true one: "The private person *has* no specialist knowledge, no particular or exceptional experience as to world politics—his thoughts and feelings would be a mere reflection of his morning newspapers and worthless both to him and to those who might some day read the story of his life". And yet, if one looks back on the past year and thinks how much one has brooded over the Far-Eastern drama—how eagerly one has read each morning's news and how one has stumbled into foreshadowing the effect of the "Rising Sun" on our Western civilisation—it is hardly fair to leave it wholly unnoticed. For instance, I watch in myself and others a growing national shamefacedness at the superiority of the Japanese over our noble selves in capacity, courage, self-control, in benevolence as well as in all that makes up good manners! They shame our Christianity, they shame our administrative capacity, they shame our inventiveness, they shame our leadership, and alas! they shame our "average sensual man". Perhaps, it makes the matter worse that they have won not by the genius of one man—which might be an accident not likely to recur again—but on the intellectual, physical and moral qualities of the whole people. They seem both more scientific and more religious than ourselves—a nobler purpose and more ably contrived processes wherewith to carry out this purpose. Their success will alter not merely the balance of power, but the balance of ideas—it will tell against Christianity as the one religion, against materialistic individualism, against autocracy, against luxury, in favour of organisation, collective regulation, scientific education, physical and mental training—but on the whole *not* in favour of democracy. They have suddenly raised the standard of international efficiency—exactly in those departments of life where we Western nations imagined ourselves supremely superior to the Eastern races. How far this shock to self-esteem will go in English society—how far it will be neutralised by the vulgar delight of seeing our ally beat our enemy—remains to be seen. But, for many a long day, the reformer will be able to quote on his side the innovating collectivism of the Japanese; the idealist, the self-abnegation of all classes of the community in a common cause. Even in one's own daily life, one is inclined towards greater persistency and more self-sacrifice. So closes 1904 and this book of the diaries.

1905

January 21*st.*—The main excitement [I write on January 21, 1905] is watching events in Russia—likely to prove the essential need for *consent* as an element in stable government. Japan is proving the superlative advantage of scientific methods in the international struggle for existence. How to combine the maximum of consent with the highest degree of efficiency is the problem before us in England: the average sensual man not wanting to be improved!

February 8th.—Dickinson, who is now trying to boss the Council's policy in *elementary* education, told Sidney quite frankly that he intended to get by *administration* what he despaired of getting by an amendment of the Act—I suppose the extinction of denominational schools through a combined policy of impossible requirements and starvation. He very naïvely added that he could not take Sidney into his confidence since he might use the knowledge to thwart him—a declaration which absolves Sidney from loyalty to the party counsels. They were most friendly with each other, but it was clear that Dickinson had got the governing *clique* to back him up and was going to keep Sidney at arm's length. However, in regard to secondary and university education, they are letting Sidney have his own way, and he is preparing some interesting situations for them to wake up to presently. The ratepayer, too, will have something to say to a policy of supersession. I have confidence that Dickinson will turn out too stupid—will fail to bring about a reaction. But it all means lack of efficiency—mutual obstruction instead of co-operation.

We have Sir Oliver Lodge staying here for two or three days. A delightful personality—large and fresh in his thought and feeling, but suffering from a bad fit of intellectual dissipation after a long life of specialism, made more acute by introduction to the Balfour-Elcho-Wyndham set—a fascinating temptation to an attractive person condemned to live in a provincial town. He is another instance of the fallacy that physical science is an outfit for the psychological and social sciences. It never occurs to us economists and political science students to imagine that our long-standing study of the complicated structure and function of society fits us to be astronomers or physicists—but the physical science man plunges head foremost into the discussion of our questions, armed with the four rules of arithmetic and the instruments of a laboratory.

For his entertainment we had a little party consisting of the Bertrand Russells, Granville-Barkers (the intellectual actor), Mackinder, Lion Phillimore, Wernher (Wernher & Beit) and Balfour. I begged the P.M. to talk to Bertrand and placed them next each other, and they got on famously—I sacrificed myself during some part of dinner to the millionaire (who is endowing London University); Lodge, Granville-Barker, Sidney and the two charming ladies kept up a lively talk at the other end. There was a subtle antipathy of Balfour to Mackinder

and Wernher—mere philistine materialist administrators he would feel
—there was sympathy between him and Russell and Barker, and of
course he and Lodge are affectionate friends and fellow synthetic
philosophers. Lodge got on with all the company—Mackinder and
Wernher chummed up and walked away together—the intellectual
young actor wrote me enthusiastically that he had walked home with
the great man. Mr. Balfour likes both the Webbs—that is clear—
finds them stimulating and attractive. To-day I took our guest to
lunch with the Courtneys—to meet John Morley, the Spenders,
George Trevelyan, etc. John Morley eyed me suspiciously, but insisted on listening to my lively talk to Spender.

February 29*th*.—Sidney gleeful as to the acceptance of his scholarship scheme—the only piece of constructive work done as yet by the
education committee of the L.C.C. Without in the least being aware
of it, the dear Progressives have let themselves in for supporting all
the existing secondary schools (under separate management, and some,
decidedly, and nearly all, theoretically, denominational) and for providing others under the direct management of the L.C.C. And the
amusing part of it is that those who, like Graham [Wallas], object to
the existing schools, will push all they know how, to get L.C.C.
secondary schools started, whereas timid Progressives, like Torrance
and the party leaders, who don't like to run up the rates for higher
education, will find themselves forced to defend the denominational
schools as the cheapest way out of the dilemma. " I can now leave the
two forms of obstruction to fight it out," chuckles Sidney, " they will
both be pushing on the machine in the direction that I want it to go."
The scholarship scheme is, in fact, going to dominate the whole policy
of the committee. Meanwhile, the five big officials have coalesced
satisfactorily and are constantly coming to Sidney for advice. So that he
really loses very little by not being chairman, and escapes both the odium
and the responsibility. " The glory of it " he is quite content to leave
to others! If the Progressives had dared to do it, they would really have
been able to control him better by placing him in the chairmanship
and then forcing him to accept the whole responsibility. And, of course,
the administration would have been more efficient and more economical. But in view of the violent suspicion of the Nonconformists
and the N.U.T., that was politically impossible.

March 5*th*.—The Wallases and Bray came to dine last night, and
the three men sat for two hours discussing education policy, whilst I
listened dreamily to Audrey's gentle chatter in the drawing-room.
Sidney and Bray tried to get Graham to enter into a *concordat*—
Sidney prepared to back him up with regard to the elementary education

if he, Wallas, would back Sidney up in secondary and university matters. But Graham will not budge from his principle of starving out the secondary schools under separate management—he will not agree to run both systems, provided and non-provided, side by side. Sidney, on the other hand, whilst ready to provide as many secondary and university institutions as the ratepayers will pay for, wants gradually to acquire sufficient control over all the others to raise their standard to the required level. However, though Graham refused to give up his principle, he agreed to consult with Sidney and Bray as to the application of it, and not to wantonly obstruct without consideration or warning. What is clear is that the present constitution of the L.C.C. as educational authority is transitional, and unstable in the last degree. The men who know most and are most patiently persistent will, however unpopular their policy may be, in the end rule the roost. The next three years, with the parliamentary election to take some of the foremost Progressives into higher spheres, and the L.C.C. elections two years hence to lose some Progressive seats, will clear off a good many of the present obstructions. But when exactly we shall feel free to go off for our eight months' trip to the Far East remains in dim obscurity —a vision of rest and refreshment at the end of many more months and years of sustained drudgery. I am beginning to hanker after a period of fallowness.

March 31*st.*—Another old friend passed away—Marie Souvestre. A brilliant woman, handsome, warm-hearted—the very soul of veracity—and keen-witted. A school mistress for nearly half-a-century, she must have counted for much in the lives of many women coming from the best of the governing class in England, America, France and Germany. But she was not only a school mistress: she was an habituée, during middle life, of intellectual society in Paris, Berlin and London: she had known most of the advanced politicians and thinkers springing from the professional and middle-class. Twenty years ago, in York House days, I used to meet her at the Chamberlains, Harrisons, Morleys—it was she who introduced me to the Creightons.

It is strange to think of that passionate nature—with her scorn of what she felt to be mean, her bitter criticism of what she did not understand, her devoted service to those she loved, her exalted enthusiasm for what was noble in her eyes—to think of that force passed away into the unknown silence of death. A few weeks ago I visited her twice, and thought I saw the hand of death on her face; she seemed quite as alive in spirit as when I first met her at Frederic Harrison's—and now where is she?

Veracity, an undeviating directness of intelligence, faithfulness and warmth of affection, were her most delightful qualities; dignity of manner and brilliancy of speech her chief ornaments. An amazing narrowness of vision for so intelligent a person; a total inability to understand religion; a dogmatism that was proof against the spirit of scientific investigation; a lack of charity to feelings with which she did not sympathise—in short, an absence of humility was, perhaps, the most disabling of her characteristics. It narrowed her influence to those whom she happened to like and who happened to like her. Others refused to listen; and with some she roused evil feelings.

It is hard for those born in the modern England to understand the passionate hatred of ecclesiasticism—of religion—which seems to dominate French free-thinkers; it is so hard not to count it as an evil thing. Yet this feeling is not mainly evil—it has in it an element of idealism—of faith in noble qualities which were, far back in history, trampled under foot by organised Christianity; and which they still believe are in danger from the existing Church. The shackling of the spirit of investigation into the processes of life, the attempt to stereotype the purpose of life—the suppression of the inner light by mere formalism, the assumption of individuals of better motives than are actually present —all these various shades of disloyalty to truth seem to these militant secularists still rampant in any body of men knit together by the religious spirit. This conviction may have a grain of truth in it, since this lack of veracity is the special temptation which besets the religious mind. But, on the other hand, the absence of religious impulse seems to leave most of these natures blind and infirm even in their intellectual judgements. Marie Souvestre was not a wise woman—she was hard on the great mass of common people—occasionally even unjust; she always insisted, like Herbert Spencer, on being judge in her own case. She could not tolerate the idea that *she* might be wrong. And it was a strange irony that she was almost as ignorant of the persistent industry, patience and humility, involved in the scientific method, as she was of the religious impulse. All knowledge appeared to her as a series of intuitions, as sparks struck by the instantaneous contact of the mind with its environ-ment—not as the slow adjustment of the order of thought to the order of things. Observation and conjecture, yes, but verification, no.

April 2nd.—Sidney is happier in his L.C.C. work than I have known him since the first Council. He has, in his special department of education, the maximum of power with the minimum of responsi-bility. He has no personal enemies on the Council, and the bulk of the Progressives, feeling that they have behaved rather shabbily in keeping him out of all prominent places, are really anxious to " oblige him " on questions of policy. The Moderates, whilst acknowledging his separate standpoint, feel him to be an ally of their best side—*i.e.* of their en-deavour to develop the neglected parts of the educational system. The officials, one and all, consult and trust him, regarding him almost as one of themselves. And as regards the future, it is rather a case of " heads you lose, tails I win ". If the Progressives, by insisting on direct administration and county provision of all education, run up the rates, then there will be a reaction in favour of the Moderates. If the Moderates come in, there will be better organisation and more delegation; if the Progressives maintain themselves, there will be more expenditure; in short, the Progressives will find it impossible not to improve the *function* and the Moderates to improve the *structure* of the educational authority—and both parties must more or less accept his policy. Meanwhile, he is completely in the background—a free-lance ready to engage in a skirmish with either side, and relieved from the worry and strain of getting things through the Council in which he is not specially interested. He is thus free to give time and thought to the book.

April 17th.—Three or four weeks, day after day, spent either amassing new material at the British Museum for our chapters on the county or in analysing our twelve boxes of material at home. Some days I have spent a good six hours at work—seeing no one until Sidney returned in the evening—just going for a constitutional after lunch or walking along the Embankment to call on Kate Courtney in the hour or so before supper. But most weeks we have had a twelve-person dinner at home; dined out twice or three times; lunched casual persons on intermediate days; and, on three occasions, we have entertained at dinner the staff of the School, with gatherings of 50 to 70 students coming in afterwards. Then my work the next day has suffered either in quality or quantity or both, and I have felt disheartened at the length and complexity of our task. Our life tends, however, to become more and more the student's life and to be less interrupted by social engagements—partly the pressure of completing these two first volumes disinclines me to accept dinners, makes me neglect calls, and absolutely prohibits evening parties other than our own. With such persons as we do see, we find ourselves on the pleasantest of terms—the result of the privilege of living with a companion who knows neither malice nor envy, nor desire to excel, nor the remotest tinge of what the world calls " snobbishness ". Sidney is simply unconscious of all the little meanness which turns social intercourse sour: he is sometimes tired, occasionally bored, but never unkindly or anxious to shine, or be admired, and wholly unaware of the absence of, or presence of, social consideration. I verily believe that if he were thrown, by chance, into a company of persons all of whom wanted to snub him, he would take up the first book and become absorbed in it, with a sort of feeling that they were good-natured enough not to claim his attention, or that they did not perceive that he was reading on the sly. And the greater personages they happened to be, the more fully satisfied he would be at the arrangement; since it would relieve him of any haunting fear that he was neglecting his social duty and making others uncomfortable. On the other hand, whether in his own house or in another's, if some person is neglected or out of it, Sidney will quite unconsciously drift to them and be seen eagerly talking to them.

H. G. Wells came for the night: he had sent us his *Utopia*. " The chapters on the Samurai will pander to all your worst instincts ", he laughingly remarked when I congratulated him. He is full of intellectual courage and initiative, and is now settling down to psychological novels —I fancy somewhat inspired by Henry James's late success.

A pleasant little dinner at the Talbots' (Bishop of Rochester) on Saturday. The P.M., the Dean of Westminster, Lady Gwendolen Cecil and ourselves. Mr. Balfour's plaint, " There is no need for the newspapers to tell me my faults, I know them all, but I can't alter them ". A long talk with the Bishop afterwards. Sidney hopeful about the future, he somewhat pessimistic. Lady Gwendolen Cecil, like her sister, Lady Selborne (whom we met at a large and fashionable dinner the other day, and with whom I talked much), exactly the same philosophy as young Algernon Cecil. Utterly sceptical of any reform of society brought about by altering the environment of individuals— the boy brought up by drunken parents in the worst slum of London, Lady Gwendolen maintained, was as likely to turn out satisfactorily as the most favoured person. " It is surely a question of experience," I suggested, " your experience of life leads to one conclusion, my experience leads me to another." But, in some subtle way, this reference to experience, as the test of our rival assumptions, did not satisfy her.

May 11*th.*—A happy three weeks with the Playnes at Longfords. Wrote about one-third of our part on the " County ", taking the two last days off for long rides in glorious weather—to Malmesbury one day, and then a lovely day in the Standish woods alone with my boy. We hid our bicycles in the leaves at the top of the beech woods and wandered down, hand in hand, to the dear old field overlooking the house—the scene of childish sorrow and joy and all the stirrings and strivings of young womanhood. The valley was shrouded in heat mist, the broad surface of the Bristol channel glimmering through and the hills behind in faintest outline—these only to the eye of knowledge. Then a lovely walk wheeling our iron round the crest of the Cotswolds to the Beacon Hill, overlooking a more glorious view of the greatest breadth of the Severn Valley bordered by the Malverns, on one side, and the Channel, on the other. A ride back through the deep lanes of the valley—cottages, churches and farms, that one knew long ago—

even some familiar faces grown old and furrowed. A delicious ending to our Easter recess!

We worked away for four or five hours a day in our little sitting-room, and chatted with the family in the intervals. There was a German nephew [1] and his wife—a young doctor—lying up with a bruised back. He was quite the typical good sort of *gebildeter* German—self-complacent, materialist, well-instructed, but appallingly ignorant of anything outside what he himself had read and observed. He was intensely nervous about his health, selfish with his excellent little wife, lacking in public spirit, or even of any notion of duty other than being a respectable doctor, father, husband. He was completely satisfied with everything German—from the German elementary education to the German Emperor, believing that Germany's pre-eminence was un-questioned in industry, in government, in knowledge, in poetry and in sentiment. Beyond the fact that he was a " nice " fellow, he had no distinction, except only a desire to improve his professional knowledge. What young English doctor, in mid-career as a consultant at a fashion-able watering-place, would dream of spending his winter months at one or other university to work under specialist professors—and yet he is considered merely a commonplace young man.

Then we had a Chinese lady and her brother down for a couple of days—the lady in native costume, the gentleman in European. They spoke English volubly but badly. They belonged to the wealthy class—the uncle the Chinese Governor of Shanghai, the father brought up to be a Mandarin but preferring the free-er position of a capitalist at large. He owned the pawnshops of Shanghai and much real estate, and had married the daughter of a large rice planter. They gave us a vision of the residences of the wealthy Chinaman; it contained within its own walls 40 maid servants, 20 men servants, 6 private secretaries and tutors, 4 tailors, all serving a family of 15, including two married sons and their babies and two unmarried daughters—the ladies and children living in the ladies' apartments in the inner walls of the establishment. These two young people represented the most emancipated of rich persons: both were supremely discontented with the government of China, the education of China, the society of China—without in the least admiring any other race or civilisation. For the Japanese they had envy and the irritation of mortified vanity at being considered their inferiors—perhaps, just a glimmer of satisfaction at their " cousins " beating the detested foreigners. They were crass materialists, regarding all religion as so much folly, fit only to eke out legal compulsion in respect to uncivilised races or classes. They had no notion of science; they were conscious there was some trick of Western civilisation which

[1] Dr. Geise. (Ed.)

they wanted to learn—which led to mechanical invention profitable to men—but the discovery of truth for its own sake was to them an unknown impulse. Honour of parents and love of children seemed their best quality, perhaps, just the first signs of philanthropy. They lacked the symptoms of health, they had no courage either physical or mental, and one would not trust their veracity. Their manners were excellent, and they were sensitive to every change of expression in those with whom they consorted—adaptable yet dignified. We have promised to visit them in China.

The little lady was the more intelligent of the two; she told us of the futility of Chinese education—how it took three years to learn the mechanical art of writing, and ten years to learn to express yourself in literature, owing to the inconceivable complication of the Chinese language. And as children they worked eight hours a day, chiefly learning books by heart—no physical exercise, no freedom, no intercourse with the world. And rich young men smoked and gambled, read and sometimes kept " seraglios "—the last was very bad, she thought. The poor worked incessantly to become rich. Some foolish persons took to " prayer ", but that occupation struck her as " only something a degree less undesirable than opium smoking ". She wanted to write a book to tell the Chinese how the Western people lived, and to get the Chinese ladies out of their habit of perpetual chatter about their dresses and their pearls. She was a good little soul, but I suspected that she said to us what she thought would please us, not her real opinions. She told us that this brother was not married—a thumping lie as she afterwards admitted—because an English missionary's wife had told her a married man was never spoken to in England!

A long talk with H. G. Wells at Sandgate: two articles of our social faith are really repulsive to him—the collective provision of anything bordering on religious or emotional training, and the collective regulation of the behaviour of the adult. As to the latter, we are not really at variance, for we would willingly accept his limitation of this intervention to all such behaviour as impinges on the non-adult (heaven knows, that little scheme would give us enough regulation of the adult and to spare). But he is obdurate as to education: no form of training must be provided out of common funds that he personally objects to. My plea for variety and experiment, for leaving the door open for new religions or morality, by permitting those who believe in the old to have it provided for their children; Sidney's plea for tolerance strikes a deaf ear. " The child is not fit for emotional training until after adolescence ", he dogmatically asserts. " There is no injustice in not giving one form of training ", he insists. But he went further than this: " I don't believe in tolerance, you have got to fight against anything being taught anybody which seems to you harmful, you have got to struggle to get your own creed taught." We all got hot and exaggerated in our arguments and were no nearer agreement when we parted.

I suppose it is inevitable that we who believe in extending the functions of the state in all directions should be keenly desirous of making this activity as catholic as possible; of safeguarding each new departure by deliberate provision for dissenters from the established view. Clearly, the whole of Liberalism in England is swinging into rigid conformity—both in the structure and formations of the social organism. As you cannot have each individual separately provided for according to his needs, therefore, you must have identical treatment to all—seems their present dogma.

June 10*th*.—The Progressives have turned Sidney off the party committee. Some of the rump are very angry with him for entangling them in secondary education. The leaders are always civil to him; the rank and file find themselves accepting his proposals; but neither the leaders nor the ordinary members really like his policy and are vexed to find themselves pursuing it. So they try to keep him down *personally*; and would, I think, be relieved to get rid of him. Sidney, meanwhile, is in the best of humours—his scholarship scheme is working admirably, and forcing by its mere weight the Council either to subsidise existing secondary schools or to build and manage new ones. It is " heads I win, tails you lose ". And, as he cannot get control of the whole machine of London education—elementary, secondary and university—and make it really efficient, he is glad enough to be *obviously* out of office, to hang loosely to the Progressive Party. It absolves him of any responsibility to the public, and of any excessive loyalty to the party. When McKinnon Wood, *I think* sincerely, expressed his regret that he had been knocked off the party committee, Sidney answered smilingly that he thought that " there was really a cleavage of opinion between himself and the party, and that therefore it was well that this should be acknowledged: he was glad to feel at liberty to take his own line, which he could hardly do if he belonged to the inner circle ". Whereupon McKinnon Wood looked thoughtful and not over-pleased. They don't want to break with him.

July 30*th*.—One or two friends we have seen in a quiet way. A Sunday with Cyril Jackson of the Education Department, in his agreeable bachelor establishment at Limpsfield—to meet us, Masterman and Beveridge (a leading Toynbee-ite), his secretary Napier and a young friend of his about to become an Indian civil servant. This latter young man (whose name I have forgotten) struck me as typical of the coming civil servant. A " double first ", clean in looks and mind, strong-willed but unselfconscious, deprecating enthusiasm, critical of ideas and projects, and above all abstemious—given up tobacco, alcohol, meat—all because the doctor who passed him for the civil service remarked that his organs were not perfectly in good order. What his views are one could not tell, since he and Napier sat silent, listening to the torrent of discussion between Masterman, Beveridge and ourselves—with Jackson intervening as an official Conservative in a party of disputing Progressives. Masterman, an attractive journalist, combines being a religionist of the high Anglican order with sentimental and pessimistic Radicalism—in theory, he is collectivist, by instinct an anarchist individualist—above all, he is a rhetorician. Beveridge an ugly-mannered but honest, self-devoted, hard-headed young reformer of the practical type, came out well in comparison with Masterman; and, from disliking him, as we had formerly done, because of his ugly manners, we approved him. There was no hope of the Liberal Party in either of these young men; but intense dislike of the Tories, and the usual anger with Balfour for remaining in.

We have slipped into a sort of friendliness with Balfour. He comes in to dinner whenever we ask him, and talks most agreeably—perhaps our vanity is flattered by his evident interest in our historical and philosophical paradoxes and enjoyment of our conversation. I have not yet discovered any consistent attitude towards private and public life which comes to the surface in dinner-party conversation: there is merely a rather weary curiosity as to other people's processes of reasoning and feeling, lit up, now and again, with a very real interest in human character—where it is distinguished. The bulk of men bore him, whether regarded as individuals or as an electorate, or a Parliament, and all the common thoughts and feelings of common folk seem to him ineffably banal—fit only for the subject-matter of Bernard Shaw's derisive wit. I raised the question, whether the derision embodied in *John Bull's Other Island*—derision unaccompanied by any positive faith or hope—counted for good? He seemed quite surprised at my doubt—thought it better to clear away humbug at any cost. I suggested that, though I personally loathed both the Irish and English " home rule " shibboleths—yet, surely, with many Irish home rulers and English Liberals, these formulas embodied honest effort towards a better state of things? " Question whether we may not be too intellectually aristocratic," I urged, " whether we may discourage right effort because it happens to express itself—not in bad grammar, because that is often picturesque, and since board schools somewhat unusual—but in fluffy thought and silly sentiment? " He acquiesced in his courteous way, but I could see he was not convinced.

October 5th.—A week or so disturbed by too much society. First the visit of the French deputies [members of the Paris Municipal Council, whom the London County Council had invited]. We cut all the parties and I had not even to go to the dinners, while Sidney felt obliged to attend. But we had long talks with the brilliant journalist quartered on us (Dausset) who suffered our voluble bad French gladly for the sake of informing himself as to English society and English public opinion. In return, he expounded to us the work of the Paris Municipal Council. " More a debating society, and that disorderly, than an administrative body ", was his verdict. " When I was president I was younger than I am now, and an enthusiast—I imagined that I was really going to help to govern Paris. What I gradually discovered was that, whenever I differed from the Préfet de la Seine, I was beaten hopelessly by his policy of passive resistance. Everything the council proposed to do or not to do was practically under his veto. He always refused to discuss the proposed policy when he disliked it. He was never ' at home '; never once did I succeed in seeing him." But this not all. Evidently it is the officials of the council who draw up all the reports—reports which M. Dausset admitted he seldom read—it is officials (many of whom are not removable without the consent of the Préfet) who execute all the orders. It would be a somewhat analogous position if the L.C.C. had to get most of its work done by the police under the Home Office. Then we gathered that all the deputies lived in terror of their constituents and he admitted voting for *les bêtises*, because he feared to lose his seat. The question arises, why he is a member on these conditions. And the general impression left by the deputies on their English hosts was that they were individuals " on the make " and there for other reasons than the good government of Paris.

Interesting to observe how intensely nervous all were about Germany—anxious to ascertain whether we genuinely intended to back them up in case of German aggression.

Mary Playne came up for ten days; and, knowing she liked to see folk, I took the opportunity to ask people to dine. George Trevelyan and his wife—excellent and interesting young people, with the charm of a strenuous and conscientious life and considerable talent, spent an evening alone with us. Among the young Liberals he is the most promising, because he has some conviction and a fervent desire for more. He is to spend the next years of his life in a history of England, 1790–1810, which is to be the glorification of Fox and rehabilitation of the French Revolution—one would think a somewhat conventional and banal task—a modernised replica of his father's book. Still, he has enthusiasm and industry, and that is better than paradoxical originality without those qualities.

On Sunday afternoon G. B. S. and Granville-Barker dropped in and spread out before us the difficulties, the hopes, the ridiculous aspects of their really arduous efforts to create an intellectual drama. Granville-Barker has suddenly filled out—he looks even physically larger than a year ago—he has grown extraordinarily in dignity and knowledge of human nature. But he dislikes the absorption in mere acting and longs to mix with persons actually in affairs or intellectually producing. G. B. S.'s egotism and vanity are not declining; he is increasing his deftness of wit and phrase, but becoming every day more completely iconoclastic—the ideal derider. In the evening we dined with the Courtneys. On Monday John Burns and Mrs. J. R. Green dropped in about 7 o'clock and stayed to share with Mary and ourselves half a pheasant! They talked at each other—Alice raging against the Liberals —John raging against the priest. Incidentally, Burns showed his dislike of the notion of a larger Labour Party, and his rooted suspicion of even his present colleagues. Keir Hardie, Crooks and Henderson " would all be out of Parliament " if he were providence. It is pitiful to see the lack of any good comradeship between these men.

On Tuesday, there dined with us Wernher (the South African capitalist), a heavy, good-natured, public-spirited and scientific-minded millionaire, Lord Lytton, Bernard Shaw and Mrs. Prothero (the mates of these three were ill)—a somewhat crooked party, that was only straightened out by sheer energy on my part into a comfortable affair. Wernher stumbled heavily along in his broken German, G. B. S. scintillated, Mrs. Prothero listened with Irish scepticism of Irish wit, Lord Lytton hung on G. B. S.'s words—looking the beautiful, fastidious young artist-aristocrat—a party of interesting types, but not mixing well. Meanwhile, I had got note after note from the Duchess of Marlborough who apparently has been seized with a whim to hear Sidney lecture and get us to dine with them afterwards. It would have been discourteous to refuse—so there was another evening of talk— the other guests being George Peel and Mrs. Craigie (John Oliver Hobbes). The Duke and Duchess corresponded exactly to the account given of them by the private secretary during our visit to Blenheim— somewhat futile young persons floating aimlessly on the surface of society, both alike quite unfit for their great position, swayed to and fro by somewhat silly motives—neither good nor bad. The little Duke is, I should imagine, mildly vicious—the Duchess has charm and, I think, goodness. I wondered how he came to be dragged by his wife to a technical lecture, and into entertaining two dowdy, middle-aged, middle-class intellectuals uncomfortably at a restaurant—for quite obviously they had come up to London on purpose. Was it G. B. S. they were after? They reminded us of H. G. Wells' " little white people " in *The Time Machine*.

On Friday we had a really entertaining and useful party—Lord Milner, the Morants, the Albert Grays, Mackinder and Alfred Cripps. This was a real success, everyone was glad to meet the others, and the conversation was sustained in subject as well as bright. I had a long talk with Milner after dinner. He has grown grim and (perhaps temporarily) bitter—obsessed too with a vision of a non-party Government without having invented any device for securing it. His grimness may be the result of fatigue and lonely work—with a life among friends and after rest, it may work off. His thesis is that the war itself, the dragging out of it, the unsatisfactory character of the settlement, the barely averted disaster—all were the result of the party system which forced half the political world to be against him. He is sufficient of a fanatic not to see that there was a genuine cleavage of opinion among the thinking people—that it was not merely a knot of cranks that disapproved his policy. He would take colonial affairs " out of politics ", but he does not suggest how. He is a strong man and an intensely public-spirited man—but he is harder and more intolerant, more distinctively the bureaucrat than when he left England. And he is sore, and bitter to opponents—not a good state of mind with which to enter politics. A little religion, or a purely intellectual pursuit, or perhaps some emotional companionship, is needed if he is to get back his sanity—his sense of proportion. So ended our week's dissipation. On all but *one* day I managed to work, though the sleeplessness which always follows on talking late made the work of poor quality. This next week has to be diverted to preparing my lecture—so alas! the book will be hung up.

The smart world is tumbling over one another in the worship of G. B. S., and even we have a sort of reflected glory as his intimate friends. It is interesting to note that the completeness of his self-conceit will save him from the worst kind of deterioration—he is proof against flattery. Where it will injure him is in isolating him from serious intercourse with intimate friends working in other departments of life —whenever he is free there is such a crowd of journalists and literary hangers-on around him that one feels it is kinder to spare him one's company—and that will be the instinct of many of his old friends engaged in administration, investigation or propaganda.

What a transformation scene from those first years I knew him: the scathing bitter opponent of wealth and leisure—and now! the adored one of the smartest and most cynical set of English " society ". Some might say that we, too, had travelled in that direction: our good sense preserve us! Fortunately, the temptation is at present slight and quite easily evaded. Curiosity about us is quickly satisfied and the smart ones subside, after one interview, into indifference. And Sidney steadily discourages my more sociable nature. " By all means be courteous but keep clear of them " is his perpetual refrain, in tone, if not in words. He is a blessed mate for me.

November 23rd.—Appointed to the Royal Commission on the Poor Law: awaiting anxiously the names of my colleagues—Charles Booth being the only one I know of.

Yesterday evening we dined with Lord Lucas (Bron Herbert that was) in his great mansion in St. James's Square: Mrs. Willie Grenfell, and Mrs. Lindsay, flippant but clever little lady, and a pleasant young Tory lawyer made up the party. Our host interests me as the son of my dear old friend Auberon Herbert; as a boy, I remember he eyed me with hostility, when I came to stay with his father twenty years ago— perhaps he thought I was going to become his stepmother! But, since he has come into the political world, first as a young Liberal candidate, now as a peer, he has cultivated our friendship. He is an attractive creature, dreamy and vague, with a charming veracity and gentleness of nature, with (for a *grand seigneur*) simple tastes and ways, and public-spirited and philanthropic impulses—the sort of ideal young aristocrat pictured in Bulwer Lytton's novels. But, from our point of view, he is no good. He is steeped in his father's individualist philosophy (he is a mere child in knowledge and thought on social and economic questions) and the only direction in which he has broken away from his father's influence is in the desire for an Empire—dragged thither by the Rosebery and millionaire associates among whom he lives. Moreover, he has no notion of work; he has great possessions and a most attractive personality. I fear that he must be written off as useless though not dangerous. His cousin, Mrs. Willie Grenfell, struck me last night as something more than the fashionable and pretty woman I took her to be. But, when I sat with her and the other smart little woman in that palatial room, I felt a wee bit ashamed of myself. Why was I dissipating my energy in this smart but futile world in late hours and small talk? Exactly at the moment this feeling was disconcerting me, the door opened and Mr. Balfour was announced. I confess that the appearance of the P.M. dissipated my regrets. It is always worth while, I thought, to meet those who really have power to alter things— should I be on the Poor Law Commission (the tempter said) if it were not for my friendship with this great one? And I collapsed into complacency. He was looking excited and fagged, on the eve of resignation. We chatted over the fire—Mrs. Grenfell, he and I—in a disjointed fashion until twelve o'clock, when Sidney and I left the tiny party to talk, perhaps more intimately.

November 29th.—Yesterday A. J. B. lunched with us, and went afterwards to G. B. S.'s new play *Major Barbara*. The vanishing Prime Minister was looking particularly calm and happy—compared to six months or even six days ago; seemed like one with a load lifted off his mind. Quite unexpectedly the conversation drifted on to the whole underlying argument of the tariff question—the possibility of continuous exports, should a prohibition tariff, say, 100% be raised against us by the whole world. Though apparently dead against ordinary protection as unsound, he seems haunted by a somewhat theoretical fear of *universal hostile* discrimination against us. I think he accepts the rate of exchange reaction as a solution of the ordinary tariff war when each country blindly raises walls against all other countries, whilst insisting on importing from other countries. But, in that extreme case, he had the support of even Sidney. He cross-examined Sidney as to the rise in the price of commodities brought about by a tariff, and discussed the whole matter with perfect frankness and ease. Sir Oliver Lodge and Sir Arthur Rucker, and a nice young Conservative lawyer—L.C.C.—were the party; after lunch he asked somewhat anxiously *who* the young man was, and looked reassured when I told him he was of the right colour. On the way to the play he told me " as a friend " all his difficulties with the Royal Commission —his refusal to have any politicians, and difficulty on finding a chairman. " George Hamilton is not the fool he looks ", he apologetically explained.

G. B. S.'s play turned out to be a dance of devils—amazingly clever, grimly powerful in the second act—but ending, as all his plays end (or at any rate most of them), in an intellectual and moral morass. A. J. B. was taken aback by the force, the horrible force of the Salvation Army scene, the unrelieved tragedy of degradation, the disillusionment of the Greek professor and of Barbara—the triumph of the unmoral purpose: the anti-climax of evangelising the Garden City! I doubt the popular success of the play: it is hell tossed on the stage— with no hope of heaven. G. B. S. is gambling with ideas and emotions in a way that distresses slow-minded prigs like Sidney and me, and hurts those with any fastidiousness. But the stupid public will stand a good deal from one who is acclaimed as an unrivalled wit by the great ones of the world.

December 2nd.—To-day, I called on the Shaws and found G. B. S. alone in his study. He was perturbed—indeed, upset by the bad acting, as he thought, of Undershaft and generally of all in the last scene— and by a virulent attack on the play in the *Morning Post*. Calvert, he said, had completely lost his nerve over Undershaft—could not understand or remember his part and was aghast at what he considered its blank immorality. I spoke quite frankly my opinion of the general effect of his play—the triumph of the unmoral purpose. He argued earnestly and cleverly, even persuasively, in favour of what he imagines to be his central theme—*the need for preliminary good physical environment before anything could be done to raise the intelligence and morality of the average sensual man.* " We middle-class people, having always had physical comfort and good order, do not realise the disaster to character in being without. We have, therefore, cast a halo round poverty, instead of treating it as the worst of crimes—the one unforgiveable crime that must be wiped off before any virtue can grow." He defended Undershaft's general attitude towards life on the ground that, until we divested ourselves of feeling (he said malice), we were not fit to go the lengths needed for social salvation. " What we want is for the people to turn round and burn, not the West End, but their own slums. The Salvation Army with its fervour and its love might lead them to do this and then we really should be at the beginning of the end of the crime of poverty."

I found it difficult to answer him—but he did not convince me. There is something lacking in his presentment of the crime of poverty. But I could honestly sympathise with his irritation at the suggested intervention of the censor—not on account of the upshot of the play, but because Barbara in her despair at the end of the second act utters the cry, " My God, my God, why hast thou forsaken me ". A wonderful and quite rational climax to the true tragedy of the scene of the Salvation Army shelter.

Meanwhile, Governments are changing in England and government of any sort is coming to an end in Russia.

CHAPTER VII

ROYAL COMMISSION ON THE POOR LAW AND THE RELIEF OF DISTRESS
1905–1909

Two events are casually noted in the concluding pages of the foregoing chapter: the one of outstanding national importance—the advent of the Liberal Government in December 1905; and the other of major significance in the life story of Our Partnership—my appointment, in November of the same year, to serve on the Royal Commission on the Poor Law and the Relief of Distress. Seeing that this book is, in the main, an autobiography and only incidentally material for British political history, I shall give premier place to the day-to-day working of this remarkable public enquiry ending in the publication, in January 1909, of the Majority and Minority Reports of the Royal Commission of 1905–9. In this recital will be included entries relating to our continued personal investigation into English local government, leading to the publication of three volumes during these very years; a ponderous volume on *The Parish and the County* in 1906, and two volumes on *The Manor and the Borough* in 1908. Hence this chapter is closely linked up with Chapter IV. describing our enquiry into English local government from the seventeenth century onwards. For it was, I venture to think, exactly this continuous six years' hard work on our own account, from 1899 to 1905, that qualified us to see further into the past, present and possible future of that unique institution—the English Poor Law—than was practicable to some of my colleagues. For the rest, the reader will find in the following pages a veritable hodge-podge of diary entries, relating to the Other One's activities on the L.C.C., the Senate of London University, the Technical Education Board and the London School of Economics, together with chance characterisations of our social and political environment, intermingled with my own meditations on the destiny of mankind.

Why did the Prime Minister (Arthur Balfour), at the close of the session of 1905, announce in reply to an evidently prearranged question in the House of Commons, that the Government had come to the conclusion that the time had come for a full enquiry into the whole question, adding with significance that there had been no such enquiry since that of 1832–34? Why did the Cabinet, on the very eve of its resignation, put itself to the trouble of choosing the members of a large and representative Royal Commission; and charge it " to enquire into (1) the working of the laws relating to the relief of poor persons in the United Kingdom; (2) the various means which have been adopted outside of the poor laws for meeting distress arising from want of employment, particularly during periods of severe industrial depression; and to consider and report whether any, and if so what, modification of the poor laws, or changes in their administration, or fresh legislation for dealing with distress, are advisable "?

Our own impression at the time was that the Commission owed its creation to the coincidence of there being, as newly appointed head of the poor law division, an energetic man of affairs (James Stewart Davy) intent on reaction; and, as President of the Local Government Board, a philosopher (Mr. Gerald Balfour) who recognised the public advantage of a precise discrimination between opposing principles. There was, in fact, in official circles, an uneasy feeling that there had been, during the last two decades, an unwilling drift away from the principles of 1834, and one which sooner or later had to be decisively stopped.

The underlying principles advocated by the Royal Commission on the Poor Law of 1832 and embodied straight away in the Poor Law Amendment Act of 1834, are herewith summarised: [1]

---

[1] For a further and more elaborate description of the principles of 1834, see *English Poor Law Policy*, by Sidney and Beatrice Webb, published in 1910. This book was an enlargement and completion of the report which I circulated to the

(1) That the public relief of destitution out of funds raised by taxation—as distinguished from the alms of the charitable—devitalised the recipients, degraded their character and induced in them general bad behaviour.

(2) That the operation of the Malthusian law of population, accentuated by the theory of a wage fund, rendered all such relief, not only futile in diminishing the miseries of the poor, but actually harmful in the creation of a wider pool of destitution.

(3) That it was imperative for a department of the national government to direct and control the actions of the local authorities concerned so as to impose on them a policy which would diminish, if not abolish, the disease of pauperism.

Hence, the famous principle of " less eligibility ". Out of these ardently held assumptions, springing from this tenaciously held principle of " less eligibility ", sprang the officially recognised policy of the Local Government Board from 1834 to 1905.

The first and most essential of all conditions, the Commissioners of 1832–34 tell us: " A principle which we find universally admitted, even by those whose practice is at variance with it, is, that his [the able-bodied person's] situation, on the whole, shall not be made really or apparently so eligible as the situation of the independent labourer of the lowest class. Throughout the evidence it is shown that, in proportion as the condition of any pauper class is elevated above the condition of independent labourers, the condition of the independent class is depressed; their industry is impaired, their employment becomes unsteady, and its remuneration in wages is diminished. Such persons, therefore, are under the strongest inducements to quit the less eligible class of labourers and enter the more eligible class of paupers. . . . Whole branches of manufacture " [to cite a much-quoted passage] " may thus follow the course, not of coal mines or of streams, but of pauperism; may flourish like the funguses that spring from corruption, in consequence of the abuses which are ruining all the other interests

Commission in July 1907, on the poor law policy of the Central Authority from 1834 to 1905, and which is referred to in the diary entries.

See also *History of the English Poor Law* in two volumes, by Sidney and Beatrice Webb.

of the places in which they are established, and to cease to exist in the better administered districts, in consequence of that better administration." The converse is the effect when the pauper class is placed in its proper position, below the condition of the independent labourer. In short, by making the alternative plainly penal, the whip of starvation was to be placed securely in the hands of the employers.

The second principle insisted on by the Report of 1834 is the principle of " national uniformity "—that is, of identity of treatment of each class of destitute person from one end of the kingdom to the other, for the purpose of reducing the perpetual shifting from parish to parish, of preventing discontent, and of bringing the parochial management effectually under the control of a government department carrying out the principles of 1834. The third principle, commonly known as the "workhouse system", that is the complete substitution of indoor for outdoor relief, was no part of the recommendations of the 1834 Report for any but the ablebodied. It was, however, adopted by the strictest of the reformers of 1834–47, and again by those of 1871–85, as the only effective method of applying the principles of less eligibility and of reducing pauperism. The workhouse, on this principle, was not to be regarded as a place of long-continued residence, still less as an institution for beneficial treatment, but primarily (if not exclusively) as a " test of destitution ", that is, as a means of affording the actual necessities of existence under conditions so deterrent that the pauper would rather prefer to maintain himself independently than accept the relief so offered.

So much, or rather so little, about the principles underlying English poor law policy during the seventy years preceding 1905. Now let us consider the make-up of the Royal Commission of 1905–9. Like its predecessor in 1934, it was to a marked degree a reforming commission, but unlike the Poor Law Commission of 1832–34, that of 1905–9 was largely composed of persons who had actually taken part in the administration of the poor law. There were on it no fewer than five guardians of the poor, four of whom were, or had been, chairmen of their boards.[1] Even more influential was the presence of the permanent heads of the Local Government Boards of England, Scotland and Ireland respectively, who were personally directing the poor law administration of the three countries, together with the senior medical inspector of the English poor law division.[2] These nine experienced poor law administrators were reinforced by half-a-dozen prominent members of the Charity Organisation Society, all of whom began the enquiry as convinced adherents of the principles of 1834; notably, the Society's general secretary, C. S. Loch; one of its founders, Miss Octavia Hill; and two other distinguished exponents of its doctrines, Mr. Hancock Nunn and Mrs. Bernard Bosanquet.[3] There were two political economists, belonging to what was then called the orthodox school, Professor William Smart of Glasgow and the Rev. L. R. Phelps of Oxford. With the Rev. Prebendary Russell Wakefield, afterwards Bishop of Birmingham, the Church of England had three representatives, and the Roman Catholic Church in Ireland one (the Bishop of Ross).[4] This predominantly *stand pat* composition of the Commission was emphasised by the appointment of a Conservative ex-Cabinet Minister as chairman: Lord George Hamilton. Out of the twenty members there were only three who belonged to the Labour and Socialist movements—Mr. George Lansbury, and Mr. Francis Chandler (general secretary of the old-established Amalgamated Society of Carpenters), and myself. But the unique characteristic of this Commission was the inclusion in it of members who had proved their capacity for the work of social investigation. There was Charles Booth,[5] who

[1] The poor law guardians were F. H. Bentham, George Lansbury, T. Hancock Nunn, the Rev. L. R. Phelps and F. Chandler (subsequently added to represent the trade union movement).

[2] Sir S. B. Provis, K.C.B., J. Patten-MacDougall, C.B., Sir Henry Robinson, K.C.B., and Dr. A. H. (now Sir Arthur) Downes.

[3] The C.O.S. members included the above-mentioned together with Rev. T. G. Gardiner and the Rev. L. R. Phelps.

[4] The Bishop of Ross (Dr. Kelly) was added to the Commission in place of the O'Conor Don, who died in 1906.

[5] The Right Honourable Charles Booth (1840–1917), shipowner and merchant, had devoted many years of thought and work, and large drafts upon his income, to

might be termed the inventor of one of the leading methods of sociological research; there were the ablest members of the Charity Organisation Society—a society whose activities were avowedly based, in a far-reaching survey of social results, on exhaustive enquiry into individual cases; and there was one of the leading researchers of the Fabian Society. The Commission was, in fact, predominantly a body of experts, either in poor law administration or social investigation. Indeed, one of the few members of the Commission who had neither an extensive knowledge of the subject, nor experience in research, was its chairman, Lord George Hamilton. Fortunately for the amenity of the Commission's internal life, and perhaps even for its efficiency as an instrument of research, this experienced politician and attractive *grand seigneur* combined exceptional personal charm and social tact with an open mind and a willingness to give free play to the activities of his fellow-commissioners. Regarded as an instrument of reform, what the Commission seemed to lack was the guiding hand of an experienced lawyer, who might have kept the enquiry strictly within the terms of reference, and insisted on all evidence being brought before the Commission as a whole, and tested by some common standard of relevance and validity; and who might, in the end, have negotiated a unanimous report on all those issues—and there proved to be many—upon which there was common agreement.[1]

statistical investigation of social conditions, for which he had a passion, and in which he became an inventor of a new technique. Public recognition of his achievements came in a privy councillorship, a fellowship of the Royal Society, and doctorates of the Universities of Liverpool, Oxford and Cambridge. For his life, see *Charles Booth—A Memoir*, 1918 (by his widow); and for an account of his great work, *Life and Labour of the People in London*, 17 vols., 1902 (of which the first volume in the original edition had been published in 1889), see *My Apprenticeship*, by Beatrice Webb, 1926, chap. v., "A Grand Inquest into the Condition of the People of London ", pp. 216-56.

I may add that he had married my cousin Mary Macaulay, daughter of Charles Macaulay, a distinguished civil servant and brother of the historian, hence my intimate connection with this great enquiry into the condition of the people of London.

[1] The Poor Law Commission of 1905–9 exceeded, in the volume of published proceedings, memoranda, reports and (especially) statistics, even the Poor Law Inquiry Commission of 1832–34. Besides the lengthy Majority and Minority Reports (Cd. 4625)—these were also published in three octavo volumes from which

The entries in the diary revealing the activities of the Royal Commission open in the first days of December 1905.

December 2nd.—A pleasant visit to Gracedieu colloguing in the old way with Charles Booth as to the proper course of the poor law enquiry. I had extracted from Davy, the assistant secretary of the L.G.B., in a little interview I had had with him, the intention of the L.G.B. officials as to the purpose and procedure they intended to be followed by the Commission. They were going to use us to get certain radical reforms of structure; the boards of guardians were to be swept away, judicial officers appointed and possibly the institutions transferred to the county authorities. With all of which I am inclined to agree. But we were also to recommend reversion to the principles of 1834 as regards policy; to stem the tide of philanthropic impulse that was sweeping away the old embankment of deterrent tests to the receipt of relief. Though I think the exact form in which this impulse has clothed itself is radically wrong and mischievous, yet I believe in the impulse, if it takes the right forms. It is just this vital question of what and which forms are right that I want to discover and this Commission to investigate. Having settled the conclusions to which we are to be led, the L.G.B. officials (on and off the Commission) have predetermined the procedure. We were to be spoon-fed by evidence carefully selected and prepared; they were to draft the circular to the board of guardians; they were to select the inspectors who were to give evidence; they were virtually to select the guardians to be called in support of this evidence. Assistant commissioners were to be appointed who were to collect evidence illustrative of these theories. And above all we were to be given *opinions* and not *facts*. Charles Booth and I consulted what line we should take. To-day at lunch I put Lansbury (the working-man on the Commission) on his guard against this policy.

At the first meeting this afternoon, Lord George laid the scheme before us: the circular had been drafted, the witnesses had been selected, the assistant commissioner had almost been appointed: it remained for us to ratify. Fortunately, the scheme did not meet with approval and

our quotations are taken—there were issued no fewer than 47 folio volumes of appendices ending with a specially elaborate " General Consolidated Index " of 1086 pages. For Scotland (Cd. 4922) and Ireland (Cd. 4630) there were also Majority and Minority Reports.

The Commission was greatly aided in its work by the ability and devotion of its secretariat, notably by its secretary, R. G. Duff, then an assistant general inspector, and subsequently a general inspector of the Local Government Board (now Ministry of Health); and by its assistant secretary, John Jeffrey, then in the Scottish Local Government Board and subsequently secretary to the Scottish Health Insurance Commission and afterwards Permanent Secretary of the Scottish Health Department.

was virtually defeated; the only point settled on is the calling of the experts of the L.G.B. for which we are all quite prepared. I suggested *all* the inspectors should be called, a suggestion to which Lord George made no answer. And no other commissioner supported me at the time —but the seed had fallen on some prepared ground. It will need all my self-command to keep myself from developing a foolish hostility, and becoming self-conscious in my desire to get sound investigation. Certainly, the work of the Commission will be an education in manners as well as in poor law. I was not over pleased with my tone this after-noon and must try to do better. Beware of showing off superior know-ledge of irrelevant detail. To be single-minded in pursuit of truth, courteous in manner, and kind in feeling—and yet not to betray one's trust for the sake of popularity and be modestly persistent in my aim must be my prayer. Meanwhile, we must get on with the book and not sacrifice our own work to what, at least, can only be co-operation in a joint task with seventeen persons, with almost as many aims—and, therefore, certain to be a partial failure.

But how interesting will be this conflict of wills. I will certainly describe it as it goes along. For instance, there are four big officials on the Commission, two from England, one each from Ireland and Scot-land respectively. The English officials think they are going to direct and limit the enquiry, the Scotch and Irish officials told us pretty plainly that they did not want any enquiry, and they had already investigated the whole subject by departmental committees! And as there were no Irish and Scotch representatives of the anti-official view the enquiry into Irish and Scotch poor law has been indefinitely postponed, and will probably hardly take place. On the other hand, Charles Booth and I want a real investigation of English administration as well as an examination into pauperism, though C. B. is more con-cerned with the question of right treatment than of prevention by better-regulated life. Lansbury, on the other hand, is willing and anxious to enquire into the initial causes of pauperism, not so keen to investigate the effect of different methods of relief. C. S. Loch wants to drag in the whole question of endowed charity, in which he has the support of Mrs. Bernard Bosanquet. She and I, and possibly Miss Octavia Hill, may combine on the question of a rate-in-aid of wages to women workers—the need for discovering how far it actually obtains —and there will be a good deal of common ground, as far as the enquiry goes, between Loch and myself. Certain other commissioners such as Smart and Phelps are going to look on, I think, and intervene as the spirit moves them.

December 15*th.*—Certainly, the procedure imposed on us by Lord George was amazing. There was no agenda; a cut and dried scheme was laid before us, we were not asked to vote on it, only to express our opinion on half-a-dozen points ranging from the hour of luncheon to the appointment of assistant commissioners. The only subject really discussed was the issue of the preliminary circular to the boards of guardians. On this point there was almost unanimity against the course proposed. Whereupon Lord George called up, out of the Commission, the guardians of the poor; and we left these five persons under the chairman's eye, sitting discussing the matter. Yesterday, I got a formal announcement that unless the commissioners dissented by post the circulars would be sent out.

This was rather intolerable. I wrote a courteous but firm dissent and enigmatically suggested that I wished for some procedure that would enable those who objected to record that objection. I did not stop there. I went and unburdened my soul to the secretary, Mr. Duff. He is an attractive and sensible young civil servant, who gave me to understand that he had been against Lord George's high-handed action. So I elaborately complained to him of the absence of agenda, of concrete resolutions, of any formal appointment and authorisation of the committee; and I claimed to have a formal procedure in future; with the circulation of all proposals, of the names of witnesses, of the précis of their evidence. Apparently, our chairman had decided against all those suggestions on the ground that " we should know too much "! " I don't want to make myself disagreeable," I ventured to add; " it is extraordinarily unpleasant for a woman to do so on a commission of men. But I don't, on the other hand, intend to hide my intentions. If a procedure and methods of investigation are adopted or slipped into the Commission, which I think incompetent to elicit the truth, it will be my obvious duty to report such procedure and to describe and analyse such methods one by one. To enable me to do this, without incurring a charge of bad comradeship, I must express, clearly and emphatically, my dissent. That is why I asked for a formal procedure for the business of the Commission." I begged Mr. Duff to report the gist of the conversation to Lord George. I await the result with some amusement, and a little anxiety. It is a new experience for me to *have* to make myself disagreeable in order to reach my ends. In private life, one can only get one's way by being unusually pleasant. In official life—at least as the most insignificant member of a Commission overwhelmingly against me in opinion—I shall only get my share of control by quietly and persistently standing on my rights as an individual commissioner and refusing altogether to be overawed by great personages who would like to pooh-pooh a woman who attempts to share in the control of affairs.

Whilst I am busy with my little teacup of a Royal Commission, a new Ministry has been formed[1] [I write on December 15, 1905]. It is a strong Government and felt to be so. All the possible actors have been included, and the parts have been skilfully allotted. Our friends the " Limps " have romped in to the leading posts under Campbell-Bannerman; Morley and Bryce being marooned on India and Ireland respectively. To put Asquith and Lloyd George and Winston Churchill dead in front of Joe on the tariff and the colonies; to place John Burns to look to the unemployed; to give Birrell the Education Office; are all apt placements. But the great *coup* is to get Haldane to take the War Office—the courtly lawyer with a great capacity for dealing with men and affairs, and a real understanding of the function of an expert, and skill in using him.

Two of the new Cabinet have already come in to talk over their new life. The very day of his introduction to the Cabinet, John Burns arrived, childishly delighted with his own post. For one solid hour he paced the room expanding his soul before me—how he had called in the permanent officials, asked them questions. " That is my decision, gentlemen ", he proudly rehearsed to me once or twice. " Don't be too doctrinaire about the unemployed, Mr. Burns ", I mildly suggested. " Economise your great force of honesty, Mrs. Webb," he rejoined solemnly, " I am a different man from what I was a week ago. You read what I say to-morrow when I stand by C. B. at the deputation. You will see I shan't give myself away." What he and the big officials will do with each other remains to be seen. To listen to him talking one would think he was hopelessly confused and blurred in his views and intentions. His best chance will be to refuse to be overwhelmed with routine administration, to devote himself to one or two points, and strike dramatic effects in one or two unconventional decisions. A sort of working-class Roosevelt is his rôle. The story goes that, when C. B. offered him the L.G.B. with a seat in the Cabinet, he clasped the Premier by the hand. " I congratulate you, Sir Henry: it will be the most popular appointment that you have made."

Yesterday afternoon Haldane came in. *He* also was in a state of

---

[1] Campbell-Bannerman accepted office on December 5, 1905. The Cabinet he formed included the leading Liberal Leaguers and the leading pro-Boers. Among the former were Asquith as Chancellor of the Exchequer; Grey as Foreign Secretary; Haldane as Secretary for War; together with Sydney Buxton, Post Office. Among the pro-Boers were Reid, afterwards Lord Loreburn, as Lord Chancellor; John Morley as Secretary for India; John Burns, Local Government Board; Lloyd George, Board of Trade; whilst Reginald McKenna, Winston Churchill, Herbert Samuel, Walter Runciman, appeared as under-secretaries. In the general election beginning January 12, 1906, the Liberals obtained 377 seats, a majority of 84 over all other parties combined. The Conservatives and Liberal Unionists secured only 157, the Irish Nationalists 83, and Labour members, 24 supporting the Liberal Party, and 29 styling themselves the Labour Party, with their own organisation and their own whips.

exuberant delight over his new task. " I chose the War Office out of three offices. Asquith, Grey and I stood together; they were forced to take us on our own terms. We were really very indifferent," he added sublimely, " Asquith gave up a brief of £10,000 to defend the Khedive's property that very week; I was throwing away an income of £15,000 to £20,000 a year; and Grey had no ambition and was sacrificing his fishing. But it was a horrid week—one perpetual wrangle. The King signified that he would like me to take the War Office; it is exactly what I myself longed for. I have never been so happy in my life ", and he beamed all over. And then he poured into my sympathetic ear all his plans. " I shall spend three years observing and thinking. I shall succeed: I have always succeeded in everything I have undertaken." I confess I was a little surprised at the naïveté of this last remark. Alas! what hideous failures the wisest of us makes. But, of course, it was merely the foam of his excited self-complacency, in the first novelty of power. He came straight from a whole day talking over matters with Arnold-Forster [preceding Secretary for War]—a thoroughly English proceeding, showing the essential solidarity of the governing class.

The lower ranks of the Government are filled with young men we know, or have known. Herbert Samuel, an old friend . . . has made a surprising advance in obtaining the under-secretaryship of the Home Office, leaving poor C. P. Trevelyan behind. Lough, McKenna, Runciman, all friendly acquaintances. We gather that as regards the non-Cabinet offices there is a sort of panel constructed by the Prime Minister, from which the Cabinet Ministers select subordinates for their respective offices. Burns said he had selected Runciman out of those submitted to him—Trevelyan and Jack Tennant being the other two—so there is still a chance for C. P. For some mysterious reason, Macnamara has refused office: it is said he could not afford to take an inferior berth or give up the editorship of the *Schoolmaster*; and he was offered no position equal to his expectations, and in that sense he is a disappointed man.

A satisfactory interview with the chairman of our Commission, arranged by the secretary whom I apparently alarmed by my rebellious attitude. For a whole hour I listened to his somewhat weak proposals, quietly insisting on a regular procedure, the appointment of a committee to consider and report on methods of investigation and the concentration of our efforts on ascertaining the facts about the relief of destitution, and not merely collecting casual opinions as to defects in law and practice. I felt strengthened by the fact that Sidney had helped me to draft a series of concrete proposals which I succeeded in making him ask me for. What upset his aristocratic mind was the notion that the Commission should appoint its own committees and regulate its own procedure. " I saw the democratic method worked out on the London School Board when I was chairman," he naïvely remarked, " and I was not impressed with its results." I tried to convince him that consent was a preliminary requirement to efficiency. " Moreover," I urged, " you will find that you practically appoint the committees even if you submit the names formally to the Commission; it may be that one or two others will be added, but when the first flush of energy has exhausted itself we shall suffer not from too large but too small a membership of the working committee." So we chatted on, getting more and more friendly. " You must remember, Lord George, that we are all rather awed by our *grand seigneur* chairman," was my parting shot, " and with a nondescript body like the Commission awe some- times gets transformed into suspicion of being bossed. With a per- tinacious spirit like C. S. Loch, for instance, this feeling might have inconvenient results."

Meanwhile, I have sent my suggestions to one or two of the com- missioners: and have had a most friendly chat with Loch who, so far as investigation goes, will, I think, be a sturdy ally.

1906

January 9th.—Second meeting of Commission went off well. The chairman introduced the motion for a committee on procedure and methods of investigation: Charles Booth (to whom I had sent my suggestions) backed it up: Loch somewhat demurred, Mrs. Bernard Bosanquet objected, seeing, I think, an insidious proposal of mine which would give the London members and the experts in investiga- tion complete control over the Commission. But the Commission on the whole was favourable. At any rate, I have made friends with the chairman, and shall now be careful not to excite the jealousy of those who feel themselves opposed to me in doctrine. The C.O.S. are far more suspicious of me than I am of them. I believe that they *do* want investigation and should be glad if we could co-operate against those who do not. But I see that, at first at any rate, they will keep both Charles Booth and me at arm's length. C. B. made a useful suggestion that no one need cross-examine Adrian [legal official of L.G.B.] until we have the proof of his evidence. The wisdom of this was quickly apparent. Adrian, a heavy, dull but conscientious official, began, in monotonous tone, to read a verbose disquisition on the law from the very beginning of poor relief to the end. The room was cold, and we all, I think, failed to take any intelligent interest in what he said. I stayed for lunch and chatted pleasantly with Lord George and then escaped and went for a walk and service at Westminster Abbey. Thory (T. G.) Gardiner came to tea and I impregnated him with our views of investigation. I stay away to-day, and see clearly that my most important work will be done outside the Commission room. I will give my best *thought* but scamp attendance.

Third meeting of Commission. I did not attend, as Adrian's evidence in chief consisted of his reading from copious notes, or long legal disquisitions, which, as it was all taken down in shorthand and served to us in printed form in two days' time, and before his cross-examination began, it was sheer waste of time to sit there listening to it. On Monday (4th meeting) the cross-examination began, and on that afternoon and the following morning I tried to make him admit that we must see and study the general and special orders, circulars, etc., for ourselves, before we could understand the body of law and regulation under which the guardians acted. In this endeavour I was stopped by the chairman and Sir Samuel Provis, and I had a little tiff across the table as to whether he, or we, should judge whether documents were important or not. But I got a specific promise from the chairman that all the documents that we needed should be at the disposal of the Commission.

However, as the Commission seemed still in a rudderless condition, at the mercy of the little clique of officials, Sidney and I prepared a memorandum on methods of enquiry, which I have asked to be circulated to the whole Commission. That done I feel that I have striven to get the enquiry on the right lines, and can now rest a bit. To reform the procedure of royal commissions would be worth delaying the completion of our book. But, up to now, I find attendance at the Commission a most disagreeable business—it is extraordinarily unpleasant when one has to force people's hands and make them attend to one by sheer ugly persistency at the cost, of course, of getting back a certain insolence of attitude on the part of hostile men.—*This is exaggeration!* (a week after).

Thought it wise to let the two secretaries see both our proof of *The Parish* and also our first draft of *The History of the Poor Law, 1689–1835.* The publication of the work before the Report of the Commission is one of the trump cards in our hand and, as our object is to make them throw up the game of obstruction to investigation, it is well to put the card on the table.

January 28th.—Hewins and his wife came to lunch here after many months' interval owing to preoccupation on all sides. Both were very depressed: he was somewhat bitter against all the Unionist leaders, even including Joe; she was merely " down on her luck "—dreary—poor little soul! The result of the election has evidently been a terrible disillusionment for Hewins: it never occurred to him that the reaction might be so complete as to keep the Tories out for six years. From his private point of view it is a catastrophe: he thought, I am convinced, that in a few years, if not immediately, he would be arranging tariffs, and tariff wars, and tariff treaties, at the Board of Trade—hurrying from continent to continent, in close and confidential intercourse with ministers and great financial personages—one long delightful intrigue with a World Empire as the result. From the public point of view, it appears to him also as a disaster. " It depends on the next six years whether or not we lose Canada: six years hence it will be too late ", he exclaimed in his mysterious way. His autumn visit to Canada has convinced him that the Canadians will range themselves under the American flag, unless we give them a substantial preference. " A great people with great resources—just chucked away through sheer ignorance and petty selfishness."

Of course, he is contemptuous of Balfour and those who surround him. But he is also irritated against Joe—for reasons I do not understand; except when there has been a gigantic fiasco, all concerned condemn " the others ". Poor Hewins, with his grand castles in the air that he has been, for the last three years, inhabiting—now lying in ruins about him! I suppose he will become a paid organiser of the protectionist cause—an occasional leader-writer in protectionist papers. Meanwhile, it is conceivable that he is right about Canada. Sidney regards it as a " mare's nest ": " if Canada leaves us because she cannot get a tariff she will leave us anyhow ".

February 5th.—The memorandum I sent in on methods of enquiry led the chairman to ask all the other commissioners for memoranda. And some six or seven responded. Whereupon all have been referred to a committee consisting of Lord George, Provis, Booth, Bentham, Smart, Loch, Phelps, Mrs. Bosanquet and myself, and we meet on Monday 12th to consider them. This morning I spent taking out all the questions which the L.G.B. witnesses had told us we ought to enquire into, with a view to trying to persuade the committee to start on a systematic survey of all the unions, with a view to more detailed investigation of some. Yesterday, Bentham—the ablest person (except perhaps Provis) on the Commission—came here, and we talked poor law from 5.30 to 11 o'clock. Result, bad headache this afternoon!

Dear Charles Booth is as delightful as ever, but he is losing his intellectual grip and persistency of purpose—is not much use on the Commission. Happily, he is unaware of it. Alas! for the pathetic strivings of age—more pitiful to the onlooker than those of youth, because without hope of amendment.

Want to get the Commission, sooner or later, to undertake:

(1) Survey of all English unions, with regard to difference of constitution and methods of administration of union.

(2) Analysis of the whence and whither of pauperism in some among them.

(3) Clear vision of course of legislation.

(4) Analysis of developments of policy of central authority.

It would be natural to begin with numbers three or four: but owing to the fact that we shall be fully occupied until next autumn in completing our book, I shall suggest beginning at the other end. We want, if possible, to superintend, or at any rate supplement, three and four.

February 9th.—About nine o'clock yesterday evening, in walked John Burns. He had an indefinable air of greater dignity—a new and perfectly fitting jacket suit, a quieter manner, and less boisterous vanity in his talk. The man is filling in with good stuff. He described the three committees of the Cabinet upon which he had that day sat— one on the Trade Disputes Bill, the other on the unemployed, and the third on the Workmen's Compensation Extension Bill. He was naïvely delighted with his share in the proceedings, especially his insistence that workmen's compensation should include provision for illness or death from unhealthy occupations. He had filled in his time with seeing all and sundry—philanthropists, Labour representatives, great employers and asking their advice. " They are all so kind to me," he said, in glowing appreciation—" especially the great employers, just the men who might have objected to my appointment." Oh! the wisdom of England's governing class!

He pulled out a set of cards, upon which he had written the measures which he had decided to bring forward in the first two years—mostly measures that the L.G.B. had long ago pigeon-holed—the abolition of overseers, further equalisation of rates in London, amendment of the Alkali Act, and finally (as a concession to the Labour Party), an amendment of the Unemployed Act of last session in the direction of greater contributions from the rates. " I want to be efficient," he said, with youthful fervour, " if you and Sidney can give me a tip I am always ready to listen. I am ready to take tips from anyone so long as they mean business in my direction." If good intentions, and a strong vigorous and audacious character, can make up for lack of administrative experience and technical knowledge, John Burns may yet be a success as President of the Local Government Board.

Altogether Sidney and I are in better spirits as to the course of political affairs than we have been for many years. We do not deceive ourselves by the notion that this wave of Liberalism is wholly progressive in character—much of its bulk is made up of sheer conservatism aroused by the revolutionary tariff policy of Chamberlain. But it looms as progressive in its direction and all the active factors are collectivist. Moreover, it is clear that Joe is going to try to outbid the Liberals by constructive social reform. It is an interesting little fact that a fortnight ago he wrote in his own hand to W. P. Reeves to beg him to send all the Acts, and literature about the Acts, relating to old-age pensions and compulsory arbitration [in New Zealand]—as if he desired to convince himself of their feasibility as an adjunct to his tariff policy. Whether or not this socialistic addition will make for the popularity of protection, it will come at any rate as pressure on the Liberals to do something for raising the standard of life of the very poor—it will bar the way to a policy of the *status quo.*

February 12th.—I sent another memorandum to the chairman sketching out the work of three committees—on statistics, local administration and central policy respectively—a scheme which in his gentlemanly way he pressed on the acceptance of the committee on procedure. The committee on statistics was agreed to, so was a committee on blue-books, etc., to which the documents of the L.G.B. might be added; and, in the course of the discussion, it became clear that a committee on local administration would, in the end, be required. But most of the members were against taking any steps towards a positive scheme until after the inspectors' evidence. Charles Booth wants one committee only; Mrs. Bosanquet objects to any but temporary committees; no members want a systematic investigation but myself. I threw out the notion of a statistical officer and an assistant commissioner to undertake the investigation into local administration —but as yet, it is not responded to. Meanwhile, Sir Samuel Provis will not agree to anyone looking through the L.G.B. documents— insists that we must call for those we want to see and not have the run of the whole. In an interview we had at the L.G.B. he lost his temper and asserted that he " would not have a picking enquiry into L.G.B. policy ". I kept my temper and we parted on friendly terms. Charles Booth blames me for having raised the hostility of the L.G.B. He may be right—the other policy would have been to wheedle my way into the place. On the other hand, if one begins by being disagreeable, one may come in the end to a better bargain. It is, however, clear that I shall not have the support of the Commission in my desire for scientific research into the past seventy years.

There is one very pleasant feature about the Commission. We are all of us after public objects, however much we may disagree as to what these objects are and how to arrive at them. There is hardly any personal vanity, or personal ambition, and no personal interest at work

331

in the Commission. A little jealousy of those who take the lead—but very little of that. And we are all getting fond of our chairman—who, like many a *grand seigneur*, can afford to be modest and unassuming.

He and his wife dined with us yesterday, meeting Rowntree (author of *Poverty*), the Barnetts, the clerk of the Westminster Board of Guardians, Mrs. Sydney Buxton and Henry Hobhouse—a most pleasant and useful party. Rowntree, who stayed the night here, is to help me to get an analysis of 1000 applications—the whence and the whither of pauperism. I am beginning to enjoy the Commission work: but the grind of combining it with our own enquiry keeps one at a low level of strength and good spirits. Book III., *Seignorial Franchise and Municipal Corporations*, is in some ways the hardest of all.

Meanwhile, Balfour has succumbed to Chamberlain, and the Conservative Party has become definitely protectionist—for the time—so long as Chamberlain lives. In so far as it commits the most *laisser-faire* party to the policy of state control and increase of taxation, we rejoice in it. Sidney still thinks that import duties are a wasteful device, though agreeing to the expediency of deepening the channels of trade between Anglo-Saxon communities. Personally, I don't believe much in the injuriousness of tariffs to a prosperous wealth-producing country like England. And, if a tariff were part and parcel of a deliberately conceived scheme of raising the standard of life by collective regulation and public expenditure, I should be willing to pay for this scheme in a slight rise in the price of commodities. And, other things being equal, I would rather pay more for commodities produced by our colonists under fair conditions of employment than fractionally less for commodities produced under unknown conditions by an oppressed people. This, as a matter of sentiment, and as an argument for bettering conditions here. However, for the next six years we have to look to the Liberal Party for any reforms. It is well that Sidney is a " free importer ". As for my private predilection " mum's the word ".

February 19th.—Dined last night with Tommy Lough (now promoted to the parliamentary secretaryship of the Education Department) and met three other minor members of the Ministry—the Lord Chancellor of Ireland, Lord Advocate for Scotland, and Solicitor-General for Ireland, as well as two or three ministerial M.P.'s. The minor Ministers were all on their best behaviour, with that peculiar combination of new-born discretion and modesty with obvious self-complacency at being within the mystic circle of the Government. Tommy Lough was great on the reforms he intended to introduce in the financial transactions of the Education Department—horror-struck at the notion of 80,000 separate cheques a year on behalf of separate institutions. " We might as well have a separate cheque for each packet of tea sold by the Tower Company." The mysteries of education are still above and beyond him. "As for the Government's intention," he whispered to me, " about education or any other matter, I know less than I did as a private member. You see I may not gossip and no one gossips with me." He added sadly, "We under-secretaries are just set down to do some departmental job and, as we know nothing of the subject, we have got to stick to it, instead of amusing ourselves in the lobby, picking up news. But it is interesting", he continued with glowing enthusiasm, " to feel yourself right inside the machine. Morant is a fine fellow and we get on splendidly—but the office from a mere business point of view *does* want reforming."

A boisterous tea dealer, whose business career has been divided between advertising packets of tea and starting doubtful companies— whose public interests are wholly Irish or working-class, who has neither literary culture nor scientific knowledge—as one of the heads of our Education Department! A rum thing is English government.

For all that I like Tommy Lough, he has energy, he is no respecter of persons, he wants, in a philistine way, to make society more prosperous and happier, and he never says what he does not think. He is a rough, ugly instrument, but so far as he cuts at all he cuts in the right direction.

February 22nd.—Had a party of young Liberals dining here last night: Herbert Samuel and Reginald McKenna, Masterman and John Simon, Massingham and Sydney Olivier. Of these Simon, the young lawyer, is by far the most brilliant—making a big income as the rising junior at the Bar. He has a conventional mind but excellent working intellect, a charming person, agreeable voice and manner. But his spirit has been broken and his whole life made arid by the loss, some three years ago, of his young wife. He declares himself already " bored " by Parliament after three days of it. " Rufus Isaacs has shown me a quiet corner to which I retire and work at my briefs." He is an individualist Liberal of the Morley type, without Morley's idealism.

I sat between the two new under-secretaries, both full of the work and dignity of office—neither of them exciting personalities, but McKenna a genuine reformer of the ordinary kind—and both as respectable and hard-working as Cabinet Ministers could desire in subordinates. Masterman exuberant in his half-cynical, half-sentimental talk; Sydney Olivier full of the possibility of going out to South Africa in an important post, all of them full of themselves and rather impatient of each other's obsessions.

This morning I took off—the first holiday for a fortnight or more. I walked along the Embankment to St. Paul's for the 10 o'clock service. The beauty of the music and the old-world charm of the words, the great space of the dome, are always the best recreation when I am weary with straining my poor little mind. I prayed for strength to order my effort rightly and keep my motives pure, to preserve the patience and persistency of purpose needed to carry through our intentions. These next three years are going to try my strength of body, intellect and character: I sometimes wonder whether I shall keep going, or whether some day I may not find that I have stopped for repair. And yet it is little that I really accomplish with all my abstinence and cutting down of all but business intercourse. Sidney can do about four times as much as I, whether measured in time or in matter.

Sidney thoroughly satisfied with the secondary education side of L.C.C. work: he gets through all his grants without opposition: he is building up a system of provided and non-provided schools side by side. He is happy in his work, as all antagonism to him personally has subsided. The little jealousies between the leading Progressives are now transferred from Spring Gardens to Westminster—and Sidney does not appear in this higher sphere. Spring Gardens has become a mere backwater in which the remaining big fish of the old gang can swim without fear of creating disturbance. Thirty-two of the Progressives, including all the leaders, now in the House of Commons! There is actually some talk of making Sidney vice-chairman of the education committee! Collins even pressed him to accept the great position: Sidney modestly put himself at the " disposition of his party " and acquiesced in the suggestion that he should work under Shepheard (who is to be promoted to the chairmanship) if the majority of the party actually desire it.[1] It is a great luxury to feel that he is beyond all question of dignity and personal position. If you are content to accept any position that is forced on you and never to compete, there is a good deal of excellent and happy work to be done in the world.

March 1st.—Meanwhile, my Royal Commission grinds slowly on. The three committees that I pressed for on the procedure committee have been appointed and have set to work: statistics, documents (on central policy and on local administration). I am trying to guide the committee on documents into making an analysis of all the documents of the central authority—statutes, orders, reports, with a view of writing a memorandum on the attitude of the state towards each class of pauper. Lord George gives me unhesitating support: my difficulty is with Sir Samuel Provis. But I had the most friendly chat with him this afternoon, and he comes to dine to meet a carefully selected party on Wednesday. Charles Booth has the statistical committee well in

---

[1] They did not wish it, so he remains chairman of the higher education committee—a post he prefers.

hand: Bentham has elaborated and improved my question as to the working constitution of the boards of guardians: I hope that investigations will be presently set on foot as to the life history of paupers in different unions. And I no longer find the association with my fellow-commissioners disagreeable. But it is a somewhat disastrous interruption of work on the book, which drags on painfully.

We are trying to avoid dining out except when it seems absolutely desirable that we should be present (*e.g.* Liberal Ministers). We wish to be on friendly terms with the administrators and to make ourselves as useful as possible. Mr. Haldane came in this morning—first to discuss with Sidney and Mackinder the organisation of London University—and, when Mackinder had left, to consult us about his scheme of army reform. So far as we could understand it, this scheme provides for a small and highly expert professional army with the militia in attendance for foreign service (a reduction of 50,000 men). Then, in the background, as material for reinforcements, in time of war, a mass of half-trained material under a semi-civil authority—probably a county authority bearing some sort of likeness to the joint committee for police —with " grants in aid " to promote extension and efficiency. Of his secretaries young Acland is attending to the labour side (contracts, etc.), Lord Lucas to Buckingham Palace, Widdows to army education, Colonel Ellison to army organisation. We are to meet all of them at dinner on Tuesday; young Acland comes to lunch to-morrow to consult Sidney about army contracts and their conditions.

A brilliant dinner for the Students' Union [London School of Economics]—A. J. B. and Sir John French as guests. One of those academic discourses from the ex-Premier in which he delights, and in which he delights his hearers. In our talk together I gathered that he is set on continued leadership: would not hear the suggestion that he should take a holiday. " It is exactly now that they are beaten and demoralised that they need me: I shall be with them as continuously as if I were Prime Minister." Like all great personages there creeps out, now and again, a little horn of egotism—a sensitiveness, more than with the ruck of men, to any depreciation of his past work and present position. He pressed me to come, both of us, to stay at Whittingehame—perhaps, we may go. I should like to talk out some matters of government with him and some aspects of the philosophy of public conduct. Is he an ingrained individualist incapable of change? Tariff reform has, at any rate, shaken the *laisser-faire* side of his philosophy.

At the meeting of Tuesday, 27th February, of the Royal Commission, Charles Booth attempted the use of the method of the interview which seemed to me illegitimate and was hotly resented by the chairman, Sir S. Provis and others. He happened to be in the chair when Preston-Thomas (inspector for South Wales District) was to be cross-examined on his printed statement. This statement concerned the district as a whole (I had urged that the inspectors should be asked to supply separate particulars about each union, but, largely because Charles Booth backed down, I was defeated and the inspector was asked to describe his district as a whole). But Charles Booth insisted on taking him right through the whole of the unions—one by one—asking him questions for which the man was not prepared and could only give hearsay evidence. Five hours were thus spent without the other members having a chance of asking questions arising out of his printed statement. I had left after lunch, but I hear that there was a hot dispute as to the relevancy of the questions and the chairman seems determined to put a stop to it. That sort of wholesale interviewing is all very well if the man is prepared and is speaking of facts within his own knowledge. But it is hardly worth the £100 which each weekly meeting of the Commission costs the national exchequer. I am inclined to think that a statement of the cost of the different methods of investigation ought to be submitted to the commissioners by the chairman—it is a case where efficiency would be actually promoted by some attention to economy. A Royal Commission drifts into stupid, lazy and costly ways through sheer inadvertence and lack of forethought as to means and ways.

The documents committee, consisting of Smart (chairman), Russell Wakefield, MacDougall, Provis and myself, met for the first time. I had circulated suggestions proposing to limit ourselves, in the first instance, to discovering what policy had been laid down by the central authority [1] as to the relief of various kinds of paupers since 1834, and proposing that the work should be undertaken by an efficient clerk under Jeffrey (clerk to the committee), according to definite plans decided on by the committee. To show what I meant, I circulated an analysis of the 1834 report, the first three statutes and two general orders, made by Mrs. Spencer. Professor Smart, on the other hand, proposed that he and Wakefield should undertake the blue-books, and that I and MacDougall should undertake the general orders and circulars—each selecting what we thought fit and doing it in the way we thought best. I was beaten, though Sir Samuel Provis supported my suggestion that the work should be done systematically under direction. The simple truth was that I had a majority against me on both counts. MacDougall, Wakefield and Provis did not want an

[1] By the term " central authority " is always meant the unbroken succession of government departments dealing with the Poor Law : first the Poor Law Commissions of 1834–48; then the Poor Law Board, 1849–71; then the Local Government Board, 1871–1930, when it was succeeded by the Ministry of Health. See *English Poor Law History*, by S. and B. Webb.

historical retrospect—they desired only to enquire into the laws of to-day—and Smart, MacDougall and Wakefield did not want the work done systematically under a deliberate plan. Seeing myself beaten, I suggested that Smart and Wakefield should do their job first and that, if that were satisfactory, we could then decide whether we would do the circulars and statutes in the same way. So the committee has adjourned for two or three months; which has the incidental advantage of leaving my Monday mornings free for our own work. The longer the Commission delays the better for me. Meanwhile, I will put Miss Longman on to the " general orders " and circulars. In all probability we shall have to do the work ourselves—a plan that has its advantages.

March 19*th*.—Attended a meeting of the Poplar Board of Guardians, held at 6.30. About 30 were present, a rather low lot of doubtful representatives of Labour, with a sprinkling of builders, publicans, insurance and other agents. The meeting was exclusively engaged in allotting the contracts for the year, which meant up to something between £50,000 and £100,000. I did not ascertain the exact amount. The procedure was utterly reckless. The tenders were opened at the meeting, the names and prices read out; and then, without any kind of report of a committee or by officials, straight away voted on. Usually the same person as heretofore was taken, nearly always a local man— it was not always the lowest tender, and the prices were, in all cases, full, in some cases obviously excessive. Butter at 1s. 2d. a lb., when the contracts ran into thousands of pounds worth, was ridiculous. Milk at 9d. a gallon—the best and most expensive meat, tea at 2s. 8d. " Give Bow a chance " was one of the relevant considerations urged successfully in favour of a change in the contractor. Will Crooks sat in the chair and did nothing to check the recklessness. Even Lansbury, by constitution a thorough-going sentimentalist, and with no other ex-perience of public affairs, protested, and was clearly ashamed of the procedure.

March 20*th*.—Two dinners, that well illustrated a subtle distinc-tion of atmosphere—one at the Asquiths, the other at the George Hamiltons. The former consisted of the Russian Ambassador, the Desboroughs, Lord Goschen, the Dickson Poynders, Mrs. Lowther (the Speaker's wife), Lord Hugh Cecil, Mrs. Lester (Mrs. Cornwallis West's sister), one or two aristocratic young men, and the Asquiths' daughter and Raymond. The large garish rooms, the flunkeys and the superlatively good dinner, gave a sort of " Second Empire " setting to the entertainment. Lady Desborough, Margot, Mrs. Lester and Lady Dickson Poynder were all very *décolletée* and highly-adorned with jewels. The conversation aimed at brilliancy—Margot's sparkling little disjointed sayings, kindly and indiscreet, Lady Desborough's somewhat artificial grace, Lady Dickson Poynder's pretty folly, Mrs. Lester's *outré* frankness, lending a sort of stagyness to the talk; we might have all been characters brought on to illustrate the ways of modern " society "—a twentieth-century Sheridan's play. They were all gushing over G. B. S., and I had to entertain the ladies after dinner with a discourse on his philosophy and personality—mostly the latter. We came away feeling half-flattered that we had been asked, half-contemptuous of ourselves for having gone. And not pleased with the entourage of a democratic Minister.

Very different the George Hamiltons. Here the party consisted of the Neville Lytteltons, Lady Arthur Russell, the Herbert Jekylls, Sir Francis Mowatt—persons belonging to much the same set as the Asquith party though of a dowdier hue. But the reception in the cosy library was homely, and the dinner without pretentiousness—the George Hamiltons treating us as if we were part of a family party— no attempt to shine, just talking about the things that interested each of us in a quiet simple way. It would have been almost impossible to show off, so absolutely sincere and quiet was the tone. And yet the conversation was full of interest and lingered willingly on each subject. After we ladies had left, Sidney said that he listened with eager interest to a long interchange of official experience between Lord George, Mowatt and Lyttelton, as to the administration of the War Office and the relations between Cabinet, War Minister and permanent staff—Jekyll and Sidney listening and occasionally intervening. And, as we drove away, we felt that we had had a restful evening, learnt something and gained stimulus from the refinement and public spirit manifest in our hosts and their guests. The Tory aristocrat and his wife were, in relation to their class, living the simple life; and the Yorkshire manufacturer's son was obviously " swelling " it, to use the vulgar expression for a vulgar thing.

April 6th.—Towards municipalisation. Edgar Speyer, the millionaire promoter of the electric tubes, and undertaker of the electrification of the underground railway, with his general manager Sir George Gibb, dined here last night to meet McKinnon Wood, and discuss a deal with the L.C.C. He wants the L.C.C. to raise five millions for him, he paying 4% and inserting a purchase clause for the whole undertaking at 21 or 40 years. A shrewd little Jew—taciturn and almost gloomy, but lighting up at the end of the evening when he thought he had impressed McKinnon Wood and Sidney. Sir George Gibb (late general manager of N.E.R.), a courtly official of great capacity and considerable charm, to whom Speyer gives £10,000 to manage his undertakings—a personage typical of the present time, when the enterprise of syndicates is managed on Civil Service lines and big officials are perpetually transferring themselves from company to company, or from company to Government, and from Government to company. McKinnon Wood and Sidney, unpaid organisers of society, Gibb and Speyer heavily-remunerated organisers—though the difference is more apparent than real since the two L.C.C. members are pensioners on the nation's industry exactly as Gibb and Speyer—the only difference being that, in Sidney's and McKinnon Wood's case, the income is small, not much more than a livelihood and working expenses. Sidney helped to bring Speyer and Wood together because he approves of the L.C.C. becoming a sleeping partner in London transport—eventually taking it over. Also Speyer may, in return, help forward the School. We are looking out for a donor of £40,000 to enlarge the building: Speyer seems the most likely of the millionaires.

Haldane has asked Sidney to join a little committee consisting of Lord Esher, Monro (L.G.B. official), and one or two military experts, with young Lord Lucas as a sort of secretary, to consider the carrying out of his scheme of " voluntary conscription ",[1] and we are trying to introduce the Secretary for War to various county and city administrators. We hope, by involving county organisations in the volunteer movement, we may pave the way for the half-time movement, by which half the working hours and all the leisure of the boys up to eighteen will be absorbed in some sort of training.

April 15th.—Decided to publish our three volumes separately: *The Parish and the County*, October 1st; *Seignorial Franchises and Municipal Corporations*, January 1st; and *Statutory Authorities for Special Purposes and some Conclusions*, May 5th. We think in that way we shall get almost continuous advertisement for the whole work for six months. There is such a mass of new stuff—both facts and theories—that the reviewer would be unable to grasp the whole. Moreover, though we do not want to hurry the work, it is essential that we get the kudos of our publication in time for the L.C.C. election and for my work on the Royal Commission.

These last three months my work has been slacker and, I fear, less good quality than last year, owing to the rival interest of the P.L.C. But we are well on with Book III., having finished the *Lord's Court and Manorial Boroughs* and beginning our analysis of *Municipal Corporations*. Most of Book IV. is done: Book V., *Some Conclusions*, is as yet but dreamt of! Toothache and nervous exhaustion somewhat spoils

---

[1] This was a phrase indignantly hurled at me by a Radical member who disapproves of Haldane and all his works.

the prospect of our Easter holiday at Longfords. But, perhaps, a few days' complete rest and more generous diet may re-establish a painless equilibrium.

April 16th.—A happy time at Longfords, and some progress with our chapter on the *City of London*—taken out of turn as the analysis and the constitution of the MS., 1835, is not yet completed by our secretaries. But there will be a stiff pull over that analysis and I must sacrifice all my other work to getting a grip of the material, which is overpowering in quantity and complexity.

Mary Playne growing every year more benign: lost all her old cynicism and worldliness—not all her old restlessness. The spirit of religion .becomes every day a more potent influence in her life—presently she will be a veritable saint. Will she end in the Catholic Church? There are signs that her inward eyes are turning that way. She prophesies great accessions to the Church universal through the virtual disestablishment of the English Church, by the Education Bill if it passes into law. The saintly Prior of Woodchester is a frequent visitor, and the unselfconscious and gentle devoutness of some neighbouring Catholics are telling on her mind. But, on the whole, I think she will remain satisfied with a mystical Christian science and conformity to the Church of England. She and I become increasingly sympathetic: we discuss, in moony fashion, the need for a new order embodying faith in a spiritual force, the obligation to love and thankfulness, and abstemiousness from all harmful, if not unnecessary, physical indulgence or vain display. We are too old and worn to start it. Some younger woman may.

Sidney thinks the Education Bill[1] a harsh measure, but takes no part in the agitation against it; does not care to discuss it since it is clear he cannot influence the result. We have no kind of influence, either on Birrell or those behind him, or on any of the parliamentary groups that are likely to carry amendments in committee. And, as we belong neither to the Church nor to the Catholics, we have no place in either of the movements in the country against it. If it is defeated, it will be through using the indifference of the bulk of parents and ratepayers to the whole question of religious education, combined with their objection to the cost of buying out the denominational schools: if that issue were separately put to the country, I think the Catholic and Church schools would be allowed to continue on the present basis. But I doubt the skill and persistency of the Church. Half, or at any

---

[1] This was the measure by which the Liberal Government sought to reverse the scheme of 1902, which placed the cost of the staffing and the incidental expenses of the Anglican and Roman Catholic elementary schools upon the shoulders of the Local Education Authority out of the rates.

rate a large fraction, like the Bill as a curb on Anglican priestcraft; whilst a powerful minority even among the clergy are really rationalists and desire the suppression of distinctively dogmatic teaching—Canon Henson for instance. The Catholics are fervent, logical and unanimous: their plea unanswerable since to them undenominational teaching is the very devil.

May 15th.—A baffling time divided between superintending two secretaries at work on the City of London records, and drafting a memorandum on the policy of the central authority of the Poor Law, 1834–47, from Miss Longman's notes.

The Royal Commission lumbers along; chaotic and extravagant in its use of time and money, each committee doing as it seems fit in its own sight. There is a lack of method and discipline with which some of us get impatient and, I fear, I sometimes offend by my easygoing ways—intervening when I ought to hold my peace. " You did not behave nicely yesterday," said Lord George in kindly reproof, " you should not have referred to current politics." So I thanked him warmly for the hint, and promised to be " seen and not heard " in future. I find it so difficult to be official in manner. However, I really will try. Dignified silence I will set before me, except when the public good requires me to come forward. Ah! how hard it is for the quick-witted and somewhat vain woman to be discreet and accurate. One can manage to be both in the written word—but the " clash of tongues " drives both discretion and accuracy away.

May 22nd.—C. S. Loch completely lost his temper yesterday at my cross-examination of Lockwood. He is always making *ex parte* statements in his questions, and yesterday he made Lockwood—a weak witness—advocate the prohibition of compounding, on the ground that the occupier, if he were conscious of paying rates, would be more severe on expenditure. So I made Lockwood say that the landlord, whatever the arrangement, really paid the rates and that the occupier would, therefore, prefer to pay the economic rent to the local authority in the form of rates, from whom he received services, than to the landlord from whom he received nil. Loch got white with rage, and protested against my questions as misleading statements of economic doctrine. All this dialectic seems to me a foolish business: but it is important to let the commissioners know that we shall challenge all the current assumptions. However, in the little tiff, the Commission was on my side. What makes him angry is that the enquiry is drifting straight into the *causes of destitution* instead of being restricted to the narrower question of *granted destitution is inevitable, how can we best prevent pauperism?* And the answer that is being extracted by our enquiry into the causes of destitution takes the form of *more regulation and more public provision without the stigma of pauperism*—probably compulsory provision which *must* be given and *cannot* be refused.

May 22nd.—An agreeable Sunday with Sir Charles Eliot, late Governor of East Africa and now Principal of Sheffield University, and Lady Elcho who had persuaded us to go thither. Poor Sir Charles, having chucked away his prospects by indiscreet and unbecoming resistance to the policy of the Foreign Office, has taken on a wholly uncongenial task. To be more or less subordinate to a second-rate town council, to be organising lectures by fifth-rate professors for clerks and unemployed young women, is somewhat riling to a distinguished diplomatist and bureaucrat of the Empire. So he takes refuge in " beasties ", spending more time in his little laboratory—describing, dissecting, and discoursing about slugs of the sea and the earth—than in the committee room or the class room. He is a strong man— observant and executive—but without subtlety or charm. Nevertheless, if I were Secretary of State I should get him back into the administration of the Empire.

Lady Elcho, a kindly sympathetic, interested but somewhat weary woman—her friendship with " Mr. Arthur ", as he is called in that set, the romance of her life, but a romance which has become somewhat faded. Now, at any rate, no sign of anything beyond old friendliness between them: " Mr. Arthur " having had a good many fancies, I imagine. We met him at dinner at her house the other night, and I was allotted to him. If it were not for the glamour that envelops a man of charm who has been Prime Minister and the leader of a great party—should I like him? One thing I know, I should dislike the set.

June 15th. Bramdean.—The last days of the Whitsun recess spent in this little country hamlet, close to Brockwood Park—whither we came for rest and work, and a sight of Georgie [Meinertzhagen] and her children. A happy peaceful time: good work done though less of it than we hoped—*The City of London*, with our wealth of material, proving a longer job than we expected.

Meanwhile, the Commission is developing in what seems a most favourable direction. They have actually given us two assistant commissioners to enquire into the connection between sweating and pauperism and have practically permitted me to select them—Steel-Maitland and Rose Squire. This is more than I should have dared to do even if I had been chairman, and is another sign of the lack of proper control of the commissioners by the chairman or staff. The commissioners have, in fact, been run away with by those commissioners who have been sufficiently pertinacious without thought of the enquiry as a whole. Charles Booth has scampered off with the statistics of to-day, I have seized upon the historical survey and have secured the marking off of sweating as a cause of pauperism. Mrs. Bosanquet has captured her own little corner of outdoor relief as a rate-in-aid of wages to women. Whether we three shall meet together in the same place, at the end of our respective enquiries, I do not know. Possibly, other commissioners feel that they are having their look in. C. S. Loch seems to have gone *caput*. But quite clearly there is no one directing purpose shaping the enquiry to a predetermined end. Which of the many conflicting or diverging purposes will prevail remains to be seen. Meanwhile, it means that, besides our own big task of history of local government, 1689–1834, we have two investigations to direct —the policy of the central authority, 1834–1906; and the connection between bad conditions of employment, or insanitary and overcrowded houses, with pauperism. All these investigations will have to go slow and be partially sacrificed the one to the other.

All this while Sidney is giving at least half his time and thought— perhaps more—to the organisation of secondary and higher education in London. This year, four wranglers (Camb.) from the L.C.C. scholars selected nine years ago! He is very happy in the success of his unseen work; all his little schemes, or at any rate the most dearly cherished of them, have come off—the scholarship ladder, the in- numerable educational institutions, secondary to university, which he has kept alive and under a semi-voluntary management; and, lastly, the London School of Economics has grown in size, significance and grace. These successes are a constant source of half-conscious satisfac- tion and make up a good part of his happiness.

Indeed, we both of us live in an atmosphere of gratitude to each other, to the community which gave us such an extraordinary good start in life, and to that undefined *providence*. There is nothing we lack in our lives, and we have far more than we deserve. Now and again, I long to rest and have time to look round and enjoy beauty, or to dissipate in purposeless thought, yet I doubt whether, with my in- grained habits of methodic work, I could be long out of the tracks without dissatisfaction and displeasure. Moreover, we have, as a matter of fact, an easy time of it, at least I have. Whenever I am really fagged I break off, lie on bed or sofa, and just let my mind go blank. It is this capacity for going blank that gives me, I think, my power for rapid and intense thought when I am in good condition. For the best intellectual effort of which a given brain is capable I suggest two habits of body are needful—abstinence in indulging appetites and the trick of complete relaxation of muscle and obliviousness of mind. With these two habits, you can get the greatest output of mental energy of which your particular brain is capable. And, with John Stuart Mill, I am inclined to think that the exercise of intellect—perhaps suffused with love—is the highest happiness of which we poor mortals are capable. " Love without intellect ", the Eastern might assert is the Nirvana. To this state I have not attained—death may it be?

. . . This long entry in my diary I have written this morning, by the open window, looking out on to the park-like meadow—a dull warm rainy grey day after a fortnight of glorious weather. Sidney has run up to London, on L.C.C. administrative business, just as I ran up on Monday for two meetings of the Commission. And, as he is away, and I have been somewhat tired, I am treating myself to a day off, or two days off, so as to go back fresh to London. Before we settle down in the Bertrand Russells' little house near Oxford six weeks hence we want to have completed *The City of London*, the memorandum on the policy of the Central Authority, 1834–1849, to have despatched Vol. I. for striking off, to have finished the records of Norwich, and, for me, to have got forward with the analysis of the constitution of municipal corporations. The last, I fear, will remain undone, which worries me. " Keep your hair on, missus " is Sidney's somewhat inelegant advice—reminiscent of the London street boy.

. . . After a 12.30 lunch I cycled off in a grey windy afternoon, up the Winchester hill along the ridge of the highland towards West Meon through fields of red clover and hay grass, under avenues of beech and fir—delighting in the sense of a holiday and in the physical vigour springing from the morning's rest. This countryside is like a beautiful but pale and somewhat stately lady—the white undertone yielded by the chalk, and the long unbroken lines of undulating down and wide stretches of valley, lack warmth and interest unless the landscape is flushed with sun or made glorious by thunder clouds. Still there is a sort of gentle unassuming sympathy—restful and meditative—in the rolling hill and dale, whilst in the high-hedged lanes, bordered with flowering broom and tall field flowers, there are delightful touches of intimacy. Always the same background of wonder, wistful wonder whether or not there is a spiritual force towards which we humans are tending, or whether we are mere animals, as we think animals to be, which are to-day and to-morrow are not—like the leaves of a tree or the blades of the grass. No more reason that we are the beginning of another and higher stage of the life force than that we are the end of this world's development, not likely to be bettered in our best types even in the one hundred million years deemed to be before our race on this earth. And we all of us—or at any rate many of us—go through this world, asking this question, perpetually, persistently, asking it and getting no answer, unless we are willing to turn our back on reason.

" I have taken service under reason," pitifully exclaimed Henry Sidgwick in explaining the pessimistic agnosticism of his later years, " I cannot now desert her." And so, in spite of every gift of artifice and nature, there remained behind all the effort of this intellectual saint, behind the love of his friends and the devotion to and from his wife, behind all the delightful intercourse and attractive surroundings of his daily existence, a background of gloom and world melancholy. Without true faith in a spiritual force, if not in personal immortality, human life seemed to Sidgwick, and seems at times to most of us, like a shallow stagnant pool of somewhat dirty water. Perhaps, it would be better for it to be entirely dried up one hundred million years before the last catastrophe? Sidney would prosaically answer: " It will not be so. Hence, we must labour to embank and cleanse waters, to drain off the overflow, stay a creeping morass." " The world can wait for political science ", bitterly moaned Professor Sidgwick. " No it cannot," urges Sidney, " for, meanwhile, lives are wrecked, and men and women and little children grow mean or suffer pain without redemption. To lessen, by one iota, physical pain or mean motive is a sufficient good for me." And he goes on his way rejoicing in his love for me, and my love for him, untroubled with the meaning of the universe, and slightly bored by those who are or think themselves so to be.

Grosvenor Rd., June 20th.—A useful little dinner here last night to help forward Haldane's territorial army scheme—R. B. H., Lord Esher, Lord Lucas and Sidney (representing the War Office committee) and Colonel Hughes (Lord Mayor of Sheffield), Sir H. Bell (Lord Lieutenant, North Riding), Bickersteth (Clerk of C.C. East Riding), Harcourt Clare (Clerk of C.C. Lancashire). After dinner Haldane enthused them all—though the clerks of the county councils were somewhat cynical as to the efficiency of the representative members of the joint committees.

July 2nd.—A freakish dinner—arranged before Lallie's death and one I did not like to put off. Balfour and Lady Elcho to meet four young Liberal M.P.'s, Masterman, Simon, Gooch and Carr-Gomm, with Sir Oliver Lodge and Beatrice Creighton thrown in. I am wondering whether Balfour will recover his position as a leader—at present there is a note of contempt in most persons' opinion of him— his charm and reputation for charm increasing the irritation at his intellectual indecision. I asked him after dinner, when we sat on the balcony, whether there had ever been a cause (apart from general good government) about which he had been really concerned. " Have you ever wished to bring about another state of affairs to what at present exists? " I insisted, perhaps somewhat rudely. " I am a Conservative," he rejoined quietly, " I wish to maintain existing institutions." Then,

345

presently, he added: " There are some things about which I have been keen: take for instance the clause in the Scotch Free Church Bill enabling the established Church of Scotland to change its formulas—freeing it from the dead hand—I worked very hard to secure that ". I sympathised and we dropped the subject. Afterwards, I wondered whether it is not exactly this basis of pure Conservatism combined with extraordinary ingenuity and resourcefulness in evading demands for advance, whether it is not this combination that leads to an appearance of shiftiness. It is characteristic that the liberty for an association to change its opinion, seemed among the most important reforms to be secured. I imagined he might have added a Catholic university for Ireland—another reform affecting the opinion or the creeds of men—all in the direction of tolerance for varieties of opinion. Perhaps faith in this sort of freedom of mental development is the most positive side of Balfour's political opinions.' Mixed up with his Conservatism and with his over-subtle opportunism there is a solid layer of Whig doctrine. By birth and tradition he is a Conservative, by conviction he is a Whig, whilst by temperament he is a manipulator, delighting in finesse. An unpopular combination just at present.

Altogether I have had this week thirty persons to lunch or dinner, as well as half-a-dozen in the afternoon—nearly all of the lot being on business of some sort. Assistant commissioners coming to be instructed in the art of investigation, and the scope of their enquiry; the secretary of the Commission to talk over the former; a German lady needing information on education, a clever woman requiring advice as to her career; also nephews, nieces. For the next six weeks my days will be taken up in much the same way, tiring and leading to little result that is apparent to oneself. But I never like to refuse to see those who think I can help them when they are in any way connected with my side of things. It all distracts one from our main work.

Dined at the house of a millionaire—Sir J. Wernher, Bath House. We went there, partly because of Sidney's connection with him over the " Charlottenburg " scheme, partly from curiosity to see inside such an establishment, partly because we both respect and like the man. He is a German giant, not unduly self-indulgent, and a real drudger at his business. But he is better than that. He is noted for generosity inside his own circle; regarding the South African commercial world as something for which he is responsible, perpetually carrying the weaker men on his back—he is good, that is to say, to his own community. He is also public-spirited in his desire for the efficiency of all industry, and the advancement of its technique. Moreover, he is obviously unconcerned with social ambition or desire to push himself by his wealth. " I have no time, even to know that I am wealthy: the only result of my millions is to make me dread being introduced to a new person lest they should begin to beg from me. The really happy person is the man with £10,000 a year, reputed to have £2000."

But, though our host was superior to his wealth, our hostess and her guests were dominated by it. . . . The company was composed, either of financial magnates, or of the able hangers-on of magnates. The setting in the way of rooms and flowers and fruit and food and wine and music, and pictures and works of art, was hugely overdone—wealth—wealth—wealth—was screamed aloud wherever one turned. And all the company were living up to it, or bowing down before it. There might just as well have been a Goddess of Gold erected for overt worship—the impression of worship in thought, feeling and action could hardly have been stronger. Always excepting Wernher himself. He looked wistful as I suggested that the fallacy of wealth was becoming apparent. " My husband and I have all the wealth we could possibly make use of without diminishing our delightful happiness. Four private secretaries on £1000 a year: a fifth would break me down. What you enjoy ", I ventured to add, " is not your wealth but the power it gives you to organise the affairs of the world." " Yes, perhaps, that is so ", he answered wearily.

A French lady factory inspector was billeted on us for the International Sociological Congress (of which we were members who did not attend). A large heavily-scented, well-dressed, clever person, with a sort of personal attraction that one could hardly associate in England with fastidious conduct—cool but agreeable in manner, direct in language, and quite clearly grasping in disposition. With extraordinary frankness she displayed to me, one by one, articles of clothing bought at absurd prices—the longest kid gloves 6 fr., an evening dress 40 fr., and a perfectly fitting grey evening cloak 29 fr.—from factories and shops which she inspected! With regard to the cloak, she explained how she had seen a model at a fashionable purveyor to smart shops in the course of her inspection, and had then and there asked the price of a similar one. " Mais, Madame, 5 frs.", the proprietor had politely suggested would be the cost of making it; 14 fr. the cloth, another 10 fr. the lace, total 29 fr. for a 250 fr. cloak. Towards us her behaviour has been extraordinary: she was asked to stay five days, and has stayed nine. To-day, when all the other congressists are departed, she is running round London with an attaché of the French Embassy with whom she seems *très amie*. Altogether, an astonishing glimpse of the possibilities of French officialism. I am wondering whether she will leave the house without borrowing money. All the same, she is not merely well-informed and hard-working, but she is cultivated, ready to tell you, and in correctly turned phrases, the whole development of legislature, metaphysical thought, French literature, the theatre, politics—doubtless superficial information but distinctly lucid and comprehensive. She is a vigorous feminist—has nothing but bad to say of the position of women in France. Frenchmen have, according to her, an innate contempt for women—both for their intellects and their conduct. And, if she is a representative type of the professional woman and advanced reformer, one is hardly surprised at a certain dislike and suspicion of anything but the conventionally pious and " innocent " lady. But she must be an exception—a product perhaps of the shoddiness of sociology.

July 17th.—Yesterday we had a field day on the Royal Commission discussing our future procedure. Various memoranda had been circulated—conflicting, overlapping and irrelevant, from the chairman, the evidence committee, the secretary, C. S. Loch and myself—a fine confusion to serve instead of a compact agenda. The chairman opened the proceedings by a long rambling statement: he had interviewed John Burns [then President of the Local Government Board], who was willing to delay dealing with the unemployed otherwise than by an extension of the Act, until the autumn session of 1908. From which Lord George deduced that our report on the whole of our reference must be in the hands of the Government by August 1908. After some preliminary sallies, we settled down to consider evidence for October. Settled by lunch time. At the afternoon sitting, we roamed over the whole field—spreading out our enquiry into the furthermost points that any individual commissioner desired to reach; Lord George always giving way with a weak protest against doing any one investigation " too thoroughly ". I confined my effort to keeping open for further consideration questions which he, or the Commission as a whole, wished to close—old-age pensions, the condition of the 200,000 children now receiving outdoor relief, the administration of relief by boards of guardians, and more important than all, the relation of poor law medical treatment to public health.

This is a new hare that I have recently started. In listening to the evidence brought by the C.O.S. members in favour of restricting medical relief to the technically destitute, it suddenly flashed across my mind that what we had to do was to adopt the exactly contrary attitude, and make medical inspection and medical treatment compulsory on all sick persons—to treat illness, in fact, as a public nuisance to be suppressed in the interests of the community. At once, I began to cross-examine on this assumption, bringing out the existing conflict between the poor law and public health authorities, and making the unfortunate poor law witnesses say that they were in favour of the public health attitude! Of course Sidney supplied me with some instances, and I hurried off to consult M.O.H.s—Dr. McCleary (Fabian), Dr. New-

348

man (infant mortality expert). As luck would have it, Dr. Downes [member of the Commission] had to give evidence and was puzzled to know what to talk about. He had dined here, and I brought forward all my instances of conflict. In the witness box, he made this conflict part of his thesis, though taking the poor law attitude and complaining of the public health authorities pauperising tendencies. With S.'s help, I drew up a memorandum emphasising all my points. Yesterday Dr. Downes, who is frightened at his own action, tried to stifle the question and to refuse to call evidence on the public health side. I purposely did not press it more than to insist on keeping the question open. I am elaborating an enquiry on my own—with funds supplied by Charlotte Shaw—so I merely said that I should, in the course of the next six months, present the Commission with a further memorandum. " You might elaborate with a few more details the one you have already presented ", said Lord George in a frightened way. And so it was left. At present I am engaged in finding a medical woman to undertake the enquiry, and on rousing the interest of the M.O.H.s throughout the country.

Meanwhile, despairing of any action on the part of the Commission, I have undertaken, unknown to them, an investigation into the administration of boards of guardians. I shall put Mrs. Spencer to analyse the documents that are pouring in to me by every post, and Miss Bulkeley shall go through minutes.

I, therefore, look forward to at least three memoranda handed in by me, (1) *Central Policy*, (2) *The Relation of Poor Law Medical Relief to Public Health*, (3) *Administration of Relief by Boards of Guardians*, as well as the report of the assistant commissioners on the relation of bad conditions of employment to pauperism. On these documents I shall base my report.

My relations to my fellow-commissioners are quite pleasant. I am completely detached from them and yet on most agreeable terms. I just take my own line, attending for just as long as it suits me, cross-examining witnesses to bring out my points and conducting the enquiries that I think important independent of the Commission's work. The lines of reform both in constitution and policy are gradually unfolding themselves to me. Whether I shall embody them in a report of my own, or give up part of my way in order to bring the whole Commission along, will be a question of expediency and delicate negotiation—about which nothing can at present be foreseen.

July 31*st*.—Out of the blue Lord Cromer wrote to ask to see Sidney. We invited him to lunch. " Shall we begin our talk now or wait until after lunch? " he opened abruptly, as he sat himself down. " What I want, Mr. Webb," he continued, on Sidney's acquiescence to proceed immediately to business, " is for you to come to Egypt for six weeks and report to me on an education system." Then he described his dissatisfaction with it—feeling that it was hollow and, perhaps, not the best suited to the natives. When he had delivered himself, Sidney quietly explained that he was not the man for the job. " I am a mere administrator making use of experts; what you want, Lord Cromer, is someone who understands the whole machinery of education—buildings, plant, curriculum, time tables, etc." " It would have been a fraud if I had taken it," Sidney said, after Lord Cromer had left, " besides we have not the time."

Lord Cromer impressed us both. He was so strong and direct, and lacking in all " side " or pretension. He had even a distinct flavour of the amateur, informal and unconventional, almost unofficial—not the suspicion of a bureaucrat. But he was evidently accustomed to rely entirely on experts for methods and processes, was deferential to Sidney exactly on those questions in which Sidney excelled him in knowledge. Beyond all things (though an attractive and somewhat sensual man) he was impersonal in his attitude, apparently quite unconcerned about the impression he was making on others. In this respect he reminded me of my father. A great administrator of the English type. The exact opposite in methods and temperament to Lord Milner.

On Saturday, a luncheon party to meet Mr. W. J. Bryan, Sydney Buxton, Horace Plunkett. Exactly the same impression as before of the wide-mouthed democrat, upright and kindly, but infantile in his administrative notions. Thought he could solve the question of administration by allotting all offices after each election to the political parties according to their voting strength. Was going to parcel out all the railways among the States—proposed to deal with trusts by making it penal to do more than 50% of the trade in one article. Sydney Buxton appeared quite a statesman comparatively. Mrs. Bryan a plain, middle-aged woman of the assertive American type, full of the shibboleths and self-deceptions of the ordinary American political metaphysician. Bryan took very much the same view as H. G. Wells of the prospects of great social reforms in America, with this difference that he is not a collectivist, all good is to come by ultra-democratic machinery—election, election, election, the cure for all evils.

August 4th. Lower Copse, Bagley Wood.—On August 1st, we arrived here after a lazy morning in London: the day after we rested. We spent yesterday writing the preface of Vol. I. This morning I started to survey the material for the chapters on the municipal corporation, and its statutory developments—the two pivotal chapters of Vol. II. Sidney busy on the article on the birth-rate and one on trade unionism for Mackinder's American encyclopaedia. Julia Faulder and

Stephen Hobhouse staying Sunday here. Before we began work Sidney drafted my letter to the M.O.H.s asking for information *re* medical relief public health enquiry. It goes out in the next few days to 600 M.O.H.s.

September 4th.—Five weeks passed like one day—all the more like one day because even the sun, moon and star-lit nights have been continuous—the darkness just sufficient for the five hours' sleep. A happy day, with no cares, no sorrow, no irritation—just the interest of our work, each other's companionship, pleasant converse with friends, and dreamy restful hours in the garden and the wood, or walking or cycling through lanes and by sleepy villages, wandering by the river or gazing at church towers and empty Oxford colleges. The net result: Vol. I. through the press; the whole material for the two pivotal chapters of Vol. II. sorted, together with our ideas as to the substance and order of these chapters; the sections on the legal instrument, the officers, the courts, court of record, court leet, court of quarter sessions, roughed out in first draft; the circular to the M.O.H.s sent out and some hundred replies received; the plan of the investigation of the relation of poor law medical relief and public health settled with Dr. Woodcock; the article on the birth-rate written (I contributing only part of the final section of it); articles on factory legislation and trade unionism finished by Sidney for Mackinder's encyclopaedia; three boards of guardians attended; five poor law institutions inspected by me —not a bad record for five weeks' holiday time. We do not feel fagged —we are both in excellent health and good spirits—having really " lazed " considerably.

Among the friends who have visited us are the Granville-Barkers; he stayed for ten days, she for Sunday. G. B. is a most attractive person, young and good-looking—good-looking in a charming refined fashion—with a subtle intellectual expression, faculties more analytic than artistic? I think with self-control, industry, freedom from vulgar desires and common fears, with varied interests, good memory, a sharp observer of human nature and above all a delicate appreciation of music, poetry and art—a medley of talents of which I do not yet see a very definite whole. He has not yet emancipated himself from G. B. S.'s influence, or found his own soul.

We took G. B. [Granville-Barker] to see Lord Milner. An old Tudor house—giving almost the impression of an inhabited ruin, a garden surrounded by a deserted backwater of the Thames—seemed a fit setting for that stern, rigid man, brooding over the South African victory or disaster. At first he was constrained, but after lunch he unbent; and, from democracy to the present Government, from the present Government to their policy in South Africa, from this to the war and its results, we drifted on until we reached intimate conversation. We tried to cheer him by suggesting that after all the friction and abuse after the war and its devastation, there still remained the two republics merged in the Empire. That was (if you believed in its rightness) a sufficient accomplishment for one man. This Government would not last more than four years, and they could undo little of the past. But he would not be comforted. " It is well for you to be optimistic," he retorted; " you say you are always in a minority, but events are moving your way; whilst my house of cards is tumbling down." And then he explained that he had started all kinds of elaborate enterprises and experimental governmental organisations of agriculture and industry in South Africa, whereby the country might really become independent of gold production; all this good work would, under self-government, certainly be dismantled—salaries reduced, officials dismissed, plant disused. He practically admitted the mistake of the introduction of Chinese labour (given the crass stupidity of the English elector and wicked lies of the Radical agitators), but he defended its introduction as inherently right on the ground that you had to create material wealth before you could give the start to higher things. " Blood and money " (the philosophy that G. B. S. tried to dramatise in *Undershaft's* character and career) had, in fact, been the underlying philosophy of Milner's government. Like Mackinder, he seems to me to enormously overestimate the value of the purely material forces, he is willing to rely on those forces though they be necessarily joined with at least a temporary demoralisation of character. Milner, though a public-spirited, upright and disinterested man, does not believe in the supremacy or even in the relevance of the spiritual side of things—goodness is a luxury to be arrived at after a course of money-getting, by whatever means, and of any blood-letting that may be necessary to the undertaking. As I listened to his feeble, forceful voice, watched his rigid face and wrinkled narrow brow, noted the emphasis on plentiful capital, cheap labour and mechanical ingenuity, I thought that perhaps, after all, there was some justification for Leonard Courtney's hard epithet " a lost mind ". A God and a wife would have made Milner, with his faithfulness, persistency, courage, capacity and charm, into a great man: without either he has been a tragic combination of success and failure. " He would have been made by being loved ", summed up G. B. as we rode away.

Among our frequent visitors have been the Ruskin Hall men, and their principal, Lees-Smith. These working-men students with their good conduct, their public spirit and their naïve enjoyment of the college life of learned leisure, were refreshing to look at and listen to. All I.L.P. in politics, enthusiastic admirers of Keir Hardie and

J. R. MacDonald, believers in the advent, as a permanent force, of the Labour Party, bitter against John Burns, Isaac Mitchell and the Liberal-Labour men—perpetually discussing, as Lees-Smith shrewdly remarked, not problems of administration but policy in its narrowest sense of getting your men *there*. Once there, the remedies for social ills would come of themselves—to them they seem almost *too* obvious to be discussed. Lees-Smith is an exceptionally attractive person, gentle and cultivated, with a strong will, high purpose, excellent manners and temper, and intelligence, lucid and slight in texture—sufficient for an instructor of the ordinary man. We have taken him on as lecturer on local government in Percy Ashley's place at the School of Economics. He has not Percy Ashley's broad knowledge, and amazing memory and capacity for work, nor his ambition, but I fancy we shall find his intellectual inferiority outweighed by his superior charm and finer moral nature. We need some moral distinction in the professoriate—at present there is a note of hard efficiency. Percy Ashley remains as lecturer on economic history: he has been promoted to an expert's place in the Board of Trade and has married a rich Jewess.

September 16*th.*—Whittingehame is an unattractive mansion, with large formal rooms and passages, elaborate furniture and heavy luxury totally without charm, somewhat cold in the fireless September phase. The atmosphere of gracious simplicity, warm welcome, intellectual interest, is all the more strikingly personal to the family that inhabits it. The four women, sisters and sisters-in-law, are in themselves remarkable—Alice Balfour neither brilliant nor very capable, but singularly loving, direct and refined, with talents both artistic and scientific wholly sacrificed to the endless detail entailed by her brother's political career and patriarchal establishment; Mrs. Sidgwick, weirdly silent but also the soul of veracity and moral refinement, open-minded, too, in a limited way; Lady Betty (Gerald's wife) a woman of quite unusual delightfulness, good to look at, sweet to listen to, original in purpose and extraordinarily gracious in disposition. Even Lady Frances, whom I expected to dislike, was attractive in her impulsive indiscretions and straightforward friendliness, with her vivid wit and large experience of political affairs. As kind as kind could be were these four women to me on the day of our arrival. In the afternoon " Prince Arthur " arrived from North Berwick—a veritable prince of the establishment —the mediaeval and saintly knight Gerald, and the boor, Eustace, completing the party. Some dozen children hovered round at intervals, but did not join us.

What shall I say of our visit? Too self-consciously Arthur's " latest friend " to be quite pleasant, the party each night becoming a watched *tête-à-tête* between us two—the rest of the company sitting round, as

Sidney said, " making conversation ". In fact, the great man is naturally enough too completely the centre of the gathering—without perhaps deserving the position of pre-eminence—all the family worshipping him and waiting on his fancies. " A Prime Minister of the ' little white people '," I said sometimes to myself, " without any guiding social purpose, floated to leadership without any strong desire to lead anywhere in particular." Charm he has—almost too obviously —a genius for destructive criticism of the logic of other people's ideas, but not the remotest desire to verify his own by testing his order of thought by the order of things. It is always theories that he is building up or pulling down in his mind, when he is not merely playing the game of office-holding or office-getting. Does he ever think of the state of affairs and wish to alter it? He was contemplating a treatise on economics. I suggested that there were only two things to be done in economics: either a mere sweeping away of fallacies—comparatively easy and somewhat futile, but a task for which he was extraordinarily fitted; or a concrete study of phenomena, say, the course of trade and the effect of different kinds of taxation on it—a task that demanded the devotion of a lifetime and, therefore, one which he could *not* undertake. But I pressed him to undertake a quite other work—a careful account of his own experience of political life and great administrative affairs— to be published after his retirement and, perhaps, even after his death. But I doubt whether he takes my suggestion either negative or positive. I learnt little about him on this visit except that he is self-absorbed and lonely, seldom consulting anyone. " Brother Arthur is independent of human companionship ", sighed Lady Betty, somewhat hurt perhaps that even Gerald was not admitted to his complete confidence. Gerald is really a more attractive nature, though far less substantial than Arthur—a dreamy, poetic, metaphysical soul, saintly in his motives and subtle in his thoughts, but with small capacity for transacting business and lacking broad sympathies. He is unspoilt—has none of the self-consciousness and egotism which lies beneath Arthur's perfect manner—has not developed the cunning of the leader, fearing deposition, or the sentimentality of the lifelong philanderer, never thoroughly in love. For philanderer, refined and consummate, is Prince Arthur, accustomed always to make others feel what he fails to feel himself. How many women has he inspired with a discontent with their life and life companion, haunted with the perpetual refrain " if only it had been so ". Not a good or wholesome record, and demoralising to the man himself—and not a worthy substitute for some sort of social fervour. But this is a harsh judgement—one aspect only of the man. Deeper down there are other and better things—but they were hidden from me in these hours of philandering!

From the glamour and charm of Whittingehame we cycled with Lady Betty to Berwick—a happy ride chatting over " brother Arthur ", Gerald and his literary and philosophical tastes, social questions—altogether the opening of a pleasant friendship. The dirty crowded railway station from which we saw her off to Whittingehame was a fit prelude to our five days in Berwick.

Dirty stuffy lodgings [at Berwick]—seven hours a day working at records in a cellar without windows and lit only by three gas jets brought us back to our work-a-day life. But the hours in the cellar passed rapidly in the fascinating pursuit of tearing the facts out of volume after volume of MS. minutes—far more voluminous and interesting than we had expected. The Berwick of to-day is a god-forsaken place, inhabited by a dull and somewhat drunken population, no municipal amenities, no leadership, the freemen demoralised by their share in the common land (about £8 a year) which serves merely as a sort of outdoor relief, the corporation no better for its £10,000 a year from rents—these simply making the rates lighter for the other landlords. All the private enterprise seems run with insufficient capital and brains; the pretty coast scenery has been spoilt by mean rows of cottages and smoky works, the only attractive feature being the ramparts made by the national Government.

A Sunday at Hutton Castle with the Jack Tennants—restful and unexciting—and then on to Alnwick. Here again we reposed in dirt—this time at the inn, but we found useful material in the records, and enjoyed the novelty of lunching with the ducal family—a courtesy we owed to Lady Frances Balfour. This glimpse of " high life " interested us. . . .

Of course, I got nothing to eat but peas and apricot tart—the six men servants, finding I did not take the regulation dishes, refused to hand me anything else, denied me the bread sauce, the plain pudding or another piece of bread. His Grace was far too much absorbed in his own dignity to note that I was unprovided with the necessaries of life. The poor man was in fact struggling to keep us at a distance, scared by the assumed attempt of these notable Socialists to get access to the records of his manor courts. He had, owing to the pressure of Lady Frances, secured for us access to the records of the Alnwick Borough (now a private company of freemen) and he was determined that he would do no more. This determination made him, at first, almost discourteous to me—which I, discovering, turned round and talked to the daughters. At the other end of the table, I heard Sidney discoursing pleasantly with the Duchess—indeed, if it had not been for ourselves it seems to me the party would have eaten its meal in heavy silence. When the Duke awoke to the fact that we were not otherwise than well-bred people, not likely to push our desires on an unwilling host, and that we were ready to talk pleasantly on other subjects, he relaxed a little, and after lunch discussed county council business with Sidney—self-important but not otherwise objectionable. Before we left, the Duchess most graciously showed us the most beautiful of the pictures and handed us on to a uniformed gentleman to show us the dungeon. It never occurred to her to introduce us to their librarian—an eminent historian of the county—whom she had told me was in the castle! As we strode away through the embattled portals of the Percys—with its pretentious magnificence—we felt we were leaving behind the atmosphere of a tomb in which several worthy and one distinguished soul (the poor Duchess) were shrinking up, day by day, into puppets walking their respective parts in the ducal establishment, with a strange combination of grandiose self-complacency and dull melancholy.

And what has been the result of the castle of the Percys on the life of the little town? That problem interested us because at Berwick there was no social leadership—but otherwise much the same condition past and present. The Percys have at any rate held up the standard of personal morality and physical self-control—they are a pious, dutiful and decorous family—prone to good works. They are public-spirited —the stupid stiff Duke being a competent chairman of the county council and an active magistrate, appearing when he ought to appear, and saying what he ought to say. Moreover, his property is well-managed; the house property which he owns in Alnwick is not only sanitary and well-built but positively charming in its varied architecture and well-kept gardens. Instead of the dirty crowded station of Berwick, there is a dignified erection to welcome the traveller, with spacious, clean public rooms. Surrounding the little town are the beautiful gardens and parklands of Alnwick Castle—much of which is open to the townsfolk. All this counts for good. On the other hand, the castle officials are, if they are of superior grade, aloof and somewhat insolently indifferent to the town life; if they are inferior, perpetually touting for shillings and sixpences to give admission to this or that sanctuary—even when it is known to be open to the public. There is a heavy atmosphere of snobbishness—all folk having their eyes fixed on the castle, fearful of its displeasure and anxious for the slightest sign of approval. And, in spite of his eminent worthiness, the Duke, who is seated on a pinnacle, is just a stupid, commonplace Englishman—made stupider and more commonplace by his lifelong entombment in the magnificence of the Percys of Northumberland.

September 22nd.—This day we begin our autumnal session and, except for three or four days' visits, shall not be away from London until Christmas. I start Mrs. Spencer on Monday on her enquiry into administration by boards of guardians; Miss Woodcock and Miss Phillips I have already started off on the medical relief and public health enquiry. Miss Longman is hard at it, preparing her memorandum on central policy (1847–71) on the plan of mine. What I have to arrange is to oversee all this investigation without interfering with my own absorption in the second volume of our work, which must come out this time next year. Refreshed by our fortnight's change we are setting out to cast, in final form, the first chapters; our work at Lower Copse having given us enough inkling of those two pivotal chapters to enable this to be done. Apart from my own enquiries, I do not intend to let the Commission take up much of my time—I shall slack it, in respect to listening to evidence, and bother neither myself nor the Commission with cross-examination. But all my self-control and new-found strength will be needed to pull this programme through.

October 1st.—First meeting of the Commission after the recess—all very friendly—to discuss our future plans. Lord George brought forward some proposals to delegate to committees the formulating of provisional general ideas which might be the basis of our report. He threw out for consideration the abolition of the boards of guardians and the creation of an authority for a larger area in order to run segregated institutions, a new machinery for determining under which class a pauper came, the drawing together of charitable agencies under a statutory authority, the possible abolition of outdoor relief, the compulsory detention of certain classes of paupers; consideration of the conditions which lead to pauperism; settlement—all these were to be considered by two committees into which the whole Commission might be divided. He invited us to discuss.

Charles Booth opened with an almost passionate denunciation of the policy of patching. He wanted to go back to the principles of 1834, start fresh from those principles and apply them drastically. This could not be done by the Poor Law Commissioners of 1835–47. They had enough to do to reduce the 15,000 parishes to 600 unions and introduce some measure of uniformity. We must at all hazard get rid of out-relief.

Mr. Phelps continued the discussion on the chairman's suggestion. He began by saying that the agreed with Mr. Booth. But he immediately started an entirely different line which will bring him, if he follows it, very much to mine. In the North of England he had found that the whole question of pauperism was a small matter: what people were thinking about was how to improve and raise the whole of the population by the advancement of public health and education. In this effort, whether or not persons were destitute, was an irrelevant issue; if it was desirable that they should be treated, then they had to be treated, whether they were rich or poor. He should favour taking large classes of cases out of the poor law.

This brought C. S. Loch to the rescue of the principles of 1834. He did not understand Mr. Phelps's suggestion, he agreed with Mr. Booth. We must have a national organisation of relief with local charitable agencies.

Bentham followed him. We must mark off for stigma the dependants of the state—there must be no blurring of the lines between persons who were supporting themselves and those that were being supported out of the rates—whether on account of old age, sickness or unemployment.

Hancock Nunn followed suit with an eloquent defence of a rigid test of destitution *plus* organised charitable agencies and provident societies. Quite a little sermon, in admirable words, did the little man give us on the principles of 1834 *plus* the C.O.S.

No other member of the Commission spoke at length: Provis warned the Commission that it would be very difficult to rearrange areas because of local jealousies; Downes protested that we had as yet no evidence warranting the abolition of the guardians. But it was evident the Commission as a whole was still on the old lines of restricting all collective provision to the technically destitute, with a view to diminishing collective expenditure on the poor. Two committees were proposed —one on indoor and the other on outdoor relief—to consider proposals. As I wanted to keep my Monday mornings free, and as I thought the time had not arrived for pushing my views, I quietly said that I did not feel sufficiently at one with the Commission to co-operate usefully in the discussion at this early stage, rather giving them to understand that I should have to have my own report. This is the line I am now taking. As I fancy they will be more anxious to meet me if I do so, even if I eventually decide to throw in my lot with the Commission or any section of it. Discussion now is premature and I think a waste of time. But it is pleasant to find that there is no tension between myself and any of the other commissioners. It is generally understood that I am undertaking a good slice of work on documents, exactly as Charles Booth is on statistics. The first part of my memorandum on central policy is to be circulated to the whole Commission.

The week before the Commission met we had a most pleasant two days with the George Hamiltons at Deal Castle. Certainly those two are the simplest-mannered, kindest and most public-spirited aristocrats I have ever come across—not intellectual but quite open-minded and anxious to understand the point of view of other classes of the community. I think we and they thoroughly like each other in private life —though the chairman finds the " trusty and well-beloved Beatrice Webb, wife of Sidney Webb " somewhat of a handful. He talked much about his former colleagues in late Conservative Governments: Dizzy is his hero—Salisbury's memory he respects, Joe he has a " sentiment " for as a warm-hearted, impulsive and forceful enthusiast —somewhat of the " vulgar boss " in his manners, but genuinely a patriot. Towards Arthur Balfour he is cool: thinks that his ingrained laziness, encouraged by his contact with the brilliant but silly " Souls ", and his tendency to regard politics as only one part of a somewhat amusing game, has resulted in devious ways, disloyal to colleagues and upsetting to the party. Also, his sense of decorum in public affairs was offended by Balfour's cliquey friendships. " When Salisbury sat at the head of the table at 10 Downing Street we were all addressed by our official designations—the Secretary for the Colonies, the President of the Board of Trade and so on. When Balfour took his place, Cabinets degenerated into cliquey conversations between ' Arthur ' and ' Bob ' and ' George '—sometimes almost unintelligible in their intimate allusions, to the outer circle of the Cabinet. I was one of the old gang of youthful friendships, but I always felt such an atmosphere to be objectionable in the conduct of great affairs by a group of men representing different interests and coming from different sections of the governing class—perhaps in some instances even hostile to one another —at any rate not on the terms of personal friendship."

Public spirit, good feeling and unselfconscious dignity, seem to me to characterise our chairman: large views or capacity for transacting business on a great scale he has not, and no inkling of technical knowledge or even much appreciation of it in others. In administration he must have been a caretaker, but a modest caretaker ready to listen to those whose character and intelligence he respected—he may therefore have arrived at some reforms and not have got much credit for them— but I suspect he usually remained in the rut.

October 18*th.*—H. G. Wells gave an address to the Fabian Society on Socialism for the middle-classes, ending up with an attack on the family. Some of the new members welcomed his denunciation, but the meeting, which was crowded, was against him, for the simple reason that he had nothing constructive to suggest. Since then I have read *The Days of a Comet*, which ends with a glowing anticipation of promiscuity in sexual relations. The argument is one that is familiar to most intellectuals—it has often cropped up in my own mind and has seemed to have some validity. Friendship between particular men and women has an enormous educational value to both (especially to the woman). Such a friendship is practically impossible (or, at any rate, impossible between persons who are attractive to each other—and, therefore, most remunerative as friends) without physical intimacy; you do not, as a matter of fact, get to know any man thoroughly except as his beloved and his lover—if you could have been the beloved of the dozen ablest men you have known it would have greatly extended your knowledge of human nature and human affairs. This, I believe, is true of our present rather gross state of body and mind. But there remains the question whether, with all the perturbation caused by such intimacies, you would have any brain left to think with? I know that I should not—and I fancy that other women would be even worse off in that particular. Moreover, it would mean a great increase in sexual emotion for its own sake and not for the sake of bearing children. And that way madness lies. This is omitting the whole social argument against promiscuity, which is the strongest. Regarding each individual as living in a vacuum with no other obligations than the formation of his or her own character, I still reject " free love " as a method of development. I suggested to Sidney for consideration whether our philosophy was not tending to the restriction of all physical desires to the maintenance of health in the individual and the race—meaning by health, the longest continued and greatest intensity of mental activity —and to the continuance of the species at its highest level of quality?

H. G. Wells is, I believe, merely gambling with the idea of free love—throwing it out to see what sort of reception it gets—without responsibility for its effect on the character of hearers. It is this recklessness that makes Sidney dislike him. I think it important *not* to dislike him: he is going through an ugly time, and we must stand by him for his own sake and for the good of the cause of collectivism. If he will let us—that is to say. I am not sure he is not getting to dislike us in our well-regulated prosperity.

Sidney's articles on the birth-rate published in the *Times* were a great popular success—a stroke for collectivism. It is strange that no one of the correspondents suggested that voluntary restriction was wrong—Bradlaugh and Besant justified at the bar of public opinion of to-day—perhaps, not of to-morrow!

The following correspondence published in the *Times*, and attached to the diary entry of November 5, 1906, needs a word of explanation. In the spring of 1889, I took what afterwards seemed to me a false step in joining with others in signing the then notorious manifesto, drafted by Mrs. Humphry Ward and some other distinguished ladies, against the political enfranchisement of women, thereby arousing the hostility of ardent women brain-workers; and, in the eyes of the general public, undermining my reputation as an impartial investigator of women's questions. When pressed by Frederic Harrison and James Knowles (the well-known editor of the *Nineteenth Century*) to write a reasoned answer to Mrs. Fawcett's indignant retort to this reactionary document, I realised my mistake. Though I delayed my public recantation for nearly twenty years, I immediately and resolutely withdrew from that particular controversy. Why I was at that time an anti-feminist in feeling is easy to explain, though impossible to justify. Conservative by temperament, and anti-democratic through social environment, I reacted against the narrow outlook and exasperated tone of some of the pioneers of women's suffrage, with their continuous clamour for the *Rights of Women*. Also, my dislike of the current parliamentary politics of the Tory and Whig " ins " and " outs " seemed a sort of argument against the immersion of women in this atmosphere. But the root of my anti-feminism lay in the fact that I had never myself suffered the disabilities assumed to arise from my sex. Quite the contrary; if I had been a man, self-respect, family pressure and the public opinion of my class would have pushed me into a money-making profession; as a mere woman, I could carve out a career of disinterested research. Moreover, in the craft I had chosen a woman was privileged. As an investigator, she aroused less suspicion than a man, and, through making the process entertaining to the persons concerned, she gained more inside information. Further, in those days, a competent female writer on economic questions had, to an enterprising editor, actually a scarcity value. Thus, she secured immediate publication and, to judge by my own experience, was paid a higher rate than that obtained by male competitors of equal standing.

November 5th.—For some time I have felt the old prejudice evaporating [I write in my diary]. And as the women suffragists were being battered about rather badly, and coarse-grained men were saying coarse-grained things, I thought I might as well give a friendly pull to get the thing out of the mud, even at the risk of getting a little spattered myself. What is, perhaps, more likely is that I shall be thought, by some, to be a pompous prig. The movement will stand some of that element now!

Times, November 5th, 1906

" SIR,—I have just received the enclosed letter from Mrs. Sidney Webb. As she generously allows me to make any use of it I like, may I beg the favour of its insertion in *The Times*?

" 'Those who have been working for many years for women's suffrage naturally regard with extreme satisfaction the adhesion to the movement of two of the ablest women who have hitherto opposed it, Mrs. Creighton and Mrs. Sidney Webb. Mrs. Creighton's change of view was chronicled in your columns about a week ago.—Yours obediently,

" MILLICENT GARRETT FAWCETT."

41 GROSVENOR ROAD
WESTMINSTER EMBANKMENT, NOV. 2

" DEAR MRS. FAWCETT,—You once asked me to let you know if I ceased to object to the grant of the electoral franchise to women. The time has come when I feel obliged to do so.

" My objection was based principally on my disbelief in the validity of any ' abstract rights ', whether to votes or to property, or even to ' life, liberty and the pursuit of happiness '. I prefer to regard life as a series of obligations—obligations of the individual to the community and of the community to the individual. I could not see that women, as women, were under any particular obligation to take part in the conduct of government.

" I have been told that the more spiritually minded Eastern readily acquiesces in the material management of his native country by what he regards as the Anglo-Saxon ' man of affairs '. In the same way, I thought that women might well be content to leave the rough and tumble of party politics to their mankind, with the object of concentrating all their own energies on what seemed to me their peculiar social obligations, the bearing of children, the advancement of learning, and the handing on from generation to generation of an appreciation of the spiritual life.

" Such a division of labour between men and women is, however, only practicable if there is among both sections alike, a continuous feeling of consent to what is being done by government as their common agent. This consciousness of consent can hardly avoid being upset if the work of government comes actively to overlap the particular obligations of an excluded class. If our Indian administrators were to interfere with the religious obligations of Hindus or Mahomedans, British rule in India would, I suppose, come to an end. It seems to me that something analogous to this is happening in the Europe of to-day with regard to the particular obligations of women. The rearing of children, the advancement of learning, and the promotion of the spiritual life—which I regard as the particular obligations of women—are, it is clear, more and more becoming the main preoccupations of the community as a whole. The legislatures of this century are, in one country after another, increasingly devoting themselves to these subjects. Whilst I rejoice in much of this new development of politics, I think it adequately accounts for the increasing restiveness of women. They are, in my opinion, rapidly losing their consciousness of consent in the work of government and are even feeling a positive obligation to take part in directing this new activity. This is, in my view, not a claim to rights or an abandonment of women's particular obligations, but a desire more effectually to fulfil their functions by sharing the control of state action in those directions.

" The episodes of the last few weeks complete the demonstration that it is undesirable that this sense of obligation should manifest itself in unconstitutional forms. We may grant that persistent interruption of public business is lowering to the dignity of public life. But it is cruel to put a fellow-citizen of strong convictions in the dilemma of political ineffectiveness or unmannerly breaches of the peace. If the consciousness of non-consent is sufficiently strong, we can hardly blame the public-spirited women who by their exclusion from constitutional methods of asserting their views are driven to the latter alternative, at the cost of personal suffering and masculine ridicule. To call such behaviour vulgar is an undistinguished and I may say an illiterate use of language. The way out of this unpleasant dilemma, it seems to me, is to permit this growing consciousness among women—that their particular social obligations compel them to claim a share in the conduct of political affairs—to find a constitutional channel.

" The reasoning involves, of course, the admission to the franchise of women as women, whether married or single, propertied or wage-earning.

" It is, I feel, due to you that I should tell you of my change of attitude, and I thought you would perhaps be interested in my reasons.—Yours very truly,

" BEATRICE WEBB."

November 21*st*.—Haldane came in for a quiet talk—during an enlarged dinner hour. He is completely absorbed in his office, thinking out the problems of army administration and attempting to adapt the experience of Germany to the character and ways of the English officer. Among other developments, there is that connected with the School of Economics—a permanent departmental committee of business magnates, distinguished soldiers, Sidney and H. J. Mackinder. We are to have forty officers to instruct in business methods, and, in return, to receive about £2000 a year. It all goes to build up the School as a national institution for administrative science, which is, perhaps, an aspect of the scheme which appeals to us more than the honour of instructing the army. On general politics, Haldane gave us the impression that the P.M. offers no lead to his Cabinet—allows each Minister to go his own way and relies on his personal popularity, and perpetual concessions, when a whip reports disaffection, to carry his huge majority in favour of the policy, or no policy, of each department. " But I see little of the House of Commons ", beamingly remarked our War Minister. " My own department takes up all my thought and time." He was very much interested in my poor law medical relief and public health enquiry; in Sidney's report as to the Progressives and London education, and the possibilities arising out of the Lords' amendments of the Education Bill. He hinted (perhaps that we might report it to our friends the churchmen) that the Government would not accept the Lords' amendments, and that, if the Lords refused to pass the Bill, the Commons would refuse to vote the education grants. Sidney said afterwards to me that this refusal of supplies would be impracticable.

Meanwhile, it looks like a *débâcle* of the Progressive forces at the March L.C.C. election. We always thought that the first Liberal Ministry would see us defeated. We are even getting anxious about the Deptford seat. But Sidney is really very unconcerned. " I have done my level best for London these last fourteen years, and, if London does not desire my services, there are plenty of causes to which I could devote my energies." He would like, for instance, to give more time both to our own research and also the School of Economics. Nevertheless, he is putting a good deal of thought into the organisation of the election, and means to make a hard fight for it. Administrative work in the afternoons exactly suits his temperament. And, during the last year or so, he has been singularly happy in the L.C.C. work. He feels without responsibility for the general Progressive policy, since they have turned him off the party committee and never consult him. And yet he has got all his pet schemes through and feels that in the last three years he has placed both university and secondary education on a thoroughly sound public foundation. " Most of my work they can't undo even if I am turned out ", he chuckles to himself. But it is sad to see the complete break-up of the old gang who have worked together so loyally and heartily these last fourteen years. For it is not only Sidney who is separated from the rest—among themselves there is no good-comradeship; and, whenever any of them talk confidentially with Sidney, it is to abuse the other. Wood, Dickinson, Collins, Benn and even Cornwall, all have their eye on the Treasury bench—and it is clear that only one will be taken. Alas! for human jealousies. What a privilege to have work—and work one loves,—without the sordid element of competition.

Dined the other night with Herbert Samuel at the House—now a sedate young Minister. Talked to Whitelegge of the Home Office about my scheme, and to young Acland about general politics. The day after A. J. B. came in for the dinner hour—tried to make him friends with Alfred Cripps, but it did not come off. The great personage dislikes my " little jewel of an advocate " and the latter feeling this dislike was singularly unattractive—both too free in his manner and too anxious to please. They touch on each other's worst sides: Alfred's self-assertiveness, and A. J. B.'s intolerance for anyone or anything that does not, at the moment, please him. But, in spite of the friction, it was a display of Prince Arthur's admirable manners—and the party went off with superficial pleasantness and ease. He hurried off when I left the dining-room. Apparently, the hard fighting with small forces is far more agreeable than thinking out an administrative policy. He is, in the main, a negative man and shines most in opposition.

November 22nd.—Lord Milner, dining here last night again, laid bare his materialist view of a nation's policy. He was upholding the Bismarckian axiom that a statesman had no right to go beyond the pecuniary or, at any rate, the material interests of his country. " It is exactly like the position of a trustee in private life. As a trustee you have no right to consider anything else than the business interests of your clients—you have no right, for instance, to satisfy some phil-anthropic impulse out of trust funds—it is positively immoral." For the time I was somewhat nonplussed: all I could retort was that you were at liberty to act according to the highest business honour and that this intangible " business honour " did, as a matter of fact, rule out a good deal of action dictated by bare pecuniary consideration. But I see now there is a more fundamental answer to this materialist view of statesmanship. Who decides that the statesman shall be the trustee of the *business interests of the community* to the exclusion of other matters? Why should he not consider himself the trustee of the national character, or the national intellect, or for that matter of the spiritual advancement of the people? The analogy of the " business trust " is a false one. Here, the character of the trust is exactly specified. It need not be so. If a child is left you, with full power to do what you think right for its welfare, still more if you were specifically required to make it into a saint, or a man of science, you might be justified in advising it to devote the whole of its energies and its property to religion, or the discovery of truth. The statesman has no *specified* trust: he is assumed to be trustee of the good of the community. He may choose to interpret the good spiritually or intellectually, or in terms of simple happiness, or in terms of wealth or in terms of Empire. All he is required to do is to state to the people what he conceives to be " the good " so that he shall not wield power on false pretences. But I see no reason to accord pre-eminence to material wealth, or to the extent of dominion, as the purpose of the statesman's trusteeship.

But though Lord Milner has a low ideal of the national purpose—and curiously enough no consciousness that there could be any other ideal—he is a strict believer in the " rules of the game "; he would, I think, be far more scrupulous in his personal methods of carrying out his ideal than many a man whose aim was higher. And, undoubtedly, he is disinterested and public-spirited. That is why my dominant feeling towards him is one of personal respect.

November 30th.—H. G. Wells, who was staying here for two nights, first justified the last chapters of *The Days of the Comet* by asserting that it was a work of art and, therefore, could not be criticised from the standpoint of morality. " When Michael Angelo displayed groups of nude figures in stone or colour, it does not follow that he desired to see all his acquaintances sprawling about without clothes "—a specious retort to my criticism. However, he afterwards admitted that he thought " free-er love " would be the future relation of the sexes when we had got over the sordid stage of the masculine proprietorship of the woman. " At present, any attempt to realise this free-er love means a network of low intrigue, assumes and, therefore, creates an atmosphere of gross physical desire—but this is only an incident of a morality based on the notion of private property in women. No decent person has a chance of experimenting in free-er love to-day—the relations between men and women are so hemmed in by law and convention. To experiment you must be base; hence to experiment starts with being damned." There is, of course, truth in this argument: it has a negative value,—detracts from the argument against free love based on the disastrous results of present-day experience. But I cling to the thought that man will only evolve upwards by the subordination of his physical desires and appetites to the intellectual and spiritual side of his nature. Unless this evolution be the purpose of the race, I despair—and wish only for the extinction of human consciousness. Without this hope—without this faith—I could not struggle on. It is this purpose, and this purpose only, that gives a meaning to the constantly recurring battles of good and evil within one's own nature—and to one's persistent endeavour to find the ways and means of combating the evil habits of the mass of men. Oh! for a Church that would weld into one living force all who hold this faith, with the discipline and the consolations fitted to sustain their endeavour.

As it is, I find myself once or twice a week in St. Paul's—listening to the music of the psalms and repeating, with childlike fervour, the words of the old Elizabethan prayers. It is this recreation that sustains me in these days of murky feeling. Perhaps I am suffering from a sort of brain fag. I long for the rest of a long and complete change of thought and scene. But there is no holiday for us until 1910.

Sidney making up his mind to retire from the L.C.C. in 1910 before we go abroad for our Sabbatical year. " I want to be rid of electioneering and all the devious ways of the elected person. Eighteen years is a fair term of service." His desires turn more and more to investigation and constructive thinking, and to the organisation of the social sciences. Administration he is willing to go on with, if those concerned are ready to have him as a co-opted colleague. " But I am weary of doing harmless things for ulterior motives: it is, after a time, irksome to distribute prizes because an election is at hand." He feels he has earned a right to be fastidious in his methods and single-minded in his aims. A luxury, I think, we elderly folk ought to be allowed.

December 14*th.*—This is an interesting vision of the Webb attitude towards religion by a learned and saintlike Dominican.[1] Clearly he has himself very much the same body of thought and feeling that is represented by that most remarkable epistle of Father Tyrrell to a Catholic professor in trouble about his soul—*A Much Abused Letter.* In this letter the passage, pp. 67-83, expressed my own faith in a spiritual force and the need for a Church—a communion of those who hold the faith—far more beautifully and completely than I could express it myself. Where I begin to doubt and differ is when he insists, pp. 83-8, on Christ as the central figure round which the faith of all races, and all ages, must necessarily revolve. Jesus of Nazareth seems to me only one and, perhaps, not the most perfect embodiment of the ideal of faith. It is, in fact, more difficult for me to accept the *Person* than the *Institution*—the person is limited by circumstances, temperament and capacity for expression, and even by the day in which he lived—the institution is indefinite in its power of experience of expression, comprehension and growth. But Tyrrell's letter is a plea for conformity to the church you are born in, not a plea for joining the Catholic Church.

December 18*th.*—A general palaver—the last day of the autumn session of the Poor Law Commission. The two committees—on indoor and outdoor relief respectively—brought up the interim reports containing certain abstract proposals—definitions of a most controversial

---

[1] This was the Dominican, Father Vincent McNabb, afterwards transferred to the headship of a more important London Monastery, who has [1937] remained an occasional friendly correspondent of " the Webbs " on public affairs.

character. These reports were apparently to lie on the table—being neither rejected nor confirmed—and the two committees proposed to continue their labours. The chairman, however, had taken fright at the thought of half the Commission accepting these abstract resolutions: it would, he suggested, shackle them in the consideration of any report he might eventually draft. So he proposed that the committees should cease to meet. This naturally did not please the one or two members of each committee who had drafted these propositions—they were delighted with their definitions and felt they were laying down the lines upon which the majority report should proceed. And it certainly did seem hard on Loch and Bentham, who had both slaved to get these propositions drafted and passed, that they should not be permitted to finish their work of determining upon what principles outdoor and indoor relief should proceed—since they had been expressly commissioned to do this. " If we don't continue meeting, all our labour will be wasted ", they plaintively remarked. I managed to make my own position clear in refusing to take part in their deliberations, and said I did not agree with either report. " But if any members of the Commission feel that they are gaining light by these discussions, why should not they go on discussing? If one committee met one Monday morning, and the other committee met the other Monday, the rest of the Commission can go on taking evidence." But the members of the committee did not like this way of looking at their labour. " If the Commission is not going to attend to our recommendations," said Bentham testily, " it is not much use our wasting our time over them." So no decision was arrived at and I assume we shall drift on as before. Meanwhile, Loch has got on the scent of my various enquiries. He objected to my circularising the M.O.H.s. I retorted that, anyhow, I had a perfect right to ask for information as an individual commissioner, and, as regards public health I had actually been deputed to prepare a memorandum. " We were not very wise when we put the matter into the hands of an individual commissioner ", Lord George sadly remarked. The odd thing is that now they are calling M.O.H.s selected by me—four for Lancashire out of twenty witnesses—and the whole enquiry is drifting in the direction of sickness as a cause of pauperism. But I shall be surprised if, sooner or later, I don't get into hot water over my special enquiries, and the means I am taking to get facts. Poor Lord George—what between Charles Booth, C. S. Loch and me, he is going to have a hard time.

1907

From the entries of the diary of 1906, the reader will have gathered that, during its first year of office, the Royal

Commission on the Poor Law drifted away from being an enquiry into the disease of pauperism, into an investigation of the disease of destitution. For, while it was clear that the only direct way of restricting relief out of the rates to the destitute, and thus diminishing pauperism, was by making their condition less eligible than that of the lowest-paid labourer, this policy not only left undiminished the mass destitution outside the poor law, but also, in the case of the infant, the child, the child-bearing mother, the sick and the mentally defective, actually increased it. Moreover, so far as the able-bodied worker was concerned, all that the deterrent policy did was to induce him to accept any job which afforded more freedom and comfort than the able-bodied " test " workhouse, which was, in fact, a penal establishment of a peculiarly repulsive character. But what if there were no jobs offering for hundreds of thousands of workers, men and women, young and old? If so, the abolition of relief, except under penal conditions, not only increased mass destitution, with its inevitable mendicancy and vagrancy, but, as many witnesses asserted, actually multiplied the number of criminals; the energetic and self-willed man preferring a life of theft or fraud, with its off-chance of prison, to the certainty of daily existence in one of the able-bodied " test " workhouses established by some boards of guardians with the approval of the Local Government Board. Hence some members of the Royal Commission insisted, in season and out, on an immediate investigation by the Commission itself, and by assistant commissioners, of all the various types of destitution.

January 10*th*, 1907.— . . . Meanwhile the evidence is coming in nicely—my paper on poor law medical relief and public health has started a ball rolling, and it promises, I think, to be a snowball. The idea of universal medical inspection and medical treatment was already afloat: all I have done is to make the Poor Law Commission into a landing-stage. The reports of the assistant commissioners are all pointing away from bad administration as *the* cause of pauperism and towards bad conditions among large classes of the population as the overwhelmingly important fact—conditions which, if we are to check destitution, must be changed, and if we do not see that destitution is checked, it is, thanks to democracy, too late in the day to check pauperism. That is the little lesson the C.O.S. will have to learn through the Commission. But, if I am to carry the majority along with me any part of the way, I shall have to be discreet—I do not altogether despair of getting my transference of poor law medical relief to the public health authorities accepted by the majority. Meanwhile, whilst I am more or less engineering the evidence in my direction, C. S. Loch is continuing his outdoor relief committee—against the strongly expressed desire of the chairman. He evidently feels that he is gaining something tangible by drafting these propositions and getting a section of the Commission to agree to them. I am clearly better out of this business: the less I say on abstract questions the better—it only irritates or frightens the bulk of my fellow-commissioners. I lack discretion in the spoken word—to that extent I lack manners.

January 28th.—The medical investigator is appointed—and turns out to be Mr. McVail, M.O.H. for Dumbartonshire—nominated obviously by my friend Jeffrey (the Scotch secretary). Certainly, the ways of the Commission are past explanation. They appoint an investigator to look after and counteract me and my machinations to transfer medical relief to the public health authority, and they appoint an M.O.H. ! I should not have dared to suggest it: it is *almost* sufficiently unfair to the other side to make me protest. And a Scotchman too, naturally biased in favour of *domiciliary treatment*.

At the palaver this morning there was a protest against any more evidence from M.O.H.s. " They are all for one scheme," one member plaintively said; " we know their view now." I compromised on printed précis from eight more—two only to be cross-examined. And, apparently, I am to have the choosing of both those who send in their statements and those who are to be called. I am completely puzzled by the collapse of the C.O.S.—it almost makes me wonder whether I am not under some extraordinary delusion. Is it that they intend to ignore the evidence as quite irrelevant to their report? In that case why don't they hurry to close the enquiry? Or are they getting converted?

February 16th.—Alone in Beachy Head Hotel with a hurricane roaring around. Came here with Sidney completely exhausted—so exhausted that he hardly liked to leave me and return to his electioneering—which is imperative. The exhaustion was brought on by the events—a most tiring five days with the Commission in Yorkshire, and a tempestuous upset in the evidence committee with regard to my special enquiries. As for the first, to a " short hour " worker like myself it was suicidal—running about from 9 A.M. to 5 P.M., then writing a report, then discussion from 9 P.M. to 11 P.M., consequently no sleep. Moreover, my inveterate social instincts always mean that I lavish entertainment on my companions. I don't simply do my work. Following on that, and partly because I was deliberately or carelessly frank about the enquiries I had on hand, I received from the chairman a somewhat curt and crude request to give up investigating on my own account—a sort of badly-delivered message from the evidence committee. I seized the opportunity to regularise the whole situation. Whilst gently complaining that my action had been discussed and condemned in my absence, I laid bare all my doings and ended up by saying politely but firmly that I intended to continue—basing myself on the practice of the Royal Commissions and select committees that I had known. " Splendid," said R. B. Haldane (to whom I submitted the correspondence), " *they* won't encounter you in a hurry again." But all this took a good deal out of me. A Sunday at the Elchos'— pleasant enough but late hours and talk—finished up my strength. I lasted out two days' Commission evidence, and a dinner to some M.O.H.s, and then fled here and completely collapsed with sleeplessness and indigestion. If it were not for my reliance on Sidney's strength, I should almost retire from business. I tremble to think how utterly dependent I am on him—both on his love and on his unrivalled capacity for " putting things through ". When he is late, I get into a panic of fear lest some mishap has befallen him. This fear of losing each other is always present—more with me, I think, than with him. " I don't think about it ", he often says. Sometimes we try to cheer each other in advance by remembering that we have had a happiness which death cannot take from us.

What has again been troubling me is the question of social engagements. I go out hardly at all, and except for business interviews at lunch and dinner entertain even less. But such society as we have, apart from professional society, is tending to become of an aristocratic and fastidious character. This partly because I like brilliant little parties, and interesting folk versed in great affairs, and partly because my reputation of knowing them helps forward the various works we have on hand. But there are grave disadvantages to this " dallying with fashion ". Least of them, perhaps, is the spiteful things that are said— partly by envious folk, partly by fanatics. More important is the drain on energy both financial and personal, that any association with the great world involves. Better clothes, fares to country houses, and most of all the exhaustion of living up to a reputation, or even of " letting myself go ". It seems ludicrous to bother about the question—the amount we do is very little—and any day we could give that little up without a pang. For all that, my conscience about it is not quite easy.

What exactly will be gained by two days' motoring with A. J. B. at Stanway? The only reply is that I have asked him to dinner to meet the two most accomplished of my M.O.H.s—the keenest for a new idea—and I have even bored him by sending him the pamphlet on poor law medical relief and public health. " It is the sort of reform that the Conservatives might bring about ", say I—and go to Stanway.

February 24th.—A week to-day, and we shall know the fate of the Progressive majority in general, and Sidney in particular. There has been a torrent of malicious denunciation of the Progressives by the " yellow " press, backed discreetly by the respectable Conservative papers. This time the Moderates are being run by the " yellow " press —almost run on commercial lines—the *Daily Mail* and the *Daily Express* taking command of the campaign. The aid of the Conservative Party has not been invoked, the L.C.C. Moderates, themselves, are completely overlooked—almost snubbed. But the Harmsworth-Pearson gang are shovelling out money, using their daily and evening papers as great advertisement sheets for the Municipal Reformers and against the Progressives. It will be an amazing testimony to John Bull's steady head if there is not a complete smash of the Progressives. How exactly Sidney stands compared to other Progressives, it is difficult to say. On the figures of past elections, he ought to be in, if there are forty Progressives left—perhaps even if there are thirty. But there is Non-conformist disaffection to his personality, a split between Liberals and Labour over the last parliamentary and borough council elections, leaving soreness; and also, the fact that he is identified with high rates —the 20s. in every £ cry which is being used as malignantly as the enemy knows how. On the other hand, he has the Church and the Catholics on his side: he is personally popular with all sections of the Progressive Party at Deptford, he has a record of long service and he is distinguished. In electioneering, I fear, I am useless to him. I loathe the whole business, the mechanical office work tires me out of all proportion to the amount I do, finally Sidney does not encourage me to sacrifice strength to it. The result is, I fear, a certain feeling of discouragement on the part of the women workers down at Deptford— very naturally they feel, " if the wife does not work, why should we? " The fact that I send down a private secretary does not quite make up for it. If he is beaten I shall regret my apathy—feel that I have been an indifferent helpmate. And a beating I think we are going to get. He is singularly calm, almost indifferent. If the London elector decides against him, he is willing to turn to other work, accepting the check as part of the day's work. Moreover, most public-spirited persons, including ourselves, think it would be better for the other side to come into office: it is clear that some Progressives have to lose seats. There would be a certain abstract justice in Sidney, who has been a bad party man, doing so. You can't both push unpopular opinions, and remain popular. It is only his skill as a manipulator that has enabled him to do it so far. It would be pleasanter if this state of things would last just three years more. But it is unreasonable to expect it.

March 3rd.—Escaped with our bare lives in the general rout. But still here they are, Phillimore and Webb—L.C.C.s again! On Wednesday, the seats were, I am convinced, lost. But we poured some three hundred Fabians into the constituency on polling day, admirably marshalled under eleven captains in eleven committee rooms, and by their dogged work we won the constituency back again by a two hundred and one hundred majority for Webb and Phillimore respectively. A narrow margin, but sufficient. From 8.30 to 8 P.M. I toiled, organising the bringing-up of the slum wards—and G. B. S., W. P. Reeves, E. Pease, Galton, the Spencers and one or two other friends did the same for the other wards. At the end, I felt singularly indifferent as to the result. We had fought hard and really it was a toss-up which ending was the best for us personally. But, now it is all over and we see that the Progressives have been completely smashed, I am proud that my man has survived in spite of his independent attitude. It is a tribute to my boy's personality. How will he find a Council run by the Moderates? And by an overwhelming majority. Not quite so satisfactory as government by a weak majority—the result we desired.

March 18th.—A nasty trick by the remaining " rump " of the Progressives—leaving R. A. Bray off the education committee. A clear case of spite. Bray was on the School Board, then on the education committee—was chairman of a sub-committee. An old member who had only recently come on to the education committee, and who had never been on the School Board, or taken an active part in education, and one new member have been put on by the selection committee. When Sidney protested, one of the committee remarked that Bray was not a good party man. Sidney was very much depressed and almost paralysed. But egged on by me he telegraphed and wrote all over the place, and is arranging for the Moderate majority to intervene, if necessary, to save Bray. That " rump " will have to be kicked and brought to heel—if we fail to give them a kicking over this business of Bray, good-bye to our influence with the Progressive Party. They are a mean lot—arranging the whole thing secretly and springing it on a hurried meeting of the selection committee—expressly and obviously hurried in order to stop Sidney's protest.

A delightful Saturday and Sunday with the Elchos at Stanway,

A. J. B. bringing down his motor. An answer to the last words of my description of the visit to Whittingehame. In his courtly devotion to Lady Elcho, in the intimate and sincere talk about men and thought that seems to be natural to him in her presence, Prince Arthur is at his best. It is clearly an old and persistent sentiment—good sound friendship, with just that touch of romantic regret that it could not have been more, that deepens sex feeling and makes such a relation akin to religious renunciation. One can believe that the relation between these two has always been at the same high level of affectionate friendship, without taint of intrigue. With this background, the intellectual camaraderie of the Conservative leader with the Webbs, dropped also its right place as a slight new thing agreeably stimulating to all concerned. Round about the central figures of the party were a dozen or so accomplished men and maidens, and intermediate between these and the distinguished elders came the fascinating Lady Desborough. " No intellect, but great organising capacity, ought to be the head of a great institution ", was my suggestion as to her characteristics to which her friends agreed. To outward appearance, she is a smart, handsome, cleverish woman—beneath it she has an iron will, excellent temper and methodic mind, but with neither wit nor reasoning power! She was an admirable foil to the beautiful-natured Mary Elcho— neglected wife, devoted and tenderly-loved mother, and adored friend —a beautiful soul in a delicately refined form. Brilliant and pleasant was the talk, as we whirled through the countryside in A. J. B.'s motor, or lounged in the famous hall of Stanway. Amused and interested we undoubtedly were (but hardly rested). What was, I think, achieved, was a wholesome settling of our new friendship. The sensationalism apparent at Whittingehame had wholly departed.

But shall we advance matters by our friendship with A. J. B.? A week ago, I had him to meet the two most eminent of the M.O.H.s, and the two most distinguished of the poor law medical officers. The dinner delighted the medical men, who found themselves subject to A. J. B.'s deferential curiosity on all scientific questions. So far it was wholly to the good, because they were more likely to become Mrs. Webb's whole-hearted allies after that most pleasant evening. But, whether the talk made the slightest practical impression on the leader himself, I could not tell. What interested him clearly was not the side of the discussion which touched the public welfare (with this aspect he was slightly bored), but the merely pathological problems, such as, the relative parts played by bacteria and constitutional tendencies in contracting of disease, the interchangeability of bovine and human tuberculosis, etc. Now and again, I fancy I interested him on the human side; but then he seemed to drift away eluding the issue—

sceptical or indifferent. No virility, either of thought or feeling, in respect to the constitution of society as it affects a human development. That makes one wonder whether, except " for the honour and glory of it ", there is any good purpose served by his friendship? (The very notion of there being a purpose in social intercourse other than amusement and recreation would repel him!) And so we may be playing an elaborate game of cross-purpose, out of which nothing can come but waste of energy—beyond gratified vanity and a little pleasure.

March 22nd.—A brilliant little luncheon, typical of the " Webb " set. Dr. Nansen (now Norwegian Minister), Gerald and Lady Betty Balfour, the Bernard Shaws, Bertrand Russells, Masterman and Lady Desborough, typical in its mixture of opinions, classes, interests—all as jolly as jolly could be—a rapid rush of talk. The present diplomat and past explorer, a fascinating Viking of simple character and romantic strength, a hero out of a saga, perhaps even too much so—with the philosophy of the secularist of 1870, holding that religion is no more than folk-lore and that there is nothing worth considering but the scientific method, the spirit of adventure and a bureaucratic government.

April 10th. Bramdean.—Two weeks and three days happy recess in these little lodgings. For two days (brilliant warm weather) we rested —spending the hours lying out of doors dreaming and reading pleasant literature—lunching and chatting with Georgie [Meinertzhagen] and her children at Brockwood, or toddling round the lanes on our cycles. As a recreation from the wear and tear of the Royal Commission and L.C.C. I plunged into mysticism—mainly Father Tyrrell's *Oil and Wine, Much Abused Letter*, Maeterlinck's *Flower*, Lodge's *The Substance of Faith*, whilst Sidney read books of all degrees and kinds borrowed from Brockwood, with intervals of the fifty volumes of L.G.B. reports that we brought down.

During these two weeks Sidney and I have been hard at work on Royal Commission business. First, we drafted a memorandum on the unemployed—getting out all the expedients that have been tried since 1834, with the evidence we need for coming to a conclusion about them. This is for the palaver on the unemployed that we are to have on the 22nd April—to decide on the course of an enquiry next winter. Then we set ourselves to finish the memorandum on the policy of the central authority—completed the period from 1847 to 1871, and began that of 1871–1906. This we expect to end in about a fortnight's time. Then, I shall have seriously to take up the memorandum on medical relief and public health.[1] I mean to make this as good as I know

---

[1] Afterwards published as *The State and the Doctor*.

how. But really the threat of it has already served the original purpose. The statements of the eight M.O.H.s that were called for are rolling in—long elaborate essays in favour of transferring poor law medical relief to public health authorities, and free medical assistance by these. Through fear of it, the Commission has appointed McVail to investigate poor law medical relief, and it is said that he will report in favour of my scheme or something like it. The Scotch evidence, largely owing to Jeffrey's keenness, seems likely to be in the same direction. There is no need for my memorandum. But they shall have it as a supplementary document.

The only set-off against me is a proposal by Duff that we should ask for a new member to be added to the Commission—a medical man —who presumably would stop this wild scheme in the interests of the private practitioner. This I doubt the chairman agreeing to. I have written to Burns to suggest that, if such a person is asked for, he might appoint Newsholme or Newman or McCleary. C. S. Loch threw out a suggestion of another investigator to look into the overlapping of medical agencies in London with a view to proving, I assume, that there is already too much medical assistance of the poor, not too little. But a proof of overlapping and extravagant granting of free medical treatment will help my argument. If, in some places, you have unsystematic lavishness, in other places, actual deficiency—all the more reason for some order in the chaos.

Meanwhile, the row over my special investigations has settled down quite satisfactorily to me. I, generously, offered to hand over my two investigators into widows with children on outdoor relief, with all the material these investigators had collected, to the Commission. This the Commission has accepted, and Miss Longman and Miss Phillips will now get comfortable salaries amounting to £7 a week in all and expenses, instead of the £2 Miss Phillips was drawing from me. The Commission has appointed an old acquaintance of mine, Dr. Williams (a lady doctor), to undertake an enquiry into all children under the poor law, and my assistants are to work under her. Responsibility for the condition of these children, and for their adequate maintenance and training, has therefore been accepted. This responsibility was refused by the Commission last summer on the ground that it rested with the parent. For the first time, these 160,000 children on outrelief become part and parcel of the so-called " children of the state ".

The enquiry into the policy of boards of guardians since 1834 goes on apace—no one objecting. But it is characteristic of the chairman's nerveless handling of the Commission's work that he would not let the minute of the documents committee, authorising me to conduct this enquiry, come up before the Commission. This minute was *ultra vires*

—as the documents committee had no authority to enquire into any-thing else but the policy of the central authority. When the storm broke over my investigations, Jeffrey, the secretary of the committee, felt it necessary to report this minute to the Commission as a whole. Lord George first delayed the report and then suppressed it! So the minute stands, and has been reported to the Commission by the secretary. " You will go on as before," whispered my friend Jeffrey, " the minute has been officially reported and you are authorised to conduct the investigation into the documents of the local authorities and to present a memorandum." And, as this is one of the enquiries that I detailed in my letter to the evidence committee, there can be no more said about the matter.

My fifth enquiry has also turned out well. This was an investigation into all the applications for relief in two unions—Hitchin and York—which began at the opening of the Commission. It was believed that Mrs. Bosanquet and Professor Smart were doing the same enquiry elsewhere. The question of such an investigation—especially in a town such as York—was brought up by C. S. Loch at our last meeting. I quietly observed that this enquiry was nearly complete—600 cases carefully investigated by a lady guardian who was also a trained enquirer. Charles Booth remembered the authorisation, and called for the results of the others. But mine were the only two that had been followed up, and were ready for consideration. So *that* material becomes part of the evidence before the Commission. . . .

What interests me as an observer of human nature is that I have become wholly indifferent to the Commission. I merely work as hard as I know how in my own direction without caring much what happens. I find myself perpetually watching my colleagues, dashing in when I see an opening—I sometimes push or squeeze through, some-times the door is jammed in my face—and I accept either fate (with equal equanimity). At first, I was so horribly sensitive to their dislike. Now I watch the chairman's expression of puzzled displeasure, or listen to C. S. Loch's rude ejaculations (I heard him say " what check " to one of my questions to a witness), and find myself calmly calculating on how much they will stand, or wondering whether Loch is really seriously ill, since he so often loses his temper. I sometimes ponder over whether this aloofness is quite a good quality. But then I recollect that, after all, I am in a minority, and that it is my business to be hostile to the Government—and if I can be comfortably and good-naturedly hostile, so much the better. With Sidney, this attitude of indifference to his colleagues on public bodies is habitual—perhaps I am merely becoming masculine—losing the " personal note " which is the characteristic of the woman in human intercourse. What is rather disconcerting is that I catch myself " playing the personal note " when it suits my purpose—playing it without feeling it. Is that a characteristic of the woman on public bodies? I do try to check myself in this mean little game; but it has the persistency of an inherited or acquired habit.

April 23rd.—Royal Commission palaver on the lines of our enquiry next autumn into unemployed question. Smart and I had each of us circulated a good memorandum—either would have been a businesslike basis for a discussion. But the chairman made up, out of ours, one of his own which sprawled over the subject without sequence or order, with the result that we found ourselves discussing relief works, the motives of Messrs. Walter Long and Gerald Balfour in bringing in the Unemployed Act, and the amounts of casual labour employed by the railway companies on bank holidays, in an equally futile way. What exactly was decided on we none of us know—something, I suppose, will appear as minutes out of the fertile brains of two secretaries and the statistical officer—all in attendance. In spite of a protest, the out-relief " labour test ", which is the standard of dealing with the able-bodied men, was excluded from the investigation to be conducted next winter. The worst of it is that I do not quite see my way to do the needful work myself. And I am blest if I know yet what to do with the able-bodied!

Meanwhile, I am more than satisfied with the course of the children's enquiry. My two young ladies and all their material have been handed over to Dr. Williams—a new investigator. The latter stayed with me yesterday to talk the whole matter over. She is exactly what I remembered—an able progressive and attractive medical woman of broad views and even broader sympathies—ready for any change that could be shown to be, in itself, desirable. She welcomes the idea of transferring medical relief to the public health authorities, and she is quite prepared to welcome the proposal to hand over the children of school age to the education authorities. I suggest that the infants would naturally go to the public health authority concerned with infant mortality. Thus, the public health authority would continue to look after the physical condition of the children of school age and the education authority the mental training of the infants. In the same way, the public health authority might take all aged and infirm persons who were not fit to receive their pension, exactly as they would take imbeciles and other non-able-bodied poor. All this might be done gradually—step by step,

April 27th.—Dined alone with Morant to talk over the handing over of poor law children of school age to the education authority—infants to the public health authority. He agreed to both, and was much pleased with the latter idea because it chimes in with his notion of taking the ordinary infants away from the school, and placing them under the public health authority. He would like to go to the L.G.B. and we must see whether it could not be managed. He says he will be forced to start a medical department because of the incapacity of the L.G.B. to do the necessary work. But we pressed on him the desirability of placing the new medical officers under the M.O.H. in each locality and, if possible, doing likewise with the central inspectors and the L.G.B.

Went for a friendly chat with McKenna at the B. of Education —also to ventilate the handing over of the children to the education authority. He was taken aback by the notion—feared it would mean additional expense. Wanted to know whether the Commission as a whole would take that view. Asked me what we proposed about old-age pensions. He was up to his neck in that question. I told him we had taken no evidence and had not discussed the matter; we thought it would be settled for us. I gathered from him that the Government plan is a non-contributory scheme—something between the New Zealand and Danish plan. How were they to limit the number of applicants to the sum they were prepared to put down? If they suggested anything below 65, they would be laughed at. Could they make character a test? I suggested not—except perhaps criminal conviction—anything less was too intangible in our densely-crowded populations. Then he suggested some proof of destitution—inability to earn. I proposed the New Zealand limit of income. How were they to discover whether a person was fit to live out of an institution? That I vigorously maintained must be settled by the public health authority—it was, in the last resort, a question of a public nuisance, a dirty or neglected old person. He took that point. " The worst of all your proposals, Mrs. Webb, is that though each one seems excellent, they all mean more expenditure. And where are we to get the money? "

At lunch at the Commission, I asked Lord George what he meant to do about old-age pensions. He replied that certainly the evidence was in favour of old-age pensions—non-contributory—but where was the money to come from? Asquith has not the money for it, he said, in a weakly tone. " That's his look-out—all we have to say is whether old-age pensions are desirable from the standpoint of character and health ", I retorted. He seemed to agree; and, apparently, he is drifting towards recommending some form of pension—in the main because he sees it is coming.

May 3rd.—Dined alone with Haldane, his two brothers and sister, to talk poor law report. He is completely absorbed in his own department—and singularly aloof in his attitude both towards Parliament and towards his colleagues. " Not a good Parliament," he remarked, " no constructive ideas, merely objections to other people's ideas. I spend very little time there ", he continued (I thought he added, but I could not be quite sure, " Nor does the Cabinet interest me "). I suggested that he, at any rate, had got his reforms over the footlights, but that it was impossible to make a success of a Government that was made up of men, either with no settled opinions, or with contrary opinions on the questions with which they had to deal. " You are not even agreed as to whether you want public expenditure, assuming it to be right expenditure, or object to it." " No," he answered in a detached tone, " we are not agreed on root questions." The only person he volunteered kindly interest in was the leader of the opposition! " I see a good deal of Balfour ", he genially remarked. " What do you think of Churchill? " he asked with a note of anxiety. I gathered that Mr. Churchill is the only man who arouses R. B. H.'s anxious interest—a mixture of respect for capacity and suspicious dislike. He feels in him the man that may push him on one side.

The same aloofness from his colleagues, and absorption in his own career, I noted in McKenna. I gather also from Morant who has seen a good deal of Birrell and McKenna and heard from them about the others, that the Cabinet is an incoherent body—intensely individualistic —each man for himself—C. B. presiding merely. There is not even a *clique* of intimate friends round the Premier, or a *clique* of enemies concerting against him, as in A. J. B.'s case. The separate individuals forming the Government have neither repulsion not attraction for each other, so I suppose the Cabinet will hold together so long as the outside pressure of a great House of Commons majority, Liberal public opinion in this country, and their separate desires to keep in office, bind them together.

R. B. H. asserted that, as with the Government, so with the public —there was no common opinion about anything—he was conscious merely of chaos and indifference leading to the massing of electors now on this side, now on that. Moved more by impatience of what was than by any clear notion of what state of affairs they desired to bring about.

The little boom in the Fabian Society continues, and Sidney and I, G. B. S. and H. G. W. sometimes ask ourselves, and each other, whether there is a bare possibility that it represents a larger wave than we think—are we, by our constructive thought, likely to attract considerable numbers of followers in the near future? If this pleasant suspicion grows, it will consolidate the Society and draw the leaders nearer together. There are no personal jealousies to keep us apart since we none of us have political ambition, and our literary spheres are wholly distinct. Indeed, as a matter of fact, we stand to gain by each other's success—each one introducing the other two to new circles of admirers. With the Shaws our communion becomes ever closer and more thoroughly complementary and stimulating—and I hope and believe it will be so with H. G. W.

Meanwhile, Sidney and I are living at the usual high pressure. We are seeing little or nothing of general society. But, whilst he is working hard at my memorandum on the central policy, I am somewhat distracted with the two days' Commission meetings, seeing M.O.H.s and other medical experts, directing our secretaries, interviewing students and generally fussing around. When I see him settling down every morning to my work, I feel rather a fraud. Just now our usual positions are somewhat reversed: it is he who sits at home and thinks out the common literary work, it is I who am racing around dealing with men and affairs! And " the book " is completely shelved until these two memoranda are out of the way.

May 15*th*.—Launched my scheme of poor law reform in strict confidence to the chairman, H. Nunn, Smart, and Thory Gardiner, C. Booth, Phelps and Sir H. Robinson. Wakefield and Lansbury are practically agreed, and Chandler will have to agree to everything we three decide on. The Bishop of Ross will probably prepare to sign an advanced report. These eight commissioners represent the largest possible contingent that I might win over—the chairman would only come if he saw I was going to get a majority without him. But to get even eight would be almost inconceivable with the packed Commission, probably four only will sign my report, and of course I might be left with Wakefield and Lansbury only. What I have to aim at is to draw up a rattling good report, vivid in statement of fact, and closely reasoned with a logical conclusion and immediately practicable proposals of a moderate character.

June 4*th*.—Sent my scheme of poor law reform to Lord Fitzalan, Alfred Cripps, Henry Hobhouse (all coming to give evidence as to areas), to F. A. Hyett, Canon Barnett and Morant and some of the M.O.H. friends. Dined with Sir V. Horsley (the great surgeon), to try and interest the B.M.A., or at any rate to stop their being hostile. What I have not got clear is the constitution and formation of the " distress committee ". We have now finished the two memoranda— as to policy of the central authority and the relation of poor law medical relief to public health. I go to Scotland with the Commission on Monday and leave Sidney at work on our book.

June 11*th*.—Sidney and I spent Sunday with the Gerald Balfours— A. J. B. joining us on Sunday morning. Took my scheme down to lay before Gerald as a past and possible future President of the L.G.B.

" If anything like this issues from the Commission, it will be as great
a reform as the 1834 Commission." On the whole, he was favourably
impressed, especially with the " stipendiary ". He agreed that curative
treatment must be applied to all classes, if we could find sufficient
administrative capacity to do it; he was sympathetic to free medical
assistance. From what he said I should think he by no means expects
to be out of office in any future Conservative Government; and,
perhaps, he expects to resume the L.G.B. Anyway, he seemed to spend
more time in considering the results of the Commission than would
have been the case if he had made up his mind to retire from politics.

I did not attempt to talk to A. J. B. about it: he regards himself
too much as the general manager of the party—the party tactician—
to even consider a purely departmental topic. Sunday evening the
brothers Balfour, Lady Betty and we two talked of many things—all
of us at our best—the central topic being political philosophy of one
kind or another. Certainly, we and they are sufficiently sympathetic to
be absolutely frank and free to range at large—Sidney is more at home
with these men than with almost any others, except G. B. S. Full of
charm and stimulus was this visit: on the whole, I prefer Gerald—a
finer and purer temperament than the greater brother. But for sheer
charm, for that delightful combination of intellect, public spirit,
artistic sense and moral refinement, this family of Balfours has no
equals. It is the oddest fact in English politics that they should be mixed
up—predominantly mixed up—with democratic politics.

Edinburgh, June 21st.—Here a fortnight with the Commission at
Edinburgh. Scotch poor law is in just as bad a mess as English poor law.
The principle of " less eligibility " more deeply rooted in the administration: that of curative treatment less understood. The boarding-out
of children the only bright spot in the system—twenty years behind us
in institutional treatment. But, on account of facts of structure, Scotland
is almost more ripe for my scheme than England.

I am not impressed with Scotch local government: there is less
capacity, public spirit and integrity in the unpaid representatives than
in England—especially those of the greater towns—more graft, I think.
On the other hand, the officials are good, perhaps better than in the
ordinary English town. Hence, the officials occupy a more predominant
position than in England. I suppose it is the deep-rooted individualism
of the Scotch—they don't believe in government; it is only when they
are actually paid for performing its functions that they take it seriously
—unpaid governmental work is left to the busybodies, to vain people
and corrupt self-interested folk.

I have been reading in the morning hours Edward Carpenter's *Art
of Creation*. Here is another helpful book—not a great work but

adequately resumes the trend towards a sort of synthesis of the scientific with the mystical spirit—opening up vistas to human thought and feeling, the vision of which gives me hope and courage, assurance in a reality underlying one's own and every other life.

" Love shining through knowledge " might be the summing-up of his teaching. . . . This little book has helped me much—has given me a lift up—has made bad feelings and silly thoughts more difficult to me, and good feelings and strenuous but peaceful thought more easy. It is strange how ideas change feelings, and feelings change outward ex-pression and action of all sorts. Ideas seem to be almost as actual as physical food, or physical poison, running their course through the body—they produce not merely states of mind, but states of body? Edward Carpenter has consoled me with his ideas, made me feel not merely morally better but physically stronger—more ready to work and to pray.

To-night, I rush back to my boy—just for two days and one night —and then begin again at Aberdeen for the inside of a week. It is hard to be away from him—apart we each of us live only half a life, together we each of us have a double life.

July 3rd.—Back from Scotland in state of exhaustion. Five days with Dr. Downes and a Scotch inspector (a kindly nonentity whom we quite unconsciously ignored—Dr. Downes and I—parcelling out the work between us). I had some long talks with my medical colleague—broke to him the coming of my report on medical assistance of the poor. He is a deep-rooted voluntaryist, timid of new things, fearful of expense, always anxious to make the existence of some little voluntary enterprise the excuse for official non-intervention—a type of official who was common twenty years ago, but is now being brushed on one side by forceful young bureaucrats eager to extend their activities. But he is apparently anxious to have a report of decided hue—something strong and vigorous in one direction or the other. He is attracted by my " stipendiary " and the notion of altering much without making a new authority or new area. On my way home, I stayed with Dr. Leslie Mackenzie, the medical member of the Scotch L.G.B.—the official of the progressive ambitious imaginative type—full of strong philanthropic feeling and an innovator. He is my most ardent supporter and the most important witness on my side—important because it is clear he had the whole idea of medical reform long before I had; he has merely been strengthened in his opinion by my independent movement towards this reform. With him also this particular proposal is only one applica-tion of the theory of mutual obligation between the community and the individual—merely one little offshoot from a general philosophy of social life. He is one of the remarkable men with whom this enquiry has brought me into contact—the other is Andrew Young, the head-master of Canongate board school—a moral genius of a man—one I should like to see more of, but shall not.

July 5th.—Had the Bishop of Stepney to lunch, also Percy Dearmer, separately to start propaganda in the Church in favour of our scheme of poor law reform. I want to make an atmosphere favourable to it—partly to influence Lord George, and partly to influence possible witnesses. The Bishop of Stepney, a wily ecclesiastic, was cautious but encouraging—he is inclined to trust us in social matters. I gave him both my memorandum on " central policy " and that on " medical relief ", to take away and read, besides having sent him my scheme. Percy Dearmer is the Fabian in Christian Social Union—an attractive, enthusiastic propagandist—easily tuned because in general harmony with us.

July 9th.—Had five medicals to meet Haldane and the Gerald Balfours to discuss my scheme—also to convert McVail, the in-vestigator, at any rate not to be hostile to it. G. B. and R. B. H. much impressed by it—the former even enthusiastic. I tried to explain to both of them the policy of clearing up the base of society—equally necessary for a sound individualist, or a sound socialist state. Nathan Raw, the head of the Liverpool poor law infirmary, told me that some of the Royal Commission had asked him to meet them at Liverpool with a view to trying to get him to make out a list of diseases that might be " dispauperised ", leaving all the rest in the poor law. Clearly the Com-mission is getting perturbed at the advance of the doctrine of free medical assistance—I gathered that this surreptitious consultation was between Bentham, Phelps, Nunn and Nathan Raw—but he would not tell me the names.

July 18th.—McKenna dined with us alone last night to discuss the old-age pension scheme. Office has hardened him—developed both capacity and cynicism. To him has apparently been entrusted the task of drafting an Old Age Pension Bill. The scheme he thrashed out with us was universal non-contributory pensions to all over 65 with less than 10s. a week from property, with sliding scale from 5s. upwards, income under 5s. not to be taken into account. No disqualification from pauperism present or future, some contribution from the rates on account of potential paupers. To be administered evidently by a stipendiary. He calculates that it will cost the national exchequer £7,000,000 to £10,000,000. He also adumbrated his Education Bill of next session which he means to pass! All denominational schools to depend on a three-quarter parents' majority, and then to be supported wholly by the Government grant and voluntary contributions; on the other hand, to be emancipated from all local control. Cowper-Temple religion to be swept away, and in its stead, hymns, prayers and Bible reading—difficult to understand exactly what he meant. He said that he hoped the Lords would throw the Bill out because if they did the Liberals would come back to power. If they passed it, there would be nothing to bind Liberal and Labour together. But I am not sure he did not express his hope to impress me with the impolicy of throwing out the Education Bill. School Medical Inspection Bill sure to pass: said he intended to appoint Newman as he heard nothing but good of him. He impressed Sidney with the rapidity of his mind and both of us with his hard businesslike tone—I think he has goodwill too, of a somewhat common sort.

July 19th. Ayot St. Lawrence.—The Bernard Shaws have lent us their little week-end house for two-and-a-half months, they having migrated to a large mansion in Wales close to the Fabian Summer School. Now we are going to set to work to finish up our volume on *The Manor and the Borough*, laid aside for six whole months in order to complete the report for the Poor Law Commission. This somewhat abstruse historical work is restful after the contriving of schemes, and the drafting of analyses, meant to affect action. And I am convinced that this intimate knowledge of what past generations of one's own race have actually done—of the motives upon which they have acted—of the potential machinery they have invented, or cast on one side, gives larger scope to one's imagination as a reformer of the present state of things. Moreover, history teaches one the impermanence during one generation, even during one decade, of any kind of social structure, and it gives one leading ideas as to what is practicable. For example, the whole theory of the mutual obligation between the individual and the state, which I find myself working out in my poor law scheme, is taken straight out of the nobler aspect of the mediaeval manor. It will come as a new idea to the present generation—it is really a very old one that has been thrust out of sight in order to attain some measure of equality in political rights. There are some who wish to attain to a socialist state by the assertion of economic equality—they desire to force the property-owners to yield to the non-property owners. I prefer to have the forward movement based on the obligation of each individual to serve, not merely by making commodities and fulfilling services, but by being healthy, intelligent and loving.

The reader of the interminable diary entries for the first eighteen months of the proceedings of the Royal Commission will have noticed that the Commission during this period was almost entirely concerned with two questions. First, we were led to enquire how far the boards of guardians were administrating the poor law according to the principles of 1834 which, so the officials of the L.G.B. assured us, had been from 1834 to 1906 the official policy prescribed by the central authority, alike for the able-bodied pauper and the non-able-bodied. The second subject emerging from the discussions and investigations of the Commission was the scheme put forward by a minority of the commissioners for taking all the non-able-bodied (the infants and children, the sick and the mentally defective) out of the poor law with its framework of repression, in order to transfer their treatment to the already existing framework of prevention, imperfectly embodied in the public health and education acts, administered by the county and county borough councils. To this it was proposed to add a national system of old-age pensions, paid for and carried out, free from any stigma of pauperism, by a department of the central government.

But the consideration of how best to treat the non-able-bodied poor was not the most important task set before us by the reference of the Commission. We had also to enquire into " the various means which have been adopted, outside of the poor laws, for meeting distress arising from lack of employment, particularly during periods of severe industrial depression; and to consider and report whether any, and if so what modification of the poor laws, or changes in their administration, or fresh legislation for dealing with distress, are available ". Successive Governments, led by Joseph Chamberlain when President of the Local Government Board in 1886, had recognised that there was a social disease of unemployment which ought, somehow or other, to be treated outside the poor law administered according to the principles of 1834. It was this question of the "disease of unemployment " that, at any rate, so far as the Socialist minority was concerned, dominated the procedure of the Commission from July 1907 to December 1908.

July 31*st*.—Final meetings of the Commission for settling the first weeks of the unemployed witnesses in October, and hearing five rural experts—the three stupid ones were in favour of the *status quo*, the two clever ones in favour of the county authority for poor law and not against distributing the services among the existing committees. At the private meeting of the Commission, a queer little episode over the reception of my report on the policy of the central authority. Lord George, before proposing that it should be circulated, made a little speech which seemed to me wholly unnecessary. In a loud high voice, he recited the circumstances under which it was drafted by an individual commissioner, and not by a committee, and explained in a somewhat ungracious way that the Commission must not in any way be bound by its conclusions, that it must not influence their report. (He apparently forgot, in his anxiety to repudiate its conclusions, to thank me for the labour of it.) I responded to the challenge by explaining that I had suggested that the documents committee should undertake the work as a committee with a salaried officer to do the drudgery, but that Sir Samuel Provis and I had been over-ruled, and that I had been forced to undertake the whole labour of the analysis and the final drafting and that, of course, it represented my opinion only, and that I had carefully stated this fact in the first paragraph. " If that be understood," said the chairman rather grumpily, " I propose that it be circulated." " Rather ungracious, the chairman's reception of your report," said the astute Sir Henry Robinson to me at lunch, " if I could get someone to draft a report like that, I should be willing to pay £500 " (Sir Henry is a consummate flatterer). " Yes," said I, pretending to be a little hurt, " I *did* think it rather unkind after having all that immense task forced on me against my better judgement! " Honestly, I thought the discomfort of the chairman and my fellow-commissioners somewhat justified. The last part of the report is a compelling document, and whether they like it or not, it will, as a matter of fact, influence their final report. And, protesting that it won't do so, will not diminish this influence. Altogether, I am satisfied with the course of events on the Commission—so far as I can see everything is working up towards my solution. Meanwhile, having my own scheme settled, I amuse myself by promoting every dissension among my colleagues, backing up every proposal that separates one from the other—my bundle of commissioners! At present they feel themselves to be bound up against me—but we shall see! What I have got to discover during the next year resolves itself into two questions: (1) Must we have a national authority for dealing with the able-bodied? (2) If national or mainly national, what must be the constitution of the body? It is the one new authority that we have to create, and I have not at present the remotest notion of how to constitute it. I have arranged to set Mrs. Spencer to work on it in October. I shall tell the documents committee that I propose to break up my report on the policy of the local authorities into classes, and that I shall present them with the report on the able-bodied about Easter of next year. This will include all past treatment of able-bodied destitution and end up with definite proposals. I shall then proceed to a report on children and finish up with one on the aged.

September 28th. Ayot St. Lawrence.—The time here has been enjoyable and unexpectedly fruitful. We have sent off the last word of *The Manor and the Borough* to the printer (we have written what equals 174 pages), we have corrected a good deal of the proof, I have organised with Mrs. Spencer the " able-bodied " enquiry and Sidney has fixed up many small jobs—we have had all three secretaries down here—the two assistant investigators (Miss Longman and Miss Phillips), Jeffrey of the Poor Law Commission, Beveridge, Pringle, [Cyril] Jackson (enquirer into " able-bodied "), the Barnetts, Leslie Mackenzie and the Granville-Barkers, and numerous young Fabians. Altogether our society has been of the useful kind—doing business—chiefly poor law—always excepting the fascinating Granville-Barker.

I gathered from Jeffrey that there has been a row about my " central policy " report—that Lord George had actually thought of not circulating it. What he has done is to issue a ukase that we are none of us to show even our own productions to other people. This I do not mean to obey—he has no right to lay it down. At present my two reports are being read by a committee of the Cabinet. Lord George has, however, issued strict orders that we are not to have copies supplied to us. But you cannot treat commissioners like children, and I shall find some way of getting all the copies I require. What is more serious is that Dr. Ethel Williams is proving incapable of methodical investigation, that she has become estranged from the two assistant investigators, that Duff is trying to baulk the enquiry. The plain truth is that the Commission is becoming deadly sick of the facts and I must be prepared for a possible wind-up in twelve months' time. Meanwhile, I think trouble is brewing between the chairman and the C.O.S. over outdoor relief—clearly my best policy is to go on quietly preparing reports on the able-bodied and keeping an eye on the material being collected by the assistant investigators on the children. About Easter I must prepare the report on the able-bodied, before the recess I must have the report on children, and later on a short one on the aged and the whole question of insurance. Whether this hemming-in of the Commission by reports will at all paralyse their activity remains to be seen—I have hopes that it will. But we shall see. In any case the game is extraordinarily exciting.

October 8th.—The first meeting of the Commission was a stormy one. The chairman took it upon himself to order the deletion of three or four paragraphs in Crooks' statement about Poplar—because they reflected on the impartiality of Inspector Davy's enquiry. Directly I got notice that this had been done, I thought it only right to stand by Lansbury and Crooks—who are fellow-Fabians. Moreover, it seemed a good opportunity to assert the right of individual commissioners to publish anything that was rejected by the Commission as a whole. So I advised Crooks to refuse to permit his statement to be mutilated, and Lansbury to protest against the chairman's action and to state his intention, if he thought fit, of inserting the whole of Crooks' statement in his report or supplementary report. At the first meeting of the Commission, the chairman made a kindly statement of the case and the correspondence was read and Lansbury made his protest. He asked me to speak: so I simply reiterated Lansbury's right to report anything he chose " on his own view and knowledge ". Thereupon Phelps cut in with the suggestion that, after all, Crooks' statement might be printed in its entirety. I quietly maintained that, if that was decided, Mr. Crooks must be informed, as he might, after all, like to give evidence. " Then you will have to get another chairman ", said Lord George. " I did not suggest that your ruling should be over-ruled, it was Mr. Phelps who did so—all I ask is that it should be definitely decided whether or not those paragraphs are to be deleted and, if they are not to be deleted, that Mr. Crooks be informed." It was referred to the evidence committee and we all quickly recovered our temper.

Meanwhile, an astonishing memorandum has been circulated from the chairman. This proposes the evisceration of the poor law by taking out the sick, the aged and the vagrant, but proposes to set up a new *ad hoc* elected poor law authority for each county and county borough. The sick are to be transferred to the public health authority, the aged to be dealt with by pensions, and the vagrants to be managed by the police. Children are not mentioned, nor are the unemployed. The whole scheme is impracticable—but it is all in the right direction and, incidentally, sweeps on one side the " principles of 1834 ". The remarkable feature about it is the adoption of the public health authority for the treatment of all sickness, though he rejects a salaried service, and favours the B.M.A. plan of free choice of doctors. This memorandum we were to discuss in an informal way. At the discussion to-day, there were present Phelps, Smart, Bentham, B. W., Lansbury, Nunn, Wakefield, MacDougall, Loch, Hill, Bosanquet, Chandler, T. Gardiner and Downes. No protest was made by the C.O.S. members against the tendency of the proposed reforms. Loch talked a good deal, but no one could gather what his proposals were—he is evidently very ill, poor fellow. There appeared to be five solid votes for my scheme, though this scheme was not mentioned: Phelps, Smart, B. W., Lansbury and Chandler—all agreed that the poor law had to be swept away; Wakefield and Nunn in a state of indecision—inclining our way; Bentham in favour of an indirectly elected *ad hoc* body, with all the old functions; Hill and MacDougall for the *status quo*; Bosanquet for an elected county *ad hoc* body, also with all the old functions; Downes in favour of a nominated body for institutions and an *ad hoc* elected smaller area for outdoor relief; and poor Loch simply fumbling. For the dissociation of medical relief from the poor law there was, I think, just a majority,—Wakefield, Nunn and the chairman joining our five, making eight out of the fourteen present. To this might be added, I imagine, the two Irishmen, making a majority of the Commission in favour of the transfer of all medical relief to the public health authority. In the course of the discussion, the chairman remarked that he had looked through McVail's draft report and that " he corroborated Mrs. Webb's conclusions as to the impossibility of maintaining the poor law as the medical authority ". It shows how well worth while it was to do that report. But it is curious to note that not a single commissioner raised the question of the children—it would be really comic to keep a poor law authority, with the deterrent principles and the stigma of pauperism, alive for the children and a few of the able-bodied! After the discussion to-day, it is clear that there is nothing between the *status quo* and my scheme.

At the meeting on Tuesday, we had as witnesses Long and Beveridge. I managed to land Walter Long on to the essentials of my scheme [1]— the county council and county borough council as the authority, and the withdrawal of some of the functions from the stigma of pauperism and the deterrent test. It is certainly amusing that the class which these Conservative statesmen wish to withdraw from the principles of 1834 is exactly the able-bodied male wage-earners! exactly the class to which *a priori* you would say the principles of 1834 were most applicable. Wishing to get Wakefield definitely on my side, I brought him home to lunch; and, when I had discovered that he was quite sound, I

---

[1] Here is a kindly account of my cross-examination of Walter Long, by the accomplished journalist, A. G. Gardiner: " There is no cross-examiner at the bar more suave or subtle than Mrs. Webb. When I was called to give evidence before the Poor Law Commission I entered the room in the midst of her examination of Mr. Walter Long. The subject was the finance of the unemployed committees. Step by step she led him unconscious to his doom with gentle, innocent-seeming questions. Suddenly he saw he was being made to admit that voluntary effort was a failure and that the rates must be used. But it was too late to retreat. With a quiet ' Thank you, that is all ', she snapped the ' bracelets ' on his wrists, folded her hands, and sat back in her chair, the picture of demure, unexultant triumph " (*Pillars of Society*, by A. G. Gardiner, pp. 204-6).

suggested that he should suggest to Phelps and Smart the circulation of something approximating my scheme and their own. " The Commission won't take it from me—it had better come from a middle party, and you and Professor Smart and Mr. Phelps are the right people to launch it." " It must be something much less elaborate than your scheme, Mrs. Webb—a few simple propositions." Acting on this suggestion, Sidney and I drafted a series of propositions beginning piano and ending piano, with the substance in the middle, and I sent three copies of these to Wakefield asking him, if he approved, to approach Smart and Phelps. I offered to sign with Lansbury and Chandler, but suggested that they were " better without us "—at any rate in the first instance. I await the result of my little machination with interest.

Meanwhile, I am trying to create " an atmosphere " in favour of the scheme. Haldane, who came in this morning, is adumbrating it in the Cabinet, but he wants me to get hold of Burns. " He is vain and ignorant, and in the hands of his officials, and opposes everything and talks so much that we find it difficult to get to business; if you could get him to take up the scheme as his own, then I could follow, but he is at the head of the department concerned, and would resent a lead off by another member of the Cabinet." What I want to secure is that, when old-age pensions are discussed next year, the " break-up of the poor law " should be quietly taken for granted by both front benches. That would be immensely impressive to Lord George and the less resolute members of the Commission—it would make it almost impracticable to set up a new authority with the stigma of pauperism and the test of destitution.

Morant came to lunch to talk over the children question—he is quite in favour of the poor law children going over to the education authority. What he really rather demurs to is heaping up the county and county borough councils with other work—medical relief, etc., so as to increase the pressure in favour of an *ad hoc* education authority. He agrees to help me with my enquiry into the poor law and industrial schools and to put on Miss Longman as an unpaid inspector. That will just suit my book.

Gerald Balfour, Beveridge, Mackinder and Dr. Newman (new head of the medical department) dined here on Tuesday to discuss the " labour exchange " and other ways of dealing with unemployment. They stayed from 7.30 to 12 o'clock—which left me rather a rag the next day. Altogether, I can foresee that this year's work is going to be straining, and I shall have to economise my strength in all directions, but the Commission's work must take the front place. I have succeeded so well up to now in my enveloping movement that I must do the job completely and tumble down humpty-dumpty so it will never get set on the wall again.

October 22nd.—Paid John Burns a visit to get some particulars about stoneyards—left my scheme with him. " I shall be going to the Home Office next summer, Mrs. Webb." " All the more reason for saying, in general terms, what you *would* have done if you had remained at the L.G.B.", I suggested. " You read my scheme and, if you agree with it, you might give a sort of lead-off to your colleagues on the question of poor law reform."

Meanwhile, Russell Wakefield has circulated the memorandum which I drew up for him (with one or two tiny alterations) as his own: he clearly did not want to share the glory of the new idea with Smart and Phelps. " Jeffrey tells me that it will be a bomb ", he said to Lansbury. " That's splendid," I rejoined sympathetically, " I only hope we shall be able to agree with it." Oh! the vanity of men! How far is it wrong to play with it?

October 29th.—Another row on over my investigations.[1] Not the able-bodied, in the very midst of which I am, not the children for whom I am quietly arranging—but the medical which is completely done with. A brilliant idea has struck Mrs. Bosanquet: why not ask Mrs. Webb for her " correspondence with M.O.H.s " upon which she has manifestly based her report on the medical services? Can we not extract something from this correspondence which will discredit her? she can hardly refuse to let us have it, as she expressly said she was glad to put the material she collected at the disposal of the Commission. Probably we shall find that the M.O.H.s were not predominantly in favour of the transfer, thought the little woman. " I shall be charmed to send the material connected with public health for inspection ", I said cheerily. That evening I looked through the correspondence, took away all letters that were at all compromising to the authors (I had to remember Provis and Downes) and a due proportion of stupid conservative ones, and bundled the letters and reports off to the Commission. To be frank, I had qualms of conscience in making any kind of selection of those I did and did not send. But it was clear that Mrs. Bosanquet was not playing the game fair. She did not want to see my correspondence in order to " inform her own mind "—which was the

---

[1] Elizabeth Haldane refers to this misdemeanour on my part in *From One Century to Another*: " Mrs. Webb did valiant service for poor law administration, but she was much criticised by some of her fellow-commissioners for getting private evidence for her own satisfaction, for not attending the meetings when she did not think it worth her while to do so, and in general organising her own activities. On the whole, she came out triumphantly, and the Minority Report, which was mainly hers, has been a sheet-anchor for the more advanced reformers " (p. 231).

only legitimate ground for the request; she wanted, as has been proved since, to incriminate me by documents which I supplied of my own free will to the Commission. So I swallowed the tacit deception and sent exactly what I thought fit—without, be it added, in any way giving the Commission to understand that I had sent them the whole or the part. I had, however, left quite enough adverse letters in the bundle to encourage Mrs. Bosanquet in her plan. In spite of the fact that I said quite distinctly that all the correspondence must be regarded as confidential, she persuaded the evidence committee to ask my permission to have the whole printed with the circular letters written to the M.O.H.s. To this request I sent a dignified refusal, pointing out that the Commission could obtain the statements of fact and opinion direct from the persons concerned. I stuck to the undeniable position that I had no authority from my correspondents to circulate their letters in a printed form which might get to the authorities concerned. I said I had no objection to the statements of fact and opinions being analysed (though I failed to see the advantage to the Commission of one year old casual letters), and the Commission could use my correspondence to put them on the track of persons whom they would like to consult. But, what relevance this mean little tricky attempt to trip me up has to a defence of the principles of 1834, I fail to see. Moreover, this particular battle of medical relief is fought and won as far as I can win it. It is my other movements they ought to be now counter-acting. Meanwhile, and it is this that has made the C.O.S. so angry, I have issued a slashing memorandum on *Some Historical Considerations Bearing on the Reconstruction of the Poor Law*, backing up the chairman's " alternative scheme " and R. Wakefield's suave proposals. The Commission's atmosphere is getting very hot, and it will be hotter before we have done. " The *status quo* or the break-up of the poor law ", I tell all the colleagues I am friendly with, is the inevitable issue. Nothing intermediate can survive discussion.

October 30th.—John Burns has become a monstrosity. He is, of course, a respectable hard-working man, who wants, when he is not blinded by vanity and malice against those who have abused him, to see straight. But this faculty of seeing facts as they are is being overgrown by a sort of fatty complacency with the world as it is: an enormous personal vanity, feeding on the deference and flattery yielded to patronage and power. He talks incessantly, and never listens to anyone except the officials to whom he *must* listen, in order to accomplish the routine work of his office. Hence, he is completely in their hands and is becoming the most hidebound of departmental chiefs, gulled by an obstructive fact or reactionary argument, taken in by the most naïve commonplaces of middle-class administrative routine.

Almost unconsciously one treats him as a non-responsible being—a creature too unintelligent to be argued with, too crazily vain to be appealed to as one self-respecting man appeals to another. What *is* the right conduct towards such a man? When issues of the gravest character are at stake, ought one to damage the chance of his taking the right course by frankness that offends him? Ought one to increase the chances of his taking the right course by ministering to his vanity—by at any rate allowing for it? Or ought one to forego all influence by merely avoiding any connection with him? Will mere genuine kindliness and charity get over the difficulty? Ought one resolutely to refuse to see a fellow-creature's faults? Ought one to treat every man as if he were a saint? Or at any rate had the makings of a saint? What casuist will answer?

November 12th. Beachy Head.—The row about my investigations developed: the chairman coming on the track of my investigations into the Unemployed Workmen's Act. Unfortunately I was, at the moment, in a state of high fever, and there ensued a somewhat angry correspondence between us—he censoring me and I asserting my right to get at facts for myself. All this has meant, on the top of a year's hard work, a bad nervous breakdown, and I am here for ten days' absolute quiet—a truce having been proclaimed in my absence on sick leave. Perhaps when I return it will all have blown over.

Meanwhile, I think, I have just saved the situation with regard to the L.G.B. public health department. For the last year I have set my heart on getting Newsholme to succeed the present man. But I had no notion that a change was imminent. Fortunately, John Burns came in to lunch about a fortnight ago to meet H. G. Wells. He casually mentioned that Dr. Power was going in December. " And are you going to appoint Newsholme? " I asked. " No, I know two better men than Newsholme—and I shall get them both too." I dared not then pursue the subject. But, after the others had gone, I went in hot and strong in favour of Newsholme. He looked pensive. " Newsholme is a publicist," he said, evidently repeating what his officials had told him: " he would do better as Registrar-General." " No, no," I said, " he is an administrative genius, with an entirely new outlook on the whole question of public health. If you appoint him, you will make your reputation as a public health reformer." He left looking thoughtful. I thought it better to strike hard, so I wrote him a long letter. I also got Morant in motion, to set Newman in motion. I believe I have just saved it—but, if so, it will have been a near shave. J. B. really wants to do right in his appointments—but how can he judge? However, he will like to make " a striking and original appointment " and I think it is all right.

But I am low and disheartened. I don't like all this intriguing. I should prefer to play with my cards on the table. It is partly remorse for my little lack of straight dealing with regard to the M.O.H.s' correspondence that has brought about my nervous collapse. Was I bound to hand over everything? Not legally certainly; but, perhaps, I ought simply to have refused to give up *any* private correspondence? I was surprised into acceding to an unwarrantable demand and then did not choose to fulfil it completely. Another time I will ask for " notice of the question " and will accept or refuse deliberately and fully.

November 15th.—Taken up a fresh position before putting in my appearance at the Commission. I have, with Sidney's help, written a kindly but dignified letter to Professor Smart begging to be released from the task of reporting on the policy of the local authorities between 1834–1907. It is clear, from what has happened lately, that such a series of reports as I intended, under this heading, would not be tolerated by the Commission, or if they were, would create an enormous amount of ill-feeling. By retiring from a position which is, at present, untenable, on the ground of wounded feelings at the ungrateful reception of the other reports, I immediately set them thinking whether they would not, after all, do well to get me to make these reports! In my letter to Smart I have given the Commission to understand that I am going on investigating, as I assume they all are, with a view to solving the problems set to us. What with offended feelings and delicate health, I shall be able to withdraw myself from the silly business of endless cross-examining, and devote my whole energy to solving the questions of able-bodied destitution. I am wondering whether Lord George will be mollified by my withdrawal from making unwelcome reports, or whether he will insist on discussing my *right* to make personal investigations.

November 26th.—Reappeared at the Commission yesterday for the general palaver. Colleagues kindly, but not specially on-coming. I gather from Jeffrey that there has been a row of an acute character between Loch and the documents committee, over my report on the " central policy ". Loch has raised the question that the documents committee has not itself reported on the central policy, and has consequently disobeyed its reference. He has not been able to complain of *my* action, as Jeffrey has pointed out that I desired the documents committee to do the work by its paid official, and that I was over-ruled and ordered to do it myself. The documents committee, meanwhile, refuses to write another report on the policy of the English central authority, no one being willing to supervise the work, and it being hardly worth while doing it again, now I have done it. It was this row that has been so disturbing to the chairman's peace, not that about the M.O.H.s' correspondence, or my new enquiry into the able-bodied.

Meanwhile, a most unexpected development has taken place. The general palaver on all the memoranda revealed the fact that I was the only person with a compact following of four or five and that various other members were veering round to me. Hence, at a certain point of the discussion, there was a call for my scheme from many quarters. To this I gracefully responded. So I am now submitting a fully formed scheme of reform—the *Break-up of the Poor Law*—in all its detail. I propose to submit myself to cross-examination, so as both to convert my colleagues, if possible, and also to learn the exactly weak points in my own armour. It is a bold move, on my part, but I think on the whole a wise one. The majority of the Commission are tired of wandering about the subject without a leader and, though I may not attract many more than I have already, the planking down of an attractive and logical scheme of reform will make the other members nervous of being contented with muddle-headed generalisations.

Beginning to prepare an atmosphere for our able-bodied proposals: Sidney put our proposals into a Christian Social Union tract (signed by Donaldson, a Leicestershire clergyman), and I am submitting them to General Booth of the Salvation Army to get that organisation on my side. One reason for attempting to rush the Commission on the *Break-Up of the Poor Law* is to clear the decks for the more revolutionary scheme of dealing with unemployment. That scheme is so drastic that I cannot conceivably get a majority, but I may get an influential minority. But its very completeness will injure my chance of getting a majority for the break-up of the poor law, if it is thrust on their attention simultaneously. It will be amusing to see how much " Webb " this Commission will stand—what exactly will be saturation point? They have absorbed a good deal already, with the transference of medical relief to public health authorities, and the county and county borough as the authority for the treatment of all destitute persons. How much more will they stand?

November 30th.—Lunched to-day with Miss Anderson, the factory inspector, to meet Smith Whitaker, the secretary, and Dr. Ford Anderson, a leading member of the British Medical Association, to discuss my medical report. Glad to find that they were not unfavourable to the transfer of poor law medical relief to the public health authority —even regarded it as inevitable—and also preferred a salaried whole-time service to a " free choice of doctor " scheme. Quite clearly my report had convinced them that something had to be done and that a greatly extended public health service was certain to come. " The question is," I ventured to suggest, " is the B.M.A. going to dominate the new service or is it not? If the Association throws itself at once on the side of the new regime then it will dominate it, if it opposes its development the new scheme will organise itself as a rival." " That is what I tell them ", said Mr. Smith Whitaker.

December 9th.—Lord George scored a great victory to-day, and I a great success. The scheme for the break-up of the poor law, which the Commission had hastily demanded, was, as is usual with my productions, received in stony silence, no reference being made to it in the course of the discussion. Lord George had circulated another memorandum denouncing my scheme as " anti-democratic ", but accepting a large part of it—transference of poor law to county and county borough councils swallowed; county stipendiary officer, the principle of curative and preventive treatment—everything, in fact, except the distribution of the services among the county council committees and the stipendiary officer for the administration of outdoor relief. In their hatred of me, all the C.O.S. members rallied to him, giving up the *ad hoc* poor law body, the principle of deterrence, the strict administration of outdoor relief—a real stampede from the principles of 1834. I insisted on taking a vote on the crucial question of a poor law statutory committee of the county council *versus* a distribution between the education committee, the health committee, etc. Lansbury and Chandler voted with me, Smart and Phelps refused to vote, all the others present (not present Booth, Robinson, Wakefield, Nunn) voted for Lord George's scheme of a statutory committee. Thereupon, I gave them to understand that we considered the issue vital and should have our minority report. Short of getting a majority report written by ourselves, this large measure of conversion to our proposals on the part of the majority, with freedom for a great report of my own, is exactly the position which I prefer. I shall lose Phelps and, perhaps, Wakefield and not gain any others. On the other hand, the report will be a thoroughly Webbian document—in tone, statement of fact, and proposals. Meanwhile, our chairman is overjoyed at the victory and received my hearty congratulations most graciously. He and I are excellent friends. With my other colleagues, there is a most distinct consolidation against me—amounting almost to boycott, at any rate, to a discourteous coldness. Honestly, I think they are somewhat justified in their dislike of me—I have played with the Commission. I have been justified in doing so, because they began by ignoring me— but it is unpleasant to be played with, especially by a person whom you want to despise.

The activity of the majority will be on the Commission: my activity will be outside it—investigating, inventing, making an atmosphere favourable to my inventions; and, where possible, getting the persons with right opinions into high places, and persons in high places in the right state of mind. The two reports on the able-bodied and the children must be finished by the summer, and we must be thoroughly equipped to turn off, on short notice, a first-rate minority report.

December 12*th.*—The next day's meeting was like pleasant sunshine after drifting storm. The chairman was enjoying an unaccustomed sense of personal power, the C.O.S. was chuckling over the defeat of my scheme, I was thoroughly complacent with having dragged the whole Commission so far in my direction whilst preserving my freedom for a minority report; others like Nunn, Wakefield, Smart and Phelps, felt that they alone were free of any decision, since they had either been absent or not voted. Perhaps it was this undeterminate party that was least comfortable. Among these and the office staff, there was a reaction in my favour—a feeling that I had been treated somewhat cavalierly in having my elaborate report peremptorily dismissed without any kind of discussion. So we all parted for the month's recess the best of friends—and, so far as I am concerned, this attitude will persist. Whether the majority will fall out among themselves and split into factions, it is impossible to foretell. Now that the pressure brought about by fear of a " Webb majority " has been removed, it is doubtful whether the chairman's party will hold together. All I have to do is to get on with my own work and leave them alone to settle their own report; merely use the Commission to get the information I need and they can give me, be pleasant with each and all of them personally, without troubling myself about the Commission as a whole. By persistent discourtesy, they have absolved me from obligations of good-fellowship.

1908

January 13*th.*—A weird Christmas recess at Hollesley Bay Colony, investigating the daily routine of the 300 men's lives, getting particulars about their former occupations and present views, having long talks with the superintendent, the works' manager, the farmer and the gangers, with a view to ascertaining the possibilities of the working colony as an element in any scheme for dealing with unemployment. The atmosphere—the impression of the place was mournfully tragic— half-educated, half-disciplined humans, who felt themselves to have been trampled on by their kind, were sore and angry, every man of them in favour of every kind of protection, protection against machinery, protection against female, boy and foreign labour, protection against Irish, Scotch and country men, protection against

foreign commodities, protection against all or anything that had succeeded whilst they had failed. There was a growing assumption in their
minds that they had the *right* to 30s. a week—in London the rate for
borough council work, though this assumption was, as yet, tall talk
to most of them. They were a faint-hearted, nerveless set of men,
their manner sometimes servile, sometimes sullen, never easy and
independent.

January 30th.—Now we have decided to take a whole four days
to discuss new editions of the chairman's memorandum defining the
constitution and powers of the central and local nominated committees.
This seems, from the standpoint of the majority, rather a slow procedure, since the whole question can be reopened when we have the
draft report before us—but the chairman seems quite unaware that
there is any distinction between casual discussions on casual memoranda
and binding decisions on the actual draft report. I propose to take little
or no part in these discussions—just stand by in a pleasant and kindly
attitude, and await events. C. S. Loch is seriously ill, which, if he
recovers, will delay matters (he will want to reopen any decision), if
he does not recover will help on the chairman with the other C.O.S.
members. About Newsholme's appointment there is a certain sullenness
on the Commission—altogether the body is in a moody leaderless
state. I do not understand where exactly they are drifting to. There is
no sign of any policy on unemployment or on any other question.

Meanwhile, we are working at high pressure, collecting our information—most of my activity being the direction of the research
conducted by our secretaries.[1] At present we can barely see the forest
for the trees—but I have ample confidence in our method. Without
Sidney's help I should not persist in this terrific effort to clear up the
whole question, to cut a way through the tangle of existing facts.
Fortunately, we have already discovered our principles of 1907, and
we have already devised our scheme of reform. What we are now
manufacturing is the heavy artillery of fact that is to drive both
principles and scheme home.

We have remitted our unemployment scheme to the leading
members of the Labour Party (barring MacDonald), and have met
with quite unexpected response—almost a promise of active support.
I have also sent this scheme with a long letter to A. J. B. and he has
suggested coming to discuss it. And Haldane and Asquith have had
the poor law scheme and we are to meet them to-night at Haldane's
house to discuss details of it. The Christian Social Union is circulating

---

[1] So far as I remember, it was Charlotte Shaw's generosity that made it possible
for us to have four or five research secretaries during this period.

both schemes as tracts and we are putting them in circulation else-where—so that they will be cropping up in altogether unexpected quarters. Shall we advance matters by all this tireless investigation, invention and propaganda—at times one gets disheartened—if it were not for the comradeship of our effort, I should be tempted to give up the struggle. It will be a real relief when the Commission is closed and we can go back to the peaceful life of research.

February 2nd. Hadleigh Farm Colony.—Here for a week-end watching the Salvation Army at work among the unemployed and un-employable. The most interesting fact is the Salvation Army itself. I have seen something of the officers in London; Colonel Lamb, Colonel Iliffe, Commander Cox and others, all belonging to the social side of the army. On the colony are some half-dozen other officers engaged in philanthropic administration, and two spiritual officers (women); two " specials " came down for Sunday—Brigadier Jackson and his wife. In respect to personal character, all these men and women constitute a *Samurai* caste, that is, they are men and women selected for their power of subordinating themselves to their cause, most assuredly a remarkable type of ecclesiastic: remarkable because there is no in-equality between man and woman, because home life and married life are combined with a complete dedication of the individual to spiritual service. A beautiful spirit of love and personal service, of content and joy, permeates the service; there is a persistent note of courtesy to others and open-mindedness to the world. The men, and some of the women, are far more cultivated than is usual with persons of the same social status—one can talk to them quite freely—far more freely than you could talk to an elementary school teacher, or trade union official; there is a curious feeling that they are, in some ways at any rate, citizens of the world. All the officers carry a power of command and have the personal dignity which springs from this, especially when it is combined with the habit of obedience. This is especially true of the officers engaged in the social work, the officers on the spiritual side have more the characteristics of the artist or public performer—more emotion and less intelligence.

How does Hadleigh differ from Hollesley? A more mixed lot of men—ex-convicts, ex-tramps, workhouse-able-bodied and men picked up in shelters, far more human wreckage, but, on the other hand, less the ordinary ruck of casual labourers. Here they are, I think, more successful in getting the men to work, there is less foul talk, perhaps less discontent and jeering. The self-devotion of the officers counts for something in raising the tone of the colonists. On the other hand, there is tremendous religious pressure—far more than I had realised. The colonists must attend the Saturday evening social and the Sunday evening religious service, whilst they are invited—almost implored—to come to prayer meetings all day on Sunday and on the other evenings. The Sunday evening service is a stirring and compelling ceremony, at which every act is used to attract the colonists to the penitent's form. Music, eloquence, the magnetic personality of the trained salvationist preachers—a personality that combines the spiritual leader with that of the refined variety artist—all these talents are lavished on the work of conversion. And would it be very surprising if the ignorant and childishly suspicious men, who make up the colonists, should imagine that they would do better, even from the worldly point of view, if they accepted the creed of their governors? The Saturday entertainment, though permeated with religious feeling, even the Sunday morning and afternoon services, did not transgress the limits of reasonable influence. But the intensely compelling nature of the appeal to become converted made to-night by Brigadier Jackson and his wife, I confess somewhat frightened me off recommending that the Salvation Army should be state- or rate-aided in this work of proselytising persons committed to their care for secular reasons! Is it right to submit men, weakened by suffering, to this religious pressure exercised by the very persons who command their labour?

The Salvation Army ritual is certainly a wonderful work of art. The men and women who conduct it are thoroughly trained performers—well modulated voices, clever gestures, all the technique of an accomplished artist, something between melodrama and the music-hall. But this technique is possessed by no mere performers. The men and women are, for the most part, real living saints, who feel intensely all they are saying and acting. To those who do not hold their faith and who look at them critically, their passionate pleadings, their dramatic gestures, their perpetual impromptus, sometimes speaking, sometimes singing, sometimes playing on various instruments, calling to each other, all this wonderful revivalist business, leaves on the outsider a feeling of amazement that these wondrous beings should be ordinary English citizens brought up in ordinary English traditions; they seem possessed with some weird faith belonging to another civilisation. And yet once the meeting is over the salvationist is a particularly shrewd, kindly, courteous, open-minded individual, eminently easy and satisfactory to do business with.

February 10*th.*—A series of political dinner parties—Haldane and A. J. B. to meet the advisory committee on army education, with the thirty young officers already at the school coming in after dinner! [I remember, on this occasion, when A. J. B. came up after dinner and saw the company of young officers, he asked with a smile, " And what am I here for to-night, Mrs. Webb? " " To show that the School is not a Socialist institution ", I laughingly replied.] Dinner with Haldane, at which I went in with Asquith, and had some talk with Winston Churchill—renewed our acquaintance; dining to-night with Sydney Buxton and on Monday with Asquith and seeing such folk as Masterman, Lyttelton and other M.P.'s. The net impression left on our mind is the scramble for new constructive ideas. We happen just now to have a good many to give away, hence the eagerness for our company. Every politician one meets wants to be coached—it is really quite comic—it seems to be quite irrelevant whether they are Conservatives, Liberals or Labour Party men—all alike have become mendicants for practicable proposals. Hence, our life has become some-what too exciting. We have the hard grind of the poor law enquiry and, on the top of it, speculative investments in the minds of rival politicians. We are inclined to plunge heavily in all parties, give freely to anyone who comes along—the more the merrier. Asquith actually asked me whether he should adumbrate the " break-up of the poor law " in the budget speech, when he introduces pensions. What effect would that little bomb have on my Commission I am wondering? Would it blow them forward or blow them back? Meanwhile, life is decidedly too exciting: it is hard to keep one's head cool and free for real downright grind. And yet it is the grind that tells far more than the gamble.

February 17*th.*—These two meetings of the Commission, the first of which is just over, settles the fate of the majority report. The majority have definitely decided to abolish the board of guardians and set up the county council and county borough council as the supreme authority. But this authority is to be exercised by a poor law statu-tory committee of the council itself, as regards institutions, and by local committees, nominated by the council, as regards outdoor relief. To-day, they decided to retain poor law medical relief in the poor law; to-morrow they will, I think, decide to throw back the unemployed into the poor law. Clearly, I cannot get them any further along my road. But there is every sign that they will " stay put " in their present position. I shall have at most four signatories to my minority report, possibly only two besides myself (Lansbury and Chandler)—Phelps contemplates the possibility of signing both! Russell Wakefield will revert to the chairman (mean dog that he is!). [This was an unjust aspersion as the event proved.] After to-morrow I shall not bother to attend their palavers and must grind at my own report as they evidently *mean* to hurry the report on to the finish before the autumn recess. They are, as a body, so light-headed and careless of form and substance that I think it conceivable that they will accomplish it. But what a document it will be! The unanimity of the Commission outside my clique is a personal triumph for the chairman, if he manages to preserve it through the actual discussion of the draft. I like the man so much that I am inclined to be pleased with his success—since it pleases him and doesn't hurt me! His one failure has been to convert the majority to any change in the *status* of medical relief. But that failure was, I think, inevitable, when once he had decided on *one* statutory poor law committee of the county council. If you withdraw one class from the authority of the committee, the whole structure falls to pieces. The reflection of my cry to abolish the poor law is viewed in the desire of the majority to alter the name into " public assistance "; they are already talking of the " old poor law " (*i.e.* the present poor law) as a thing of the past, which is to be superseded by a completely transformed service. The spirit of change possesses them, without any clear conception of whither they wish to go.

February 18th.—Half the morning's discussion on the unemployed question. Unanimity in favour of a system of labour exchanges—really half-hearted on the part of the C.O.S., regarded as a safe futility, not compulsory or nationally managed. Such relief as is given to be doled out by the public assistance authority. What was interesting was Loch's proposal to abolish the class of " able-bodied " altogether, with all the L.G.B. restrictions on the relief of this class, and to let the relieving authority deal with each case " on its merits ". " But this goes against the fundamental principles we have adopted in favour of uniformity and classification ", protested poor Lord George. " Would not the system of treating each case on its merits be rather difficult to work with nominated committees spending the county rate? " I asked innocently of Sir Samuel Provis. " Impossible ", was the reply.

What, however, is clear, is that the C.O.S. party are desperately anxious to slur over everything which distinguishes one destitute person from another destitute person—the category of the destitute is to be kept absolutely separate from the rest of the population. Yesterday it looked like a possible report by the end of this summer; to-day we were again in the morass of unsettled opinions, and were surrounded by big controversies. A majority report became again a nebulous affair —but with this extreme muddleheadedness on the part of the chairman and most of the members, there is no saying where the Commission may be dragged by the C.O.S. faction. Just at present they are in the ascendant. Having given way to the chairman as regards the constitution of the authority, they are forcing him to accept their policy with regard to each class of destitute person, *i.e.* rooted objection to the curative policy and determination to stand by the principle of merely *relieving destitution*, whether that destitution be due to childhood, age, illness, unemployment or vagrancy.

Note that the curative principle is absolutely inconsistent with national uniformity of treatment. The only possible sphere for the principle of uniformity is the economic sphere: the question whether a person is within the income-limit for treatment at the public expense, or treatment without charge, or treatment in the home (the latter assumes that outdoor relief is economically pernicious and must be guarded against).

February 22nd. Leeds.—Off on a tour round able-bodied work-houses and labour yards in Lancashire and Yorkshire—an unpleasant and costly business (Commission won't allow me even my travelling expenses), but necessary to my work. The Sheffield " test " house and " test " yard represent the most deterrent poor law practice. But it is interesting to note that neither the master of the workhouse, nor the superintendent of the yard, feel satisfied that they are doing more than shift the problem for others to deal with. It is a horrid business: ah me! When will all this wicked misery cease—misery that leads to wicked-ness and wickedness that leads to misery? An abomination. Oh! ye politicians, what a work before you if you could only be forced, every-one of you, to realise the needlessness of this abomination.

March 11th.—Winston Churchill dined with us last night, together with Masterman, Beveridge, Morton: we talked exclusively shop. He had swallowed whole Sidney's scheme for boy labour and unemployment, had even dished it up in an article in *The Nation* the week before. He is most anxious to be friendly and we were quite willing to be so. He and Masterman seem to be almost sentimental friends. Rhetoricians both are, but Winston has a hard temperament, with the American's capacity for the quick appreciation and rapid execution of new ideas, whilst hardly comprehending the philosophy beneath them. But I rather liked the man. He is under no delusions about himself. And I am not sure that he is not beginning to realise the preposterousness of the present state of things—at any rate he is trying hard to do so, because he feels it necessary that he should do so, if he is to remain in the Liberal ranks. Will he remain in the Liberal ranks?

March 17th.—Two more palavers over a wonderful scheme of Mrs. Bosanquet's for medical relief. A fantastic constitution—" cycle upon epicycle " of nominated committees, all to start going a scheme of provident associations to which the whole world below a certain wage limit is eventually to belong. But I pricked the bubble by reminding them that " free choice of doctor " by destitute persons meant some millions of compensation to the 3500 poor law medical officers. Moreover, they could not make up their own minds, whether or not these provident associations were to be subsidised out of the rates, and whether any kind of compulsion was to be exercised on poor persons to belong to them; eventually they decided *against* all four conditions of success; *i.e.* free choice of doctors by destitute persons, subsidy from the rates, compulsion to belong, most important of all, prohibition of free medical treatment by hospitals and charitable agencies. So the whole business fell to the ground. " A profitless meeting ", said Sir Henry Robinson to me angrily. " Here I have been called all the way from Ireland to discuss a silly memorandum, and we have come to no conclusions." He did not appear on the following day, and I thought it not worth while to put in an appearance. Apparently, they were all very angry with each other and the second day's discussion ended in a quagmire. Such resolutions as they did pass have been circulated, though apparently neither Provis nor Robinson believe that they bind the majority of the Commission. I gather that there are to be no more palavers until Easter: yet the report is to be ready by August! But the atmosphere is quite peaceful, and we are the best of friends among ourselves.

March 24th.—Gave A. J. B. my poor law scheme whilst we were staying at Stanway. Lord Elcho had read it and been captivated by it, and begged me to hand it on, in A. J. B.'s presence. " If he will really read it and remember to return it to me ", I graciously remarked. " I promise on both counts, Mrs. Webb." So having reported to H.M. Government, I report to H.M. Opposition (A. J. B. kept it for some weeks and returned it with an encouraging letter).

Meanwhile, the L.C.C. with its Moderate majority has plumped down in its statement of evidence on my side, much to the dismay of the majority. And an enterprising journalist has adopted the L.C.C. scheme to the whole country and issued it as a forecast of the Commission's report. Fortunately it is *not* exactly my scheme, as the minor local authorities (metropolitan borough councils and urban district councils) are retained for outdoor relief and there is no stipendiary. But the children are to be managed by the education authority, and the sick by the health authority, etc. etc. The chairman is much perturbed and begs us to be discreet. If the forecast had been inspired (which it had not), it could not have been more discreetly indiscreet—more likely to raise the right sort of expectations. Will they persist in their stupid plan? The coils are winding round them—they must be beginning to feel a bit stuffy—though they look quite happy and self-complacent. No sign of a draft report.

For my part I have returned to the anti-Commission state of mind. The meetings seem no longer to concern me; and, if I look in after lunch, it is only to show that I bear no ill-will. Moreover, the Commission has run dry, both in evidence and in capacity for palavers—on two successive Tuesdays we have not met at all, and Monday's meetings have been very perfunctory and ill-attended. Sidney and I are hard at work on the treatise on " able-bodied destitution ", its prevention and treatment, and we foresee that for the next six months or a year we shall be absorbed in preparing the various reports arising out of the Commission. Just at present, the bulk of the work is falling on him, as I feel dreadfully tired—habitually tired, not ill—merely physically and mentally weary. Owing to his blessed strength and capacity, I can lie back in these times, just giving him all the suggestions and help that I can, and waiting calmly for returning strength. And, in order to store the strength up, we are not entertaining or being entertained; one day after another passing in its regular routine of early hours, simple meals and regulation work—I just luxuriating by the side of my boy, encouraged and encouraging.

Matters are disconcertingly slack on the Commission. A draft of the headings of the report has been prepared—a most extensive document covering the whole field of poor law and unemployment. The sort of report which would take us six months to *write*. If Lord George really means to have a report of that sort, we shall be discussing it this time next year—at least we shall if the Commission gets out of its chronic state of paralysis. I don't believe we shall have the completed draft by October. There is the possibility of the C.O.S. rucking up and going back in favour of an *ad hoc* authority, when they realise that municipalisation means distribution of services. They have already broken away from the chairman, as to London. Also, they may begin to see that they had better play for delay so that this Government shall not touch the question. On the whole, I incline to think that this Government will *not* be able to do either poor law or unemployment. In some ways it would be better that they should not, if we can get Morant settled at L.G.B. and both front benches impregnated with the idea of the break-up. But as Sidney says, " A Bill in the hand is better than a Bill in the bush. . . ."

April 22nd. Kilteragh, near Dublin.—Four days with Horace Plunkett in his charming and restful home—the perfect ease of a most comfortable but easygoing bachelor establishment, seeing officials and his little clique of the Irish Agricultural Organisation Society. He is the same dear, good man—painstaking and with delicate insight into human nature—but not wanting in little human weaknesses. He is, at present, smarting at his dismissal and at the iconoclastic disposition of the Russell-Birrell administration. Hence, he is dead on all their doings and trying to nullify their action as they have nullified his. For instance, he is fomenting opposition to Birrell's Catholic University Bill on the ground of its unworthy governing body; he is trying to discount, in advance, the report of the Commission on the congested districts. On the whole, as far as I understood his contention, I agree with his dislike of the mechanical and materialist views of social reform which the English Liberal metes out to the Irish. Mechanical relief is to them the only alternative to *laisser-faire*. Plunkett, like ourselves, wishes to grow a new set of obligations for the individual in return for increased state aid. How far he has been too nervous in taking action, too anxious to put education in front of assistance—one cannot say.

April. Rian Hotel, Co. Galway.——A pleasant and useful time with eight or nine colleagues at Dublin—chairman, Phelps, Bentham, Downes, Robinson, Bishop [of Ross], Smart, H. Nunn, MacDougall— all most friendly. The chairman is quite satisfied that the Commission, as a whole, has accepted the resolutions agreed to as a final basis for the report, and is now beginning to write it, with the help of his three secretaries. He believes he can get the whole draft ready for discussion by the end of July—and that he will get it passed by the middle of August. If necessary he proposes to adjourn to Deal. " We must settle it before we part: if we don't we shall come back in October with new ideas, and shall have to begin all over again." Such is the stability of these proposals. But the other members of the Commission are not so confident. Phelps, it is true, thinks we shall muddle through somehow, and intends to stick to the chairman and the majority, whatever they propose. But Downes is determined to abide by the boards of guardians, and will have his own report. H. Nunn is going for the abolition of outdoor relief and a minor authority, made up of charitable agencies, to grant admission to institutions. Robinson and Smart feel wholly un- committed and are attracted by my scheme—Robinson determined not to put his name to anything that is unworkable and fantastic. MacDougall is resolved, like Downes is for England, to stand on the *status quo* for Scotland, though he is indifferent as to what happens in the other kingdom. The Bishop does not think he can sign my report, as our ideas are " so fundamentally opposed " on the family—but he also feels himself uncommitted by the resolution. Meanwhile, the chairman thinks his greatest difficulty will be Loch, and I believe I have Wakefield in addition to Lansbury and Chandler, so that it is difficult to see where exactly is the majority on which the chairman relies! The members may be paralysed by their own inability to draft a report and their fear of tumbling into my arms, into accepting the chairman's draft. But my impression is that the end of August will see us in a morass of conflicting ideas.

Meanwhile, Morant has had my scheme reprinted with another front page, to circulate to experts and no doubt the Cabinet. Directly

I get back, we must put all else on one side and devote ourselves to the general report. Every word of the report must be devised to lead to the conclusion. It must be a work of art in the best sense, admirably adapted to its " end ", the conversion of the reader to the " break-up of the poor law ".

May 3rd.—Henry Robinson (the Vice-President of the L.G.B. of Ireland), who is escorting our party, is one of the most agreeable companions I have ever run across. He comes of an Irish garrison family that has produced a bevy of admirals, governors and army officers of considerable distinction. He was bred, with his brother, for the public service. He is tall and thin, with a retreating forehead, large ears, straight dark hair, long foxy nose, and somewhat foxy expression in his dark grey eyes. He has an agreeable and accomplished manner and a most pleasant faculty of mimicry and an endless flow of Irish stories. He knows his Ireland through and through, and looks at its life with kindly good sense. His enemies say he is " slim " and a " time server ". So he is, but he has developed these qualities, without a lack of uprightness, and with a measure of good intention. So far as I have carried my investigation, during our long motor rides together, I have discovered no kind of preference for one state of society over another. After trying to elicit a positive principle, or a positive prejudice, I asked him outright what kind of society he desired in Ireland, assuming he had complete power to bring it about. A dull look came into his grey eyes—giving the impression of a sort of film—an expression of deadness which he has whenever one gets away from the facts of to-day, and after a moment's silence he said, " Well, Mrs. Webb, I have lived all my life at concert pitch, and I really never thought of all these questions in which you are interested. What has concerned me is to keep my successive chief secretaries out of trouble." To keep the chief secretary out of trouble in all matters coming within the purview of the Irish L.G.B. is, in fact, Robinson's chief aim. He looks at each successive chief secretary, both with regard to his past pledges, the exigencies of his party in England, and with regard to Irish affairs, as a problem to be solved. He naturally prefers the Unionist chiefs as these have a freer hand—they can ignore their own allies and need have no consideration for the " Irish Party "; but I could not discern any real personal opinion as to reform, one way or the other, except a preference for law and order. His only personal concern is the agreeableness of the holder of the office—he liked Balfour and Long and he likes Birrell; he detested Wyndham, Hicks-Beach; found Bryce a bore, and so on. He has the characteristics of all very clever officials; he seems indiscreet and is a monument of discretion.

Just now he is thinking a good deal of the probable successor to

Antony Macdonnell. This last, he says, like all Indian administrators coming to Ireland, has been a complete failure—not one of his schemes has come off. He came as a great land expert, and intended to take up and reform each department of Irish administration on Indian lines. But he found the law, the customs, the habits of the people wholly different. Moreover, he was face to face with a new factor—one he had never before encountered—the democratic institutions of Great Britain, which baffled and perplexed him; which he began by ignoring and which, therefore, were always straight in his road stopping his way. So poor Antony is now a broken man, broken in health, broken in spirit and much worsened in fortune. And he is on the point of resigning. Who is to succeed him? The next to succeed is an old man—Dougherty—with one year to run, and he may and probably will be appointed for next year. But who next? asks H. R. If it were not for politics, undoubtedly Robinson would get the place. But he is reputed a Unionist, and the Irish nationalists detest him. Will Birrell dare, if he should be in office, to make him under-secretary in spite of nationalist pressure? That is the question.

H. R. has told me much about Irish local government and the doings of various chief secretaries; but from these casual sketches, it is difficult to construct even an outline of what happened. I cannot even make out whether the countryside is better or worse for all this subsidising activity—there is less misery but more dependence. Feeling the impossibility of getting any kind of knowledge—even the most casual—from my trip, I have taken it as a holiday jaunt at the Treasury expense, with just the excuse of investigation to give a flavour to our touring. These days of motoring and steaming along coasts, and between islands, have been a most delightful rest to me. The beauty of the scenery, the freshness and pathos of Irish life, the complete break into the continuous routine grind of the last two years, have done me a world of good. But this very enjoyment shows how hopelessly irresponsible I feel with regard to Irish affairs—no more responsible than if I were travelling in Norway or Sicily. For the misery is genuine—the men, women and children who crouch in those filthy huts and toil hour by hour on those bog lands in a listless fashion, are in this their beloved country hopeless and helpless with regard to this world's affairs. There is heaven and there is America—and, according to whether they are the children of this world or of the next, they desire to escape to one or the other. Until this escape opens to them, they are drearily indifferent to varying degrees of squalor and want—mechanically day after day they toil, but they do not struggle to survive the ordeal. In the West of Ireland, one realises for the first time the grim fact of the existence of a whole community on the margin of cultivation. All the expedients resorted to seem but to prolong the misery of the mortally sick.

May 5th. Mallarany.—The last day of the Irish holiday. Yesterday, we continued our unblushing jaunt at the Treasury's expense by a most delightful steam in the Congested Districts' boat to Clare Island, and afterwards up Killary Bay—the most beautiful part of the Connemara scenery. At Clare Island we shipped a loquacious priest, Father Nally, a rebel against the authority of Bishop or Irish party—a denouncer of the " Gombean Man " who now rules these western coastal islands. I suggested to him a co-operative store run by the district board, or the abolition of prosecutions for debt so as to destroy the credit system. I am not sure that the abolition of debt is not the best measure for these folk—to force them to rely on character among neighbours for fulfilling their obligations.

I seem to have converted both Robinson and Downes to the notion that the alternatives before the Commission are the *status quo* and my scheme. That is what I have aimed at—steadily to press to that conclusion. Professor Smart has maintained throughout the little trip what Robinson called " a mad dog " habit of wandering off by himself, jotting down little facts about the countryside—the number of public-houses in a village street, the character of the crops on the wayside, and every other morsel of disjointed fact that he can pick up—in the intervals of heavy eating. He is a dull fellow without intellectual purpose—and with precious little intelligence, with all the less attractive qualities of the Scotchman. The gentle Downes, the lively Robinson and I have made up a jolly party, and we all part with regret from each other's company.

Directly I get back we must start on the general report—every word must tell. If every word in every sentence tells towards the conclusion, then I can afford to circulate it freely to my colleagues, without fear that some of it shall be taken and the rest left.

May 15th.—Yesterday we met for the last time before adjourning for the chairman to write the report. This he believes, he and the secretaries, with Mrs. Bosanquet and Professor Smart's help, will accomplish by the first week in July. He then proposes to sit every day until the report is passed; even into August; it will then be handed over to someone to smooth out inconsistencies and we shall meet to sign it in October. Meanwhile, the minority and minorities, or partial dissentients, will be expected to produce their documents equally ready for signature in October.

Meanwhile, Morant has provided me with some 100 copies of my scheme for breaking up the poor law, which he has had printed for his own consideration. I have sent or given it in confidence to Asquith, Lloyd George, Haldane, Winston Churchill, McKenna, Sydney Buxton, Runciman, Harcourt, H. Samuel, John Burns, McKinnon Wood of the present Government, and Balfour, Long, Austen Chamberlain, Lyttelton, Gerald Balfour, of the late Government, and to a select few important civil servants, journalists and local administrators. I have a notion that, when we have got our " unemployed " scheme drafted in its final form, we will get Winston Churchill to print it at the Board of Trade and do ditto with that. Such big schemes require careful consideration by many brains, they have to sink in to the minds of those likely to carry them out, if they are to become practical politics within a generation.

May 19th.—I had a talk with John Burns at the L.G.B. about the Commission and the possibility of his bringing in a big poor law scheme. He went over the scheme of the " break-up of the poor law " very carefully. When we came to the able-bodied, I explained that you could either revert to the principles of 1834 and establish an able-bodied " test " workhouse under police committees, or go forward towards a great national authority for the unemployed. " That's no good, Mrs. Webb: I should prefer to make the police the authority for vagrants and able-bodied men. Now the rest of your scheme I see clearly." He brought up the name of Morant, evidently to see what I should say. I again assured him that Morant was the only man who could carry out the job, and bring order into the L.G.B. He is clearly considering the matter and said that, any day, I might hear of great changes. He is clearly uncomfortable about his loss of popularity in the Liberal ranks, but consoles himself with cuttings from the *Daily Mail* and *Express*.

From John Burns we went to lunch alone with R. B. Haldane and found him as friendly as ever. Clearly his *bête noire* is Lloyd George—and after him Winston Churchill—the young generation knocking at the door. He is full of confidence in his Territorial Army and in all the reforms he has brought about at the War Office. " I shall have finished my work there in eighteen months and then I should be prepared to take on the L.G.B." I impressed on him that Asquith must see to the appointment of Morant at the L.G.B. (Burns by the way actually suggested Sidney, but I pooh-poohed the idea as impossible on account of his views), and told him how delighted we should be to have him at the L.G.B. Both Burns and Haldane declared that it would be impossible to bring in a big poor law scheme next session, even if the Commission did report by December or January. This would certainly be so, unless the report were practically unanimous. If two or three courses were suggested, there would have to be a year's consideration of the alternatives opened out by the Commission.

What interested me, somewhat sadly, in both these men, was the manner in which their own personalities and their own careers loomed large before them; with Burns, blocking out everything else; with Haldane, detracting from the charm of his public-spirited intelligence. This was shown in both cases by an extraordinary anxiety to prove to us that they were the important factors in the Government, and to run down other members of the Cabinet. Probably every poor mortal suffers from this obsession with self; but actors and actresses, and politicians, seem really plagued by it. Fine-natured men like Haldane, fastidious-natured men like A. J. B., neither of whom, as *littérateurs* or as lawyers or as doctors, would be self-conscious, are in their character as politicians teased by the spirit of competitive fame.

July 27th.—Exactly two months since I have reported progress. Three weeks we spent happily at the Playnes', then a fortnight in London, then four weeks at the Hermitage, Luton, all the time working day in day out at the report, and not yet nearly finished Part I., *The Non-Able-bodied*. To survey the whole field and lead up, step by step, to the break-up of the poor law, in such a way as to make any other policy impossible, is a very big task. Whether we shall not overreach ourselves in the elaborateness of our statement and our argument, is a serious question. Many people will think so. But so momentous a change—one needing so large an expenditure of thought and money—can only be brought about by an exhaustive process. Anyway, when it is finished we can throw over any parts which seem really superfluous—and on this we may take advice. Meanwhile, I have sent all we have written to be printed at the request of the secretaries of the Commission who seem most anxious for the privilege of reading it. After considering this anxiety, we decided that, on the whole, it would suit us better to have it in print.

Our stay in the cottage of the millionaire, whilst we were composing this great collectivist document, was really rather comic. Sir Julius Wernher wrote in May to offer us " The Hermitage ", a pleasant little house in its own grounds, but in his park, for as long as we cared to accept it. From the extreme corner of the millionaire's park, we surveyed a machine for the futile expenditure of wealth. Wernher himself is big in body and big in mind, and even big in his aims. To make wealth was his first aim; to carry on great enterprises because he delights in industrial construction was his second aim, and now to advance technology and applied science has been his latest aim. It was over the establishment of the London " Charlottenburg " scheme that Sidney came across him, and found him the best of fellows according to his own lights. Hence, we felt free to accept his hospitality. Part of the minor convention of his life has been the acquisition of a great country mansion, with an historic name as counterpart to Bath House, Piccadilly. This was no doubt to please his " society "-loving wife—a hard, vainglorious woman, talkative and badly bred, but not otherwise objectionable. The family spend some Sundays at Luton Hoo and a few months in the autumn, but all the rest of the 365 days the big machine goes grinding on, with its 54 gardeners, 10 electricians, 20 or 30 house servants and endless labourers for no one's benefit, except that it furnishes dishonest pickings to all concerned. The great mansion stood, closed and silent, in the closed and silent park—no one coming or going except the retinue of servants, the only noises the perpetual whirring and calling of the thousands of pheasants, ducks and other game that were fattening ready for the autumn slaughter. At the gates of the park, a bare half-mile distant, lay the crowded town of Luton— drunken, sensual, disorderly—crowded in mean streets, with a terrific infant mortality. The contrast was oppressingly unpleasant, and haunted our thoughts as we sat under the glorious trees and roamed through wood and garden, used their carriages, enjoyed the fruit, flowers and vegetables, and lived for a brief interval in close contact with an expenditure of £30,000 a year on a country house alone.

September 15*th.*—After another six weeks at the little house in Herefordshire, and four days at the Fabian Summer School, we are again back in London. Not yet finished the " non-able-bodied " report, though nearly through with it. Meanwhile, I am again in disgrace with the Commission, this time somewhat seriously. As part of the newspaper campaign for " the break-up of the poor law ", we gave our poor law scheme to Amery[1] of the *Times*, telling him he could use the idea, but was *not* to mention either our names or the Royal Commission. About the middle of August, there appeared special articles on the breaking-up of the poor law, giving the whole scheme— the last part verbatim. This really indiscreet use of our composition roused Lord George Hamilton to fury, and he fired off angry letters denouncing a breach of confidence. The last of these letters is not only amazingly indiscreet, but contains a malicious fib. There are no two separate series of propositions before the Commission, there is only his draft report. He stuck this statement in in order to make it appear that there had been a breach of confidence; and, of course, to anyone who knows the make-up of the Commission the evil one must be the Webbs, in the combined capacity of commissioner and publicist. To this attack, there was no public rejoinder possible. I circulated a letter to the Commission saying that neither Sidney nor I had contributed the articles, but that we had circulated freely our scheme of reform, and that the writer had evidently had a copy of it beside him. I was

[1] Afterwards the Rt. Hon. L. Amery, member of Conservative Cabinets.

worried about the business, but Sidney remained imperturbable. Of course, the publication in the *Times*, together with Lord George's indiscreet letter, have boomed the scheme enormously, the *Morning Post, Standard* and many provincial papers accepting it as the obvious reform. The net result of our indiscreet, or, as some would say, unscrupulous activity, has been to damage the Webbs but to promote their ideas. We seem destined to use ourselves up in this breaking-up of the poor law—the fate of capacity and good intentions combined with bad manners! And the worst of my temperament is, that I have far more audacity than I have passive courage—I do this thing with splendid dash and then tremble with fear afterwards. All of which means nervous strain. Fortunately, there is always Sidney to fall back on with his genuine indifference to what the world says. " They say, what say they, let them say ", might be his motto—except that he is unaware of his indifference, it is too complete.

The *Times* episode breaks, I think, finally any friendly relations with my colleagues—with all except Chandler, Lansbury and possibly Wakefield. Fortunately, no further co-operation is necessary—I am known to be writing the minority report, and they will be discussing the majority report. I already announced my intention in the spring of not joining in their discussions, and shall only put in a formal appearance on the first days. Afterwards, I shall leave the guerilla warfare to Lansbury and Chandler. What we want now is some months' delay to perfect our report, both in form and substance—we want, in fact, till Easter. So far as I hear from Lansbury, who has been abroad with Loch, Nunn and Bentham, there is a great desire to finish the business by Christmas, partly to be rid of it, partly to counteract the Webb propaganda by definite contrary proposals. If they are really both united and determined, they could do it. We should then have to consider whether we would issue our " non-able-bodied " report with this, and issue the " able-bodied " separately, or hurry through with both in a less perfected form than would be desirable. Probably, however, they will *not* finish their discussion by Christmas and will adjourn for re-drafting. Even when the majority proposals are in their final shape, there will be dissentient paragraphs and supplementary reports to be drafted and printed. But I shall have to keep in the best training, refuse to worry over the coldness of my colleagues, or the censorious remarks of other people, with my mind fixed on the one aim (whatever happens to the Webbs). The position is unpleasant, but it will be soon over.

The Fabian Summer School has become an odd and interesting institution. Two or three houses on the mountainous coast of North Wales are filled to overflowing for seven weeks with some hundred Fabians and sympathisers—a dozen or so young university graduates and undergraduates, another strain of lower middle-class professionals, a stray member of Parliament or professor, a bevy of fair girls, and the remainder—a too large remainder, elderly and old nondescript females, who find the place lively and fairly cheap. The young folk live the most unconventional life, giving the quaker-like Lawson Dodd, who rules the roost, many an unpleasant quarter of an hour—stealing out on moor or sand, in stable or under hayricks, without always the requisite chaperone to make it look as wholly innocent as it really is. Then the gym costume which they all affect is startling the methodist Wales, and the conversation is most surprisingly open. " Is dancing sexual? " I found three pretty Cambridge girl graduates discussing with half-a-dozen men. But mostly they talk economics and political science in the intervals of breaking off the engagements to marry each other they formed a year ago. Meanwhile, there is some really useful intellectual intercourse going on between the elders, and between them and the younger ones. The Cambridge men are a remarkable set— quite the most remarkable the Fabian Society has hitherto attracted— fervent and brilliant.

I had seven of the Cambridge Fabians to stay with me on their way to Wales. Two are remarkable men—Keeling and Dalton—the one a fervent rebel (who reminds me of sister Holt in his generous vitality and incontinent intelligence), and the other an accomplished ecclesi- astical sort of person—a subtle wily man with a certain peculiar charm for those who are not put off by his mannerism. The other five were, I think, commonplace—Schloss, Strachey, Brooke [1] (a poetic beauty) and Shove—perhaps Dudley Ward was a little over the line of medium capacity and character.

October 2nd.—Sidney and I are living at the highest pressure of brain-work. We are working against time on the report—fearing lest the majority should agree to their report before Christmas. Sidney has to give six lectures on " currency " at the School in November—a subject with which he is not familiar: he has also to help Reeves to get into the saddle.

There is the usual medley of business at the L.C.C., the Central Unemployed Body and Fabian Society, and we have to write the chapter on social movements for the *Cambridge Modern History*. To enable me to fill my part of the work, I am living on the most rigorous hygienic basis—up at 6.30, cold bath and quick walk or ride, work

[1] This was the afterwards famous Rupert Brooke who put me off the track of his distinction by delivering a super-conceited lecture on the relation of the uni- versity man to the common herd of democracy. Also I am poetry blind like some persons are colour blind.

Ben Keeling was killed in the war; Hugh Dalton is now a member of the Labour Party (December 1923).

from 7.30 to 1 o'clock, bread and cheese lunch, short rest, another walk, then tea and work until 6 or 6.30, sometimes as much as seven hours' work in the day. I feel it is too much, and am sleeping badly from brain excitement. But short of breaking down, I must continue at it until Christmas. After the report is done with we *must and will* have a complete rest—Egypt or Italy—somewhere where we shall rid our minds of the whole business.

October 5th.—First meeting of the Commission after the recess. I came in when they were just beginning business. A letter from me offering the " infant mortality " material had been circulated and lay on the table. But they evidently did not intend to discuss it while I was there. The chairman somewhat haltingly described the difficulties in drafting the Majority Report, and desired a general discussion on its reception by the Commission. The Bishop endorsed it fully: R. Wakefield and H. Nunn hedged; Lansbury and Chandler stated their general objection to it, but would move amendments; Bentham agreed, with minor amendments; Smart pleaded that the whole report, including his long-winded history, should be retained and not curtailed; Phelps dryly agreed to it generally; ditto Provis, Loch, Bosanquet and Gardiner. Dr. Downes and Miss Hill stated that they were not in agreement as to the machinery and constitution. No member objected to the doctrines contained in it, but everyone held themselves free to alter it. Settled that we are to meet twice a week, and that we are to try and get finished by Christmas, so far as discussion is concerned, leaving one month to get the report revised and out before the session begins. There was coldness towards me, and Lansbury says they are very angry both at the *Times* episode and at the length of my report. They were not pleased with the offer of the " infant mortality " material[1] and will, I think, refuse to receive it. Lansbury and Chandler are going to attend all the sittings and move some amendments. I shall seldom intervene. We have now a clear three months to complete our report in, that ought to suffice to make a really good job of it. On the whole, I doubt the majority getting through by Christmas—if they do it will be an odd document.

October 16th.—Meanwhile, we are seeing something of Ministers. On Sunday we lunched with Winston Churchill and his bride—a charming lady, well bred and pretty, and earnest withal—but not rich, by no means a good match, which is to Winston's credit. Winston had made a really eloquent speech on the unemployed the night before

---

[1] The statistics of infant mortality for a certain number of workhouses were actually compiled and analysed for me by Dr. (afterwards Sir Arthur) Newsholme, the principal medical officer of the L.G.B.

and he has mastered the Webb scheme, though not going the whole length of compulsory labour exchanges. He is brilliantly able—more than a phrase-monger I think—and he is definitely casting in his lot with the constructive state action. No doubt he puts that side forward to me—but still he could not do it so well if he did not agree somewhat with it. After lunch Lloyd George came in and asked us to breakfast to discuss his insurance scheme.

On Friday, we fulfilled the engagement at 11 Downing Street, meeting Haldane, Blain of the Treasury, two secretaries, Harold Cox and, after breakfast, Winston. We had a heated discussion with the Chancellor about the practicability of insurance against invalidity; tried to make him see that the state could not enter into competition with the friendly societies and insurance companies, that it could hardly subsidise a voluntary scheme without becoming responsible for the management, and that any insurance scheme would leave over all the real problems of public assistance. I tried to impress on them that any grant from the community to the individual, beyond what it does for all, ought to be conditional on better conduct and that any insurance scheme had the fatal defect that the state got nothing for its money— that the persons felt they had a right to the allowance whatever their conduct. Also, if you did all that was requisite for those who were uninsured, there was not much to be gained by being insured, except more freedom. No; insurance against unemployment had the great advantage that you could offer more freedom to the person who insured compared with the person whom you maintained and forced to accept training. Hence, insurance against unemployment *might* be subsidised by the state as a sort of " set off " to the trade unionists to get them to accept " maintenance with training " for all the others.

He is a clever fellow [Lloyd George], but has less intellect than Winston, and not such an attractive personality—more of the preacher, less of the statesman. Haldane intervened, as the peace-maker, and suggested that insurance had to be part of a big scheme with conditional relief for those at the bottom, and insurance for those struggling up. We begin our report on the unemployed to-morrow—it must be finished by the end of November—which means sharp work with our tendency to elaboration.

November 15*th.*—The Prime Minister wrote about a fortnight ago to Lord George Hamilton to ask for the evidence taken before the Commission. Without any notice, Lord George brought the matter before the Commission and persuaded those who were present to refuse to supply the evidence, but to offer the draft report after it had passed the drafting committee. Lansbury happened to be present, and after the resolution had been passed stated that he assumed the minority would be at liberty to send their report when they considered it sufficiently ready. This seemed to take the chairman by surprise, but the Commission reluctantly agreed that our dissent should be *sent by the secretary* after it had been discussed by the Commission, thus keeping in their hands the power to withhold it until they could find a day to discuss it in. I happened to meet McKenna the next morning outside the Commission office, he gleefully told me that the Cabinet was going to get the evidence. " Don't be too sure of that," I said, " you will get neither the evidence nor my report—only their own silly nonsense." On Saturday, Haldane came round in his motor. " I have come to ask you whether you would object to our seeing your report? " " Certainly not ", I replied. " I feel quite at liberty to give you all I have as I understand that the majority are sending you their draft— but get the evidence and the investigators' reports ", I added. " Asquith has written again for it, and he quite hopes to get it." " Well, if they *don't* give it you, I shall feel free to do so, as I know John Burns has had some of it—I saw it on his table a year ago." This morning Haldane again appeared. " I want another copy of your report: I have given mine to a young man to master,[1] and I want one for myself. Also *could* you possibly give the Cabinet a loan of the evidence? " " I will get you Lansbury's, if possible." Poor dear ninnies of a Commission: a futile refusal producing the worst impression. And not to realise that the Government had only to ask me for it!

Haldane explained that he had been deputed by the P.M. to get up the whole subject, with a view to drawing up a comprehensive scheme of reform. They would bring in some portions of it next year and the year after (I understand Winston's labour exchanges, and Lloyd George's invalidity pensions), and go the year after that to the country on the whole scheme. He was rather woolly about it. But we chaffingly told him that, if the Liberals did not " break-up the poor law ", we would give the whole business to the tariff reformers—they were in want of a good social reform cry wherewith to go to the country. My own idea is that the Liberals will adumbrate the scheme, but the Tories will carry it out. Which I should prefer in many ways—there would be no nonsense about democracy!

About a fortnight ago, we were invited to breakfast at the Board of Trade. We found assembled some half-dozen of the Labour M.P.'s —Shackleton, Barnes, Curran, Henderson, Appleton, the principal officials of the Board of Trade, Winston and Lloyd George and

---

[1] The young man turned out to be Harold Baker, a brilliant Oxford graduate, at that time a frequenter of political society. He reported, so I was once told, against the minority, and in favour of the Majority Report, which accounts for the coolness of the Liberal Cabinet towards poor law reform in the last years of the administration.

Masterman. After breakfast, we sat round a table and discussed this agenda for a couple of hours—Winston using us· to explain the theory of labour exchanges to the Labour men. They were cordial, but strongly urged that the organisation for casual labour by labour exchanges should not be given them as a provision for unemployment.

We are working at terribly high pressure. The way seems clear as regards the organisation of the labour market—the difficulty lies in the character of the provision we make for those thrust out by this very organisation. Having ascertained our surplus and isolated it, how are we going to treat it? That's the question. *We* answer, training. But the Labour men laugh at the notion of training adult men. They want employment at good wages, not to interfere with ordinary employment. In despair, when they realise the danger of displacement of the ordinary workers by unemployed labour, they sometimes suggest unemployed benefit paid by the state *with no conditions*. That is, of course, under the present conditions of human will, sheer madness, whatever it may be in good times to come.

The difficulty of solving the question oppresses me. I dream of it at night, I pray for light in the early morning, I grind, grind, grind, all the hours of the working-day to try to get a solution. Our task is made more difficult by the obligation to carry Lansbury, Chandler and Wakefield with us. I have got to satisfy those men, both in our statements of fact and in our proposals. And there is the consciousness of being hurried and scurried by that blessed old Commission, which is bungling through its report at a great rate, though it seems to order almost as much to be rewritten as it accepts as final. Also, though in a way the fight between my colleagues and myself adds to the excitement and amusement, it also adds to the strain. Their last little pin-prick is to suggest that I am only to have one proof to work on. " Tell the chairman ", I said to Jeffrey yesterday, " that on the day that I am refused the number of proofs that I think necessary for efficient working the report goes off to my private printer, *and if that happens I will not be responsible for the consequences.*"

The poor old Commission—and it is getting more old and weary, if not actually senile, with every week's sitting. It is floundering about in its morass of a report. Everyone is disgusted with the report but no one dares get up and openly rebel. " What is the alternative? Mrs. Webb's draft dissent from the chairman's draft report ", says one disconcerted commissioner to the other. For our document stares at them in a fine blue cover; and, though it is only Part I., yet there it is, 300 pages of reasoned stuff with a scheme of reform at the end. Their report is still in scraps, and each week makes these scraps more discordant with each other. The majority commissioners are getting so tired and irritated with each other that they may break up any day. But I guess they will stick together in so far as mere formal signing is concerned.

Are all men quite so imbecile as that lot are? I sit and watch them and wonder. They play about, altering commas and capitals and changing the names of things, but leaving to mere accident whether or not the vagrants or the mentally defective are to be dealt with under the poor law. What puzzles me is that Provis goes into fits of laughter,[1] and Loch is beginning to be hysterically hilarious, when the chairman is more than usually muddled and inconsequent. I should have thought that a report which everyone is waiting for is not quite a laughing matter. On the other hand, they talk quite seriously of their scheme coming into existence, in so many months, and discuss for hours the interim arrangements. As they have not yet settled their scheme, in a form that is intelligible, their discussion seems somewhat " previous ". If I ever sit again on a Royal Commission, I hope my colleagues will be of a superior calibre—for really it is shockingly bad for one's character to be with such folk—it makes me feel intolerably superior.

To these entries of the 1908 diary I add two from that of January 1909, a somewhat cat-like description of the last scenes of the Royal Commission on the Poor Law and Unemployment of 1905–9.

January 1st, 1909.—Our report is finished and we await only the revise of the majority, so as to correct our references and keep in or omit our criticism according to their decision to keep in or omit the paragraph on " The Break-up of the Poor Law ". On Saturday, we are all to attend and be photographed and sign a blank piece of paper. So ends the Commission of 1905–9. I am in a state of complete exhaustion, made worse by nervous apprehension of more indiscretions in the press in the interests of the dissentient minority. The Minority Report has been pretty considerably read, and one or two copies are flying about. However, my colleagues will now melt back into the world at large, and we shall know each other no more. The relation has not been a pleasant one, for either side.

---

[1] After his retirement I became a colleague of Sir Samuel Provis in the Statutory Committee for Pensions of Disabled Soldiers, and we became warm friends. Hence, when the reconstruction committee appointed a sub-committee to recommend as to poor law reform, Provis and also Lord George Hamilton were among my colleagues, and the report of that committee, which was in favour of the break-up of the poor law, was drafted by Sir Samuel Provis, Sir Robert Morant and myself, and accepted by the committee. This reform was, however, not carried out until the Poor Law Amendment Act of 1929.

January 17th, 1909.—A scrimmagy meeting on Saturday ended the Royal Commission as far as I am concerned. I was dead beat, and in that state gave Duff a bit of my mind as regards the procedure of the Commission. We are all commanded to sign. But the report from which we had to sign our dissent is still in the making—a new piece of it came round to-day, which apparently is to be inserted into the *signed* document without any meeting of the signatories. It happens to be a somewhat vital part, as it lays down the principle that all applications are to be made, in the first instance, to the " voluntary aid committee " !

Meanwhile, everything looks favourable for the reception of the Minority Report. The majority are counting on the reviewers never getting to that document, and damning it as Socialist. We naturally are taking care, so far as we can, that they get at it—not later than to the Majority Report. We believe that the Majority Report will get a bad reception from all sides. We shall see.

Now I am resting for a week with sister Playne before pulling myself together and clearing up all the mess left over by the report. Then we are going off for a month's holiday. The next months may be stormy. " You have declared war," wrote one of the inspectors of the Local Government Board, " and war this will be."

CHAPTER VIII

THE PLUNGE INTO PROPAGANDA
1909–1911

THE next two years, from the spring of 1909 to the summer of 1911, when we started on our second tour round the world, were spent in an incessant propaganda of the legislative and administrative proposals of the Minority Report of the Poor Law Commission. For this purpose, in May 1909, we inaugurated the National Committee for the Promotion of the Break-Up of the Poor Law, a cumbrous and equivocal title which was changed in the following year to the National Committee for the Prevention of Destitution. This association was presided over by the senior signatory of the report, the Dean of Norwich (Russell Wakefield, afterwards Bishop of Birmingham), with myself as honorary secretary, and the Other One as chairman of the executive committee.

We started out with a small staff of paid assistants and rapidly enrolled a large body of voluntary organisers, journalists and lecturers, together with some 20,000 members, contributing an income for office expenses of over £5000 a year. Within this organisation were not only leading Labour men and Socialists, but also distinguished persons belonging to the Conservative and Liberal parties; also Nonconformist ministers, Anglican dignitaries, and even Catholic priests. In short, the National Committee claimed to be a non-party organisation.

Here it may be well to note that this plunge into propaganda entailed two grave consequences which, if we had realised at the time, might have deterred us from taking this new departure. First and foremost, our research into social institutions had to be suspended: the history of English Local Government during the nineteenth century which we had planned to write in 1899 was never completed, except the history of the English Poor Law, for which my member-ship of the Royal Commission on the Poor Law enabled us to collect a mass of new material.

The second untoward consequence is less easy to explain. Perhaps it may be summarised in the axiom, you cannot at one and the same time exercise behind-the-scenes influence over statesmen, civil servants and newspaper editors, while you yourself engage in public propaganda of projects which these eminent ones may view with hostility or suspicion.

Thus during 1909–11 we lost touch with Liberal Cabinet Ministers, and later on with the Conservative leaders and superior civil servants. Thereby hangs another tale to be told in a future volume: our rapidly increasing participation in the Labour movement, largely brought about by our success as propagandists of a definite scheme of social reorganisation. This led to the Other One's active participa-tion, during the Great War, in the consolidation of the Labour Party as His Majesty's Opposition; with the result that he himself became a Labour M.P.; then a member of the two Labour Cabinets; and eventually one of the Labour representatives in the House of Lords. Being wise after the event, I sometimes regret this turning-point in Our Partner-ship. Personally, I should have preferred a life of continued research and non-party social intercourse. But has one, however free one may seem from other people's orders, any real choice between rival calls to action? Is the future as irretrievably fixed as the past seems to be viewed by the historian? Is the career of every mortal settled in advance by character and circumstance? Who knows?

1909

The first entries in the MS. diary after the final meeting for the signature of the two reports reveal utter exhaustion of body and mind, followed by balked self-esteem, blank disappointment at the superior publicity and approval ac-corded by the press to the Majority over the Minority Report. A restful six weeks' holiday in Italy swept away these unhealthy symptoms and I returned to the daily work of *Our Partnership*, happy and self-confident, with just a spice of renewed combativeness.

January 17*th*.—Looking back on those autumn months [I write early in January] I wonder how I managed to come through it—it was sheer will power induced by prayer. Every morning I trudged out between 6.30 and 7.30—an hour of sharp physical exercise combined with intense prayer for help to solve the problem before us each morning. And solutions *did* come to me in those morning walks. How they came I do not know; but, by the time I sat down to work, the particular knot was undone. Now I am in a state of collapse because there is nothing to pray for, nothing particular to do, which seems *beyond* my power—for which I need inspiration. Perhaps, there will be another call. I must be strong enough to answer: " Yes, we will come and do it ".

February 5*th*.—Still in the depth of depression—the reaction from the pressure of the last eight months. But already I am beginning to foresee that presently I shall revive, and that I shall find myself back again in the quiet atmosphere of the student's life, with no public responsibilities, and with none of those horribly difficult questions of conduct that have been a sort of nightmare to me since I joined the Royal Commission. The plain truth is, that the position of a minority on a hostile Royal Commission is rather intolerable; it has no chance of fighting openly. With no publicity, no appeal from the decision of a preponderant majority, with no regular procedure, so that it is impossible even to know what is being done, leave alone oppose it, the minority is thrown back on the device of working outside the Commission and in defiance of it. Throughout the whole business, Lord George has considered the Commission analogous to a Government of which he was Prime Minister, and those who agreed with him, Secretaries of State, and the minority members sort of Under-Secretaries to be told as much, or as little, as he chose and to obey orders. This has led me to look elsewhere for my forces, and to undermine and circumvent the commissioners' will by calling in those forces. This, of course, has not been nice on my side, and I have from time to time felt horribly miserable about it—especially, I am afraid, when I have been found out. Such are the infirmities of half-civilised human nature! Sidney, of course, takes a different view and has no kind of qualms: he is *self-less* and does not mind doing what he decides it is right to do, whatever other people may think about it. And in all these ways he has a robust conscience. It is immaterial to him whether or not he is found out, or even whether or not he is rightly or wrongly accused. " If I have not done this particular thing," he says cheerily, " I have done something else just as bad, so rough justice is done. *I think I am quite right to do it, or I should not do it* ", he adds.

February 18th.—The day after the reception of the reports of the Poor Law Commission. We turned out to be quite wrong as to the reception of the Majority Report. So far as the first day's reviews are concerned, the majority have got a magnificent reception. We have had a fair look in, but only in those papers which had got to know of the existence of a Minority Report before the issue late on Wednesday night. If we had not taken steps, we should have been submerged completely, by the great length of the Majority Report, coupled with their revolutionary proposals, the largeness of their majority and the relative weight of the names. Roughly speaking, all the Conservative papers went for the majority proposals, and the London Liberal papers were decidedly for ours. We secured, in fact, belligerent rights, but not more than that. The majority hold the platform. Perhaps we feel a trifle foolish at having crabbed the Majority Report to our family and intimate friends, and exalted our own. That has certainly not proved to be the estimate of public opinion.

We have had an amusing little encounter with the majority over the separate publication of our report—by the Fabian Society and Longmans. We thought we had the copyright: or that Sidney had it. I told the Royal Commission staff that we intended to publish immediately after the Royal Commission published. A few days before the publication, the Fabian Society received a peremptory letter from the Treasury solicitor forbidding the publication of the Minority Report as an infringement of the crown copyright. This was, I think, clearly instigated by Lord George or Duff; and it was apparently unwarranted bluff, as there is a Treasury minute (1887) permitting re-publication unless the public has been notified otherwise. We did not know of this minute, and got a bit flustered. But an appeal to Haldane settled the matter, and the Treasury letter was withdrawn. Both editions were published on Thursday, the day on which the Reports were reviewed in the press. It is a most interesting experiment in book-selling.

10,000 Minority Report: encumbered with
    Majority Report! and notes and references
    in a ponderous blue-book.   5s. 6d.

3000 ditto: without references, Fabian pocket
    edition, two vols.   3s.

1500 ditto: again without notes and references,
    Longmans bound, two volumes.   12s. 6d.

It is scarcely conceivable that separate publication of the Minority Report can injure the blue-book sale of the whole report, but will this amazingly cheap blue-book injure sales of the cheap edition, or stop the 12s. 6d. edition selling?

In another fortnight we sail for Italy for a good five or six weeks' holiday. We need it to refresh us from the hard grind of these years, and to cleanse the thoughts that are in us—at least, I do—at present, I am morbidly sensitive, quite unworthily so.

February 22nd.—I am recovering my equilibrium slowly. It is always interesting to analyse one's mistakes and successes. In our depreciation of the Majority Report and our false expectation of its failure to catch on, we overlooked the immense step made by the sweeping-away of the deterrent poor law, *in name, at any rate,* and, to some extent in substance, by municipalising its control. Every now and again, I realised this; but then, when I considered the chaotic proposals of the Majority Report, I lost sight of it in my indignation at their attempt to present a new appearance while maintaining the old substance underneath. In a sense, the Majority Report meant success to our cause, but not victory to ourselves. However, I am inclined to think the distinction between the two reports—the fact that only by re-distribution of the services can you obtain curative and restorative treatment—will become gradually apparent to the nation. What is certainly most surprising is the absence of any kind of protest from the adherents of the old order—the believers in the principles of 1834— against the iconoclastic effect of the Majority Report. That the principles of 1834 should die so easily is certainly a thorough-going surprise. Even the *Spectator* acquiesces.

April 20th.—Home again after the most refreshing six weeks' holiday. It began badly. The life on board the steamer was horribly unpleasant for the first two days, and boresome, though wholesome, for the last six days. The three days at Naples before we had acquired the habit of the tourist were chaotic; we were real innocents abroad, not knowing exactly what to do with ourselves. But the three weeks at Rome were unexpectedly delightful. Our bedroom at the Hotel Flora looked straight on to the tops of the pines of the Borghese Gardens, to the northern hills of the Campagna. The ruins, the sculptures, the Campagna and the Alban hills, all yielded hours and days of interest and enjoyment. A pleasant little circle of Italians—the Scipio Borgheses, Contessa Pasolini, Count Balzani, Marchesa de Vita, the Sodarinis, and various Monseigneurs and other cultivated men and women, belonging to the " White " and the " Black " sets, just gave the touch of intimacy with native things that prevents one from sinking into the guide-book attitude and feeling the mere tourist. Then four heavenly days at Assisi, a week with the Playnes in Florence, revelling in the pictures I loved so well thirty years ago, a not unpleasant journey home pondering on all the beauty we had seen, on the movements in the old world of Rome, its republica, its empire, its mediaevalism, its renaissance and its nationalism, and its church, and we are back to find our little home cleaned up and re-decorated and our work awaiting us.

Above all, I have a completely rested brain, and the Commission, with all its hateful friction, has practically ceased to concern me. Good intention is now dominant, and I have recovered the habit of prayer. What I have to avoid is all silly worry and self-consciousness. We have to go straight for our object, to clean up the base of society, single-minded, without thought of ourselves or what people think of us or our work. Sidney has this talent of unselfconscious effort—" the soldier's pay if not the victor's meed "; he is always content; our pay, he suggests, is a very handsome one. But I need deliberately to oust from my mind other feelings. Now that I am strong again and my brain thoroughly re-created with new thoughts and feelings, rested by thoughts about great things, unconnected with my own little spark of life, I can go back to my daily work with real enjoyment in the routine grind, and without thought of any other reward than the doing of the work itself, in loving companionship with my boy, and kindly intercourse with fellow-workers. We may have another fifteen or twenty years of working life; may we use these years well, with zeal, discretion, kindliness and straightforward integrity.

So far as we can foretell [I enter a few days later] the work of the next eighteen months will consist of (1) propaganda of the Minority Report, (2) bringing out of books connected with these proposals, and also (3) finishing up our eighteenth-century study of English local government. We are starting a committee for pushing the Minority Report; and we are lecturing considerably; five days next week in the big north-country towns, and odd lectures in London, Oxford, etc.— all before we go for a week to the Fabian School in Wales. Beyond this work I mean, during the next ten months, to turn my attention on to the Fabian Society and the London School of Economics, and to cultivate the young people who are members of either organisation— more especially the Fabian Society. There is coming over the country a great wave of reaction against Liberalism and Labour, and the Fabian Society will probably lose in membership. The Minority Report, and the kudos which the Society has got out of it, will stay that reaction but not wholly prevent it. By our personal influence we have to keep the flag flying—the flag of steady, persistent pressure for levelling up the bottomest layer of society. We think in the Minority Report we have a clear consistent scheme which can be worked out by any sensible and well-intentioned body of administrators. The wave of political reaction need not prevent this—the Conservatives are, for this purpose, quite as good as the Liberals and we have as much influence over them.

May 15th.—Enter the National Committee for the Break-Up of the Poor Law. Started on our campaign for forming public opinion. My first attempt at organisation. I am trying a new experiment—an executive committee for consultative purposes and a secretariat of young men and women who will initiate policy and carry it out, I acting as chairman, and reporting to the executive committee. We start, with very little money and a good deal of zeal, on a crusade against destitution. It is rather funny to start at my time of life, on the war-path, at the head of a contingent of young men and women. What I have got to aim at is to make these young people do the work, acting as moderator and councillor, and occasionally suggesting new departures for them to carry out. I have to teach them how to work, not work myself. All the same, it is a horrid nuisance: I long to get back to the quiet life of research and pleasant friendship, long days and weeks in the country, which we enjoyed before the Royal Commission came in to upset our life.

June 18th.—A month's grind at preparing forms, letters, membership cards, leaflets, tracts and other literature, for the National Committee. It looks as if Sidney and I will be absorbed in directing the propaganda—probably entirely, for three or four months at any rate—and for most of our time for the next year or so. What I am trying to set on foot is a real comradeship in this crusade—an intensive culture of the membership with a view to enrolling others and getting everyone to give of their best. My band of volunteers are devoted; and we are trying to do the utmost with a small sum of money—£600. I have a vision of a permanent organisation growing out of the temporary propaganda; an organisation to maintain the standard of life in all its aspects, and to co-ordinate voluntary effort with the action of the public authorities responsible for each service. Time will show. Meanwhile, we have been quite strangely dropped by the more distinguished of our acquaintances and by the Liberal Ministers in particular. I have never had so few invitations as this season, and this in spite of the advertisement of the Minority Report. No doubt this is partly due to our growing reputation for being absorbed in our work, but largely, I think, because there is a return of active fear of Socialism, and of being assumed to be connected with Socialists, though Lord George

Hamilton's bad word (and I hear he " foams at the mouth " whenever I am mentioned) counts. Altogether I am rather in disgrace with the great folk!

June 18*th.*—In response to an invitation to dine, Haldane called yesterday—excused himself from dining here and asked us to come and dine that very evening with Elizabeth and himself alone. Last evening we told him, in a friendly way, of our new plunge into propaganda, and suggested that a crusade against destitution was a really fine complement to " the Great Budget ". He welcomed neither the news of our work, nor the reference to the magnitude of his colleagues' success. Both displeased him. We gathered from what he said, or left unsaid, that he had become indifferent, if not actually hostile, to the minority scheme, or felt that the Cabinet intended to be so. There does not seem to be any chance of the majority scheme being accepted—rather an inertia and a willingness to accept John Burns' assurance at the Local Government Board, that the *status quo* was the best of all possible worlds. Haldane actually stood up for J. B. as an efficient Minister!

A curious little episode at this dinner. The conversation drifted on to religious teaching in secondary schools, and I casually remarked that I liked a definitely religious atmosphere and the practice of prayer as part of the school life. " Nonsense—Mrs. Webb ", blurted out the usually calm Elizabeth, with a sort of insinuation in her voice that I was not sincere. I fired up and maintained my ground; and, in a moment of intimacy, asserted that prayer was a big part of my own life. Whereupon both the Haldanes turned round and openly scoffed at me, Haldane beginning a queer kind of cross-examination in lawcourt fashion as to what exactly I prayed to, or prayed about, and Elizabeth scornfully remarking that prayer was mere superstition. It was a strange outburst met by another vehement assertion on my part that the two big forces for good in the world were the scientific method applied to the process of life, and the use of prayer in directing the purpose of life. Being well-bred persons, we all saw our mistake—I in introducing a note of too great intimacy, and they in scoffing at it. But the jar produced between us lingered through the remaining part of the evening, and I went away with somewhat hurt feelings.

What the ill-success of that evening proved to me was that my instinct to keep clear of the Liberal Ministry was a wise one; it would have been better if I had *not* invited Haldane and had *not* accepted his *pis aller* invitation. For some reason which we do not appreciate, the Haldanes are constrained or estranged. Possibly because they feel obliged to go back on their former agreement with the Minority Report; possibly because they have heard that we admire Lloyd George and Winston Churchill and openly state that they are the best of the party (I always put in a saving clause for Haldane, out of old affection).

Unfortunately, our estrangement from the Whigs does not mean comradeship with the Radicals: we are wrong, and likely to become wronger, with Lloyd George and Winston Churchill over immediate issues. We do not see our way to support their insurance schemes. We shall not go against them directly, but we shall not withdraw our criticisms in the Minority Report. If their schemes can be carried out we should not much object. Both have good consequences. But we still doubt their practicability, and some of the necessary conditions strike us as very unsatisfactory. The *unconditionality* of all payments under insurance schemes constitutes a grave defect. The state gets nothing for its money in the way of conduct, it may even encourage malingerers. However, we shall honestly try not to crab the Government schemes: they are thoroughly well-intentioned.

We remain friends with the Balfours. Arthur dined here a day or two ago and was as friendly as ever. Gerald has accepted the presidentship of the Students' Union of the London School of Economics—a very kindly action. But then they are not in office (!) and any agitation for the Minority Report does not affect them except that it may be an inconvenience to the Liberals and, therefore, welcome—so says the cynic. I am inclined to believe in their genuine friendliness.

As a set-off to the estrangement from the Liberal leaders, many Progressives who have shunned both us and the Fabians are trooping in to the National Committee—Leonard Hobhouse, J. A. Hobson, G. P. Gooch, Graham Wallas, Gilbert Murray, H. G. Wells and others—and the Liberal editors are friendly.

What I have to keep intact is my health and my nerve. All this office organisation, writing ephemeral tracts, preparing speeches and talking to all sorts of different persons, is soul-destroying; excites but does not satisfy. There is none of that happy alternation of strenuous work and complete rest which made such a pleasant life. However, the life of agitator lies before me for many months, perhaps years.

June 22nd.—I met Winston on the Embankment this afternoon. "Well, how do you think we are doing, Mrs. Webb?" "*You* are doing very well, Mr. Churchill, but I have my doubts about your Cabinet: I don't believe they mean to do anything with the poor law." "Oh! yes, they do", said Winston. "You must talk to Haldane about it, he has it in hand. We are going in for a *classified* poor law." I muttered something about *that* not being sufficient, which he half understood and then turned the conversation. I had obtained the clue to Haldane's displeasure. He and Asquith have decided against *the break-up of the poor law*. We have a formidable fight before us. They are contemplating, not the majority scheme, but a new poor law authority of some kind or another. We shall have to fight hard, and we may be beaten. We must not talk big, or boast or brag. We must just go persistently on, taking every opportunity of converting the country. Meanwhile, the less we see of the Liberal Ministry, the better. We had better not *know* they are against us.

We had further information that the Liberal Ministers have settled on London to start their new poor law. We shall see!

July 6th.—A pleasant episode: delighted to get my doctorate, and from Manchester, the birthplace of my family as members of the governing class. Dear old Father, how pleased he would have been.[1]

July 22nd.—We are living in a veritable turmoil. The little office we took is crowded with literature and active workers: members are streaming in and a good deal of money. Sidney and I spend our lives writing, talking, organising. After all, we are not far off the end of our working life; and, if we could really start a great social drainage scheme before we leave the scene, it would be something for which to die content. It is no use shrinking from this life of surface agitation—

[1] " There were ringing cheers as Mrs. Webb ascended the platform and was presented by Professor Alexander for the degree of Doctor of Letters. Whatever changes in the structure or the methods of industry and society, Professor Alexander said, the future may hold in her lap, they prepare the way not least to a prudent and beneficent result who, like the lady whom I have the honour to present to you, set themselves the task of tracing the growth and the tendency of the forces which are now at work. Trying her young wings over the field of co-operation, she spread them, in the company of her distinguished husband, for a wider and more sustained flight, in order to survey the history of trade unionism, the present operation of the principle of collective bargaining, and its scope and possibilities for the future; and later, with an even greater courage of enterprise, to take in, in one comprehensive view, the whole history and condition of English local government. Let timorous politicians complain that these studies by their persuasiveness of interpretation insinuate a particular ideal of political reform, and warn us that ' Subtle wiles are in her smiles, to set the world a-wooing '; it is for us rather to praise their learning, their devotion to enquiry, the large and luminous sweep of their observation. Of her report upon the poor law I cannot tell whether it is destined to be known hereafter as the report of the minority of a commission or as the judgment of the majority of a people. (Applause.) But, individualists or socialists or Fabians, we are all of us Fabians in the tribute of admiration which we pay to the breadth, the consistency, the singleness of conception displayed by its authors. In all these vast undertakings she has maintained with pertinacious modesty that her own share in the joint labour is less than an equal one. But I crave your permission, Mr. Vice-Chancellor, to follow a world unconvinced in counting this belief of hers in the class of illusions generated by the affections. (Laughter.)

" Though we cannot claim her as one of our own former students, she belongs to a family associated intimately with the life of Manchester, whose tradition of eminent public service she has continued and enlarged. And it is therefore a daughter of our own house whom I ask you to inscribe upon our rolls when in the name of the Senate I present to you Beatrice Webb for the degree of Doctor of Letters in this University " (*Manchester Guardian*, July 5, 1909).

from this perpetual outgiving of personality—we have just got to use ourselves up at it. I have taken to it too late to make more than a mediocre success, but I have our joint name as a sort of jumping-off place. It is a curiously demoralising life, if one did not realise the essential conditions of it and guard one's mind from taking them otherwise than conditions that all agitators are subject to—the subservient and foolish admiration of followers. Just as during those last months of the Commission I was working in the atmosphere of perpetual hostility and disparagement, here I am working in the atmosphere of admiration and willing obedience to my will. One has to accept this atmosphere, even to foster it, otherwise an organisation does not flourish. But one must be perpetually reminding oneself that the attitude of followers does not depend on one's own excellence but on the exigencies of leadership.

July 23rd.—As I sat in my office this morning—the three rooms crowded with volunteers—Bentham [a leading member of the majority of the Commission and chairman of the Bradford Board of Guardians] was announced. I gave him the warmest welcome, introduced Colegate [the secretary] to him, and asked him what we could do for him. He seemed almost dazed with the bustle of the office. " I wanted to see your literature ", he said. " You seem as busy here as if it were a general election." " Perhaps it is ", I laughingly replied. " I wish we had someone to organise our side—like you; no member of the Majority cares enough about it." He seemed much perturbed by Willis-Bund's leaflet [the chairman of the Worcestershire County Council who had been converted to our report] and by Shackleton's adhesion [a Labour M.P., afterwards a Government official], collected all the literature he could get hold of, paid for it, and retired, after I had shown him our third room full of stock and literature. Now they have realised that we are at work, what will the majority do? Will they start a rival organisation, or will they issue a manifesto warning the world against us; or will they subside into apathy?

We have three forces against us besides the *status quo* or 1834 school: the *British Medical Journal*, the British Medical Association (*i.e.* the inferior medical practitioners fearing the encroachments of preventive medicine in physic-mongering); the busy-body relief-of-distress philanthropist who likes the " voluntary aid committee " of the majority; and the Hegelians, led by Bosanquet, clinging to the " category of the destitute "! On our side we have organised Labour, the Liberal press, the officials of the new preventive services, and a large section of the disinterested public who long for a radical and comprehensive scheme for *preventing destitution*, and many administrative minds of all creeds and political views. We also have the huge unpopularity of the poor law with its stigma of pauperism. If we can stop any re-establishment of a poor law authority for a couple of years, I think we shall win; we shall commit the country to a policy of complete communal responsibility for the fact of destitution. For many years that responsibility will be imperfectly fulfilled, but it will never again be repudiated. That will be an immense step forward, worth a big sacrifice of time and energy—the best way to spend the remainder of our two little lives.

There won't be much left of us when this work is done! Seventeen years to-day we were married: another such period, and probably only one will be left, *if* one. If only we could look forward to going out together, hand in hand, as we have pressed through the active period of our lives, trying each day to complete some little part of the common task, but always close together in body and mind, day and night, night and day. This union in death is too great a prize to win—in nature's way?

Sidney has also been thoroughly happy, partly because our comrade-ship has never been so complete. Hitherto, we have had only one side of our work together: our research and book-writing. But, this last year, we have organised together, spoken together, as well as written together. And he has been extraordinarily generous in not resenting, in the very least, my having nominally to take the front place, as the leading minority commissioner, and ostensible head of the National Committee. Fortunately, in spite of his modesty, everyone knows that he is the backbone of the " Webb " firm, even if I do appear, on some occasions, as the figure-head.

September 27th.—The whole political world is convulsed with excitement as to whether or not the Lords will throw out the budget. No one quite knows what will happen to the finances of the country if they do—the tea duty and the income-tax will lapse, and unless the Government takes some extraordinary measures the public revenue will be in the most amazing confusion. That in itself seems to prove that the constitution does not provide for the Lords throwing out a budget! Hence, wiseacres who are not party men, like Courtney and Sidney, say the Lords won't throw out the budget. On the other hand, two considerations drive them to do so—the exigencies of tariff reform, and the fear of future onslaughts on their power over money bills. All advance in Socialism might, perhaps even must, take the form of money bills, now that the cleavage between parties is chiefly a cleavage with regard to the ownership of property. Hence, if the Lords do *not* throw out the budget, they admit that they are powerless to fulfil their main function—the protection of property and the *status quo*. On the other hand, by throwing out the budget they raise the old, old issue of the right of the Commons to tax the commonalty—an issue that dates back to Charles I and Hampden; they also set themselves against the rapidly growing feeling against great holdings of land and capital by individuals. And, if the country declares overwhelmingly against them, they may lose their veto, not merely over money bills but over all legislation whatsoever. In forcing the Lords to fight on a budget, and a budget which taxes land and great accumulations of capital, the Liberals have chosen the only position from which they may win a victory. And, even if they were to lose, they have a splendid question upon which to work up democratic fanaticism against a *tax-the-food-of-the-people* Government. I am inclined to think that, whatever the result of an election on the budget, it will land the Lords in their last ditch. But have they an alternative?

Meanwhile, our agitation booms along in its own little way. Our membership rises rapidly; a good deal of fluff of course, but a good deal of good material mixed in with it. The manufacture of this movement is really like the manufacture of the School of Economics—it depends on untiring ingenuity in organising power, perpetually inventing new devices, stepping from stone to stone. Though the blatant budget agitation overshadows our propaganda in the public mind, I am not altogether sure that this is not something of an advantage. We don't seem to belong to any party—and each party is inclined to look at us beneficently. We are, in fact, creeping into the public mind much as the School of Economics crept into the University, into the City, into the railway world, into the Civil Service, into the War Office— before anyone was aware of it. Our little office, wedged between the Fabian office close on its right, and the London School of Economics a few yards to its left, is a sort of middle-term between avowed Socialism and non-partizan research and administrative technique. The staff of the three organisations and the active spirits of their management are all the same persons, and they exchange facilities with the utmost freedom. It is only in London that this triangular activity of the Webbs could occur—London with its anonymity, with its emphasis on personal likings, and its contempt for intellectual principles—a state of things which favours a rapid but almost unconscious change in the *substance* of the structure of society.

On the day before his great Bingley Hall meeting A. J. B. dined here. I had to meet him five men—Sir Gilbert Parker, J. W. Hills (M.P. for Durham), Major Wardle, all Conservatives who have joined our Committee, Dr. Macdonald, president of the British Medical Association, and Dr. Newman of the Education Department. We really had a brilliant talk, and sat over dinner until 10.15 o'clock, continuing the discussion upstairs. It all raged over the principles of the Minority Report, and A. J. B. egged us on, evidently vastly interested and amused. I believe he is *with us*, but he is naturally very discreet. Anyway, his presence and obvious intimacy was a proper sight for my two friendly Conservative M.P.'s and my unfriendly Tory president of the British Medical Association.

October 3rd.—Winston and his wife dined here the other night to meet a party of young Fabians. He is taking on the look of the mature statesman—*bon vivant* and orator, somewhat in love with his own phrases. He did not altogether like the news of our successful agitation. " You should leave the work of converting the country to us, Mrs. Webb, you ought to convert the Cabinet." " That would be all right if we wanted merely a change in the law; but we want ", I added, " to *really change* the mind of the people with regard to the facts of destitution, to make them feel the infamy of it and the possibility of avoiding it. That won't be done by converting the Cabinet, even if we *could* convert the Cabinet—which I doubt. We will leave that task to a converted country! "

In the course of the evening he took a fancy to my organising secretary, Colegate, and told him to apply to the Board of Trade. And I have secured a position for Fred Keeling. Winston Churchill said that anyone, if really recommended " on my honour ", he would take on. I felt justified in recommending Keeling and Colegate.[1]

November 14th.—We are carrying on a raging, tearing propaganda, lecturing or speaking five or six times a week. We had ten days in the North of England and in Scotland—in nearly every place crowded and enthusiastic audiences. In Scotland, our special end was to establish the Scottish National Committee; that is a somewhat difficult task as we have no personality as yet in the movement except, perhaps, that gentle and intellectual Professor James Seth. And the Scottish people are cautious and wait to have the credentials of a new movement before they join. But so far as interested and enthusiastic audiences are concerned, and large sales of literature at our meetings, we could hardly have done better. In some ways Scotland is more ripe for our scheme than England. The school boards are far keener than the education committees to take full reponsibility for the children, and the fact that the children of able-bodied parents cannot be legally relieved out of poor rates adds to this tendency. The public health authorities have already been charged with phthisis. Its unemployed and vagrancy problems are outside the poor law at present, and could hardly be thrust into it as the majority proposes.

[1] As managers of Labour Exchanges which he was just starting.

November 14th.—We had a delightful three days at Whittingehame with Arthur Balfour, Lady Betty, Miss Balfour and Professor Lodge. Sidney had far more talk with A. J. B. than ever before. He was more than sympathetic about the Minority Report. I made him read the whole of the latter part of the Scottish Report and he asked Sidney what could be said against the minority scheme; it almost seemed self-evident. Of course, we must not build too much on such sympathetic sayings from a man of Mr. Balfour's temperament. But it means that, if the Liberals did bring in a new poor law, they would probably be opposed by the Labour Party and by the front opposition bench only too glad to find itself advanced. The odd thing is that, this being the attitude of the leader of the opposition, the *Times* should continue so bitterly hostile as it showed itself in its leader about the Scottish Report. The *Morning Post* is already beginning to tack—but it is the only Unionist paper that is ever decently impartial towards the Minority Report and its authors.

A. J. B. is much concerned with all the crude promises about tariff reform as a cure for unemployment that are being made by his following —from his tone I should think there had been ructions.

November 22nd.—As usual, A. J. B. has capitulated to the tail and repeated the shibboleth that tariff reform will diminish unemployment. What can be the attraction of leadership when you are led!

December 1st.—Another two spells of lecturing—Sheffield, Leeds, Bradford and Hereford last week, Bristol, Newport, Cardiff this week, Worcester, Birmingham, Manchester next week, a wearing sort of life, but we do seem to be impressing the Minority Report on those who are interested in the poverty problem.

Meanwhile, we are on the eve of the great political match—Lords *v.* Commons. I am inclined to think the Lords are in for a bad beating; and, through them, the tariff reformers are going to get a set-back. To the onlooker it looks rotten business for the very section of the party— the extreme tariff reformers—who have pushed the Lords over the precipice. Tariff reform would have won handsomely at the next general election coming in its ordinary course. But, allied with Lords and land monopoly, I cannot conceive that the tariff reformers will get any better result than some considerable reduction of the Government majority—which will leave the Government in power for another five years, and Lloyd George and Winston Churchill in command of the Government majority with the backing of the Labour Party.

We feel now much more content with the prospects of an election. We have sixteen thousand members and we are printing one hundred thousand questions for candidates. Whatever happens, John Burns leaves the Local Government Board. He will probably lose his seat, but anyhow, the fact that, if he remains at the Local Government Board and Winston at the Board of Trade, neither of them can draw the £5000 salary, means that there will be a general post of Ministers. If by any chance the Tories come in, we think that the personal friendship of A. J. B. and Lyttelton, combined with the anxiety of the tariff reformers for an advanced programme, will entail a continuation of the breaking-up process, even if they do not deliberately adopt the whole scheme straight away.

Sir R. Morant came to supper with us the other day. Apparently, if the Liberals do come back, Winston means to go to the Local Government Board and to take Morant with him, with the intention of carrying out the Minority Report. Morant is printing our Bill, at his private press, and is getting to work to study the question. He is nervous that J. B. will appoint the legal expert in Adrian's place before leaving, but I hardly think that likely. Altogether everything looks most promising. But there is a good eighteen months' grind, before we can get free of this agitation.

December 10*th.*—When at Birmingham for our Town Hall meeting we stayed a night with Clara Ryland and met Beatrice Chamberlain. The family is fully satisfied that they are in for a great victory. Apparently the " Master " regards the passing of the budget as a real disaster—as beginning a method of raising money that leads straight away from tariff reform and straight into Socialism. I thought I detected both in Clara Ryland and Beatrice Chamberlain a growing feeling for the protection of property—a growing fear of encroachments on the wealth of the wealthy which I had not noticed before. Hence, rather than pass the budget they are willing to risk a re-invigorated Liberal Party. And, unlike A. J. B., they have no sort of doubt that a tariff reform Government will recommend itself to the people—they have not the shadow of a fear that they would have growing up underneath such a Government an exasperated body of discontent, based on a really revolutionary propaganda against a propertied class and a hereditary second chamber. It seems to me that the welding together of old Radicalism and modern Socialism, which this pro-budget-anti-Lords movement means, will get more and more dangerous the longer it lasts—and it is bound to last until it gets its Government into power. On that reasoning, a victory for tariff reform, *unless it were absolutely overwhelming*, would be the most dangerous issue of the present campaign for Conservatism. Partly because moderate counsels will prevail, we prophesy the return of the Liberals with a much reduced majority—sufficient to pass the budget but not sufficient to permanently handicap the House of Lords *for all purposes.*

December 20th.—We are all awaiting breathlessly the issue of the great battle. The progressives of all shades are in mind united, however Labour and Liberal Party exigencies may make them fight among themselves in particular cases. To the outside observer, it is amazing that the Lords should have dared democratic feeling at one and the same time on the political and economic side! Those who have led them, men of the type of Hewins, Milner, Garvin, Curzon (encouraged by the old politician of Highbury [1]), have apparently relied on the ignorance and snobbish prejudice of the non-political elector—the man *without social purpose* of any kind—the reader of the *Daily Mail* and *Express* intent only on keeping all he has, and leading his life undisturbed by social obligations. No one knows how big this class is, how many persons are actually without any social purpose and can be swayed by vulgar cries of alarm for their property or their personal freedom, or by admiration for the " sporting Lord ". We believe that English public opinion is still sound and healthy, and that there will be at the polls a considerable majority in favour of steady popular control over the life of the community. Even if the polls go against us, the battle will have only just begun and will be of the longest and bitterest that England has experienced since the first Reform Bill. The wisely moderate man should dread a Tory victory. The whole Liberal Party would become extremists. There would be no turning back for the Greys and the Haldanes, the lines would be drawn; political Radicalism would be finally merged into " economic collectivism "; the Fabian Society would be, in fact, triumphant. Perhaps it is an instinctive perception of this fact that has made both Courtney and Henry Hobhouse throw in their lot with the Liberals. The moderate men must, if wise, desire a moderate Liberal victory. That alone will keep the Liberals, for another spell, from falling into the arms of the Socialists.

New Year's Eve, 1909. *Southsea.*—Sidney had to come and speak for Sanders (the Fabian candidate for Portsmouth), so I came too, for three days' walking in the Isle of Wight, a rest before beginning the new year's work.

Very happy we have been since the close of the Commission and our Italian holiday. Since we took up this propaganda we have had a straightforward job, with no problems of conduct, but with a great variety of active work; organising office work, public speaking and personal persuasion of individuals, work which absorbs all one's time without any severe strain on one's nerves. I enjoy it because I have the gift of personal intercourse and it is a gift I have never, until now, made full use of. I genuinely *like* my fellow-mortals whether as individuals, or as crowds; I like to interest them, and inspire them, and

[1] Joseph Chamberlain. [Ed.]

even to order them in a motherly sort of way. Also, I enjoy leadership. Everyone has been kind and appreciative; and money has come in when I asked for it, and volunteers have flocked round us. Of course, we have had a clear field and have just romped in. Our two sets of opponents—the *status quo* and the *majority*—prefer being, until just lately, inert. Now both the one and the other are up and doing. The guardians who have been spending their time in denouncing the Majority Report, are now concentrating all their guns on the " break-up committee " and the Minority Report—the majority commissioners are forming a committee to fight us, and the *British Constitutional Association* is spending all the force it possesses on taking the field against us. So that we shall have this year to fight the forces we have called out. But I think we are getting our defences into good order and are preparing a new campaign, offensive as well as defensive. A good deal depends on the larger political fight; if the Liberals come in, they must take up a modified version of the Minority Report; if the Conservatives come in, we have nothing to depend on but A. J. B.'s personal friendship, and, if they are in with a small majority, the desire of the tariff reformers to get hold of something advanced. If the Tories get in with a large majority, the rank and file reactionaries could either prevent anything being done, or would prefer the Tory report. On the other hand, in such a case, we should have the whole of the Liberal Party wheeling into our movement and probably nothing would be done until they came back again to do it. So we think the game is with us, in the end, on all eventualities; *if we continue to fight in the country* so as to keep the question alive.

From the last entries in the diary of 1909 it will be apparent that we no longer had the field of propaganda to ourselves. During the first year of our propaganda we had been far too optimistic. In the first article of the first number of our monthly *The Crusade*,[1] we had blithely asserted that " the Majority Report, with its proposals to thrust the unemployed and the underfed school children back into the poor law, to give non-elected bodies uncontrolled power over public funds, and to reinstate the old poor-law system under a new name,

---

[1] *The Crusade*, being the organ of the National Committee of the Prevention of Destitution, first appeared in February 1910 (12 pages), and continued under the editorship of Clifford Sharp as a monthly of larger and larger size until February 1913 (35 pages). On the last page of *The Crusade* of February 1913 appeared the first advertisement of *The New Statesman*, a weekly review of politics and literature to begin on April 12th, 1913, of which Clifford Sharp was appointed the editor.
The Crusade during these two years contains many articles by distinguished medical men, education officials and social researchers.

is to all intents and purposes dead ". And we add: " The character of the membership [of the National Committee for the Break-up of the Poor Law] is, perhaps, even more satisfactory than its size, for it shows that the ordinary party cleavages do not apply to the question of poor-law reform, and that men and women of all parties, classes and creeds are ready and anxious to combine for the purpose of inaugurating a serious and determined campaign against destitution. . . . Our real opponents are the party of the *status quo*, a party which, though as weak in controversy as we could wish, has behind it all the forces of political inertia. It is always easier in this country to resist changes than to bring them about."[1] Unfortunately, that vital fact was exactly what Lord George Hamilton and his colleagues had discovered and acted on.

Hereafter, wherever we penetrated, by word or by script, we were confronted by a powerful organisation doing likewise in an opposite direction. This new association—the National Poor Law Reform Association—presided over by Lord George Hamilton, included not only the members and supporters of the Majority Report but also the far more formidable representatives of the existing boards of guardians. Moreover, this organised opposition to our proposals had the official support of the President of the Local Government Board, John Burns, together with the newly appointed permanent head, Horace Monro, and the staff of local government inspectors, all of whom were dead against any tampering with the structure and working of the existing poor law.

" I do not ask or expect all joining this organisation to consider themselves pledged to every proposal of that report [the Majority Report of the Royal Commission] ", stated Lord George Hamilton. ". . . We propose only one authority, with power to give relief from public funds; the minority propose five authorities, with separate objects and separate sets of officials, and each such authority is to be under the control of a different department of the state.

" We propose to deal with the family as a whole; the

[1] See *The Crusade against Destitution*, February 1910, p. 2.

minority propose to disintegrate it by sending each item of it to a separate committee.

" We propose to place the granting of relief and its recovery in the hands of the authority who gives relief; the minority propose to separate the two functions. The giving of relief is to be in the hands of an elected authority; its recovery is to be subsequently adjudicated upon by a paid official in the employ of the authority giving the relief. All who have experience of these matters know what this means —the recovery will be *nil*, and in a short time all relief given will become gratuitous.

" The majority, whilst admitting that deterrence under our existing system has been pushed too far, propose to retain it in the sense that those who are helped out of public funds, in consequence of an inability to maintain themselves or their dependants, should not be in a position of perfect equality with those who maintain others as well as themselves. The minority would obliterate any such distinction.

" We propose that those requiring relief should apply and prove their application. The minority propose that each authority should send out an army of officials to search out and enforce relief upon all who in nurture, medical attendance, and general surroundings, are not up to the standard which that particular authority may consider to be necessary. The relief given to all such individuals will not be confined to a period of want, but is to be given in anticipation of it and subsequently to it."

Such being the character of the forces arraigned against us, we quickly realised that we must change the direction of our propaganda from a destructive to a constructive policy; from " the break-up of the poor law " to " the prevention of destitution ". Only in this way could we walk round our opponents and ally ourselves with another form of governmental authority, the education and public health departments of the county and county borough councils, with their medical officers of health, their directors of education, school visitors, inspectors and teachers, nearly all of whom were in favour of extending their sphere of beneficent social service.

Here, also, we found supporters in Whitehall to counterbalance the weight against us of John Burns and his Department;—Robert Morant of the Education Department and his energetic medical officer George Newman, and even the gifted Arthur Newsholme, recently appointed chief medical officer for that home of reaction, the Local Government Board.

This change of tactics, embodied in the new title, the National Committee for the Prevention of Destitution, compelled us to explain exactly what we meant by destitution. Destitution, we argued, was being without one or other of the necessaries of life, in such a way that health and strength, and even vitality, is so impaired as eventually to imperil life itself. Nor is it merely a physical state. It is, indeed, a special feature of destitution in modern urban communities that it means not merely a lack of food, clothing and shelter, but also a condition of mental degradation. Destitution in the desert may have been consistent with a high level of spiritual refinement. But destitution in a densely-crowded modern city means, as all experience shows, not only on-coming disease and premature death from continued privation, but also, in the great majority of cases, the degradation of the soul. Massed in mean streets, working in the sweating dens, or picking up a precarious livelihood by casual jobs, living by day and by night in overcrowded one-room tenements, through months of chronic unemployment or persistent under-employment; infants and children, boys and girls, men and women, together find themselves subjected—in an atmosphere of drinking, begging, cringing and lying—to unspeakable temptations to which it is practically inevitable that they should in different degrees succumb, and in which strength and purity of character are irretrievably lost. Anyone acquainted with the sights and sounds and smells of the quarters of great cities, in which destitution is widely prevalent—especially anyone conversant with the life histories of families below the " poverty line "—learns to recognise a sort of moral malaria, which undermines the spiritual vitality of those subjected to its baleful influence and, whilst here and there a moral genius may survive, saddened but otherwise unscathed, gradually submerges the mass of each generation as it grows up, in coarseness and bestiality, apathy and cynical scepticism of every kind. When considerable numbers of people in such a condition are found together—still more when they are practically segregated in cities of the poor— this means that the community of which they form part is, to that extent, diseased. It is in this sense that we are entitled to say that destitution is a disease of society itself.

1910

January 8th.—A set-back for the Webb influence. John Burns has appointed Monro to succeed Provis, and his own private secretary Jerred to succeed Monro, and thus ruined the Local Government Board as a possible instrument of reform. This is serious, and curiously unexpected. All we know about it is that we understood that J. B. had been bound over by Asquith *not* to appoint a successor to Provis without his (Asquith's) consent, and Morant clearly expected to go there. It is an interesting constitutional point as to whether the P.M. has a right to veto big appointments. Lowell, in his big book on the constitution, states that he has. From our standpoint, it means one of two things. If Asquith has consented to these appointments, the Liberals do *not* intend to break up the poor law in a big way, however much they may nibble at the subject. If Asquith has *not* consented, it will widen the rift between J. B. and Winston backed up by Asquith, and may lead to J. B. being excluded from the Cabinet in the reconstruction. This depends on how much Asquith cares for unquestioned supremacy, or whether he merely wants to keep the two parties in his Cabinet balancing and counteracting each other.

Meanwhile, we have to go steadily on converting the country to the *philosophy* of our scheme. The application of it will follow (whatever persons are in power) on the conversion of men of intelligence and good intention.

January 27th.—After the elections. The coalition back with something over 100 majority, a clear anti-Lords majority and, abstracting the Irish, a majority for the budget.

What is remarkable is the dividing of England into two distinct halves each having its own large majority for its own cause—the south country, the suburban, agricultural, residential England going Tory and tariff reform, and the north country and dense industrial populations (excluding Birmingham area) going Radical-Socialist, self-conscious Radical-Socialist. The conversion of Lancashire from chronic Conservative to Liberal-Labour is a big fact; the fidelity of Scotland, in spite of the scare of Socialism, to the anti-Lords-pro-budget party is another asset for our party. On the other hand, tariff reform has got hold of large masses of working-men and lower middle-class men and has become the shibboleth of the upper and upper-middle classes.

On the Saturday before the polling we went to tea with Haldane, who has been seriously ill with gout in the eye. He and Elizabeth were most friendly. From what he said he seems to have looked forward to some such result as has happened. Interesting to hear from a Conservative dame, who was calling, that Lord George Hamilton felt certain of a Conservative majority of forty over all parties. That is why, perhaps, he went out of his way to insult Lloyd George as " a little Welsh solicitor "—which has pretty well done for his blessed report as far as Liberals are concerned. Imagine my insulting Carson or Milner!

We are considering mending our fences on the tariff reform side. The more active spirits see that they must find something that will take with the industrial classes, other than tariff reform. By sheer ignorance they *might* plunge on *poor law reform*, we must see to it that they do not do so. These troubled waters are somewhat disturbing to our little bark: but if she be skilfully steered into the right currents of party interests, she will get all the quicker into harbour.

February 15*th*.—A week-end at Stanway with A. J. B., the Salisburys, Hugh Cecil and George Wyndham. A real " Hotel Cecil " party. All these, including the leader, were anxious to understand the reason of the rout in Lancashire and Yorkshire. We naturally improved the occasion and tried to awaken them to the evil consequences of letting tariff reform be associated with anti-social reform. But Hugh Cecil (who is an attractive creature) was already desperately alive to the peril to their souls from any alliance with reformers of our colour. We shall not get the tariff reform party to take up the Minority Report; all we shall do is to prevent them from throwing their whole weight *against it*. To many of the more upright minds, failure at the polls would be the lesser evil compared with the downward course towards a collectivist organisation. They have a *blind* fear of any increase of social responsibilities; and, if they are to accept any measure of it, they would positively prefer to hide their heads in the sand and *refuse to see it*. Arthur Balfour is, if anything, attracted by our scheme; but he is too unconcerned and sceptical to be more than *negatively beneficent*.

Lord George Hamilton has issued his call to arms against the minority. It is interesting to note that he cannot muster a committee in favour of the majority scheme: he has had to include persons like Charles Booth, Bailward,[1] Clay,[2] Lord Cromer and all definitely pledged to an *ad hoc* elected poor law authority. He explicitly states that membership of his anti-minority committee does not entail agreement with the machinery of the Majority Report. We have, in fact, forced the majority back to the *status quo*; after they have smashed this up by their unanimous condemnation.

Sometimes, in moments of physical depression, I wonder whether we can keep up this agitation, all of which revolves round our joint personality. On Friday, I start off for six days' continuous lecturing in the west country, whilst Sidney is dashing about in other parts of the country. Shall we be able to keep it up?

February 25th. Plymouth.—A sleepless night after the six lectures in seven days. What is worse is that my last lecture, the most important one at Plymouth, was only a qualified success owing to very great fatigue. Once or twice I lost control of the big audience—I was too utterly fagged to keep the verve of the lecturer right to the end. And, now and again, I felt I might suddenly give way and faint or collapse— it was an effort of sheer will-power to keep myself on my feet and talking. However, the difference between a lecture which one feels to be first-rate (as I felt the lectures at Exeter and Falmouth) and a lecture that one feels was a failure, is not so marked to others as it is to oneself; the one not so good, and the other not so bad as it appears to the speaker himself. What I most fear is that I may lose my nerve if I have that unpleasant sensation that I had the other night at the Exeter P.S.A. of coming over faint in the midst of what I am saying.

March 1st.—Another five days' continuous lecturing in Lancashire. On the whole, very successful.

Meanwhile, there have been political crises that have disposed of

---

[1] One of the most prominent members of the new organisation was W. A. Bailward, who declared that: "Speaking generally the Majority Report would enormously extend the functions of state relief, and it would, in fact, bring about a sort of system of state-organised charity which would probably eventually be almost wholly dependent upon public funds. . . . I end as I began, by saying that there are, in my opinion, only two possible policies for the future. The one is that of independence, upon which the reforms of 1834 were based. The other that of the Minority Report, which frankly adopts universal provision by the state. The majority try to steer a middle course. I think that they will fail. I cannot help thinking that the majority of guardians will prefer the old policy, under which this country has made such enormous strides, under which the great friendly societies have been born and flourished, under which rural able-bodied pauperism has practically disappeared " (*Poor Law Conferences*, 1911–1912, pp. 183, 187).

[2] Sir Arthur Clay, a well-known artist; his son, Sir Felix Clay, married my niece Rachel Hobhouse.

most persons' respect for the Liberal leaders. It is almost inconceivable
that Asquith should have gone off to the South of France, with no
clear idea of what he was going to propose to Parliament as the Liberal
policy. But, from what one gathers, that seems to have been the case.
At the subsequent Cabinets, Grey insisted on introducing the policy of
reforming the House of Lords; a policy which no one but he himself
had even mooted during the election. In this he was backed up by
Haldane and opposed by Lloyd George and Churchill (?). Partly out of
jealousy of the two Radical leaders, the Cabinet gave way to him. No
attempt was made to gauge the opinion of the three groups upon whom
Asquith depends for his Government's existence.

The King's speech came like a thunderclap over the head of the
whole of the progressives—and after a moment's stupefaction, produced
an ultimatum from Redmond, a threat from the Labour Party, and
vigorous expostulations from the advanced Radicals. Thereupon more
Cabinet meetings and a sudden retreat on to the position advocated by
the *Daily News* and *Nation*—a complete capitulation to the advanced
party. There is a wild rumour that the King intervened in favour of
the Veto Bill and not reform. But Asquith has shown himself careless,
unintelligent and cowardly—without foresight or firmness. It is a great
triumph for Winston and Lloyd George who have behaved with
loyalty and discretion, whilst letting it be quietly understood that they
disagreed with the King's speech policy, and had opposed the complicated policy of attempting to reconstitute the House of Lords.

Sidney lunched with Haldane the Sunday before the King's speech
and his host then adumbrated the policy of " reform " [of House of
Lords] *versus* " veto ". " If you do that," Sidney remarked, " you
will be preparing for yourselves an ignominious funeral." But R. B. H.
turned a deaf ear. I gathered that Haldane had not grasped the policy
of the Minority Report though he suggested that the Cabinet was
favourable to it. It is clear that, if we had left it to the Cabinet to
decide yea or nay, mere jealousy of Lloyd George and Winston might
have turned the scales against the minority in favour of a new poor law.
By the time any Government is ready to tackle the question, no other
course but to break-up shall be open to them.

This week Sidney quietly slips out of the L.C.C. to which he has
devoted so much time, thought and feeling. The last three years the
L.C.C. has been rather dead to him. The Progressive movement,
which the Fabian Society started in 1889, has spent itself. The
machine that has been created goes grinding on all in the right direction
—but it has become more or less automatic. A fresh impetus will, I
think, come from our propaganda, from the new principle of the
national minimum and the joint responsibility of the individual and

the community, for a given standard of individual life. Possibly he may return to the Council to carry out such a programme—but for the present we can do more by persuading the country at large than by administration of London's municipal business.

March 13*th.*—We met the Prime Minister, Grey and Birrell at dinner the other day, interesting to note that we had met none of these personages since they were in office—Grey I had not seen for years. We neither of us spoke to any of them, though it was a small party— Asquith was somewhat marked in his non-recognition of either of us. He is much older, and, in a sense, commoner, in appearance; at dinner he was talking scandal with Mrs. Crawshay about " the Pasolini " who has recently eloped (the daughter-in-law of our friend in Rome). After dinner he was ogling Lady Ripon of fashionable and fast fame. Grey looked the same charming aristocrat that he has always been— slim in figure, and young and refined in expression—but somewhat of a " stick " in general attitude. Birrell was the same jovial *littérateur*— pleasantly sparkling about nothing with a group of admiring women. I was quite entertained with a thoughtful Russian—Count Constantine Benckendorff[1] at dinner, and Raymond Asquith afterwards. But it was a somewhat odd sensation to see these three Ministers for the first time since they were in office, and to be conducting an agitation in the country which must eventually affect their policy, and yet not have even a good-day from them! Each of them would, I think, have been supremely bored to have exchanged one little word about poor law or any other social-economic question. Contrasting it with the talk down at Stanway, even with the interest shown in all these questions by Lord Salisbury and George Wyndham, the Liberal Ministers' indifference, not to say distaste, is amazing and makes one wonder what exactly is happening to the leaders of the Liberal Party. Here we are making the bed they will have to lie in—and yet they seem wholly unconcerned with this happening. Strange!

I went to Granville-Barker's *Madras House* this afternoon. After listening to this and to G. B. S.'s *Misalliance*, one wonders whether these two supremely clever persons are not obsessed with the rabbit-warren aspect of human society? G. B. S. is brilliant but disgusting; Granville-Barker is intellectual but dull. They both harp on the mere physical attractions of men to women, and women to men, coupled with the insignificance of the female for any other purpose but sex attraction, with tiresome iteration. That world is not the world I live in, or indeed, think to exist outside a limited circle—at the top and

---

[1] Son of the Russian Ambassador: after the October Revolution he served for a time the Soviet Government in a diplomatic capacity.

at the bottom of the social strata. In the quiet intermediate area of respectable working-class, middle-class and professional life, and in much gentle society, there is not this over-sexed condition. The women are almost as intelligent as, and certainly a good deal more spiritual than, the men, and their relations to the other sex are those of true friendship and intelligent comradeship in the transaction of the affairs of life, and in the enjoyment of the interests and beauty of life. *The male and the female have become the man and the woman.* It is mischievous to be perpetually drawing society as being worse than it is, just because most persons are stupider than such clever mortals as G. B. S. and Granville-Barker, and fail to express their good thoughts and feelings otherwise than in stereotyped and banal phrases which bore these clever ones.

At Exeter, for instance, I stayed with a commercial traveller in a one-servant house. He was a very ugly man, with a red nose and great unshapely, protruding ears; he did not eat nicely, and his accent was harsh. But he was full of goodwill and public spirit, and had wide intellectual and artistic interests. His wife was a gentle pious lady of sound sense and discretion and charming manners, and his daughter played Chopin to me for two hours on end, and gave me a vivid and broadminded account of the life of her sister as a Chinese missionary. They all lived together in affectionate, happy harmony, and had endless friends in Exeter of like temperament and interests. Of course, their house was dull-coloured and dowdy, and not over-clean; the food was of the plainest and had the look of being always on the table. But where was the rabbit warren? Their thoughts and feelings were in the main engaged in spiritual, intellectual, artistic or philanthropic matters. In this set the women folk were treated exactly like the men folk— and all were Christian gentlefolk, in spite of belonging to the lower middle-class. Neither G. B. S., nor Granville-Barker, seems to realise that these people represent the English middle-class far more truly than their surreptitious or avowed polygamists, with women running after them, that they are so fond of producing on the stage as representative of English society. Let us hope that future historians will not take the play, even of the new school of intellectuals, as really representing English society as a whole at the beginning of the twentieth century.

Where I think G. B. S., Granville-Barker, H. G. Wells and many other of the most modern authors go wrong, from the standpoint of realism in its best sense, is their complete ignoring of religion. By religion, I mean the communion of the soul with some righteousness *felt to be outside and above itself.* This may take the conscious form of prayer: or the unconscious form of ever-present and persisting aspirations—a faith, a hope and a devotion to a wholly disinterested purpose. It is this unconscious form of religion which lies at the base of all Sidney's activity. He does not pray, as I often do, because he has not acquired so self-conscious a habit. But there is a look in his eyes when he patiently plods on through his own and other people's work, when he unwittingly gives up what other people prize, or when he quietly ignores the spite or prejudice of opponents, that tells of a faith and a hope in the *eventual* meaning of human life—if not for us, then for those who come after us. He refuses to put his aspiration into words, because he would fear the untruth that might be expressed in those words—he has a dread of being even remotely irrational or super-stitious. But, for all that, he believes.

Not one of G. B. S.'s men or women, or Granville-Barker's or H. G. Wells's, have either the conscious or unconscious form of religion. The abler of these puppets of their thoughts deny it; the stupider are oblivious of it—a few are blatant hypocrites. And, that being so, there is nothing left for them to be but intellects or brutes—and for the most part they are both. It is strange that, whatever these clever men may think and feel themselves, they don't perceive that there *is* such a thing as religion and that it is a force which moulds many lives and makes the mere rabbit warren an inconceivable horror.

March 15*th.*—Sidney and I went to Galsworthy's *Justice*—a great play, I think—great in its realistic form, great in its reserve and restraint, great in its quality of pity. Its motive, that all dealings with criminals should be treatment *plus* restraint in the interest of the com-munity, are all worked in with the philosophy of the Minority Report. But what is to be done with the incurable?

April 12*th.*—Last Friday was a great day for the National Com-mittee, our Bill being discussed in a crowded House by A. J. B., Asquith and Burns (besides picked men on all three sides). The first-named was extraordinarily friendly; the second coldly appreciative; the last as hostile as he dared be. The Labour Party gave the Bill a full-blooded support—the rank and file Liberals are obviously inclined to it. But the net impression of the debate was that, though the majority proposals were dead, the *status quo* had the hot approval of J. B., and that Asquith was sceptical of the possibility of change, and A. J. B. hesitating as usual. One big advance has been the sweeping away by A. J. B. of the Socialist bogy and the intimation to the Conservative press that the Conservative Party does not want to be pledged against the Minority Report scheme in the country. That was real kind of A. J. B.! And, I think, wise from the standpoint of his party.[1]

[1] " The whole scheme of the minority report was brought before the House of Commons on Friday, April 8, 1910, by Sir Robert Price, where it attracted an

Next session we shall have a litter of Bills embodying the different parts separately, while keeping one complete one on the stocks.

April 28th.—Enter Royal Commission No. 3.

At four o'clock yesterday afternoon a messenger came from Lloyd George asking Sidney to let him submit his name to H.M. as one of the commissioners of the new Development Act, and to announce it that very evening in Parliament. Sidney naturally accepted the honour —rather liking the prospect of new work. So enters Commission No. 3 —this time an executive and permanent Commission in all probability. I bargained that it should not prevent our Eastern travel a year hence.

May 19th.—The King's death has turned politics topsy-turvy— and robbed the Liberals of their cry. Whether they will be able to get up the steam again seems very doubtful. London and the country

unusually large attendance of members, and elicited speeches from the Prime Minister (H. H. Asquith), the President of the Local Government Board (Mr. John Burns) and the leader of the Opposition (Mr. Arthur Balfour). No division could be taken " (*Hansard*, April 8th, 1910).

". . . After his speech and Wyndham's, A. J. B., Long, Lyttelton and myself retired to Balfour's room to consider our attitude to a private members' bill which embodies the policy of the Minority Report of the Poor Law Committee. Balfour, who had not read it or given much consideration to it but who had seen the Webbs, was the most favourably inclined to it. The rest of us, who had gone a little deeper into it, were agreed that it would not do, though I confessed to having been greatly attracted by it before I studied it. I think that our line will be that the first work for parliament (and quite enough for one parliament) is to carry out the recommendations on which both the majority and minority are agreed. These alone will work an enormous change and require all the care parliament can give to them. The popular and sound objections to the minority scheme in its entirety are: (1) That it would cost about 50 millions! (2) That it established an intolerable bureaucratic tyranny. Five separate inspectors from the Local Authority might descend on any working man's home and carry off himself, his wife or any or all of his children to a municipal institution, feed, clothe or otherwise care for them, utterly ignoring both parental rights and parental responsibility, whilst it would rest with a sixth inspector not appointed by or under the control of the Local Authority to decide without appeal whether any and, if so, what part of the cost of this public assistance should be recovered from the family. And all the inspectors might act without any call for help from the individual, without there being any destitution and without there being anything in the nature of a criminal act or default on the part of the parents. (3) The whole tendency of the report is to make the position of the State-aided better than that of the ordinary decent working man taxed to support them.

" ' The Webbs ', said Vivian to Lyttelton, ' carry you on logically and imperceptibly from one point to another; but when you look at the whole, it's moonshine! ' " Not a bad criticism " (The Rt. Hon. Sir Austen Chamberlain, K.G., P.C., M.P., *Politics from Inside*, pp. 238-9, March 30th, 1910).

" A curious episode: last Friday week Burns rose as soon as Asquith sat down after speaking in the Poor Law discussion. Everyone was surprised at this unusual arrangement of ministerial speeches, especially as Asquith had fairly covered the departmental ground, giving the departmental statistics, etc.

" ' But no one ', said Asquith to Balfour subsequently, ' was more amazed than I was. Burns hadn't said a word to me about it! ' What a Cabinet! " (*ibid.* p. 253, April 17th, 1910).

generally is enjoying itself hugely at the royal wake, slobbering over the lying-in-state, and the formal procession. Any collective thought and feeling is to the good; but the ludicrous false sentiment which is being lavished over the somewhat commonplace virtues of the late King would turn the stomachs of the most loyal of Fabians. But is it possible for a *crowd* to be anything but exaggerated in its manifestations, with a popular press playing up to it? " The crowd on the press " and the " press on the crowd ".

One year of our organisation over. We have been at the job continuously lecturing, organising, writing—one long-sustained exposition. And we mean to spend another year at it. Here again, there is a curious process of action and reaction. We have made a following, and now our followers are making us into professional leaders. " How shall we be able to retire? " is what I ask myself. The office with its eleven salaried persons, and its twenty or thirty volunteers, the corps of four hundred lecturers, the three thousand five hundred contributing members, the twenty-five thousand non-contributing members, the twenty or so branches, make up a machine which at present depends on us for its motive force. It is clear that we are making great headway in the country, we are rolling up a great body of enthusiasm. And it is all centring round our joint personality. Will it be possible for us, when we think the idea is safely launched, simply to step back and say —cease, or go on without us?

What we have to do in the next twelve months is to construct machinery that will go on without us! At any rate for a time. We must consolidate, and not merely roll on.

One great success we have had is at the St. James's Hall lectures— six successive Mondays we have had a full house of good material— majority of men of the governing and professional classes—we have actually cleared a profit of three hundred and fifty pounds!

Meanwhile, the co-operators have declared in our favour, and even the friendly societies are unexpectedly in our favour.

May 24th. Edinburgh.—It is better to be dead beat after making a success than dead beat after making a failure—or, to put it more correctly, when one *feels* one has made a success—because I daresay the feeling of success is as exaggerated as that of failure. But holding a big meeting of Scottish ministers for an hour's lecture and answering of questions is a feat of endurance—the giving out of vital energy.[1]

The question is: Where is this going to end? Having discovered in myself the faculty of the preacher and the teacher, shall I be able to withdraw to the life of research?

---

[1] This was the Church Assembly presided over by the Master of Polwarth.

May 27th.—It is just one year since we started the National Committee and we have had one long grind of lecturing and organising. We go now for a month's holiday before directing the Fabian Summer School and entering on another campaign of talking and office organisation. It is well to take stock of our undertaking.

We have done what we set out to do. A year ago, the Minority Report was one among many official documents; now it is a movement which is obviously spreading from one section to another. The co-operative movement is the last of the great Labour organisations to join us; we have practically the whole of the social service side of Nonconformity, and a large and increasing section of the Church. Two Cabinet Ministers have been willing to preside at our meetings, and we were able to prevent a Tory ex-Cabinet Minister (Walter Long) from speaking for the Majority Committee; while Mr. Balfour was extraordinarily favourable to us in the debate of our Bill.

And we do seem to be attracting the devoted service of a large body of volunteers. We are moving out of our five little rooms into more spacious offices, and we are developing a highly-organised staff out of salaried workers and some thirty or forty unpaid office-helpers and some four hundred lecturers.

I am trying to construct out of the volunteers a subordinate organisation—an interesting experiment. There is the executive of fifty members with its three committees—finance, meetings and membership, and literature. These are the spending committees which Sidney and I run. Then there is the office committee of the six staff officers presided over by Sanders of the Fabian Society, to whom we give a small honorarium. But, besides this ordinary organisation, I have now a volunteers council with a press committee, a social committee, a propaganda committee, and an office improvement committee, which revolves round myself and Mrs. Surrey Dane. We ought also to have a lecturers' council revolving round [C. M.] Lloyd and Mrs. Carter. Our difficulty is with our local branches, which are always getting into debt or relapsing into vacuum. We have *not* solved the question of branch organisation—even the Scottish branches being insolvent and raising barely enough money to pay postage and stationery.

Now the question is: Can we develop this organisation into a really big national movement to do away with destitution as a chronic and wholesale state of millions of our people? Here seems an opportunity. The Minority Report has the extraordinary advantage of being a platform at once concrete, comprehensive, and yet unconnected with any one political party. It has a philosophic basis in the whole theory of an enforced minimum of civilised life: and yet it is part and parcel of an urgently-needed reform which must come up for consideration by whichever party is in power. But, at present, the whole organisation depends on us—and is limited by the defects of our joint-personality and the prejudices which this personality arouses. So long as this is the case, the life of the movement will be precarious; not merely because our strength and means might fail, but because the distrust and dislike of us might blaze out into a powerful hostility to the spread of the philosophy which lies at the base of the minority scheme. Sidney and I *are* Socialists; there is no denying the fact. In Scotland, this fact has prevented the Minority Report making any substantial headway with the upper and professional classes, and that means no money for propaganda. Owing to our social prestige and Sidney's administrative reputation—largely owing to Arthur Balfour's personal friendship—this stigma of socialism has not stood in our way in England. But, at any time, the fear of Socialism might deplete our moneyed membership, and then our organisation would necessarily collapse. The problem before us in the next few months is: Can we give this organisation an existence independent of our leadership—exactly as we have done in the case of the London School of Economics? If not, it will have its day—a quite vigorous and useful day—and then be wound up with the first instalment of the reform of the poor law on the lines of the Minority Report. Of course, we *might* fail even to carry this—but that amount of failure I do not contemplate. We have already made it impossible, either to set up a new poor law or to maintain for an indefinite time the present state of things.

I often wonder whether I like this life of propaganda or not. I enjoy the excitement of successful leadership, I like the consciousness of the use of faculties which have hitherto been unused—the faculty for public speaking and the faculty for organisation. On the other hand I feel harassed—I don't like financial responsibilities, I am perpetually haunted by the fear of failure to live up to the position I am forced into. And I grudge the quiet study and thought with its output of big books. I sometimes wonder whether the expenditure of money and energy on mere passing propaganda is as socially useful as research. And I positively dislike the feeling of being dragged along by the movement we have created—almost mechanically dragged along—not able to refuse to respond to a demand we have ourselves stimulated. And, now and again, I wonder with regard to the unemployment scheme whether we could really carry it through. One ought never to propose any public action which one could not, *if called on*, carry out. About the non-able-bodied part of our scheme, I am supremely confident that we are almost *blatantly right*. But, with regard to certain parts of the unemployment scheme, I am not quite so sure—*e.g.* the regularisation of government work and the technique of training establishments both give me pause. Also, I am convinced that Sidney underestimates the expense. However, that last point does not upset me—the more of the national wealth we can divert from the rich to the regular outgoings of the poorest class, *so long as it is accompanied by an increase in personal responsibility on the part of these benefited classes*, the wholesomer for the state. Only one does not like to mislead the public, even for its own good!

July 8th.—A vigorous holiday in Switzerland: walking with Colegate and Lloyd or both—perhaps rather too vigorous for an old lady like myself. But, though it tired my body, I believe it really rested my mind. Now that we are immersed in this movement we cannot get the old half-term holidays in the country. So long as we are in England we stand to be shot at by all our followers and opponents. It is rather a breathless business—a perpetual sense of insufficiency to meet the demands of a perpetually growing clientèle. A reading public has to wait until the author produces the book; and is wholly unknown to the author, not only before the book is produced but, except in rare cases, after it is produced. But, when once one takes to organising public opinion, there is no peace; the unconverted, the half-converted, even the converted are bombarding one for arguments, additional facts, counter-arguments, and orders for personal service to the cause. We have risen to the opportunity which the Royal Commission has opened out before us for the conversion of England.

During the next nine months we have to consolidate our following into a sufficiently self-sufficing organisation to go on without us. The month we were away a certain amount of disorganisation set in, which showed that very unstable equilibrium which exists at present. If we can give the organisation an independent life, nine or ten months' absence a year hence will be all to the good. It will permit it to settle down on its own foundations instead of depending so much on us. Can we do this?

July 12th.—Lord George Hamilton has scored two points against the Webbs. First he has, through his personal friendship with Lord Belper and the Duke of Northumberland, turned the poor law committees of the County Councils Association away from the Minority Report proposals which our friend Chapman had got them to accept. This is largely due to Henry Hobhouse who, in a quiet way, has always been hostile to us, especially to me, and who proposed a scheme of his own with marked majority features. We have advised Chapman to amend and accept it, as it is of the utmost importance that the County Councils Association should seem willing that the county councils should take over the work. Moreover, even H. H.'s scheme proposes that the feeble-minded, the vagrants and the unemployed, should be taken out of the poor law, that the medical services should be unified under the county medical officer, and that the poor law school should be handed over to the education committee. That is good enough for a beginning, and the fantastic constitution of the county poor law board, the body which is to manage the rest, could not pass any Cabinet. The other matter is more serious—though it does not concern the poor law. My late chairman has persuaded Lord Balfour of Burleigh and his Departmental Committee on Royal Commissions to recommend that there should be no more minority reports of the Webb brand! It is odd that Royal Commissions have been going on muddling about all these seventy years, but that no enquiry is made into their procedure until a Labour-Socialist group puts forward a really powerful report upon which a popular movement can be based! No one suggests that the Minority Report is not worth the printing bill. As a matter of fact, the Government have sold more Minority Reports than Majority, in spite of our sale of twelve thousand. So the country thinks the report valuable. In fact, its *power* is exactly the reason why future ones are to be suppressed before they are born. It is rather a mean proceeding. But our enemies have got into a panic—highly complimentary no doubt, but inconvenient. Another sign of this was a three-column review of the Minority Report in the *Times* with a leader calling attention to it— all to the effect that the Minority Report *was* the French Revolution in another form! This gave us an opportunity for a column-and-a-half answer in our best style of modest moderation.

August 19th. Caermeddyg Llanbedr.—Half through the very exhausting performance of directing the Fabian Summer School.

On the whole more satisfactory than I expected. The first fortnight, with the somewhat remarkable party we had here and the many interesting and influential persons who had congregated at the National Conference [on the Prevention of Destitution], was really profitable from the standpoint of propaganda and personal influence. But I cannot say that even this fortnight was exactly enjoyable. To keep house for twenty persons and be accessible to another hundred, as well as lecturing three or four times in the week, is a strain on nerves. Since our more especial friends and supporters have left, we have been surrounded by a miscellaneous crowd—all kindly and well-bred and interested, but not exciting in themselves, and some of them ugly and crude in mind and manners. Still, my dominant impression is the well-bredness of this extraordinarily mixed assembly—I.L.P. organisers, M.O.H.s, teachers, minor officials of all sorts, social workers, literary men, journalists and even such out-of-the-way recruits as auctioneers and unregistered dentists—all living in extremely close quarters, and yet not getting on each other's nerves through a too great disparity of speech and behaviour. It is a wonderful instance of the civilising effect of a common purpose and a common faith. Of course, every now and again one longs to escape for a day or two; the whirl of constant talk and discussion and the answering of questions is too much for physical or mental comfort. Sidney is simply splendid—his perpetual courtesy and kindness and willingness to be helpful to all and sundry without distinction of persons. And, I suppose, one gains facility of experience and thrashes out one's own thoughts.

What appalls me is the fear that we may never be able to get quit of leadership again. Is our existence going to be one perpetual round of talking and organising for the rest of our working lives? It is a terrifying prospect! The two of us, taken together, seem to constitute a leader at the time when the English political world is singularly without definite leadership on social and economic questions. And no one has yet attempted to make a political movement without being in politics or desiring to be in politics. I wonder whether it will succeed?

We have planned a big effort for the second National Conference to be held in London next Whitsun. We mean to run it on the constructive side of the Minority Report, and to run it in sections—all sitting concurrently—*unemployment, public health, care of children*, etc. This little start down in Wales has whetted our ambition, and we have secured a nucleus of persons who will assist in getting it up. We have all the winter to work it up, and we mean to make it a real big affair. Meanwhile, we have a hard winter's lecturing before us as well as settling our National Committee on a permanent basis.

September 4th.—Within sight of the end of our six weeks' directorship of the Fabian School—only one more week and the ordeal is over.

The attempt to attract university Fabian Societies has failed and, perhaps, we alone are to blame. We quite casually decided to put on the programme—Conference of University Fabian Societies—without much consulting these societies as to time, place or subjects, and without getting sufficient college celebrities to attract any number of the members. A little group of half-a-dozen Cambridge men—Hugh Dalton, Rupert Brooke, James Strachey, Clifford Allen, Foss—came for a week, and Clifford Allen has stayed on as our guest. One or two other university or ex-university Fabians dribbled in from Edinburgh, Manchester, London—but at the most liberal calculation there cannot be more than forty or fifty university men and women here. Hence, the rather elaborate programme of two discussions every day has been a frost bordering on the ridiculous. We have had interesting and useful talks with these young men: but the weather, being detestable, must have made the trip appear rather a bad investment for them, and they are inclined to go away rather more critical and supercilious than they came. Quite clearly we must not attempt it again unless we can ensure the presence of twenty or thirty leading dons and attractive celebrities. "They won't come, unless they know who they are going to meet", sums up Rupert Brooke. And I gathered that, even if they *did* come, they would only talk together and to us. So that it would not be much use. They don't want to learn, they don't think they have anything to learn. They certainly don't want to help others; unless they think that there is something to be got in the way of an opening and a career, they won't come. The egotism of the young university man is colossal. Are they worth bothering about?

Apart from this specific failure, what is apparent from this six weeks' experience is that there are two conceptions of the school which are really incompatible with each other—the Webbs' conception, and that of the general manager, Miss Hankinson. She and Miss Atkinson desire a co-operative country holiday—made up, in the main, of organised games, excursions and evening entertainments—with a few lectures and discussions thrown in to give subjects for conversation. Our conception is that of an organised school—teaching, learning and discussing, with some off days, and off hours, for recreation and social intercourse. This involves getting at least one hundred to one hundred and twenty persons, and having a real bond of union based on a particular philosophy of life, with many specialised sections—like the several parts of the Minority Report.

For the first fortnight *our* conception was carried out; for the second fortnight there was a rather unsatisfactory compromise. But this third fortnight has been practically given over to Miss Hankinson's pleasuring—and the lectures and discussions have suffered in consequence. Moreover, the sixty or seventy members left have not constituted an audience that is much worth addressing. If there had been no pretension in the last fortnight to be anything in particular, there would have been no note of failure. But, pretending to be a University Fabian Societies' conference, the failure has been obvious. And, as I began, so I end by saying that we are to blame. We presumed on a greater importance and popularity than we possessed with the university Fabians.

One thing stands out as the net result. If we again think of undertaking this sort of business, we must run it deliberately ourselves, with our own staff. Miss Hankinson is most valuable as an organiser, but she is, in a sense, too much of the expert, and will not carry out any policy but her own. Secondly, six weeks is far too long—we must limit the session to a fortnight or three weeks—at most four weeks. Thirdly, we must try and solve the question of a compromise between studiousness and a certain amount of carefully devised entertainment. It is *not* desirable to exclude games, exercise, music, but these must not be permitted to absorb the whole energies of any section of the company. And for this reason I am rather against having professional gymnastic instructors (?), or letting any lively man or woman absorb a large part of the company in a play or a pageant. Exercise, like walking, cycling, golf, bathing, tennis, are all right if they are taken when convenient. But regular lessons or highly organised games, the learning of parts in plays, and the preparation of dresses and scenery, become an occupation in themselves and turn the mind away for good and all from listening to lectures and quiet fireside discussion. Hence, another time we must, somehow or other, select our staff and even our guests, and take a great deal more trouble to plan out an intellectually varied bill of fare, and a far more *technical* and *specialised* kind of discussion which will attract a better type.

To sum up the result: National Conference was an *unqualified* success: the Fabian Summer School partially a financial success, and, I think, a moral success, because we have raised the standard of manners and intellectual atmosphere. Some most valuable friends made, among whom Alfred Ollivant [the well-known novelist] will, I think, prove the best. And finally, a considerable increase of general interest in the Minority Report among some three hundred men and women of more than average intelligence and good-will. Against this we have to set the disappointment of perhaps half-a-dozen persons with the School, together with the harmless but somewhat absurd failure of the Fabian University Conference. Taken as a whole, the experiment has been worth trying, for it has taught us a good deal and has been, *as regards its main purpose* (the promotion of our crusade), decidedly successful. Points to be remembered:

1. Sessions should be two, three or at most four weeks.
2. August the best month.
3. Fee for lectures should be *separate*, and the payment of it should constitute the qualification for residence. (When lectures are thrown in they are regarded as necessary evils and discipline, instead of being the main purpose.) This latter device has selective effect on guests.
4. The whole staff should be under the direction of one head, and should be inspired with the same purpose as the director.
5. The character of the exercise, etc. and all provisions for entertainments should be deliberately organised by the director.
6. The boarding arrangements should be differentiated with regard to *quiet*, accommodation and extra luxuries, according to the diverse wishes of the guests. Of all the differentiations *quiet and freedom from noise* is the *most* important. Some people delight in noise. Would it

be possible to exclude the more boisterous, larky entertainments and substitute, or at any rate include, something of the nature of religious music—or time for meditation? Could you have this and keep the bracing free thought of the Fabian Summer School?

7. Every member of the conference or school should be *formally* introduced to the director and should have an opportunity for some little personal intercourse.

8. Seminars or special classes, to which admission might be considered a privilege, might sometimes take the place of the *second lecture* of the day (technique of public speaking or investigation, metaphysics).

9. Careful attempts should be made respecting literature and sale of literature.

The director ought to have a *secretary* whose business it is to get to know every person and find out whether that person is comfortably settled, and is getting what they want out of the School. The general manager should be restricted to the special province of catering, etc., and the secretary should consider herself as a whole-time official. There should be organisers of games, etc.—there should be a business secretary as well as a social secretary.

A certain selective process should be applied to the guests—proper proportions between men and women, exclusion of undesirable or completely careless people, due admixture of persons of high standing at the same table or in the same house. Persons of high standing should be always persons of good-will and friendly to the School. The purely critical element must not be allowed to set the tune. It has been a misfortune that C. H. Norman, an enemy of Webbs and the Minority Report, settled himself at Caermeddyg. We could not prevent it because the custom of the School is that every guest chooses his own accommodation. The three or four critical *Cambridge* Fabians were also a bad element: on the other hand, Lady Betty Balfour was wholly advantageous.

Finally, there is the financial basis. Quite clearly here, as elsewhere, education of the university type cannot be made self-supporting. The fees or the boarding arrangements cannot pay for the intellectual direction and the lectures—I doubt whether it can be made to cover the necessary machinery for the smooth running of the School in respect to social intercourse and housekeeping. It may be possible to get a few persons to give their time and thought—but holidays are very sacred institutions with English persons; the more leisure they have, the less they will devote to other people (we have not merely given our services but we have been paying guests the whole time). Hence, I do not see that any experiment could be likely to succeed without a fund set apart for the educational side of the School.

The last days of the School have left the pleasantest impression. E. D. Simon and Dr. Saleeby—some thirty or forty pleasant men and women—delightful weather, lively discussions—all this has contributed to a feeling of successful accomplishment. Lawson Dodd is enthusiastically hopeful of a great future for the School, and we complete our directorate amid mutual congratulations with the staff. The one unpleasant result is persistent neuralgia—a bad beginning to a busy autumn.

Perhaps one of the important results of the School is the alliance between ourselves and Dr. Saleeby. The eugenists have always been our bitter opponents on the ground that all attempts to alter environment are not only futile, but positively mischievous, as such improvements in environment diminish the struggle for existence and retard the elimination of the unfit. Eugenics have, in fact, been used as a weapon against Socialism. Dr. Saleeby, who is one of the most prominent of the apostles, now joins not only the National Committee, but the Fabian Society. We spent two days talking with him and eventually proved to him that changes in the environment were a necessary accompaniment to even negative eugenics, whereas *positive* eugenics can only be brought about by collective control and collective expenditure. He has even invented the term preventive engenics, which includes all action against racial poisons and all checks to the deterioration of good stocks by bad environment.

September 17th.—Position in the political world is most unsatisfactory for the progressive movement. The financial basis of the Labour Party has been smashed by the Osborne Judgement.[1] The Labour members are being attacked by a considerable section of the I.L.P. The trade union movement is distracted by the insurrection of large bodies of its members against their officials—the insurrection which involves repudiation of agreements made by the officials. Meanwhile, Tom Mann, recently returned from Australia, is preaching general trade unionism and the general strike, and running down political action. And behind it all there is the likelihood of a compact between the front benches which will keep the Liberal Cabinet in power, in spite of the Labour and Irish parties, till after the coronation, and bring the tariff reformers back in strength at the next election. It looks as if Asquith and Co. had rucked up, and were determined to ally themselves with the Tories rather than let themselves be goaded by Labour. However, there will be old-age pensions, the budget, and a weakened House of Lords as the net result. No break-up of the poor law. I

[1] See " The Osborne Judgement ": *The History of Trade Unionism,* 1920 edition, p. 608, by Sidney and Beatrice Webb.

doubt the passing of the insurance schemes. Neither Labour nor the Tories will accept them. And, if Labour breaks away, many Radicals will follow. The Liberal Cabinet will have to depend on Tory support; and will, therefore, if it remains in, sit still. More probably there will be an explosion in November, and an election in January. Balfour may come in: but not with a *bona fide* tariff reform majority. In fact, my impression is that tariff reform itself has lost ground these last months and that a Conservative majority will be simply an anti-Liberal Cabinet majority. The time might come for a genuine Socialist Party—if we had this sort of smash-up of the Liberal Party.

October 6th.—A. J. B. has done for the chances of a Tory Party at the next election, if this takes place in January, by his Edinburgh speech—a courageous and sincere speech but one of complete scepticism on the constructive side, and a non-possumus attitude towards the Osborne Judgement and payment of members. Now is Asquith's chance! Break up the Conference,[1] and go to the country on House of Lords and Labour representation. The North Country and Scotland would be absolutely firm.

October 9th. Auchterarder.—Started on our autumn campaign. After lecturing at Bournemouth and Southampton, I returned to London for three days and then journeyed to Hull, Middlesbrough and Darlington, arriving here on Saturday and leaving again for Inverness on Monday. I felt ill when I left for Hull, and on the day I travelled to Middlesbrough I thought the end had come, and that I should find myself the next day in bed with a bad breakdown. But, by fasting and prayer (this literally!), I pulled through, and to-day for the first time I feel decently fit for the work—though not over-much so. Splendid meeting at Middlesbrough—speaking for one hour to two thousand persons, with questions afterwards. Small but influential meetings at Darlington and Hull. Now I am spending the Sunday with the Haldanes before opening the Scottish campaign at Inverness and Edinburgh.

I find the Haldanes as kindly as ever; the dear old lady is very frail—Elizabeth is the same sturdy, kind and direct woman. R. B. H. is rapidly ageing and looks as if he were on the verge of another breakdown. He is terribly stout and pasty, and eats enormously and takes no exercise. He is worried and depressed about his War Office administration—in a very different state of mind from the buoyant self-confidence and delight with which he undertook it. He is conscious of hostility to his beloved Territorials from the National Service League, of indiffer-

[1] The Constitutional Conference between leaders on both sides of the House, which broke down (Oct. 16th) on the Irish question. (Ed.)

ence from his own party, and of limpness and inefficiency in the W.O. itself. " I can't depend on my orders being carried out—there is slackness directly I turn my back."

He takes the same philosophically cynical but good-natured view of the progressive politics. He is really in favour of the Osborne Judgement and against payment of members—but he is prepared to come down with many qualifications on the advanced side. He would like the party to stay in for another year, and then make way for the Tories, and then come in again in five years' time. He would like the Conference [on the Prevention of Destitution] to succeed. He is inclined to take a benevolent view of a Tory Government; he is contemptuous of the Labour Party and altogether sceptical about the growth of Socialism. His eyes are still fixed on the city as an index of public opinion. All this is not very hopeful. On the other hand, both from my talk with him and with Elizabeth, I gather that they are favourable to the Minority Report. " Both Asquith and Lloyd George want me to go on the Local Government Board, if there is another Liberal administration, and to carry out a large reconstruction." He would evidently be prepared to give us the substance so long as he could keep some semblance of compromise with those favourable to a poor law authority. But I should very much doubt whether our old friend had very much longer to work in the world of edibles—there will be another flare-up presently which may attack something more vital than the eyes. After such a warning as his illness last year— within an inch of total blindness—it is strange he should go on eating himself into the grave, or at any rate into permanent invalidity.

What makes one despair is the atmosphere in which these leaders live. Their lives are so rounded off by culture and charm, comfort and power, that the misery of the destitute is as far off as the savagery of central Africa. To R. B. Haldane the irritation at " Form 4 " in the mind of the landlord is a far more *real grievance* than the absence of employment or the virtual starvation of a family. They don't realise either the misery itself or the possibility of preventing it. And the atmosphere of Cloan is practically identical with that of Whittingehame—there is no difference at all in the consciousness of the front benchers. What differs is the rank and file behind them—one made up of reactionaries, and the other of progressives. But as a set-off, the Tory front bench has complete control of their party and they have no effective opposition to any of their schemes, *if they are progressive*, whilst the Liberal front bench has always the Tories and the House of Lords to stem their progress. So really I don't know from what party we shall get the most. We may have, in the end, to establish a real Socialist Party if we want rapid progress.

Edinburgh. October 1*0th*-11*th*.—2 P.M. Sleepless! Made a failure of the opening lecture of the Edinburgh course. I had prepared it very carefully—spent the whole day at it. I found my St. James's Hall lecture did not do for Scotland and so had to construct an entirely new one. Unfortunately, the task of preparing it exhausted my remaining strength, and consequently I did not give the lecture I had prepared, but ground out a mechanical reflection of it. Once or twice I wondered whether I could go on—I kept repeating myself and I was conscious of my best friends in the audience being disappointed and concerned at my evident fatigue. However, I daresay it was not so bad as it seemed to me—*some* of the value was there.

On this tour I have had two successes, Middlesbrough and Inverness; two quite decent performances, Hull and Darlington; one failure, Edinburgh. What concerns me is whether I shall get through, especially the one on unemployment, and the one on voluntary agencies. Ah me! What a grind it is, this propaganda; research is not in it. *Shall I pull through?* That is the question which frightens me. This cursed sleeplessness, especially when I have not got my boy with me just to tell me it is all right. " The soldier's pay, if not the victor's meed." But sometimes to march, march, march is wearisome, and one feels one will fall on the way.

October 19*th*.—A bomb thrown into the School by the railway magnates led by Lord Claud Hamilton! A demand for Sidney's resignation of the chairmanship of the School of Economics, in the form of resignation of the position of governor and an implied threat to withdraw the railway class and denounce the School as " socialistic ". The ostensible reason is a speech by Sidney some six weeks ago to the railway servants—the *real* reason is the Minority Report campaign, as the *Times* let out in a leader which actually drew me into the business. The Hamiltons know that we care for the School and that it is our child, so to speak. George Hamilton has also some silly notion that Sidney gains *social status* by being chairman!

It is an awkward corner to turn. We *do* value our connection, and *authoritative* connection with the School, and if Sidney were to retire presently from the chairmanship it would endanger the tie. On the other hand, we value more the continued prosperity of the School so long as it remains unbiassed and open to collectivist tendencies. Moreover, Sidney will be going away for a year presently. And there *is* a danger that, as we succeed more and more in our agitation and as we develop the other parts of our programme, the hostility to us will grow and would make the position untenable. The question therefore arises whether it would not be better to accept the situation gracefully and not stand for re-election in December. If when we come back we return to the life of administration and research, then we can resume our connection. If, on the other hand, we are still in the toils of agitation, we are likely to become more and more prominent and be more and more hated. What is desirable is to keep a good majority on the governing body to back up Reeves. We have put an imprint on the School which it will not easily lose. It is always sad when a favourite child grows up and *seems* to escape influence and control. But one has had one's day and we must not repine. In some ways, the School has been too successful, it has outgrown our tutelage. Still I think it will retain the Webb method of concrete investigation, and the Webb bias in favour of expert administration in all human affairs.

November 5th. Grosvenor Road.—The Claud Hamilton episode seems to be closed. The governors met, and (though there was an undercurrent of disapproval of Sidney's speech) passed a unanimous resolution of confidence in Sidney. There seems a possibility of the return of the four errant knights of individualism. I don't think that the School has been damaged. But clearly, if, when we come back, we are to continue an agitation on a great scale as at present, we shall have to drop into the background in the School's life.

The Scottish tour has, I think, been an unqualified success. We have got through the whole programme and the new lectures on *voluntary agencies, unemployment* and *education,* which I was rather dreading, were the most successful of those which I gave. Indeed, the one drawback was the repetition of the old lectures on the break-up of the poor law in different parts of the country. It is very difficult to invent a new way of stating the old thing.

One Sunday we spent at the Yarrows (who afterwards subscribed one hundred pounds); another we spent at Whittingehame, with that most charming of families. A. J. B. and I had a long argument as to whether the stately charm of Whittingehame was compatible with either feeling or knowing about the problem of destitution. As a " holy-day " it is extraordinarily refreshing, there is a delightful atmosphere of intimacy, a freedom to say anything to anybody—to be yourself. Sidney feels it just as much as I do—so evidently do the other guests. But Lady Betty realises that it is gained at the expense of aloofness from the world, from the countryside, from the world of experts and administrators, even from the world of Conservative politicians. A. J. B. works hard as a politician, is nearly always in his place, dominates his front bench, but, save for this work, he is as aloof from all intercourse as if he were a lonely college don. Gathered around him are his family, his intimate friends, and every now and again a new-comer chosen for some personal charm or interest. Within this circle all is friendliness, frankness and equality, without it, all men and women are kept at an equally remote distance, not from any feeling of superiority, A. J. B. is far too philosophical to be conscious of class—but merely from sheer indifference—" No doubt these people are as nice as any others, but life is not long enough to think of knowing them ", is the sort of attitude he takes towards the whole world outside the little circle of friends.

November 30th.—The autumn lecturing is well-nigh over—only four more lectures before Christmas—another four in January (put off on account of election) and we shall have carried out the whole pro-gramme of eighty meetings for the two of us in two-and-a-half months. I am not much the worse for it except for a threatening of neuritis of the leg which I hope to walk off. I have had a varied experience—all types of meetings from gatherings of seventy to one hundred and fifty persons, all keen supporters, to great popular meetings of two thousand strong. Everywhere, I see an opening for a different kind of propaganda —conferences of experts on the various kinds of preventive agencies on the lines of the Minority Report. Exactly as the poor law and the guardians have their conferences, we must organise a meeting place where medical officers, teachers, inspectors, labour exchange officials, working-class representatives and voluntary agencies may discuss and resolve with regard to the new preventive authorities. To the teachers must be devoted the next three months.

Meanwhile, we are again in the turmoil of an election. The sensa-tional counter-stroke of the Lords is a clever dodge which will, if it does not succeed, do much to damage their prestige as sober folk. The violent abuse by the Tory press of the Liberals and Lloyd George, on the ground of Socialism and Irish nationalism, is an old game which everyone tires of. But it is hardly to be expected that the Liberals will do more than hold their own. If they do not lose at the election it will be a triumph, and the Lords will have to go as a permanent drag on progressive legislation. If they gain seats, then we are in for a time of rapid changes in our direction. The tariff reformers will become very desperate; they will have played every card and will have either to wait for the inevitable reaction or invent some more taking programme. At present they refuse as a party to declare themselves for any specific proposal except the silly business of occupying ownership of land. " They all say ", remarked our one devoted tariff reform M.P., J. W. Hills, " they are in favour of social reform, but when you urge them to declare in favour of any single item they shrink back with a cry ' That is Socialism! ' In which of course they are right."

The big thing that has happened in the last two years is that Lloyd George and Winston Churchill have practically taken the *limelight*, not merely from their own colleagues, but from the Labour Party.

They stand out as the most advanced politicians. And, if we get a Liberal majority and payment of members, we shall have any number of young Fabians rushing for Parliament, fully equipped for the fray—better than the Labour men—and enrolling themselves behind these two Radical leaders.

December 1st. The eve of the election.—Balfour's sudden advocacy of the referendum, whatever effect it may have, at the eleventh hour of the election, completely alters our constitutional system. Now that a responsible party has proposed the referendum, it will have to come; unless, of course, the responsible party were to drop it, which it will not. It is a bad method of government if the country could trust its representatives to play fair. But elections have been run on such rotten issues lately that the referendum may be the only way out of the difficulty. And, from the point of view of the leader of a party, it has one inestimable quality. It delivers him from the domination of a political sect that has got hold of the caucus. That advantage must appeal to A. J. B., who has been suffering from having had tariff reform foisted on him. It is the last move in his duel with Chamberlain; it is a final checkmate to tariff reform. And it is a superlatively fine stroke in his duel with Asquith—though it may be it has been delivered too late for this time.

What other effect will the referendum have on our political life? If we have it coupled with the payment of members, it will hasten the advent of a class of expert representatives paid to carry out the will of the people. It will be the death knell of the caucus supported only by small and energetic minorities capable of making themselves troublesome to the elected representatives. It will, therefore, delay some types of social reform—the more recondite advances in social control—unless the advocates of these can get them *accepted by both parties*. And will it not delay indefinitely women's suffrage?

For us it points to increased propaganda among all classes of the community. Also, we must devote more energy to a propaganda of the *ideas* of the Minority Report apart from its shibboleth. And, hence, we must push forward with the conception of conferences, and the elaboration of *The Crusade* into a technical journal. Sidney and I have exhausted the effect of our own lecturing and writing—at any rate in the big centres of population. Now we must get other people at work —ostensibly unconnected with the Minority Report, but all preaching the same doctrine and developing the technique of the same purpose—the abolition of extreme poverty.

December 10th.—Sidney and I are both feeling weary and somewhat dispirited. In spite of all our work the National Committee does not seem to be gaining many new members and our friends are beginning to melt away. One wonders whether we have not exhausted the interest in the subject, and whether our dream of a permanent organisation inspiring a large sustained movement on a broad philosophical basis, is possible at present? Is public opinion ripe for a synthesis taking the place of chaotic endeavours of public authorities and voluntary agencies? We shall go on steadily for another six months, devoting ourselves for the next two months to collecting money sufficient to carry the National Committee through our absence, and to organising the National Conference at Whitsun. If we fail, we shall have to cut down the work of the Committee to an expenditure of some £2000 a year—of this income, I think, we are pretty well secure for another two years. That will mean dropping the enlarged *Crusade* and dismissing half our staff and giving up our political propaganda. It will also mean the abandonment of all notion of a permanent organisation. As far as we personally are concerned, probably that would be a pleasanter prospect than the development of the National Committee into a big and permanent business. I should regret it because, I think, a permanent organisation would have immense value, and also on the lower ground that some of my staff would be on their beam ends. One never likes to have attracted men and women into work which ends in a *cul-de-sac*, though of course I warned each of them that the job would be probably temporary. In case we had to wind up the National Committee, I should throw the remnant and some of our energy into revivifying the Fabian Society. Whether that would be possible with E. Pease as secretary I do not know.

But whilst I am depressed on some counts, I am supremely grateful that I have been able to struggle through, with no nervous breakdown, the severe ordeal of this autumn's lecturing. An attack of influenza, or even a bad cold, might have made the Scottish tour a costly fiasco: and it would have been serious to have not been able to fulfil our North Country and Midlands engagements. Sidney too has gone on with his lecturing and all his other work—a quite incessant activity—and though strained and weary sometimes, on the whole happy in the intensity of our comradeship.

December 30th. Fishers' Hill, Woking.—We are spending a fortnight in the charming house of the Gerald Balfours, lent us whilst they are at Whittingehame. I have been lazing (Sidney working as usual), alternating long walks, twelve to fifteen miles, across the Surrey hills with days writing casual letters, reading, and talking to a succession of young friends we have had with us. . . .

During the next six months we have to get through three tasks—(1) make the position of the National Committee secure, both financially and constitutionally so that it will outlast our ten months' absence; (2) organise the first of a series of National Conferences; (3) write a short book on *The Prevention of Destitution*, summing up the lectures we have given in the last eighteen months. If we succeed in carrying out this programme we can go away with a clear conscience. I think it is even best that we should go away so as to see whether the movement has independent life.

1911

January.—The general election has brought the Liberals back with far greater power because they have not lost but slightly gained on balance. They have also got a clear mandate in favour of the " veto " and " home rule ", payment of members and a complete reform of the constitution. As Lloyd George said to the press interviewers, we are in for a period of rapid social reconstruction unless foreign complications turn the nation away from its quarry. Whether the complete supersession of the poor law will be one aspect of that reconstruction depends on whether or not John Burns stays at the Local Government Board. And the schemes of insurance are not really helpful to our scheme. Doling out weekly allowances, and with no kind of treatment attached, is a most unscientific state aid; and, if it were not for the advantage of proposing to transfer the millions from the rich to the poor, we should oppose it root and branch. As it is, we shall stand by quietly suggesting criticisms of the schemes to the Labour Party and the Conservatives. The unemployment insurance might bring inadvertently the compulsory use of the labour exchange, and the standardisation of the conditions of employment. But the sickness insurance as expounded in the communicated scheme of the *Times* (January 4th) is wholly bad, and I cannot see how malingering can be staved off except that the amount given is so *wholly inadequate* that it will be only the very worst workmen who will want to claim it and remain out of work (the low-paid women, by the way, and the inhabitants of Irish and Scottish country districts, may find it better than their wages, especially as it will be impossible to prevent their doing home-work). The invalidity scheme may be only an extension of old-age pensions, to which there could be no objection. What the Government shirk is the extension of *treatment* and *disciplinary supervision*— they want merely some mechanical way of increasing the money income of the wage-earning class in times of unemployment and sickness. No attempt is made to secure an advance in conduct, in return for the increased income. What we should like would be for Lloyd George to make the financial provision, but to find his scheme so criticised that he had to withdraw it for reconsideration. Of course, we are handicapped in our criticism by the fact that Lloyd George and Winston are the most favourable to the supersession of the poor law, and that it is these Ministers who are responsible for the insurance schemes. We have to dance on eggs without cracking them—we shall have to try and invent some way out for Lloyd George.

January 16*th*.—We are organising the Whitsun National Conference with great care, whilst keeping our names well out of it. Our draft prospectus has met with universal approval, and it looks as if the conference would take on considerably. Our object is two-fold: (1) to provide opportunities for discussion between the different experts and stimulus to each department of prevention; (2) to give out to the public the new synthesis, in a non-partizan and expert form—by making all the authorities engaged in preventive works, aware of themselves and each other, and the public aware of them and expectant of great thing . It is a bold idea to exclude the poor law from a conference on destitution! Then I should like, having started this Conference, to gradually transfer the whole staff and organisation of the National Committee to this Conference organisation. In this way we shall get a much wider circle of adherents to the policy of prevention than is possible by the Minority Report campaign. We want, in fact, to slip out of this movement, or at any rate from the leadership of it. After our Eastern tour I should like to get back to our research and finish up all those volumes. And there may have come the time for a big campaign for a Socialist Party with a self-conscious collectivist programme. Payment of members and election expenses may entirely revolutionise English politics. Hosts of able young men, well trained in Fabian economics and administrative lore, will be crowding into the political arena, and if they succeed in squeezing themselves through a many-cornered election they will make Parliament hum! The young men are with us.

March 6*th. Eastbourne*.—Let our house for one year to the William O'Briens, in order to get it off our hands for our Eastern tour, and retired first to a little house here for five weeks, then to Luton Hoo for two-and-a-half months.

It is a relief to get out of London with its perpetual whirl of talking and organising, and occasional lecturing. After two lectures this next week I am free to turn to the writing of our little book on *The Prevention of Destitution*, summing up all our lectures of the last two years to be left as a legacy to the National Committee for the next session's propaganda.

Since Xmas we have been seeing a good many political personages—we have had both Haldane and Churchill to dinner; we have breakfasted with Lloyd George and had A. J. B. to meet various M.O.H.s

The front bench Liberals have, in fact, been softening towards us—partly because we are going away, and partly because we could, if we chose, wreck their schemes of insurance by rousing the Labour hostility to them. What we are trying to achieve is to direct the sickness insurance scheme into a big reconstruction of public health. It is clear that public opinion has got firmly into its silly head that insurance has some mystical moral quality, which even covers the heinous sin of expenditure from public funds. It is an amazingly foolish delusion—the only moral advantage of insurance was its voluntary character; when that is superseded by compulsory contributions all the moral characteristics vanish, and you are left with a method of provision which is provocative of immoral motives. But there comes a time when it is useless to argue with an obsession of the public mind; you have to accept it, and by skilful devising of the scheme see that it does as little harm as possible. In the public health scheme, which we have put into the hands of the M.O.H.s to press on Lloyd George and to give to leading politicians in the three parties, we have accepted the contributory side of insurance and attempted to supersede the provision characteristic of insurance, by the provision characteristic of public health administration. We talked to Lloyd George about it, and then suggested that he should see persons who were more expert than ourselves—the little group of M.O.H.s who are in our confidence. Meanwhile, the scheme is published simultaneously under Lyster's name in the *British Medical Journal*, *Public Health Journal* and *The Crusade* of this month. It has been given to all the Cabinet Ministers favourable to our views; to A. J. B. and the Labour Party and to Llewellyn Smith and other officials.

March 7th.—Last night I was dead tired when I gave my last lecture in London. To-morrow I have to speak to the Free Church Council at Portsmouth. After that I am free from this strain of public speaking. For the remainder of our time in England I shall be writing and, to a small extent, organising. And then our holiday, that supreme luxury of the propertied brain-worker! If the National Conference turns out a success, I believe we shall have practically converted England to the obligation of preventing destitution. What will remain is seeing that the obligation is fulfilled by the different public authorities, and the voluntary agencies attached to them. But oh! I am tired—deep down tired. I shall just last out, but not more than last out.

The Fabian Society is going through a crisis, not of dissent, but of indifference. Sidney thought that, as he was leaving England, he had better resign for a year. Thereupon G. B. S. not only announces his intention of resigning, but persuades some half-a-dozen others of the old gang to resign also. All with the view to making room for young men who are not there! Clifford Sharp, who is a loyal and steadfast member of the executive, is in despair, and Sidney is remaining on if G. B. S. and the others persist in going. Charlotte Shaw told Sharp that G. B. S. had got sick of the Fabian Society and cared for nothing but his own productions, that he felt himself too important to work in harness with anyone else. It is largely her fault as she has withdrawn him from association with us and other Fabians in order not to waste his intellectual force in talk and argument. It is clear to me that the Fabian Society has to get a new impetus, or gradually dwindle to a mere name. I am not sure that the time may not have arrived for a genuine Socialist Party with a completely worked-out philosophy, and a very detailed programme. When we come back from the East we will see how the land lies. If the prevention of destitution movement is safely in other hands, I am not sure whether we had better not throw ourselves into constructing a party with a religion and an applied science. In that case, I should devote half the year to public speaking and organising, and half the year to thinking and writing.

March 8th, 4 a.m.—The non-brain-worker has little conception of the misery of the over-excited brain. Yesterday night I lay right through the long hours twisting every domestic detail or incident of our organisation into a giant of evil, a monster of unpleasant things. And it is in the night that I suffer from remorse for lack of consistency between conduct and conviction. All my little self-indulgences—the cup of tea or occasional coffee after a meal, the regular five or six cigarettes consumed daily, the extra expenditure on pretty clothes—all seem sins from which I can never shake myself free. Ought one ever to do anything that is against an ideal of perfect health, equality of income and the noblest use of money? When the morning comes and one returns to the rough and tumble of a hard day's work, or the necessities of human intercourse, these scruples seem mere weaknesses, and one goes forward without thought of justification with the habits and customs of one's daily life. Still, there lies at the back of one's mind a discontent with these compromises, a longing to be completely at peace with one's own ideal even in the smaller details of life. To a great extent Sidney and I are at peace with our ideal—in all the larger determinations of our life we do conform to our perception of what is best for the community, and we have the extraordinary joy of complete agreement as to this purpose. But I still fail in some of the minor matters because I am not sufficiently convinced of the wrongness of the action to overcome my self-indulgence. As for Sidney, he sweeps on one side as irrelevant and foolish all consideration of these trifles! By nature and training economical in personal expenditure, abstemious without being faddy, untroubled by vanity or large appetite, he goes on his way of sane temperance, without temptation or scruple, and with one settled opinion that he wants *me* to indulge myself to the top of my bent! He is the most perfect of lovers, by night and by day, in work and in play, in health and in sickness!

March 12th. Eastbourne.—Sidney has gone up to London, summoned by the M.O.H.s to counsel them what next to do. They had a formal interview with Lloyd George, Buxton and Masterman, at which Lloyd George explained his scheme of wholesale subsidy to friendly societies; and, for the excluded residuum, an artificial friendly society managed by the state nominees, with far lower benefits relatively to the contributions. They report that Masterman seemed a bitter opponent of the public health administration, and that he even suggested that the poor law was not " half bad ". Lloyd George, having explained his scheme, asked the M.O.H.s to consider it and send him a memorandum on it, and he would see them again. So they wrote begging Sidney to meet them and draft the memorandum. They have now their chance. Alone among medical men they have been consulted. It is characteristic of the public contempt for the medical profession that it should be so, a contempt largely justified since the B.M.A. has only one idea—to protect the pecuniary interests of the worst type of medical man by a futile insistence on free choice of doctors by the beneficiaries of state insurance—an obvious administrative absurdity, as absurd as free choice of teachers by the school children or their parents, rather more so, as the parents would be a better judge of a teacher than of a medical man as they would have *far less reason for choosing a bad one.*

The whole attitude of the Government about the destitution question, together with the leaderless state of the democratic movement, makes me feel more strongly every day that our duty, when we return, *may be* to throw ourselves into the democratic movement. Hitherto Sidney and I have kept ourselves almost exclusively for the work of expert guidance of the expert. Sidney has had a repulsion for public speaking and public agitation, partly because he is impatient of stupidity, and partly because he really hates putting himself forward; he far prefers working quietly in the background and he does not like the intercourse entailed by leadership. The life he really enjoys is to sit in a room and draft things for other people, and then to spend his spare time reading endless books and being with me without anyone there to bother him. Added to that he would like to go on writing great books of wisdom and research, and enjoy the mild pleasure of an academic reputation. Popular approval he does not enjoy, it bores him; he has no glow of satisfaction at the applause at a public meeting. He is the ideal " man at the desk "—thinking, devising, scheming and drafting ideas and devising actions for subordinates to carry out, and other public speakers to advocate. And this is in spite of the fact that he is a most persuasive advocate and speaker himself; and, if he had chosen to push forward, might have been a notable leader of public opinion and acknowledged as such in his own generation. There may still rise up some master-man in the Labour Party or the Fabian Society, or the leaders of the Liberal Party may prove themselves to have both conviction and knowledge. But unless this does happen, I am afraid we are doomed to offer ourselves as officers of the larger crusade to conquer the land of promise.

April 21st. The Hermitage, Luton Hoo.—In retreat here, toiling at our book on destitution and finding the task a tediously stale one. But we had to present the old story in a new form, with all the main objections answered and all the new developments noted. Moreover, with the National Conference at hand, it was all-important to have a book coming out entitled *The Prevention of Destitution*, giving the minority scheme in a non-controversial form—a textbook practically for the persons who attend the Conference, or for future Conferences. Having patented the name, and then getting it adopted as the name of a larger article of commerce than we can provide, we proceed to suggest that our patent is that larger article of commerce! And the odd thing is that few are taken in, but they all believe the others are taken in! Here is Lord George Hamilton accepting the vice-presidency of the Conference, and C. J. Hamilton reading a paper at one of the sections. I imagine that they have not the remotest objection to the ideas of the Minority Report, which are rampant in each one of the sections—all they desire is that we should not get the credit of them—that they should not be *credited* to the Minority Report. And, of course, we are only too glad to oblige them. If we were quite certain that our proposals would be accepted if we withdrew ourselves and our book, we would retire at once, and for good and all, and devote our energies to pushing on further up in the Socialist movement. In fact, that is what we rather hope may happen during the next year or so.

May 13th.—The splendid reception by all parties of Lloyd George's scheme of sickness insurance is a curious testimony to the heroic demagogy of the man. He has taken every item that could be popular with anyone, mixed them together and produced a Bill which takes some twenty millions from the propertied class to be handed over to the wage-earners *sans phrase* to be spent by them, as they think fit, in times of sickness or unemployment. If you add to this gigantic transfer of property from the haves to the have-nots the fact that the tax is to be collected in the most costly and extravagant fashion, and that the whole administration of the fund is to be put into the hands of the beneficiaries who are contributing only one-third, there is enough to make the moderate and constitutional Socialist aghast.

The first asset he started with was the word *insurance*. To the governing class insurance has always meant the voluntary contributions of the persons benefited—a method of raising revenue which has saved the pockets of all other persons. During the controversy about old-age pensions, insurance gradually acquired a compulsory element, and the Conservative Party became pledged to raising money from wage-earners, employers and the general taxpayer, as an alternative to non-contributory pensions. Hence, by using this word Lloyd George secured the approval of the Conservative section of the community. Then there were the friendly societies who stood in the way. So he puts them into possession of the whole machinery of distribution: a fund that is mainly contributed by non-beneficiaries is to be wholly administered by the beneficiaries. This scheme has the adherence of the friendly society world and of the larger part of the working class.

" What is a communist? " " A man who pockets your shilling and forks out his twopence." When one knows the liability to malingering, even in a friendly society in which all members stand to lose by the misconduct of one member, when one thinks of all the diatribes levied at unconditional outdoor relief, one is simply amazed at the " Simple Simon " of upper and middle-class optimism.

Now the question is: Can he hustle it through this session? If he does not, the scheme won't survive the criticism of all the interests imperilled by it. He has extraordinary luck. The Coronation shortens the time, distracts the attention, and makes everyone inclined to a sentimental gift to the working-class. The Parliament Bill paralyses the opposition—they dare not oppose any popular scheme. The Labour and Irish parties stand to gain—the Liberals are naturally averse to even criticising their leader's magnificent demagogy. If the Cabinet backs him up, the scheme will go through. The only way of stopping it would be for all the outraged interests to make the ordinary M.P. feel that he would lose votes heavily. But they have precious little time to organise this pressure.

Sidney, on the whole, wishes the Bill to go through. I am not sure that I do. He believes that the big and difficult matter is to get the money voted, and that the inanities of both the method of raising the revenue, and the character of the provision given, could and will be altered by subsequent legislation. I fear the growth of malingering and the right to money independently of the obligation to good conduct. I cannot dismiss my rooted prejudice to relief instead of treatment. Anyway, our duty is clear—just to say what we think about it. In our chapter on insurance in our forthcoming book we have done this faithfully. And, by the time it comes out, the Bill will have been read a second time, and we shall be out of the country. But where are the professional champions of sound administration?

The Unemployment Bill is on quite a different basis. If it is carried through, it will lead to increased control of the employer and the wage-earner by the state. We are not against this, so long as this control is exercised on the wage-earners' behalf. On the other hand, it might smash up trade unions and not give anything in return. I should imagine the opposition will concentrate on this far more statesmanlike proposal, just because it is statesmanlike. Public opinion takes the sloppy and sentimental schemes and dislikes anything that looks like increased efficiency and control. Even the propertied class are ready to spend public money, but they are not ready to exact the corresponding conduct, even when it is the conduct of the non-propertied class on whom the money is being spent. Administrative nihilism has its partizans; slovenly administration has its adherents; good administration has no public opinion on its side. That is the principal danger in front of us.

If only we could have a leader, or a body of opinion, that would undertake to redress the whole of the grievances and yet insist on redressing them in such a way as to improve conduct.

One result of the Sickness Insurance Bill, if it passes into law as now drafted, is that it will sweep away innumerable voluntary agencies —act as a great scavenger. We shall have a sort of bastard organisation, neither a properly constituted organ of the state, nor a voluntary agency. The only good feature being that it will be in such a state of unstable equilibrium that it will tumble the Government of the country sooner or later.

May 26th.—George Lansbury was down here consulting with us about the amendment or postponement of Lloyd George's rotten scheme of sickness insurance. The more we examine, the less we like it, both for what it does and what it omits to do. We have written in our new book what is virtually a scathing indictment of insurance in general and the Government scheme in particular—but it will come out after the Bill is well in committee and will probably not be much attended to except by our own followers. Lansbury told us that Masterman came up to him after Lloyd George's triumphant exposition of his scheme with a pleasant jeering expression: " We have spiked your guns, eh? " showing that he is hostile to the whole conception of the Minority Report and that the Government schemes are intended as an alternative method of dealing with the question of destitution. John Burns also goes about saying that insurance has finally " dished the Webbs ". All of which is interesting. What remains to be seen is whether the Minority Report has come too late to stop insurance, or whether the Government scheme of insurance has come too late to stop the Minority Report! The issue is fairly joined—complete state responsibility with a view of prevention, or partial state responsibility by a new form of relieving destitution unconnected with the poor law, but leaving the poor law for those who fall out of benefit. It is a trial of strength between the two ideas. In our new book we have said our say. By the time we get back from our holiday, the matter will probably be settled one way or the other—possibly for a generation. However, if the nation finds sickness increasing and premiums going up, they may turn more quickly than we expect to prevention. And it is still possible that opposition may grow to Lloyd George's scheme and that, if he cannot get it through this session, he will have to abandon it altogether. On the whole, I should prefer the scheme abandoned rather than passed in its present form. But we do not feel inclined to agitate against it.

June 3rd.—Probably my last entry in this tag-end of a period of my life, finishing with the National Conference on the Prevention of Destitution [1]—a great success, doing credit to Robert Harcourt and John W. Hills, Clifford Sharp, and the staff and volunteers. " What organisation is at the back of this? " was the question which everyone asked each other. We kept ourselves carefully in the background—the three secretaries evidently desired us to do so, and we were only too glad to be relieved from attendances and responsibility. Sidney will write the preface to the proceedings and then we are quit of the whole business. I have advised Sharp to steer the National Committee into the National Conference, and see what subscribers to the old organisation he can keep for the new. When we come back next spring we shall have to decide what is to be done—whether we are to close up or go on, or to divide the work between the National Conference and the Fabian Society. We shall know, too, how this insurance is going to affect us. If it is carried, it alters the whole situation and we shall have

---

[1] This remarkable Albert Hall meeting, which opened the National Conference for the Prevention of Destitution, in Whitsun Week, 1911, was presided over by an old friend of the Webbs, the Bishop of Southwark (Dr. Talbot). The following resolution :

> " the formation of a National Conference of a non-party and non-sectional character, to promote the working of the various agencies for the prevention of destitution . . . as a valuable means of bringing together municipal representatives and social workers from all parts of the country "

was proposed by Mr. Arthur Balfour, seconded by Sir John Simon (then Solicitor-General) and supported by Mr. Ramsay MacDonald. To get these three leaders of the three political parties to formally adopt the policy of the national minimum of civilised life, was an apparent success for our cause. But looking back on it, I am inclined to think that it was a little too clever. It lost us the friendship of the Conservative leader, and did little to gain us any general support from the Liberal and Labour leaders, neither of whom were our personal friends.

to begin a new kind of propaganda. And, even if it does not pass, the issues have been so much bigger that the Minority Report propaganda sinks into insignificance for the present. I think it will rise up as the only alternative to a hopeless muddle.

A. J. B. spoke with his usual charm and distinction at the Albert Hall meeting. But he held himself back considerably and appeared less friendly than he has done before. In talking with me at the Cripps's dinner, he was inclined to be pleased with Lloyd George's Bill (before I explained matters to him), he thought it excellent to make the wage-earners " pay ", and he thought it would be unpopular! (Oh! ye politicians!) Everywhere among the governing class one meets the naïve delight at making the men pay—a delight which makes them overlook all the other circumstances—the heavy state contributions, the cost of collection, the absence of prevention, the exclusion of the weakest, and even the danger of malingering—all these real evils are to be cancelled by the extracting of the pennies from the workman's disposable income, extracting them so that he shall feel extraction.

Can I sum up the success or failure of this plunge into propaganda by word and by script? For this purpose, I must answer two separate and distinct questions: Did we get the specific recommendations of the Minority Report actually implemented by law and administration? Moreover, in making these recommendations, were we right or were we wrong in assuming that they would or could, without any more fundamental change in the structure of society, lead to the prevention of mass destitution in all its forms, whether due to old age or sickness, illiteracy or unemployment, so as to ensure to the workers by hand and by brain steady progress in health and happiness, honesty and kindliness, culture and scientific knowledge, and the spirit of adventure?

First, was the Minority Report carried out by Parliament and the Government? So far as immediate events were concerned, our propaganda ended in failure. For another eighteen years the defenders of the *status quo* maintained their position all along the line. Indeed, during the next few years, propaganda to retain and enlarge the powers of the boards of guardians altogether eclipsed the allied propaganda for the Majority Report. This aspiration to become the sole authority dealing with all classes of necessitous persons was emphatically endorsed by Charles Booth in his presidential address to the Central Poor Law Conference of 1912. " It is essential ", stated this experienced philanthropist, " that the elective character of the boards of guardians should be retained, and that the authority of the guardians and their responsibilities should suffer no diminution." He urged the guardians not to shrink " from any consistent development in the work or its responsibilities; holding that, whatever may be the cause of distress—whether moral, mental or physical, depravity, incompetence, or ill-health, or pure misfortune—its public relief lies within the proper sphere of the poor law ". The poor law, as established by the Royal Commission of 1834 and administered by directly elected boards of guardians, under the supervision of the poor law department, first of the Local Government Board, and then by the newly established Ministry of Health, remained intact and practically unaltered until the Local Government Act of 1929.[1]

Meanwhile, in 1911–12, there was established by Act of Parliament a system of compulsory insurance, financed by a triangle of taxation, deduction from wages, contribution from employers and a Treasury grant. This Insurance Act was divided into two sections, unemployment and sickness: Part I., dealing with unemployment, being passed through Parliament in December 1911, and Part II., dealing with sickness, during the following session of 1912. Neither of these measures are to be found in the Minority proposals. If not actually opposed by the National Committee for the Prevention of Destitution, this way of taking the destitute out of

[1] We note, in our *History of the English Poor Law*, that our agitation " powerful as it became, was destined to be unfruitful in the political field. The Liberal Cabinet remained unfriendly to any legislative reform of the poor law, to which the Minister primarily concerned (Mr. John Burns from 1906 to 1914) was resolutely opposed. Meanwhile Mr. Lloyd George, the most powerful force in the government, had become enamoured of an entirely distinct method of dealing with poverty, and was pressing forward the vast scheme of sickness insurance, to which the initial experiment in unemployment insurance promoted by Mr. Winston Churchill was eventually attached. Although these schemes of social insurance left untouched both the evils and the cost of the poor law, and thus gave the go-by to all the proposals of the Royal Commission, they presently absorbed the whole attention, not only of the Cabinet and the legislature, but also of the public. All the steam went out of the movement for extinguishing the boards of guardians and transferring their powers to the county and municipal authorities and to the national government, whether according to the prescriptions of the majority or those of the minority " (pp. 722-3)

the poor law received a very half-hearted support. To us the compulsory insurance with automatically distributed money allowances, during illness or worklessness, with free choice of doctor under the panel system, would not and could not prevent the occurrence of sickness or unemployment. Indeed, the fact that sick and unemployed persons were entitled to money incomes without any corresponding obligation to get well and keep well, or to seek and keep employment, seemed to us likely to encourage malingering and a disinclination to work for their livelihood.

But some of the proposals embodied in the Minority Report were carried out by the Liberal Government in the next few years. A non-contributory old-age pension scheme, financed by the Treasury, opened its payments in January 1909: a measure advocated by the Other One in 1890 and popularised a few years later by Charles Booth. And here I come to a paradoxical event which certainly we had not foreseen. The section of the Minority Report which was most vehemently denounced, alike by the defenders of the *status quo* and by the Majority Reporters, was our detailed plan for taking the able-bodied out of the penal poor law and transferring them to a Ministry of Labour designed not to prevent able-bodied pauperism, but to prevent the cause of this type of destitution—unemployment and under-employment, as well as low wages and long hours. And I must admit our opponents were justified. The 280 pages of Part II. of the Minority Report concerned with the able-bodied was a far more revolutionary document than Part I. dealing with the old, the sick, the disabled and the mentally deficient, for the good reason that it was a direct challenge to the epoch-making report of the Royal Commission on the Poor Law of 1834; which, it will be remembered, was almost exclusively concerned with the abolition of able-bodied pauperism, and not with the prevention of able-bodied destitution. Moreover, our propaganda of this new scheme for preventing unemployment and under-employment was apparently effective. " The history of modern unemployment policy ", states an authoritative writer on British unemployment policy, " really begins before the Great War. This is not so much because of the extent of the pre-war problem, as because there was a fundamental change in the attitude of the community towards its unemployed citizens about the years 1909 to 1911. It was then that the new sense of social responsibility took shape in the creation of a national system of employment exchanges and a limited experiment in compulsory unemployment insurance. The former were to reduce unemployment to the minimum, whatever the state of the labour market; the latter was to compensate the genuine worker for unavoidable interruptions of wage-earning." [1]

Our main proposal—the axle round which all our other recommendations turned—was the creation of a national authority for the exclusive purpose of organising the labour market, so as to prevent unemployment and under-employment as well as enforcing a minimum standard of earnings and hours by factory legislation and wages boards. " The task of dealing with unemployment is altogether beyond the capacity of local authorities having jurisdiction only over limited areas ", the Minority Report dogmatically asserts. The first step in this direction taken by the Liberal Government was the establishment of a national system of labour exchanges in the spring of 1909, as a department of the Board of Trade, a seemingly harmless proposal which had been endorsed by the majority commissioners. These labour exchanges proved to be the thin edge of the wedge which ultimately lifted the destitute able-bodied out of the poor law. In 1916, a Ministry of Labour was created which took over from the Board of Trade all questions relating to labour, whether regulative or administrative. But neither the labour exchanges, nor unemployment insurance with its continuously enlarged sphere and increasing benefits, sufficed to prevent the wholesale able-bodied destitution which arose during the great depression of 1929–33. Hence the National Government took the final step of taking the able-bodied out of the poor law, by passing the Unemployment Act of 1934; Part I, establishing the Unemployment Assistance Board,

[1] *British Unemployment Policy since 1930*, by Ronald C. Davison, 1938. 136 pp.

to relieve all able-bodied persons who had fallen out of benefit, an authority more or less under the control of the Ministry of Labour; and Part II., constituting the Unemployment Insurance Statutory Committee, which was " to advise the Government and Parliament how to make the insurance scheme financially self-contained, and self-adjusting, without legislation, and to block the channel of indefinite borrowing from the Treasury ".[1]

Meanwhile, by the Local Government Act of 1929, the boards of guardians were abolished and all their duties and powers relating to the non-able-bodied destitute persons were transferred to the county and county borough councils, these authorities being enjoined, somewhat haltingly, to deal with the children and the sick through their education and public health committees, with the co-operation of a newly established public assistance committee, in so far as money allowances were concerned. Hence, it is only the non-able-bodied person who is now within the poor law, and that to an ever-decreasing extent, according to the capacity and public spirit of the local authority concerned.[2]

And now for the second question: Were we right, or were we wrong, in assuming that our recommendations would or could, without any more radical change in the structure of society, lead to the prevention of mass destitution in all its forms?

The sole purpose of the Minority Report, so we told listeners and readers, was to secure a national minimum of civilised life (note the word minimum) open to all alike, of

---

[1] *The Unemployment Insurance Statutory Committee,* by Sir William Beveridge (" Politica " Pamphlet No. 1).
[2] In our epilogue to volume ii. of *English Poor Law History: The Last Hundred Years,* we observe: " In a thousand pages we have followed the doings of these Destitution Authorities, and estimated the successes and failures, from 1834 to 1928, of the deterrent Poor Law that they were set to administer. We are grateful to Mr. Baldwin's Cabinet for enabling us to finish the story with dramatic completeness. For in this Epilogue we recount the sentence of death passed by Parliament in December 1928 on the century-old Boards of Guardians. Is there not also a policy, conscious or unconscious, implicit in this upsetting of existing institutions? Can it be doubted that the transfer of the obligation to relieve the destitute, from the ' Guardians of the Poor ' to the Local Authorities primarily concerned, each in its own sphere, with the prevention of destitution, finally disposes of the ' Principles of 1834 '? " (p. 985).

both sexes and all classes, by which we meant sufficient nourishment and training when young, a living wage when able-bodied, treatment when sick, and a modest but secure livelihood when disabled or aged. Could these conditions be obtained without altering fundamentally the existing system of wealth production, distribution and exchange; without sweeping away the landlords and the capitalists, and penalising the profit-making motive? We implied, if not openly asserted, that they could. How otherwise should we have sought the support of Conservative and Liberal leaders and of the majority of the working-class who certainly were not at that time convinced Socialists? And in doing so were we sincere? I think we were. In the years before the Great War, and for some time afterwards, we did not foresee the collapse of Western Civilisation: that is, of the strange and mutually destructive trilogy of the Christian religion, profit-making capitalism and political democracy. To-day, it is crystal-clear that the code of conduct taught by Jesus of Nazareth, and presumably accepted by the Christian churches, is hopelessly inconsistent with the dominance of the profit-making motive in the direction of production, distribution and exchange; whilst the addition of political democracy to a capitalist system of industry, sooner or later, leads to class war, hidden or naked. But, though we ourselves were convinced Socialists, we did not assert, or even imply, in our propaganda that the proposed enforcement of a national minimum of life for all the inhabitants, all the time, was impracticable under profit-making capitalism. Rightly or wrongly, we believed in " the inevitability of gradualness ". We were content to leave the future to take care of itself.

First, about our proposals with regard to the non-able-bodied. In so far as the infants and the children, the sick, mentally deficient, and aged were concerned, I think our proposals, if fully implemented, could, even under capitalism, prevent the occurrence of mass destitution and secure a minimum standard of life for all the persons concerned. But this result would depend on whether the capitalist system could or would supply the large sum needed for the requisite development of these social services. To-day, this is not the case. There are literally millions of infants and children in the United Kingdom growing up without either the nutriment or the training for regular employment and effective citizenship in adult life. There is a vast amount of preventable disease due to bad housing, poisoned atmosphere, noise and dirt, and the maintenance and treatment afforded by the sickness insurance and panel practice are totally inadequate and of bad quality.

The pension provided for old age is so low that many aged persons who have led respectable and hard-working lives find themselves compelled to seek extra assistance from the poor law. Meanwhile, in every period of trade depression, wages tend to be reduced and hours lengthened, so that the able-bodied who are in employment can afford to spend less on their dependants. Indeed, according to the most influential economists, whether in the City or in the universities, the only way of meeting a chronic state of trade depression has been by deliberate measures to lower the money wage or to raise prices; either policy resulting in a lower standard of life, whether in respect to nourishment, housing or recreation. Finally, there has arisen in the offing, so the statisticians tell us, the menace of a declining birth-rate, which, if not checked by generous endowment of child-bearing and rearing, may lead, if not to the gradual extinction of our race, to lost leadership among the nations of the world. But there is one comforting thought for the authors of the Minority Report. Whether or not the plenty can be produced or will be distributed under a capitalist system of society, our proposal to take all the non-able-bodied out of the poor law and transfer them to deliberately organised social services, administered by the central and local authorities, has proved to be the right road to a better state of things. For, whether we have a capitalist, a Socialist or a Communist organisation of production, distribution and exchange, it is imperative to have all the various classes of non-able-bodied persons dealt with on the lines of preventive service rather than on those of a stigmatised poor law relief. In short, so far as the non-able-bodied are concerned, the supersession of the penal poor law by highly specialised preventive social services, is to-day accepted as a sound principle by public opinion whether Conservative, Liberal or Socialist.

No such complacence can be justified in respect of Part II. of the Minority Report on the destitution of the able-bodied. Here, I admit, we unwittingly misled public opinion. We asserted in the Minority Report, and reaffirmed in our propaganda during 1909–11, that, without any substantial change in the social and economic order, the mass destitution arising from unemployment could be prevented. " *We have to report that, in our judgment, it is now administratively possible, if it is sincerely wished to do so, to remedy most of the evils of unemployment;* [1] to the same extent, at least, as we have in the past century diminished the death-rate from fever and lessened the industrial slavery of young children. It is not a valid objection that a demonstrably perfect and popularly accepted *technique,* either with regard to the prevention of unemployment or with regard to the treatment of the unemployed, has not yet been worked out."

" That unemployment, even under present industrial conditions, is to a very large extent preventable was perhaps the most unexpected and certainly the most welcome piece of information which the Minority Report of the Poor Law Commission had to give to the world. Practically all previous writers, with the exception of Mr. Beveridge, whose book on unemployment appeared a few weeks before the reports of the Royal Commission, accepted the phenomenon of unemployment as an inevitable accompaniment of capitalism

---

[1] *Report of the Royal Commission on the Poor Law and Relief of Distress,* 1909, *Vol. III.: Minority Report,* p. 685. The following note is added to the text of the report: " if . . . by a solution is meant that no man able and willing to work should come to degradation or destitution for want of work, then a solution is not indeed within sight, but by no means beyond hope. Its direction is certain, and its distance not infinite. . . . It is a policy of industrial organization, of meeting deliberately industrial needs that at present are met wastefully because without deliberation. Fluctuations of demand are now provided for by the maintenance of huge stagnant reserves of labour in varying extremities of distress. There is no reason in the nature of things why they should not be provided for by organized reserves of labour raised beyond the reach of distress (*Unemployment: A Problem of Industry,* by W. H. Beveridge, 1909, p. 236)."

and competitive industry, and confined their attention to the problem of how to provide for the ' out-of-work ' and his family. The minority commissioners, however, after a more extensive and searching investigation than had ever before been undertaken, came to the conclusion that unemployment was mainly due to defects of industrial organisation which it is fully in the power of the state to remedy, if and when it chooses. As a consequence of this new knowledge *we are now as a nation morally responsible for the continued existence of the great army of ' out-of-works ' in our midst in a far more direct and unmistakable sense than ever before.*" [1]

To-day (1938) we look back on two decades of continuous mass unemployment in times of good trade, never falling below one million, and at the peak of the last depression in 1933 rising to near three millions of workers actually unemployed, which, including dependants, means nearly nine million persons destitute of livelihood. What is even more disturbing is the appearance of a new type of the disease, unknown or at any rate undetected prior to the Great War: what has been termed *long unemployment*. To quote the authoritative report of the Pilgrim Trust on *Men without Work* (1938): " There is a ' hard core ' of long unemployment which will not be resolved by recovery alone, in every town of this country, however prosperous, however diversified its range of industries or however much its main industry benefits from industrial trends, and wherever it is situated. The problem is of increasing social importance throughout the country and is not entirely bound up with the problem of economic activity and depression." And further on in this report: " It is evident that this hard core of long unemployment carries within itself another hard core of very long unemployment which proves even more obstinate to re-employment than the hard core itself. In the summer of 1935, out of 100 long unemployed men 8 were very long unemployed, but within a year this number had doubled to 16. It is a vivid reminder of the changed conditions when it is realised that in 1936 the number of men who had been

[1] Article by Sidney Webb in *The Crusade*, January 1911.

without work for fully five years was the same as the number of men before the depression who were unemployed and had been without work in the previous year. The ' hard core within the hard core ' in 1936 was the same size as the total hard core of 1929. Evidently this ' hard core within the hard core ' consists of thousands of men who are being passed on from year to year and finally accumulate in that remotest of all backwaters, ' five years or more out of work '. . . . It seems desirable ", the report continues, " to get a clearer insight into the working of this paradoxical fourth factor; that long unemployment tends to be self-generating, and that the longer a man stands in the queue, the less likely he is to get out of it again; and that long unemployment (in addition to age, a home in a depressed district, and connection with a contracting industry) is in itself a bar to re-employment."

Moreover, the most intractable group of this " hard core " of unemployment are found to be not the " too old to be taken on ", but young men in their twenties, who have never yet been regularly employed, and who are adapting themselves in body and mind to a life of idleness—of undeveloped bodies and vacant minds. " Yet this problem of the young unemployed man remains serious, perhaps the most serious of all the problems of the long unemployed. It is especially aggravated by the conditions of Liverpool, the depression, the casual character of much employment and the low standard, material and non-material, at which the Liverpool long unemployed are living. . . . What is most depressing ", sum up the authors of the report, " is to find from the figures of both Category II. and of Category III. that the young men are those who are most ready to accept long unemployment. It is hard to exaggerate the importance of this for the future. One other point must be mentioned here concerning the attitude of these young men. That association with an unemployed community, which can be so powerful a factor in reconciling a man to unemployment, is present probably more extensively here than in any other age group. Though they tend not to belong to specific organisations, the number who spend most of their time with other young men who are also out of work is large. In Liverpool these associations take chiefly the form of 'cellar clubs'. In Leicester, it is the ordinary unemployed club which the young men patronise. But, whatever the form, we find this feature regularly through the various areas into which the sample took us. It suggests at once one of the reasons for their continual unemployment, and also perhaps the possibility of a more effective institutional approach to them than has been made in the past."[1]

It is this pernicious adaptation of the individual to his environment—this thoughtless manufacture of a parasitic class —that leads to a tragic paradox. For, in spite of there being nearly three million unemployed, the enterprising employers in the most progressive industries bitterly complain of a shortage in skilled and reliable labour which prevents fulfilment of pressing orders at home and from abroad.

Confronted with this dismal tragedy of mass unemployment, with its constantly increasing core of manufactured parasitism, it is futile to suggest that the recommendations of the Minority Report of the Poor Law Commission of 1906–9, even if fully implemented, would or could prevent mass destitution of the able-bodied. Labour exchanges for the better organisation of the demand and supply of labour, subsidised trade union insurance for organised workers, maintenance with training for those who fall out, or are never included in the insurance scheme, with a modicum of public works during temporary depressions, might have

---

[1] An even more striking testimony is given by Sir Ronald Davison, whose admirable book on the unemployed I have already quoted, in a communication to the fortnightly *News Letter*, December 3rd, 1938, which is the organ of the National Labour Party: "Unheeded by the general public, a terrible malaise is spreading among many thousands of our younger unemployed. They are being degraded to an almost sub-human way of life, not merely through lack of work, but also as the direct result of our relaxed systems of allowances and doles, doles without end and without conditions. Human nature, or a large part of it, cannot stand the strain of an easy-going official system which freely offers perpetual maintenance, even though a pittance, without exacting any return in self-help and without imposing any ultimate sanction. History has proved in the past and we are proving again to-day that such a system is bound to be abused. But my point in this article is that we are proving it on the bodies and souls of some 100,000 men still under 35 years of age and that we are too complacent about it. The ruin is steadily increasing. Some, alas! perhaps over a third of these men, are already irretrievably damaged, yet we do nothing. Many of us, including our politicians, simply turn away from the forbidding problem."

sufficed to prevent the destitution of the able-bodied during the rapidly expanding capitalist system in Europe and the U.S.A., characteristic of the last decade of the nineteenth century and the first decade of the twentieth century. Where we went hopelessly wrong was in ignoring Karl Marx's forecast of the eventual breakdown of the capitalist system as the one and only way of maximising the wealth of the nations. Karl Marx foresaw that the exploitation of land and labour by the private owners of the means of production, distribution and exchange would lead inevitably and universally to a corruption and perversion of the economic system; that it would divide the community into two nations, the rich and the poor; that it would concentrate power in the hands of the wealthy, and keep the wage-earners and the peasants in a state of poverty and dependence; that it would produce a disastrous alternation of booms and slumps, with a permanent army of unemployed persons, tragically deteriorating in health and happiness, skill and character. This profit-making motive may even lead to the destruction of natural resources, and turn forests and fertile plains into sand-swept deserts. But this was not all. Intent on securing new markets, new lands and minerals, new peoples to exploit, the profit-making motive would lead surely and inevitably, not to the peaceful emulation between individual capitalists to lower prices and improve quality for the community in which they live, but to a trustified and imperialist capitalism crushing out the little man, restricting production at home when it suited them, and transferring capital and brains to undeveloped countries where better prices could be obtained. Moreover, whilst the early nineteenth-century capitalists were almost to a man free-traders and pacifists, the City of London and the manufacturers of certain centres became not only protectionists but imperialists, instigating successive Governments to use force in the conquest of lower races in Asia and Africa. What a significant fact was the appearance of the South African millionaire gold-diggers, who dominated London " society " as well as the City, in the last years of the nineteenth century. I must admit that even the Webbs

accepted their gracious hospitality in return for their bene-
factions to the London University, the London School of
Economics and the Imperial College of Science! Finally,
the rule of the capitalist and the landlord has proved to be
hopelessly inconsistent with political democracy. There can
be no permanence of social peace in a situation in which we
abandon production to a tiny proportion of the population,
who own the means of production, and yet give the workers
the political power to enforce demands on the national income
which capitalism has neither the ability nor the incentive to
supply. This hopeless contradiction between the economic
power of the few and the political power of the many is
shown in its most vivid form in the problem of the treatment
of the involuntarily unemployed. How far is it practicable to
relieve the destitution of the able-bodied, according to the
principles of a minimum standard of civilised life under
profit-making capitalism? Are you, by giving sufficient nutriment, decent housing, not to mention the amenities of
civilised life, to millions of unemployed persons and their
descendants, making the conditions of the workless more
attractive and secure than those of the regularly employed
worker? Can the capitalist system in the period of its decadence, when there are no longer fresh markets, fresh lands and
lower races to exploit, afford the high wages, shorter hours,
and holidays with maintenance, which would make the conditions of the regularly employed persons more agreeable
than that of the man on the dole, or still more than the
family claiming public assistance assumed to be full maintenance? If not, the core of permanently unemployed persons
will grow steadily larger with each successive depression of
trade; the alternative is to throw back the able-bodied into
a penal poor law. Is it likely that political democracy will
accept a return to the able-bodied " test " workhouse and
the stone-yard?

At this point I break off my argument, otherwise I should
be anticipating future chapters of *Our Partnership*. But, in
case I should not live to finish this autobiography, here is a
short indication of the successive stages of our conversion to

the Marxian theory of the historical development of profit-making capitalism. It may be recalled that Marx held that though, as an alternative to feudalism, the free enterprise of the profit-making capitalist was the most efficient way of increasing the wealth of the nation at the end of the eighteenth and the beginning of the nineteenth century, it inevitably passed first through a period of stabilisation, and then into the period of trustified imperialist capitalism, which would restrict production and create the paradox of masses of unemployed capital with a host of unemployed men.

First, on our return from our Far Eastern tour in June 1912, we discovered that our propaganda of a national minimum of civilised life within the capitalist system was out-of-date. In the three great political democracies of the United Kingdom, France and the U.S.A., the workers were, from 1912 to the outbreak of the Great War, in open revolt. Anarchist workers in the U.S.A. were blazing out into multitudinous strikes and were being suppressed by armed forces, the leaders being hung or sentenced to life imprisonment; whilst, in France and Great Britain, the syndicalist and the guild socialist movement was promoting general strikes in all the main industrial activities, in order to secure complete "workers' control" as an alternative to the rule of the capitalist profit-maker. Then came, in the autumn of 1914, the Great War, ostensibly started to protect a little state against absorption by a big Empire; but, in fact, the outcome of a long-standing bitter struggle between capitalist states; some having extended dominions and colonies, others wanting new territories, new markets and new native populations to exploit for the purpose of making profit for their financiers, manufacturers and traders. There followed the disastrous peace of Versailles, breaking up defeated Empires, annexing their colonies, and imposing impossible reparations which could only be paid by the exportation of capital from the victorious countries to the victims. . . . It was in the years immediately following the disastrous war, and still more disastrous peace, that we published our first indictment of the capitalist system *The Decay of Capitalist Civilisation*, supplemented by our forecast of *A Constitution for the Socialist Commonwealth of Great Britain*.

The next event to disturb our faith in a modified capitalism was the great depression of trade which began in the 'twenties, first in Europe, and then in 1929 with even greater intensity in the United States of America, a depression which shows every sign of being recurrent, each depression leaving a larger residuum of permanent unemployment, judged by the statistics of unemployment, home production and foreign trade. Meanwhile there had arisen out of a tumultuous but successful revolution a new social order, in a vast territory, one-sixth of the earth's surface, with 160 millions of inhabitants, of many races, languages and religions—the Union of Socialist Soviet Republics. A detailed examination and description of this new social order, in two ponderous volumes published in 1935, entitled *Soviet Communism: A New Civilisation*, was the final and certainly the most ambitious task of " Our Partnership ". Whether we were right or whether we were wrong in acclaiming Soviet Communism with its multiform democracy, its sex, class and racial equality, its planned production for community consumption, and above all its penalisation of the profit-making motive and insistence on the obligation of all able-bodied persons to earn their livelihood by serving the community, the event will prove: perhaps I ought to substitute *will have been proved* or disproved before *Our Partnership* is published and read, or not read, by students of social institutions.

NOTE TO BIOGRAPHICAL INDEX

THIS volume, like its predecessor *My Apprenticeship*, is much more than a mere personal record; it is a slice of English social history during a deeply interesting and important period, and so is bound to be used as a standard work of reference by students for many years to come. In the course of the years which it covers, the Webbs' work and interests brought them into contact with an enormous number of persons of importance in Society, in politics and in the social services, many of whom will be but names even to the present generation, or, if they are remembered at all, their connection with the events of 1892 to 1912 will have been forgotten. In order, therefore, to help make this book of permanent value as a record, to save its readers from the burden of hunting in elderly works of reference—and to avoid littering the text with innumerable footnotes—the Editors decided to add to it a biographical index, compiled by one of them, of everyone mentioned in its pages whom it has proved possible to trace; some have proved to date untraceable and their names are omitted. The notes which follow are not, of course, biographies; but it is hoped that they will date and identify for students the persons mentioned, and, in the case of well-known figures, indicate their special connection with Beatrice's life and work.

Every endeavour has been made with the generous help of others to check the facts. Errors, however, will have undoubtedly crept in, particularly in the present rather difficult circumstances, and we shall welcome any additions or corrections for future editions.

M. I. C.

BIOGRAPHICAL INDEX

ABERDEEN and TEMAIR, ISHBEL MARIA, Marchioness of (1857–1939). Sister of Lord Tweedmouth and wife of the Marquess of Aberdeen who was Governor-General of Canada and Lord-Lieutenant of Ireland. Lady Aberdeen was a public figure, President of the International Council of Women from 1893 to 1899 and from 1904 to 1936, and of several other bodies.

ABRAHAM, MARY (Mrs. Tennant) (1870–1946). Factory inspector, at one time Superintending Inspector of Factories; an authority on factory legislation and women's problems and member of several Government commissions. Married, as his second wife, Harold John Tennant, q.v.

ABRAHAM, WILLIAM (1842–1922). Known as " Mabon ", and celebrated as a Methodist preacher and for his fine singing voice, Abraham, the miners' leader from the Rhondda, was first elected to Parliament for that area in 1885, and held it for many years, first as Lib-Lab and then as Labour.

ACLAND, SIR ARTHUR HERBERT DYKE (1847–1926). Liberal politician and educationalist, grandfather of the present Sir Richard Acland. M.P. for Rotherham, Vice-President of the Privy Council Committee on Education and Cabinet Minister, 1892–95; in this capacity he did much to promote higher education, through the Science and Arts Department, effective inspection and better conditions in schools. After his retirement he devoted himself to the cause of co-operation—his wife was a leading co-operator—and education, particularly adult education; he established the Acland scholarships.

ACLAND, SIR FRANCIS DYKE (1874–1939), " young Acland ". Liberal politician; M.P. successively for Richmond, North Cornwall and Tiverton; Chairman of the Devon County Education Committee. Parliamentary Private Secretary to Haldane, 1906–8; afterwards held vari-ous under-secretaryships. Father of Sir Richard Acland.

ACWORTH, SIR WILLIAM MITCHELL (1850–1925). Barrister and railway economist; member of several commissions of enquiry into railway affairs.

ADLER, DR. CYRUS (1863–). American scholar and authority on Jewish history and comparative religion. One of the editors of the *Jewish Encyclopaedia*.

ADRIAN, ALFRED DOUGLAS (1845–1922). Civil servant; Assistant Secretary to Local Government Board, 1883–89, and its legal adviser, 1899–1910.

ALEXANDER, SAMUEL (1859–1938). The philosopher; from 1893 to 1924 Professor of Philosophy in Manchester University; especially effective in marrying philosophy with modern scientific thought.

ALLAN, WILLIAM (1813–74). Founder, with William Newton, of the Amalgamated Society of Engineers, the new model Union of its time, and forerunner of the present Amalgamated Engineering Union. Allan was elected its general secretary in 1851 and retained this position until his death. He was, however, primarily interested in administration and though he built up a very strong organisation, he took less part in the moulding of opinion in the mid-century than men like Newton and Applegarth.

ALLEN, CLIFFORD, afterwards Lord Allen of Hurtwood (1889–1939). Fabian Socialist, and member of the I.L.P. Secretary and General Manager of *Daily Citizen*, 1911–15. Pacifist and conscientious objector (absolutist) during first world war; imprisoned three times. Chairman of I.L.P., 1922–26; promoter of *Socialism in Our Time* programme; sided with MacDonald in 1931 crisis.

ALTGELD, JOHN PETER (1847–1902). American politician, served in the Civil War on the Union side. Governor of Illinois, 1893–97, and pardoned

494

the Chicago anarchists; prison reformer and bimetallist.

AMERY, LEOPOLD STENNETT (1873–). Secretary for India in the National Government of 1931. On editorial staff of *The Times*, 1899–1909; in his youth a Fabian Socialist.

ANDERSON, ADELAIDE MARY (1868–1936). Australian-born factory inspector. Principal woman inspector of factories under the Home Office, 1897–1921; during the inter-war years did much work for the International Labour Office in China, and wrote several books.

ANDERSON, ELIZABETH GARRETT (1836–1917). First English woman doctor, friend of Emily Davies of Girton College and sister of Mrs. Fawcett. A pioneer of women's rights and founder of the hospital which bears her name.

ANDERSON, DR. JOHN FORD. Doctor, with a large general practice in Hampstead, medical officer to the Haverstock Hill Provident Dispensary. During the period of the Royal Commission on the Poor Law he was a member of the Council of the British Medical Association.

ANSON, SIR WILLIAM REYNELL (1843–1914). The distinguished jurist, author of *The Law and Custom of the Constitution*. Parliamentary Secretary to Board of Education, 1902–5.

APPLETON, WILLIAM ARCHIBALD (1859–1940). Trade Unionist, a lacemaker by craft, then Secretary to the Lace-makers' Union, 1896–1907, and from 1907 Secretary of the General Federation of Trade Unions; never in Parliament. He was a strong supporter of the Lloyd George insurance proposals.

ARNOLD, SIR ARTHUR (1833–1902). Liberal, Chairman of the L.C.C., 1895–97, and President of the Free Land League.

ARNOLD-FORSTER, HUGH OAKLEY (1855–1909). Tory politician and author, grandson of Arnold of Rugby, adopted son of W. E. Forster of the 1870 Education Act; much interested in education and social questions. Secretary of State for War, 1903–5.

ASHBEE, C. R. (1862–1942). Architect, designer and town planner; Founder

and Director for twenty-five years of the Guild of Handicrafts. His wife was Janet Elizabeth Forbes.

ASHLEY, SIR PERCY WALTER LLEWELLYN (1876–1945). Historian who became a civil servant. Lecturer at London School of Economics till 1906, then joined Board of Trade and became Assistant Secretary, 1918–28, and Secretary to Import Duties Advisory Committee, 1932–39. Wrote text-books on local government.

ASQUITH, EMMA ALICE MARGARET, " MARGOT " (*d.* 1945). Countess of Oxford and Asquith, leading spirit of the " Souls " and London political hostess of Beatrice's early married life. (See her autobiography.) Notwithstanding their political connections, Mrs. Webb did not like Mrs. Asquith, and the sentiment was reciprocated.

ASQUITH, HERBERT HENRY (1852–1928). Earl of Oxford and Asquith, Liberal Prime Minister, 1908–16. Asquith in the years between 1895 and 1905 was a friend of Haldane's and one of the Liberal imperialist group which the Webbs hoped to make use of for Socialist purposes. Beatrice never, however, felt for Asquith the instinctive sympathy which she had for Balfour the Tory.

ASQUITH, RAYMOND (1878 – 1916). Eldest son of the Prime Minister, killed in action. He married a daughter of Lady Horner, *q.v.*

ATKINSON, MABEL. Fabian, journalist on the *Daily News*, and lecturer on economics, on which she wrote a text-book with a Miss McKillop. Very active in the Fabian Society and its Women's Group before the first world war. She married an Australian named Palmer, but they soon separated; and in 1920 she left England to lecture in economics at the University of Durban.

AUSTIN, MICHAEL (1855–). Irish Nationalist and Trade Unionist, M.P. for West Limerick, 1892–1900. Member of the Royal Commission on Labour; signed the Minority Report.

BACON, SIR HICKMAN (1855–1945). Premier baronet of Britain. Very much interested in the Webbs' projects.

BAILWARD, WILLIAM A. Member of the Charity Organisation Society and a Poor Law Guardian for Bethnal

Green; wrote many papers for Poor Law Conferences. One of them (dated 1898) was entitled "Are Workhouses Unduly Attractive?"

BAKER, HAROLD TREVOR (1877–). Sometime Warden of Winchester College. Before the first world war he was a Liberal politician, M.P. for Accrington, 1910–18, and Financial Secretary to the War Office, 1912–13.

BALDWIN, STANLEY, Earl Baldwin of Bewdley (1867–). Prime Minister, 1923–24, 1924–29 and 1935–37.

BALFOUR, ALICE BLANCHE (1850–1936). Sister of Arthur Balfour, the Prime Minister.

BALFOUR, ARTHUR JAMES (1848–1930). Earl Balfour, philosopher and Tory politician, Leader of the Commons, Prime Minister from 1902 to 1905. Beatrice very much appreciated Balfour's mind and manners.

BALFOUR, LADY ELIZABETH EDITH (1867–1945). Daughter of the Earl of Lytton and wife of Gerald Balfour. "Lady Betty" was a well-known Society hostess and interested in many causes.

BALFOUR, EUSTACE (1854–1911). Brother of Arthur Balfour.

BALFOUR, LADY FRANCES (1858–1931). Daughter of the Duke of Argyll and wife of Eustace Balfour; wrote several memoirs.

BALFOUR, GERALD WILLIAM (1853–1945). Politician, brother of Arthur Balfour, Chief Secretary for Ireland, 1895–1900, and holder of various other offices; member of the Royal Commission on Trade Unions. A popular man of great social charm.

BALFOUR, JABEZ SPENCER (1843–1916). Famous in the 'nineties as promoter, with two men called Hobbs and Wright, of the fraudulent "Liberator" Society, which failed in 1892. Balfour fled to the Argentine, but was subsequently sentenced to fourteen years' penal servitude, a large public subscription being raised for his victims. Prior tò the crash he was well known as Radical M.P. for Tamworth and Burnley, and had a country seat in Oxfordshire.

BALFOUR OF BURLEIGH, ALEXANDER HUGH BRUCE, sixth Baron (1849–1921). Representative peer for Scotland from 1876, Parliamentary Secre-

tary to Board of Trade, 1889–92, and Secretary for Scotland, 1895–1903. Chairman of innumerable commissions, of which the most important was the 1916–17 Commission on Commercial and Industrial Policy after the war.

BARNES, GEORGE NICOLL (1859–1940). Engineer, one of the up-and-coming local secretaries of the A.S.E. in the early 'nineties; became its General Secretary from 1896 to 1908. In 1906 Barnes was elected Labour M.P. and held his seat until 1922. He entered the war-time Coalition Government, was Minister of Pensions between 1916 and 1918, and a member of the War Cabinet from 1917, after Henderson's resignation. He opposed the Labour Party's break with the Coalition, and this cost him his influence in the movement.

BARNETT, SAMUEL AUGUSTUS (1844–1913) and HENRIETTA OCTAVIA ROWLAND (1851–1926). Canon and Mrs. Barnett, so long connected in the public mind with Toynbee Hall, Whitechapel—of which Canon Barnett was Warden from 1884 to 1906—with the Hampstead Garden Suburb, the Children's County Holiday Fund and the Charity Organisation Society, were friends of Beatrice in the days of her East End enquiries. (See *My Apprenticeship*.) She disagreed with them over the social policy of the C.O.S., and in the 'nineties the Barnetts also severed connection with that organisation.

BARRY, SIR JOHN WOLFE (1836–1910). Consulting engineer, employed in construction of Tower Bridge and other important works. Member of the Royal Commission on the Port of London, 1900–2.

BATTERSEA, CYRIL FLOWER, first Baron Battersea (1843–1907). M.P. for Brecknock, 1880–85, and for Luton, 1885–92; held minor office in 1886. He married Constance (*d.* 1921), daughter of Sir Anthony de Rothschild.

BEACHCROFT, MRS. CHARLOTTE, afterwards Lady Beachcroft, wife of Sir Melville Beachcroft, an original member of the L.C.C. and its Chairman, 1909–10.

BEIT, ALFRED (1853–1906). South

African financier and diamond merchant. Partner in firm of Wernher, Beit and Co. Life Governor of De Beers Consolidated Mines. Director of Rand Mines, Rhodesian Railways and other companies. One of the rich men whom Beatrice tried to " milk " for particular projects.

BELL, SIR HUGH (1844–1931). The great coal and ironmaster of the Tyne area, director of Brunner Mond, Dorman Long, the L.N.E.R., etc. His wife (*née* Frances Oliffe) was author of many books, including the social study entitled *At the Works.*

BELL, JAMES. Town Clerk of Leicester, 1894–1902.

BELPER, HENRY STRUTT, second Baron (1840–1914). Chairman of Nottingham County Council and Quarter Sessions.

BENN, SIR JOHN WILLIAMS (1850–1922). Member of the L.C.C. from its formation until his death; Chairman in 1904, and connected with all its activities. Liberal M.P. for Devonport, 1904–10.

BENTHAM, F. H. Chairman of Bradford Poor Law Guardians, member of the 1905 Royal Commission on the Poor Law, and editor of the *Poor Law Conferences,* 1910–11.

BENTHAM, JEREMY (1748–1832). The founder of the school of Philosophic Radicalism, to which the early Fabians owed so much.

BERENSONS, The. Relatives of Bernhard Berenson, the American art critic, who married a sister of Alys Russell and Logan Pearsall Smith.

BESANT, ANNIE (1847–1933). Annie Besant, married young to a clergyman, left him on becoming a convert to Secularism and birth control, for which she and Charles Bradlaugh were the most popular and effective propagandists in the 'seventies. In the early 'eighties she became a Socialist; she was an early member of the Fabian Executive, one of the seven contributors to *Fabian Essays* in 1889, and a brilliant speaker and lecturer for Socialism; in 1888 she led a successful strike of miserably-paid matchgirls at Bryant & May's. In 1889 she suddenly abandoned Socialism for theosophy and became a passionate advocate of Indian nationalism.

BEVERIDGE, WILLIAM HENRY, Lord Beveridge (1879–   ). The author of the Beveridge Report. Originally a civil servant, he was Director of Labour Exchanges at the Board of Trade; during the first world war served in the Ministry of Munitions and the Ministry of Food. Director of the London School of Economics, 1919–37, and Master of University College, Oxford, 1937–45.

BICKERSTETH, JOHN JOSEPH (1850–1932). Son of the Bishop of Durham and married to a daughter of Lord Ashburnham. Clerk of the Peace and Clerk to the East Riding County Council from 1889.

BIRRELL, AUGUSTINE (1850–1933). Liberal politician, lawyer and writer of biography and *belles lettres.* President of the Board of Education, 1905–7, and Chief Secretary to the Lord-Lieutenant of Ireland, 1907–16. His wife was a Locker by birth and widow of the Hon. Lionel Tennyson.

BIRTWISTLE, THOMAS. One of the first Trade Union secretaries to be selected by competitive examination. He was Secretary of the Lancashire Weavers from 1861 to 1891, and in the following year, although he was very old, he was appointed inspector under the new Factory Act as being the only man who understood the methods of wage-payment in the weaving trade.

BLACKIE, JOHN STUART (1809–95). Philosopher and humanist. Professor of Greek at Edinburgh University, 1852–82.

BLAIN, WILLIAM (*d.* 1908). Civil servant; Assistant Secretary to the Treasury, 1907, and Auditor of the Civil List.

BLAND, HUBERT (1856–1914). Socialist. Journalist and author, a founder-member of the Fabian Society, whose Honorary Treasurer he remained from 1884 to 1911. Bland was married to E. Nesbit, the writer of many children's books; they had an unorthodox and interesting household which was enjoyed by many young Fabians.

BOOTH, CHARLES (1840–1914). Shipowner and manufacturer who carried through at his own expense the great eighteen-volume enquiry into the

extend, however, to the projects of Socialists. She is buried in Westminster Abbey.

BURNETT, JOHN (1842–1914). General Secretary of the Amalgamated Society of Engineers after the death of William Allen, and member of the Parliamentary Committee of the Trades Union Congress from 1876 to 1885. In Trade Union history he is chiefly memorable as leader, in 1871, of the successful strike of the North-East coast engineers for the nine-hour day. In 1886 he became Labour Correspondent to the Board of Trade, and in that capacity prepared a number of reports on strikes and lockouts; later he was made Chief Labour Correspondent.

BURNS, JOHN (1858–1943). The " Man with the Red Flag ", most prominent of the " new " Trade Unionists and chief leader of the 1889 Dock Strike. Burns was elected to the L.C.C. in 1889 and to Parliament as a Socialist in 1892. At first the Webbs had high hopes of Burns; but his desire to play a lone hand grew on him more and more. He would not co-operate with Keir Hardie, and when President of the Local Government Board in 1906 proved to be a bitter enemy of the Webbs in the Poor Law agitation. He left the Government in 1914 on account of his pacifist principles.

BUXTON, SYDNEY CHARLES, Viscount Buxton (1853–1934). Radical politician, friend of Acland and Haldane. Member of the London School Board, 1876–82, and of the conciliation committee on the 1889 Dock Strike; author of the Fair Wages resolution, responsible for 1911 Copyright Act and (in part) for the first National Insurance Act. President of the Board of Trade, 1910–14. Married to Constance (d. 1892), daughter of Lord Avebury.

CADOGAN, GERALD OAKLEY, sixth Earl (1869–1933). Lord Cadogan sat on the L.C.C. for one year only, from 1895 to 1896; he seems none the less to have had some influence. He was a hereditary Trustee of the British Museum.

CALVERT, LOUIS (1859–   ). Actor; played with Henry Irving, Sir Frank Benson and many others; formed his own company in 1890. His first Shaw part (in 1905) was that of Broadbent in *John Bull's Other Island*; he played an enormous number of parts.

CAMPBELL, MRS. PATRICK (d. 1940). The actress. See Bernard Shaw's published correspondence with her.

CAMPBELL-BANNERMAN, SIR HENRY (1836–1908). The Liberal Prime Minister of 1906. The Webbs tended to under-rate Campbell-Bannerman; their Liberal Imperialist friends, such as Asquith and Haldane, before the 1906 election were planning to shelve him. See Haldane, *Autobiography*.

CANTERBURY, ARCHBISHOP OF, RANDALL THOMAS DAVIDSON (1848–1930). Bishop of Westminster, 1895–1903, and Archbishop, 1903–19. A progressive in many ways, the Archbishop endeavoured to mediate during the 1926 General Strike, but was refused permission to broadcast.

CARNEGIE, ANDREW (1835–1919). The Scot who became an American millionaire, fathered the United States Steel Corporation and founded public libraries and the Carnegie Trusts.

CARPENTER, EDWARD (1844–1929). Socialist, humanitarian and anarchist, friend of William Morris, Walt Whitman and Havelock Ellis. Author of *Civilisation, Its Cause and Cure* ; *Love's Coming of Age*, etc.

CARR–GOMM, HUBERT WILLIAM CULLING (1877–1939). Liberal politician, M.P. for Rotherhithe, 1906–18; at one time private secretary to Campbell-Bannerman.

CARSON, SIR EDWARD, afterwards Lord Carson (1854–1935). The violent Ulster Tory lawyer, who with F. E. Smith (Lord Birkenhead) played the chief part in organising resistance to the Home Rule Bill in 1913–14.

CARTER, MRS. FLORA. Social worker, daughter of Sir Alexander Ogston, the head of the University of Aberdeen; her husband died of tuberculosis a year or so after their marriage. She was one of the chief office organisers in the Webbs' campaign against the Poor Law.

CAUSTON, RICHARD KNIGHT, later Baron Southwark (1843–1929). Gladstonian Liberal politician, director of Joseph Causton & Sons, M.P. for West Southwark, 1888–1910.

COURTNEY, LEONARD HENRY, Baron Courtney of Penwith (1832–1918). Husband of Beatrice's sister Kate, political economist, leader-writer to *The Times*, and Liberal parliamentarian. He was Under-Secretary to the Treasury in 1882, but disagreed with Gladstone over Home Rule and became a Liberal Unionist. He led the anti-war party at the time of the Boer War, and thereafter pursued an independent liberal pacifist line of his own. In 1892 he narrowly missed the Speakership of the House of Commons. Courtney was blind for many years before his death; the *D.N.B.* calls him " the greatest British statesman, since Cobden, of those who have never held Cabinet office ".

COWEY, E. (*d.* 1903). Of the Yorkshire miners; a Trade Unionist of the old school.

COX, ADELAIDE (*d.* 1943). Commissioner of the Salvation Army; an officer therein from 1881 to her death. For twenty-four years chief helper to Mrs. Bramwell Booth in the Women's Social Work of the Army, and in command of it from 1912 to 1926. A Poor Law Guardian (Hackney).

COX, HAROLD (1859–1936). Lecturer on economics and journalist. At first a Fabian Liberal, collaborated with Sidney Webb and was secretary of the Cobden Club, 1899–1904; later became a strong anti-Socialist and anti-Liberal.

CRAIGIE, MRS. PEARL MARY TERESA (1867–1906). The novelist once famous as " John Oliver Hobbes ". Born of American parents settled in London, she published her first novel in 1891.

CRANE, WALTER (1845–1915). Painter, designer and decorator. Socialist, Fabian, friend and collaborator of William Morris, and with him in the Socialist League.

CRAWSHAY, MRS. A society lady who lived almost next door to Lady Horner, and was a great friend of hers.

CREIGHTON, BEATRICE (1874–). Daughter of the Bishop of London and a close friend of Beatrice. She became a Deaconess of St. Hilda's, Ootacamund.

CREIGHTON, LOUISE (1850–1936). Wife of the Bishop of London, and herself a well-known writer on historical subjects. A lady with a " salon " and a very determined character.

CREIGHTON, MANDELL (1843–1901). Bishop of London, 1897, historian, first President of the London School of Economics. Mandell Creighton was a very old friend of Beatrice, who admired both his character and his intellect. (See *My Apprenticeship*.)

CRIPPS, CHARLES ALFRED (1852–1941), Lawyer, married Beatrice's sister Theresa (1852–93). Entered Parliament as a Tory in 1895, and in 1914 was created Baron Parmoor. On the outbreak of war, however, he resigned from his party on pacifist grounds, and with his second wife (Marian Ellis) played a leading part in the subsequent pacifist and internationalist movement. He was Lord President of the Council in the Labour Governments of 1924 and 1929 and father of Sir Stafford Cripps. Beatrice was very much interested in his character, about which she changed her mind several times.

CRIPPS, SIR RICHARD STAFFORD (1889–). President of the Board of Trade in the 1945 Labour Government. Advocate, son of C. A. Cripps, Lord Parmoor. Ambassador to U.S.S.R., 1940–42, and head of 1943 mission to India; Minister of Aircraft Production in war-time Coalition, 1942–1945.

CRIPPS, WILLIAM HARRISON (*d.* 1923). Brother of Lord Parmoor. Surgeon, St. Bartholomew's Hospital, and Chairman of Metropolitan Electric Supply Company; married as his first wife Blanche, elder sister of Beatrice.

CROMER, EVELYN BARING, first Earl (1841–1917). The administrator of Egypt; son of Henry Baring, M.P., of the great banking family. Commissioner for the Egyptian Public Debt, 1877, he began in 1883 his administration of Egypt, which lasted until 1907. In 1916 he was made Chairman of the Dardanelles Commission, but died before the Report was complete.

CROOK, WILLIAM MONTGOMERY (1860–). Liberal politician and journalist; on the staff of the *Methodist Times*, 1892–98, and editor of the London *Echo*, 1898–1900. From 1895 to 1898

Crook was the Secretary of the Eighty Club, a group of young Liberals founded by Haldane and others in 1880.

CROOKS, WILLIAM (1852–1921). Trade Unionist and Socialist, member of the Coopers' Union, early Fabian. Mayor of Poplar, 1891, and Chairman of the Poplar Board of Guardians, 1898–1906. Labour M.P. for Poplar, 1903 till his death. A moving speaker on social conditions.

CUNNINGHAME - GRAHAM, ROBERT BONTEEN (1852–1936). One of the most colourful personalities of the early Socialist movement, artist, author, son of a Scottish landowner. He first stood for Parliament as a Liberal of the extreme left, but soon afterwards joined the Social Democratic Federation, sat for North Lanark from 1886 to 1892, and played an active part in all the S.D.F.'s attempts to agitate for the London unemployed in the 'eighties. With his friend John Burns he was imprisoned for six weeks for breaking through the police cordon in Trafalgar Square on " Bloody Sunday ", 1887.

CUNYNGHAME, SIR HENRY HARDYNGE (1848–1936). Civil servant, Assistant Under-Secretary, Home Office, 1894–1913. Secretary to Parnell Commission on riots at Featherstone Colliery, etc.

CURRAN, PETER (1860–1910). Socialist and Trade Union leader, member of the I.L.P., organiser of the Gas Workers' and General Labourers' Union from 1891, and first Chairman of the General Federation of Trade Unions. Labour M.P., 1906–10.

CURZON, GEORGE NATHANIEL, Marquess Curzon of Kedleston (1859–1925). The Empire-builder, Viceroy of India, 1899–1905; Foreign Secretary, 1919–22.

DALTON, HUGH (1887–   ). Chancellor of the Exchequer, 1945; at the date of this book student of King's College, Cambridge, and a leader of the Cambridge Fabian Society.

DAUSSET, LOUIS JEAN JOSEPH (1866–   ). Senator for the Seine; *Agrégé des lettres* and professor of rhetoric, Paris. Paris Municipal Councillor, 1900–22, and President, 1901–2,

rapporteur général du budget de la Ville, Paris, 1908–19; *président du Conseil général de la Seine*, 1919–20.

DAVEY, HORACE, Baron Davey of Fernhurst (1833–1907). Lawyer and Liberal politician, Solicitor-General, 1886; became Lord Justice of Appeal. Chairman of the Committee which drew up the constitution of the University of London, 1897, and member of the Senate.

DAVIES, MRS.—not Miss—MARY (1855–1930). Distinguished soprano, retired from concert-singing to devote herself to teaching; became president of the Welsh Folk Song Society.

DAVISON, SIR RONALD CONWAY (1884–   ). Civil servant, Board of Trade and Ministry of Labour until 1928; then retired in order to become writer and lecturer on social questions, particularly unemployment and unemployment insurance.

DAVY, SIR HUMPHRY (1778–1829). The great inventor was director and professor at the Royal Institution from 1801 onwards.

DAVY, SIR JAMES STEWART (1848–1915). Civil servant, sternest upholder of " the principles of 1834 " in the Poor Law, which, as an inspector, he put forward in evidence before the Commission of 1888. Became Chief Inspector, 1905, and endeavoured to guide the 1905 Royal Commission. (See S. and B. Webb, *English Poor Law History*.)

DEARMER, REV. PERCY (1867–1936). Broad Churchman, Fabian and social reformer. Vicar of St. Mary's, Primrose Hill, 1901–15; Secretary of London Christian Social Union, 1912–15; later Canon of Westminster. Chairman of the League of Arts from 1920; wrote, edited and contributed to a great many publications.

DESBOROUGH, WILLIAM HENRY GRENFELL (1855–   ). Created Baron Desborough in 1905. Tory M.P. for Salisbury, Hereford and Wycombe (1900–5), member of the Tariff Commission of 1904. His wife, *née* Ethel Fane, was co-heiress to the barony of Butler, a noted Society hostess, and one of Mrs. Asquith's " Souls ".

DEVONSHIRE, SPENCER COMPTON CAVENDISH, eighth Duke (1833–1908). Liberal politician of many years' standing. Lord President of the Council, 1895–1905, and as such President of the Privy Council Committee on Education until the establishment in 1902 of the Board of Education.

DICKINSON, WILLIAM H., Lord Dickinson (1859–1924). Liberal M.P., elected to L.C.C. as Progressive, 1889; Deputy Chairman, 1892, and subsequently Chairman. An ardent internationalist, Dickinson joined the Labour Party in 1930, but left on the formation of the National Government in the following year.

DIGGLE, REV. J. R. Chairman of the London School Board, 1885–94, defeated in that year. Diggle was a London curate until he left the Church in 1879 on his election to the London School Board. The fight of the Progressive Party against the policy of the Church in education, known as " Diggle-ism ", raged for a long time.

DILKE, SIR CHARLES WENTWORTH (1843–1911). The Liberal Imperialist politician, author of *Greater Britain*.

DILKE, EMILIA FRANCES (1840–1904). Lady Dilke's first husband, Mark Pattison, the Rector of Lincoln College, died; and in 1885 she married Sir Charles Dilke. Lady Dilke was a distinguished author and journalist on painting, sculpture and architecture, but she entered Beatrice's life through her interest in the conditions and organisation of working women. She was Chairman of the Women's Trade Union League and one of its principal speakers.

DILLON, JOHN (1851–1927). Irish Nationalist, M.P. for Tipperary and East Mayo. Leader of the anti-Parnellite faction in the Irish Party; after its reunion became lieutenant to Redmond, and leader after the latter's retirement in 1918. His wife (*d.* 1907) was Elizabeth Mathew.

DISRAELI, BENJAMIN (1804–81). Prime Minister, 1868 and 1874–80.

DODD, FREDERICK LAWSON (1868–). Dentist, Surgeon to Royal Dental Hospital, London. Played a prominent part in the Fabian Society in the days of this book, more particularly as he belonged to a profession in which Socialists have not been

numerous. First Chairman of the Fabian Society's Summer School, and at one time its Honorary Treasurer.

DONALDSON, FREDERIC LEWIS. Archdeacon of Westminster. An enthusiastic Christian Socialist, Vicar of St. Mark's, Leicester, from 1896 to 1918; one of the first members of the Christian Social Union and Chairman of its Leicester branch for many years; a founder of the Church Socialist League and its Chairman, 1913–16; made Canon of Westminster by the first Labour Government.

DONNELLY, SIR JOHN FRETCHEWILL DYKES (1834–1902). Started his career as a soldier, served in the Crimean War and retired as a Major-General. After his retirement became secretary to the Science and Arts Department, 1884–99.

DOUGHERTY, SIR JAMES BROWN (1844–1934). Liberal politician. Under-Secretary to the Lord-Lieutenant of Ireland, and Clerk to the Privy Council in Ireland; M.P. for Londonderry City, 1914–18.

DOWNES, SIR ARTHUR HENRY (1851–1937). Doctor and administrator. Senior Medical Inspector for the Poor Law under the Local Government Board, 1889 onwards; member of many departmental committees and of 1905 Royal Commission on the Poor Law.

DUFF, ROBERT HAROLD AMBROSE GORDON (1871–1946). Civil servant, mainly in Local Government Board; private secretary to its President, 1903–5. Secretary to 1905 Royal Commission on the Poor Law, and appointed General Inspector, 1909. Subsequently Secretary to the Mesopotamia Commission and to the Maclean Committee on Local Government.

DUGDALE, MRS. ALICE (1843–1902). Daughter of Sir Charles Trevelyan and in 1893 widow of William Stretford Dugdale. She was a connection of the Potter family, and her son later married Blanche, daughter of Eustace and Lady Frances Balfour.

DUKE, SIR HENRY EDWARD (1855–1939). Lord Justice Duke, afterwards Lord Merrivale. Lawyer, Recorder of Devonport, 1897–1914. Tory M.P. for Plymouth. Chief Secretary for Ireland, 1916–18.

EDGEWORTH, FRANCIS YSIDRO (1845–1926). Economist and statistician; from 1891 Professor of Political Economy, University of Oxford. Assisted London School of Economics in its early days.

EDWARDS, ALLEN CLEMENT (1869–1928). Liberal politician and journalist, writer for the *Daily News*. A Fabian for many years and author of several Fabian Tracts.

ELCHO, LORD. Hugo Richard Wemyss Charteris, later 11th Earl of Wemyss (1857–1937). M.P. for Haddington, 1883–85, and for Chiswick, 1886–95. His wife (*d.* 1937) was Mary Constance Wyndham, grand-daughter of Lord Leconfield, a Society lady and one of the hostesses of the " Souls ").

ELIOT, SIR CHARLES NORTON EDGE-CUMBE (1864–1931). Diplomat; Commissioner and Commander-in-Chief, British East Africa Protectorate, 1900–4; resigned and became Vice-Chancellor (not Principal) of Sheffield University, and in 1913 Principal of University of Hong Kong. Later Ambassador to Japan.

ELLISES. The last Leicester representative of this family, William Henry Ellis, moved to Hucknell in the next-door county, where his son, Francis Newman Ellis (1855–1934) became a colliery director and Sheriff of Nottingham.

ELLISON, SIR GERALD FRANCIS (1861–   ). Soldier, Secretary to War Office Reconstruction Committee, 1904; Private Secretary to Haldane, 1905–8, and Director of Organisation, Army Headquarters, 1908–11.

ENSOR, ROBERT CHARLES KIRKWOOD (1877–   ). Journalist, Fabian, political theorist and historian; member of L.C.C., 1910–13. Leader-writer on *Daily News* and *Daily Chronicle*, 1906–30, now " Scrutator " of the *Sunday Times*. Author of *England, 1870–1914*, etc.

ESHER, REGINALD BALIOL BRETT, second Viscount (1852–1930). Secretary to the Office of Works, 1895–1902. The friend of Edward VII, wrote Memoirs in four volumes. A friend of Haldane's; chairman of the War Office Reconstruction Committee, 1904.

FARADAY, MICHAEL (1791–1867). The great scientist was taken on by Sir Humphry Davy as his assistant at the Royal Institution, and was its superintendent at the time of his death.

FARRER, KATHERINE EUPHEMIA. Wife of Baron Farrer, a Vice-Chairman of the L.C.C.

FAULDER, JULIA (1880–1921). Daughter of Beatrice's sister Blanche Cripps and wife of Tom Faulder, surgeon.

FAWCETT, MILLICENT GARRETT (1847–1929). Sister of Elizabeth Garrett Anderson and wife of Henry Fawcett, the blind Postmaster-General. The leader for many years of the constitutional movement for women's suffrage.

FELS, JOSEPH (1854–1914). Millionaire Socialist and single-taxer; built up the huge Fels-Naptha plant which sold its products all over the world. Afterwards Fels came to England, made friends with Keir Hardie and George Lansbury and other Socialist leaders, and became very interested in the Back-to-the-Land Movement. He bought 1300 acres of land at Hollesley Bay and 600 at Maylands (both in Essex), for the settlement of unemployed men as agricultural workers, and gave generously to many social movements.

FISHER, MRS. ARABELLA, *née* Buckley. Secretary to Sir Charles Lyall; her brother later became Lord Wrenbury. She was one of the friends of Beatrice's girlhood, and "encouraged me in my lonely studies".

FITZALAN, EDMUND BERNARD FITZ-ALAN-HOWARD, first Viscount (1855–   ). Son of the Duke of Norfolk. Tory M.P. for Chichester, 1894–1921, a Lord of the Treasury, 1905, and Chief Whip, 1913–21.

FOSS, W., of Emmanuel College, Cambridge, Secretary of the Cambridge University Fabian Society in the autumn of 1909.

FOWLER, SIR HENRY, later Viscount Wolverhampton (1830–1911). Liberal politician and leading Wesleyan. President of the Local Government Board, 1892–94.

FOXWELL, HERBERT SOMERTON (1849–1936). Professor of Political Economy, University College, London, and owner of a unique library of books on political and social questions —now in the possession of the University of London. Foxwell's political views were strongly conservative, and his appointment as lecturer to the London School of Economics helped to give the lie to the suggestion that the Webbs intended to use that body as a vehicle of crude Socialist propaganda.

FRAMPTON, SIR GEORGE JAMES (1860–1928). The sculptor who made the Edith Cavell Memorial as well as many statues of Queen Victoria, Queen Mary and other works. One of the art advisers to the London Technical Education Board.

FRENCH, SIR JOHN DENTON PINKSTONE, later Earl French of Ypres (1852–1925). Commander-in-Chief in France, 1914–15, and in England, 1915–18.

GALTON, FRANCIS W. (1867–). Fabian Socialist; joined Morris's Socialist League in 1885 and the Fabian Society in 1891. Secretary to the Webbs, 1892–98, and to London Reform Union, 1898–1918. General Secretary to Fabian Society, 1920–39.

GARDINER, ALFRED G. (1865–). The Liberal writer and journalist, editor of the *Daily News* from 1902 to 1919, and author of many penportraits of the men and women of his day.

GARDINER, REV. THORY GAGE (1857–). Churchman, Co-operator, and Poor Law administrator. Secretary to Education Committee of the Co-operative Union, 1891–95. Member of Charity Organisation Society and of several Boards of Guardians; served on Royal Commission on the Poor Law, 1905. Residentiary Canon of Canterbury.

GARNETT, DR. WILLIAM (1850–1932). Mathematician, physicist and educationalist. Planned the Durham College of Science, Newcastle, of which he became Principal and Professor. Secretary and adviser to the London Technical Education Board, 1893–1904, and Education Adviser to L.C.C., 1904–15.

GARVIN, JAMES LOUIS (d. 1947). The journalist, editor of *The Observer*, 1908–42, and of the 1929 *Encyclopaedia Britannica*; author of the three-volume Life of Chamberlain.

GIBB, SIR GEORGE STEGMAN (1850–

1925). Solicitor, professional man and arbitrator. General Manager L.N.E.R., 1891–1906, and its Chairman, 1906–10. Managing Director, London Underground Railways, 1906–10, Chairman of the Road Board, 1910–19, a member of the war-time Committee on Production, 1915–18.

GLADSTONE, HERBERT, Viscount Gladstone (1854–1930). Son of the Liberal leader. Chief Liberal Whip, 1899–1906, and Home Secretary, 1906–1910, during the early part of the suffrage agitation; he was then sent out to South Africa as Governor-General.

GLADSTONE, WILLIAM EWART (1809–1898). Gladstone (whose last Premiership was from 1892 to 1894) represented the part of the Liberal tradition with which the Webbs had least sympathy. He was very old when they entered politics, and neither the modified Socialism of the Newcastle Programme nor the modified Imperialism of Haldane and his friends had any appeal for him.

GOMME, SIR GEORGE LAWRENCE (1853–1916). In the service of the Metropolitan Board of Works until 1889, when he was transferred to its successor, the L.C.C., whose Clerk he was from 1900 to 1915. Gomme was also an antiquary of some note.

GOOCH, GEORGE PEABODY (1873–). The Liberal historian, Fellow of Trinity College, Cambridge, joint-editor of the *Contemporary Review* and of the *Cambridge History of British Foreign Policy*; author of many books on history and on the problems of peace and democracy.

GORE, CHARLES (1853–1932). High Church leader, Christian Socialist and social reformer, Bishop of Worcester, 1902–5, of Birmingham, 1905–1911, and of Oxford, 1911–19.

GORST, SIR JOHN ELDON (1860–1911). Liberal M.P. who went over with Joseph Chamberlain to Liberal Unionism. Vice-President of the Privy Council Committee on Education, 1895–1902; hence responsible for the piloting through Parliament of the 1902 Education Act.

GOSCHEN, GEORGE JOACHIM, first Viscount (1831–1907). The Liberal

BIOGRAPHICAL INDEX

anti-Home Ruler, became Liberal Unionist. Chancellor of the Exchequer, 1886–92, and First Lord of the Admiralty, 1900–5; a strong supporter of University Extension.

GRANVILLE-BARKER, HARLEY GRANVILLE (1877–1946). The actor and dramatist, author of *The Madras House*, *The Voysey Inheritance*, etc. In 1894 entered on management at the Royal Court Theatre, and later the Savoy. Fabian and associate of Shaw in the early years of the century; his wife at that time was the actress Lillah McCarthy.

GRAY, SIR ALBERT (1850–1928). Lawyer, Counsel to the Chairman of Committees in the House of Lords from 1896 onwards. His wife was Sophie, daughter of S. Wells Williams of the U.S. Legation, Peking.

GREEN, ALICE SOPHIA AMELIA (*d.* 1929). Wife of John Richard Green, the historian of England, and herself a writer on historical subjects. A member of the Frederic Harrison group, and a friend and neighbour of the Webbs. She was a passionate Irish Nationalist, and became a member of the first Senate of the Irish Free State. Of her Beatrice wrote in her diary: " She chose me as a friend, and not I her, but she was good to me in the springtide of my good fortune, and she was one of the first to appreciate and like Sidney ".

GREEN, JOSEPH FREDERICK (1855–1932). Originally a curate, became a Positivist, Fabian and Secretary of the International Arbitration and Peace Association from 1886 to 1917. It that year, however, he became violently opposed to all attempts to end the war, and, in the ensuing general election, stood as National Labour candidate against Ramsay MacDonald, beat him and became P.P.S. to Sir Eric Geddes of " Geddes Axe " fame.

GRENFELL, MRS. WILLIE, see DESBOROUGH.

GREY, EDWARD, Viscount Grey of Fallodon (1862–1933). Liberal politician, Foreign Secretary from 1906 to 1916. Grey was one of the group of Liberal Imperialists in the early years of this century, which included Asquith and Haldane. See his auto-

biography. His wife, who died in 1906, was a Widdrington from Northumberland.

HALDANE, ELIZABETH SANDERSON (1862–1937). Sister of Haldane of Cloan and herself a distinguished public woman, writer on philosophy, ethics and Scottish history, and the first woman magistrate in the whole of Scotland.

HALDANE, RICHARD BURDON, Lord Haldane of Cloan (1856–1928). Lawyer, philosopher, leader among Liberal collectivists and Liberal Imperialists, educationalist, Army reformer, and lifelong friend of the Webbs. Most noted as effective founder (with the Webbs) of the modern University of London, and as Secretary of State for War and subsequently Lord Chancellor in the 1906 Liberal Government (from which he had to resign upon accusation of pro-German sympathies), Haldane became gradually converted to Labour and was Lord Chancellor to the first Labour Government of 1924. The " dear old lady " mentioned on p. 461 was Haldane's mother; she lived to be 100.

HALL, SIR BENJAMIN, afterwards Baron Llanover (1802–67). Whig politician, first returned to Parliament for Monmouth Boroughs in 1831; in the new House sat for Marylebone, and supported many projects for reform. In 1855, as Chief Commissioner of Works, he brought in the Bill which established the Metropolitan Board of Works, and settled the area of the present L.C.C.

HAMILTON, CHARLES JOSEPH (1878–). Economist; Professor of Economics at Calcutta, 1912–18; and later at Patna University, India.

HAMILTON, LORD CLAUD JOHN (1843–1925). Son of the Duke of Abercorn and grandson of the Duke of Bedford; Tory M.P. for various divisions, 1865–88, and 1910–18. Chairman of the Great Eastern Railway.

HAMILTON, SIR EDWARD WALTER (1847–1908). Civil servant, Treasury, from 1870; rose to be Joint Permanent Secretary, 1902.

HAMILTON, LORD GEORGE FRANCIS (1845–1927). Tory politician who held a number of offices between 1874 and 1903. Chairman of the London School Board, 1894–95, and of the Royal Commission on the Poor Laws, 1905–9. His wife was Maud, daughter of the Earl of Harewood.

HAMMILL, FREDERICK (1856–1901). Engineer from the North-East coast and member of the A.S.E. An early Fabian, and a prominent worker with Keir Hardie in the I.L.P.

HANKINSON, MARY. Socialist and prominent member of the Fabian Women's Group. By profession a gymnastic instructor in schools. Miss Hankinson was for many years manager of the Fabian Summer School and captain of its cricket team.

HARBEN, HENRY DEVENISH (1874–). Socialist and Fabian of many years standing, member of Executive Committee, 1911–20. As a recruit from the Liberal League organised a Fabian enquiry into land problems, which was published as *The Rural Problem*. Harben had many arguments with the Webbs and the Fabian Society before the last war, but remained their firm friend and admirer.

HARCOURT, LEWIS, Viscount Harcourt (1863–1922). Son of Sir William Harcourt; Liberal M.P. for Rossendale, 1904–17, and First Commissioner of Works, 1905–10.

HARCOURT, ROBERT VERNON (1878–). Brother of Lewis Harcourt, and a more Radical Liberal. M.P. for Montrose Burghs, 1908–18; journalist, and also wrote plays.

HARCOURT, SIR WILLIAM (1827–1904). Liberal politician ; imposer, as Chancellor of the Exchequer in the 1892 Government, of the first death duties, and author of the phrase " we are all Socialists now ". Leader of the Commons in Rosebery's Adminstration. The rivalry between him and Lord Rosebery accounted for much of the weakness of Liberal leadership around the turn of the century.

HARDIE, JAMES KEIR (1856–1915). The Scottish miners' leader who founded the I.L.P. and was the chief influence in the formation of the Labour Representation Committee which became the Labour Party. Hardie—whom John Burns so strongly disliked— stands for the emotional appeal of Socialism in the British working-class

movement; but his mind was out of tune with the Webbs, and they never really got on terms with him.

HARKNESS, MARGARET. A second cousin of Beatrice's and about the same age. Daughter of a parson, she ran away from home to work with the Salvation Army, became a Socialist and joined the S.D.F., earning her living as a free-lance journalist. Beatrice found her " greatly improved " by social work. (MS. diary, 1883.)

HARMSWORTH, ALFRED CHARLES WILLIAM (1865–1922). Lord Northcliffe of *Answers* and the *Daily Mail*. The founder of modern popular journalism.

HARRISON, AMY (Mrs. Spencer). One of the Webbs' earliest secretaries, married another—see note on p. 153 of this book; also wrote on factory legislation.

HARRISON, CHARLES (1835–97). Liberal politician, solicitor and advocate of leasehold enfranchisement. M.P. for Plymouth; elected to L.C.C. in 1886 and became Vice-Chairman and member of its Parliamentary Committee.

HARRISON, FREDERIC (1831–1923). The Radical leader of the English Positivists, free thinker and staunch supporter of Trade Unionism in the latter part of the nineteenth century. Harrison never succeeded in converting Beatrice to Positivism, but he and his wife were among her oldest friends. (See *My Apprenticeship*.)

HARRISON, JANE ELLEN (1850–1928). The distinguished classical scholar and archaeologist; author of *Prolegomena to the Study of Greek Religion*.

HART, SIR ISRAEL (1835–1911). Chairman of Hart & Levy, wholesale manufacturers of Leicester, four times Mayor of Leicester; presented the city with a free library and an ornamental fountain.

HARVEY, ALFRED SPALDING (1840– 1905). Originally a civil servant, in 1880 Harvey left to become secretary to the banking house of Glyn, Mills, Currie & Co., and retained this position until his death: he was a member of two Royal Commissions and was often consulted by the Treasury. He was a strong Liberal and free-trader and welcomed economic education on those lines.

HARVEY, THOMAS EDMUND (1875–). Progressive Radical, Warden of Toynbee Hall, 1906–11, Member L.C.C., 1904–7, M.P. for West Leeds, 1910–18, for English Universities, 1937. A Quaker, wrote many books on Quakerism, religious and social subjects.

HAWKSLEY, BOURCHIER F. (d. 1916). Solicitor whose firm acted for the Chartered Company of South Africa.

HEADLAM, REV. STEWART DUCK-WORTH (1847–1924). Christian Socialist, founder of the Guild of St. Matthew, and a Fabian of many years standing. Member of the London School Board, 1886–1904, and of the L.C.C. (Progressive) from 1907 till his death.

HENDERSON, ARTHUR (1863–1935). An ironmoulder by trade, " Uncle Arthur " Henderson first entered Parliament as Labour in 1903; and was Treasurer and then for many years Secretary to the Party, whose organisation was largely of his building. He was a member of Asquith's and Lloyd George's War Cabinet, until forced out in 1917, Home Secretary in the first Labour Government, and in the second as Foreign Secretary made a great effort to bring peace to Europe; after the fall of the Government he was President, until its final failure, of the Disarmament Conference. Henderson's friendship with the Webbs, which became very close, did not really begin until the war period.

HENSON, HERBERT HENSLEY (1863–1947). The Churchman and author. Canon of Westminster and Rector of St. Margaret's, 1900–12. Afterwards Bishop of Hereford and Bishop of Durham.

HERBERT, AUBERON EDWARD WILLIAM MOLYNEUX (1838–1906). Son of the Earl of Carnarvon, brought up a Tory, became first a Liberal, and then a republican, agnostic and strong supporter (in the 'seventies) of Charles Bradlaugh and of Arch's Agricultural Labourers Union; took up farming and vegetarianism. This amiable and eccentric writer was a friend of Beatrice's youth. (See My Apprenticeship.)

HERBERT, AUBERON THOMAS (" Bron "), afterwards Lord Lucas (1876–1916). Son of Auberon Herbert; a vigorous young Liberal politician who held two or three offices, but was killed in action in the first world war.

HEWINS, WILLIAM ALBERT SAMUEL (1865–1931). Economist, first Director of the London School of Economics, but resigned in 1903 on his conversion to Tariff Reform, and became for fourteen years secretary of the Tariff Reform Commission. Entered Parliament as a Tory in 1912.

HIBBERT, SIR JOHN (1824–1908). Liberal politician who held various offices from 1872 onwards. President of the County Councils Association and a critic of the Webbs' local government policy.

HICKS-BEACH, MICHAEL EDWARD, later Earl St. Aldwyn (1837–1916). Tory politician, first held office in 1868. Secretary for Ireland, 1886–87, and Chancellor of the Exchequer, 1885 and 1895–1902.

HILL, OCTAVIA (d. 1912). The pioneer of modern Housing Management, which she first undertook in 1864. Beatrice's early work as a rent-collector was following in her steps. Octavia Hill was a philanthropist, but no Socialist; she was a pillar of the Charity Organisation Society. In 1905 she was appointed a member of the Royal Commission on the Poor Law.

HILLS, JOHN WALLER (1867–1938). Tory M.P. for Durham City, 1906–1922, and afterwards for Ripon. One of the Progressive group of Tories, with a strong interest in social questions.

HOBHOUSE, HENRY (1854–1937). Liberal Unionist, M.P., married to Beatrice's elder sister Margaret; member of the Royal Commission on Secondary Education. Chairman of the Somerset County Council, 1904–1924, in which capacity he had a strong influence on the policy of the County Councils Association.

HOBHOUSE, LEONARD TRELAWNY (1864–1929). Sociologist and political theorist. Professor of Sociology in the University of London, and author of many standard books; wrote much for the Manchester Guardian. A cousin of Henry Hobhouse and therefore a friend and helper of the Webbs.

On his death the Fabian leaders were astonished to find that he had left £10,000 for Fabian purposes, to be spent in ten years. Half of this sum went to pay travelling Hutchinson Lecturers; the other half founded the London School of Economics.

HUTTON, SIR JOHN (1842–1903). Chairman of L.C.C., 1892–95.

HUXLEY, THOMAS HENRY (1825–93). The great scientist was professor at the Royal Institution as well as the Royal College of Surgeons.

HUYSMANS, CAMILLE (1871–   ). Belgian Socialist politician, Prime Minister to the Coalition Government of 1946. Huysmans entered international politics in 1905, as Secretary to the Second International, and at the end of the first world war played the chief part in its reorganisation; he was strongly opposed to both German and Russian Communists. The Webbs had a high opinion of his abilities, and it was at his request, in his official international capacity, that they wrote *A Constitution for the Socialist Commonwealth of Great Britain*.

HYETT, SIR FRANCIS ADAMS (1844–1941). Gloucestershire landowner; Deputy Chairman of Quarter Sessions, 1886–1904, and Chairman, 1904–20. Vice-Chairman, Gloucestershire County Council, 1904–18, and Chairman, 1918; also wrote bibliographical and other monographs.

ILIFFE, WILLIAM H. (d. 1938). Lieutenant Commissioner of the Salvation Army, and an officer in the Army from 1886 (?) to his death. He served in India, was at one time in charge of the Army's Land Colony at Hadleigh and of its Boxsted Small Holdings Settlement, and later commanded its Men's Social Work throughout Great Britain.

IRVINE, SIR WILLIAM HILL (1858–1944) is almost certainly the individual referred to. He was a British-born Australian politician, Attorney-General and later Premier of Victoria, afterwards Attorney-General to the Commonwealth and Lieutenant-Governor of Victoria, 1918–35.

ISAACS, RUFUS DANIEL, afterwards Marquess of Reading (1860–1935). The lawyer and politician. Attorney-General, 1910–13, at the time of the Marconi scandal.

JACK, JAMES M. (1848–1912). Secretary of the Associated Ironmoulders of Scotland.

JACKSON, BRIGADIER, afterwards Colonel (d. 1930). In the Salvation Army from 1886 to 1930. For many years Chief Accountant at the Army's headquarters, and later its Auditor-General. He was only a visiting officer at the Hadleigh Colony, but went there often as conductor of the International Staff Songsters — also an Army venture.

JACKSON, SIR CYRIL (1863–1924). Educational administrator; head of Education Department, Western Australia, 1896–1903, then Chief Inspector of the Board of Education until 1906. Member of London School Board, 1891–96, and of L.C.C. (Progressive), 1907–13; Chairman, 1915. One of the expert investigators employed by the 1905 Royal Commission on the Poor Law; and member of many commissions.

JAMES, WILLIAM (1842–1910). The American philosopher and psychologist, brother of Henry James.

JAMESON, SIR LEANDER STARR (1853–1917). "Dr. Jim" of the Jameson Raid, which he organised while administrator of Rhodesia for the Chartered Company of South Africa. After the South African War he was Premier of the Cape from 1904 to 1908, and in 1913 was made Chairman of the British South African Company.

JEFFREY, SIR JOHN (1871–1947). Civil servant, joined as boy clerk in 1888. 1905–9, Assistant Secretary to Royal Commission on the Poor Law, subsequently Secretary to Scottish National Health Insurance Commission, Scottish Board of Health, Department of Health for Scotland, and from 1933 to 1937 Permanent Under-Secretary for Scotland.

JEKYLL, SIR HERBERT (1846–1932). Soldier (retired 1901), Private Secretary to the Earl of Carnarvon and to Lord Houghton. Assistant Secretary, Board of Trade, 1901–11. His wife was Agnes Graham, daughter of William Graham, M.P.

JEPHSON, ARTHUR W. (1853–1935). Canon of Southwark. Member of

London School Board, 1885–1903; member of L.C.C., 1904–6.

JERRED, W. T. Civil servant, transposed to Local Government Board from Dublin, 1897. Private secretary to Burns, 1906, and Assistant Permanent Secretary, 1911.

JEUNE, LADY MARY, afterwards Lady St. Helier (d. 1931). Society lady and social worker. One of the " Souls ". Married first to a brother of Lord Stanley of Alderley, afterwards to Sir Francis Jeune.

JOHNSONS, of Leicester. There were several prominent citizens of this name, two (Joseph, d. 1837, and Robert, d. 1842) being sons of Joseph Johnson, who in 1775 was Mayor of the un-reformed Corporation. Both were freemen and chamberlains of the Corporation. Later Thomas Fielding Johnston (1828–1921), " gentleman ", of Stoneygate, was a member of the Council from 1861 to 1870.

JONES, BENJAMIN (1847–1941). Leading co-operator, manager for many years of C.W.S. London branch; wrote the best-known book on Co-operative Production. Beatrice made his acquaintance at the time of her studies in co-operation before her marriage. (See My Apprenticeship.) He quarrelled with the Co-operators in 1902.

KAUTSKY, KARL (1854–1928). Leading theoretician of the German Social-Democratic Party. Wrote much on Marxism, war and social history. Kautsky had a vehement controversy with Lenin concerning the dictatorship of the proletariat, which he strongly opposed. Editor of Neue Zeitung, and of German Foreign Office archives after 1918.

KEELING, FREDERIC HILLERSDON (1886–1916). " Ben " Keeling was one of the founders of the Cambridge Fabian Society in 1905–6. On leaving Cambridge he took up social research. Was for a time manager of the Leeds Labour Exchange and later assistant editor of the New Statesman. He was killed in France.

KEKEWICH, SIR GEORGE WILLIAM (1841–1921). Civil servant, Secretary to the Education Department, 1890–1900, and later to the Board of Education.

KER, WALTER PATON (1855–1923). The distinguished literary critic. Professor of English Literature at University College, London, and of Poetry at Oxford.

KIMBERLEY, LORD (1826–1902). Liberal politician. Leader of the Liberal Party in the House of Lords from 1897 to 1902 and in 1899 Chancellor of the University of London. His successor (d. 1932) was one of the earliest peers to join the Labour Party.

KIMMINS, CHARLES WILLIAM. Educationalist; Inspector of Schools under L.C.C. Technical Education Board, and Director of University Extension in London. Chief Inspector of Education, L.C.C., 1904–23; member of the Senate of the University of London from 1900 onwards.

KINGSLEY, MARY (1862–1900). Explorer, niece of Charles Kingsley.

KNOWLES, SIR JAMES THOMAS (1831–1908). Architect who laid out Leicester Square, editor of Contemporary Review from 1870 to 1877, when he founded and edited The Nineteenth Century; Founder in 1869 of the Metaphysical Society, which included a large number of distinguished persons.

KROPOTKIN, PRINCE PETER ALEXEIE-VITCH (1842 – 1921). Greatest of anarchist-communists, he was born into one of the oldest families of Russia, and having seen on his travels the misery of the peasantry, he joined the First International and became a follower of the anarchist leader Bakunin. After being imprisoned in Russia and in France he escaped to England, where he stayed until he returned to Russia after the Revolution. Kropotkin's Communism, as expressed in books like Mutual Aid, had a strong influence on English Socialists at the end of the last century.

KRUGER, STEPHEN PAUL (1825–1904). " Oom Paul ", inveterate enemy of the British Government after he had been dismissed from his official post in 1878. President of the Transvaal Republic from 1883, and moving spirit of the Boer War.

LABOUCHERE, HENRY (1831–1912). " Labby " of Punch. Liberal M.P. for Northampton, 1880–1906; proprietor and editor of Truth when Truth was a Radical journal.

McCLEARY, GEORGE FREDERICK (1867–). Doctor and public health expert. Deputy Senior Medical Officer, Ministry of Health, and Principal Medical Officer to the National Health Insurance Commission; M.O.H. for Battersea. Specialist in maternity and child welfare, and an authority on population.

MACDONALD, DR. J. A. Doctor; district Poor Law Officer at Taunton; from 1907 onwards held high office in the British Medical Association.

MacDONALD, JAMES RAMSAY (1866–1937). Labour Prime Minister, 1924 and 1929–31; then Prime Minister in the National Government until 1935. During the period of this book MacDonald was a writer and lecturer on Socialism, member of the I.L.P., and first Secretary of the Labour Representation Committee; he resigned from the Fabian Society at the time of the Boer War. The Webbs never really liked or trusted MacDonald, nor he them.

MACDONALD, MARGARET ETHEL (1870–1910). Wife of Ramsay MacDonald, daughter of Dr. Gladstone, a professor of chemistry and member of the London School Board—and herself a steadfast worker for women's labour organisations. Her death at so early an age was a disaster in more ways than one.

MACDONNELL, SIR ANTONY PATRICK, later Lord Macdonnell (1844–1925). Indian and Irish administrator, Lieutenant-Governor of Accra and Oudh, organiser of Indian famine relief in 1897, and author of the famous Famine Report. In 1903 he became Irish Under-Secretary under Wyndham with special administrative powers, but his indiscretions led to Wyndham's resignation, and though he remained in office until 1908 he lost his special powers.

McKENNA, REGINALD (1863–1933). Liberal politician; Financial Secretary to the Treasury, 1905–7, thereafter President of the Board of Education, First Lord of the Admiralty, Home Secretary, and Chancellor of the Exchequer (1915–16). After retirement from politics he became Chairman of the Midland Bank.

MACKENZIE, SIR LESLIE (1862–1935).

The distinguished doctor and public health practitioner. M.O.H. for Kirkcudbright and Wigtown, and for Leith; medical member of Scottish Local Government Board, 1904–19, and of Scottish Board of Health, 1919–28.

MACKINDER, SIR HALFORD JOHN (1861–1947). Geographer, Reader in Geography, University of Oxford, 1887–1905; Reader and afterwards Professor, University of London, 1900–25. Director of London School of Economics, 1903–8; member of many Government committees.

McNABB, FATHER VINCENT (d. 1943). Dominican priest, born at Portaferry, County Down; an untiring worker and preacher in the cause of social and economic morality; the first Dominican father to become an extension lecturer for the University of London. He continued lecturing for more than twenty years until his death, and wrote many books, pamphlets, and articles on Christianity, literature, etc.

MACNAMARA, THOMAS JAMES (1861–1931). Elementary school teacher who became a Liberal politician. Member of London School Board, 1896–1902, and M.P. for North Camberwell, 1900–18; Coalition Liberal in 1918 election and Minister of Labour, 1920–22. A strong Nonconformist, and editor of The Schoolmaster from 1892 to 1907.

MACROSTY, HENRY W. Civil servant; member of the Fabian Executive from 1895 to 1907; Assistant Director of the first Census of Production, 1907; writer on trusts and combines.

McTAGGART, JOHN McTAGGART ELLIS (1866–1925). Hegelian philosopher; Fellow of Trinity College, Cambridge.

McVAIL, JOHN CHRISTIE (1849–1926). Scottish doctor; M.O.H. for Stirling and Dumbarton. Examiner in medical jurisprudence and public health for Scottish Universities. President, Society of M.O.H.s of Great Britain; on General Medical Council. Medical investigator for the 1905 Royal Commission on the Poor Law.

MAETERLINCK, MAURICE (1862–). The Belgian playwright and mystic published his L'Intelligence des Fleurs,

MERRIMAN, JOHN XAVIER (1841–1926). South African politician, entered the Cape Parliament in 1869, and obtained office in 1881. Merriman was a member of the Committee on the Jameson Raid and drew up its report; subsequently he was a member of the National Convention for Union (of South Africa) and Prime Minister from 1908 to 1910 in the United Government.

MERZ, JOHN THEODORE (1840–1920). Scientist and engineer, of a well-known Newcastle family. Wrote a monumental work on the development of European thought in the nineteenth century, stressing the importance of the growth of science and scientific method.

METCHNIKOFF, ILYA (1845–1916). The Russian biologist who became assistant director of the Pasteur Institute at Paris, and did much work on the possibility of prolonging life by preventing intestinal putrefaction. Beatrice, who had a lifelong interest in dieting, was naturally influenced by Metchnikoff's work.

MILL, JOHN STUART (1896–73). The great Utilitarian philosopher who bridged the gap between Benthamism and Socialism, sat as an Independent for Westminster from 1865 to 1868, and introduced into Parliament the first petition for Women's Suffrage. The social philosophy of the Fabians owed a great deal to Mill.

MILNER, ALFRED, Viscount Milner (1854–1925). Journalist and civil servant; Under-Secretary for Finance in Egypt, 1889–92, then Chairman of the Board of Inland Revenue till 1897. A member of the Rhodes school of Imperialists, as High Commissioner for South Africa from 1897 to 1901, Milner bears responsibility for much of the policy which led to the South African War.

MITCHELL, H. ISAAC (1867–   ). A leading official of the Boilermakers' Society and wrote its history. He subsequently became an official of the Labour Department of the Board of Trade.

MONRO, SIR HORACE CECIL (1861–   ). Civil servant; entered Local Government Board, 1884; was secretary to several Presidents. Assistant Secretary to the Board, 1897–1910, and Permanent Secretary, 1910–19.

MONTEAGLES, The. THOMAS SPRING RICE, second Baron Monteagle (1849–1926), and his wife Elizabeth Butler (d. 1908), daughter of the Bishop of Meath and sister of Lady Prothero.

MORANT, SIR ROBERT LAURIE (1862–1920). Civil servant; chief author of the 1902 Education Act. Morant started his career by laying (as tutor to the Crown Prince) the foundation of an educational system in Siam; on returning to England he entered the Education Department in 1895 and wrote special reports for Sir Michael Sadler. In 1902 he became private secretary to the Duke of Devonshire and in 1903 Permanent Secretary to the Board of Education, where he had great influence. Differences with his colleagues led him to leave in 1911 and to become Chairman of the National Health Insurance Commissioners, and in 1919 Secretary to the new Ministry of Health.

MORGAN, JOHN HARTMAN (1876–   ). Lawyer and journalist; wrote for *Daily Chronicle* and *Manchester Guardian*; Liberal candidate in 1910 election; published many books on legal and political subjects. He married Helen Mary Cracknell.

MORLEY, ARNOLD (1849–1916). Liberal politician. Chief Liberal Whip, 1886–1893, and Postmaster-General, 1892–1895.

MORLEY, JOHN (1838–1916). Lord Morley of Blackburn, biographer of Gladstone, Secretary of State for India during the Morley-Minto reforms, resigned from the Asquith Cabinet in 1914 on pacifist grounds. Morley was a close friend of the Leonard Courtneys (q.v.), although not of the Webbs.

MOWATT, SIR FRANCIS (1837–1919). Civil servant; appointed Clerk in the Treasury, 1856; Assistant Secretary, 1888, and Permanent Secretary, 1888–1903; member of many Royal Commissions. Alderman L.C.C., 1903, and member of the Senate of London University.

MUNDELLA, ANTHONY JOHN (1825–1897). Progressive Radical politician. Originally a hosiery manufacturer in Nottingham, Mundella set up the first conciliation board in industry; he supported the New Model Unionism of Allen, Applegarth, etc., and worked continuously for Parliamentary reform, for universal education and for Factory and Housing Acts. As President of the Board of Trade in 1886 he established its Labour Department and he was a member of the 1891 Royal Commission on Labour.

MUNRO FERGUSON, RONALD CRAUFURD (1860–1934). Later Viscount Novar. Large Scottish landowner and Liberal politician; M.P. for Leith, 1886–1914; at one time Private Secretary to Lord Rosebery.

MURRAY, GEORGE GILBERT AIMÉE (1866–   ). Gilbert Murray, Professor of Greek, translator of Euripides; Liberal and internationalist; Chairman of the League of Nations Union until there was no longer a League of Nations.

MURRAY, GRAHAM, Viscount Dunedin (1849–   ). Scottish lawyer and Tory politician. Secretary of State for Scotland, 1903–5. Chairman, 1903–6, of the Royal Commission on Trade Union Law, set up as a result of the Taff Vale judgment.

NANSEN, FRIDTJOF (1861–1930). The explorer who nearly reached the North Pole in the *Fram* in 1893. He became Professor of Oceanography at Oslo, director of the repatriation of prisoners after the first world war, when he introduced the " Nansen " passport; and High Commissioner for Relief in the Russian famine of 1921.

NAPIER, SIR ALBERT EDWARD ALEXANDER (1881–   ). Youngest son of Lord Napier of Magdala; lawyer, Assistant Secretary in the Lord Chancellor's Office, 1919–44, and Permanent Secretary since 1944. At the time of this book he was private secretary to Cyril Jackson (*q.v.*) and lived in his house at Limpsfield.

NAPIER, THOMAS BATEMAN (1854–1933). Lawyer, County Court Judge, Derbyshire, from 1912 onwards. Ph.D. of London University, on its Senate in 1895; member of L.C.C. (Progressive), 1893–1906, and three times chairman of its Parliamentary Committee.

NASH, VAUGHAN (1861–1932). Jour-nalist who became a civil servant. Nash's interest in Trade Unionism and social questions began early; with Llewellyn Smith he wrote the standard history of the 1889 Dock Strike; he was on the editorial staff of the *Daily Chronicle* and the *Daily News*. In 1905 he became private secretary to Campbell-Bannerman and subsequently to Asquith; and was Secretary to the Ministry of Reconstruction in 1917–1919.

NEVILL, LADY DOROTHY FANNY (*d.* 1913). Daughter of the third Earl of Oxford, married R. M. Nevill, a grandson of the Earl of Abergavenny. She was a great Society hostess, and wrote entertaining memoirs.

NEWMAN, SIR GEORGE (1870–   ). Doctor and public health administrator. Chief Medical Officer to Ministry of Health, 1919–35, and to Board of Education, 1907–35. Chairman of the Health of Munition Workers Committee during the first world war, member of many Government committees, and author of Government Reports and other publications.

NEWSHOLME, SIR ARTHUR (1857–   ). Doctor and public health administrator; for many years Principal Medical Officer to the Local Government Board. Author of many books and important Government Reports.

NORMAN, CLARENCE HENRY (1886–   ). Expert shorthand writer and author, and a Fabian Socialist. Conscientious objector during first world war; twice imprisoned; on Executive of No-Conscription Fellowship.

NORTHUMBERLAND, HENRY GEORGE PERCY, seventh Duke (1846–1918). M.P. for North Northumberland, 1868–85. Lord-Lieutenant of the County and Custos Rotulorum, Chairman of Northumberland County Council and Chancellor of the University of Durham. The Duchess (*d.* 1913) was Lady Edith Campbell, daughter of the Duke of Argyll.

NUNN, THOMAS HANCOCK (1859–1937). Member of the Charity Organisation Society, a Poor Law Guardian and member of the 1905 Royal Commission on the Poor Law; signed the Majority Report. A pioneer in the development of voluntary Councils of Social Welfare.

O'BRIEN, WILLIAM (1852–1928). The Irish nationalist and journalist, M.P. for Cork, 1910–18; his wife was a Frenchwoman, Sophie Raffalovich.

O'CONOR DON, CHARLES OWEN, " the O'Conor Don " (1838–1906). Irish landowner and Liberal politician, M.P. for Roscommon, 1860–80; member of many Government Committees and Commissions.

OLIVIER, SYDNEY (1859–1943), Baron Olivier. Lifelong friend of Sidney Webb, whom he met first as a young civil servant in the Colonial Office. One of the seven Fabian Essayists and a pillar of the early Fabian Society. Acting Governor and later Governor of Jamaica (1907–13); wrote *White Capital and Coloured Labour*, and other books on the problems of native emancipation. In the 1924 Labour Government Olivier was Secretary of State for India.

OLLIVANT, ALFRED (1874–1927). Novelist, earlier held commission in Royal Artillery. His best-known work is *Owd Bob* (1898).

OWEN, ROBERT (1770–1858). The great educationalist, factory reformer and Socialist. Beatrice was unsympathetic to Owen for the greater part of her life, disliking both his millennialism and his ideals of producers' co-operation—which she did not accept as a practical possibility until her visit to the U.S.S.R. See the criticism of Owen in *The History of Trade Unionism*.

PAGET, Family of. John Paget, J.P. (1811–98), is the best illustration of Beatrice's point. He was son of Thomas Paget of Humberstone in Leicestershire, but came to London, became a metropolitan police magistrate for 25 years and a London clubman. Another Leicester John Paget (1808–92) became a landowner and distinguished agriculturist in Hungary.

PANKHURST, EMMELINE (*d.* 1928). The leader of the militant suffragettes. Earlier (with her husband, Dr. Pankhurst) a strong Fabian and pacifist; later a violent supporter of the first world war.

PARKER, SIR GILBERT (1862–1932).

Canadian-born traveller and novelist, author of *The Seats of the Mighty*, etc., M.P. for Gravesend, 1900–18. Chairman of Imperial South African Association and of Small Ownership Committee; at the beginning of the first world war was in charge of British publicity in U.S.A.

PARRY, SIR CHARLES HUBERT HASTINGS (1848–1918). The composer; Professor of Music at Oxford, 1899–1908. His wife, Maud, was an enthusiast for " left wing " causes.

PASSMORE EDWARDS, JOHN (1823–1911). Philanthropist, Radical and pacifist; in his early days a Chartist and editor of an Anti-Corn Law League journal, later edited the *Echo* (first halfpenny newspaper) from 1876 to 1896 and became President of the London Reform Union. Founded free libraries, hospitals, convalescent homes and supported many Radical causes; declined a knighthood.

PATTEN-MACDOUGALL, SIR JAMES (1849–1919). Barrister and civil servant; legal secretary to Lord Advocate, 1886, 1892, 1894; Vice-President, Scottish Local Government Board, 1904–9, and Deputy Clerk Register for Scotland, 1909–19. Member of the 1905 Royal Commission on the Poor Law.

PEARSON, SIR CYRIL ARTHUR (1866–1921). One of the makers of modern popular journalism, founded *Pearson's Weekly* in 1890 and the *Daily Express* in 1900. In 1912, having become blind, he retired from journalism, founded St. Dunstan's and devoted himself to promoting the welfare of the blind.

PEASE, EDWARD R. (1857–   ). One of the founders of the Fabian Society, which held its earliest meeting in his rooms. He was General Secretary of the Society between 1889 and 1914, and its Honorary Secretary both before and after that date, retiring finally in 1939. See Pease, *History of the Fabian Society*.

PEEL, HON. ARTHUR GEORGE VILLIERS (1868–   ). A descendant of Sir Robert Peel; a Treasury clerk who afterwards wrote biography and political works; a governor of the London School of Economics.

PERKS, SIR ROBERT WILLIAM (1849–

1934), "Imperial Perks". Railway engineer and lawyer; Wesleyan (Treasurer of the Wesleyan Twentieth-Century Million Fund); Liberal M.P., 1892–1910. Perks, the Founder and Treasurer of the Liberal League, was the wire-puller *par excellence* of the Liberal Imperialist group (the "Limps") formed by Haldane and his friends; but the Webbs did not find him congenial.

PERRY, SIR EDWIN COOPER (1856–1938). The distinguished physician, consultant to Guy's Hospital. Much interested in the University of London, of which he was Vice-Chancellor, 1917–19, and thereafter Principal Officer.

PERTHES, FRIEDRICH CHRISTOPH (1772–1843). German Liberal and Nationalist, who founded a famous publishing house at Gotha. Justus Perthes, the geographical publisher, was his uncle.

PHELPS, LANCELOT RIDLEY (1853–1936). Fellow and Tutor of Oriel College, Oxford, and Provost, 1914–1929. Interested in social reform; a Poor Law Guardian and member of the C.O.S. and of the 1905 Royal Commission on the Poor Law.

PHILLIMORE, MRS. LUCY ("Lion"), *née* Fitzpatrick. Wife of R. C. Phillimore. A prominent member of the Fabian Society and associated with many causes.

PHILLIMORE, ROBERT CHARLES (1871–1919). Eldest son of the first Lord Phillimore, one of the rich young adherents of the Webbs in their early work. Member of L.C.C. for Deptford, 1898–1910 and 1913–19.

PHILLIPS, MARION (1881–1932). Australian-born, she came to the London School of Economics and became an investigator for the 1905 Royal Commission on the Poor Law; then took up work in the Labour movement, and became in 1918 Chief Woman Officer to the reorganised Labour Party.

PLAYNE, ARTHUR (1845–1913). Country squire and owner of a cloth mill in Gloucestershire, married to Beatrice's third sister, Mary.

PLUNKETT, SIR HORACE CURZON (1854–1932). The great promoter of the Irish Co-operative movement; founded in 1894 the Irish Agricultural Organisation Society. M.P. for Dublin County, 1892–1900, and Commissioner for the Congested Districts Board, Ireland, 1891–1918. In later years Plunkett became a much closer friend of the Webbs and took them for their first ride in an aeroplane.

POLLOCK, SIR FREDERICK (1845–1937). The distinguished judge and legal authority, editor for many years of the *Law Reports*. Member of the 1891 Royal Commission on Labour.

POWER, DR. W. H. Doctor and public health specialist. Chief Medical Officer to the Local Government Board until 1907.

POYNDER, SIR JOHN POYNDER DICKSON, later Lord Islington (1869–1936). Tory landowner and politician, member of L.C.C. (Moderate), 1898–1904, M.P. for Chippenham, 1892–1910; held various minor offices. His wife was Anne, daughter of Lord Napier of Magdala.

PRESTON-THOMAS, HERBERT. Civil servant in Local Government Board; entered the service in 1859, and in 1894 was appointed Inspector under the Poor Law.

PRICE, SIR ROBERT JOHN (1854–1926). Liberal M.P. for East Norfolk, 1892–1918.

PRINGLE, REV. JOHN CHRISTIAN (1872–1938). For many years secretary to the Charity Organisation Society; during 1902–9 was assistant curate in East End parish. Expert investigator (on distress due to unemployment) to 1905 Royal Commission on the Poor Law.

PROTHERO, SIR GEORGE WALTER (1848–1922). The historian; Professor of History at Edinburgh University, 1894–99; editor of the Cambridge Historical Series and co-editor of the *Cambridge Modern History*; a member of the British Peace Delegation, 1919. Best known to Beatrice, however, as the editor of the *Quarterly Review*. His wife was Mary Frances Butler, daughter of the Bishop of Meath; they had a large circle of literary, scientific and political friends.

PROVIS, SIR SAMUEL BUTLER (1845–1926). Lawyer and civil servant;

Permanent Secretary to Local Government Board, 1898–1910. Member of 1905 Royal Commission on the Poor Law.

PYCROFT, ELLA. Social worker, worked with Beatrice in her early days as a rent collector for St. Katharine's Buildings. (See *My Apprenticeship*.) Subsequently turned her attention to education and became chief organiser of domestic economy under the Technical Education Board of the L.C.C.

RAMSAY, SIR WILLIAM (1852–1916). Chemist, Professor of Chemistry at University College, London, 1887–1912. In 1904 he received the Nobel Prize for chemistry.

RATHBONES. The great Liverpool family of merchants and philanthropists, founded by William Rathbone (1757–1809), whose son William (1787–1868) was Mayor of Liverpool and a great benefactor of education. The late Eleanor Rathbone, the protagonist of family allowances, was granddaughter to the second William, and the family includes many well-known names.

RAW, NATHAN (1866–1940). Doctor and tuberculosis expert; M.P. (Tory) for Wavertree, 1918–22. Head of various asylums and hospitals, O.C. first Western General Hospital, Lancashire.

REDESDALE, ALGERNON BERTRAM FREEMAN - MITFORD (1837 – 1916), first Baron Redesdale, diplomatist and M.P.

REDMOND, JOHN ARTHUR (1851–1918). The Irish Nationalist, leader first of the Parnellites and then of the reunited Nationalist Party from 1900 to his death.

REEVES, WILLIAM PEMBER (1857–1932). Director of the London School of Economics, 1908–19. Reeves was a New Zealander who became Minister of Labour, Education and Justice in the colony, and resigned to come to London as Agent-General; from 1905 to 1909 he was its High Commissioner. Socialist and Fabian, wrote books on State experiments in Australia and New Zealand, etc., father of Amber Blanco White. His wife, *née* Magdalen Stuart Robison, was a social investigator, author of the famous *Round About a Pound a Week*.

REID, ROBERT THRESHIE, later Lord Loreburn (1846–1923). Lawyer and Liberal politician; Lord Chancellor, 1905–16.

RHODES, CECIL (1853–1902). Rhodes of South Africa, whose estate founded the Rhodes Scholarships. Though they did not take the pacifist line during the Boer War, the Webbs never accepted Rhodes' imperialism.

RICHARDS, HENRY CHARLES, K.C. (1851–1905). Lawyer; Tory M.P. for Finsbury from 1895, had previously fought hard against Bradlaugh at Northampton; frequent speaker in favour of the Constitution.

RIPON, FREDERICK OLIVER ROBINSON, 2nd Marquess of (1852–1925). Large landowner in Yorkshire and Liberal politician, friend of Rosebery; at one time Liberal leader in the House of Lords. He married Constance Gladys, widow of the Earl of Lonsdale.

RITCHIE, CHARLES THOMSON, Baron Ritchie (1838–1906). Tory politician, M.P. from 1874 onwards, held various Government posts, rising to Chancellor of the Exchequer, 1902–3. As President of the Local Government Board (1886–92) played a considerable part in the formation of the London County Council.

ROBERTS, SIR OWEN (1835 – 1915). Magistrate; Clerk for forty years to the Worshipful Company of Clothfounders, and thereafter its Master; Lieutenant for the City of London and High Sheriff of Carnarvonshire.

ROBERTSON, JOHN G. (1867 – 1933). Professor of German Language and Literature, University of London.

ROBINSON, SIR FREDERIC LACY (1840–1911). Inland Revenue official, 1857–1902, during his last ten years Deputy Chairman of the Commissioners. Thereafter member of L.C.C. (Moderate).

ROBINSON, SIR HENRY AUGUSTUS (1857–1927). Vice-President, Local Government Board for Ireland, from 1898 until its abolition. Member of 1905 Royal Commission on the Poor Law.

ROBINSON, JOSEPH ARMITAGE (1858–1933). Churchman and author. Professor of Divinity at Cambridge,

Morant; thereafter Vice-Chancellor of the University of Leeds. Father of Michael Sadleir, the novelist and publisher.

SALEEBY, DR. CALEB WILLIAM (1879–1940). Doctor, eugenist, Fabian, divorce law reformer, etc. Founder of the Sunlight League, and propagandist and organiser for a large number of associations connected with hygiene, sociology and racial health.

SALISBURY, JAMES EDWARD HUBERT GASCOYNE-CECIL (1861–1947), fourth Marquess, son of the third, first took office in 1909 as Under-Secretary for Foreign Affairs, and thereafter held many other posts, ending his political career as Lord Privy Seal, 1924–29, and Leader of the House of Lords, 1925–29.

SALISBURY, ROBERT ARTHUR TALBOT GASCOYNE-CECIL, Marquess of Salisbury (1830–1903), " the Markiss " as *Punch* called him. Three times Conservative Prime Minister, retiring in 1902 to be succeeded by Arthur Balfour.

SALT, HENRY STEPHENS (1851–1937). Eton master, writer, humanitarian, vegetarian, Fabian, Socialist; secretary for thirty years of the Humanitarian League. Salt married a relative of J. L. Joynes, another Eton master who was a Socialist and friend of William Morris, and served humanitarian causes all his life; his best-known book is his autobiography, *Seventy Years Among Savages*.

SAMUEL, HERBERT LOUIS, Viscount Samuel (1870–   ). An intimate friend of the Webbs in the early years of this century. First held office in the Liberal Government of 1906; High Commissioner for Palestine, 1920–25; Home Secretary in the National Government, 1931–32, and leader of Liberal Parliamentary Party, 1931–35.

SANDARS, JOHN S. (1869–1934). Private secretary to Arthur Balfour from 1892 to 1905.

SANDERS, WILLIAM STEPHEN (1876–1942). Fabian Socialist who started life as a farmer's boy and later became a Fabian lecturer under the Hutchinson Trust. Secretary of the Fabian Society, 1914–20, and Honorary Treasurer thereafter. L.C.C. Alderman, 1904–10, and Labour M.P. for North Battersea, 1929–31.

SAUER, J. W. (d. 1913). South African lawyer and politician. Colonial Secretary to the Cape Government under Rhodes; after the Union became Minister of Railways and subsequently of Agriculture. Sauer described himself as a " philosophic radical " and refused a knighthood.

SCHILLER, FERDINAND CUNNING SCOTT (1864–1937). The leading English Pragmatist philosopher: not a Hegelian, as stated in the text.

SCHLOSS, DAVID F. Civil servant, on the staff of the Labour Department of the Board of Trade; prepared important Reports on *Gain-sharing* and on *Profit-sharing and Co-partnership*. Schloss also wrote on *Methods of Industrial Remuneration* and pioneer studies in unemployment, and lectured for the Fabian Society.

SCHREINER, WILLIAM PHILIP (1857–1919). South African politician; Attorney-General to the Cape Government, 1893, and its Prime Minister from 1898 to 1900. From 1914 to 1919 he was High Commissioner for South Africa: his sister was Olive Schreiner, the novelist, author of *The Story of an African Farm*.

SELBORNE, LADY. Lady Beatrix Maud Cecil, daughter of the Marquess of Salisbury and wife of the second Earl of Selborne, the Liberal politician.

SELLICKS, ALFRED (1845–1902). Woolwich member of the A.S.E. and delegate to national conferences of that organisation.

SETH, JAMES (1860–1925). Professor of Moral Philosophy, University of Edinburgh, from 1898; and co-editor of the *Philosophic Review*.

SHACKLETON, SIR DAVID JAMES (1858–1940). Trade Unionist and Labour M.P. who became a civil servant. A cotton operative, President of the Weavers' Amalgamation, he was elected to Parliament as Labour M.P. for Clitheroe in 1902; in 1910 he became Labour Adviser to the Home Office, and was later Permanent Secretary to the Ministry of Labour.

SHARP, CLIFFORD DYCE (1883–1935). Journalist and Fabian; editor of *The Crusade*, and of the *New Statesman* from its foundation until 1931. He married the daughter of Hubert Bland, treasurer of the Fabian Society.

SHAW, FLORA LOUISE (*d.* 1929). Author and journalist, friend of Rhodes and Joseph Chamberlain; Special Commissioner for *The Times* in South Africa. In 1902 she married Sir Frederick Lugard (Lord Lugard, the great colonial administrator).

SHAW, GEORGE BERNARD (1856–   ). Playwright, Socialist, very early member of the Fabian Society, to which he introduced Sidney Webb. Editor of *Fabian Essays*, and one of the " Big Four " who ran the early Fabian Society. Shaw, whom Beatrice Webb described as a " Sprite ", was the lifelong friend of both of them, as well as being the Fabian Society's most brilliant pamphleteer. See Shaw, *Early History of the Fabian Society.*

SHAW-LEFEVRE, GEORGE JOHN, Baron Eversley (1832–1928). Liberal politician; as Postmaster-General, 1882–84, introduced the sixpenny telegram. First Commissioner of Works and later President of the Local Government Board in Rosebery's government of 1892–95, in which capacity he carried the first London Equalisation of Rates Act. Sat on the L.C.C. as a Progressive.

SHEPHEARD (not Shepherd), A. J. Member of L.C.C. (Progressive), 1901–13.

SHIPTON, GEORGE (1839–1911). By trade a builder, Shipton's chief claim to fame is his long secretaryship of the London Trades Council in the latter days of the Junta. (See Webb, *History of Trade Unionism.*) He gave evidence before the 1874 Royal Commission on the Labour Laws, which produced important and far-reaching changes. He was an opponent of Burns and Tillett and the " New Unionists ", but eventually became converted to the regulation of hours of work by law.

SHOVE, GERALD FRANK (1887–1947). Economist; lecturer in economics at Cambridge University and Fellow of King's College; in early days a strong left-wing Socialist and Syndicalist.

SIDGWICK, ELEANOR MILDRED (1845–1936). Widow of Henry Sidgwick and sister of Arthur Balfour the Prime Minister; Principal of Newnham College, 1892 – 1910, and Bursar, 1880–1919.

SIDGWICK, HENRY (1838–1900). The philosopher, influenced by John Stuart Mill, who wrote text-books on ethics and political economy. A strong advocate of higher education for women; promoted Newnham College, Cambridge.

SIMON, ERNEST DARWIN, afterwards Baron Simon of Wythenshawe (1879–   ). Manufacturer of gas engines; Liberal, later Labour politician and expert on housing and local government. Member of Manchester City Council, 1911–25, and Lord Mayor, 1921. Twice Liberal M.P. for Withington, author of several books on housing, city government, democracy, etc. Chairman of B.B.C., 1947.

SIMON, JOHN ALSEBROOK, first Viscount (1873–   ). Lawyer, Liberal and then , National Liberal politician; M.P. for Walthamstow, 1906–18, and thereafter for other divisions. Solicitor-General, 1910–13; Foreign Secretary, 1931–35; Lord Chancellor, 1940–45. His first wife, Ethel Mary Venables, died in 1902, after three years of marriage.

SMART, WILLIAM (1853–1915). Economist; Professor of Political Economy at Glasgow University from 1896 to his death; author of Smart's *Economic Annals of the Nineteenth Century.* Member of 1905 Royal Commission on the Poor Law.

SMITH, FRANK S. (1854–1940). Furnishing trades worker who became a journalist and Salvationist. Lifelong Socialist and member of I.L.P.; close friend of Keir Hardie. Member of L.C.C. (with intermission) from 1892 to 1913.

SMITH, LOGAN PEARSALL (1865–1946). Writer of books, of essays and belles-lettres, of which *Trivia* is the best known. Brother of Alys, first wife of Bertrand Russell, and a friend of the Webbs from their early married days.

SOMERSET, LADY HENRY (1851–1921). Unhappily married when quite young, Lady Henry Somerset ran away from her husband. The social ostracism thus incurred turned her mind to philanthropic work; she became an ardent temperance advocate (Chairman for a time of the World Women's Temperance Organisation) and interested herself in the problem of " fallen " women.

SOUVESTRE, MARIE (d. 1905). Brilliant French intellectual, daughter of the French Academician Émile Souvestre, in the last quarter of the nineteenth century owned and ran a fashionable boarding-school, first at Fontainebleau and then at Wimbledon. Mlle. Souvestre was a radical free-thinker, intimate with the set which surrounded the Frederic Harrisons; Beatrice in youth greatly admired her intellect.

SPENCER, FREDERICK HERBERT (d. 1946). One of the Webbs' earliest secretaries, who rose to become Chief Inspector to the L.C.C. (See note on p. 153 of this book.)

SPENCER, HERBERT (1820–1903). The philosopher who was Beatrice's earliest friend and preceptor and who so violently disliked her conversion to Socialism. (See the amusing account in *My Apprenticeship*.)

SPENCER, LORD (1835–1910). Liberal peer; First Lord of the Admiralty, 1892–95.

SPENDER, E. HAROLD (1864–1926). Liberal journalist; editor between 1891 and 1914 in succession of the *Pall Mall Gazette*, the *Daily Chronicle*, the *Manchester Guardian* and the *Daily News*; brother of J. A. Spender, the biographer of Asquith. Spender was a Fabian, and his London editorships afforded many good openings for Fabian facts and propaganda. His wife was Violet Hilda Schuster.

SPEYER, SIR EDGAR (1862–1932). Millionaire, partner in Speyer Bros. in three countries, Germany, America and England; became director of the London house in 1887; responsible for electrification of London railways. Speyer was also a patron of music and art and one of the founders of the Whitechapel Art Gallery.

SPICER, SIR EVAN (1849–1937). Of a well-known philanthropic family, Liberal, Congregationalist and interested in education. Alderman of L.C.C., 1889 onwards, and its Chairman, 1906–7.

SQUIRE, ROSE ELIZABETH (1861–1938). Civil servant. Inspector of Factories, Home Office, 1896, and Senior Woman Inspector, 1903; Principal in Home Office, 1921–26. Special Com-missioner to 1905 Royal Commission on the Poor Law.

STACY, ENID (d. 1903). One of the most effective women speakers and lecturers in the 'nineties. A Socialist from Bristol, she joined the Fabian Society in 1891, became lecturer to the Hutchinson Trust and a member of the Council of the I.L.P. She married a Socialist curate in Newcastle, the Rev. P. E. T. Widdrington; but unfortunately died very young.

STAMFORD, WILLIAM GREY, ninth Earl (1850–1910). Married Elizabeth Theobald. He was a strong churchman, a Chairman of the Charity Organisation Society, and member of the councils of many religious organisations.

STANLEY, ARTHUR PENRHYN (1815–1881). Dean of Westminster from 1864 to his death. The famous " Dean Stanley ", who defended Dr. Jowett and Bishop Colenso against the orthodox. A connection of Lord Stanley of Alderley.

STANLEY, EDWARD LYULPH, Lord Stanley of Alderley, later Lord Sheffield (1839–1925). Educationalist and authority on social questions, sat on Government Commissions on housing, etc. Member of London School Board, 1876–85 and 1886–96. M.P. for Oldham, 1880–85.

STEADMAN, W. C. (1851–1911). Secretary of the Barge-Builders' Union, and in 1905 Secretary to the T.U.C. Sat on L.C.C. for many years representing Stepney; Lib-Lab M.P. for Tower Hamlets, 1898–1900, and for Central Finsbury, 1906–10. An early Fabian.

STEEL, MRS. FLORA ANNIE (1847–1929). The popular novelist—mostly on Indian themes. She lived in India until 1889, and was inspector of schools in the Punjab.

STEEL-MAITLAND, SIR ARTHUR HERBERT DRUMMOND RAMSAY (1876–1935). Tory politician; M.P. for Birmingham seats, 1910–29; Minister of Labour, 1924–29. Special Commissioner to 1905 Royal Commission on the Poor Law.

STEPHEN, SIR LESLIE (1832–1904). The Rationalist, first editor of the *Dictionary of National Biography* and author of *The English Utilitarians* and

BIOGRAPHICAL INDEX

English Thought in the Eighteenth Century, etc. Father of Virginia Woolf.

STEYN, MARTINIUS THEUNIS (1857–1916). South African politician. Attorney-General to the Orange Free State, 1889, and its President from 1896 to 1900. At first he was friendly to Great Britain, but joined with the Transvaal Republic at the outbreak of war.

STONE, SAMUEL. The first Town Clerk of Leicester after the Municipal Corporations Act, 1835. Stone was both Town Clerk and Clerk to the Magistrates from 1836 to 1872.

STOREY, JOHN. Town Clerk of Leicester, 1874–94.

STRACHEY, LIEUTENANT-GENERAL SIR RICHARD (1817–1908). Distinguished Indian Army officer and administrator, Secretary to the Government of the Central Provinces during the Mutiny; was subsequently member of the Council for India. President of the Famine Commission, 1878–80, and held many other offices. Lytton Strachey was one of his five sons, and St. Loe Strachey of the *Spectator* his nephew. Lady Strachey was a daughter of Sir John Grant of Rothiemurchus; she wrote poetry and memoirs.

STRACHEY, JAMES B. The psychoanalyst, brother of Lytton Strachey. As an undergraduate of Trinity College joined the Cambridge University Fabian Society in 1908.

STUART, SIR JAMES (1843–1913). Professor of Mechanics at Cambridge, 1875–89; Liberal M.P. for Hoxton, 1885–1900, and for Sunderland, 1906–10. Founded the University Extension system at Cambridge.

STURGE, MILDRED. Of an old Quaker family, of whom three sisters married three brothers, Stephens by name, all descended from one great-great-grandfather. Mildred Sturge became Mrs. Arthur Stephens, and had six children.

SUTHERLAND, MILLICENT, Duchess of Sutherland. Wife of the fourth Duke (who *d.* 1913). Author, social worker and Society hostess; a prominent and distinguished lady in her day.

SWEET-ESCOTT, SIR ERNEST BICKHAM (1857–1942). Colonial administrator, entered the service in 1881 and rose to be Governor of British Honduras, 1904–6, of the Leeward Islands, 1906–1912, and Governor of Fiji and High Commissioner and Consul-General for Western Pacific, 1912–18.

TALBOT, EDWARD STUART (1844–1934). Bishop of Rochester, 1895–1905, of Southwark, 1905–11, and of Winchester, 1911–23. A moderately high churchman who supported many social reforms and worked for agreement among the various sections of Church opinion.

TENNANT, HAROLD JOHN (1865–1935). Liberal politician; Private Secretary to Asquith, who married his sister Margot; held various offices. His wife was May Abraham, the inspector of factories.

TERRY, ELLEN (1847–1928). The actress. See Bernard Shaw's *Letters to Ellen Terry.*

THESIGER, FREDERIC AUGUSTUS. Baron Chelmsford (1827–1905). Soldier, served in Crimean War, Indian Mutiny, Kaffir and Zulu Wars. Lieutenant of the Tower, 1884–89.

THESIGER, FREDERIC JOHN NAPIER, afterwards Viscount Chelmsford (1868–1933). Member of the London School Board, 1900–4, and of L.C.C. (Moderate), 1904–5. Viceroy of India, 1916–21, and First Lord of the Admiralty in the first Labour Government. His wife was Frances Charlotte Guest, a daughter of Lord Wimborne.

TILLETT, BENJAMIN (1860–1943). One of the principal organisers of the Transport Workers. Started work in a brickyard, subsequently served in the Navy and in merchant shipping. As Secretary of the Tea Porters' Union, Tillett played a considerable part in the 1889 Dock Strike, and became Secretary of the Dock, Wharf, Riverside and General Workers' Union. He ran the London Dock Strikes of 1911 and 1912, and prayed on Tower Hill that "God would strike Lord Devonport dead". Labour M.P., 1917–24 and 1929–31.

TORRANCE, SIR ANDREW M. (*d.* 1909). Member of L.C.C. (Progressive), 1889–1907. Liberal M.P. for Central Glasgow, 1906.

TOWNSHEND, CHARLOTTE PAYNE (*d.* 1944). Fabian, the "Irish millionairess with green eyes ", who became the wife of Bernard Shaw. (See Shaw's *Letters to Ellen Terry*, etc.)

TREVELYAN, SIR CHARLES PHILIPS (1870–). Eldest son of Sir George Otto Trevelyan. At first a Liberal M.P., holding office in the last Liberal Government, but resigned in 1914 on pacifist principles, and became a strong pacifist and internationalist. Joined the Labour Party, and was President of the Board of Education in the Labour Government of 1929.

TREVELYAN, GEORGE MACAULAY (1876–). The historian and Master of Trinity College, Cambridge, younger brother of the above. His wife was Janet Penrose, daughter of Mrs. Humphry Ward.

TREVELYAN, ROBERT CALVERLEY (1872–). Poet and man of letters. Younger brother of Sir Charles Trevelyan, and associated with him in the Webbs' Socialist and Poor Law projects.

TUCKWELL, GERTRUDE. Niece of Lady Dilke. Honorary Secretary of the Women's Trade Union League, 1892–1904, and thereafter Chairman. Miss Tuckwell was one of the most fervent promoters of Trade Unionism among women, and of labour legislation. She was for many years Honorary Treasurer of the British Section of the International Association for Labour Legislation; she was also one of the first women magistrates.

TWEEDMOUTH, EDWARD MARJORIBANKS, Baron Tweedmouth (1849–1909). Rich Liberal landowner and politician, held various offices. When First Lord of the Admiralty (1906–8) he wrote an indiscreet letter to the Kaiser which led to the termination of his political career.

TYNDALL, JOHN (1820–92). The great scientist who succeeded Faraday in 1867 as Superintendent at the Royal Institution.

TYRRELL, GEORGE (1861–1909). Father Tyrrell, the modernist priest who in 1906 was turned out of the Society of Jesus for an unorthodox " Letter to a Professor of Anthropology ". Writer of many books and articles, and a strong influence in the early twentieth century.

VANDERVELDE, ÉMILE (1866–1939). For many years leader of the Belgian Labour Party and President of the Labour and Socialist (" Second ") International. His best-known book is *Le Socialisme contre l'État*. Several times a Minister in Belgian Governments.

VINCENT, SIR WILLIAM WILKINS (1843–1916). Hat and cap manufacturer of Leicester; member of the Town Council from 1891; Mayor in 1902 and 1910.

VIVIAN, HERBERT (1865–1940). Traveller and journalist; correspondent for *Morning Post*, *Daily Express*, *Daily Mail*; strongly Conservative in politics.

WAKEFIELD, REV. HENRY RUSSELL (1854–1933). Broad churchman, member of the London School Board, 1897–1900; Rector of St. Mary's, Bryanston Square, 1894–1909, and Bishop of Birmingham, 1911–24. Chairman of the Central Committee on the Unemployed, member of the 1905 Royal Commission on the Poor Law, where he signed the Minority Report.

WALLAS, AUDREY (1859–1934), née Ada Radford. Wife of Graham Wallas and herself a writer.

WALLAS, GRAHAM (1858–1932). Sociologist, author of *Human Nature in Politics* and other books, and lecturer at the London School of Economics. With Webb, Shaw and Olivier, Wallas made up the " Big Four " of the early Fabian Executive, on which he sat from 1888 to 1895. He was a member of the London School Board from 1894 to 1904, and of the L.C.C. from 1904 to 1907.

WARD, DUDLEY (1885–). Banker and expert on bridge; Director and Manager of British Overseas Bank. In Treasury during the first world war and represented it at the Peace Conference and the 1921 Brussels Conference.

WARD, MARY AUGUSTA. Mrs. Humphry Ward (1851–1920), the author, her most famous novel being *Robert Elsmere*. Mrs. Humphry Ward was a strong opponent of women's suffrage and in 1889 induced Beatrice to sign a letter to the Press objecting to it. (See *My Apprenticeship*.)

WELBY, REGINALD EARLE, first Baron

1937. Previously Clerk in House of Commons, 1892–1901, and Secretary of Transvaal Education Department.

WILLIAMS, DR. ETHEL MARY NUCELLA (1863–   ). Doctor; President of the British Federation of Medical Women, in practice in Newcastle-on-Tyne from 1913. Active in local government, education and women's emancipation; Treasurer of the first Socialist Medical League.

WILLIAMS, JOSEPH POWELL (1840–1904). Liberal-Unionist politician; M.P. for South Birmingham. Chamberlain's right-hand man, Chairman of the Management Committee of the Liberal-Unionist Association.

WILLIS-BUND, JOHN WILLIAM BUND (1842–1928). Chairman of Worcester County Council and Worcester Quarter Sessions, and of Cardigan Quarter Sessions.

WILSON, JAMES HAVELOCK (1858–1929). Creator in 1887 of the National Sailors and Firemen's Union, which for many years was a vigorous fighting Union. Wilson, however, disliked the I.L.P. type of Socialism; elected to Parliament in 1892 as a Lib-Lab he refused to co-operate in any way with Keir Hardie, and during the first world war, on his instigation, members of his Union refused to carry MacDonald, Henderson and others to meet Russian Socialists and to discuss the re-formation of the International. Thereafter Wilson broke completely with the Labour Party.

WIMBORNE, LADY. Daughter of the seventh Duke of Marlborough and wife of Ivor Bertie Guest, Baron Wimborne. A famous Society hostess.

WOOD, SIR EDWARD (1839–1906). Boot and shoe manufacturer of Leicester; member of the Town Council from 1880 to his death, and Mayor in 1888, 1895, 1901 and 1906.

WOOD, THOMAS MCKINNON (1855–1927). Liberal politician, member of the L.C.C., 1892–97; Chairman, 1898–99, and Leader of the Progressive Party. Liberal M.P., 1906–1918; Parliamentary Secretary to Board of Education, 1908.

WOODCOCK, DR. Her Christian name was not Julia. The only woman Dr. Woodcock on the Medical Register at the date mentioned was Dr. Louisa Woodcock of Portman Square, an eye specialist.

WOODS, SAMUEL (1846–1915). A Lancashire miner by origin, Woods was a Trade Unionist of some note, Secretary to the London Trades Council from 1894 to 1904, and Lib-Lab M.P. from 1892 to 1895 and from 1897 to 1900. He was one of the four delegates sent by the T.U.C. to take part in the Conference of 1900 which resulted in the formation of the Labour Party.

WYNDHAM, GEORGE (1863–1913). One of the more brilliant of the aristocratic Tory politicians, a descendant of Lord Edward Fitzgerald and private secretary to Balfour for five years. From 1900 to 1905, Chief Secretary for Ireland, passed Irish Land Purchase Act; but died young.

YARROW, SIR ALFRED FERNANDEZ (1842–1932). Founder and Chairman of Yarrow & Co., shipbuilders, on the Clyde. His wife was née Minnie Florence Franklin.

YOUNG, ANDREW (1858–   ). Socialist schoolmaster, co-operator. Head for 27 years of North Canongate School, Edinburgh; Edinburgh Town Councillor. Labour M.P. for Partick, 1923–24.

INDEX

Liverpool, Local Government Enquiry, 162-3, 187
Llewellyn Smith, Sir Hubert, 78, 80, 470
Lloyd, C. M., 452, 454
Lloyd George, Rt. Hon. David, 283, 411, 418, 430, 436, 444, 446, 450, 462, 465; Board of Trade, President, 325 n.; and Boer War, 217-18; and National Insurance Scheme, 417, 418, 429-30, 468-9, 469-70, 472, 473-6, 478 n.
Local Administration, confusion of, 66 n.
Local Government Act (1929), 478, 481
Local Government Enquiry, 147 et seq.; historical, 149-53; visits to: Leeds, 157-8; Leicester, 165-8; Liverpool, 162-3, 187; Manchester, 159, 160-62; Newcastle-on-Tyne, 169-70; Plymouth, 163-4; Torquay, 164-5; York (East Riding), 148-9, 157-8
Local Veto, 124, 126, 200
Loch, Sir Charles S., Poor Law Commission, 320, 323, 327, 329, 341, 343, 348-9, 368, 370, 377, 389, 395, 399, 416, 420; supports principles of 1834, 358
Lockwood, Henry, 341
Lodge, Sir Oliver, 300-301, 314, 436
London Building Act, 58 n.
London County Council, 58 et seq.
  Constitution and Administration, 58-76, 149, 285; Deputy Chairmanship, 73, 73 n.; List of Committees on which S. W. served, 82 n.; Progressive Party Committee, 308; Selection Committee, 286-8
  Education Committee, Authority for Education, 63, 183, 250-51, 285; campaign for, 259-66, 279-81, 285, 293; case for, 252-5; newspaper articles by S. W., 257-8, 283-4; scholarship scheme, 295, 301-2, 343; S. W.'s influence, 303-4, 364-5
  Elections: (1889), Progressive victory, 59; (1892), S. W. elected, 13, 17, 27, 57, 60; (1895), Progressive decline, 69-74, 121-3; (1898), Progressive success, 74-6, 144-5; (1901), 212-13; (1904), 271, 276, 282-7; (1907), Progressive débâcle, 372-3; (1910), S. W. retires, 317, 446-7
  Technical Education Board, 76 et seq.; constitution, 78-9; history and function, 76-84, 100; scholarship ladder, 78-81; S. W. addresses scholars, 138; chairman, 18, 36, 78, 91, 101, 203,

229-30, 229-30 n., 235 n., 240, 247, 260, 263; vice-chairman, 181, 271; superseded by Education Committee, 264-5
London County Council, History of, Gibbon and Bell, 73 n.
London Day Training College, 80
Londonderry, Lord, 251, 262
London Dock Strike (1889), 20
London Education, S. W., 177, 279-81
London Education Act (1903), 183, 252-5, 256, 281, 293
London Education Bill (1903), campaign for, 183, 250-51, 259-63; newspaper articles by S. W., 257-8, 258 n.; opposition to, 260-63; passage through Parliament, 264-5
London Programme, The, S. W., 58, 61-62, 61 n., 62 n.
London Reform Union, 61, 65-7
London School Board, 78, 83, 287, 327; elections, 65, 67, 67 n.; superseded by L.C.C., 63, 76, 229, 241
London School of Economics, 84 et seq.
  History and Growth, action by S. and B. W., 9, 86-8; appointment of first director, 87-9; Hutchinson Trust, 84-6, 132, 195, 242; subsequent development, 94, 133, 145, 163, 168, 189, 195-6, 224-5, 229-30, 243, 282, 287, 294, 339, 427, 453, 489
  Library of Political Sciences, 92-3, 133
  Mansion House Meeting, 213-14
  Special Courses—Army, 363-4, 401-2; railway, 246, 294; railway magnates demand S. W.'s resignation, 463-4
  Students' Union, 175; B. W. President, 246; addresses scholars, 263-4; dinner, 335-6
  University status, 95, 181, 185, 195
London "society", 146, 195, 211-12, 291, 294
London Trades Council, 20, 79, 125-6
London Unification Commission (1893), 83
London University, 95 et seq.; historical, 95-9, 233-6; reconstruction: action by S. W. and Haldane, 99-102, 185, 489; case for, 236-9; Senate, S. W. member, 181, 195, 203, 225
London University Act (1898), 100-102, 235 n.
London University: A Plan and a Forecast, S. W., 236-9
London University Commission (1900), 196

INDEX

THE END